Re-Reading Education Policies

EDUCATIONAL FUTURES
RETHINKING THEORY AND PRACTICE
Volume 32

Scope
This series maps the emergent field of educational futures. It will commission books on the futures of education in relation to the question of globalisation and knowledge economy. It seeks authors who can demonstrate their understanding of discourses of the knowledge and learning economies. It aspires to build a consistent approach to educational futures in terms of traditional methods, including scenario planning and foresight, as well as imaginative narratives, and it will examine examples of futures research in education, pedagogical experiments, new utopian thinking, and educational policy futures with a strong accent on actual policies and examples.

A C.I.P. record for this book is available from the Library of Congress.

ISBN 978-90-8790-829-4 (paperback)
ISBN 978-90-8790-830-0 (hardback)
ISBN 978-90-8790-831-7 (e-book)

Published by: Sense Publishers,
P.O. Box 21858, 3001 AW
Rotterdam, The Netherlands
http://www.sensepublishers.com

Printed on acid-free paper

Re-Reading Education Policies

*A Handbook Studying the Policy Agenda
of the 21st Century*

Edited by

Maarten Simons
Catholic University Leuven, Belgium

Mark Olssen
University of Surrey, UK

Michael A. Peters
University of Illinois at Urbana-Champaign

SENSE PUBLISHERS
ROTTERDAM/BOSTON/TAIPEI

TABLE OF CONTENTS

TABLE OF CONTENTS

QUALITY, ACCOUNTABILITY, CONTROL

TEACHER PROFESSIONALISM

MAARTEN SIMONS, MARK OLSSEN & MICHAEL A. PETERS

HANDBOOK ON MATTERS OF PUBLIC CONCERN

Introduction & Overview

Critique as ethos

This book is a collection of papers that study and discuss current education policy challenges from a variety of perspectives. Although the term is clearly too broad, these papers are part of the field of study that is commonly referred to as '*critical education policy studies*'. Perhaps today the term critical has become devoid of meaning – and there are probably no researchers who wouldn't call themselves, or their research, critical. Notwithstanding this "trivialisation", we do want to maintain the term critical here (Masschelein, 2004). However, critical does not refer to how the researcher of education policy relates to her research (methodology, data, results, peers...). Indeed, in that sense, all research is expected to be critical. Neither is the term used here to characterise the kind of analytical framework that informs the research usually thought of as critical social or political theory.

In our vernacular critical first of all indicates a particular engagement with, or relation to, the domain that is being studied. What we have in mind is a critical *attitude* or *ethos*, and thus a way of relating to the present. The contributions in this collection articulate that such a critical research ethos can take different forms. Approaches would vary from bringing attention to aspects of policy that are often taken for granted, to contributing to the formulation of new policy agendas. Of course, to think of critique as the adoption of an ethos is not to say that such an ethos will have no implications for the kinds of framework or methodology that are used. However, there is more at stake for scholars than the theoretical or analytical framework that they adopt. Their work seems to articulate a form of public concern. We will flesh out this particular critical perspective by introducing the concept 're-reading'.

Re-readings

As the title of the handbook indicates, what these papers share, despite the variety of approaches and methodologies, is a critical attitude that could be equated with the term re-reading. The concept of re-reading refers to the following issues:

– re-reading suggests the importance of taking as a point of departure *current* challenges: problems for governments, proposed policy solutions, power mechanisms or emerging practices and tensions (for example, how do policy makers, political parties, organisations 'read' the problems and challenges they want to address, what kind of discourses emerge, and which measures and instruments are proposed or implemented?);

– re-reading not only focuses on policy texts, but adopts a *broad perspective* that includes readings of policy instruments, procedures and strategies. Re-reading also involves recognition of the subtle and contingent mechanisms of power and knowledge production;

– re-reading contemporary readings of policy is a critical activity that aims to *de-familiarise* the current ways in which policies pose problems, offer and implement solutions and justify agendas. It draws attention to the ways in which power is exercised in both society and education and focuses on how problems are defined in these areas;

– the critical potential of re-reading takes on board a *variety of approaches*. Such approaches include attempts to reveal underlying forms of rationality, identify unspoken interests, focus on unintended consequences, point out contradictions, or map the field of contingencies;

– motivated by a concern for ideas pertaining to the role of education in society, re-reading brings new attention to issues bound up with policy, politics and power. We use the expression '*the public, and its education*' to outline the field that incorporates such critical commitment (the reasons for adopting this expression will become clear).

If one assumes that the policy agenda represent a politics of reading, these papers aim at a re-reading of the politics of reading. Taking the policy agenda as a point of departure does not mean, however, that we adopt a limited notion of education policy, for policies must not only be seen as relating to the formal agenda of state governments. At a theoretical and analytical level, this handbook adopts a rather general notion of policy that takes on board processes, practises, and discourses at a variety of levels, in diverse governmental and non-governmental contexts, and considers policy's relation to power, politics and social regulation. Thus from this point onward, the term education policy will be used as a general term to address topics of power, politics, government, and policies (in a strict sense) surrounding education.

From a handbook on matters of fact...

In contrast to regular handbooks, the contributions are not ordered according to the theoretical approach adopted, the part or stage of the policy process focused on, or the methodological issues discussed. The contributions are written and ordered in view of a selection of policy challenges: globalisation, knowledge society/economy, lifelong learning, equality/democracy/inclusion, accountability/control/efficiency and teacher professionalism. We treat the six challenges selected, although this does not exhaust the field of possible considerations, as constitutive of the policy agenda. For each challenge we attempt to include a diverse range of critical approaches. At the end of this introduction, a general overview of these challenges is presented. Here, we focus first on the consequences of a form of ordering based on challenges.

Rather than discussing theories and methodologies in detail, the papers that are included report the *results* of critical education policy analyses. The aim of the handbook is to show, and hence to illustrate, what critical education policy analysis is about by presenting actual re-readings. In order to further this goal, the contributors to this handbook have been explicitly asked to limit theoretical and methodological discussions in their papers in favour of presenting, in as much detail as possible, their re-readings of policy readings. For those who are interested in exploring the topics addressed in more detail, and the theoretical and methodological background, a short list of further readings is included in each paper. Additionally, the introduction (Part 1 and 2) discusses some of the theoretical and methodological approaches that are adopted.

Our preliminary remarks about this book's intended scope may have already indicated that this is not a regular handbook, although it is also not a reader that collects state of the art research in a particular domain of study. Perhaps a few words of clarification are needed, because these topics are not just about terms and definitions, but relate closely to the scope of the handbook.

Academic handbooks are commonly conceived of as reference works that offer easy access to a particular topic, discipline or field of practice/study. In that sense, scientific or scholarly handbooks aim at offering useful state-of-the-art information in order to orient readers in their role as students or (future) scholars in a particular domain. In this respect, handbooks have a clear educational function. They aim at passing on knowledge of issues related to the main concepts, theories, approaches, methods, and current and future challenges so as to enable people to gain access to the domain or discipline, and to become well informed participants. In view of this aim, the information collected in many academic handbooks presents both factual and procedural knowledge, that is, research results upon which the field of study at a particular moment agrees, and mainly methodological knowledge about how to approach a factual reality that constitutes the field of study.

An early example of such handbooks is perhaps Immanuel Kant's critical work on (theoretical, practical, aesthetic) *Reason* at the end of the eighteenth century. In his search for the universal conditions under which the use of reason is legitimate, and grounding human autonomy beyond tradition and religion, Kant's critical work actually functions as a kind of meta-handbook. This work includes the guidelines or limits determining for mankind what can be known, what must be done and what may be hoped for – and thus also indicates the limits beyond which people are lost in respect to knowledge, morality and aesthetics. Handbooks in this enlightenment tradition, one could say, function as a type of 'entrance gate' to a discipline or field of study. And, at the same time, through the vehicle of a handbook the field of study strengthens its disciplinary borders, and in some cases, is able to constitute itself as a 'mature' discipline. Indeed, there is a politics involved in handbooks for they constitute what knowledge in a particular field is, who the main representatives are, and how one should look at the discipline's past and future. In short, 'knowledge oriented handbooks' play a clear role in the demarcation, internal organisation, external proliferation and teaching of disciplines. Additionally, due to this bundling of roles, handbooks are instruments of what could be called disciplinary mechanisms, professionalisation, scientific socialisation, or the politics of academic knowledge.

... to a handbook on matters of concern

This is, however, not what we have in mind with this handbook. As mentioned earlier, this book does not aim to provide access to a discipline or field of study. Instead, current policy challenges orient the structure and content of the book. Re-reading as an ethos or attitude first of all implies a particular relation of the researcher towards her present and her society. The point of departure is a particular involvement with the present, and with what is going on in the present of which the researcher is herself a part. Loosely adopting the terminology of Latour (2004a), which we will discuss in more detail throughout the introduction of this book (Part 1 & 2), we see the contributors as involved with matters of concern. They are not just talking and writing about matters of fact. The distinction between concern and fact is not however a new version of the theoretical distinction between value and fact.

Matters of concern are *things* that create a public, not in view of finding agreement (on facts or values), but by gathering people for whom something is at stake. In this way, the book hopes to "make things public", that is, to help to constitute "matters of public concern" by transforming what policies or researchers regard as matters of fact into "an issue to talk about" (Latour & Sanchez-Criado, 2007, p. 368). There is a clear echo here of the opening sentence of Dewey's *The Public and Its Problems* (1927/1954, p. 3): "If one wishes to realise the distance which may lie between 'facts' and the meaning of 'facts', let one go to the field of social discussion." It is Dewey (1927/1954, 15-16) who suggests connecting the public with the notion of fact when he defines the public as follows: "The public consists of all those who are affected by the indirect consequences of transactions, to such an extent that it is deemed necessary to have those consequences systematically cared for," and he adds, "The essence of the consequences which call a public into being is the fact that they expand beyond those directly engaged in producing them" (ibid., 15-16). Thus, people are transformed into a public when confronted with issues that are not being taken care of by the private or official institutions and experts in a given society. Whereas matters of fact and problems are always already being taken care of – by the available expertise and agencies in society – matters of concern, because no-one can claim them, can become everyone's concern, and therefore a public concern. These are "issues" that can "spark a public into being" (Marres, 2005). In line with this, we think all contributors to this book would agree that accompanying their investigations is a commitment to what we want to call 'the public, and its education'. The involvement of critical scholars in these issues ensures that their work is always a kind of "collective experiment" – it inaugurates the question about how we are going to live together (cf. Latour, 2004b).

Perhaps, and we are deliberately mixing highly diverse intellectual traditions here, the notion public concern could be situated alongside the Habermasian notion of "interest", and particularly the idea of an "emancipatory interest", or the idea of the "orientation towards mutual understanding" (Habermas, 1971, 1982). Also, Foucault's (2000, p. 239) notion of books and courses as "invitations" or "public gestures" could be regarded as the expression of a similar commitment. The texts collected in this book can function as public gestures and invitations, not just because these are gestures to a public of contemporaries but most importantly because integral to these gestures is the creation of public issues. To put it another way, what is at stake is perhaps a type of Foucauldian "curiosity"; a curiosity that is not in the first place knowledge-oriented, but about "care" (derived from the Latin *cura* in curiosity/*curiosité*) and concern for the present and to "live the present otherwise" (Foucault, 1980). Maybe a public gesture and concern comes close to what Derrida (2001) regards as one's "profession of faith", or the unconditional orientation towards justice motivating academic work in the humanities and social sciences. Or, to draw on the terminology of Rancière (2005), one could say these papers are "demonstrations of equality" or "democratic acts." They are raising a voice with regard to the policy agenda, although that voice has no part in the current "police order" according to the present distribution of parts (Rancière, 2005). As Fairclough (2001) argues, it seems as if "the public sphere is cut off from struggles over the public sphere", and that in view of this consideration it is important to reconsider "how we research, how and where we publish, and how we write." The collected papers could be regarded indeed as rethinking the public role of research.

From yet another perspective, one could say that what these papers share is the attempt to ask questions in a society that, as Bauman (2000, p. 5) states after Cornelius Castoriades, "stopped questioning itself":

> Not asking certain questions is pregnant with more dangers than failing to answer the questions already on the official agenda; while asking the wrong kind of questions all too often helps to avert eyes from the truly important issues. The price of silence is paid in the hard currency of human suffering. Asking the right questions makes, after all, all the difference between fate and destination, drifting and travelling. Questioning the ostensibly unquestionable premises of our way of life is arguably the most urgent of the services we owe our fellow humans and ourselves.

Whether these papers ask the "right questions", or merely, and often equally valuably, are "an exercise in asking and prompting the asking of questions – without the pretence that is asking the right questions (…)" (ibid., p. 5), the act of asking questions could be regarded as a public act, that is, opening up a space to think about our destination. This is perhaps at stake in the activities Bourdieu had in mind when talking about the "collective intellectual", and "working collectively to invent collective structures for invention" in the current international context (Bourdieu, 2001/2008, p. 383; 2000/2008, p. 387).

Despite the highly diverse theoretical and analytical frameworks, the authors cited in the previous paragraphs clearly share an involvement with their present moment. It is a concern that is often only articulated in the margins of their work, and phrased in a language and with a timbre that often differs from that of their 'main' work. Perhaps this concern is formulated at those moments and places where their scholarly work becomes both highly personal (it is rooted in their concern with their present) and public (it is a commitment that needs to be made public).

In sum, the term critical refers first of all to a very specific *ethos* or way of relating to one's present, and holding to the belief that the future should not be the repetition of the past. Hence re-reading is not just about wanting to know facts about policy and education, but foremost about being concerned with what is going on, and about developing knowledge and building theories in view of that concern. Because re-reading confronts what policies take for granted or want to achieve with *us*, the commitment is not merely personal but also public (and political). And we should stress again that there are evidently theoretical differences and discussions, but having disagreement with regard to matters of fact is not the same as having disagreement surrounding matters of concern.

Education and our limits

Being *concern*-oriented this book hopefully has an educational value. Its hope is to "make things public" (Latour, 2005), to play a role in the creation of matters of public concern, and to invite readers to share these concerns and to elaborate on them in various ways. As discussed previously, this book can indeed be used as *hand*-book. Again, the educational value of such a book does not reside primarily in the entrance it gives to a homogeneous and disciplinary space filled with matters of fact. Its educational meaning is hopefully first and foremost related to its transformational potential, that is, its potential to transform the reader's *ethos*. Using a Foucauldian expression here, the book could be regarded as a "medium" or "equipment" to transform *logos* into *ethos* starting from present public concerns (cf. Foucault, 2001; Rabinow, 2003). In other words, we hope that the educational value of this work resides in its ability to transform someone's assumptions about, or actions in, the world; or to transform one's world into a heterogeneous space of matters of concern constituted by diverse voices regarding policies that act upon *us* today.

It is important to say something about the editorial 'politics of selection': the selection of challenges/chapters and the selection of contributions. First, we think that a handbook becomes more than the sum of its parts. Within the scope of our handbook, this means that we hope that the gathering of articles in this collection will create new concerns. Second, we are well aware, and whilst writing this preface we became even more aware, that the selection of both challenges and contributors is limited in many ways. This is invariably due to the editors' limited re-reading of what is going on today and who is concerned with what is going on today. There are practical reasons for this limitation, but also reasons related to our reading of the research literature. For instance, this collection is insufficiently 'global', not to say that the editorial reading was focused mainly on concerns in Western parts of the world. Also racial and gender issues lack sufficient attention. Despite what is lacking from our handbook, we hope the book nevertheless presents something of what is at stake in our world today.

In the final paragraphs of this preface, we present a short overview of the introduction chapters, an overview of the selected challenges and some important acknowledgments.

Introduction chapters part 1 & 2

In the introduction of this book, we will clarify our particular scope in more detail. Part 1 of the introduction aims at positioning contemporary critical education policy studies in a broader intellectual and social context. The emergence of the policy orientation in social and political sciences will be taken as a point of departure, in order to describe the specificity of what we want to call the 'critical education policy orientation'. Next, some of the concerns of this research orientation will be outlined; the moral and political stance related to education and society, the broad interest in education, power, politics and policy and the articulations of critical advocacy. Part 2 of the introduction discusses some of the challenges critical policy studies have been facing in the recent past and today. In line with this overview, the second part of the introduction presents an overview of models and tools that can be used for research, as well as a short introduction to the main approaches.

Public concerns: An overview

We mentioned earlier that the papers should be regarded as being *concern-oriented*. Instead of introducing each of the contributions, we limit ourselves here to a short overview of the selected concerns.

Globalisation
The point of departure for the contributions of this section is the way education policy and governing bodies read the challenges of globalisation, and in the European context, the challenges related to Europeanisation. Increasingly, processes of globalisation and Europeanisation are mentioned when formulating policy objectives and/or to justify policy measures, such as: improving student and teacher mobility in order to increase global competition; further decentralisation, deregulation and privatisation in order to organise global markets in education; restructuring curricula, degrees and systems of accreditation in view of new student populations; monitoring and improving performance through international benchmarking, governance by numbers, World Bank requests; and learning from examples of good practice. Through re-reading these challenges and their solutions, the contributions critically examine and assess the assumptions, consequences or tensions pertinent to them. Some of the following issues are

stressed: the erosion of national state government and its consequences for education as a public good, the impact of World Bank policies, the contradictions emerging in the field of education due to new modes of global regulation, and the questionable assumptions concerning education in a global (market) environment.

The knowledge society
Education is regarded as playing a major role in the further development of knowledge societies and economies, and policies try to enable educational institutions to take up this role. The measures include institutional restructuring, reorganisation of curricula, the implementation of information and communication technology and changed patterns in knowledge production, the changed role of education and research in societies, and new modes to manage and assess higher education and research. The contributions in this section examine governmental reflections upon the relationship between society and education, how policy objectives are formulated and justified and what sort of solutions are proposed and implemented. They seek to promote a de-familiarisation with common policy conceptions, measures and modes of governance, based on an analysis of, for instance, the impact of an economic agenda on the aims of education and research, the challenges with regard to the position of teachers, the role of the OECD and World Bank, and challenged public-private distinctions.

Lifelong learning
National and regional governments increasingly regard one of their tasks as the promotion of, and investment in, lifelong learning, and the organisation of an adequate infrastructure that allows each and all to learn throughout their lives. These policies on lifelong learning are regarded as a necessity to support individual and collective well-being in the emerging knowledge society and economy. The contributions in this section reflect, for example, on the rhetoric on lifelong learning, tensions between personal and collective (and vocational-economic and socio-cultural) interests, the construction of the lifelong learner (in the European context), and shifts in the conception of lifelong learning.

Equality, social inclusion and democracy
Within the welfare state, education policy and social policy were closely linked, that is, from the viewpoint of social justice, education was regarded as a tool in the promotion of social equality and the democratisation of society. Due to the dominance of neoliberal strategies such as marketisation, the concern for social justice is increasingly pushed aside. When social concerns are still part of the education policy agenda, the challenges are often formulated in a new way (e.g. inclusion-exclusion, optimal mobilisation of human recourses, democratic deficit) and new measures are proposed or implemented (e.g. stimulating parental/student involvement and participation, investment in social skills and citizenship competencies, empowerment). The contributions of this section focus on the tensions between educational concerns with regard to social justice and equality, governmental interests and strategies to mobilise human capital, new conceptions

of social justice, identity and equity, and the links between educational reasoning and exclusion.

Quality, accountability, control
In past decades, the notion of 'quality of education' has been of major importance to justify education policies. However, it has been noticed that this concern for quality is mainly about an obsession with (financial) efficiency and effectiveness (e.g. attainment targets, standards, and the optimal performance of teachers and schools). Closely related to policies in the name of quality are policies aiming at increasing accountability (e.g. holding schools or teachers accountable for their performance, stimulating managerial and market accountability). From an educational perspective, the contributions in this section discuss the consequences of these modes of regulation, emerging contradictions (between quality and equality), the dominant rationales behind and politics related to quality assurance, accountability and control, and adoption of these new control mechanisms by teachers and schools.

Teacher professionalism
In many countries and regions the professionalisation of teachers has become an explicit policy target, and thus no longer merely the responsibility of autonomous, specialised institutions. Closely related to the challenges of quality and accountability (e.g. standards for teacher training institutions, performance appraisal in schools) and lifelong learning (e.g. sustainable employability), professional work in schools is the target of regulation and control. Hence, in terms of controlling and developing professionalism, and supported by specific teacher training discourses, governments actually change the scene of teaching and the role of teachers. The contributions in this section bring about a de-familiarisation with these policy ideas and regulations on professionalisation, and focus on issues such as de-professionalisation, reduced autonomy, managerialism, micro-politics and the political and discursive constitution of teacher professionalism.

Acknowledgements

Allow us to close this preface with an expression of our gratitude. First, we need to thank the Flemish Research Council (FWO) and the University of Leuven (Belgium) and in particular the Group Human Sciences for offering Maarten Simons research grants to prepare the book, together with Mark Olssen at the University of Surrey (UK) and Michael Peters at the University of Illinois at Urbana-Champain (US). Additionally, we must express our gratitude to the University of Wisconsin at Madison (US) and the Department of Curriculum and Instruction for the Honory Fellowship (supported by the University of Leuven, Belgium, Group Human Sciences) that enabled Maarten Simons to work on completing the introduction and to edit the manuscript. Special thanks must be expressed to Tom Popkewitz for help with orientation issues in a field of study that is not "exactly" a field of study. Last but not least we want to thank Ilse Geerinck,

Karine Hindrix, Judith McFarlane, Liselotte Vandeperre, Anneleen Verckens, Joris Vlieghe and Bartel Wilms for their support during the editorial work.

Some of the chapters appearing in this book have been published elsewhere, and appear with the much-appreciated permission of the original publishers. The original reference and publisher is mentioned clearly in these papers.

REFERENCES

Bauman, Z. (2000). *Globalization: The human consequences.* Cambridge: Polity Press.

Bourdieu, p. (2008). *Political interventions: Social science and political action.* London: Verso.

Derrida, J. (2001). *L'université sans conditions.* Paris: Galilée.

Dewey, J. (1927/1954). *The public and its education.* New York: Holt.

Fairclough, N. (2001). The discourse of new Labour: Critical discourse analysis. In M. Wetherell, S. Taylor, & S. Yates (Eds.), *Discourse as data. A guide for analysis* (pp. 229–266). London: Sage Publication.

Foucault, M. (1980). Entretien avec Michel Foucault. In D. Defert, F. Ewald, & J. Lagrange (Eds.), *Dits et écrits IV 1980–1988* (pp. 104–110). Paris: Gallimard.

Foucault, M. (2000). Interview with Michel Foucault. In M. Foucault (Ed.), *Power: Essential works of foucault, Vol. III* (J. D. Faubion, Ed., & R. Hurley et al., Trans.) (pp. 239–297). New York/London: Penguin.

Foucault, M. (2001). *L'herméneutique du sujet. Cours au Collège de France (1981–1982).* Paris: Gallimard.

Latour, B. (2004a). Why has critique run out of steam? From matters of fact to matters of concern. *Critical Inquiry, 30,* 225–248.

Latour, B. (2004b). *Politics of nature: How to bring the sciences into democracy.* London: Harvard University Press.

Latour, B. (2005). From Realpolitik to Dingpolitik or how to make things public. In B. Latour & p. Wiebel (Eds.), *Making things public. Atmospheres of democracy* (pp. 14–41). Karlsruhe and Cambridge: ZKM & MIT Press.

Latour, B., & Sanchez-Criado, T. (2007). Making the 'Res Public'. Ephemera. Theory & Politics in Organization, 7(2), 364–371.

Masschelein, J. (2004), How to conceive of critical educational theory today? *Journal of Philosophy of Education, 38*(3), 351-367

Marres, N. (2005). Issues spark a public into being. A key but often forgotten point of the Lippmann-Dewey debate. In B. Latour & p. Wiebel (Eds.), *Making things public. Atmospheres of democracy* (pp. 208–217). Karlsruhe and Cambridge: ZKM & MIT Press.

Rabinow, p. (2003). *Antropos today. Reflections on modern equipment.* Princeton, NJ: Princeton University Press.

Rancière, J. (2005). *La haine de la démocratie.* Paris: La fabrique.

INTRODUCTION CHAPTERS

MAARTEN SIMONS, MARK OLSSEN & MICHAEL PETERS

RE-READING EDUCATION POLICIES

PART 1: The Critical Education Policy Orientation

INTRODUCTION

The aim of this first part of two introduction chapters is to discuss features of critical studies of education policy within the broader field of policy studies. The point of departure is the so-called "policy orientation" in social research, and the emergence of policy analysis and its concern within the welfare state. The genre of critical education policy studies at the beginning of the 1980s was mainly rooted in the research tradition interested in the power, politics and social regulation in and around schools, and particularly confronting the crisis of the welfare state. Echoing the term 'policy orientation', we want to introduce the notion *critical education policy orientation* to describe the distinctive scope of these studies. In this chapter we will not present either detailed definitions of or illuminate linkages between the main concepts in research traditions. The aim instead is to offer some general overviews of approaches and discussions.

The first section of the introduction presents a short overview of the so-called policy orientation; the emergence of policy sciences, the role of policy research in the welfare state, the challenges posed to rationalist conceptions of policy making, and the emergence of a critical concern with education policy, power and politics in education. In the second section we give a classical account of the different approaches adopted in policy studies in order to describe the emergence of the critical education policy orientation in the third section. The fourth section explores this orientation in more detail by focusing on three main features: the underlying educational, social and/or moral concern, the broad conception of education policy, and the forms of critical advocacy adopted. In the concluding section of this chapter we have chosen to discuss the particular limits of policy research by exploring the challenges posed to the role of research and knowledge within democratic societies. While this first part of the introduction limits itself to the recent past of critical education policy research, Part 2 will discuss current challenges and offers an overview of some of the theoretical and analytical frameworks that are used in research.

THE POLICY ORIENTATION: A BRIEF OVERVIEW

Depending on the lenses adopted, the history of research on policy is either a long history or quite a short history. One could go back to the advice given to the

M. Simons, M. Olssen and M.A. Peters (eds.), Re-Reading Education Policies: A Handbook Studying the Policy Agenda of the 21st Century, 1–35.

princes, or even to the ancient moral and political philosophies pertaining to the organisation of city states. Or one could focus on the *Polizeiwissenschaften* ('police sciences') in eighteenth century Europe, the gradual emancipation of the social sciences with a strong political and state-centred interest from moral philosophies in the nineteenth century, the economic and defence related studies and calculations during the World War II, and finally the emergence and development of 'policy sciences' in the second part of the twentieth century.

Within the limited scope of this introduction we will adopt the short term perspective here, particularly attending to the policy orientation in the social sciences after World War II. This orientation referred to the social science focus on public policy both as a domain of study and as a practice in need of scientific knowledge to improve itself (cf. Wagner et al., 1991; Parsons, 1995). Despite the fact that the roots of critical studies of education policy are very diverse, it is worth mentioning this brief history of the policy orientation. In fact, an overview of the *problem solving* policy orientation helps to understand the different background of what could be regarded as the *critical* education policy orientation. In this overview we will switch between discussing the broader social and political context of the development of policy research, and the theoretical developments within policy research.

a) The policy sciences

It was the book *The Policy Sciences*, edited by Lerner and Lasswell in 1951, that can be regarded as programmatically setting the scene for the social sciences' orientation to public policy in the welfare state. Especially after the devastating effects of World War II, with the expansion of communism and the economic crisis, social scientists in the West were eager to actively support the development of the western democratic state and its public policy. Lerner and Lasswell's book thus expresses western social scientists' commitment to improve the social and democratic basis of the state by studying issues related to such phenomena as full employment, equality, and peace, and to optimise the effectiveness of public administration and organisational structures.

It is important to stress here that the role of policy sciences was defined in close relation to a particular belief in the role of public policy. In Parson's (1995, p. 6) words, this involves a change in "(...) the role of the state (...) to manage the 'public' and its problems so as to deal with those aspects of social and economic life which markets were no longer capable of solving." The policy orientation thus assumed that the modern, democratic state and in particular its public policy, are in need of specialist knowledge to improve its functioning or to reach its goals. The particular Lasswellian policy orientation of the social sciences can be summarised in terms of five characteristics[1]:

– they are multi-disciplinary given the nature of the complex social problems, and they should focus on the general picture instead of addressing small, *ad hoc* problems, and combining work from sociology, law, economics, politics...;

- the policy sciences include a value orientation, and it is important to clarify the values implied in policy and those embraced by the scientist. Furthermore, the scientist should say clearly which solution is better than others, although the research itself should be conducted objectively;
- there is a clear focus on the context, that is, the attempt to recognise the contextuality of the policy process, policy options and policy outcomes and hence, using not only quantitative methods but qualitative methods as well;
- the orientation has two components: "the development of a science of policy forming and execution" and "the improving of the concrete content of the information and the interpretations available to policy makers" (Lasswell, 1951 in Wagner et al., 1991, p. 8). The first component refers to the "analysis of the policy process" and the second one includes the "analysis in and for the policy process" (Parsons, 1995, p. xvi). The distinction comes close to the often used, although scrutinised, distinction between analysis *of* policy and analysis *for* policy (see further below);
- the integration of knowledge, the organisation of teaching and the organisation of new institutions to bring policy scientists and policy makers into contact, and hence to actually contribute to the optimisation of public policy and consequently to the democratisation of society.

These characteristics clearly indicate on the one hand the academic belief in the development of social science knowledge relatively independent from particular, ad hoc interests, and on the other hand the instrumental and political belief that such knowledge could be utilised in the process of policy making and problem solving in society and in state administration. Indeed, in later work, Lasswell introduces the term "policy process", regards problem-solving as a main focus of public policy, and stresses that the distinctive scope of the policy scientist is that s/he is "problem-oriented" (Lasswell, 1970 in Parsons, 1995, p. 19). The particular focus on the 'analysis of the policy *process*' should be regarded as an alternative to the classical political scientists' focus on constitutions, administration, legislatures, etc.

Except for Lasswell's formulation of the stages in the policy process in 1956, and related to what he later would call "the decision process", there are the important contributions of Herbert Simon, Charles Lindblom and David Easton during the 1950s and 1960s (Parsons, 1995, pp. 21–29; Deleon, 1999, pp. 20–21). With respect to decision making, in the field of policy as well as in other fields, Simon focused on the "bounded" character of rational decision making, especially in organisations, taking into account both intellect and affect, through the stages of "intelligence, design and choice." As an alternative to the rational models of Lasswell and Simon, Lindblom introduced the idea of "incrementalism" in relation to the policy process. Questioning whether policy making could fit into a model, he developed the "science of muddling through." Lindblom stressed that decision-making and change is often incremental, not theoretically driven, and involves trial and error. Finally, it is important to mention the influence of Easton, who developed a model of the "political system", and the "intra-societal" and "extra-societal" environment, in order to analyse the process of policy making and the outputs of policy in a broader context. This combination of the stages or cycle model and the system approach became an often used tool in the analysis of public policies (cf. Wielemans & Berkhout, 1999).[2]

Notwithstanding the many theoretical differences and discussions, the policy sciences seem to inscribe themselves in the enlightenment project. They aim at the re-organisation of society through policy measures taken on the basis of scientific problem-solving rationality (see also Wittrock et al., 1991, pp. 28–29; Hammersly, 1994). Although there is a clear value-orientation, such as democratic values and the prevention of coercion, the epistemological and methodological assumptions of Lasswell and his contemporaries are clearly positivistic (that is, it is possible to reveal the nature of policy and decision making based on objective, empirical data or logical reasoning) and instrumental (to engineer policy based on positive knowledge of how it should be). This is foremost the case for the component 'analysis of and in the policy process', often referred to as policy analysis *strictu senso*, and to a lesser extent to the more academic and substance oriented 'analysis of the policy process'.[3]

b) Policy studies and the welfare state

Despite these programmatic statements, we should keep in mind that the policy sciences came to full development in the United States and Europe only during the 1960s and early 1970s. This development cannot be disconnected from the emergence of the "full-blown, interventionist welfare state" that follows the stage of the "late liberal state" and the "early restricted welfare state" (Wittrock et al. 1991, p. 79). Clearly, there has always been a connection between state power on the one hand and knowledge on the other hand. With the welfare state in the second part of the twentieth century an alliance between a particular kind of power and a particular kind of knowledge took shape (cf. Rose, 1999). The interventionist state relied on social planning, and indeed expected social scientists to support the general plans for social and economic change. Social scientists on their part aimed at giving their research relevance through welfare policies. In this context, "political arithmetic" emerged as a discipline. Not theoretically oriented, the discipline was mainly concerned with collecting data to support public policy, and hence inscribing itself in a social-democratic agenda of reform (Saha, 1997, p. 108; Hammersley, 1994, p. 141).

The close relation between policy and research is exemplified by the so-called 'educational planning', emerging at the end of the 1960s and defined by Coombs (1970, p. 14) as:

> Educational planning, in its broadest generic sense, is the application of rational, systematic analysis to the process of educational development with the aim of making education more effective and efficient in responding to the needs and goals of its students and society. Seen in this light, educational planning is ideologically neutral.

Educational planning hence regards itself as a system-based and strongly economically oriented analytical approach offering the necessary information basis for
social and education policy and modern administration. Claiming it is ideologically
neutral, educational planning considers itself to be an indispensable calculating tool
in the development of the welfare state. Also worth mentioning here is the
orientation towards education policy in the context of comparative educational
research, or at least the attempt to use comparison as a tool to generate adequate
information for planning (see Zajda, 2005).

Although it is beyond the scope of this introduction to compare the context of
the United States with the contexts in other countries (see Wittrock et al., 1991), it
helps to picture the scene by mentioning some differences. It is important to keep
in mind that the state in the US could rely upon a well-developed empirical and
applied oriented social science base that was related to the universities. In Europe
on the other hand the academic establishment and development of the social
sciences, in particular those with a clear policy orientation and relevance, arose
from the very start in close relation to the urgent governmental request for expertise.
Nevertheless, in Europe there was actually a rather strong academically based field
of study on administration and state bureaucracy. Despite the important national
differences, one could say that from the 1960s onwards welfare reform and
intellectual reform become clearly connected in an atmosphere of social planning.
Social policy scientists and politicians seemed to share the same agenda and
worked closely together (cf. John, 1998, pp. 4–5).

By the end of the 1970s however, that 'contract' and consensus on definitions of
problems came to an end. There was at least some hesitation from scientists and
scholars to having a close interaction with policy makers. The contradictions of the
supported welfare reforms, and their limited impact, opened up room for scholars
to take distance and in addition generated new themes and topics for policy
sciences. At the same time, the neoliberal and neoconservative policies (under
Reagan and Thatcher) started actively questioning the role and value of the social
sciences, and in particular those closely linked to the welfare state. As a result: "In
most European countries it can no longer be assured, as seemed the case in the
1960s, that the spheres of policy making and research have a common concept of the
nature of societal problems and of the role of research in ameliorating them"
(Wittrock et al., 1991, p. 59).

Despite the less evident relation, the social sciences increasingly became
exposed to "state-directed science policies" (policies they helped to create or at
least supported during the 1960s), and related initiatives such as "new policy-
oriented research institutions" and "the expansion of markets for ministerial
contract research" (Wagner et al., 1991, p. 11). In view of this close connection,
the agenda setting and funding of much policy-oriented social research was largely
in the hands of governments particularly applying the Lasswellian component
'analysis in and for the policy process.' Other critical social scientists, still
concerned with a policy orientation, were not without influence and played a role
in the (academic) margins. Here, the sociology of education, and particularly
critical studies relying on Marxist and Weberian intellectual traditions, started to

play an increasing role in the critical and social analysis of education policy and politics. Additionally, with the advent of the 'new sociology of education', and new concepts on power and politics, the tradition of political arithmetic and quantitative, statistical policy analysis was discussed.

In relation to these critical movements, it is important to make a short reference to the elaboration of critical theory by Horkheimer in the 1930s and 1940s (and later on by Adorno, Marcuse, Habermas and others) (see Horkheimer, 1931, 1939). The intention of this theory, displaying parallels to Lasswell's project in the US, was the development of interdisciplinary social research that would meet the criteria of genuine Enlightenment science. Its aim was to combine empirical work and philosophical reflection, yet at the same time having a clear political engagement, and playing an emancipatory role. However, there was no explicit orientation to public policy, and no project supporting state policies in changing society. Relying on a Marxist background, the social reform agenda here was not predominantly state or policy orientated, but was linked with social movements, cultural change and education, and subscribed to a universalistic, enlightenment agenda. Or, as Wittcock et al. indicate, "Horkheimer's point of departure was an explicit rejection of pragmatic epistemology, which he argued would prove incompatible with the preservation of such integrity [the universalistic claims of knowledge inherent in the tradition of the Enlightenment]" (ibid., p. 62).[4] During the sixties and seventies, critical social theory and political philosophy came to be focused on education policy, as part of broader social and political reform projects. It is important to mention however that policy was not often the main research focus. Policy and the problematic of 'the state' played a role in the broader debates on the role of education in social control and equal opportunities and/or reproduction of inequality (cf. Saha, 1997, pp. 106–107) (see further below).

This short historical overview indicates how the policy orientation originated in the United States, and that the interest for education policy was part of the broader concern of scientists and policy makers to improve the information basis for welfare states policies: "For over century and a half, Americans have translated their cultural hopes and anxieties into demands for public school reform" (Heck, 2004, p. 3). Much of the education policy analysis in the United States, however, focused on improving decision making and applying quantitative, functionalist and policy-directed approaches. From the 1960s onwards there also emerged a clear focus on the broader context of the policy process, but this research was mainly concerned with evaluation and improvement. In the field of the political sciences in the United States, it is important to mention as well the research domain of the 'politics of education.' Research in this domain studies "the set of interactions that influence and shape the authoritative allocation of values" focusing on the concepts government, power, conflict and policy. As a field of study relying on political science concepts and behavioralist theories it became of central importance (Scribner & Englert, 1977, pp. 22–23).[5]

Most research on education policy in Europe was located within educational administration, public policy studies and comparative education. From the late 1970s onwards a substantial amount of critical research on education policy was done in the field of the new sociology of education – gradually labelled as "education policy sociology" (Ozga, 1987) – as well as in other fields of social, political and educational theory (Kogan, 1975; Prunty, 1985; Dale, 1989; Troyna, 1994a/b). Additionally, in both Europe and the United States, social and historical research on curriculum and social control became gradually oriented towards the problematic of the state and state governance. However, the impetus of the critical involvement towards education policy featured not only in academic debate but also in the changed political and social context of the 1980s. Indeed, the crisis of the welfare state, and of a particular kind of welfare policy, seemed to give rise to critical studies applying itself more straightforwardly on education policy (see further below).

At this point in the overview, we will switch from a focus on the social and political context of policy research to a focus on its theoretical and conceptual context.

c) The limits of rationalist conceptions

Different perspectives have been developed from the 1970s onwards in reaction to the technicist and positivist line of policy analysis, and the rationalist conception of policy making and the policy process (Parsons, 1995, pp. 434–455). Often, these perspectives have been attempts to link up again with the broader Lasswellian program of a "science of *democracy*." A short overview will clarify more precisely what is at stake.

Critical rationalists hold to a position in between that of the rational model of the policy process and that of an incrementalist viewpoint. Etzioni for instance develops the idea of an "active society" that is self-critical, where the public is involved in testing assumptions and developing knowledge and a community-based moral order. Dror holds more strongly to the rational model of policy making, however he includes "extra-rational" elements in his model in order to promote understanding of policy making and public policy decision making.

The *political rationalists*, including researchers such as Lindblom and Hogwood, criticise the position of rationalist policy analysis, and argue that policy analysis should not replace the political process but complement political argumentation and discussion:

> The quality of public policy depends on a vast network of thought and interaction, in which professional policy analysts play a small role. (...) In principle, those who analyse public policy can help to challenge aspects of the policy-making process that obstructs wise policy making, can help to broaden the range of changes under consideration, and can help to deepen political debates about problems, opportunities, and policy options (Lindblom & Woodhouse, 1993, p. 137 in Parsons, 1995, p. 438).

According to Parsons, the *forensics* developed a third kind of critical reaction towards the rational model of the policy process. For them, policy analysis is more similar to "legal investigation" than about using rational, scientific techniques to find the truth. For example, policy analysis is concerned with "telling stories" (Rein), and what is important in this viewpoint is the persuasiveness of arguments. Others argue that policy analysis should be regarded as a kind of jurisprudential analysis (Dunn), and claim that it is rational to the extent that it is possible to develop a framework and rules to test arguments and make choices. What these approaches have in common is that positivistic assumptions are left behind and the adoption of post-positivistic, interpretative approaches is preferred (cf. Fischer, 1998; DeLeon, 1997; see also Taylor et al., 1997, p. 38).

Also, *managerialists* criticise the overly rational model of the policy process and policy making. They do so by introducing new analytical techniques from the business sector. By the 1990s, the management orientation has become dominant and in its form as New Public Management it has overtaken to a large degree public policy (Pollitt, 1990). In view of that development, policy analysis has become integrated as a technique within the general framework of public sector management, and supporting or replacing political decision making. Current versions of evidence-based policy are closely linked up with this management orientation (see further below). Similar to rationalist views on policy making, one of the major opponents of the managerial point of view is politics in public policy and decision-making:

> What managerialism shares with the rationalist mentality is a belief that *'politics'* is not an effective mode of decision-making. Managerialism (especially when allied to 'public choice' theory) in this sense represents an on-going search to take decision-making out of the world where there are conflicts over values and beliefs into a realm where decisions can be made in a more rational (non-political) way (Parsons, 1995, p. 454, italics in original).

Finally, *critical theorists* refer to a group of scholars (Forester, Considine, Fischer, Dryzeck among others) who support the idea that policy analysis should be driven by a strong commitment to social change and equality. The basic premise is that decision making should be an open process, where knowledge and claims are open to critique and promote empowerment of citizens. In line with some of the ideas of Lasswell on democracy as well as with critical theory, and in particular the work of Habermas on communicative action, scholars announce the "argumentative turn in policy analysis" (Fischer & Forester, 1993; see also the forensics). Furthermore, the importance of argument and the focus on assumption is linked to a commitment to openness, critique and emancipation.

Dryzeck for instance stresses in line with Habermas the importance of communicative rationality as an alternative for instrumental rationality. Rational policy analysis, according to Dryzeck, is a particular kind of instrumental rationality. He disagrees however with the two common alternatives of the rational and instrumental model: political rationality (and the incrementalist position) and market rationality (and the managerial position). Instead, he proposes a communicative rationality where "the only remaining authority is that of a good argument" in an open discussion on an equal basis, and where instrumental, strategic or power-related and economic interests play no decisive role (Dryzek,

1990, p. 15). According to Dryzek, the insistence on the public character of decision-making, open debate and democratic values is close to the original inspiration of Lasswell and his idea of a policy science that is actually a science of democracy.

d) The problematic of education policy, politics and power

Based on the previous historical sketch and the listing of approaches, we have some grounds to start describing the problematic within which the critical interest for education policy emerged. The problematic will be outlined along four dimensions: the focus on the policy context and critical advocacy, the reliance on sociology of education and political theory, the concern for education and public policy, and the critical stance towards knowledge-policy alliances.

Firstly, the distinction between the 'analysis of the policy process' and the 'analysis for and in the policy processes' can be regarded as a first general attempt to bring some order in the studies of public policy: the understanding of policy, policy making and its content and related institutions and procedures on the one hand, and the concern for improving policies, decision making and problem-solving on the other hand. The research that can be placed under the general banner of critical education policy studies shares the first concern. However, in line with the critical theorists discussed earlier, there is also a commitment to actually influence education policymaking, focusing on both democratic procedures and content. But contrary to rationalist approaches, most critical studies do not embrace the problem-solving attitude and refuse to rely on how policies frame problems (cf. Marshall & Gerstl-Pepin, 2005). Furthermore, these studies do not share a rigid positivist and instrumental distinction between on the one hand policy analysis/studies (focusing on means and optimal allocation with a neutral stance towards aims or goals) and on the other hand policy advocacy (where the focus is on the sphere of values and goals) (Prunty, 1985; Taylor et al., 1997, p. 18). Concerned with the moral and social role of education and accepting the political and cultural dimension of both policy means and ends, these critical studies often combine analysis and critical advocacy.

Secondly, it is important to keep in mind that education policy was and still is a domain that is not ranked highly on the research agenda of political scientists. This is described by Raab (1994, pp. 19–20) as follows:

> It is possible that a certain academic disdain has left research on education, and perhaps particularly on schooling, mainly to the 'mere' teachers and their educators who were steeped in its practice, placing it out of contention as a 'serious' political science. Although education is now an issue area of the first rank on governmental and party agendas, and in public debate, it remains the case that few political scientists with an inclination to policy studies have it clearly in their sights.

This remains to a large extent a common attitude in the second part of the 1990s as well as the beginning of the twenty-first century. The central role attributed to education in the 'knowledge society and economy', and the transformation of education policy and governance in a global context, increasingly seems to open up education policy for political scientists. Nevertheless, when we refer to critical studies in education policy we are mainly speaking about the research that is rooted in the new sociology of education or critical political theory tradition, as well as the research of educationalists with a policy inclination. This specific background adds a particular dimension to education policy studies as we will describe below.

Thirdly, and in line with the previous remark, there is a particular interest among researchers in the field to consider education policy as part of public policy, or even the other way around; because of the interest in 'education and the public' they orient their research towards politics and policy. In the context of education the term public can of course have different meanings; referring to the sector or domain, the source of funding, the mode of access, the type of control, the nature of the problems of policy, the aim of education, and so on. Clearly, what is assumed in all these welfare definitions of 'public' is that education is a justified domain for policy intervention. Additionally, it is assumed that changing policy is the way to reform education and to change society accordingly. The close relation between academic and political agendas in the 1960s is a clear example of this assumption. But the tension between these agendas in the 1980s and 1990s could also be regarded as an example. In fact, the critical orientation towards education policy was very closely linked with advocating a new, progressive policy agenda. And at this point, it is important to remember that these studies incorporated mainly "a critical and sometimes politically committed sociology", and that "adherents ignored or rejected 'mainstream' political science and policy studies perspectives that were deemed positivist or wedded to powerful controlling interests" (Raab, 1994, pp. 20–21).

Fourthly, part of the emergence of critical research focusing explicitly on education policy from the 1980s was the questioning of the assumptions and strategic use of instrumental research on policies (Prunty, 1985; Young, 1999, pp. 678–679). First, and embracing some of the alternative approaches to the rational approach mentioned earlier, critical studies focus on the context of decisions and how problems are constructed or framed. Similarly, the view that planning and implementation can easily be managed based upon knowledge is scrutinised, as is the idea that deciding on the optimal solution for policy problems is a value-free activity. Second, the alliances between rational policy research on the one hand and education policy making on the other hand become themselves the object of critical studies. For example, the 'ideologies' of positivist, behaviourist and instrumental research have been questioned because they are used by policy makers to criticise those being governed for their irrational behaviour, or because these studies, while ignoring values, in fact support the status quo (Prunty, 1985, p. 133). Thus the relation between policy and research, and between power and knowledge, becomes itself an important focus for critical studies.

In order to contextualise the critical approaches in the study of education policy, it is helpful to switch again to the problematic of general frameworks adopted in policy studies.

GENERAL FRAMEWORKS FOR POLICY STUDIES

A useful way to grasp the diversity of policy studies is to list the analytical framework or frames of analysis that have been employed. We draw upon the classification of eight frameworks by Parsons (1995), although there are other often similar classifications (e.g. Bobrow & Dryzek, 1987; John, 1998; Heck, 2004; Howlett & Ramesh, 2003). In this overview, the focus is on policy studies in general. Critical studies of education policy are discussed afterwards.

- welfare economics
- public choice
- information processing
- social structure
- political process
- comparative politics
- management
- political philosophy

Scholars often combine several frameworks, yet it is useful to discuss the distinctive focus of each of them (Parsons, 1995, pp. 32–54).

Welfare economics, which mainly inspires analysis for and in the policy process, is rooted in the idea that markets are not always able to distribute recourses efficiently, and that in view of market failures political institutions can intervene to correct social problems. Against this background, welfare economics is basically concerned with finding the most efficient way to intervene based on cost-benefit analysis. In other words, the main concern here is to generate knowledge that promotes the organisation of welfare policies in an 'economic' way.

Public choice theory can be regarded as a strong version of rational choice theory. Economic actors are regarded as calculating agents who are focussed on the maximisation of satisfaction/utility. Public choice theory assumes that political actors, that is politicians, civil servants as well as voters, are "rational utility maximisers" (Buchanan) who are guided by self-interest and thus do not act, as naively believed, on behalf of a kind of public interest. In view of this perspective, the policy process and policy making is explained in terms of rent-seeking behaviour, and in terms of actors who seek power, prestige and popularity. The resulting extension of state and welfare provision is criticised for distorting the more optimal handling of allocation through markets. Hence, what is proposed is the application of economics to political science. Thus the main concern is to judge public policy in terms of rational, that is economic, choices.

According to Bobrow and Dryzek, the analysts within the framework of *information processing* "share an interest in how individuals and organisations (...) arrive at judgements, make choices, deal with information, and solve problems" (Bobrow & Dryzek in Parsons, 1995, p. 35). This framework is not restricted to a single academic discipline; it uses insights from psychology, information science, artificial intelligence and organisational behaviour. The focus on the psychological component in policy-making and the "psycho-pathologies of power" by Lasswell is an important perspective here, as well as the ideas of Herbert Simon on "bounded rationality" and the way decision making and problem solving takes place within given cognitive limits. Hence, the approaches within this framework are concerned with the analysis of the role of information in decision making, with a view to optimising policy making through optimising decision making.

The *social structure* framework refers to the contribution of sociological theory to policy analysis, and consequently it covers a very broad field. The field ranges from the analysis of social problems (and particularly the construction of social problems in lifecycle approaches), the analysis of power in society and organisations, and the sociology of knowledge studying the role of knowledge in institutions, politics and policy. Additionally, particularly in the United States, functionalist sociology influenced research of the policy process. The concern of this framework is to look at the social dimension of policies and policy making, and to explain and/or understand policies, their making and their effects in relation to social structures.

The *political process* framework collects approaches that look at the political context of policies and politics in policy and policy making. Parsons distinguishes between six approaches:

- stagist approaches: the analysis of policy as a process with different stages, from agenda to evaluation (e.g. Jones, Hogwood);
- pluralist-elitist approaches: the analysis of the distribution of power among (elite) groups and how they influence or make policy (e.g. Dahl, Lindblom, Lukes);
- neo-Marxist approaches: the analysis of ideology, hegemony, repression and contradictions in policy-making, and the link between different levels in the political/policy system (e.g. Miliband, Poulanzas, Offe);
- sub-system approaches: the analysis of policy-making at the level of networks, communities and the influence of sub-systems and their institutions (e.g. Rhodes, Atkinson & Coleman, Baumgartner & Jones, Sabatier & Jenkins-Smith);
- policy discourse approaches: the analysis of policy-making at the level of language, discourse and communication (e.g. Fischer, Forester);
- institutionalism (economic, sociological or political): analysis of the constitutional and institutional spaces and arrangements in which policy takes place, and relying on economics (e.g. transaction cost economics, agency theory), organisational sociology (Di Maggio & Powell, March & Olsen, Selznick) or political theory and historical accounts (Skocpol, Hall).

The *comparative public policy* framework includes different approaches to the study of public policy by comparing 'what, why, how and with what effects' different governments 'do something or do not'. In these comparisons, different approaches are adopted: socio-economic approaches regard public policy as the result of economic and social factors, party government approaches study the role of party competition and partisan control, class struggle approaches focus on how political forms of class struggle result in particular policies, neo-corporatist approaches take organised interests as points of departure in explaining differences in policy, and institutionalist approaches focus on the role of the state and social institutions.

The most pronounced impact on policy studies comes from the *managerial* framework. Important here is the application of managerial thought and techniques to public administration. This happened under the impetus of the financial crisis at the end of 1970s and consequently the transformation of public policy by public management interests and the adoption of techniques and procedures commonly used in the private/profit sector. The work of Drucker (1954, 1964, 1969) and the technique of Management by Objectives played a significant role here, as did the ideas of Osborne and Gaebler (1992) on "entrepreneurial government" and the revolutionary restructuring of the US public sector, called the "American Perestroika." By the end of 1980s, there is the rise of what is called New Public Management, a general term referring to the application of techniques such as written contracts and performance agreements, short term employment contracts, new and multiple forms of accountability, client/customer orientations, and so on. Hence, this framework includes both a strong reform agenda and an analytical gaze that looks at public policy problems in terms of managerial problems related to efficiency, effectiveness, economy, objectives and clients.

Finally, public policy has been discussed in great detail and for a long time by *political philosophers* and *social theorists*. It is impossible to mention the ethical, methodological, normative and theoretical discussions in detail here; even distinguishing main approaches would be difficult. Additionally, it is important to keep in mind that the empirical policy sciences typically proclaim themselves as emancipated from these speculative theories and philosophies. Nevertheless, the framework still plays an important role, and specific philosophies, theories and methodologies often inspire approaches within the frameworks mentioned earlier.

In line with Parsons (1995, pp. 41–54) we could mention Machievelli and Bacon as the first modern theorists reflecting on the rationale and aims of the art of governing. Furthermore, it is worth mentioning the utilitarianism of Bentham and Mill for they introduced an utilitarian calculus in regard to social and political frameworks, and in a way they are the predecessors of cost-benefit analysis during the twentieth century. The pragmatists Dewey and James could be mentioned as articulating conceptions of democracy and problem solving, and as clearly inspiring the Lasswellian program of the sciences of democracy. Political theorists and philosophers such as Rawls and Nozick, with their view on justice, property and the (re)distribution of good/justice, undoubtedly encouraged approaches which link policy studies to broader themes of social justice and the scope and limits of social/reform policies. Another example is Hayek, whose ideas as a (neo)liberal juridical and economic theorist on the free market and on human freedom and the limits of social planning strongly influenced current versions of public management and public choice theory, and played a role in the neoconservatism of Thatcher and Reagan. Still another inspiration is the work of social theorists such as Etzioni on communitarianism and Habermas on communicative rationality. Part of their influence is related to stressing again the democratic dimension of public policy and its creation, and accordingly redefining the critical role of the policy analysis. Also worth mentioning is the work of so-called post-structuralist authors such as Foucault, with his conception of power-knowledge regimes, and his analysis of governmentality. Giddens' ideas on structuration and Bourdieu's conception of discursive policy fields and different forms of capital reproduction, have been influential as well. They played a role in developing analytic tools to focus both on structure and agency in relation to policy making.

FRAMEWORKS FOR EDUCATION POLICY STUDIES

The previous overview of approaches is not exhaustive, but we think it sufficiently illustrates the broad and very diverse intellectual background of research on public policy. This classification also helps to explore the approaches adopted by studies of *education* policies, and particularly the *critical* versions herein. For this exploration, we note Floden's (2007) distinction as a kind of meta-classification. Mainly referring to the United States context, Floden et al. identify three approaches in education policy analysis: economics, organisation theory and critical theory (cf. Fuhrman et al., 2007).

The *economic* approach includes the approaches listed earlier as welfare economics, public choice, perspectives within information processing theories, and some of the managerial perspectives. The main concern here is the rational analysis of the costs and benefits of education policy, as well as more general concerns with the economics of education. *Organisational theory* includes neo-institutional perspectives, perspectives focusing on decision making, and different perspectives on politics and conflict regarding organisation and administration, as well as the conventional and rational managerial and rational choice theories. The focus here is on the analysis and evaluation of organisational, administrative and political structures and procedures. The first two approaches are thus concerned with optimal organisation and administration on the one hand and rational/economic education policy analysis on the other hand.

The third approach mainly relies on frameworks within the social perspective approach, political process approaches and political philosophy and theory. Floden (2007) refers to this approach as *critical theory* in a broad sense. An important impetus here was the new sociology of education.[6] This new sociology of education, inspired by phenomenology, western Marxism and symbolic interactionism included a shift from statistical, quantitative research methods to qualitative, ethnographic methods. Hammersly (1994, pp. 142–144) distinguishes between three strands: critical ethnography (Keddie, Willis, and later feminist and antiracist approaches), qualitative curriculum evaluation and the teacher-action research movement (Stenhouse, Hamilton, Elliot among others) and interactionist ethnography (for example the work of Woods, Hargreaves, Ball, Hammersley).

The kind of critical policy orientation that emerged within these traditions was not only concerned with public policy (and what governments do), but the broader politics of education inside and outside schools. In other words, it oriented itself towards the politics of and within policy and the state with a view to understanding issues of power surrounding education. In line with the broadened field of study, these scholars not only petitioned policy makers and educational administrators with their research, but combined academic work, policy engineering and social criticism (Hammersley, 1994). Relying on research in school organisations and classroom interaction, and often closely related to teacher education programs, scholars started to address the work of teachers, the field of teacher education and the actors at other local levels of the education system.

In the United States context, as well as in Europe, neo-Marxist inspired forms of resistance theory (Aronowitz, Giroux) were developed and adapted from the end of the 1970s. Other important developments are critical curriculum theory (Apple), and poststructuralist inspired studies of governance through knowledge and subjectivation (Popkewitz), alongside the classic 'politics of education' field that was rooted in political theory and developed along the lines of micropolitical perspectives, political culture approaches and neo-institutionalism.[7] In the United Kingdom, Australia and New Zealand the critical orientation towards education policy was rooted in, for example, a critical ethnography of policy trajectories and forms of exclusion through knowledge definition and teaching methods (Ball, Bowe, Whitty, Edwards, Gewirtz) and various strands of cultural Marxism and critical theory (Prunty, Ozga, Codd, Lingard). Additionally, from political theory, new versions of Marxist political theory (and state/conflict) theory have been developed in order to understand education policy and state governance (Dale), as well as state-centred comparative approaches (Green, Neave). Later on, there were several elaborations of French post-structuralist perspectives, and combinations with critical theory and Marxism (Marshall, Peters, Pongratz, Lindblad, Olssen, Usher, Edwards).[8]

In short, these studies distance themselves from the kind of education policy analysis or policy research that was oriented towards the improvement of existing policies and administration, the evaluation of reform programs and the support or development of (public) management tools and procedures. Instead, these studies examine the development of education policy, its content and justifications, the impact of its broader social context and its relation to power and politics in schools. Their aim is to reveal contradictions, tensions, or general patterns and contingent or structural assemblages (see Marshall & Peters, 1999 for an overview).

Despite the diversity, and despite what has been referred to as a condition of "theoretical eclecticism" (Ball, 1997; Ozga, 2000; Taylor, 1997; Vidovich, 2002), what these studies share is the concern to put education policy in a broader social context or the context of social and political regulation. In fact, one could argue that the critical involvement with education policy is rooted in the older scholarly concern with education, power and with social regulation. When this kind of research, as a next step, started to focus on the overt and hidden form of power and politics related to the state and state governance, public policies came into view. Of course, during the 1960s, critical scholars had an interest in policy too, but either regarded it as an integral part of the criticised state apparatus or as a useful instrument to reform education and society. During the 1980s policy becomes itself an object of critical studies, and was no longer only regarded as a tool for social reform or a function of the oppressive state. This clarifies the point that the critical focus on policy can not be disconnected from the focus on politics and power, and ultimately, from values and debates on the social role of education.

Broadly speaking policy refers here to matters of interest, conflict and power, or to the games played in structured arenas and the effects or power of discourses. For instance, one can ask whose values start to play a role in education policy, how values and power are related to policy knowledge and how they are symbolised, which sorts of conditions lead to the imposition of these specific values, discourses and/or ideologies, and how a value-loaded policy text is debated and used in the practice of schooling and what the political contexts of the texts might be (cf. Taylor et al. 1997, p. 21). Or, one can focus on the historically assembled cultural configurations that generate the emergence of political arenas where particular challenges are framed as policy problems and where policy solutions are accordingly being discussed (Popkewitz, 1996). In short, the concern with education policy in this line of research is part of a focus on the broader politics of education, knowledge and culture, as well as the politics and power within education.

Despite the diversity between and debates among scholars with a critical education policy orientation, we do think it makes sense to speak about a kind of *critical education policy orientation* emerging at the end of the 1970s and beginning of the 1980s. Yet, the term policy is then used very broadly, it includes power, politics and policies, and is related to a concern for education in society – that is, 'the public and its education'. At one level, this is far removed from Lasswell's policy orientation, and the problem solving focus mentioned in the beginning of the chapter. However, at another level the critical education policy orientation is perhaps still close to that program, for underlying Lasswell's orientation towards public policy was a concern with democracy.[9] In the next section of the chapter, we will explore the critical orientation in more detail by discussing its main features.

THE CRITICAL EDUCATION POLICY ORIENTATION

Before the 1980s scholars in the sociology of education were mainly concerned with the study of the school and classroom (drawing upon interactionist and various kinds of behaviourist, positivistic approaches) or the economy (relying on functionalist, structuralist and neo-Marxist theories) (Ball, 1994a, p. 1; Torres & Antikainen, 2003). The educational reforms during the 1980s and 1990s, and specifically the confrontation with the neoliberal and neoconservative governments in the United States, United Kingdom and Australia and New Zealand, acted as a "catalyst" for the development of a new "genre of policy studies" (Troyna, 1994a, p. 3; Trowler, 1998). As mentioned earlier, perhaps this is not only a genre of policy studies, but is also a genre within the longstanding scholarly concern with power and politics within education.

Focusing on the context and impact of the educational reforms, and relatively ignored by regular political and social scientists, educationalists and sociologists of education hence developed from the 1980s onwards their own particular policy orientation (see Prunty, 1984, 1985). Although this orientation was not grounded in a firm disciplinary basis, there are several features characteristic of the research conducted during the 1980s and 1990s. We will discuss the following features: a) the educational, moral and social concerns underlying the policy studies, b) the broad conception of policy, including politics, the mechanisms of power and the relation with the wider social context, and c) the diverse forms of critical advocacy. For each of these features, we will give some illustrations of theoretical approaches that will clearly articulate the diversity of the field of study. Other examples of approaches are discussed in Part 2 of the introduction.

a) Educational, moral and social concerns

The first characteristic is the involvement with issues of equality in education, the public role of education, social justice and critical pedagogy. These moral and political commitments appeared to be very strong in confrontation with policies that actively and explicitly sought to re-organise schooling based on the market and on managerial principles such as freedom of school choice, privatisation and deregulation, new forms of accountability and standardised curricula. Prunty expresses these concerns clearly when he argues from a "radical humanist" and "critical theory" perspective:

> (...) A critical analysis would be overtly political. The personal values and political commitment of the critical policy analyst would be anchored in the vision of a moral order in which justice, equality and individual freedom are uncompromised by the avarice of a few. The critical analyst would endorse political, social and economic arrangements where persons are never treated as a means to an end, but treated as ends in their own right (Prunty, 1985, p. 136).

Throughout the 1980s and 1990s other educationalists and sociologists developed a similar point of view, adding to this general description of the critical policy orientation. The common term used to refer to these studies in the United Kingdom, Australia and New Zealand was "education policy sociology", defined as a sociology "rooted in the social science tradition, historically informed and draw[ing] on qualitative and illuminative techniques" (Ozga, 1987, p. 14; Ball, 1990; Bowe et al., 1992; Trowler, 1998; Whitty, 2002). The description indicates clearly that these studies broke with the classical rational and instrumental tradition in policy analysis. They aimed to arrive at a comprehensive understanding of education policy making and its impact by adopting theories and methods from critical social theory. Moreover, the definition stipulates a view of research which aims at illuminating the practice of education and education policy making. Different focuses have been developed here. A quick overview would be helpful to clarify what was and is at stake.

Troyna (1994b) for example argued that the perspective on education policy should be broadened; it should not be limited merely to sociological research but should be regarded as part of "critical social research'. The latter, according to Troyna, drawing upon the work of Lee Harvey (1990) in this respect, is "guided by a commitment to go beyond the surface realities", and moreover "aims to identify those elements which have the potential to change things" (Troyna, 1994b, p. 72). In line with this broadening of the approach, Troyna argued that antiracist and feminist perspectives should be included, to "provide genuine support (...) in the struggle against the structural oppression of discernible groups" (ibid., p. 82). The term critical thus refers to both a particular theoretical and political stance.

In a similar way, although focusing less on the political struggle, Ball (1994a) stresses that the notion critical should not be limited to the use of a single theoretical framework or method, but should first and foremost be linked with a reflexive attitude on the part of the researcher and his/her particular concern with the broader social and educational context. Additionally, Ball emphasises the importance of focusing on the effects of policy making, thus combining research on the formulation and the implementation of policy. In view of this project:

> The task then, is to examine the moral order of reform and the relationship of reform to existing patterns of social inequality, bringing to bear those concepts and interpretive devices which offer the best possibilities of insight and understanding (Ball, 1994a, p. 2).

At the beginning of the 1990s several researchers stressed the importance of theory building. Additionally, they pleaded that the broader social, economic and political context of education policy making should be taken into account, and they warned against merely ad hoc research (Ozga, 1990; Dale, 1994; Ball, 1994b; see further below). However, there seems to be an agreement on the critical scope of the studies. The critical scope is clearly linked up with the specific role of education in society.

In this regard, writers like Prunty (1985, p. 136) and Taylor et al. (1997) state very clearly that as education and schooling have a particular moral dimension, and as discussions of values are always involved, the study of education policy is to a certain extent always critical (cf. Prunty, 1985; Lingard et al., 1993; Wielemans & Berkhout, 1998). It is argued that education cannot be disconnected from moral ideas about the individual and collective purposes of education, or from more abstract ideas about social justice and the cultural and political order. In a similar vein, Apple (1979) states that education is not a "neutral enterprise", and "that by the very nature of the institution, the educator was involved, whether he or she was conscious of it or not, in a political act" (p.1), and that what is needed is a "progressive articulation of and commitment to a social order that has at its very foundation (...) the maximisation of economic, social, and educational equality" (p. 11). Clearly, there is no agreement on what education should be about, and even at first sight equivocal terms such as democracy, participation and freedom are heavily debated.

In view of this, the point of departure for a large number of studies is that social and moral assumptions on education become visible in political debates and struggles especially at the level of the policies themselves:

Clearly, then, a major task of critical policy analysis must be to investigate the ways in which key terms are used, and the extent to which particular policies and practices are consistent with our moral vision for education. In this way, critical analysis is overtly political – it is anchored in a particular vision of a moral order (Taylor et al., 1997, p. 19).

Additionally, based on this overt political scope and in agreement with Prunty, the authors argue that "policy analysis needs to concern itself with the question of how progressive change might occur and the desirability of alternative policy options" (Taylor, 1997, p. 38). In a similar way, Ball states that policy and policy choices are related to a political agenda, that such an agenda can not be disconnected from values and ideologies, hence: "policies cannot be divorced from interests, from conflict, from domination or from justice" (Ball, 1990, p. 3).

It is important to note that the scholar's moral and political commitment to education can also take another form. Worth mentioning here is the critical orientation that is not directed in the first place towards policy (and state government) but towards education or schooling. This is the domain of critical and radical pedagogy, and related theories about the political and emancipatory role of education. Aronowitz and Giroux for example state that schools are sites of public service, promoting "critical literacy" and "cultural power" (Aronowitz & Giroux, 1994, p. 127). What is needed are "radical pedagogues" who acknowledge the "necessity of struggle in sites other than those influenced and controlled by the state" and who create "oppositional public spheres" for "transformative intellectuals – that is, intellectuals who are part of a specific class and/or movement and who serve to give it an awareness of its own function not only in the economic but also in the social and political fields" (ibid., pp. 130–131). The focus on schools as being not only a reproductive setting, but also a productive site, that is, a partly autonomous cultural institution of struggle, is linked with a reform agenda at school level (McLaren, 1989). In short, the focus here is not top-down, regarding policy reform as the main route to change society. Instead, the focus is bottom up, approaching education as the main site of change in society, including change of oppressive policies and the state apparatus.

Evidently, not all researchers within the genre of critical education policy studies define 'critical' in the same way, or draw the same consequences for the political, social or educational significance of their research. The section on critical advocacy will elaborate on these issues. At this point, we want to present some of the options taken regarding the concern that motivates critical research.

The concern can be articulated rather explicitly and straightforwardly. Using the words of Ozga (2000), policy research should not merely be research for policy but research into policy, and more specifically on the consequences of policy, on issues of power and politics surrounding education and on social justice, equality and individual freedom. However, a critical concern can also be more implicit, that is, part of the research process itself. Critical research can show for instance that what is taken for granted is part of a very particular configuration of power and knowledge (Popkewitz, 1991; Popkewitz & Brennan, 1998; Usher & Edwards, 1994). The term critic here does not refer to what should be done in education, society and by policy, but tries to open up new spaces for thought and action. And additionally, Popkewitz argues:

> To make the naturalness of the present as strange and contingent is a political strategy of change; to make visible the internments and enclosures of the commonsense of schooling is to make them contestable (Popkewitz, 2008, p. xv).

Despite the differences in intellectual strategies, what these studies share is that the scholarly orientation towards policy and power is embedded in a social, moral and/or educational concern. That is precisely one of the reasons why education policy is investigated in relation to power and politics, as we will elaborate in more detail in the next section.

b) Policy, power, politics and the wider context

A common view in policy analysis is to make a sharp distinction between politics on the one hand and policy and policy making on the other hand (cf. Prunty, 1985; Taylor et al., 1997; Lingard & Ozga, 2007; Ozga & Lingard, 2007). Politics then is regarded as a messy field of interests, conflicts and power, which is mainly concerned with discussing goals, strategic options and agendas. Policy on the other hand refers to the domain of rational decision making, as well as the efficient allocation of resources and optimal outcomes. The critical orientation in the study of policy clearly questions this distinction, and particularly the exclusion of politics from the sphere of policy. We will explore the roots and implications of the broad conception of policy in the following paragraphs by listing some examples.

Let us take the ideas of Prunty as the first example. The background of his concern, in line with the new sociology of education developed in the 1970s, is how oppression works in schools, especially through the three "message systems" identified by Bernstein (1971): "curriculum (what counts as knowledge), pedagogy (what counts as valid transmission of knowledge) and evaluation (what counts as valid realisation of knowledge)" (Prunty, 1985, p. 136). What is assumed in this type of research is that decisions on "what counts as knowledge" involves power and conflicts based on interests. Research along these lines allows the researcher to examine what happens in schools, and how this is linked with more general mechanisms of economic and social reproduction. Based on this, the focus is on the question of how administration and policies play a role in political mechanisms of power, conflict, interest and control/reproduction. Thus a rather particular critical policy orientation emerges here, clearly articulated by Prunty (1985, p. 135) as follows:

> (…) It must be recognised that much of the power and control exerted by the school administrator over classroom practice issues from, and is legitimated by, educational policy. Hence, many educational structures and procedures are manifestations of policy, and much of the school's administrator's work has to do with ensuring that policy is followed.

The orientation towards policy is thus rooted in the concern with both macro and micro mechanisms of reproduction in education, and ideas about alternative forms of schooling. This broad conception of policy becomes much clearer when we run quickly through some of the definitions and descriptions found in the literature.

In line with Easton and Anderson, Prunty defines policy very broadly as "the authoritative allocation of values", and he assumes that "on the bottom line, policy is the legitimation of values." He goes on: " (...) It draws our attention to the centrality of power and control in the concept of policy, and requires us to consider not only whose values are represented in policy but also how these values have become institutionalised" (ibid., p. 136). Additionally, and in line with Dye, some scholars add that the study of policy should focus on what is done, but also on what is not being done or on non-decision making (cf. Taylor et al., 1997, p. 22). Hence, the politics of education policy also plays a role in what is not being done. In a similar way, and explicitly mentioning the political dimension of policy, Codd offers the following definition:

> Policy (...) is taken to be any course of action (or inaction) relating to the selection of goals, the definition of values or the allocation of resources. Fundamentally, policy is about the exercise of political power and the language that is used to legitimate that process (Codd, 1988, p. 235).

In view of this, Rizvi (2006, p. 198) suggests not only focusing on how different policies work and on the effects of policies, but to focus as well on how the authority is developed and secured for governments to steer society, to deploy power and to develop policies.

At this point it is worth mentioning the versions of critical policy research embedded within political theory and more specifically critical theory and Marxist state theory. Dale (1989), for example, studies the "politics of education", that is, the way the broader social, economic and cultural context gives rise to particular state politics and education policies. His concern is how the needs of the economy and social expectations are translated into a policy agenda for schools, what the role of the state is in these translations, and he develops a critical policy orientation as an answer to the limited scope of classic reproduction theories (Dale, 1994, p. 37). Dale thus suggests focusing on the 'politics of education' next to the more narrow field of 'educational politics', that is, how actors within the field determine the policy agenda.

Several other conceptions of policy are worth mentioning, including cultural political perspectives, studies on the historic assemblage of social regulation, critical theory, system theory and public regulation.

In the United States, a critical orientation towards education policy came to development from the end of the 1970s onwards. More precisely, the focus shifted to the problematic of the state and the state's role in social regulation. In view of the perspective on power and conflict in schools, Giroux for instance suggests that schools no longer be viewed in line with Althusser's deterministic conception as being merely part of the "Ideological State Apparatuses" (Giroux, 1981, p. 18). His culturalist approach acknowledges the relative autonomous role of culture, interaction and knowledge production in social settings (Giroux, 1983). Additionally, in elaborating the classic sociological perspective that focused mainly on social control and reproduction, Apple focuses on the role of the state apparatus, and its relative autonomy.

Indeed, Apple observed at the beginning of the 1980s there had been no real interest in the role of the state in education except for the "predominantly liberal research on the 'politics of education'" (Apple, 1982, p. 29; pp. 120–134). The latter refers in the United States to a sub-discipline within the political sciences which focuses on the "authoritative allocation of values" (Scribner & Englert, 1977, pp. 22–23). Critical policy studies seek to take distance from this line of research. A scholarly concern with shifts in (federal) welfare policies emerges, particularly related to the Reagan/Bush administration. This critical orientation towards the state remains embedded within the broader interest in power and hegemony in schools. As mentioned earlier, the studies are often related to critical and radical pedagogy, rooted in the work and projects of Paulo Freire (1970) in Brazil and other versions of Central and South-American emancipatory education.

Though not directly involved in these discussions, one could argue that Popkewitz's approach in line with Foucault and Bourdieu, is another attempt to rethink and reconceptualise the problem of social regulation and consequently the problematic of the state (Foucault, 1996, p. 27; cf. 1991). In his research the relation between 'the state' and 'civil society' is not the point of departure. According to Popkewitz: "(...) These set of distinctions accept political rhetoric as the presupposition of analysis rather than making the rhetoric itself the focus of what is to be understood and explained." And hence he formulates his purpose as "an attempt to locate the state in the problematic of regulation (Popkewitz, 1996, p. 27). The main focus, and contrary to functionalist or Marxist accounts, is to study the production of actors, images and ideas, and their assemblage as a construction of governing; "this assemblage is neither evolutionary nor structural, but historically contingent" (ibid., p. 47). Concerned with the forms of power surrounding knowlegde and education, genealogical research includes a particular orientation to political and policy discourses.

A complete overview is beyond the scope of this introduction, but it is worth mentioning more European orientations towards politics and education policy. First, it is important to keep in mind the distinction between policy and politics is difficult to make in the French, German, Italian or Spanish languages. The notion 'policy' can not be translated, at least not in relation to 'politics' as is the case in English. The terms political and politics are mainly used, as well as broad conceptions of administration (cf. Parsons, 1995, pp. 13-14). With regard to education a strong social research tradition emerged in Germany focusing particularly on power and control in schools and society in parallel with the critical theory of Adorno and Habermas (Pongratz, 1989; Sünker & Krüger, 1999). Equally important in the German context are the system theoretical accounts of education (by Luhmann and others). In contrast to critical social theory, many of these theoretical accounts claim a sort of neutrality. The studies address manifestations of the logic of differentiation in society, including the consequences for the educational and political system (cf. Oelkers, 1989; Tenorth, 1992; Hermann, 1993; Vanderstraeten, 1997). In France, in line with the early work of Bourdieu and Passeron, and the genealogical work of Foucault, there has been an interest in the politics in and around schooling and the impacts of different kinds of public regulation and public action (except for research in education administration and *politique publique*) (van Zanten, 2005, Boussaguet et al., 2004; and for the French speaking part of Belgium: Maroy, 2006). The early sociological work of Bourdieu and Passeron, which assumed little room for policy to change education and society, played however a major role in the educationalist and intellectual distrust towards the field of policy and policy making (van Zanten, 2004).

The previous overview sufficiently indicates that the critical policy orientation as we define it here is not restricted to the analysis of public policy, or the policy produced by government. Based on the introduction of Lingard and Ozga (2007, p. 2) to the *RoutledgeFalmer Reader in Education Policy and Politics,* we will end this section with a useful overall picture of the domain of study:

- Education policy, as a field, in respect to schooling at least, deals with all texts, apart from curricula, which seek to frame, constitute and change educational practices (...);
- Education policy includes all sectors of education, (...) it includes policy produced in parts of the state other than education ministries;
- The totally pedagogised society (...) demands (...) the extension and refocusing of its [policy research] gaze (...);
- (...) We also include the processes involved in the production of policy text and those involved in its practice in our definition of education policy (...);
- [We] recognise that contestation is usually involved at all stages of production and implementation, as well as in relation to the discourses which frame the actual written text;
- (...) Policy texts are usually heteroglossic in character, discursively suturing together differing interests to achieve apparent consensus and legitimacy (...);
- If we work with a broad definition of politics as practices and discourses to do with power (in its structural sense, i.e., as concentrated and congealed, as well as in its poststructural sense, i.e. as dispersed, relational and practical forms) and questions of who benefits from particular social arrangements, then education policies are evidently political.

Thus critical policy studies focus both on the "politics of education policy" and on "education policy as politics" (Lingard & Ozga, 2007, p. 3). The former refers to the broader context of power, social arrangements and discourses around education within the national and global context. Policy here is regarded as part of the broader political context and social structures. The latter focuses on how state policy involves politics (interests, conflicts, power and control) in its formulation and implementation. Here, politics is approached as part of policy.

This is close to Dale's distinction between the 'politics of education' and 'education politics.' According to Dale, the latter can not be explained and understood in detail without understanding "the agenda for education and the processes and structures through which it is created" (Dale, 1994, p. 35). Although Dale has clearly some of Ball's work in mind here, Ball himself agrees with the need to find an optimal balance between both. The following description summarises precisely what is at stake:

> (…) The problem always remains that by focusing on the figures which move across the policy landscape we may neglect the geomorphology of the landscape itself and changes in its terrain and substructure. On the other hand, a preoccupation with dominant modes of political rationality and global economic forces may lead to a misleading neglect of transformative activities and the possibility of surprise. It is the interplay between figure and landscape that is important theoretically and empirically (Ball, 1994a, p. 118).

c) Critical advocacy

The final characteristic of the critical education policy orientation we want to explore is its strong progressive commitment towards education and society. Prunty is clear about this: "We contend that an *educational* policy analysis must attend simultaneously to the workings of the school and the workings of society" (Prunty, 1985, p. 135, italics in original). Thus the analysis of education policies is at the same time a commitment to try to have an impact on education policy and to support education reforms that lead to a more equal and less coercive society (cf. Taylor et al., 1997). In its original formulation it is an attempt to criticise what was called conservative education policy, that is, policy supporting educational systems that reproduce inequality and maintain specific cultural and moral formations. What it supports is progressive education policy, that is, policies explicitly aiming at education reform in view of social equality. In other words, the analytical focus on the politics of education policy is linked to the attempt to develop counter-politics in view of a more socially just and liberating allocation of values through policy.

There are clearly different approaches regarding 'critical advocacy.' The continuum of Gordon et al. (1977) is a helpful point of departure to say more about these differences (cf. Codd, 1988, pp. 235–236; Parsons, 1995, pp. 55–56). In line with the Lasswellian distinction between knowledge for the policy process and knowledge about the policy process, Gordon et al. (1977) make a distinction between "analysis *of* policy" and "analysis *for* policy." The latter refers to the kind of analysis that provides information for policy making, while the former includes the critical examination of past and existing policies.

Analysis for policy can take two different forms: 'information for policy' and 'policy advocacy.' Policy advocacy includes research that wants to influence the policy agenda, and hence to make specific policy recommendations. Information for policy is about the analysis that wants to provide information and data (on policy options for example) to assist the formulation or revision of policies.

- Analysis for policy

    o   Information for policy

    o   Policy advocacy

- Analysis of policy

    o   Policy determination and effects

    o   Policy content

Analysis of policy can take the form of 'analysis of policy determination and effects' and 'analysis of policy content.' The first kind of analysis is concerned with how policy is made, why, when and for whom, as well as with the effects of policies (on groups) and its impact (on a given problem and in view of social concerns). The analysis of the policy content focuses on the development of a particular policy (in relation to earlier policies) or on the values, assumptions and ideologies at stake in the policy process and content.

Many scholars however question the value of this classification. Prunty (1985) explicitly argues that critical education policy analysis is not only about an analysis of the content of policies and its effects, but underlying it is a strong concern for critical policy advocacy. As mentioned earlier, the advocacy concern is actually about the moral and social dimension of education, and the political commitment for progressive education reforms. In a similar vein, Taylor et al. (1997, pp.18–21) and Lingard and Ozga (2007, p. 6) hold to the idea that policy advocacy should be a main component of critical policy analysis. However, it is worth stressing once again that their understanding of policy advocacy is quite different from the kind of technical advocacy (strictly speaking not advocacy for it is limited to means) in rational policy analysis.

In order to be able to explore in more detail the scope of critical advocacy, we shall discuss first some assumptions of the traditional approach. Young (1999) distinguishes four characteristics of the traditional approach to education policy studies:

— Education policy studies are concerned with the process of educational changes or reforms (planning, implementation, examination, and/or evaluating); they assume reforms are deliberate processes that can be planned and managed (sequential, incremental, and/or political);
— Education policy studies assume that action is driven by goals or preferences (and actually equate this with what rationality is about);
— Education policy studies assume that knowledge for decisions and for implementation is obtainable, cumulative and communicable to others;

– Education policy studies hold to the idea that policies and their results can be evaluated; that in evaluation problems can be identified and that accordingly solutions can be given.[10]

What is taken for granted in this approach is that education policy studies are neutral with regard to the policy option or content, and are merely supportive. Codd (1988, p. 238) discussed this approach as the "technical-empiricist model of policy analysis." The model assumes that policy analysis is about facts on the means of policy or the nature of the policy problem while politics considers the goals of policy, the problem formulation and the implied values. In this model, there is no real form of policy advocacy (Taylor, 1997, p. 174), but there is primarily an empirically based technical support of policy making in the policy process itself (formulation, decision, execution, implementation). In such a model, the focus is on improvement in terms of efficiency and effectiveness.

Most critical policy studies do not agree with this objectivistic and technical-empirical relationship to the field of policy making. In fact, in line with the broad conception of education policy, these studies lead to different forms of critical advocacy. Some aim at policy recommendation, while others want to inform readers about the effects of policies or about taken for granted arenas in social governance. Despite the differences we propose to understand them as different genres of critical advocacy.

An attempt to describe the specificity of critical advocacy at yet another level is the distinction between "policy science" and "policy scholarship" (Grace, 1984; cf. Ozga, 1994, pp.3–4, Ball, 1997, p. 264). Borrowed from Brian Fay (1975) and his influential book *Social Theory and Political Practice*, Grace makes this distinction:

> Policy science (...) is a form of social and educational analysis which attempts to extract a social phenomenon from its relational context in order to subject it to close analysis. Following the models of natural science from which it is derived, it is relatively uninterested in the history or cultural antecedents of the phenomena under investigation. (...) Policy scholarship resists the tendency of policy science to abstracts problems from their relational settings by insisting that the problem can only be understood in the complexity of those relations. In particular, it represents a view that a social-historical approach to research can illuminate the cultural and ideological struggles in which schooling is located. (...) Whereas policy science excludes ideological and value conflicts as 'externalities beyond its remit' (...) (Grace, 1995, pp. 2–3).

The critical education policy orientation is clearly part of policy scholarship. The policy scholar is someone who can inform policy makers and the public, and at that level there is a possible advocacy role. However, the role of the scholar is not about clear-cut prescriptions on means or policy engineering along the assumptions of the technical-empiricist model. Ball's refinement of the distinction between scholarship and science by adding four additional figures illustrates the differences even better (Ball, 1995, 1997; cf. Humes & Bryce, 2003, pp. 183–184).

The *policy scholar* is the intellectual who can inform policy making, however without providing clear prescriptions or instructions. The latter are instead regarded as a major aim of *policy science*, and include the component of policy engineering in particular (that is, policy advocacy understood in its technical sense). The policy engineer wants to give the most efficient and effective procedure or course of action in order to be able to come to a solution or to realise a policy aim.

The *interpretative social scientist* with a policy orientation (relying on case studies and ethnographic research for example) wants to point out the correct meaning of what is going on in the social world, or the correct understanding of social and education policy processes. As this kind of research often relies upon modern epistemological assumptions, its relation to the context of policy making (and education in general) remains to a large extent instrumental. Consequently, it can be argued that this research often functions as a tool in justifying existing practices.

Critical social science regards theory itself as a tool in the process of social change, and hence moves beyond the 'conservative' tendency within classic interpretive social science. However, as mentioned earlier, its role of advocacy is not restricted to informing governments about reform policies, but should be situated as well at the level of teachers, teacher educators and curriculum. According to Ball (1995), the figure of the 'reflective practitioner' (Schön) who combines professional development, classroom change and curriculum reform, could be regarded as exemplary.

A fifth figure is the *policy entrepreneur*, that is, someone "who is committed to the application of certain technical solutions [to] organisations and context which are taken *a priori* to be in need of structural and/or cultural change" (ibid., p. 265, italics in original). The entrepreneur is driven by belief and acts with a view to selling applications, including having the networking and story-telling skills for doing this. Reform applications with a goal of organising "education for citizenship" could be regarded as part of the package of the policy entrepreneur.

However, Ball seeks to define a sixth figure to describe the role and aim of policy research in current societies. We can call this the figure of the *policy theorist*. He or she provides answers to the epistemological challenges of post-structuralism and the current pluralist social world, and who also takes up the difficult work of intellectually-based social criticism. In contrast to the traditional rational policy science and managerial and technical policy entrepreneurship, this approach pleas for theory as a tool to "defamiliarise the present practices and categories, to make them less self-evident and necessary, and to open up spaces for intervention of new forms of experience" (Ball, 1995, p. 266). Theory is not to be understood as offering explanations for knowledge-based change, but first and foremost as a vehicle for the "cultural critic" by offering new perspectives, and opening up spaces for "edifying conversation" (ibid., p. 268).

Such a 'post-structural' option however, is not generally agreed on (cf. Troyna, 1994b, p. 82). Some will argue that a much more overt and committed form of informing the policy process and politics is needed. In line with Flyvbjerg (2001, p. 166) and his plea to "transform social science to an activity done in public for the public", Humes and Bryce (2003, p. 182) suggest that policy scholarship should "concentrate on problems that matter to local, national and global communities and this will involve focusing on issues of values and power." This democratic form of social criticism is regarded as indispensable in preventing the isolation of the academic world, or for preventing the advocacy role of critical policy studies to become sterile, contingent or relativist (and endlessly stuck in self-critique, leading to intellectual paralysis and postponed decision making).

It is not our aim to picture this debate in detail, or to take a position. What we want to stress here is that the figure of the policy theorist remains valuable because it clarifies that, even if modernist forms of advocacy are radically questioned, underlying critical policy research is still a deep commitment to influence the social and political world. Critical policy theorists put forward neither technical advice, policy selling, agenda setting, nor social criticism, but "offer new perspectives and edifying conversations" at the level of cultural life. Yet, it is still an orientation to, and concern with 'the public, and its education'.

A final illuminating attempt to locate the intellectual scope and the social and political role of the critical policy orientation is the distinction of Dale (1994) between the critical analysis of the 'politics of education' and 'applied sociology of educational politics' and, related to this, the distinction between 'critical theory' and 'problem solving'. Although much more is at stake in this discussion, these distinctions are useful in exploring critical advocacy.

The concern of Dale, shared with several other scholars in the field (Ozga, 1994; Raab, 1994; Ball, 1994b; Popkewitz, 1984; Apple, 1979), is that "questions of short-term, practical application" risk displacing theoretical questions. This is actually the case with a large number of education policy studies which Dale refers to as "applied education politics" (Dale, 1994, p. 32). According to Dale, it is important to question the prevalence of education politics over politics of education and the related insistence on problem solving instead of critical theory. Politics of education is "the process and structures through which macro-societal expectations of education as an institution are identified and interpreted and constituted as an agenda for the education system" (ibid., p. 36).[11] In contrast, education politics refers to "the processes whereby this agenda is translated into problems and issues for schools, and schools' responses to those problems and issues" (ibid., p. 35). In Dale's view, education politics can not be understood sufficiently without linking it with the politics of education. The risk is, according to him, taking the policy agenda for granted and, as a consequence, an inability to obtain any distance from the way problems and policies are framed.

According to Dale, and drawing upon the work of Robert Cox, this is connected with adopting the common problem-solving approach in contrast to a reliance on critical theory. The former "takes the world as it finds it", "with the prevailing social and power relationships and the institutions into which they are organised, as the given framework for action" and with a view to making "these relationships and institutions work smoothly by dealing effectively with particular sources of trouble" (Cox, 1980, p. 129 in Dale, 1994, p. 39). Critical theory by contrast "stands apart from the prevailing order of the world and asks how that order came about" and is "directed towards an appraisal of the very framework for action, or problematic, which problem-solving accepts as its parameters (Cox, 1980, p. 129 in Dale, 1994, p. 39). Dale does not want to say that critical studies of education policy and the politics of education should not be concerned with intervening in and informing policy makers. They can even play a role in finding solutions. The point is that, relying on critical theory, the concern and focus is not to make the existing system, procedures or practices more efficient and effective by offering solutions for problems identified elsewhere. In other words, the critical policy orientation is not rooted in the concern for problem solving, but is concerned with obtaining the larger picture within which policy problems take shape.

The previous discussion between education politics and politics of education refers partly to the discussion between the approach of Dale in contrast to the approach of Ball, and to the difference in theoretical and methodological assumptions. But both seem to agree that the critical orientation to education policy is not about solving problems per se. It is foremost concerned with putting the way policies 'read' the world and define problems in a broader context, and hence not taking the problems for granted. Additionally, the orientation includes being sensitive to how policies themselves create the problems to which they are an answer, and acknowledging that often problems are framed with specific solutions in mind (cf. Dale, 1989, p. 35; Yeatman, 1990, 158; p. Ball, 1994b, p. 118). However, as Gale remarks, this should also apply to the work of critical analyst, and therefore: "(…) we must be careful not to simply fill predetermined theoretical buckets with policy data" (Gale, 2001, p. 384). In other words, the attempt to re-read policy agendas also includes an awareness of and critical attitude towards one's own role as scholar in the policy and political fabric.

In sum, the distinction between problem solving and critical theory mirrors the distinction between policy science and policy scholarship, and refines the general opposition between analysis for policy and analysis of policy. Again, research with a critical policy orientation is highly diverse, combining both analysis of policy and analysis for policy (cf. Lingard & Gale, 2007, p. 18). The meaning of the term 'for policy' does not imply that critical studies are carried out for policy makers, based on their problem definition and in view of their goals, but that critical research is concerned with 'change' or 'acting upon' the world and existing discourses. Whether acting upon or critical advocacy take the form of overt social criticism, political commitment, informed public debate, offering perspectives or seeking to achieve educational and social reforms based on critical pedagogy depends largely on the critical *ethos* and the related theoretical intuition. Yet, we propose to conceive of them as different genres of critical advocacy concerned with 'the public, and its education'.

CONCLUSION: THE CRITICAL EDUCATION POLICY ORIENTATION AND ITS LIMITS

As a conclusion to this part of the introduction we shift our attention to some specific limits of the critical policy orientation. An important aspect of the limits of policy studies is the question of the role of policy researchers in democratic societies, and more broadly, the tension between research and democracy. The tension between both can be summarised in the typical modern conception that policy research is based on the 'power of truth' or 'the facts that speak', while democracy is about the 'power of the people' or 'the opinions of people.'[12] In today's societies, the authority of the researcher's knowledge and policy advocacy is no longer taken for granted (cf. Ozga, 2000). Moreover, in line with the evidence based policy movement it seems that policy-makers themselves have become policy experts relying on facts regarding decision making and policy objectives.

Modern approaches to policy assumed a distinction between the field of democracy and the field of informed decision-making. The distinction is similar to the distinction between ('often messy') politics and ('possibly rational') policy making. Inspired by critical theory, scholars however started to focus on the relation between politics and policy making, as well as on politics as part of policy making and policy making as part of the political context. One step further, and in line with for example Habermas, Yeatman or Rancière, is to bring the link between democracy and politics/policy to the foreground. Democracy could be regarded as an un-gendered fundamental process *within* the process of policy and politics:

> This opens policy up to the appropriate participation of all those involved all the way through points of conception, operational formulation, implementation, delivery on the ground, consumption and evaluation, rather than separating policy from politics, which has the effect of protecting and sustaining bureaucratic logics of practice from democratic possibilities (Ozga & Lingard, 2007, p. 67).

In a radical form, however, the recognition of the democratic process *within* policy and politics actually questions the role of 'policy advocacy based on research', or at least, forces policy analysts but also critical education policy scholars to re-examine the democratic value of their intellectual position and advocacy. In this context, and possibly merging 'theory' and 'politics', Yeatman introduces an extended and deliberately normative definition of the "policy activist" as someone who:

> (...) champions in relatively consistent ways a value orientation and pragmatic commitment to what I have called the policy process, namely a conception of policy which opens it up to the appropriate participation of all those who are involved in policy all the way through points of conception, operational formulation, implementation, delivery on the ground, consumption and evaluation (Yeatman, 1998, p. 34).

It is beyond the scope of this introduction to discuss these challenges in detail, but we do think it is important to mention them. What has become clear today is that the authority granted to the critical policy researcher in the welfare state is being challenged. This forces us the rethink the idea of a science of democracy (Lasswell), and the implied tension between science and democracy. And rethinking this idea, we can consider a shift from welfare advocacy to democratic advocacy. Indeed, re-reading education policies in view of gathering people around matters of concern – the focus of this handbook - could be regarded as a democratic act or an act of public advocacy. It is about gathering people around issues in education as a public, and hence turning education into a matter of public concern. This critical ethos is not in opposition to democracy, but is perhaps a way of living a democratic life, and a way to be concerned with or to be part of 'the public and its education.'

NOTES

[1] This summary is based on the work of Parsons (1995), Wagner et al. (1991), Colebatch (1998), and Howlett & Ramesh (2003), although they each use a slightly different list of characteristics.

[2] Although the clear dominance of US scholars in the field, Parsons mentions the influence of scholars outside the US: Geoffrey Vickers and Yehezkel Dror (Parsons, 1995, pp. 25–26). Vickers contribution lies in his focus on the role of values and judgements (related to social cooperation) in the policy process, while Dror developed a modified form of decision-making in his critique of the rational models, and by taking distance from the incrementalist position of Lindblom.

[3] The term policy analysis is sometimes used as a general term including analysis for policy and analysis of policy, while the term policy studies is used to refer to policy analysis combined with so-called program evaluation (evaluation of large scale social programs in the 1960s) (cf. Nagel, 1999).

[4] Horkheimer describes the idea of critique in the following terms: "By criticism, we mean that intellectual, and eventually practical, effort which is not satisfied to accept the prevailing ideas, actions, and social conditions unthinkingly and from mere habit; effort which aims to coordinate the individual sides of social life with each other and with the general ideas and aims of the epoch, to deduce them genetically, to distinguish the appearance from the essence, to examine the foundations of things, in short, really to know them." (Horkheimer, 1939)

[5] For a detailed overview of the development of the field of politics of education: Mitchell & Goertz, 1990; Scribner, Aleman & Maxcy, 2003.

[6] With regard to this influence, Shaha (1997, p. 108) states: "Perhaps the most important aspect of the 'new' sociology of education was that it directed attention to the study, using mainly qualitative methods, of classroom interaction, classroom language, and the curriculum, the last having been a hitherto neglected field for sociological research (…). During the 1970s and 1980s the 'new' sociology of education stood in opposition to the 'old' and was manifested particularly in resistance theory and social and cultural reproduction theories."

[7] By adopting the approaches of the latter, the education of politics field has been overshadowed by the policy analysis and evaluation field (Scribner, 1977; Mitchell & Goertz, 1990; Scribner et., 2003; cf. Heck, 2004, p. 17).

[8] For an overview and illustrations: Olssen, Codd & O'Neill, 2004.

[9] Democracy actually starts to play a rather prominent role in critical theory (of education policy), for instance in line with the work of Yeatman, Bourdieu and Rancière (see also conclusion of this chapter). Of course, these authors question precisely the instrumental relation between 'science' and 'democracy'.

[10] See also Pring (2000) for a (similar) listing of features of conventional research in the physical and social sciences, and Humes and Bryce (2003) for a discussion on the assumptions on the relation between research, practice and policy.

[11] The "macro-societal expectations" refer to the outcome and specification of the three core problem of the capitalist state: "the support of the accumulation process", "the maintenance of a social context not amenable to the continuation of that accumulation process" and "the legitimation of the system" (Dale, 1994, p. 36; cf. Dale, 1989).

[12] It is interesting to refer in this context to Wildavsky (1987, pp. 12–13), who states in his book *Speaking truth to power: The art and craft of policy analysis*: "(…) Speaking truth to power remains

the ideal of analysts who hope they have truth, but realise they have not (and, in a democracy, should not have) power. No one can do analysis without becoming aware that moral considerations are integral to the enterprise. After all, analysis is about what ought to be done, about making things better, not worse. I have never been sympathetic to the view that facts and values, except as intellectual constructs, either are or ought to be kept separate in action."

REFERENCES

Apple, M. (1979). *Ideology and curriculum*. London & Boston: Routledge & Kegan Paul Ltd. Publishers.

Apple, M. (1982). *Education and power*. New York: Routledge & Kegan Paul Ltd. Publishers.

Aronowitz, S., & Giroux, H. (1994). *Education still under siege*. Westport, CT: Bergin & Garvey.

Ball, S. J. (1990). *Politics and policy making in education*. London: Routledge.

Ball, S. J. (1994a). Researching inside the state: Issues in the interpretation of elite interviews. In D. Halpin & B. Troyna (Eds.), *Researching education policy: Ethical and methodological issues* (pp. 107–120). London: Falmer Press.

Ball, S. J. (1994b). *Education reform: A critical and post-structural approach*. Buckingham: Open University Press.

Ball, S. J. (1995). Intellectuals or technicians? The urgent role of theory in educational studies. *British Journal of Educational Studies, 43*(3), 255–271.

Ball, S. J. (1997). Policy sociology and critical social research: A personal review of recent education policy and policy research. *British Educational Research Journal, 23*(3), 257–274.

Bernstein, B. (1971). On the classification and framing of educational knowledge. In M. F. D. Young (Ed.), *Knowledge and control* (pp. 47–69). London: Collier Macmillan.

Brobrow, D. B., & Dryzek, J. S. (1987). *Policy analysis by design*. Pittsburgh, PA: University of Pittsburgh Press.

Boussaguet, L., Jacquot, S., & Ravinet, P. (2004). *Dictionnaire des politiques publiques*. Paris: Les Presses de Sciences-Po.

Bowe, R., Ball, S., & Gold, A. (1992). *Reforming education and changing schools: Case studies in policy sociology*. London: Routledge.

Colebatch, H. K. (1998). *Policy*. Buckingham: Open University Press.

Codd, J. (1988). The construction and deconstruction of education policy documents. *Journal of Education Policy, 3*(3), 235–247.

Coombs, P. H. (1970). *What is educational planning? Fundamentals of educational planning 1*. Paris: UNESCO International Institute for Educational Planning (IIEP).

Cox, R. (1980). Social forces, states and world orders' millennium. *Millennium: Journal of International Studies, 10*(2), 126–155.

deLeon, P. (1997). *Democracy and the policy sciences*. Albany, NY: SUNY Press.

deLeon, P. (1999). The stages approach to the policy process: What has it done? Where is it going? In P. A. Sabatier (Ed.), *Theories of the policy process* (pp. 19–34). Boulder, CO: Westview Press.

Dale, R. (1989). *The state and education policy*. Buckingham: Open University Press.

Dale, R. (1994). Applied education politics or political sociology of education? Contrasting approaches to the study of the recent education reform in England and Wales. In D. Halpin & B. Troyna (Eds.), *Researching education policy: Ethical and methodological issues* (pp. 31–41). London: Falmer Press.

Dryzek, J. S. (1990). *Discursive democracy: Politics, policy, and political science*. Cambridge: Cambridge University Press.

Drucker, P. (1954). *The principles of management*. New York: Harper & Row.

Drucker, P. (1964). *Managing for results: Economic tasks and risk-taking decisions*. New York: Harper & Row.

Drucker, P. (1969). *The age of discontinuity. Guidelines to our changing society*. New York: Harper & Row.

Fischer, F. (1998). Beyond empiricism: Policy inquiry in postpositivist perspective. *Policy Studies Journal, 26*(1), 129–146.

Fischer, F., & Forester, J. (Eds.). (1993). *The argumentative turn in policy analysis and planning*. Durham: Duke University Press.

Floden, R. (2007). Philosophical issues in education policy research. In S. Fuhrman, D. Cohen, & F. Mosher (Eds.), *The state of education policy research* (pp. 3–18). Malwah, NJ: Lawrence Erlbaum Associates.

Flyvbjerg, B. (2001). *Making social science matter. Why social inquiry fails and how it can succeed again*. Cambridge: Cambridge University Press.

Freire, P. (1970). *Pedagogy of the oppressed*. New York: Continuum.

Fuhrman, S., Cohen, D., & Mosher, F. (Eds.). (2007). *The state of education policy research*. Malwah, NJ: Lawrence Erlbaum Associates.

Gale, T. (2001). Critical policy sociology: Historiography, archaeology and genealogy as methods of social analysis. *Journal of Education Policy, 16*(5), 379–393.

Giroux, H. (1981). *Ideology, culture and the process of schooling*. Philadelphia: Temple University Press.

Giroux, H. (1983). *Theory and resistance in education: A pedagogy for the opposition*. Westport, CT: Bergin & Garvey.

Gordon, I., Lewis, J., & Young, K. (1977). Perspectives on policy analysis. *Public administration bulletin, 25*, 26–30.

Grace, G. (1984). Urban education: Policy science or critical scholarship? In G. Grace (Ed.), *Education and the city* (pp. 3–59). London: Routledge/Kegan Paul.

Grace, G. (1995). *School leadership: Beyond educational management. An essay in policy scholarship*. London: Falmer.

Hammersley, M. (1994). Ethnography, policy making and practice in education. In D. Halpin & B. Troyna (Eds.), *Researching education policy: Ethical and methodological issues* (pp. 139–153). London: Falmer Press.

Harvey, L. (1990). *Critical social research*. London: Allen & Unwin.

Heck, R. H. (2004). *Studying educational and social policy: Theoretical concepts and research methods*. Mahwah, NJ: Erlbaum Associates.

Hermann, U. (1993). *Aufklärung und Erziehung. Studien zur Funktion der Erziehung im Konstitutionsprozess der bürgerlichen Gesellschaft im 18. und frühen 19. Jaherhundert in Deutschland*. Weinheim: Deutscher Studien Verlag.

Horkheimer, M. (1939). The social function of philosophy. In *Critical theory. Selected essays (1982)*. New York: Continuum. [http://www.marxists.org/reference/archive/horkheimer/1939/socialfunction.htm]

Horkheimer, M. (1931). The present situation of social philosophy and the tasks of an institute for social research. In *Between philosophy and social science. Selected early writings (1995)*. Cambridge, MA: MIT Press. [http://www.marxists.org/reference/archive/hork heimer/1931/present-situation.htm]

Howlett, M., & Ramesh, M. (2003). *Studying public policy: Policy cycles and policy subsystems* (2nd ed.). Toronto: Oxford University Press.

Humes, W. M., & Bryce, T. G. K. (2003). Post-structuralism and policy research in education. *Journal of Educational Policy, 18*(2), 175–187.

John, P. (1998). *Analysing public policy*. London: Cassell.

Kogan, M. (1975). *Educational policy making*. London: Allen and Unwin.

Lingard, B., Knight, J., & Porter, P. (1993). *Schooling reform in hard times*. London: Falmer Press.

Lingard, B., & Gale, T. (2007). The emergent structure of feeling: What does it mean for critical educational studies and research. *Critical Studies in Education, 48*(1), 1–23.

Lingard, B., & Ozga, J. (2007). Reading education policy and politics. In B. Lingard & J. Ozga (Eds.), *The Routledge Falmer reader in education policy and politics*. London: Routledge.

Maroy, C. (2006). *École, regulation et marché*. Paris: PUF.

Marshall, J., & Peters, M. (Eds.). (1999). *Education policy. The international library of comparative public policy*. Cheltenham: Edward Elgar Publishing Limited.

Marshall, C., & Gerstl-Pepin, C. (2005). *Re-framing educational politics for social justice*. Boston: Allyn and Bacon.

McLaren, P. (1989). *Life in schools: An introduction to critical pedagogy in the foundations of education.* New York: Longman.

Mitchell, D. E., & Goertz, M. E. (1990). *Education politics for the new century: The twentieth anniversary yearbook of the politics of education association.* New York: Falmer.

Nagel, S. (Ed.). (1999). *Policy analysis methods.* Commack, NY: New Science Publishers.

Oelkers, J. (1989). *Reformpädagogik: eine kritische Dogmengeschichte.* Weinheim: Juventa.

Olssen, M., Codd, J., & O'Neil, A. (2004). *Education policy.* London: Sage.

Osborne, D., & Gaebler, T. (1992). *Reinventing government: How the entrepreneurial spirit is transforming the public sector.* New York: Plume.

Ozga, J. (1987). Studying education through the lives of policy makers: An attempt to close the micro-macro gap. In S. Walker & L. Barton (Eds.), *Changing policies. Changing teachers* (pp. 138–150). Milton Keynes: Open University Press.

Ozga, J. (1990). Policy research and policy theory: A comment on Halpin and Fitz. *Journal of Education Policy, 5*(4), 359–362.

Ozga, J. (2000). *Policy research in educational settings: Contested terrain.* Buckingham: Open University Press

Ozga, J., & Lingard, R. (2007). Globalisation, education policy and politics. In R. Lingard & J. Ozga (Eds.), *The RoutledgeFalmer reader in education policy and politics* (pp. 65–82). London: Routledge.

Parsons, W. (1995). *Public policy: An introduction to the theory and practice of policy analysis.* Cheltenham: Edward Elgar.

Pollitt, C. (1990). *Managerialism and the public services: The anglo-american experience.* Oxford: Blackwell.

Pongratz, L. A. (1989). *Pädagogik im Prozess der Moderne. Studien zur Sozial- und Theoriegeschichte der Schule.* Weinheim: Deutscher Studien Verlag.

Popkewitz, T. S. (1984). *Paradigm and ideology in educational research: The social functions of the intellectual.* London: The Falmer Press.

Popkewitz, T. (1991). *A political sociology of educational reform: Power/Knowledge in teaching, teacher education, and research.* New York: Teachers College Press.

Popkewitz, T., & Brennan, M. (Eds.). (1998). *Foucault's challenge: Discourse, knowledge and power in education.* New York: Teachers College Press.

Popkewitz, T. (1996). Rethinking decentralization and state/civil society distinctions: The state as a problematic of governing. *Journal of Education Policy, 11*(1), 27–51.

Popkewitz, T. (2008). *Cosmopolitanism and the age of school reform: Science, education and making society by making the child.* New York: Routledge.

Prunty, J. J. (1984). *A critical reformulation of educational policy and polic' analysis.* Geelong, Victoria: Deakin University Press.

Prunty, J. (1985). Signposts for a critical educational policy analysis. *Australian Journal of Education, 29*(2), 133–140.

Pring, R. (2000). *Philosophy of educational research.* London & New York: Continuum.

Raab, C. (1994). Where we are now: Reflections on the sociology of education policy. In D. Halpin & B. Troyna (Eds.), *Researching education policy: Ethical and methodological issues* (pp. 17–30). London: Falmer Press.

Rizvi, F. (2006). Imagination and the globalisation of educational policy research. *Globalisation, Societies and Education, 4*(2), 193–205.

Rose, N. (1999). *The powers of freedom. Reframing political thought.* Cambridge: Cambridge University Press.

Saha, L. J. (Ed.). (1997). *International encyclopedia of the sociology of education.* Oxford: Elsevier Science Ltd.

Scribner, J. D. (Ed.). (1977). *The politics of education. The seventy-sixth yearbook of the national society for the study of education.* Chicago: University of Chicago Press.

Scribner, J. D., & Englert, R. M. (1977). The politics of education: An introduction. In J. D. Scribner (Ed.), *The politics of education* (pp. 1–29). Chicago: University of Chicago Press.

Scribner, J. D., Aleman, E., & Maxcy, B. D. (2003). Emergence of the politics of education field: Making sense of the messy center. *Educational Administration Quarterly, 39*(1), 10–40.

Sünker, H., & Krüger, H.-H. (Eds.). (1999). *Kritische Erziehungswissenschaft am Neubeginn?!*. Frankfurt/M.: Suhrkamp.

Taylor, S. (1997). Critical policy analysis: Exploring contexts, texts and consequences. *Discourse: Studies in cultural politics of education, 18*(1), 23–35.

Taylor, S., Rizvi, F., Lingard, B., & Henry, M. (1997). *Educational policy and the politics of change*. London: Routledge.

Tenorth, H.-E. (1992). *Geschichte der Erziehung: Einführung in die Grundzüge ihrer neuzeitlichen Entwicklung*. München: Juventa.

Torres, C. A., & Antikainen, A. (Eds.), (2003). *The international handbook on the sociology of education. An international assessment of new research and theory*. Lanham, Boulder, New York and Oxford: Rowman and Littlefield Publishers.

Trowler P. (1998). *Education policy: A policy sociology approach*. London: Routledge.

Troyna, B. (1994a). Reforms, research and being reflexive about being reflexive. In D. Halpin & B. Troyna (Eds.), *Researching education policy: Ethical and methodological issues* (pp. 1–14). London: Falmer Press.

Troyna, B. (1994b). Critical social research and education policy. *British Journal of Educational Studies, 42*(1), 70–84.

Usher, R., & Edwards, R. (1994). *Postmodernism and education: Different voices, different worlds*. London: Routledge.

Vanderstraeten, R. *(1997)*. Circularity, complexity and educational policy *planning*. A systems approach to the *planning* of school provision. *Oxford Review Oxford Review of Education, 23*(3), 321–332.

van Zanten, A. (2004). *Les politiques d'éducation*. Paris: PUF.

van Zanten, A. (2005). Bourdieu as education policy analyst and expert: A rich but ambiguous legacy. *Journal of Education Policy, 20*(6), 671–686.

Vidovich, L. (2002). *Expanding the toolbox for policy analysis: Some conceptual and practical approaches*. Occasional Paper Series (2), Comparative Education Policy Research Unit, Hong Kong: City University of Hong Kong.

Wagner, P., Weiss, C. H. W., Wittrock, B., & Wollmann, H. (Eds.). (1991). *Social sciences and modern state*. Cambridge: Cambridge University Press.

Wielemans, W., & Berkhout, S. (1999). Towards understanding education policy: An integrative approach. *Educational Policy, 13*(3), 402–420.

Wildavsky, A. (1987). *Speaking truth to power: The art and craft of policy analysis* (2nd ed.). Brunswick, NJ: Transaction Publishers.

Wittrock, B., Wagner, P., & Wollmann, H. (1991). Social science and the modern state. In P. Wagner, Peter, C. H. Weiss, B. Wittrock, & H. Wollmann (Eds.), *Social sciences and modern state* (pp. 28–85). Cambridge: Cambridge University Press.

Whitty, G. (2002). *Making sense of education policy: Studies in the sociology and politics of education*. London: Paul Chapman.

Yeatman, A. (1990). *Bureaucrats, femocrats, technocrats: Essays on the contemporary Australian state*. Sydney: Allen & Unwin.

Yeatman, A. (1994). *Postmodern revisionings of the political*. New York: Routledge.

Yeatman, A. (1998). *Activism and the policy process*. St Leonards: Allen & Unwin.

Young, M. (1999). Multifocal educational policy research: Toward a method for enhancing traditional educational policy studies. *American Educational Research Journal, 36*(4), 677–714.

Zajda, J. (Ed.). (2005). *The international handbook of globalisation and education policy research*. Dordrecht: Springer.

MAARTEN SIMONS, MARK OLSSEN & MICHAEL PETERS

RE-READING EDUCATION POLICIES

PART 2: Challenges, Horizons, Approaches, Tools, Styles

INTRODUCTION

Part 1 of the introduction explored the emergence of the so-called critical education policy orientation, and explored three features of this orientation: acknowledgement of the educational, moral and social concerns in debates on education, the focus on power, politics and regulation in education, and the adoption of a specific form of critical advocacy towards society and policy. This part of the introduction discusses the current state of affairs, and aims both at giving access to theoretical discussions and analytical frameworks and offering some overviews of specific and hopefully useful tools and approaches.

The first section explores some of the challenges critical education policy studies are facing today in view of the challenges of contemporary society and regarding theory and methodology. We will clarify that in confrontation with these challenges the critical orientation is in need of "de-parochialisation" (Dale, 1994; Lingard, 2006) and a "recalibration of critical lenses" (Robertson & Dale, 2008). The second section sketches the (meta-)theoretical horizons of critical policy research in order to discuss the main approaches adopted by critical education policy scholars (and in the contributions of this book): cultural political economy, critical discourse analysis, policy field analysis, governmentality study, micropolitical analysis, feminist theory, post-colonial theory and philosophical analysis. The third section discusses some classifications and analytical tools that are being used to examine education policy. In the concluding section of the chapter, different styles of critical policy research are distinguished in order to emphasise the idea that when policy makers become *critical* there is perhaps an urgent need for critical scholars to become *concerned*.

THE NEW IMPETUS FOR A CRITICAL EDUCATION POLICY ORIENTATION

The first part of the introduction chapter described the appearance of the critical policy orientation during the 1980s and 1990s, emerging as it did in close relation with the education reforms of that time. In this section we discuss the challenges at both the level of society and theory that seem to give a new impetus to critical policy research. Six sets of challenges will be discussed: a) parochialism and cosmopolitanism, b) globalisation, c) the role of state government, d) neoliberalism, third way policies and social justice, e) theory development, f) evidence based policy, and g) critical and concerned research.

M. Simons, M. Olssen and M.A. Peters (eds.), Re-Reading Education Policies: A Handbook Studying the Policy Agenda of the 21st Century, 36–95.

a) Old fashioned parochialism and trendy cosmopolitanism

The first set of challenges relates to a tension in studies of education policy concerning whether these studies are guided by research interests in *education* or whether the main focus is on *policy* (cf. Halpin, 1994, Raab, 1994a). Part of this is the question whether education policy is regarded as a distinctive domain of study in need of specific research and theorisation or whether it is important to embrace the broader domain of policy, politics and social or cultural theory, and to rely on research and methodologies developed elsewhere. At an even more general level, there is a discussion whether education policy should be a distinctive focus or whether the focus on policy should be regarded as part of the broader interest in power in education and society.

According to Dale (1994, p. 32), there is a tendency to "disciplinary parochialism" – implying that scholars sometimes regard education and its research tools as highly distinctive. Hence scholars rarely go beyond disciplinary boundaries, and if they do they merely incorporate other approaches instead of using them to rework and reorient their own distinctive discipline.[1] Additionally, and this is also stressed by Lingard (2006) and Lingard & Ozga (2007), a kind of parochialism is noted with regard to education as a policy domain or sector. This is related to what Robertson and Dale (2008) call "methodological educationalism." From the viewpoint of educationalists education is often confined to the formal education sector. Consequently, the policy focus is limited through one's formal educational lenses. Through "institutional parochialism" (Dale, 2005), or the tendency within educational studies to take the existing education system as their focus, a similar narrowing of research takes shape. An additional limitation here is to focus mainly on the overt conflicts and interests in policy and politics, and on instrumental and governmental forms of power. What is being disregarded here is the broader field of power relations and how policies are dispersed across both discursive and non-discursive practices (Popkewitz, 1996). Taking into account the current state of affairs, several other kinds of parochialism are worth mentioning (cf. Lingard & Gale, 2007).

In today's societies, practices and discourses on the knowledge society and lifelong learning are clearly challenging the education and school oriented vocabularies (e.g. Biesta, 2006; Fejes & Nicoll, 2008). The least one could say is that term 'education' today has become something that has to be clearly defined, especially in relation to the fields of learning and work. Additionally, the sector of vocational education, often framed within human capital investment approaches, is increasingly interwoven with socio-economic policies (e.g. Dale & Robertson, 2007). As a consequence, the notion 'education policy' itself is in need of careful definition. Furthermore, technological advancements in society and education (such as in ICT) correlate clearly with new patterns of power, regulation and inclusion/exclusion, and lead to new ways of organising public space and distributing common goods, and to new opportunities to stabilise or change society (e.g. Burbules & Callister, 2000). Hence, there is a need to become attentive to new forms of power, and new forms of resistance and public action. Finally, it is important to focus on the changed context of research itself. Cases in point are the current tendency to orient research on education towards meeting the needs of evidence based practice and policy (Ozga, 2000), and the often limited internationalisation of the research agenda (Appadurai, 2001). This demands a careful reflection upon the relation between critical education policy research and the evidence oriented science apparatus, as well as reflection on the very meaning of academic research in a global context. With regard to the latter, we can agree with Appadurai (2001, p. 15) of the need for a "de-parochialisation of the research ethic – of the idea of research itself." (see further below)

It is evident that parochialism with regard to one's own discipline while facing these developments results in an impoverished critical policy orientation. More importantly, such theoretical and epistemological limitation can have a political downside. "Methodological statism and nationalism", that is limiting one's analysis to state policies and politics within the state and assuming a fixed linkage between government and territory in a single nation, actually re-enforces a given state of affairs at the national and international level (Robertson and Dale, 2008). Hence, Lingard claims in line with Bourdieu that the "rejection of epistemological innocence is central to the deparochialising project and a disposition of epistemological diffidence" (Lingard, 2006, p. 291).

However, most scholars today re-focus their lenses. Perhaps there is another risk here: questioning different types of parochialism from the viewpoint of a fashionable 'academic cosmopolitanism'. The embraced cosmopolitanism is often tainted with implicit assumptions of universally shared global orientations and criticism. It leads to the assumption that we all think and act the same, suffer from the same kind of policy diseases and are in need of the same medicine. In view of these assumptions, it is vitally important that critically oriented research is attentive to the limits of academic cosmopolitanism as well (see Appadurai, 2001; Popkewitz, 2008).

We want to conclude this section on parochialism by mentioning possible challenges to the often taken for granted 'welfare connection' between education and policy itself. The connection being made between education and policy is traditionally a two-way connection; on the one hand studying the policy context of education but on the other hand studying how policies could be used to improve education and its role in society. The background for this critical orientation is clearly the modern welfare state that conceives of education as a major component of public policy. The general principles of welfare policy, often taken for granted by critical scholars, are 'the change of education through change of public policy' and 'the change of society through change of education'.[2] What we want to stress is the importance of being aware of a sort of 'critical/advocacy parochialism' at the level of these principles. Facing the crisis of the welfare state and state government, these principles are no longer evident. Or to formulate this in a positive way, a major challenge will be to discuss what 'the public, and its education' is about in today's global context, and how education and policy are related and should be related.

b) Research scripts for the global scene

A second important set of challenges is related to globalisation. As a social phenomenon, this term is generally used to refer to the economic, political and cultural processes leading to new practices, connections and discourses at the supranational level, and consequently related to processes that modify local identities and perceptions of space and time. In Giddens' words: "Globalisation can thus be defined as the intensification of worldwide social relations which link distant localities in such a way that local happenings are shaped by events occurring many miles away and vice versa" (Giddens, 1990, p. 64). Held et al. specifically stress the "widening, deepening and speeding up of worldwide interconnectedness in all aspects of contemporary life" (Held et al., 1999, p. 2). Next to action at the distance and interconnectedness, globalisation includes a number of other developments: new modes of production/development, new forms of communication and new technologies leading to "time-space compression" (Harvey, 1990, p. 350; Bauman, 1998); network patterned social structures reflecting new social and political identities (Castells, 1996); new modes of governance, new processes of and actors/agencies in policy making and the formation of "competitive" or "performative" states (Cerny, 1997; Yeatman, 1994; Dale, 1999; Ball, 1998).

Many of these developments are acknowledged in studies with a critical policy orientation. Indeed, many scholars have meanwhile subscribed to what Bourdieu refers to as "the policy of globalisation": "I deliberately say a 'policy of globalisation', and do not speak of 'globalisation' as if it were a natural process." In revealing his specific theoretical commitment he continues: "This policy is to a large extent kept secret, as far as its production and distribution is concerned. And a whole work of research is needed at this point, to reveal it before it can be put into practice" (Bourdieu, 2001a/2008, p. 380). Meanwhile, several aspects of the policy and politics of globalisation have become a concern for critical investigation: the impact of globalisation (including new supranational organisations, new forms of internationalisation, Europeanisation, etc.), globalisation effects, new forms of policy borrowing and the changed role of the state, global framing of education policy and politics, the formation of a global policy field, the role and impact of the World Bank, OECD (and PISA), GATS, the relation between travelling and embedded policies ... (Halpin, 1994; Taylor et al., 1997; Dale, 1999; Burbules & Torres, 2000; Tikly, 2001; Robertson, 2005; Rizvi, 2004; Ozga & Lingard , 2007; Henry et al., 2001; Ozga, Seddon & Popkewitz, 2006).

The global framing of policy and politics thus clearly broadens the research domain of critical studies: researchers 'globalise' their agenda and broaden the often state-oriented methodological and theoretical approaches. Two further challenges linked up with globalisation are worth mentioning: 1) international comparisons and 2) globalised advocacy.

1) The field of comparative education research is traditionally characterised by a strong focus on education policy and politics (Noah, 1984; Bray, 2003). Historical as well as empirical studies within this field attempted to portray differences in educational structures and outcomes as related to differences in educational

administration, education policy and the political context and culture in a country. Many of these cross-national studies were typically aligned with educational planning at the level of state government, and were intended to meet the need for well-informed policy borrowing (Halpin & Troyna, 1995).

From the 1960s onwards, empirical cross-national research became conducted or organised by international organisations (UNESCO, World Bank, OECD). From the 1990s the data collected by these organisations clearly gained political prominence (Henry et al., 2001). This data collection is part of the emerging global policy field that focuses on the collection and distribution of information on performance and best practices. Additionally, the specific global governance mechanisms that are emerging are linked up with national policy trends towards deregulation and devolution. What takes shape in this new strategic governance field is "government by numbers" (Rose, 1999; see also Desrosieres, 1998, Porter, 1995) and "steering by evaluation" (Lindblad & Popkewitz, 2000; Power, 1997). Importantly, within this strategic and comparative policy field nation states come to see themselves, and particularly their policy objectives, policy domains and resources for policy legitimisation, in a new way (Henry et al., 2001; Lawn & Lingard, 2002). The global field is constituted as a market of national education systems with policy makers obsessed with competitive self-improvement (Haahr, 2004; Simons, 2007).

What we want to stress at this point is that a particular kind of global policy analysis and comparative education has become part of the assemblage of the global policy field (Dale, 2006, p. 184). Indeed, as Nóvoa & Yariv-Marshal (2003) clarify, the actual comparison of states and modes of international benchmarking have become modes of governance and policy. Thus critically positioning oneself towards this global regime of power and knowledge and including popular comparative education research is an important challenge for scholars. Critically oriented research indeed has to come to terms with the practice of comparison, and the underlying assumptions regarding commensurability and the role of modern states. In dealing with these challenges, Dale (2006) suggests that critically orientated researchers follow Santos here and shift from a modern and state based and oriented focus on "comparison" to "translation." Focusing on mechanisms of translation at different levels and in different contexts is regarded as a way to expand the critical research imagination and go beyond forms of parochialism.

2) The second challenge related to globalisation has to do with the critical advocacy component. The questions that emerge today are: who to address critically in the global policy field, who are the important actors in the global field, how to address actors that are often not identifiable as classic education workers, how to inform a global public opinion, and to ask what is 'the public' in a global context and how are issues of global justice to be addressed? (cf. Bourdieu, 2001/2008, 2000/2008) Acknowledging the importance of these questions, Appadurai suggests discussing radically the Western assumptions on research ethics and effective critique. Additionally, he stresses the importance of world-wide collaboration and new forms of dialogue for the globalisation and democratisation of knowledge on globalisation and democracy. In his view, these

forms of collaboration and dialogue can support "grassroots globalisation" or "globalisation from below", and play a role in shaping alternative "social imaginaries" (Appadurai, 2001, p. 20). Acknowledging the importance of new imaginaries of and new knowledge for informed citizenship, it is suggested that current challenges related to globalisation are framed in terms of the "right to research" and the "democratisation of this right to research" (Appadurai, 2006). This critical focus on the global policy field however not only links the global and the local, but also opens up a perspective that focuses on the 'gap' between the North and the South, and broadens the often Western (and state based) conception of social justice (Arnove & Torres, 1999; Tikly, 2001).

The previous set of challenges clearly indicates that the critical education policy orientation is gaining a new momentum from what is called globalisation. Rizvi nicely summarises what is at stake:

> If national policies, which have been the objects of our research efforts, have themselves acquired international, transnational and global dimensions, then we need to ask how this has become so, and what implications this has for thinking about national policy programs, local policy initiatives and inter-nationalising policy dialogue. It is this research agenda that is, in my view, fundamental to the globalisation of education policy research. But beyond this, it is essential to our attempts to develop an alternative education policy agenda to neo-liberalism, which demands not only fine sounding policies but also the creation of an alternative social imaginary committed to strong democracy and global justice (Rizvi, 2006, p. 203).

c) The new state of the old state

One particular challenge that is related to the previously discussed globalisation challenges is worth mentioning: the role of the nation state in education policy, and the re-emergence of the problematic of the state in the global policy field. We will start the exploration with a short outline of the discussion between Marxism and pluralist (elitist) approaches to education policy.

To put it very broadly, pluralist approaches assume there is a plurality of values and power distributed throughout society, and they assume that governments attempt to represent through the policy process as many interest groups as possible (Parsons, 1995, p. 134). While the pluralist approach focuses mainly on the distribution of power, elitist approaches conceive of power as something that is concentrated, and they focus on how governments act along the values and interest of particular elite groups (ibid., p. 248). One could say that neo-Marxist (conflict) approaches take this elitist position further and claim that basically groups who play a major role in the capitalist economy have a hold on government and education policies. To put the latter in more classic terms: "political legal and ideological apparatuses are grounded in conditions within the material economic infrastructure" (Turner & Mitchell, 1997, p. 24). Of course, there are various strands of neo-Marxist theory, differing for instance with regard to the level of autonomy of the state apparatus and the ideological role of culture and intellectuals (cf. Aronowitz & Giroux, 1994, pp. 65ff).

In order to discuss the challenges posed by globalisation, we will explore how these approaches take shape within the field of education policy studies. Firstly we will discuss some examples in the United Kingdom and Australia, and then some examples from scholarly work in the United States.

The difference between the pluralists and the elitists is connected to the debate in the 1990s between *state-centred* approaches and approaches of the policy *process and cycle* (Vidovich, 2002). The state-centred approaches examine the role of state apparatuses and ideologies in capitalist societies, and on how education is organised and governed. The policy process approach addresses the role of actors and their interests in different stages of the policy process which leads to particular decisions and policy measures.[3] The debate is represented in Dale's (1989) focus on the (macro) politics of education and on the role of the state on the one hand and Ball's (1990; 1994a/b) focus on the (micro) politics involved in education policies within the state on the other hand. The first type of research discusses the changing production structures, the functional division of labour in the coordination of education and the role of the state, while the second type of research considers policies in changed societal and cultural patterns, taking into account the readings and meanings of local actors, and the emerging discourses and trajectories. In sum, there is a theoretical (political) perspective on structures, divisions and tasks, next to an analytical (sociological) approach of trajectories and meanings. There have been attempts to transcend both perspectives however. It is suggested for instance that the focus should be on the relative autonomy of the state as a kind of strategic terrain where actors struggle inside the policy process and over policy texts. In line with this, Lingard (1993, 1995) speaks about the micro-politics at the level of the state, which is an acknowledgement of pluralism in the context of administration, bureaucracies and other state terrains. Focusing on intermediate "policy networks", and in line of neo-pluralist approaches, Raab also (1994a/b) seeks to transcend the old tensions between state and policy actors, and between macro and micro.

In the United States, an analogous development and discussion can be noticed. Embracing neo-Marxist assumptions, Torres (1989) for instance develops a political sociological framework to explain public and education policy-making in capitalist and developing countries. Similarly, within Apple's neo-Marxist framework there is an emphasis on the role of the state. However, in his emphasis on the role of the state Apple explicitly criticises so-called liberal pluralist approaches (Apple, 1982 p. 29; pp. 120–134). These pluralist approaches assume that policies represent a diversity of interests, but Apple suggests instead that the focus should be on the concentration of interest and power in relation to the accumulation of power, and on the ideological meaning of cultural struggles (around the school and curriculum).[4] One could argue that the work of Popkewitz (1996, p. 27; cf. 1991) represents another approach. His focus on the emerged systems of reasoning and the power of these knowledge systems is another attempt to rethink and reconceptualise the problem of social regulation and consequently the problematic of the state. Contrary to functionalist and/or Marxist accounts, his

Foucauldian inspired "political sociology" approach studies the social production of actors, images and ideas, and their contingent assemblage.[5] The focus here is on how the state emerges as an actor within a particular system of reasoning.

During the 1990s the problematic of the state has been lifted out of these discussions, and gradually has been reframed. In this context, it is worth mentioning two developments: 1) the introduction and use of the term governance and 2) the practical and theoretical repositioning of state government.

1) Except for normative uses, the term governance is used as an analytical lens to look at power and regulation mechanisms beyond common policy and government practices: the processes of governing and bottom-up decision making by people at different levels of both governmental and non-governmental organisations; non-hierarchical (private/public) networks of governing; specific ways of coordination analytically distinguished from the agents and institutions involved in governing and the act of governing or steering itself (Kooiman, 1993; Rhodes, 1997; Stoker, 1998; Jessop, 2000). In line with this, the term refers as well to actual changes in the organisation of society, and particularly the changed role of state government in relation to the emergence of new practices of regulation and coordination both locally and globally. Authors such as Rosenau argue that what takes shape is "governance without government" (Rosenau, 1992). An illustration of this development is seen at the level of international organisations and the networks of private and public collaboration in regions in the European Union (Dale, 1999). Elaborating on this, policy scholars attempt to describe the repositioning of governments and states in accordance with the new patterns and networks of governance. The state, here, is regarded as a regulator, and as responsible for "metagovernance" or "coordination of coordination" (Maroy, 2004; Dale, 1997; see also Jessop, 2000).

Despite the above mentioned diversity, a common concern underlying the use of the term governance is to disconnect the question of power and regulation from the question of government and particularly from the problematic of the state. Accordingly, it becomes possible to rethink the question of government and the state in relation to new practices of governance. State government can be regarded as something that is part of a broader system of education governance. Thus the term governance, both as part of an analytical perspective or as a term indicating new developments in society, may support the viewpoint of the critical policy scholar.

2) The second development worth mentioning in order to understand the new way the problematic of the state is posed is related to globalisation. The opening up of the black box of globalisation indeed puts some of the traditional theoretical tensions to the background, or at least, leads to a reformulation of the problematic of the state (Burbules & Torres, 2000; Bottery, 2000; Lingard, 2000; Rizvi, 2004; Ozga & Lingard, 2007; Ball, 1998; Dale, 1999). Dale (2008) for instance suggest that the nation-state should not be located at the level of the *explanans* but the *explanandum*, and that scholars should take into account different overlapping "scales of politics and policy." The focus on scales, and distinguishing between the local, regional, national and international, is regarded as a way to resist what is

called "spatial fetishism" by Benner (1999). Spatial fetishism refers to the tendency to approach the global as a new, but self-evident additional component in the social context and hence ignoring differences at the level of scales and forms of re-scaling.

Different approaches have been developed with regard to state government and state policies at the level of the explanandum. Ball (1998) suggests remaining attentive to processes of "re-contextualisation" and to the role of local politics and cultures in the translation of "global and generic" solutions. Relying on Bourdieu, Lingard (2005) suggests the emerging global policy field should be analysed, as well as cross-field effects within the state (see Lingard & Rawolle, 2004; Lingard et al., 2005a/b; Rawolle, 2005). In a similar vein, Ozga and Lingard (2007, p. 69) point at the emergence of the "globalised education policy field situated between global pressures and local vernacular education policy responses", and they propose to study in detail "vernacular globalisation" (Appadurai, 1996). The concern here is not only with "travelling policies", that is, with how policies get globally dispersed. Equally important is to examine how global policies are connected with "embedded policies." Addressing a similar concern, Arnove and Torres (1999) discuss the "dialectic between the global and the local." From still another perspective, Popkewitz (1996) speaks of the "international circulation of ideas" and Lindblad & Popkewitz (2004) suggest focusing on "travelling policies." The latter means that it is revealing to take for instance a close look at the controversies around 'educational restructuring' that are produced in different national contexts. A specific case is current policy research with regard to the European Union. Here, scholars start to focus on the new policy actors that enter the scene, how member states are being re-positioned, and how they come to develop national education policies embedded within a competitive European framework (Lawn & Lingard, 2002; Haahr, 2004; Simons, 2007). In line with Bourdieu, Lingard (2006, p. 293) argues that it is the amount of "national capital" possessed by a nation that should be regarded as a major factor in determining the space of resistance within a global context and the degree for autonomy for the development of policy within the nation.

In sum, what these critical studies share is an attempt to rethink the problematic of the state in view of the emergence of globalised policies and education restructuring discourses. Elaborating on the observed shift from the so-called "welfare state" to the "competition" (Yeatman, 1993; Cerny, 1997), "evaluative" (Neave, 1998) or "performative" (Ball, 2000) state, there is special attention to the way state government reformulates, justifies and develops education policies and becomes an actor among other actors in the global field of governance. Indeed, it is noticed that far from retreating, the post-welfare state develops new ways of governing. A case in point is the state's role in organising output control in education and in setting the framework for entrepreneurial freedom, quality assurance and choice (see Hudson, 2007). This leads to the next set of challenges: the many guises of post-welfare policies.

d) Right way solutions adopted by third way policies

Although dating back to the end of 1970s, and intrinsically bound with the development of the critical orientation to education policy (see part 1 of the introduction), scholars remain attentive to the conditions of what is often referred to with the term neoliberalism. Harvey attempts to grasp the elusive term as follows:

> Neoliberalism is in the first instance a theory of political economic practices that proposes that human well-being can best be advanced by liberating individual entrepreneurial freedoms and skills within an institutional framework characterised by strong private property rights, free markets, and free trade. The role of the state is to create and preserve an institutional framework appropriate to such practices (Harvey, 2005, p. 2).

While Harvey mainly focuses on theoretical developments, other authors try to grasp conditions and consequences of neoliberalism for education and education policy. Scholars study for instante the educational restructuring included within neoliberal policies, that is, "schooling reform in hard times" (Lingard, Knight & Porter, 1993). Topics being discussed are: the politics of quality assurance systems and standardisation; the impact of policies on parental choice, diversification and increased school autonomy; the effects of new forms of responsibility and accountability; and the politics and effects of decentralisation and marketisation (e.g. Whitty et al, 1993; Whitty et al., 1998; Kenway et al., 1993; Apple, 1993; Gewirtz et al., 1995; Weiler, 1990; Lauglo, 1995; Marginson, 1997; and for support of particular neoliberal reforms: Chubb & Moe, 1990; Tooley, 1996).

We will not discuss the critical study of neoliberalism in detail here. We want to limit ourselves to discussion of four less obvious challenges that are becoming more pressing at the start of the twenty-first century: 1) the adoption of neoliberal tools within the Third Way policies, 2) the need to reformulate ideas of social justice, 3) the renewed attention for pedagogy and teacher professionalism/teacher education, and 4) the critical sensitivity for master signifiers such as neoliberalism and globalisation.

1) Throughout the 1990s, the scholarly interest in new modes of government and social regulation continued. An interesting observation was that aside from so-called liberal policy makers, also social democrats and 'third way' political administrations came to rely on policy measures previously classified under the general term neoliberalism (Rose, 1999; Olssen et al., 2004; Tomlinson, 2005; Ball, 2008). Measures related to output control, managerialism and responsabilisation did not disappear with the change of political coalitions. The result is that in contrast to the 1980s and the early 1990s, and at least in the United Kingdom and several other European countries, policy scholars are no longer merely describing the policies of so-called neoliberal and neoconservative administrations. Instead they are clearly spotlighting continuities at the level of policy measures and mechanisms (Furlong, 2005; Tomlinson, 2005; Ball, 2008).

As a consequence, critical advocacy becomes directed to those policy makers that at an ideological level represented the progressive alternative.

2) The widespread use of measures and policy options previously associated only with neoliberalism, actually leads to a situation where social democracy can no longer be identified with social justice, and neoliberalism can no longer be used as a synonym for social injustice. The challenge here is to open up the black box of social justice, and to rethink critically the idea of social justice and equity as promoted through education policy. Seddon, for instance, stresses the importance of being extremely careful with identifying post-welfare education and the impact of neoliberal policy measures with "unjust education" (Seddon, 2003). Instead, it is suggested to go beyond the large categories such as neoliberalism, social democracy and third way policy, and to adopt an adequate perspective that enables analysis of policies in their contexts as well as analysis of the specific practice of social justice.

3) The new developments in policy and education are not just analysed at the level of theories, assumptions and ideologies and evaluated against the background of social justice, democracy and freedom (Apple, 2003; Giroux, 2004; Olssen et al., 2004). In the wake of current education policies, and this can be regarded as the third challenge, there is a specific focus on issues related to teacher professionalism and pedagogy. Current developments are analysed at the level of local discourses, the related technologies and practices and the effects on teachers and students (Ball, 2003; Webb, 2005, 2006). The concern here is the impact of managerial, market-related and performance-oriented reforms on teaching and pedagogy, on the professionalism and autonomy of teachers, on teacher education policy and school leadership (cf. Ball, 1998, 2003; Whitty, 2002; Furlong, 2005; Cochran-Smith, 2005; Hargreaves, 2000; Smyth, 2002; Avis, 2003, Menter et al., 2006). These studies could be regarded as evaluation and implementation studies; however their orientation is clearly critical. Their aim is to evaluate the implementation and effects of current reform policies, not in the first place to improve policy making, but to critically assess the impact on the values assumed in professionalism and pedagogy.

4) A final challenge relates to the role of so-called master signifiers today. We mentioned earlier that most critical studies of education policy no longer take notions such as globalisation, the state, neoliberalism or social justice for granted. Scholars acknowledge that the notions in themselves have little analytical or explanatory value. However, it is one thing to open up the conceptual problematic or to articulate and make explicit the meaning of these terms or the practices and discourses implied. Another critical approach is to regard the notions themselves as being part of global policy discourses. Nóvoa (2002) speaks for instance about "planet speak", a sort of "worldwide bible" and the circulation of "magical concepts" that are the roots of all evil or the solutions for all problems. In line with this, Lindblad and Popkewitz (2004) refer to neoliberalism, as well as educational restructuring, as planet-speak and "elevator words" (Ian Hacking) relating different practices in order to create objects, to identify problems and to create ways to talk about them and to offer solutions. According to these writers, the challenge is to

analyse the discourses *on* globalisation, neoliberalism and the changed state, where and how they emerged, and how they work (rather than just analysing the dominant discourse *of* neoliberalism).

e) Between theoretical inspiration and inspired theories

Clearly not disconnected from social and political developments, new challenges at the level of theory building, methodology and data use arise. Several issues are explored here: 1) the relation between the theoretical and the empirical, 2) the importance of specific concerns, 3) new theories and methods, and 4) the use of quantitative data.

1) During the early 1990s many authors noticed that critical studies often addressed specific policies, and then proceeded to study these cases in an ad hoc fashion (Ozga, 1990; Lingard, 1993; Troyna, 1994; Raab, 1994b; Dale, 1994; Ball, 1990, 1994a/b). The main concern of these writers is that this ad hoc focus actually troubles genuine theory building. There are several points of view here. Some scholars express the concern that the qualitative methodology used (such as case-studies based on interviews and observation), and the focus on micro-politics at micro-levels do not allow us to get a picture of the broader context of education policy (for instance, the politics of education) (Dale, 1994; Troyna, 1994; Hatcher & Troyna, 1994). However, from the side of the qualitative, micro-oriented research that is criticised here, the diagnosis is different. Their concern is that policy research in education is often "commentary and critique" and lacking "empirical research" (Ball, 1990, p. 9). Empirical research and taking particular policies and their trajectories as a point of departure, as well as drawing upon social theories of the post-modern condition, are regarded as essential in explanatory and sociological theory building – something that Ball (1994a/b) regards as an important challenge as well. Thus from different perspectives the development of critical *sociological* theories of education policy is recommended as a major task.

In contrast to these perspectives, Halpin (1994, p. 201) stresses the importance of non-sociological theories as well as the elaboration of theories on the implementation of policies (and theorising what works and what doesn't work and for what reasons). Additionally, he proposes that the conception of supportive research methods should be broadened to include discourse analysis and fine grained content analysis beyond actor and intention focused observation, interviews and text analysis (cf. Taylor et al, 1997, p. 43). In short, it is suggested to broaden the definition of what valuable theories and valuable methods concerning education policy and politics are expected to be.

2) Perhaps it is crucial to mention that for scholars with a critical policy orientation the definition of theory should take one important issue into account. The point of departure for critical studies is often neither situated at the level of theory, nor a well defined ad hoc case. The point of departure instead seems to be a particular concern, yet clearly not disconnected from theoretical perspectives and existing cases. The definition of a valuable theory hence is inspired by this

commitment, and develops in relation to the scholar's involvement with the present. In short, if the term critical research addresses the relation of concern between the researcher and society, or between the researcher and her present, then critical research of education policy can never be either solely theory-oriented or merely applied. The critical orientation is embedded in a matter of concern, and in view of such a specific concern the theoretical and the practical are intertwined.

3) Except for challenges regarding the role of theory, critical policy studies are challenged by ongoing developments at the level of theories and methods. We limit ourselves to the outline of some influential developments. From the 1980s onwards, the problematic of gender and racism is regarded as highly important in studies of education policy and politics, and is related to the need to have theoretical and methodological tools to address these topics (Troyna, 1994; Ferguson, 1984; Henry & Taylor, 1993; Giroux, 1997; Marshall & Anderson, 1995; Marshall, 1999). Next, and in close relation to globalisation, there is the emergence of postcolonialism and specifically the critique of adopting Western points of view in (comparative) theory and politics, embedded within discourses, concepts and ways of looking (Young, 2003; Rizvi, 2004; Tikly, 2001). At a more general epistemological and meta-theoretical level, post-structuralism, anti-foundationalism and post-positivist methodologies have been part of the debate since the 1990s. The debate involved the questioning of modern assumptions regarding knowledge, truth, facts, theory, critique etc., and related to this, the modern role of critical scholarship (Cherryholmes, 1998; Usher & Edwards, 1994; Scheurich, 1994: Peters, 1996; Humes & Bryce, 2003). In view of previous developments, some new lines of study emerged. Instead of looking at texts, intentions and interpretation, scholars shifted attention to the study of policy as discourse, the politics of policy discourses, or discourses as politics. And instead of actor or subject oriented approaches, scholars adopted approaches focusing on the discursive constitution of types of (gendered) subjects and subjectivities, and local struggles of resistance around this constitution (Butler, 1990).

An example is the Foucauldian-inspired approach of "social epistemology", where speech and the use of particular concepts such as 'youth at risk' are regarded as the effect of (productive) power (Popkewitz & Brennan, 1998, p. 9). In line with this, there is a cultural history approach (Popkewitz et al., 2001) incorporating a focus on the "cultural politics of text." Research in line with the cultural history approach does not take policy agencies and their interests as given entities, but studies how discourse constitutes, for example, the relation between state and university departments (Heyning, 2001). Another example is the attempt to combine materialist approaches and post-structuralist approaches in line with Foucault (Fairclough, 1989; Olssen, 1999). The attempt here is to locate the power of discourses within a particular cultural and economic reality, and thereby combine discourse analysis with social analysis. Another perspective is "political spectacle theory" (Edelman, 1988). As an elaboration of symbolic interactionism, political spectacle theory focuses on the symbolic forms in the political process. Education policy as political spectacle is located at the intersection of governance, media and economy, and is analysed at the level of symbolic language. In line with this orientation to the symbolic, the following issues can be addressed: "casting political actors as leaders, allies, and enemies; dramaturgy (staging, plotting, and costuming); the illusion of rationality; the illusion of democratic participation, disconnection between means and ends; and distinguishing the action on stage from the action backstage" (Smith et al., 2004, p. 12). Ultimately, the scholar is interested in the struggles and dominant interest behind the spectacle.

The main focus of the debates around new theories and methodologies during the 1999s was the modernist-postmodernist discussion, and particularly discussions about relativism-universalism, foundationalism-antifoundationalism, inductive-deductive, and construction-deconstruction approaches. These arguments are not closed or decided today; however, it seems the discussion is no longer central to academic debates. Studies with a critical education policy orientation remain driven principally by major social concerns posed by challenges such as globalisation, neoliberalism and managerialism. Perhaps, this moves the meta-discussions about the assumptions of theory and methodology to the background, or connects the discussion at least to specific questions posed by society. At this point it is worth mentioning two relatively new concerns: the need for alternative conceptions of education, pedagogy, democracy and social justice.

It is striking to see how both old and new philosophies and theories inform the critical education policy perspective. Their mixed usage seems to surpass the modernism-postmodernism debate. For instance, Foucault's work on governmentality or Bourdieu's work on policy fields is elaborated in combination with empirical methods (Masschelein et al., 2007; Fejes & Nicoll, 2008; Lingard et al., 2005a/b). The need for a straightforward and positively formulated critical and/or normative stance towards social and political developments in general, and towards education policy and politics specifically is also prominent. Examples are: education and the question of democracy, participation and recognition (in line with Habermas, Fraser, Benhabib, Honneth, Rancière), social justice, education policy, capabilities or capacities for social practice (in line with Sen, Nussbaum), teaching, politics and the dimension of responsibility, freedom, justice and virtues (in line with Levinas, Lyotard, Derrida, Bauman), and practical wisdom, *phronesis* and education (MacIntyre). Additionally, scholars express a renewed interest in the moral and social role of 'education and pedagogy', and critical discussion of the dominant practices and discourses on lifelong learning (Biesta, 2006). It should be noted however that in critically orientated policy studies these theories and philosophies are mentioned, discussed or applied, but are not often guiding and orienting the policy research.

4) Regarding the concern with quantification, some more background information should be given. Within education policy studies, traditionally there is a tension between the use of *quantitative* and *qualitative* methods. The critical policy orientation during the 1980s and 1990s, at least those studies rooted in new sociology of education approaches, mainly relied upon qualitative methods.[6] As mentioned earlier, the newer methods are also qualitative, for example (critical) discourse analysis (Codd, 1988; Ball, 1994a/b; Taylor, 1997). The methods that are used rely on interpretation and qualitative data, and critical scholarship seems to

turn itself away from quantitative research methods (such as large data-bases on school input and outputs, longitudinal research programs etc.) (Apple, 1996, p. 127). Additionally, and this is currently enforced by recent evidence-based policies, critical scholars often identify quantitative research methods with instrumental policy analysis and with classic political arithmetic. From this perspective, any type of quantification seems to become a critical concern, instead of a possible valuable method for critical education policy research. There are voices, however, to include quantitative methods in critical education policy research. As Halpin (1994, p. 199) claims:

> (…) interpretative approaches favoured by many education policy analysts often inform very well the thinking of members of their intellectual communities, but fail to penetrate the minds of policy makers who are seeking answers to more prosaic, but nonetheless important questions about the relative merits of different proposals for reform and improvement.

In line with this, Lauder et al. (2004) talk about a new kind of "political arithmetic" that is part of critical scholarship and that gathers and discusses quantitative data on effects in relation to social justice aims (cf. Gale, 2001, p. 382). In a similar vein, Luke argues for critical policy researchers to start playing an active and constructive role in "redressing" the numeric data in policy making (Luke, 2003, p. 98). Instead of criticising the data as such, he suggests paying attention to the narratives linked up with numeric evidences in current policy making, and giving support to new narratives and to contextualise numeric data in new ways (see further below).

f) Research that works and unemployed research

Another set of important challenges arises from the changed relation between research and policy making, particularly with the advent of so-called "evidence based policy" and related movements of "evidence-based practice" in teaching during the 1990s (Young et al., 2002). Governments have always relied on particular knowledge in decision making. What is currently referred to as evidence based policy clearly includes a particular kind of public policy, a particular kind of evidence, and a particular need for research on education. Governments adopting procedures of New Public Management and looking for ways to render themselves and professionals accountable to citizen-consumers are permanently seeking for performance-oriented re-structuring, and hence, for particular evidence.

What counts as evidence today is mainly related to the achievement of targets and examples of best performance, and on the identification of procedures, options and measures that have proven to be efficient or effective in view of these targets and performance indicators. The required evidence is thus regarded as knowledge on 'what works' (Davies et al., 2000). For instance, in line with the No Child Left Behind Act (2001) in the US one of the concerns of public policy is implementing programs that have 'scientifically' proven to lead to improved scores on standardised tests (Luke, 2003, p. 89). The concern with evidence today thus is a concern with 'what works' or with what contributes to 'excellent performance'.

One reason for the increased governmental influence on education research and on the actual instrumental value of outcomes in education research is clearly the strategic role of education and lifelong learning in the knowledge society and particularly the knowledge economy (Ozga et al., 2006; Ozga & Lingard, 2007, p. 78). The current knowledge society seems to be a "totally pedagogised society" (Bernstein, 2001) where educational, social and economic policies are converging (Ball, 2008). Thus, the investment in education, and different types of investment in human capital, is more then ever linked up with economic policies. Against this strategic background, the so-called semi-professional diversity of teachers' *personal* judgement should give away to programs and procedures that have *proven* to result in high performance. As a result, a specific kind of research on education and learning becomes of strategic importance. Especially in the United States and the United Kingdom the needs of governments for evidence on 'what works' has a considerable impact on education research. There are debates however on whether this link between policy and research, and the implied expectations towards both policy and research, are tenable and justified (Hammersley, 2002; Ozga, 2000).

Additionally, we should consider the emergence of the new global policy field in discussing these issues. This field is to a large extent an assemblage of particular research on 'what works' and 'excellent performance' in education. Thus, education governance is increasingly linked with data collection and numbers on performance indicators, which in reality leads to the development of patterns of "governing by numbers" or "policy as numbers" (Rose, 1999; Ball, 1998; Lindblad & Popkewitz, 2000; Henry et al., 2001; Lawn & Lingard, 2002; Simons, 2007; Grek, 2009). There is a politics involved in the presentation of examples of excellent performance and international comparisons, and policy makers rely on the media not just to inform citizens about new policy measures but actually to shape policies. The "mediatisation of education policy" clearly plays a role here (Lingard & Rawolle, 2004).

Confronted with evidence based policy or the "governmental re-articulation of *analysis for policy*", critical scholarship faces different challenges (Lingard & Ozga, 2007, p. 6, italics in original). It makes scholars increasingly aware of their own position in the making of policy, and thus asks for a kind of "epistemic reflexivity" focusing on one's relation to the needs of government and one's role in the "politics of research" (Usher & Edwards, 1994, p. 181). Within the current politics of research, critical scholars have to position themselves towards the regular policy research arena that became analysis *for* policy, towards all sorts of meta-research that investigates how to improve the arena of policy-oriented research, and towards diverse types of education research assessment tools that measure the impact of one's research. As a consequence, the critical education policy scholar is no longer only oriented towards the field of education policy, but also towards the evidence-producing research fabric that is part of policy.

Noticing these developments, Ozga (2000, 2007) suggests looking for new relationships between governing, policy and research (cf. Ozga & Lingard, 2007). What is suggested is to hold to the idea that critical policy scholarship includes a particular kind of critical advocacy, relying on a particular conception of equality and social justice. Thus instead of withdrawing oneself from the evidence based policy context, Ozga & Lingard (2007, pp. 78–79) suggest looking for new ways to relate to both education and research policies and to resist dominant modes of research steering:

> Pressures for research steering in education are very high because of the instability and fluidity of the knowledges that it produces, and because less 'managed' research activities may, indeed, have considerable value in the creation of active, independent and creative thinkers and learners. There is, thus a considerable contradiction at the heart of the research steering process, and this opens up spaces for research to rediscover and render explicit its national capital, in terms that are not entirely set by globalising pressures and practices.

Specifically speaking, Ozga (2000) proposes to "remove policy from its pedestal" and to form research communities by bringing together academics and practitioners and their concerns (cf. Vidovich, 2007). There is the suggestion that researchers should look for optimal ways to govern and organise education, which then *inform* policy making and provide resistance to the dominant evidence based policy agenda that is oriented to 'what works' (Ozga, 2000; Lingard & Gale, 2007). Along similar lines, Luke suggests that researchers should not criticise the ideology of evidence based policy as such. Based on the observation that evidence used in policy making is always wrapped in narratives, selectively used and overtly discussed, he argues that it is always possible to re-appropriate and redress the use of evidence in policy development:

> As a research community, we need to move towards a richer, more multidisciplinary approach to education analysis and policy development – beyond the crude league tables and single-dimension test score analysis, and beyond critique that explicates the ideological contradictions of these policies but struggles to remake schools and systems in communities' and student's interests (Luke, 2003, p. 98).

Hence, Luke suggests to put different 'evidences' on the table and to engage researchers, educational workers and policy makers in the development of "new narratives, new pathways and new policies" (ibid., p. 98).

A stronger version of critical advocacy is perhaps Bourdieu's plea for "collective intellectuals." Bourdieu underlines the scholar's role in the development of "rational utopias" in collaboration with (new) social movements and (international) trade unions. The development of these utopias could be based on the "social costs of economic violence, as a way of laying the foundations for an economics of happiness" (Bourdieu, 1997/2008, pp. 292–293). Closely related to this, Halpin argues in line with Giddens for a "utopian realism." Halpin's idea is to go beyond the ideological stance in terms of *either-or* (for example, either neoliberalism or Marxism/socialism) in the direction of a more pragmatic stance holding to the *and-also* position, yet to hold to the utopianism included in third way politics for example (Halpin, 1999).

In sum, the critical scholar indeed runs the risk of being unemployed in the large evidence-producing fabric, yet there are certainly other ways to put this research to work.

g) Critical policymakers and concerned scholars

Finally, we wish to briefly focus on the set of challenges arising from the critical ethos that inspires scholarly and policy work. In the last section of this chapter we return to these challenges in more detail.

One major aim of critical policy studies is to reveal how practices, problems and ideas that are taken for granted are in fact part of hidden or not clearly visible social, political or cultural constellations. Critical studies assume that through awareness of contingency ('things are not necessary this way'), and by taking into account the legitimate rules, goals and/or courses of action, people would be able to liberate themselves and that this would lead to the construction of a more free, just, democratic society. This assumption can be re-formulated as follows: critical thought assumes that facts and problems are socially constructed, that this construction involves power, and that awareness of this construction (based on critical studies) opens up a space for re-construction (cf. Latour, 2004).

Due to these assumptions, critical policy scholarship opposes those ways of thinking that take facts and problems for granted. Indeed, critical scholarship opposes instrumental ways of thinking, such as problem solving theory. Problem solving is about finding the most efficient and effective way to solve problems, and does not imply an awareness of the construction or contingency of the problems. The opponent of critical theory, according to Robertson and Dale (2008) and in line with Robert Cox, is thus problem solving theory. From the perspective of critical scholars, the problem solving way of thinking is naïve in that there is no awareness of the power and politics involved at the level of the problem-formulation and definition. Several critical scholars question the basic assumptions of the critical project however. What they notice is that its assumptions seem to have become common sense outside the academic sphere of critical theory.

Latour, for instance, sees a remarkable overlap in critical attitude between his own critical research on the construction of scientific facts (revealing how what is taken for granted as fact or object by scientists is socially constructed) and the current attitude of policymakers. Policymakers, he notices, have come to adopt a similar attitude when they argue that particular problems or facts should not be taken for granted. Latour mentions the example of policymakers arguing that global warming is a scientific or policy construct, and that there is politics and power in the definition of this problem (Latour, 2004). In short, it is seems as if policy makers have become critical. Additionally, critical thinkers and social movements – for instance those concerned with climate change – seem to adopt the problem solving attitude. They try to convince everyone to regard the problem as a fact and to find solutions as quickly as possible.

In a similar vein, Robertson and Dale argue the new status of problem-solving in the changed relation between states and global actors such as the IMF/World Bank, WTO and OECD. According to them, what these actors do is not characterised by problem *solving* but by problem *framing*:

> (…) The way we see the prescriptions and advice of international organisations is not so much as *problem solving contributions*, but as *problem defining and framing interventions*. Essentially, it is through these agencies that states learn what their problems 'really' are (Robertson & Dale, 2008, italics in original).

Indeed, Robertson and Dale raise the question why the World Bank's education strategies, and its explicit attempt to reform education and governance, to frame or shape problems and to construct the world, should not be regarded as a mode of critical theory itself. Thus facing these strategies of problem framing and the problem solving strategies, the classical assumptions of critical theory are clearly challenged. Robertson and Dale (2008) however do not propose getting rid of critical theories, but advocate redefining them, for instance by developing a theory that addresses the following issues: how power and discourses work at the level of problem framing and reality shaping policies and politics; how actors strategically adopt problem solving theories; and how to articulate in more detail one's framework for social justice. The latter refers to what we called a matter of concern that motivates the critical policy orientation (see introduction and overview of this book). In the words of Robertson and Dale that underlying concern is an engagement "to advance and enable a socially transformative agenda for critical education policy analysis." Their perspective comes close to the suggestions of scholars we discussed earlier, such as Ozga's plea for new research communities and Luke's argument to broaden the evidence used in current evidence policy making.

In the conclusion of this chapter we will return to the now crucial challenge posed by policy makers. At this point we underline the importance of being attentive to the assumptions of the critical orientation and of being especially attentive to its basic concern. In our view, questioning the assumptions of critical policy scholarship should not lead to radical questioning its *concern*.

AN OVERVIEW OF THEORETICAL HORIZONS AND APPROACHES

This section presents an overview of approaches adopted in studies critically oriented towards politics, power and policies in education: state theory, critical discourse analysis, field theory, governmentality, micro-politics, post-colonial theory, feminist policy analysis, and philosophical analysis. Often these approaches are combined, but we think it is helpful to discuss them separately. For a good understanding, it is necessary to first sketch the general theoretical horizons the approaches have sprung from.

a) Mapping horizons

We will start with a short overview of the main frameworks or paradigms in social theory: functional, utilitarian, conflict and interactionist theorising (Turner, 1991; Turner & Mitchell, 1977, pp.22ff). The paradigms will be complemented by a short sketch of critical theory and post-structuralism.

Functional, utilitarian, conflict and interactionist theorising

The main aim of *functional* theorising is an analysis of education taking into account the effects on or consequences for society. For example, education is regarded as a source of social integration or as having a selection and allocation function. *Utilitarian* theorising starts from the assumption that actors have clear hierarchies of values (for desired resources), and calculate what is needed (that is, costs) in order to secure their highly valued preferences. This economically oriented perspective analyses education in terms of 'rate of return on investment in education' in line with Human Capital Theory or in terms of 'decision making processes in the educational market' (school choice, school vouchers) in line with Public Choice Theory.

The two traditions that actually form the horizon for a lot of critical policy studies are conflict and interactionist theorising.

Conflict theorising starts from the assumption that the unequal distribution of resources in society fosters a particular understanding of education, its organisation and development. There are many different versions here, although a broad distinction between Marxian-inspired and Weberian-inspired conflict theories is useful in order to grasp their scope.

Marxian-inspired theories focus on how schools through ideology reproduce class relations and the unequal distribution of material resources. In line with the work of Althusser (1971), scholars focus on the reproductive role played by the "superstructure" that consists of a "political-legal repressive apparatus" and an "ideological state apparatus." In line with Gramsci (1971) there is a focus on the role of ideology or cultural ideas and symbols, of intellectuals in creating and reproducing hegemony at the cultural level, and of teachers reproducing this hegemony in classrooms. In both lines of elaboration, education and the state are regarded as arenas for ideological struggle that are ultimately rooted in the material relations of production or the struggle around the distribution of material resources.

The Weberian-inspired conflict theories also focus on the role of education and the state in reproducing inequality, yet their main focus is on the formation and role of status groups in reproduction mechanisms. These studies broaden the class concept and concentrate on the status conflicts surrounding honour, prestige and cultural capital. The work of Bourdieu and Passeron (1964/1979, 1970/1977) has been influential here. In short, their work focuses on the role of education in producing and reproducing different kinds of capital: economic capital (money, objects), social capital (positions, affiliations), cultural capital (skills, tastes, preferences) and symbolic capital (legitimating codes). The assumption is that capital is unequally distributed and that a social class is constituted based on the total amount of capital and on the configuration of the different kinds of capital. Each class has its own "culture" or "habitus", that is, "the largely unconscious perceptions, choices, preferences, and behaviours of members within a given level and configuration of economic, social, cultural, and symbolic capital" (Turner & Mitchell, 1977, p. 26). Education, and in particular educational credentials, play an important role in the production of types of capital, but also in the reproduction of inequality because mediation occurs through the "habitus" (received in the family, peer group) and the school structure (valuing particular amounts/kinds/configurations of capital). In sum, Weberian inspired theories allow a focus on the role of elite groups in the unequal distribution of resources, chances, and skills.

Interactionist modes of theorising focus on face-to-face interactions in schools and classrooms, and on how meaning is constituted in these local contexts. In the literature, four distinct versions of interactionist theory are distinguished (Turner, 1991). Symbolic interactionist theories and role theories concentrate on the self-conception of teachers and students, the definition of the situation, the playing of roles and the production and maintenances of definitions of the situation (e.g. Hargreaves). Dramaturgical interactionism, in line with Goffman, studies the context of interactions by focusing on presentations of self, lines of conduct, strategies, rituals, and the framing of the situation. Interactionist structuralism, in line with Bernstein, pays attention to how linguistic codes in schools lead to different forms of socialisation (for example, the restricted code of lower-class students). Finally, interactionist phenomenology reveals that what is taken for granted, and what is supposed to be an objective reality, is actually produced in interaction and hence socially constructed. Research on the assumptions of the superiority of abstract knowledge to everyday knowledge (Young) and the implicit use of class labels in evaluating students (Keddie) are examples.

Although not really to be situated at the same level of the previous modes of theorising (functional, utilitarian, conflict, interactionist), it is important to mention on the one hand critical theory (in line with the Frankfurt School) and on the other hand post-structuralism (Honneth, 2006; Peters, 1996; Humes & Bryce, 2003).

Critical theory

Critical theory is regarded as an influential attempt to develop Marxist thought. It originated at the Frankfurt Institute of Social Research during the 1930s through the work of Horkheimer, Marcuse, and Adorno, and later Habermas and Honneth. The aim of Horkheimer was to integrate all kinds of empirical social research and philosophical thought into a general materialistic theory of society. For Horkheimer, the following question should orient all research at the institute in Frankfurt: "How do the psychic mechanisms come about which make it possible for tensions between social classes, which are forced to become conflicts because of the economic situation, to remain latent?" (Horkheimer in Honneth, 2006, p. 242) Underpinning this program for social empirical research was a belief in changing social relations and social progress by means of political revolutions.

Later versions of critical theory, for instance in line with Adorno and the description of society as a "totally administered society", noticed a negative model of development, and thus no longer assumed social progress and the potential of political change.

From the 1960s onwards, the work of Habermas gave a new impetus to critical theory. In his discussion with Marxism, Habermas stresses the importance of language and particularly its role as a medium for understanding, and hence as playing a major role in social reproduction. Later on, Habermas (1981) develops his theory of the rationality of communicative action. In this theory, he draws attention to the emancipatory potential of communication based on mutual understanding, in contrast to the colonising effects of strategic and instrumental rationalities (mediated through power, money, efficiency calculation). The Habermasian version of critical theory assumes that modernity is an "unfinished project," and his support of social democratic policies contributes to the further development of an straightforward orientation to education policy. It should also be noted that Habermas' critical reading of the so-called postmodernists, including for instance Foucault and Derrida, has been influential. Specifically his sharp attack on what he calls the "crypto-normativity" and "ethical relativism" of the "young conservatives" was picked up by critical policy scholars (Habermas, 1985). From the side of the so-called postmodernists, the 'modernist' Habermas however was criticised for imposing universalism. We will return to this debate after introducing the term post-structuralism.

Post-structuralism

Although the term post-structuralism is loaded with negative connotations, and although most authors given the label post-structuralist did not appreciate the label, we can briefly outline some of the topics discussed under this banner (cf. Gottweis, 2004).

Firstly, post-structuralists share a focus on language. This focus however is beyond a structuralist conception of language on the one hand and beyond a representational and intentional conception on the other hand. In line with Ferdinand de Saussure, the linguistic structuralists analyse language, society and culture as a closed system of signs and conventions, and examine language use within specific social contexts. Post-structuralists, instead, analyse the production and change of meaning in how language works, for example, in terms of text working on text, or the assemblage of discursive formations. Language and text are not analysed in relation to the speaker/writer (and his/her intentions), neither is it conceived of in relation to a reality it wants to represent. Instead, the focus is on the use of language and on the interpretations by the readers. However, and in contrast to Habermas, attention is not placed on the pragmatic and linguistic dimension of language, on the validity claims in argumentative discourse and on the implied social bonds. Instead, the French theorists commonly referred as post-structuralists conceive language in terms of events, discursive practices and formations (Foucault, 1969), intertextuality and the infinite play of signifiers (Derrida, 1961), or language games and narratives (Lyotard, 1979; 1983). An important assumption is that the social order is at once a discursive order, and that this order is not to be analysed in structural or binary (linguistic or materialistic) models and neither is it to be analysed in relation to an objectivity or given outside.

This shift towards language has put the notion 'discourse' in the centre of many sociological disciplines, including those of education theory and sociology of education (Codd, 1988; Ball, 1994b). For example, policy text is analysed as part of discourses that frame issues in a particular way as policy problems by using specific concepts, words, and ways of arguing, and hence constituting a specific arena within which to propose and discuss solutions. The focus is on the power of language, and in a Foucauldian framework, on how knowledge (in terms of *savoir* or general forms of knowing) and power (in terms of a complex of forces or steering mechanisms) are linked up in discourses (Foucault, 1982).

Secondly, and in line with the particular conception of language, there is no focus on the underlying structures or powerful actors in order to explain or describe the social fabric and education policy. In line with Foucault, the focus is on the historically contingent formation of assemblages and regimes, and not, as in conflict and structural theories, on how elite groups or material conditions are leading to a particular discourse, and how this discourse has an ideological or hegemonic effect. It is important however to keep in mind that the popular term 'discourse' is used in several theories.

In line with Foucault (1969, 1972), discourse refers to a discursive formation or order, that is, the historically shaped rules and practices for things to be said and known (and things not to be said and known). In 1970s, Foucault suggests analysing regimes of power-knowledge by focusing on how discourses work and how related forms of power work (Foucault, 1971, 1975, 1976). However, in Habermasian critical theory discourse is used in a different way. In Habermas' attempt to develop a discourse ethics the term refers to the practice of argumentative communication and the assumptions of validity within communicative reasoning (Habermas, 1981). Combining Foucauldian insights and conflict theories, Fairclough (1992, 1995, 2003) as one of the founders of critical discourse analysis (CDA) uses the term discourse to analyse how language shapes social practices and how these social practices in turn influence discourses (see further below). Here, the focus is on the ideological role of discourse, that is, the way language plays a major role in power struggles. Thus although there seems to be a common focus on the social and political dimension of language, it is important to keep in mind that the fashionable term discourse is often used in different ways and with highly diverging theoretical assumptions.

Thirdly, within post-structuralist thinking, there is on the one hand a critical reading of so-called modern social and political theories and on the other hand the development of an alternative critical scholarly position. Alongside the work of Foucault and Derrida strong criticism of deterministic and foundational reasoning in social, historical, and educational theory emerged. What is criticised is the assumption that specific conditions (for instance, unequal distribution of material resources), particular people or groups (for instance, policy makers or classes) or agencies (for instance, the state) determine social and cultural life, power and state structures and even people's subjectivity (Peters, 2001; Olssen et al., 2004). In line with Foucault and Derrida, there is a spatial focus on discursive events, contingent assemblages, and dispersed practices. However, there is not only a discussion at a theoretical, epistemological and methodological level between anti-foundationalist thinkers and so-called modernist scholars. What complicates things is that each camp turns the other into a research object itself.

Foundational and deterministic social thought and the assumption of a single cause or an underlying structure/subject is criticised itself for being part of a discursive formation with power effects (Blake et al., 1998; Usher & Edwards, 1994; Popkewitz & Brennen, 1998; Simons et al., 2005). The belief in foundations, underlying modern critical theory, is regarded itself as an effect of power relations. From the other camp, post-structuralists are blamed for justifying the existing power constellations, due to their ignorance of the role of actors and underlying material conditions and/or because they lack a normative point of view outside power to be able to judge hegemonic forms of power (see Habermas, 1985; Zippin, 1998; Olssen, 1999). This discussion is also repeated at the level of critical positions. From the perspective of Marxist conflict theory or critical theory, the critical potential of the historicising and de-naturalising analysis in line with Foucault is regarded as limited. Indicating that things are problematic or contingent but not explaining why they are problematic or need to change, or without offering explicit norms for social or political change, is regarded as relativistic and politically flawed or even dangerous (Habermas, 1985). Furthermore, the post-structural line of analysis is unmasked as being paradoxical for it explains how subjects and agents are constituted but assumes at the same time that there is still room for change. However, from the position of the post-structuralists, the use of norms is regarded as a foundational way of reasoning, leading to speaking for others and continuing the existence of power formations. Additionally, the focus on the classic institutions of power (such as The State, The School, The Economy) is criticised for not being able to describe how power actually works locally, and how discourses are interwoven with power mechanisms (Foucault, 1982). Furthermore, the act of showing that things can be changed and focusing on the contingency of what is assumed to be universal is regarded as a critical position in its own right, and it iw stressed that focusing on the production of subjects through power is not the same as assuming there is no agency.

In this introduction, we are not going into this discussion in depth. The reason for this is not only the limited space available. One of the reasons for not taking up this debate again is that we think the debate no longer 'colonises' the current research of scholars. The 'discursive arena' of policy research has changed. As mentioned throughout the introduction, there seem to be indications that this debate is no longer omnipresent, or at least that there is a shift from the theoretical and epistemological discussions of the 1990s to discussions mainly driven by new social and political developments. While the current discussions do not ignore theoretical interests, underlying them is a commitment to education and society. In other words, and drawing on the language of Latour (2004), there are indications of a shift from discussions around matters of fact (that divide and isolate scholars) to discussions on matters of concern that bring people together and generate 'public interest'.

The previous observation does not mean however there is a convergence or homogenisation of theoretical approaches in policy research. The next section will show that several different approaches are adopted.

b) Mapping approaches

The following overview of approaches does not attempt to be exhaustive and does not attempt to discuss each selected approach in detail. Despite the risk of oversimplification, we do think a brief outline is helpful as an introduction to the current orientations towards policy.

Cultural political theory

An influential background for critical education policy studies is state theory, and particularly the theoretical focus on the role and functions of the state in capitalist societies (Offe, 1984; Dale, 1989, 1994; Jessop, 1990; Bonal, 2003). Of growing importance is the work of Bob Jessop (2002, 2007) and his attempt to develop a "cultural political economy", that is, an attempt to understand the dynamics of capitalist societies by attending to the constitutive role of cultural production through economic and political imaginaries. In this respect, he criticises a deterministic analysis of the role and function of the state by combining system theories (and the focus on structures) and conflict theories (and the focus on cultural conflict and strategy). Jessop (2000a) suggests analysing the role of the state along four dimensions.

Firstly, in view of the need for capital accumulation, Jessop proposes to analyse the state's role in economic policy. Secondly, the state's role in social policy is linked up with social reproduction, and the reproduction of labour forces. Thirdly, capitalist societies are characterised by the scalar organisation of both policies in order to guarantee relatively stable periods of accumulation. Here, "spatio-temporal fixes" strategically allocate tasks to specific scales (local, national, regional…) and to specific periods in order to settle contradictions and dilemmas of capital accumulation in capitalist societies (such as market failures). Finally, the necessity of regulation in capital relations, the emerging contradictions and dilemmas in accumulation and the temporal fixation of these problems open up space for governance (ongoing management, muddling through or crisis management). This governance or coordination can take the form of coordination through imperative, by the state, a more anarchist coordination by the market, or a self-organising coordination through networks. The focus on the cultural or semiotic level in what Jessop calls a "strategic-relational approach" enables him to analyse how within a specific system particular identities, actors and strategies are produced and privileged, and how these strategies are actually deployed by actors.

Relying on this framework, scholars have developed a particular perspective to analyse education and the governance of education within local and global political economies (see the contributions of Dale, Robertson, Fahey et al.). Within the "cultural political theory of education", education is approached as a major site for cultural and social reproduction, and hence constituted in relation to specific local, national, regional, international policy settlements and modes of regulation. In addition, education policy can be approached at the level of economic and political imaginaries, and related to forms of state coordination. In order to understand education policy in a broad sense, one can also look at the interconnection of state coordination with market and network coordination, as well as how the coordination of matters related to education is divided over different scales.

Finally, and related to the critical agenda, this approach allows a focus on the contradictions in and around education and its governance, and shows how the contradictions and preferred strategies reveal power patterns and social inequalities. Jessop (2000b) describes, for example, how knowledge within the European knowledge economy is regarded as both a private and public good, leading to highly contradictory policies.

Critical discourse analysis

As mentioned earlier, the critical study of education policy often addresses policy as discourse although the term discourse is used within many approaches. Except for a stricter Foucauldian usage which we will discuss later, Critical Discourse Analysis (CDA) of Fairclough is influential (Codd, 1988; Ball, 1994b; Janks, 1997; Edwards & Nicoll, 2001; Luke, 1997, 2002; Gewirtz et al., 2004; Taylor, 2004). The point of departure for Fairclough is to analyse the actual language used in texts and to combine this analysis with a focus on discursive and social practices within which the actual text plays a role.

> In seeing language as discourse and as social practice, one is committing oneself not just to analysing texts, nor just to analysing processes of production and interpretation, but to analysing the relationship between texts, processes, and their social conditions, both the immediate conditions of the situational context and the more remote conditions of institutional and social structures (Fairclough, 1989, p. 26).

All text thus belongs to a discursive practice or order of discourse, that is, a specific way of speaking and including distinctive modes of representing, genres and styles.[7] The discursive is argued to be dialectically linked up with social practices. For example, within school institutions texts could be analysed as part of an instructional-psychological and managerial order of discourse, and as actually influencing social relations in schools, while the school is at the same time conditioning the text and discourses.

In view of these assumptions, Fairclough suggests three levels of analysis: the analysis of text, the analysis of the order of discourse and the analysis of social practices. At the level of discourse, language plays an ideological role, that is:

"(…) the struggle over language can manifest itself as a struggle between ideologically diverse discourse types" (Fairclough, 1989, p. 90). Social struggles are linked up with struggles over language and critical discourse analysis can reveal how practices are ideologically maintained, strengthened or resisted. Important here, and clearly related to the approach of Jessop, is the assumption that texts are "overdetermined" by other social elements. As a result, the linguistic analysis of texts immediately leads to the discussion of issues related to social relations and institutions (Fairclough, Jessop & Sayer, 2004). However, the term overdetermination does not imply that the analysis of text can be displaced by a form of social analysis.

Relying upon this framework, scholars oriented towards education policy can look at policy texts as struggles over language and as dialectically linked to a particular organisation of society (see the contributions of Seddon, Nicoll, Lingard & Rawolle, Bradford & Hey). We will list some of these perspectives.

Firstly, the analysis of policy at the level of discourse enables scholars to focus on dominant discourse types (managerialism for example) within policy texts, and on how realities and identities, and writer and reader positions are being constituted. In line with Fairclough, one can focus on how discursive operations (such as marketisation), attempt to address the readers as individual persons (synthetic personalisation) and how dominant discourses and positions exclude, marginalise or silence others.

Secondly, critical discourse analysis allows a combination of detailed textual analysis at the level of policy texts with an analysis of the broader economic and political context and institutions (Luke, 1997). Here, scholars can focus on the emergence of discourses (for instance, the knowledge-based economy), how these discourses become hegemonic, how they are recontextualised (that is, starting to play a role in new fields) and finally, how they are operationalised (that is, how they shift from mere imaginaries to actually transforming social reality and being materialised) (Fairclough, 2005).

Thirdly, critical discourse analysis can include a specific interest in the rhetoric of policy, and specifically in how discourses are 'technologised' (based on the technical use of forms of communication) in view of influencing social practices by persuasion. The use of concepts, images and phrases in policy talk, and the included genres and styles, can be analysed in terms of explicit strategies or spin aimed at ideologically influencing readers and listeners.

Leaving behind some of the critical theory assumptions of Fairclough, a further step is to focus radically on what language does, without assuming a distinction between truth and rhetoric/ideology, argument and persuasion, language and reality. This implies that a scholar does not position himself as someone who reveals the truth, but as someone who launches so to speak a counter-language or counter-rhetoric (see contribution of Nicoll).

Finally, critical discourse analysis can include different critical attitudes towards policy and society. Fairclough (2005) suggests distinguishing between three forms of critique that are relevant to critical discourse analysis: "Whereas ideological critique focuses on the effects of semiosis on social relations of power, and rhetorical critique on persuasion (including 'manipulation') in individual texts or talk, what we might call 'strategic critique' focuses on how semiosis figures within the strategies pursued by groups of social agents to change societies in particular directions." Perhaps a fourth form of critique can be added here. In line with acknowledging the rhetoric within each form of discourse, and thus including one's own discourse as a researcher, there is room for a 'tactical critique': explicitly launching a counter-discourse as critical policy scholar.

Policy field analysis

The work of Bourdieu has played a major role in sociology of education for a long time. The use of his work in critical education policy scholarship is relatively recent. This is partly related to a shift in his thinking and his political activism during the 1990s. While his former work is mainly focusing on the straightforward reproduction of societal inequality through schooling, in his latter work Bourdieu focuses more explicitly on the role of politics and policy and on the impact of actors in maintaining or being able to change social reproduction (van Zanten, 2005). This openness to change is related to his critical analysis of globalisation policy, the dominant role of economic neo-liberalism herein, and the opportunities to inaugurate counter-movements.

Bourdieu's political optimism is based on the idea of "reflexive sociology" or "sociology of the sociology", that is, a sociology that adopts a "self-socio-analysis" of the intellectual project in view of mutually enriching the theoretical and empirical through a kind of "philosophical fieldwork" (Bourdieu, 2004/2007). Bourdieu develops the idea of the "collective intellectual" as an elaboration of this approach (Bourdieu, 1997/2008, pp. 292–293). The collective intellectual seeks to create new forms of collaboration among researchers and between the field of research and the field of practice, and she attempts to bridge the field of critical research and politics. As a collective intellectual himself, Bourdieu attempts to develop the concept of rational utopias in conjunction with his idea concerning "the victims of neoliberalism." Through rational utopias, he supports the transformation of victims to become actors of social change.

Interest is growing in the adoption of the ideas of Bourdieu in elaborating a distinctive approach to education policy as a social field (Lingard & Rawolle, 2004; Lingard et al., 2005b; Rawolle, 2005). Bourdieu defines a social field as follows:

> A field is a structured social space, a field of forces, a force field. It contains people who dominate and people who are dominated. Constant, permanent relationships of inequality operate inside this space, which at the same time becomes a space in which the various actors struggle for the transformation or preservation of the field. All the individuals in this universe bring to the competition all the (relative) power at their disposal. It is this power that defines their position in the field and, as a result, their strategies (Bourdieu, 1998, pp. 40–41, quoted in Lingard & Rawolle, 2004, p. 365).

From this point of view, different social fields can be distinguished each having their own logic and each seeking to uphold a relative autonomy against intrusion from other fields: the journalistic and artistic fields, the political field and academic fields (Wacquant, 2006). Also policy and education policy in particular can be approached and analysed in terms of a relative autonomous social field, although clearly influenced by and influencing other fields. Within the education policy field, like in all other fields, agents struggle and compete over (cultural, economic, and social) capital and strategise in order to secure their own position and social power. The *habitus* of agents, that is, a "durable, transposable disposition" that functions "as a matrix of perceptions, appreciations, and action", informs practice and enacts the structure of the field. The field itself meditates between habitus and practice (Bourdieu, 1980/1990, p. 53). From the perspective of field theory, the aim is to analyse both the structures and relations within fields and the disposition and schemata of perception of the agents who inhabit the fields. This double focus can be regarded as an attempt to reconcile the objective and subjective, structure and agency, objective structures and mental structures or, at a theoretical level, a structural and phenomenological approach.

There are different dimensions to be distinguished in the policy studies that approaches education policy as a field and education as an arena of strategic struggles based on different status positions (see the contributions of Lingard & Rawolle, Lawn & Grek, Seddon, Bradford & Hey, Apple, Suncker, Giroux and Marginson).

At a rather general level, it is possible to elaborate and reframe the distinction between "context of influence", "context of production" and "context of practice" in the well-known policy process model (Bowe et al., 1992; Ball, 1994b) (see further below). From the viewpoint of fields one could focus on the struggles in the policy field around production, as well as on the influence from other fields and the intrusion of the policy field in other fields. Additionally, and discussing the effects of policies, it is possible to grasp the social logic or the mental structures generated among teachers or students.

Secondly, in studying the constitution of the logic of the education policy field and its transformations, it is interesting to examine specifically "cross-field effects." One could focus for example on how the journalist field (or media) and the economic field have an effect on the education policy field, or on how the logic and techniques of the economic field transforms the academic field and the field of (higher) education (Lingard & Rawolle, 2004).[8]

Thirdly, field theory can be particularly useful in addressing globalisation policies, especially in terms of the emergence of a "global policy field." By addressing cross-field effects on different scales and by taking into account different time frameworks, it becomes possible to analyse the conflicts and struggles around education policy (Lingard, 2006, p. 293). Additionally, it is possible to focus on the different strategies adopted by nations based on their respective "national capital" in the global field, and on how the neoliberal logic of globalisation combined with the mediatisation of policy leads to reduced autonomy in the national education policy field.

Finally, the policy orientation inspired by field theory is accompanied by a particular critical ethos. The main critical endeavour is to grasp the struggle over preserving or upholding the existing distribution of capital and the debates over identities and hierarchies. Ultimately, the goal is to picture "symbolic violence", that is, the imposition of systems of meaning that justify existing structures of inequality. We mentioned earlier that in line with Bourdieu, the critical scholar can develop a stance as collective intellectual and contribute to new social imaginaries.

Governmentality studies

As with Bourdieu, the work of Foucault has already played for a rather long period a role in educational research and social and political theory of education. It is impossible to give an overview of all the – philosophical, historical, sociological – uses of Foucault in educational research.[9] Yet, it seems that the teaching of Foucault on "governmentality" during his courses at the Collège de France in 1977-1978 and 1978-1979 has given a new impetus to critical education policy studies.[10] Within the scope of this introduction we are necessarily limiting ourselves to an exploration of the relevance of the study of governmentality in the critical study of education policy.[11] Governmentality is a neologism referring to a perspective on the assembly of particular rationalities and forms of thought ('mentalities') with specific technologies and strategies to govern (Dean 1999; for a slightly different interpretation see Sennelart, 2004). 'To govern' here is understood in a very broad sense: the structuring, guiding or shaping of people's behaviour in very different contexts and in very different areas (including the structuring or shaping of human beings as subjects).

We will picture very shortly Foucault's own account of forms of governmentality from the seventeenth century onwards until the emergence of neoliberal governmental rationalities in the second part of the twentieth century. Contrary to the previous approaches this historical overview is needed in order to be able to discuss the perspective on governmentality from a more analytical viewpoint and in order to give a short overview of the governmentality orientation towards education policy.

A main characteristic of the birth of the modern nation state, according to Foucault (1981, 1978), is not the "etatisation of society" but the "governmentalisation of the state." This means that he conceives the state as a complex of centralizing governing relationships and mechanisms aimed at steering people (both as individuals and population). As a result, the birth of the modern state as a "governmental state" implies the emergence of a particular rationalisation of the role of the state, its tasks and responsibilities as well as its objectives and the entities to be governed. Furthermore, Foucault (2004a/b) elaborates in detail how the governmental state and its rationalities and mentalities have continually transformed throughout history. Firstly, a governmentalisation in the name of state reason in the early modern period. This is followed in the modern era by processes of governmentalisation in the name of individual freedom and security, and finding its intellectual rationalisation in the reflections on political economy. Next, he discribes the governmentalisation in the name of the social in the twentieth century and culminating in the 'social state'. Foucault (2004a) notices a new crisis in the problematic of how to govern during the second part of the twentieth century, which inaugurated a new phase in the governmentalisation of the state. Meanwhile many scholars (Gordon 1991, Rose 1999, Dean 1999, Olssen et al. 2004, Simons, 2007) have elaborated on this. Their findings indicate that the role of the state is no longer rationalised as a central agency of government that should intervene in society in the name of the social in order to align individual freedom and social welfare (Rose 1996). Instead, it is argued that the state today is increasingly regarded as a managerial agency that should enable an entrepreneurial type of freedom through for example marketisation, investment in human capital and in collaboration with other agencies of governance (both local and global, public and private) (Olssen & Peters, 2005).

Drawing upon Foucault's historical accounts of governmentality, scholars have elaborated the term governmentality into an analytical perspective enabling investigation of past and current forms of government. From a Foucauldian perspective, government is to be regarded as a form of "conduct of conduct" (Foucault 1982, p. 237) or a more or less calculated and rational attempt to direct human conduct by the application of particular technical means. As Dean (1999, p. 23) explains, an "analytics of government (…) takes as its central concern *how* we govern and are governed within different regimes, and the conditions under which such regimes emerge, continue to operate and are transformed." The assemblage and operation of these regimes of government can be analysed by focusing on three related dimensions: the governmental rationality or program at stake, the *techne* of government being used, and the type of governable subject involved (Foucault 1978a/b). Governmentality studies are not aimed at explaining the particular agency and underlying motives of the actors in government. The focus of an analytics is, as explained by Rose (1999, p. 21), the space of thought and action for a particular self-government or conduct to emerge and hence the "conditions of possibility and intelligibility for certain ways of seeking to act upon the conduct of others, or oneself, to achieve certain ends."

There are several adoptions of the perspective on governmentality within the study of education (Popkewitz & Brennan, 1998; Weber & Maurer, 2006; Masschelein et al, 2007; Fejes & Nicoll, 2008) and several components in the elaboration of the governmentality orientation towards education policies can be distinguished (see the contributions of Fejes, Pongratz, Popkewitz, Fendler, Foss Lindblad & Lindblad, Olssen, Ball, Wain).

At a rather general level, and not strictly related to governmentality, Foucauldian concepts and tools have been developed which focus on policy as a social practice and discourse: policy archaeology (and the focus on discursive formations in policy) and policy genealogy (and the focus on implied power relations, changes in discursive formations and the resulting exclusions) (Scheurich, 1994; Gale, 2001). More sociological and historical approaches are developed along these lines, but each is seeking to focus on the cultural politics within education policy and the regulation of schools (Varela, 2001).

Secondly, and more closely related to the governmentality perspective, are the attempts to analyse the governing regime and the conditions of possibility for policy texts, policy problems and solutions, and actors and their self-understanding to emerge. Again, Foucault's idea of governmentality does not provide a theoretical framework nor fixed methodological guidelines, neither should governmentality be regarded as a domain of practice. Instead, the term is foremost a *perspective* on governing and being governed. What is assumed is that people are governed in a particular way, and that it is possible to analyse how this government (its rationality or technology) and one's own role in becoming governable (that is, one's conduct or self-government) emerged at a particular moment in time (Simons & Masschelein, 2007). As indicated earlier, the perspective of governmentality analyses the interrelation of three components. One can focus on the governmental rationality, that is, the mode of reasoning about how and why government takes place, the implied grid of visibility for policy problems, solutions and entities to be governed to appear, and the mode of justifying authority and presenting the *telos* of government. Additionally, one can focus on the *tekhnē* of government. This encompasses the instruments, procedures, techniques and tools that are combined and used in order to accomplish the governmental objectives. Finally, there can be a focus on the side of the governed, that is, the way the subjectivity of those who are governed (for instance, teachers, but also schools) is made up. The assumption is that in order for people and organisations to be governable they have to come to understand themselves in a particular way, to experience particular issues as relevant and to govern themselves and 'practice their freedom' accordingly.

Thirdly, we can mention two further extensions in critical studies on education policy relying on the governmentality perspective: the inclusion of technologies of the self and the focus on processes of governmentalisation both globally and locally. While Foucault seeks to relate in governmentality both 'political technologies' (to steer people and regulate society) and 'technologies of the self' (adopted by people to constitute oneself as a subject and to govern oneself accordingly), the primary focus in education policy research has been on political technologies. Meanwhile, there is an interest to examine in more detail how 'conduct' takes shape at the local level, that is, through what kind of technologies of the self people work upon the self and transform themselves (as teacher for instance) into governable subjects. In terms of Hacking (2004), this should not be regarded as an attempt to link the macro and micro level, but to combine "the abstract" and "the concrete", and their enactment. The perspective of governmentality additionally seeks to open up the research domain by addressing processes of governmentalisation both locally (e.g. public-private partnerships at regional and local levels) and globally (e.g. transnational organisations) (Perry & Maurer, 2003; Ong & Collier, 2004; Larner & Walters, 2004). Instead of addressing current developments in Europe, for instance, in terms of the "etatisation of Europe" there are attempts to describe the "governmentalisation of Europe" and the role of education therein (Masschelein and Simons, 2003; Walters & Haahr, 2005). Closely related to the extension of the perspective of governmentality to 'global technologies' and 'technologies of the self', the field of study also seeks to develop its methodological apparatus. It wants to go beyond discourse analysis and includes methods from critical anthropology and critical discourse analysis.

Finally, the governmentality-inspired orientation in education policy is motivated by a particular critical attitude. Foucault (1982, pp. 231–232) used the concept "(historical) ontology of the present" in order to describe in a general way the critical attitude underlying his research, and explains this can be understood as a critical concern or care for the present (Foucault 1980, p. 108, cf. Rajchman 1991, p. 141). The aim is to draw precise attention to what is familiar today and to what is often invisible due to this familiarity (Foucault 1978a, pp. 540–541). What is needed to achieve this aim is a kind of "cartography" (Deleuze 1986) that "maps" (Flynn 1994) the present or, as Rose (1999, p. 57) puts it, an "empiricism of the surface" focusing on what is said and what allows it to be said. Thus what is at stake, according to Rose (1999, p. 20) is "introducing a critical attitude towards those things that are given to our present experience as if they were timeless, natural, unquestionable" and "to enhance the contestability of regimes" that seek to govern us. Foucault indeed explains that critique is "the art of not being governed like that and at that cost" (Foucault, 2007/1978, p. 45), and hence, the study of processes of governmentalisation if often motivated by an ethos of "de-governmentalisation" (Gros, 2001, pp. 520–523).

Micropolitics, feminist theory, postcolonial theory and philosophical analysis

Each of the following approaches deserves a more detailed elaboration, but because they are often linked up with the previously discussed approaches we think a limited elaboration is justified.

The micropolitical approach relies on interactionist assumptions and conflict theory, and is often combined with biographic research and critical ethnographic approaches (Young, 1999). The micropolitical approach plays a major role in a critical orientation towards how power actually works in schools, as well as towards the problematic of policy implementation (see the contribution of Kelchtermans). Blase (1991, pp. 1–2) defines micropolitics as follows:

> Micropolitics is about power and how people use it to influence and protect themselves. It is about conflict and how people compete with each other to get what they want. It is about cooperation and how people build support among themselves to achieve their ends.

Instead of describing schools in structuralist or functionalist ways, this approach focuses on the school as an "arena of struggle", and on how schools are built through the interactions of people (Ball, 1987). Drawing upon this perspective, it is also possible to describe the development of "micropolitics at the state level", that is, how the arena works at the level of politicians, state officials and other representatives (Lingard, 1995). Additionally, the micropolitical approach is adopted to understand how education policy is filtered through the micropolitics of schools, and thus questioning rationalist and instrumental assumptions of policy making and policy makers (Kelchtermans & Ballet, 2002).

Another important approach is feminist theory and post-colonial theory, and particularly their orientation towards education policy. Davies (1997) distinguishes the following versions of feminism: liberal feminism (focusing on issues of equal rights and access), radical feminism (questioning maleness and the male symbolic and cultural order), socialist feminism (focusing on the relation between capitalist societies, patriarchal structures and ideologies), and feminist poststructuralism (analysing male/female and gender issues through discourse). Socialist and poststructuralist feminist theories especially play a role in critical education policy studies (cf. Ferguson, 1984; Ozga & Gewirtz, 1994). These theories offer tools to critically examine how inequality in capitalist structures is a gendered inequality, and how policy texts actually reproduce gender inequality through the words, images and examples that are used. Another influential account is Marshall's (2000, p. 128) "feminist critical policy analysis":

> (…) Assuming that hegemonic policy arenas are managed and controlled primarily by, and for, white males, defines how women's needs and perspectives are marginalised, so policy analysis must be pursued differently.

In view of this, Marshall suggests focusing on the feminist, gender and race philosophies that are part of policies, in order to analyse the policy discourses and their ideological function, and particularly on the counter-narratives and counter-discourses that emerge. From a Foucauldian perspective, Pillow (1997, p. 146; 2003) coins the term "feminist genealogy" and elaborates an approach that "focuses specific attention upon the discursively structured, raced, gendered and sexed body." Furthermore, she claims that "feminist genealogy locates the work of genealogy as critique within the body, a methodology that embodies policy analysis" (ibid., p. 147). Often linked up with race and gender theories is the post-colonial perspective, summarised by Rizvi (2004, p. 160) as follows:

> (…) A point of view of knowledges developed outside the dominant hegemonic orientation of the West. It is a perspective concerned with developing a set of guiding principles of political practice morally committed to identifying and transforming the conditions of exploitation in which large sections of the world's populations live out their daily lives.

Last but not least, it is important to explore the philosophical analysis of education policy. From the viewpoint of more empirically orientated approaches, philosophical analysis and reflection is often regarded as mere commentary. Because it can be an approach in its own right, it is worth mentioning two types of philosophical analysis.

Firstly, policy research can involve a hermeneutical approach. Hermeneutics is the philosophical tradition that regards understanding and interpretation as major activities in social life (Ödman & Kerdeman, 1997). In line with Gadamer (1960), this means that the scholar attempts to grasp the meaning of the text (and text can include artefacts and experiences) by taking into account the context in which the text emerged as well as the scholar's own cultural background and pre-understanding. The act of interpretation implies that the meaning of something only reveals itself in relation to the culture or tradition in which it emerges. Understanding takes shape in a kind of circular tension between the familiar and the strange, and the past and the future, with a view on grasping the deep assumptions of social life. The guiding principle here is the so-called 'hermeneutical circle'; the parts of the text need to be related to the whole to gain meaning, but the whole only reveals itself through the parts. An example of a hermeneutical approach to policy making, combined with a conceptual Wittgensteinian focus on rule-following, is the focus on the "politics of interpretation" (Peters & Marshall, 1996). The approach suggests conceptually analysing the definition of a policy problem in relation to the rules of the context in which it emerged, to gradually try to understand the deeper assumptions and values implied in these rules, and to evaluate them in view of emancipatory interests.

Secondly, philosophical analysis of education policy can take the form of policy deconstruction. The term deconstruction today seems to cover almost all so-called post-modern French theory. Here, we use the term however in a specific way, that is, in line with the work of Derrida (1961/1967, 1967). While hermeneutics assumes the possibility of the understanding of the meaning of a text, deconstruction is a kind of 'strategic device' that assumes the text is an endless play of signifiers (and that meaning consists in what Derrida refers to as *différance*). Understanding in this respect can only result from the act of deconstruction itself – there is no understanding without translation, interpretation, or negotiation. What is exposed through deconstruction are the texts' assumptions regarding (metaphysical) presence and internal logics. In sum, and to put it very broadly, deconstruction reveals that taken for granted concepts, objects and distinctions exist in language and receive their meaning through language, and hence, can not be taken in their pure or given form. Policy deconstruction thus involves a reading of policy texts by revealing how accepted concepts and arguments work through contradictions and silences. In line with Edwards (see his contribution in this book), deconstructive reading should be regarded at once as a form of re-writing in the margins. Deconstruction does not aim at revealing the truth behind the (policy) text, but is the event where concepts, arguments and words in policy texts lose their evidence through adding comments in the margins.

AN OVERVIEW OF CLASSIFICATIONS AND OTHER TOOLS

In order to develop some further familiarity with critical education policy studies, we think it is useful to list some of the classifications and analytical or heuristic tools that have been and are being used. Some of these tools are the operationalisation of approaches discussed in the previous section. The listing is necessarily limited.

a) Historical classifications and typologies

Historical ideal types

Firstly, we will discuss an example of a historical classification that is based on a country's political context (Neave, 1995; Wielemans & Roth-van der Werf, 1997). The rationale behind this (state-centred) classification is that education policy can be described with regard to the degree of centralisation/decentralisation. It is assumed that within each country there have been discussions concerning to what extent central government controls and organises education, or whether control and organisation is in the hands of lower levels of government and/or private organisations. Based on this rationale, and comparing states within the European context, the authors distinguish three *historical* models or ideal types: the *centralising, Jacobin state*, the *central state and diversity of initiatives*, and the *non-interventionist, facilitating* state.

The main feature of the first historical type is the central control of the state with regard to education (and issues related to structure, curriculum, and employment...) and with a view to safeguarding ideological neutrality. The policy context in France and Sweden is a fine example of this. In view of social equality, the state wants to bring about a kind of uniformity and installs several centralised control mechanisms to monitor uniformity and equality. The second type is characterised by a strong central state control over curriculum, teachers and structure as well, however in collaboration and agreement with lower levels of government and/or private agencies. The underlying idea, exemplified in countries like Belgium and the Netherlands, is that the school system should reflect the value pluralism and specifically reflect the diversity of ethical and religious convictions. The non-interventionist facilitating state model is characterised by a minimal centralised intervention, and governance is mainly about facilitation and looking for collaboration with local authorities. The former situation in the UK is traditionally regarded as an example of this 'bottom up' philosophy that takes into account and promotes educational diversity.

As ideal types that mainly address the European context, these models have limited analytical value in a study of the current state of affairs. However, they still promote understanding of the historical roots of current developments in education policy within different countries. For instance, it is illuminating to take into account the French historical context of centralisation and uniformisation in order to understand current reactions related to managerial tendencies. Additionally, these models remain instructive in describing how different traditions in education policy are influenced by the arrival of (travelling) 'globalisation policies', the emergence of 'competition states', new forms of decentralisation/deregulation, and by new forms of centralisation or 'remote control' (Weiler, 1990; Lauglo, 1995; Neave, 1998; Ball, 1998; Ozga & Jones, 2006; for an approach towards "decentralised centralism", see Karlsen, 2000). The classifications thus help us to remain attentive to national political and cultural differences in framing policy challenges (Cribb & Gewirtz, 2007).

Education policy periodisation
The second example is a historical classification as well, however it focuses not on the political context but on the general characteristics of education policy (Idenburg, 1971; Coombs, 1970, p. 20ff; Wielemans & Roth-van der Werf, 1997). Addressing the modern state (and particularly in Europe), this classification distinguishes between three periods in education policy. The period before the Second World War is described as a period of *distributive-allocative* education politics. In the relatively static industrialised societies, where the Church monopoly regarding education was broken in most countries, the main objective was to distribute and allocate available resources to organise and fund education, and to take 'incidental' policy measures regarding distribution and allocation.

After the Second World War, the need emerged for a more planned education policy, and to face broader challenges in public policy and social reform. This period is generally referred to as the period of *constructive* education policy. In this constructive period between the Second World War and the 1980s four phases are distinguished.

Until the end of the 1950s education policy was focused on "reconstruction." School reconstruction was part of the large social and economic programs aimed at rebuilding society. However, with the challenge of economic progress and demographic change, the need was soon felt to actively intervene in education as part of broader public and economic policy, mainly in order not to slow further growth. The second phase in constructive education policy is the phase of "manpower planning." Here, education is regarded as "investment expenditure" (instead of merely a "non-productive sector") and education policy and labour market policy became closely connected. The third phase, from the middle of the 1950s onwards, was characterised by education policy wanting to address the increased demand for education. This "rampant expansion phase" was the result of changes in demographic conditions, caused by new processes of democratisation and parents regarding education as the main route for their children to have a better job and better life. In line with the reorganisation of schools to give access to larger populations, there were proposals for substantial reforms, for instance reforms of the curriculum and the examination system. However, by the end of the 1960s, educational reform became part of broader contestation movements among students, teachers, and labour unions. Characteristic of this fourth phase of constructive education policy – the "innovation phase" – is that education policy makers start to acknowledge the need for permanent structural and organisational reform and for reform at the level of the curriculum and pedagogy. The idea of "rolling reform" arises, and thus the belief that reform is not achieved once and for all, but is a continuous challenge for policy makers.

The four phases of constructive education policy are all part of the development of the welfare state and planned public policy in the second part of the twentieth century. With the crisis of the welfare state and the rise of neoliberal and neoconservative ideologies and politics at the end of the 1970s, a new period emerged: *government at a distance*. With questioning social planning and public policies in view of the self-organising forces within society and the freedom and responsibility of individual citizens, the constructive forms of education policy are questioned too. However, and despite some of the *laissez faire* rhetoric, deliberate attempts to steer education through education policy and politics are not disappearing. Closely related to New Public Management, new policies are developed on deregulation, regionalisation, marketisation and consumer choice, as well as on management by objectives and performance accountability. Education policy is no longer about direct steering. However steering at a distance, through targets and new forms of consumer accountability, is steering nevertheless.

This historical classification is illuminative for it helps to place education policy and politics, and the notion of education policy itself in a broader context. But it is important to remain attentive to geographical differences and to new developments. It could be argued for instance that by the end of the 1990s the emergence of a global policy field inaugurates a new period.

Periodisation based on shifts, ruptures and state forms
In relation to current developments, a third historical overview can be introduced (Table 1). This overview is more detailed and integrates elements of the previous classifications. In his policy history of English education policy, Ball makes a distinction between four periods "marked off from one another by *ruptures*, related to more general political *shifts* (…)" and "(…) each of these ruptures is also associated with changes in the *forms and modalities of the state* (how it is organised and how it works" (Ball, 2008, pp. 55–56, italics in original). Although the overview focuses on the English education policy context, it has heuristic value for understanding education policy in other countries. Particularly interesting is the shift from the neoliberal state to the managerial and competition state. Most of the contributions in this handbook can be regarded indeed as an attempt to reshape the critical policy concern in its confrontation with the neoliberal state and with the transition to the emerging managerial and competition state.

Types of policy
A fourth sort of classifications is concerned with listing types of policy (Prunty, 1985, pp. 137–138; Taylor et. al, 1997, pp. 33–35; Parsons, 1995, p. 132; John, 1998, p. 7). These classifications are somewhat reductive and do not take into account contextual differences. However, they are worth mentioning in our exploration of the field of study.

In line with the work of Lowi (1972), a distinction could be made between *distributive, redistributive, regulatory* and *constituent* policy issues. The first type of policies is about the straightforward allocation of new resources to society at large or to those without specific entitlements. When the policies are targeted, for example when addressing a specific part of the student population (and in view of changing the distribution of existing resources), they are called redistributive. Regulatory issues involve the regulation and control of activities, such as the control of competition. Constituent policy issues include the setting-up or reorganisation of existing resources.

Table 1. Ball's overview of shifts, ruptures and the state (England) (Ball, 2008, p. 57)

Shift	Rupture	State
1870-1944		
Political problems of management of urban working-class migrations and imperial industrial development and trade	Break with liberal resistance to state education and welfare	Modern (or interventionist) state
1944-1976		
Postwar economic growth and the expansion of the middle class	Move to universalist welfare state education – national system locally administrated	Welfare state
1976-1997		
Economic crisis, mass unemployment and shift from Fordist to post-Fordist regime of accumulation and the first stage of de-industrialisation	Break from emerging comprehensive national system and the end of professional autonomy for teachers and schools	Neoliberal state
1997-2007		
Assertion of the knowledge economy and new forms of work	End of a national system, locally administrated	Managerial or competition state

In close relation to the previous distinction, and specifically focused on social justice issues, is the distinction between *regulatory* and *deregulatory* policies. The former explicitly aim at regulating society (through prohibition, for instance), while the latter are related to minimal government/state intervention, and to the promotion of market forces.

Another distinction is between *symbolic* and *material*. Material policies are supported by the provision of resources and financial commitments for securing implementation, while symbolic policies lack these resources. Symbolic policies (such as statements and policy declarations) are often the first step in much broader political programs and/or focused at legitimising particular viewpoints and setting agendas.

Next, the distinction has been made between *rational* and *incremental* approaches towards policy development and decision making. The first approach regards policy making as a rational process based on a clear rational input. The incrementalists claim that policies are rooted within earlier policies, political contexts and practices.

Another classification makes a distinction between *substantive* and *procedural* policies. The former refers to policies that are mainly based on the aims and goals of what governments want to do (that is, general declarations about the desirable state of affairs), and do not address in detail how actors should proceed. Procedural policies are policies that rely on a detailed plan, guidelines for implementation and the allocation of resources.

Finally, policies can be characterised as being more *top-down* or *bottom-up*. Top-down policies are formulated at a central level (for instance the department of education), while bottom-up policies are rooted in existing practises or locally based requests for change.

Reform technologies
A final classification we want to mention here discusses the different "policy technologies" that are being used in education reform (Table 2).

Table 2. The language of reform technologies (Ball, 2008, p. 42)

	Market	Management	Performance
Subject positions	Consumers Producers Entrepreneurs	Manager(s)/Leaders(s) Managed/workforce Teams	Appraisee Comparator
Discipline	Survival Income maximisation	Efficiency/effectiveness Corporate culture	Productivity Targets Achievement Comparison
Values	Competition Institutional interests	'What works'	The performative worth of individuals Fabrication

According to Ball, these technologies "involve the calculated deployment of forms of organisation and procedures, and disciplines or bodies of knowledge, to organise human forces and capabilities into functioning systems" (Ball, 2008, p. 41). Each reform technology involves particular subject positions, draws upon specific disciplines, incentives and procedures, includes a particular set of values and provides a new language. This classification at the level of technologies is helpful to grasp the local mechanisms of policy steering, and to look at policy levels and discourses often not associated with policy making. Additionally, this classification has an analytical value for it can be used for example to describe the operation of these technologies, their linkages and effects in particular contexts.

b) Analytical tools

We will discuss five analytical tools. The first is a set of questions that provides a general orientation for policy analysis. The second is a model of the policy cycle. The third tool is a state-centred model that allows analysis of the division of labour in the governance of education, and a set of questions that operationalises a state-centred approach. And the last analytical tool is a model of policy historiography and archaeology/genealogy. Each of these tools will briefly be outlined.

Questions
Kenway (1990) suggests to focus on education policy from the viewpoint of three kinds of questions: *what, how* and *why* questions. Her point of departure is that policies and their texts should be regarded as a 'temporary settlement' between different forces in society, the state and related discursive regimes. For Kenway, 'what' questions provide a focus on the approach to education that is implied in policies. The approach to education is to be situated at the specific organisation of three message systems: curriculum, pedagogy and assessment (Bernstein, 1971). Secondly, the question 'how are such proposals organised?' should be asked. Organisation can refer to issues of funding, staffing, authority and administration. Finally, and at a more explanatory, sociological level, the question 'why a particular approach and organisation are selected?' should be answered: why this policy, on whose terms, what are the grounds for justification, whose interests are involved, and how were such interests negotiated? Taylor et al. include two additional questions: "Why now? Why is this particular policy on the agenda at this particular time?" and "What are the consequences?" (Taylor et al., 1997, p. 39). The first additional question opens up a perspective to the broader social and political context within which policy is produced, while the second question addresses the impact of policies, for example regarding issues of social justice.

Contexts, trajectories and cycles
Bowe and Ball (with Gold) (1992) suggest analysing the policy process as a non-linear and interactive trajectory taking into account three contexts: the context of *influence* (where actors struggle over the construction of policy discourses), the context of *policy text production* (where policies are represented in texts including

contradictions) and the context(s) of *practice* (where interpretation and recreation of policy take place). Each context consists of arenas of action in terms of struggle, compromise and ad hocery. The contexts are "loosely coupled" without "one simple direction of flow of information between them" (ibid., p. 26). This trajectory focus is used to look at policy both as a text emerging within a particular context and as a process involving conflict, interests and consensus. By regarding the different contexts in terms of an arena the model acknowledges the politics within policy as text and process.

Ball adds a fourth and fifth context: the context of *outcomes* and the context of *political strategies* (Ball, 1994b, p. 26). The former is addressing the impact of policies related to justice, equality and individual freedom, and hence the relation between the first order outcomes (context of practice) and second order outcomes. Analysis of the political strategies is related to what we earlier called critical advocacy and is based on the general evaluation of different outcomes of policies.

In line with Bourdieu, Lingard (2000) elaborates on this heuristic tool by focusing on the role of the global context, that is, the new "global policy field" and "cross-field effects" (e.g. mediatisation of education policy) (cf. Lingard & Rawalle, 2004; Lingard et al., 2005a). In his critic examination of the model, Rizvi stresses the importance of exploring the "context of authority" in policy making. He suggests researchers elaborate how the context of state authority is rooted in national "social imaginaries" and how new neoliberal, global imaginaries reorganise authority and conditions for policy making (Rizvi, 2006). Thus, each of the contexts (influence, production and practice) can be enlarged by including global fields next to national fields, by addressing the relationship between global and national contexts, and by taking into account the new imaginaries within which authority is rooted.

A similar distinction in terms of contexts is made by Taylor et al. (1997), although focusing in more detail on the discursive nature of policy and policy making, the broader context of policy making and the relations between different contexts/levels in the policy process (Taylor, 1997). Regarding policy making as "an arena of struggle over meaning or as 'the politics of meaning' (Yeatman, 1990)" a distinction is made between the *context, text* and *consequences* (ibid., p. 26). The context of a specific policy includes the study of: economic, social and political factors; influences of pressure groups and social movements; and the study of the historical background including past initiatives upon which new policies are built. The study of the text includes a focus on the politics and related tensions and ambiguities within the policy text, and, for instance, the presence of particular discourses and/or ideologies (on gender for example). Consequences refer to interpretation and implementation of policies at different levels and over different periods of time, and to the politics surrounding the translation of policies.

Division of labour in governance
The third analytical model is derived from a particular version of state theory (Offe, 1984; Dale, 1989, 1994; Jessop, 1990; Dale & Robertson, 2007; Robertson & Dale, 2008). The main concern here is to understand the division of labour in

education governance. The point of departure is that in capitalist societies, the state faces three core problems: "the support of the accumulation process", "the maintenance of a social context not amenable to the continuation of that accumulation process" and "the legitimation of the system" (Dale, 1994, p. 36; cf. Dale, 1989). In other words: the state is faced with supporting capital accumulation, at the same time protecting society and its order from the impact of the economic process, and offering legitimation for itself and the capitalist system. The assumption is that these core problems are always being translated in "macro-societal expectations" and that this translation occurs in such way that institutional structures and traditions that are nationally available, including education, can be used as responses to the problems. Thus the problems of the state, as well as the problems for which education is suggested to give an answer, are regarded as being constructions based on available structures.

Table 3. Pluri-scalar governance of education (Robertson, Bonal & Dale., 2002,p. 478)

SCALE OF GOVERNANCE				
Supra-National				
National				
Sub-National				

INSTITUTIONS OF COORDINATION	GOVERNANCE ACTIVITIES			
	Funding	Ownership	Provision	Regulation
State				
Market				
Community				
Household				

In view of this model, education policy has to be regarded as a kind of settlement regarding contradictory problems that are mediated by particular state structures. In order to analyse these settlements, it is suggested the focus should be on the functional division and coordination of labour in the governance of education (Table 3). Additionally, the scale at which governance tasks are divided as well as the division of labour across sectors should be taken into account (Robertson & Dale, 2008). The notion pluri-scalar governance refers to the combination and coordination of activities, actors/agents and scales through which education is constructed and delivered in national societies (Robertson et al., 2002; Dale, 2005). The essential activities of governing education are funding, ownership, provision and regulation. The actors or institutions that can play a role in the coordination are the state, the market, the community and the household. The governance can take place at a subnational, national or supranational scale.

This analytical model is clearly concerned with the analysis of the 'politics of education' in capitalist societies, and oriented to 'education politics' as specific events within governance structures. In contrast, the policy cycle models discussed earlier are concerned with the 'education politics' that are part of particular specific policies, and focus on 'politics of education' in terms of influences or conditions. We will not engage here in the polarised debate concerning both models during the 1990s – 'researching into the state' versus 'merely applied education politics', or 'state-control/centred' versus 'policy cycle' perspectives (Gewirtz, 2002; Halpin & Troyna, 1994; Taylor, 1997). We want to mention here that despite the theoretical and methodological differences, there are several attempts to combine these analytical models and/or to elaborate them (for example, Vidovich, 2002, 2007; Gale, 1999, 2003). Vidovich (2002) for instance suggest modifying the policy cycle model and the focus on micro agency by incorporating a focus on macro constraints, the influence of the global context and by focusing on each of the contexts (influence, production, practice) of the policy cycle at all levels (macro, intermediate and micro).

It is beyond the scope of this introduction to elaborate such adaptations in detail. Instead, we want to outline briefly a specific operationalisation of the state-centred perspective that takes into account policy trajectories and contexts. In their study of the reform under the Labour Government in Australia during the 1990s (and in comparison with other countries as well) Lingard, Knight and Porter (1997, p. 18) list the following questions:

– In what way do these policy developments conceptualise education: as the politics of consumption [individual and social needs] or as the politics of production [with prime importance given to profitability in the economic sector]? (...)
– Where is the emphasis: on increasing human capital in the national interest – or improving the situation of those disadvantaged in the social formation?
– What solution, if any, do policy developments offer towards providing economic constraints upon the provision of educational services: corporate managerialism for a more efficient and effective state – or privatisation which moves provision increasingly out of the state and into the private schools?
– What is the justification for devolution: does it make schooling more effective and democratic through school-based decision-making and community participation – or does devolution ensure the efficient and effective delivery of clearly defined educational services to school communities through administrative rather than political devolution?
– What is the role of equity and social justice in this approach to both policy-making and policy?

Policy historiography, archaeology, and genealogy
The final (meta-)model or classification of critical education policy analysis that we want to discuss here is the model of "policy historiography" elaborated by Gale (Gale, 2001, for further elaboration, see Gale, 2003; Olssen et al., 2004, pp. 53-58). In line with the what, why and how questions, it includes three "overlapping historical lenses with which to 'read' and 'write' policy research": policy historiography (referring here to a particular lens), policy archaeology, and policy genealogy (Gale, 2001, p. 384). This model is based loosely on the Foucauldian approach of history, and on Scheurich's post-structuralist methodology of policy archaeology developed in line with Foucault's work (Scheurich, 1994). Each of these perspectives correlates with a specific set of research questions:

Policy historiography:
- What were the 'public issues' and 'private troubles' within a particular policy domain during previous periods and how were they addressed?
- What are they now?
- What is the nature of the change from the first to the second?
- What are the complexities in these coherent accounts of policy?
- What do these reveal about who is advantaged and who is disadvantaged by these arrangements? (Gale, 2001, p. 385)

Policy archaeology:
- Why are some items on the policy agenda (and not others)?
- Why are some policy actors involved in the production of policy (and not others)?
- What are the conditions that regulate the patterns of interaction of those involved? (ibid., pp. 387–388)

Policy genealogy:
- How [do] policies change over time?
- How [might] the rationalities and consensus of policy production be problematised?
- How [are] temporary alliances formed and reformed around conflicting interests in the policy production process? (ibid., pp. 389–390)

Each perspective tells a particular story about policy (and policy making): "Policy historiography [is coupled] with the substantive issues of policy at particular hegemonic moments, policy archaeology with conditions that regulate policy formations, and policy genealogy with social actors' engagement with policy" (Gale, 2001, p. 385). Of central importance here is the focus on 'temporary policy settlements', that is, the discursive frame at a particular historical moment and the geographical location within which a specific policy is produced, their possible hegemonic character and their relation to other past and waiting settlements.[12] According to Gale, and drawing on Mill, part of such a settlement is "how personal troubles are dealt with as public issues and how public issues are expressed in personal troubles" (ibid., p. 381). In view of this, policy historiography (in its specific meaning) studies the conditions of a policy settlement, while the archaeological perspective looks at the particular parameters of a settlement. Policy genealogy is focused on the particularities and realisations within a settlement and the role of actors. Focusing on the substance of hegemonic policy settlements, its conditions, the actors involved and strategies deployed, this (meta-)classification is concerned with critical advocacy. Advocacy can be situated at the level of a "radical democracy", where all policy actors are acknowledged, and that aims at establishing conditions for new conversations, new collective commitments and creative possibilities (Gale, 2001; 2003).

CONCLUSION: CRITICAL STYLES AND PUBLIC CONCERNS

In the concluding section of the introduction, we want to return to the general scope of the handbook in order to explore different styles of critique, and the commitment to public concerns.

Styles of critique

The contributions collected in this book aim at the re-reading of challenges offered by the current policy agenda. Re-reading today's policy agenda is regarded as a critical activity that involves a moment of de-familiarisation. The goal is a de-familiarization with the current way policies pose problems, offer and implement solutions and justify agendas, or with the way that power is exercised in society and how problems are framed. The previous sections clarified in detail that the critical potential of re-reading can be related to a variety of approaches: revealing an underlying rationality, identifying unspoken interests, focusing on unintended consequences, pointing at contradictions, mapping the field of contingencies. What motivates these approaches is a commitment to education and society. De-familiarization thus involves a concern with what can be captured in the general expression 'the public, and its education'. In other words, the act of critical re-reading and the moment of de-familiarization opens up a new space for thought and action. This space should be regarded as a public space because the type of questions emerging here constitute 'a public', that is, these questions affect people and transform education into their concern – even if it is decided afterwards to reformulate what is at stake in terms of private interests. There are different ways, however, to open up this public space. We want to introduce the term 'styles of critique' to explore these differences.

Generally speaking, the term critical in relation to education policy research can be located at three levels. The term can be used to qualify the relation the scholar has towards her own or someone else's research. Critical then refers to the use of research methods, the use of research data, or the approach of someone else's research in reviews. At this level, every researcher is expected to be critical. The term critical can also be used at the level of the theoretical or analytical framework that is used in research. Scholars relying on critical theory or other normative theories of society are called critical. There is, however, another level where the term critical is used: the relation of the scholar to her present. It is at this level that we want to locate the critical policy orientation that is explored throughout the book.

Critique here is first of all about an *attitude* or *ethos*, that is, a way of being involved with one's present and with what is at stake in one's society. Being involved with one's present or being attentive to what is going on in one's society actually disrupts what is going on or the course of history (of policy, of capital accumulation, of discourse...). The present is the moment where one finds oneself as a scholar confronted with the question whether *this* present should be the moment of inaugurating change. In sum, critique is the attitude that involves an act of re-reading resulting in a moment of de-familiarization, and opening up a space for new thought or action in between past and future. When situating critique at the level of the scholar's ethos, perhaps different styles of being critical could be distinguished. The notion style then refers to the specific form of one's attitude, that is, the form of one's relation to one's present.

The critical scholar can take an attitude of *unmasking*, that is, opening up a space for public concern by describing the effects of policy measures on existing power relations in society or the way policy discourses are linked up with power configurations. This is in line with what Fairclough labelled as ideological critique. The attitude of *revealing* (or rhetorical critique) is concerned with rhetoric in education policies, and thus with how language is used by actors to justify decisions or to persuade other actors. *Repositioning* could be regarded as a third style of critique, and aims at positioning oneself in a different way towards policy and the included discourses. Opening up a space for new ways of acting is the main concern here. Finally, *reformulation* is about regarding education policy as something that can and should be tactically re-written. Creating new ways of thinking and speaking is a major concern here.[13]

Public concerns

We discussed in the previous sections that critical thought assumes that policy facts and problems are socially constructed, and that awareness of this construction opens up a space for re-construction. Here, we want to explore in more detail this assumption and specifically the scope of critical studies in an age where policy makers became critical. Indeed, among policy makers there is an awareness that they 'read' the world in a particular way. Consequently, for policy makers re-reading their own reading or one's opponents' reading becomes in itself a political strategy. Some examples can illustratie this.

The use of spin in policy making and the strategic adoption of impression management indicates that in the field of policy the construction and re-construction of facts/images is a deliberate strategy (Gewirtz et al., 2004). There is thus a general awareness of the politics of policy problem definition, and it is actually used deliberately as a policy strategy. Another example is Foucault's analysis of neoliberal governmentality. He stresses that the 'constructivist perspective' is a core component of neoliberal ways of reasoning. Part of neoliberalism is to approach the market for instance not as a natural domain (as in classic liberal rationalities), but as a construction (cf. Foucault, 2004a/b). It is precisely this constructivist rationality which opens up spaces to justify the role of state regulation in creating the market, and which actually support marketisation and the constructing and reconstruction of problems as deliberate technologies to govern the public sector.

Still another example is mentioned by Lyotard. He notices that critique has become part of the liberal-capitalist system (1992, p. 28; 1996, p. 6ff). Critique and emancipation are no longer referring to something outside the system (it is hard to imagine an alternative for the current system, according to Lyotard) but is a strategy within the system leading to further differentiation and hence the system's survival. In a similar line, Dale (2006, p. 180) stresses in reference to Santos that in today's context where social regulation is mainly ceded to the market, social emancipation is about market freedom. A final example is the shift from public policy and the *social reform* agenda towards new public management and the *innovation* or *restructuring* agenda. In new public management, restructuring or change is the rule so to speak. There is a shift from structural change in view of social reform towards permanent change in view of efficiency, effectiveness or increased performance. The latter involves a 'critical' awareness about permanent construction and reconstruction in a way similar to the critical scholar's awareness. One could even go a step further by stating that in times of restructuring, being for example 'an old style teacher' is progressive (Lindblad & Popkewitz, 2004, p. xxix).

In sum, problem solving, and the attitude to accept the problems as they are formulated, no longer seem adequate to describe what happens in the context of policy and politics. Hence, critical theory no longer seems adequate to describe the assumptions of policy makers and policies. Confronted with this state of affairs – that is, with policy makers 'behaving critically' – Latour offers us a way out that is worth exploring. According to Latour, critical theory has focused too much on matters of fact and on questioning what is behind what people take for granted. What is falling out of sight, according to Latour, are matters of concern and the gathering and assembling involved in matters of concern. He argues for a new kind of realism:

> My argument is that a certain form of critical spirit has sent us down the wrong path, encouraging us to fight the wrong enemies and, worst of all, to be considered as friends by the wrong sort of allies because of a little mistake in the definition of its main target. The question was never to get away from facts but closer to them, not fighting empiricism but, on the contrary, renewing empiricism. What I am going to argue is that the critical mind, if it is to renew itself and be relevant again, is to be found in the cultivation of a stubbornly realist attitude – to speak like William James – but a realism dealing with what I will call matters of concern, not matters of fact (Latour, 2004, p. 231).

Oriented towards matters of concern the critic is not in the first place revealing what is behind the taken for granted policy problems, but contributing to the transformation of current policy problems in matters that affect people:

> The critic is not the one who lifts the rugs from under the feet of the naïve believers, but the one who offers the participants arenas in which to gather (Latour, 2004, p. 246).

Precisely in being orientated to and helping to develop matters of concern the critical scholar is playing his/her political role, because something that is of concern unerringly brings people together; not only because they necessarily share opinions about what is important, but also, and often primarily, because the matter of concern divides them:

> (...) We don't assemble because we agree, look alike, feel good, are socially compatible or wish to fuse together but because we are brought by divisive matters of concern into some neutral, isolated place in order to come to some sort of provisional makeshift (dis)agreement (Latour, 2005).

In line with this, one could think of the critical policy studies as interested in making things public through helping to create and support matters of concern. Hence, the specificity of Latour's proposal seems to reside in his idea that research should be linked up with matters of concern, and not in the first place with matters of fact. In other words, for the critical policy scholar the thing she investigates is from the very start a matter of concern. Although research with a critical policy orientation undoubtedly always has been familiar with this idea, a reminder does no harm – especially because there seems to be an ever present tendency or 'academic reflex' to look at this critical commitment as a matter of fact in need of rational justification.

NOTES

[1] Raab nuances this statement with regard to the 1970s and 1980s and the influence of critical sociology and sociology of knowledge in educational studies (Raab, 1994b, p. 21).

[2] Although, as mentioned earlier, some scholars question the role of the state apparatus in change processes, and regard education in its form as radical pedagogy to be the site for inaugurating social and political change.

[3] This discussion is related to discussions between approaches that focus on the *macro*-level or *micro*-level, *bottom-up* and *top-down* approaches, and approaches of policy *formation* or approaches of policy *effects* and *outcomes* (Raab, 1994a/b).

[4] In contrast to Dale, Apple shares with Ball the interest in a (Marxist) ethnography and in understanding cultural struggles. Nevertheless, Apple's interest is not in the first place the politics and conflicts in policy trajectories and processes (as is Ball's), but the power and conflict in and around the school and curriculum.

[5] Similar to Ball, Popkewitz has an interest in the productive forces of knowledge and discourses and the relational view on power, however he takes it further in bracketing (at the theoretical/analytical level) the role of actors, agencies or structures in explaining a particular assemblage. At the level of the descriptions of surface mechanisms and divisions, he is closer to Dale, however, without holding to the latter's neo-Marxist assumptions.

[6] For instance, with regard to policy research in the UK, three (qualitative) orientations are distinguished (Maguire & Ball, 1994, pp. 278–281). First, elite studies based on life history methods in order to grasp longer policy trends (e.g. Gewirtz & Ozga, 1990) or based on interviews with key-informants in view of current developments in education policy (e.g. Ball, 1990). Second, trajectory studies that follow a specific policy cycle including the context of influence (based on interviews for instance), the micropolitics within the state and as part of the production of policy text, and finally the context of practice, that is the phase of implementation (based on case studies) (e.g. Edwards et al., 1989; Henry & Taylor, 1995). The third orientation is implementation research focusing on the interpretation of policy texts and their translation into practices, based on participant observation methods and interviews as part of critical ethnography.

[7] Fairclough uses the concept discourse in two ways (Fairclough, 2005). Firstly, discourse refers to semiotic elements (next to non-discursive elements), while secondly, discourse is used to indicate a way of representing, next to a style and genre. Hence, an 'order of discourse' (first meaning) combines specific styles, genres and discourses (second meaning).

[8] Lingard & Rawolle (2004, pp. 368–369) make a distinction between five cross-field effects: effects at the level of structures of the field, effects related to the impact of an event, systematic effect in underlying values, temporal effect or effects limited in duration and hierarchical and vertical effects occurring in fields that are asymmetrically related.

[9] See, for instance: Pongratz, 1989; Ball, 1990; Marshall, 1996; Popkewitz & Brennan, 1998; Olssen, 1999, 2006; Peters, 2004; Baker & Heyning, 2004; Peters & Besley, 2007; Simons & Masschelein, 2007.

[10] Except for interviews, course summaries and transcripts of a few of Foucault's courses, the sociologically oriented work of Burchell et al. (1991), Barry et al. (1996), Lemke (1997), Rose (1999), Dean (1999) and Bröckling et al. (2004) have been particularly important as resources for the field of study related to governmentality. It could be expected that the recent publications of Foucault's courses and the English translations will increase this interest (Foucault, 1997, 1999, 2001, 2004a/b, 2008), as will any future publication of the courses.

[11] One can rightly refer to these studies as a kind of new subdiscipline within the humanities (Dean, 1999, p. 2). However, the term discipline may not be fully appropriate since it might mask the huge diversity of these studies, both in terms of research domain and in terms of method (Rose, 1999, p. 9). What they share, however, is an interest in actual forms of governmentality, minimally conceived of as the strategies of governing people and governing ourselves.

[12] The term settlement is widely used, however, often in slightly different ways: Seddon, 1989; Kenway, 1990.

[13] It could be interesting to elaborate these styles with Hacking's distinction between six grades of commitment (Hacking, 1999, p. 19).

REFERENCES

Althusser, L. (1971). Ideology and ideological state apparatuses. In *Lenin and philosophy, and other essays* (pp. 136–170). London: New Left Books.

Apple, M. W. (1982). *Education and power*. New York: Routledge & Kegan Paul Ltd. Publishers.

Apple, M. W. (1993). *Official knowledge: Democratic education in a conservative age*. New York: Routledge & Kegan Paul.

Apple, M. W. (1996). *Education and cultural politics*. New York: Teachers College Press.

Apple, M. W. (2003). *The state and the politics of knowledge*. London: RoutledgeFalmer.

Arnove, R., & Torres, C. (1999). Introduction: Reframing comparative education: The dialectic of the global and the local. In R. Arnove & C. Torres (Eds.), *Comparative education: The dialectic of the global and the local* (pp. 1–23). New York: Rowman & Littlefield.

Appadurai, A. (1996). *Modernity at Large: Cultural dimensions of globalization*. Minneapolis, MN: University of Minnesota.

Appadurai, A. (2001). Grassroots globalization and the research imagination. In A. Appadurai (Ed.), *Globalization* (pp. 1–21). Durham, NC: Duke University Press.

Appadurai, A. (2006). *The right to research. Globalisation, societies and education, 4*(2), 167–177.

Aronowitz, S., & Giroux, H. (1994). *Education still under siege.* Westport, CT: Bergin & Garvey.

Avis, J. (2003). Rethinking trust in a performative culture: The case of education. *Journal of Education Policy, 18*(3), 315–332.

Baker, B., & Heyning, K. (2004). *Dangerous coagulations? The uses of Foucault in the study of education.* New York: Peter Lang.

Ball, S. J. (1987). *The micro-politics of the school.* London: Routledge.

Ball, S. J. (1990). *Politics and policy making in education.* London: Routledge.

Ball, S. J. (1994a). Researching inside the state: Issues in the interpretation of elite interviews. In D. Halpin & B. Troyna (Eds.), *Researching education policy: Ethical and methodological issues* (pp. 107–120). London: Falmer Press.

Ball, S. J. (1994b). *Education reform: A critical and post-structural approach.* Buckingham: Open University Press.

Ball, S. J. (1997). Policy sociology and critical social research: A personal review of recent education policy and policy research. *British Educational Research Journal, 23*(3), 257–274.

Ball, S. J. (1998). Big policies/small world: An introduction to international perspectives in education policy. *Comparative Education, 34*(2), 119–126.

Ball, S. J. (2000). Performativities and fabrications in the education economy: Towards the performative society? *The Australian Educational Researcher, 27*(2), 1–24.

Ball, S. J. (2003). The teacher's soul and the terrors of performativity. *Journal of Education Policy, 18*(2), 215–228.

Ball, S. J. (2008). *The education debate. Policy and politics in the twenty-first century.* London: Policy Press.

Barry, A., Osborne, T., & Rose, N. (Eds.), (1996). *Foucault and political reason: Liberalism, neo-liberalism and rationalities of government.* London: University College of London Press.

Bauman, Z. (1998). *Globalization: The human consequences.* Cambridge: Polity Press.

Bernstein, B. (1971). On the classification and framing of educational knowledge. In M. F. D. Young (Ed.), *Knowledge and control* (pp. 47–69). London: Collier Macmillan.

Bernstein, B. (2001). From pedagogies to knowledge. In A. Marais, I. Neves, B. Davies, & H. Daniels (Eds.), *Towards a sociology of pedagogy. The contribution of Basil Bernstein to research.* New York: Peter Lang.

Biesta, G. J. J. (2006). *Beyond learning. Democratic education for a human future.* Boulder, CO: Paradigm Publisher.

Blake, N., Smeyers, P., Smith, R., & Standish, P. (1998). *Thinking again: Education after postmodernism.* New York: Bergin & Garvey.

Blase, J. (1991). The micropolitical perspective. In J. Blase (Ed.), *The politics of life in schools: Power conflict and cooperation* (pp. 1–18). Newbury Park: Sage.

Bonal, X. (2003). The neo-liberal educational agenda and the legitimation crises: Old and new state strategies. *British Journal of Sociology of Education, 24*(2), 159–176.

Bottery, M. (2000). *Education, policy and ethics.* London: Continuum.

Bourdieu, P., & Passeron, J. C. (1964/1979). *The inheritors: Students and their culture.* Chicago: University of Chicago Press.

Bourdieu, P., & Passeron, J. C. (1970/1977). *Reproduction in education, culture, and society.* London: Sage.

Bourdieu, P. (1980/1990). *The logic of practice.* Cambridge: Polity Press.

Bourdieu, P. (2004/2007). *Outline of a self socio-analysis.* Chicago: University of Chicago Press.

Bourdieu, P. (2008/1997). Neoliberalism as conservative revolution. In P. Bourdieu (Ed.), *Political interventions: Social science and political action* (pp. 288–293). London: Verso.

Bourdieu, P. (2001/2008). Scholars and the social movement. In P. Bourdieu (Ed.), *Political interventions: Social science and political action* (pp. 380–383). London: Verso.

Bourdieu, P. (2000/2008). How to effectively establish the critical attitude. In P. Bourdieu (Ed.), *Political interventions: Social science and political action* (pp. 384–388). London: Verso.

Bowe, R., Ball, S., & Gold, A. (1992). *Reforming education and changing schools: Case studies in policy sociology*. London: Routledge.

Bröckling, U., Krasmann, S., & Lemke, T. (Eds.). (2000). *Gouvernementalité der Gegenwart. Studien zur Ökonomisierung des Sozialen*. Frankfurt am Main: Suhrkamp.

Bray, M. (Ed.). (2003). *Comparative education: Continuity traditions, new challenges, and new paradigms*. Dordrecht: Kluwer Academic Publishers.

Burbules, N., & Callister, T. (2000). *Watch IT: The risks and promises of information technology for education*. Colorado, CO: Westview.

Burbules, N., & Torres, C. A. (2000). Globalization and education: An introduction. In N. Burbules & C. A. Torres (Eds.), *Globalization and education: Critical perspective* (pp. 1–26). New York: Routledge.

Burchell, G., Gordon, C., & Miller, P. (Eds.). (1991). *The foucault effect: Studies in governmentality*. Chigago: University of Chicago Press.

Butler, J. (1990). *Gender trouble: Feminism and the subversion of identity*. Routledge: New York.

Castells, M. (1996). *The rise of the network society*. Oxford: Blackwell.

Cerny, P. (1997). The paradoxes of the competition state, the dynamics of political globalisation. *Government and opposition, 32*(2), 251–274.

Cherryhomes, C. H. (1998). *Power and criticism: Poststructural investigations in education*. New York: Teachers College Press.

Chubb, J., & Moe, T. (1990). *Politics, markets and America's schools*. Washington, DC: Brookings.

Cochran-Smith, M. (2005). The new teacher education: For better or for worse? *Educational Researcher, 34*(7), 3–17.

Codd, J. (1988). The construction and deconstruction of education policy documents. *Journal of Education Policy, 3*(3), 235–247.

Coombs, P. H. (1970). *What is educational planning? Fundamentals of educational planning 1*. Paris: UNESCO International Institute for Educational Planning (IIEP).

Cribb, A., & Gewirtz, S. (2007). Unpacking autonomy and control in education: Some conceptual and normative groundwork for comparative analysis. *European Educational Research Journal, 6*(3), 203-213.

Dale, R. (1989). *The state and education policy*. Buckingham: Open University Press.

Dale, R. (1994). Applied education politics or political sociology of education? Contrasting approaches to the study of the recent education reform in England and Wales. In D. Halpin & B. Troyna (Eds.), *Researching education policy: Ethical and methodological issues* (pp. 31–41). London: Falmer Press.

Dale, R. (1997). The state and the governance of education: An analysis of the restructuring of the state-education relationship. In A. H. Halsey, H. Lauder, P. Brown, & A. Stuart Wells (Eds.), *Education. Culture, economy and society* (pp. 273–282). Oxford: Oxford University Press.

Dale, R. (1999). Specifying globalisation effects on national policy: Focus on the mechanisms. *Journal of Education Policy, 14*(1), 1–17.

Dale, R. (2005) Globalisation, knowledge economy and comparative education. *Comparative Education, 41*(2), 117–149.

Dale, R. (2006). From comparison to translation: Extending the research imagination? *Globalisation, Societies and Education, 4*(2), 179–192.

Dale, R., & Robertson, S. (2007). Beyond 'Isms' in comparative education in an era of globalisation: Political and methodological reflections. In A. Kazamias & R. Cowan (Eds.), *Handbook on comparative education*. Rotterdam: Springer.

Davies, B. (1997). Gender theories in education. In L. J. Saha (Ed.), *International encyclopedia of the sociology of education* (pp. 62–67). Oxford: Pergamon.

Davies, H. T. O., Nutley, S. M., Smith, P. C. (Eds.). (2000). *What works? Evidence-based policy and practice in public services*. Bristol: The Policy Press.

Dean, M. (1999). *Governmentality. Power and rule in modern society.* New Delhi: Sage.

Deleuze, G. (1986). *Foucault.* Paris: Minuit.

Derrida, J. (1961/1967). *De la grammatologie.* Paris: Minuit.

Derrida, J. (1967). *La Voix et le Phénomène.* Paris: PUF.

Desrosieres, A. (1998). *The politics of large numbers.* Harvard: Harvard University Press.

Edwards, R., & Nicoll, K. (2001). Researching the rhetoric of lifelong learning. *Journal of Education Policy, 16,* 103–112.

Edwards, T., Fitz, J., & Whitty, G. (1989). *The state and private education: An evaluation of the assisted places scheme.* London: Falmer Press

Edelman, M. (1988). *Constructing the political spectacle.* Chicago: University of Chicago Press.

Fairclough, N. (1989). *Language and power.* London: Longman.

Fairclough, N. (1992). *Discourse and social change.* Cambridge: Polity Press.

Fairclough, N. (1995). *Critical discourse analysis: The critical study of language.* London: Longman.

Fairclough, N. (2003). *Analyzing discourse.* London: Routledge.

Fairclough, N. (2005). Critical discourse analysis. *Marges Linguistiques, 9,* 76–94

Fairclough, N., Jessop, B., & Sayer, A. (2004). Critical realism and semiosis. In J. Joseph & J. Roberts (Eds.), *Realism, discourse and deconstruction* (pp. 23–42). London: Routledge.

Fejes, A., & Nicoll, K. (2008). *Foucault and lifelong learning: Governing the subject.* London: Routledge.

Ferguson, K. (1984). *The feminist case against bureaucracy.* Philadelphia: Temple University Press.

Flynn, T. (1994). Foucault's mapping of history. In G. Gutting (Ed.), *The Cambridge companion to Foucault* (pp. 28–46). Cambridge: Cambridge University Press.

Furlong, J. (2005). New labour and teacher education: The end of an era. *Oxford Review of Education, 31*(1), 119–134.

Foucault, M. (1969). *L'archéologie du savoir.* Paris: Gallimard.

Foucault, M. (1971). *L'ordre du discours.* Paris: Gallimard.

Foucault, M. (1975). *Surveiller et Punir. Naissance de la prison.* Paris. Gallimard.

Foucault, M. (1976). *Histoire de la sexualité 1. La volonté de savoir.* Paris: Gallimard.

Foucault, M. (1978a). La philosophie analytique de la politique. In D. Defert, F. Ewald, & J. Lagrange (Eds.), *Dits et écrits III 1976–1979* (pp. 534–551). Paris: Gallimard.

Foucault, M. (1978b). La 'gouvernementalité'. In D. Defert, F. Ewald, & J. Lagrange (Eds.), *Dits et écrits III 1976–1979* (pp. 635–657). Paris: Gallimard.

Foucault, M. (1980). Entretien avec Michel Foucault. In D. Defert, F. Ewald, & J. Lagrange (Eds.), *Dits et écrits IV 1980–1988* (pp. 104–110). Paris: Gallimard.

Foucault, M. (1981). 'Omnes et singulatim': Vers une critique de la raison politique. In D. Defert, F. Ewald, & J. Lagrange (Eds.), *Dits et écrits IV 1980–1988* (pp. 134–161). Paris: Gallimard.

Foucault, M. (1982). Le sujet et le pouvoir. In D. Defert, F. Ewald, & J. Lagrange (Eds.), *Dits et écrits IV 1980–1988* (pp. 222–243). Paris: Gallimard.

Foucault, M. (1997). *'Il faut défendre la société'. Cours au Collège de France (1975–1976).* Paris: Gallimard/Le Seuil.

Foucault, M. (1999). *Les Anormaux. Cours au Collège de France (1974–1975).* Paris: Gallimard/Le Seuil.

Foucault, M. (2001). *L'Herméneutique du sujet. Cours au Collège de France (1981–1983).* Paris: Gallimard/Le seuil.

Foucault, M. (2004a). *Naissance de la biopolitique. Cours au Collège de France (1978–1979).* Paris: Gallimard/Le seuil.

Foucault, M. (2004b). *Sécurité, territoire, population. Cours au Collège de France (1977–1978).* Paris: Gallimard/Le seuil.

Foucault, M. (2008). *Le gouvernement de soi et des autres. Cours au Collège de France (1982–1983).* Paris: Gallimard/Le seuil.

Foucault, M. (1978/2007). *The politics of truth.* Semiotext(e): Los Angeles.

Gadamer, H.-G. (1960). *Wahrheit und Methode. Grundzügen einer philosophischen Hermeneutik.* Tübbingen: Mohr.

Gale, T. (1999). Policy trajectories: Treading the discursive path of policy analysis. *Discourse: studies in the cultural politics of education, 20*(3), 393–407.

Gale, T. (2001). Critical policy sociology: Historiography, archaeology and genealogy as methods of social analysis. *Journal of Education Policy, 16*(5), 379–393.

Gale, T. (2003). Realising policy: The who and how of policy production. *Discourse: studies in the cultural politics of education, 24*(1), 51–65.

Gewirtz, S., Ball, S., & Bowe, R. (1995). *Markets, choice and equity in education.* Buckingham: Open University Press.

Gewirtz, S., & Ozga, J. (1990). Partnership, pluralism and education policy: A reassessment. *Journal of Education Policy, 5*, 37–48.

Gewirtz, S. (2002). *The Managerial school: Post-welfarism and social justice in education.* London: Routledge.

Gewirtz, S., Dickson, M., & Power, S. (2004). Unravelling a 'spun' policy: A case study of the constitutive role of 'spin' in the education policy process. *Journal of Education Policy, 19*(3), 321–342.

Giddens, A. (1990). *The consequences of modernity.* Cambridge: Polity Press.

Giroux, H. A. (1997). *Pedagogy and the politics of hope: Theory, culture and schooling.* Boulder, CO: Westview Press.

Giroux, H. A. (2004). *The terror of neoliberalism.* Boulder, CO: Paradigm.

Gordon, C. (1991). Governmental rationality: An introduction. In G. Burchell, C. Gordon, & P. Miller (Eds.), *The Foucault effect: Studies in governmentality* (pp. 1–51). London: Harvester Wheatsheaf.

Gottweis, H. (2003). Theoretical strategies of poststructuralist policy analysis: Towards an analytics of government. In M. A. Hajer & H. Wagenaar (Eds.), *Deliberative policy analysis. Understanding governance in the network society* (pp. 247–265). Cambridge: Cambridge University Press.

Gramsci, A. (1971). *Selections from the prison notebooks.* London: Lawrence and Wishart.

Grek, S. (2009). Governing by numbers: The Pisa 'effect' in Europe. *Journal of Education Policy, 24*(1), 23-37.

Gros, F. (2001). Situation du cours. In M. Foucault (Ed.), *L'herméneutique du sujet. Cours au Collège de France (1981–1982)* (pp.488–526). Paris: Gallimard.

Habermas, J. (1981). *Theorie des kommunikativen Handelns.* Frankfurt am Main: Suhrkamp.

Habermas, J. (1985). *Der philosophische Diskurs der Moderne. Zwölf Vorlesungen.* Frankfurt am Main: Suhrkamp.

Haahr, J. H. (2004). Open co-ordination as advanced liberal government. *Journal of European Public Policy, 11*, 209–230.

Hacking, I. (1999). *The social construction of what?* Cambridge: Harvard University Press.

Hacking, I. (2004). Between Michel Foucault and Erving Goffman: Between discourse in the abstract and face-to-face interaction. *Economy and Society, 33*, 277—302.

Halpin, D. (1994). Practice and prospects in education policy research. In D. Halpin & B. Troyna (Eds.), *Researching education policy: Ethical and methodological issues* (pp. 198–206). London: Falmer Press.

Halpin, D. (1999). Utopian realism and a new politics of education: Developing a critical theory without guarantees. *Journal of Education Policy, 14*, 345–361

Halpin, D., & Troyna, B. (Eds.). (1994). *Researching education policy: Ethical and methodological issues.* London: Falmer Press.

Halpin, D., & Troyna, B. (1995). The politics of education policy borrowing. *Comparative Education, 31*(3), 303–310.

Hammersley, M. (2002). *Educational research, policymaking and practice.* London: Paul Chapman.

Hargreaves, A. (2000). Four ages of professionalism and professional learning. *Teachers and Teaching: Theory and Practice, 6*(2), 151–182.

Harvey, D. (1990). *The condition of postmodernity: An enquiry into the origins of cultural change.* Cambridge, MA: Blackwell.

Harvey, D. (2005). *A brief history of neoliberalism.* New York: Oxford University Press.

Hatcher, R., & Troyna, B. (1994). The 'Policy Cycle': A ball by ball account. *Journal of Education Policy, 9*(2), 155–170.

Held, D., McGrew, A., Goldblatt, D., & Perration, J. (1999). *Global transformations: Politics, economics, and culture.* Stanford, CA: Stanford University Press.

Henry, M., & Taylor, S. (1993). Gender equity and economic rationalism: An uneasy alliance. In B. Lingard, J. Knight, & P. Porter (Eds.), *Schooling reform in hard times* (pp. 153–175). London: Falmer Press, London.

Henry, M., & Taylor, S. (1995). Equity and the AVC pilots in Queensland - a study in policy refraction. *The Australian Educational Researcher, 22*(1), 85–106.

Henry, M., Lingard, B., Taylor, S., & Rizvi, F. (2001). *The OECD, globalisation and education policy.* Oxford: Pergamon.

Honneth, A. (2006). Frankfurt school. In W. Outhwaite (Ed.), *The Blackwell dictionary of modern social thought* (2nd ed., pp. 241–244). Oxford: Blackwell Publishing.

Hudson, C. (2007). Governing the governance of education: The state strikes back? *European Educational Research Journal, 6*(3), 266–282.

Humes, W. M., & Bryce, T. G. K. (2003). Post-structuralism and policy research in education. *Journal of Educational Policy, 18*(2), 175–187.

Idenburg, P. H. (1971). *Theorie van het onderwijsbeleid.* Groningen: Wolters-Noordhoff.

Janks, H. (1997). Critical Discourse Analysis as a Research Tool. *Discourse: Studies in the Cultural Politics of Education, 18*(3), 329–340.

Jessop, B. (1990). *State theory: Putting the capitalist state in its place.* Cambridge: Polity.

Jessop B. (2000a). The crisis of the national spatio-temporal fix and the tendential ecological dominance of globalizing capitalism. *International Journal of Urban and Regional Research, 24*(2), 323–360

Jessop, B. (2000b). *The state and the contradictions of the knowledge-driven economy.* Department of sociology, Lancaster University. Retrieved from http://www.comp.lancs.ac.uk/sociology/soc044rj.html

Jessop, B. (2002). *The future of the capitalist state.* Cambridge: Polity.

Jessop, B. (2007). *State power: A strategic-relational approach.* Cambridge: Polity

John, P. (1998). *Analysing public policy.* London: Cassell.

Karlsen, G. E. (2000). Decentralised centralism: Framework for a better understanding of governance in the field of education. *Journal of Educational Policy, 15*(5), 525–538.

Kelchtermans, G., & Ballet, K. (2002). The micropolitics of teacher induction. A narrative-biographical study on teacher socialisation. *Teaching and Teacher Education, 18*(1), 105–120.

Kenway, J. (1990). *Gender and education policy: A call for new directions.* Geelong: Deakin University Press.

Kenway, J., Bigum, C., & Fitzclarence, L. (1993). Marketing education in the post-modern age. *Journal of Education Policy, 8*(2), 105–122.

Kooiman, J. (Ed.). (1993). *Modern governance: New government-society interactions.* London: Sage.

Larner, W., & Walters, W. (Eds.). (2004). *Global governmentality: Governing international spaces.* London: Routledge.

Latour, B. (2004). Why has critique run out of steam? From matters of fact to matters of concern. *Critical Inquiry, 30*(2), 225–248.

Latour, B. (2005). From Realpolitik to Dingpolitik or how to make things public. In B. Latour & P. Wiebel (Eds.), *Making things public. Atmospheres of democracy* (pp. 14–41). Karlsruhe and Cambridge: ZKM & MIT Press.

Lauder, H., Brown, P., & Halsey, A. H. (2004). Sociology and political arithmetic: Some principles of a new policy science. *British Journal of Sociology, 55*, 4–22.

Lauglo, J. (1995). Forms of decentralisation and their implications for education. *Comparative Education, 31*(1), 5–29.

Lawn, M., & Lingard, B. (2002). Constructing a European policy space in educational governance: The role of transnational policy actors. *European Educational Research Journal, 1*(2), 290–307.

Lemke, T. (1997). *Eine Kritik der politischen Vernunft. Foucault's Analyse der modernen Gouvernementalität*. Berlin/Hamburg: Argument.

Lingard, R. (1993). The changing state of policy production in education: Some Australian reflections on the state of policy sociology. *International Studies in the Sociology of Education, 3*(1), 2547.

Lingard, B. (1995). Gender policy making inside the state. In B. Limerick & B. Lingard (Eds.), *Gender and changing educational management* (pp. 136–149). Rydalmere: Hodder Education.

Lingard, B. (2000). It is and it isn't: Vernacular globalization, educational policy, and restructuring. In N. Burbules & C. A. Torres (Eds.), *Globalization and Education*. New York: Routledge.

Lingard, B. (2006). Globalisation, the research imagination and deparochialising the study of education. *Globalisation, Societies and Education, 4*(2), 287–302.

Lingard, B., & Gale, T. (2007). The emergent structure of feeling: What does it mean for critical educational studies and research. *Critical Studies in Education, 48*(1), 1–23.

Lingard, B., & Ozga, J. (2007). Reading education policy and politics. In B. Lingard & J. Ozga (Eds.), *The RoutledgeFalmer reader in education policy and politics* (pp. 1–8). London: Routledge.

Lingard, B., & Rawolle, S. (2004). Mediatizing educational policy: The journalistic field. Science policy and cross-field effects. *Journal of Education Policy, 19*(3), 361–380.

Lingard, B., Rawolle, S., & Taylor, S. (2005a). Globalizing policy sociology in education: Working with Bourdieu. *Journal of Education Policy, 20*(6), 759–777.

Lingard, B., Taylor, S., & Rawolle, S. (2005b). Bourdieu and the study of educational policy: Introduction. *Journal of Education Policy, 20*(6), 663–669.

Lingard, B., Knight, J., & Porter, P. (1993). *Schooling reform in hard times*. London: Falmer Press.

Lindblad, S., & Popkewitz, T. (Eds.). (2000). *Public discourses on education governance and social integration and exclusion. Analyses of policy texts in European contexts*. Uppsala Reports on Education 36.

Lindblad, S., & Popkewitz, T. (Eds.). (2004). *Educational restructuring: International perspectives on travelling policies*. Greenwich, CO: Information Age Publishers.

Luke, A. (2003). After the marketplace: Evidence, social science and educational research. *Australian Educational Researcher, 30*(2), 87–107.

Lowi, T. (1972) Four Systems of Policy, Politics and Choice. *Public Administration Review, 33*, 298–310.

Lyotard, J.-F. (1979). *La condition postmoderne*. Paris: Les Éditions de Minuit.

Lyotard, J.-F. (1983). *Le différend*. Paris: Les Éditions de minuit.

Lyotard, J.-F. (1992). *Het onmenselijke: causerieën over de tijd* (I. van der Burg, F. van Peperstraten, & H. van der Waal, Trans.). Kampen: Kok Agora.

Lyotard, J.-F. (1996). *Postmoderne fabels* (I. van der Burg, Trans.). Kampen: Kok Agora.

Maguire, M., & Ball, S. J. (1994). Researching politics and the politics of research: Recent qualitative studies in the UK. *Qualitative Studies in Education, 7*(3), 269–285.

Maroy, C. (2006). *École, regulation et marché*. Paris: PUF.

Marginson, S. (1997). *Markets in education*. Sydney: Allen and Unwin.

Marshall, J. D. (1996). *Michel Foucault: Personal autonomy and education*. Dordrecht: Kluwer.

Marshall, C. (1999). Researching the margins: Feminist critical policy analysis. *Educational Policy, 13*(1), 59–76.

Marshall, C. (2000). Policy discourse analysis: negotiating gender equity. *Journal of Education Policy, 15*(2), 125–156.

Marshall, C., & Anderson, G. (1995). Rethinking the public and private spheres: Feminist and cultural studies perspectives on the politics of education. In J. D. Scribner & D. H. Layton (Eds.), *The study of educational politics: The 1994 commemorative yearbook of the politics of education association (1969–1994)* (pp. 169–182). Washington, DC: Falmer Press.

Masschelein, J., Simons, M., Bröckling, U., & Pongratz, L. (Eds.). (2007). *The learning society from the perspective of governmentality*. Oxford: Blackwell.

Menter, I., Brisard, E., & Smith, I. (2006). Making teachers in Britain: Professional knowledge for initial teacher education in England and Scotland. *Educational Philosophy and Theory*, *38*(3), 270–286.

Neave, G. (1995). *The core functions of government. Utrecht.* ARO Working document, 29, June 1995, pp. 8–11

Neave, G. (1998). The evaluative state reconsidered. *European Journal of Education*, *33*(3), 265–284.

Noah, H. (1984). Use and abuse of comparative education. *Comparative Education Review*, *28*(4), 550–562.

Nóvoa, A. (2002). Ways of thinking about education in Europe. In A. Nóvoa & M. Lawn (Eds.), *Fabricating Europe: The formation of an educational space* (pp. 131–156). Dordrecht: Kluwer.

Nóvoa, A., & Yariv-Marshal, T. (2003). Comparative research in education: A mode of governance or a historical journey? *Comparative education*, *39*(4), 423–438.

Ödman, P.-J., & Kerdeman, D. (1997). Hermeneutics. In L. J. Saha (Ed.), *International encyclopedia of the sociology of education* (pp. 67–75). Oxford: Pergamon.

Offe, C. (1984). *Contradictions of the welfare state*. Cambridge, MA: M.I.T. Press.

Olssen, M. (1999). *Michel Foucault. Materialism and education*. Westport, CT: Bergin & Garvey.

Olssen, M. (2006) *Michel Foucault: Materialism and Education.* Updated Edition. Boulder, CO.: Paradigm Publishers.

Olssen, M., Codd, J., & O'Neil, A. (2004). *Education policy*. London: Sage.

Olssen, M., & Peters, M. (2005). Neoliberalism, higher education and the knowledge economy: From the free market to knowledge capitalism. *Journal of Education Policy*, *20*(3), 313–347.

Ong, A., & Collier, S. J. (Eds.). (2004). *Global* assemblages: *Technology, politics, and ethics as anthropological problems*. Oxford, UK: Blackwell Publishing

Ozga, J. (1990). Policy research and policy theory: A comment on Halpin and Fitz. *Journal of Education Policy*, *5*(4), 359–362.

Ozga, J. (2000). *Policy research in educational settings: Contested terrain*. Buckingham: Open University Press.

Ozga, J., & Gewirtz, S. (1994). Sex, lies and audiotape: Interviewing the education policy elite. In D. Halpin & B. Troyna (Eds.), *Researching education policy* (pp. 121–136). London &Washington: The Falmer Press.

Ozga, J., & Jones R. (2006). Travelling and embedded policy: The case of knowledge transfer. *Journal of Education Policy*, *21*, 1–17.

Ozga, J., & Lingard, R. (2007). Globalisation, education policy and politics. In R. Lingard & J. Ozga (Eds.), *The RoutledgeFalmer reader in education policy and politics* (pp. 65–82). London: Routledge.

Ozga, J., Seddon, T., & Popkewitz, T. S. (Eds.). (2006). *Education research and policy: Steering the knowledge-based economy. World yearbook of education 2006.* London: Routledge.

Ozga, J. (2007). Knowledge and policy: Research and knowledge transfer. *Critical Studies in Education*, *48*(1), 63–78.

Parsons, W. (1995). *Public policy: An introduction to the theory and practice of policy analysis*. Cheltenham: Edward Elgar.

Perry, R., & Maurer, B. (Eds.). (2003). *Globalization under construction: Governmentality, law, and identity*. Minneapolis, MN: University of Minnesota Press.

Peters, M., & Marshall, J. (1999). Educational policy analysis and the politics of interpretation. In J. Marshall. & M. Peters (Eds.), *Education policy*. Cheltenham, Glos: Edward Elgar.

Peters, M. (1996). *Poststructuralism, politics and education*. London: Bergin & Garvey.

Peters, M. (2001). *Post-structuralism, Marxism and neo-liberalism: Between theory and politics*. Lanham, MD: Rowman and Littlefield.

Peters, M. (2004). Why Foucault? New directions in Anglo-American educational research. In L. Pongratz et al. (Eds.), *Nach Foucault. Diskurs- und machtanalytische Perspectiven der Pädagogik*. Wiesbaden: VS Verlag Für Sozialwissenschaften.

Peters, M. A., & Besley, T. (Eds.). (2007). *Why Foucault? New directions in educational research*. New York: Peter Lang.

Pillow, W. S. (1997). Decentering silences/troubling irony: Teen pregnancy's challenge to policy analysis. In C. Marshall (Ed.), *Feminist critical policy analysis: A perspective from primary and secondary schooling* (pp. 134–152). London: Falmer Press.

Pillow, W. S. (2003). Bodies are dangerous: Using feminist genealogy as policy studies methodology. *Journal of Education Policy, 18*(2), 145–159.

Pongratz, L. A. (1989). *Pädagogik im Prozess der Moderne. Studien zur Sozial- und Theoriegeschichte der Schule*. Weinheim: Deutscher Studien Verlag.

Popkewitz, T. (1991). *A political sociology of educational reform: Power/knowledge in teaching, teacher education, and research*. New York: Teachers College Press.

Popkewitz, T. (1996). Rethinking decentralization and state/civil society distinctions: The state as a problematic of governing. *Journal of education policy, 11*(1), 27–51.

Popkewitz, T., & Brennan, M. (Eds.). (1998). *Foucault's challenge: Discourse, knowledge and power in education*. New York: Teachers College Press.

Popkewitz, T., Franklin, B. M., & Pereyra, M. A. (Eds.). (2001). *Cultural history and education: Critical essays on knowledge and schooling*. New York: Routledge Falmer.

Popkewitz, T., & Brennan, M. (Eds.). (1998). *Foucault's challenge: Discourse, knowledge and power in education*. New York: Teachers College Press.

Popkewitz, T. (2008). *Cosmopolitanism and the age of school reform: Science, education and making society by making the child*. New York: Routledge.

Porter, T. (1995). *Trust in numbers the pursuit of objectivity in science and public life*. Princeton, NJ: Princeton University Press.

Power, M. (1997). *The audit society rituals of verification*. Oxford: Oxford University Press.

Prunty, J. (1985). Signposts for a critical educational policy analysis. *Australian Journal of Education, 29*(2), 133–140.

Raab, C. (1994a). Theorising the governance of education. *British Journal of Educational Studies, 42*(1), 6–22.

Raab, C. (1994b). Where we are now: Reflections on the sociology of education policy. In D. Halpin & B. Troyna (Eds.), *Researching education policy: Ethical and methodological issues* (pp. 17–30). London: Falmer Press.

Rajchman, J. (1991). *Truth and Eros: Foucault, Lacan and the question of ethics*. London: Routledge.

Rawolle, S. (2005). Cross-field effects and temporary social fields: A case study of the mediatization of recent Australian knowledge economy policies. *Journal of Education Policy, 20*(6), 705–724.

Rhodes, R. (1997). *Understanding governance*. Buckingham: Open University Press.

Rizvi, F. (2004). Debating globalization and education after September 11. *Comparative Education, 40*(2), 157–171.

Rizvi, F. (2006). Imagination and the globalisation of educational policy research. *Globalisation, Societies and Education, 4*(2), 193–205.

Robertson, S., Bonal, X., & Dale, R. (2002). GATS and the education services industry: The politics of scale and global reterritorialization. *Comparative Education Review, 46*(4), 472–496.

Robertson, S. (2005). Re-imagining and rescripting the future of education: global knowledge economy discourses and the challenge to education systems. *Comparative Education, 41*(2), 151–170.

Robertson, S., & Dale, R. (forthcoming, 2008). The World Bank, the IMF and the possibilities of critical education. In M. Apple & L. Gandin (Eds.), *International handbook of critical education*. New York: Routledge. Retrieved from http://www.bris.ac.uk/education/people/academic Staff/edslr/publications/21slr/

Rose, N. (1996). Governing 'advanced' liberal democracies. In A. Barry, T. Osborne, & N. Rose (Eds.), *Foucault and the political reason: Liberalism, neo-liberalism and rationalities of government* (pp. 37–64). London: UCL Press.

Rose, N. (1999). *The powers of freedom. Reframing political thought*. Cambridge: Cambridge University Press.

Rosenau, J. N. (1992). Governance, order, and change in world politics. In J. N. Rosenau & E.-O. Czempiel (Eds.), *Governance without government: Order and change in world politics* (pp. 1–29). Cambridge: Cambridge University Press.

Scheurich, J. (1994). Policy archaeology: A new policy studies methodology. *Journal of Education Policy, 9*(4), 297–316.

Seddon, T. (2003). Framing justice: Challenges for research. *Journal of Education Policy, 18*(3), 1–24.

Senellart, M. (2004). *Situation de cours*. In M. Foucault (Ed.), *Sécurité, Territoire, Population: Cours au Collège de France (1977–1978)* (pp. 381–411). Paris: Gallimard.

Simons, M. (2007). "To be informed": Understanding the role of feedback information for Flemish/European policy. *Journal of Education Policy, 22*(5), 531–548.

Simons, M., Masschelein, J., & Quaghebeur, K. (2005). The ethos of critical research and the idea of a coming research community. *Educational Philosophy and Theory, 37*(6), 817–832.

Simons, M., & Masschelein, J. (2007). The learning society and governmentality: An introduction. *Educational Philosophy and Theory, 38*, 417–430.

Smith, M. L., et al. (2004). *Political spectacle and the fate of American schools*. New York: Routledge.

Smyth, J. (2002). Unmasking teachers' subjectivities in local school management. *Journal of Educational Policy, 17*(4), 463–482.

Stoker, G. (1998). Governance as theory: Five propositions. *International Social science Journal, 50*(155), 17–28.

Taylor, S. (1997). Critical policy analysis: Exploring contexts, texts and consequences. *Discourse: Studies in Cultural Politics of Education, 18*(1), 23–35.

Taylor, S., Rizvi, F., Lingard, B., & Henry, M. (1997). *Educational policy and the politics of change*. London: Routledge.

Taylor, S. (2004). Researching educational policy and change in 'new times': Using critical discourse analysis. *Journal of Education Policy, 19*(4), 433–451.

Tikly, L. (2001). Globalisation and education in the postcolonial world: Towards a conceptual framework. *Comparative Education, 37*(2), 151–171.

Tooley, J. (1996). *Education without the state*. London: Institute for Economic Affairs.

Torres, C. A. (1989). The capitalist state and public policy formation: A framework for a political sociology of educational policy-making. *The British Journal of Sociology of Education, 10*(1), 81–102.

Troyna, B. (1994a). Reforms, research and being reflexive about being reflexive. In D. Halpin & B. Troyna (Eds.), *Researching education policy: Ethical and methodological issues* (pp. 1–14). London: Falmer Press.

Tomlinson, S. (2005). *Education in a post-welfare society* (2nd ed.). Buckingham: Open University Press.

Turner, J. H. (1991). *The structure of sociological theory*. Belmont, CA: Wadsworth.

Turner, J. H., & Mitchell, D. E. (1997). Contemporary sociological theories of education. In L. J. Saha (Ed.), *International encyclopedia of the sociology of education* (pp. 21–31). Oxford: Pergamon.

Usher, R., & Edwards, R. (1994). *Postmodernism and education: Different voices, different worlds*. London: Routledge.

van Zanten, A. (2005). Bourdieu as education policy analyst and expert: A rich but ambiguous legacy. *Journal of Education Policy, 20*(6), 671–686.

Varela, J. (2001). Genealogies of education: Some models of analysis. In T. S. Popkewitz, B. M. Franklin, M. A. Pereyra (Eds.), *Cultural history and education: Critical essays on knowledge and schooling*. New York: Routledge/Falmer.

Vidovich, L. (2002). *Expanding the toolbox for policy analysis: Some conceptual and practical approaches*. Occasional Paper Series (2), Comparative Education Policy Research Unit. Hong Kong: City University of Hong Kong.

Vidovich, L. (2007). Removing policy from its pedestal: Some theoretical framings and practical possibilities. *Educational Review, 59*(3), 285–298.

Wacquant, L. (2006). Pierre Bourdieu. In R. Stones (Ed.), *Key contemporary thinkers* (new ed., pp. 261–267). London & New York: Macmillan.

Walters, W., & Haahr, J. H. (2005). *Governing Europe. Discourse, governmentality and European integration.* London & New York: Routledge.

Webb, T. P. (2005). The anatomy of accountability. *Journal of Education Policy, 20*(2), 189–208.

Webb, T. P. (2006). The choreography of accountability. *Journal of Education Policy, 21*(2), 201–214.

Weber, S., & Maurer, S. (2006). *Governementalität und Erziehungswissenschaft:Wissen – Macht – Transformation.* Wiesbaden: VS Verlag für Sozialwissenschaften.

Weiler, H. (1990). Comparative perspectives on educational decentralization: An exercise in contradiction? *Educational evaluation and policy analysis, 12*(4), 433–448.

Whitty, G., Edwards, T., & Gewirtz, S. (1993). *Specialisation and choice in urban education: The city technology college experiment.* London: Routledge.

Whitty, G., Power, S., & Halpin, D. (1998). *Devolution and choice in education: The school, the state and the market.* Buckingham: Open University Press.

Whitty, G. (2002). *Making sense of education policy.* London: Paul Chapman.

Wielemans, W., & Roth-van der Werf, G. J. M. (1997). *Onderwijsbeleid in Europees perspectief.* Leuven/Heerlen: Garant/Open Universiteit.

Yeatman, A. (1990). *Bureaucrats, femocrats, technocrats: Essays on the contemporary Australian state.* Sydney: Allen & Unwin.

Yeatman, A. (1994). *Postmodern revisionings of the political.* New York: Routledge.

Young, M. (1999). Multifocal educational policy research: Toward a method for enhancing traditional educational policy studies. *American Educational Research Journal, 36*(4), 677–714.

Young, R. (2003). *Postcolonialism: a very short introduction.* Oxford: Oxford University Press.

Young, K., Ashby, D., Boaz, A. & L. Grayson (2002). Social science and the evidence-based policy movement. *Social Policy & Society, 1*(3), 215–224.

Zipin, L. (1998). Looking for sentient life in discursive practices: The question of human agency in critical theories and school research. In T. S. Popkewitz & M. Brennan (Eds.), *Foucault's challenge: Discourse, knowledge and power in education* (pp. 316–347). New York: Teachers College Press.

GLOBALISATION

XAVIER BONAL & AINA TARABINI

GLOBAL SOLUTIONS FOR GLOBAL POVERTY?

The World Bank Education Policy and the Anti-Poverty Agenda

INTRODUCTION

During the last decades the World Bank (WB) has been without any doubt the most significant subject of globalisation processes in education and development. Political and economic transformations have transformed the Breton Woods institutions as actors with the ability to shape and even impose agendas to less developed countries. Since the beginning of the eighties the World Bank influence on education has expanded enormously, both quantitatively and qualitatively. This expansion has afforded it a quasi-monopoly in the area of international aid for educational development. Changes in the economic world order, shifts in educational multilateralism and internal crises in institutions such as UNESCO resulted in the dominance of institutions such as the IMF or the World Bank in shaping the international agenda for development (Mundy, 1999, p. 40).

Curiously, the World Bank's prominence in education over the last two decades has coincided with the application of structural adjustment policies in both Latin America and Africa. Against a background of prescribing policies of extreme austerity, lending in the educational sector and other social policy areas has increased. This change can be explained by the priority that the World Bank has given to institutional reform, an essential aspect of these adjustment programmes and a fundamental condition for granting loans (Mundy, 2002, p. 488). As a result, although the adjustment programmes have led to drastic reductions in basic subsidies, the financing allocated for sectorial reform has increased. This is a key point in understanding the World Bank's capacity to influence the direction of education policy in developing countries. Although, in quantitative terms, educational financing channelled through the Bank may represent a relatively small percentage of a country's domestic educational budget, the conditional nature of these credits increases their influence on the administration and management of educational systems. The ideological capacity of the WB in shaping national policies has located education as one of the clearest examples of the supranational leverage in domestic policies.

The pressures, criticisms and evident failure of the adjustment programmes have, however, caused modifications to certain important aspects of the World Bank's agenda. Substantial changes in the Bank's rhetoric have been observed since the beginning of the decade, even as regards its strategy for programme design and evaluation.[1] The incorporation in 1990 of the "Education for All"

M. Simons, M. Olssen and M.A. Peters (eds.), Re-Reading Education Policies: A Handbook Studying the Policy Agenda of the 21st Century, 96–111.

programme, the creation of a Social Adjustment Unit charged with assessing the social impact of stabilisation policies (Samoff, 1994), the influence of the work of Amartya Sen on human development, the engagement of Joseph Stiglitz in 1997 as chief economist at the World Bank (and the development of the so-called *Post-Washington Consensus*), and, above all, the priority of the fight against poverty are all factors that explain the reorientation of some of the Bank's strategies and priorities. Clearly, the new order of priorities demonstrates that education has remained one of the "strong" areas of World Bank policy, as shown by some of its strategic documents (World Bank, 1995, 1999a, 1999b, 2001a). In the struggle against poverty, education appears as one of the key mechanisms for facilitating the social insertion and employment of excluded communities, providing them with the abilities that they require to be individually independent.

The aim of this chapter is to make a critical assessment of the explicit strategies of the World Bank's education policies aimed at fighting poverty since the implementation of the *Structural Adjustment Programmes* (SAPs). The introduction of SAP locates the World Bank as a subject of globalisation of education. Within the ambiguous terrain of assessing what globalisation is and what type of effects it generates on economic, social and political relations (Hay, 1999), the WB appears to be a real subject embedded of political and economic capacity to generate global changes in educational discourses and practices. Actually, the WB procedures and objectives can be considered an extreme case of globalisation of education: as an international organisation, the WB has shown an enormous capacity to generate convergence in policy processes and "desirable" policy goals (though effects may differ depending on national conditions). Although the aim of the objective is ambitious, we will present two main phases of the World Bank rhetoric on education and poverty: the one embedded in structural adjustment programmes and the post-Washington Consensus of the nineties with a special reference on the most recent strategies that have put the struggle against poverty at the forefront of the Bank's policies and loans; that is, the *Poverty Reduction Strategy Papers* (PRSPs). The chapter not only pretends to introduce a critical perspective in order to analyse the WB's discourses and proposals in the fight against poverty but also to identify the main failings that underline the positive and hoped-for relationship between investment in education and the reduction of poverty. A re-reading of the WB's proposals therefore will be addressed, exploring its main limitations and omissions.

EDUCATION AND POVERTY ALLEVIATION UNDER THE WASHINGTON
CONSENSUS

The "Washington Consensus" term was coined by Williamson (1993) in the early nineties to refer to the economic policy agenda that the IMF, the WB and the US Executive Board were undertaking in Latin America during the eighties. That agenda included a number of policy 'recommendations' to be followed by developing countries in order to achieve the necessary stabilisation of their economies and institutional reforms that would facilitate the insertion of those countries into the competitive global economy. In broad terms, the Washington Consensus approach recommends that governments should reform their policies by following a number of measures. As Gore (2000) argues, these measures should: (a) pursue macroeconomic stability by controlling inflation and reducing fiscal deficits; (b) open their economies to the rest of the world through trade and capital account liberalisation, and (c) liberalise domestic product and factor markets through privatisation and deregulation (Gore, 2000, pp. 789–790).

During the eighties, the Washington Consensus appeared as the *paradigm* for economic development. It substituted former approaches, especially those based on Keynesian economics and modernisation, in which the state intervention was crucial to stimulate economic demand through direct investment. Clearly shaped by neo-classical economics, the Washington Consensus pursued economic stabilisation (control of inflation rates, control of balance of payments deficit, public expenditure reduction and so on) through strong adjusting measures, and claimed the retreat of the state as an economic actor that disturbed the efficient allocative role of market forces. This paradigm made the state almost disappear from the scene of structural change for development. The role of the state was reduced to generate the necessary conditions for a market-led economy (mainly through privatisation and deregulation of markets). Market economics were supposed to make the economy competitive enough to overcome the initial difficulties brought about by adjustment policies and to generate the necessary growth rate to insert developing countries into the new economic order.

Multilateral organisations like the International Monetary Fund and the World Bank became global agents for spreading the neo-liberal paradigm of development. During the eighties, both institutions were able to impose the Washington Consensus agenda to many developing countries through loan conditionality. Their hegemonic position within the international market of financial assistance for development and the extreme dependency of highly indebted countries on international loans, mostly to refund external debt interests, shifted completely the relationship between the Bretton Woods institutions and borrowing countries. Through programs like *Structural Adjustment Facilities, Extended Fund Facilities* or *Structural Adjustment Loans*, both the IMF and the WB were able to impose the neo-liberal paradigm of development to borrowing countries, whatever the previous social and economic conditions were. In Latin American, for instance, the imposition of loan conditionality entailed a dramatic structural policy change, from Import Substitution Industrialisation (ISI) to export-oriented models of development (Gwynne & Kay, 2000). That is, a development model based on state protectionism of strategic industries was forced to disappear and be substituted by a free market model in which non-subsidised industries should openly compete in the global market of free trade.

A number of empirical studies have shown that the programs extended by the WB and the IMF were associated with increased poverty, increased inequality of income and slow economic growth (Stewart, 1995; Cornia et al. 1997; Chossudovsky, 1998). The failure of Structural Adjustment Programs (SAPs) as appropriate recipes for development is illustrated by a simple fact: since the mid eighties, third world countries have become net capital exporters to northern countries (Chossudovsky, 1998, p. 51), that is, they have paid more than they have received. Debt repayments account for more than capital transfers to the third world (counted as loans, direct foreign investment and development assistance).[2] Of course, not only International Financial Institutions (IFIs) are responsible for this failure. Actually, it is always difficult to provide an accurate evaluation of the reasons why certain programs were wrongly designed or implemented. National problems (governmental corruption, bureaucratic inefficiency, and so on) might added difficulties to the implementation of IFI's agenda. Whatever the concrete causes, the global result was the economic and social devastation of third world countries during the eighties (the "lost decade", in Latin America).

Under the hegemony of the Washington Consensus, the priority of macro-economic stabilisation, pro-export policies and commercial and economic liberalisation are considered to be factors that are fundamental to economic growth. From the earliest signs of growth, once a preliminary adjustment period has passed, the effects of growth on the reduction of poverty are considered to be "automatic." Indeed, throughout the 1980s it is unusual to find any analysis or discussion in the World Bank's documentation regarding the greater or lesser redistributive impact of its Structural Adjustment Programmes (SAPs). As Mundy (2002) pointed out, "it is widely assumed that market-led growth resumed and government distortions were eliminated, the demand for the labour of the poor would increase, ensuring their enhanced buying power and economic betterment" (Mundy, 2002, p. 488). This "trickle-down" effect is even sufficiently powerful to alleviate the effects of a reduction in public expenditure in education or other social policy areas. It is assumed that the improvements in efficiency resulting from a reduction in the public sector and an increase in private provision will in themselves generate employment and, as a consequence, facilitate social integration in the most disadvantaged social sectors. As a result, the World Bank's main prescriptions are aimed at drastically reducing the public sector, at deregulation and at privatisation. This model for the automatic reduction of poverty ignores the relationship between inequality and economic growth. If, under the chairmanship of Robert McNamara (1968-81), this was based on a contradictory relationship between both factors (and therefore the need to establish priorities for intervention, accompanying them with compensation policies), the dominant neo-liberal orthodoxy of the World Bank's policy during the 1980s meant that no specific agenda was developed in relation to policies for redistribution or the struggle against poverty.

The reverse effects that SAPs had both on education and especially on poverty, goes a long way towards explaining the progressive abandonment of a stricter neo-liberal orthodoxy and the adoption of a development agenda that includes strategies which are complementary to a market-led model of economic growth. It is in the context of adjustment crisis and the emergence of strong critiques to the Bank's policies that a new discourse on education and poverty must be interpreted.

THE POST-WASHINGTON CONSENSUS: A NEW AGENDA FOR FIGHTING AGAINST POVERTY?

In the late eighties the Washington Consensus was experiencing difficulties in face of a number of criticisms. The rise of poverty and subsequent complaints about structural adjustment effects led to demands of adjustment with a human face (Ilon, 1996). Simultaneously, the success of East Asian economies opened claims for a different role of the state in development (Fine, 2001, p. 139). In Latin America, the Economic Commission for Latin America and the Caribbean (ECLAC)'s neostructuralism[3] tried to establish a "Southern Consensus" to challenge the neo-liberal assumptions of the Washington Consensus and claimed for a context-based strategy of industrialisation to ensure the integration of national economies into the global economy (Gore, 2000, p. 796). The work of Joseph Stiglitz as Chief Economist to the WB in the late nineties, and a number of lectures of Amartya Sen at the WB, opened a new debate about development and generated conditions for a Post-Washington Consensus. Fine (2001) describes the features of the Post-Washington Consensus as follows:

> First, it is sharply critical of the Washington Consensus and seeks an alternative in which state intervention is greater in depth and breadth. Second, it rejects the analytical agenda of state versus market, arguing that the two are complements and can work together and not against one another. Third, if less explicit, it poses an alternative agenda for development economics and policy debate, seeking to establish the appropriate role of the state in view of market imperfections. Fourth, it also brings the social back into the analysis as the means of addressing, and potentially correcting, market imperfections – rather than simply creating them as for the Washington Consensus for which the world would be a better place if it were made more and more, if not completely, like the market (Fine, 2001, p. 139).

Interestingly enough, and as Fine argues, in policy terms the Post-Washington Consensus does not differ radically from the Washington Consensus. State interventionism is still restricted to market imperfections, which are now recognised, but this is different from the Keynesian state model of development, in which the state plays a more active role in tax policy and resource allocation. The state is still seen as captured by rent-seeking agents, that is, as a space inducing clientelism, a major obstacle for bringing structural change. Thus, it is questionable that the Post-Washington Consensus brings a new agenda for policy development and educational development. A review of some education policy papers published in the late nineties (World Bank, 1999a & 1999b) shows new objectives and commitments for education; social aspects have clearly more relevance than it had in previous statements. However, it is questionable the extent to which new objectives and commitments for education challenge the basic principles of economics of education that sustain the rationale of WB education policy. Basic features of WB education policy, like the rates of return rationale for educational investments, the importance of private education, or the marginalisation of vocational education and training, remain unaltered.

In fact, since the 1980s, the WB relies heavily on rates of return to education as the only rationale for educational investment (World Bank, 1995; Bennell, 1996). Since then, financing basic education has become the first priority of the WB's intervention, at the cost of technical and even secondary and higher education. This political priority has given credibility to the Bank in two aspects: first, it relies on apparently irrefutable arguments legitimated by the dominant paradigm of economics of education[4]; secondly, it makes the Bank appear as an institution concerned with the struggle against poverty and educational opportunities (Bonal, 2002). However, the rates-of-return rationale has also legitimated other priorities in policy making. It has justified arguments in favour of more user participation in the financing of post-basic education and has opened the door for an increase of the private sector in educational supply. The current WB's objectives and commitments for education not only maintain the top priority on primary education but also the recommendations for increasing the role of the private sector in secondary and tertiary education. As the World Bank (2006) points out:

> Greater attention must also be given to the role of the private sector in education provision, given the large numbers of children in low-income countries without access to primary education and the significant unmet demand for higher education in many countries (...) Public provision of good-quality primary education at no cost to parents or children is the cornerstone for achieving the Millennium Development Goals, but there is room and need—in low- and middle-income countries alike—to promote increased private participation in education. The aim is to help meet demand; improve education quality (international assessments show that some private school students consistently outperform public school students); increase private sector access to public funding; promote teacher training for primary and secondary education; and support system wide capacity building at tertiary and vocational levels (World Bank, 2006, pp. 33–34).

However, the post-Washington Consensus does frame a new rhetoric on education and poverty reduction. The *World Development Report 2000/2001, Attacking Poverty* sets out the World Bank's desire to set itself up as an institution charged with overseeing "global welfare", along with the strategies and priorities that should support this objective. The World Bank's greater receptiveness to the social implications of economic growth in its analysis of development is especially clear in chapter 3 of the report: "Growth, inequality and poverty." This is an extensively documented chapter, which assesses the relationship between these three variables on the basis of questions such as "Why are similar rates of growth associated with different rates of poverty reduction?" (World Bank, 2001a, p. 51). Far from offering an unequivocal reply to this question, the World Bank's discourse abandons the classic incompatibility between growth and equality, acknowledging that:

> Recent thinking – and empirical evidence – weaken the case for such a trade-off: lower inequality can increase efficiency and economic growth through a variety of channels. Unequal societies are more prone to difficulties in collective action, possibly reflected in dysfunctional institutions, political instability, a propensity for populist redistributive policies, or greater volatility in policies – all of which can lower growth. And to the extent that inequality in income or assets coexists with imperfect credit markets, poor

people may be unable to invest in their human and physical capital, with adverse consequences for long-run growth (World Bank, 2001a, p. 56).

Even so, in the same chapter, the World Bank hastens to assure us that:

This is not to say that every pro-equity policy will have such desired effects. If the reduction in inequality comes at the expense of the other factors conducive to growth, the gains from redistribution can vanish. Expropriation of assets on a grand scale can lead to political upheaval and violent conflict, undermining growth. And sometimes attempts to redistribute income can reduce incentives to save, invest, and work (World Bank, 2001a, pp. 56–57).

Certain important points can be derived from this chapter when interpreting the model used by the World Bank to attack poverty: a certain resistance to accepting the majority of analyses that underline the positive relationship between growth, equality and the reduction of poverty[5], the tendency to attribute the fact that growth benefits the entire population and effectively reduces poverty to internal (domestic) factors rather than to the design of its own policies or recommendations, and the importance given to education as a key strategy for permitting social inclusion. The other chapters in the report confirm the tendency towards a less orthodox approach by the World Bank. They offer recommendations for the reorientation of public spending (with allocations that offer more benefit to the poorer sectors), mechanisms aimed at making the markets function more favourably for the poor, proposals for target interventions in social programmes, improvements in administrative efficiency, stimuli for direct participation in the decision-making process by the most disadvantaged sectors, initiatives for involving all types of organisations in a coalition against poverty, strategies for generating and mobilising social capital in development projects and strategies for reducing the vulnerability of the poor. The range of strategies and priorities is broad.

In this context, certain changes could be seen in the direction of the World Bank's education policies. The most significant change was undoubtedly in the Bank's desire to establish new mechanisms for determining the credits to be borne in mind in a regional or local context. New terminology, which included expressions such as "Comprehensive Development Framework" (World Bank, 1999a), reflected the integral nature that the World Bank's interventions attempted to acquire under the management of James Wolfensohn. This was an attempt to integrate sector-based strategies (in education, health and infrastructure) with broader programmes whose design was always preceded by evaluations of the context in which they were to be applied. This new approach also required changes to be made to the World Bank's intervention methodology. Over recent years, the World Bank has sought the assistance of NGOs and other international bodies when designing, planning and implementing its projects. It has also resorted to a system of dialogue, holding direct consultations with the potential beneficiaries of its projects and members of civil society in its borrower countries and regions[6]. This is intended to establish more participatory planning systems that are better adapted to real local circumstances.

These new trends mean that education policy has been completely adapted to a development agenda which is more flexible and which, above all, adopts selective actions in respect of target groups as a new strategy for intervention. Within the educational sphere, the global priorities established by the World Bank centre around four areas: basic education for the poorest sectors and for girls; intervention programmes for early child development and health in education; the use of innovative methods in education (distance education, use of new technologies) and the so-called "systemic reform" (in curricula and assessment, management and the financing of education). Each of these strategies is applied selectively in different countries (particularly in Africa) and enjoys the collaboration of NGOs and other bodies (World Bank, 1999a, p. 30).

Thus, WB policy documents during the nineties showed that the Bank's conception of poverty changed. The incorporation of the Human Development Index, which measures nutritional status, educational attainment and health status, shows a difference with the conventional understanding of poverty as per capita income (Pender, 2001, p. 406). However, it is less clear that these changes altered loan conditionality based on the priority of fighting poverty. Actually, strategies against poverty do not necessarily entail a paradigmatic change in WB education policy. On the one hand, attacking poverty can be understood as a state strategy to account for a market imperfection: to compensate for the failure of the trickle down effect of the market, the state uses emergency services to attend the most damaged sectors of society – see Robertson and Dale (2002) on the use of local states of emergency by the neo-liberal state. Poor sectors of society become *target* groups in a state logic of intervention that manages risk and uncertainty. Moreover, according to Ilon (2002) the WB's concern on poverty is based exclusively in an economic logic, which means, to avoid the risks that poverty generates for markets' stability and growth.

On the other hand, strategies against poverty do not necessarily entail a redistributive economic and social policy. A policy to ensure basic needs for the poorest can be addressed without locating redistribution as the main priority for education policy, neither changing the trickle down logic of the market as the means to ensure redistribution. Actually, in the WB education policy discourses redistribution as a prior objective only appears when dealing with the finance of post-compulsory education, a discourse that provides the rationale to legitimate more user-pay share and the concentration of public spending in basic education. Progressive or regressive redistributive effects of expanding the private sector of education are never considered by the WB policy papers.

In policy terms, what the new strategies meant for an education policy against poverty was the "targeting the poor" approach. Identifying the poor and concentrating resources and efforts on providing them with the opportunity to gain access to different markets became the predominant political strategy. This new approach had a rapid effect on the loan portfolios of the World Bank and the IMF, to the extent that, by the end of the 1990s, so-called "emergency social funds" formed 50% of all structural adjustment credits (Mundy, 2002, p. 492).[7]

The rapid expansion of targeting programmes has led to a number of debates regarding the advantages and disadvantages of selective action as compared with more universalist policies. Discussions centre around the underlying philosophies of the various policy options (what type of action is socially more just), the value of one type of action over another in specific political contexts and problems relating to the coverage, selection and implementation costs of each type of policy.[8] Moreover, according to Mkandawire (2005) the current debate on the choice between targeting and universalism is couched in the language of "efficiency." That is, targeting is presented as the best strategy in order to maximise the benefits of resource allocation in a context of budget constrains; as the most efficient strategy to guarantee simultaneously poverty reduction and economic growth.

Educational targeting in fact is presented as more efficient than any other strategy in order to guarantee the access of poor people into the school and, consequently, to increase their human capital and their chances of breaking the inter-generational cycle of poverty. It is justified on the bases of the need to compensate the social sectors that have not been able to take advantage of the opportunities provided by economic growth and educational expansion by helping in their *empowerment* and activation. It is presented, in short, as the key mechanism for guaranteeing the "activation" of poor people, thus contributing to the increase of labour productivity, economic growth and social development (Tarabini, 2007).

THE POVERTY REDUCTION STRATEGY PAPERS

The consolidation of the anti-poverty strategy of the World Bank and its aim to locate the struggle against poverty as the main mission of the Bank took the form of the Poverty Reduction Strategy Papers (PRSP). PRSP were introduced in 1999 by the World Bank and the International Monetary Fund and, as Ruckert (2006) points out, are one of the main new policy tools for the Post Washington Consensus be articulated.

The PRSPs are instruments which aim is to describe a country "macroeconomic, structural and social policies and programs over a three year or longer horizon, to promote broad based growth and reduce poverty, as well as associated external financing needs and major sources of financing" (World Bank, 2001b). Formally speaking, the content of each document is elaborated by the developing countries themselves, trying to reflect their specific needs and features. Principles that underline the PRSP must include a result-oriented strategy (with targets that can be monitored); a comprehensive strategy (incorporating macroeconomic, structural and social policy aspects); a country driven strategy (that is, it should be oriented differently according to the special features of the country) and a participatory strategy (based on partnership between IFIs, governments, and other actors, like NGOs). Education is one of the major elements of the PRSP (Caillods and Hallak, 2004). PRSP include "good practices" for the sector and recommendations for investment in education that focus on the most vulnerable groups.

However, the World Bank itself provides the guidelines for developing countries to prepare their PRSP. The World Bank published *Sourcebook for Poverty Reduction Strategies* that is intended to be "a guide to assist countries in the development and strengthening of poverty reduction strategies." The sourcebook contains a very detailed chapter on education policy to draw the best educational practices for poverty reduction. As it is stated in the document: "[the education chapter] provides diagnostic tools and research findings that can help countries identify the policies and programs likely to have the most powerful impact on education opportunities and outcomes for poor children and illiterate adults within their country context" (Aoki, Bruns et al., 2002, p. 233). The chapter is organised in four main parts. The first one presents a rationale for investing in education as part of a general strategy for poverty reduction. The second one focuses on how to elaborate a diagnosis of the education system performance. The third part is related to policies and defines a number of "best practices" and "benchmarks" for fighting against poverty. The last one focuses on implementation, financing and evaluation.

Without any doubt, the educational chapter is clearly guided by human capital theory. The main thesis stands that in order to empower the poor and increase their capacity to create income, the strategy should remove obstacles and facilitate access to education and training for the poor. According to this view, primary education continues to have a central role. It remains understood as the area with the highest rate of return and therefore, the educational level to be prioritised. Moreover, the strategy puts an important emphasis on targeting the poor, and recommends educational policies to be directly addressed to poor students and families. The strategy makes a special reference to conditioned cash transfer programmes as one of the good educational policies to follow in the struggle against poverty. According to Caillods and Hallak (2004), what seems to be missing in PRSP is a theory concerning teaching and learning: "the PRSPs do not discuss the teaching and learning strategies most likely to facilitate participation of the poor and ensure real learning" (Caillods & Hallak, 2004, p. 18). Reducing poverty requires that the poor do not only attend school, but that they do really learn and acquire relevant skills to overcome their poverty condition.

PRSPs are supposed to be nor compulsory and neither conditional. However, several elements cast doubt about this theoretical premise:

First of all, all PRSP have to carry out the same general principles, following the *Sourcebooks for Poverty Reduction Strategies* instructions and recommendations. The *Sourcebooks* (Klugman 2002a, 2002b) are professedly to reflect the thinking and practices associated with the Comprehensive Development Framework, the World Development Report 2000/2001 and the good international practices related to poverty reduction. As a result, four priority areas are identified as imperatively necessary for bringing both economic growth and poverty alleviation to developing countries. These areas have turned into conditions that have to be met before concessional lending for a PRSP can be approved (Ruckert, 2006). The four areas are the following ones, p. 1) Macroeconomic and structural policies to support sustainable growth in which the poor participate, 2) Improved governance, including public sector financial management, 3) Appropriate sectoral policies and programs and 4) Realistic costing and appropriate levels of funding for the major programs (Klugman, 2002a, p. 16). The *Sourcebook* specifies that the particular content of each area will differ across countries. However, the areas themselves are expected to appear in any PRSP, being the framework for all discussions about it.

Secondly, the content of a country's PRSP have to be compatible with the framing prescriptions of the respective Country Assistance Strategy (CAS) of the World Bank and Poverty Reduction and Growth Facility (PRGF) of the International Monetary Fund (Weber, 2004). Both the CAS and the PRGF are supposed to reflect the country's priorities and specific circumstances. PRSP priorities, therefore, are not able to contradict the general framework and the specific targets and indicators that the CAS and the PRGF identify as central in achieving the stated outcomes.

Thirdly, the European Union (EU) decided to base its five year assistance programmes in African, Caribbean and Asian Pacific countries on PRSPs, declaring that: "The framework and basic tool for European development cooperation is the poverty reduction strategy paper (PRSP), which aims to promote country-driven policies with local ownership and partnership. All countries wishing to receive EU aid are required to develop a PRSP, and EC policy is to fund only activities covered within a country's PRSP" (European Comission, 2003, p. 5). At the same time, key bilateral donors like the Netherlands and the United Kingdom orientate their assistance strategies on the basis of the PRSPs.

Finally, the PRSPs are considered by the Executive Boards of the IMF and World Bank as the basis for concessional lending from each institution and debt relief under the joint Heavily Indebted Poor Countries (HIPC) Initiative. Financial flows of aid, whether linked to the reduction of debts, grants or concessional loans have been linked to the adoption by recipient countries of a comprehensive poverty reduction strategy (Caillods & Hallak, 2004, p. 6). Moreover, having an approved PRSP is a condition for being considered in the *Education for All* (EFA) Fast Track Initiative (FTI)[9]. PRSP becomes the framework for the IFIs development assistance to lending countries.

These circumstances put clear the PRSPs do not only recommend but also prescribe and shape policies to be implemented by developing countries. In fact, the IFI's final decisions in supporting or disapproving national PRSPs remains quite ambiguous (Ruckert, 2006): "While the shift to country ownership will allow substantially more leeway in terms of policy design and choices, acceptance by the Bank and the IMF boards will depend on the current international understanding of what is effective in lowering poverty" (Klugman, 2002a, p. 4). Moreover, all the PRSPs documents and guidelines written by the World Bank or the IMF Staff highlight the need of setting an 'enabling environment' for the implementation of the full PRSP process. Far from being neutral this "environment" is based on the same criteria underlining the implementation of the Structural Adjustment Plans.

Craig and Porter (2003) argue that PRSPs sort the action priorities in the following way: "global economic integration first, good governance second, poverty reduction following as a result, underpinned by limited safety nets and human capital development" (Craig and Porter, 2003, p. 53). The main thesis of the authors is that this prioritisation represents a refinement of the liberal political project and specifically a mode of "inclusive liberalism." With the idea of "inclusive liberalism" the authors aim to identify a more eclectic strategy that introduces the importance of poverty reduction along with classical neo-liberal principles and policies. The main criticism of Craig and Porter to this new strategy is its silence with regard to power structures and inequalities. The PRSP consolidate a technical and apolitical approach to poverty that more than changing policy contents, it changes the labels. This idea fits with what some authors understand as the logic of Post-Washington Consensus: to complete, correct and complement the reforms of a decade ago but not to reverse them (Gwynne, 2004).

In fact several authors argue that anti-poverty policies applied within the "second generation reforms" do not represent, at all, the end of neo-liberalism.[10] Some authors (Booth, 2003; Driscoll & Evans 2005; Stiglitz, 1998) that argue that Post Washington Consensus represents a fundamental rupture in development thinking and a progressive move away from neo-liberalism. On the contrary, according to authors like Cammack (2004), Soederberg (2005) or Robertson et al. (2007), anti-poverty policies are the best strategy of the World Bank and International Monetary Fund to maintain the neo-liberal model. As Soederberg pointed out: "(…) the Poverty Reduction Strategy Papers are not about doing away with conditionality, but should be seen instead as direct responses to the above mentioned threats to neo-liberalism, which are, in turn, targeting at reconfiguring and deepening neo-liberal domination over the growing number of the poor in the South" (Soedeberg, 2005, p. 339).

CONCLUSIONS: THE MISSING ASPECTS OF THE RELATIONSHIP BETWEEN EDUCATION AND POVERTY

This paper has focused on the main principles that have underlined the World Bank education policy since the 1980s with regard to its effects for fighting poverty. A review of some of the key WB policy papers has shown the evolution of both discursive rhetoric and specific strategies for fighting poverty. Interestingly enough, the anti-poverty agenda has gain more and more space in the World Bank discourse for development and has become recently as the main mission of the Bank. However, as some authors have pointed out, even under the post-Washington consensus policies, the poverty alleviation approach remains framed by a political economy that always locates the objective of poverty reduction as a consequence of economic growth. Although there are extensive and important debates around the role that social inequalities can play to help poverty reduction strategies, that is, if reducing inequalities makes easier also to reduce poverty, the WB usually undervalues its role compared to the importance given to growth-led policies. The balance allows us to detect serious limitations in the role that the World Bank has assigned to educational development in order to achieve the poverty reduction target (one of the central goals of the *Millennium Summit*).

Nevertheless, it is also interesting to turn our view to the taken for granted understanding of the education and poverty relationship that is embedded in all different poverty reduction strategies developed by the World Bank. And it is clear that the WB strategies stress the positive effect of education to combat poverty but fail to take into account the effects of poverty on education. This omission, which persists throughout the various approaches to education policy, not only conditions the central importance of education as a mechanism for breaking the inter-generational poverty cycle, it also explains why, on so many occasions, the policies designed for the most disadvantaged groups give such poor results. Social policies designed to "activate" the poor often place the need for intervention in the category of "cultural deprivation" while at the same time ignoring a set of objective obstacles that restrict any real possibility of the poor developing sustainable forms of investment, such as investment in human capital itself. When these obstacles are recognised, however, the strategy consists of facilitating access to markets that must adapt to the social and economic conditions of the excluded groups (World Bank, 2001b), which completely disregards the limitations that any market has in adapting to the needs of the poor, as well as the limitations of the poor themselves as regards subsistence via access to the formal markets.

But the exclusion processes associated with globalisation[11] have a particular impact on the most vulnerable sectors, which are increasingly concerned with day-to-day survival and find themselves less able to benefit from policies that are designed to "activate" them and provide them with the means necessary for their social inclusion. If escaping from poverty requires more than 10 years' schooling, who is in a position to visualise this objective? If the benefits of additional years in primary schooling are reduced, what use is it to remain at school when the cost of schooling is rising and at the same time people are getting poorer? If the school systems are becoming increasingly socially polarised, what use is the ability to gain access to the system with the least social value? If the working conditions of the teaching staff deteriorate, and with them educational standards, what quality of education is reserved for the poorest sectors?

There are, therefore, grounds for reviewing the minimum material conditions in which poor families can effectively invest in human capital over the long term and that will provide us with systems that enable us to determine when education policy can actually be effective as a strategy for combating poverty.

NOTES

[1] See Fine (2001), Pender (2001) and Bonal (2002) for a critical evaluation of the limits and possibilities of the World Bank's reorientation of its discourse.

[2] The transfer from Third World to First World countries is four times superior to the Marshall Plan to reconstruct Europe after World War II. In the mid eighties total net transfer to the First World accounted for 250 billion dollars (Hoogvelt, 2001, p. 180).

[3] Neostructuralism defines development as an integral process and takes into consideration not only economic elements but also social and political structures as well as institutional, cultural and psychological factors.

[4] In any case the consistence of the rates of return analysis is only apparent. There are many practical problems (missing data and especially, the over-estimation of benefit rates as a consequence of excluding significant variables in the calculation). See Bennell (1996) for a critique on the use and abuse of rates of return.

[5]   See the article by Dagdeviren *et al.* (2002) for a mathematical model of the relationship between growth, equality and poverty. See also ECLAC's simulations for Latin America (ECLAC, 2002, p. 49 *et seq.*).

[6]   See Ilon (2002) for a critique of those strategies.

[7]   An excellent critique of emergency social funds can be found in Cornia (2001).

[8]   See for example Offe (2002), Filgueira (2001), Brodershon (1999) and Coraggio (1995).

[9]   In 2002, the Education for All – Fast Track Initiative (FTI) was launched as a global partnership between donor and developing countries to ensure accelerated progress towards the Millennium Development Goal of universal primary education by 2015.

[10] The neoliberal theory was mainly formulated by Milton Friedman's Chicago School.,This theory motivated concrete policies of adjustment in many states. These policies included the radical break with the role of the state as the engine of economic growth, the reduction of controls and restrictions in the foreign trade, the adjustment of the exchange rates, the abolition of interventions in the domestic markets and the liberalisation of the financial markets.

[11] Although there is an extensive debate with regards to the impacts of globalisation on inequality there are growing evidences that globalisation has led to dynamics of exclusion both at a national and international scale. See for example Wade and Wolf (2002).

REFERENCES

Aoky, A., Bruns, B., Drabble, M., et al. (2002). Chapter 19. Education. In J. Klugman (Ed.), *A sourcebook for poverty reduction strategies. Volume II: Macroeconomic and Sectoral Approaches.* Washington, DC: World Bank.

Bennell, P. (1996). Using and abusing rates of return. *International Journal of Educational Development, 16*, 235–248.

Bonal, X. (2002). *Plus ça change.* The World Bank global education policy and the post-Washington consensus. *International Studies in Sociology of Education, 12*, 3–21.

Booth, D. (2003). PRSPs - Introduction and overview. *Development Policy Review, 21*(2), 31–159.

Brodersohn, V. (1999). Focalización de programas de superación de la pobreza. In UNICEF, *Derecho a tener derecho: infancia, derecho y política social en América Latina.* Montevideo: Instituto Internacional del Niño (IIN) i Unicef.

Caillods, F., & Hallak, J. (2004). *Education and PRSPs. A review of experiences.* UNESCO: IIPE.

Cammack, P. (2004). What the World Bank means by poverty reduction and why it matters. *New Political Economy, 9*(2), 189–211.

Chossudovsky, M. (1998). *The globalisation of poverty. Impacts of IMF and World Bank reforms.* London: Zed Books.

Coraggio, J. L. (1995). Las *propuestas del Banco Mundial para la educación: ¿Sentido oculto o problemas de concepción? O Banco Mundial e as Politicas de Educaçao no Brasil.* Açao Educativa: Sao Paulo.

Cornia, G. A. (2001). Social funds in stabilization and adjustment programmes: A critique. *Development and Change, 32*, 1–32.

Cornia, G., Jolly, R., & Stewart, F. (1997). *Adjustment with a human face* (Vol. 1). Oxford: Clarendon Press.

Craig, D., & Porter, D. (2003). Poverty reduction strategy papers: A new convergence. *World Development, 31*(1), 53–69.

Dagdeviren, H., Van Der Hoeven, R., & Weeks, J. (2002). Poverty reduction with growth and redistribution. *Development and Change, 33*, 383–413.

Driscoll, R., & Evans, A. (2005). Second-generation poverty reduction strategies: Opportunities and emerging issues. *Development Policy Review, 23*(1), 5–25.

ECLAC. (2002). *Panorama Social de América Latina 2001–2002.* ECLAC: Santiago de Chile.

European Commission. (2003). *The European Union and the South: A new era. The international responsibilities of an enlarged European Union.* Conference organized by SID-Netherlands and EADI. 3-4 Novembre. Retrieved from http://www.sidint.org/files/report/EU_and_the_South-Conference_Report.pdf

Filgueira, F. (2001). *Entre pared y espada: la ciudadanía social en América Latina (II).* Instituto Internacional de Gobernabilidad: Biblioteca de Ideas.

Fine, B. (2001). *Social capital versus social theory.* London: Routledge.

Gore, C. (2000). The rise and fall of the Washington consensus as a paradigm for developing countries. *World Development, 28*(5), 789–804.

Gwynne, R., & Kay, C. (2000). Views from the periphery: Futures of neoliberalism in Latin America. *Third World Quarterly, 21*(1), 141–156.

Gwynne, R. (2004). Structural reforms in South America and Mexico: Economic and regional perspectives. In R. N. Gwynne & C. Kay (Eds.), *Latin America transformed. Globalisation and modernity* (pp. 39–66). London: Edward Arnold.

Hay, C. (1999). *What place for ideas in the structure-agency debate? Globalisation as a process without a subject.* Paper presented at annual conference of the British International Studies Association, University of Manchester, 20–22 December.

Hoogvelt, A. (2001). *Globalisation and the postcolonial world. The new political economy of development* (2nd ed.). London: MacMillan.

Ilon, L. (1996). The changing role of the World Bank: Education policy as global welfare. *Policy and Politics, 24*, 413–424.

Ilon, L. (2002) Agent of global markets or agent of the poor? The World Bank's education sector strategy paper. *International Journal of Educational Development, 22*, 475–482.

Klugman, J. (Ed.). (2002a). *A sourcebook for poverty reduction strategies. Volume I: Core techniques and cross-cutting issues.* Washington, DC: World Bank.

Klugman, J. (Ed.). (2002b). *A sourcebook for poverty reduction strategies. Volume II: Macroeconomic and sectoral approaches.* Washington, DC: World Bank.

Mkandawire, T. (2005). *Targeting and universalism in poverty reduction, Programme Paper, 23.* Geneva: United Nations Research Institute for Social Development (UNRISD).

Mundy, K. (1999). Educational multilateralism in a changing world order: Unesco and the limits of the possible. *International Journal of Educational Development, 19*, 27–52.

Mundy, K. (2002). Retrospect and prospect: Education in a reforming World Bank. *International Journal of Educational Development, 22*, 483–508.

Offe, C. (2002). *Wasteful welfare transactions.* Paper presented at the IX Basic Income European Network International Congress, 12–14 September, Geneva.

Pender, J. (2001). From 'Structural Adjustment' to 'Comprehensive Development Framework': Conditionality transformed? *Third World Quarterly, 22*(3), 397–411.

Robertson, S., & Dale, R. (2002). Local states of emergency: The contradictions of neo-liberal governance in education in New Zealand. *British Journal of Sociology of Education, 23*(3), 463–482.

Robertson, S., Novelli, M., Dale, R., Tikly, L., Dachi, H., & Alphonce, N. (2007). *Globalisation, education and development: Ideas, actors and dynamics.* DFID: London.

Ruckert, A. (2006). *Towards an inclusive-neoliberal regime of development: From Washington consensus to the post-Washington consensus.* Canadian Political Science Association conference 1–3 June, York University, Toronto.

Samoff, J. (Ed.). (1994). *Coping with crisis. Austerity, adjustment and human resources.* London: Cassell.

Soederberg, S. (2005). Recasting neoliberal dominance in the global South? A critique of the monterrey consensus. *Alternatives, 30*, 325–364.

Stewart, F. (1995). *Adjustment and poverty.* London: Routledge.

Stiglitz, J. E. (1998). *Towards a new paradigm of development: Strategies, policies and processes.* Prebisch Lecture, 19 October, UNCTAD, Geneva.

Tarabini, A. (2007). The spread of targeted educational policies in Latin America: Global thesis and local impacts. *International Studies in Sociology of Education, 17*(1/2), 21–43.

Wade, R., & Wolf, M. (2002). Debate: Are global poverty and inequality getting worse? *Prospect, 72,* 16–21.

Weber, H. (2004). Reconstitutuing the "Third World"? Poverty reduction and territoriality in the global politics of development. *Third World Quartely, 25*(1), 187–206.

Williamson, J. (1993). Democracy and the 'Washington Consensus'. *World Development, 21,* 1329–1336.

World Bank. (1995). *Policies and strategies for education: A World Bank review.* Washington, DC: World Bank.

World Bank. (1999a). *Education sector strategy.* Washington, DC: World Bank.

World Bank. (1999b). *Educational change in latin America and the Caribbean.* Washington, DC: World Bank.

World Bank. (2001a). *World development report 2000/2001. Attacking poverty.* Washington, DC: Oxford University Press.

World Bank. (2001b). *Reviewing poverty reduction strategy program.* Retrieved from http://www.worldbank.org/developmentnews/stories/html/080601a.htm.

World Bank. (2006). *Education sector strategy update.* Washington, DC: World Bank.

FURTHER READINGS

Craig, D., & Porter, D. (2003). Poverty reduction strategy papers: A new convergence. *World Development, 31*(1), 53–69.

Gore, C. (2000). The rise and fall of the Washington consensus as a paradigm for developing countries. *World Development, 28*(5), 789–804.

Ilon, L. (2002). Agent of global markets or agent of the poor? The World Bank's education sector strategy paper. *International Journal of Educational Development, 22,* 475–482.

Mundy, K. (2002). Retrospect and prospect: Education in a reforming World Bank. *International Journal of Educational Development, 22,* 483–508.

Robertson, S., Novelli, M., Dale, R., Tikly, L., Dachi, H., & Alphonce, N. (2007). *Globalisation, education and development: Ideas, Actors and Dynamics.* DFID: London.

Xavier Bonal
Sociology Department
Autonomous University of Barcelona

Aina Tarabini
Sociology Department
Autonomous University of Barcelona

LEON TIKLY

GLOBALISATION AND THE QUEST FOR SOCIAL JUSTICE IN AFRICAN EDUCATION

INTRODUCTION

The chapter will focus on the African continent[1] and consider the main challenges facing education in the global era. The decision to focus on Africa is because as a region it is increasingly being left behind by the globalisation process (Scholte, 2006). The analysis of the chapter is also informed by ongoing research undertaken by the author in collaboration with colleagues that is based on the continent (Tikly et al., 2003; Robertson et al., 2007; Barrett & Tikly, 2008, Ngcobo & Tikly, forthcoming, for example). Most recently this has been in the context of a research programme consortium on Implementing Education Quality in Low Income Countries (EdQual) which has an African focus and seeks to understand the key processes of teaching, learning and school management that impact on the quality of eudcation. The chapter will consider the role of education, however, from a 'social justice' perspective and in this way will contribute to the emerging debate about the meaning of global social justice albeit form an educational perspective. According to Steger (2005) discourses around social justice are part of an emerging ideological landscape distinctive to the global era. He contrasts these with a 'market globalism' as well as more recent post 9/11 'imperial globalism' as well as with a range of religious fundamentalist ideologies that taken together are reshaping the ideological terrain beyond the boundaries of traditional political ideologies such as liberalism and Marxism. Market globalism, in particular with its roots in a rampant neo-liberalism has been important in shaping education policy in sub-Saharan Africa and we will return to this below. The chapter will commence with a discussion of the meaning of social justice in the global era and in the context of a discussion of the postcolonial condition. Attention will then turn to a consideration of the nature and impact of economic, political and cultural globalisation on education on the continent. This will provide a basis for setting out the key challenges for education in the global era.

SOME STARTING POINTS

It is important to make explicit the theoretical starting points. Firstly, the chapter is informed by a 'postcolonial' perspective on African education. The basis for such a perspective has been spelt out at length elsewhere (Tikly, 1998, Crossley & Tikly, 2004, for example). Put briefly what it entails is that we place centre stage the continuing implications of Europe's expansion into Africa, Asia, Australasia and

M. Simons, M. Olssen and M.A. Peters (eds.), Re-Reading Education Policies: A Handbook Studying the Policy Agenda of the 21st Century, 112–142.

the Americas from the fifteenth century onwards, not only as a means to understand the subsequent histories of these parts of the world but as a defining moment in European history and in the formation of contemporary global markets (Hall, 1996). In order to understand Africa's position in the global world and the implications of this for education we need to take seriously the changing economic realities of the continent since colonial times. We also need to enquire into the political legacy of colonialism including Africa's changing relationship with the rest of the world and the role of indigenous elites in perpetuating inequalities along the grounds of class, race and gender. At a cultural level, we need to take account of issues relating to ethnicity and language and the role of cultural norms and values that impact heavily on education but are also deeply embedded in the colonial past. In order to delve into these areas we need to combine old and new forms of analysis and critique – from political economy as well as from the cultural turn in the social sciences.

For many scholars writing from a postcolonial perspective, the work of Antonio Gramsci on hegemony and counter-hegemony and of Michel Foucault on the discursive basis of colonial rule have been particularly influential in this respect (see Appadurai, 1992; Young, 2001, for example). The attraction of Gramsci's work lies in his non-reductionist approach to understanding the nature of social reality and the role of cultural as well as economic and political factors in understanding change. The ttraction of Foucault's work lies in his understanding of the constitutive role of colonial practices and institutions including education in moulding or constituting colonial and postcolonial identities.

The chapter is also informed, however, by more recent work on social justice. Nancy Fraser provides a thought-provoking analysis of social justice in relation to globalisation that has relevance for Africa. She argues that "the acceleration of globalization has altered the scale of social interaction" and that "questions of social justice need to be reframed" (Fraser, 2006, p. 1). She highlights the limited applicability of the western state model as a framework for considering non-western contexts and that understanding issues of social justice requires taking account of the broader economic, political and social contexts. Fraser's ideas have the following implications. Firstly, rather than assuming that issues of education and social justice will take a similar form to those in the west, it is important to base the argument on an analysis of the African context. Secondly, just as important as the issues themselves is an understanding of the process by which some voices get heard in educational debates whilst those of others remain marginalised.

Fraser usefully draws attention to three dimensions of social justice that will be referred back to later on. The first, *redistribution* relates to issues concerned with access to resources. In our case this equates with access by all to a quality education and the potential outcomes that arise from this. Access to and ideas about what counts as a quality education, however, are contested in the context of neo-liberalism and the increasing marketisation of education as we will argue. The second dimension, that of *recognition*, means first identifying and then acknowledging the claims of historically marginalised groups. In the African context given the widespread nature of poverty and disadvantage it could be argued that this includes most learners! Some groups are however, more disadvantaged than others including women, rural dwellers, victims of HIV/AIDS orphans and vulnerable children refugees, cultural, linguistic, religious, racial and sexual minorities and indigenous groups. Issues of recognition concern the extent to which the needs of these groups are catered for in understandings of the quality of education including the formal and hidden curriculum and the way that schools are resourced. The third dimension, that of *participatory justice* includes the rights of individuals and groups to have their voices heard in debates about education and to actively participate in decision making. Importantly, for Fraser and indeed for the argument developed here, this is a prerequisite for realising issues of redistribution and recognition. It will be suggest that in the African context, given the scarcity of basic resources redistributive issues tend to predominate in the education debate over those of recognition and participation compared to similar debates in the west. It is argued, however, that whilst issues of redistribution are clearly central, they are inseparable from those of recognition and participation.

Before proceeding, a few riders are necessary. Careful consideration needs to be given before applying the concept of social justice to the African context. Firstly, the origins of the term lie outside of Africa in the European enlightenment and in the development of western humanism. These events coincided with particularly brutal periods in African history including the advent of western colonialism and the slave trade.[2] It is important to acknowledge this history whilst also recognising that indigenous understandings of justice have been present on the continent since pre-colonial times (Ramose, 2006) and how ideas of social justice have often lain at the heart of struggles against colonialism and slavery. Indeed, there has been a recent upsurge in interest in social justice as a concept on the continent and this is reflected in a range of new initiatives and publications.[3] Secondly, it is also important to acknowledge the enormous diversity of views around social justice issues in Africa and, as is the case elsewhere in the world, their often contested and contradictory nature.[4] A third caveat, in applying a social justice framework to Africa relates to the relative predominance of redistributive issues over those of recognition and participation compared to similar debates in the west. In this respect Susan George (2003) has argued that the deepening of poverty and inequality under globalisation is the most profound obstacle to realising global rights. In the African context it will be suggested that whilst issues of redistribution are clearly central, they are inseparable from those of recognition and participation.

IMPACT OF GLOBALISATION ON SUB-SAHARAN AFRICA: UNDERSTANDING GLOBALISATION

Scholte (2002, p. 4) reports that the terms 'globalize/globalise' and 'globalism' first appeared in the 1940s, and that globalisation first entered the dictionary of American English in 1961. It became a key analytical tool within the academy from the early 1980s. Since then, equivalent terms have emerged in a range of countries and in almost all of the major languages (see also Robertson et al., 2007).

During the course of research into *Globalisation and Skills for Development in Rwanda and Tanzania* (Tikly et al., 2003) the research team learned of a Swahili word, *Utandawazi* that is commonly used to capture local conceptions of globalisation. This fuses two words that relate to the concepts of 'network' and 'openness'. This indicates the increasing local significance of globalisation as a concept, but also the importance of the influence of language and context in shaping conceptualisations of globalisation itself. Thus when the team spoke to senior government officials and donors they would tend to emphasise issues such as 'attracting foreign the direct investment' or 'promoting export-led growth'. When talking to subsistence farmers, tea, pickers and cattle herders deep in the rural areas, however, the emphasis was more on protecting their livelihoods from the threat posed by cheap imports, opening up regional markets for their own goods and providing a safety net for them and their families, for example through fixed prices and subsidies for basic commodities. All of the African respondents were concerned about the possibly negative affect on African traditions and values posed by the largely western content of the internet. Despite differences, however, the prevailing view, reflected too in regional and national policy initiatives is that globalisation is irreversible and that the key point is how to make it work in the interests of Africa and of the continent's poor.

Put simply globalisation refers to the growing interconnectedness of the world and the extent to which, according to Giddens, "local happenings are shaped by events occurring many miles away and vice versa" (Giddens, 1990, p. 64). For Held et al. (1999) globalisation is best understood as an unfolding set of *processes* rather than a single 'condition'. These processes and how they relate to Africa will be explored in more detail below. With respect to technology, for example, it has involved a revolutionary process associated with the invention of the micro-chip. This has led in turn to the advent of the computer, e-mail, mobile phones, the internet etc. which have profoundly affected people's lives. It has also led to changes in the production process in the economy because it has enabled trans-national corporations (TNCs) to become more flexible in their production processes, outsourcing production to wherever in the world it is most profitable and the idea of 'just in time' production, facilitated at the push of a button. It has also facilitated the rapid movement of finance, goods and people around the world. These movements have happened in the context of the dominance of capitalism as a global system and of market driven, neo-liberal policies aimed at opening up borders and markets for goods and services. The problem for many African countries is that they lie at the periphery of these processes. Although there is variation with some countries such as South Africa, Namibia, Botswana and Mauritius now classified as middle income countries, the overall economic picture is bleak.

A term often associated with these developments is that of the *knowledge economy*. Originally coined by Daniel Bell (1973) to describe the shift form industrial to post-industrial societies, and more recently developed as an idea by Manuel Castells (1996) and his network society thesis. The core argument is that knowledge is *a new factor of production* that can be contrasted with traditional factors such as land (natural resources), labour (human effort) and capital goods (machinery) (Robertson et al., 2007. Of relevance for our purposes is that large sections of the globe, including Africa, are increasingly on the periphery of these processes. This is reflected, for example, in recent data on access to telephones and to the internet in different regions of the world which gives an indication of the spread of these technologies and the nature of the digital divide.

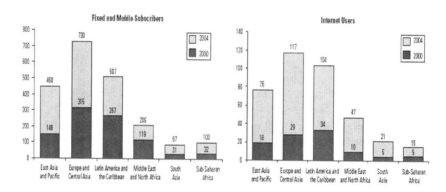

Figure 1. Telephone (fixed line and mobile) and internet access per region (per 1000 people) (source: World Bank, 2006)

This knowledge divide has been exacerbated by the so-called 'brain drain' which has affected many low income countries including those of Africa. According to the *International Organization for Migration* (IOM), Africa has already lost one third of its human capital and is continuing to lose its skilled personnel at an increasing rate, with an estimated 20,000 doctors, university teachers, engineers and other professionals leaving the continent annually since 1990. There are currently over 300,000 highly qualified Africans in the Diaspora, 30,000 of which have PhDs (IDRC, 2004). The reasons for this brain drain are complex but include poor pay and conditions of service in Africa compared to wealthier countries as well as contextual factors like a higher standard of living and greater security and political stability and freedom of speech. One implication is dependence by African governments on outside 'experts'. Africa spends US$4 billion per year (representing 35% of total official development aid to the continent) to employ some 100,000 Western experts performing functions generically described as technical assistance. For example, 90% of private firms in Gabon are managed by expatriates (IDRC, 2004).

For authors such as Castells (1993) and Amin (1997), the implication of the new technologies has been to consign much of sub-Saharan Africa to the so-called emerging 'Fourth World' and "from a structural position of exploitation [under colonialism] to a structural position of irrelevance [under globalisation]" (Castells, 1993, p. 37). During the colonial era Africa's economic relationship with the industrialised countries was based principally on the export of raw materials including minerals and agricultural produce. Now, however, the development of new materials has undermined the market for primary commodities. Africa has also suffered because high income countries restrict the continent's ability to sell its products in their countries. As a consequence, Africa's share of world exports has dropped from more than 3.5 percent in 1970 to about 1.4 percent at the end of 2002 (World Bank, 2005, p. xx) whilst its share of world trade has fallen from 6% to less than 2% the same period (CFA, 2005). African countries also find it difficult to attract foreign direct investment which is low in absolute terms compared to other low income regions and strongly focused on resource-based industries like diamonds and oil. A key barrier for investors is political instability and a poor infrastructure including transport and power (CFA, 2005). The upshot is that much of the manufacturing associated with the new forms of production is taking place in Asia and elsewhere in the world and the high levels of economic growth associated with financial deepening and the increased trade in new commodities and financial services have principally benefited western and newly industrialised nations who are integrated into these new global networks.

A further key dimension of economic globalisation has been the development and influence of the Bretton Woods institutions, the World Bank and the IMF and their role in promoting neo-liberal, market driven policies linked to the market globalism mentioned above. During the 1980s, structural adjustment policies as they were known impacted heavily on many countries of sub-Saharan Africa (although in some instances such as South Africa, many aspects of structural adjustment have also been self-imposed (Marais, 1997)). The main ingredients of these policies are cuts in government expenditure, trade liberalisation policies, currency devaluation, reduction of price controls, a shift to export oriented policies, revised fiscal policies to increase government revenue, user charges for public services like education and increased privatisation. Structural adjustment policies relate to the new market principle because they are intended to make countries more competitive through lowering production costs (through cuts in social welfare and reduced unit costs) and through making Africa more attractive to foreign investors (by means of trade liberalisation, reduced tax and other macro-economic reforms).

For authors such as Hoogvelt (2001) and Chossudovsky (1997), however, the impact of structural adjustment has been economic catastrophe, the slowing down and even reversal of human development – in short what Chossudovsky has described as "the globalisation of poverty" (1997, p. 34). In Hoogvelt's analysis, structural adjustment policies served a dual function, namely, to enable the periphery of the world capitalist system to be 'managed' in the interest of the core countries; and, to more effectively extract an economic surplus from it. In this respect she argues that "structural adjustment has helped to tie the physical economic resources of the African region more tightly into servicing the global system, while at the same time oiling the financial machinery by which wealth can be transported out of Africa and into the global system (Hoogvelt, 2001, p. 171). More recently, the international financial institutions have been advocating 'adjustment with a human face'. User fees for some services such as basic education and health have in many countries now been abolished. Through the impact of initiatives such as the *Heavily Indebted Country Initiative* (HIPC), countries are also being encouraged to pursue 'pro-poor' policies although there has to date been a negligible impact on levels of poverty on the continent. Table 1 summarises some of the key facts and figures relating to Africa's position in the global economy.

Table 1. Africa in a globalised world (adapted from Robertson et al., 2007, Commission for Africa, 2005)

Integration of African countries in the global economy

• With 11 percent of the world's population (700 million people), Sub Saharan Africa accounts for only about 1 percent of the global gross domestic product (GDP) (World Bank, 2005, p. xx).

• Africa has seen its share of world trade fall from 6% in 1980 to less than 2% in 2002. Africa has suffered because developed countries restrict Africa's ability to sell its products in their countries as well as other 'supply side' barriers (CFA, 2005).

• Share of world exports that dropped from more than 3.5 percent in 1970 to about 1.4 percent at the end of 2002 (World Bank, 2005, p. xx).

• Flows to investment in Africa by foreign investors are average for all low-income countries if measured as a percentage of Africa's income (2-3%) but are low in absolute terms. It is strongly focused on high value resource-based industries like oil and diamonds (CFA, 2005).

• Large sums of money depart Africa in the form of capital flight estimated at $15 billion a year. About 40% of the stock of African savings is held outside the continent (CFA, 2005).

• As a percentage of GDP, Africa's share of remittances is higher than that of either the East Asia or Pacific region or the Europe or Central Asia region. However, in cash terms, Africa receives less in remittances than does any other low-income region (CFA, 2005).

• Over the last few years, nearly half of all aid money to Africa has returned to the developed world in debt repayments; that is to say that for every dollar received in aid, nearly 50 cents has gone straight back to the developed world in debt payments. (CFA, 2005).

• Measured as a share of donor countries' incomes, aid has halved since the 1960s. However, Africa now receives around 5% of its income from aid, which is a much bigger proportion than other low-income regions get (CFA, 2005).

Inadequacy of growth on the continent

• The GDP per African has fallen by 13 percent, compared to 1981 (World Bank, 2005, p. xx).

• Between 1980 and 2002, sub-Saharan Africa's population grew from 238.3 to 689 million people – an increase of 80%. This population is moving into towns at a very rapid rate placing a huge strain on infrastructural investment for housing, water, supply and sanitation (CFA, 2005).

• Sub-Saharan Africa needs an annual growth rate of income per capita of 5% for 10 years to achieve the Millenium Development Goals [MDG] target of halving poverty. The actual growth rate since 2000 has been 1.6% (UNDP, 2005, p. 66).

- Despite an overall gloomy picture, there is considerable diversity between African countries. 24 countries in sub-Saharan Africa had 5% or more economic growth in 2003 and falls in poverty are directly associated with growth (CFA, 2005).

Informalization of labour and unemployment

- Informal employment in Africa increased from 44% to 48% between 1980-89 and 1990-1999 (ILO, 2004, p. 42).
- Open Unemployment increased from 13.7% in 1990 to 14.4% in 2002 (ILO, 2004, p. 42).

Inequality in Africa

- Thirty four of the world's forty-eight poorest countries in the world and twenty-four of the thirty-two countries ranked lowest in human development are in Africa (World Bank, 2005, p. xx).
- Extreme poverty has doubled from 164 million people in 1981 – 314 million today (World Bank, 2005, p. xx).
- Per capita income levels in sub-Saharan Africa decreased between 1980 and 2001 from 3.3 to 1.9 per cent (UN, 2005, p. 47).
- Average per capita income is US$342 per person (excluding South Africa) but wide variance: $100 per head in Burundi to over $7000 in the Seychelles (World Bank, 2005, p. xx).
- Poverty and hunger are deepening in sub-Saharan Africa with the number of poor people expected to rise from 315 million in 1999 to 404 million by 2015 (CFA, 2005).
- Some 34% of the population are malnourished – almost double the figure in the rest of the low-income world and hunger kills more people than all of the continent's infectious diseases put together (CFA, 2005).
- Average life expectancy in Africa is only 46 years compared to 63 years in South Asia and 69 in South East Asia (CFA, 2005).
- Whereas thirty years ago the average income in Africa was twice that of both East and South Asia the situation is reverse now and the average African income lags behind that of people in all other regions of the world (CFA, 2005).

Implications for human development

- Sub-Saharan Africa – 25 million people are infected with HIV in Sub-Saharan Africa, out of a global total of 38 million (UNESCO, 2005, p. 26). Fewer than 4% of people in need of antiretroviral treatment for HIV are receiving drugs (ibid., p. 27).
- Each year nearly 1 million African pupils lose a teacher to the HIV/Aids epidemic (World Bank, 2005, p. xxi).
- About 150,000 African children die per month as a result of malaria (World Bank, 2005, p. xxi).
- Health expenditures averaged only $13 per head in Sub-Saharan Africa, excluding South Africa, and were below $10 per head in 16 countries (World Bank, 2005, p. xxi).
- Illiteracy was 35 percent in 2003 (World Bank, 2005, p. xxi).

Political instability and insecurity.

- In 2000, 20 out of 45 SSA countries were directly involved in armed conflict (Obidegwu, 2004, p. 2).
- Of the 49 countries in Sub-Saharan Africa, at least 19 of them (excluding Namibia, South Africa, and Zimbabwe) have been involved in internal armed conflicts (Obidegwu, 2004, p. 2).

- Over 800,000 people were killed in the genocide in Rwanda in three months in 1994 (Obidegwu, 2004, p. 2).
- 200,000 people killed in Burundi since violence erupted in 1993 (Obidegwu, 2004, p. 2).
- Democratic Republic of the Congo (DRC), formerly Zaire, has witnessed the mother of all complex violent conflicts since the mid 1990s with an estimated 3.5 million lives lost in this continuing tragedy (Obidegwu, 2004, p. 2)
- It is estimated in 2000 that about 14 million people have been uprooted from their homes by conflict in Africa (Obidegwu, 2004, p. 2)

Politically, globalisation has involved a transformation in the way that our world is governed. Since the end of the cold war we have witnessed the emergence of one true superpower – the United States of America. Since the end of the Second World War we have also seen the emergence of the multilateral organisations such as the World Bank, the IMF, the World Trade Organisation and the United Nations. With differing governance structures and mandates the UN and its agencies sometimes project alternative priorities to those of the financial institutions and countries are often caught between sometimes conflicting agendas. In relation to education policy, for example, whilst the World Bank and IMF have over the years tended to project an 'efficiency' view of education, the UN and its agencies have projected a more rights based approach although there has been increasing convergence around education's role in a poverty eradication agenda (see Robertson et al., 2007).

In September 2000, the United Nations (UN) held a Millennium Summit at which all the members of the United Nations made a commitment to work toward a world in which the elimination of poverty and sustained development had the highest priority. The Millennium Declaration was signed by 147 heads of state and passed unanimously by the members of the UN General Assembly. The resulting eight *Millennium Development Goals* (MDGs) – which range from halving extreme poverty to halting the spread of HIV/AIDS as well as providing universal primary education, by the target date of 2015 – grew out of that declaration. The MDGs enjoy the support of all the multilateral agencies including the World Bank as well as governments and donors to education. The new consensus is also evident in the *Fast Track Initiative* which was originally established by the World Bank to fund the MDGs. Funding the MDGs, however, remains a cause for concern. As indicated in table 1 above, existing rates of growth are a fraction of those required if African governments were to fund the MDGs themselves, whilst aid to African governments which has declined in proportion to the GDP of donor countries since the 1960s and has dropped by 8.4% in real terms in 2007 is currently insufficient for bridging the gap (CFA, 2005; UNESCO, 2008; UN Millenium Project, 2005).

We have also witnessed the development of the regional level of governance including such influential bodies as the European Union, the North American Free Trade Agreement, the Association of East Asian Nations for example. In Africa this has included the newly formed African Union as well as sub-regional structures like the *Southern African Development Community* (SADC) *Southern African Development Community* (SADC), the *Economic Community of West*

African States (ECOWAS), the *Common Market for East and Southern Africa* (COMESA). These regional structures have facilitated processes of free trade at a regional level but also sought to project a distinctive regional identity. The *New Partnership for African Development* (NEPAD) is the official programme of the African Union (AU). It promotes a vision of greater regional co-operation in promoting good governance and pro-poor growth. Also important in this regard is the concept of the Mbeki-introduced concept of the *African Renaissance* which seeks to reassert a positive African economic and cultural message onto the global stage after Africa's marginalization and suppression during the colonial era. A range of specifically educational bodies and initiatives have also sprung up at a regional level and are having an ever-increasing influence on policy as our recent research has shown (Tikly et al., 2003).

Globalisation has also brought about changes at the level of the nation state. Whilst some commentators have argued that the nation state has lost power and influence, others maintain that it is more a case of its role having changed in the global era. Given what Ankie Hoogvelt (2001) describes as the "new market discipline" states are increasingly expected to play a key role in increasing a nation's global competitiveness. This is achieved through measures such as attracting foreign direct investment, encouraging export-led growth and promoting free trade and commerce particularly in those areas in which the nation is perceived to have a competitive advantage. Becoming globally competitive has also meant becoming more 'efficient' in the way that the economy has managed, including cutting back on government subsidies and spending, privatising state enterprises, encouraging public private enterprises, decentralising services nearer to the point of service delivery etc. Education and skills are often considered key in a nations ability to become competitive. Interestingly in this regard, rather than relinquishing power to regional bodies, many countries have in fact tightened control over key areas of education including the school curriculum and assessment whilst at the same time decentralising control over other key areas to schools and governing local communities and introducing a quasi-market with the aim of making schools more efficient and accountable although this had mixed implications for both so-called parental 'choice' and equity. Roger Dale (1999) has provided a fascinating account of how these policies are spread at a global, regional and national level creating a degree of uniformity in the trajectory of national policies. States in different parts of the world are perceived to have been more or less successful in implementing these policies.

A key difficulty in the African context relates to the particular form of the state which grew out of the colonial era and was designed principally to serve colonial interests. In the postcolonial era it has variously been described as "personal rule," "elite accommodation" and "belly politics" and as a "shadow" or "neo-patrimonial state" (Boas, 2003). As in other parts of the world, the state has proved a key mechanism for accumulation both under colonialism and subsequently and the emergence of national and global elites as well as for the maintenance of the status quo through the state apparatus. Holders of positions of power can also use their position to demand goods, cash and labour without recourse to violence and can supplement their salaries with bribes (practices that also have their origins in colonial times). The resulting phenomenon of weak states but strong regimes provides a source of contradiction within the African state system. Although there have been strides towards greater democracy in recent years in many African countries, some of the contradictions of the postcolonial state remain resilient. Critically, the state often also lacks capacity to formulate and to implement policy in the national interest and this reinforces dependency on outside experts and advisors who may not have a clear grasp of local realities. One response to these realities has been for outside donors and multilateral agencies to promote the so-called 'good governance' agenda. Some also suggest, however, that 'good governance' should not necessarily rely on Western models (Cheru, 2002; Ake, 2001). Cornwell argues that the greater accountability of African leaders ought to involve the creation of voluntary neighbourhood governments and rural grass roots movements that produce alternative institutions of decision making, drawing on customary notions of justice, fairness and political obligation (Cornwell, 1998, p. 14).

Related to this is the observation often made that globalisation is based on the dominance of western cultural norms and values. It is worth reflecting on this briefly. At the level of knowledge for instance, it is often argued that the Western *episteme* (or ground base of knowledge as it has developed in the various disciplines) predominates. In fact one commentator has gone so far as to suggest that "the real power of the West is not located in its economic muscle and technological might. Rather it resides in its power to define (…)."(Sardar, 1999, p. 44). A key issue in this regard is the need to develop knowledge and ways of conducting research that are relevant for the African context and for solving Africa's many problems (Ntuli, 1998). An example that Sardar gives is the extent to which so much of our Western thinking since the enlightenment is often premised on an individualistic and competitive view of human nature. He contrasts this with other, more collective/communal ways of thinking in other cultural traditions including Chinese and African traditions. A great deal of care is needed here lest we fall into simplistic stereotypes. Nonetheless, for Sardar these underlying assumptions profoundly shape the way we think in disciplines such as economics, politics and education and even inform our views of what it means to be 'developed' and what 'progress' entails. Other commentators have also commented on how the western view of human nature is also shaped by interactions and perceptions of non-Europeans during the colonial encounter (Young, 2001). The kinds of ideologies that were used to justify European domination including forms of biological and cultural racism continue to cast a long shadow in today's world and are reflected in western perceptions of Africans as being 'under-developed' or 'backward'. As many feminists have pointed out, the view of human nature in western thought has also often been one defined by men in their own image and to support their own interests. A key challenge implied by the *African Renaissance* idea is to project a view of African norms and values onto the world stage. For critics of the idea, however, the difficulty is that the view projected is often an elitist and patronising one reflecting dominant interest on the continent rather than those of the poor and historically marginalised. In relation to this kind of critique, the question is whose norms and values exactly are we talking about here? Those of urban elites, or of rural dwellers, of men or of women, of indigenous groups or speakers of minority languages? Which norms and values are truly 'African' in this sense? The struggle for supporters of the concept such as Cheru (2002) and Tikly (2003a) is that it needs to be articulated in a way that truly reflects diversity on the continent and the interests and aspirations of ordinary Africans rather than simply elites.

Globalisation, through the medium of the mass media including now the internet has also involved the spread of western consumer culture. As was discussed in relation to Rwanda and Tanzania above, however, the impact of this culture is sometimes resisted and modified. Key to the spread of western cultural forms has been the dominance of European languages such as English, Spanish, French and German. It is estimated that 80% of the world's computer data is stored in English. English is also the language of much international business and diplomacy. As Mazrui (1999) has pointed out though, no country has successfully globalised in the post World War Two period without also developing their own language/s of mass communication so that they are capable of expressing the most sophisticated and abstract scientific concepts. This is true, for example, of Japan and some of the other so-called Asian tigers. Language rights are becoming ever more complex in the global era. Part of this complexity is to do with the way that colonial boundaries were drawn up more with the interests of colonisers in mind than in recognition of the realties of linguistic and ethnic diversity. For Phillipson (1999), the complexity is around the use and recognition of different dialects and forms of English, besides standard English. For Rassool (1999) it is about recognising language rights in trans-national settings, such as the language rights of refugees or migrants. Speakers of minority languages may be particularly disadvantaged by blanket language policies that promote either a global language or a local majority language (Brock-Utne et al., 2004; Trudell, 2005). They may perceive learning in these languages as a threat to their culture (Aikman, 1995) and certain ethnic groups, including pastoralists and nomads, find formal education alien and even hostile to their culture (e.g. Tshireletso, 1997; Dyer, 2001).

The above overview of globalisation as it impacts on Africa draws attention to some overarching features. Firstly, the processes of globalisation do not represent a 'level playing field' in the sense that clearly there are winners and losers. Amongst the winners are the US and its allies in North America and Western Europe, the so-called Asian tigers and Australasia as well as more recently some provinces of China and some cities in India and other emerging economies. Integration into the core of the global economy for these regions, however, has had contradictory effects for poverty and inequality and for the environment (Wade, 2004). Large sections of the postcolonial world, however, including parts of South America, South Asia and Africa remain largely peripheral to globalisation processes and are increasingly being left behind by them (Scholte, 2006).

Secondly, as Held et al. (1999) point out, the various processes themselves (economic, political, cultural etc.) are partial and uneven in their effects. That is to say they do not apply uniformly across the whole globe and affect all people in the exactly the same way. As Held et al. argue, "political and economic elites in the world's major metropolitan areas are much more tightly integrated into, and have much greater control over, global networks than do the subsistence farmers of Burundi" (Held et al., 1999, p. 16). You only have to look at some of the inner city areas of London or New York to see pockets of the so-called 'Fourth World' on our doorstep (Amin, 1997). Furthermore, dominant global economic interests are these days to a lesser extent identified with nation states or even with elites within nation states but are increasingly *trans-national* in their composition (Robinson, 2001). This emerging class is tied to TNCs and to global financial firms and funds although it is not of a piece and represents competing mercantilist interests linked to different sections of global capital, regional trading blocks and political interests (Hoogvelt, 2001).

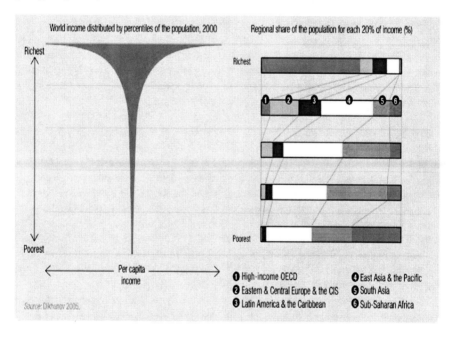

Figure 2. Where the Money Is (source: UNDP, 2005, p. 35)

According to the *United Nations Development Programme* (UNDP) global income distribution resembles a champagne glass. At the top, where the glass is widest, the richest 20% of the population hold three-quarters of world income. At the bottom of the stem, where the glass is narrowest, the poorest 40% hold 5% of world income and the poorest 20% hold just 1.5%. The poorest 40% roughly corresponds to the 2 billion people living on less than $2 a day. We can see growing gaps between the wealthiest 20 countries and the poorest. The poorest countries in the world have stood still, while the richest have increased GDP per capita by over 300% (UNDP, 2005: 36). A large number of the poorest countries are in Africa.

Finally, dominant global forces and interests are contested. This is evident, for example in the relationship between some parts of the Islamic world and the global 'war on terror'. It is also evident in the development of global civil society and in international campaigns against poverty and debt and around environmental issues and against corporate-led globalisation etc. Having considered Africa's position in relation to globalisation attention will now turn to the role of education first of all in supporting the present status quo and subsequently as a potential means for realising social justice goals.

THE COLONIAL AND ANTI-COLONIAL LEGACY IN AFRICAN EDUCATION IN RELATION TO GLOBALISATION

Formal education systems emerged in Africa as an aspect of the spread of global religions, especially Islam and Christianity. These brought with them systems of schools and universities. These interacted with and often disrupted and displaced indigenous forms of education, ceremonies, skills and crafts training. Formal schooling really developed and intensified, however, with the advent of European colonialism (Rodney, 1972). The significance of colonial education for our discussion is fourfold.

Firstly, it provided a key mechanism and template for the spread of contemporary forms of education. The form that colonial education systems took in sub-Saharan Africa depended on the form of colonialism adopted, e.g. 'classical' or 'internal' colonialism (Altbach & Kelly, 1978)[5] and on the nature of the educational programme of the colonising power (England, France, Belgium, Portugal, Germany etc.) which differed in some important respects (White, 1996). Nonetheless, colonial education spread a common structure of schooling throughout the region. It was bureaucratic in nature and characterised by highly teacher centred and authoritarian approaches to teaching and learning (including the widespread use of corporal punishment) with an emphasis on rote learning and examinations. In this respect, colonial forms of schooling and the pedagogies and forms of knowledge that they engendered have proved remarkably resistant to change. The picture below shows a typical primary school in Africa today. The teacher is standing at the front of rows of obedient children. The methods of teaching like the curriculum are formal and rigid. Discipline is enforced with the help of a rod held across the teacher's knee.

Secondly, because colonial education was generally limited to basic education and was never universal it provided only a limited human resource base upon which postcolonial governments could build their reconstruction efforts. Colonial education was also highly selective and elitist in the opportunities it offered for secondary and higher education and was, therefore, implicated in the formation of indigenous elites who in turn have become part of the emerging global elite. Thirdly, colonial education has been instrumental in ensuring the dominance of western cultural norms and values at the expense of indigenous ones. The colonial curriculum with its roots in the Graeco-Roman tradition was often divorced from local realities and indigenous forms of knowledge. Further, colonial education was instrumental in the globalisation of English and other European languages. In undermining local languages and cultures, colonial education was complicit in a process of cultural bifurcation in which those who had access to such education often became disconnected and even sometimes looked down on their own cultural origins whilst never being fully accepted into European society. This phenomenon is described by Franz Fanon in his (1967) book *Black Skin, White Masks*.

A primary school in Ghana (photo taken by author)

Finally, however, colonial education has provided an important seedbed for local *resistance* to colonialism. Many leading intellectuals and revolutionaries during the heyday of national liberation struggles on the sub-continent were products of colonial education.

Some Western intellectual traditions such as Marxism have also inspired and influenced African revolutionary thinking. In this respect, much of the critical edge within comparative education owes a debt to the thinking of anti-colonial and postcolonial scholars and activists over the years including the likes of Nelson Mandela, Julius Nyerere, Ngugu Wa Thingo, Mahatma Ghandi, Paulo Freire and many others. These thinkers have not only produced devastating critiques of colonial education but have also provided a vision of how education, broadly conceived, can be a tool in the creation of a more socially just society within a postcolonial world order. Thabo Mbeki's more recent calls for an *African renaissance* as an alternative to western global hegemony build on and develop these and other intellectual currents.

Products of colonial education (source: Mangan et al., 1988)

SOCIAL JUSTICE AND THE CHALLENGES FOR AFRICAN EDUCATION IN THE GLOBAL ERA

In this section the aim is to draw out aspects of the above analysis for education and in relation to the discussion of social justice at the beginning of the chapter. The ideas are partial and tentative rather than comprehensive and are intended as a contribution to an ongoing dialogue about education on the continent.

Redistributive justice and a quality education for all

Earlier it was suggested that redistributive justice in education equates with access by all to a quality education and the potential outcomes that arise from this. On the one hand, education can contribute to economic growth through providing the skills required for African countries to become globally competitive. Basic education has been correlated with improved economic growth and productivity including agricultural productivity (Appleton & Balihuta, 1996) and individual economic welfare (Hannum & Buchmann, 2005). On the other had it can also contribute to the creation of sustainable livelihoods in the fight against poverty and disease. Here Sen's concept of "capabilities" as a basis for understanding the range of cognitive (skills and acquired knowledge) and affective (emotional, attitudinal) outcomes that contribute to a person's well being, i.e. that enable learners to become economically productive, healthy, secure and active citizens is useful (Sen, 1999; Barrett & Tikly, 2008). In this sense education has a critical role to play within local communities through providing access to information that can support the feasibility and diversity of sustainable livelihoods and can give communities access to their rights (Lawrence & Tate, 1997). Unfortunately, the picture regarding participation in primary schooling remains bleak as table two below illustrates.

Table 2. Participation in education and training in sub-Saharan Africa

• African has the lowest school life expectancy of any region. A child in Africa can expect to attend school (including primary, secondary and tertiary education) for 7.8 years compared to a world average of 10.5 and an average for all low income countries of 9.9 years (UNESCO, 2005, p. 38). • The gross enrolment ration (GER) in pre-primary education is the lowest for any region at 5.6% compared to a global average of 48.6% and an average for low income countries of 34.3% (UNESCO, 2005, p. 302). • The region has the lowest GER in primary education of any region at 91% in 2002 with the largest number of children primary school age out of school children (40, 370). Primary education on the continent has the highest drop out rate for any region (40.5% compared to 25.5% for all low income countries) and the lowest transition rate to secondary education (53.8% compared to 84.5% for all low income countries) (UNESCO, 2005, p. 44). • Africa also has the lowest GER for any region in secondary education at 28.4% and in 2002 compared to a global average of 65.2% and an average for all low income countries of 58.3% (UNESCO, 2005, p. 342). At 2.5% Africa has the lowest GER of any region in tertiary education. This compares with a global average of 21.2% and an average for low income countries of 11% (UNESCO, 2005, p. 350).

African governments have provided support for the *Dakar framework*[6] and for the *Millennium Development Goals* (MDGs) relating to education, namely:
– Ensure that all boys and girls complete a full course of primary schooling
– Eliminate gender disparity in primary and secondary education preferably by 2005, and at all levels by 2015

According to the latest *Education for All Global Monitoring Report*, however, only four countries in sub-Saharan Africa have a high chance of achieving the first goal whilst sixteen have a low chance. Eight others are either at risk or at serious risk of not achieving the goal at all. All African countries missed the gender parity goal in 2005. In spite of promises to support basic education, aid commitments are stagnating and remain far short of what is required to achieve universal primary education (UNESCO, 2008).

Although lack of access is a general issue affecting hundreds of thousands of African children, the situation is worse for some groups than for others. For example, it is alarming that in Africa girls can expect to stay in school for only six years compared to eight years for boys (UNESCO, 2002). Poor educational outcomes and low participation rates become more pronounced at the secondary and tertiary levels and in vocational education. The focus of the MDGs on the access of girls and women to education is not only a question equal rights. It also has wider benefits in relation to health and welfare including the fight against HIV/AIDS and greater control by women over their own fertility (see also DfID, 2000; Hannum & Buchmann, 2005; Lloyd et al., 2000; Benefo, 2005). Citing recent research (Abu-Ghaida & Klasen, 2004), the CFA, for example, argues that "Countries which are not on track to meet the gender parity MDG target in education (and nearly half of those are in Africa) will have child mortality rates one and a half per cent worse than countries with better education systems, and they will also have two and a half per cent more underweight children" (CFA, 2005, p. 181).[7] Educating women and girls can also contribute to their alleviation from poverty and can have wider economic benefits.[8] It has a positive effect on overall labour supply through increasing the amount of time women work (UNESCO, 2003). Finally, educating mothers through adult literacy programmes has been linked with improving their children's attendance and performance at school (UN Millenium Project, 2005).

Those with special education needs, including physical disabilities, are often excluded as already overstretched and under-resourced schools fail to meet their needs (UNESCO, 2005). Orphans (including AIDS orphans) and other vulnerable children are more likely to be excluded. A death of a parent has been related to a delay in starting primary education and lowered attendance of girls (Ainsworth et al., 2002).

The conflicts that have blighted the continent in recent years have had a big impact on issues of access and social justice (see Robertson et al., 2007). A recent UNDP (2005) report, for example, observed that half of all primary schools were closed or destroyed during Mozambique's civil war between 1976 and 1992. Furthermore, the UNDP state that countries in conflict are likely to spend less on education, and parents are less likely to send girls to school for fear of violence (Kirk, 2004). Similarly, poor children are far more likely to be deprived of education and affected by conflict than wealthier children (Seitz, 2004).

The debate however, is wider than access to primary education. Tackling youth and adult illiteracy through adult literacy programmes is also important for realising social justice goals (UNESCO, 2006). There is much debate in the literature over the precise meaning of literacy[9] although there is less dispute over its benefits. It is seen not only as a fundamental human right but as central to economic growth, sustainable development, individual and community empowerment and the fostering of democracy. Thus it is tragic that whereas in most other parts of the world the number of illiterates has declined, in Africa there has been an increase from 108 million in 1970 to 141 million in 2004 and that of the 30 countries most at risk of not achieving the target of having illiteracy by 2015, 21 of these are in Africa (UNESCO, 2006). Part of the reason for this is the relatively low priority accorded to literacy programmes and adult education in government and donor spending priorities.

Similarly there are pressures for increasing access to pre-primary education where the foundations for learning in later life are laid. Africa currently has the lowest enrolment in this sector of any region (see table two above). There are also growing demands for access to secondary and tertiary education given the role these levels can play in supporting sustainable development including the provision of middle and higher order skills. In the case of higher education the development of an indigenous capacity for research is considered essential for tackling Africa's problems and breaking the chains of dependency on the West (AU, 2005; Tikly et al., 2003). Furthermore, as we have seen, globalisation has contributed to the informalisation of labour. In Africa, as Afenyadu et al. (1999), Tikly et al. (2003) and King & McGrath (2002) point out, a very significant proportion of school leavers are likely to enter into the *jua kali* informal sector which is the mainstay of many local economies. In this respect, these authors ask whether some basic vocational skills ought to be included under the heading 'basic education'. Similar arguments are advanced about access of children and adult learners to basic agricultural and other livelihood skills such as various kinds of crafts. What emerges form this discussion is that a one size fits all approach to funding education does not work. Rather, given limited resources, defining funding priorities needs to be linked to an analysis of needs in different countries.

The issue of access, however, does not stop at getting learners into formal education. A key feature of social injustice in education on the continent is the poor quality of education that is experienced by many learners. As Ilon (1994) has argued, there is a growing gulf in educational opportunities between emerging global elites and the rest of the population. According to Ilon, "a national system of schooling is likely to give way to local systems for the poor and global systems for the rich" (Ilon, 1994, p. 99). Within this highly differentiated environment, a top tier will benefit from a private education that will make them globally competitive; a middle tier will receive a 'good' but not 'world class' education, whilst the majority, third tier, will have a local, state education that will make them "marginally competitive for low-skill jobs" (ibid., p. 102). EdQual's *School Effectiveness and Education Quality* (SEEQ) project has identified huge variations in the quality of education not only between but within countries and it is likely that these will intensify as countries strive for universal primary education and already overstretched resources are stretched further (Yu, 2007). The quality of education is important for several reasons. For example, there is evidence from the wider literature that improvements in the quality and relevance of education can ultimately have a beneficial impact on enrolments and on continuation rates (Bergmann, 1996; Lloyd et al., 2000; UNESCO, 2005) as well as leading to improved cognitive and affective outcomes.

The poor quality of education is related to a range of factors chief amongst which are an under-qualified, poorly paid and motivated teaching force (which has also been depleted due to the impact of HIV/AIDS) (CFA, 2005; AU, 2005 for example). There is also a crippling lack of basic resources in many schools including teaching materials and text books. This is exacerbated by the problem of large class sizes especially given recent growth in enrolments. Many schools have a poor infrastructure including a lack of electricity, water and basic sanitary facilities. In terms of teaching and learning, there is a perceived lack of relevance of the curriculum. Curricula are often irrelevant both in terms of local realities and needs but also with respect to meeting national needs. Thus whereas many countries are adapting curricula to promote generic skills such as critical thinking, problem solving and communication, many curricula in African countries remain locked in the colonial past. A perceived lack of relevance is compounded by the prevalence of teacher centred and authoritarian teaching. A key problem in implementing quality initiatives and bringing about change is a lack of capacity for leading and managing education throughout the system including a lack of leadership skills and low levels of community involvement at a local level. Issues of quality in higher education are further exacerbated by the brain drain and a poor research infrastructure.

At the regional level both NEPAD and the Blair-led Commission for Africa (CFA)[10] make several recommendations to improve education quality (see CFA, 2005 for example). NEPAD, in particular, makes proposals to address the digital divide and there are several NEPAD initiatives in the area of ICTs as well as a range of similar initiatives.[11] There is a growing consensus about the potential benefits of ICT use in supporting a more student centred, problem based and collaborative approaches to teaching and learning and to assessment (Haddard & Draxler, 2002; Hawkins, 2002; World Bank, 2004). However, to achieve these benefits and to transform learning, ICT use has to be integrated into national policy and into practice in schools. In this respect, according to UNESCO, most African countries are still at the 'emerging' stage of development (Farrell and Wachholz 2003) and the upshot is that many learners continue to be denied access to even basic ICT skills.[12]

Debates about access to quality education are bound up with the privatisation and marketisation of education on the continent. Privatization and marketisation has been a feature of education policy in low-income countries since the 1980s (Whitty, Power & Halpin, 1998; Bullock & Thomas, 1997) although the degree of marketisation has varied considerably across the continent (Bennell, 1997). The increase in privatisation is related to the influence of neo-liberal ideas in contemporary globalisation. In most African countries, marketisation has involved encouraging the policy of charging user fees, a proliferation of private schools and universities and the development of a limited notion of 'choice' for some students in the urban areas.

Privatisation has major implications for social justice. For example, the introduction of user fees had disastrous consequences for primary and secondary school enrolments during the 1980s and early 1990s in many countries. The policy of encouraging private provision in secondary and tertiary education since the 1980s has led to increases in enrolments at these levels throughout sub-Saharan Africa (secondary school enrolment, for example has risen from 24% in 1999 to 32% in 2005, whereas tertiary enrolments have increased from 4.4 to 5.1% during the same period) (UNESCO, 2008). Enrolments lag significantly behind the rest of the world however. Private education has also been associated with growing educational inequality in countries such as Tanzania (Lassibille, Tan & Sumra, 1998) and the quality of private schools compared to government schools in Africa has been extremely variable (Kitaev, 1999). The African Union argues that the privatization of higher education poses risks for what it describes as the "fulfilment of the broad mission of a university, spanning critical thinking, knowledge generation, innovation, production of different skills, 'an enlightened citizenry', laying the foundation for democracy, nation building, and social cohesion" (AU, 2005, p. viii).

The proposed marketisation of higher education through the introduction of a *General Agreement on Trade in Services* has proved controversial in many low income countries (see Tikly, 2003b). The implication of African countries signing up to such an agreement would be to open up the provision of education to a range of international suppliers with western, industrialised countries having a distinct market advantage. The recently adopted *Accra Declaration on GATS and the Internationalization of Higher Education in Africa* calls for an internationalization process that is mutually beneficial, and called on African governments to exercise caution on further GATS commitments in higher education until a more informed position is arrived at on how tradable, trans-national education can best serve national and regional development priorities. In the same vein, higher education institutions expressed concern (AAU, 2004) that market forces alone are inadequate to ensure that cross-border education contributes to the public good and by implication social justice.

Recognising diversity in education

Other issues relating to education quality are less widely recognised in the literature but are also important in relation to Fraser's second dimension of social justice, namely the need to identify and then acknowledge the claims of historically marginalised groups. This is evident for example in relation to meeting the needs of girls and women in education. Some commentators have argued that the curriculum needs to become more girl friendly, for example by making some subjects more accessible to females (FAWE, 2003). A key issue is the lack of women in senior positions within institutions and at a national policy making level. An important consideration for teenage girls is the availability of appropriate sanitary facilities (UNESCO, 2005). For organizations such the *Federation of African Women in Education* (FAWE) which champions the education of girls and women on the continent, gender issues need to be tackled in a holistic way and must be mainstreamed into all areas of policy and practice (FAWE, 2003). Furthermore, girls and women are more likely to experience gendered abuse in African schools (FAWE, 2003; Leach et al., 2003) and teenage girls may expose themselves to sexual risk in order to fund their education (Vavrus, 2003; Vavrus, 2005). Girls also face particular difficulties in accessing some areas of the curriculum, such as science and mathematics and technology education (Swainson, 1998). Children, who suffer abuse and neglect at home, may be especially vulnerable to bullying and abuse by teachers or fellow students at school (Leach et al., 2000).

Similar arguments are advanced in relation to support for orphans and vulnerable children (OVC). For example, those living in remote rural areas are more likely to attend schools with a poor infrastructure. AIDS orphans are more likely to fall into this category as well as suffering, together with learners, who are HIV positive, the stigma attached to the disease.

A growing area for curriculum reform is the development of life skills programmes which include the provision of HIV/AIDS education and the teaching of citizenship. The quality of education with respect to the practice and teaching of human rights and citizenship is particularly important for refugees and those living in contexts of violence. In relation to this last group, Bush & Saltarelli (2000) describe how education has two faces, and its negative side can promote rather than reduce the chances of violent conflict. The authors argue that the negative face shows itself in the uneven distribution of education to create or preserve privilege, the use of education as a weapon of cultural repression, and the production or doctoring of textbooks to promote intolerance (Bush & Saltarelli, 2000, p. vii). Davies (2004) discusses the multiple ways that school systems might reproduce social inequalities, increase tension and be a catalyst for war. One example of this relationship is pointed out by the UNDP who highlight how school exclusion as a result of poverty contributed in Sierra Leone to young people joining the rebel armies.[13]

Issues of education quality in Africa are intimately tied up with culture and language. For example, the CFA argues that "Education systems are often based on inherited curriculum content that is limited to conventional academic subjects (...). Curricula should be designed with regional histories, cultures and languages in mind" (CFA, 2005, p. 187). Elsewhere in the report there is a suggestion that development must be African-led and informed by African values. Whilst these ideas fit with some of the earlier perspectives outlined, as argued they need to be more adequately developed. Part of this relates to the question of participation which will be discussed below and which voices are actually heard and recognised in the debate about values.

A key tension is around whether African-led development is best served by using indigenous or European languages as the medium of instruction (ADEA, 2005). On the one hand, the use of a global language as a medium of instruction can help to diffuse ethnic tensions through providing a *lingua franca*. Furthermore, the acquisition of English in particular is recognised by many as important for gaining access to power and prosperity. English as a medium of instruction is favoured by many parents as evidenced by the growth of English medium private schools. It is also cheaper to obtain suitable learning materials in English and is sometimes seen as a 'neutral' medium in a multilingual setting (ADEA, 2005, p. 1). On the other hand, no country has successfully advanced scientifically without significantly developing indigenous language/s. Examples here include global success stories such as Japan and Korea (Mazrui, 1999). Furthermore, there are pedagogical and psychological benefits to learning in ones own language, especially in the early years. These advantages feed into more critical perspectives which see the spread of European languages as vehicles for western consumer culture and as an aspect of neo-colonialism (see Brock-Utne, 2001; Brocke-Utne et al., 2004; Phillipson, 1999; Pennycook, 1995; Watson, 1999, Moodley, 2000, for example).

Faced with conflicting perspectives and complexity, African countries are increasingly adopting a phased bilingual or even trilingual approach, favouring indigenous languages in the early years and global languages such as English in the later years (Heugh, 2005). In some countries, such as South Africa, choice of languages for learning are left up to individual school communities within broad national guidelines. The *Great Lakes Initiative* has specifically identified overcoming the deep ethnic divisions caused in part by the legacy of the colonial language issue as fundamental to securing regional co-operation and peace. Many regional initiatives, including the CFA and NEPAD and the AU, are committed to developing and promoting African languages but shy away from detailed policy recommendations about how this commitment can be realised in practice. The problem is that the resources, training and political will required to support such a policy are often lacking (Brock-Utne et al., 2004) and schools often to revert to English as the 'default' medium.

Participatory justice

The third aspect of social justice discussed here, namely, the right of different groups including those less powerful and historically marginalised to have a say in educational decision-making is a pre-requisite for the other two. It is also arguably the most complex to conceive of and to realise. In the wider literature issues of 'participation' are often framed in terms of community participation in schooling; the need to make leaders more accountable to the communities they serve; and, as a means to mobilise additional resources for education. A lack of participation is often identified in the literature as contributing to the poor quality of education (UNESCO, 2005). These aspects are undeniably important although it is suggested that the existing debate around participation is somewhat limited given the nature of the colonial legacy and of the challenges posed by globalisation. In the context of the postcolonial state and in particular in relation to some postcolonial regimes that spring all to easily to mind, issues of accountability need not stop at the level of the school. For example, a more educated citizenry is better able to make leaders accountable to them. This could, arguably be a reason why some postcolonial regimes seem content to keep their populations in ignorance! In this sense participation is fundamentally a political issue about the need for popular involvement in decision making and which voices, including those of women, of the urban and rural poor, of linguistic and cultural minorities to have their voices heard and their rights acknowledged.

It is also an issue, however, that goes right to the heart of the reform effort. This is on the one hand to acknowledge that many governments are increasingly committed to bringing about reforms to education that are aimed at benefiting the most disadvantaged sections of society, for example through implementing the MDGs or in some cases a more relevant curriculum. Sometimes as in the case of Tanzania after independence or the new South Africa, for instance, this is itself a result of popular pressure for access to quality education which is seen as a means out of grinding poverty for many parents. It may also often be the result of pressure from the international community. Effecting change in these contexts requires taking seriously issues of participation because as scholars of the change process remind us, reform requires both top down leadership and bottom up pressure and ownership if it is to succeed and the latter relies on participation. Implementation of change relies on detailed awareness by policy makers and planners of local contexts and realities that may either facilitate or provide barriers to change (see Fullan, 1999; Samoff et al., 2003, for example). A lack of active ownership of the change process by those most closely affected by it denudes policy makers and planners of this knowledge. This observation is *writ large* in Africa where the change process from colonial times has been technicist, top down and bureaucratic in orientation relying heavily on outside expertise. Furthermore, many of the policies are themselves 'borrowed' from other, often high income countries. The history of reform in Africa is littered with examples of failed or staled reforms, a good recent one being attempts to implement curriculum change in South Africa and elsewhere on the continent (Jansen, 2005; Chisholm, 2005). These efforts have usually involved a commitment to move away from authoritarian, teacher centred curricula, based on rote learning of facts to one that seeks to develop critical thinking, problem solving, communication and other generic skills that are considered important in the global era. They have often foundered, however, because policy makers have not fully understood the extent to which more traditional ways of teaching and learning and the underlying view of education itself have been so deeply entrenched since colonial times along with the other barriers that may hinder implementation.

Findings from recent work on effective leadership in township and rural schools in South Africa provides a complex picture of both the processes and the benefits of participation at a local level (Ngcobo & Tikly, forthcoming). In this research the authors focused on schools that despite operating in contexts of extreme disadvantage were successful at raising the achievement of their learners even compared to well-resourced schools in the area. They had also proved effective in implementing change in the eyes of the communities they served and of local government officials. Issues of participation were critical for how these schools were run. In the contexts of South Africa's transition to democracy many of the principals demonstrated a genuine commitment to involving teachers, learners and the community in decision making, partly in response to historic demands. They were, however, also not afraid to lead form the front in implementing the change agenda. Key here was the emphasis that these leaders placed on what we describe as 'the basics', i.e. getting teachers and pupils to arrive on time, suitably prepared to teach and to learn; ensuring that the resources required for effective teaching and learning were in place; and, ensuring discipline. At times it required balancing participative 'transformational' approaches with more 'transactional', top down ones. Sometimes, in the context of ongoing urban warfare and high levels of drug taking and crime it involved getting involved in local politics to broker the safety of learners and teachers.

Mostly, however, it involved a 'values led' style of leadership in which the purpose of the reform and the underlying values were clearly communicated and understood. This often involved an educative effort, especially given sometimes high levels of illiteracy. Many of the principals emphasised ongoing professional learning for staff to equip them for change. They would spend long hours talking to parents about their role in preparing their children for school, ensuring that they are adequately nourished, that they have a place to do their homework and enough light to read their books. It also forms of distributed leadership – bringing out the leadership potential and efficacy in others to realise change including teachers, parents, learners and other members of the local community through harnessing the popular commitment to education. It is in this wider context that issues of accountability and resource mobilisation need to be understood. Principals would mobilise resources from the community in the form of voluntary contributions but were impeccable in the way that they accounted for these and this gained the trust of the community. In this and other respects, like working long hours and being punctual and so they 'walked the talk'.

CONCLUSION

Critical education policy analysis has an important role to play in bringing issues of social justice to the fore in Africa as elsewhere in the world. A good deal of contemporary debate on African education is dominated by the intellectual financial complex of the World Bank and the global financial institutions and donors and draws largely on development economics and related disciplines. It tends, therefore to be 'technicist' in nature and lacking a critical edge when it comes to the impact of globalisation and the role of global institutions and indigenous elites. The present chapter has sought to sketch out the contours of the issues facing African education drawing on more critical perspectives and approaches. Of particular importance for the future, however, is the need to foster critical analysis and research emanating from the African continent itself that can reflect the experiences and aspirations of educators, parents and learners on the continent as well as the voices of grass roots organisations.

It has been argued in this chapter that social justice concerns lie at the heart of the educational debate. Indeed they can be seen as a sine qua non for realising the vision of an *African Renaissance* that also seeks to build on the aspirations of generations of anti-colonial activists and thinkers who have placed issues of education and justice at the heart of their change agendas. The problems of realising change in Africa are certainly deep seated and at times appear intractable. Despite these problems our ongoing research has also revealed enough commitment, passion and dedication from practitioners, learners and parents to know that with the right leadership and support from the international community change is possible. Of relevance here Antonio Gramsci's advice that in seeking change one must maintain simultaneously a pessimism of the intellect and an optimism of the will.

NOTES

[1] There is always a danger of treating Africa as if it is a single entity and not to acknowledge the huge differences within and between African countries. I will try to avoid doing this. In this chapter, the focus is on sub-Saharan Africa although even here there is enormous variation in contexts as we shall see.

[2] Specifically the origins of social justice lie in the thinking of writers such as John Rawls who himself drew on a longer tradition going back to the Jesuits and encompassing the liberalism of John Locke, the utilitarianism of Jeremy Bentham and John Stuart Mill and the moral philosophy of Emanuel Kant.

[3] See for example, *Pambazuka News* which is a pan-African initiative that provides a weekly forum for discussing social justice issues on the continent, including educational issues! (http://www.pambazuka.org/en/) Accessed 11 April 2007.

[4] For example, just as some western norms and values sit uneasily with some principles of social justice so too do some African ones. This is evident for example, in the practice of female circumcision, in patriarchal attitudes to women, in homophobia and in the suppression of indigenous and other minority groups. Further, some individuals and groups who may support some social justice goals, e.g. racial equality, may hold deeply conservative views in relation to other issues, e.g. the role of women in society.

[5] In classical colonialism the colonising power remained principally based in the colonisers own country in the metropole. This was the case in much of Africa. Internal colonialism occurred where the colonising power were based within the same geographical boundaries as the colonised, e.g. in South Africa under apartheid.

[6] The Framework was adopted by the World Education Forum Dakar, Senegal, 26-28 April 2000. It sets out global and regional frameworks for achieving a quality education for all (http://unesdoc.unesco.org/images/0012/001211/121147e.pdf) Accessed 22/4/08.

[7] Following in the same vein, the CFA recommends that "in their national plans African governments must identify measures to get girls as well as boys into school with proper allocation of resources. Donors should meet these additional costs" (CFA, 2005, p. 185).

[8] Providing girls with one extra year of education has been estimated to boost their eventual wages by 10 to 20 per cent (Dollar & Gatti, 1999).

[9] The definition offered here is that adopted by the UNESCO GMR team: "A person is functionally literate who can engage in all those activities in which literacy is required for effective functioning of his group and community and also for enabling him to continue to use reading, writing and calculation for his own and the community's development" (UNESCO, 2006, p. 30).

[10] The Commission for Africa was launched by British Prime Minister Tony Blair in February 2004 with the aim of taking a fresh look at Africa's past and present and the international community's role in its development path.

[11] Besides the NEPAD e-school initiative there are several other initiatives: *Catalyzing Access to ICT in Africa (CATIA)* (http://www.catia.ws); *Global E-school and Community Initiative (*http://www-wbweb4.worldbank.org/disted/)*; Leland Initiative- Africa Global Initiative (*URL:http: //www.usaid.gov/regions/afr/lelnad/).

[12] Related to the above point is that older, non-digital ICTs also have an important role to play in supplementing teacher knowledge and providing increased opportunities for disadvantaged learners. Whilst digital technologies might transform education in the longer term, an exclusive focus on newer ICTs is likely to disproportionately benefit elites who have access to them and have the effect of exacerbating the digital divide at least in the short term.

[13] A survey of ex-combatants in Sierra Leone found that an overwhelming majority of those who joined the brutal rebellions were youths who had been living in difficult conditions prior to the onset of the war and that half had left school because they could not afford the fees or because the school had shut down (UNDP, 2005, p. 159).

REFERENCES

Abu-Ghaida, D., & Klasen, S. (2004). *The costs of missing the millennium development goal on gender equity*. IZA Discussion Paper 1031. Bonn: IZA.

Afenyadu, D., King, K., McGrath, S., Oketch, H., Rogerson, C., & Visser, K. (1999). *Learning to compete: Education, training and enterprise in Ghana, Kenya & South Africa*. DfID Education Paper 42. London: DfID.

ADEA. (2005). Learning, but in which language. *ADEA Newsletter, 17*(2), 1.

AU. (2005). *Revitalizing higher education in Africa: Synthesis report.* Accra: Department of Human Resources, Science and Technology.

Ainsworth, M., Beegle, K., & Koda, G. (2002). *The impact of adult mortality on primary school enrolment in Northwestern Tanzania.* Washington: The World Bank.

Ake, C. (2001). *Democracy and development in Africa.* Ibadan: Spectrum.

Aikman, S. (1995). Language, literacy and bilingual education: An Amazon people's strategies for cultural maintenance. *International Journal of Educational Development, 15*(4), 411–422.

Altbach, P., & Kelly, G. (1978). *Colonialism and education.* London: Longman.

Amin, S. (1997). *Capitalism in the age of globalization.* London: Zed Books.

Appadurai, A. (Ed.). (1992). *The social life of things: Commodities in cultural perspective.* Cambridge: Cambridge University Press.

Appleton, S., & Balihuta, A. (1996). Education and agricultural productivity: Evidence from Uganda. *Journal of International Development, 8*, 415–444.

AAU. (2004). *Accra declaration on GATS and internationalization of higher education in Africa.* Participants Declaration, at the Workshop on the Implications of WTO/GATS for Higher Education in Africa, 27th–29th April. Accra: AAU.

Barrett, A., & Tikly, L. (2008). *Education quality: Research priorities and approaches in the global era.* Paper presented at the 52 conference of the Comparative and International Education Society, Teachers College, Columbia University, New York, 17–21 March 2008.

Bell, D. (1973). *The coming of post-industrial society: A venture in social forecasting.* New York: Basic Books.

Benefo, K. D. (2005). Child schooling and contraceptive use in rural Africa: A Ghanaian case study. *Population Research and Policy Review, 24*(1), 1–25.

Bennell, P. (1997). Privatisation in sub-Saharan Africa: Progress and prospects during the 1990s. *World Development, 25*(11), 1785–1804.

Bergmann, H. (1996). Quality of education and the demand for education - evidence from developing countries. *International Review of Education, 42*(6), 581–604.

Boas, M. (2003). Weak states, strong regimes: Towards a 'real' political economy of African regionalization. In J. Grant & F. Soderbaum (Eds.), *The new regionalism in Africa.* Aldershot: Ashgate.

Brock-Utne, B., Desai, Z., & Quorro, M. (2004). *Researching the language of instruction in Tanzania & SA.* Oxford: One world.

Bullock, A., & Thomas, H. (1997). *Schools at the centre: A study of decentralisation.* London: Routledge.

Bush, K. D., & Saltarelli, D. (2000). *The two faces of education in ethnic conflict: Towards a peace-building education for children.* Florence: Innocenti Research Centre, UNICEF. Retrieved April 22, 2008, from http://www.unicef-icdc.org/publications/pdf/insight4.pdf

Castells, M. (1993). Economy and the new international division of labour. In M. Carnoy, M. Castells, S. S. Cohen, & F. H. Cordoso (Eds.), *The new global economy in the information age.* London: MacMillan.

Castells, M. (1996). *The rise of the network society.* London: Blackwell.

Cheru, F. (2002). *The African renaissance: Roadmaps to the challenge of globalization.* London: Zed Books.

Chisholm, L. (2005). The politics of curriculum review and revision in South Africa in regional context. *Compare, 35*(1), 35–100.

Chossudovsky, M. (1997). *The globalization of poverty: Impacts of IMF and World Bank reforms.* London: Zed Books.

Cornwell, R. (1998). The African renaissance: The art of the state. *Indicator SA, 15*(2), 9–14.

Crossley, M., & Tikly, L. (2004). Postcolonial perspectives and comparative and international research in education: A critical introduction. *Comparative Education, 40*(2), 147–156.

CFA [Commission for Africa]. (2005). *Our common interest.* London: CFA.

Dale, R. (1999). Specifying globalisation effects on national policy: Focus on the mechanisms. *Journal of Education Policy, 14*(1), 1–17.

Davies, L. (2004). *Education and conflict: Complexity and chaos.* London: RoutledgeFalmer.

DfID. (2000). *Eliminating world poverty: Making globalisation work for the poor, white paper on international development.* London: DfID. Retrieved January 7, 2006, from http://www.dfid. gov.uk/Pubs/files/whitepaper2000.pdf

Dollar, D., & Gatti, R. (1999). *Gender inequality, income, and growth: Are good times good for women?* World Bank Policy Research Report on Gender and Development, Working Paper Series No. 1. Washington, DC: World Bank.

Dyer, C. (2001). Nomads and education for all: Education for development or domestication? *Comparative Education, 37*(2), 315–327.

Fanon, F. (1967). *Black skins, white masks.* New York: Grove Press.

Farrell, G., & Wachholz, C. (Eds.). (2003). *Meta-survey on the use of technologies in education in Asia and the Pacific (2003–2004).* Bangkok: UNESCO. Retrieved January 7, 2006, from http://www.unescobkk.org/ips/ebooks/documents/metasurvey/

FAWE. (2003). Engendering EFA: Is Africa on track. *FAWE News, 11*(January-June). Retrieved September 2, 2008, from http://www.violencestudy.org/a195

Fraser, N. (2006). *Research interest.* Retrieved April 22, 2008, from http://www.newschool.edu/ GF/polsci/faculty/fraser/, last accessed 22/4/08.

Fullan, M. (1999). *Change forces: The sequel.* Brighton: Falmer.

George, S. (2003). Globalizing rights? In M. J. Gibney (Ed.), *Globalizing rights. The Oxford amnesty lectures 1999* (pp. 15–33). Oxford: Oxford University Press.

Giddens, A. (1990). *The consequences of modernity.* Cambridge: Polity.

Haddad, W. D., & Draxler, A. (2002). *Technologies for education: Potential, parameters and prospects.* Paris/Washington, DC: UNESCO/The Academy for Educational Development.

Hall, S. (1996). When was the postcolonial? Thinking at the limit. In I. Chamber & L. Curtis (Eds.), *The postcolonial question: Common skies, divided horizons.* London: Routledge.

Hannum, E., & Buchmann, C. (2005). Global educational expansion and socio-economic development: An assessment of findings from the social sciences. *World Development, 33*(3), 333–354.

Hawkins, R. (2002). *Ten lessons for ICT in education in the developing world.* Harvard: CID. Retrieved April 22, 2008, from http://www.cid.harvard.edu/cr/pdf/gitrr2002_ch04.pdf

Heugh, K. (2005). The case for additive bilingual/ multilingual models. *ADEA Newsletter, 17*(2), 11–12.

Held, D., McGrew, A., Goldblatt, D., & Perraton, J. (1999). *Global transformations: Politics, economics and culture.* Cambridge: Polity Press.

Hoogvelt, A. (2001). *Globalisation and the postcolonial world: The new political economy of development.* London: MacMillan.

ILO [International Labour Organization]. (2004). *A fair globalization: Creating opportunities for all, the world commission on the social dimensions of globalisation.* Geneva: ILO.

Ilon, L. (1994). Structural adjustment and education - adapting to a growing global market. *International Journal of Educational Development, 14*(2), 95–108.

International Development Research Centre (IDRC). (2004). *Brain drain: Facts and figures.* Retrieved April 22, 2008, from http://web.ncf.ca/cp129/factsandfigures.pdf

Jansen, J. (2005). Targeting education: The politics of performance and the prospects of 'Education for all'. *International Journal of Educational Development, 25*(4), 368–380.

King, K., & McGrath, S. (2002). *Globalisation, enterprise and knowledge: Education, training and development in Africa.* London: Springer.

Kirk, J. (2004, November). Promoting a gender-just peace: The roles of women teachers in peace-building and reconstruction. *Gender and Development,* 50–59. Retrieved April 22, 2008, from http://www.oxfam.org.uk/what_we_do/resources/downloads/gender_peacebuilding _and_reconstruction_kirk.pdf

Kitaev, I. (1999). *Private education in sub-Saharan Africa: A re-examination of theories and concepts related to its development and finance.* Paris: UNESCO.

Lassibille, G., Tan, J., & Sumra, S. (1998). *Expansion of private secondary education: Experiences and prospects for Tanzania.* Working Paper Series on Impact Evaluation of Education Reforms 12. Washington, DC: World Bank.

Lawrence, J., & Tate, S. (1997). *Basic education for sustainable livelihoods: The right questions.* New York: UNDP.

Leach, F., Machakanja, P., & Mandoga, J. (2000). *Preliminary investigation of the abuse of girls in Zimbabwean junior secondary schools.* London: DfID.

Leach, F., Fiscian, V., Kadzamira, E., Lemani, E., & Machakanja, P. (2003). *An investigative study of the abuse of girls in African schools.* Education Research Report No. 54. London: DfID.

Lloyd, C. B., Mensch, B. S., & Clark, W. (2000). The effects of primary school quality on school dropout among Kenyan girls and boys. *Comparative Education Review, 44*(2), 113–147.

Mangan, J. (Ed.). (1988). *Benefits bestowed? Education and British imperialism.* Manchester: Manchester University Press.

Marais, H. (1997). *South Africa: Limits to change: The political economy of transformation.* London: Zed.

Mazrui, A. (1999). *The African renaissance: A triple legacy of skills, values and gender.* Paper presented to The African Renaissance - From Vision to Reality conference, 23rd November, The Barbican Centre, London.

Moodley, K. (2000). African renaissance and language policies in comparative perspective. *Politikon, 27*(1), 103–115.

Ngcobo, T., & Tikly, L. (forthcoming). Key dimensions of effective leadership: A focus on township and rural schools in South Africa. *Journal of Education Management, Administration and Leadership.*

Ntuli, P. (1998, Winter). Who's afraid of the African renaissance? *Indicator South Africa,* 15–18.

Obidegwu, C. (2004). *Post-conflict peace building in Africa: The challenges of SocioEconomic recovery and development.* Africa Region Working Paper No: 73, World Bank.

Pennycook, A. (1995). English in the world/The world in English. In J. Tolleffson (Ed.), *Power and inequality in language education* (pp. 34–58). Cambridge: Cambridge University Press.

Phillipson, R. (1999). The globalization of dominant languages. *Education in Africa, 8,* 199–216.

Ramose, M. B. (2006). The king as memory and symbol of African customary law. In M. Hinz (Ed.), *The shade of new leaves: Governance in traditional authority: A Southern African perspective* (pp. 351–374). Berlin: LIT Verlag.

Rassool, N. (1999). *Literacy for sustainable development in the age of information.* Clevedon: Multilingual Matters.

Robertson, S., Novelli, M., Dale, R., Tikly, L., Dachi, H., & Alphonce, N. (2007). *Globalisation education and development: Ideas, actors and dynamics.* London: DfID.

Robinson, W. I. (2001). Social theory and globalisation: The rise of a transnational state. *Theory and Society, 30*(2), 157–200.

Rodney, W. (1972). *How Europe underdeveloped Africa.* London: Bogle-L'Ouverture Publications.

Samoff, J., Sebatane, E. M., & Dembélé, M. (2003). *Scaling up by focussing down: Creating space to expand education reform.* Paris: ADEA.

Sardar, Z. (1999). Development and the locations of eurocentricism. In R. Munck & D. O'Hearn (Eds.), *Critical development theory* (pp. 44–62). London: Zed.

Scholte, J. A. (2002). *What is globalisation? The definitional issue – again.* CSGR Working Paper 109/02. Centre for the Study of Globalisation and Regionalisation, University of Warwick.

Scholte, J. A. (2006). *Globalisation: Crucial choices for Africa in ESRC, from: Africa after 2005: From promises to policy forum and report by the ESRC and Development Studies Association.* London: Church House, Westminster.

Sen, A. (1999). *Development as freedom.* Oxford: Oxford University Press.

Seitz, K. (2004). *Education and conflict: The role of education in the creation, prevention and resolution of societal crises - consequences for development cooperation.* Eschborn: German Technical Cooperation/ Deutsche Gesellschaft für Technische Zusammenarbeit (GTZ).

Steger, M. (2005). Ideologies of globalisation. *Journal of Political Ideologies, 10*(1), 11–30.

Swainson, N. (1998). *Promoting girls' education in Africa - the design and implementation of policy interventions.* Education Research Paper No. 25. London: DflD.

Tikly, L. (1998, July). *Postcolonialism and education.* Paper presented at the WCCES Congress, University of Cape Town.

Tikly, L. (2003a). The African renaissance, NEPAD and skills formation: policy tensions and priorities. *International Journal of Educational Development, 23*(5), 543–564.

Tikly, L. (2003b). GATS, globalisation and skills for development in low-income countries. In R. Carr-Hill, K. Holmes, P. Rose, & T. Henderson (Eds.), *Education and the general agreement on trade in services: What does the future hold?* Report of the fifteenth CCEM preliminary meeting, Thursday, 29 May. London: Commonwealth Secretariat.

Tikly, L., Lowe, J., Crossley, M., Dachi., H., Garrett, R., & Mukabaranga, B. (2003). *Globalization and skills for development in Rwanda and Tanzania.* London: DflD.

Trudell, B. (2005). Language choice, education and community identity. *International Journal of Educational Development, 25*, 237–251.

Tshireletso, L. (1997). They are government's children: School and community relations in a remote (Basarwa) settlement in Kweneng district, Botswana. *International Journal of Educational Development, 17*(2), 173–188.

UNDP. (2005). *Human development report 2005: International cooperation at a crossroads: Aid trade and security in an unequal world.* New York: UNDP. Retrieved April 22, 2008, from http://hdr.undp.org/reports/global/2005

UN Millennium Project. (2005). *Investing in development: A practical plan to achieve the millennium development goals.* Retrieved April 22, 2008, from http://www.unmillenniumproject.org/reports/fullreport.htm

UNESCO. (2002). *Is the world on track? Global monitoring report 2002.* Paris: UNESCO.

UNESCO. (2003). *EFA global monitoring report 2003/4: Gender and education for all: The leap to equality.* Paris: UNESCO.

UNESCO. (2005). *Education for all: The quality imperative - EFA global monitoring report 2005.* Paris: UNESCO.

UNESCO. (2006). *Literacy for life – EFA global monitoring report.* Paris: UNESCO.

UNESCO. (2008). *Education for all by 2015: Will we make it? EFA global monitoring report.* Paris: UNESCO.

Vavrus, F. (2003). *Desire and decline: Schooling amid crisis in Tanzania.* New York: Peter Lang.

Vavrus, F. (2005). Adjusting inequality: Education and structural adjustment policies in Tanzania. *Harvard Educational Review, 75*(2), 174–201.

Wade, R. H. (2004). On the causes of increasing world poverty and inequality, or why the Matthew effect prevails. *New Political Economy, 9*(2), 163–188.

Watson, K. (1999). Language, power, development and geopolitical changes: Conflicting pressures facing plurilingual societies. *Compare, 29*(1), 5–22.

White, B. W. (1996). Talk about school: Education and the colonial project in French and British West Africa. *Comparative Education, 29*(issue), 9–25.

Whitty, G., Power, S., & Halpin, D. (1998). *Devolution and choice in education: The school, the state and the market.* Buckingham: Open University Press.

World Bank. (2004). *Technology in schools: Education, ICT and the knowledge society.* Washington, DC: World Bank. Retrieved April 22, 2008, from_http://www1.worldbank.org/education/pdf/ICT_report_oct04a.pdf

World Bank. (2005). *Africa-development indicators.* Washington, DC: World Bank.

World Bank. (2006). *Information and communications for development: Global trends and policies.* Washington, DC: World Bank.

Young, R. (2001). *Postcolonialism: An historical introduction.* Oxford: Blackwell.

Yu, G. (2007). *Research evidence of school effectiveness in Sub-Saharan African countries.* Retrieved April 22, 2008, from http://www.edqual.org/research/seeqlit2007.pdf

FURTHER READINGS

Chossudovsky, M. (1997). *The globalization of poverty: Impacts of IMF and World Bank reforms.* London: Zed Books.

Robertson, S., Novelli, M., Dale, R., Tikly, L., Dachi, H., & Alphonce, N. (2007). *Globalisation education and development: Ideas, actors and dynamics.* London: DfID.

Sen, A. (1999). *Development as freedom.* Oxford: Oxford University Press.

Tikly, L., Lowe, J., Crossley, M., Dachi., H., Garrett, R., & Mukabaranga, B. (2003). *Globalization and skills for development in Rwanda and Tanzania.* London: DfID.

Young, R. (2001). *Postcolonialism: An historical introduction.* Oxford: Blackwell.

Leon Tikly
Graduate School of Education
University of Bristol

CARLOS ALBERTO TORRES & RICHARD VAN HEERTUM

GLOBALISATION AND NEOLIBERALISM

The Challenges and Opportunities of Radical Pedagogy

INTRODUCTION

Globalisation is one of the most debated topics inside and outside academia today. Neoliberals, as propagators of the dominant paradigm, see it as a natural process that liberates markets, improves economies and sets the foundation for democracy to emerge and flourish. Opponents see it as a bulldozer riding over cultures, economies and the peoples of the global South. Many others wade in the murky waters between the two camps recognising the dialectic nature of this complex phenomenon. Consensus does appear to exist that globalisation profoundly influences the social, political and economic spheres across the globe and that efforts to stop the process are largely futile.

In this article, we re-read globalisation through the lens of critical theory. We first expand the notion of globalisation to encompass its multifaceted nature. We then look at it within the context of neoliberalism and its project of 'market liberation,' government retrenchment and the dismantling of the social safety net. We conclude by exploring the role of social movements in educational reform and the central role formal and informal education play within these social movements.

We argue that critical theory offers valuable tools to deconstruct educational reforms undertaken under the auspices of neoliberalism and global competitiveness including the call for privatisation and school choice, professionalism and deskilling of teachers, standardisation and accountability and the movement to more closely align schooling with the imperatives and interests of the market. Educational reforms in this vein, while often framed within traditionally progressive notions of education, challenge long-established ideas of education and the public good. They do promote individual choice, access, student autonomy and collaboration, but appear to be largely driven by market forces and an attempt to make schooling about sorting and training alone. Lost are more expansive notions of holistic education that incorporate creativity, citizenship and democracy, cultural sensitivity and the development of the whole student as constitutive, opening their minds to the world around them and providing the tools to critically reflect on it.

We then turn to the role critical theory can play in challenging these reforms and re-establishing the primacy of education for democracy and social justice. We foreground the challenges and opportunities faced by those dedicated to progressive educational reform and ways that theory can inform practice at the local, national and global levels. In our analysis, we explore the contradictory nature of 'globalisation,' particularly when framed within the context of current U.S. and European foreign

M. Simons, M. Olssen and M.A. Peters (eds.), Re-Reading Education Policies: A Handbook Studying the Policy Agenda of the 21ˢᵗ Century, 143–162.

policy, economic and social turmoil in many regions and the shrinking commitment to civil society in advanced economies.

GLOBALISATIONS: EXPLORING THE CONTRADICTIONS

Globalisation clearly varies from one country to the next, with some more heavily influenced by outside forces and others just beginning to experience global power at the local and national levels. Its influence also varies between the Global North and South with the former in many cases benefiting from its push toward market liberation while the South tends to suffer under its influence, even as it provides opportunities for export driven economic growth (as in China and India). Here we would like to briefly highlight another aspect of the diverse forms it sometimes takes, re-reading globalisation as comprising four related forms: including the popularly conceived neoliberal version, one ostensibly working to spreads human rights and democracy, a third tied to terrorism and anti-terrorist policies and finally the loose confederation of organisations and individuals grouped under the label of 'anti-globalisation.'

The first form of globalisation, often described as *globalisation from above*, is framed by the pervasive neoliberal ideology. Neoliberals call for an opening of national borders to increase commodity and capital exchange, the creation of multiple regional markets, the elevation of free markets over public goods and state intervention, the proliferation of fast-paced economic and financial transactions, and the establishment of transnational governing systems that supersede the nation-state. The movement is to privatise public goods and service, under the premise that markets are superior to governments as mediators of social relations. 'Selective deregulation' and 'market liberation' are thus the mottos of this version of globalisation.[1]

Another form of globalisation represents the antithesis of the first, often described as *globalisation from below* or *anti-globalisation*. We see the latter as a misnomer given that the various groups and movements aimed at challenging neoliberal versions of globalisation are not opposed to increased international integration in general, but to specific elements of the process that tend to cause increased inequality, loss of national autonomy, corporate interests trumping the common good and a general worsening of conditions for the average global citizen. Globalisation from below is largely manifest in individuals, institutions, and social movements actively opposed to what they perceived as corporate-driven globalism. For these individuals and groups, 'no globalisation without representation' is the dominant motto.

A third form of globalisation pertains more to rights than to markets, working to spread human rights to all. With the growing ideology of human rights taking hold of the international system and international law, many traditional practices deeply sewn into the fabric of particular societies (from religious to cultural practices) are now being called into questioned, challenged, forbidden, or even outlawed. Advancement of cosmopolitan democracies and plural citizenship is the theme of this version of globalisation, which appears to have both positive and negative aspects that are often difficult to disentangle.[2]

A final form of globalisation is the ongoing international war on terror. This new form of globalisation has been prompted in large part by the events of September 11th – interpreted by many as the globalisation of the terrorist threat – and the subsequent reaction of the United States. The anti-terrorist response has been militaristic in nature, resulting in two coalition wars led by the U.S. against Muslim regimes in Afghanistan and Iraq. Yet, the overall theme of this process transcends its military aspect to emphasise security and control of borders, people, capital, and commodities; in some cases reversing the opening of markets and high-paced commodity exchanges while simultaneously serving as the foundation for arguments on democracy and market liberation as the only legitimate way to counteract the breeding of terrorism and dangerous rogue states ruled by dictators like Saddam Hussein. Security as a precondition of freedom is the theme of this form of globalisation. Not surprisingly, its nemesis, terrorism, endorses the motto that only violence and chaos can bring radical change.

There are thus multiple instantiations of globalisation that affect different groups in different ways. In its most basic form, however, we believe globalisation is best defined by Anthony Giddens (1999) as "the intensification of worldwide social relations which link distant localities in such a way that local happenings are shaped by events occurring many miles away and vice versa." We next turn to a deeper analysis of globalisation from above, or neoliberalism, and its ramifications for education before concluding with an analysis of globalisation from below and its potential to alter debates on educational reform across the globe. We first offer a brief overview of critical theory.

CRITICAL THEORY AS A METHODOLOGY OF ANALYSIS

Critical theory emerged from the Frankfurt School and their attempt to place Marxism in dialogue with Freudian psychoanalysis, Nietzschean philosophy and Weberian sociology. Witnessing the emergence of a new form of capitalism structured around the administered society and the rising significance of the cultural industry, they sought to move beyond the surface of social life to explore its deeper structural and psychological conditions and the ways these were implicated in domination and control. The group started as a loose connection of German philosophers and intellectuals working at the Institute for Social Research in the 20s and 30s. Led by Max Horkheimer and Theodor Adorno, they were the first to systematically analyse and critique popular culture – studying a *cultural industry* that worked to establish the centrality of production and a system of values, needs, desires, lifestyles and institutions that reinforced and expanded the prevailing rationality of first Fascism and then the U.S. capitalist society in the Fordist era of mass production.

One member of the Frankfurt school, Herbert Marcuse, argued that the media and technology contained their own discourse that prevails over the ability to think negatively and question the validity of the system in which one resides (Marcuse,

1964). By erecting a *technological society* that integrated individuals into an administered world of circumscribed thought and behaviour, a meme of conformity or "one dimensionality" prevailed. In this mode, the ability to think negatively, or outside the strictures of the system, became all but impossible and one was forced to instead conform to a naturalised set of needs and wants in line with capitalist logic. The central features of this mode of thought were repression of values, aspirations and ideas inconsistent with the prevailing operational attitudes and rationality. Technology and media had in his mind developed their own rationality and become powerful forces for control and domination. Globalisation can be seen in a similar light today, with many simply accepting it as the natural continuation of the growth of capitalism.

Habermas (1962) saw the culture industry performing this function in the political arena as well, arguing that the public sphere had been transformed from facilitating rational debate and the free exchange of disparate opinions to a source shaping, constructing and limiting public discourse to reside within a relatively narrow continuum that limited the diversity of opinions and worked to stultify free thought and debate. Political ideologies became identification with one of the prevailing modes of thought, consumed through increasingly specialised media outlet that reinforce those ideas without dissenting viewpoints. Opinions were manufactured, packaged and then sold to the public without critical analysis or open debate and people increasingly accepted these packages and called them their own, or through a sense of futility or cynicism disengage from politics altogether.[3]

The Frankfurt School thus offered a model of analysis that centred on ideological critique toward unearthing the deeper political and economic interests that underwrote cultural production and state activity. They utilised an approach that situated analysis within the larger context of social, political and economic life, exploring the role of various social institutions and structures in the development of normative values, desires and needs. The approach is transdisciplinary, incorporating sociology, political economy, history, political science, philosophy and psychoanalysis. It explored social phenomena from a variety of optics seeking to deconstruct culture toward emancipating people from a capitalist society that continued to exploit, dominate and alienate in the name of instrumentalised notions of progress.

Critical theorists are committed to penetrating objective appearance and exploring the underlying social relations the surface often conceals. They rejected rationality that subordinated human consciousness and action to the imperatives of universal law and instead highlight the contradictions, alienation and subjugation that existed below the cohesiveness and universality of functionalist traditions (Giroux, 1983). By looking at the relationship between political domination and culture, subjectivity, and consciousness, Frankfurt School theorists hoped to critique the social order as part of a radical project for change that offered a normative vision of what society should be like. Adorno and Horkheimer, as two of the leading members of the Frankfurt School, were among the first to recognise the dialectic nature of objectivity and offer a trenchant critique of positivism and its over-reliance on science, reason, and objectivity.

In the most general sense of progressive thought the Enlightenment has always aimed at liberating men from fear and establishing their sovereignty. Yet the fully enlightened earth radiates disaster triumphant (Adorno & Horkheimer, 2002).

They argued that instrumental rationality had penetrated all aspects of quotidian life and that science had become a vehicle of social domination and control that actually denied the critical faculty of reason in deference to the empirically provable fact. In their view, science had fallen prey to the scientific method and analysis had become separated from the questions of ethics and ends, instead focusing solely on description, classification, and means. Positivism thus ushered in a paradigm that always stopped short of critique, and was forever stuck in describing the world as it was seen, heard, and felt.

Horkheimer offered dialectical social theory as an alternative to the over-reliance on the scientific method (Kellner, 1989). Dialectical social theory is founded on empirical evidence but is underwritten by values and a normative political standpoint to attack injustice, suffering, and alienation. It assails the notion of 'value free,' or objective, research and calls for the centrality of critique – based on a symbiotic relationship between theory, morality, and politics. It is further underwritten by an ethical foundation based on minimising the unhappiness of the poor and suffering and maximising the happiness of all. This involves locating the socio-historical sources of suffering and injustice and working to overcome them.

Jurgen Habermas (1973) furthered this line of reasoning by arguing that adherence to reason alone eliminated the ability to hope, to take a position, to desire, to strive for happiness, and to dignify all other aspects of human experience that did not fit into the scientifically observable fact. In Habermas' view, science had separated reason from desire and suffering, and had increasingly centred itself on production, technological 'progress,' and efficiency alone. As a result, anything associated with transcending reality was deemed nonsensical and outside the scope of scientific study. In the end, he felt, science had abandoned its role in aiding the progress of humanity.

Critical theory thus offers a methodological approach that explores social phenomena within a broader perspective that takes it outside its situated particularity and places it in the larger social, economic and political spheres. It grounds itself in critique as a foundational principle and imbues ethics into the very heart of its work. In analysing the multifaceted forms and manifestations of globalisation and its effects on education, it allows a more interdisciplinary, complexified analysis that can escape the limitations of a particular field of study or perspective. Instead it explores globalisation and education as phenomena with cultural, political and economic aspects that interact in diverse ways in diverse settings. It seeks to move beyond analysis that celebrates globalisation tout court or those who see it as merely a product of capitalist expansion and consolidation. A critical theory of globalisation instead analyses the positive and negative aspects of the key global phenomenon of our age and ways we can work to mitigate and challenge its deleterious effects on the individual and larger society.

147

CRITICAL THEORY, EDUCATION & POLICY CRITIQUE

Critical theory first emerges in education in a serious analytical way with the work of Paulo Freire, a Brazilian educator who gained international acclaim with the publication of his book *Pedagogy of the Oppressed* in the early 70s. In that book and his other work, Freire attempted to critique traditional education and pedagogy, particularly what he called *banking education* and its adherence to a subject-object relationship between teacher and student. Freire instead advocated a problem-posing education that centred on dialogue and using student's cultural knowledge and experience to help move students toward critical consciousness and hope and empowerment for social change. His work inspired the critical pedagogy movement that followed in this country, led by Michael Apple and Henry Giroux among others, who used the tools of critical theory to offer a systematic critique of schooling and its role in reproducing class, race and gender inequalities.

These critical social theorists see education as a key site for their work, given the role that schools, colleges, and universities play in social reproduction and preparing citizens for participation in the broader society (Giroux, 1983; Morrow & Torres, 2002; Rhoads & Valadez, 1996; Tierney, 1993; Torres, 1998, 2002). For them, critical theory provides valuable tools to explore the relationship of knowledge, schooling and the social order and the role schools play in spreading ideology, maintaining or challenging social inequality and serving democracy. Critical theorists in this sense use inquiry as a means for challenging forms of oppression and marginality that limit full and equitable participation in public life (Habermas, 1973; Horkheimer, 1972; Marcuse, 1972). Thus, a key contribution of critical theory in education is the belief that research ought to serve an emancipatory goal. That is, and we paraphrase Karl Marx here, social scientists should not simply interpret the world, but use their inquiry as a vehicle for improving, reforming, or revolutionising social life. Critical theory thus provides *theoretical* tools that are then used by theorists in advocating for educational reform, critical pedagogy, or other radical or progressive pedagogical practices that can advance democratic ideals and practices and address social inequalities.

In looking specifically at educational research, Freire advocating critical hermeneutics as a way out of the impasse of strict positivism and absolute relativity. He employed a reinterpretation of phenomenological epistemology to this end, arguing that we can reach a provisional and generalisable knowledge that can be used constructively in the struggle to define and reinvent the world (Freire, 1970, 1998a, 1998b).[4] This new knowledge is tied to everyday life, rather than universalising principles, with dialogue and experimentation leading people to produce new knowledge based on collective lived experience. In the process, research creates a space where individuals become conscious of the social, cultural, and political world around them, as well as the power relations that underwrite those realities. The knowledge created by this 'experiential' research that has a provisional and collective nature, tied to place and time, and to larger issues of culture, language, and social structures, highlighting the centrality of intersubjectivity and the social nature of all knowledge and reality.[5] Adherents of Freire thus often critique the positivist tradition that dominates much educational research today, looking to go beyond 'objective' research to incorporate broader social critique and political engagement into their research and offer normative alternatives that can address and challenge ongoing problems in education (Van Heertum, 2005). One of those concerns is a continued critique of neoliberalism and its fatalistic exodus from hope, a theme that became central to Freire in his later work (see for example *Pedagogy of Freedom* (1998)).

Praxis, or the combination of theory and practice, thus informs all the work in this area, with critical theory and critical pedagogy intimately tied together in challenging hegemonic discourse in education. In thinking about democratic possibilities and an action agenda for education, we take the work of John Dewey and Paulo Freire as starting points for advancing a critical analysis of education in a global age. Dewey (1916) had a particular vision of democratic life that entailed much more than the right to vote. He saw democracy as people actively engaging in meaningful social relations and participating in decisions that have an impact on their lives. There is thus a strong *relational* tone to Dewey's vision, meaning that democracy is dependent upon the quality of social relations forged among individuals and groups. A passage from his classic work *Democracy and Education* highlights this conception: "A democracy is more than a form of government; it is primarily a mode of associated living, of conjoint communicated experience. The extension in space of the number of individuals who participate in an interest so that each has to refer his own action to that of others, and to consider the action of others to give point and direction to his own" (Dewey, 1916, p. 93). Dewey believed education was essential to democracy – providing citizens with the tools and knowledge necessary to actively engage in civil life, work collaboratively for social change and make decisions that transcended individual interest to consider the public or common good.

Dewey's vision of democracy challenges all citizens to take part in decisions that affect their lives, balancing our own interests with the interests of others, a position that is challenged by the neoliberal ideology we will discuss below. Given the role that economic policies play in the lives of citizens, Dewey's democratic vision calls for citizen input at the local, national, and global level. But where is the democratic space within the context of corporate-driven forms of globalisation, where public spheres are increasingly distanced from the nexus of decision making and global trade organisations and multinational enterprises (MNEs) define the terms of world economic (and tangentially political and social) affairs? Indeed, a fundamental criticism coming from a variety of social movements, including those who gathered in the streets of Seattle in 1999 to protest the meetings of the World Trade Organisation (WTO), is the lack of representation and use of open and democratic processes in the construction of global relations. How can average citizens and workers influence global processes when they and their representatives are absent from the table? This analysis increasingly extends to schools, as organisations like the World Bank dictate the form and content of education in countries across the globe, undermining state and local control and the power of the people to define their own educational goals and practices.

Similar to Dewey, Paulo Freire's work in education focused on advancing social justice and democracy. Freire was deeply touched by the lives of quiet desperation that so many lower and working-class citizens throughout his native homeland of Brazil experienced. He envisioned education as a grassroots process, and believed that engaging people in their communities was essential to elevating literacy and raising consciousness. Self-empowerment was vital to the pedagogical project spelled out in *Pedagogy of the Oppressed*, and he believed that average citizens could take charge of their own lives, and ultimately, develop the critical skills necessary to write their own histories. His vision saw education as an emancipatory or libratory practice that could serve the cause of social transformation, challenging the fatalism at the heart of the new global order. In this sense, critical theory informs practice as the analytical tools become the foundation for critical pedagogy, an approach that builds on the analytical insights, ethical imperatives and dedication to social transformation of critical theory to alter the social order to more readily serve the needs and wants of humans outside the strictures of markets and instrumental rationality.

Within the policy realm, critical theory provides tools to explore the underlying social, political and economic forces that currently dominate global debates on educational policy and practice. It allows researchers and scholars to highlight the interests represented by current reforms and the ways these interests often undermine broader notions of education for democracy, social justice and the common good. Ultimately, critical theory provides a powerful analytical model for exploring the ways globalisation affects the lives of teachers and students inside and outside the classroom and an inspiration to challenge current educational reforms that work against their interests. In the next sections, we explore the dominant ideology of globalisation today, namely neoliberalism and its effects on education in the United States and abroad.

NEOLIBERALISM & THE WITHERING STATE

In this section, we provide an overview of neoliberalism through the lens of critical theory, exploring power dynamics and the socio-historical impetus that underlie the contemporary global economic and political order. Neoliberalism designates a new state formation that has emerged in the past three decades. It is tied to reforms first implemented in the neoconservative governments of Margaret Thatcher and John Major in England, Ronald Reagan in the United States, and Brian Mulroney in Canada.[6] Neoliberal governments promote open markets, free trade, reduction of the public sector, decreased state intervention in the economy, and the deregulation of markets. In the context of developing countries, neoliberalism has been philosophically and historically associated with structural adjustment programs, whether initiated locally or though international pressure from groups like the International Monetary Fund (IMF), World Bank and World Trade Organisation. It takes traditional liberal notions of free markets and *laissez-faire* economic policy and expands them to a global context, where free trade and liberal democracy are described as the best way to realise global prosperity and international peace.

A central aspect of the model is a drastic reduction in the state sector, especially via the privatisation of state enterprises, the liberalisation of salaries and prices, and the reorientation of industrial and agricultural production toward exports. In the short run, the purpose of these policy packages is to reduce the size of the fiscal deficit, public debt, inflation, exchange rates, and tariffs. In the long run, structural adjustment is based on making a county more amenable to foreign investment and business interests, on the premise that exports are the best engine of development. Thus structural adjustment and stabilisation policies seek to free international exchange, reduce distortions in price structures, do away with protectionism and unions, and facilitate the influence of the market in the Latin American and other global economies (Bitar, 1988).

The prevailing premises of the economic restructuring of advanced capitalism and the premises of structural adjustment are highly compatible with the neoliberal models. They imply the reduction of public spending, reduction of programs considered wasteful, sale of state enterprises, and mechanisms of deregulation to avoid state intervention in the business world. Together with the aforementioned, it is proposed that the state should participate less in the provision of social services (including education, health, pensions and retirement, public transportation, and affordable housing) and that these services should be privatised. The notion of 'private' (and privatisations) is glorified as part of a free market. It implies total confidence in the efficiency of competition because the activities of the public or state sector are seen as inefficient, unproductive, and socially wasteful. In contrast, the private sector is considered to be efficient, effective, productive, and responsive. In contrast to the model of the welfare state in which the state exercises a mandate to uphold the social contract between labour and capital, the neoliberal state is decidedly pro business, supporting the demands of the corporate world. Nevertheless, as Schugurensky rightly points out, this departure from state interventionism is differential, not total (Schugurensky, 1994). It is not possible to abandon, for symbolic as well as practical reasons, all of the state's social programs. It is necessary to diffuse conflictive and explosive areas in the realm of public policy.

That is why there are programs of social solidarity in Costa Rica and Mexico, or why Brazil and other Latin American countries have passed legislation that protects street children. The modification of the schema of state intervention is not indiscriminate but is a function of the differential power of the clientele, which leads to policies of solidarity among the poorest of society as well as subsidies and the transfer of resources for the middle and dominant sectors, including those who are fundamentally against protectionism. Furthermore, the state does not wholly abandon the mechanisms of discipline and coercion, nor populist strategies of distribution of wealth (or promises of such), in order to obtain legislative consensus or win elections.

A central element for understanding the development of neoliberalism is the globalisation of capitalism. Critical theory developed as a model to explain changes in capitalism that had altered the dynamics of class relations and foregrounded ideology, the state and culture as important tools in its consolidation and acceptance. With globalisation and neoliberalism, the welfare state that was arguably established to save capitalism from the great depression is being systematically dismantled. One could argue that this is due in large part to the collapse of an alternative to capitalism and liberal democracy, namely the end of communism. Globalisation, which one should note is not really a new phenomenon but one that has expanded and accelerated dramatically in recent years through the opening of global markets, the successful spread of American culture across the planet and the ascendancy of technology that facilitates both process, marks a turning point in the development of capitalism, expanding commodification and markets beyond national borders.

This process, predicted to some extent in Marx's *Grundrisse*, alters the principles away from imperialist expansion and national competition to a global economic order dominated by multinational corporations and international organisations largely operating beyond the power of nation states and even international law. This process has been analysed by theoretical currents tied to the New Left in the United States (e.g., Paul Baran and Paul Sweezy) or by Claus Offe (1984) as "late" or "disorganised" capitalism. From a postmodern perspective, Fredric Jameson (1991) defines the characteristics of postmodernism as "the cultural logic of late capitalism," arguing that we have not entered a period of complete rupture, but one underwritten by the further expansion and consolidation of capitalist logic in the cultural and political spheres The important element to retain is the idea of globalisation in a post-Fordist world (where the service industry replaces manufacturing as the dominant mode of production in advanced economies), with production and power diffused and natural borders, cultures and identities becoming increasingly destabilised and porous. Critical theory then becomes useful in exploring the power dynamics at play in what popular discourse claims as an inevitable and essentially positive global transformation.

GLOBALISATION & EDUCATIONAL REFORM

In this section we offer a more specific and detailed analysis of two aspects of globalisation that have affected educational systems across the globe. The first relates to neoliberalism and its views on education. The second relates to mass migration from the global South to advanced economies in the U.S. and Europe and their effects on educational policy. Within the educational realm, neoliberal policy is defined by a push toward standardisation, professionalism, testing/ accountability regimes and the decentralisation and privatisation of education (Macedo, Dendrinos, & Gounari, 2003). It involves the infusion of business models and logic at all levels of education and the stressing of training and sorting as the primary function of schooling. Lost is the more holistic notion of education that involves the formation of good citizens that can contribute not only to the economy but the public good (Apple, 2001; Dewey, 1916; Giroux, 2003). Weakened is the notion that schools can create more tolerant and socially able adults that are well-adjusted and prepared to deal with their familial and social responsibilities. Largely disabled are efforts to cultivate the imagination, to critically engage with the world and see it in diverse ways and to teach students the rudiments of democratic participation and civic engagement. And disavowed are efforts for education to serve the project of social transformation.

At the heart of the paradigm however is the notion that teachers, teaching and teachers unions are one of the greatest barriers to global prosperity. As Lois Weiner has pointed out, a 2004 World Bank Draft Report *World Development Report 2004: Making Services Work for Poor People*, makes this claim explicit arguing "unions, especially teachers union, are one of the greatest threats to global prosperity" and that unions have "captured governments holding poor people hostage to demands for more pay" (Compton & Weiner, 2008). The report suggest that teachers should be fired in large numbers if they strike or refuse reduced pay and that governments should implement a policy of privatising services, charging user fees (essentially parents pay to send their children to school), devolving control of schools to neighbourhoods and greatly reducing public funding for schools at all levels. Many of these policies have been implemented across Latin America and beyond, often by making loans and aid contingent on these economic restructuring plans. In Argentina, Adriana Puiggros and Torres (1997) have argued that these policies have caused great harm to student from the poorer strata of society.

The move to attack teachers and teacher unions relates to the underlying logic of neoliberalism and its project of market liberation – essentially transforming schools to serve as the primary institution of sorting and training in the economy. This explains the overall neoliberal model of education, which really entails deskilling teachers, focusing instruction on tests and specific knowledge, using outside experts and funding to ensure business interests trump all others in the school and pushing outside the U.S. to weaken or abolish teachers unions (Apple, 2004; Kozol, 2005). In the United States, ex-Secretary of Education Rod Paige went as far as calling the NEA a "terrorist organisation."

At a deeper level, it can be argued that the neoliberal agenda attacks schools as ideological institutions that could challenge the discourses and rationality behind neoliberalism itself. (Weiner, 2008) If this claim is true, it would explain the move to weaken the power of teachers and establish teacher-proof curriculum, to call for neutrality and apolitical classrooms all the way through to the university (such as David Horowitz's Academic Bill of Rights movement in the U.S.) and to standardise curriculum and use high stakes testing to all but erase time for education outside its vocational and job training aspects. By undermining teacher autonomy and authority, neoliberal advocates ensure that education serves the needs of global competition and segmented labor needs in different countries and among different classes within a country. Carmen Luke (Luke & Luke, 2000) thus describe two fundamental shifts in pedagogy resulting from the ongoing neoliberal educational reforms: "To refocus on teachers and teaching, what is most interesting are not the most overt aspects of such reforms – the change in systems-level administration and school management to fit mercantile practices and new age metaphors – but rather the ways in which teaching has increasingly been appropriated both by curriculum and instructional commodities and the extent to which teachers have moved toward consumer-like behaviour."

This is accompanied by attempts to undermine the political power of unions in general and teachers in the classroom, by disavowing the relationship between politics and education and advocating objectivity and neutrality across the curriculum. Freire (1998) once warned: "Washing our hands of the conflict between the powerful and the powerless means to side with the powerful, not to be neutral." The educational system in the United States and across much of the globe stand in jeopardy of doing just that by attempting to eradicate politics and real critical thinking from the classroom at all levels and by ensuring inequalities along the lines of gender, race, nationality and class continue to persist and grow. Jonathon Kozol outlined in *Savage Inequalities* (1991) and the more recent *The Shame of the Nation* (2005), that class and race still define the access and opportunity available to students – undermining a central promise of democracy and freedom. (see also Anyon, Year and Bowles and Gintis, 2005). Outside the U.S., these trends are only amplified in many cases. By disavowing the connection between education and politics, neoliberal advocates dismantle the role education can play in awakening students to their surroundings and allowing them to critically engage with that world. Rather the new paradigm assumes ideas are dangerous and works to protect students from any knowledge that might challenge the current order of things.

This relates to a second major implact of globalisation, which is arguably the movement of large poor populations from Latin America and Africa to the U.S. and Europe. Debates across the West center on the changing demographics of their countries and how to deal with the cultural and political shifts those changes entail. In the United States, the large infusion of students from Mexico and Central and South America have amplified concerns about racial bias in education and growing social segregation inside and outside schools. Research by Richard Valencia, Angela Valenzuela, Orfield and Yunn, Kozol and a host of others has highlighted the ways in which schools are underserving these immigrant populations leading to dramatic underachievement and drop out rates.

Yet since neoliberalism embraces inequality as a powerful engine for economic growth and vitality, the commitment to equal access and opportunity is little more than a rhetorical tool to undermine broader analysis and critique of the failure to educate large swaths of the population. Knowledge in this sense loses its power as an emancipatory vehicle, replaced by a relatively anti-intellectual notion of schooling. School gives us the facts, knowledge and skills necessary for professional success (or at least efficiency). All other aspects of human development are secondary – including health, safety, artistic appreciation and talent, social skills, tolerance, civic understanding and the like. Students are taught that knowledge is useful toward an end, with that end rarely related to their personal growth or emancipation from social inequality or discontent. Much of this change occurs under the auspices of globalisation and the need to train the future corps of workers that will ensure continued economic competitiveness (Reich, 1992). Essentially neoliberal reforms thus redefine schools as largely vocational education centres that serve the needs of 'consumers' to acquire the best education possible for future economic success, while in reality reproducing class and racial inequalities through their sorting practices (e.g., sorting, special education, high stakes testing) (Oakes, 1986; Valencia, 2002).

These two trends come together in the push to reinforce the idea that neoliberal globalisation is both positive and inevitable. The extrication of politics from the classroom together with the deskilling and disempowering of teacher and the increased standardisation of curriculum all work to infuse business logic into the classroom while undermining efforts to open the minds of students and get them to critically challenge their surrounding and the social order. As Apple (2004) has long pointed out the hegemonic ideology that underwrites curriculum often provides messages intent on showing the inevitability of current social, political and economic order. In the process, the role of education in expanding the imagination and fostering hope is largely cut off. When schools are forced to treat knowledge as an instrumentalised commodity, they are closing off the hope necessary to act and intervene in the world. In Freire's last book, *Pedagogy of Freedom* (1998), he argued that neoliberal reforms have taken hope away from children, teaching them that all they can do is adapt to the system and compete for access to the best schools and then best jobs available to them. He felt as if schools were doing little to activate the natural curiosity of children, instead focusing on static, standardised content that didn't relate to their daily lives or cultural experiences. The result is a cynicism to the possibility of change (Torres, in press; Van Heertum, 2008).

Looking specifically at higher education, the impact of globalisation upon colleges and universities is both direct and indirect. An example of a direct effect is the way in which national economies are restructuring their systems of support for higher education as a consequence of shifting economic priorities and structural adjustment policies mandated from above. Indirect effects include the manner in which the war on terror has come to limit academic freedom and the transnational flow of scholars and students, or the way in which academic culture at some Latin American universities is shifting from a collectivist orientation to ideals associated with individualism. This is coupled with attempts to infuse market logics into higher education, undermining its mission as an independent source of knowledge and inquiry. This fits with the general critique above, attempting to limit the effectiveness of universities as sites of contestation to the global order.

Increased entrepreneurialism in post-secondary education, especially in the most developed countries, has been led by efforts to expand revenue (or simply replenish losses from decreasing state and federal support) through a variety of profit-seeking endeavours, including close collaboration with businesses in research, satellite campuses and extension programs around the world. This has been coupled with recent efforts to bring accountability regimes similar to *No Child Left Behind* to the university level, ensuring increased homogeneity and standardisation and disempowering professors and counter-hegemonic ideas. On top of this, many universities in the wealthiest countries are actively involved in shaping the nature of higher education in less developed countries, as is the case with a program funded by the United States Agency for International Development (USAID) in which U.S. colleges and universities received funds to assist in the development of

Iraqi higher education and in developing a stronger private higher education sector in Afghanistan (Del Castillo, 2003). In these latter two instances, we see clear connections between neoliberalism and the U.S.-led war on terrorism, with two countries identified by U.S. officials as breeding grounds for terrorism on the receiving end of heavy doses of 'American-style' higher education. And privatisation is also driving research and development agendas at universities, especially in the U.S.[7]

In sum, neoliberal globalisation has attempted to undermine the broader goals of education, pushing it to serve as the primary source of sorting and initial training for corporations. It has also attempted to undermine the ideological and political power of education, specifically disempowering teachers and teacher unions. In many cases, neoliberal reforms have limited access and opportunity along class and racial lines including limiting access to higher education through the imposition of higher tuition and reduced government support to institutions and individuals. Critical theory helps researchers go beyond the rhetoric of neoliberal, free markets and trade advocates to explore the interests served and the broader social impact on oppressed and underserved populations. It allows theorists to deconstruct the logic of educational reforms that appear to be progressive in nature and recognise their underlying power dynamics and deleterious results. In re-reading globalisation and education, it allows us to explore the logic that underwrites educational reforms across the globe and the powerful interests they serve. It also allows us to craft a program of educational reform that can challenge globalisation from above, a topic to which we now turn.

CRITICAL THEORY, SOCIAL MOVEMENTS & THE FUTURE OF EDUCATION

Critical theory commenced as a theoretical project to modernise Marxist theory to adapt to the changing nature of capitalism and the growing importance of the administered society and cultural industry to its consolidation. With contemporary globalisation, the culture industry and ideology continue to maintain their importance, though the centre of power moves away from the nation state and toward multinational corporations and their institutional supporters (IMF, World Bank, WTO, etc.). Critical theory provides tools to deconstruct this movement and consider its broader implications to social, political and economic life, but it also offers a path toward social action, based on its critical analysis of the underlying inequality and undemocratic nature of globalisation from above. The *cacerolazos* of Buenos Aires are a telling indicator of the level of dissatisfaction and hopelessness afflicting the lives of average citizens today.[8] As globalisation advances and the discrepancy between the poorest and wealthiest of our societies widen, as access to decision-making bodies dwindles, and as the educational differences between the rural and the urban and the lower and upper classes expands, tensions will continue to surface. We witnessed these tensions in the streets of Seattle during meetings of the World Trade Organisation in 1999, and in 2001 at the World Economic Forum in Davos, the G-8 summit in Genoa and in Buenos Aires, where Argentina's economic collapsed under the direction of the

IMF led thousands of citizens to carry their misfortune and discouragement into the streets.

Yet globalisation as defined by the neoliberal project is not inevitable. Grassroots movements and sound analysis and criticism have altered the strategies of those individuals and organisations seeking to advance a corporate-driven model of global trade relations. Clearly, leaders of the neoliberal project see the growing resistance among workers, intellectuals, human rights advocates, environmentalists, students, citizens, and the economically disenfranchised. Efforts from agents of *globalisation from below* are thus altering the nature of the debate and challenging the push of neoliberal reforms at all levels, including in the educational realm where neoliberals appear to see great peril. These social movements are both using the tools of progressive and radical education and simultaneously working to offer educational reforms of their own. De Sousa Santos (2004), for one, presents a strategy for rescuing the university from the forces of neoliberalism and globalisation. He calls for democratic and emancipatory tactics that embrace elements of today's university – including service to the public not bound by the revenue-generating potential of users – and "confronting the new with the new," imploring universities to embrace innovative practices that avoid the tendency for blind resistance to neoliberal globalisation or attempt to turn back to some mythical university of the past that had significant democratic shortcomings. He calls for a "new institutionalisation" in which he argues that universities must build connections across institutions at the national level, suggesting that their public benefit may be best produced through networks. And he believes they must implement more democratic strategies, both internally and externally and create a more participative system of evaluation.

We believe efforts in a similar vein must begin at the K-12 level, working to combat neoliberal notions of education as a source of sorting and training to reiterate more holistic and transgressive goals. We thus believe an action agenda is necessary to challenge the hegemony of neoliberal globalisation and its powerful influence on schooling, the university, the state, and the market. Here we turn to the work of Paulo Freire (1970) and his deployment of "generative themes." Freire established the notion of generative themes as a way to educate communities by using well-researched and crafted images that displayed local problems related to larger structural issues. (Torres 1998b). Freire's notion of generative themes may provide us with a reasonable set of guiding principles for action against neoliberalism, based on a re-reading of globalisation that focuses on issues central to critical theory, including the dialectical nature of reality, the use of science to reduce suffering and increase happiness and an ethical imperative to challenge systems of domination and oppression (Morrow and Torres, 2000). Included below are themes that we believe best capture the challenges and possibilities of globalisation from below to educational reform (Torres, in press; Rhoads & Torres, 2005).

Anti-hegemonic globalisation. The need for universities, social movements, scholars, intellectuals, and communities to confront the dilemmas of the global and the local should not distract us from a most pressing concern: to challenge authoritarian neoliberal globalisation and its hegemonic discourse of inevitability through networks, institutions, and practices that can change the intensity and dynamics of social interaction, and the actual lives of people in impoverished societies. This involves challenging the narratives of neoliberal globalisation, particularly the fatalistic idea of *un pensamiento único* (the only possible thinking) so prevalent among economists and policymakers who, following rational choice models and game theory, have come to conclude that in a post-Fordist society the only possible theoretical model and social order is neoliberal economics and liberal democracy. This consensus has been ratified and consolidated by a diverse group on the left and right, including neoconservative governments that have implemented neoliberal reforms, as explicated by Michael Apple in many of his books and articles (Apple, 2001, 2004). Challenging, defying, and demystifying this technocratic approach to social sciences (particularly economics) and policy is the most important generative theme of contemporary struggles, focusing on forging the sort of decentred unity Apple has advocated in recent years bringing together the diverse groups that form the fragmented left and challenging the commonsensical idea that globalisation and neoliberal reform are inevitable.

Freedom is emancipation, not tutelage. One of the most important insights of a critical analysis of educational policy is that the attempt to highlight representative democracy as the only viable model is also an attempt to create freedom that is controlled and circumscribed; essentially used as a device of elites to dominate and control the masses. What we have come to see is that representative democracy often represents a dictatorship of capital, or at least the dictatorship of the economic elites. There are other alternatives, starting with a liberal notion of participatory democracy that will exploit the limitations of representative democracy and enhance the quality and texture of democratic life (Torres, 1998), or in a more radical vein, the notion of radical democracy as practiced in the implementation of participatory budgeting for more than a decade in Porto Alegre, Brazil. A renaissance of democracy emerges as a central concern in the context of education and the larger society. Movements toward reforming campaign finance and elections, to increase transparency and accountability, as well as attempts to create better ways to increase the connections between education and citizenship, or between citizenship and the practice of democracy, are essential to this work. We must also work to link the university with social movements opposing hegemonic globalisation and schooling with the broader debates on globalisation and the roles, purposes and goals of education in general.

Defence of public education. It is clear that the defence of public education is one of the central concerns of innumerable social movements and public declarations, from the World Social Forum, World Educational Forum, student strike at UNAM, student protests over tuition around the world and teacher union protests. For those who still view participatory democracy as viable, a robust defence of the importance of public support and public goods must be waged. We must also defend the achievements of some of the most cherished ideals of the democratic pact including equality, freedom and solidarity, and not allow the hegemony of neoliberalism to erode these essential ideals by redefining the citizen as merely a consumer.

Defence of the democratic state. Given the intense dynamics between the local and the global, the nation-state takes on even greater importance within the context of globalisation. Yet, it is clear that without resorting to a serious defence of the principles of representation and participation in the democratic state, we may not be able to implement the generative themes outlined above. The state plays an important role in altering the nature of public education and cannot be subsumed by discourses of the individual or small group autonomy. This is not to undermine these movements or the importance of the local, just to recognise the essential role the democratic state will play in the realisation of a more holistic, just and emancipatory education for all.

A planetarian multicultural citizenship. This is perhaps the most important action to be undertaken by schools and universities as part of their responsibility to the public good. With increased immigration, and the slippage of cultures and languages in local communities and national societies, it is imperative to work toward a cosmopolitan democracy based on a planetarian multicultural citizenship. Indeed, as utopian as this model may sound – and remembering that many of the most astute and critical social scientist like Immanuel Wallerstein (2001) have called for a science of "utopistics" – there are really few options but to create new social and human horizons. We need to seek these new trajectories through pedagogical models that facilitate novel encounters between humans and nature. We need a new model of relationships between the mind and body, one that moves beyond the logocentric characteristic of European and North American white cultures. We need a new model for building and sustaining global relationships, one not based on the threat of a nuclear holocaust, but rooted in ideals anchored to a more peaceful world.

The responsibilities of educational institutions to the survival of the planet, to social justice and democracy and to peace and solidarity among individuals and communities cannot simply be a subject of study within ivory tower walls. The knowledge and ideals advanced by our greatest minds must impact our societies, our social policies, and indeed global practices. Consequently, we call for a transformation of education across the globe with schooling becoming a source of social action that can transcend economic rationality and reengage with the long, hard struggle for the good life and good society. This involves a new vision of education and the will and collective action necessary to struggle toward its realisation.

Critical theory provides powerful analytical tools to go beyond the generally accepted assumptions of globalisation and neoliberalism to the forces that are leading this radical transformation of the social order. In re-reading globalisation in this vein, we see the interests served by the process and the ways it undermines social justice and democracy and undermines the opportunities and quality of life of large proportions of the global economy. Critical theory also reminds us of the power people have to intervene in the world and the ways the ideology of inevitability becomes a profound tool of the economic and social elite in their pursuit of global domination and control. In this sense, critical theory can serve as the inspiration for critical pedagogy and other social and educational movements to challenge globalisation from above and reaffirm the global struggle for social justice, democratisation and a common good outside the instrumental rationality of markets and consumption.

NOTES

[1]   See Stiglitz (2002) and Reich (1992) for explanation of neoliberalism and its underlying logic. Stiglitz does provide some critique of neoliberal globalisation, though he does argue for the advantages of free markets and largely unfettered global trade.

[2]   See for example Hardt & Negri's argument in *Empire* that human rights NGOs often serve as the legitimating agents for the use of military force and foreign policy that often hurt the very "victims" they seek to help (Hardt & Negri, 2000).

[3]   For further articulation of this relationship, see Van Heertum's *The fate of democracy in a cynical age,* which offers an in depth analysis of cynicism and its relationship to cultural influences like education and the media (Van Heertum, 2007).

[4]   Positivism tends to dominate educational research today, founded on a fervent dedication to objectivity and value-neutrality in research (Van Heertum, 2005). On the opposite end of the spectrum is absolute relativity, based on post-structural critiques of objectivity and a belief that no universal knowledge claims are valid. Freire attempts to situate research between these two extremes, arguing for a knowledge that is true in a particular time and place and its relationship to larger social, political and economic truths that can be substantiated conditionally (Torres & Morrow, 2002).

[5]   Intersubjectivity refers to the belief that reality and our sense of self are built through communication and our relationship to other individuals and their subjective experience. This contradicts traditional notions of identity or consciousness that rely on a subject looking out on an object world and creating subjectivity through that subject-object relationship. Ultimately, it places language and communication at the center of metaphysics and ontology.

[6]   Neoliberalism refers primarily to economic policy imperatives of market liberation (domestic and foreign), privatisation, deregulation and the shrinking of the federal governments role in overseeing the economy. Neoconseratives tend to follow neoliberal social policy but are also involved in efforts to return to an idealized past of gender inequality, racial segregation and family values, security and religious moral certitude. Neoconservativs are also often associated with geopolitical programs to spread democracy and free markets, as in the revised justification for the Iraq War that started in 2003. Ironically, it is thus neoconservatives who started the push for neoliberal reforms. See Apple (2006) for further articulation of the similarities and differences between neoliberals and neoconservatives and the ways in which the two have worked together to implement a number of educational reforms.

[7]   The quest by U.S. colleges and universities to acquire funds for research and development activities is discussed in much detail by Slaughter and Rhoades (2004), as they highlight the "academic capitalist knowledge/learning/consumption regime."

[8]   Cacerolazo is a popular form of protest where large groups of people congregate and make noise by banging pots, pans and other utensils to draw attention and disrupt normal social life. In Argentina in 2001 and 2002, groups of largely middle-class protesters formed outside banks to protest the freezing of their savings and an arbitrary conversion of accounts to pesos at a devalued rate. Protesters again emerged in more diffuse, random fashion in 2002 as a protest against increased public service fees. In both cases, the protests surrounded policies associated with structural adjustment and the subsequent damage to the Argentinean peso (which devalued dramatically) and economy as foreign investment fled the country.

REFERENCES

Adorno, T. W., & Horkheimer, M. (2002). *Dialectic of enlightenment.* New York: Continuum.

Apple, M. (2006). *Educating the right way: Markets, standards, god, and inequality.* New York: Routledge Falmer.

Apple, M. (2004). *Ideology and curriculum.* New York: RoutledgeFalmer.

Apple, M., & Beane, J. (1995). *Democratic schools.* Alexandria, VA: Association for Supervision and Curriculum Development.

Bitar, S. (1988). Neo-conservativism versus neo-structuralism in Latin America. *CEPAL Review, 34,* 45.

Compton, M., & Weiner, L. (2008). *The global assault on teaching, teachers and their unions: Stories for resistance.* New York: Palgrave MacMillan.

Del Castillo, D. (2003). American colleges are offered grants to aid in revival of Iraqi higher education. *The Chronicle of Higher Education.*

Dewey, J. (1916). *Democracy and education.* New York: The Free Press.

Freire, P. (1970). *Pedagogy of the oppressed.* New York: The Continuum International Publishing Group, Inc.

Freire, P. (1998a). *Pedagogy of freedom.* Lanham, MD: Rowman & LittleField Publishers, Inc.

Freire, P. (1998b). *Politics and education.* Los Angeles: UCLA Latin American Center Publications.

Giddens, A. (1999). *Runaway world: How globalisation is reshaping our lives.* New York: Routledge.

Giroux, H. (1983). *Theory and resistance: A pedagogy for the opposition.* South Hadley, MA: J. F. Bergin.

Giroux, H. (2003). *Public spaces, private lives: Democracy beyond 9/11.* Lanham, MD: Rowman & Littlefield.

Habermas, J. (1962). *The structural transformation of the public sphere: An inquiry into a category of bourgeois society.* Cambridge, MA: MIT Press.

Habermas, J. (1973). *Theory and practice.* Boston: Beacon Press.

Hardt, M., & Negri, A. (2000). *Empire.* Cambridge, MA: Harvard University Press.

Hooks, B. (1994). *Teaching to transgress: Education as the practice of freedom.* New York: Routledge.

Horkheimer, M. (1972). *Critical theory.* New York: Seabury Press.

Jameson, F. (1991). *Postmodernism or, the cultural logic of late capitalism.* Durham, NC: Duke University Press.

Kellner, D. (1989). *Critical theory, marxism and modernity.* Baltimore: John Hopkins University Press.

Kozol, J. (1991). *Savage inequality: Children in America's schools.* New York: Harper Collins.

Kozol, J. (2005). *The shame of the nation: The restoration of apartheid schooling in America.* New York: Three Rivers Press.

Luke, A., & Luke, C. (2000). A situated perspective on cultural globalisation. In C. A. Torres & N. Burbules (Eds.), *Globalisation and education: Critical perspectives.* New York: Routledge.

Macedo, D., Dendrinos, B., & Gounari, P. (2003). *The hegemony of English.* Boulder, CO: Paradigm Publishers.

Marcuse, H. (1964). *One-dimensional man: Studies in the ideology of advanced industrial society.* Boston: Beacon Press.

Marcuse, H. (1972). *Counterrevolution and revolt.* Boston: Beacon Press.

Morrow, R., & Torres, C. A. (2002). *Reading Freire and Habermas: Critical pedagogy and transformative social change.* New York: Teachers College Press.

Oakes, J. (1986). *Keeping track: How schools structure inequality.* New Haven, CT: Yale University Press.

Offe, C. (1984). *Contradictions of the welfare state.* London: Hutchinson.

Reich, R. (1992). *The work of nations: Preparing ourselves for 21st century capitalism.* New York: Vintage.

Rhoads, R., & Valadez, J. (1996). *Democracy, multiculturalism, and the community college: A critical perspective.* New York: Garland.

Rhoads, R., & Torres, C. A. (2005). *The university, state and market: The political economy of globalisation in the Americas.* Stanford, CA: Stanford University Press.

Schugurensky, D. (1994). *Global economic restructuring and university change: The case of Universidad de Buenos Aires.* University of Alberta.

Stiglitz, J. (2002). *Globalisation & its discontents.* New York: W.W. Norton & Co.

Tierney, W. G. (1993). *Building communities of difference: Higher education in the 21st century.* Westport, CT: Bergin & Garvey.

Torres C. A. (1997). *Latin American education: Comparative perspectives.* Boulder, CO: Westview.

Torres, C. A. (1998). *Democracy, education and multiculturalism: Dilemmas of citizenship in a global world.* New York: Rowman & Littlefield Publishers, Inc.

Torres, C. A. (2002). Globalisation, education and citizenship: Solidarity versus markets? *American Educational Research Journal, 39*(2), 363–378.

Torres, C. A. (In Press). *Education and neoliberal globalisation.* New York: Routledge.

Van Heertum, R. (2005). How objective is objectivity? A critique of current trends in educational research. *Interactions: UCLA Journal of Education and Information Studies, 1,* 2.

Van Heertum, R. (2008). *The fate of democracy in a cynical age: Education, media and the evolving public sphere.* Los Angeles: University of California.

Wallerstein, I. (2001). *The end of the world as we know it: Social sciences for the twenty-first century.* Minneapolis, MN: University of Minnesota Press.

FURTHER READINGS

Apple, M. (2001). *Educating the right way: Markets, standards, god, and inequality.* New York: Routledge Falmer.

Giddens, A. (1999). *Runaway world: How globalisation is reshaping our lives.* New York: Routledge.

Hardt, M., & Negri, A. (2000). *Empire.* Cambridge, MA: Harvard University Press.

Stiglitz, J. (2002). *Globalisation & its discontents.* New York: W.W. Norton & Co.

Torres, C. A. & Burbules, N. (2000). *Globalisation and education: Critical perspectives.* New York: Routledge.

Carlos Alberto Torres
University of California Los Angeles

Richard Van Heertum
University of California Los Angeles

KA HO MOK

WHEN SOCIALISM MEETS GLOBAL CAPITALISM

Challenges for Privatising and Marketising Education in China and Vietnam [1]

INTRODUCTION

Both China and Vietnam have experienced significant social and economic changes since the adoption of the market-oriented reforms to transform their economies in the late 1970s in China and in the late 1980s in Vietnam. Since the late 1970s, the economic reform in China has significantly transformed the society not only in the economic aspect but also in social and political dimensions. Embracing the market economy has made China possibly the largest manufacturing powerhouse globally. With consistent and steady GDP growth in the last two decades, China has become one of the major economic powers in Asia (So, 2003; Saich, 2004). After the accession to the World Trade Organisation (WTO) in 2001, China has begun to integrate with the global market. More importantly, China's proactive approach in establishing free trade zones with the neighbouring countries has enhanced its geo-political influences in Asia (Cai, 2005; Liu, 2005). Similar to China, Vietnam has undergone a transition from state socialism to market socialism. The adoption of the policy of *doi moi* (renovation) in 1986 is usually considered as the beginning of the economic reform in Vietnam. However, the geopolitical events since 1989 are probably the real breakthrough in Vietnam's socio-economic transition as those events have dissipated the salience of Cold War concerns in Asia and therefore have reinserted Vietnam into regional and world markets. These changes have greatly speeded Vietnam's market transition and have consequently pushed the Communist Party to reconstitute the state-society relations in Vietnam (London, 2003). The present chapter sets out in the wider socio-economic contexts briefly outlined above to examine how the market transition taking place in China and Vietnam has led to changes in education governance, with particular reference to discuss how China and Vietnam approach the challenges of global capitalism by transforming the socialist education model into a more market-oriented one. After discussing changes in education governance, this chapter will critically examine major challenges of governance confronting these two governments when education is increasingly privatised and marketised.

Despite the disagreements and diverse interpretations of globalisation impacts on state capacity in governance, the growing impact of globalisation has caused a number of modern states to rethink their governance strategies in coping with rapid social and economic changes. In order to enhance the global competitiveness, a growing number of modern states have searched for new forms of governance in

M. Simons, M. Olssen and M.A. Peters (eds.), Re-Reading Education Policies: A Handbook Studying the Policy Agenda of the 21ˢᵗ Century, 163–183.

lines with the ideas and practices of neo-liberalist approach. Theories of "new governance" propose that modern governments are adapting to radical changes in their environments by turning to new forms of governance which are "more society-centred" and focus on "co-ordination and self-governance" (Peters, 1995; Pierre, 2000, pp. 2–6). Instead of relying solely upon government bureaucracy in terms of delivery of goods or services, there has been a massive proliferation of tools and policy instruments such as dizzying array of loans, loan guarantees, grants, contracts, insurance, vouchers, etc to address public problems (Salamon, 2002). Like countries in their western counterparts, Asian states have launched public policy and public management reforms along the lines of ideas and practices of marketisation, privatisation, corporatisation, and commercialisation. Privatisation has been a common theme in evolving patterns of government-business relations in some countries (for example, Malaysia and South Korea) (Gouri et al., 1991; World Bank, 1995). Pressures for broad governance changes have been strong, coming to a head in the financial crisis of 1997 in Asia. A feature of these pressures is the presence of influential international agencies such as the IMF and the World Bank. Their preferred models of governance reflect many of the same tendencies noted above: a less interventionist and arbitrary state; a strengthening of juridical "forms of regulation (often associated with fundamental legal reform), more disaggregated and decentralised forms of government, including partnerships and a stronger 'co-production' role for civil society groups; and a preference for market-like mechanisms over bureaucratic methods of service delivery" (World Bank, 1995). Hence, it is not surprising that strategies, measures and policy instruments in line with the global neo-liberal orthodoxy of pro-competition are introduced and adopted by Asian states to transform the way public sector is managed (Cheung and Scott, 2003; Mok & Forrest, 2008). Having discussed the wider policy context of the present chapter, let's now examine how the doctrines and practices of neo-liberalism affected the way education is governed in China and Vietnam.

CHANGES IN SOCIAL POLICY PHILOSOPHY: IMPACTS ON EDUCATION POLICY

The adherence to market principles and practices has affected not only the economic sphere but also the way social welfare and social policy is managed. Since the late 1970s, the principle of fully-subsidised in social policy during the Mao's era was abandoned and the implementation of policies in line with decentralisation and marketisation has altered the way social policy/social welfare is managed in China. Social welfare and social services used to be dominated by the state provision and financing, are now increasingly run on market principles (Guan, 2001; Wong & Flynn, 2001; Mok, 2005). In order to cut welfare burdens and promote economic efficiency of the state sector, social policy provision, social security and social protection has experienced significant restructuring. Nowadays, Chinese citizens have to become self-reliance and they need to pay for the major social services such as health, education and housing (Wong & Flynn, 2001; Wong, Gui & White, 2004). As Cook (2002) has rightly suggested, the Chinese citizens nowadays no longer enjoy "iron rice bowl" and "social security" especially when major social responsibilities have gone to individuals and families. Hence, it is not surprising to hear the popular complaints among Chinese citizens about the three new mountains being left by the state to them, namely, bearing more financial burdens for education, health and housing (Zhu, 2005).

In the new socialist market economy context, the old way of "centralised governance" in education has been rendered inappropriate (Yang, 2002). Acknowledging that over-centralisation and stringent rules would kill the initiatives and enthusiasm of local educational institutions, the Chinese Communist Party (CCP) called for resolute steps to streamline administration, devolve powers to units at lower levels so as to allow them more flexibility to run education. As early as 1985, the CCP issued the *Decision of the Central Committee of the Chinese Communist Party of China on the reform of the Educational System* which marked the beginning of a process of educational reform and gradually aligned the educational system with the newly emerging market economy. The documents called for the devolution of power to lower levels of government and a reduction in the rigid governmental controls over schools (CCCCP, 1985). Since then, the state has started to diversify educational services, allowing and encouraging the non-state sector to establish and run educational institutions. Meanwhile, the state has deliberately devolved responsibility and power to local governments, local communities and other non-state actors by providing a necessary framework for educational development (Hawkins, 2000; Ngok & Chan, 2003). The *Outline for Reform and Development of Education in China* issued in 1993 restated the reduction of centralisation and government control in general as the long-term goals of reform (CCCCP, 1993). The government began to play the role of "macro-management through legislation, allocation of funding, planning, information service, policy guidance and essential administration." The retreat of the central state provided space for local states as well as non-state actors to take more responsibilities for education provision, financing and regulation. Therefore, non-state bodies started to provide education in the formal education sector, thereby leading to the emergence of *minban* (people-run) schools and colleges.

While maintaining its control over the ideologies, the Vietnamese government has effectively shifted an increasing burden of the costs of social services from the state onto individual households. Similar to China, the Vietnamese Government has decided to engage with the global economy, especially when it has become a member of World Trade Organisation (WTO). Before the entry to the WTO, there were still debates in Vietnam whether running education and providing education could make profits. Nonetheless, the Education Law issued in 2005 no longer prohibits educational activities going commercialised. Following the principles of General Agreement on Trade in Services (GATS), the Vietnamese Government has begun to regard higher education a commodity; thereby a spontaneous and immature education market has begun to emerge (Pham, 2006).[2] Actually, education provision and financing has begun to change when the policy of "socialisation" (*xa hoi hoa*) was adopted since the early 1990s. Central to the socialisation policy is the shifting of costs from the state onto society in Vietnam, thereby social service provision is no longer purely welfare entitlements but citizens have to make financial contributions when making use of these social services. Similar to China, the Vietnamese Government realises depending upon the state's subsidies would never satisfy people's pressing educational needs, diversifying educational finances and proliferating educational providers has therefore become an increasing popular trend (Banh, 2006). It is against such a policy context that the Vietnamese Government began to allow the emergence of "semi-public" and "non-state" provision of social services, and meanwhile it undertook cost-recovery and cost-reduction measures in various social services. Today, the principle of cost-sharing has been deeply embedded in different social policy areas and its impacts have consolidated the emergence of a hybrid welfare regime in Vietnam (London, 2003; Bélanger & Liu, 2004).

Given the new challenges generated from rapid socio-economic developments in the market transition, the socialist model of education, which is characterised by centralised power, bureaucracy and subsidies, is no longer able to meet the requirements for the new development (Nguyen & Sloper, 1995). Realising the difficulty to separate the higher education development from the economic development of the country, the Vietnamese Government has therefore changed its governing philosophy of higher education (Overland, 2006). Decree No. 90/CP issued in 1993 stipulated that all people have the right to pursue higher education and thus led to a tide of massification of higher education in the country. For example, total higher education enrollment grew from 162,000 in 1993 to 1.3 million in 2003, while the number of higher education institutions has grown from 120 in early 1990s to 224 in 2004 (IIE, 2005, p. 5; Hayden & Lam, 2007, p. 74). Following up the massification of education, the Vietnamese Government has sought for the diversification of educational provision because it cannot solely bear the financial burden of an expanded tertiary education. Since the establishment of the first non-public university in 1988, non-public higher education has been continuously increasing its role and function in Vietnam's higher education system (Ngo, 2006, pp. 243–244). The entry to the WTO has further liberated the education market in Vietnam and private higher education is expanding in the country.

Reshuffling the monopolistic role of the state in educational provision, reforms in educational structure in China and Vietnam have made education a mixed economy of private and public consumption (Cheng, 1995; London, 2003). Both communist authorities have begun to realise that education is a sort of investment and an important structural component of socio-economic infrastructure in the knowledge-based economy. Realising depending upon the state alone would never satisfy the strong demands for education in the new socio-economic settings, the proliferation of education providers and diversification of education finance have become increasingly popular during the market transition (Loc, 2006; Chen & Li, 2002; Ngok & Kwong, 2003). Despite the ideological debates on whether education should be commercialised, the leaders in China and Vietnam have been pragmatic in allowing non-state sectors including the private sector and the market to provide education (Yang, 1997; Mok, 2000; Pham & Fry, 2002). As a result, education institutions at all levels are active in establishing collaborations with sectors from diverse backgrounds, involving the public and private sectors as well as overseas institutions. With the emergence of self-financing students and non-state education providers (including private and foreign ones), education in China and Vietnam has been undergoing the processes of marketisation and privatisation (Borevskaya, 2003; Mok, 2000; Ngok & Chan, 2003; Pham & Fry, 2002; London, 2003; IIE, 2005). The following part will examine how the Chinese and Vietnamese Governments have transformed the education sector by adopting far more pro-competition policy instruments in lines with privatisation and marketisation strategies.

CHANGES IN PRACTICES: PRIVATISATION AND MARKETISATION IN EDUCATION

The shifting of educational costs onto individual households

Despite the intentions to increase government's investment in education, the introduction of "fee-paying" principle in the last two decades has significantly directed the way social policy/social welfare is managed in these transitional economies. Departing from the socialist model in which education was a free public service solely provided by the state, the governments in China and Vietnam have significantly reduced their financial contributions to education. In China, for example, the state financial support to higher education had actually declined from 93.5% to 50% in 1990 to 2002 respectively (Chen, 2006). With the continual decline in the central government's allocations to education, educational financing and provision has been heavily relied upon the financial abilities of local govern-ments and individual contributions. Coinciding with "multiple channels" in financing, the state describes the use of a mixed economy of welfare as a "multiple-channel" (*duoqudao*) and "multi-method" (*duofangfa*) approach to the provision of educational services during the "primary state of socialism" (*shehui zhuyi chuji jieduan*), indicating a diffusion of responsibility from the state to society (Mok, 1996; Cheng, 1990). The introduction of a "fee-paying" principle has significantly affected higher education financing in China. Early in the 1980s, the plan for fee-charging students was regarded as "ultra-plan", implying that the in-take of these "self-supporting" students was beyond the state plan (Cheng, 1996). But after the endorsement of a socialist market economy in the CCP's Fourteenth Congress, the State Education Commission officially approved institutions of higher education admitting up to 25% students in the "commissioned training" or "fee-paying" categories in 1992. In 1993, 30 higher learning institutions were selected for a pilot study for a scheme known as "merging the rails", whereby students were admitted either because of public examination scores or because they were willing and able to pay a fee though their scores were lower than what was formally required. In 1994, more institutions entered the scheme and the fee-charging principle was thus legitimised (Cheng, 1996). The structural change in the financing of education in China is more obvious in higher education. Before the 1990s, the number of fee-paying students was only a very tiny group but it has been increasing since the adoption of the "user charge" principle. The percentage of fee-paying students of higher educational institutions in Shanghai increased from 7.5% in 1988 to 32.1% in 1994, showing a huge jump in "self-financing" students (Yuan & Wakabayashi, 1996).

Now, all university students have to pay tuition fees and the user-pays principle has been made the foundation of Chinese education. According to a recent report, the tuition fees in higher education have increased by 24 folds, jumping from an average tuition of 200 *yuan* per student in 1986 to about 6,000 *yuan* in 2006. Zhu Qingfang, a renounced sociologist who has been monitoring Chinese urban residents' consumption patterns, repeatedly reports the heavy financial burden for parents in financing children's education. More recently, at least one-third of the household consumption in urban China has been allocated to education, health insurance and housing. In 2004 alone, education expenditure constituted around 7.8% of the total expenditure of urban residents in China. Comparing the urban household educational expenditure of 2004 with that of 2000, it increased by 41%, with an annual growth rate of 9% in the last few years. In the last ten years, Chinese urban residents had paid around 2000 billion *yuan* to education ministries/departments at different levels (Zhu, 2005, p. 94). In urban Zhejiang, one of the most economically prosperous area in China, per capita education expenditure in year 2003 was around 802 *yuan*, increased by 4.2 times when compared to the figure of 1995 or an increase by 8.6% when compared to the figure of the previous year. Another study regarding education expenditure conducted by Zhejiang provincial government also suggests an ordinary urban household in the province had to spend around 10,398 *yuan* annually for children's education in 2005. Using the price of the year 2004, one source even suggests a cumulative sum of fees being paid to an ordinary Chinese student from kindergarten to university is around 14,000 *yuan* (Dai, 2005). One recent report even suggests that now a four-year bachelor's degree can carry a price tag of up to 60,000 *yuan*, this amount would take a farmer in some underdeveloped areas more than 30 years to generate (Li, 2007). Therefore, a number of university presidents and educationalists in China criticise the government for denying its responsibility in educational financing and has not kept its promise in its commitment in educational development (*Mingpao*, 8 March 2006).

In Vietnam, cost recovery has been implemented under the theme of "socialisation" of education. The term "socialisation" is directly translated from the Vietnamese term "*xa hoi hoa*", which has a meaning of mobilising the whole society to make contributions to the national education under the state guidance (Bui et al., 1999, citied in Loc, 2006). Under this principle, the introduction of tuition fees has been justified for cost recovery. Like China, the policy of fee-charging was first introduced in the higher education sector in 1987 by allowing higher education institution to admit free-paying students in excess of the centrally planned quota. Thereafter, the number of fee-payment students grew quickly. By 1999, the number of fee-paying students grew four times larger than the number of regular students (Ngo, 2006, p. 230). As for the school sector, school fee was introduced in 1989 and was applied to students in grade four and five in primary schools and all students in secondary schools. In 1993, the government decided to waive the tuition fee for primary attendance, but in return it increased the charge for secondary schools students. In addition to tuition fees, local governments also charge various compulsory payments, such as registration fee, contributions to school maintenance and renovation fund, contributions to school purchasing and so on, from students (London, 2003, p. 153; Bélanger & Liu, 2004, p. 27).

Since the introduction of fee-charging policy, household expenditures on education have significantly increased in Vietnam (Bray, 1996). In the early 1990s, individual households were responsible for 67% and 72% of the costs of lower and upper secondary education respectively, while household source accounted for around 50% of the costs of primary education. Nevertheless, the same figures in China were around 20% for secondary education and around 30% for primary education. These substantial contributions from individual households made household costs on education in Vietnam the second highest in Southeast Asia after Cambodia (Bray, 2002; Bélanger & Liu, 2004). Moreover, family expenditures on education have increased much more than those on other social services like healthcare and housing, hence adding tremendous financial pressures onto families for meeting children's education needs. According to the Vietnam Living Standard Surveys of 1992–93 and 1997–98 conducted by the World Bank, household expenditures on education increased from 2.7% of total household expenditures in 1993 to 6.4% in 1998, a 141% growth within five years, whereas the proportion of household expenditures on healthcare and housing recorded a decrease during the same period. As a consequence, the poorest households had to spend around 60% of their non-food budget on a child in lower secondary school, while upper secondary education became unaffordable to these families because the cost had exceeded their non-food annual budget. Even for the richest households, 30% of their non-food budget had to spend on education expenditure (Bélanger and Liu, 2004, p. 27). Despite the government's efforts for launching fee exemption schemes for children from families with difficult economic circumstances, the high tuition fees have remained as a major barrier discouraging children from poor families to attend schools (General Statistical Office, 2000).

The growing importance of the 'privateness' in education

The growing prominence of the "privateness" in education is another prominent feature captured in China's transitional economy. In late 1993, the *Program for Reform and the Development of China's Education* stipulated that the national policy was actively to encourage and support social institutions and citizens to establish schools according to laws and to provide right guidelines and strengthen administration (CCCCP, 1993). Article 25 of the *Education Law* promulgated in 1995 reconfirmed once again that the state would give full support to enterprises, social institutions, local communities and individuals to establish schools under the legal framework of the People's Republic of China (PRC) (SEC, 1995). In short, the state's attitude towards the development of non-state-run education can be summarised by the phrase "active encouragement, strong support, proper guidelines, and sound management" (*jiji guli, dali zhichi, zhengque yindao, jiaqiang guanli*). Under such a legal framework, coupled with the "decentralisation" policy context, educational providers have proliferated, particularly when the Chinese state in an effort to expand capacity encouraged all democratic parties, people bodies, social organisations, retired cadres and intellectuals, collective economic organisations and individuals subject to the Party and governmental policies, actively and voluntarily to contribute to developing education through various forms and methods (Wei & Zhang, 1995, p. 5).

In 2005, Hu Jin, Head of the Department of Education Planning and Development of the Ministry of Education, People's Republic of China (MOE), reported on current developments of private/*minban* higher education at a press conference, indicating that by the end of 2004, there were 1.4 million students enrolled in these institutions, which accounted for 10.4% of the national total, representing an increase of 3.16%.[3] According to Hu, approximately 1,300 private/*minban* higher education institutions had developed by 2004, of which 228 have received official authorisation to grant diplomas and 23 have been authorised to offer undergraduate degrees (China Education and Research Network, 2005). Another report suggests that of the 1,260 private/*minban* higher education institutions, 50 of them have become so-called "*wanren daxue*", meaning that each of them has enrolled over 10,000 students (Lin, 2006). Officials from the MOE also project that future higher education expansion will take place through the private/*minban* sector (China Education and Research Network, 2005). Despite the fact that the private/*minban* higher education sector remains small when compared to the large public sector, the private share of enrolments has been spectacular in terms of the growth rate especially when viewed in a socialist political context. Seen in this light, education provision has obviously been diversified in the post-Mao period, especially with the increase in the privateness and the popularity of these market initiatives in higher education governance (Lin, et al., 2005; Mok, 2005; Levy, 2006).

More importantly, the rise of private/*minban* sector in China's education has developed towards a hybrid of public and private. Two types of *minban* higher education, including second-tier colleges and transnational programmes jointly offered by Chinese and foreign partner, are typical examples of the public-private blurring. Second-tier colleges refer to the extension arm of public (national) universities, which are run as "self-financing" entities and operated in terms of "market" principles. Considering conventional *minban* colleges lacking "self-discipline" and posing difficulties for management, such kinds of publicly-owned but privately-run higher education institutions are established as alternatives for achieving the policy objectives of increasing the higher education enrolment rate (Lin, 2004; Lin et al., 2005; Shi et al., 2005). But, with their characteristics of fee-charging under the market mechanism, second-tier colleges also serve as revenue generating projects with a background of deceasing government financial support. It is against this wider policy context that these sorts of "quasi *minban*" institutions have become increasingly popular in China. By 2005, there were 344 second-tier colleges throughout China, enrolling 540,000 undergraduate students (Chen and Yu, 2005, p. 167).

Furthermore, China joined the World Trade Organisation (WTO) and subscribed to the GATS agreement. These actions represent the post-Mao leaders' recognition for by permitting competition in the market of ideas and knowledge products, which provides a framework to rationalise the global trade in knowledge (Altbach, 2004). This provides an ideological rationale for the rapid development of international public-private partnership of higher education, such as jointly offered academic programmes by local and foreign institutions, in China (Huang, 2005). In 2003, the government has issued the *Regulations of the People's Republic of China on Chinese-Foreign Cooperation in Running Schools*. This document not only provides details on governing transnational higher education, but also more importantly, allows overseas institutions of higher learning from making a profit from these joint programs (State Council, 2003). It is against such a policy context that developing international public-private partnerships in running higher education programmes has become increasingly popular in China. By 2004, there were 745 joint programmes provided in Chinese institutions in collaboration with overseas partners. As the higher education sector in China is still dominated by public sector in term of provision, most of local providers are public universities, thereby representing a growing trend of private-public partnerships in higher education provision in China (MOE, 2006).

The emergence of private education in Vietnam began at pre-primary level in the 1990s. The Ministry of Education and Training's Decision No. 124 stated to "guide, manage, and encourage the foundation of self-financing preschool" (cited in London, 2003, p. 151). Later in 1993, the state in its Resolution 90 further introduced a set of rules to allow the establishment of "non-public" schools, including "semi-public" (*ban cong*) and "people-founded" (*dan lap*). According to available data, 5% of lower secondary students, 50% of kindergarten students, 34% of upper secondary students, and 11% of tertiary students studied in non-public schools in 2001 (Loc, 2006). Currently, non-public education institutions include three types, namely "semi-public" (*ban cong*), which refers to those owned by the state but managed by public authorities at various levels and operated upon the cost from tuition fees; "people-founded" (*dan lap*), which means that the institutions are owned and managed by non-government organisation or private associations and operated upon the cost from tuition fees; and "private" (*tu lap*), which are owned and managed by private individuals (IIE, 2005, p. 8).

As for higher education sector, Thang Long University is the first non-public university in Vietnam and was established as an experiment in 1988. Although the operation of the University met many difficulties, its establishment represents the beginning of privatisation, marketisation and commercialisation of higher education in Vietnam. After the experiment on Thang Long University, a number of non-public universities have been established (Hoang and Sloper, 1995; Pham and Fry, 2002). At present, non-public education has occupied a significant proportion in higher education sector. In 2004, there were 137,122 students enrolled in non-public institutions, which accounted for 15.3% of the national total.

In terms of the numbers of institutions, there were 224 higher education institutions, among which 24 were non-public institutions, and 7 and 17 were semi-public and people-founded respectively (Ngo, 2006, p. 243). According to the Higher Education Reform Agenda (HERA) issued by Ministry of Education and Training (MOET), the non-public higher education sector should further expand in order to enrol 40% of the total number of tertiary students by 2020 (Hayden & Lam, 2007, p. 79).

In addition, the Vietnamese government has started to open the door to outside education providers. As discussed earlier, rejoining the regional and international market is critically important for the development of transnational education in Vietnam. For instance, Vietnam re-established a normal diplomatic relation with the US in 1997. Thereafter, bilateral trade between the two countries has continuously grown. Today, the US is one of Vietnam's largest trading partners and English becomes increasingly important in the country. In many universities, English is the most popular choice for the students in their selection of learning a foreign language. Meanwhile, privately run language schools have become popular throughout the country and a number of overseas investors have actively started and run English-language institutes to meet the pressing needs for learning English (Overland, 2006). Indeed, foreign education programs run either by foreign institutions or through cooperation between overseas and local institutions have been expanding quickly. For example, the University of Hawaii provides MBA program in partnership with Hanoi School of Business; Washington State University provides MBA program with the National Economics University; University of Houston, Clear Lake offers undergraduate degrees with the Hanoi University of Technology; Troy State University offers undergraduate degree in collaboration with the International College of Information Technology and Management (IIE, 2005, p. 18). The establishment of the Royal Melbourne Institute of Technology in 2001 was a milestone of the emergence of private and foreign sector in education. The Institute is the first wholly foreign-owned degree awarding institution in Vietnam. Its programs include information technology, engineering and business (Overland, 2006). Recognising the proliferation of foreign education, the Vietnamese Government promulgated Decree No. 06/2000/ND-CP in 2000 in order to provide a regulatory framework and also incentive for foreign investment in education and training, whereas in 2001 the government has regulated the entry of foreign education programs into the local market by requiring that only those existing institution with license in their home countries can apply for launching program in Vietnam (IIE, 2005, p. 18). After joining the WTO, the Vietnamese Government has begun to change its laws in allowing overseas institutions to run education for making profit notwithstanding the unfinished debates on the nature of education as public or private goods. It is against this new policy context that more for-profit education institutions have emerged in Vietnam to offer transnational education programmes (Pham, 2006; Ashwill, 2006).

Up to this point, we have discussed how education has privatised and marketised in China and Vietnam. Such transformations are not without problems, especially when we critically examine the social and political consequences of these changes during the market transition in China and Vietnam. The rapid quantity growth in education has resulted in the problems of quality assurance, while the reliance upon market forces in meeting people's educational needs has also intensified the inequalities in education in these Asian economies. The intensified inequalities in education have clearly shown the private-public tension in education provision and financing. Let us now turn to examine these major challenges resulting from the privatisation and marketisation of education in China and Vietnam.

CHALLENGES FOR PRIVATISING/MARKETISING EDUCATION

Unresolved debates on the private and public nature of education

Despite the fact that the Chinese and Vietnamese Governments have joined the WTO and have tried to honour their commitments in following the principles of GATS, we have witnessed the unresolved debates on the public and private nature of education. Comparing the development of private education in China with that of Vietnam, we can argue that China has been at a more advanced stage of development especially when the private/*minban* education has evolved since the mid-1980s (Mok, 2000). It is particularly true when comparing the legal foundation for private education of these countries, which has shown China, has a more established foundation for private/*minban* education. For example, the *Law of the People's Republic of China on Promotion of Privately-run Schools* promulgated in 2002 has provided a legal framework on private education in China (Ministry of Education, 2002). The breakthrough in the document is that of allowing education investor to make profit through provision of private/*minban* education. In addition, as mentioned earlier, the *Regulations of the People's Republic of China on Chinese-Foreign Cooperation in Running Schools* promulgated in 2003 also gives the green light to the profit-making in the collaboration between local and foreign institutions (Ministry of Education, 2003). Nonetheless, our recent research on private/*minban* education in China has indicated that the education market in China is a 'governed market', whereby the market is highly regulated by the state. The growing prominence of second-tier/affiliated colleges run on a self-financing principle has shown how the Chinese government has attempted to create its own education market to constrain the development of the conventional private/*minban* education institutions because the ministry of education has the final decisions regarding the academic qualifications of the programmes offered by the conventional private/*minban* institutions, as well as determining the profit level for the private/*minban* colleges (Mok & Ngok, 2008).

In contrast, in Vietnam, even though the *Education Law* in 2005 has provided a general legal basis for the governance of non-public education sector, it did not end the debate on the profit-making issues in education. Article 66 of the document states that people-founded and private education institutions have financial autonomy and allows the investors to divide the profits according to their capital contribution, whereas Article 20 states that "making use of education activities for profit is forbidden" (cited in Hayden and Lam, 2007, p. 77). Indeed, practically investors of private education institutions in Vietnam might keep the profit, while technically their investment is considered as a donation to the public good because non-public university also belongs to "the people." This becomes a factor restricting private investment on education in Vietnam (Overland, 2006a). Despite that the MOET has recently issued two provisional regulations on governing non-public education, relevant legal framework is criticised as "not yet well-developed" and private university is run without transparency and accountability (Ngoc and Ashwill, 2004; Ngo, 2006). Yet, it is recognised that previously the responsibilities of individual institutions and their relationship with the state were defined on a case-by-case basis. The ambiguity of the situations provides space for individual institutions to exercise autonomy (Ngo, 2006). Perhaps, the Vietnamese authorities intend to reserve the grey areas in order to provide more space for the survival of private education institutions, as many of them claim that they are operating in an extremely difficult situation (Overland, 2006; Overland, 2006a). Despite the unresolved tensions whether education is a private or a public goods, the Vietnamese Government has recently amended its laws to allow institutions to run for-profit education since Vietnam as one of the WTO members has to honour the regulations of GATS. Putting these observations together, although there have been newly enacted laws governing private education in China and Vietnam the actual implementation of the policies has shown the unresolved tensions whether institutions could make profits for running education and the unfinished ideological debates on whether education is a public or private goods.

Unresolved dilemma between quantity and quality

The rapid expansion of education by means of privatisation and marketisation has raised the concerns for quality assurance. It is beyond doubt that both China and Vietnam have experienced great economic success through the adoption of market reforms and continuous integration with the global economy. For example, China recorded a double-digit economic growth (estimated at 10.7%) in 2006, while Vietnam also achieved a high GDP growth rate (estimated at 8.2%) (CIA, 2007). The economic growth has generated an increase of both public and private expenditure on education, especially when education is seen as a sort of investment on human capital (OECD, 1998), which has been shown by the growth of enrollment rate at various levels in these two countries (UNESCO Institutes for Statistics, 2007). Despite the growth in quantity, there have been concerns raised about the assurance of educational quality with the rapid increase in enrollments through the means of privatising and marketising education. For example, the number of university students rose 3.96 times from 1993 to 2002 but the number of teachers only rose only 1.47 times in Vietnam during the same period. This makes the ratio of teacher students reaches to 1/29, one of the highest in the world, indicating an insufficient supply of teachers catering for the increase of student enrolments (Pham & Fry, 2002, p. 138). In addition to the shortage of teaching staff, the qualification of teaching is concerned as well. Despite the fact that English is becoming more popular and commonly taught in Vietnam's universities now, many university teachers do not speak the language but are forced to adopt English as a medium of instruction (Overland, 2006). Similarly in China, many *minban* education institutions tend to employ more part-time and retired faculty members and therefore it is difficult to assure the quality of teaching. This is particularly true because there is not yet a well-developed quality assurance system of teaching in China and Vietnam (Chan, 2007).

Nevertheless, if we look at the top tier part of the education sectors, we can recognise the differences between the two countries. In China, the government has shown its intention of building world class universities and offer generous financial support to those selected institutions. For example, from 1996 to 2000, more than 10 billion *yuan* was invested onto 99 universities under the "211 project" and the two key universities, Peking University and Tsinghua University were granted 1.8 billion *yuan* of extra budget under the "985 scheme" in 1999 (Ngok and Guo, 2007, p. 31). These have substantially shown China's ambition of and commitment to developing world-class universities in the country. In Vietnam, two national universities, namely Vietnam Nation University in Hanoi and Vietnam Nation University in Ho Chi Minh City, are granted ministerial-level status and significant financial and administrative autonomy from the MOET (Hayden & Lam, 2007). We can expect that their leading role is similar to that of Peking University and Tsinghua University in China in order to build a top-tier international university in Vietnam. In addition, Vietnam has recently started to establish collaborations with other countries such as Singapore and the US, on education (*The Straits Times*, 26 April 2007; Cathcart, 2006). However, according to a recent article published in *the Chronicle of Higher Education*, Vietnam's higher education system is "20s, even 30 years, out of date... the country does not have a single university considered to be international quality. It lacks a credible research environment, produces few PhDs and is locked in Soviet-style pedagogy" (Overland, 2006). Indeed, when we recognise that the Royal Melbourne Institute of Technology, the only foreign-owned universities in Vietnam, are requested to teach Ho Chi Minh thought and "Scientific Socialism" but University of Nottingham Ningbo China adopts programmes entirely the same with those in the Nottingham UK, we might be able to identify the differences between the two countries in terms of their levels of internationalisation and academic standards (Overland, 2006; University of Nottingham Ningbo China, 2007).

Unresolved tensions between efficiency and equality in education

The making use of market forces in education has brought improvements to education in China and Vietnam. By examining the recent statistics regarding the improved literary level and enrolment rate of these socialist countries, the UNESCO has recently remarked that China and Vietnam have made significant achievements in raising the education standards, with school education is achieving universal, higher education is developing toward mass education (UNESCO Institutes for Statistics, 2007). However, these achievements are not evenly shared among different social groups and geographical regions in these Asian economies.

Unsurprisingly, rich households and regions enjoy larger improvements than poor households and regions do, hence having widened social inequalities in these two socialist counties. Indeed, inequality between rich and poor as well as urban and rural has become one of the most challenging problems in the growing prominence of the privateness in China's education (Mok & Lo, 2007).

Realising the educational inequalities have become intensified, both the Chinese and Vietnamese governments recognise the importance of providing basic education to the citizens, hence, the school education sector has attracted relatively more state funding than that of higher education. In China, with a continual increase in state funding to elementary education in recent years, the net enrolment rate of primary school children grew up to 99% in 2005, while the gross enrollment rate of junior secondary schools reached 95% (China Education and Research Network, 2006). Since the promulgation of the *Compulsory Education Law* in 1986, the nine-year compulsory education has been implemented. Given that primary and secondary have been universalised in many urban areas and economically developed coastal areas, the Chinese government has allocated extra resources to create more educational opportunities in rural areas during the 10th Five Year Plan (2001–2005). In late 2005, the State Council decided to further reform the funding system of school education in rural areas, with the nine-year compulsory education funded by the general public finances (China Education and Research Network, 2006). Among the various tasks in the 11th Five Year Plan (2006–2010), the consolidation of nine-year compulsory education in rural areas has been given high priority with the implementation of the "Two Basics" project to universalise nine-year compulsory education and to eradicate illiteracy among the middle and young aged groups in the western part of China. Regarding educational finances, the government decided to waive all the tuition and miscellaneous fees of students from rural areas of western China in 2006 in order to release parents' from heavy burden of educational expenses. It is anticipated that the same policy will be introduced to the central and eastern parts of the country in 2007 (China Education and Research Network, 2006). However, it is realised that those disadvantaged groups such as new urban immigrants in China are still being neglected and discriminated in the current education system. Being regarded as temporary immigrants or 'floating population', these new urban immigrants cannot obtain the similar social status as their urban counterparts because they are still classified as rural citizens without an urban household registration. Although some local schools in cities accept these temporary migrant children, their parents have to pay for the education endorsement fee (*jiaoyu zanzhu fei*), which is considerably high (Cao, 1997).

In Vietnam, the government has addressed the increasing burden of higher education financing that parents and individuals have experienced since 1989. In response to the high fee problems, the government has introduced several national programs to exempt poor household from paying tuition fee. Eligibility was based on a poverty line set by the state. But, the programs were less than effective owing to the extremely harsh conditions in poor rural areas. Therefore, the government has turned to poverty reduction in order to narrow down the regional disparity. In

1993, the Ministry of Labour, Invalids, and Social Affairs (MOLISA) set national poverty lines in aid of the poor communities and households. During the Eighth Party Congress in 1996, the Vietnamese authorities have decided to secure the free access to basic education for the poor people by including this policy into the outline of objectives of hunger eradication and poverty reduction. The programs aim to erase illiteracy by exempting or reducing school fees as well as providing grant and scholarships to students from poor rural families. As reported in 1999, the MOET had committed over 834 billion *dong* over three years, an amount equal to about 2% of the annual education budget during the period. By the end of 1998, the government established 6,958 hunger eradication and poverty reduction boards at commune level in order to assure local authorities would follow the criteria set by the central government in mapping the poverty households. However, these programs only benefited those families fall into the low-income group. And, the poverty-line set was criticised to be too low. Moreover, the exemption can partially help students from poor families only. Their families still need to bear other expenditure on education, such as living cost, transport and so on, which are heavy burden to those families in harsh living conditions (London, 2003, p. 166–168). Indeed, although enrolment rate has significantly increased in the last decade, the drop-out rate is also alarming. A study on schooling in Vietnam indicates that the higher cost of secondary education compared to primary education is one of the reasons for explaining the considerately high drop-out rate. The study also points out that dropping out as an interruption to schooling would seriously jeopardise the progression from primary education to lower secondary education (Bélanger & Liu, 2004, p. 36-37). In short, despite the effort by the central government in China and Vietnam, inequality of access to education is still a significant problem in the two countries.

Furthermore, when looking at the issue on educational inequality within the context of cultural value, it is clear that the influence of the traditional Confucianism with emphasis on learning and stressing the importance of a willingness to exert effort to master school work is becoming increasingly popular among Asian parents (Cummings, 1996). The positive impact of such a traditional value has certainly reinforced people to look for better education and created a conducive environment for the rise of private education. Nonetheless, the same cultural values would also disadvantage those who are unable to pay for private education, especially when increasing pressure is placed on parents to give their children the best education despite the overwhelming financial burdens. For wealthy families, they are free to send their children for after school classes and activities without financial constraints. However, it is very difficult for families from relatively poor socio-economic backgrounds to pay a few thousands *yuan* in China or a few hundreds US dollars in Vietnam per year on after-school education for their children. Given that results of these extracurricular activities would increasingly affect the formal education of children as well as their career development, the growing prominence of after-school education, as a sort of commercialisation of education, has made the whole education systems more competitive. More sociologically important of all, this is a problem about how to address the contradictions between rapid economic growth and the intensified social inequality/ regional disparity. From a political perspective, it is about the ideological dilemma between socialism and capitalism. How to resolve the unresolved tensions between educational efficiency and equality is becoming an increasingly important political challenge confronting both the Chinese and Vietnamese governments.

CONCLUSION: BRINGING THE 'PUBLIC' BACK IN EDUCATION?

Our above discussion has shown that the communist authorities in China and Vietnam have recognised the importance of being committed to developing education in order to catch up with other developed economies. Nonetheless, government investment on education had only occupied 2.3% of GNP in China, while the figure in Vietnam was 2.7% in the mid-1990s. Such state investments in education were considerately low when comparing to the average investment rate of other countries in East Asia (3%) or other less developed regions such as in Africa (5.6%), Latin America (4.5%) and South Asia (4.3%). Nevertheless, observers forecasted that the proportion should be raised in China (Bray, 2002, p. 6–8). Realising the low level of state's educational investment, the State Council of the People's Republic of China has most recently decided to increase government funding to education. It is against this context that the 11th Five Year Programme Guidelines on Education (2006–2010) calls on governments at all levels to make the development of education a strategic priority and "to commit to a public education system that can be accessed by all" (cited in Li, 2007). Conversely, despite the fact that the Vietnamese government has shown its intention to further develop education, it substantially charges more for educational services and has led to an open debate in the National Assembly and the media (Luong, 2006, p. 151).

In addition, we have discussed how both the Chinese and Vietnamese governments have introduced new policy measures to help citizens who come from lower socio-economic background to get access to education; the success of these new policies depends heavily upon how the local governments have genuinely implemented the policies issued by the central government. In China, the attempts to de-privatise and de-marketise education governance reflect the Hu-Wen administration's determination to rectify the mistakes resulting from the quest for 'GDPism'. But whether the senior Chinese leaders would have the capacity to implement the proposed changes and turn the heavily market-driven social policy paradigm deeply embedded in the post-Mao era into a more humanistic approach is still subject to question. In this connection, de-privatisation and de-marketisation is less a matter of reversal-cum-reconstruction in the context of new thinking about the limits to privatisation and marketisation strategies, but more an exercise in 'damage control' by which private and para-state organisations operating in the market are subject to new forms of regulation and some direct measures of subsidy are introduced to address the plight of the very poor However, heightened public investment in the rural and non-coastal areas is introducing a potentially contradictory 'dual-track' system in which marketisation may only be delayed: the incentives and legal framework for marketisation will likely see the private sector grow in these parts of the country, just as it did in the coastal regions, as more funds are injected into the system (Painter & Mok, 2007).

Similarly, the attempts to reduce the pace of the marketisation of education in Vietnam have not been able to stop the momentum, especially after Vietnam has entered the WTO. With the increase of the involvement of the overseas partners, the education market has expanded rather than contracted. In this regard, I would argue the fundamentals have not significantly altered even when both governments have taken initiatives to reverse the privatisation and marketisation in education. We should not underestimate the tensions between different levels of governments, with a diversity of stakeholders competing for their vested interests in a privatised and marketised education context. It is clear that the present Chinese and Vietnamese authorities have tried to address the tensions and contradictions between rapid economic growth and worsening social inequalities. However, in the case of education, we have argued that any attempted reversal from the market-driven approach to a more state-centred, welfare-based approach would exceed the capacities of the state. Tensions and contradictions in education policy provide just one case among many others in contemporary China and Vietnam of a core political dilemma: how to uphold socialist ideologies in a neo-liberal policy setting, in order to preserve the legitimacy of the ruling political parties.

In conclusion, we have discussed how the education governance in China and Vietnam has been challenged by the growing pressures of globalisation. We have also critically examined some major governance challenges and policy implications when higher education is becoming increasingly privatised and marketised. The present comparative study has clearly shown how the two selected transitional economies in Asia have struggled to cope with the challenges of global capitalism. The adoption of far more pro-competition and market-oriented strategies in reforming higher education sectors in China and Vietnam has brought about negative social costs of privatisation. As being socialist countries, the governments in China and Vietnam have to properly and appropriately tackle the intensified tensions between global capitalism and socialist ideals.

NOTES

[1] This chapter is a revised version of the article published in *Policy Futures in Education, 6*(5).

[2] Being a socialist transitional economy, Vietnam has been experiencing significant social, economic and political changes when the present regime has decided to adopt an open door policy in engaging in market-oriented reforms. Following the model of China, Vietnam has started economic reforms and people's livelihood has improved significantly. After experiencing the economic success resulting from opening up to the global market place, the Vietnamese government has chosen to become one of the WTO members notwithstanding with the heated debates about the pros and cons for getting the entry of WTO. Being a WTO member, Vietnam is then subject to the regulations of the organisation and has to honour the GATS in opening up its higher education sector.

[3] Since China is still a socialist country, the notion of private education is not politically acceptable. It is against this socio-political context that schools that are run and financed by non-state sectors or actors are named as "*minban*" education or "people-run" schools in order to avoid the controversy in

Chinese politics. With the *minban* labels, we can easily find education provision has proliferated and funding sources diversified in China today. For details, see Mok and Ngok (2008).

REFERENCES

Altbach, P. G. (2004). Globalisation and the university: Myths and realities in an unequal world. *Tertiary Education and Management, 10*, 3–25.

Ashwill, M. A. (2006). *US institutions and fertile ground in Vietnam's expanding higher education market.* Paper presented at the International Forum on 'WTO Entry and Vietnam Higher Education Reform, 11–12 December 2006, Hanoi, Vietnam.

Banh, T. L. (2006). *State management reform for Vietnam higher education.* Paper presented at the International Forum on 'WTO Entry and Vietnam Higher Education Reform, 11–12 December 2006, Hanoi, Vietnam.

Bélanger, D., & Liu, J. (2004). Social policy reforms and daughters' schooling in Vietnam. *International Journal of Educational Development, 24*, 23–38.

Borevskaya, N. (2003). The private sector in the Chinese educational system: Problem and prospects. *Far Eastern Affairs, 31*(4), 89–107.

Bray, M. (1996). *Counting the full cost parental and community financing of education in East Asia.* Washington, DC: The World Bank.

Bray, M. (2002). *The costs and financing of education: Trends and policy implications.* Manila and Hong Kong: Asian Development Bank and Comparative Education Research Centre, the University of Hong Kong.

Cai, B. K. (2005). China's peaceful development and relations with East Asian neighbours. In S. H. Saw et al. (Eds.), *ASEAN-China relations: Realities and prospects.* Singapore: Institute of Southeast Asian Studies.

Cao, H. (1997). Where to put their school desks? *China New Digest, 315*, 3–6.

Cathcart, M. (2006). Asia's Possibilities. *Connection*, Fall, 13.

Central Committee of the Chinese Communist Party [CCCCP]. (1985). *The decision of the central committee of the communist party of China on the reform of educational structure.* Beijing: People's Press.

Central Committee of the Chinese Communist Party [CCCCP]. (1993). The programme for educational reform and development in China. *Zhonghua Renmin Gongheguo Guowuyuan Gongbao, 2*, 58–66.

Central Intelligence Agency, US [CIA]. (2007). *The world factbook.* Retrieved from https://www.cia.gov/library/publications/the-world-factbook/index.html.

Chan, D. (2007). The impact of globalisation on the educational developments in China: Policy and challenges. In J. Y. S. Cheng (Ed.), *Challenges and policy programmes of China's new leadership.* Hong Kong: City University of Hong Kong Press.

Chen, B., & Li, G. (2002). Minban gaodeng jiaoyu ziketiqu yanjiu baogao (The research report on people-run higher education). In B. Chen & G. Li (Eds.), *Minban Jiaoyu de Gaige yu Fazhan (Minban reform and development of people-run education).* Beijing: Jiaoyu Kexue Chubanshe.

Chen, C. G., & Yu, Q. Y. (2005). *Zoujin Dazhonghua: 21 Shijichu Guangzhou Shi Gaodeng Jiaoyu Fazhan Yanjiu (Towards Massification: Research on Guangzhou's Higher Education Development in Early 21st Century).* Guangzhou: Jinan daxue chubanshe.

Chen, X. (2006). *High-risk enterprises: Will universities go bankrupt.* Retrieved from www.dajun.com.cn/daxuepc.htm.

Cheung, A. B. L., & Scott, I. (Eds.). (2003). *Governance and public sector reform in Asia.* London and New York: RoutledgeCurzon.

Cheng, K. M. (1990). Financing education in mainland China: What are the real problems? *Issues and Studies, 3*, 54–75.

Cheng, K. M. (1995). Education – decentralisation and the market. In L. Wong & S. MacPherson (Eds.), *Social change and social policy in contemporary China.* Aldershot: Avebury.

Cheng, K. M. (1996). Markets in a socialist system: Reform of higher education. In K. Watson, S. Modgil, & C. Modgil (Eds.), *Educational dilemmas: Debate and diversity*. London: Cassell.

China Education and Research Network. (2005). Retrieved from www.edu.cn/20050301/3129836.shtml.

Cook, S. (2002). From rice bowl to safetynet: Insecurity and social protection during China's transition. *Development Policy Review, 20*(5), 615–635.

Cummings, W. (1996). Asian values, education and development. *Compare, 26*(3), 287–304.

Dai, J. L. (2005). Resident's life: Moving towards the society of overall well –to-do level. In B. Ren (Ed.), *2005 blue book of Zhejiang*. Hangzhou: Hangzhou Publishing House.

General Statistical Office. (2000). *Vietnam living standards survey 1997–1998*. Hanoi: Statistical Publishing House.

Gouri, G., Shankar, T. K., Reddy, Y. V., & Shams, K. (1991). Imperatives and perspectives. In G. Gouri (Ed.), *Privatisation and public enterprise*. New Delhi: Oxford and IBH Publishing.

Guan, X. P. (2001). China's social policy in the context of globalisation. In Social Policy Research Centre, Hong Kong Polytechnic University (Ed.), *Repositioning of the state: Challenges and experiences of social policy in the Asia pacific region*. Hong Kong: Joint Publishing Co. Ltd.

Hawkins, J. N. (2000). Centralisation, decentralisation, recentralisation: Educational reform in China. *Journal of Educational Administration, 38*(5), 442–454.

Hayden, M., & Lam, Q. T. (2007). Institutional autonomy for higher education in Vietnam. *Higher Education Research & Development, 26*(1), 73–85.

Hoang, X. S., & Sloper, D. (1995). An entrepreneurial development: Thang Long University. In D. Sloper (Ed.), *Higher education in Vietnam: Change and response*. New York: St. Martin's Press.

Huang, F. T. (2005). Qualitative enhancement and quantitative growth: Changes and trends of China's higher education. *Higher Education Policy, 18*, 117–130.

Institute of International Education [IIE]. (2005). *Higher education in Vietnam update – May 2004*. Hanoi: Institute of International Education.

Leung, J. C. B. (1994). Dismantling the 'iron rice bowl': Welfare reforms in the people's republic of China. *Journal of Social Policy, 23*(3), 341–61.

Levy, D. (2006). *New private realities in Chinese higher education*. Retrieved from www.albany.edu/dept/eaps/prophe/publication/News/SummaryAsia.

Li, R. (2007, January 27). Casualties of the rush to profit from schooling. *South China Morning Post*.

Lin, J. (2004). China: Private trends. *International Higher Education, 36*, 17–18.

Lin, J. (2006). *Private universities in China: Expansion and challenges*. Paper presented at the AAS annual meeting, 6–9 April, Marriott, San Francisco.

Lin, J., Zhang, Y., Gao, L., & Liu, Y. (2005). Trust, ownership, and autonomy: Challenges facing private higher education in China. *The China Review, 5*(1), 61–82.

Liu, X. C. (2005). Strengthening ASEAN-China cooperation in the ASEAN regional forum. In S. H. Saw et al. (Eds.), *ASEAN-China relations: Realities and prospects*. Singapore: Institute of Southeast Asian Studies.

Loc, N. (2006). *Viet Nam's education in the transitional period*. Retrieved from www. apecknowledgebank.org/resources/downloads/06_hrdwg1_057.pdf.

London, J. D. (2003). Vietnam's mass education and health systems: A regimes perspective. *American Asian Review, 21*(2), 125–158.

Luong, H. V. (2006). Vietnam in 2005: Economic momentum and stronger state-society dialogue. *Asian Survey, 46*(1), 148–154.

Mingpao. (2006, March 8).

Ministry of Education, China [MOE]. (2006). *List of Chinese-foreign cooperation in running schools programmes*. Retrieved from www.jsj.edu.cn/mingdan/002.html.

Mok, K. H. (1996). Marketisation and decentralisation: Development of education and paradigm shift in social policy. *Hong Kong Public Administration, 5*(1), 35–56.

Mok, K. H. (2000). Marketizing higher education in post-Mao China. *International Journal of Educational Development, 20*, 109–126.

Mok, K. H. (2005). Riding over socialism and global capitalism: Changing education governance and social policy paradigms in post-Mao China. *Comparative Education*, *41*(2), 217–242.

Mok, K. H., & Lo, Y. W. (2007). Embracing the market: The impacts of neo-liberalism on China's higher education. *Journal for Critical Education Policy Studies*, *5*(1).

Mok, K. H., & Ngok, K. L. (2008). One country, diverse systems: Politics of educational decentralisation and challenges for regulatory state in post-Mao China. *China Review*, *8*(2), 169-199.

Mok, K. H., & Forrest, R. (Eds.). (2008). *Changing governance and public policy in East Asia.* London: Routledge.

Ngo, D. D. (2006). Viet Nam. In *Higher education in South-East Asia.* Bangkok: UNESCO Asia and Pacific Regional Bureau for Education.

Ngoc, M. L., & Ashwill, M. A. (2004). A look at non-public higher education in Vietnam. *International Higher Education*, *36*(Summer), 16–17.

Ngok, K. L., & Chan, K. K. D. (2003). Towards centralisation and decentralisation in educational development in China: The case of Shanghai. In K. H. Mok (Ed.), *Centralisation and decentralisation: Educational reforms and changing governance in Chinese societies.* Hong Kong: Comparative Education Research Centre, University of Hong Kong.

Ngok, K. L., & Guo, W. Q. (2007). The quest for world class universities in Cjhina: Critical reflections. *Journal of Comparative Asian Development*, *6*(1), 21–44.

Ngok, K. L., & Kwong, J. (2003). Globalisation and educational restructuring in China. In K. H. Mok & A. Welch (Eds.), *Globalisation and educational restructuring in the Asia Pacific region.* Basingstoke: Palgrave Macmillan.

Nguyen, D. Q., & Sloper, D. (1995). Socio-economic background of Vietnam since 1986: Impact on education and higher education. In D. Sloper (Ed.) *Higher education in Vietnam: Change and response.* New York: St. Martin's Press.

Organisation for Economic Co-operation and Development [OECD]. (1998). *Human capital investment: An international comparison.* Paris: Centre for Education Research and Innovation, Organisation for Economic Co-operation and Development.

Overland, M. A. (2006). Higher education lags behind the times in Vietnam: Outdated thinking in the classroom hampers the country's reform efforts. *The Chronicle of Higher Education*, *52*(4), 37.

Overland, M. A. (2006a). Higher education lags behind the times in Vietnam: Outdated thinking in the classroom hampers the country's reform efforts. *The Chronicle of Higher Education*, *52*(4), 36.

Painter, M., & Mok, K. H. (2007). *Reasserting the public in public service delivery in China: The de-privatisation and de-marketisation of education?* Paper presented at the international conference on the Role of the State in Public Service Delivery, 27–28 September 2007, Lee Kuan Yee School of Public Policy, National University of Singapore, Singapore.

Pham, L. H., & Fry, G. W. (2002). The emergence of private higher education in Vietnam: Challenges and opportunities. *Education Research for Policy and Practice*, *1*, 127–141.

Pham, D. N. T. (2006). *WTO/GATS Implications and Vietnam higher education development.* Paper presented at the International Forum on 'WTO Entry and Vietnam Higher Education Reform, 11–12 December 2006, Hanoi, Vietnam.

Peters, G. (1995). *The future of governing.* Lawrence, KN: University Press of Kansas.

Pierre, J. (Ed.). (2000). *Debating governance.* Oxford: Oxford University Press.

Saich, T. (2004). *Politics and governance in China.* Basingstoke: Macmillan.

Salamon, L. M. (Ed.). (2002). *The tools of government: A guide to the new governance.* Oxford: Oxford University Press.

Shi, Q. H., et al. (2005). *Affiliated colleges and private education development in China: Take independent colleges as an example.* Retrieved from www.ocair.org/files/presentations/Paper2003_04/forum2004/ChinaHE.pdf.

So, A. (2003). Introduction: Rethinking the Chinese developmental miracle. In A. So (Ed.), *China's developmental miracle: Origins, transformations, and challenges.* Armonk, NY: M.E. Sharpe.

State Council. (2003). *Regulations of the people's republic of China on Chinese-Foreign cooperation in running schools*. Beijing: State Council.

State Education Commission [SEC]. (1995). *Education law*. Beijing: State Education Commission.

The Straits Times. (2007, April 26);

UNESCO Institutes for Statistics. (2007). *Data centre*. Retrieved from http://stats.uis.unesco.org/unesco/TableViewer/document.aspx?ReportId=143&IF_Language=eng

University of Nottingham Ningbo China. (2007). *The University's website*. Retrieved from http://www.nottingham.edu.cn/index.php

Wei, Y. T., & Zhang, G. C. (1995). *A historical perspective on non-governmental higher education in China*. paper presented to the international conference on Private Education in Asia and the Pacific Region, University of Xiamen, Xiamen.

Wong, L., & Flynn, N. (Eds.). (2001). *The market in Chinese social policy*. Basingstoke: Palgrave.

Wong, L., White, L., & Gui, X. S. (2004). *Social policy reform in Hong Kong and Shanghai*. Armonk, NY: M.E. Sharpe.

World Bank. (1995). *Higher education: The lessons of experience*. Washington, DC: The World Bank.

Yang, R. (1997). The debate on private higher education development in China. *International Higher Education*, Fall, 1–4.

Yang, R. (2002). *The third delight: Internationalisation of higher education in China*. London: Routledge.

Yuan, Z. G., & Wakabayashi, M. (1996). Chinese higher education reform from the 'state model' to the 'social model': Based on a Sino-Japan comparative perspective. *Forum of International Development Studies*, 6, 173–200.

Zhu, Q. F. (2005). Social and economic indicators: Analysis and assessment. In X. Yu, et al. (Eds.), *Analysis and forecast on China's social development 2006*. Beijing: Social Sciences Academic Press.

FURTHER READINGS

Chan, C. K., Ngok, K. L., & Philips, D. (2008). Education policy. In *Social Policy in China: Development and Well-being*. Bristol: Policy Press.

Hayden, M., & Lam, Q. T. (2007). Institutional autonomy for higher education in Vietnam. *Higher Education Research & Development*, 26(1), 73–85.

Levy, D. (2006). New private realities in Chinese higher education. Retrieved from www.albany.edu/dept/eaps/prophe/publication/News/SummaryAsia.

London, J. D. (2003). Vietnam's mass education and health systems: A regimes perspective. *American Asian Review*, 21(2), 125–158.

Mok, K. H. (2007). Local responses to a global agenda: Changing state-education relations in Mainland China. In, W. F. Tang & B. Holzner (Eds.), *Social change in contemporary China*, Pittsburgh, PA: University of Pittsburgh Press.

Pham, D. N. T. (2006). *WTO/GATS Implications and Vietnam higher education development*. Paper presented at the international forum on WTO Entry and Vietnam Higher Education Reform, 11-12 December 2006, Hanoi, Vietnam.

Ka Ho Mok
Faculty of Social Sciences
The University of Hong Kong, Hong Kong

MAREK KWIEK

GLOBALISATION

Re-Reading its Impact on the Nation-State, the University, and Educational Policies in Europe

INTRODUCTION

The paper re-reads the complex and changing relationships between the university and the nation-state, and between national and supranational (EU-level) educational policies in Europe.[1] It is focusing on long-term consequences of globalisation-related pressures on European nation-states with respect to national educational policies. It assesses the indirect impact of globalisation on European universities (via reformulating the role of the nation-state in the global economy), and a direct impact of Europeanisation – as a regional response to globalisation – on universities (via new EU-level discourse on the changing role of universities in knowledge economy). New educational policies promoted at the EU-level are viewed as de-linking the nation-states and public universities. The paper re-reads the changing institution of the nation-state and its changing educational policies in the context of globalisation (sections 2 and 3) and in the specific, regional context of Europeanisation (section 4). It follows from presenting three major positions taken in the literature with respect to transformations of the nation-state under globalisation to presenting the process of de-linking traditional universities and the nation-state and its practical dimension at the EU level at which the role of universities is viewed from the perspective of larger social and economic agenda (called the Lisbon strategy for growth and jobs). The major lesson to be drawn from this re-reading exercise is that there are complex and often contradictory relationships between globalisation as a process affecting the nation-states, changing national educational policies, and national and EU-level policies – which all transform the future role(s) of European universities. In sum, current challenges European universities face, and current policy solutions European governments suggest, are best viewed in the overall context of globalisation. National governments are responding to both globalisation and Europeanisation: policies and strategies they produce, instruments they use, and contradictions they cope with are best re-read in this context.

Historically, modern states came to be nation-states because they triumphed in war, were (relatively) successful economically and won legitimacy in the eyes of their populations and other states (Held, 1995, pp. 71–72). The sovereignty of the state meant also – in the European context – the sovereignty of national educational policies and full state support for nation-state oriented universities (from their inception, especially in a German-inspired so-called 'Humboldtian' model, as

M. Simons, M. Olssen and M.A. Peters (eds.), *Re-Reading Education Policies: A Handbook Studying the Policy Agenda of the 21ˢᵗ Century, 184–204.*

modern institutions closely linked to modern nation-states). The university used to provide the modern nation-state with "a moral and spiritual basis" and professors were the representatives of the nation (Delanty, 2001, p. 33). National education systems in Europe were created as part of the state forming process which established the modern nation-state. They were born when states based on absolutistic or monarchical rule gave way to the modern nation-state: the history of national education in Europe is thus very much the history of the "nation state in formation" (Green, 1997, p. 131). National education systems contributed to the creation of civic loyalties and national identities and became guardians for the diversity of national languages, cultures, literatures and consciousness. The modern university and the modern nation-state went hand in hand, or were parts of the same wide process of modernisation. Consequently, reconfigurations of the modern nation-state in Europe today – caused by both globalisation and Europeanisation processes – are bound to affect the modern institution of the university. State-sponsored mass education has been the primary source of socialisation facing the individual as citizen of a nation-state. Individuals were given access to 'knowledge' and the opportunity of becoming 'educated' – together with the identification with, and participation in, the state as a national project. European nation-states were engaged in authorising, funding and managing education systems, including higher education, to construct unified national polities.

Under the pressures of globalisation (and European integration, speaking of Europe), the above historical assumptions no longer work, and the relationships between (public) universities and nation-states are changing; the modern pact is being widely questioned by both sides: (until recently, national) mission-bound universities on the one hand and fund-providing states on the other. The reliance of both institutions on each other is no longer evident; universities are becoming increasingly self-reliant (and self-supporting), and states are under global pressures to reformulate their tasks and priorities, including their funding priorities in social services provided by the welfare state. Traditional (largely) nation-state oriented and (mostly) welfare-state supported public universities are in new settings: if reformulations to the state's roles and capacities are significant, so will be reform-ulations of the roles of universities. The university becomes radically delinked from the nation-state – and in the European context, new EU higher education policies are being developed which put lifelong learning (and the lifelong learner) in the center of the project of the integrated European Union. The focus on the EU education policy plane today – as discussed in section 4 below – seems to be on the de-nationalised European *lifelong learner* – rather than on the *citizen* of traditional European nation-states.

GLOBALISATION AND THE NATION-STATE

It is crucial to see both the changing historical relationships between the university and the nation-state and the current impact of globalisation on the institution of the state. Following the classification of David Held and his colleagues from their magisterial *Global Transformations* book (Held et al., 1999), in the debate on globalisation it is possible to distinguish between three broad schools of thought: the hyperglobalisers, the sceptics and the transformationalists. We will use this classification in a much more narrow sense, associating the three intellectual camps with the three positions taken today with regard to the impact of globalisation on the nation-state and referring to them as globalists, skeptics and moderates. The three stances will need a reformulation with regard to the issue of the present and the future of the nation-state: those who pronounce its demise, those who maintain that generally nothing substantial has changed in recent decades, and those who see the transformation of the nation-state as fundamental (but not deadly to it).[2]

Indirectly, through discussing globalists', sceptics' and the moderates' views on the future of the nation-state, we will get a continuum of possible answers to the question of the future of nation-state oriented higher education systems. It is hard to say which of the two close relationships the institution of the modern university has (its relationship to the nation-state or its being a part of the welfare state), will be more important for the future role(s) of the institution in the long term. Transformations to both aspects of the state are long-term processes and right now, on more practical grounds, the reformulation of the welfare state seems to be affecting universities more immediately and more directly (leading in higher education to financial austerity, privatisation, deregulation etc). In the future, though, the other dimension of transformations to the state, namely, the questioning of the autonomous role of the nation-state in a global setting (its 'end', 'hollowing out', 'withering away', 'demise', 'decline', 'collapse' etc, in various current formulations) may have even greater effects on the university, both in terms of reformulating its social purpose and missions – and in terms of future public funding for both teaching and research. The three theoretical positions taken with respect to the nation-state under global pressures lead to three different scenarios of the future of traditional public nation-state oriented (and welfare state supported) universities.

For the globalists, recent historical and political developments, and globalisation processes in particular, open a new epoch in human history, a radically new, post-national world order: "a new age" has just taken place and consequently we need "a new beginning" in our thinking (Albrow, 1996, p. 2). The collapse of communism in Eastern Europe brings an end to the "age of the nation-states" (and re-opens the issue of the future of welfare state) with the very idea of a nation being perhaps "only an ephemeral political form, a European exception." This is no surprise, we are entering a "new age" (Guéhenno, 1995, p. x, 4, xiii). There will be no national economies (products, technologies, corporations or industries); consequently, citizens of nation-states are no longer in the same economic boat called the 'national economy' and they are not bound together by the same economic fate (Reich, 1992, pp. 3–8). The economy becomes "borderless" and what occurs under the influence of global forces is the "end of the nation-state": nation-states appear to have been merely a transitional form of organisation for managing economic affairs (Ohmae, 2000, p. 210).

The social and political consequences of the shift of balance between the state and the market are as far-reaching as those of the industrial revolution in the past. States are collectively retreating from their participation in the ownership and control over industry, services and trade as part of state policies. Susan Strange stresses that today it is increasingly doubtful that the state in general can still claim loyalty from its citizens substantially greater than their loyalty to family, to the firm or to their political party. People from stable political societies do not expect to have to sacrifice their lives for anyone except for their families. In short, the claim that there is a difference of degree between the loyalty to the authority of the state and the loyalty to other forms of authority cannot be sustained. Consequently, the state "is becoming (…) just one more source of authority among several, with limited powers and resources" (Strange, 1996, pp. 72–73).

The paradox of the global age is that the populations in general want to continue to be recognised as nations but nation-states are no longer able to protect their citizens from the uncertainties of the outside world: it is as impossible to "control" the world around them as it is to "ignore" it (Guéhenno, 1995: 138ff). In this context, most of the forces unleashed by globalisation are very hard to control for individual countries. Kenichi Ohmae, one of greatest management gurus at the end of the 1980s, claims in *The End of the Nation State: The Rise of Regional Economies* that the old world has "fallen apart." The nation-state has begun to "crumble" and the older patterns of linkages between nations have begun to lose their dominance. Current changes are fundamental: nation-states have lost their role as "meaningful units of participation in the global economy of today's borderless world." Nation-states today have much less to contribute to the global economy and much less freedom to make contributions. In the past, they may have been efficient engines of wealth production but in the new world order they have become "remarkably inefficient engines of wealth distribution" (Ohmae, 2000, p. 207). They are "inescapably vulnerable" to economic choices made elsewhere – by people and institutions over which they have no practical control at all.

The sceptics hesitate whether, generally, anything new has happened to the nation-state with the advent of globalisation. Most of the sceptics refer to the statistical data of world flows of trade, investment and labour from the 19th century onwards and claim that the contemporary levels of economic interdependence are not historically unprecedented. Most of them rely on an economic conception of globalisation, equating it with an integrated global market. They conclude that contemporary globalisation is exaggerated. They consider the globalist thesis as "fundamentally flawed" and "politically naïve" since it underestimates the power of national governments to regulate international economic activity; they tend to disregard the presumption that economic internationalisation might lead to the emergence of a new, less state-centric world order; and they point to the growing centrality of governments in regulating and promoting cross-border economic activity. They reject the 'myth' that the power of national governments or state sovereignty is being currently undermined by economic internationalisation or global governance and argue against the thesis of a convergence of macroeconomic and welfare policies across the globe. As Held et al. conclude, "rather than the world becoming more interdependent, as the hyperglobalisers assume, the sceptics seek to expose the myths which sustain the globalisation thesis" (see Held et al., 1999, pp. 5–7).

John Gray, a British postliberal political philosopher, differs considerably from other skeptics. His theses are not economic and his views are not economics-based but philosophical. He pronounces the "passing of social democracy" and views European social democracy as "belong[ing] to the past" (Gray, 1998, pp. 87, 99, 64). Where Gray grasps the nettle, as opposed to several other sceptics discussed here, is his clear realisation that we are no longer living in closed economies. Social democracy, especially European welfare state regimes, presupposes closed economies. Many of the core policies of social democracy, Gray rightly argues, just cannot be sustained in open economies. In open economies, Gray argues, egalitarian principles will be rendered unworkable – by the freedom of capital, including "human capital", to migrate (Gray, 1998, pp. 87–89). Therefore, under current economic conditions, Continental Keynesianism is a "dead end" and European social models cannot survive in their current forms. Next sceptics, Paul Hirst and Grahame Thompson, stay mostly in the realms of economics and they present an argument against the idea that the international economy has become or is becoming "globalised." The major problems with globalisation they point out are that there is no proof of the emergence of a distinctly 'global' economic structure; that there have been earlier periods of internationalised trade, capital flows and monetary systems, especially before the First World War; that truly global transnational corporations are relatively few; and, finally, that the prospects for regulation by international cooperation, for the formation of trading blocks and for the development of new national strategies that take into account internationalisation are not exhausted (Hirst & Thompson, 1996, p. 196). Sceptics tend to reject the hypothesis put forward by globalists that what we are witnessing is the emergence of a new, less state-centric world order. They stress the growing centrality of states. States are not the "victims" of globalisation but its "midwives" (Weiss, 1998). Neither global governance nor economic liberalisation and internationalisation seems to be undermining the sovereignty of nation-states and their autonomy in determining the course of national welfare, tax and social policies.

Finally, the third position – that of the moderates – with respect to the impact of globalisation on the nation-state is the one I find especially convincing. This is the position with respect to the future of the nation-state which will guide my re-reading of the future of nation-state oriented university. In moderates, under the impact of current patterns of globalisation, the power of the nation-state is 're-positioned', 're-contextualised', 'transformed', 're-constituted', 're-engineered', 're-structured', 'dis-placed', 're-articulated', 're-located', 're-embedded', 'de-centered', 're-configured', 're-shaped', 'eroded' etc. Consequently, the traditional relationships between the nation-state and the modern university are substantially different in this perspective.

The moderates do not expect the arrival of a single world society nor do they find evidence for global convergence in economics, politics and culture. On the contrary, they stress "new patterns of global stratification" in which some states and societies are becoming central, and others marginal in the global order. At the core of their convictions, as Held summarises them, is a belief that globalisation is reconstituting the power, functions and authority of national governments (while economic activity becomes increasingly deterritorialised due to production and finance acquiring global and transnational dimensions). They reject both "the hyperglobalist rhetoric of the end of the sovereign nation-state and the sceptics' claim that 'nothing much has changed'." Territorial boundaries have become "increasingly problematic", and sovereignty, state power and territoriality stand today in a "more complex" relationship than in the epoch during which the modern nation-state was forged. New non-territorial forms of economic and political organisation have emerged such as e.g. multinational corporations, transnational social movements and international regulatory agencies. The world is no longer purely state-centric or even primarily state-governed – as authority has become increasingly diffused among public and private agencies at all levels. Globalisation brings about, rather than the "end of the state", a whole spectrum of adjustment strategies: the power of national governments is being "reconstituted and restructured" in response to the growing complexity of the processes of governance (Held et al., 1999, p. 9). Jan Aart Scholte describes the moderate stance as the one from which "globalisation is indeed a distinctive and important development in contemporary world history. However, its scale and consequences need to be carefully measured and qualified. Nor is globalisation the only, or always the most significant, trend in today's society" (Scholte, 2000, p. 18).

Saskia Sassen in *Losing Control? Sovereignty in an Age of Globalisation* and *Globalisation and Its Discontents* argues that the growth of a global economy plus new telecommunications and computer networks have profoundly reconfigured institutions fundamental to the processes of governance and accountability in the modern state. State sovereignty and the institutional apparatus in charge of regulating the economy (central banks, monetary policies) are being "destabilised" and "transformed" under the pressures of globalisation and new technologies (Sassen, 1996, p. xii). Economic globalisation has transformed both the territoriality and sovereignty of the nation-state but the state itself has been deeply involved in the implementation of the laws and regulations necessary for economic globalisation. Globalisation has therefore been accompanied by the creation of new legal regimes, especially for international commercial arbitration, along with institutions that perform ratings and advisory functions.

The nation-state itself (in Western advanced democracies) is becoming reconfigured as it is directly involved in this emerging transnational governance system. The state legitimates a new global doctrine about its new role in the economy – and what is central to this doctrine is a consensus among states to continue globalisation, to further the growth of the global economy (Sassen, 1996, p. 23). The powers historically associated with the nation-state have been taken on by global financial markets on the one hand and the new covenants on human rights on the other. They are very different from each other. Global capital markets represent a "concentration of power capable of influencing national government economic policy and, by extension, other policies as well" (Sassen, 1996, p. 42). This is exactly the point in which tax policies, welfare policies and, by extension, educational and research and development policies are influenced and transformed. Historically, educational policies were largely national policies; currently, they seem to be a part of much broader, and mostly economic, policy packages. Education and research, and higher education and university research in particular, are not isolated islands. They are under constant scrutiny, as a small part of national economic policies. Sassen calls the function that global capital market exercises on national governments "disciplining" and concludes: "when it comes to public spending, governments are increasingly subject to outside pressures" (Sassen, 1996, p. 48, see also 2003). Public spending on both higher education and research and development – especially in the European transition countries – is not an exception: the general pressure in underfunded transition economies is to find more private funds for both education (e.g. through various forms of cost-sharing) and research and development (through increasing academic entrepreneurialism bringing more non-core non-state income) rather than consider increasing public funding.

Another moderate, Manuel Castells, in his trilogy, *The Information Age: Economy, Society and Culture*, argues that "a crisis of legitimacy is voiding of meaning and function the institutions of the industrial era. Bypassed by global networks of wealth, power, and information, the modern nation-state has lost much of its sovereignty. By trying to intervene strategically in this global scene the state loses capacity to represent its territorially rooted constituencies" (Castells, 1997, p. 354). The modern nation-state seems to be losing on both fronts, global and domestic, vis-à-vis global actors and vis-à-vis their citizens. State control over space and time is bypassed by global flows of capital, goods, services, technology, communication, and information such that national identity is being challenged by the plural and hybrid identities of citizens. The nation-state is doomed because it is increasingly powerless in controlling monetary policies, deciding its budget, collecting its corporate taxes and fulfilling its commitments to provide social benefits to its citizens. In sum, the state has lost its economic power, even though it retains some regulatory capacity, as in Saskia Sassen's diagnoses about the state basically having one final thing to do: producing new legal regimes for the global age in national settings (Castells, 1997, p. 254).

Such authors as Fritz Scharpf and John Gerard Ruggie stress the idea that the economic space of the nation-state and national territorial borders no longer coincide. Consequently, the postwar social contract between the state, market, and labour does not work anymore as it was designed to work within closed national economies. Scharpf argues that in the history of capitalism, the decades following the Second World War were "unusual in the degree to which the boundaries of the territorial state had become coextensive with the boundaries of markets for capital, services, goods and labour" (Scharpf, 2000, p. 254). Investment opportunities existed mainly within *national* economies and firms were mainly challenged by *domestic* competitors. "The 'golden years' of the capitalist welfare state came to an end" (Scharpf, 2000, p. 255). The social contract which had allowed the nation-states in advanced capitalist countries to be accompanied by a welfare state originated right after the Second World War. With the advent of globalisation, it is eroding. This post-war compromise assigned specific policy roles to national governments – which governments are increasingly unable, or unwilling, to perform today. One of the indirect effects of globalisation is its impact on the ability of the state to "live up to its side of the post-war domestic compact" (Ruggie, 1997, p. 2). In the approach of both Scharpf and Ruggie, the impact of globalisation on the nation-state is through undermining the founding ideas behind the post-war welfare state: through liberalisation and the opening up of economies, nation-states begin to lose their legitimacy provided, in vast measure, by a social contract valid in closed, national economies. Out of the three scenarios of the future of the nation-state under the pressures of globalisation, the scenario of the moderates is the one I am strongly favouring. The remaining two perspectives would provide grounds for a different re-reading of the future of public universities in Europe. In the following section, I am assuming substantial transformations, recontextualisations and relocations of the nation state which result in substantial transformations, recontextualisations and relocations of the nation-state oriented, modern university.

THE NATION-STATE AND THE MODERN UNIVERSITY

The processes of globalisation seem to be affecting the traditional modern institution of the state simultaneously on many levels, from regional and subnational to national and supranational. The two crucial dimensions of the state in transition are its relation to the welfare state on the one hand and its relation to the nation-state on the other. Both dimensions are closely linked to higher education, especially to its elite segment, the institution of the university; which, in Europe, has been mostly state-funded as part of the well-developed post-war Keynesian welfare state apparatus (I am viewing higher education in Europe as part of the welfare state, following e.g. Nicholas Barr from his *The Economics of the Welfare State*, 2004, pp. 321–348), and which has been closely related to the modern construct of the nation-state.

Anthony Giddens provides the following definition of the nation-state: "a nation-state is (...) a bordered power-container (...) the pre-eminent power-container of the modern era" (Giddens, 1987, pp. 116, 120). The nation-state, in the course of the 19th century, had become an irresistible political form on a global scale. The social world discussed in sociology (but also in the political sciences, political philosophy and political economics) is less and less related to the above definition, and globalisation and its practices make the discussions on the classical world of sovereign nation-states increasingly irrelevant to its current theoretical concerns. The view of current states as "bordered power-containers" seems to be increasingly untenable both in theory and in practice (as Ulrich Beck stresses, "the whole conceptual world of national sovereignty is fading away – a world that includes the taming of capitalism in Europe by the post-war welfare state", Beck 2000b, p. 17). The container theory of society is no longer able to explain the complexities of the new world order in which intergovernmental agencies, political and economic cartels, economic unions, transnational corporations, military alliances etc. play an increasingly important role and in which the nation-state is becoming "progressively less important" in world organisation (Giddens, 1987, p. 282).

The importance of the need to revise our theoretical thinking and to reorient ourselves conceptually and intellectually to the new "global order" has been shown by analysts of globalisation from the above disciplines. In practical terms, the consequences of abandoning the power-container view of society and the premises of the world organised through sovereign territorial nation-states are far-reaching. The advent of globalisation may bring about the erosion of the state as we know it i.e. the traditional nation-state described by the sociological container theory of society we have been familiar with. The central premise of (Beck's) national modernity is already overturned – namely, the idea that "we live and act in the self-enclosed spaces of national states and their respective national societies" (Beck, 2000a, p. 20).

While discussing current transformations of the institution of the modern state, we need to bear in mind the institution of the modern university, born at roughly the same time, as an intellectual (and ideological) product of the same project of modernity. Transformations to the modern university are better understood in the context of transformations to the modern state. Since, as Guy Neave put it, the modern university was always "the Nation-State university" (Neave, 2001, p. 16). Gerard Delanty reminds us about the "pact" between the modern university and the state: "in return for autonomy, it [university] would furnish the state with its cognitive requirements." The global process of the retreat of the state from the position of provider to that of regulator "fundamentally alters the historical pact between knowledge and the state" (Delanty, 2001, pp. 2, 103).

Modern states developed as nation-states – political apparatuses, "distinct from both ruler and ruled, with supreme jurisdiction over a demarcated territorial area, backed by a claim to a monopoly of coercive power, and enjoying legitimacy as a result of a minimum level of support or loyalty from their citizens", argued David Held in his *Democracy and the Global Order* (Held, 1995, p. 48). And modern universities in large parts of Continental Europe developed as nation-state universities. The most prominent innovations for the concept of the state include territoriality, control of the means of violence, as well as an impersonal structure of power and legitimacy. It is only with the system of modern states that exact borders have been fixed. Holding a monopoly on force and the means of coercion only became possible with the breaking down of rival centres of power and authority. An impersonal structure of power was not possible as long as political rights, obligations and duties were tied to religion and traditional elites. Finally, human beings as "individuals" and "peoples" had won a place as active participants in the new political order. As Held went on to argue,

> the loyalty of citizens became something that had to be *won* by modern states: invariably this involved a claim by the state to be legitimate because it reflected and/or represented the views and interests of its citizens (Held, 1995, pp. 48–49).

Although Held does not mention the theme, the modern legitimacy of the state brings us closer, in the 20th century, to the beginnings of the idea of the welfare state. Modern states have certainly won the loyalty of their citizens (as well as achieved social and political stability) when they gradually introduced not only political rights, but also social benefits; including pension schemes, state-subsidised (if not free) higher education and affordable health care. The welfare state became a fully-fledged reality in Europe throughout the quarter of a century following the end of the Second World War.

But the legitimacy of, and loyalty towards, modern liberal democratic welfare states is under severe stress today and the whole idea of a post-war "social contract" between the state and its citizens is widely debated. Increasingly, there are differences between the "national interests" of particular nation-states and their citizens on the one hand and the corporate interests (economic interests) of particular transnational companies on the other, so states are torn between purely economic decisions which often undermine their traditional legitimacy and purely political decisions which could contribute to maintaining their legitimacy. There is an increasing awareness of the artificiality, or at least of the constructed nature, of nation-state citizenship. As Mike Bottery argues, it is only at the present time that "the political body defining the terms and boundaries of citizenship is something called 'the nation-state'" (Bottery, 2003, p. 102). The loyalty of citizens of nation-states is closely related to a bilateral agreement, although never fully codified, between citizens and the state. Should the nation-state be threatened, so also will its role as primary guarantor of citizenship rights. It is very unclear indeed why – along with the (possible) dismantling of the welfare state and the (possible) end of the postwar "social contract" between governments, unions and workers, the decline in the capacities, capabilities and willingness of nation-states to provide some traditionally (sometimes even fully) state-funded welfare services – national loyalty should not be decreasing. And if it is decreasing anyway, for some structural reasons, it is hard to say why the whole modern paradigm of the close relationships between higher education (civic, national education) and the nation-state should not be substantially weakened. In the present re-reading of these relationships, I am strongly suggesting their weakening, especially in the additional context provided by the emergent EU-level educational policies discussed below.

The new order endorsed the right of each state to autonomous and independent action. As Held comments, "in this conception, the world consists of separate political powers pursuing their own interests, backed by diplomatic initiatives and, in the last instance, by their organisation of coercive power" (Held et al., 1999, p. 38). But today we experience the end of the Westphalian model, the end of the traditional world order of nation-states and the traditional relationships between them. In his strong formulation of 1995, "the modern state (...) [is] unable to determine its own fate" (Held, 1995, p. 92), which was later modified and quantified in a magisterial introduction to the globalisation debate which he co-authored with his colleagues (Held et al., 1999). The Westphalian order and the sovereign state evolved in a "symbiotic partnership": rulers recognised each other's sovereignty and, in turn, the consolidation of the Westphalian state system reinforced the primacy of the sovereign territorial state (see McGrew, 1997, pp. 4ff). Since the Second World War the modern nation-state has become "the principal type of political rule across the globe", and it has acquired a political form of liberal or representative democracy (Held et al., 1999, p. 46). Globalisation, if it is indeed reconstituting the nature of sovereign states, has profound implications for modern democratic theory and practices which have been constructed upon the foundations of the Westphalian order.

In Europe, the sovereignty of the state meant also the sovereignty of national educational policies and full state support for nation-state oriented universities (from their inception as modern institutions bound by a "pact" with modern nation-states). The historic function of the modern university – the transmission of national cultures, the inculcation of national consciousness in citizens of nation-states, forging national citizenship, the formative purpose and mission of supporting national ideas and ideals, mainly through the humanities and social sciences – seems up for grabs today. The modern university and the modern nation-state in Europe (especially in its Humboldtian version) were major agents of the same modernisation process in Europe. The crucial step in the historical development of European universities is what Guy Neave termed the process of their nationalisation – bringing the university formally into the public domain as a national responsibility. With the rise of the nation-state, the university was set at the apex of institutions defining national identity. The emergence of the universities in Berlin and in Paris marked the termination of the long process for the incorporation of the university to the state (Neave, 2001, pp. 25–26).

The process of the "nationalisation" of the university in Europe settled the issue of what the role and responsibilities of the modern institution in society should be. The emergent nation-state defined the social place of the emergent modern university and determined its social responsibilities. The nation-state determined the community to which the university would be answerable: it was going to be the national community, the nation. The services and benefits the unitary and homogeneous nation-state gradually, and over the passage of time, placed at the disposal of society went far beyond education and included e.g. generous healthcare systems and old-age pension schemes. Nowadays, as the reduction of the welfare state in general progresses smoothly (e.g. through new legislation) in most parts of the world, social contracts with regards to these (and possibly other) areas of state benefits and state-funded services may have to be renegotiated, significantly changing their content. Globalisation seems to be changing the role of the nation-state: the nation state is gradually losing its power as a direct economic player and at the same time it is losing a significant part of its legitimacy as it appears not to be willing, or able, to provide the welfare services seen as the very foundation of the post-war welfare state (I am viewing higher education as both public services and part of the public sector). It is important, I believe, to see higher education policies in the context of larger welfare state policies (which I am doing in more detail elsewhere, see Kwiek, 2007b): higher education is a significant (and most often significantly fund-consuming) part of the public sector and a part of the traditional welfare state that is now under severe pressure, though perhaps under less pressure than the two main parts of it, healthcare and pensions. In more theoretical than practical terms, these phenomena had their powerful impact on thinking about public services, including public higher education, in Central Eastern Europe.[3]

DELINKING THE NATION-STATE AND THE UNIVERSITY: RECENT EU EDUCATIONAL POLICIES

The modern university in Europe (especially in its German-inspired "Humboldtian" version) has been closely linked to the nation-state. With the advent of globalisation, and its pressures on the nation-states, universities are increasingly experiencing their de-linking from both the traditional needs of the nation-state (inculcating national consciousness in citizens of the nation-state etc) and from its financial resources. They increasingly need to rely on the "third stream income" – especially non-core non-state income and earned income. In Europe, the overall social and economic answer to globalisation has been the strengthening of the European integration, and the policy agenda of this regional response to globalisation is called the Lisbon strategy for more growth and jobs. European universities, as well as governments of EU member states, find it useful to refer to this strategy in redefining the role(s) of educational institutions under both globalisation and its regional response, Europeanisation. Consequently, a recent decade brought about substantially new ways of thinking on universities on the level of the European Commission of the European Union. Emergent EU educational policies are increasingly influential as the university reforms agenda is viewed as part of wider Lisbon strategy reforms. The EU member states – national governments – are adopting not only the Lisbon strategy but also the social and economic concept of the university implied in it and consistently developed in subsequent official documents of the European Commission. The EU member states, for the first time in the fifty years of the history of the European Union, need to balance their educational policies between the requirements of new policies strongly promoted by the EU and the requirements of their traditional national systems (in the four first decades, higher education in general was left in the competence of the member states; today it is viewed by the European Commission as being of critical importance to the economic future of the EU and in need of EU-level intervention). Additionally, national educational policies are under strong globalisation-related (mostly financial) pressures, as all other social services of the "European social model."

In this new ways of thinking, the traditional link between the nation-state and the modern university has been broken; moreover, higher education in the EU context has clearly been put in a post-national (and distinctly European) perspective in which interests of the EU as a whole and of particular EU member states (nation-states) are juxtaposed. The reason for the renewed EU interest in higher education is clearly stated by the European Commission: while responsibilities for universities lie essentially at national (or regional) level, the most important challenges are "European, and even international or global" (EC 2003a, p. 9). The major challenges facing Europe – related to both globalisation and demographics, such as losing its heritage and identity, losing out economically, giving up the European

Social Model etc – should be, according to a recent influential *Frontier Research: The European Challenge* report, met through education, knowledge, and innovation:

> The most appropriate response to these challenges is to increase the capacity of Europe to create, absorb, diffuse and exploit scientific and technical knowledge, and that, to this end, education, research and innovation should be placed much higher on the European policy agenda (EC 2005b, p. 17).

Thus recent years have brought about intensified thinking about the future of public universities in Europe, from a distinct EU perspective. Regional processes for the integration of educational and research and development policies in the European Union add a new dimension to the nation-state/national university issue discussed in the preceding sections. On top of the discussions about the nation-state (and the welfare state), we are confronted with new transnational ideas on how to revitalise the European project through education and how to use European universities for the purpose of creating in Europe a globally competitive knowledge economy. For the first time in the 2000s new ways of thinking about higher education were formulated at an EU level – and were accompanied by a number of practical measures, coordinated and funded by the European Commission. Higher education, left at the disposal of particular nation-states in recent decades in Europe, returns now to the forefront in discussions about the future of the EU.

Consequently, Europe in the 2000s has been undergoing two powerful integration processes, initially separate but recently increasingly convergent. The former is the Bologna process, gradual production of the common European Higher Education Area (started by the Bologna Declaration signed in 1999) by 45 Bologna-signatory countries (reaching far beyond the 27 EU member states and ranging geographically from the Caucasus to Portugal). Its main goals include the adoption of a system of easily readable and comparable degrees, the adoption of the three cycles of studies – undergraduate, graduate and doctoral, the spread of credit transfer systems enabling student mobility, and the promotion of pan-European quality assurance mechanisms. The latter is the Lisbon strategy for growth and jobs, adopted by the EU countries in 2000 and simplified and re-launched in 2005: currently, it has only two targets – total (public and private) investment of 3% of Europe's GDP in research and development and an employment rate of 70%, both to be reached by 2010. Increasingly, the goals of the Bologna process are being subsumed under the goals of the Lisbon strategy. The European Commission stresses that the divergence between the organisation of universities at the national level and the emergence of challenges which go beyond national frontiers has grown, and will continue to do so. Thus a shift of balance is necessary, the arguments go, and the Lisbon strategy in general, combined with the emergence of the common European Research Area (co-funded by EU research funds totaling 51 billion EUR for 2007-2013) in particular, provide new grounds for policy work at the European level, despite restrictions on engagement of the European Commission in education – leaving the area of education in the competences of the member states – as defined by the Maastricht Treaty on the European Union (1992) (see Kwiek, 2004, 2006b).

In recent years the project of European integration seems to have found a new leading legitimising motif: education and research for the "Europe of Knowledge." A crucial component of the Europeanisation process today is its attempt to make Europe a "knowledge society" (and "knowledge economy") in a globalising world. "Education and training" (a wider EU category) becomes a core group of technologies to be used for the creation of a new Europe; the creation of a distinctive and separate "European Higher Education Area" as well as a "European Research (and Innovation) Area" is the goal the EU has set itself by a deadline of 2010. The construction of a distinctive European educational policy space – and the introduction of the requisite European educational and research policies – has become part and parcel of EU "revitalisation" within the wide cultural, political and economic Europeanisation project (see Lawn, 2003).

We are witnessing the emergence of a "new Europe" whose foundations are being constructed around such notions as, on the one hand, "knowledge", "innovation", "research", and on the other – "education" and "training." Education in the EU, and especially lifelong learning, becomes a new discursive space in which European dreams of common citizenship are currently being located. This new "knowledge-based Europe" is becoming increasingly individualised (and de-nationalised), though; ideally, it consists of individual European learners rather than citizens of particular European nation-states. The emergent European educational space is unprecedented in its vision, ambitions and possibly its capacity to influence national educational policies. In the new knowledge economy, education policy, and especially higher education policy, cannot remain solely at the level of Member States because only the construction of a new common educational space in Europe can possibly provide it with a chance to forge a new sense of European identity, as well as be a practical response to globalisation pressures, the arguments presented by the European Commission go. "Europeans", in this context, could refer directly to "European (lifelong) learners": individuals seeking knowledge useful in the knowledge economy. The symbol of this new Europe is not "the locked up cultural resources of nation states, but the individual engaged in lifelong learning" (Lawn, 2001, p. 177); not the nationally-bound and territorially-located citizen of a particular member state but the individual with an individuated "knowledge portfolio" of education, skills, and competencies. European citizenship is being discursively located in the individual for whom a new pan-European educational space is being built. The individual attains membership in this space only through knowledge, skills and competencies. At the same time, the economic future of Europe is believed to increasingly depend on investing in knowledge and innovation and on making the "free movement of knowledge" (the "fifth freedom", completing the four freedoms of movement of goods, services, people and capital) a reality (EC, 2007, p. 14); "science and technology" are "the key to Europe's future", as the title of an EC communication runs (EC, 2004); and "the success of the Lisbon strategy hinges on urgent reforms" of higher education systems in Europe, as another title runs (EC, 2003b).

The idea of Europe, as well as the core normative narratives and major discourses that hold Europeans as Europeans together, is being redefined; and this new education space (being constructed through the emergent European educational and research policies) in which the new European identity is being forged seems crucial. Through prioritising the idea of "lifelong learning" in the Lisbon strategy and in the EU agenda of "Education and Training 2010" (see EC, 2000a), learning becomes redefined as an individual activity, no longer as closely linked with national projects as in the times of founding (Neave's) "Nation-State universities" already referred to. The new "learning society" comprises more and more "(European) learning individuals", wishing and able to opt in and opt out of particular European nations and states (Kwiek, 2007b). Consequently, one of the key concepts in the Bologna process for the integration of European higher education systems is no longer employment but employability, a transfer of meanings through which it is the individual's responsibility to be employed, rather than the traditional responsibility of the state, as in the Keynesian "full employment" welfare model.[4]

The process of creating the European Higher Education Area and the simultaneous emergence of the European Research Area have one major common dimension: that of a redefinition of missions of the institution of the university (even though universities were at first neglected as places for research in EU thinking – for instance, in the first EU communication on the subject, "Towards a European Research Area", universities and higher education in general were not even mentioned, see EC, 2000b). Both teaching and research are undergoing substantial transformations today. The institution of the university is playing a significant role in the emergence of the common European higher education and common European research spaces, but in none of these two processes, is the university seen in a traditional modern way – as discussed in the context of the emergence of the modern university in traditional European nation-states. It is evolving together with radical transformations of the social setting in which it functions (the setting of "globalisation" and, regionally, "Europeanisation"). Globalisation is the overriding notion in most major European discussions about the role(s) of higher education and research and development, the notion behind the Lisbon strategy, especially when combined with such accompanying new notions as the "knowledge economy" and the "knowledge society" – and in respect of the traditional contexts of economic growth, national and European competitiveness and fighting unemployment. The Lisbon "strategy for growth and jobs" is a regional (European) response to the challenges of globalisation. As globalisation seems to be redefining the role of the nation-states in today's world, it is indirectly affecting higher education institutions. In this context – and thus indirectly – globalisation pressures are behind new higer education policies which promote competitiveness of nations (and regions) through education, research and innovation. Globalisation affects the proposed policy solutions in higher education of both national governments and the European Commission.

The impact of globalisation on EU-level educational policies and strategies, and increasingly on ensuing national policies and strategies, is substantial. Higher education is viewed, assessed, and measured in the context of both globalisation and Europeanisation. Globalisation, indirectly, for instance through a large Lisbon Strategy for growth and jobs, fundamentally alters the lenses through which universities are viewed, assessed, and measured. Its most evident impact on universities is the overall sense that (predominantly public) universities in Europe need profound transformations if Europeanisation is to be a successful response to globalisation. Consequently, the overall picture on reading recent EU documents, reports, working papers and communications is that the relationship between government and universities is in need of profound change. The two most recent documents, "Mobilising the Brainpower of Europe: Enabling Universities to Make Their Full Contribution to the Lisbon Strategy" (EC, 2005a, see Kwiek, 2007a) and "Delivering on the Modernisation Agenda for Universities: Education, Research and Innovation" (EC, 2006a) make clear that radical transformations of university governance are expected by the European Commission to make possible their full contribution to the Lisbon Strategy. Universities are urged to consider fundamentally new arrangements (new "contracts") with societies and governments are urged to consider establishing new partnerships with universities, with a shift from state control to accountability to society (EC, 2005a, p. 9). As explained clearly in an EU issue-paper on university governance: "coordinated change is required both in systems regulation and in institutional governance in order to mobilise the enormous potential of knowledge and energy of European universities to adapt to new missions" (EC, 2006a, p. 1). The policy lesson for the EU member states is that substantial changes in governance are needed: according to new university/ government contracts envisaged by the EU, universities will be responsible and accountable for their programs, staff and resources, while the state will be responsible for the "strategic orientation" of the system as a whole – through a framework of general rules, policy objectives, funding mechanisms and incentives (EC, 2006a, p. 5).

European universities have "enormous potential" but this potential "is not fully harnassed and put to work effectively to underpin Europe's drive for more growth and more jobs." Research is no longer isolated activity and emphasis in research is shifting from individual researchers to "teams and global networks" (EC, 2006a, p. 3). Therefore universities need autonomy and accountability; and full institutional autonomy to society at large requires new internal governance systems, based on strategic priorities, professional management of human resources, investment and administrative procedures (EC, 2006a, p. 5). From a larger perspective, as the title of another EU communication recently put, the implementation of the Lisbon Strategy requires "fostering entrepreneurial mindsets through education and learning" (EC, 2006c), from primary to secondary to higher education. With reference to the latter, the document promotes the commercialisation of ideas and development of new technologies by students and researchers (EC, 2006b, p. 9).

Consequently, universities under globalisation pressures face an imperative need to "adapt and adjust" to a series of profound changes Europe has been undergoing (EC, 2003a, p. 6). They must rise to a number of challenges. They can only release their potential by undergoing "the radical changes needed to make the European system a genuine world reference" (EC, 2003a, p. 11). They have to increase and diversify their income in the face of the worsening underfunding:

[A]fter remaining a comparatively isolated universe for a long period, both in relation to society and to the rest of the world, with funding guaranteed and a status protected by respect for their autonomy, European universities have gone through the second half of the 20th century without really calling into question the role or the nature of what they should be contributing to society (EC, 2003a, p. 22).

But it is clearly over now. Thus the fundamental question about European universities today is the following: "Can the European universities, *as they are and are organised now*, hope in the future to retain their place, in society and in the world?" (EC, 2003a, p. 22, emphasis in original). It is a purely rhetorical question in the context of the whole communication on the "role of universities in the Europe of Knowledge": the universities in Europe – as they are and as they are organised today – will *not* be able to retain their place. Restructuring is necessary, and a much wider idea of European social, economic and political integration applied to the higher education sector, expressed in the ideals of a common European higher education area, comes in handy. The university's goal is the creation of an area for research where scientific resources are used "to create jobs and increase Europe's competitiveness" (EC, 2000a, p. 1) which is a radical transformation of modern university missions, in its close relationships with the nation-state, especially in the Humboldtian tradition – national loyalty, national consciousness, almost and ideological arm of the nation-state (Kwiek, 2005 2006a, 2006b). The impact of globalisation – and of Europeanisation – on education policy is thus fundamental: there is a new interplay of changing policies at the EU member states level (national education policies), at the EU level (Lisbon Strategy and the Bologna process) and at a global level (global education policies promoted by e.g. the OECD and the World Bank) and universities are influenced, directly or indirectly, by all of them at the same time.

TENTATIVE CONCLUSIONS

The paper re-reads a wider context for rethinking the changing relationships between the university and the state in Europe under globalisation pressures on the state. Globalisation is viewed as a major factor influencing the transformations of the state today, in its two major dimensions: the nation-state and the welfare state. As the nation-state is changing, the argument goes, so is the modern university, most often very closely linked to the state in major European variants of higher education systems. The modern university becomes radically delinked from the nation-state – and in the European context, new EU higher education policies are being developed which put lifelong learning (and the lifelong learner) in the center of the project of the integrated European Union. The individualised learner, the product of both globalisation and Europeanisation, is contrasted in the EU discourse on the future university missions with a traditional citizen of the nation-state, formed by the modern university which was born together with the nation-state. These challenges and chances seem to be clearly seen in the emergent EU discourse on the university in which both universities and students are delinked from the nation-states; while universities are expected to be linked to the Lisbon strategy of more growth and more jobs, and more competitiveness of the European Union economy, students are expected to be more linked to the new project of the "Europe of Knowledge" than to traditional, individual national projects of particular European nation-states.

The present re-reading of both wider global trends (the impact of globalisation on the nation-states) and more narrow regional trends (the impact of the Europeanisation on national educational policies in Europe) is intended to show that universities could also be viewed in large social and economic contexts. Education policy studies need to critically develop these fundamentally new contexts if they intend to trace possible university futures. Directions for future research include such topics as the future of the (various forms of) European Social Model, the impact of new European policies on new national strategies for academic entrepreneurship and cost-sharing, gradual Europeanisation (and de-nationalisation) of large-scale research programs, the privatisation of social services and further reformulation of the role of the welfare state in knowledge economies, the impact of both the Lisbon Strategy and the Bologna process on the education sector, and the competition of the EU in research and innovation with other regions. Additional perspectives, not applied in the paper, would include economics in further welfare research, European studies in further European integration research, political sciences in further European governance research, and sociology in the academic profession and academic institutions research.

NOTES

[1] The present paper presents arguments which are developed in more detail in my book (Kwiek, 2006a).

[2] As to the globalists, I am referring to Jean-Marie Guéhenno, Kenichi Ohmae, Martin Albrow, Robert B. Reich, and Susan Strange; as to the skeptics, I am referring to Paul Hirst and Grahame Thompson, Linda Weiss, and John Gray; finally, as to the moderates, I am referring here to Anthony Giddens, Saskia Sassen, Manuel Castells, Jan Aart Scholte, as well as David Held, Anthony McGrew, David Goldblatt and Jonathan Perraton.

[3] In Poland, the theoretical impact was already translated into changed national legislation in the case of the pensions reform and health care reforms at the end of the 1990s. To discuss transformations of higher education in CEE countries is to discuss a much wider political and economic process of transformations towards market economies; the accompanying reforms of the public sector seem unavoidable, and higher education figures in this sector prominently. In Poland, bold reforms of the public sector began in the second half of the 1990s, starting with pensions (the introduction of a World Bank-supported multipillar system), healthcare (decentralization of funding and partial privatization), and primary and secondary education (decentralization of funding). Current discussions at the EU level on the introduction of tuition fees in (largely tax-based) higher education systems in Europe, reflected by current (2008) Polish discussions of tuition fees, introduce the theme of privatization, new in the EU context (see Kwiek, 2008a, 2008c).

[4] The difference between *employment* and *employability* is crucial: the latter term transfers the responsibility for a graduate's future away from the state and towards the individual concerned. Especially in the context of "lifelong learning", one's "employability" clearly depends on one's "knowledge 'portfolio'" (Martin Carnoy). In the new situation in which "job" becomes "permanently temporary", "workers are gradually being defined socially less by the particular long-

term job they hold than by the knowledge they have acquired by studying and working. This knowledge 'portfolio' allows them to move across firms and even across types of work, as jobs get redefined" (Carnoy, 1999: 33). The responsibility becomes somehow *privatized* and *individualized*: given that the opportunities for studying, training and retraining are there, it is simply the individual's "fault" not to be "knowledge rich", not to have the right knowledge "portfolio."

REFERENCES

Albrow, M. (1996). *The global age. State and society beyond modernity.* Oxford: Blackwell.

Barr, N. (2004). *Economics of the welfare state.* Oxford: Oxford University Press.

Beck, U. (2000a). *What is globalisation?* (P. Camiller, Trans.). Cambridge: Polity.

Beck, U. (2000b). *The brave new world of work.* (P. Camiller, Trans.). Cambridge: Polity.

Beck, U. (1999a). *World risk society.* Cambridge: Polity.

Bottery, M. (2003). The end of citizenship? The nation-state, threats to its legitimacy, and citizenship education in the twenty-first century. *Cambridge Journal of Education, 33*(1).

Carnoy, M. (1999). *Globalisation and educational reform: What planners need to know.* Paris: UNESCO (International Institute for Educational Planning).

Castells, M. (1997). *The power of identity. The information age. Economy, society and culture* (Vol. II). Oxford: Blackwell.

Delanty, G. (2001). *Challenging knowledge. The university in the knowledge society.* Buckingham: SRHE and Open University Press.

EC. (2007). *Strategic report on the renewed lisbon strategy for growth and jobs.* Brussels COM (2007) 803 final.

EC. (2006a). *Delivering on the modernisation agenda for universities: Education, research and innovation.* Brussels COM (2006) 208 final.

EC. (2006b). *Implementing the community lisbon programme: Fostering entrepreneurial mindsets through education and learning.* Brussels COM(2006) 33 final.

EC. (2005a). *Mobilising the brainpower of Europe: Enabling universities to make their full contribution to the lisbon strategy.* Brussels COM(2005) 152 final.

EC. (2005b). *Frontier research: The European challenge.* Brussels: European Commission.

EC. (2004). *Science and technology, the key to Europe's future – guidelines for future European union policy to support research.* Brussels. COM(2004) 353 final.

EC. (2003a). *The role of universities in the Europe of knowledge.* Brussels COM(2003) 58.

EC. (2003b). *'Education & training 2010'. The success of the lisbon strategy hinges on urgent reforms.* Brussels COM(2003) 685 final.

EC. (2000a). *A memorandum on lifelong learning. Commission staff working paper.* Brussels. SEC(2000) 1832.

EC. (2000b). *Towards a European research area.* Brussels COM (2000)6.

Giddens, A. (1987). *The nation-state and violence.* Berkeley and Los Angeles: University of California Press.

Gray, J. (1998). *False dawn. The delusions of global capitalism.* New York: The New Press.

Green, A. (1997). *Education, globalisation and the nation-state.* London: McMillan Press.

Guéhenno, J.-M. (1995). *The end of the nation-state.* (V. Elliott, Trans.). Minneapolis, MN: U. of Minnesota Press.

Held, D. (1995). *Democracy and the global order.* Cambridge: Polity Press.

Held, D., & McGrew, A., Goldblatt, D., Perraton, J. (1999). *Global transformations. Politics, economics and culture.* Cambridge: Polity.

Hirst, P., & Thompson, G. (1996). *Globalisation in question. The international economy and the possibilities of governance.* Cambridge: Polity Press.

Kwiek, M. (2008a, March). On accessibility and equity, market forces and entrepreneurship: Developments in higher education in central and eastern Europe. *Higher Education Management and Policy, 20*(1).

Kwiek, M. (2008b, forthcoming). Academic entrepreneurship and private higher education in Europe (in a comparative perspective). In M. Shattock (Ed.), *Enterepreneurialism in universities and the knowledge economy. Diversification and organisational change in European higher education.* Maidenhead: Open University Press.

Kwiek, M. (2008c). The many faces of privatization in higher education in Poland. Its impact on equity and access. In J. Knight (Ed.), *Financing higher education: Access and equity.* Rotterdam: Sense Publishers.

Kwiek, M. (2007a). The European integration of higher education and the role of private higher education. In S. Slantcheva & D. C. Levy (Eds.), *Private higher education in post-communist Europe. In search of legitimacy.* New York: Palgrave.

Kwiek, M. (2007b). The university and the welfare state in transition. Changing public services in a wider context. In D. Epstein, R. Boden, R. Deem, F. Rizvi, & S. Wright (Eds.), *World yearbook of education 2008: Geographies of knowledge, geometries of power.* New York: Routledge.

Kwiek, M. (2006a). *The university and the state. A study into global transformations.* Frankfurt a/Main and New York: Peter Lang.

Kwiek, M. (2006b). *The classical German idea of the university revisited, or on the nationalization of the modern institution.* Poznan: Center for Public Policy Research Papers Series. Vol. 1. Retrieved from www.cpp.amu.edu.pl

Kwiek, M. (2005). The university and the state in a global age: Renegotiating the traditional social contract? *European Educational Research Journal, 4*(4).

Kwiek, M. (2004, December). The emergent European educational policies under scrutiny. The Bologna process from a central European perspective. *European Educational Research Journal, 3*(4).

Lawn, M. (2003). The 'Usefulness' of learning: The struggle over governance, meaning and the European education space. *Discourse: Studies in the cultural politics of education, 24*(3).

Lawn, M. (2001). Borderless education: Imagining a European education space in a time of brands and networks. *Discourse: Studies in the cultural politics of education, 22*(2).

McGrew, A. (Ed.). (1997). *The transformation of democracy? Globalisation and territorial democracy.* Cambridge: Polity Press.

Neave, G. (2001). The European dimension in higher education: An excursion into the modern use of historical analogues. In J. Huisman, P. Maassen, & G. Neave (Eds.), *Higher education and the state. The international dimension of higher education.* Amsterdam: Pergamon Press.

Ohmae, K. (2000). The end of the nation state. In F. J. Lechner & J. Boli (Eds.), *The globalisation reader.* Oxford: Blackwell.

Reich, R. B. (1992). *The work of nations.* New York: Vintage Books.

Ruggie, J. G. (1997). *Globalisation and the embedded liberalism compromise: The end of an era?.* Max Planck Institute for the Studies of Ssocieties. Working Paper 97/1.

Sassen, S. (1996). *Losing control? Sovereignty in an age of globalisation.* New York: Columbia UP.

Sassen, S. (2003, February). Globalisation or denationalization? *Review of International Political Economy, 10*(1).

Scharpf, F. (2000). Negative integration: States and the loss of boundary control. In C. Pierson & F. G. Castles (Eds.), *The welfare state reader.* Cambridge: CUP.

Scholte, J. A. (2000). *Globalisation. A critical introduction.* New York: Palgrave.

Scholte, J. A. (2002). *What is globalisation? The definitional issue – again.* Centre for the Study of Globalisation and Regionalisation at the University of Warwick. Working Paper. No. 109/02.

Strange, S. (1996). *The retreat of the state. The diffusion of power in the world economy.* Cambridge: CUP.

Weiss, L. (1998). *The myth of the powerless state.* Ithaca, NY: Cornell University Press.

FURTHER READINGS

Delanty, G. (2001). *Challenging knowledge. The University in the knowledge society.* Buckingham: SRHE and Open University Press.

EC (European Commission). (2003). *The role of universities in the Europe of knowledge.* Brussels COM(2003) 58.

Held, D., McGrew, A., Goldblatt, D., Perraton, J. 1999). *Global transformations. Politics, economics and culture.* Cambridge: Polity.

Lawn, M. (2003). The 'Usefulness' of learning: The struggle over governance, meaning and the European education space. *Discourse: Studies in the Cultural Politics of Education, 24*(3).

Sassen, S. (1996). *Losing control? Sovereignty in an age of globalisation.* New York: Columbia UP.

Marek Kwiek
Center for Public Policy
Poznan University, Poland

BOB LINGARD & SHAUN RAWOLLE

RESCALING AND RECONSTITUTING EDUCATION POLICY

The Knowledge Economy and the Scalar Politics of Global Fields

INTRODUCTION

Globalisation has seen a new scalar politics emerge (Brenner, 2004, Robertson et al., 2006), reconstituting relations between nations and international organisations and provoking the emergence of a range of global fields. Bourdieu (2003), for example, speaks of a global economic field which has resulted from politics played by certain individuals, groups, businesses and organisations and a related performative construction of globalisation read only as neo-liberal market capitalism on a global scale in the post Cold war era. Bourdieu's observation rejects a reification of globalisation, reinforcing the work of Dale (1999) and Robertson et al. (2006). All argue the necessity to understand the mechanisms of globalisation and how it works and has effects. In this chapter we also argue the need to document and understand how globalisation works through discourses, organisations and individuals and its consequent effects within nations. Tikly (2004) has made the point that globalisation effects work their way through and into different nations in different ways and illustrates his point in terms of the differences between nations of the global north and those of the global south. The impact of globalisation therefore requires empirical investigation in a way that is sensitive to both national differences and global commonalities. We suggest, drawing on Bourdieu (2003), that one way that such differences may be understood is through the amount of 'national capital' possessed by a given nation, which will be a significant factor in the nature and extent of such mediation. This view of national capital is akin to factors such as democratic governance, national levels of education and so on. Such factors help to secure a given nation's positioning within geo-politics and help mediate pressures from above the nation. It is the growing importance of this hybrid mix of global and national factors that we refer to as a rescaling of educational politics, into which national policies and their effects are increasingly drawn and reconstituted in a global field of comparison.

In this chapter we take what Held and McGrew (2002) call a "transformationalist" view of globalisation, in that we recognise that politics and processes beyond the nation have seen a reframing of both the state and policy processes within the nation. This is an account which rejects any suggestion of a straightforward emergent post-national politics, but rather one which accepts that globalisation of various kinds has produced new state modalities and production rules for policy and policy processes within nations. The nation-state nonetheless remains

M. Simons, M. Olssen and M.A. Peters (eds.), Re-Reading Education Policies: A Handbook Studying the Policy Agenda of the 21st Century, 205–219.

important in political and policy terms, but has been reconstituted in the context of globalisation. Indeed, in some ways we would argue the nation-state now functions strategically in relation to a number of global fields and international organisations. Additionally, as part of the rescaling of policy production, we have seen the emergence of a global education policy field (Lingard, Rawolle & Taylor, 2005), acting *inter alia* as a global field of comparison.

The broad changes discussed in this chapter hold similarities with recent work that identifies a move from government to governance, from hierarchy to networks (Atkinson & Coleman, 1992, Rhodes, 1997). Using a different metaphor to identify these changes, Appadurai (2006) speaks of "vertebrate politics" to describe familiar hierarchical and bureaucratic forms of government and "cellular politics" to refer to the new more horizontal networked forms of governance. We argue that, inevitably, both forms continue simultaneously, adding complexity to the processes of policy and requiring the development of new methodologies for the study of its effects. We see the latter form of cellular politics as related to a post-Westphalian challenge to national sovereignty or at least a reconstitution of it. Again we see this as operating simultaneously with older nation-based Westphalian international relations, where nation-states remain significant in relationships between nations and between nations and a broad range of international organisations. Mann (2000) has spoken about a number of socio-spatial networks which operate simultaneously today; he describes these as local, national, international (relations between nations), trans-national (pass through national boundaries) and global. In this chapter, we are concerned with the interweaving of the national with the global in relation to policy conceptualisation and policy processes and with an emergent global education policy field. This takes us beyond concerns with policy borrowing and policy learning which operate in international, Westphalian ways, and which remain important, to a consideration of the emergent global policy field in education.

This chapter deals with two empirical cases of policy production, set against these new scalar politics and as exemplars of them. We draw upon these empirical cases rather than outline the data. The first empirical case deals with knowledge economy policy, an idea which is an exemplary example of a globalised policy discourse (Taylor et al., 1997) and which the OECD was central to proselytising through an influential 1996 document on the topic. This part of the chapter documents and analyses how knowledge economy policy came to be rearticulated in Australia and as such considers national mediation of the Australian knowledge economy policy, *The Chance to Change* (Batterham, 2000). This analysis also demonstrates not only specific national mediation of a globalised policy discourse, the interplay between global and national educational policy fields, but also mediatisation of the policy process in the sense of the role of the field of journalism in its production (Fairclough, 2000) and cross-field effects (Rawolle, 2005). The second case deals with what we call an emergent global education policy field (Lingard, Rawolle & Taylor, 2005). Here we document the significance of a global articulation of policy as numbers (Rose, 1999) and comparison as new form of governance (Novoa & Yariv-Mashal, 2003) and the ways in which these two help constitute the global education policy field through the creation of a global space of equivalence, a commensurate space of measurement (Porter, 1995, Desrosieres, 1998). The analysis in both cases uses the work of Bourdieu, which we have argued is useful to education policy analysis (Lingard, Taylor & Rawolle, 2005, Lingard & Rawolle, 2008), as has van Zanten (2005). The cases are essentially about understanding the new scalar politics of education policy production and the emergent global education policy field and how it works through cross-field effects in the national field. In this sense, the macro level concern of the chapter is with the rescaling and reconstitution of the production rules for education policy in the context of globalisation. A second level concern is to demonstrate the usefulness of Bourdieu to understanding these new scalar politics in education policy.

KNOWLEDGE ECONOMY: MEDIATISATION AND REARTICULATION IN AUSTRALIA

Our argument in this section is that one of the effects of globalisation on nations can be identified through the development of national policies that adopt, adapt and utilise policy discourses and concepts from international organisations such as the OECD. In this section we focus on the knowledge economy. But, to come back to one of our framing arguments, we suggest that the specific effects of policy concepts such as the OECD's 'knowledge-based economy' should be understood relative to national pressures and policy problems for which they are offered as solutions. This is the interplay of the global and the national, the interplay of an international organisation and the nation-state in a Westphalian way, but in a context where international competitiveness is seen as the *raison d'etre* for education policy. To this end, we focus on Australia's adoption of a policy version of the knowledge economy, which acted as a meta-policy, collecting and coordinating a range of diverse fields, from intellectual property law, higher education, school education, research and innovation. The event that we focus on is Batterham's Review, a policy review established in 1999 by the federal government, initially framed around the potential that Australia's science, engineering and technology industries could play in economic growth. The end point of this review was the production of a final report, *The Chance to Change* (Batterham, 2000), which promoted the adoption of a meta-narrative around Australia's future, based on the potential of knowledge production and innovation, one that went beyond the securing of market fundamentals. This marked a significant anomaly for readings of the policy direction of the Howard Government (1996-2007), whose approach to education in particular was typically associated with neo-liberalism (Marginson, 2002, 2004, 2006).

The policy use of the knowledge economy emerged during the 1990s, alongside other competitor concepts such as the knowledge society, and the more recent development of knowledge cultures (see Kenway et al., 2006; Peters with Besley, 2006). There were two fundamental connections between these competitor concepts developed and proselytised by international organisations such as the OECD and the World Bank. The first connection was a problematisation of knowledge production, and how the governance of institutions related to the production, development and exploitation of knowledge should be managed. This problematisation related to the link between changes in the way that knowledge was produced and social and economic problems facing nations around the world. The second connection was in providing a rationale and rhetorical defences for planned investments in different levels of knowledge production, from school education, higher education, research and industry, relative to the local and national paths of development of these institutions. This defence is crucially important as a distinction from neo-liberal policy developments, in that it highlighted the possible futures that could only emerge from sustained investments in these institutions. The formation of quasi-markets may be a mechanism for such investments, but only in the pursuit of desirable, imagined economic futures. What distinguishes knowledge-economy policies from neo-liberal policies is a normative goal for investment shaped by policy agents, drawn from Government, industry and the private sector involved in creating an imaginary of a desirable future. This kind of knowledge policy can be represented as 'creating policy imaginaries'. In neo-liberal policy development, setting such future imaginaries represents an intervention in markets, which are viewed as a normative end in themself. Such planning is antithetical to Hayekian inspired neo-liberal policy developments.

Ironically, the emergence of these competitor concepts in a global field of policy producers connected together and made visible the very different literatures and assumptions in economics, knowledge management and sociology that underpinned each concept's development. Though semantically similar and used in similar ways in policy aphorisms (Lingard & Rawolle, 2004), the conceptualisation of the knowledge economy and the knowledge society mark divergent disciplinary paths taken by different strands of intellectual thought around the significance of different forms of knowledge and knowledge production. In short, the knowledge economy focuses on the importance of different institutions to innovation, and to the development of systems that embed and enable innovation to take hold. In contrast, the policy conceptualisation of the knowledge society focuses on the different social consequences that result from an increased focus on skills, education and technological development, including social exclusion, social capital and their distribution across and within nations. Given these differences, there is a separate issue of the use-value of each policy concept for nations employing them. The location and use of policy concepts such as the knowledge economy in global and national policy fields refracts the meaning ascribed to them in disciplinary traditions according to the logics of practice of each level of policy field. In brief, such policy fields act as a social space of competition, within which agents compete for certain stakes, such as the priority of social problems, and follow a set of social rules. We argue that the national differences between policy fields also act to inflect the associations of national policy discussions around knowledge production.

There are two interconnected ways that the knowledge economy links to globalisation. The first connection is in the kinds of processes identified in knowledge economy policy documents and academic literature around the knowledge economy. Though there are many processes, we will deal with only one example related to flows of ideas and people (a broader discussion of these developments is discussed in Peters with Besley, 2006). The growth of different information and communication technologies, and in particular the computer technology revolution, enabled increased interconnectivity between people engaged in knowledge production in different nations around the globe. This has resulted in an increasing rate of knowledge production in multiple disciplinary fields, and movement of researchers to nations and locations of research strength (the 'brain drain' and 'brain gain'). Concurrent with this growing potential to produce knowledge has been a commensurate growth in interest in securing and protecting intellectual property rights, so that the transfer of knowledge is not free, but incurs a cost on consumers of knowledge, and a benefit to producers. One of the major outcomes of this move has been a 'globalisation of regulation' (Drahos and Braithwaite, 2000), exemplified through policies such as the *Agreement on Trade Related Intellectual Property Rights* (TRIPS), which attempts to coerce different nations to accept the legal validity of US patents and copyrights. As Story (2002) has argued, education is something of a 'sleeping giant' in discussions around TRIPS. These processes involving flows of ideas and people can also be found in discussions of globalisation (Appadurai, 1996). Such moves, founded principally on new economic stakes in applications of new knowledge and emerging ways to structure knowledge production, invoked the OECD and other researchers to claim that a distinct and new economic field was emerging, and increasingly important for national economic growth and global economic competitiveness: the knowledge economy. One of the effects of this emergent economic level is that the capacity of individuals to understand, consume, produce and benefit from new knowledge becomes crucial to a nation's economic future. Hence, education becomes a much more prominent location for policy intervention, because of its role in developing the capabilities of individuals necessary to be a part of the knowledge economy.

The second connection of the knowledge economy with globalisation is much more direct and relates to the role that international organisations such as the OECD have started to play in representing relevant policy problems for nations and offering their own policies as solutions. The development and promotion of the knowledge-based economy by the OECD highlights the distinctly activist stance such organisations have increasingly favoured (Henry et al., 2001, Rizvi and Lingard, 2008), not only within internationally less powerful nations, but also within affluent nation-states such as Australia. Such involvement of international organisations in national policy developments would appear to compromise the sovereignty of nation-states in dealing with policy and political problems. These two connections between globalisation and the knowledge economy illustrate both the development of policy conceptualisations by international organisations and the underlying social problems that changes in knowledge and knowledge production provide for national governments.

Despite the connections between knowledge production and globalisation, these do not, on their own, explain the way that individual nation-states come to adopt policies related to the knowledge economy, and the effects of these policies. At best, they are pre-conditions for the national adoption of knowledge policies, and offer broad explanations of the policy terrain around knowledge production at the time when nations adopt particular versions of policy concept. In order to understand the local effects of knowledge economy policies, we now turn to a brief outline of a case study of the emergence of knowledge economy policies in Australia. Batterham's Review provides one instance of the emergence of knowledge economy policies in a national context (Australia), and the subsequent translation of knowledge economy discourse to a specific set of national circumstances (Peters with Besley, 2006).

In developing this argument, we draw on Bourdieu's theory of social fields, which highlights the connections between different social fields, including policy fields, and what we refer to as 'cross-field effects' (Lingard & Rawolle, 2004; Rawolle, 2005, 2008; Lingard, Rawolle & Taylor, 2005). While there is not room for an extended treatment of how policy can be understood in relation to social fields (see Rawolle, 2008), for now we will use fields as a nomenclature for different social areas, in which agents compete for specific stakes. In the discussion that follows, we will discuss the 'field of print journalism', indicating the space of competition between journalists in national newspapers in Australia, the 'field of policy', the 'field of politics', the 'field of higher education' and the 'field of business'. Cross-field effects are used here as a way of highlighting the effects that policy developments produce in fields beyond the policy field and vice versa. We will focus specifically on a subclass of cross-field effects which we call 'looping effects', drawing on Ian Hacking (1997, 1995, 2003, 2004) and its development in some research by one of us (Rawolle, 2008). What we call looping effects are cross-field effects that result from agents in one field (for example, the policy field or the field of print journalism) diagnosing specific social problems which involve the naming groups of agents, a categorising of their roles and an imperative to intervene and change the practices of some named groups. The reason these are described as looping effects is that the reactions of groups of people to their diagnosis are in fact the effects in practice. This model represents one kind of causal mechanism to explain and explore some policy effects.

In thinking about what the concept of the knowledge economy allows policy makers to do, we make the argument that policy development "is an attempt to arbitrate in matters where there are disputes within fields or between fields that have led to tensions between fields and pressures within fields" (Rawolle, 2008, p. 7). From this perspective, it is necessary to describe the specific tensions and pressures between different fields in which Batterham's Review can be represented as an intervention, and from which Australia's version of the knowledge economy emerged. Without understanding these tensions and pressures, it would be difficult to study and explain the kinds of cross-field effects produced by Batterham's Review.

The major source of tensions that Batterham's Review sought to resolve were provoked by a series of newspaper reports from a range of journalists and newspaper that documented considerable dissatisfaction with the government's funding of research, higher education and innovation. These were carried in the field of print journalism, but reflected concerns from the fields of higher education, business, science and industry. While some of this dissatisfaction resulted from the government's seeming refusal to offer increased funding, one recurring theme was that, on measures used by the OECD, Australia's performance in knowledge production and innovation was falling behind other OECD and competitor countries. Through the practices of journalists, Australia's policies on higher education were drawn into a global policy field through emerging themes carried in articles. The effects of comparisons with other nations were a perceived decline in Australia's capacity to compete with other OECD nations in knowledge based industries. This is the globe as a commensurate space of measurement linked to the emergent global education policy field, which we will discuss in the next section of this chapter. Yet, despite the seemingly comprehensive decline in Australia's position on these OECD measures, when Batterham's Review was announced, the terms of reference were limited to the extent to which Australia's science, engineering and technology capabilities could contribute to the economy.

The diagnosis offered by Batterham's terms of reference suggested that the 'science base', inclusive of Australia's science, engineering and technology institutions, was the vital connection between innovation, knowledge production and the community, rather than other aspects of education or even other disciplines in higher education. Throughout the course of Batterham's Review, however, emerging themes carried in newspaper articles continually challenged these limited terms of reference. Consistently these terms of reference were challenged with updated figures released by the OECD, adding additional pressure on the national field of politics from an international organisation, and drawing the mediatised policy debate into a global field of comparison. Notably, though, the diagnosis of problems in the terms of reference held looping effects on the kinds of journalists who wrote reports and articles about Batterham's Review. Reporting about Batterham's Review was initially limited to science journalists and business journalists, and then subsequently higher education journalists. It was only after the consultation phase of Batterham's Review had been concluded that a wider section of journalists contributed to coverage; this occurred once the backing of the Prime Minister (then John Howard) highlighted the potential political importance of the review.

The continual reworking and challenge of journalists throughout Batterham's Review highlighted some ways that the field of print journalism was able to re-represent the diagnosis offered by the terms of reference and to offer alternative diagnoses. This is one aspect of the mediatisation of policy, indicating the way that the logic of the field of print journalism acted on and influenced the field of policy over the duration of Batterham's Review. Yet, Batterham resolved the tensions between the field of politics and the field of print journalism by offering an alternative diagnosis, with direct associations with the OECD's knowledge-based economy policy. In dealing with the emerging themes from the fields of print journalism and the field of politics, Batterham represented the problem to be a series of blockages that prevented innovation from occurring. One location of these blockages was represented as the government viewing funding to the science base and other knowledge institutions as an expenditure without returns, while Batterham argued that such funding should be viewed as an investment with specific and measurable returns. Another location of these blockages was the lack of incentives for interactions between people situated at different points within Australia's innovation system, so that much new knowledge produced in Australia's research institutions did not have an avenue for commercialisation. Batterham's resolution was to aim for increased funding, with the intention of keeping Australia competitive with other OECD nations, but to be strategic in the allocation of funds so that the benefits of funding research funding would lead to commercialisation and more researchers staying in Australia.

What this case has demonstrated is how policy production in Australia around the concept of knowledge economy was mediated by the field of journalism, demonstrating particular cross-field effects, namely looping effects. This can be seen to be the mediatisation of policy production in Fairclough's (2000) sense, in that it suggests "a new relationship between politics, government and mass media... which means that many significant political events are now in fact media events" (p. 3) and is an important development in the production of contemporary policy. The case also shows how comparative indicators from the OECD in relation to Australia's investment in the science base was a factor in the final policy outcome, as was the need to justify investment in the science base and higher education. This latter justification was framed by and linked to the globalised discourse of science and education investment as being central to the global competitiveness of the national economy, a discourse proselytised by a range of international organisations, including importantly in this case, the OECD. We would note as well the more policy activist role of an international organisation such as the OECD in the context of globalisation and the rise of supranational entities such as the EU and the emergence of a global education policy field, to a consideration of which we now turn.

AN EMERGENT GLOBAL EDUCATION POLICY FIELD

The previous case dealt with the interplay of the global and the national in policy production in a number of ways. In this section we will consider in broad outline the features of what we see as an emergent global education policy field, which operates in addition to the relationships considered in the previous section, as part of the rescaling of policy production accompanying globalisation. Our specific usage of field here is derived from Bourdieu's concept of field to refer to a space of relations with particular logics of practice, requiring particular habitus and involving contestation over various capitals. This emergent global education policy field, the skeletal features of which will be outlined here, is an important element of the rescaling of education policy, just as the Batterham case provided evidence of the ways that nations today in policy production have to position themselves strategically in relation to the global and are also positioned by globalisation. The outline of the global education policy field ostensibly draws on two research projects (Henry et al., 2001, Grek et al., forthcoming).

As the global economic field has emerged in the post Cold War era and as globalisation has performatively and politically been constructed as neo-liberal economics with more power granted to the market and less to the state (Bourdieu, 2003), education has become a central economic policy tool for nations. Education as the production of the requisite human capital for a knowledge economy is seen as central to national economic policies and national economic well-being. This broad framing of education has witnessed some policy convergence across the globe, but always reframed by what Appadurai (1996) calls 'vernacular globalisation' to pick up on the ways in which global pressures – globalisation from above – are always mediated to a lesser or greater extent by local and national politics, cultures and histories – globalisation from below. This economistic reframing of education policy has also seen a need within nations for comparative performance data and comparative indicators in relation to national education and training systems (Brown et al., 1997) as a measure of likely economic prosperity and success of economic policies. This is where a globalised version of what Rose (1999) has called policy as numbers comes into play and which is intimately linked to the global education policy field.

In the context of globalisation, the nation-state has been restructured under New Public Management, which now steers at a distance by setting broad strategic goals and then 'ensuring' their achievement through a plethora of outcomes and indicator measures. This reinforces Rose's (1999) argument about policy as numbers linked to various forms of accountability and quality control. Our argument here, though, is that this policy as numbers approach within nations has now also been globalised, as a way of nations measuring and comparing their educational performance globally against that of other nations. We would also argue that the OECD, seeking a new role for itself in the context of globalisation, has also moved to establish itself as the international organisation par excellence in terms of international educational indicators and measurement of educational performance globally (Rizvi and Lingard, 2008). This globalised policy as numbers is central to the global education policy field.

In a most insightful paper, Novoa and Yariv-Mashal (2003) have argued that comparison has become central to contemporary forms of governance and that comparison today is global as well as operating inside nations and at both levels works through numbers. In their terms, the 'national eye' today governs through comparison with the assistance of the 'global eye', a globalised policy as numbers. At another level, all of this data, national and international, which is reflective of policy as numbers, is also linked to the rise of what Power (1997) has called the "audit culture", which accompanies quality assurance and the steering at a distance of the new public management, which has eviscerated the old bureaucratic structures of the nation-state. These data can also be seen to be a central component part of what Nigel Thrift (2005) has called "knowing capitalism", the ways today management and social science knowledges, discourses and data have become important sources as capitalism seeks to manage risk and use knowledge about itself as tools for managing the system, which is permanently "under construction" (p. 3). In many ways though, this knowing has thinned out what is regarded as being central to know, particularly in the field of education policy. As Power (1997) notes, management literatures have become more significant in relation to the audit explosion than social science ones, and the system is now managed more through the gaze of top-down quality and audit procedures reliant upon numbers and indicators than inspection at the site of practice. The point here, though, is that such audit now has a global framing as well – the global eye is important and evident in the global education policy field and also assists the national eye in governance.

As indicated earlier, in talking about the rescaling of politics in the context of globalisation we must avoid reifying globalisation. How then has a global education policy field been created: who are the players and organisations involved? We believe some insights can be gained from a brief consideration of the histories of statistics and their imbrication with the emergence of state administrative structures and that an analogy can be made to the emergence of a global education policy field though globalised policy as numbers.

Histories of statistics have demonstrated the interwoven connections between the emergence of state administrative structures at the national level – what Latour (1987) has called a "centre of calculation" – and the development of standardised methodologies and related cognitive schemes inherent in statistics (Porter, 1995, Desrosieres, 1998). Desrosieres (1998, p. 8), for example, observes: "As the etymology of the word shows, statistics is connected with the construction of the state, with its unification and administration." Both Porter and Desrosieres demonstrate the symbiotic relationship between the modern state and statistics. The unification of the space which is the nation, its constitution as a "space of equivalence" (Desrosieres, 1998) is central to policy as numbers through statistics, indicators and the like. Indeed, Porter (1995, p. ix) argues that "quantification is a technology of distance." Similarly Desrosieres (1998, p. 324) points out:

> The construction of a statistical system cannot be separated from the construction of equivalence spaces that guarantee the consistency and permanence, both political and cognitive, of those objects intended to provide reference for debates. The space of representativeness of statistical descriptions is only made possible by a space of common mental representations borne by a common language, marked mainly by the state and the law.

There are at least two binaries at work in relation to statistics/numbers and these spaces of equivalence. On the first, Desrosieres (1998) talks about the realist/non-realist debate to pick up on questions of validity and reliability.. Whatever one's epistemological position (objectivist or relativist), the point to note here though, is that "the measures succeed by giving direction to the very activities that are being measured" (Porter, 1995, p. 45). Porter (1995) also writes about a second binary, notably, the standardisation/accuracy debate. He suggests that: "There is a strong incentive to prefer precise and standardisable measures to highly accurate ones. For most purposes, accuracy is meaningless if the same operation cannot be performed at other sites" (p. 45). Rose (1999) also argues, in a Foucauldian fashion, that numbers, indicators, statistics are inscription devices, which in some ways constitute that which they seek to represent. Single numbers, he suggests, also 'black box', that is, render invisible the judgements and so on which go into the technical construction of a scale. Such statistics, numbers and indicators make a space legible for governing.

Now, our argument here is that the creation of a global education policy field has occurred, or perhaps more accurately is occurring, through creation of a global space of equivalence in relation to student education performance and to a whole raft of educational indicators. The OECD in its more recent activist phase in global education policy processes has established a niche as the centre of technical excellence for international educational indicators and for international comparative measures of student performance. This globalised policy as numbers has begun to constitute the globe as a space of equivalence for measuring the performance of national education systems. This makes the global space legible and as such helps constitute a global education policy field. The creation of the global education policy field thus has occurred in ways analogous with the symbiotic relationships between statistics, state administrative structures within nations and the constitution of the nation as a space of equivalence. This is the post-Westphalian character of this aspect of the rescaling of politics and policy production in education.

Elsewhere we have elaborated the story of the OECD's educational indicators which are published annually now in *Education at Glance* (Henry et al., 2001) and which also seek to deal with input-outcomes relationships in education systems. The OECD is also involved with the World Bank, and UNESCO in the creation of *World Education Indicators*, a project which seeks to create indicators in education for nations of the global south, as a complement to its educational indicators which deal largely, but not wholly, with its thirty member nations. We would also note the alignment of statistical categories across the OECD, Eurostat, the EU's statistical agency and UNESCO.

The OECD's *Programme for International Student Assessment* (PISA), which was established by the OECD in the late 1990s in the broad global policy context outlined earlier, has been conducted three times now (2000, 2003, 2006) and seeks to measure students' literacy, numeracy, science literacy and problem solving capabilities and potential for lifelong learning at the end of compulsory schooling (approximately aged 15 years). In 2006, 57 countries participated, while in 2009 the number will be almost 100. These tests, commissioned from experts and expert agencies, purport to be non-curricula based. In a way they constitute the globe as a space of equivalence with the emphasis being upon standardised measures rather than on accuracy of measurement, even though we would concede that the tests are probably as technically good as they could be, as is the analysis of them. However, their policy use as points of comparison within nations gives priority to their standardisation over their accuracy.

The global education policy field then is being constituted through a globalised approach to policy as numbers. We have tentatively and skeletally outlined the way these processes are occurring and paid attention to the role that the OECD has played in relation to its emergence. However, more empirical research and theorising are required into this specific element of the rescaling of education policy production. Consideration would also need to be given to policy as numbers approaches at other supranational levels, for example, in the indicators work in relation to education within the EU (Grek et al., forthcoming). There are also a range of other international comparative measures of educational performance. However, we have concentrated in this brief case study on the OECD's indicators and PISA work, because it is the OECD which has sought to create a global space of equivalence through both.

DISCUSSION AND CONCLUSION

In this chapter we have begun to outline the contours of the new scalar politics as evident in the new production rules for education policy and in the strategic education policy work of nations today. In so doing, we have also sketched the emergent global education policy field.

The first policy case presented an account of the ways in which national policy fields draw on the resources offered by the global education policy field as a template for designing national policies, and as a way of attempting to resolve tensions between national fields. The focus of this case was on the OECD's concept of a knowledge based economy. This case outlined ways in which both the field of policy and the field of print journalism drew on the scale of policy and numbers of comparison offered within the global education policy field to challenge the then government's representation of problems related to knowledge production. The role of the field of print journalism over the course of this review illustrated what, after Fairclough (2000), we called the mediatisation of policy, in that media coverage offered alternative diagnoses of problems facing knowledge production in Australia, but also introduced emerging themes around the importance of global comparisons of performance for the Batterham review. We would argue that the mediatisation of education policy is a relatively new phenomenon, which also requires more research in critical education policy studies.

The second case of this paper proposed an argument more directly about the development and importance of an emergent global education policy field, which acts as a global field of comparison, in which the performance of nations is reduced to a limited range of numbers and indicators. Testing, indicators and metrics developed by international organisations take on a much broader political significance as a result of the emergence of this field, which is constituted by their policy as numbers work, and which reconstitute national education policy against and within a new scale of equivalence, while simultaneously removing traces of values and conflict embedded in the development of the relevant numbers and metrics. This global space of equivalence is central to the global education policy field, which is an important instance of the new scalar politics and Post-Westphalian practices affecting education policy production rules today.

Both cases have also demonstrated how globalisation has affected international organisations and their modus operandi. Specifically, we have illustrated the more activist role of the OECD in proselytising global education policy discourses such as knowledge economy (and lifelong learning) and in relation to the constitution of the global educational policy field.

The final point we would make is that Bourdieu's bundles of concepts including social field, habitus, capitals and logics of practice can be usefully applied in education policy studies (Lingard, Taylor & Rawolle, 2005, van Zanten, 2005, Lingard & Rawolle, 2008). This has been illustrated through consideration of education policy as a field and through the concept of cross-field effects in the first policy case and in the concept of the global education policy field in the second. The concept of logics of practice, which defines any given social field, would also seem to have real purchase for understanding education policy as a field and its rescaled character, as well as failures of implementation across fields, including global and national fields.

REFERENCES

Appadurai, A. (2006). *Fear of small numbers an essay on the geography of fear.* Durham, NC: Duke University Press.

Appadurai, A. (1996). *Modernity at large: Cultural dimensions of globalisation.* Minneapolis, MN: The University of Minnesota Press.

Atkinson, M., & Coleman, W. (1992). Policy networks, policy communities and the problems of governance. *Governance, 5,* 154–180.

Batterham, R. (2000). *The chance to change: Final report.* Canberra: Australian Government Printing Service (AGPS).

Bourdieu, p. (2003). *Firing back against the Tyranny of the market.* London: Verso.

Brenner, N. (2004). *New state spaces urban governance and the rescaling of statehood.* Oxford: Oxford University Press.

Brown, p. , Halsey, A. H., Lauder, H., & Stuart Wells, A. (1997). The transformation of education and society: An introduction. In A. H. Halsey, H. Lauder, p. Brown, & A. Stuart Wells (Eds.), *Education: Culture, economy and society.* Oxford: Oxford University Press.

Dale, R. (1999). Specifying globalisation effects on national policy: A focus on mechanisms. *Journal of Education Policy, 14*(1), 1–17.

Desrosieres, A. (1998). *The politics of large numbers: A history of statistical reasoning.* Cambridge: Harvard University Press.

Drahos, p. , & Braithwaite, J. (2000). The globalisation of regulation. *Electronic Journal of Intellectual Property Rights,* Working Paper 02/00.

Fairclough, N. (2000). *New Labour, New Language.* London: Routledge.

Grek, S., Lawn, M., Lingard, B., Ozga, J., Rinne, R., Segerholme, C., et al. (forthcoming). National policy brockering and the construction of the European education space in England, Sweden, Finland and Scotland. *Comparative Education.*

Hacking, I. (1975). *The emergence of probability.* Cambridge: Cambridge University Press.

Hacking, I. (1995). The looping effects of human kinds. In D. Sperber, D. Premack, & A. J. Premack (Eds.), *Causal cognition: A multidisciplinary approach.* Oxford: Clarendon Press.

Hacking, I. (2003). Inaugural lecture: Chair of philosophy and history of scientific concepts at the Collège de France, 16 January 2001. *Economy and Society, 31,* 1–14.

Hacking, I. (2004). Between Michel Foucault and Erving Goffman: Between discourse in the abstract and face-to-face interaction. *Economy and Society, 33,* 277–302.

Held, D., & McGrew, A. (2002). *Globalisation/Anti-Globalisation.* Oxford: Polity Press.

Henry, M., Lingard, B., Taylor, S., & Rizvi, F. (2001). *The OECD, globalisation and education policy.* Oxford: Pergamon.

Kenway, J., Bullen, E., Fahey, J., & Robb, S. (2006). *Haunting the knowledge economy.* London: Routledge.

Latour, B. (1987). *Science in Action: How to follow scientists and engineers through society.* Cambridge: Harvard University Press.

Lingard, B., & Rawolle, S. (2004). Mediatising educational policy: The journalistic field. Science policy and cross-field effects. *Journal of Education Policy, 19*(3), 361–380.

Lingard, B., & Rawolle, S. (2008). *The sociology of Pierre Bourdieu and researching education policy.* Unpublished paper.

Lingard, B., Rawolle, S., & Taylor, S. (2005). Globalising policy sociology in education: Working with Bourdieu. *Journal of Education Policy, 20*(6), 759–777.

Lingard, B., Taylor, S., & Rawolle, S. (2005). Bourdieu and the study of educational policy: Introduction. *Journal of Education Policy, 20*(6), 663–669.

Mann, M. (2000). Has globalisation ended the rise and rise of the nation-state? In D. Held & A. McGrew (Eds.), *The global transformations reader.* Cambridge: Polity Press.

Marginson, S. (2002). Nation-building universities in a global environment: The case of Australia. *Higher Education, 43,* 409–428.

Marginson, S. (2004, April). They make a desolation and they call it F.A. Hayek: Australian universities on the brink of the Nelson reforms. *Australian Book Review,* 28–35.

Marginson, S. (2006). Dynamics of national and global competition in higher education. *Higher Education, 52,* 1–39.

Novoa, A., & Yariv-Mashal, T. (2003). Comparative research in education: A mode of governance or a historical journey? *Comparative Education, 39*(1), 423–438.

Peters, M. A., & Besley, A. C. (2006). *Building knowledge cultures: Education and development in the age of knowledge capitalism.* New York/Oxford: Rowman & Littlefield.

Porter, T. (1995). *Trust in numbers: The pursuit of objectivity in science and public life.* Princeton, NJ: Princeton University Press.

Power, M. (1997). *The audit society rituals of verification.* Oxford: Oxford University Press.

Rawolle, S. (2005). Cross-field effects and temporary social fields: A case study of the mediatisation of recent Australian knowledge economy policies. *Journal of Education Policy, 20*(6), 705–724.

Rawolle, S. (2008). *When the knowledge economy becomes the chance to change: Mediatisation, cross-field effects and temporary social fields.* PhD Thesis, The University of Queensland.

Rhodes, R. (1997). *Understanding governance.* Buckingham: Open University Press

Rizvi, F., & Lingard, B. (2008). The OECD and global shifts in education policy. In R. Cowen & A. Kazamias (Eds.), *International handbook of comparative education.* Dordrecht: Kluwer Academic Publishers.

Robertson, S., Bonal, X., & Dale, R. (2006). GATS and the education service industry: The politics of scale and global reterritorialisation. In H. Lauder, p. Brown, J. Dillabough, & A. H. Halsey (Eds.), *Education, globalisation & social change.* Oxford: Oxford University Press.

Rose, N. (1999). *Powers of freedom: Reframing political thought.* Cambridge: Cambridge University Press.

Story, A. (2002). Don't ignore copyright, the 'sleeping giant' on the TRIPS and international educational agenda. In p. Drahos & R. Mayne (Eds.), *Global intellectual property rights: Knowledge, access and development.* London: Macmillan.

Taylor, S., Rizvi, F., Lingard, B., & Henry, M. (1997). *Educational policy and the politics of change.* London: Routledge.

Thrift, N. (2005). *Knowing capitalism.* London: Sage.

Tikly, L. (2004). Globalisation and education in the postcolonial world: Towards a conceptual framework. *Comparative Education, 37*(2), 151–171.

van Zanten, A. (2005). Bourdieu as education policy analyst and expert: A rich but ambiguous legacy. *Journal of Education Policy, 20*(6), 671–686.

FURTHER READINGS

Bourdieu, p. (2003). *Firing back: Against the Tyranny of the market*. London: Verso.

Brenner, N. (2004). *New state spaces urban governance and the rescaling of statehood*. Oxford: Oxford University Press.

Lingard, B., & Ozga, J. (Eds.) (2007). *The RoutledgeFalmer reader in education policy and politics*. London: Routledge.

Peters, M. A., & Besley, A. C. (2006). *Building knowledge cultures: Education and development in the age of knowledge capitalism*. New York: Rowman & Littlefield.

Porter, T. (1995). *Trust in numbers: The pursuit of objectivity in science and public life*. Princeton, NJ: Princeton University Press.

Rizvi, F., & Lingard, B. (2008). The OECD and global shifts in education policy. In R. Cowen & A. Kazamias (Eds.), *International handbook of comparative education*. Dordrecht: Kluwer Academic Publishers.

Bob Lingard
School of Education
The University of Queensland, Australia

Shaun Rawolle
School of Education
Charles Sturt University, Australia

KNOWLEDGE SOCIETY

HEINZ SÜNKER

SOCIETY, KNOWLEDGE AND EDUCATION

INTRODUCTION

"Which knowledge, which society" is the question André Gorz (2004, p. 87) brings to the fore when dealing with problems of social analysis based on relating knowledge, value and capital.[1] He argues very strongly in favour of an approach which mediates knowledge production and material production – especially in times where allegedly immaterial production has gained overweight in comparison to material production.[2] Gorz' position of 'knowledge capitalism' can be linked to a question Henri Lefebvre put more than 30 years ago, "What should one call today's society?" (1972, p. 69), in the context of his analysis of everyday life in the modern world. Having discussed a variety of suggestions, Lefebvre arrived at his own conclusion: "a bureaucratic society of planned consumption" (Lefebvre, 1972, p. 88).This was supposed to define what was characteristic of the appearance of social relationships, that is to say, the current societal formation.

Therefore the aim of this paper is to assess the meaning and the reality of speaking about a 'knowledge society' or better: 'knowledge capitalism' and its possible consequences for education, i.e. analysing the 'new' relationship between education and society, consequences for education policy and education practise.[3] Since the time of Lefebvre's analysis the suggestion has been made, in more or less well-founded socio-theoretical debates, that, with reference to the present or the future, we should speak of a "knowledge society" (cf. Beck, 2000; Thurow, 2000; Stehr, 2001; Weingart, 2001). These debates also include contributions that focus on the implications of acceptance of this new concept of "knowledge society" for "education" [4](cf. European Commission, 1995; Rosenbladt, 1999; Stross, 2001) and consequently attempt to specify the general problem of what and how children should "learn" (cf. Gagnon, 1995) by referring to the question "what is new in times of a knowledge society?"

Here one should first of all remember the origins and contexts of discussions that can be understood as the precursors of central present views of problems, change in society and "change in the method of knowledge production" (Weingart, 2001, p. 11; cf. Nowotny, 1999). These include articles about the "Structure of Scientific Revolution" (Kuhn, 1967; cf. Weinberg, 1998), about the "Knowledge Society" (Lane, 1966), "Science and Capital" (AK-Fraktion, n.d.), "Scientific-Technical Progress and Political System" (Hirsch, 1970), and "Technology and Capital" (Vahrenkamp, 1973), in which the capitalist shaping of machinery and the

M. Simons, M. Olssen and M.A. Peters (eds.), Re-Reading Education Policies: A Handbook Studying the Policy Agenda of the 21st Century, 220–234.
© 2009 Sense Publishers. All rights reserved.

role of scientific-technical intelligence became a topic, for analysis about "Science and Social Reproduction" (Rolshausen, 1975), and the "Richta Report" (Richta, 1972), in which convergence theoretically orientated questions of the relationship between technical progress and industrial society were discussed. In addition there were questions about the fundamental problem of the social synthesis of mental and manual work (Sohn-Rethel, 1970), "The Manufacture of Knowledge" (Knorr-Cetina, 1984) and the "Anthropology of Recognition. The Development of Knowledge as the Epic Theatre of a Cunning Reason" (Elkana, 1986). Finally, there is the analysis of a new type of society in the form of the reflexive modern world (Beck et al, 1996). At the end of this development, both chronologically, and perhaps systematically, are the so-called "science wars" (Sokal, 1996).[5]

In order to evaluate all these debates and approaches, as well as their scope in regard to questions that are practical for democracy (cf. Elkana, 1986, p. 350), it is valid to refer to a central leitmotif of critical theory that Anna Siemsen formulated 50 years ago, thus connecting educational theory, social analysis and critical policy analysis[6]:

> I see the cause [of fascism and Stalinism] as coming much more from the fact that our consciousness has been exclusively technically orientated, has achieved enormous success in the area of nature domination and material technology and instead totally neglected the area of social relationships. The objective consequence of this has been the decline and the chaotic confusion of our social relationships, which may politically emancipate humans, but which socially isolates them. (...) The individual is seen to be isolated from society. He or she sees that this is only used or misused against him or herself, and thus feels opposed to it. For the individual the 'struggle for existence' is only a competition with its own kind in which any means is allowed. Until, finally, the insufferableness of this state and of this attitude towards awareness leads him or her to escape to any kind of social relationship, be it the blind submission to a state leadership, a party or a fuehrer (Siemsen, 1948, p. 5).

Bringing this problem to the fore includes, too, the task of dealing with connections between modes of societalisation and education[7]. Since the beginning of the new sociology and politics of education debate (Bowles/Gintis, 1976; Cole, 1988; Wexler, 1990) there is a main topic called "correspondence and contradiction in education theory" (Cole, 1988). In these discourses social tasks of education were mediated with governance structures embedded in social relations of production. This task has been seen as strongly connected with the production of historically specific standards of the qualification of the work force.[8] The attempt of "making sense of education policy" (Whitty, 2002) in contemporary times ends up in the analysis of processes of marketisation and commodification of education. These analyses furthermore deal with "class strategies and the education market" (Ball, 2003), the new status of citizens as consumers (Whitty, 1998) and the international cheering of school autonomy and choice (Radtke & Weiss, 2000; Sünker, 2006a: chap. 2).[9]

THE RISE OF THE KNOWLEDGE SOCIETY

In the classical framing, which focuses on the development of a rise of the knowledge society, the wording, according to Lane (1966) is:

> As a first approximation to a definition, the knowledge society is one in which, more than in other societies, its members: (a) inquire into the basis of their beliefs about man, nature, and society; (b) are guided (perhaps unconsciously) by objective standards of veridical truth, and, at the upper levels of education, follow scientific rules of evidence and inference in inquiry; (c) devote considerable resources to this inquiry and thus have a large store of knowledge; (d) collect, organize, and interpret their knowledge in a constant effort to extract further meaning from it for the purposes at hand; (e) employ this knowledge to illuminate (and perhaps modify) their values and goals as well as to advance them. Just as the "democratic society" has a foundation in governmental and interpersonal relations, and "the affluent society" a foundation in economics, so the knowledge society has its roots in epistemology and the logic of inquiry (Lane, 1966, p. 650; cf. p. 661).

In this context Drucker, in his text *The Rise of the Knowledge Society* (1993), analyses developments whose object is social change and a radical change in the role of knowledge in and for the modern age. At the centre of this radical change in the significance for individual life and social contexts is the transition from 'being' to 'doing'. Against this background knowledge changes, for him, from a private to a public commodity (Drucker, 1993, p. 53).

Drucker reconstructs three phases of this development whereby the first phase is related to the Industrial Revolution around 1750 and consists of the fact that knowledge is applied through a new type of relationship to tools, processes and products. The second phase begins in 1880 and is connected to what Drucker calls the "revolution of productivity." The new significance of knowledge is expressed in the fact that it refers to work, structures, procedures and contents of the work process. The last phase of this development begins after the Second World War and is centred in knowledge being applied to knowledge itself; at the core it concerns what Drucker calls the Management Revolution. In all, it is crucial for Drucker that the change in the significance of knowledge, which he feels began 250 years ago, has transformed society as well as the economy (Drucker, 1993, p. 65) and is overall to be evaluated as progress. Here the fact that this development goes hand in hand with increasing social inequality and leads to a further impoverishment of great parts of the population (cf. Beck, 2000; Thurow, 2000) is forgotten, overlooked and underrated.

Drucker goes as far as to claim that with this development, knowledge is given the power to create a new society. At the end, however, is the question that is crucial and new for him: "What constitutes the educated person in the knowledge society?" (Drucker, 1993, p. 70). He is also presented with the task of clarifying what it means to be an educated person (ibid., p. 71). Consequently, one must state that, for Drucker, the rise of the knowledge levels include obviously a particular historical relationship between knowledge, education and personality.

WORK, OWNERSHIP AND KNOWLEDGE: ON THE KNOWLEDGE SOCIETIES

More than ever before knowledge is the foundation and guide of human action in all areas of our society. This has extensive social consequences that are practically irreversible. In industry production this development is expressed for example in the fact that particularly in knowledge based production a high portion of the costs account for the category of 'knowledge' (Stehr, 1994, p. 11, trans. Jane Farrar).

According to Stehr's analysis it is crucial that one can speak of an advance in scientific awareness for all essential areas of life in modern-day society. It concerns dimensions and processes that were mentioned in the introduction and that refer to:

– scientification as the scientific pervasion of all areas of life and activity, as well as the concept of the knowledge society;
– professionalisation, that is to say, a suppression of traditional forms of knowledge through scientific awareness, the complex 'scientific knowledge and ability';
– the differentiation of a system of scientific and educational politics;
– the production of knowledge in the context of education in a specific sector of production;
– the reformation of dominant structures in the context of technological/ technocratic developments;
– the emergence of expert power, that is to say, transformation processes in the context of the legitimation of power;
– knowledge about the analysis of social processes and, thus, a new foundation for emancipation and social control (Stehr, 1994, p. 36; cf. Weingart, 2001, p. 332).

Fundamental for Stehr and his analysis is the fact that knowledge is increasingly becoming a constituent of modern society, which means that the social constitutive mechanism is determined by knowledge, and, as the case may be, that the identity of the present social formation is determined by knowledge (Stehr, 1994, p. 28; cf. also Stehr, 2001, p. 119). The evaluation of the "generally growing importance of knowledge as the resource and basis of social activity" (Stehr, 1994, p. 39) is a consequence of this. This idea, which is later interesting for educational theory, is concretised by the assumption that chances for action of small individual groups of people are widespread (ibid., p. 451).[10] This thought is also interesting because Stehr emphasises that one cannot talk of a comparable amplification of the capacity for action of social institutions (see later).

At the same time Stehr emphasises the contradictoriness of the new constellations. He expresses that knowledge must always be (re)produced and that actors must always appropriate it; so if the chance arises, the actors can put a stamp on knowledge, so to speak. This appropriation process is said to leave marks on knowledge. In the course of this activity becoming a matter of course, actors would acquire new cognitive abilities, deepen existing efficiency in their work with knowledge and improve the overall efficiency of their contact with knowledge, which would then make it possible for them to increasingly critically treat offerings of knowledge and to implement new possibilities for action. However, the social distribution of knowledge has no zero sum qualities.

Especially relevant for the question of use and misuse of knowledge for human goals, i.e. against power structures, is Stehr's assessment: With the increase in the extent of the social scope of knowledge there is, for example, no simple linear increase in the content of knowledge achieved, but rather more likely a type of explosive or geometric progression of the capacity for action and, thus, an expansion in the knowledge of many individuals and groups. Therefore this expansion – and this can be decisive for democracy as a praxis – leads to a situation in which it is no longer only a few actors who control relevant capacities for action, as in the past, but rather, many actors would have some influence on the possibilities of action determined for them. Against this possibilities for defending a 'principle of hope', i.e. competencies of the people to govern their own life, Stehr warns. This general expansion in the social distribution of knowledge does not at all mean that the average citizen, voter, consumer, patient or pupil suddenly develops a strongly pronounced feeling that every day contexts are transparent and understandable or even controllable (see Giddens, 1990, p. 146). In other words: the general expansion of the social possibilities of action should not be misunderstood as the elimination of fear, risks, chance, arbitrariness, luck and generally of circumstances of action on which the individual barely has a grasp (Stehr, 1994, p. 516, cf. also pp. 20, 467).

THE INFORMATION AGE

The beginning of Castells' three-volume work[11] provides the description of a task that it is necessary to analyse the emergence of a new social structure manifesting itself in various forms which are based on the diversity of cultures and institutions on our planet. This new social structure is said to be connected to the emergence of a new type of development, called "informationalism" by Castells; this form is said to have formed historically through the restructuring process of capitalist production methods at the end of the twentieth century: "The theoretical perspective that underlies this research approach assumes that societies are organized by processes produced by people, which are then structured in a historically defined way through the relationships between production, experience and power" (Castells, 1996, p. 14).

In this analytical approach it is relevant that the understanding is that the processes to be verified concern developments in the context of capital relationships that express themselves purely in the endless search for money and more money through the production of goods and more goods (ibid., p. 474).[12] Crucial for this level of development, which Castells labels "network society", is the attempt at a global coordination of capital while work is individualised and, thus, supposed to be atomised. This leads to the deciding consequence that the struggle between different capital fractions and a weakened working class is subordinated to an even more fundamental contradiction between the pure logics of capital flow and the cultural values of human experience (ibid., p. 476).

According to Castells' analysis the present societal formation concerns a new form of capitalism, characterised by the globalisation of central economic activities, organisational flexibility and a greater power of work management in the form of the product of labour (ibid., p. 337).

Even though it concerns a strengthened and hardened form of capitalism regarding the aim of the realisation of capital, this is incomparably more flexible than any previous form as far as the means are concerned. It concerns an information-based capitalism that abuts innovation-induced productivity and globalised competitiveness with regard to the ability to produce wealth and to selectively acquire it. Thereby, according to Castells, this form of capitalism is more than ever before embedded in culture and produced through technology. However, now culture and technology are dependent of the specific ability of knowledge and information to act on the basis of knowledge and information; this happens in a network of global correlated interrelations (ibid., p. 338).

Under these new conditions of production, work (always to be thought of as the product of labour) is redefined in its production role and thereby strictly defines itself according to the characteristics of the worker:

> The crucial difference here refers to what I call generic labour versus self-programmable labour. The critical point when distinguishing both of these types of labour is education, the ability to achieve a higher level of education; this means that it concerns knowledge and information embodied in education. Thereby the concept of education must be distinguished from that of technologies. Technologies can quickly become obsolete through technological and organizational changes. Education, in distinction to looking after children and pupils, represents a process through which people, that is to say, work capacity, develop the ability to constantly redefine the necessary abilities for a given task; it also concerns abilities to provide oneself with access to the sources to learn these techniques. An educated person, at least in a corresponding organization environment, can reproduce themselves in regards to the endlessly changing tasks of the production process (Castells, 1998, p. 341).

In conclusion this view means that education represents the key qualification in the product of labour (Castells, 1998, p. 345).

In contrast to an analytical approach, which could to be understood as structure functionalistic, Castells is essentially interested in the question of alternatives for the dominant form of societalisation. According to his approach, these alternatives arise from identity-forming processes to which the organising principles of the analysed society are external. Possibilities for alternative developments can be found in social movements and cultural projects (ibid., p. 351). This perspective considers the insight into the necessity for breaking off from institutionalised social logics. Castells reinforces this view that such a separation is necessary by including historical experiences that are related to the twentieth century and which are characterised by the fact that up until now technology and industrialisation have been used by people to massacre each other in terrible wars. Since then the new technological power has reached a stage in which humanity could end life on Earth (ibid., p. 353). When Castells speaks of the fact that there is an extraordinary gap between our technological overdevelopment and our social underdevelopment (ibid., p. 359) he thus incorporates a leitmotif in the evaluation of social relationships which, as Siemsen's analysis has already shown, is and remains significant for critical social analysis.

EDUCATION, SOCIETY AND EMANCIPATION

A crucial point of reference for the emancipation problem, i.e. the question of the subject of survival as well as the perspective of surviving, affecting at the same time the core of critical education science or critical pedagogy (cf. Sünker & Krüger, 1999), forms the "institution question" from both the perspective of critical social science as well as education theory: when Stehr claims that the capacity for action of social institutions is not able to be expanded and when Castells finds in an even clearer way that it is only when going beyond institutionally formed social logics that the chance to form autonomous identities arises, then this may serve the purpose of a socio-scientifically orientated interfacing of Heydorn's idea, formulated in educational theoretical interest, which says: in light of the present social relationships institution and maturity form an insurmountable contradiction (Heydorn, 1979, p. 317).[13]

This is formulated by Heydorn on the model and at the end of a presentation of dialectics of the institutionalisation of education in European history (cf. Sünker, 2006a: chap. 7); in this concept the relationship of education, work and reflexivity plays a crucial role.[14] In the future of fundamental changes in the work process new technical and organisational demands that are placed on production promote the radical spread of democratic, that is to say, emancipatory principles in the economy (Bowles & Gintis, 1987, p. 179). However, this development must be supported by an increase in awareness of the conditions of social life (cf. the arguments of Siemsen and Castells) as well as of a new kind of technological competence whose core exists in the knowledgeable critique of technocratic rule (cf. Fischer, 1990; Heydorn, 1980b, p. 145; Hörning, 2001), which would mean that the reflexive aspect of knowledge would indeed be given priority.

With this background Kern & Schumann (1984) demand in their study *The End of Labor Division*, as a consequence of their new production concepts (and this difference to Drucker's technically founded belief of progress is to be emphasised), firstly, a generalisation of the recently required production intelligence and secondly, a politicisation, as well as raising awareness of this systematically induced need. The fact that this problem does not present anything new historically, that is to say, in the context of bourgeois capitalist social development, is referred to by Heydorn's view of Enlightenment educational theory and production education, an idea that makes the historical contingence of this relationship clear (cf. Sünker, 2006a: chap. 7)

> An educational concept is only as progressive as the powers that represent it, and, at the same time, lead a direct political battle to change society. This is the only way that education possibilities are actualized and education becomes an important moment in the discussion. Education for its own sake is not capable of very much, it is not clever common sense. The concept of production education receives its possibility for liberation through a conscious middle class ready for revolution that was temporarily able to connect with the rising proletariat. In the moment in which this requirement was omitted, production education became its opposite, it stabilized the existing authority. Without transcending categories, without the formal, abstract clamp on material things, a coordination system of understanding, became a means by which to keep people's nose to the ground like that of a pig without direct struggle (Heydorn, 1980b, p. 109, trans. Jane Farrar).

In this context the incapability of alteration, subject to mutual agreement of awareness education firstly arises for reflexive, that is to say, positions of educational theory, social sciences and industrial sociology that do not serve the ruling interests. In its substance this means gaining a conscience of history and presence; this finds an essential foundation in the fact that knowledge and experience determine the beginning of the struggle against the prevailing conditions. In this sense one may say: "The new revolutionary subject that is the only one concerned is a knowledgeable subject" (Heydorn, 1979, p. 334, trans. Jane Farrar; cf. Sherover-Marcuse, 1986); consequently, education as an essential approach for overcoming power and rule contains a "revolution of awareness" (Heydorn, 1979, p. 337) which is particularly necessary as Castells' analysis has shown, in light of the permanent "production revolutionising"; for the relationship between production and awareness education is able to be characterised in the present by the fact that production has reached what have been unknown possibilities up until now and has stayed behind 'these possibilities' more and more:

> The production of humans' capacity for action against the technical revolution is the foremost problem of education; it includes the revolutionary change in conditions. Liberation of awareness through education thus poses the question of how delays in awareness which are destructive to humans can be stopped from material production (Heydorn, 1980b, p. 164, trans. Jane Farrar; cf. Sonnemann, 1969).

In order to make the background of this argumentation clear it is useful to refer to the practical philosophical constellation within which Heydorn moves and within which the possibility of subject constitution is generally connected to achievements of awareness (cf. Adorno, 1973; Bourdieu, 1987; Sünker, 1989). This includes the fact that overcoming the separation of upbringing and education, as well as that of domination and freedom, essentially occurs as that of individuals as well as of all humans who work on their conscience and on the 'world'. Therefore it is not only complementary but also supports the level of the social organisation of work and technology as well as the form and content of social relationships, giving it crucial importance.

The education of awareness refers to this as dialectic and thus does not manifest itself in the paradigm of awareness philosophy (cf. Sünker, 1989).[15] A similar social policy deals with the question of overcoming alienation, which is thought to be a revolutionisation of work, recreation and needs and whose aim exists in the development of radical democracy (Heydorn, 1980a, p. 295; cf. Heller, 1978; Laclau/Mouffe, 1985; Lefebvre, 1987; Meiksins Wood, 1995; Gorz, 2004). The universality, that is to say, the comprehensive nature of this approach lies for Heydorn in a view of the present situation in which education has gained generality and refers to the fact "that the moments of education overcome their class historical disunity and can become universal in a liberated way" (Heydorn, 1980b, p. 291; cf. Thompson, 1983, p. 238; Sünker, 2006a: chap. 3, 5). This position still includes the concept of a radically altered emancipation process in a broad sense, which is beneficial to the relationship between culture and economy, thus referring to the form and content of the work process as well as to the relationship between general education and occupational training: "The economic and the aesthetic concept, imago and historical process have reached the limits of their previous possibilities; this condition allows them to find each other transformed" (Heydorn, 1980b, p. 122, trans. Jane Farrar; cf. Marcuse, 1987, p. 37).

Even though up until the present a spreading diffusion of the new production concepts and a hesitant change from work structures on the basis of a new type of relationing of subjectivity and technology may have been concerned (Kern & Schumann, 1984), and even though up until now it has only been an idea that capitalists are outdated in their social function (Bowles & Gintis, 1987, p. 213; cf. Schweickart, 1996), the perspective remains that democracy can only survive if it spreads to the areas of social life that have so far been dominated by the prerogative of capitalist ownership structures (Bowles & Gintis, 1987, p. 211). This perspective and the social developments that accompany it are derived from the view that the question of the social organisation of work in its capitalist formation is on the agenda today because a change in the form of distribution alone is not adequate in terms of carrying out the democracy and maturity perspective (Bowles & Gintis, 1987, p. 71; cf. Meszaros, 1989, p. 351). Furthermore, it leads to the challenge of rethinking Marx's idea of the "association of free individuals" (cf. Theunissen, 1978a, p. 472ff.; Berman, 1988, p. 90ff.; Meiksins Wood, 1995, p. 290-291) as well as grasping Marx's utopia of "travail attractive, self-realization of the individual" (Marx, n.d., p. 505; cf. Heydorn, 1980b, p. 165). In this context knowledge would have a new position in relieving the life of everyone and unburdening the conditions of material production.

Regarding the discourses about knowledge society, in a materialistic turn this would mean, from an educational political, educational practical and educational theoretical perspective, not only to adhere to the conception of education for everyone, but rather to demand it. With respect to the present social relationships in their consequences for upbringing and education one could say that three functions are concerned here – labour, civil status and private life, for whose fulfilment it is valid to recognise:

> Schooling for work is a 'conservative' function, demanding disciplined mastery of tasks from the world of work as it is, not as we wish it to be, and objective testing of student competence. Schooling for citizenship, in contrast, is a 'radical' activity, egalitarian and sceptical in style, mixing the hard study of history and ideas with free-swinging exchange on public issues. The school nurtures teamwork and thorny individualism, at once the readiness to serve and the readiness to resist, for nobody knows ahead of time which the good citizen may have to do. To educate the private person, the school must detach itself much of the time from the clamor of popular culture. It must be conservative in requiring students to confront the range of arts, letters and right behavior conceived in the past, toward the liberal end that their choices be informed and thereby free (Gagnon, 1995, p. 74).

If, in the new "order of knowledge", as Weingart writes (2001, p. 351), "the social distribution of experimental learning as a method of action" and an "increase in reflexivity" are concerned, and if, at the same time, it is obvious that "the majority of social activities are still not involved with the production, [but] rather the reproduction of knowledge itself" (Stehr, 1994, p. 463), then the contradictions in education[16] that exist in the classical demands once again worsen. Therefore today the concern is whether one, like critical education science or critical pedagogy, will overcome previous "part emancipations", qualitatively redefining emancipation (Schweppenhäuser, 1973, pp. 404, 407) and recognising "that maturity can only be achieved together; otherwise it is not achievable at all" (Heydorn, 1980b, p. 162, trans. Jane Farrar). This is the call for education for all and this is also to break through the logics of the reproduction of social inequality with the help of the education system, i.e. overcoming selective educational systems (Farnen & Sünker, 1997; cf. Vester, 1998).[17]

The necessity for maturity and competent action, as well as emancipation, thus arises from both the adoption of the Enlightenment tradition and from the analysis of Europe's catastrophic history, particularly that of Germany, in this century. Bacon's view, according to which knowledge is power, could, finally, be understood as a self-critique of instrumental reason (cf. Horkheimer, 1974) and be made profitable.

This is related to the task of new and renewed theoretical efforts to analyse forms and formations of social relationships in their consequences for people's private as well as social lives today and to extract from it chances of 'pedagogical work' based on an educational scientific approach and analysis, becoming a crucial basis for democratisation processes that aim for the democratisation of all areas of life. Included here is the task of differentiating between types of knowledge, of knowledge production and of knowledge use. (cf. Elkana, 1986, pp. 255–257). Included here, too, is the challenge to mediate these knowledge related questions to a conceptualisation of education (*Bildung*) relevant for today. In a time when a main argument with respect to participation in society and access to participation is based more powerfully than ever on education (educational credentials) than used to be the case (cf. Bourdieu, 2001, pp. 36–40, pp. 283–292) it is especially important that we discuss class divisions and social inequality anew – beyond the 'digital divide'.

When knowledge society in reality is knowledge capitalism we have to deal with both the traditional and the new problems of capitalism, i.e. problems arising from the processes of the realisation of capital. The quest for surplus value today is strongly linked with – as referred to in the beginning of this paper – changes in the mode of societalisation and changes in the method of knowledge production. Education as a means for democracy is under siege but education could make use of this new mode of knowledge production, too: in the shape of educating all in the interests of all.

NOTES

[1] In sociology and philosophy of science – and sometimes in sociology of knowledge – there is a long lasting debate on social history and the history of knowledge and science: see Gideon (1948) and Bahr (1983) for 'mechanization' and 'machinery'; Pichot (1995), Burke (1997) and Kintzinger (2003) for the 'social history of knowledge (production)'; Canguilhem (1979), Bachelard (1980) and Böhme (1993) for questions of the 'philosophy of science'.

[2] Gorz shows very clearly in his social analysis that the main problem still today is the subsumption of knowledge under Capital (2004, pp. 37–49). Beyond this answer it seems worth considering that 'knowledge society' relates to a large extent to what was called in the late 1960s and early 1970s 'technocratic society'; both approaches incorporate the attempt to escape the class problem, i.e. the problem of dealing with domination.

[3] This is the social site of questions of changing types of governance in society and education, too (cf. as one prominent example Lemke 1997).

[4] 'Education' here is dealt with and used in the meaning of the German concept of 'Bildung' (cf. Peters, 2006; Sünker, 2006a).

[5] With this contextualisation I essentially refer to socio-scientific debates. Therefore questions of other disciplinary orientations whose theme are the contexts of 'Knowledge, Truth and Action' are ignored; see with respect to Kant and his understanding of philosophy as a 'form of knowledge' the work of Picht (1999), with respect to Hegel see Theunissen (1978a, b); for theology see Rad (1970) and for the study of literature see Schlaffer (1990).

[6] In the context of policy analysis this consideration can be connected with an idea formulated by Adorno (1998, p. 93): "But democracy has not become naturalized to the point where people truly experience it as their own and see themselves as subjects of the political process. Democracy is perceived as one system among others, as though one could choose from a menu between communism, democracy, fascism, and monarchy: but democracy is not identified with the people themselves as the expression of their political maturity."

[7] And this means, too, to deal with the classical problem of social change and educational change(s) (cf. Sünker, 2005).

[8] With respect to the special case 'Germany' with a highly social selective three-tiered-system in education and very special politics of education see Sünker (2006: chap. 1).

[9] This leads eventually to serious class-based consequences in childcare practises (Vincent/Ball, 2006) and to contradictory discourses on children's rights and in conceptualisations of politics of childhood (Moran-Ellis/Sünker, 2008).

[10] Ruling powers try to subvert these possibilities in hegemonic struggles via – at least – processes of expropriating the awareness of the people (Kilian, 1971; Chomsky, 2000). Additionally to this, it seems necessary to analyse what Plessner called the 'temptability/susceptibility of the bourgeois

mind' (Verführbarkeit des bürgerlichen Geistes, Plessner, 2003; cf. Bollenbeck, 1999) or the representatives of the Frankfurt School analysed as the transition from capitalism to fascism (Sünker 2006b).

[11] For Castells' social analysis of the consequences for social politics see Stern's fundamental analysis (1999); a summary of Castells' approach can be found in Castells (2000).

[12] For an outline of Marx's analysis and for the context of the money and capital theory see Reichelt (1970), Müller (1977) and Postone (1996).

[13] See also another view of Heydorn (1979, p. 32): 'Education as an institution is ready to be used against itself in order to signal the dissolution process of domination under the symbol of the human being who has become aware; the material conditions are ready to let capitalism and domination perish together. Education is the opportunity by which to make social suffering productive, to comprehend the withholding as a historical challenge. It relies on the historical movement that helps it but it is itself a power inside this movement, an essential part, like never before (...) education is becoming what it was at the beginning: self help' (trans. Jane Farrar).

[14] With reference to these three points the question of professionality and professionalisation processes in the 'knowledgeable society' could be discussed; cf. here Weingart (2001, p. 337 onwards).

[15] This a main topic in Habermas' study on modernity (1985).

[16] Here, it is necessary to refer to the title of the main study in the history and theory of education from Heydorn (1979): 'On the contradiction between education (Bildung) and Domination'.

[17] Here it must be fully emphasised once again that 'knowledge society' per se has nothing to do with the democratising or overcoming of class relationships; it concerns much more the opposite: 'Indeed, most people are worse off today than 30 years ago, and the advance of knowledge has played a role in their impoverishment' (Beck, 2000, p. 42); Thurow also speaks in the context of the knowledge-based economy of 'rising inequality' and of the destruction of sociality (p. 27) – with consequences that allow him to place the USA next to Algeria (p. 28).

REFERENCES

Adorno, T. W. (1973). *Negative dialectics*. New York/London: Continuum.

Adorno, T. W. (1998). The meaning of working through the past. In T. W. Adorno (Ed.), *Critical models. interventions and catchwords* (pp. 89–104). New York: Columbia University Press.

AK-Fraktion der Roten Zellen München (n.d.). *Wissenschaft und Kapital*. München: AK-Fraktion der Roten Zellen München.

Bachelard, G. (1980). *Die Philosophie des Nein. Versuch einer Philosophie des neuen wissenschaftlichen Geistes*. Frankfurt: Suhrkamp.

Bahr, H.-D. (1983). *Über den Umgang mit Maschinen*. Tübingen: Konkursbuchverlag.

Ball, St. (2003). *Class strategies and the education market. The middle classes and social advantage*. London/New York: Routledge/Falmer.

Beck, A. (2000). The knowledge business. *Social Policy, 31*, 42–49.

Beck, U., Giddens, A., & Lash, S. (1996). *Reflexive modernisierung*. Frankfurt: Suhrkamp.

Berman, M. (1988). *All that is solid melts into the air*. New York: Penguin.

Böhme, G. (1993). *Am Ende des Baconschen Zeitalters. Studien zur Wissenschaftsentwicklung*. Frankfurt: Suhrkamp.

Bollenbeck, G. (1999). *Tradition, Avantgarde, Reaktion. Deutsche Kontroversen um die kulturelle Moderne 1880–1945*. Frankfurt: Fischer.

Bourdieu, P. (1987). *Sozialer Sinn*. Frankfurt: Suhrkamp.

Bourdieu, P. (2001). *Meditationen. Zur Kritik der scholastischen Vernunft*. Frankfurt: Suhrkamp.

Bowles, S., & Gintis, H. (1976). *Schooling in capitalist America*. London: Routledge and Kegan Paul.

Bowles, S., & Gintis, H. (1987). *Democracy and capitalism. Property, community, and the contradictions of modern social thought (With a new introduction by the authors: The politics of capitalism and the economics of democracy)*. New York: Basic Books.

Burke, P. (1997). *A social history of knowledge*. Cambridge: Polity Press.

Canguilhem, G. (1979). *Wissenschaftsgeschichte und Epistemologie*. Frankfurt: Suhrkamp.

Castells, M. (1996). *The information age. Vol. I. The rise of the network society*. Oxford: Blackwell.

Castells, M. (1998). *The information age. Vol. III. End of millennium*. Oxford: Blackwell.

Castells, M. (2000). Elemente einer Theorie der Netzwerkgesellschaft. *Sozialwissenschaftliche Literatur Rundschau, 23*(41), 37–54.

Chomsky, N. (2000). *Chomsky on miseducation* (Introduced by D. Macedo, Ed.). Lanham, MD: Rowman and Littlefield.

Cole, M. (Ed.). (1988). *Bowles and Gintis revisited. Correspondence and contradiction in education theory*. London: Falmer.

Drucker, P. F. (1993). The rise of the knowledge society. *The Wilson Quarterly, 17*(2), 52–71.

Elkana, Y. (1986). *Anthropologie der Erkenntnis. Die Entwicklung des Wissens als episches Theater einer listigen Vernunft*. Frankfurt: Suhrkamp.

European Commission. (1995). *Lehren und Lernen. Auf dem Weg zur kognitiven Gesellschaft*. Brussels: European Commission.

Farnen, R., & Sünker, H. (Eds.). (1997). *The politics, sociology and economics of education. Interdisciplinary and comparative perspectives*. Houndmills: MacMillan.

Fischer, F. (1990). *Technocracy and the politics of expertise*. Newbury Park, CA: Sage.

Gagnon, P. (1995). What should children learn? *Atlantic Monthly, 276*, 65–78.

Gideon, S. (1948). *Mechanization takes command*. Oxford: Oxford University Press.

Gorz, A. (2004). *Wissen, Wert und Kapital. Zur Kritik der Wissensökonomie*. Zürich: Rotpunkt.

Habermas, J. (1985). *Der philosophische Diskurs der Moderne*. Frankfurt/M.: Suhrkamp.

Heller, A. (1978). *Philosophie des linken Radikalismus. Ein Bekenntnis zur Philosophie*. Hamburg: VSA Verlag.

Heydorn, H. J. (1979). *Über den Widerspruch von Bildung und Herrschaft*. Frankfurt: Europäische Verlagsanstalt.

Heydorn, H. J. (1980a). Überleben durch Bildung. In H. J. Heydorn (Ed.), *Ungleichheit für Alle* (pp. 282–301). Frankfurt: Syndikat.

Heydorn, H. J. (1980b). Zu einer Neufassung des Bildungsbegriffs. In H. J. Heydorn (Ed.), *Ungleichheit für Alle* (pp. 95–184). Frankfurt: Syndikat.

Hirsch, J. (1970). *Wissenschaftlich-technischer Fortschritt und politisches System*. Frankfurt: Suhrkamp.

Hörning, K. H. (2001). *Experten des Alltags. Die Wiederentdeckung des praktischen Wissens*. Weilerswist: Velbrück.

Horkheimer, M. (1974). *Eclipse of reason*. New York: Continuum.

Kern, H., & Schumann, M. (1984). *Das Ende der Arbeitsteilung. Rationalisierung in der industriellen Produktion*. München: C. H. Beck Verlag.

Kilian, H. (1971). *Das enteignete Bewusstsein*. Neuwied: Luchterhand.

Kintzinger, M. (2003). *Wissen wird Macht. Bildung im Mittelalter*. Ostfildern: Jan Thorbecke.

Knorr-Cetina, K. (1984). *Die Fabrikation von Erkenntnis*. Frankfurt: Suhrkamp.

Kuhn, T. S. (1967). *Die Struktur Wissenschaftlicher Revolutionen*. Frankfurt: Suhrkamp.

Laclau, E., & Mouffe, Ch. (1985). *Hegemony and socialist strategy. Towards a radical democratic politics*. London: Verso.

Lane, R. E. (1966). The decline of politics and ideology in a knowledgeable society. *American Sociological Review, 31*, 649–662.

Lefebvre, H. (1972). *Das Alltagsleben in der modernen Welt*. Frankfurt: Suhrkamp.

Lefebvre, H. (1987). *Kritik des Alltagslebens. Grundrisse einer Soziologie der Alltäglichkeit* (Afterword to this edition by B. Dewe, W. Ferchoff, & H. Sünker, Ed.). Frankfurt: Fischer Taschenbuch Verlag.

Lemke, T. (1997). *Eine Kritik der politischen Vernunft. Foucaults Analyse der modernen Gouvernementalität*. Hamburg: Argument.

Marcuse, H. (1987). *Konterrevolution und Revolte*. Frankfurt: Suhrkamp.

Marx, K. (n.d.). *Grundrisse der Kritik der Politischen Ökonomie*. Frankfurt: Europäische Verlagsanstalt.

Meiksins Wood, E. (1995). *Democracy against capitalism. Renewing historical materialism.* Cambridge: Cambridge University Press.

Meszaros, I. (1989). *The power of ideology.* New York: New York University Press.

Moran-Ellis, J., & Sünker, H. (2007). *Giving children a voice: Childhood, power and culture.* In J. Houtsonen & A. Antikainen (Eds.), *Symbolic power in cultural contexts. Uncovering social reality* (pp. 75–92). Rotterdam: Sense.

Müller, R. W. (1977). *Geld und Geist. Zur Entstehungsgeschichte von Identitätsbewußtsein und Rationalität seit der Antike.* Frankfurt: Campus.

Nowotny, H. (1999). *Es ist so. Es könnte auch anders sein. Über das veränderte Verhältnis von Wissenschaft und Gesellschaft.* Frankfurt: Suhrkamp.

Peters, M. (2006). Preface. In H. Sünker (Ed.), *Politics, bildung and social justice. Perspectives for a democratic society* (pp. VII–IX). Rotterdam: Sense.

Pichot, A. (1995). *Die Geburt der Wissenschaft. Von den Babyloniern zu den frühen Griechen.* Frankfurt: Campus.

Picht, G. (1999). *Von der Zeit.* Stuttgart: Klett-Cotta.

Plessner, H. (2003). Die verspätete Nation. Über die Verführbarkeit des bürgerlichen Geistes. In H. Plessner (Ed.), *Die Verführbarkeit des bürgerlichen Geistes. Gesammelte Schriften VI* (pp. 7–23). Frankfurt: Suhrkamp.

Postone, M. (1996). *Time, labor and social domination. A reinterpretation of Marx critical theory.* Cambridge: Cambridge University Press.

Rad, G. v. (1970). *Weisheit in Israel.* Neukirchen-Vluyn: Neukirchner Verlag.

Radtke, F.-O., & Weiss, M. (Eds.). (2000). *Schulautonomie, Wohlfahrtsstaat und chancengleichheit.* Opladen: Leske & Budrich.

Reichelt, H. (1970). *Zur logischen Struktur des Kapitalbegriffs bei Karl Marx.* Frankfurt: Europäische Verlagsanstalt.

Richta, R. (1972). *Technischer Fortschritt und industrielle Gesellschaft.* Frankfurt: EVA.

Rolshausen, C. (1975). *Wissenschaft und gesellschaftliche Reproduktion.* Frankfurt: Suhrkamp.

Rosenbladt, B. v. (Ed.). (1999). *Bildung in der Wissensgesellschaft.* Frankfurt: Suhrkamp.

Schlaffer, H. (1990). *Poesie und Wissen.* Frankfurt: Suhrkamp.

Schweickart, D. (1996). *Against capitalism.* Boulder and Oxford: Westview Press.

Schweppenhäuser, H. (1973). Zur Dialektik der Emanzipation. In M. Greiffenhagen (Ed.), *Emanzipation* (pp. 387–410). Hamburg: Hoffmann & Campe.

Sherover-Marcuse, E. (1986). *Emancipation and consciousness.* Oxford and New York: Blackwell.

Siemsen, A. (1948). *Die gesellschaftlichen Grundlagen der Erziehung.* Hamburg: Oetinger.

Sohn-Rethel, A. (1970). *Geistige und körperliche Arbeit. Zur Theorie der gesellschaftlichen Synthesis.* Frankfurt: Suhrkamp.

Sokal, A. B. (1996). Transgressing the boundaries: Toward a transformative hermeneutics of quantum gravity. *Social Text, 14*(1 & 2), 217–252.

Sonnemann, U. (1969). *Negative Anthropologie. Vorstudien zur Sabotage des Schicksals.* Reinbek: Rowohlt.

Stehr, N. (1994). *Arbeit, Eigentum und Wissen. Zur Theorie von Wissensgesellschaften.* Frankfurt: Suhrkamp.

Stehr, N. (2001). *Wissen und Wirtschaften.* Frankfurt: Suhrkamp.

Stern, M. (1999). Gesellschaftsanalyse und Soziale Arbeit heute. *Sozialwissenschaftliche Literatur Rundschau, 22*(38), 5–22.

Stross, A. M. (2001). Die 'Wissensgesellschaft' als bildungspolitische Norm? *Sozialwissenschaftliche Literatur Rundschau, 24*(42), 84–100.

Sünker, H. (1989). *Bildung, Alltag und Subjektivität.* Weinheim: Deutscher Studienverlag.

Sünker, H. (2005). 'New people' and 'Old structures': Max Adler and Siegfried Bernfeld on society, education and change. *Policy Futures in Education, 3*, 184–193.

Sünker, H. (2006a). *Politics, bildung and social justice. Perspectives for a democratic society.* Rotterdam: Sense.

Sünker, H. (2006b). Kritische Theorie und Analyse des Nationalsozialismus. In M. Heinz & G. Gretic (Eds.), *Philosophie und Zeitgeist im Nationalsozialismus* (pp. 67–86). Würzburg: Königshausen and Neumann.

Sünker, H., & Krüger, H. (Eds.). (1999). *Kritische Erziehungswissenschaft am Neubeginn?* Frankfurt: Suhrkamp.

Theunissen, M. (1978a). Begriff und Realität. Hegels Aufhebung des metaphysischen Wahrheitsbegriffes. In R.-P. Horstmann (Ed.), *Seminar: Dialektik in der Philosophie Hegels* (pp. 324–359). Frankfurt: Suhrkamp.

Theunissen, M. (1978b). *Sein und Schein. Die kritische Funktion der Hegelschen Logik.* Frankfurt: Suhrkamp.

Thompson, P. (1983). *The nature of work.* Basingstoke: Macmillan.

Thurow, L. C. (2000). Globalization: The product of a knowledge-based economy. *Annals of the American Academy of Political and Social Science, 570,* 19–31.

Vahrenkamp, R. (Ed.). (1973). *Technologie und Kapital.* Frankfurt: Suhrkamp.

Vester, M. (1998). Was wurde aus dem Proletariat? Das mehrfache Ende der Klassenkonflikte: Prognosen des sozialstrukturellen Wandels. In J. Friedrichs, R. M. Lepenies, & K. U. Mayer (Eds.), *Die Diagnosefähigkeit der Soziologie* (pp. 164–206). Opladen: VS Verlag für Sozialwissenschaften.

Vincent, C., & Ball, S. (2006). *Childcare, choice and class practises. Middle-class parents and their children.* London/New York: Routledge.

Weinberg, S. (1998, Winter). Wissensrevolutionen. *Lettre International,* 64–67.

Weingart, P. (2001). *Die Stunde der Wahrheit? Zum Verhältnis der Wissenschaft zur Politik, Wirtschaft und Medien.* Weilerwist: Velbrück.

Wexler, P. (1990). *Social analysis of education. After the new sociology.* New York/London: Routledge

Whitty, G. (1998). Citizens or consumers? Continuity and change in contemporary education policy. In D. Carlson & M. Apple (Eds.), *Power/knowledge/pedagogy. The meaning of democratic education in unsettling times* (pp. 92–109). Boulder, CO: Westview.

Whitty, G. (2002). *Making sense of education policy.* London: Paul Chapman.

FURTHER READINGS

Ball, S. (2003). *Class strategies and the education market. The middle classes and social advantage.* London/New York: Routledge/Falmer

Berman, M. (1988). *All that is Solid Melts into the Air.* New York: Penguin.

Burke, P. (1997). *A social history of knowledge.* Cambridge: Polity.

Castells, M. (1996). *The information age. Vol. I. The rise of the network society.* Oxford: Blackwell.

Whitty, G. (1998). Citizens or consumers? Continuity and change in contemporary education policy. In D. Carlson & M. Apple (Eds.), *Power/Knowledge/Pedagogy. The making of democratic education in unsettling times* (pp. 92–109). Boulder, CO: Westview.

Heinz Sünker
Department of Bildungs- and Social Sciences
University of Wuppertal, Germany

SUSAN L. ROBERTSON

'PRODUCING' THE GLOBAL KNOWLEDGE ECONOMY

The World Bank, the Knowledge Assessment Methodology and Education

INTRODUCTION

If globalisation was the policy buzz of the 1990s to the point that we could breathe it in the air, its 21st century equivalent must surely be the 'knowledge-based economy'. Like globalisation, knowledge is viewed as both a new problem and panacea for our times. If we don't have enough of it, we are told we are destined to become third world countries. If we are not yet a knowledge economy, or are not 'in transition' to becoming one, then organisations like the Organisation for Economic and Cooperative Development (OECD) and the World Bank (WB) are on hand to guide us in the right direction; the self-appointed 'midwives' giving birth to this bright new future.

The problem with this kind of buzz – like 'white noise'- is that it conceals more than it reveals. Like 'globalisation talk', for example, our attention is all too easily diverted from its profoundly western roots (Harvey, 2006; Connell, 2007). It is therefore important that we ask questions like: *Who are the actors? What is being globalised?* and *Who stands to gain?* from the production of this kind of (knowledge-based) economy?

The idea of knowledge is a particularly slippery one. It is a concept so utterly familiar and 'good for us' that it has made its appearance on the policy and political circuit with seemingly very little resistance. For this reason, making sense of 'knowledge economy talk' through a critical 're/reading' of a longer standing project which had its genesis in the crisis of Atlantic Fordism in the late 1960s, is important. Pushed forward by political and economic forces, including the World Bank, the Organisation for Economic and Cooperative Development (OECD) and the World Economic Forum, interested nation states (cf. USA, UK) and regions (EU), this particular economic imaginary – a knowledge based economy – is increasing being mobilised rhetorically to inform the scope, direction, pace and outcome of development in the 21st Century around the globe, including education, as a sub-set of activities within this field of power.

This chapter examines the early role of the OECD in initiating and creating the framework for this project, and the World Bank's emulation of this framing in its Knowledge For Development Program (K4D) beginning in 1999. My specific focus is on the World Bank's instrument, the Knowledge Assessment Methodology (KAM), which is now being used by the Bank to diagnose, direct and produce a particular version of a 'knowledge-based economy' within the developed and

M. Simons, M. Olssen and M.A. Peters (eds.), Re-Reading Education Policies: A Handbook Studying the Policy Agenda of the 21st Century, 235–256.

developing world. In this imaginary, education is formulated in a very particular way; as investments in science and technology, upper secondary and higher education, and research and development, whilst other ways of thinking about education, such as the development of the individual through social and cultural knowledge, is made absent.

The theoretical framing for this analysis is informed by a 'critical, cultural political economy of education' (CCPEE) approach. CCPEE sees education, not as a pre-given container or universal and unchanging category of social relations and life-worlds, but as simultaneously a complex terrain and outcome of discursive, material and institutionalised struggles over knowledge, status and credentials that take place at multiple scales and over time. It locates education within a wider ensemble of capitalist and other social relations that directs, albeit in contradictory ways, the form and function of education over time. It takes the cultural turn seriously by examining the role of semiosis in constituting 'education' subjects and objects; for instance as it shapes the ideational, representational and institutional moments in education strategies, structures, subjects and subjectivities (Jessop, 2004; Jessop and Sum, 2006). CCPEE also deploys a strategic relational approach to understanding the structured and structuring role of education in political economies more generally (Jessop, 2001, p. 5), and the global political economy in particular (Dale, 2000). This involves:

> (…) examining how a given structure may privilege some actors, some identities, some strategies, some spatial and temporal horizons, some actions over others; and the ways, if any, in which actors (individual and/or collective) take account of this differential privileging through 'strategic-context' analysis when choosing a course of action (Jessop, 2004, p. 162).

CCPEE also argues that education, a key site of cultural production and social reproduction, is directly and indirectly shaped by combinations of economic, political and intellectual forces who manipulate power and knowledge in order to re/produce new boundaries, geometries and temporalities in a spatio-temporal fix to displace or defer capitalism's crisis tendencies (Jessop, 2000). Taken together, CCPEE enables us to unravel and reveal the complex (and contradictory) ways in which discourses/ideas (such as growth, development, knowledge), actors/institutions (such as the World Bank, OECD, nation states) and material capabilities/power (resources, aid) are being mobilised to strategically and selectively advance an imagined, new, knowledge-based economy and its material re/production, within which education is now being re/constituted in particular ways.

Anchored in this analytical framing, I advance my analysis in four parts. In part one I trace the genealogy of the idea of a knowledge-based economy by focusing, first, on the work of those social scientists in the 1960s and 70s who were engaged in imagining the development of a post industrial society. Part two explores the OECD's early engagement with this idea, while part three examines the World Bank's take-up of the idea in the mid-1990s under the presidency of James Wolfensohn. At this point the Bank, under fire because of its austere structural adjustment policies, reinvented itself as a 'knowledge bank', establishing the

Knowledge for Development Programme (K4D). By 2004 it had begun work on a Knowledge Assessment Methodology (KAM) that would enable the Bank to measure countries progress (or not) toward realizing an imagined knowledge-based economy. Part four concludes by returning to the question: whose agendas and interests are being advanced through the KAM as a particular political project? I also reflect on the emerging contradictions, dilemmas and tensions embedded in this new strategic re/structuring of the production of knowledge.

CONSTRUCTING 'THE KNOWLEDGE-BASED ECONOMY' – THE GENEALOGY OF A PROJECT

Contemporary hegemonic knowledge economy discourses have their roots in arguments developed by a group of intellectuals, futurologists and information economists writing in the 1960s and 70s; that industrial societies were evolving into what they referred to as either knowledge economies; post-capitalist economies; or post-industrial societies (cf. Machlup, 1962; Drucker, 1969; Bell, 1973). This evolutionary thesis was added to by writers in the 1990s, the most prominent being Manuel Castells (1996) and his proposal that we are now living in a network society. At the core of these arguments is that knowledge is *a new factor of production*. This is contrasted with classical arguments that posited that land (natural resources), labour (human effort) and capital goods (machinery) were the three main factors of production.

As the sub-title of Bell's *The Coming of the Post-Industrial Age: A Venture in Social Forecasting,* indicates, this work was rather speculative. Perhaps as a consequence, Bell's thesis was greeted with considerable scepticism amongst the academic community (see Webster, 2002), not least because of its technological determinism and assumed teleology of the economy. Nonetheless, it received a great deal of attention in the popular press and amongst policymakers, as well as from international organisations, like the OECD.

There are several core propositions to Bell's arguments:

- all societies evolve, moving from pre-industrial to industrial to post-industrial;
- in this evolutionary cycle, work moves from being muscle-based to mind-based;
- post-industrial societies are more dependent upon 'theoretical' knowledge or the knowledge of professionals, such as scientists, engineers, teachers, health workers; and
- post-industrial societies generate greater degrees of wealth than industrial societies.

Understanding Bell's conception of 'knowledge' is also important for we see here the significance attached to knowledge as a form of property and capital. As he noted:

Knowledge is that which is objectively known, an *intellectual property*, attached to a name or group of names and certified by copyright, or some other form of social recognition (e.g. publication). This knowledge is paid for in the time spent in writing and research; in the monetary compensation by the communication and educational media. It is subject to a judgement by the market, by administrative or political decisions of superiors, or by the peers as the worth of the result, and as to its claim on social resources, where such claims are made. In this sense, knowledge is part of the social overhead investment of society, it is a coherent statement, presented in a book, article, or even a computer program, written down or recorded at some point for transmission, and subject to some rough count (Bell, 1973, p. 176).

By patenting various kinds of knowledge, from processes, procedures and products as diverse as new turbine machinery, seeds, or DNA, value can be realised. This, in turn, creates economic value and economic growth. More recently, knowledge producing sectors in the form of 'education services' have been added to the list of 'products' that are now traded in the global economy.

In order to better understand the World Bank's approach to the idea of a knowledge-based economy we need to look, first, at its early framing by the OECD, whose specific mandate was to act as a knowledge broker for the developed economies on economic development.

The OECD was influenced by the early debates on knowledge by Bell and others. During the 1970s the OECD adopted the idea of an 'information society' (Mattelart, 2003, p. 113). It enlisted the expertise of a range of economists concerned with mapping and measuring information, including Marc Uri Porat the Franco-American economist, who later produced a nine volume study of the definition and measurement of the information economy for the US government. The concept of a knowledge-based economy was added in the 1990s. However, it took another decade for this idea to stabilise into the master discourse we know today.

Interest in ideas like 'knowledge based economies' can also be better understood if set against the wider crisis the Atlantic Fordism in the 1970s, where developed economies, such as the USA and UK, began to experience a sharp decline in their share of the production of manufactured goods (Jessop & Sum, 2006). It was a crisis of capitalism that sought to displace or defer capitalism's crisis tendencies, by producing new boundaries, geometries and temporalities that would in turn open the way for renewed economic growth. However, as Castells observes:

> (...) this is a brand of capitalism that is at the same time very old and fundamentally new. It is old because if appeals to relentless competition in the pursuit of profit and individual satisfaction (deferred or immediate) is its driving engine. But it is fundamentally new because it is tooled by new information and communication technologies that are the roots of new productivity sources, of new organisational forms, and of the formation of a global economy (Castells, 1996, p. 32).

Crises also encourage strategic and semiotic innovation (Jessop, 2004). Between 1992-5 Danish evolutionary economist, Ake-Bengt Lundvall (as Deputy Director of the OECD Directorate for Science, Technology and Industry) worked on the OECD's 'knowledge management' programme. Lundvall launched the idea of a 'learning economy' arguing that: (i) learning does not just come from R&D but from a myriad of routine activities in production, distribution and consumption; and most importantly, (ii) learning comes from interacting (Lundvall, 1992).

Lundvall's work progressed, but with difficulty. To begin with, the OECD did not have the funds to support the development of indicators. It therefore forced a compromise by encouraging Lundvall to build on old data sets. Lundvall's work was also proving difficult to implement and hard to sell to national policymakers - the funders of the OECD. This caused unease within the OECD about the direction being taken by Lundvall. As a result, Dominic Foray, initially a consultant to the OECD during the early 1990s was bought in. Foray, however, critiqued Lundvall's work as unoriginal and offered an alternative theory; that it was the *distribution* and *use* of knowledge that was the most important for the knowledge-*base*.

Godin (2006) argues that the first step in the generalised use of the concept of 'the knowledge economy' in the OECD came in 1995 with a document written by the Canadian delegation to an OECD meeting – where 'the knowledge economy' was in its title. The paper discussed two themes: 'new growth theory' and 'innovation'. 'New growth theory' had been developed by Romer (1989, p. 1) and others as a way of getting beyond the 'narrow growth accounting models' of classical economics where were focused on the traditional factors of production: labour, capital, materials and energy.

New growth theory now identified the knowledge base – as crucial. New growth theory articulated with human capital theory which the OECD had embraced in the 1960s following the publication of Becker's book *Human Capital* in 1964 (invested in via education, training, medical treatment and so on). New growth theory had finessed human capital theory, arguing it was the nature of the knowledge base (innovation, research, quality learning) *and* its distribution across the population that was the most critical. Importantly, these elements were also policy levers, making it easier for policymakers to specify policies in more precise terms. By linking knowledge and education together, these two theories were to provide the bedrock for the OECD's work on the development of this new economy.

The Canadian proposal also articulated well with the work of Lundvall and others in the OECD who had sought to take account of more components in an economy. On the innovations theme, the paper argued innovation needed to be dynamic, and that indicators needed to be developed (beyond input and output measures – such as R&D expenditures, patents, publications) that measured processes. In other words, indicators were needed to measure the *distribution* of knowledge within key institutions and the *interactions* forming the system of innovation.

The OECD began work on developing new indicators that built upon existing ones to measure inputs, stocks, flows, networks, learning, international trade, employment, structural change, and so on. By 1999, 32 indicators were reported on. In 2000 more were added. The effect of producing statistics to measure the knowledge base of the economy in turn stabilised the concept of a Knowledge-Based Economy (KBE), despite the fact that there was a pervading view, even amongst its supporters, that " (…) measuring knowledge itself is more challenging, if not impossible" (Foray & Gault, 2003, p. 18). According to Godin (2006, p. 19), this was important as it "helped crystallise the concept by giving it empirical content."

By 2005 the OECD's KBE concept had become further conceptually refined and most importantly, it had become an umbrella concept that contained a particular set of institutional arrangements. In her introduction to an OECD/ National Science Foundation (NSF) Conference on 'Advancing knowledge and the knowledge economy', OECD Deputy Secretary-General, Berglind Asgeirsdottir stated:

> The development of the knowledge economy is dependent on four main 'pillars': innovation, new technologies, human capital and enterprise dynamics. I have chosen to illustrate the important factors shaping the knowledge economy as a 'Greek temple' with four pillars. The 'economic fundamentals' are the base on which the four pillars are standing. The four pillars are also illustrating that for the knowledge economy to develop and grow, it is not enough to focus on a single policy or institutional arrangement. A whole range of policies and coordinated actions to create the right conditions are necessary. The 'policy mix' must be based on a comprehensive strategy suited to each country or circumstance and will include the four pillars 'innovation', 'new technologies', 'human capital' and 'enterprise dynamics'. At the top of the Greek temple, I have put 'globalisation', which is a driver that influence all four pillars and four key factors that are becoming increasingly mobile and global under the globalisation process: 'research and development', 'Internet', 'highly skilled' and 'multi-national companies' (Asgeirsdottir, 2005, p. 1)

This representation of the knowledge economy with its four pillars was identical to the World Bank's K4D depiction of the knowledge economy.

GLOBALISATION, DEVELOPMENT AND KNOWLEDGE – THE WORLD BANK'S APPROACH

In the Spring of 2004, the first newsletter of the World Bank's K4D programme was launched. In it the Bank argued: "(…) knowledge, and its application, are now widely acknowledged to be one of the key engines of economic growth" (World Bank, 2004, p. 1). This assertion attests to the stabilisation of the concept. Again in 2007 the Bank continued to insist that:

> This 'knowledge revolution' manifests itself in many different ways: there are closer links between science and technology; innovation is more important for economic growth and competitiveness; there is increased importance of education and life-long learning; and more investment is undertaken in intangibles (R&D, software and education) which is even greater than investments in fixed capital. And of course there is the ICT

explosion which brings worldwide interdependency and connectivity (World Bank, 2007, p. 1).

Though the World Bank's process of early formulation of the idea of a knowledge economy has been different to the OECD, there appears to have been sufficient corroboration for each agency to arrive at identical means of representing the knowledge economy – a stylised Greek temple made up of four pillars with the knowledge economy and globalisation its protective roof.[1]

The World Bank's foray into the 'knowledge' arena began in the early 1990s. The World Bank was the first cooperation agency to explore the implications of 'knowledge' both for its own activities as an organisation and also for its clients (King, 2002). This ambitious work began in 1996 under the leadership of World Bank President, James Wolfensohn, where it reinvented itself as 'the Knowledge Bank'. Its 1998 World Development Report (WDR), *Knowledge for Development*, laid the foundations for much of the Bank's work over the next decade. The WDR placed knowledge at the centre of the work of the Bank's activities, so that in the education sector the focus was now shifted away from the primary school as the site/agent/mover of change to (embrained) 'knowledge' as a means of growth. In policy terms, this meant a shift away from focus on teaching as the central activity, to the conditions for learning for the child and meta-learning for countries through the use of indicators and benchmarks to guide performance and generate strategic knowledge (cf. World Bank, 2003).

What made this report and the ongoing programme of work different was the seriousness with which education was now taken – as a key factor in technological creation, adoption, and communication. This policy move entailed that low-income country's reorient their attention to basic education to include not only investments in basic education, *but* upper secondary and tertiary.[2] These ideas were more widely taken up in later World Bank's reports on education where they argued that:

A knowledge economy relies primarily on the use of ideas rather than physical abilities and on the application of technology rather than the transformation of raw materials or the exploitation of cheap labour. It is an economy in which knowledge is created, acquired, transmitted and used more effectively by individuals, enterprises, organisations and communities to promote economic and social development. (…) The knowledge economy is transforming the demands of the labour market in economies throughout the world. In industrial countries, where knowledge based industries are expanding rapidly, labour market demands are changing accordingly (World Bank, 2003, p. 1).

A series of initiatives were developed by the Bank to realise the ambition of the WDR. This included Knowledge4Development (K4D), a 'knowledge sharing' programme for those working inside the Bank dedicated to revamping staff learning. According to King:

The sheer scale of the coverage on the Bank's website of knowledge sharing, knowledge initiatives, knowledge management, knowledge economies and knowledge resources is difficult to exaggerate. It stands in marked contrast to the explicit treatment of knowledge in most other bilateral and multilateral agencies (King, 2002, p. 312).

The Bank's K4D argument was that the increased importance of knowledge provided great potential for countries to strengthen their economic and social development by providing more efficient ways of producing goods and services, and delivering them more effectively and at lower costs to a greater number of people. Combined with the liberalisation of trade policy, the knowledge revolution was to lead to greater globalisation and increased international competition. To capitalise on the knowledge revolution to improve competitiveness and welfare, the Bank argued that developing countries needed to build on their strengths and plan appropriate investments in human capital, effective institutions, relevant technologies, and innovative and competitive enterprises. However, the Bank also raised the danger of a growing 'knowledge divide' [rather than just a 'digital divide'] between those advanced countries generating most of this knowledge, and developing countries - many of whom were failing to tap the vast and growing stock of knowledge because of their limited awareness, poor economic incentive regimes, and weak institutions.

The objective then of the World Bank K4D programme was to:

(...) stimulate social and economic development in client countries by building their capacity to access and use knowledge as a basis for enhancing competitiveness and increasing welfare. The K4D programme is intended to help countries understand their strengths and weaknesses with respect to knowledge as a means to identifying appropriate policies for improvement of the country's performance and to give direction to the country's ambitions. Working closely with the World Bank's regional and sector teams, K4D works with client countries to create a framework for achievable action over a reasonable time period. To be effective, this work must be supported by the creation of the necessary capacity to deliver – namely, people and organisations with the skills, competencies and understanding capable of taking things forward, and supported by access (online and face-to-face) to networks of expertise and experience from across the world (World Bank, 2007).

There was, nevertheless, a very particular set of 'knowledges' being privileged in the K4D programme: Western science and technology, enabled by ICTs and the institutional structures that supported a liberal market economy. As King argues (2002), this was pretty much business as usual for the Bank. What was different was, on the one hand, a shift in the language of development, and on the other hand, the embrace of digital technologies as the means to enable developing countries to catch-up. As King observed:

WDR also draws heavily on the older faith about the role of science and technology in development, and on what has been learnt about technology transfer and adaptation for over 30 years. Arguably, the word 'knowledge' has to some extent replaced what was written about 'technology' and technological capability in earlier decades, but the information and communication technology revolution is what now makes the difference in terms of outreach, potential and impact of this now globally-accessible knowledge (King, 2002, p. 313).

Like the OECD, the World Bank's K4D programme is based on four pillars:

- An *economic and institutional regime* that provides incentives for the efficient use of existing and new knowledge and the flourishing of entrepreneurship.
- An *educated and skilled population* that can create, share, and use knowledge well.
- An *efficient innovation system* of firms, research centres, universities, think-tanks, consultants, and other organisations who can tap into the growing stock of global knowledge, assimilate and adapt it to local needs, and create new technology.
- *Information and Communication Technologies (ICT)* that can facilitate the effective communication, dissemination, and processing of information.

The K4D programme is delivered through what it calls 'product lines': (i) 'Knowledge Economy Policy Services' for clients, including policy reports and policy consulting advice on various aspects of the knowledge economy; (ii) enhanced assessments designed to meet the needs of different client countries; (iii) 'Knowledge Economy Studies' designed to bring together global learning and experience on the knowledge economy, such as on innovation systems; and (iv) 'Learning Events' to build knowledge and skills and to facilitate exchange of experience and good/best practice on the knowledge economy (see Appendix 1 for a list of countries and types of assessments undertaken between 2003 and 2007).

Like the OECD, the Bank's approach to knowledge for development to produce a knowledge-based economy was also influenced by classical human capital theory *and* new growth theory. Human capital theory had long been used by the World Bank to justify its investments in education. However, new growth theory was now reflected in education policy. For instance the Bank's *Lifelong Learning for the Global Knowledge Economy* (2003) report embraced the need for investment in education shaped by rates-of-return analyses (human capital theory) as well as new pedagogical approaches, such as 'learning-by-doing' and 'learning-to-learn' (that is, new growth theory) (Robertson, 2005). Taken together, the turn to 'knowledge' by the Bank was ambitious and breathtaking in scope, though as King (2002) also observes, the Bank's hyperbole about knowledge management and sharing was not always matched in practice.

THE WORLD BANK AND THE KAM – HOW IT WORKS

We can get a good sense of the World Bank's strategic and selective framing of what it means to be a knowledge economy, as well as the tools being used by the Bank to help shape a country's strategies, by looking at the content of the *Knowledge Assessment Methodology* (KAM). The KAM is simultaneously the centrepiece and underpinning architecture of the Bank's K4D programme. It is an interactive, diagnostic and benchmarking tool that provides a preliminary assessment of countries and regions 'readiness for the knowledge economy' (World Bank, 2007). The KAM enables countries to benchmark themselves with neighbours, competitors, or other countries they wish to learn from on the four pillars of the knowledge economy. It is therefore a tool aimed at promoting 'learning' amongst developing and developed countries about the elements that constitute the Bank's version of a knowledge economy. Learning through comparisons with others (normalisation), and making appropriate policy changes is seen as producing a nation's knowledge-based economy. Dale (1999) identifies this kind of mechanism of globalisation as 'emulation' which can be contrasted with the earlier structural adjustment approaches of the Bank largely built around the imposition of policies and programmes.

Since its launch, the KAM has undergone a series of refinements (Chen and Dahlman, 2005). In 2004, 121 countries were included in its database with 76 structural and qualitative variables available as measures of knowledge-based economies. In 2006 the KAM was re-launched, this time with 128 countries and 80 variables. By 2007, four further countries were added. The KAM currently consists of 81 structural and qualitative variables for 132 countries to measure their performance on the four Knowledge Economy (KE) pillars: Economic Incentive and Institutional Regime, Education, Innovation, and Information and Communications Technologies. Variables are normalised on a scale of zero to ten relative to other countries in the comparison group. The KAM also derives a country's overall *Knowledge Economy Index* (KEI) and *Knowledge Index* (KI) based on an aggregation of the 14 key variables (see below).

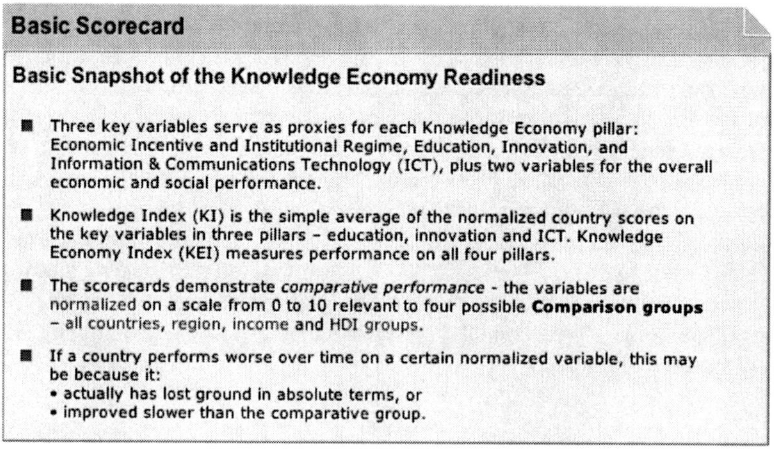

Basic Scorecard

Basic Snapshot of the Knowledge Economy Readiness

■ Three key variables serve as proxies for each Knowledge Economy pillar: Economic Incentive and Institutional Regime, Education, Innovation, and Information & Communications Technology (ICT), plus two variables for the overall economic and social performance.

■ Knowledge Index (KI) is the simple average of the normalized country scores on the key variables in three pillars – education, innovation and ICT. Knowledge Economy Index (KEI) measures performance on all four pillars.

■ The scorecards demonstrate *comparative performance* - the variables are normalized on a scale from 0 to 10 relevant to four possible **Comparison groups** – all countries, region, income and HDI groups.

■ If a country performs worse over time on a certain normalized variable, this may be because it:
• actually has lost ground in absolute terms, or
• improved slower than the comparative group.

Figure 1. Mode 1 – Basic Scorecard data (Source: World Bank, 2007)

Variable	Finland (Group: All)	
	actual	normalized
Annual GDP Growth (%)	2.30	1.85
Human Development Index	0.947	9.15
Tariff & Nontariff Barriers	2.00	7.13
Regulatory Quality	1.74	9.70
Rule of Law	1.96	9.55
Researchers in R&D / Mil. People	7832.00	9.89
Scientific and Technical Journal Articles / Mil. People	1000.38	9.69
Patents Granted by USPTO / Mil. People	164.38	9.55
Adult Literacy Rate (% age 15 and above)	100.00	8.41
Gross Secondary Enrollment	109.40	9.15
Gross Tertiary Enrollment	89.50	9.92
Total Telephones per 1,000 People	1407.00	8.79
Computers per 1,000 People	481.10	8.33
Internet Users per 1,000 People	628.50	9.39

Figure 2. Mode 1 – Basic Scorecard data for Finland (World Bank, 2007)

The KAM is available in six different modes. Mode 1, a *Basic Scorecard* (see Figures 1 and 2) uses fourteen key variables as proxies to benchmark countries on the four KE pillars and derive their overall KEI and KI indexes. The scorecard allows comparisons for up to three countries for 1995 and the most recent available year. Using the interactive website tool, it is possible to generate rapid and colourful depictions of a country's 'knowledge-economy' status over time, in relation to others, and regionally. Mode 2, *Choose Variables* allows the use of any combination of the 81 variables and to compare up to three countries or regions for the most recent available year (see Figures 3, 4 and 5).

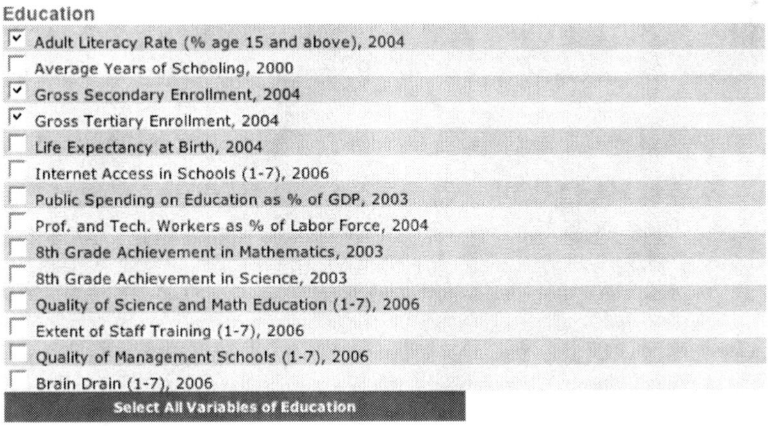

Education
- ☑ Adult Literacy Rate (% age 15 and above), 2004
- ☐ Average Years of Schooling, 2000
- ☑ Gross Secondary Enrollment, 2004
- ☑ Gross Tertiary Enrollment, 2004
- ☐ Life Expectancy at Birth, 2004
- ☐ Internet Access in Schools (1-7), 2006
- ☐ Public Spending on Education as % of GDP, 2003
- ☐ Prof. and Tech. Workers as % of Labor Force, 2004
- ☐ 8th Grade Achievement in Mathematics, 2003
- ☐ 8th Grade Achievement in Science, 2003
- ☐ Quality of Science and Math Education (1-7), 2006
- ☐ Extent of Staff Training (1-7), 2006
- ☐ Quality of Management Schools (1-7), 2006
- ☐ Brain Drain (1-7), 2006

Select All Variables of Education

Figure 3. Mode 'Choose Variables' – in this case the education pillar (World Bank, 2007)

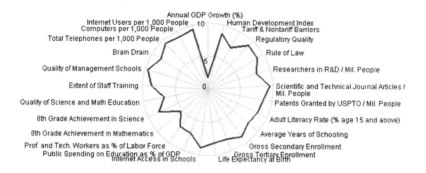

Figure 4. Mode 'Choose Variables' – in this case the education in the UK pillar (World Bank, 2007)

Education	Tanzania	
	actual	normalized
☑ Adult Literacy Rate (% age 15 and above), 2004	69.40	2.12
☑ Average Years of Schooling, 2000	2.71	0.85
☑ Gross Secondary Enrollment, 2004	5.90	0.00
☑ Gross Tertiary Enrollment, 2004	1.20	0.24
☑ Life Expectancy at Birth, 2004	46.20	0.91
☑ Internet Access in Schools (1-7), 2006	2.50	1.55
☑ Public Spending on Education as % of GDP, 2003	2.20	0.53
☑ Prof. and Tech. Workers as % of Labor Force, 2004	2.35	0.00
☑ 8th Grade Achievement in Mathematics, 2003	n/a	n/a
☑ 8th Grade Achievement in Science, 2003	n/a	n/a
☑ Quality of Science and Math Education (1-7), 2006	2.90	1.38
☑ Extent of Staff Training (1-7), 2006	3.10	2.33
☑ Quality of Management Schools (1-7), 2006	3.30	1.64
☑ Brain Drain (1-7), 2006	2.60	2.43
Select All Variables of Education		

Figure 5. Mode 'Choose Variables' – in this case the education in Tanzania (World Bank, 2007)

Mode 3, *KEI and KI Indexes* presents performance scores of all countries on the KEI and KI indexes, as well as on the four KE pillars, in a sort-able table format (see Tables 6 and 7 for top 10 and bottom 10 countries on the four pillars). Mode 4, *Over Time Comparison*, demonstrates a country's progress on the Knowledge Economy pillars and indexes from 1995 to the most recent year (see Table 8). Mode 5, *Cross-Country Comparison*, allows bar-chart comparison of up to 20 countries on their KEI and KI indexes while demonstrating the relative contribution of different KE pillars to the countries' overall knowledge readiness. Finally, mode 6 – *World Map* (see Figure 9), provides a colour-coded map for a global view of the worlds' 'readiness' for becoming knowledge-based economies in 1995, and the most recent year.

Rank		Country		KEI	KI	Economic Incentive Regime		Innovation	Education	ICT
1	+4	Denmark		9.23	9.37	8.82		9.42	9.20	9.48
2	●	Sweden		9.22	9.49	8.41		9.72	8.98	9.77
3	-2	Finland		9.12	9.24	8.79		9.71	9.16	8.84
4	+11	Iceland		8.83	9.03	8.25		9.07	8.78	9.24
5	+2	Norway		8.80	8.89	8.54		8.86	9.21	8.59
6	-3	United States		8.74	8.90	8.26		9.42	8.38	8.91
7	-1	Australia		8.74	9.02	7.89		8.82	9.15	9.11
8	+1	Netherlands		8.73	8.80	8.51		8.63	8.67	9.08
9	-5	Canada		8.68	8.73	8.51		9.05	8.52	8.63
10	●	United Kingdom		8.67	8.77	8.36		8.62	8.44	9.25

Figure 6. Comparison of top 10 countries over four pillars (Source: World Bank, 2007)

122	+5	Bangladesh	X	1.20	1.35	0.76	1.63	1.57	0.83
123	-1	Mali	X	1.15	0.45	3.27	0.50	0.45	0.41
124	+5	Burkina Faso	X	1.07	0.47	2.87	0.73	0.24	0.46
125	-18	Nepal		1.05	0.92	1.44	0.85	1.36	0.57
126	+5	Mozambique	X	1.04	0.54	2.52	0.42	0.28	0.93
127	+5	Angola	X	1.02	0.98	1.16	1.29	0.74	0.91
128	-25	Djibouti	X	0.88	0.86	0.93	0.00	0.87	1.71
129	-3	Lao PDR	X	0.85	0.91	0.66	0.15	1.86	0.72
130	●	Ethiopia	X	0.72	0.51	1.37	0.61	0.81	0.10
131	-14	Eritrea	X	0.72	0.58	1.14	0.23	0.87	0.64
132	-7	Sierra Leone	X	0.44	0.29	0.89	0.27	0.34	0.27

Figure 7. Comparison of bottom 10 countries over four pillars (Source: World Bank, 2007)

The KAM works as a strategic selection device as well as relationally; that is against an imagined 'perfect' knowledge economy for which a value of, for instance 10, is assigned, while its absence is denoted by the other end of the continuum, for instance 0. Many of the indicators require a judgement about where a country is in relation to others; a judgement made by the K4D programme officers.

We can now run through the four pillars and 81 indicators to indicate the essential elements and ideas of this imagined knowledge economy. A knowledge-based economy is: open to global trade; moving in the direction of creating a services sector; has few bans on imports and licensing (as measured by the Heritage Foundation's Trade Policy Index); strong protections in place for intellectual property; the transaction costs (time and money) to start a business are low, and there is a limited number of market-unfriendly policies. In relation to governance, the rule of law to ensure contracts is enforced; governments are effective (such as the civil service is independent); and there is a measure of political stability and limited corruption. In relation to the innovation system, Foreign Direct Investment is welcomed, there is a system to ensure payments for royalties and intellectual property across borders; science and engineering enrolments are strong; there are a large number of researchers involved in R&D; total expenditure on R&D are high; companies collaborate with universities; venture capital is available; publications in scientific journals, and patent applications are high; and there is evidence of value being added higher up the value chain.

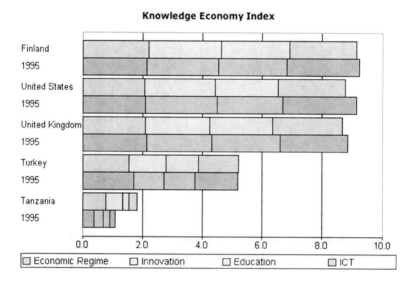

Figure 8. Over-time comparision of selected countries, Finland, USA, UK, Turkey and Tanzania (Source: World Bank 2007)

In the area of education (see also Figure 3 above), measures include the adult literacy rate, the average years of schooling (for 15 years and above); secondary and tertiary enrolments are high; life expectancy at birth is high; schools have access to the internet; the state funds education; there is a high level of achievement on international mathematics and science tests (such as TIMMS); teachers receive ongoing training; schools are assessed as well locally-managed; and the talented individuals of a country stay rather than leave. Gender receives a special focus, with indicators on females in the labour force; females elected to Parliament; and the numbers of females enrolled in secondary school and tertiary education. Finally, a knowledge economy embraces information and communication technologies as indicated by the number of telephones, landlines, computers, internet connections, televisions and newspapers circulated per capita; the bandwidth and cost of connection to the internet; e-government; e-business; and ICT expenditures as a % of GDP.

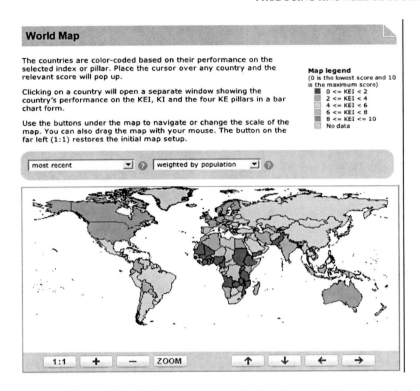

Figure 9. World map of knowledge economy countries by colour code (Source: World Bank 2007)

ANALYSING THE KAM

There are three ways in which we can begin to open up the KAM to closer inspection. First, we can review the indicators themselves and what it is they 'represent' as modalities of selectivity. Second, we can view the KAM as a selective tool, deployed to produce a particular kind of economy. This means asking what kind of imagined economy is being discursively and materially 'produced', whose interests are being selectively and strategically advanced, and what are the roots of this project? Third, we might ask: how is 'education' specified in this project, for whom, and with what likely outcome? In the conclusion I also ask: what form do the contradictions of capitalism take in this new imagined society, and how might these be revealed in the agendas of education policymakers in the 21st Century?

Indicators of what?

The KAM draws upon existing data-bases and indexes from the international organisations, such as World Bank data-bases, OECD national accounts data, the

Human Development Index (United Nations Development Programme), unemployment rates from the *International Labour Organisation* (ILO), and the Global Competitiveness Index from the *World Economic Forum* (WEF). It also draws upon indexes from think-tanks, such as the right wing Heritage Foundation on the existence (or not) of tariffs and other forms of protectionism. These actors can be characterised by their commitment to neo-liberal economic policies. These databases and indexes provide measures of 'economic performance' (such as GDP growth over time) and measures of 'human development' (as in the Human Development Index (HDI)).

However, many of these indicators and indexes are based upon data that are inadequate. As a result, their translation into indexes is problematic. Sagar and Najani's (1998) discussion of the problems of the HDI are instructive here. While the HDI was welcomed by many in the development community because it opened to door to a wider discussion on development beyond the economic, very early on the HDR noted there was some way to go in refining the content and method used in the Index "(…) before the HDI could be confidently used to interpret reality and make policy decisions" (Sagar & Najani, 1998, p. 25). However, this refinement did not occur. As a result, we see Mexico and Switzerland being represented as having very similar HDIs. Small wonder that Sagar and Najani argue the Index is deeply flawed and a long way from representing what is going on in the real world. Similarly, Pyatt (2003) shows that there are major errors in household survey data and national accounts data-bases, both of which underpin OECD and World Bank instruments. This makes, for instance, the *Living Standards Measurement Study* (LSMS) unreliable, and World Bank dependence on them problematic.

Data-bases and statistics – like all representations of the world – tend to present themselves as truths, concealing their politics and forms of strategic selectivity. As Cusso and D'Armico (2005, p. 199) note:

> (…) according to OECD or the World Bank, more emphasis should be placed on the comparability of education outputs than on the measurement of the development of mass education. Moreover, indicators should be used not only to compare the characteristics of national education systems but also to compare underlying political decisions. The latter would be evaluated based on performance criteria established by external assessments. This new kind of comparability, which was justified by the quest for data quality, is, in a sense, less robust from a statistical point of view, but more ambitious in terms of objectives and consequences. This comparability has also been accompanied by the reshaping of international decision-making.

Similarly, Godin's (2002) work referred to earlier shows how the OECD's statistics framed a very particular understanding of the knowledge economy; one tied to science and technology. Taken together, the international agencies use of statistics and indicators to drive national development in directions that suit particular interests demonstrate the powerful way that these agencies are penetrating nation-state space and directing the realising a more tightly interwoven global-political economy.

Whose knowledge economy?

As Jessop argues (2004, p. 167), crises encourage semiotic as well as strategic innovation. As I have argued earlier, the idea of a knowledge-based economy had its material and ideological roots in the 1960s and 70s as a result of the crisis of Atlantic Fordism. This ideas was taken up in the 1970s by the OECD, however, it did not gain traction until the 1990s when the OECD committed significant resources to the development of its knowledge programme.

This project was significantly buoyed by the idea that the services sectors (health, education, banking, insurance and so on) might also be the basis for generating a competitive advantage for the developed economies. This idea was supported by the work of think-tanks, and lobbying by interests in the services sectors – such as the coalition for services' unions, particularly in the USA (Mundy & Iga, 2003).

The US's competitive edge, at the high value-added end of the commodity chain, prompted a concerted effort to develop the material and ideological base for a new accumulation strategy centred on the widening and deepening of the services sector, the extension of intellectual property rights, and the means to protect those rights internationally in order to return value to economies like the US. These ideas and strategies also contributed to the formation of the *World Trade Organisation* (WTO), and the creation of new agreements, such as the *Trade Related Intellectual Property Services Agreement* (TRIPS) and *General Agreement on Trade in Services* (GATS) which materialised in 1995 (Robertson, Bonal and Dale, 2002). Taken together, they represented the creation of institutional structures and instruments to advance this new economy project – a services-oriented, high-valued added, knowledge-based economy. However, this new economy requires the borders that had protected services sectors (largely public) to be removed. It also demanded new institutions be established that would return value to those producers who claimed it as intellectual property (May, 2004).

We can see from the KAM indicators that intellectual property, its protection by states, and the institutional means for returning value across borders, is a key feature. The KAM is, therefore, a strategically-selective tool that advances the interests of capital in the developed economies. This framing of the economy also underpins the hope for a new long wave of accumulation for the developed economies. Put another way, the knowledge-economy narrative is *not* about developing countries becoming knowledge-based. Rather, it is tool for putting into place the ideological and institutional means to enable the developed economies, in particular the USA, to generate value from knowledge services globally. The KAM prioritises the ideological and structural means for developing a globally-integrated post-Fordist macro-economic order, secured through WTO regulations. It also "(...) reflects a neo-liberal policy for productive capital that safeguards US super-profits behind the cloak of free trade in intellectual property" (Jessop, 2004, p. 170).

This chapter also reveals the ways in which the World Bank, along with the OECD and the WTO (as regulator), represent themselves as the mid-wives of this new economy; as institutions helping give birth to a country's transition from an industrial to a knowledge economy. However, as Jessop (2004, p. 166) also observes, to produce a new social formation, something *more* is required; it "(...) also depends critically on institutional innovation intended to reorganise an entire social formation, and the exercise of political, intellectual and moral leadership" (Jessop, 2004, p. 166). The combination of forces of the big international agencies (OECD, World Bank, World Trade Organisation) along with strategic coalitions within nation states, have advanced a formative agenda for institutional innovation to realise a new global economy and social formation.

The idea of a knowledge-based economy is also a particularly powerful discursive and strategic tool for the World Bank and OECD. It not only enables the rethinking of social, material and spatio-temporal relations among economic and extra-economic activities, institutions and systems, but the master narrative of knowledge provides a useful cloak for these international agencies because it appeals to the 'knowledge is progress/ive' ideals that continue to dominate the development industry societies imaginary. Who can be against knowledge, and by implication, knowledge-based economies? Who can be against knowledge for development? However as we have seen this is an imaginary that works in the interests of the developed economies and capital, with its need to protect profits and realise value from intellectual property whilst at the same time expanding into new services markets globally. It is structural adjustment cloaked in a consensual, progressive mantle.

What education?

How then, is education represented in the KAM? Whilst a major pillar of the knowledge-based economy imaginary, education is now constructed as 'investment' and 'performance' in adult literacy, science, mathematics and technology, including scientific publications in these areas. This represents an extension of western high modernity, with its faith in science, technology and law, now aided by new technologies to direct and hasten development. It is argued that only science and technology will produce the innovations and patents for the new economy and to the extent that education can produce more scientists, engineers and technologists, it is in turn valued. In this reformulation, education is now completely subordinated to the economy, like any other commodity-producing sector. The emancipatory potential implied in the formulation, 'knowledge for development', is emptied out, leaving little more than instrumental knowledge.

The KAM indicators also ignore important aspects of education in low-income countries that have been central to the *Millennium Development Goals* formulated by the UN; access to education as a universal right; the level of completions of schooling (quality issues) and alternative trajectories for developing knowledge and skills that are more appropriate to regional and local conditions (see Robertson et al., 2007). The combination of human capital and new growth theory, with their focus on education outputs and knowledge production through innovation, also gives the World Bank greater leverage over education. Read in conjunction with the World Bank's 2003 Report, *Lifelong Learning for the Global Knowledge*

Economy, we can see that developing countries in particular are being faced with new ways of embedding neo-liberal interventions in their economies. For instance, in order to widen access to education to realise a knowledge-based economy, the World Bank is financing innovative forms of provision that favour for-profit firms delivering education in low-income countries (cf. Robertson, 2005).

CONCLUSIONS

In this chapter I have set out to better understand the construction and use of the World Bank's Knowledge Assessment Methodology as a tool which is discursively and materially producing and institutionalising a very particular kind of economic imaginary; a global knowledge-based economy. The Critical Cultural Political Economy of education approach deployed in this re-reading of economic development policy makes this globally-structuring development both visible and therefore readable in ways that nationally-anchored approaches to education policy tend to overlook. This approach reveals the strategic *and* selective approach to knowledge that is being advanced by the KAM. Through this mechanism, it is possible to see the way in which the interests of the developed economies and fractions of capital are advanced by the World Bank and the OECD, and reinforced at regional, national and institutional scales of policymaking and practice.

I have also argued that the material and ideological roots to this hegemonic imaginary can be found in the crisis of capitalism in the developed economies (USA, UK, Australia, Canada) when capital and the state agents sought to deepen and widen the services sectors globally in order to more freely trade in the services sectors globally, and to extend intellectual property rights. International agencies, such as the OECD and World Bank, have been important actors in helping launch this master narrative.

A CCPEE approach is also attentive to the contingencies, contradictions and dilemmas produced by political projects, for it is the production of crises and the need for repair and renovation that are at the heart of the dynamics of change. There are evident fundamental and profound contradictions of this form of capitalism both for accumulation and for ongoing social stability. For instance: (i) the dominant assumptions of the KAM are Western-centred 'northern' knowledges; the knowledge of *modernity* (science, progress). It therefore excludes the knowledges and values of more than two-thirds of the world, exposing it to the critique of hyper-colonialism and imperialism; (ii) by prioritising competitiveness, the KAM might be oriented to the production of new and valuable knowledges *but* also converts them into Intellectual Property, limiting both the possibility of their development (e.g. ICT), and their potential benefits (HIV/AIDS drugs) to the rest of the world. The struggle around the production of lower cost generic drugs to help fight global diseases like AIDS, for instance, reveals that intellectual property is highly contested; (iii) exploiting 'tacit knowledge' through codification enhances a competitive edge for capitalists *whilst* at the same time it undermines the dynamic nature of knowledge for capitalist development, a point well made by Stiglitz on the economics of information (2000); (iv) the emergence of knowledges ('know who', 'know what', 'know that') disguises the class-based nature of the KBE project, as new hierarchies are produced globally, making evident the asymmetrical distribution of knowledge and its consequences across the globe. Arocena and Sutz (2002) have called this a new learning divide; (v) benchmarks and indicators create hierarchies, however their leakiness and lack of robustness make them open to critique and in need of constant renovation and repair, reducing their effectiveness as legitimator in capitalist societies; and (vi) it is also important to remind ourselves that, historically, education has been notoriously difficult to pin down as a factor of production, despite the interest in doing so by human capital and new growth theorists. As new growth theorist, Paul Romer (1989) noted, we can say education matters, but the question is what kind of education? The answer, of course, lies in the fact that, as Dore (1976) reminded us many years ago, it is not possible to generate a causal relationship between education and growth, beyond the fairly commonsensical understanding that literacy is important. Dore outlines at least 10 competing explanations for the relationship between education, earnings and growth, all of which continue to resonate today. Similarly, it is notoriously difficult to 'predict' and re/produce the conditions for generating new innovations, patents and intellectual property, as the OECD have found. Systems, though structured and structuring, are also open, contingent and potentially plural, making prediction and certainty problematic.

Finally, and in conclusion, we might also argue (and indeed we can see some evidence for this) that the specification of 'the knowledge based economy' has opened up the knowledge question for both scrutiny (whose knowledge?) and challenge (what about other knowledges?) in ways in which education systems had tended to contain and close it off. This is all for the good, in my view, and for this reason we might continue to see knowledge on the agenda not only for education policy analysts *and* critical academics, but *also* subaltern groups for some time to come.

NOTES

[1] There are regular movements of key personnel from the OECD to the World Bank and vice versa. For example, Kurt Larsen, a Senior Researcher with the Education Directorate of the OECD and author of key reports on the cross border supply of higher education and knowledge management, joined the K4D team in 2005.

[2] See World Bank, 2003 report on *Lifelong Learning for the Global Knowledge Economy*, Washington: World Bank.

REFERENCES

Arocena, R., & Sutz, J. (2002). *Innovation systems and developing countries*. DRUID Working Paper 02-05, Aalborg University, Department of Business Studies.

Asgeirsdottir, B. (2005). *Opening keynote address by OECD Deputy Secretary-General to the "Advancing knowledge and the knowledge economy"* OECD/NSF Conference 10–11 January 2005.

Bell, D. (1973). *The coming of the post-industrial society: A venture in social forecasting*. Middlesex: Penguin.

Castells, M. (1996). *The rise of the network society*. London: Blackwell.

Chen, D. C., & Dahlman, C. (2005). *The knowledge economy, the KAM methodology and World Bank operations*. Washington, DC: World Bank.

Connell, R. (2007). The northern theory of globalisation. *Sociological theory*, *25*(4), 368–385.

Cusso, R., & D'Armico, S. (2006). From development comparativism to globalisation comparativism: Towards more normative international education statistics. *Comparative Education*, *41*(2), 199–216.

Dale, R. (1999). Specifying globalisation effects on national policy: Focus on the mechanisms. *Journal of Education Policy*, *14*, 1–17.

Dale, R. (2000). Globalisation and education: Demonstrating a 'common world culture' or locating a 'globally structured agenda'? *Educational Theory*, *50*(4), 427–448.

Dore, R. (1976). Human capital theory: the diversity of societies and the problem of quality in education. *Higher Education*, *5*, 79–102.

Drucker, P. (1969). *The age of discontinuity: Guidelines to our changing society*. London: Heinemann.

Foray, D., & Gault, F. (2003). *Measuring knowledge management in the business sector: First steps*. Paris: OECD.

Godin, B. (2002). Rhetorical numbers: How the OECD constructs discourses on S&T. *Technology in Society*, *24*, 387–413.

Godin, B. (2006). The knowledge-based economy: Conceptual framework of buzzword. *Journal of Technology Transfer*, *31*, 17–30.

Harvey, D. (2006). *Spaces of global capitalism: Towards a theory of uneven development*. London: Verso.

Jessop, B. (2004). Critical semiotic analysis and cultural political economy. *Critical Discourse Analysis*, *1*(2), 159–74.

Jessop, B., & Sum, N.-L. (2006). *Beyond the regulation approach: Putting capitalist economies in their place*. Cheltenham, UK: Edward Elgar.

Jessop, B. (2001). Institutional (re)turns and the strategic relational approach. *Environment and Planning A*, *33*(7), 1213–1237.

Jessop, B. (2000). The state and the contradictions of the knowledge-based economy. In J. R. Bryon, P. W. Daniels, N. D. Henry, & J. Pollard (Eds.), *Knowledge, space, economy*. London: Routledge.

King, K. (2002). Banking on Knowledge: The new knowledge projects of the World Bank. *Compare*, *32*(3), 312–326.

Lundvall, B.-Å. (1992). *National innovation systems: Toward a theory of interactive learning*. London: Pinter Publishers.

Machlup, F. (1962). *The production and distribution of knowledge*. Princeton, NJ: Princeton University Press.

Mattelart, A. (2003). *The information society: An introduction*. London: Sage.

May, C. (2004). Capacity building and the (re)production of intellectual property rights. *Third World Quarterly*, *25*(5), 821–837

Mundy, K., & Iga, M. (2003). Hegemonic exceptionalism and legitimating bet-hedging: Paradoxes and lessons from the US and Japanese approaches to education services under the GATS. *Globalisation, Societies and Education*, *1*(3), 281–319.

Pyatt, G. (2003). Development and the distribution of living standards: A critique of the evolving data. *Review of Income and Wealth*, *49*(3), 333–358.

Robertson, S., Novelli, M., Dale, R., Tikly, L., Dachi, H., & Alphonce, N. (2007). *Globalisation, education and development: Ideas, actors and dynamics*. London: DfID.

Robertson, S. (2005). Re-imagining and rescripting the future of education: Global knowledge economy discourses and the challenge to education systems. *Comparative Education*, *41*(2), 151–170.

Robertson, S., Bonal, X., & Dale, R. (2002). GATS and the education service industry. *Comparative Education Review*, *46*(4), 472–496.

Romer, P. (1989). *Human capital and growth: Theory and evidence*. NBER Working Paper, Cambridge, Massachusetts.

Sagar, A., & Najam, A. (1998). The human development index: A critical review. *Ecological Economics*, *25*, 249–264.

Stiglitz, J. (2000). *Knowledge as a global public good* [last accessed on 13th March, 2008 at http://www.worldbank.org/knowledge/chiefecon/articles/undpk2/index.htm]

Webster, F. (2002). *Theories of the information society* (2nd ed.). London and New York: Routledge.

World Development Report (WDR). *Knowledge for development.* Washington, DC: World Bank.

World Bank. (2003). *Lifelong learning for a global knowledge economy.* Washington, DC: World Bank.

World Bank. (2004). 1 K4D. *Newsletter, 1*(1), 1.

World Bank. (2007). *Knowledge for development* [http://web.worldbank.org/WBSITE/EXTERNAL/WBI/WBIPROGRAMS/KFDLP/EXTUNIKAM/0,,menuPK:1414738~pagePK:64168427~piPK:64168435~theSitePK:1414721,00.html?, last accessed on 23rd July, 2007]

APPENDIX 1

Table 1. World Bank Knowledge Economy Assessments Carried Out – 2003-2007(Source: World Bank K4D Newsletters 2004-2007)

	Benchmark *basic*	Enhanced *intermediate*	Comprehensive *Comprehensive*
El Salvador	2003		
Slovakia	2004		
Turkey	2006	2003	
Morocco	2004		
Tunisia	2004		
India		2004	2005
China			2004
Mexico			2004
Korea			2006
Ethiopia		2006	
Japan			2005
Finland			2006
Chile			2006

FURTHER READINGS

Chen, C. & Dahlman, C. (2005). *The Knowledge Economy, The KAM Methodology and World Bank Operations.* Washington, DC: World Bank.

Godin, B. (2006). The knowledge-based economy: conceptual framework or buzzword. *Journal of Technology Transfer,* 31, 17-30.

Jessop, B. (2004). Critical semiotic analysis and cultural political economy. *Critical Discourse Analysis, 1*(2), 150-74.

King, K. (2002). Banking on knowledge: the new knowledge projects of the World Bank. *Compare, 32*(3), 312-26.

Robertson, S. Bonal, X. & Dale, R. (2002). GATS and the Education Service Industry. *Comparative Education Review, 46*(4), 42-96.

Susan L. Robertson
Centre for Globalisation, Education and Societies
University of Bristol, UK

TERRI SEDDON

KNOWLEDGE ECONOMY

Policy Discourse and Cultural Resource

INTRODUCTION

The idea of a knowledge economy or knowledge society is a key theme in contemporary education policy. It foregrounds the place of knowledge in economic production and wealth creation and, on the basis of this reading of economic history, projects particular concepts, classifications, norms and values which are woven into future scenarios for societies. This slippage, from an assessment of changes in the economy to imperatives for society, frames measures to achieve these preferred ways of organising and governing education and society.

My aims in this chapter are, firstly, to show how the process of reading society as economy is made possible by a particular construction of 'knowledge economy'. These discursive practices represent a world, the world of knowledge economy, and through narratives, provide the cultural resources – the concepts, images and imaginaries – that can be used in world making. Secondly, I consider the way different actors deploy these cultural resources in making worlds for learning. My argument is that while governments and other elites use these cultural resources to redesign education systems, they are also used by professionals and practitioners to both defend their established educational practices and to pursue other ideas of a good society.

I approach this agenda from a position at the interface of a critical sociology of education and work, and the sociology of knowledge. My perspective recognises the obduracy of social structures and relations of possession-dispossession, domination-subordination, and also the significance of discursive practices and cultural politics in framing social action and identities. It focuses on the active participation of individuals and groups in their own formation as social beings in contexts that are pre-given. They are positioned and ordered discursively but also 'construct themselves into' dominant cultural expectations and work to reconstruct those cultural and structural norms at the 'points at which change is possible', 'where chains chafe most' and where 'accommodations have been made' (Haug et al., 1987).

The analysis involves two methodologies, critical discourse analysis and socio-historical analysis of education reform. The discourse analysis is used to re-read two policy texts published in the proceedings of a 1994 OECD conference. The first text is the synthesis paper, prepared as a commentary on the conference (Foray & Lundvall, 1996). The second more applied policy text (Miller, 1996), drawn from the same conference proceedings, creates a discursive bridge between the

M. Simons, M. Olssen and M.A. Peters (eds.), Re-Reading Education Policies: A Handbook Studying the Policy Agenda of the 21ˢᵗ Century, 257–276.

discourse of knowledge economy and education reform agenda. The implications of these discursive constructions are then tracked into local spaces, Australia and a small training provider in Melbourne (VICRTO). This part of the paper draws on my policy and ethnographic research in schools, Institutes of Technical and Further Education (TAFE, like US Community Colleges or UK Colleges of Further Education), private and community providers, and multi-agency social partnership initiatives. These interview-based studies provide empirical evidence of the processes and effects of education and training reform in Australia since the early 1990s. The details of VICRTO are based on an interview-based case study conducted in 1999 (Seddon, 2001). VICRTO had a small staff, comprising three managers, eight teachers (mostly working part-time) and three office staff. Quotes are drawn from the managers and 2 teachers.

The chapter begins by briefly outlining the conceptual framework that informs this reading of knowledge economy. The re-reading develops through three sections. The first section interrogates Foray and Lundvall (1996) to show the construction of knowledge economy discourse. The second section documents the translation of these discursive practices into practical reforms. Finally, I show how professionals at VICRTO mobilise the discourse of knowledge economy to build another space for learning.[1]

APPROACHING CRITICAL POLICY ANALYSIS

The idea of a knowledge economy is a key theme in contemporary education and training. Its significance is evident in its effects as a "travelling policy" that has been embedded within diverse local spaces with far-reaching effects in terms of national policies, and institutional change (Alexiadou & Jones, 2001; Ozga et al., 2006). A recent cross-national study found that in all 30 countries reviewed the aim of creating a knowledge-based economy and knowledgeable citizens was seen to be important for national economic and political systems, whether the countries were developed or developing, democracies or dictatorships (Kuhn, 2007). As Kuhn suggests, this idea is not only widely embraced but also pervasively embracing so that it seems that 'the world wants to become' a knowledge-based economy/society. In this embrace, other ideas about a good society and the models and measures to realise them are dispersed and rendered invisible/impossible.

Critical education policy research provides a way of problematising the pervasiveness, impact and global reach of the knowledge economy idea. This research tradition builds on theories of power that offer ways of understanding processes of domination and constraint within societies. These theories developed historically through analysis of centred sovereign power, particularly studies of the nation-state. But state-centric theories are problematised by contemporary social changes that are increasing global interconnectivity and decentering sovereign power exercised through centralised states. These historical changes raise questions about the best way of understanding power in relation to (a) conflict, opposition, disorder and (b) authority, control, compliance.

Allen (2003) identifies three main traditions in theorising power. Instrumental conceptions of power emphasise power-over a social space through domination and constraint. This is the familiar view of power anchored in a centred identity, a state or leader that holds power as property that can be delegated. A counterview, less anchored in identities where power is concentrated, emphasises power as an effect and enabler of social action. In this view, power is in constant formation. Power is a medium for social action, whose effects are determined by the mobilisation of resources and sustainability of relationships. Finally, 'post-power' theories build on and extend Foucault's theorisation of power-knowledge-space. This approach focuses on discourses, the social practices that are always also practices of knowledge and power. It emphasises the way knowledge practices are also governing practices that frame authority to speak and be heard, constitute social ordering and govern self-regulating identities.

The analysis of policy has become increasingly significant as older notions of centralised and sovereign power have been challenged. In education this problem-atising of instrumental power and state-centric theorising has been developed through research on problem-taking and problem-making. Early work focused on the way problems are framed and ideas mobilised towards particular ends by being operationalised through a range of objects, institutions and relationships (Young, 1971). In this respect, policy becomes an "authoritative allocation of values" (Prunty, 1984). More recently, critical policy researchers have used notions of discourse to interrogate this process of problem taking/making. Seeing policy as discourse focuses attention on the way power operates through micro-practices of power-knowledge in which language is a medium for, and also mediates, social action (Ball, 1990). Yet this approach, with its emphasis on governing practices and self-regulation can encourage a kind of discursive determinism which over-states governability and downplays evidence of ungovernability. These debates within critical education policy highlight the need for analysis of policy discourse alongside theorisations of power that acknowledge the continuing significance of the state, instrumental power and mobilisations through forms of collective action.

POLICY AS DISCOURSE

The idea of 'policy-as-discourse' foregrounds the symbolic dimensions of policy processes while also acknowledging the way they are materialised as tangible things. These social practices encompass activities, subjects and social relations, instruments, objects, time and place, forms of consciousness, values and discourse, which are all dialectically related. Each element is distinct but also embraces and internalises the others in a way that is not reducible to one another (Fairclough 2001). This dialectics of discourse constructs and constitutes entities (knowledge and things) that are also identities (webs of meaning and ways of being in the world). It permits consideration of "what can be said, and thought, and about who can speak, when where and with what authority" (Ball, 1990, p. 17–18).

From this perspective, policy making and implementation is a process of producing knowledge, which is always also an effect of power. "Discourses are more than ways of thinking and producing meaning. They constitute the 'nature' of the body, unconscious and conscious mind and emotional life of the subjects they seek to govern" (Weedon, 1987, p. 108). Ideas, norms, values are constituted through socio-politically positioned performances because of the way language is mobilised through activities (ways of doing), representations (ways of thinking), and the constitution of particular identities (ways of being). These discursive practices form a social space as a symbolic order of discourse. This is a space of ordered relationships among different ways of making meaning that become embodied in different identities that are also entities.

The idea of the 'knowledge economy' has become powerful because it frames, and names, an order of discourse anchored in a particular web of meanings and ways of being. Knowledge economy discourse is, for instance, embedded in a powerful narrative about social change that is driven by economic processes. This story about historical changes in our social ecology provides a way of understanding the world as a basis for imagining the future. These understandings play out in everyday practices that construct institutional arrangements, power relations and a particular ordering of social positions, which mark out social inclusions and exclusions.

The policy-as-discourse approach has become influential because it reveals the way discursive practices delimit and construct knowledge and therefore shape possibilities in thinking and acting. This approach has been particularly helpful in understanding contemporary changes in education. The argument is that particular economic discourses have been mobilised to justify and drive education reform. These discourses privilege the individual and individual choice, which justifies a neo-liberal reconfiguration of schooling based on market, rather than state, coordination.

Yet policy as discourse research builds on particular theorisations of power that construct and constrain understandings about the use and effects of policy discourse. For instance, Bacchi (2000) argues that research on policy as discourse has framed the consideration of policy effects and policy use to pre-given understandings of relations of domination. Discourse users are identified as dominant groups who deploy policy discourse as they drive market reforms in education. Subaltern groups are identified as subject to policy discourse and therefore perform policy effects. The binary construction of powerful-powerless is lined up with the binary of policy use-policy effect. The effect of the analytical frame is to confirm a story about the power of the powerful and, in the process, fail to properly unpack agency and the space for challenge within policy discourses.

These critiques of policy-as-discourse refocus attention on agency and its embodiment within orders of discourse. Subaltern as well as dominant groups deploy discourses for political purposes. Revealing these effects requires research that focuses more sharply on the relationship between discursive effects and non-discursive factors in policy processes (Bacchi, 2000, p. 53). It turns attention to the way agency is constituted through embodiment, discursive closure, and the interplay of structure and agency in processes of subjectification, knowledge production, and the intersection between self-work and social stratification (Stehr & Meja, 2005; McLeod & Yates, 2006).

The way these processes of embodiment have been understood draws variously on the vocabulary of power and political philosophy rooted in Nietzsche and on the vocabulary of property and political economy rooted in Marx. The result is a debate that recognises the interplay of power in knowledge production but offers different explanations. Some favour property-like dispositional interpretations (e.g. Bourdieu) that emphasise 'having knowledge'. Others prefer more fluid actionist power-knowledge interpretations (e.g. Foucault) that favour "doing things with words" (Pels, 2005).

These different explanations of agency within policy discourses suggest different patterns of closure that support social action. On the one hand, webs of meaning and ways of being may be materialised as a social space and a distinct order of discourse that is evident through the discursive framing of rules, laws, norms, programs. On the other hand, the order of discourse may be materialised as things, including knowledge, available as cultural resources.

This double character of policy is particularly clear in knowledge economy discourse. The idea that knowledge is a factor of production and central to wealth generation depends upon the mobilisation of the thing-like aspects of knowledge (as human capital, intellectual property) as a basis for designing reform measures (indicators, expert systems, regulatory requirements, legal frameworks). Simultaneously, the economic framing of these understandings constructs a social space with an order of discourse that positions these activities in a hierarchy, which values practices in terms of their compliance and contribution to influencing, innovating, individualising and economising social practices.

Research that investigates agency within policy discourses needs to consider how the lived effects of discourse intersect with real bodies as they live the effects of discursive conventions and their materialisations. Such research must be sensitive to contextualisation in time and space because agency confronts pre-given structures that increasingly have their effects across local, national and global scales. Yet these structures are social and symbolic identities/entities that are not fully fixed. Human embodiment depends upon particular ways of doing social participation and appropriating the cultural resources of a society. These engagements form knowing bodies and also build capacities for action in ways that are always located in particular contexts or time-spaces. Yet ideas can travel, whereas skills are embodied in people who live in particular ways in particular places. Dissonances arise as these things in motion confront "the pre-existing world of structures, organisations and other stable social forms" (Appadurai, 2001, p. 5). Women and men engage with these contradictions and paradoxes on a day-to-day located basis. These knowing bodies constituted discursively within particular time spaces live these contradictions by harmonising everyday activities in conformity to dominant discourses and also by engaging actively with cultural resources to construct alternative imaginaries, innovations and activist subjectivities (Haug, 1992).

From this perspective, the knower, an embodiment of knowledge, becomes a resource for social action, but their deployment or capacity to act depends upon the social and intellectual conditions that prevail. Capacities for action are framed by the prevailing order of discourse. They are also stratified by life chances, style and social influence because they depend upon access to the stock of knowledge (Stehr & Meja, 2005). They are affected by the way subjects live discursive effects alongside habitual dispositions everyday. In this way, capacities to act are affected by the way subjects are positioned and attend to the harm they experience (Bacchi, 2000) as well as the lives they value (Sen, 1999).

My argument in this paper is that the mobilisation of knowledge economy discourse *constructs* webs of meaning and ways of being that establish an order of discourse. It makes a world, the world of knowledge economy, by creating an ordered space of action by telling stories. These stories create closure through framing and materialising social spaces as bodies (knowledge and things) that seem property-like. The stories provide concepts and categories that constitute cultural resources and knowers which are mobilised to *translate* ideas into practices. Yet these processes are interrupted by the way knowers are embedded in social and cultural orderings of time-spaces. And because governing practices are always incomplete, cultural resources are deployed in dissonant ways that build and also question the world of knowledge economy, as identities-entities *negotiate* alternative futures, in practice and in imagination.

In the remainder of this chapter I illustrate these processes of constructing, translating and negotiating knowledge economy. The next section documents the construction of knowledge economy discourse by re-reading a policy text that helped construct the imagined world of knowledge economy.

CONSTRUCTING THE 'KNOWLEDGE ECONOMY'

In 1994, an OECD conference was held in Copenhagen, It was jointly organised by the Danish Ministry of Business and Industry and the OECD *Directorate for Science, Technology and Industry* (DSTI). The conference documented trends towards a knowledge-based economy. The synthesis draws the emerging themes into an argument for the knowledge-based economy, its key characteristics and drivers.

The synthesis paper, prepared by Foray and Lundvall (1996), provided a commentary on the conference. This text has been selected for discourse analysis because its significance in the conference authorised its discursive construction of knowledge economy. The authority of this text was further endorsed by the standing of its authors. Foray and Lundvall are both economists, men who have had close affiliations with the OECD. Lundvall, in particular, has been central to the construction of the idea of a knowledge-based economy. In 1994, at the time of the conference, Lundvall (2007) was Deputy Director at DSTI. Foray (2007) was Research Director at the *Centre National de la Recherche Scientifique* (CNRS) and Professor at the *Institut pour le Management de la Recherche et de l'Innovation* (IMRI) of the University of Paris-Dauphine (from 1993 to 2000). From 2000-2004 he was Principal Analyst at OECD.

These biographical details give an indication of the kind of social ecology and identity from which these authors are writing. Their significance lies in their disciplinary background and their association and standing within OECD, an institution with a particular commitment to high economic growth, employment, financial stability and the expansion of world trade (OECD, 1996). Their institutional location contributes to the reach and authority with which they speak. It is illustrated by their involvement in the 1994 conference, their roles as discussants and by the extent to which their work is taken up by the wider academic-policy community. LogEc, a website that provides access statistics for Economics working papers, journal articles and software, indicates that over the last 12 months (2006-7) Lundvall has had almost 19000 abstract downloads and over 7000 full working paper downloads. Foray has had almost 6000 abstract, and 1870 full paper, downloads (LogEc, 2007).

The 1994 conference, which drew around 250 representatives from government, academia and business, claimed "wide agreement across all layers of society on the crucial role of knowledge in economic production, and the wide scope for policy action in the area" (OECD, 1996, p. 3). Yet this support for the idea of a knowledge-based economy, agreed by conference participants (but extrapolated to 'all layers of society'), also recognised the threat that negative public perceptions of science and technology, and resistance to innovation, held for realising an economy based on knowledge. This recognition underpins the slippage between the idea of an economy/society based on knowledge. As the Danish Prime Minister (Rassmussen, 1996, p. 7) noted in opening the conference:

> Let there be no doubt that the benefits of new technologies and a new pattern of global trade will by far exceed the costs. We must, however, realise that there are costs involved in adapting and adjusting to this new reality. However, our challenge is not to slow down an inevitable development. On the contrary, policies in the OECD countries should facilitate structural change and simultaneously alleviate the burden on those who are negatively affected.

The message of the conference was that there is no alternative to the knowledge economy. Yet the recognition that community concerns and hardship could threaten this developmental trajectory, provided a rationale for addressing citizens and governance to facilitate change. These themes were elegantly captured in Foray and Lundvall's text, which sets an agenda for building and rationalising the knowledge economy.

A WORLD-MAKING NARRATIVE

Policies are a space of stories but, unlike other social spaces, the stories projected are simple, uni-linear narratives. These narratives coalesce to construct an order of discourse based on networked themes and ways of making meaning. The knowledge economy discourse constructed by Foray and Lundvall has three key elements: a genealogy which tells a story about contemporary societies and how we got there; an ecology which represents the web of relationships that knit together humans, their internal and external relationships, and their participation in socio-technical systems that operate at different scales; and an imaginary which projects a possible future and specifies what has to happen to get there.

A genealogy

The synthesis paper begins by acknowledging but questioning the trans-historical significance of knowledge in economic life. The authors argue that, for theoretical, historical and political reasons, it is necessary to recognise that knowledge has a different status now from the past. The premise of this story is that "we are in a period of radical change … it is especially pertinent moment of time to focus on learning and on the knowledge base" (p.13).

In developing this case, the text constructs an analytical distinction. There is a long view across the span of human history in which "human competence is at the core of economic development in *any society*" (p.12 – emphasis included). There is also a historically specific view which "draws attention to the new characteristics of the economy which make it legitimate to speak of a new historical era – the knowledge-based economy, the learning economy or the information society – where the economy is more strongly and more directly rooted in the production, distribution and use of knowledge than ever before" (p.12).

The authors anchor and authorise this assumption about the significance of knowledge in the economy. They justify their claim by referring to: economists' views of competence in society and the increasing significance of knowledge in the economy; the ICT revolution which was already well established in established ideas about the information society, post-industrial society; and economic research which documents the changing patterns of industry and its implications for knowledge, learning and change. While acknowledging these long-term trends, the synthesis concludes by reiterating the premise that we are at a historical discontinuity:

> (…) reducing historical description and documentation to these long-run trends would result in a theory of a continuous and regular trajectory of technological change, underestimating the fact that we are in the midst of a radical socio-economic transformation, entailing the emergence of new forms of economic, social and industrial organisation, where new learning processes, as well as new modes of production and distribution of knowledge, are becoming crucial (p.17).

An ecology

In establishing the genealogy of the knowledge economy, the authors map an ecology of human society and economy by representing things and relationships as concepts and facts. Already they have established that knowledge and economy are related, technologies are pervasive and developing rapidly, and these processes have effects in human lives, particularly in the rate of learning and change. This broad-brush ecology is further delineated by the introduction of specific concepts and distinctions that establish the framework leading the argument to its logical conclusion – that there is no alternative to a knowledge economy.

A variety of concepts and classifications are used to develop the argument:

Economy: defines the landscape because economy is elided with, and used as a proxy for, society. This economy (and society) is defined as a knowledge economy. As Kenway, Bullen, Fahey, and Robb (2006) suggest, this discursive strategy obscures society and the social by privileging the economy.

Two sectors: This landscape can be seen in different ways. Knowledge production is located and sourced in the "knowledge-intensive part of the economy" (p.25). This innovation system is a "separate sector in charge of production of new knowledge or the handling and distribution of information." Yet knowledge is also generated through everyday "routine activities in economic life, taking the form of learning-by-doing, learning-by-using, and learning-by interacting" (p.13). The interface between the two is the information marketplace (p.15) within which knowledge is transacted between economic agents. The authors later associate these sectors, respectively, with codified and tacit knowledge. The critical transaction is the codification of tacit knowledge as a resource for innovation.

Classifications of organisation: This knowledge market is defined in terms of concepts that the authors justify using economic research. These concepts narrate, and therefore construct, the system of knowledge, production, distribution and exchange that comprises:

- Primary & secondary sectors (e.g. US Dept of Commerce): "industries that participate directly in the information market-place and includes virtually all the information activities listed above" (p.15), and those information activities that occur outside the information marketplace as part of manufacturing for non-information products;
- Categories of information activity (Machlup): Identified as education, communications media, information machines, information services, and other information activities;
- Information processing activities (OECD, 1996): Identified in developing input accounting systems based on the activities of information producers, processors, distributors, infrastructure providers;
- Labour inputs oriented to particular end uses (Eliasson): which identified labour in relation to function and quality and shows that the knowledge economy affects not only specified information-activities, but all sectors of the economy, including "the so-called low tech sectors" (p. 16).

Classifications of knowledge: What is transacted within this knowledge market distinguishes between "knowledge as more or less complex information, and knowledge as a set of skills and competences" (p. 19). This identifies knowledge products:

- Know-what: "Knowledge about facts (…) Information that can be broken down into bits" (p.19).
- Know-why: "Scientific knowledge of principles and laws of motion in nature, in the human mind and in society" (p.19). Knowledge that is important in technological innovation in the form of new developments and incremental improvements in practice.
- Know-how: Skills and "the capability to do something." Not restricted to 'practical people' but also required by scientists.
- Know-who: A mix of skills including social skills which involves information about "who knows what and who knows how to do what." This knowledge depends upon relationship-building, "the formation of special social relationships with the expertise involved which makes it possible to get access and use their knowledge efficiently" (p. 20).

This classification of knowledge is further elaborated by distinguishing codified and tacit knowledge on the basis of its accessibility and ease of use:

- Codified knowledge: is information, particularly know-what and know-why, chunked-up knowledge that can be easily stored and transmitted. It is "typically expressed in a format that is compact and standardised in order to facilitate and reduce the cost of such operations" (p. 21). It is also amenable to exchange within the information marketplace but such transactions are not simple because of the nature of this commodity.
- Tacit knowledge: is knowledge that has not been stated in explicit and codified form and is therefore not easy to transmit, or transact. It includes skills, knowledge of the know-how and know-who kind. It is embedded in practice and framed by rules that are not explicit, and often not recognised or even communicable.

Classifications of people: The two sector economy based in primary and secondary production of knowledge for the information market, plus the source of these different knowledges, constructs different kinds of identities. These are:

- Experts, scientists, and the scientifically trained: These knowledge workers are associated with the primary sector producing and distributing knowledge for and within the information marketplace. They are particularly located in specialist knowledge organisations, like universities. They develop know-what and know-why through academic learning.
- Practical people, skilled workers: These people have developed their knowledge primarily through practical experience, supported by manuals and basic skills in the field of application. Their knowledge develops through master-apprentice relationships. In this respect, scientists are practical people as well as being scientifically trained, while other people depend more upon practical engagement in learning relationships for their skill development. Know-who is a subset of these practical skills but can become a specialised form of human capital when it is extended to working and facilitating translations across boundaries between different knowledge codifications. "The skills necessary to understand and use

the local codes will often be developed only by those allowed to join the network and take part in the process of interactive learning" (p. 24).
- Less-skilled workers, unskilled workers, "working poor"(p. 26), "excluded workers" (p. 27), "weaker players" (p. 28), the "unemployed and unemployable" (p.28): These people are evident because of labour market polarisations which are explained by globalisation, technological change and institutional changes in the labour market, firm behaviour and industrial relations (p. 26). The range of representations indicates the political sensitivities surrounding this category of persons and the author's efforts to speak into these political complexities.

These concepts and classifications are 'world-making'. They construct the world of the knowledge economy as an ecosystem, a dynamic and complex whole in which people, organisations, countries, technologies, relationships and processes work together as a complex system.

This ecosystem is centred on knowledge, and its production, distribution, and exchange. The production of new knowledge, innovation, is fundamental to sustainability and at the core of productive life. What is at stake in the sustainability of the knowledge economy is the system and hierarchy of capitalist economies and states that enables profit making and its private appropriation.

The boundaries of this ecosystem appear ambiguous. They do not follow conventional organisational boundaries but cut across individuals, firms, countries, and regions giving the impression of a globally interconnected world. In this ambiguous space, the synthesis paper intervenes. The particular concepts and narratives deployed, like primary and secondary knowledge production and an (open) information marketplace, construct boundaries that connect across familiar spatial scales (e.g. international, national, local). Defining these boundaries on a world-scale repositions organisations and individuals so that some (e.g. universities) are positioned as globally networked players, while others are remaindered as an external, secondary, domain dealing in non-information products and as the residual population.

This world of the knowledge economy is all-embracing. This is because the development of concepts, based on scientific evidence from economics, is knitted into a complex historical narrative that is anchored in a representation of contemporary social ecology. This discursive construction frames understandings that discourage the imagining of alternative worlds. This discouragement is compounded by the institutional authority of this policy text (in the OECD, its networks with advanced economies and their governments), its incessant repetition (e.g. Lundvall's 18000 abstract downloads in 2007) and pervasive global uptake (Kuhn, 2007). The knowledge economy discourse also obscures social life beyond the economy because society is absorbed into an economic model. Its simple representation based on definable concepts and classifications is easily projected and grasped in imagined form and easily adopted in translating between policy and real effects. As Kenway, Bullen, Fahey and Robb (2006) argue, non-capitalist economic discourses anchored in social life persist but only as echoes that haunt the knowledge economy.

TRANSLATING POLICY IMAGINARIES

In constructing the imagined world of knowledge economy as a shared resource for the global policy community, policy-as-discourse brings interpretation to closure through framing and codification. Concepts and narratives become available as cultural resources that can be used in making the real world of knowledge economy.

The translation of these cultural resources into action agendas is a critical part of applied policy work. However it is affected by how and who does the translation. In this section of the chapter, I consider the translation accomplished by Riel Miller's (1996), a policy analyst working for the OECD whose paper was also published in the OECD Copenhagen conference proceedings. In the following section, I consider an alternative translation by staff at VICRTO.

Constructing a future of learning and forgetting

Foray and Lundvall (1996) project the imagined world of knowledge economy into the future. They bring interpretation to closure by weaving the concepts and narratives of knowledge economy genealogy and ecology into four development stories that construct the knowledge economy as a discursive space that privileges learning and forgetting.

This narrative of learning and forgetting draws, firstly, on the story of ongoing 'economic growth' through "expansion of the knowledge sector; change in the nature of the bias of technological change; and acceleration of change" (p. 17). It uses the historical record and economic research to reveal an economy driven by innovation. Knowledge sharing arrangements, consolidated through collaborations and networks, is shown to optimise innovation, establishing 'knowledge networks' that blur familiar boundaries as the organisational motif of the knowledge economy.

Secondly, the story of 'knowledge development' constructs a "new dynamic in the formation of tacit and codified knowledge" (p.13). It tells how a 'knowledge stock' is generated, not as ideas, but as codified knowledge, that is tangible and exchangeable entities, and as tacit knowledge. It also claims that the effects of codification prompts problem-solving that generates new tacit knowledge as innovation. This results in an incremental increase in know-how and creates the basis for 'knowledge flow'.

These constructions also tell a moral tale that establishes the desirability of this process of knowledge production. The authors describe this knowledge-building process as the "most fundamental aspect of learning ... the spiral movement, where tacit is transformed into codified knowledge, followed by a movement back to practice where new kinds of tacit knowledge are developed." (p.13) This spiral movement, "at the very core of individual and organisational learning" (p.22) constitutes innovation – the source of profit, which is realised through the codification and materialisation of knowledge into tradable goods and services.

The message is that innovation, growth and competitiveness depend upon human capital and its mobilisation through flexible organisations that can learn. Competence and skill acquisition, at all scales – individuals, organisational, national – rests on learning. The premise is that innovation happens when learning is unfettered, positively directed towards economic innovation and its returns, and when new learning displaces old learning. Innovation therefore depends upon unfettered and entrepreneurial learning and also upon unfettered and entrepreneurial forgetting. Change requires individuals and groups to relinquish old practices, ways of acting and relationships in a pro-active way based on assessment of returns from innovation. *"Forgetting* is a crucial and necessary element in the process of creative destruction. Unless we can forget the old ways of doing things, new procedures will be blocked" (p. 19).

Finally, this positively endorsed story of innovation is linked to the management of learning and development (that is, learning and forgetting) at all scales – individual, organisational, system, society. This means addressing threats to unfettered learning and forgetting through strategies that address resistance to change, disengagement from profitable work and social exclusion that threatens the ecology of the knowledge economy. The strategies include speeding up change to drive growth and competitive advantage; creating a sheltered sector (to warehouse those people who are resistant and excluded); providing access to networks and skill formation through human resource development policies; and slowing down change where there are mutual costs arising from 'hyper-acceleration'.

Miller (1996) takes up this agenda aimed at building the knowledge economy by managing learning and forgetting (i.e. learning and development) as a resource for applied policy making. In his contribution to the 1994 OECD conference, he translates Foray and Lundvall's concepts into an agenda for institutional redesign in education. This institutional design centres on the idea of human capital as a managed resource, which is optimised through individual and organisational (eg. employer) investment decisions.

Miller's policy imaginary constructs a particular reading of the relationship between human capital and social institutions. He defines human capital as "the more elusive kinds of knowledge that are embodied in human beings." The challenge in building the knowledge economy is therefore to mobilise this human capital in terms of property-like "actual competences, the specific attributes of a person's human capital" (p. 70). This mobilisation of human capital depends upon investment decisions that have the effect of managing learning and forgetting.

Where these processes are located frames the kind of human capital decisions that are made. Sites where decision-making structures are not formalised (households, workplaces) produce practical knowledge based in "thousands of decisions and experiences" (p. 70). It creates the kind of tacit knowledge that Foray and Lundvall represent and value as the source of innovation. More formalised decision-making structures (schools, traditions) establish incentives and organisational imperatives that "shape how and what we learn, remember and forget" (p. 70). They create knowledge stocks as a mixture of codified and tacit knowledge. These institutional arrangements, Miller explains, were developed for old economies. They no longer fit the requirements of the knowledge economy, which depends upon "innovation, creativity and adding your point of view to the product in order to increase its value" (p.70).

This imagined future privileges the importance of changes in knowledge (i.e. flow) as learning (acquisition) and forgetting (decomposition) rather than knowledge stocks that are sustained through remembering. Realising value from this new knowledge dynamic requires "human capital investment systems that accurately capture the capacities or competences accumulated as we live, work and continuously learn" (p.70). It also requires good information about these knowledge stocks. Such information can inform investment decisions that maximise innovation through the management of knowledge acquisition ('learning' through skill development and recruitment) and capital depreciation (forgetting through disinvestment, downsising, restructuring, labour replacement, redeployment and renewal).

Technologies of effective knowledge codification are needed to inform human capital investment decisions. Indicators, signs and symbols that represent knowledge stocks (fixed human capital) and flows (human capital changes through learning and forgetting) provide good information because they are focused on people learning by doing. What counts are the signs of competence. Not just the capacity to act (which may not be realised or may be directed perversely) but the capability of individuals to perform learning and forgetting in an institutional order that valorises practical knowledge.

In this way, Miller dismisses the learning and signage of the old economy as certification 'framed by the classroom', focused on the acquisition of knowledge content as its indicator of success. Rather than using old-styled qualifications as markers of educational achievement, the knowledge economy finds "more supple, content-related and transparent signals" and positional goods useful. These responsive signs and personal styles are rooted in reputational capital that is available through networks and knowledge sharing.

The institutional design that Miller presents confronts established education and training. Building on Foray and Lundvall (1996), he constructs an order of discourse that valorises the information needs of those knowledge users who make investment decisions. This discursive ordering privileges practical and applied learning over that occurring in formal education institutions with well-established organisational boundaries. It affirms learning across boundaries through knowledge sharing networks that support intra-cultural and cross-cultural knowledge-building where organisational and cultural boundaries are blurred (and where forgetting is optimised).

The politics of these proposals are clear. Building the world of knowledge economy requires systems that generate and read the new signage of learning and forgetting that is anchored in performance and reputation. In this way human capital can be managed to maximise value, that is profitability, and a sustainable knowledge economy order. The agenda that Miller articulates advocates institutional re-design that will "clear away vexsome bottlenecks" and "may pose a serious threat to the rents collected by certifying institutions" (p. 73), as it reconstructs education and training for a performative world.

Building a learning economy-society

Knowledge economy discourse, and its agenda of innovation through learning and forgetting, has been mobilised by governments in practical "didactic" (Miller, 1996, p. 69) interventions that build their economy-society of learning and forgetting. This is pursued through re-engineering education and training as performative information systems via the reconfiguration of rules, incentive structures and disciplinary imposts.

In Australia, since the mid-1980s, Commonwealth and State governments have energetically pursued market reform of education across all education and training sectors (Marginson, 1997). These changes constructed student as user and customer, industry as user and decision-maker, and educators and their institutions as customer service providers. It encouraged a view of students as human capital products, which are 'delivered' to meet industry needs, and a notion of teaching as 'delivery'.

While all education and training sectors have been affected by these trends, Institutes of Technical and Further Education (TAFE), particularly in Victoria, have been driven hardest in terms of institutional responsiveness and low cost. The measures used to engineer these changes included shifts in governance, the imposition of technologies and technologised learning and assessment, funding constraints and regulatory requirements which required TAFE Institutes to return annual productivity dividends. National training reform created an entrepreneurial vocational education and training (VET) sector marked by: a concern with competence (bits of human capital capability) not curriculum-based training; an assessment and credentialing regime which focused on recognition rather than development of competence; *Recognition of Prior Learning* later termed *Current Competence*; proliferation of on-line learning to facilitate delivery of training any where, any time. This system of signage that governs required outcomes has spawned competency standards, performance indicators, quality mechanisms, and price signals that are constructing the world of education as a textual, rather than lived, reality.

In 1996, Miller described these efforts by Australia in training reform as "one of the most comprehensive and ambitious efforts to improve human capital information and decision-making systems" (p. 74). In 2007, the Commonwealth Minister for Vocational and Further Education described Victorian TAFE Institutes as 'outstanding performers' that 'lead the way' nationally in autonomy and flexibility, in employer satisfaction, and in education export income (Robb, 2007).

NEGOTIATING A PLACE FOR LEARNING

Yet while the knowledge economy discourse travels globally, its take up occurs in local spaces. Here knowledge economy discourses confront local discourses that have already constructed structures and cultures of place, and localised work and learning imperatives (Farrell & Fenwick, 2007). While governments took up the knowledge economy discourse in their efforts to make a world of performative learning and forgetting, professionals found themselves inside this performative world, trying to find ways of surfing through change from within (e.g. Seddon, 2008). The constraints of this chapter limit the elaboration of these processes but I provide a window on these processes in one local place by outlining that activities of a Victorian training provider.

VICRTO was established by a small group of adult educators. They had all worked in the TAFE sector and community education for 25 to 30 years. But in the late 1980s, partly in response to the market reform and funding squeeze in TAFE Institutes, they took up externally funded project work associated with industry restructuring. While these teachers and managers had backgrounds in adult literacy and basic education, they found themselves working together in manufacturing to support enterprise-based reform through developing human capital. Their task was to support adults develop literacy and numeracy skills, justified partly by the employees need to know occupational health and safety signage and also by competitive pressures in manufacturing.

Their work in industry was framed within knowledge economy discourse and its developing systems of competence, performance, recognition, and signage in a competitive entrepreneurial context. They learned to play this game well and were recognised for their distinctive approach to training. Yet, the work offered professional rewards and provided a kind of escape from the accelerating change in TAFE. Describing themselves as 'refugees from TAFE' suggests one way of making a place for learning within the knowledge economy. Many other TAFE employees also escaped from hyper-acceleration, through retirement, resignation, off-campus teaching, industry-based projects and international work.

Yet fickle project work, depending on soft money, did not support their work of turning their particular take on knowledge economy discourse into a sustainable place for learning. They turned to the network of employers, managers and unions they had consolidated through their project work for advice. Drawing on shared understandings of learning and what serious learning could do in an industry context, they decided to form a private company – flavour of the month in knowledge economy terms.

Their aim was to provide training to industry as a way of realising their professional educational goals. As one manager noted,

> (...) a lot of people thought we were nuts because we'd go out there and talk visions and education with companies, and we do – well we put it in their terms – but what we're talking about is an educational vision not a training-type vision. We saw a whole range of people out there who needed training and what they were getting was not suitable (...). It was a question of saying, all right, that's the way we want to go.

This distinction between an 'educational vision' and a knowledge economy 'training-type vision' is a window into an alternative order of discourse. As the informant notes, it is performed in a lexicon and style that is familiar to industry, but it represents the renegotiation of webs of meaning and ways of being to affirm an order of discourse that privileges life and valued living, sustainable sociality and citizenship, and the importance of collective happiness.

This educational vision sees learning broadly but not as 'lifelong learning' with its totalitarian insistence that we learn all the time, about everything, exhaustively and exhaustingly all through our lives. Rather this broad idea of learning is about learning for living and living together. Informants capture it as a commitment to living that they want for themselves. As a teacher said, they

> (...) reflect in our work-lives the way we live our lives. We have developed a philosophy that motivates us rather than profit. We try to be a workplace that tolerates employees who have other things in their lives. And we use the workplace to support people.

Here learning is not acquisition of transactable human capital, but about building capacities for action that are embedded within networks of affiliation that support generous socio-cultural engagement. Another manager explained, "what capacities are being built? Its values. Values in action. But capacities for what? I think it is for building a better world. The capacity is oriented to an end. And I think that all the staff can see that the world could be a better place than it is."

The challenge at VICRTO was to sustain this educational vision for learning within a basically hostile environment. Their solution was to construct and consolidate a localised order of discourse that countered the absorption of pleasures and priorities into competitive economic goals. Rather than 'learning and forgetting' the group holistically orchestrated learning and remembering in ways that addressed changing circumstances. Building on their own individual, collective and network histories, they put this philosophy at the core of their operations so that it was institutionalised across their business practices and embedded in their ways of working and procedures.

In doing this work they felt that it was important not to be constrained by institutional boundaries, but it was also necessary to not blur boundaries that differentiated roles and responsibilities, interests and imperatives, and cultures. The knowledge economy encouragement of blurred boundaries destroys the map that allows people to locate themselves within social life, to know how power works, how they can participate, and how they can access the knowledge that enables their participation. They worked with a relatively flat organisational structure, but everyone knew that the 'buck stopped with the CEO'. They knew that there were codes of conduct that they had to meet to be recognised and accepted within particular contexts and communities. They had to be 'business-like', 'accountable', 'efficient', but knew that you can perform this conduct, by dressing right and play-acting for the serious purpose of enhancing communication.

The consolidation of self-boundaries, coupled with openness to collaboration and dialogue, provided a powerful basis for anchoring VICRTO as an identity-entity and protecting its holistic educational vision for training in industry. This anchoring extended into a wider network of education, industry, government and university-based professionals who shared their ordering of meanings. The organisation drew on this network for support, advice, ideas and challenges that enriched its narrative space but also built its own stories of genealogy, ecology and preferred futures. Informants recalled their own personal histories – being a migrant girl in a private school, smelling the grease on a father's overalls, arguing at the kitchen table and realising that 'I just hate bullies' – as ways of accounting for their personal-professional priorities and their commitment to sustain 'applied adult education' – an order of discourse that supports holistic educational work in industry but is in tension with the wider ordering of knowledge economy.

Making a place for learning and remembering in this small company meant managing vision and values through contradiction, engaging in the cultural work that constructed their own space for meaning making, and also reaching out to others with different cultures but similar commitments to learning. Such work forged the bonds that supported sociality and sustained shared commitments. As one of the managers reflected, "it is not in anyone's interest for our facade to be cracked. If it is cracked it will weaken the organisation and the politics we represent."

TOWARDS A POLITICS OF LEARNING AND REMEMBERING

This paper has argued that through its stories, knowledge economy discourse creates webs of meaning and ways of being that construct an imagined world, the knowledge economy. In making this world, it generates and authorises cultural resources – concepts, categories, ideas and knowers that are mobilised in design measures to make the real world through learning and forgetting. This imagined world confronts lived experience as a kind of disruption that does violence to human commitments and sociality. It subsumes society into economy and market relations (Marginson, 1997). It obscures non-economic aspects of social life that persist as ghosts haunting the knowledge economy (Kenway *et al.*, 2006).

The embrace of this knowledge economy discourse is a coercive imprint that is felt heavily, particularly in education. Yet it is never complete. Translating discursive practices into action agendas is opened up when cross-cutting discourses are interrupted and negotiated in the light of cultural anchorings. Creating a space for stories based on learning and remembering, rather than learning and forgetting, supports discursive practices that fumble towards learning for living. Within the interstices of the knowledge economy's textualised reality there are reaffirmations of humanist values and human sociality that work with and against knowledge economy discourse (Casey, 2006).

Where does this re-reading of knowledge economy discourse leave us in terms of further research in the field of critical education policy? There are I think 3 lessons. First, analysis of education policy is part of a longer intellectual tradition that has analysed power, its character and effects, to inform a number of different theorisations. Each theoretical approach offers a helpful but inevitably partial perspective. This means that it is necessary to locate each particular analysis of education policy in this longer history of ideas in order to understand the discursive effects of particular theorisations. This strategy increases the likelihood of research which captures the rich cross-cutting effects of different manifestations of power in education. Second, and in this vein, this chapter is a contribution to current debates within education policy about ways of analyzing policy and politics after globalisation. The further reading highlights other approaches being examined in this debate. Finally, there is a need to complement critical policy analysis with grounded empirical research. This can document the effects of policy, its deployment by different users, their creative engagement and negotiation of power and therefore reveal the emergent politics of education that contribute alongside and in tension with policies to building educational futures.

NOTES

[1]   I acknowledge the support of Australian Research Council, National Research and Evaluation Committee and the Victorian Office of Training and Technical Education in funding these projects. I would like to thank Anita Devos, Allie Clemans, Damon Anderson and John Pardy for helpful suggestions in preparing this paper.

REFERENCES

Allen, J. (2003). Power. In J. Agnew, K. Mitchell, & G. Toal (Eds.), *A companion to political geography* (pp. 95–108). Malden, MA: Blackwell.

Alexiadou, N., & Jones, K. (2001, September). *Traveling policy/local spaces*. Paper presented at the Congrès Marx International III, Le capital et l'humanité, Université de Paris-X Nanterre-Sorbonne, France.

Appadurai, A. (2001). *Globalisation*. Durham, NC: Duke University Press.

Bacchi, C. (2000). Policy as discourse: What does it mean? Where does it get us? *Discourse, 21*(1), 45–57.

Ball, S. (1990). *Politics and policy making in education*. London: Routledge.

Casey, C. (2006). Work and workers in the learning economy. In M. Kuhn (Ed.), *Towards a knowledge-based economy? Knowledge and learning in European education research* (pp. 149–169). New York: Peter Lang.

Fairclough, N. (2001). Dialectics of discourse. *Textus, XIV*(2), 231–242.

Farrell, L., & Fenwick, T. (Eds.). (2007). *Educating the global workforce*. World Yearbook of Education 2007. London: Routledge.

Foray, D. (2007). *Biographical details*. Retrieved July 8, 2007, from http://advancing knowledge.com/bios_Dominique_Foray.htm

Foray, D., & Lundvall, B.-A. (1996). The knowledge-based economy: From the economics of knowledge to the learning economy. In OECD (Ed.), *Employment and growth in the knowledge-based economy* (pp. 11–32). Paris: OECD.

Haug, F. (1992). *Beyond female masochism: Memory-work and politics*. London: Verso.

Haug, F., et al. (1987). *Female sexualisation: A collective work of memory*. London: Verso.

Kenway, J., Bullen, E., Fahey, J., & Robb, S. (2006). *Haunting the knowledge economy*. London: Routledge.

Kuhn, M. (2007). *Towards a knowledge-based economy? Knowledge and learning in European education research*. New York: Peter Lang.

LogEc. (2007). *LogEc: Access statistics for participating RePEc services*. Retrieved July 8, 2007, from http://logec.repec.org

Lundvall, B.-A. (2007). *Biographical details*. Retrieved July 6, 2007, from http://72.14.235.104/ search?q=cache:YWbuRd-C76IJ:www.mariajoaorodrigues.eu/lisbonagenda/group/cvs/CV_bal_06. doc+Bengt+Lundvall&hl=en&ct=clnk&cd=7&gl=au

Marginson, S. (1997). *Markets in education*. Cambridge: Cambridge University Press.

McLeod, J., & Yates, L. (2006). *Making modern lives: Subjectivity, schooling and social change*. Albany, NY: SUNY.

Miller, R. (1996). Towards the knowledge economy: New institutions for human capital accounting. In OECD (Ed.), *Employment and growth in the knowledge-based economy* (pp. 69–80). Paris: OECD.

OECD. (1996). *Employment and growth in the knowledge-based economy.* Paris: Author.

Ozga, J., Seddon, T., & Popkewitz, T. (Eds.). (2006). *Education research and policy: Steering the knowledge-based economy.* World Yearbook of Education 2006. London: Routledge.

Pels, D. (2005). Mixing metaphors: Politics of economics of knowledge? In N. Stehr & V. Meja (Eds.), *Society and knowledge: Contemporary perspectives in the sociology of knowledge and science* (pp. 269–298). New Brunswick, NJ: Transaction Publishers.

Prunty, J. J. (1984). *A critical reformulation of educational policy analysis.* Geelong: Deakin University.

Robb, H. A. (2007). *Positioning Australia in a supercycle of change.* Speech by the Minister. Minister for Vocational and Further Education to the Minerals Council of Australia - Minerals Week Seminar, 30 May 2007. Retrieved April 17, 2008, from http://www.andrewrobb.com.au/news/default.asp?action=article&ID=215

Seddon, T. (2001). Exploring capacity-building: From functionalist to political analysis. *Australia and New Zealand Journal of Vocational Education Research, 9*(2), 61–86.

Seddon, T. (2008, April). *Crafting capacity in VET: The VET workforce in context.* Keynote presentation at the 11th AVETRA annual conference, Adelaide, Australia. Retrieved April 15, 2008, from http://www.avetra.org.au/AVETRA%20WORK%2011.04.08/P4%20-%20Terri%20Seddon.pdf

Sen, A. (1999). *Development as freedom.* Oxford: Oxford University Press.

Stehr, N., & Meja, V. (2005). *Society and knowledge: Contemporary perspectives in the sociology of knowledge and science.* New Brunswick, NJ: Transaction Publishers.

Weedon, C. (1987). *Feminist practice and poststructuralist theory.* Oxford: Blackwell.

Young, M. (Ed.). (1971). *Knowledge and control.* London: Collier-Macmillan.

FURTHER READINGS

Allen, J. (2003). Power. In J. Agnew, K. Mitchell, & G. Toal (Eds.), *A companion to political geography* (pp. 95–108). Malden, MA: Blackwell.

Boden, R., Deem, R., Epstein, D., Rizvi, F., & Wright, S. (Eds.). (2008). *Geographies of knowledge, geometries of power: Higher education in the 21st century.* World Yearbook of Education 2008. London: Routledge.

Dale, R. (1999). Specifying globalisation effects on national policy: A focus on the mechanisms. *Journal of Education Policy, 14*(1), 1–17.

Hardy, I., & Lingard, B. (2008). Teacher professional development as an effect of policy and practice: A Bourdieuian analysis. *Journal of Education Policy, 23*(1), 63–80.

Marginson, S. (1999). After globalisation: Emerging politics of education. *Journal of Education Policy, 14*(1), 19–31.

Ozga, J., & Jones, R. (2006). Travelling and embedded policy: The case of knowledge transfer. *Journal of Education Policy, 21*(1), 1–17.

Resnik, J. (2007). Discourse structuration in Israel, democratisation of education and the impact of the global education network. *Journal of Education Policy, 22*(3), 215–240.

Terri Seddon
Faculty of Education
Monash University, Melbourne Australia

JOHANNAH FAHEY, JANE KENWAY & ELIZABETH BULLEN

THE KNOWLEDGE ECONOMY, SCHOLARLY WORK AND THE GIFT ECONOMY

Rival and Non-rival Goods [1]

INTRODUCTION

Policy-makers around the world have developed policies that fuse various ideas about the relationship between knowledge, information, learning, the economy and society. Such policies identify the rise of knowledge intensive productivity, the globalisation of economic activity, and the networked character of economies and cultures as key features of the global knowledge economy (Castells, 1996; Marginson, 2002).[2] Knowledge economy and associated discourses have become powerful levers and drivers of policy in such international and supranational bodies as the OECD (2004) and the European Commission (2003). They are also used extensively in national policy – in the UK – Department of Trade and Industry (2005), Australia – Commonwealth of Australia (2004), Canada – Government of Canada (2002), and Ireland – Government of Ireland (2005) particularly – and by international organisations assisting developing nations (World Bank, 2005). Such policies typically represent knowledge economy initiatives as the way to economic prosperity, scientific progress, social inclusion and unprecedented global inter-connectivity, premised on the increasing commodification of knowledge.

This chapter exposes some of the limitations, contradictions and weaknesses in economic conceptualisations of knowledge as a commodity by evaluating the status of scholarly knowledge as a public good via the notion of the gift economy. Given that "one of the primary challenges for gift theory has been to distinguish between gift exchanges and market exchanges", it offers a lens through which to "discriminate between gifts and commodities" (Osteen, 2002, p. 229). Drawing on several theories of gift exchange primarily informed by Marcel Mauss' *The Gift: the form and reason for exchange in archaic societies* (first published 1925), we will investigate the scholarly community as a gift community. A gift community is bound together in the obligatory circulation of meaningful objects, its members obligated to give, to receive, and to repay. This chapter argues that socially and ethically obligated exchange needs to be seen not as a contingent addendum to knowledge economy policy, but as the positive manifestation of an inevitable 'other' of commodity exchange.

KNOWLEDGE AS A COMMODITY

In the knowledge economy we see the privileging of knowledge that can be commodified, codified, quantified and applied. Knowledge becomes economically

M. Simons, M. Olssen and M.A. Peters (eds.), Re-Reading Education Policies: A Handbook Studying the Policy Agenda of the 21ˢᵗ Century, 277–292.

valuable when it is reconceptualised as a commodity or good. However, knowledge behaves differently from other commodities, in part because it is symbolically constructed, not physically manufactured (although we acknowledge there are physical carriers of knowledge, such as paper, CDs, etc.). To explain the properties of knowledge as a good, we will compare it to the properties of goods as they are conventionally defined, using the distinctions between 'rival' and 'non-rival', 'excludable' and 'non-excludable', and 'private' and 'public' goods.

Romer, a key New Growth economic theorist, defines a purely rival good as having the property "that its use by one (...) person precludes its use by another" (1990, pp. 73–4). In terms of material goods, if two people share an object, then each person's potential physical use of it is reduced. Rival goods are a precondition for the economic notion of 'scarcity' as their depletion through consumption becomes the basis of a system of supply and demand that regulates a capitalist economy. As a symbolically constructed good, knowledge can be used by any number of people at the same time without it being depleted, and with no loss of benefits. In other words, one person's consumption of knowledge does not reduce the amount of knowledge available for others, meaning that its use-value "does not diminish when that knowledge is shared" (Jessop, 2000, online). Indeed, it could be argued, that knowledge is essentially an inexhaustible resource that is actually enhanced through use or consumption. Knowledge, therefore, is a non-rival good: "its use by one ... person in no way limits its use by another" (Romer, 1990, p. 74).

To transform knowledge into a commodity for trade and profit, it "first has to be made artificially scarce by being turned into a privately-owned commodity" (Kundnani, 1998-1999, p. 52). In other words, it must be made 'excludable', which means that "the owner can prevent others from using it" (Romer, 1990, p. 74). One of the key ways in which the owner of a good maintains a monopoly over and profits from a private good is by charging people 'rent' for its use and, conversely, excluding non-payers. Private goods are goods that are commercially exploitable (through trade and profit) in a capitalist market. Public goods, by contrast, are understood to be non-rival and non-excludable. A good is non-excludable if it is impossible to selectively exclude others from using it, if it is difficult to have monopoly ownership of that good, and to make people pay for its use. From the economists' perspective, the provision of a public good "cannot be guaranteed at an optimal level in the marketplace" and so "to make up for this market failure" (Callon, 1994, p. 401), provision needs to be achieved by other means, typically through state support.

The level of state investment in public goods (for instance, libraries, galleries and museums) is dependent on the perceived benefits of those goods to a community or nation as a whole (Kaul, Grunberg et al., 1999). In its statement on global public goods at the 2002 *World Summit for Sustainable Development*, the European Commission identifies knowledge as one of the five such goods. According to its criteria, global public goods are those that "bring advantages to society as a whole" and to which "every individual has an equal entitlement" (European Commission, 2002, p. 1), implying that knowledge is a non-excludable. Knowledge "has the potential to be enjoyed by all, regardless of whether the end user has paid for [it] or not" (European Commission, 2002, p. 1). However, elsewhere the European Commission promotes knowledge as precisely a private, excludable good.

At the 2005 European Council, the heads of state affirmed their commitment to "increasing the potential for economic growth and of strengthening European competitiveness by investing above all in knowledge, innovation and human capital" (European Commission, 2005, p. 3). In *Building the ERA of knowledge for growth*, knowledge is linked to "social cohesion" and "social sustainability", and the chance for Europe to "strengthen its model of society" (European Commission 2005, p. 2). However, it is also fundamental to the aim of making "Europe the most dynamic and competitive, knowledge-based economy in the world" (European Commission 2005, p. 2), strategies for which involve fostering private investment in research and development and, increasingly, positioning knowledge as a private good via intellectual property rights. The latter, designed to protect "the investment which firms make in research and development by guaranteeing them a monopoly on the exploitation of knowledge arising out of their research" (Kundnani, 1998-1999, p. 52), renders the knowledge outcome excludable—a commodity available only to those who pay for its use. In broader terms, given that making money from knowledge is its essence, it follows that the knowledge economy will inevitably involve the privatisation of the intellectual commons and the potential exclusion of non-payers from the common pool of knowledge.

As Jessop points out, the European Commission's approach to knowledge betrays "contradiction[s] between knowledge as intellectual commons and [knowledge] as intellectual property" (2000, online). It conceives of it as both a private and public good, and as serving social and market interests. Compromises between competing interests and definitions may mean that knowledge takes the form of a mixed good, being both public and private, or that policy bodies adopt profoundly contradictory policies, as the case of the European Commission indicates. Knowledge is also vulnerable to contestation over its meaning and value. In the present stage of the knowledge economy, one of the sites of contestation is in the area of intellectual property rights. Whilst knowledge may be a public good and non-rival in its conceptual form, it can be excluded from other public users via intellectual property legislation.

INTELLECTUAL PROPERTY RIGHTS AND THE KNOWLEDGE ECONOMY

In the knowledge economy, knowledge can produce financial and other benefits. Individuals identify their ownership of knowledge using 'Intellectual Property' (IP). Intellectual Property Rights (IPR) is "the term used to refer to the system of law in place designed to allow people to protect and exploit their IP." There are four categories of IPR: "patents (for inventions); trademarks (for brand identity); designs (for product appearance); and copyright (for material such as literary and artistic outputs, music, films, sound recordings, broadcasts, software and multimedia)" (Epstein, Kenway & Boden, 2005, p. 49). IPR converts knowledge into a private good.

IPR are central to innovation – the commercialisation of new knowledge – which is pivotal in knowledge economy policies. OECD policy, for example, endorses a strong IPR régime. According to an OECD discussion paper, IPR provide "a powerful *incentive* for creating things" (2003, p. 13, emphasis added). In other words, it is the possibility to profit from new ideas that encourages knowledge production in the first place. This is an often-repeated claim made on behalf of IPR, but it is not uncontested. Arguments can be mounted that the history of knowledge production (such as basic research and creative endeavour) suggests that it is not motivated by the financial protection offered by IPR. It could also be argued that universities, rather than IPR *régimes*, have been the key to innovation. Furthermore, even where IPR play a role in innovation, this role is overshadowed by the fact that those companies profiting from it often initially rely on public knowledge produced by universities (Drahos & Braithwaite, 2002). Although shortcomings in measuring innovation through the production of IPR are acknowledged in some policy circles and are being addressed (OECD, 2003), the overall trajectory is still the same. Knowledge production in universities is increasingly coming under the sway of IPR regimes. Government funding tied to IPR puts pressure on universities to participate in the privatisation of the intellectual commons (Drahos & Braithwaite, 2002) at the expense of academic freedom, the pursuit of knowledge for its own sake or as a public good and, moreover, the character and constitution of the academic community.

In terms of knowledge networks, when knowledge is a tradable asset, so too are its associated human relationships. These are conceived instrumentally and commercially, in other words, in terms of use and exchange value. Other people or groups are evaluated in terms of what they can trade. They may be valued because they can back-fill the knowledge or the status that a particular knowledge network lacks and needs in order to competitively bid for resources. It is perhaps a misinterpretation in policy of the nature of an academic community that is at the heart of the problem. What is being suppressed in this misunderstanding is an acknowledgment that academic and other knowledge communities also have the potential to function as gift economies, although they do not always function in this manner.

THE GIFT ECONOMY

In *The Gift: the form and reasons for exchange in archaic societies*, Mauss argues that members of a gift community are bound together in the obligatory circulation of meaningful objects.[3] Members are obligated in three ways: to give, to receive, and to repay for reasons of community, solidarity and status. The obligation towards another, to return without diminishing social relationships, is the key to understanding the gift. It is this force that makes the gift "one of the bases of social life" (Mauss [1925] 1990, p. 2). Gift exchange binds objects and subjects in a symbolic and reciprocal relationship that de-limits their movements according to social and ethical codes.

Mauss develops his theory of the gift economy around a principle of reciprocity. He asks, "What power resides in the object given that causes its recipient to pay it back?" (1990, p. 3). He derives his understanding of this force from the Maori concept of *hau*, the 'spirit' of a specific person that is transferred in part to the objects they give. Mauss (1990, p. 33) states:

> [O]bligation (...) takes the form of interest in the objects exchanged; the objects are never completely separated from the men [sic] who exchange them; the communion and alliance they establish are well-nigh indissoluble.

As part of the giver is embodied in the given object, it is not something that can be alienated from its place within a particular social network. Mauss (1990, p. 12) explains that "to give something is to give part of oneself (...) [one gives] away what is in reality part of one's nature and substance, while to receive something is to receive part of someone else's spiritual essence." In gift exchange, the *hau* can leave a person through the medium of the gift, but can only do so in a temporary way through a process of circulating within a group, and it must then return to its point of origin. This return can only be realised "through the medium of an object given in exchange for the original gift" (Yan, 2002, p. 67). In this way the continuous exchange of gifts serves to fulfil the obligation to give, to receive, and to repay in a gift economy.

At the heart of any gift giving is the 'good gift'. According to Fennell (2002, p. 94), "A good gift is something like an act of recognition, in which the donor makes her knowledge of the recipient known to the recipient, who in turn may come to recognise something new about herself, or the donor, or the relationship." The 'good gift' then partakes in knowledge of, and being known by, the recipient. When a gift is presented to another, and when that gift has attached to it some form of knowledge about the other, what is being affirmed is a form of social or communal contract. Objects cannot be "given as gifts outside of the group without threatening the very social identities that underpin their inalienability" (Osteen 2002, p. 235). The act of giving away an object associated with a specific person or group demonstrates a fundamental paradox in a gift economy. Gift giving involves a separation from, and continued belonging to, the giver. Objects that are exchanged in a gift economy are imbued with the spirit of: the person giving, the people who are linked into the circulation and history of that object, and the community and related communities. We might argue that this process reverses Marx's theory of commodity fetishism. In a commodity economy, the people who produce the things are transformed and appear to be objective characteristics of the things themselves (Marx, 1915). In a gift economy, by contrast, the things that people give contain the subjective characteristics of the giver and the social identity of their community. As Osteen suggests, "in a gift economy, objects are personified; in a market economy, persons are objectified" (2002, p. 233).

Marx asserts that commodity exchange moves from the margins to the "interior of the community, exerting a disintegrating influence upon it" (1971, p. 50). We could also say that commodity exchange exerts a disintegrating influence on the *spirit* and the social bonds of a community. When objects are sold in a commodity economy, the ownership rights of the object are transferred to the new owner. Therefore, the object is fully disassociated or 'alienated' from the original owner. In contrast, "gifts are concrete representations of social relations" (Osteen 2002, p. 2). As 'inalienable' objects, gifts serve to nurture the *spirit* and cement the social bonds of community. Gregory (1982, p. 19) maintains the aim of gift giving is to acquire relationships rather than money, social capital rather than economic capital:

> The gift economy, then, is a debt economy. The aim of a transactor in such an economy is to acquire as many gift-debtors as she possibly can and not to maximise profit, as it is in the commodity economy. What a gift transactor desires is the personal relationships that the exchange of gifts creates, and not the things themselves. [4]

Whereas people are required to accumulate economic power by amassing incomings in capitalism, the giver in a gift economy aims to amass social credit amongst their group through expenditure. In this sense, gift exchange inverts the fundamentals of commodity exchange. Where there is gift exchange, at least according to Gregory, there can be no commodity exchange. [5]

Two major assumptions underpin a gift economy: a social system of obligation and awareness of the reciprocity of the gift. We may also say that such assumptions do not consider society and the spiritual from a distance. These things are not objects for a disinterested person's consideration. Neither does knowledge belong only to the individual. It belongs to the social and 'spiritual' realm, to which it must always return. These are the constitutive elements of knowledge in a gift economy. Social knowledge starts with the idea that all members of that society are socially obligated, or potentially socially obligated, that they are all in relations, or have contracts with each other of debt and credit. Spiritual knowledge pertains to the idea that the object is imbued with a particular essence when it is exchanged that is derived from the gift-giver and their community. As this spirit cannot be alienated from the original gift-giver and their community, the gift itself is compelled to return to its place of origin. In a gift economy, knowledge is forever tied to the individual and the community; so too is its expression, or the material products of its expression. Here we find a key distinction between knowledge within a gift economy and knowledge within a commodity economy. As Gregory maintains "commodities are *alienable* objects transacted by aliens; gifts are *inalienable* objects transacted by non-aliens" (1982, p. 43, original emphasis). In the following discussion, we consider scholarly communities as gift economies.

UNIVERSITY KNOWLEDGE COMMUNITIES AS GIFT COMMUNITIES

According to Stiglitz, "initial knowledge is a key input into the production of further knowledge" (1999, p. 312). In other words, new knowledge arises from working on, and with, the ideas of others. In terms of an intellectual community such as the university, the academic receives knowledge from others, adds their own intellectual contribution, and then returns this transformed knowledge to their community. One way this happens is through the publication of research literature.

As we stated earlier, the use of knowledge as a non-rival good does not reduce the amount of knowledge available for others. We suggested that knowledge is essentially an inexhaustible resource that is actually enhanced through consumption. The publication of research literature facilitates the circulation of knowledge, and the continuance of an intellectual community. In this respect, there are parallels to be made between the way the circulation of knowledge sustains an intellectual community, and the way the circulation of gifts maintain a gift community. Research literature disseminates ideas that have been re-worked, or refined, and given back to the intellectual community. Research obeys the logic of gift exchange insofar as it entails receiving the gift of knowledge from others, and then giving the gift of knowledge back in return in the form of publications.

A scholarly community has well-developed protocols for fulfilling the three obligations of the gift by: giving (contributing new knowledge through research publications); receiving (using initial knowledge to produce new knowledge); and repaying debt (citation). Citation rules and practices are community building because individuals acknowledge others within that community. Citation rules and practices establish, continue and develop relationships within a body of knowledge and define that disciplinary community to itself and to the outside. As such, they can be thought of as one aspect of a gift economy characterised as a 'debt economy'. Such practices involve, importantly, the idea that the thing given is not alienated from the person or the group. By participating in the three obligations of the gift, the academic contributes to the maintenance of the terms of exchange of knowledge. Indeed, a gift community is in large part defined by the presence of obligated social relationships. Anyone who fails to enact the three obligations is "effectively denying that he or she is in a social relationship" (Carrier, 1995, p. 21), and is consequently affirming the end of that relationship. While it may well be the case that not all scholarly communities operate in this manner – for example, contemporary performative and audit cultures in the academy individualise effort and undermine trust (Strathern, 2000) – it can nonetheless be argued that the gift ideal is what holds the real together. The three obligations are the ways that the community re-affirms itself to itself.

If an intellectual community is dependent on a gift economy, then it follows that knowledge economy policy needs to understand knowledge in terms of the gift as well as the commodity. This means that it needs to advocate on behalf of the one who gives, receives and repays knowledge for reasons of obligation to knowledge itself, and solidarity towards an on-going intellectual community. As Frow (1997, p. 104) explains:

> Gift exchange is at the core of social cohesion, or rather it represents a social generosity that is absent from other, more 'contractual' or 'mechanical' forms of social solidarity. One of the main functions of the theory of the gift has accordingly been to provide an account of altruism or of non-exploitative reciprocity as the basis of community.

The idea that the gift is the property of no one and the property of all implies that knowledge as a gift belongs to the intellectual commons. The circulation of knowledge conceived of as a form of gift exchange sits uneasily against the dominant knowledge economy paradigm of commercialism and economic self-interest. However, support for such a system of knowledge exchange can be witnessed in the endorsement of Open Access [OA], particularly in terms of research literature. This has arisen in response to a worrying trend in scholarly publishing, as we will now explain.

SCHOLARLY PUBLISHING AND OPEN ACCESS

Scholarly publishing (particularly in peer-reviewed journals available online through institutional subscription) is perhaps the key contemporary avenue for the circulation of knowledge within academic communities. Of concern is scholarly publication where knowledge goods become excludable to various populations, not just to a general public, but also to sections of the scholarly community, including those in different geographical regions where costs might be prohibitive. While the legal basis of the exclusion is the assignment of copyright, this does not necessarily mean that access need be restricted. The main issue is that the assignment of copyright to publishers then allows journals to charge all users a fee to access the work; or in some cases, even to access the abstract. At the heart of issue are the abuse of IPR and the commercialisation of knowledge.

The big publishing houses are currently "amassing huge electronic archives of intellectual property" and "buying each other up, merging and accumulating all the world's books, archives, research, journals into an ever-decreasing number of corporations" (Australian Broadcasting Corporation, 2001, online). Why? The answer is the potential for profit, and there is much profit to be made. For North American research libraries, journal costs rose by 320% between 1986 and 2006 (Association of Research Libraries, 2008, online). Of course, the more journals the publishing house has, the more it is able to charge. And once it has a monopoly in a particular field, the opportunities for additional charges increase. There is potential for viewing, sharing and downloading opportunities to be further restricted and thus to be increasingly costly. In essence, we are seeing the increasing commodification and privatisation of public knowledge in the digitising and globalising intellectual bazaar.

While this process may enhance the distribution of knowledge, access may become more and more restricted as it becomes more and more costly. Thus, while the knowledge economy can capitalise on the non-rival status of knowledge, its push to exclude is self-defeating. Of equal concern is the fact that the control of knowledge slips yet further from the hands of those who produce it, and from those who fund those who produce it, namely tax-payers. Whilst publishing houses have increased their profits, university libraries have simultaneously cancelled journal purchases while accepting costly, and perhaps even unnecessary, 'Big Deal' journal bundles. This places pressure on Library funds to reduce expenditure elsewhere, most obviously in other areas of scholarly publishing (Johnson, 2004).

Although academics write and peer review the articles that go into the research journals (usually without payment), their university then has to pay to view them.

University libraries spend a large percentage of their acquisitions budget on electronic journal subscriptions. The irony here is that universities – and tax-payers in the case of public universities – are paying for knowledge three times: to produce it, to review it and then to purchase it. Publicly funded knowledge is turned into an excludable good. Those outside the university sector and, indeed, those in poor institutions and poor countries around the world find themselves excluded from ready access to knowledge.

Academics, librarians, and extended coalitions, have recognised the threat that this commercial régime poses to them. Velterop (2005, p. 7), an academic who has developed a practical guide to Open Access for scholarly societies, states:

> The currently prevalent model of subscription-based journals is not achieving the goal of optimising the return on the research investment that the world makes. Limited access means limited use, limited impact, and limited benefits for (...) society at large.

Perhaps the best example of the academic resistance to the commercialisation of knowledge can be found in the support for OA research literature. This endorsement can be seen as an assertion of the research community as a gift community. OA literature is digital, online, free of charge, and free of most copyright and licensing restrictions.

The term 'open access' was first defined in the 'Budapest Open Access Initiative' [BOAI] (2002), the result of a meeting in Budapest of supporters of OA who were brought together by the Open Society Institute in late 2001.[6] Its members include academics and a broad range of representatives from libraries, publishing coalitions, and scientific associations. The 'Berlin Declaration' followed this in 2003 and the fifth conference in the 'Berlin Declaration' tradition took place at the end of 2007 (see Berlin 5, 2008, online). The original Initiative, which focuses primarily on peer-reviewed journal articles, characterises OA research literature according to its:

> free availability on the public internet [the norm], permitting any users to read, download, copy, distribute, print, search or link to the full texts of these articles, crawl [sic] them for indexing, pass them as data to software, or use them for any other lawful purpose, without financial, legal or technical barriers. (BOAI, 2002, online)

Open Access provides a means through which an academic community can continue to flourish along the lines of a gift economy. By making knowledge freely available, and easily and equitably accessible to the public, it fulfils the three obligations of the gift: to give, to receive, and to repay. OA is a ground-swell movement emanating from the academic community in reaction to the negative impacts of the commercialisation of knowledge. It removes price barriers (subscriptions, licensing fees, pay-per-view fees) and permission barriers (most copyright and licensing restrictions). OA does not close knowledge off from the intellectual commons by making knowledge an excludable commodity. Rather, it "closes [the] gaps in access to knowledge" (Velterop, 2005, p. 7) by making it available for all. The only way to sustain the intellectual commons (for the present and the future) is to give back to it as much, if not more, than one has taken; and to not preclude others from similar use. OA to knowledge is a "good gift" that sustains the academic community as it "enables the building of databases and knowledge-bases" (Velterop, 2005, p. 7).

INTO THE REALM OF THE GOVERNMENTAL

We are currently seeing governmental bodies beginning to pay attention to activist projects which promote the free exchange of knowledge as a gift. However, as we will explain, although Open Access is now on policy-makers' agendas, there are still those who seek to question how truly open access to knowledge will become. We look at the case of Research Councils UK (RCUK), which according to its website, enables the seven research councils in the United Kingdom "to work together more effectively to enhance the overall impact and effectiveness of their research, training and innovation activities, contributing to the delivery of the Government's objectives for science and innovation."

A position statement issued by the RCUK in 2006 outlines its views on the dissemination of and access to research outputs. In summary, it is committed to the following principles:

- Ideas and knowledge derived from publicly-funded research must be made available and accessible for public use, interrogation and scrutiny, as widely, rapidly and effectively as practicable.
- Published research outputs must be subject to rigorous quality assurance, through effective peer review mechanisms.
- The models and mechanisms for publication and access to research results must be both efficient and cost-effective in the use of public funds.
- The outputs from current and future research must be preserved and remain accessible for future generations (RCUK, 2006, online).

The Research Councils were the first public funding agencies in the world to mandate Open Access with regard to the results of Council-funded research, with access to this research literature facilitated by Internet technologies. The European Research Council released its guidelines for open access in 2008 (2008, online). The RCUK advocates communication, access and availability of research literature through e-print repositories and open access journals.

E-print repositories are either institutional or subject-based digital collections of research literature. Institutional repositories preserve the intellectual output of a single university or a multiple institution community of colleges and universities. According to Crow (2002, p. 3), a Senior Consultant for the Scholarly Publishing & Academic Resources Coalition (SPARC), they:

> provide a critical catalyst (...) in reforming the system of scholarly communication by expanding access to research (...) [and] have the potential to serve as tangible indicators of an institution's quality (...) [and] the

relevance of its research activities, thus increasing the institution's visibility, status and public value.

Institutional repositories can therefore be thought of as the building blocks of the academic community as a gift community. Ideally, they will become part of "a global system of distributed, interoperable repositories that provides the foundations for a new disaggregated model of scholarly publishing" (Crow, 2002, p. 4). As they centralise, preserve, and make freely accessible a university's intellectual capital, they do not diminish social relations, but rather consolidate them by affirming the scholarly community, academic solidarity, and academic status.

The RCUK also maintains it will ensure that published research remains of a high quality by instituting rigorous peer review, further recommending that e-print repositories make a clear distinction between published research that has and has not been peer-reviewed. In most research disciplines, the editors and referees who perform peer review donate their labour without expecting payment. In this respect, peer-review of publications (in both OA journals and conventional journals) by members of the academic community is another form of gift giving, whereby altruism and non-exploitative reciprocity become the basis of a gift community.

The Research Councils further recommend the adoption of an 'author-pays' publication model. SPARC acknowledges that the term 'author-pays' is misleading. However, in the 2006 RCUK position statement, this remark is further qualified by the fact that "it is for authors' institutions to decide whether they are prepared to use funds for any page charges or other publishing fees" (2006, p. online). Therefore, Open Access does not necessarily convert the user-pays system (endorsed by big publishing houses) to an author-pays system; rather, the OA publication model is funded by the public to ensure knowledge remains a public good. The final point made by the RCUK is in the interests of long-term preservation, whereby the British Library and other Legal Deposit Libraries are acknowledged as having a critical role to play in the preservation of digital publications.

SPARC (2005, online) responded to the original RCUK position statement by saying:

> The policy is superb. It has four primary strengths. First, it mandates OA and does not merely request it. Second, it applies to all publicly-funded research, not just biomedicine. Third, it gives authors some flexibility about the OA archive in which to deposit their work. Fourth, it offers to pay fees at OA journals that charge fees.

Not surprisingly, the Association of Learned and Professional Society Publishers (ALPSP) responded more cautiously. Their chief concern was that the immediate publication of OA research literature in e-print repositories might economically weaken peer-reviewed journals. They stated "any new model which has the potential to 'siphon off' a significant percentage of otherwise paying customers will, understandably, undermine the financial viability of [peer-reviewed journals'] value-adding activities" (2005, online). Some examples include: "commissioning editorials, reviews and opinion pieces which put the original research articles in context…; ensuring maximum visibility of the journals' content, through secondary databases, search engines and elsewhere; [and investing] in robust and sophisticated journal delivery platforms" (2005, online). They further suggested that "alternative licensing and business models (…) are necessary if the system is not to be gravely damaged" (2005, online). In this context, economic concerns are privileged over social relationships. By advocating that OA proves itself as "a viable business model" (2005, online), a misunderstanding of the possible ways in which an academic community can function is again reinforced.

CONCLUSION

Gift theory calls into question the knowledge economy's future direction. The notion of Open Access, particularly the push towards OA research literature, operates according to key features of a gift economy. In this system of exchange, if knowledge is used then its use must also be repaid, or returned to the site of circulation (i.e. go back into e-print repositories and open access journals). In a gift economy, there is an obligation to return to the community what one has taken, with interest. Through OA, the academic community is joined together in a non-commodified and obligated way. What belongs to this gift community is given, and yet stays within that community. The part of oneself that the academic gives away is their knowledge, that which substantiates their status in the academic community in the first place. In this context, the gift is the property of no one and the property of all. We have shown that knowledge as a gift functions as a public good and belongs to the intellectual commons. Knowledge as it is conceived of in the knowledge economy functions as a commodity or private good determined by intellectual property.

Knowledge economy discourse asserts a need to commodify knowledge and to protect knowledge profits through intellectual property rights. We have argued that these rights will essentially restrict access to knowledge to those who can afford to pay. These rights will harm academic standards, slow the circulation of research, and diminish the pool of available knowledge. In effect, what they will do is destroy the substance that they wish to exploit: knowledge. We have suggested that resistance is presently gathering against this process involving free and open access to research literature using the Internet. As the Budapest Open Access Initiative states, "An old tradition and a new technology have converged to make possible an unprecedented public good" (2002, online).

We have raised the idea that the aim of the gift giver in an intellectual gift economy, such as the OA community, is to acquire as many intellectual-debtors as possible, not to maximise private profit, as it is in the commodity economy. In other words, the aim of gift giving is to acquire relationships rather than money, social capital not economic capital. To demonstrate this notion we have mobilised Gregory's suggestion that the gift economy is a debt economy (1982). What a gift transactor desires is an intellectual community, the intellectual relationships that the exchange of gifts creates and not the things themselves. The ideal subject of knowledge economy discourse, the *technopreneur*, finds such notions incomprehensible and even reprehensible.[7] Debating if and how these two different subject positions might accommodate each other is vital to the future of knowledge production.

The application of gift theory calls into questions the knowledge economy's current economic course, challenges its narrow and reductionist logic, and confronts its underlying assumptions. The gift economy recognises a system of exchange based on: the accumulation of social capital instead of financial capital; the subject who gives, receives and repays for reasons of social obligation and community solidarity; the subject who gains status and power through the act of giving; a community whose aim is to acquire relationships rather than money; and a community whose values are social rather than individual.

NOTES

[1] The authors express their appreciation to the Australian Research Council for funding the project that this chapter arises from, to Routledge for giving us permission to produce an updated version of a chapter from Kenway, Bullen and Fahey with Robb, S. (2006), and to Simon Robb from the University of South Australia for his early work on this chapter.

[2] 'Knowledge economy discourse' and 'the knowledge economy' are used throughout this article as interchangeable terms. Both terms refer to the economic dogma of contemporary capitalism.

[3] One of the persistent concerns in theories of the gift, and one that we will not pursue here, is that of the 'potlach' or 'waste'. Our concern here is with co-operative rather than competitive gift exchange. Our focus is on those activities in a gift economy that are primarily motivated by the desire of its members to enhance that community. Rivalrous gift exchange, as expounded by Mauss (1990) in his discussion of the 'potlach' and by Bataille (1988) in terms of destruction, sacrifice and waste have more to do with claims for individual power and prestige within the community.

[4] For critiques of Gregory's theories, see Mirowski, 2001; Frow, 1997; Laidlaw, 2002.

[5] For our purposes we rely on Gregory's analysis; however we are aware that this is the source of a contentious debate. Gregory views gift exchange and commodity exchange as diametrically opposed; Mirowski makes a distinction between the 'gift' and 'exchange' but suggests they are mutually dependent (see Callari, 2002).

[6] The Bethesda Statement and the Berlin Declaration on OA followed the Budapest Open Access Initiative in 2003.

[7] The technopreneur is both a subject and agent of innovation policy. For more, see Kenway, Bullen and Fahey with Robb (2006).

REFERENCES

Australian Broadcasting Corporation. (2001). *Knowledge indignation: Road rage on the information superhighway.* Radio National: Background Briefing, 12 August. Online. Retrieved February 21, 2008, from <http://www.abc.net.au/rn/talks/bbing/stories/s345514.htm>

Association of Learned and Professional Society Publishers (ALPSP). (2005). *Dissemination of and access to UK research outputs: Response from the Association of Learned and Professional Society Publishers (ALPSP) to the RCUK position paper.* ALPSP. Online. Retrieved February 21, 2008, from <http: // www.alpsp.org/RCUK/Response.pdf >

Association of Research Libraries. (2008). *ARL statistics.* Online. Retrieved February 21, 2008, from <http://www.arl.org/stats/annualsurveys/arlstats/arlstats06.shtml>

Bataille, G. (1988–1991). *The accursed share: An essay on general economy* (R. Hurley, Trans.). New York: Zone Books.

Berlin 5-Open Access: From Practice to Impact:Consequences of Knowledge Dissemination. (2008). Online. Retrieved February 21, 2008, from <http://www.aepic.it/conf/index.php?cf=10>

Budapest Open Access Initiative. (2002). Online. Retrieved February 21, 2008, from <http://www.soros.org/openaccess/read.shtml>

Bullen, E., Kenway, J. & Robb, S. (2004b). Can the arts and humanities survive the knowledge economy? A beginner's guide to the issues. In J. Kenway, E. Bullen & S. Robb (Eds.), *Innovation and Tradition; The arts, humanities, and the knowledge economy*. New York: Peter Lang.

Callari, A. (2002). The ghost of the gift: The unlikelihood of economics. In M. Osteen (Ed.), *The question of the gift: Essays across disciplines*. London and New York: Routledge.

Callon, M. (1994). Is science a public good? Fifth Mullins Lecture, Virginia Polytechnic Institute, 23 March 1993. *Science, Technology and Human Values, 19*(4), 395–424.

Carrier, J. G. (1995). *Gifts and commodities: Exchange and western capitalism since 1700*. London and New York: Routledge.

Castells, M. (1996). *The rise of the network society*. Oxford: Blackwell.

Commonwealth of Australia. (2004). *Backing Australia's ability - building our future through science and innovation*. Canberra: Commonwealth of Australia.

Crow, R. (2002). *SPARC institutional repository checklist & resource guide*. Washington, DC: Scholarly Publishing and Academic Resources Coalition.

Department of Trade and Industry [UK]. (2005). *Innovation report: Competing in the global economy: The innovation challenge*. Retrieved February 21, 2008, from http://www.innovation.gov.uk/innovationreport/

Drahos, P. (1996). *A philosophy of intellectual property, applied legal philosophy series*. Dartmouth: Aldershot.

Drahos, P., & Braithwaite, J. (2002). *Information feudalism: Who owns the knowledge economy?* London: Earthscan Publications Ltd.

Epstein, D., Kenway, J., & Boden, R. (2005). *Academic support kit: Writing for publication*. London, Thousand Oaks, New Delhi: Sage.

European Commission. (2002). *The EU at the WSSD: EU focus on global public goods*. Online. Retrieved February 21, 2008, from<http://ec.europa.eu/environment/wssd/pdf/publicgoods.pdf >

European Commission. (2003). *Choosing to grow: Knowledge, innovation and jobs in a cohesive society* . Luxembourg, Office for Official Publications of the European Communities.

European Commission. (2005). *Building the ERA of knowledge for growth*. COM (2005) 118 final. Luxembourg, Office for Official Publications of the European Communities.

European Research Council. (2008). *Guidelines for Open Access*. Online. Retrieved February 21, 2008, from <http://www.earlham.edu/%7Epeters/fos/2008/01/oa-mandate-from-european-research.html>

Fennell, L. A. (2002). Unpacking the gift: Illiquid goods and empathetic dialogue. In M. Osteen (Ed.), *The question of the gift: Essays across disciplines*. London and New York: Routledge.

Frow, J. (1997). *Time and commodity culture*. Oxford: Clarendon Press.

Government of Canada. (2002). *Knowledge matters: Skills and learning for Canadians* (Hull, Human Resources Development Canada). Retrieved February 21, 2008, from http://www.innovation strategy.gc.ca

Government of Ireland. (2005). *Ireland now a Knowledge Economy*. Retrieved February 21, 2008, from http://www.idaireland.com/home/index.aspx?id=625

Gregory, C. A. (1982). *Gifts and commodities*. London and New York: Academic.

Jessop, B. (2000). *The state and the contradictions of the knowledge-driven economy*. Lancaster: Department of Sociology, Lancaster University. Online. Retrieved February 21, 2008, from <www.lancs.ac.uk/fass/sociology/papers/jessop-state-and-contradictions.pdf >

Johnson, R. K. (2004, March). *Open access: Unlocking the value of scientific research*. Paper presented at The New Challenge for Research Libraries: Collection management and strategic access to digital resources, Oklahoma.

Kaul, I., Grunberg, I., & Stern, M. A. (1999). Defining global public goods. In I. Kaul, I. Grunberg, & M. Stern (Eds.), *Global public goods: International cooperation in the 21st Century*. Oxford and New York: Oxford University Press.

Kenway, J., Bullen, E., Fahey, J. with Robb, S. (2006). *Haunting the knowledge economy*. London: Routledge, International Library of Sociology.

Kenway, J., Bullen, E., & Robb, S. (Eds.). (2004a). *Innovation and tradition: The arts, humanities and the knowledge economy*. New York: Peter Lang.

Kundnani, A. (1998–1999). Where do you want to go today? The rise of information capital. *Race and Class, 40*(2–3), 49–72.

Laidlaw, J. (2002). A free gift makes no friends. In M. Osteen (Ed.), *The question of the gift: Essays across disciplines*. London and New York: Routledge.

Marginson, S. (2002). What's wrong with the universities? *Arena Magazine, 61*, BB3–BB16.

Mauss, M. (1990). *The gift: The form and reason for exchange in archaic societies* (W. D. Halls, Trans.). New York: W. W. Norton (first published 1925).

Marx, K. (1971). *A contribution to the critique of political economy*. Moscow: Progress Publishers (first published 1859).

Mirowski, P. (2001). Refusing the gift. In S. Cullenberg, J. Amariglio, & D. F. Ruccio (Eds.), *Postmodernism, economics and knowledge*. London and New York: Routledge.

Organisation for Economic Co-operation and Development (OECD). (2004). *Innovation in the knowledge economy: Implications for education and learning*. Paris: Centre for Educational Research and Innovation.

Organisation for Economic Co-operation and Development. (2003). *Creativity, innovation and economic growth in the 21st century: An affirmative case for intellectual property rights*. Paris: OECD.

Osteen, M. (2002a). Gift or commodity? In M. Osteen (Ed.), *The question of the gift: Essays across disciplines*. London and New York: Routledge.

Osteen, M. (Ed.). (2002b). *The question of the gift: Essays across disciplines*. London and New York: Routledge.

Research Councils UK (RCUK). (2006). *Research Councils UK, updated position statement on access to research outputs*. London: RCUK. Online. Retrieved February 21, 2008, from <http://www.rcuk.ac.uk/access/default.htm>

Romer, M. (1990). Endogenous technological change. *Journal of Political Economy, 98*(5), 71–102.

Scholarly Publishing and Academic Resources Coalition (SPARC). (2005). *Open access newsletter*. Issue No. 87. Online. Retrieved February 21, 2008, from <http://www.earlham.edu/ ~ peters/fos/newsletter/07-02-05.htm >

Stiglitz, J. E. (1999). Knowledge as a global public good. In I. Kaul, I. Grunberg, & M. A. Stern (Eds.), *Global public goods: International cooperation in the 21st century*. Oxford and New York: Oxford University Press.

Strathern, M. (Ed.). (2000). *Audit cultures: Anthropological studies in accountability, ethics and the academy, European association of social anthropologists*. London and New York: Routledge.

Velterop, J. M. (2005). *Open access publishing and scholarly societies: A guide*. New York: Open Society Institute.

World Bank. (2005). *Knowledge for development* [K4D]. Retrieved February 21, 2008, from http://web.worldbank.org/WBSITE/EXTERNAL/WBI/WBIPROGRAMS/KFDLP/0,contentMDK:20269026~menu PK:461205~pagePK:64156158~piPK:64152884~theSitePK;461198,00.html

Yan, Y. (2002). Unbalanced reciprocity: Assymmetrical gift giving and social hierarchy in rural China. In M. Osteen (Ed.), *The question of the gift: Essays across disciplines*. London and New York: Routledge.

FURTHER READINGS

Gregory, C. A. (1982). *Gifts and commodities*. London and New York: Academic.

Kenway, J., Bullen, E., Fahey, J., & Robb, S. (2006). *Haunting the knowledge economy*. Routledge: International Library of Sociology.

Kenway, J., Bullen, E., & Robb, S. (Eds.). (2004a). *Innovation and tradition: The arts, humanities and the knowledge economy*. New York: Peter Lang.

Mauss, M. (1990). *The Gift: The form and reason for exchange in archaic societies* (W. D. Halls, Trans.). New York: W. W. Norton (first published 1925).

Osteen, M. (Ed.). (2002). *The question of the gift: Essays across disciplines*, London and New York: Routledge.

Johannah Fahey
Education Faculty
Monash University, Australia

Jane Kenway
Education Faculty
Monash University, Australia

Elizabeth Bullen
School of Communication and Creative Arts
Deakin University, Australia

MICHAEL A. PETERS

KNOWLEDGE ECONOMY AND SCIENTIFIC COMMUNICATION

Emerging Paradigms of 'Open Knowledge Production' and 'Open Education'

INTRODUCTION

On February 14 2008 Harvard University's Faculty of Arts and Sciences adopted a policy that requires faculty members to allow the university to make their scholarly articles available free online. The new policy makes Harvard the first university in the United States to mandate open access to its faculty members' research publications (Suber[1]) and marks the beginning of a new era that will encourage other U.S. universities to do the same. Open access [OA], to use Suber's definition, means "putting peer-reviewed scientific and scholarly literature on the internet, making it available free of charge and free of most copyright and licensing restrictions, and removing the barriers to serious research." As Lila Guterman reports in *The Chronicle of Higher Education News Blog* "Stuart M. Shieber, a professor of computer science at Harvard who proposed the new policy, said after the vote in a news release that the decision 'should be a very powerful message to the academic community that we want and should have more control over how our work is used and disseminated.'"[2] Open access has transformed the world of scholarship and since the early 2000s with major OA statements starting with Budapest in 2002, the movement has picked up momentum and developed a clear political ethos. Harvard's adoption of the new policy follows hard on the heels of open access mandates passed within months of each other – theU.S. National Institutesof Health (NIH) and the European Research Council (ERC). As one blogger remarked: "open archiving of peer-reviewed journal literature [is] now on an irreversible course of expansion"[3] not only as U.S. universities follow Harvard's lead but also as open archiving makes available learning material to anyone including students and faculty from developing and transition countries. Harvard's adoption of the open archiving mandate is similar in scope to the step taken by MIT to adopt *OpenCourseWare* (OCW) in 2001. These initiatives are part of *emerging knowledge ecologies* that will determine the future of scholarly publishing challenging commercial publishing business models and raising broader and deeper questions about content development processes as well as questions of resourcing and sustainability.

The Ithaca Report commissioned by the U.S. Association of Research Libraries, *University Publishing In A Digital Age* (2007) indicates that there have been huge

M. Simons, M. Olssen and M.A. Peters (eds.), Re-Reading Education Policies: A Handbook Studying the Policy Agenda of the 21st Century, 293–318.

changes in creation, production and consumption of scholarly resources with the "creation of new formats made possible by digital technologies, ultimately allowing scholars to work in deeply integrated electronic research and publishing environments that will enable real-time dissemination, collaboration, dynamically-updated content, and usage of new media" (p. 4). As the report goes on to mention alongside these changes in content creation and publication "alternative distribution models (institutional repositories, pre-print servers, open access journals) have also arisen with the aim to broaden access, reduce costs, and enable open sharing of content" (p. 4).[4]

We can consider open publishing, open access and archiving as parts of the wider movement called *Open Education* that builds on the nested and evolving convergences of open source, open access and open science, and also emblematic of a set of still wider political and economic changes that ushers in 'social production' as an aspect of the global digital economy, an economy that is both fragile and volatile as the current world credit and banking crisis demonstrates so well.

Consider the recent writer's strike in Hollywood held by the Writers Guild of America (WGA) which voted to settle its 100-day strike against the Alliance of Motion Picture and Television Producers (AMPTP) on the basis of a three-year contract that gives the WGA jurisdiction over projects created specifically for the Web, provides payment for 'ad-supported streaming' over the Internet, increases payment for residuals on downloaded movies and television shows, and includes a two percentage of the distributor's Web stream revenue. As Michael Wolff, media commentator and contributing editor for *Vanity Fair* puts it:

> The epochal point is that Hollywood, which has been the center of the culture, the coolest place, the ruler of the *Zeitgeist*, is out of it. It's on the industrial sidelines. It's just a bunch of crabby managers and a sullen workforce in a dysfunctional relationship in a declining industry, quarreling over an ever smaller piece of the pie.

Why? Because as Wolff argues the value of the story keeps going down and the era and cult of the Hollywood writer is over. In an age of user-generated content the narrative has lost its power, at least as an unbroken storyline. Besides the iamge has supplanted the text-based narrative and time is against plot and plot development—there is now only time for the momentary blast of images.

> Cheap production technology, no-barrier-to-entry distribution, and a Niagara of "product" (65,000 new videos are uploaded on YouTube daily) mean the entire Hollywood story-development complex is now in a daily competition with do-it-yourself writers. Hollywood product itself is remade, reduced to clips, bites, fractals, and mixes. Sitting through an entire feature film more and more feels like an unreasonable commitment. (We use DVRs to fast-forward, to pause, to hold for some other time—anything not to have to watch something from beginning to end.) The narrative is disposable. Video games, whose 2007 receipts of $8.7 billion rival Hollywood's $9.7 billion box-office take, are anarchically unplotted. And while Hollywood is getting

larger and larger fees from licensing its characters (born of those tortured three acts) for video games, the more video games become the entertainment model, the less patience my son and his friends will invariably have for conventional story lines. Not only is reality TV a network solution for lowering costs, but it works too because it busts scripted, plotted formulas. Movies as displays of visual virtuosity more and more become pure technology plays. The *Zeitgeist* is expressed through engineering (most of which is not created in Hollywood), not through the story. If you don't have story, that great collaboration of writers, re-writers, directors, producers, agents, executives, publicists, managers, stars, and the retinues – however painful and abusive and exploitive that process might be – do you have Hollywood?

The present decade can be called the 'open' decade (open source, open systems, open standards, open archives, open everything) just as the 1990s were called the 'electronic' decade (e-text, e-learning, e-commerce, e-governance) (Materu, 2004). And yet it is more than just a 'decade' that follows the electronic innovations of the 1990s; it is a change of philosophy and ethos, a set of interrelated and complex changes that transforms markets and the mode of production, ushering in a new collection of values based on openness, the ethic of participation and peer-to-peer collaboration.

This chapter first briefly charts the history of systems of scientific communication before focusing on the serial crisis and the economics of publishing. Against this background the chapter reviews the strengths and potential of the open access movement, including statements by research and research-related organisations concerning the possibilities of 'open science'. In the final two sections the chapter theorises the term 'open knowledge production' identifying its major characteristics, and outlines the notion and practice of 'open education' as an emergent paradigm.

HISTORY SCIENTIFIC COMMUNICATION SYSTEMS

The history of scientific communication, even in the post-war period, is a mammoth undertaking where technological developments and the new paradigm of open knowledge production seem to outstrip our capacity to give an adequate account of them. There is so much experimentation by way of new electronic journals launched and new projects being established that it is near impossible to document even the range in its diversity let along theorise its main characteristics and implications for modes of scientific communication. One source, perhaps the most comprehensive, provides a bibliography on scholarly electronic publishing that runs to 1,400 items in English under such categories as: economic issues; electronic books & texts; electronic serials; general works; legal issues; library issues; new publishing models; publisher issues; repositories, e-prints and AOI (America Online) (Bailey, 2006; see also 2001).

The history of electronic scientific communication itself is now nearly twenty years old if we date the process from the appearance of the first electronic journals.

The electronic revolution of those first utopian years in the early 1990s with predictions of the collapse of the traditional print-based system, the demise of academic publishers, and the replacement by electronic journals has not yet come to pass. As Valauskas (1997, n.p.) argues "electronic scholarly journals differentiate themselves from printed scholarly journals by accelerated peer review, combined with mercurial production schemes (...). The sheer interactive nature of digital journals (…) and the ability to access the complete archives of a given title on a server make that sort of publishing a significant departure from the long established traditions of print." He concludes "electronic scholarly journals are indeed different from traditional print scholarly journals, but not as radically different as some would argue. They are different in terms of process, but not in terms of the ancient traditions of peer review and verification." At the same time, while slower than originally thought there are certainly revolutionary changes taking place that I will refer generically to as 'open knowledge production', a term that might be said to embrace open source, open access, open 'science' (referring to systematic knowledge), open courseware and open education.

To begin let us remind ourselves that the history of scientific communication demonstrates that the typical form of the scientific article presented in print-based journals in essay form is a result of development over two centuries beginning in seventeenth century with the emergence of learned societies and cooperation among scientists. *Journal des Sçavans*, the first journal, was published in Paris in 1665 (Fjällbrant, 1997) as a twelve page quarto pamphlet, appearing only a few months before the *Philosophical Transactions of the Royal Society*, the oldest journal in continuous production.[5] The development of the journal and scientific norms of cooperation, forms of academic writing and the norm of peer review was part and parcel of the institutionalisation of science first with the development of the model of the Royal Society that was emulated elsewhere in Europe and the US, and then later institutionalisation received a strong impetus from the emergence of the modern research university beginning with the establishment of the University of Berlin in 1810 in the reforms of von Humboldt. This institutionalisation of science necessarily also was a part of the juridical-legal system of writing that grew up around the notion of a professional scientist and academic, the notion of the academic author, the idea of public science or research, the ownership of ideas and academic recognition for the author who claimed originality for a discovery, set of results or piece of scholarship (Kaufer & Carley, 1993).

Over 180 years later the form, style and economics of scientific communication was to undergo another set of changes to its socio-technical ecology and infrastructure. The pre-history of the emergence of electronic forms of scientific communication can be traced back at least to Ted Nelson's notion of 'hypertext' which he coined in 1963 and went on to develop as a hypertext system. It is also a pre-history that reveals the development of networking and network publishing in the Advanced Research Projects Agency Network (ARPANET) launched by the U.S. Department of Defense in 1969 and in the Education Resources Information Center (ERIC) launched by the U.S. Department of Education's Office of

Educational Research and Improvement and the National Library of Education.[6] In this context it is important to recognise that the concept of 'information' emerged from the combination of the development of modern military intelligence (breaking codes, deciphering messages, encoding information, resolving conflict of sources etc.) and the development of new communication technologies, often also strongly related to the military context and the cooperation between the military and business sector, for instance, the U.S. Advanced Research Projects Agency (ARPA) developed in response to Sputnik, the contribution of RAND corporation (a nonprofit research-based policy organisation) to packet switching through its research on the control of missiles and the ARPANET constructed in 1969 linking the University of California at Los Angeles, SRI at Stanford, University of California at Santa Barbara, and University of Utah.

Here some account of the impact of computers on writing is required including the shift from: literacy to orality and the way that computers re-introduce oral characteristics into writing; linearity to connectivity; fixity to fluidity; and passivity to interactivity (Ferris, 2002). Jay David Bolter's (1991) *Writing Space: The computer, hypertext and the history of writing* is the seminal text that explores the computer's place in the history of symbolic (textual) media. The consequences of the networking of science and culture have yet to be worked through fully yet certainly as Bolter points out the new definition of literacy is synonymous with computer literacy and while it is the case that the computer signifies the end of traditional print literacy it does not signify the end of literacy. The Web has now spawned a whole set of new media genres and forms and the Internet has been accepted into education enthusiastically and in a way that previous technologies like television were not. We have not begun to identify systematically the way these new media forms and the development of visual literacy have and will impact upon scientific communication but already there have been some telling signs (see Woolgar, 2000; Nentwich, 2003).

THE ECONOMIC CONTEXT AND THE SERIALS CRISIS

A media industry overview conducted by Morgan and Stanley in 2002 revealed a US$7 billion market for global STM (science, technology and medicine) publishing broadly divided into scientific publishing (with libraries as major markets) and medical publishing (with hospitals and practitioners as major markets) with Reed as the market leader. The report indicated that scientific publishing is the fastest-growing media subsector of the past 15 years and that since "1986 the average price of a journal has risen by 215% while the number of journals purchased has fallen by only 5.1%" (Morgan & Stanley, 2002, p. 2).

The report concludes that the nature of the industry is unlikely to change although it will experience a cyclical slowdown due to budget cuts, large publishers will enjoy economies of scale through 'bundling' and margins will expand for those publishers with successful online platforms.

Table 1. Global Scientific Publishing Market Players 2001 (Source: Simba, Morgan & Stanley 2002, p. 2)

	2001 Revenues (US $mn)	2001 Market Share (%)
Reed Elsevier (Elsevier Science)	1,055.3	23.3
American Chemical Society	357.3	7.9
Thomson	259.0	5.7
John Wiley & Sons	243.6	5.4
Inst of Electrical & Elect. Engineers	200.3	4.4
Wolters Kluwer	169.3	3.7
McGraw-Hill	146.2	3.2
Taylor & Francis	144.6	3.2
Springer-Verlag	44.0	1.0
Others	1,916.9	42.3
Total Scientific Market	4,536.4	100.0%

The European Commission's (2006, p. 5) report *Study on the Economic and Technical Evolution of Scientific Publication Markets in Europe* corroborates and updates the Morgan & Stanley report confirming:

The core STM (science, technology and medicine) publishing market is estimated between USD 7 billion and USD 11 billion, while in 2001 OECD countries allocated USD 638 billion to R&D. In the last 30 years, the prices of scientific journals have been steadily increasing. Between 1975 and 1995, they increased 200%- 300% beyond inflation.

The report goes on to record that as of 1995, publishers started to adopt digital delivery modes and to provide online access to their journals, but while the new technologies and the internet have dramatically improved the accessibility of scientific publications for researchers the actual access to the literature still relies on their library's ability to pay subscriptions.

The report outlines the broad market trends from 1995 which is taken as the approximate start of the 'electronic revolution' including the following main features that have remained constant since about 1975:

– the increasing reliance on journals as the main channel for dissemination of scientific knowledge, with a growth that parallels the growth of research produced;
– the dominance of the 'reader-pay' or 'library pay', as opposed to the 'author-pay' model of journal dissemination;
– the existence of many publishers in the market, with two big groups of publishers: For-profits (FP) and Not-for-profits (NFP), the latter group including learned societies and university presses;
– the very fast growth of some big FP publishers, through new journal introduction, through the running of journals from learned societies, and through mergers (EC, 2006, p. 7).

In 1987 *New Horizons in Adult Education*, perhaps the earliest electronic journal, was established by the Syracuse University Kellogg Project[7] and in 1989 *Psycoloquy*[8] was established by Stevan Harnad the same year that the Newsletter on Serials Pricing was launched and there was serious talk of a crisis in scholarly communication which has grown ever more insistent. The origins of the crisis are the increasing volume and high cost for print journals and books together with loss of control in the marketplace and through copyright.[9]

United Kingdom House of Commons Science and Technology Select Committee (2004) determined that in face of the high and increasing prices of journals imposed by academic published that the Government should develop a strategy to improve the provision of academic publications. The issue at stake is put succinctly quoting statistics from The Chartered Institute of Library and Information Professionals:

> Whilst the volume of research output and the price of scientific journals has been steadily increasing – one respected source cites average journal price increases of 58% between 1998 and 2003 – library budgets have seen funding decreases (Introduction, http://www.publications.parliament.uk/pa/cm200304/cm select/cmsctech/399/39904.htm).

The concern is that the results and profits of government investment in public good science are being increasingly diverted to the publishers' shareholders.[10] The Select Committee on reviewing technological developments, that have fundamentally changed the way that scientific articles are published making it feasible to published free online and acknowledging that several new models have emerged around the movement known as 'Open Access', recommends:

> that all UK higher education institutions establish institutional repositories on which their published output can be stored and from which it can be read, free of charge, online. It also recommends that Research Councils and other Government funders mandate their funded researchers to deposit a copy of all of their articles in this way. The Government will need to appoint a central body to oversee the implementation of the repositories; to help with networking; and to ensure compliance with the technical standards needed to provide maximum functionality. Set-up and running costs are relatively low, making institutional repositories a cost-effective way of improving access to scientific publications (Summary, http://www.publications.parliament.uk/pa/cm 200304/cmselect/cmsctech/399/39903.htm).

The Committee also suggests that the UK Government become a proponent for change internationally leading by example.[11] The report was seen in some quarters as an important step forward in the global movement for open access to scientific and medical literature. The Government response was luke-warm: it was not convinced of the 'serials crisis' arguing that consortia can make a big difference and, in general, it supported the concept of 'healthy' competition in the publishing industry.[12]

THE OPEN ACCESS MOVEMENT

The EC report also provides a useful summary of the Open Access Movement beginning with SPARC's (Scholarly Publishing and Academic Resources Coalition) launch in 1998.[13] SPARC on its website advertises itself as 'an international alliance of academic and research libraries working to correct imbalances in the scholarly publishing system' and provides the following self-description.

SPARC (the Scholarly Publishing and Academic Resources Coalition), launched in 1998 as an initiative of the Association of Research Libraries, is an alliance of 222 academic and research libraries working to correct imbalances in the scholarly publishing system. These imbalances have driven the cost of scholarly journals (especially in science, technology, and medicine) to insupportably high levels, and have critically diminished the community's ability to access, share, and use information. At the core of SPARC's mission is the belief that these imbalances inhibit the advancement of scholarship and are at odds with fundamental needs of scholars and the academic enterprise (from its 2007 Program Plan).

The movement, its complexity and its momentum can best be represented by a timeline of developments. Clearly no one paper or indeed book can give a complete picture of its developments and with every passing day the overall picture becomes more complex.

Open Access Timeline [14]

Pre-1990 ERIC (1966), Project Gutenberg (1971), New Horizons in Adult Education (1987), Psycoloquy (1989)
1990 Electronic Journal of Communication, Postmodern Culture, Bryn Mawr Classical Review
1991 Surfaces, Behavior and Brain Sciences, Ejournal
1992 First Symposium on Scholarly Publishing on the Electronic Networks
1993 Aboriginal Studies Electronic Data Archive, Education Policy Analysis Archive
1994 Digital Libraries Initiative, Electronic Journal of Sociology
1995 Stanford Encyclopedia of Philosophy
1996 Electronic Publishing Trust for Development[15]
1997 Research Papers in Economics
1998 SPARC, The International Consortium for the Advancement of Academic Publication[16]
1999 Declaration on Science and the Use of Scientific Knowledge[17] (UNESCO)
2000 PubMed Central (PMC), BioMed Central, Public Library of Science[18]
   Public Library of Science petition
2002 Budapest Open Access Initiative,[19] Creative Commons[20]
2003 Bethesda Statement on Open Access Publishing[21], Berlin Declaration on Open Access to Knowledge in the Sciences and Humanities,[22] US Public Access to Science Act
2004 U.K. House of Commons Science & Technology Report, Wellcome Trust Reports, OECD's Declaration On Access To Research Data From Public Funding[23]
2005 Policy on Enhancing Public Access to Archived Publications Resulting from

NIH-Funded Research, The Open Knowledge Foundation[24]
2006 US Research Council's Statement on Open Access,[25] EC Commission Report,
Launch of Open J-Gate[26]

What these reports and declarations have in common is a statement of commitment to the principles of open access and open knowledge production. By 'open access' the Budapest Open Access Initiative (BOAI) means:

> free availability on the public internet, permitting any users to read, download, copy, distribute, print, search, or link to the full texts of these articles, crawl them for indexing, pass them as data to software, or use them for any other lawful purpose, without financial, legal, or technical barriers other than those inseparable from gaining access to the internet itself. The only constraint on reproduction and distribution, and the only role for copyright in this domain, should be to give authors control over the integrity of their work and the right to be properly acknowledged and cited (<http://www.soros.org/openaccess/read.shtml>).

As the BOAI public statement on its website puts it, "[p]rimarily, this category encompasses (...) peer-reviewed journal articles, but it also includes any unreviewed preprints that [scholars] might wish to put online for comment or to alert colleagues to important research findings." Typically these statements and declarations also make reference to the serials crisis, the economics of academic publishing and to an emerging global intellectual property (IP) regime that expands and looks after the interests of IP owners without the same or sufficient regard for the rights of users, especially in the Third World. More activist associations provide histories of the open access movement and develop alliances across a variety of organisations involved with scientific communication including libraries and their associations, research institutions, universities and university consortia, learned societies, open access journals, small university presses, government and state agencies, and publishers. There is general concern about the extent of new IP regulations, increased duration of copyright, and the extension of IP to new areas of activity including databases and software. There is also strong concern for questions involving the governance of the Internet, the protection of its intellectual commons, and the way that private interests are being allowed to muscle in and enclose some areas of the public domain (Höök, 1999; Jacobs, 2006; Willinski, 2006).[27]

Most of these statements also place their faith in the promise of open access and the architecture of the Internet to distribute and disseminate public knowledge. Thus the Statement of the Libraries & Publishers Working Group runs

> We believe that open access will be an essential component of scientific publishing in the future and that works reporting the results of current scientific research should be as openly accessible and freely useable as possible. [28]

The Statement then itemises a set of proposal for libraries and journal publishers aimed at encouraging the open access model. The Statement of Scientists and Scientific Societies Working Group from the same source reads:

> Scientific research is an interdependent process whereby each experiment is informed by the results of others. The scientists who perform research and the professional societies that represent them have a great interest in ensuring that research results are disseminated as immediately, broadly and effectively as possible. Electronic publication of research results offers the opportunity and the obligation to share research results, ideas and discoveries freely with the scientific community and the public.

In the Preface to the Berlin Declaration on Open Access to Knowledge in the Sciences and Humanities there is a recognition of the way the Internet has changed scientific practice focusing on how the Internet has emerged as a "functional medium for distributing knowledge" that will also significantly "modify the nature of scientific publishing as well as the existing system of quality assurance":

> The Internet has fundamentally changed the practical and economic realities of distributing scientific knowledge and cultural heritage. For the first time ever, the Internet now offers the chance to constitute a global and interactive representation of human knowledge, including cultural heritage and the guarantee of worldwide access. [29]

The Association of College & Research Libraries (ACRL) 'Principles and Strategies for the Reform of Scholarly Communication', issued August 28, 2003 defines scholarly communication as:

> The system through which research and other scholarly writings are created, evaluated for quality, disseminated to the scholarly community, and preserved for future use. The system includes both formal means of communication, such as publication in peer-reviewed journals, and informal channels, such as electronic listservs. [30]

The Principles then examines the system in crisis mentioning specifically increasing prices, commercialisation and economic pressures facing university presses and the humanities, creeping licensing agreement and the expansion of copyright, long-term preservation and access to electronic information, and the way that powerful commercial interests have been successful at the national level in limiting the public domain and reducing principles of fair use. It goes on to stipulate a set of principles and strategies.

Both the OECD [31] and the UN World Summit on the Information Society [32] emphasise the importance of shared knowledge and the significance of the international exchange of data, information and knowledge for the advancement of scientific research and innovation, and for meeting the development goals of the Millennium Declaration. In addition, open access is recognised as having the potential to maximise the value derived from public investments in science, help with training researchers, increase the scale and scope of research and enhance the participation of developing countries in the global science system. The World Summit goes further by politically linking open access and open knowledge production to principles of democracy and to fundamental human rights of freedom of expression and opinion under the United Nations. Furthermore it emphasises the role of governments in the promotion of ICTs for development, the importance of the information and communication infrastructure as an essential foundation for an inclusive information society. There are a broader set of arguments that predate open access, open knowledge production systems and open education that argue for the necessity of open information to democracy more broadly (see Peters, 2007a).

OPEN KNOWLEDGE PRODUCTION

Open knowledge production is based on the open source model that follows principles of encouraging the active sharing of all forms of information and knowledge enabled by the economics of file-sharing that permits the addition of new users without depleting the original stock of ideas. Indeed, 'open knowledge' is based on the understanding that the use, reuse and modification of digital content does not diminish its value but operates expansively to enhance and develop ideas through sharing, reuse and modification. What is more, open knowledge production systems at the level of code are open to the same development through open use and modification by any user, often implying democratisation of users and their anonymity. The 'product' is what undergoes successive refinement over a number of 'generations' without explicit authorship or ownership. While certain models of openness have prevailed and/or been theorised the models have themselves been based on an ideology of political and methodological individualism. This section briefly discusses the concept of the 'open society' as it was developed by Karl Popper. His notion became important both politically and epistemological especially during the Cold War period. It was also accompanied by a view of the open market and the doctrine of free trade as promoted by Friedrich von Hayek. Some economists, like Joseph Stiglitz wants to draw parallels and connections between knowledge as a global public good and open institutions. Commons-based peer production is a clear example of a form of open knowledge production which conforms precisely to the criteria outlined above and the emerging paradigm of 'open education' also follows this same form of open collaboration and innovation that springs from new architectures of participation and a new political economy of knowledge.

(i) The Open Society

Whatever the historical origins the term 'open' has now become associated with 'open knowledge production', although Benkler (2006) and others also use other terms such as 'commons-based production'. In any event, the term open has resonance with systems theory, cybernetics and with open systems. In systems theory an open system is defined as a system where matter or energy can flow into and/or out of the system which is thus in continuous interaction with its environment. In computer science open systems are computer systems that provide some combination of interoperability, portability and open software standards. The term openness as developed from systems theory especially as adopted and modified in economics, sociology and politics can mean 'open' markets, 'open' science and 'open' institutions. In this sense openness is opposed to secrecy and associated also with both participation and self-governance. Often the case is made for the openness of markets and political systems in Eastern Europe following the demise of the closed system of Soviet authoritarianism although there is no conclusive data on the empirical relation between liberalisation in the political and economic senses (i.e., 'free trade', 'open capital markets' or globalisation and democracy). As Eichengreen & Leblang (2007, p. 4) argue:

> The idea that globalisation promotes the diffusion of democratic ideas goes back at least to Kant (1795). Schumpeter (1950), Lipset (1959) and Hayek (1960) all argued that free trade and capital flows, by enhancing the efficiency of resource allocation, raise incomes and lead to the economic development that fosters demands for democracy. Within modern political science, the connections between economic and political liberalisation is one of the foundational topics of international political economy.

This kind of understanding, for instance, underlies The Open Society Institute (OSI), a foundation created in 1993 by George Soros[33] to support his foundations in Central and Eastern Europe and the former Soviet Union established to help countries make the transition from communism. The OSI

> aims to shape public policy to promote democratic governance, human rights, and economic, legal, and social reform. On a local level, OSI implements a range of initiatives to support the rule of law, education, public health, and independent media. At the same time, OSI works to build alliances across borders and continents on issues such as combating corruption and rights abuses.(http://www.soros.org/about/overview)

The concept of the 'open society' was given its first formulation by Henri Bergson (1977, orig. 1932) in *The Two Sources of Morality and Religion* as an outgrowth of his *Creative Evolution* (orig. 1911). He described two sources of morality, one open whose religion is dynamic, the other closed whose religion is static. Only the former is both creative and oriented towards progress; it is genuinely universal and aims at peace.

Some years later Karl Popper (1945) wrote *The Open Society and its Enemies* while a political exile in New Zealand during 1937 to 1943. It was an influential two volume work that criticised historicism (Plato, Hegel and Marx) and provided a defense of the principles of liberal democracy. His aim in this work was not unrelated to his doctrine of fallabilism, especially in relation to the social sciences and its powers of prediction, and the promotion and defense of the critical ethos in science. The relationship of Popper and his ideas to Hayek is still a largely unwritten story; Hayek was responsible for championing Popper's appointment at the London School of Economics and cited him first in his early *Economics and Knowledge* 1936 paper which established the field of the economics of knowledge and heralded the 'knowledge economy'. There is some evidence that Hayek's attack on central planning strongly influenced Popper's attack on historicism and closed societies (Caldwell, 2003).

There are some general arguments for making the association between the open society and the knowledge economy. Joseph Stiglitz, the renegade ex-Chief Economist of the World Bank who resigned over ideological issues draws an interesting connection between knowledge and development with the strong implication that universities as traditional knowledge institutions have become the leading future service industries and need to be more fully integrated into the prevailing mode of production. He asserts: "We now see economic development as less like the construction business and more like education in the broad and comprehensive sense that covers, knowledge, institutions, and culture" (Stiglitz 1999a, p. 2). Stiglitz argues that the "movement to the knowledge economy necessitates a rethinking of economic fundamentals" because, he maintains, knowledge is different from other goods in that it shares many of the properties of a 'global' public good. This means, among other things, a key role for governments in protecting intellectual property rights, although appropriate definitions of such rights are not clear or straightforward. It signals also dangers of monopolisation, which Stiglitz suggests, given the economies of scale to be achieved, may be even greater for knowledge economies than for industrial economies. In more technical terms knowledge is non-rivalrous, that is, knowledge once discovered and made public, operates expansively to defy the normal 'law' of scarcity that governs most commodity markets. Knowledge in its immaterial or conceptual forms – ideas, information, concepts, functions and abstract objects of thought – is purely non-rivalrous, that is, there is essentially zero marginal costs to adding more users. Yet once materially embodied or encoded, such as in learning or in applications or processes, knowledge becomes costly in time and resources. The pure non-rivalrousness of knowledge can be differentiated from the low cost of its dissemination, resulting from improvements in electronic media and technology, although there may be congestion effects and waiting time (to reserve a book, or download from the Internet). Stiglitz argues that these knowledge principles carry over to knowledge institutions and countries as a whole. If basic intellectual property rights are routinely violated, the supply of knowledge will be diminished. Where trust relationships have been flagrantly violated learning opportunities will vanish. Experimentation is another type of openness, which cannot take place in closed societies or institutions hostile to change. Finally, he argues that changes in economic institutions have counterparts in the political sphere, demanding institutions of the open society such as a free press, transparent government, pluralism, checks and balances, toleration, freedom of thought, and open public debate. This political openness is essential for the success of the transformation towards a knowledge economy (see Peters, 2007b).

(ii) Commons-based Peer Production

The terms 'open knowledge' and 'open knowledge production' are now well accepted in the literature to refer to a range of related models of 'peer production' and 'peer governance' that provide an emerging alternative to traditional proprietary models of knowledge production. The concept of 'open' and 'openness' deserves special attention because it has come to christen a range of related activities concerned with the advantages of decentralised distributed networks that characterise what Benkler (2006) calls "commons-based peer production" and increasingly defines the political economy of the digital networked environment. The concept of 'openness', for example, has been applied to:

- open source
- open access
- open content
- open communication
- open archives
- open urls
- open learning
- open courseware
- open education

Typically, as we saw with the BOAI definition, the concept 'open' is sometimes associated with 'free' although Richard Stallman prefers the term 'free' in relation to both 'free software' and Free Software Foundation.[34] Stallman provides the following definition of 'free':

Free software is a matter of the users' freedom to run, copy, distribute, study, change and improve the software. More precisely, it refers to four kinds of freedom, for the users of the software:

- The freedom to run the program, for any purpose (freedom 0).
- The freedom to study how the program works, and adapt it to your needs (freedom 1). Access to the source code is a precondition for this.
- The freedom to redistribute copies so you can help your neighbor (freedom 2).
- The freedom to improve the program, and release your improvements to the public, so that the whole community benefits (freedom 3). Access to the source code is a precondition for this. (http://www.gnu.org/philosophy/free-sw.html)

Stallman distinguishes 'free' from 'open'. While criteria for the latter was derived from his definition of free, it is something less than free and attempts to avoid the ethical question. He explains:

In 1998, a part of the free software community splintered off and began campaigning in the name of 'open source.' The term was originally proposed to avoid a possible misunderstanding of the term 'free software,' but it soon became associated with philosophical views quite different from those of the free software movement (…). Nearly all open source software is free software; the two terms describe almost the same category of software. But they stand for views based on fundamentally different values. Open source is a development methodology; free software is a social movement. (http://www.gnu.org/philosophy/open-source-misses-the-point.html)

This may have been the case at the end of the 1990s but today the notion of openness as it applies to the new convergences of open source, open access and open knowledge production has clearly taken on the hue of a political and social movement. Open access and open knowledge production, sometimes also referred to A2K (access to knowledge) and P2P (peer-to-peer), now customarily refers to knowledge creation and sharing as well a range of other topics such as framing human rights and development, political economy of trade treaties and intellectual property, peer production and education, digital right management, and open archives (OA), OA publishing and libraries, among others.

In a study of how social production transforms markets and freedom, Benkler (2006, p. 1) begins his authoritative work with the following words:

Information, knowledge, and culture are central to human freedom and human development. How they are produced and exchanged in our society critically affects the way we see the state of the world as it is and might be; who decides these questions; and how we, as societies and polities, come to understand what can and ought to be done. For more than 150 years, modern complex democracies have depended in large measure on an industrial information economy for these basic functions. In the past decade and a half, we have begun to see a radical change in the organisation of information production. Enabled by technological change, we are beginning to see a series of economic, social, and cultural adaptations that make possible a radical transformation of how we make the information environment we occupy as autonomous individuals, citisens, and members of cultural and social groups (…). The change brought about by the networked information environment is deep. It is structural. It goes to the very foundations of how liberal markets and liberal democracies have coevolved for almost two centuries.

Benkler is not alone is making what seem like extravagant claims. His work rests on and is in turn reinforced by a range of scholars mostly working in the related areas of informatics, international law and political economy, including James Boyle, Hal Abelson, and Lawrence Lessig (see Peters, 2007). They concur that the role of nonmarket and nonproprietary production promotes the emergence of a new information environment and networked economy that both depends upon and encourages great individual freedom, democratic participation, collaboration and interactivity. This "promises to enable social production and exchange to play a much larger role, alongside property – and market based production, than they ever have in modern democracies" (Benkler, 2006, p. 3). Peer production of information, knowledge, and culture enabled by the emergence of free and open-source software permits the expansion of the social model production beyond software platform into every domain of information and cultural production.

Open knowledge production is based upon an incremental, decentralised (and asynchronous), and collaborative a development process that transcends the traditional proprietary market model. Commons-based peer production is based on free cooperation, not on the selling of one's labor in exchange of a wage, nor motivated primarily by profit or for the exchange value of the resulting product; it is managed through new modes of peer governance rather than traditional organisational hierarchies and it is an innovative application of copyright which creates an information commons and transcends the limitations attached to both the private (for-profit) and public (state-based) property forms.[35]

As Michael Bauwens' P2P Foundation acknowledges there are and have been many thinkers and scholars who have expressed similar ideas in terms of the "High-tech Gift Economy" (Richard Barbrook[36]), "the Public Domain" (James Boyle[37]), "Copyright, Commodification and Culture" (Julia Cohen[38]), "Peer Governance and Democracy" (Erik Douglas[39]), "Connective Knowledge" (Stephen Downes[40]), and "An Economic Theory of Infrastructure and Commons Management" (Brett Frischmann, 2005). There is a clear link of this set of ideas to those that employ ecological nor environmental models to talk about the commons such as "Freedom In The Commons" (Yochai Benkler[41]), "the Second Enclosure Movement" (James Boyle), "Circulation of the Commons" and "Immaterial Labor" (Nick Dyer-Witheford[42]) and "the Tragedy of the Commons" (Garreth Harding[43]). Others have sought to provide, in addition, an evolutionary thesis concerning societal evolution and/or changed states of consciousness, including "the movement from tribes to networks" (David Ronfeldt[44]), "the Participatory Worldview" (David Skrbina[45]), and "the Enactive Theory of Consciousness" (Evan Thompson[46]). Finally, some scholars have sought to link open knowledge or commons-based production to a political system and especially to Marxism including "Socialist Individualism" (Magnus Marsdal[47]), "The DotCommunist Manifesto" (Eben Moglen[48]), "the Tradition of Civil Socialism" (Bruno Theret[49]) and "Sharing Culture" (Raoul Victor[50]). This list is quite useful but also potentially difficult to decipher and interpret; three sets of ideas outlining the economics of open knowledge production systems, reinterpreting this phenomenon in terms of ecological or environmental models, shifts in evolutionary consciousness, and its exemplification of political models. The first set of conceptual links to ecological nor environmental models is now well established across the literature whether it be in political economy, law, sociology, psychology, or some combination of all four (see Peters, 2007b). The second set of links to evolutionary models also in some way can be considered an extension of the first set and is a powerful paradigm in psychology (computational models of cognition), philosophy (connectionist epistemology) and anthropology.[51] The third set that emphasise political models seems particularly problematic with scholars from both Marxist and Liberal traditions of political economy claiming open knowledge production systems for their own, even though the principles they articulate are overlapping.

The Foundation for P2P Alternatives[52] provides the following brief sketch that outlines the relationships between these different set of ideas:

- that technology reflects a change of consciousness towards participation, and in turn strengthens it
- that the networked format, expressed in the specific manner of peer to peer relations, is a new form of political organising and subjectivity, and an alternative for the political/economic order, which though it does not offer solutions per se, points the way to a variety of dialogical and self-organising formats to device different processes for arriving at such solutions; it ushers in a era of 'nonrepresentational democracy', where an increasing number of people are able to manage their social and productive life through the use of a variety of networks and peer circles
- that it creates a new public domain, an information commons, which should be protected and extended, especially in the domain of common knowledge creation; and that this domain, where the cost of reproducing knowledge is near zero, requires fundamental changes in the intellectual property regime, as reflected by new forms such as the free software movement
- that the principles developed by the free software movement, in particular the General Public License, provides for models that could be used in other areas of social and productive life
- that it reconnects with the older traditions and attempts for a more cooperative social order, but this time obviates the need for authoritarianism and centralisation; it has the potential of showing that the new egalitarian digital culture, is connected to the older traditions of cooperation of the workers and peasants, and to the search for an engaged and meaningful life as expressed in one's work, which becomes an expression of individual and collective creativity, rather than as a salaried means of survival
- that it offers youth a vision of renewal and hope, to create a world that is more in tune with their values; that it creates a new language and discourse in tune with the new historical phase of 'cognitive capitalism'; P2P is a language which every 'digital youngster' can understand
- it combines subjectivity (new values), intersubjectivity (new relations), objectivity (an enabling technology) and interobjectivity (new forms of organisation) that mutually strengthen each other in a positive feedback loop, and it is clearly on the offensive and growing, but lacking 'political self-consciousness'.

There is no doubt that there exist relationships between these different sets of ideas and the emerging information environment based upon a new form of open knowledge production and that these connections have strong implications for a kind of informational democracy (Peters, 2007). Whether the same set of relationships between these ideas can be extended to shifts of consciousness understood in ecological or evolutionary terms, or whether they imply a certain kind of political system or even spirituality is best treated as a set of working hypotheses at this stage. The actual complexity of establishing theoretical relationships between these different sets (rather than assuming them) is staggeringly difficult.

THE EMERGING PARADIGM OF 'OPEN EDUCATION'

'Open education' has emerged strongly as a new paradigm of social production in the global knowledge economy. In the last year or so four major reports have documented existing developments and new tools and technologies, heralded the utopian promise of 'openness' in global education extolling its virtues of shared commons-based peer-production and analysed the ways in which it contributes to skill formation, innovation and economic development.

The powerful Washington-based Committee for Economic Development[53] released its report *Open Standards, Open Source, and Open Innovation: Harnessing the Benefits of Openness*[54] in April 2006 examining the phenomenon of 'openness' in the context of today's digital economy highlighting the key attributes of accessibility, responsiveness, and creativity and commenting on the relevance of three areas of open standards, open-source software, and open innovation. The report by the Digital Connections Council of the Committee For Economic Development built on three earlier reports dating from 2001: *The Digital Economy and Economic Growth* (2001), *Digital Economy: Promoting Competition, Innovation, and Opportunity* (2001) and *Promoting Innovation and Economic Growth: The Special Problem of Digital Intellectual Property* (2004).[55] These reports emphasised intellectual property issues involved with file-sharing and peer-to-peer networks and the way that "heavy-handed enforcement of intellectual property rules and reliance on business practices designed for the trade of physical goods can stifle the collaboration and innovation that is vital to the growth of the digital economy." What is perhaps of greatest interest in the present context is the emphasis in the new report on what they call 'open innovation' – new collaborative models of open innovation, originating outside the firm, that results in an "architecture of participation" (Tim O'Reilly)- and to a lesser extent their definition of 'openness'. This is what the report says about "open innovation":

> Open innovation can be seen in the growing use of digital software tools tied to computer-controlled fabrication devices that allow users to design an object and then produce it physically. As the costs of these digital design tools decrease, users are able to innovate, breaking the model of manufacturers being the source of innovation and customers simply consuming them. The openness model, the antithesis of a 'not invented here' attitude, encompasses not only manufacturers and users, but suppliers whose innovations should be welcomed by the companies they supply (Executive Summary, 3004, p. 4).

The report goes on to mention "the extraordinary increase in 'peer production' of digital information products" which are produced by individuals without any expectation of monetary gain and commenting that "sophisticated commercial firms are harvesting the benefits of openness." (ibid., p. 4). In this same context they mention the movement of "open science" promoted by the National Institutes of Health (NIH) and the model of open courseware on which they comment:

> Advocates for more openness contend that openness will result in greater innovation than would be achieved by restricting access to information or allowing first creators to exert greater control over it. Such a belief in the value of tapping the collective wisdom is profoundly democratic (ibid., p. 5).

What is remarkable about this set of statements is the link between firm innovation, what we might all open education and the emergence of the paradigm of social production (more about this concept later).

In 2007 three substantial reports were released that reviewed open education as a movement and assessed its benefits: The OECD's (2007) *Giving Knowledge for Free: The Emergence Of Open Educational Resources*[56]; Open e-Learning Content Observatory Services (OLCOS) project and report entitled *Open Educational Practices and Resources*[57]; *A Review of the Open Educational Resources (OER) Movement: Achievements, Challenges, and New Opportunities* (Eds. Atkins, Brown & Hammond, 2007), a report to The William and Flora Hewlett Foundation.[58] These three reports share similar emphases each focusing on 'openness' and the promise of the new technologies and their educational benefits. The OECD report focuses on four questions:

- How can sustainable cost/benefit models for OER initiatives be developed?
- What are the intellectual property rights issues linked to OER initiatives?
- What are the incentives and barriers for universities and faculty staff to deliver their materials to OER initiatives?
- How can access and usefulness for the users of OER initiatives be improved? (OECD, 2007, pp. 3–4, Foreword)

The Executive Summary gives us a flavor of the potential of OE[59] and the utopian educational promise that graces these three reports:

> An apparently extraordinary trend is emerging. Although learning resources are often considered as key intellectual property in a competitive higher education world, more and more institutions and individuals are sharing digital learning resources over the Internet openly and without cost, as open educational resources (OER) (ibid., p. 9).

The report then concerns itself with the following questions: What are open educational resources? Who is using and producing OER and how much? Why are people sharing for free? What are the provisions for copyright and open licences? How can OER projects be sustained in the long run? alongside a set of policy implications and recommendations.

The OLCOS report, by comparison, focuses on: Policies, institutional frameworks and business models; Open Access and open content repositories; and Laboratories of open educational practices and resources, warning against instituting open education within the dominant model:

OER are understood to be an important element of policies that want to leverage education and lifelong learning for the knowledge economy and society. However, OLCOS emphasises that it is crucial to also promote innovation and change in educational practices. In particular, OLCOS warns that delivering OER to the still dominant model of teacher centred knowledge transfer will have little effect on equipping teachers, students and workers with the competences, knowledge and skills to participate successfully in the knowledge economy and society. This report emphasises the need to foster open practices of teaching and learning that are informed by a competency-based educational framework. However, it is understood that a shift towards such practices will only happen in the longer term in a step-by-step process. Bringing about this shift will require targeted and sustained efforts by educational leaders at all levels (OLCOS, p. 12).

In Chapter 4 'Competences for the knowledge society' the report opines "priority must be given to open educational practices that involve students in active, constructive engagement with content, tools and services in the learning process, and promote learners' self-management, creativity and working in teams" and "introduces the idea of value chains of open educational content which emerge when teachers and students re-use available content and make enriched and/or additional material (e.g. use cases, experiences, lessons learned, etc.) available again to a larger community of practice" (ibid., p. 37). The report defines a competency-focused, collaborative paradigm of learning and knowledge acquisition where "priority is given to learning communities and development of knowledge and skills required for tackling and solving problems instead of subject-centred knowledge transfer." (ibid, p. 37) For the purposes of this paper and audience I quote further from the report:

> We believe that, to acquire the competences and skills for personal and professional achievement in the knowledge-based society, the learner's autonomy, personal mastery and self-direction must be acknowledged and innovative approaches implemented that foster self management, communication and team skills, and analytical, conceptual, creative and problem solving skills. However, there is of course a huge difference between identifying required competences and operationalising them for inclusion in the concrete practices of teaching and learning at different educational levels (ibid., p. 39).

The report then lists the following skills of "digital competence":

– Ability to search, collect and process (create, organise, distinguish relevant from irrelevant, subjective from objective, real from virtual) electronic information, data and concepts and to use them in a systematic way;
– Ability to use appropriate aids (presentations, graphs, charts, maps) to produce, present or understand complex information;
– Ability to access and search a website and to use internet-based services such as discussion fora and e-mail;

– Ability to use ICT to support critical thinking, creativity and innovation in different contexts at home, leisure and work (ibid., p. 39).

The report to The William and Flora Hewlett Foundation is perhaps, the most comprehensive even although it follows similar lines of investigation to the others but frames the report in terms of Amartya Sen's work with the plan to develop "a strategic international development initiative to expand people's substantive freedoms through the removal of 'unfreedoms.'" What is impressive about this report is not only the inventory of open education projects (the incubation of high-quality specialised open resources) but also its attempt to conceptualise the issues and to move to a new understanding of openness in terms of an ethic of participation (and the design of "open participatory learning infrastructure") that supports the role of technology in emphasising the social nature of learning and its potential to address questions of the digital divide in developing countries.

There is much else that deserves attention in these reports. While they touch on conceptual issues to do with openness and document aspects of the contemporary movement of open educational resources they do not provide a history of 'openness' in education – it has a long, complex and significant history that influences conceptions of its wider purposes – or make the necessary theoretical links to the wider political literature. The reports, it might be argued, are too wedded to a technological account of open education and to an engineering notion of information that blind them to the criticisms that have been and can be mounted against various conceptions of 'openness', 'information' and the cybernetic society based upon it.

CONCLUSION

This chapter has outlined the relationship between the knowledge economy and scientific systems of communication demonstrating that the form, substance and organisation of the system - its technology - strongly influences the form, development, access and distribution of knowledge. In this chapter I have sought to provide the basis for understanding not only the current political economy of scientific knowledge, its economic context and associated serial crisis but also to explain the emerging paradigms of open knowledge production and open education as related instances of a new social mode of knowledge production based on the ethic of sharing, peer production and new technological architectures of participation in an age of mass collaboration. This is an approach to the political economy that is both material and historicist: knowledge and the value of knowledge as Marx and Wittgenstein affirm are rooted in social relations; and knowledge, as both Foucault and Lyotard demonstrate, cannot be separated from relations of power. New systems of open knowledge production embrace the elements of knowledge as a global public good and encourage new forms of distributed knowledge organisation that challenge aspects of the 'old' knowledge economy and contradict the neoliberal policy prescriptions based on the revival of *homo economicus* and its assumptions of individuality, rationality and self-interest.

Open knowledge systems and open learning systems, by contrast, are based on assumptions of *sharing* or *collaboration, distributed* or *collective intelligence,* and the *ethic of participation* often for nonprofit and altruistic motives. In essence, 'open knowledge economy' provides a completely different model to the neoliberal knowledge economy and also challenges the underlying neoliberal ideas of ownership, authorship, human capital, and intellectual property rights, as well as principles of the access, distribution, and creation of knowledge. Future research needs to map the emerging contours of open knowledge production systems, open education and open science but also to devise ways of enhancing, promoting and protecting it in order to realise its full global public promise. There is a need for theoretical studies of how distributed knowledge systems alter 'the knower', knowledge and the act of knowing just as there is a practical need for software engineers and technologists to work collaboratively with educationalists to devise new pedagogical visions and learning platforms that harness the potential of the new architectures associated with Web 2.0. Finally, educational policy scholars must work with national and international policy makers in education, and directly with teachers, students, and community groups especially in developing countries to embrace, develop, devise and evaluate the virtues of openness and open education.

NOTES

1   See Peter Suber's blog at http://www.earlham.edu/~peters/fos/fosblog.html.
2   See http://chronicle.com/news/article/3943/harvard-faculty-adopts-open-access-requirement.
3   See the comment by Ray English on the same site.
4   The Association of College and Research Libraries (ACRL) recently released their research agenda for scholarly publishing around eight themes: The impact and implications of cyberinfrastructure; Changing organisational models; How scholars work; Authorship and scholarly publishing; Value and value metrics of scholarly communications; Adoptions of successful innovations; Preservation of critical material Public policy and legal matters. See http://www.acrl.ala.org/scresearchagenda/index.php?title=Main_Page.
5   See the journal's website http://www.pubs.royalsoc.ac.uk/index.cfm?page=1085 where it is recorded 'The Royal Society was founded in 1660 to promote the new or experimental philosophy of that time, embodying the principles envisaged by Sir Francis Bacon. Henry Oldenburg was appointed as the first (joint) secretary to the Society and he was also the first editor of the Society's journal *Philosophical Transactions.*' The first issue appeared in 1665 and included Oldenburg's correspondence with some of Europe's scientists as well an account by Robert Boyle of a Very Odd Monstrous Calf. Subsequent early issues include 'articles' by Robert Hooke, Issac Newton and Benjamin Franklin. The entire archive is available online.
6   ARPANET was discontinued in 1990 while ERIC advertises itself as 'the world's largest digital library of educational literature' with free access to more than 1.2 million bibliographic records of journal articles http://www.eric.ed.gov/.
7   The journal is now titled *New Horizons in Adult Education & Human Resource Development* and run from the College of Education at Florida International University <http://education.fiu.edu/newhorizons/>.
8   < http://psycprints.ecs.soton.ac.uk/>. In 1990 three online journals were launched: *Electronic Journal of Communication* < http://www.cios.org/www/ejcmain.htm>, *Postmodern Culture*

<http://www3.iath.virginia.edu/pmc/contents.all.html>, and *Bryn Mawr Classical Review* <http://ccat.sas. upenn.edu/bmcr/>.

9   See, for instance, the statements of the Universities of Connecticut and Iowa State respectively, <http://www.lib.uconn.edu/about/publications/scholarlycommunication.html>, <http://www.lib.iastate.edu/libinfo/reptempl/origins.html>.

10 "Between 1986 and 2004, journal expenditures of North American research libraries increased by a staggering 273%, with the average journal unit cost increasing by 188%. During this same period, the U.S. Consumer Price Index rose by 73%, meaning that journal costs have outstripped inflation by a factor of almost 4" (see the website Scholarly Communication at UIUC http://www.library. uiuc.edu/scholcomm/journalcosts.htm)

11 The full report Scientific Publications: Free for all? is available as a pdf file at <http://www.publications. parliament.uk/pa/cm200304/cmselect/cmsctech/399/399.pdf>.

12 A full account of the process and the UK Government's response is given by Steven Harnad at <http://www.ecs.soton.ac.uk/~harnad/Hypermail/Amsci/4131.html>. Harnad comments that the Committee originally had a vague remit to reform publishing but went on to discuss problems associated with journal publishing, affordability, pricing and accessibility, recommending author self-archiving.

13 <http://www.arl.org/sparc/>

14 I have focused on major reports including all the EC report's significant events. The most detailed timeline is that by Peter Suber of which this is but a small selection. See his website at <http://www.earlham.edu/~peters/fos/timeline.htm>.

15 < http://www.epublishingtrust.org/>

16 < http://www.icaap.org/>

17 < http://www.unesco.org/science/wcs/eng/declaration_e.htm>

18 < http://www.plos.org/index.php>

19 < http://www.soros.org/openaccess/>

20 < http://creativecommons.org/>

21 < http://www.earlham.edu/~peters/fos/bethesda.htm>

22 < http://oa.mpg.de/openaccess-berlin/berlindeclaration.html>

23 < http://www.oecd.org/document/0,2340,en_2649_34487_25998799_1_1_1_1,00.html>

24 < http://okfn.org/>

25 < http://www.rcuk.ac.uk/cmsweb/downloads/rcuk/documents/2006statement.pdf>

26 http://www.openj-gate.com/ 'an electronic gateway to global journal literature in open access domain' (Informatics India Ltd), as of March 22 2007 it indexed 3913 open access journals.

27 See Intellectual Property Reform and Open Knowledge, http://www.soros.org/initiatives/ information/focus/access/grants/reform.

28 Bethesda Statement on Open Access Publishing, June 20, 2003http://www.earlham.edu/~peters

29 Berlin Declaration on Open Access to Knowledge in the Sciences and Humanities, October 22, 2003 http://oa.mpg.de/index.html

30 http://www.ala.org.

31 Organisation for Economic Co-operation and Development (OECD) Declaration on Access to Research Data From Public Funding, January 30, 2004 <http://www.oecd.org>.

32 UN World Summit on the Information Society Declaration of Principles and Plan of Action, December 12, 2003

33 Soros became acquainted with Karl Popper's ideas on the open society when he was at the London School of Economics and writing a number of books defending the open society including *Open Society: Reforming Global Capitalism* (2000); *The Crisis of Global Capitalism: Open Society Endangered* (1998); *Underwriting Democracy* (1991); and *Opening the Soviet System* (1990).

34 < http://www.fsf.org/>.

35 I based this formulation on Michel Bauwens' P2P Foundation work at the P2P Foundation <http://p2pfoundation.net/3._P2P_in_the_Economic_Sphere>.

36 <http://www.firstmonday.dk/issues/issue3_12/barbrook/>.

[37] <http://www.law.duke.edu/pd/papers/boyle.pdf >.
[38] <http://papers.ssrn.com/sol3/papers.cfm?abstract_id=663652 >.
[39] <http://www.p2pfoundation.net/Peer_to_Peer_and_the_Four_Pillars_of_Democracy>.
[40] <http://www.downes.ca/cgi-bin/page.cgi?post=33034>.
[41] <http://www.law.duke.edu/shell/cite.pl?52+Duke+L.+J.+1245/>.
[42] <http://www.geocities.com/immateriallabour/withefordpaper2006.html>.
[43] <http://dieoff.org/page95.htm>.
[44] <http://www.rand.org/pubs/papers/P7967/P7967.pdf>.
[45] <http://www.bath.ac.uk/carpp/davidskrbina/summarycontents.htm>.
[46] <http://www.philosophy.ucf.edu/pcsfetz1.html>.
[47] <http://www.autodidactproject.org/other/marxind2.html>.
[48] <http://www.cabinetmagazine.org/issues/10/dot_communist.php>.
[49] <http://fr.pekea-fr.org/?p=11&c=2-3-Theret.html>.
[50] <http://www.oekonux-konferenz.de/dokumentation/texte/Victor.html>.
[51] There are a number of dominant precedents for this work including that of the so-called Cybernetics Group sponsored by the Macy Foundation series of conferences beginning in 1946 (Feedback Mechanisms and Circular Causal Systems in Biological and Social Systems) and including Gregory Bateson, Julian Bigelow, Frank Fremont-Smith, Kurt Lewin, Warren McCulloch, Margaret Mead, John von Neumann, Northrop, Arturo Rosenblueth, Claude Shannon and Norbet Weiner, among others (see Heims, 1993; Dupuy, 2000). Bateson's (1972) *Steps to an Ecology of Mind* is one of the classics to emerge but see also more recently Piero Scaruffi's (2006) *The Nature of Consciousness* that attempts a synthesis of Philosophy, Psychology, Computer Science, Mathematics, Biology, Neurology and Physics, at http://www.thymos.com/nature/preface.html or Ken Wilber on 'integral psychology'.
[52] <http://p2pfoundation.net/Main_Page>.
[53] See the website http://www.ced.org
[54] See http://www.ced.org/docs/report/report_ecom_openstandards.pdf
[55] Digital versions are available on their website at http://www.ced.org/projects/ecom.shtml
[56] Available electronically at http://www.oecd.org/document/41/0,3343,en_2649_201185_3865949 7_1_1_1_1,00.html
[57] Available at http://www.olcos.org/cms/upload/docs/olcos_roadmap.pdf
[58] Available at http://www.oerderves.org/wp-content/uploads/2007/03/a-review-of-the-open-educational -resources-oer-movement_final.pdf
[59] I prefer the term OE to OER because it embraces the notion of *practices* as well as the notion of sharing educational resources and also because it gels with open source, open access, and open science (as well as open innovation).

REFERENCES

Atkins, D. E., Brown, J. S., & Allen, L., Hammond, A. L. (2007). *Review of the Open Educational Resources (OER) movement: Achievements, challenges, and new opportunities.* Report to The William and Flora Hewlett Foundation. Retrieved from http://www.hewlett.org/NR/rdonlyres/5D2E3386-3974-4314-8F675C2F22EC4F9B/0/AReviewoftheOpenEducationalResourcesOERMovement_BlogLink .pdf

Bailey, C. W., Jr. (2001). Evolution of an electronic book: The scholarly electronic publishing bibliography. *The Journal of Electronic Publishing, 7*(2). Retrieved from http://www.press.umich.edu/jep/07-02/bailey.html

Bailey, C. W., Jr. (1996–2006). *Scholarly electronic publishing bibliography.* Houston, TX: Author. Retrieved from <URL:http://sepb.digital-scholarship.org/>

Benkler, Y. (2006). *The wealth of networks: How social production transforms markets and freedom.* New Haven, CT and London: Yale University Press.

Bergson, M. (1977). *The two sources of morality and religion*, (R. Ashley Audra & C. Brereton, with the assistance of W. Horsfall Carter, Trans.). Notre Dame, IN: University of Notre Dame Press [1935].

Bergson, M. (1998). *Creative evolution* (A. Mitchell, Trans.). New York: Dover [1911]).

Björk, B.-C. (2007). A model of scientific communication as a global distributed information system. *Information Research, 12*(2). Paper 307. Retrieved from <http://InformationR.net/ir/12-2/paper307. html>

Bolter, J. D. (1991). *Writing space: The computer, hypertext, and the history of writing*. Hillsdale, NJ: Erlbaum.

Caldwell, B. (2003). Popper and Hayek: Who influenced whom? *Cahiers d' Épistémologie, Groupe de Recherche en Épistémologie Comparée*. Retrieved from <http://www.unites.uqam.ca/philo/pdf/ Caldwell_2003-01.pdf>

CERI. (2007). *Giving knowledge for free: The emergence of open educational resources*. Paris: OECD. Retrieved from http://www.oecd.org/document/41/0,3343,en_2649_201185_38659497_1_1_1_1,00.html

Dupuy, J.-P. (2000). *The mechanisation of the mind: On the origins of cognitive science* (M. B. Debevoise, Trans.). Princeton University Press.

Eichengreen, B., & Leblang, D. (2007). Democracy and globalisation. Retrieved from http://socsci. colorado.edu/~leblang/Site/Research_files/Globalisation%20and%20Democracy2007.pdf

European Commission. (2006). *Study on the economic and technical evolution of scientific publication markets in Europe*. Retrieved from http://ec.europa.eu/research/science-society/pdf/scientific-publication-study_en.pdf

Ferris, S. P. (2002). Writing electronically: The effects of computers on traditional writing. *The Journal of Electronic Publishing, 8*(1). Retrieved from http://www.press.umich.edu/jep/08-01/ferris.html

Fjällbrant, N. (1997). *Scholarly communication - historical development and new possibilities, IATUL*. Retrieved from http://www.iatul.org/conference/proceedings/vol07/papers/full/nfpaper.html

Frischmann, B. (2005). An economic theory of infrastructure and commons management, *Minnesota Law Review, 89*, 917–1030.

Geser, G. (Ed.). (2007). Open Educational Practices and Resources. OLCOS Roadmap 2012. Open e-Learning Content Observatory Services (OLCOS), European Commission. Austria: Salzburg Research/ EduMedia Group. Retrieved from http://www.olcos.org/cms/upload/docs/olcos_roadmap.pdf

Heims, S. J. (1993). *Constructing a social science for postwar America: The cybernetics group, 1946–1953*. MIT Press.

Höök, O. (1999). Scientific communications: History, electronic journals and impact factors. *Scandinavian Journal of Rehabilitation Medicine, 31*(18), 3–7.

Jacobs, N. (Ed.). (2006). *Open access: Key strategic, technical and economic aspects*. Oxford: Chandos Publishing Ltd.

Kaufer, D. S., & Carley, K. M. (1993). *The influence of print on sociocultural organisation and change*. Hillsdale, NJ: LEA.

Morgan & Stanley. (2002). *Scientific publishing: Knowledge is power*. Retrieved from http://www. econ.ucsb.edu/~tedb/Journals/morganstanley.pdf

Nentwich, M. (2003). *Cyberscience: Research in the age of the internet*. Vienna: Austrian Academy of Sciences Press.

Peters, M. A., & Araya, D. (2007a). Network logic: An ecological approach to knowledge and learning. In M. McKenzie, H. Bai, P. Hart, & B. Jickling (Eds.), *Fields of green: Philosophies of educational praxis* (forthcoming).

Peters, M. A., & Araya, D. (2007b). Networks, information politics, and the new paradigm of social production. In P. Smeyers (Ed.), *Educational research/networks and technologies*. Dordrecht: Springer.

Peters, M. A. (2007a). The political economy of informational democracy. In C. Kapitzke & M. A. Peters (Eds.), *Global knowledge futures*. Rotterdam: Sense.

Popper, K. (1945). *The open society and its enemies* (2 Vols.). London: Routledge.

The Ithaka Report. (2007). *University publishing in a digital age* (L. Brown, R. Griffiths, M. Rascoff, Preface: K. Guthrie, Eds.). Retrieved July 26, 2007, from http://www.ithaka.org/ strategicservices/ Ithaka%20University%20Publishing%20Report.pdf

United Kingdom House of Commons Science and Technology Select Committee Tenth Report. (2004). Retrieved from http://www.publications.parliament.uk/pa/cm200304/cmselect/cmsctech/399/39903.htm

Valauskas, E. (1997). Waiting for Thomas Kuhn: First Monday and the evolution of electronic journals. *The Journal of Electronic Publishing*, 3(1). Retrieved from http://www.press.umich.edu/jep/03-01/FirstMonday.html.

Wittenberg, K. (2007, Winter). *Credibility of content and the future of research, learning, and publishing in the digital environment* (Vol. 10, Issue 1). Ann Arbor, MI: Scholarly Publishing Office, University of Michigan, University Library. Retrieved from http://hdl.handle.net/2027/ spo.3336451.0010.101

Wolff, M. (2008, March). The plot sickens. *Vanity Fair*. Retrieved from http://www.vanity fair.com/ culture/features/2008/03/wolff200803

Woolgar, S. (Ed.). (2000). *Virtual society? Technology, cyberbole, reality*. Oxford: Oxford University Press.

FURTHER READINGS

Benkler, Y. (2006). *The wealth of networks: How social production transforms markets and freedom.* New Haven, CT & London: Yale University Press.

Peters, M. A., & Besley, A. C. (2006). *Building knowledge cultures: Education and development in the age of knowledge capitalism.* Boulder, CO & Oxford: Roman & Littlefield.

Peters, M. A., Murphy, P., & Marginson, S. (2008). *Creativity and the global knowledge economy.* New York: Peter Lang.

Peters, M. A., & Roberts, P. (2008). *The virtues of openness: Education. literacy and scholarship in a digital Age.* Boulder, CO: Paradigm Publishers.

Willenski, J. (2005). *The access principle: The case for open access to research and scholarship.* Cambridge, MA: MIT Press.

Michael A. Peters
Educational Policy Studies
University of Illinois, Urbana-Champaign, US

ROSEMARY DEEM

'MANAGING' ACADEMIC RESEARCH IN UNIVERSITIES OR CAT-HERDING FOR BEGINNERS

Unintended Institutional Consequences of Recent Research Policy in the UK [1]

INTRODUCTION

The paper explores some of the institutional, structural and cultural consequences of attempts by universities to 'manage' academic research, which is becoming an institutional practice in many countries, as the significance of research activity to the status and global positioning of universities continues to grow in importance (Marginson & Sawir, 2005; Marginson, 2006). The example of the management of research in UK universities is used as a case study vehicle for this exploration, enquiring into what it means to manage research in contemporary universities and how academics respond to this, as well as the consequences for the integrity of academic work.

To what extent is research management linked to wider requirements for academic efficiency and accountability and to national system-wide policies on higher education, such as the introduction of research quality evaluation systems like the UK Research Assessment Exercise (which periodically subjects academics' research outputs, infrastructure and culture to discipline-based peer review)? Research management is usually undertaken by both career administrators (for example someone who heads up a central research management unit) and academics with, leadership and management roles (such as vice- rectors or vice-presidents for research). There are several reasons why research management is becoming more evident in higher education. These include the crucial place of research in the global positioning of the world's top research universities, the importance of research funding to universities' overall financial health (especially publicly funded institutions facing a decline in the unit of resource) and the growing prominence of large collaborative interdisciplinary research projects. Interestingly, recent research and science policy documents in the UK do not mention institutional research management but it does seem likely that it has arisen as a consequence of both UK-wide research policy developments and through the permeation of higher education by new managerialism (Boudon, 1982; Hood & Peters, 2004; Deem, Hillyard & Reed, 2007). New managerialism is an ideological approach to the management of publicly funded service organisations which has been widespread in its application in western countries and which focuses on markets, quality audit, targets, league tables, performance management, the pursuit

M. Simons, M. Olssen and M.A. Peters (eds.), Re-Reading Education Policies: A Handbook Studying the Policy Agenda of the 21st Century, 319–336.

of efficiency and effectiveness, devolved budgets (for example, from the central university level to faculties or academic departments) and 'doing more with less' (for instance, teaching many more students with the same number of academic staff). The case of academic research management demonstrates how national policy on the quality evaluation and audit of university research (particularly where as in the UK, the outcomes of quality evaluation are linked to differential funding outcomes) can lead to academics losing control of key elements of the research process, such as what to research (and with whom) and where to publish. As Lucas has noted, the "research game" that arises from policies such as the periodic UK Research Assessment Exercise (peer quality assessment by subject/discipline, of research outputs, research income, research students and research culture/ infrastructure) means that academics are no longer in the driving seat in planning and carrying out research or in disseminating the outcomes (Lucas 2006).

Despite this, leading and managing academics is not always easy. Indeed it is sometimes described by manager-academics and university career administrators (e.g finance or human resource directors) as being akin to 'herding cats'. The focus in this paper is on how universities attempt to manage their research at the meso and macro organisational level, through such roles as Department and Faculty Research Directors and Pro-Vice Chancellors/Vice-Rectors/Vice-Principals for research, why they do this and what the possible consequences are. The paper also considers departmental, faculty and central administration of research activity, including the work of central units which specialise in the management of research, consultancy and entrepreneurial and enterprise activity. The paper draws on theories about the permeation of universities by new managerialism (Deem, Hillyard & Reed, 2007) and on the tensions between academic self governance and managerial governance (Kehm & Lanzendorf, 2006); the growth of audit cultures (Strathern 2000), the varieties of strategic activity found in higher education (Jarzabkowski, 2005a) and recent research on the management and leadership of higher education, including a project directed by the author (Deem, Hillyard & Reed, 2007) and studies undertaken by the Leadership Foundation for Higher Education (Petrov, 2007; Smith & Adams 2007).

The question of where the direction and administration of the research of others fits in relation to new managerialism is an interesting one. Kehm and Lazendorf (2007) in their discussion of academic and managerial institutional and system self-governance see these two phenomena as analytically separable. Whilst the former "is constituted by professional communities and their mechanisms of consensus building, based on strong egalitarianism balanced by authority of reputation, (...) institutionalised in the form of collegial decision-making bodies", managerial self-governance "is characterised by the existence of formal hierarchical leadership positions (...) the roles of rectors and deans are redefined by strengthening their capacity to take decisions" (ibid., p. 16) and there is often a shift in how such individuals are appointed, away from elections by other academics or rotating fixed term appointments towards formal appointment systems by university senior management teams. In practice, however, particularly in relation to research management and leadership, it may not be that easy to separate out the dividing line between an academic *qua* academic and an academic who has taken on a leadership role (for example, as a dean or vice-president), as such individuals may have multiple identities which are utilised in different contexts (Deem, Hillyard and Reed, 2007).

Institutional research management and administration is also sometimes described as having strategic elements but what does this mean? A study of university strategising (Jarzabkowski, 2005a) as a "situated, socially accomplished activity constructed through the actions and interactions of multiple actors" (ibid., p. 7) notes that strategy is often regarded as a coherent activity, both in the literature and by those who undertake it. Her research, using longitudinal case studies of 3 different UK universities, found that there are a number of different elements of university strategy. Pre-active strategising concerns informal, localised, bottom-up activity in a particular group (such as an academic department), which has not yet been adopted at organisational level. If it is to become a strategy, it has to gain legitimacy (consent from academics) and become organisation-wide (Jarzabkowski, 2005a, pp. 160–1). Procedural strategising involves establishing legitimacy for an activity by "embedding it in the formal administrative practices of an organisation" (ibid., p. 161) and such activities may have high structural legitimacy (in the form of structural changes to the organisation such as the creation of interdisciplinary research institutes) but lack interpretative legitimacy (that is, academics may not understand why such units have been created), whereas something that is innovative may have high interpretative legitimacy (those academics involved understand the reasons behind its creation) but low structural legitimacy (any change to organisational structure might be not fully implemented as the innovation is still developing). Interactive strategising involves "establishing high level interpretative legitimacy for an activity through face-to-face interaction between top managers and others in the community" (ibid., p. 161). Often this is undertaken for a new activity. Finally, integrative strategising involves "establishing both high interpretative and high structural legitimacy for an activity" (ibid., p. 162). Research strategies might come in all these guises, from departmental based initiatives that are pre-active to an integrative strategy on study leave and a procedural strategy on how to make research funding bids.

Before examining what UK universities are actually doing in respect of research management, it may be useful first to sketch the recent policy background at a system level.

RESEARCH, UNIVERSITY REFORM AND THE UK HIGHER EDUCATION SYSTEMS

The UK which actually consists of four separate higher education systems (with only one entirely privately-funded university)[2] has been at the forefront of global reforms to higher education for more than three decades (Kogan & Hanney, 2000). As is noted in a comparison of system level research governance in four EU countries, the UK has moved since the 1980s from having relatively little higher education regulation to having a high level of it from the 1990s onwards (Leisyte, de Boer and Enders, 2006), whilst at the same time the emphasis on hierarchical self-governance involving lay governors of university boards and senior managers/ leaders has also increased. Consequently it could be argued that the trust which used to exist between senior academic leaders and other academics has declined (Deem, Hillyard & Reed, 2007). A number of UK HE reform policies have specifically concerned university research, including quality audit (Lucas, 2006), which institutions and academics should undertake research (Deem, 2006b; Deem & Lucas, 2007) and the governance of research (Leisyte, 2007). At the same time, since the 1980s, all the UK HE systems have undergone massification of their student intake, with a related expansion in the number of universities, particularly in 1992 when the polytechnics acquired university status (Pratt, 1997; Pratt, 1999). There has also been the development of a more arms-length and contested relationship with the state (Kogan & Hanney, 2000) and in several periods, a reduced contribution (a so called efficiency-gain) from the public purse. Competition between institutions for students, staff and research monies has significantly increased, corporate management has been introduced, giving more decision-making power to lay members of governing bodies and leading to the reconstruction of Vice Chancellors as Chief Executives rather than lead academics. At the same time, there is also a strong emphasis in many institutions on performance management of staff by manager-academics (Deem, Hillyard & Reed, 2007). Higher education has ceased to be free to UK domiciled undergraduate students since the late 1990s and many ostensibly publicly-funded UK universities now rely for their financial health on private funding from applied research/consultancy and international student fees. There is also regular audit of academic standards in teaching programmes and degree awards by the *Quality Assurance Agency*.

Many of the higher education reform policies have affected the basic research undertaken by academics. For example, massification has produced higher teaching workloads and worsened staff-student ratios, leaving less time for research. Selective research funding has encouraged a split between research-intensive and teaching-intensive institutions and between academics who both teach and research and those who only teach. The most prominent system-wide reform affecting research has been the introduction of regular research quality audits whose outcomes are linked to substantial funding for those who are successful. This began in 1986 and 1989 with research selectivity exercises, which from 1992 onwards became known as the *Research Assessment Exercise* (RAE). Successive RAEs in 1992, 1996, 2001 and 2008 have used subject and discipline based peer panels of academics to make quality judgements about the outputs, funding, research students, research cultures and infrastructures and research esteem of academic researchers.

The RAE has been controversial from its inception, both in terms of the processes used in the assessment of quality and in respect of the impact of the outcomes on academics and their institutions. After the 2001 exercise, in the results of which over half of all academic staff entered were in departments obtaining the two highest quality grades (5 and 5*) there were government calls for reform. A review process, chaired by Sir Gareth Roberts (a former rector), reported in 2003. The review made a number of suggestions for change. These included focusing on those departments and institutions which believed themselves to be the most successful in research (with alternative funding streams for those less research-focused), greater comparability across subject panels and more transparency in determining their academic membership, paying greater attention to research infrastructure (such as support for new researchers) and replacing the single quality grade for each submission with a quality profile for each academic submitted (Roberts, 2003). The comparability across panels and the replacement of a single grade by a graded profile of outputs, research culture and infrastructure and esteem factors (e.g. international plenaries, journal editing etc) have been incorporated into the 2008 Exercise.

In 2006, further proposals from the UK government and the higher education funding bodies were made, this time suggesting a replacement for the RAE, a Research Excellence Framework using metrics on research income, postgraduate research student numbers, and bibliometric indicators of quality and impact. For science, technology, engineering and medicine this is planned to be in place by 2010-11, with a combination of metrics and light touch peer review (not yet defined in any document but presumably referring to the retention of subject based panels of academics who might read a small proportion of academic outputs instead of the high proportion read in the 2008 RAE) retained for the social sciences and arts/humanities to be introduced in 2013-14. A consultation on the new framework in early 2008 showed overwhelming support from universities and academics who responded for retaining a peer review element for all disciplines. The merits of a metrics based system (which still rests heavily on peer review of funding applications, journal papers and peer citations) and its effects on different universities, are the subject of considerable debate (McKay, 2003; Weingart, 2005; Sastry & Bekhradnia, 2006). But it is undeniable that the RAE has become an elaborate academic Bourdian game-playing activity (Lucas, 2006) as well as introducing an increasingly bureaucratic emphasis to research. The RAE has further enhanced the status of researchers in higher education *vis a vis* teachers, widened the gap between the elite universities and others, led to heated policy debates about the relationship between teaching and research (Deem, 2006b; Deem & Lucas, 2007) and ensured that many UK universities are obsessed by both their national RAE rankings *and by* international rankings, including Shanghai Jiao Tong and the Times Higher (Marginson, 2006).

At the same time as quality audit of research has been developing, other policy changes are also in train. In 1992 under a Conservative government, a new government office was created, the Office for Science and Technology, which had as its main concerns science policy and research, while English higher education *per se* remained the preserve of a separate Education government Department. In 1993 a White Paper *Realising Our Potential* tried to establish a new strategy for publicly-funded applied research, giving a strong signal that universities should not just see their research as a curiosity-driven activity, funded mainly by government research councils (Great Britain: Chancellor of the Duchy of Lancaster 1993).

In 1997, Lord Dearing led a review of higher education (initiated by a Conservative administration but implemented by a Labour government), which whilst failing to solve universities' immediate financial crisis with which it had been tasked with investigating, said more about student finance, widening participation and learning and teaching than research (National Committee of Inquiry into Higher Education 1997), although the significance of research to economic competitiveness was noted. The Dearing Review also made recommendations on strengthening and streamlining institutional governance and suggested greater collaboration between universities and industry. For some time after its initial election in 1997, the 'New Labour' Government focused on the teaching elements of higher education and on widening the social base of university degree participation. However, it also had its eyes on the costs to the public purse of research and sought ways to limit the cost of supporting basic research. In 1998 New Labour issued a White Paper *Our Competitive Future: Building the Knowledge Driven Economy*, which echoed the Dearing Review's emphasis on learning to learn and stressed the dawn of a learning society in which research and higher education would play a key role. It proposed a ten year programme of government support to enable the UK to close the performance gap with its main competitors by exploiting a modern knowledge-driven economy (Department for Trade and Industry, 1998).

In 2001, a new White paper on science policy appeared, entitled *Excellence and Opportunity – a science and innovation policy for the 21st century* which stressed the role of research in growing the economy, and the importance of excellent science in shaping innovations in the private sector (Department for Trade and Industry, 2001). In 2003, a further White Paper *The Future of Higher Education in England* was produced by New Labour but this time it came not from the DTI but from the Department for Education and Skills. Amongst its recommendations were a greater separation between teaching and research, with institutions deciding which best reflected their mission, recommendations on variable fees for undergraduates and new rules for acquiring university status (with the previous requirement for postgraduate research degree awarding powers removed) (Department for Education and Skills, 2003). Most of these recommendations were subsequently included in the 2004 Higher Education Act. The early 2000s also saw a further shift in the basic versus applied research debate, with the publication of the *Lambert Review of Higher Education/Industry Links* (Lambert Committee on Business-University Collaboration, 2003), a development extending the concern apparent since the 1993 White Paper about how the burden of paying for university research could be shifted from public to private sources and how research outcomes could be made much more useful to industry and commerce. Universities themselves, struggling to do all that was required of them, were in any case increasingly looking to non-government research income as a way of boosting their flagging finances and also exploring other ways to exploit research, from intellectual property rights and spin-off companies to technology transfer. The New Labour government also reminded universities of the importance of their research in order to underpin a dynamic economy, in a 2004 document about world-class education (Department for Education and Skills, 2004).

A potential source of extra research money for universities arose in 2005 when the UK Research Councils announced the introduction of Full Economic Costing

(FEC) for all research grants. This meant that universities would receive an 80% overhead on all staff costs on Research Council funded grants (previously only 46%) and the full cost of academics who are directors or co-directors of funded projects rather than just teaching buy-outs. However, many other research funders, including charities, businesses and the European Commission do not pay FEC, so the benefits remain limited and may also have deterred some potential funders. FEC, in combination with the RAE, has also made bidding for research council funds much more competitive. But FEC has increased the argument for institutional oversight of research activity.

In 2006 the final report of the Leitch Review of Skills *Prosperity for all in the global economy – world class skills* was published, emphasizing how crucial skills for employment (from generic skills such as team work and computer literacy to specific skills such as plumbing) are to the UK's competitiveness and urging more attention to the development of skills in schools, further and higher education and in employment (Leitch, 2006). This review was not about universities *per se* but the importance of both generic and specific skills being part of HE's portfolio (for instance more programmes run as a collaboration between higher education and industry) was emphasized. The Leitch Review may partly explain another recent development in England. From 1992 onwards, oversight of research by government was split between two government departments, the Department for Trade and Industry whose Office for Science and Technology controlled the research funding councils and UK science policy and the Department for Education, which was responsible for higher education in England. However, following Gordon Brown's appointment as New Labour's Prime Minister in succession to Tony Blair in June 2007, research and higher education were transferred to a single Department, the Department for Innovation, Universities and Skills (DIUS), with schools moved to another new Department (Schools, Children and Families). DIUS's name drives home the science/HE/innovation link.

This brief over-view of recent higher education policy in the UK points to the growing importance of higher education/industry collaboration, greater recognition of the significance of scientific research to the knowledge economy and the [3] development of a research audit culture in the last three decades. It is not surprising that in the wider context of a greater emphasis on management and leadership in higher education over that period, (Deem, 2004; Deem, Hillyard & Reed, 2007) research is now seen as far too important to be left up to academics themselves. Such is the permeation of a climate of management into UK universities that overt management of research has now become commonplace. We now turn to a more detailed examination of this management.

ACADEMIC MANAGEMENT OF RESEARCH

What do academics managers and leaders do when they 'manage' research and what does it involve? What are its challenges? The focus in this section is on Pro Vice-Chancellors (Vice-rectors/Vice-Presidents) for Research, Department and Faculty Research Directors. As Jazarbkowski notes, strategic activities which succeed need both structural and interpretive legitimacy. No-one doubts that managing academics is a challenging activity, whatever aspect of academic work is involved. In a UK Economic and Social Research Council funded study of 137 manager-academics in 16 UK universities conducted in 1998-2000,[4] many of our respondents told us that managing academics was very difficult. One Vice Chancellor expressed it as follows:

> managing academics is slightly more difficult, as with managing a herd of cats (...) it's not a job you should take on if you're an individual that's going to lose a lot of sleep over what's going on in the institution.

> (VC, Albus University) [5]

Not only is managing academics like herding cats. In addition, some mechanisms used in other organisations to manage staff simply do not work on academics, particularly in relation to research, as this Pro Vice Chancellor pointed out:

> In practice somebody who doesn't meet their performance indicator or their performance target, I mean you could actually kind of spend a whole lifetime destroying the morale of an institution and achieve very little. To actually get rid of somebody who is hopeless is virtually impossible. It's fine in Business, you say, "Yeah, you sell a hundred thousand packets of Kleenex by the next account date or you've had it." You can't say to an academic (...) "If you haven't done that article by next year you're out." (...) And if you try to do it and change it and get, put in performance indicators (...) you're in danger of creating a culture in which is there is no goodwill at all, in which you know, "I've done my one article for this year, thank you very much, end of story."

> (Pro-Vice-Chancellor, Riverside University)

Although analysts of changes to professions in recent decades, particularly those professions employed in the public services, point to the erosion of trust and discretion and the replacement of trust with accountability (Evetts 2006), persuasion remains a dimension of managing academics:

> they will use their judgement to go for a conference which they think is in their academic or research interests, you know, and so therefore you can usually trust them to do that. Presumably they are not going on holiday, well they might be, but very few of them will actually, you will soon find that out (...).

> (Pro-Vice-Chancellor, Cleeworth University)

At the same time there are also some general trends in the management of universities which affect *how* academics are managed and *who* manages them. As well as a general growth in senior management teams in UK universities (Deem, Hillyard & Reed, 2007), one senior role that has expanded a great deal in recent years is that of the Pro-Vice-Chancellor [PVC] (or Vice-Rector). Where once universities would have had simply a single deputy working with their institutional leader (rector), now many universities have several. These PVC posts are usually part of the institution's senior management team and they tend to have a specific portfolio (for example responsibility for research,, teaching and learning or resources) as well as a more general role deputising for the VC or rector.| It is rare for PVCs to have line management responsibilities or to be budget holders, unlike heads of department, for example. Smith and Adams (2007) note in an interim report on a study of 50 Pro-Vice-Chancellors in 2006-7, that those who undertake the PVC role in the UK share three characteristics: a concern with common standards of quality and maintaining their institution's 'brand', a responsibility for ensuring regulatory compliance (for instance on academic standards) and balancing competing institutional pressures and an interest in strategic change tempered by reference to the particular values of academe (Smith and Adams, 2007). Smith and Adams also observe that PVCs act as key facilitators in relation to institutional boundaries and also broker relationships with academics rather than relying on executive and budgetary power. Thus, in Jazrbkowski's (2005) terms, PVCs work particularly hard at the interactive aspects of strategic activity.

The majority of pre and post-1992 UK universities now have a PVC with a research portfolio. Sometimes it is combined with responsibility for research students or entrepreneurial activities. Research PVCs are usually keen to retain some kind of research credibility as academics in their own right (for example supervising doctoral students or writing academic papers), which they may feel protects them from allegations that they are simply enacting managerialist governance.

Typically, UK Research PVCs develop institutional research strategies, nurture institutional research themes (sometimes as a focus for selective internal investment), chair institutional research committees, try to improve the quality of the research done and the research outputs produced, attempt to raise the RAE scores of departments and increase the number of successful grant applications and endeavour to generate more income from knowledge exchange and commercial exploitation of research results. Whilst it is often hard to get academics to take on roles such as Head of Department [HoD], with "reluctant heads" being common (Deem, Hillyard & Reed, 2007), it is seldom difficult to fill PVC posts in research. Indeed, as Petrov et al. (2007) noted in their recent research involving 150 interviews in twelve UK universities, this was thought to be so for all PVC roles, which are well paid, high status, often have no line management responsibilities attached, seldom have direct budget responsibilities and can pave the way to becoming a Vice Chancellor if that is desired. By contrast with the challenges of a HoD dealing with frequent anxieties about money, students, teaching and staffing problems, or a Dean faced with competing demands on a shrinking budget, PVCs can work on strategic matters and do more interesting things with their time.

Are PVCs for research an example of managerial rather than academic self-governance? They seem closer to the managerial end of the spectrum in the sense that they are at the top of a clear hierarchy and are expected to take decisions about institutional research direction. But conversely, most PVCs for research have an academic background and may well still be highly active as researchers in their own right. Furthermore, do PVCs enhance research activity or just promote the profile of what is already there? Since the academic 'cats' are still largely autonomous, if there are more successful grant applications, publications are more favourably cited and income from consultancy and knowledge exchange increase, to whom is that attributable? Can it be traced to institutional integrative strategies or to a myriad of pre-active local strategies? Might the successful outcomes that do occur have happened irrespective of the central strategies? If things don't improve but get worse, is that the fault of the PVC Research or a failing of the research strategies (or their perceived legitimacy), or simply that many academics have failed to get their act together?

We know from studies of the impact of the RAE on UK academics that some resent the extent to which they perceive their academic freedom as having been compromised by the RAE's audit processes (e.g in being persuaded to do certain kinds of research rather than others or being pushed to find funding even for research that may not 'need' it) or feel that certain kinds of research and also notably, teaching, are devalued by the emphasis given to the RAE (Harley, 2002; Lucas, 2006). The RAE is largely responsible for the huge amount of attention paid to research in UK higher education. It also helps account for the growth of academic posts concerned with the management of research and the growth of research administration in general. How have academics responded to this? Academics in the UK could be seen as being less resistant to externally imposed changes and reforms than academics in some other countries (Huisman, de Boer & Goedegebuure, 2005). Basic research itself is not necessarily threatened by research management (it could be argued that it is better supported than before) but it may be that basic unfunded research, lone scholar research and risky research are perceived as being or are, discouraged in favour of funded and applied research, research in teams and research that pursues well-trodden paths.

The work of faculty and department research directors has developed in parallel with the work of research PVCs. The range of things faculty and department research directors are responsible for, whilst confined to a more local remit, are not dissimilar to the PVC Research role. That is, they formulate research strategies, develop research themes, chair faculty or department research committees, try to improve the quality of the research done and the research outputs produced, attempt to raise RAE scores of departments and increase the number of successful grant applications. Are these posts also an example of managerialist governance? The roles stem from a similar premise, that individual academics cannot be left to their own devices in relation to research. Compared with other roles in departments and faculties, such as programme leadership or responsibility for students, research roles tend to have higher status and people actually want to do them rather than having to be cajoled into doing them. Furthermore anyone undertaking these roles generally has to have research credibility in their own field. So they may represent a hybrid of academic and managerial governance. Nevertheless, the greater management of research at department and faculty level may be an attempt to turn research into a routine (rather than a creative) activity that can be managed in the same way as endeavours to manage) teaching (for example through timetabling of exact teaching slots, allocation of teaching responsibilities, approval of new units, oversight of curricula and monitoring of exam results and student course evaluations.

ADMINISTRATIVE RESEARCH MANAGEMENT

If academics in senior leadership and management roles find academics somewhat challenging to manage, administrators can find academics even more frustrating. In our ESRC *New Managerialism* research (Deem, Hillyard & Reed, 2007), senior administrators whom we interviewed talked of the problems that they encountered in trying to deal with academic staff:

> the academic teams, someone once said it was like herding cats. You know, it's difficult to get the same degree of cohesion because a disparate group of academics have different loyalties; there's a loyalty to their discipline, the loyalty to the department and then there's the bigger, sort of budgetary unit, whatever it's called and then the institution, whereas administrative staff tend to be much more institutionally loyal

> (Finance Director, Gardenfield University)

> trying to manage anything involving academics is like trying to herd cats (…) It means that you've got this whole group of people who are all independent thinkers and will do things if they think it will suit them (...) but you know, they won't do it just because you say so

> (Senior Administrator, Pathside University)

Career administrators, particularly those that have come into academe from the private sector, can find the management of academics rather different from and more challenging than those of their own staff. However, the extent of the challenge depends on what they require of the academics they deal with and *vice versa*. Some of the administrative jobs connected to research at the department level, whilst demanding, offer a straightforward service that (most) academics are happy to use. The remit of research administration at department/faculty level usually involves alerting academic staff to calls for funding, helping with the mechanics of bidding for research funds, including finances, collating and monitoring the production of research outputs, administering meetings about research and helping to run research events. The work may be informed by department or institutional strategies, and may offer examples of pre-active and procedural strategies (e.g. on research grant applications).

However, central research administration is a different matter and those engaged in this may face some of the same problems as those already noted in relation to Pro Vice Chancellors. It is now fairly commonplace for universities to have central units concerned with aspects of research management and the exploitation of research outcomes. These units contain a range of expertise from RAE and research policy analysis to advance intelligence about funding prospects, contracts, intellectual property rights and technology transfer. Some administrators have a strong academic background themselves, whilst others may have worked for research councils or HE funding bodies, or be from the private sector. As Langley has pointed out, the UK government does not recognise research administration as a specific university function, there is no proper career structure for UK research administrators and no professional qualification for which they can study (Langley, forthcoming), unlike in the USA. So the status and occupational identity of research administrators in the UK remains uncertain, as Collinson (2007) notes.

Furthermore, the tendency for academics to feel loyalty and commitment mainly to their basic unit (Henkel 2000) means that anything provided at a higher level is more likely to be regarded with suspicion. Those central roles that involve dealing with phenomena such as approving contracts, intellectual property rights, technology transfer or the RAE, may invoke an ambivalent attitude from academics, either because there is an inability to separate the message and the messenger (as for example, in the case of the RAE) or because the legitimacy of the task or of the person performing it, are questioned. Just as Gallacher (unpublished) has noted in her study of the boundaries between learning support, library and information management support staff and academic staff [6], that the latter do not recognise the former as having a right to an equal voice (even when the administrators concerned have comparable academic qualifications, which may increasingly be the case), so similar questions and issues of equality, credibility and legitimacy are raised about central research administrators. Collinson, from research with university research administrators, has also raised questions about the occupational identities of such administrators and how they maintain legitimacy (Collinson, 2007). Furthermore, whilst department level research administration is often welcomed, central research administration is likely to be perceived at best as bureaucratic and at worst as a symptom of managerialism. It may also be seen as a problematic use of resources. Such responses, even if not universal, make it difficult for research administrators to do their job properly and may reinforce their sense of trying to herd cats. It can also make it hard to embed research strategies, so that in some institutions there may be a prevalence of pre-active localised strategic activities and some procedural strategising but few institution-wide strategies recognised as having both structural and interpretive legitimacy. There may be a bigger problem with interpretive legitimacy, which is about values and beliefs. Central research administration is likely to be viewed as something that gets in the way of academic self-governance. It may be seen (rightly or wrongly) as favouring applied over basic research, as being more supportive of science than social science and as being more interested in big collaborative funded projects than pushing back the boundaries of knowledge. But despite this, central research administration continues to grow in the UK and elsewhere. The institutional stakes in relation to research success are high and the unintended consequences of government policy and global competition continue to exert themselves.

CAN ACADEMIC RESEARCH BE 'MANAGED' AND WHAT ARE THE CONSEQUENCES FOR BASIC ACADEMIC RESEARCH?

With the greater emphasis on research in UK universities as underscored by many government policies, so research as an activity has come to be seen as too important to be left to academics alone. But unlike many aspects of teaching, such as at institutional level, timetabling, allocation of precise teaching responsibilities, approval of new programmes and monitoring of student progress and assessment outcomes, or at system level, the inspection of academic standards and specification of levels of qualifications and codes of practice for degree programmes from undergraduate to doctoral level by the Quality Assurance Agency for higher education) research does not lend itself as easily to such precise management. As we found in our ESRC study of new managerialism, (Deem, Hillyard & Reed, 2007), both academics and those in academic leadership and management roles agree that research is much less routinised, more creative and individualised, less predictable and not as easily subjected to the same kinds of fairly rigid timetables as teaching. Whereas an academic can be ordered to teach a particular course (albeit this does not guarantee the quality) ordering someone to do research, write a paper or prepare a funding bid is unlikely to achieve the desired result and indeed may produce a kind of rule-following that can prove counterproductive. However, some aspects of the research *process*, from gathering intelligence on the coming trends in research or on the impact of publications through to support in the submitting of successful research bids, *can* be managed, as can things like patents and intellectual property rights. Furthermore, there can also be attempts to specify where research outputs are published. This process management may take a minimal form, such as advice on costing projects or be much more invasive and involve, for instance, the employment of professional grant writers. What is less likely to be involved in universities is the day to day quality monitoring of research, that occurs in organisations which commission rather than undertake research, although attention to research ethics, project management and the careers and training of contract researchers and arranging external reviews of research activity may all be undertaken. There is a clear issue, as we have already seen, about the level at which help with the research process should take place. For instance, academics from Manchester University, which came top in an August 2007 Times Higher Educational Supplement analysis of grant success in UK universities, attributed some of their success to research administration being devolved to the level of academic departments (Radnofsky, 2007). Finally, the oversight of RAE submissions and development of administrative capacity in gathering intelligence about and analysing research policy, both national and international, can also be invaluable and tend to add rather than detract from the contribution to research made by academics.

We have seen that the current approach to research activity in UK universities, both in respect of academics who take on research leadership roles and for administrators who are involved in research administration, is one that relies heavily on local interventions and support at the level of the basic academic unit (which allows for at least the appearance of the retention of academic self-governance) but at a central level utilises a more hierarchical and managerial approach to research. New roles in research leadership, for both academics and administrators, have been created at all levels of universities, and new organisational sub-units have been established. Research strategy development has accompanied this creation of new roles. Yet despite, or perhaps because of the growth of managerial governance in UK higher education (Leisyte, de Boer & Enders, 2006; Deem, Hillyard & Reed, 2007), academics remain challenging to lead and manage.

As workloads and stress increase among academic staff working in UK higher education (Kinman & Jones, 2003; Tytherleigh, Webb, Cooper & Ricketts, 2005) so research comes to be regarded as something which needs protecting from outside intervention, as a private activity often done in individuals' spare time (but then claimed by the institution). Indeed research on academics' motivation suggests that being able to research is one of the key reasons for wanting to pursue an academic career (Metcalf, Rolfe, Stevens & Weale, 2005). The analysis presented here has suggested that the pressures on academic research in the UK are to a large extent the product of policy shifts (albeit ones in which academics and university leaders have been complicit) and that overt research management and administration are symptoms of this rather than the cause.

CONCLUSION

The paper has examined the case of overt institutional management of research by taking the case of the UK, exploring how national policy changes and international developments such as league tables of institutional research achievements have led to much greater surveillance of and intervention in academic research. Such trends are certainly not confined to the UK and are increasingly be found in a variety of higher education systems. The UK itself has experienced considerable reform and change in its public higher education systems over the past three decades, much of it directed towards increasing efficiency, productivity and accountability. During that time, the size and number of universities has grown, the social background of students has changed (and fees for undergraduates introduced), an audit culture for both research and teaching has been established, institutions have found themselves in competition for students, staff and research funding, and the emphasis on managing and leading academic activities in universities has considerably increased, heralding a shift from academic governance towards more hierarchical and corporate management. Much greater government regulation of higher education has been introduced than ever before, at the same time as the unit of resource for universities from public funds has (mostly) been declining. So far as research is concerned, successive attempts since 1986 to measure the quality of research outputs and reward the most successful departments and institutions with more public funding have put pressure on universities to raise the quality and extent of their research activity. Science policy over the last two and a half decades has emphasized the significance of research to the national economy and international competitiveness and to the so-called 'learning society', and has stressed that higher education should collaborate more with industry on applied research and ensure that the results of its research are utilized in practical contexts (knowledge exchange, spin-off companies). Declining public funding has sent institutions searching for new sources of money, in the form of applied research and international student fees. League tables of universities, both national and international, have become a pre-occupation of both government and heads of universities.

As research has become more and more crucial to universities' status and financial health, so research leadership, management and administration (alongside other aspects of administration, leadership and management, such as quality assurance of teaching) has been enhanced as well. This takes many forms, both at the basic unit level and at the centre of the university, and as we have seen, includes both academics (such as Pro Vice Chancellors for research, and Faculty and Departmental Research Directors) and administrators (at department, faculty and central levels). Whilst department level direction and administration of research is often acceptable to academics, central direction and administration, whether by Pro Vice Chancellors or administrative staff, is more likely to be perceived as hierarchical managerialist governance. Research strategies at the local level may be more welcomed than central ones, even if the former lack structural legitimacy, as they are more likely to have an interpretive legitimacy. The question of legitimacy is also applicable to research administrators, who in the UK, despite often having academic credentials, lack a clear career structure and postgraduate qualification opportunities and hence may find themselves disregarded by some academics.

As UK universities have increased in size and complexity, so the challenges of managing and leading academics have become more evident. Research policy and audit, coupled with the increasing global research competitiveness of leading world universities have increased the need for institutions to ensure that academics are more efficient in their conduct of research and that research activity is made fully accountable. This has also put pressure on the kinds of research that academics are encouraged to carry out. Unfunded research done by individuals is receding in importance as funded team-based research and applied research have grown in significance, and the research activities of individuals are much more subject to surveillance than they once were. Similar trends are happening in many other countries too. The academic cats will probably go on refusing to be herded and may continue to resist losing the creative potential of their research by handing control over to others but in the UK, it may already be too late to save this important aspect of academic autonomy. Perhaps, for some other countries, it may not be too late to heed the warning of what is to come.

Acknowledgements

I should like to thank David Langley for a very interesting discussion about research administration in the UK and Jo-Anne Baird for a helpful conversation about the differences between managing research in a university and in government and quasi-government bodies involved in commissioning research. I'd also like to thank Lesley Dinsdale and Kerry Vernon for providing good examples of what excellent research administration/support and policy intelligence should be like.

NOTES

[1] An earlier version of this chapter was presented at the Consortium of Higher Education Researchers Conference on 'The Research Mission of the University' at University College, Dublin, Ireland 30th August to 1st September 2007.

[2] The UK higher education systems comprise 89 universities (counting the Federal universities of Wales and London as two institutions) and 168 other higher education institutions. In 2006 the median income per institution was £80m and the median institutional size by student enrollment, 12,280, with 109,625 full time across the whole UK HE sector Universities UK. Higher Education in Facts and Figures. Universities UK Retrieved October 2006 from http://bookshop.universitiesuk.ac.uk/downloads/Facts_2006.pdf.

[3] This study was a UK Economic and Social Research Council funded study investigating how UK academics, manager-academics, and career administrators perceive the management of higher education and the extent to which it is believed to have been permeated by new managerialism. This research was conducted at Lancaster University, England, by a team directed by the author, in eleven learned societies and sixteen UK universities between 1998 and 2000. The methods used included focus groups with learned societies, interviews with manager-academics and career administrators and four institutional case studies where the views of 'managed' employees (from secretaries and technicians to academics) were compared with those of manager-academics such as rectors and deans.

[4] For this and other respondents' institutions we used pseudonyms.

[5] Cathryn Gallacher is Assistant Director of Information Services at Bristol University and currently completing a part time PhD on this topic. She can be contacted on C.Gallacher@bristol.ac.uk

REFERENCES

Boudon, R. (1982). *The unintended consequences of social action*. Basingstoke: Macmillan.

Collinson, J. A. (2007). Get yourself some nice, neat, matching box files! Research administrators and occupational identity work. *Studies in Higher Education, 32*(3), 295–309.

Deem, R. (2004). The knowledge worker, the manager-academic and the contemporary UK University: New and old forms of public management. *Financial Accountability and Management, 20*(May 2), 107–128.

Deem, R. (2006b). Conceptions of contemporary European universities: To do research or not to do research? *European Journal of Education, 41*(2), 281–304.

Deem, R., Hillyard, S., & Reed, M. (2007). *Knowledge, higher education and the new managerialism: The changing management of UK universities*. Oxford: Oxford University Press.

Deem, R., & Lucas, L. (2007). Research and teaching cultures in two contrasting UK policy locations: Academic life in education departments in five English and Scottish universities. *Higher Education, 54*(1), 115–133.

Department for Education and Skills. (2003). *The future of higher education*. London: HMSO.

Department for Education and Skills. (2004). *Putting the world into world class education. Department for education and skills*. Retrieved August, from http://www.globalgateway.org.uk/Default.aspx?page=624

Department for Trade and Industry. (1998). *Our competitive future: Building the knowledge driven economy: Analysis and background, Cm 4176*. London: HMSO.

Department for Trade and Industry. (2001). *Excellence and opportunity – a science and innovation policy for the 21st century*. London: HMSO.

Evetts, J. (2006). Trust and professionalism: Challenges and occupational changes. *Current Sociology, 54*(4), 515–532.

Great Britain Chancellor of the Duchy of Lancaster. (1993). *Realising our potential: A strategy for science, engineering and technology: A government White Paper*. London: HMSO.

Harley, S. (2002). The impact of research selectivity on academic work and identity in UK universities. *Studies in Higher Education, 27*(2), 187–206.

Henkel, M. (2000). *Academic identities and policy change in higher education.* London: Jessica Kingsley.

Hood, C., & Peters, B. G. (2004). The middle aging of new public management: Into the age of paradox? *Journal of Public Administration Research and Theory, 14*(3), 262–287.

Huisman, J., de Boer, H., & Goedegebuure, L. (2005). *New public management at Dutch Universities. A clash of cultures or peaceful practice?* Unpublished paper presented at the Society for Research into Higher Education Annual Conference, University of Edinburgh, UK, 13th–15th December.

Jarzabkowski, P. (2005a). *Strategy as practice - an activity-based approach.* London: Sage.

Kehm, B., & Lanzendorf, U. (Eds.). (2006). *Reforming university governance: Changing conditions for research in four European countries.* Bonn: Lemmens/Verlag.

Kinman, G., & Jones, F. (2003). Running up the down escalator: Stressors and strains in UK academics. *Quality in Higher Education, 9*(1), 21–38.

Kogan, M., & Hanney, S. (2000). *Reforming higher education.* London: Jessica Kingsley.

Lambert Committee on Business-University Collaboration. (2003). *Lambert review of business-university collaboration.* London, UK: HM Treasury. Retrieved February 2007, from http://www.hm-treasury.gov.uk/media/EA556/lambert_review_final_450.pdf

Langley, D. (forthcoming). Leadership in the management of research. *Engage*

Leisyte, L. (2007). *University governance and academic research.* Doctoral Thesis, University of Twente, Twente, Netherlands.

Leisyte, L., de Boer, H. F., & Enders, J. (2006). England: The prototype of the 'Evaluative State'. In B. Kehm & U. Lanzendorf (Eds.), *Reforming university governance: Changing conditions for research in four European countries* (pp. 21–58). Bonn: Lemmens.

Leitch, S. (2006). *Leitch review of skills: Prosperity for all in the global economy - world class skills.* HM Treasury. Retrieved August 2007, from http://www.hm-treasury.gov.uk/media/6/4/leitch_finalreport051206.pdf

Lucas, L. (2006). *The research game in academic life.* Maidenhead: Open University Press & the Society for Research into Higher Education.

Marginson, S. (2006). Dynamics of national and global competition in higher education. *Higher Education, 52*(1), 1–39.

Marginson, S., & Sawir, E. (2005). Interrogating global flows in higher education. *Globalisation, Societies and Education, 3*(3), 281–310.

McKay, S. (2003). Quantifying quality: Can quantitative data ("Metrics") explain the 2001 RAE ratings for social policy and administration? *Social Policy and Administration, 37*(5), 444–467.

Metcalf, H., Rolfe, H., Stevens, P., & Weale, M. (2005). *Recruitment and retention of academic staff in higher education. National institute of economic and social research & department for education and skills.* Retrieved August 2005, from http://www.niesr.ac.uk/pubs/searchdetail.php? PublicationID=645

National Committee of Inquiry into Higher Education. (1997). *Higher education in the learning society.* HMSO. Retrieved June 2006 from http://www.leeds.ac.uk/educol/ncihe/

Petrov, G. (2007). *No more heroes? Rhetoric and reality of distributed leadership in higher education.* Unpublished paper presented to the South West Higher Education Research Network, University of Bristol, Graduate School of Education, 19th June. Retrieved August 2007, from http://www.bristol.ac.uk/education/research/networks/henetsw

Pratt, J. (1997). *The polytechnic experiment 1965–1992.* Buckingham: Open University.

Pratt, J. (1999). Policy and policymaking in the unification of higher education. *Journal of Education Policy, 14*(3), 257–269.

Radnofsky, L. (2007, August 24). Manchester leads the cash bonanza. *The Times Higher Educational Supplement,* p. 6.

Roberts, S. G. (2003). *The Roberts report on the future of the research assessment exercise.* Higher Education Funding Council for England. Retrieved February 2007, from http://www.ra-review.ac.uk/reports/roberts.asp

Sastry, T., & Bekhradnia, B. (2006). *Using metrics to allocate research funds.* Oxford: Higher Education Policy Institute.

Smith, D., & Adams, J. (2007). Changing roles of the Pro-Vice Chancellor. *Engage,* (7), 14.

Strathern, M. (2000). *Audit cultures: Anthropological studies in accountability, ethics and the academy.* London: Routledge.

Tytherleigh, M. Y., Webb, M., Cooper, C. L., & Ricketts, C. (2005). Occupational stress in UK higher education institutions: A comparative study of all staff categories. *Higher Education Research & Development, 24*(1), 41–61.

Universities UK. (2006). *Higher education in facts and figures.* Universities UK. Retrieved October 2006, from http://bookshop.universitiesuk.ac.uk/downloads/Facts_2006.pdf

Weingart, P. (2005). Impact of bibliometrics upon the science system: inadvertent consequences? *Scientometrics, 62*(1), 117–131.

FURTHER READINGS

Collinson, J. A. (2007). Get yourself some nice, neat, matching box files! Research administrators and occupational identity work. *Studies in Higher Education, 32* (3), 295-309.

Deem, R. (2004). The knowledge worker, the manager-academic and the contemporary UK University: new and old forms of public management. *Financial Accountability and Management 20* (2 May), 107 -128.

Harley, S. (2002). The Impact of Research Selectivity on Academic Work and Identity in UK universities. *Studies in Higher Education, 27* (2), 187-206.

Leisyte, L., H. F. de Boer & J. Enders (2006). England: the prototype of the 'Evaluative State'. In B. Kehm & U. Lanzendorf (eds.), *Reforming University Governance: changing conditions for research in four European countries* (pp. 21-58). Bonn: Lemmens

Marginson, S. (2006). Dynamics of national and global competition in higher education. *Higher Education, 52* (1), 1-39.

Rosemary Deem
Graduate School of Education
University of Bristol, UK

LIFELONG LEARNING

KENNETH WAIN

LIFELONG LEARNING AND THE LEARNING SOCIETY

Critical Reflections on Policy

INTRODUCTION

The notion of a 'learning society' played a fundamental role in the policy literature of lifelong education/learning over roughly three decades, from the 1970s to the beginnings of the year 2000. Nowadays it has virtually disappeared from the policy scene (at least within the European context where I am focusing this critique), replaced by the more fashionable expression 'knowledge-based economy and society' about which much is being written. In this opening statement I am signalling two phases for the notion; a first when it originally found its home in the UNESCO-based lifelong education policy literature of the 1970s, a second where it reappeared in the 1990s, after more than a decade and a half of neglect, in the European Union's policy literature on lifelong learning. The reader will note that, in distinguishing the two phases I use different expressions namely lifelong *education* and lifelong *learning*. Recently Field (2006, p. 11) has described the second as "a slightly different formulation" of the first. But the difference is, in fact, politically very significant. In the European context the dropping of education for learning achieved with the now universal dominance of the expression 'lifelong learning' marks a crucial shift from the UNESCO agenda couched in humanistic terms where the last object is the growth, human and democratic, of individuals and societies, and in a negative evaluation of capitalist societies as venues for such growth (Gelpi, 1992; Suchodolski, 1976) to one, the EUs, couched mainly in the economic language of human capital theory where the individual is a consumer of skills and information in an open learning market. The UNESCO literature itself described its lifelong education discourse as preoccupied with *being* (Faure, 1972) as against a contemporary consumerist discourse preoccupied with *having*. In this chapter I will follow a critical analysis of the changing fortunes of the notion of the learning society within the lifelong learning policy literature of both organisations, and within a body of theoretical literature that grew around it in the late 1990s when its popularity peaked, with some reflections on how I view its future.

THE NOTION PROPOSED

Elsewhere (2004) I have traced the fortune of the notion of the learning society through its history from those early 1970s when it appeared in the Faure report

M. Simons, M. Olssen and M.A. Peters (eds.), Re-Reading Education Policies: A Handbook Studying the Policy Agenda of the 21ˢᵗ Century, 337–354.

Learning to Be (1972) to its virtual demise today. Faure concluded with a long section titled 'The Learning Society'. The early UNESCO-based literature on the notion that followed conceived it in terms of a policy of *mobilising* learning in the interest of its humanistic-democratic agenda. The assumption that the learning society does not yet exist, that it is still to come, gave the writing a distinctly utopian flavour (one factor that led to its eventual fall from favour in the late 1970s and early 1980s). To become learning societies, it was argued by the UNESCO-based theorists of the lifelong education movement in those early 1970s, societies needed to *institutionalise* the notion and practice of lifelong education, re-conceptualise the *whole of learning* (formal, non-formal and informal) as both a lifelong and a *lifewide* process.[1] Labelled the *maximalist* notion of a learning society this idea was regarded as revolutionary at the time, which it truly was. It was pointed out in the literature that the idea that one's education is a lifelong enterprise was common to different cultures and widespread, and encouraged as an enlightened personal initiative in many societies. Western philosophers have regarded it as endemic to a liberal education in the sense that a liberal education is lifelong *by definition* (Peters, 1966).[2] It was the democratisation of the idea that was new and revolutionary; the proposal that the education of all should be a lifelong enterprise rather than for the enlightened few. And this view, in turn, came from growing agreement world-wide that in the fast-changing world of the last quarter of the twentieth century lifelong learning is a need for all – indeed that it will grow into necessity, into a matter of personal survival, for all. The UNESCO-based lifelong education theorists went the extra step of proposing its public provision, its institutionalisation in the notion of the learning society. They proposed that the learning society should occupy the place that mass schooling has hitherto occupied in modern societies as the focus, the 'master-concept' as it was put, for policy-making in education at national and international levels.

Thus, unlike competing conceptions of lifelong learning held by other international organisations like the OECD ('recurrent education'), the Council of Europe (*'education permanente'*), and other understandings in vogue in the Anglo-saxon world (further and continuing education) at the time, the UNESCO-based lifelong education theorists did not, at the beginning, identify it purely and simply with adult education and training (see Wain, 2004).[3] They extended its policy discourse to re-conceptualise the whole of the educational enterprise as a lifelong process extended temporally over the life-span of the individual and spatially over the whole of society. Schooling would, in their understanding, have no *a priori* privileged status in this scenario; it would have to be re-conceptualised simply as a phase in the individual's life and a function of the learning society. In short, the lifelong education theorists understood the learning society as a comprehensive project taking *all* kinds of learning into account in all the locations where it occurs; in the formal sites of schools, colleges, training institutes, universities, and so on, but also in the non-formal sites of homes, neighbourhoods, clubs, work-places, leisure centres, etc., and informally or experientially also where learning occurs unconsciously by interaction with one's environment social or physical (the architecture of what surrounds us, in the broad meaning of the term). More than a straightforward report as commonly understood, the Faure Report of 1972 was a 'manifesto' for the learning society of the future, a call to action, with a leftists political core. From it stemmed a political discourse which militated for a radical participatory democracy with a scientific humanist culture (see Wain, 2004). A discourse to which writers and educators of the lifelong education movement in the immediate post-Faure years, sensitive as they were to the point that a learning society could just as well be an instrument of oppression as one of emancipation, contributed a whole literature.

That discourse, however, and with it the notion of the learning society itself, fell out of favour with the arrival of a second strain of writing within the movement that emerged in the late 1970s. Reacting to the criticisms made against the post-Faure *utopian* thrust of the earlier first strain, the thrust of the second was *pragmatic* (see Ireland, 1978; Wain, 1987, 2004). The criticism made against the first utopian strain was that it was excessively theoretical, that its utopia idealised a Western political model of the learning society, and that the object of the theory was covertly hegemonic, its intention to impose the model on the 'third world' or economically less developed parts of the world. The 'pragmatist' writers of the second strain abandoned the 'philosophical' or theoretical project of constructing utopian models of the learning society for the consumption of international conferences and workshops for experts, in favour of a pragmatic approach that would study the possibility of lifelong education approaches in different localised political and socio-cultural environments through the social sciences. In this way it was also hoped that UNESCO could move from a controversial politics of manifestos to one of investigative study and practical action. The lifelong education literature, accordingly, became historical, sociological, and comparative rather than 'philosophical' and theoretical. Strategically, the pragmatists abandoned the maximalist approach of institutionalising lifelong education in the far-reaching way of their predecessors, which had assumed a strong involvement by the state in partnership with non-formal or voluntary learning agencies and replaced it with a non-revolutionary approach encouraging ongoing autonomous localised action by enlightened communities or radical individual, non-professional 'educators'. The impetus for this approach came from the Italian director of the lifelong education unit at UNESCO in Paris, Ettore Gelpi. With it the connection between lifelong and adult education which (as I noted above) was there from the start in the other venues where the idea of lifelong learning had also caught on, became close also in the UNESCO literature. There, it corresponded with a perception shared by Gelpi with Paul Lengrand (1975) that real, significant, emancipatory, changes to educational practice is possible only in adult education settings; that it was beyond schools and professional teachers, because of the inherently conservative nature of the latter. The difference between the two thinkers and adult educators was that while Lengrand, writing earlier, pinned his faith on the coming into existence of an emancipatory adult education movement creating new, non-formal, revolutionary institutions, Gelpi pinned his faith on the solitary educator experimenting with new ideas and practices in the non-restrictive environments of non-formal learning.

REPROPOSED

Having virtually disappeared through the later 1970s and 1980s, the expression 'learning society' received a new lease of life in Europe in the early 1990s when its reappearance coincided with a renewed interest in lifelong learning generated from a different source, mainly employers and governments, and within a different ambience, namely in the work and employment sector. Born with it was the subsidiary notion of the 'learning organisation'. In 1994 the *European Round Table of Industrialists*, in a vocabulary reminiscent of Faure but with a very different agenda, published a report named *Education for Europeans: Towards the Learning Society* which wanted 'to raise a *cry of alarm* to alert society to the educational gap,' between the needs of industry and the work force and the present educational provision in schools (Cornelis, 1994, p. 6, italics in original). The cry was immediately echoed in different EU countries. In the same year (1994) in Britain, for instance, the Economic and Research Council (ERC) funded a two million pound research programme forthrightly entitled in terms of its purposes *The Learning Society: Knowledge and Skills for Employment* also with a predictably economic and industrial agenda. Its remit was to seek out the links between learning and economic success, between training and competitiveness, and between education, innovation and wealth creation (Ball in Bradshaw, 1995, p. 22). This was the new agenda for lifelong learning that was typically put about by the employers and government policy-makers in Europe. It was not, however, uncontested, even in Britain itself. That same year saw the appearance of Stewart Ranson's book *Towards the Learning Society* (1994), and, again in 1994, in collaboration with John Stewart, *Management for the Public Domain: Enabling the Learning Society*. Both books challenged the economic and work-orientated thrust the employers were giving to the notion of the learning society at the time. Ranson, on his own and with Stewart and others, supported the idea of a learning society as a 'learning democracy' with a strong social orientation instead.

Like Faure's utopian learning society which tended in the same political direction, the learning democracy would have a strongly participative political agenda "supported by a framework of national governance" (Ranson, 1994, 114). Its foundation would be 'a strong system of local democracy' that would allow "citizens from many backgrounds to play an active part in developing their communities, including the education institutions which meet their demands"' (ibid., p. ix). Ranson et al.'s was basically a return to the style of theorising embraced by the utopian lifelong education writers of the early 1970s. Later, in other articles like the one he wrote with Jane Martin and John Nixon (1997) and Glenn Rikowski and Michael Strain (2001), he elaborated more on the notion of a learning democracy. "The predicament we face" today, he said with his co-authors in the first article, "is that although the problems confronting society are public and require a public solution, our society has developed institutions that are not constituted to encourage an active public domain" (Ranson et al., 1997, p. 121). The revival of a public domain that would be the heart of a learning democracy became for these authors the main object of a learning society, and the obvious place to turn to for help for a project of this kind is Habermas. Unsurprisingly, therefore, the learning democracy described in the article writtern with Martin and Dixon had Habermas's theory of communicative rationality at its heart. In another article of the period, John Quicke (1997), also drawing on Habermas, similarly theorised the learning society as a participative democracy with a strong ethos of community and civic cooperation. Quicke shared Ranson et al.'s view that contemporary policy in education was dominated by the neo-liberal discourse of the 1980s which foregrounded a combination of 'free market ideas and neo-conservative authoritarianism,' underpinned by an ethos of choice, diversity and equity in educational governance (Quicke, 1997, p. 139) instead of by civic cooperation, participation and justice (Ranson et al., 1997).

Not surprisingly, given its adoption by the European employers and business lobby, it was not long before the expression 'learning society' attracted the interest of the EU Commission. It appeared in the title of an important official document in 1995, an EU white paper, *Teaching and Learning: Towards the learning society* which replicated the emphasis on employment and employability given to it in the lifelong learning discourse at work in the employment and economic camp. With a gesture of compromise, however, it included democratic citizenship and social cohesion on its agenda for future lifelong learning policy.[4] It is important that the lifelong learning discourse in the white paper, and that which emerged generally in the 1990s was, as I remarked earlier, couched largely in the vocabulary created by the writers of the lifelong education movement of the 1970s and 1980s with the significant difference, referred to in my introduction, that it abandoned the normatively-loaded word 'education' for the normatively-neutral 'learning' and had a different political agenda in that the concerns for democratic citizenship and personal growth that were peripheral to the white paper were central for the movement. Writers of the UNESCO-centred movement, like Suchodolski (1976) had often referred to the learning society as an 'education-centred society' with a view of rendering their emancipatory agenda explicit. Another difference was power. The EU Commission, unlike UNESCO and the other organisations of the 1970s that sponsored lifelong learning policies but that could only produce reports and make recommendations to governments, is a decision-making body with independent power and real leverage on the national policies of the EU member states (see Field, 2001).

Probably because the expression 'learning society' came to them from the sectors of employment and business, most of the writers who used it in the second half of the 1990s were oblivious to its earlier history. In 1996, for instance, the *Open University* produced a book in collaboration with the publishers Routledge named *The Learning Society: Challenges and Trends*. The book edited by Peter Raggatt, Richard Edwards and Nick Small had just one chapter (Hendrik van der Zee's) that dealt explicitly and directly with the notion of the learning society. The other chapters (reflecting the persisting prejudice of identifying lifelong learning and its related terms with adult learning) were about adult learning and training and the contemporary condition of adult *education* in Europe.. Their authors compared the past when adult education had "operated within a liberal paradigm in which adult educators saw themselves as engaged in the transformation of the social condition," with an emerging reality that reflected significant drops of investment in the field of adult liberal education everywhere in favour of more targeted funding justified "in terms of economic benefits flowing from a more highly educated and skilled society" (Raggatt et al., 1996, p. 3). Some also noted a current trend to justify this decline in the funding of adult liberal education by casting it as part of the leisure and entertainment market, a private good that, as such, should be financed personally. Other articles in Raggatt et al.'s book described the growing marginalisation of vulnerable groups of adults from the emerging 'learning society'. But there was no engagement by the editors with the notion of the learning society as such, as a concept, in their Introduction to the book notwithstanding its promising title: "From adult education to a learning society?." They simply limited themselves to the observation that the "learning society" is "today's vocabulary" (1996, p. 1) .

But 'today's vocabulary' was not unambiguous, to the contrary it was highly contested. In the same year that the white paper was published, 1995, Christina Hughes and Malcolm Tight published an article dismissing the learning society as a 'myth' (which it necessarily was in its utopian form) with no corresponding contemporary reality. But, they added, it was not the less powerful for that reason because of the powerful lobby that propagated it; a "wide coalition of interests, including politicians, employers and educators" (Hughes & Tight, 1995, p. 290). In 1997 Richard Edwards writing on his own, in a book named *Changing Places? flexibility, lifelong learning and a learning society*, gave the notion another political dimension. Like Ranson et al., and Quicke, and many of the critics in Raggatt et al., he expressed his fear over the dominant emerging 'myth' of the learning society; a vision that harnessed lifelong learning policies "in ways that are prejudicial to some of the equity goals of supporters of alternative visions of such a society," where the policy agenda was directed "predominantly to equip individuals globally to compete ever more strenuously against each other in the market for qualifications" (Edwards, 1997, p. 21).

Edwards opened with a quotation from Michel Foucault to signal his own particular approach to the learning society. Rather than theorise a counter-programme to the dominant emerging one he critically described (as did Ranson and Quicke, for instance), he analysed the discourse that had come to dominate the education and training of adults in recent years on Foucaultian lines. What an analysis of this kind "makes possible in the discussion of a learning society and lifelong learning," he held, "is an examination of who is setting the agendas, how, what those agendas are and where and how they are contested" (ibid., p. 7). This sceptical-*critical* approach to the learning society is radically different from both the utopian-*theoretical* approach of the first strain of writers/activists of the lifelong education movement and the reformative-*pragmatic* approach of the second strain. Rather than regard the learning society as a society yet to come; still in the making and to be theorised, it regards *every* society as *ipso facto*, in itself, a learning society. The question it raises is what kind? Different from the orthodox, reformative, social scientific methodology of the second strain pragmatists a Foucaultian, genealogical, analysis concerns itself with unmasking power. Following a line similar to but independently of Field, I have shown elsewhere (2004) that Foucault's genealogies could be read as unmasking the 'agendas' and power technologies at work in modern learning societies mobilised for the purpose of policing and disciplining their members rather than for their education.

Though he devoted a large part of his book to analysing the 'regime of truth' underpinning the current discourse of lifelong learning, Edwards only turned his attention to the learning society proper in his last chapter, the shortest. Meanwhile he had simply tagged 'and a learning society' onto everything he had said about lifelong learning up to that point. In this last chapter he described the "learning society" as a notion that "has been rewritten over time and in which different meanings have been ascribed," tracing it back not to Faure or to other roughly contemporary uses of the term but to the *British Economic and Social Research project* mentioned earlier, and to the EU 1995 white paper (Edwards, 1997, p. 173). His conclusion was that though the notion had received much rhetorical support it was still largely unexamined in terms of its practical applications. It did no more, he concluded like Hughes and Tight, than provide "a large banner behind which a range of differing bodies can walk, apparently in some form of solidarity" (Edwards, 1997, p. 175). Nevertheless, he was, usefully, able to distinguish three contemporary discourses which cast the learning society: (a) as an *educated society* tied to a vision of universal provision and democratic participation, (such as Faure's et al. in the 1970s and, to a lesser extent, Ranson's et al. in the 1990s), (b) as a *learning market* tied to an economic, individualistic, consumerist, and largely managerialist agenda, and (c) as *learning networks* conceived as a heterogeneous interactive space of overlapping, interrelated, local, regional, national, international, global societies, with nomadic members participating "in a range of neo-tribal networks with which they identify and through which that identity is constituted" (Edwards, 1997, p. 182). He associated his own sympathies with the last; with a landscape of different local micro-narratives of learning societies (as against the single master-narrative of *the* learning society) that produce a "diversity of knowledges' in a range of different settings" (ibid., p. 183).

In 1998 Edwards was part of a team (that also included Raggatt) that produced a research report for the UK *Department for Education and Unemployment* (DfEE) titled *Recent Thinking in Lifelong Learning.* The report devoted an opening section to 'Visions of a Learning Society' but its bulk was about 'Realising the Vision' rather than elucidating it politically. Again, the notion was described as a "catch all solution to a wide range of social issues with wide ranging appeal for politicians, educators and industrialists" (Edwards et al., 1998, p. 25). But, despite this absence of focus, the report held, policy was still possible based on the existence of 'broad agreement' among the parties concerned on a number of key practical principles germane to the notion like increasing access to and participation in learning, providing continued opportunities for learning, and recognising and valuing other forms of learning (non-formal and informal) than the traditional academic kind. Beyond this, however, the report concurred with Edwards's earlier assessment that "the learning society reveals itself to be a highly contested and problematic concept which embraces many different interpretations" (ibid., p. 25).

Michael F.D. Young echoed this conclusion in his book published in the same year as the report. "Despite the frequently ideological and rhetorical character that they have taken," he claimed (justifying his interest in them), both the idea of lifelong learning and that of the learning society were important because they marked "real social changes" (Young, 1998, p. 2). Like the report of Edwards et al. he described the learning society as "a *contested concept* in which the different meanings given to it not only reflect different interests but imply different visions of the future and different policies for getting there," and declared that he wanted to develop a concept of a learning society that is an improvement on some of the sloganised and rhetorical ways in which it has been used up to now (ibid., p. 140-141, italics in original). Like Edwards (1997) he did not date the concept's origin and first definition to the Faure report (1972) but, unlike Edwards, to Hutchins's (1970) book which, unlike Faure, tied it with the policy of part-time adult education for all, and, like Faure, with a humanistic agenda (with the object of 'becoming human'). Hutchins had also anticipated Faure's maximalist politics of directing all the institutions of the society to these ends. Young, on his part, rejected Hutchins' approach as "little more than another idealistic utopia of the kind that educationalists are so fond of," and that they could theorise *ad infinitum* (the same judgement he would have meted on Faure), and promised more concrete policies (ibid., p. 141).

His narrative of the reappearance of the notion of the learning society in the 1990s was more or less similar to the one I have been relating in this chapter. He described how it first 'began to be used not only by educational theorists but by business and management experts, as well as by governments of the left and right,' then its transition to the current discourse, describing it as a case of 'a utopia becoming an ideology' supporting the agenda of business, then he criticised, on lines similar to those of Edwards and of various contributors to Raggatt et al.'s book (1996) how it justified different "inequalities by masking the extent to which modern societies, as well as depending upon the population's knowledge and skill, are also based on growing inequalities of power and wealth" (ibid., p. 141). He also noted that Hutchins' legacy had not died among utopian progressive educationists where it survived as a rationale "for the democratisation of education and the broadening of access to learning opportunities," in constant competition with this economic model promoted by business and management theorists (ibid., p. 141). For his part, however, he declared himself as out of sympathy with visionaries as with genealogists. He conceded that "what kind of learning society and for whom?" is a "crucial question," but opted for a pragmatic, reformist, approach to it rather than an utopian or sceptical (ibid.,p. 141). Starting from the actual policies/strategic actions that govern learning in contemporary society he identifies three very different models of a learning society at work in it from those of Edwards (1997); the *schooling model* which "starts from the criterion of high participation in full-time post-compulsory education as a feature of a learning society," the *credentialist model* which "takes as the criterion of a learning society the notion that everyone should, if possible, have a qualification that indicates their capabilities," and the *access model*, which "focuses on individual learners and their opportunities for access to learning" (ibid., p. 142).

Critical of all three models for not focussing directly "on learning relationships nor on learning processes but on participation in institutions, gaining qualifications, and on access to learning opportunities for individuals" (ibid., p. 150), he proposed a model of his own which he called the *educative or connective model* which "focuses on the form of learning and in particular the relationship between learning and economic life" (ibid., p. 142). The connective model would, unlike the other models, put learning processes and relationships at the heart of a learning society. Young went on to discuss the changes or reforms to the contemporary system which would be required to bring it into operation; to the traditional curriculum and learning institutions, to the regimes of qualification, to the relationship between learning and production, and to our concept of learning itself. The reconceptualisation of these areas of policy that he proposed would "be of use in giving practical reality to three important ideas: that a society of the future will embody an education-led economy rather than an economy-led education (...) that a curriculum of the future [will be] defined by the kind of learning needs we envision that young people preparing to be adults in the twenty-first century will need (...) [that] work in a learning society could become, as Gramsci once hoped, an educational principle" (ibid., p. 155). The question that arises immediately from these proposals is why we should regard this vision of the learning society as any less utopian than Hutchins', or any less ideological than Faure's. In short, he is unable to avoid the political question 'what kind of learning society and for whom?'

ABANDONED

In sum, the intense debate on the learning society between the middle and the end of the 1990s struggled politically with the notion's policy implications, while, judged on the basis of its actuality, the learning society was regarded (as it had been in the 1970s) as little more than an utopian theory or still-to-be-fulfilled myth. As we saw, there were numerous thinkers around at this time (Ranson, Quicke, etc.) who were ready to give this myth political form; to theorise it as an inclusive and socially just learning democracy, or as decentred, rhisomatic learning networks. Others, however, opted for a different approach. Edwards et al., as we saw, presented a strategy that would dispense with the need for theory by translating the notion of the learning society into a set of strategic commitments to learning policies negotiated between different stake-holders. But the sense of referring to these collective commitments as the commitments of a learning society seems dubious because they do no more than give expression to a more general commitment to lifewide as well as lifelong strategies of learning, which is not necessarily a commitment to a learning *society*. Young, also unhappy with the utopian approach to the notion and similarly committed to a pragmatic approach instead, tried a compromise by creating a model rather than a theory of a learning society. But though models are theoretically less constricting than theories, they do not escape being political any more than do theories. The 1995 EU white paper itself, which had helped put the notion up for debate to begin with, had avoided offering any substantive elaboration of its cryptic support for an agenda that included democratic citizenship and social inclusion besides its emphasis on economic and work-related concerns.

Meanwhile, the turn of the century brought a further shift in the policy discourse of the European Union on lifelong learning. As was pointed out at the beginning of the chapter the notion of the learning society was virtually abandoned and replaced with that of the "knowledge-based economy and society" (EU Memorandum, 2000). The Commission's Memorandum on lifelong learning of 2000 circulated to all the member and candidate countries, went well beyond the 1995 white paper and other policy documents in between in constituting an explicit and concrete attempt to harmonise thinking and to structure action in lifelong learning policy-making, and to standardise the policy vocabulary of lifelong learning across Europe. The year following, 2001, the Commission reminded all member states that the Lisbon European Council of March 2000 had "set the European Union the strategic goal, reaffirmed at the Stockholm European Council in March 2001, of becoming the most competitive and dynamic knowledge-based society in the world" (EU Commission, 2001, p. 6). The white paper had, in fact, already used this expression in its pages, but the more usual expression in use in the EU's policy literature since then is the Memorandum's "a knowledge-based *economy and society*" in that order and with my italics, rather than simply to a "knowledge-based society" (EU Memorandum, 2000, p. 3). The strategic goal of achieving such an economy and society, the communication went on, involves as its more specific objectives: (a) offering tailored learning opportunities to individual citizens at all stages of their lives; (b) promoting employability and social inclusion through investment in citizens' knowledge and competences; (c) creating an information society for all; and (d) fostering mobility of learners and resources (EU Commission, 2001, p. 6). These strategies articulate the changing political agenda underpinning the Commission's lifelong learning policies and the move away from the politics of the learning society. The extent of the success to which it has succeeded in this intention since then is reflected now, in late 2007, as I write this chapter for this book, which, responding as it does to present realities, plans a section (Section III) on 'The Knowledge Society and the Knowledge Economy' but makes no mention at all of 'The Learning Society.' Such a thing would have been unthinkable in the middle to late 1990s.

The adoption of 'knowledge-based economy and society' brings the Commission's policy language in line with the growing orientation of its lifelong learning agenda away from the EU's earlier socio-political goals identified in the 1995 white paper; i.e., those of democratic citizenship and social cohesion, and closer to its more overt socio/economic agenda for the new millennium. Notwithstanding its claim that "a noticeable shift towards more integrated policies that combine social and cultural objectives with the economic rationale of lifelong learning is taking place", the Commission's language is clear; a knowledge-based society is purely a means to an end, the end being a competitive economy (EU Memorandum, 2000, p. 9). What probably made the change of orientation more possible than it would otherwise have been was the transformation in the political language of the New social democrat Left in Europe at the turn of the millennium as it moved towards the political centre and adopted neo-liberal ideas about society and the economy. It created consensus on responsibilising individuals in an open learning market. Young gave a growing tendency to locate learning in the individual, as one reason for his interest in the learning society. "Learning is too important," he had remarked, "to be left to those learning theorists whose mistaken assumption is that learning is an individual phenomenon that must be abstracted from the contexts in which it takes place so that it can be a topic for specialised psychological study" (Young, 1998, p. 2). The danger to the social dimension of learning today captured in the idea of a learning society, however, whatever it may have been at his time of writing, comes not from the psychologists but from the policy-makers. Signified in the collapse of the notion of a learning society, its source is ideological rather than scientific as I shall argue when I return to the politics of the New Left below.

Of course there could be different ways of understanding the statement that the individual learner should be placed at the heart of the politics of lifelong learning. It could be argued, for instance, that it is perfectly compatible with the 1970s discourse of lifelong education which emphasised the self-directed learner as the lifelong learner. But the self-directed learner was conceived in that discourse as *a part of*, not *apart from*, a learning society; one with the skills, ability, and the disposition to exploit and extend the resources of a learning society with a political agenda based on the principles of solidarity and participatory democracy and on the politics of a welfare state – a learning society that recognises learning as a lifelong right for all irrespective of age. More than a *society that learns* (an idea that is perfectly compatible with a society that is radically individualist or atomist), the learning society of the lifelong education theorists was, as I said earlier, a society *mobilised* for learning; a society in which solidarity with others in their learning needs and efforts was of the essence. It required all within the society to recognise what their contribution to the 'mobilisation effort' would be, what the 'challenges' being mobilised against were, and a central agency, the government, to coordinate action with its partners conceived of not, as in the contemporary lifelong learning language, as business and capital but as non-formal organisations and local communities, autonomous learning movements and spontaneous collective initiatives for collaborative learning. The enemy was helplessness, the danger of alienation to the 'being' of individuals, to their feeling overwhelmed in the fast changing world of late capitalism, rather than to their 'having', to the exercise of their powers as consumers, and to national economic competitiveness. "It is tempting to conclude, as some have done," Field remarks, "that the semantic shift from 'lifelong education' to 'lifelong learning' marks a sharp turn towards vocationalism and away from emancipation [Boshier, 1998]" (Field, 2001, p. 12). I would associate myself with those 'some' he refers to. I would argue, with them, that the shift from 'learning society' to 'knowledge-based society and economy' in the same policy discourse, marks the same turn.

Indeed, in 1997 Quicke had identified a rugged individualism with a "particular mix of neo-liberal free market ideas and neo-conservative authoritarianism," at the heart of the emerging lifelong learning policy discourse with the political discourse of the New Right of the time (Quicke, 1997, p. 139). But, the emerging discourse of the New Left social democrat parties also signalled, as I remarked earlier, a broad political consensus with the Right on their mutual allegiance to the free market, and this, in turn, led it to endorse the same politics of rugged individualism Quicke referred to. Translated into policy it responsibilised the individual squarely for her own lifelong learning. This ideological shift in the politics of the New Left, in my view, sealed the fate of the notion of a learning society in the policy language of the Commission. Articulated theoretically by such as Anthony Giddens, the political language of the New Left expresses disenchantment with the old welfare state and favours a "social investment state" instead; one "operating in the context of a positive welfare society" (Giddens, 1998, p. 117). "The guideline" for this new state, Giddens says, "is investment in human capital wherever possible, rather than the direct provision of economic maintenance" (ibid., p. 117). In it "the contract between individual and government shifts, since autonomy and the development of self – the medium of expanding individual responsibility – become the prime focus," for policy (ibid., p. 128). The state, on its part, partners employers and the individuals financially to invest in "learning accounts" driven by the individuals themselves (Wain, 2004). The thrust of this policy approach is very clear; it explains the more general politics of self-dependence, of responsibilising individuals for their lives, that underpins the New Left's political thinking. The "overall aim" of government policy Giddens says is "to help citizens pilot their way through the major revolutions of our time: *globalisation, transformations in personal life* and our *relationship to nature*" (ibid., p. 64). This is how the writers of the lifelong education movement intended their policies in lifelong education too. But the 'prime motto' of the social investment state is to be not (like that of the welfare state) to each according to his or her needs but "*no rights without responsibilities*" (ibid., p. 65). Membership in the learning society thus conceived stops being an automatic *right* for all, as it was in the earlier emancipative policy discourse on the learning society from Faure onwards, it becomes something that must be *earned* individually.

The degree to which this thinking has caught on in the whole of Europe was reflected in a EURYDICE survey (2000) prepared for the Commission to present as a document for the Lisbon Council of 2000. Reporting on the contribution of education systems to policies of lifelong learning in the member states of the EU, and referring to the 1995 white paper as "the essential source of reference on Community policy in the area of lifelong learning," the survey document identifies the white paper as having already "placed the responsibility of the individual at the heart of the process" (EURYDICE, 2000, 10). That makes one wonder, however, as I remarked earlier, about the title of the white paper which, misleadingly it would seem (at least according to this reading), indicates not the individual but the learning society at 'the heart of the process'. In any case, the Commission's later communication of 2001 referred to earlier confirmed "*the centrality of the learner*", together with "*equality of opportunity*" and "*high quality and relevance,*" as its political principles (EU Commission 2001, p. 9, emphasis in the original). The last points to a principle of performativity, where quality and relevance are measured against the criteria of efficiency and effectiveness, that is alive everywhere in the EU policy discourse of lifelong learning; a principle which is reflected in the yen to measure and benchmark all learning including the informal or experiential, and which, in turn, reflects a managerialist mentality (a yen to manage people and knowledge) to go with the rugged individualism. This individualism has eclipsed any other notion of equality than that defined as equality of *consideration* in the investment of state and employers in individual knowledge and competencies, an investment which is, in turn, regulated by its anticipated benefit to the economy. Richard Bagnall refers to an "economic determinism" at the heart of this outlook "articulated in recent years in human capital theory," where "the value of education and learning are reduced to – calculated and constructed as – assessments of their contribution and cost to individual, local, national, regional or global economic well-being" (Bagnall, 2000, p. 21).

Equality of opportunity is in any case a very different principle of justice than need and solidarity and perfectly compatible with the discourse of rugged individualism. A policy of mere openness of access to the opportunities for learning and knowledge available is cynical if the barriers that render that access impossible for many people remain. Various contributors to Raggatt et al.'s book list these people as minority ethnic groups, the long-term unemployed, those in unskilled and semi-skilled occupations, women with dependent children, people living in rural areas, older people. They point to the extent to which these significant groups are already marginalised from the available learning resources of our societies. They are likely to be even more so in knowledge societies conceived as learning markets and with what is on offer determined by market criteria – knowledge societies, in other words, that regards learners not as 'students' but as consumers of open or distance learning packages. The discourse of solidarity and equity is out of place in such societies. The only subsidies that are likely to be available for those in need are those that make a good economic return on the investment. Add this way of thinking to the 'she shall only be helped who is able and willing to help herself' mentality ('no rights without responsibilities') of the new social investment state, and the prospects for the vulnerable and helpless are indeed bleak while issues of equity of distribution do not even arise.

Of course, the inequalities in a learning market are more exacerbated by the digital divide; the divide between those who have access to (and the skills and knowledge to operate) the communication and information technologies that are supposed to open the market for all and that are so powerful that lifelong learning is sometimes simply identified with open learning, and those who do not. The Commission's sensitivity to this very basic inequality is reflected in the need it expresses to create 'an information society for all'. The knowledge-based society is an information society, its public sphere is, theoretically, an informed sphere. In this respect, however, van der Zee notes the subtle but crucial shift of meaning from the notion of learning as the *acquisition* of knowledge (learning being acquired knowledge) which underpins the idea of a learning society to the notion of information as the *availability* of knowledge that underpins the information society. An information society, he points out, "is still not an informed society" (van der Zee, 1996, 64). To the contrary, he says, the contemporary evidence is that people, who are the users of information, are taken out of the equation in the emerging information society and feel defeated under the pressure from technology and the economy. "If we don't take action," he warns, "an inhuman, highly technocratic society lies ahead of us see" (ibid., p. 64). 'Taking action,' in the mid-1990s when he wrote, meant militating for a learning society at the heart of which, as he put it, is people not information, people who can make their own critical sense out of the information available.

CONCLUSION

So where are we left today with respect to the notion just over a decade after the appearance of van der Zee's chapter? The conclusion of my narrative is that, in the policy literature in particular, the notion is dead, or practically so. Notions die when they fall or are taken out of use and the expressions that embody them disappear. This is what, in my analysis claims, has happened to the notion of the learning society. Although the odd article still crops up here and there with the term 'learning society' in its title or content, the literature on the subject virtually dried up after the period of intensity in the mid to late 1990s I described earlier. In my view, the facility with which the older discourse of emancipation that underpinned the early theorising of the learning society and the work of some writers in this period has been set aside in favour of this 'economic determinism' referred to by Bagnall (2000) owes itself significantly to events in Europe after the final collapse of Communism (the last surviving totalitarian/revolutionary ideology/system of the twentieth century) in the early 1990s, which collapse led to a crisis of identity in the politics of the Left in the West. This crisis coincided with what Lyotard (1999) describes as a growing 'postmodern' climate of scepticism towards the master narratives that had sustained the modern world and that has led to the dominance instead of the (apparently) 'non-ideological' master narrative of performativism to which all, including the New Left, can, and do presently, subscribe. This state of affairs makes any thought of a comeback for any theory of a learning society with an emancipative agenda more than unlikely in practical terms, in the foreseeable future at least.

In this situation there are different alternatives possible for the notion of such a society. One can persist in proposing it against the postmodern trend, in the effort to revive its emancipative political agenda in the utopian form of old, of the Faure report, Ranson et al., etc., in an oppositional language game to the current language game of lifelong learning, acknowledging its status as a myth, but a myth worth fighting for, a banner for a new movement to militate under, either revolutionary or reformist. Or one can accept that the term has outlived its time and use and relegate it to history as a once coherent notion in a language game that is now dead and no longer part of our world of policy, theory, and action – this would also rule out the politics of reform in its name described by Young. Or, again, one can adopt it in a Foucaultian way as an analytic tool to understand the evolving knowledge-based society as an economy of learning institutions and practices where the knowledge created, disseminated, and negotiated is always inextricably tied with technologies of power that tend to be masked, often subtly and in the interests of oppression or manipulation.

A Foucaultian approach would suggest an activism that is rather different from that advocated by Edwards in 1997 or writing with Robin Usher in 1999 where he repeated his distinction of the three discourses he had made earlier in his book in order to critically eliminate the first two, "the view of a learning society as an 'educated society' (...) cast in modernist terms," i.e., as a master narrative of truth and justice, and in postmodernist terms as a 'learning market', in order to elaborate and justify their joint preference for a society of learning networks (Edwards & Usher, 1999, p. 264). The authors pointed out, with some justification, that hitherto "learning societies have been considered largely as coterminous with nation states," and argued that "the notion of society as a bounded entity," a homogenous political space, has "come to be seen as problematic" in the new postmodern globalised world (ibid., p. 265). In this respect, drawing on Baudrillard (mainly) and Debord, they highlighted the role the communications technologies have played in creating this world, describing how the media, in particular, have created a "society of signs", of spectacle and simulacra, that challenges "much current thinking regarding a learning society" (ibid., p. 266), by destroying the idea of a homogeneous and bounded public space, and bringing forms of learning to the fore "which barely feature in dominant discourses of a learning society" (ibid., p. 269). In a postmodern world, Edwards and Usher claimed, we must conceive of a learning society as such; as a "society of signs" which needs to be critically scrutinised, and as "a sociality of interactive spaces or communities of practice with multiple and shared sentiments, collective bonds and customs," which people "sign on" to in order to participate (ibid., p. 265). Baudrillard's (1983) own hypothesis about the state of mesmerised stasis of the 'society of signs' whose members are seduced by the media into fascinated silence rules out this form of action within it. Still, despite this pessimism, his work twinned with Foucault's, could, as I have suggested elsewhere (2004), serve the purposes of critical analysis (the purposes of 'scrutiny' referred to by Edwards and Usher) in an approach that regards the notion of a 'learning society' not in terms of some future state to be achieved but as the actual state of present-day postmodern societies with the political features described above. The strategy of finding subversive emancipative spaces within these societies by creating interactive learning networks of the kind Edwards and Usher suggest, could be one way to respond to the more sinister forms the politics of performativism may take in them. Foucault, on his part, would want the nodes of resistance in any such networks to have a more temporary, responsive, tactical nature instead. His would be a tactics of concrete temporary alliances rather than a strategy of enduring 'communities of practice'.

NOTES

[1] The report *Learning to be* prepared for UNESCO by a committee chaired by Edgar Faure and published in 1972 was the culmination of a debate within the organisation that had started in the first half of the 1960s. At that time, UNESCO had adopted lifelong education as the 'master concept' for its policy discourse in education and training. Though there had already been some earlier writings on the subject, the Faure report launched a body of literature that sought to articulate a philosophy of lifelong education together with its policy implications to which the notion of the learning society was central. Though the individual contributors to this literature, writers like R.H. Dave, Paul Lengrand, Bogdan Suchodolski, A. J. Cropley and, later on, Ettore Gelpi, never constituted themselves formally as a movement, their writings were consistent enough to merit that name.

[2] Difficulty has, however, been encountered with accommodating the idea of lifelong education, as, by definition a permanently unfinished enterprise, with that of the 'educated person' which was central to liberal thinking right into the 1980s, For being an educated person, as John White (1982) has argued, signifies a point of arrival or completion – the point at which one becomes such a person.

[3] While the notion of lifelong education regarded education as concurrent with life the other notions understood the relationship education/life differently. Recurrent education was already tied with the interests of the workplace at the time. It saw lifelong learning as an on/off affair with periods of adult education (requiring special 'educational leave' for workers) alternating with periods of non-education. On the other hand, further and continuing education was about topping up or 'adding on' on schooling through different courses. Both strategies were designed to build on traditional compulsory schooling while lifelong education was about a strategic re-consideration of schooling not as *preparatory* to adult learning but as part of the learning society.

[4] The white paper concludes the last section of its "five general objectives for action"(1995, p. 9) by saying that "at least as much emphasis" should be placed "on the personal fulfilment of its citizens, men and women alike, as it has up to now placed on economic and monetary issues" (1995, p. 11). But this 'emphasis' is not actually reflected in the white paper.

REFERENCES

Bagnall, R. G. (2000, Jan-Feb). Lifelong learning and the limitations of economic determinism. *International Journal of Lifelong Education, 19*(1), 20–35.

Ball, C. (1995). Learning does pay. In D. C. A. Bradshaw (Ed.), *Bringing learning to life*. London, Washington, DC: The Falmer Press.

Baudrillard, J. (1983). *In the shadow of the silent majorities*. New York: Semiotext(e).

Cornelis, F., et al. (1994). *Education for Europeans: Towards the learning society*. Brussels: European Round Table of Industrialists.

Edwards, R. (1997). *Changing places? Flexibility, lifelong learning and a learning society*. London, New York: Routledge.

Edwards, R., Raggatt, P., Harrison, R., McCollum, A., & Calder, J. (1998). *Recent thinking in lifelong learning*. United Kingdom: Department for Education and Employment (DfEE) Research Report No. 80.

Edwards, R., & Usher, R. (1999, September). A society of signs? Mediating a learning society. *British Journal of Educational Studies, 47*(3), 261–274.

European Union Commission White Paper. (1995). *Teaching and learning: Towards the learning society*. Brussels: European Union.

European Union Commission Staff Working Paper. (2000). *A memorandum on lifelong learning*. Brussels: European Union.

European Commission Communication. (2001). *Making a European area of lifelong learning a reality*. Brussels: Europea Union.

Eurydice European Unit Survey. (2000). *Lifelong learning: The contribution of education systems in the member states of the European union*. Brussels: EURYDICE.

Faure, E., et al. (1972). *Learning to be*. London: Harrap.

Field, J. (2001, January-April). Lifelong education. *International Journal of Lifelong Education*, *20*(1/2), 3–15.

Field, J. (2006). *Lifelong learning and the mew educational order*. Stoke on Trent, Stirling (USA): Trentham Books.

Furter, P. (1977). *The planner and lifelong education*. Paris: UNESCO.

Gelpi, E. (1992). *Complessita umana*. Florence: McColl Publisher.

Giddens, A. (1998). *The third way: The renewal of social democracy*. Oxford: Polity Press.

Hughes, C., & Tight, M. (1995). The myth of the learning society. *British Journal of Educational Studies*, *XXXXIII*, 290–304.

Ireland, T. D. (1978). *Gelpi's view of lifelong education*. Manchester: Manchester University Press.

Lengrand, P. (1975). *An introduction to lifelong education*. London, Sydney: Croom Helm.

Lyotard, J. F. (1999). *The postmodern condition: A report on knowledge*. Manchester: Manchester University Press.

Peters, R. S. (1966). *Ethics and education*. London: Allen & Unwin.

Quicke, J. (1997). Reflexivity, community and education for the learning society. *Curriculum Studies*, *5*(2), 139–161.

Raggatt, P., Edwards, R., & Small, N. (1996). *The learning society: Challenges and trends*. London, New York: Routledge/The Open University Press.

Ranson, S. (1994). *Towards the learning society*. London, New York: Cassell.

Ranson, S., & Stewart, J. (1994). *Management for the public domain: Enabling the learning society*. London: The Macmillan Press.

Ranson, S., Martin, J., & Nixon, J. (1997). A learning democracy for cooperative action. *Oxford Review of Education*, *23*(1), 117–131.

Ranson, S., Rikowski, G., & Strain, M. (2001). Lifelong learning for a learning democracy. In D. Aspin, J. Chapman, M. Hatton, & Y. Sawano (Eds.), *International handbook of lifelong learning*. Dodrecht, Boston, London: Kluwer Academic Publishers.

Suchodolski, B. (1976). Lifelong education – some philosophical aspects. In R. H. Dave (Ed.), *Foundations of lifelong education*. Oxford: Pergamon Press.

van der Zee, H. (1996). The learning society. In P. Raggatt, R. Edwards, & N. Small (Eds.), *The learning society: Challenges and trends*. London, New York: Routledge & Open University Press.

Wain, K. (1987). *Philosophy of lifelong education*. London, Sydney: Croom Helm.

Wain, K. (2001). Lifelong learning: Small adjustment or paradigm shift? In D. Aspin, J. Chapman, M. Hatton, & Y. Sawano (Eds.), *International handbook of lifelong learning*. Dodrecht, Boston, London: Kluwer Academic Publishers.

Wain, K. (2004). *The learning society in a postmodern world*. New York: Peter Lang.

Wain, K. (2007). Lifelong learning and the politics of the learning society. In D. Aspin (Ed.), *Philosophical perspectives on lifelong learning*. Dordrecht: Springer.

White, J. (1982). *The aims of education restated*. London: Routledge & Kegan Paul.

Young, M. F. D. (1998). *The curriculum of the future from the 'New sociology of education' to a critical theory of learning*. London, Philadelphia: Falmer Press.

FURTHER READINGS

Dohman, G. (1996). *Lifelong learning: Guidelines for a modern education policy.* Bonn: Federal Ministry of Education, Science, Research and Technology.

Edwards, R. (1997). *Changing places? Flexibility, lifelong learning and a learning society.* London, New York: Routledge.

Raggatt, P., Edwards, R.., & Small, N. (1996). *The learning society: challenges and trends.* London, New York: Routledge/The Open University Press.

Ranson, S., & Stewart, J. (1994). *Management for the public domain: Enabling the learning society.* London: The Macmillan Press.

Wain, K. (2004). *The learning society in a postmodern world.* New York: Peter Lang.

Young, M. F. D. (1998). *The curriculum of the future from the 'New Sociology of Education' to a critical theory of learning.* London, Philadelphia: Falmer Press.

Kenneth Wain
Faculty of Education
University of Malta, Malta

ANDREAS FEJES

FABRICATING THE LIFELONG LEARNER IN AN AGE OF NEOLIBERALISM

INTRODUCTION

Lifelong learning is an important contemporary theme in many countries and international organizations, in particular in the European Union and the OECD. It is promoted via national and international policies as a solution to the particular challenges of the contemporary age that must be overcome. It is used as a means to promote change and in this it promotes further change; within socio-political systems of governance, institutions for education and training and in our very understandings as citizens in society. Lifelong learning is therefore a significant phenomenon of our times and one that warrants close scrutiny. This chapter thus takes up questions of lifelong learning and the significance of such change. Drawing upon the work of Foucault, it is possible to address such issues, in particular, examining lifelong learning as part of the practices of governing in the twenty-first century, exploring the techniques through which such governing takes place and subjectivities are brought forth.

The aim of this chapter is, thus, to re-read policy discourses on lifelong learning drawing on Foucault's concept of governmentality. More specifically, I want to analyse what kind of rationality of governing is created today in relation to the lifelong learner. What future should be created, how should such a future become a reality, what lifelong learner should be created and how will such a subject be governed? These questions will be elaborated on by analysing the practices of adult, higher, and popular adult education using a historicising approach inspired by Foucault's concept of genealogy (Foucault, 1977; 2003a). The analysis has been made on a discursive level where questions of a 'reality' per se have been omitted. Instead, my starting point is that social reality can only be apprehended through discourse. Thus, my analysis has focused on discourse and techniques, how it regulates what is and what is not legitimate to say, how it constructs ideas of what is good and bad, etc. Through the analysis I want to question the increasingly taken-for-granted ideas about lifelong learning and problematize them as being historically related to the problem of governing within the changing contours of the present.

With the help of the Foucauldian concepts, I analyze and re-read governmental white papers concerning education and popular education for adults produced during the 20th century and at the beginning of the 21st century in Sweden. Thus, I am able to problematize ideas – mentalities – of how the subjectivity of the lifelong learner 'should' be governed during the 20th century, to consider how these have

M. Simons, M. Olssen and M.A. Peters (eds.), Re-Reading Education Policies: A Handbook Studying the Policy Agenda of the 21ˢᵗ Century, 355–368.

been formulated at different times and emerged in new linguistic forms. This analysis will make visible how power operates to exclude as it includes. Through the analysis I want to create a space for reflection on what policymaking does to our subjectivities on a discursive level.

A GOVERNMENTALITY APPROACH

Today, there is a growing focus on the idea of neoliberalism as both an ideology and as an economic theory, which was not the case 30 years ago. In relation to the emergence of neo-liberalism in Thatcher's Great Britain during the 1980s, we could see how some researchers (e.g. Nikolas Rose, 1999) started to find 'new' or different analytical tools as a way to analyse such changes in governing practices. One of the strengths of governmentality was and is that it widens the commonly used concept of 'government'. Nor is it only concerned with governing through lawmaking, the police, decisions in governmental organisations, etc. Governmentality also concerns our everyday life; all the relations we are involved in, not least one's relation to oneself. The concept covers 'the whole range of practices that constitute, define, organize, and instrumentalize the strategies that individuals in their freedom can use in dealing with each other' (Foucault 2003a, p. 41).

The notion of governmentality is made possible through Foucault's (1980) view of power. There is no subject such as the nation-state, who has and uses power against someone else. Power is not the property of an object. Rather, power is relational. It circulates everywhere, operating through relations of power. Taking such a stance makes it possible to analyse government as something more complex than the government of the nation-state. It relates the government of ourselves, the government of others and the government of the state (Dean, 1999), which makes it possible for us to show the complexity of the conduct of government. The focus is not on social, economic and political circumstances that shape thought. Instead, the focus is on how thoughts operate in the taken-for-granted ways we do things and on neo-liberalism; instead of being seen as an ideology, it is seen as a way of reasoning about governing – it is a mode of governing. Thus, governmentality helps us to understand the modern forms of the exercise of power and its different practices of governing. Within a time of neoliberal governmentality, freedom is a prerequisite for government, where those who try to control and limit the freedom of others, are themselves free individuals (Burchell 1996).

More specifically, what is analysed in a governmentality analysis are liberal rationalities of governing. This chapter is structured around four questions that might be posed in a governmentality analysis (Foucault, 1983; Dean 1999): What is the thing to be governed? What is the telos of governing (why govern)? How should governing be conducted? What rationality of governing is constructed? After discussing each question, the chapter ends with a discussion (for a more elaborate discussion on governmentality and a Foucauldian-inspired approach to lifelong learning, see Fejes & Nicoll, 2008).

FABRICATING THE LIFELONG LEARNER AND THE TELOS OF GOVERNMENT

A central question for governmentality analysis is: what is the thing to be governed, i.e. what is the substance to be governed (Foucault, 1983; Dean, 1999)? One could say that it is the material to be worked upon (*what to govern*). For example, Foucault argues that in a general way, the ethical substance today is feelings, which are to be worked upon. It could also be the 'soul' in today's penal discourses. In this chapter I argue that it is the 'desire and will to learn' that is the substance to be worked upon, e.g. you should desire to become a lifelong learner through self-work upon your 'soul'.

Lifelong learning for all has become an increasingly important feature of long-term policy in Sweden. This idea is best understood as a process of individual learning and development throughout a person's entire life, from the cradle to the grave – from learning in early childhood to learning during retirement. It is an all-embracing concept that refers not only to education in formal settings, such as schools, universities and adult educational institutions, but also to the "lifewide" learning in informal environments, both at home and at work (Ministry of Education, 1999, p. 10).

We can see how there is an idea that everyone needs to work on their relation to themselves as a way of positioning themselves as specific kinds of learners – those who are learning all the time. Such a construction should be desired by everyone, and thus I argue that the substance to be governed (fostered) is the desire and the will to learn. According to the texts, learning is not only related to formal settings, but also to non-formal and informal settings such as family life and leisure time. We are always learning and should desire to always learn. Such a construct is related to the question of why govern? Why is there a need for lifelong learners?

According to different texts, Sweden and Europe need to have a highly educated population if they are to be able to compete with the surrounding world. It is argued that Europe must become

> the most competitive and dynamic knowledge-based economy in the world, capable of sustainable economic growth with more and better jobs and greater social cohesion. At the meeting it was confirmed that the union has taken the step in to the knowledge age, with all it implies for cultural, economic and social life. How we learn, how we live and work – all this is rapidly changing. This not only implies that the individuals have to adapt to changes, but also that established patterns of behaviour have to change (Ministry of Education 2000, p. 44).

As can bee seen, it is stated that we are living in a society undergoing rapid change where knowledge is an increasingly important factor in life. The future is constantly changing, and we cannot know anything about the future except that it changes. Further, the speed of transformation of knowledge and information is increasing and somehow such a situation must be handled. According to policy texts, a country becomes competitive by developing its citizen's knowledge and information-processing skills. Further, other countries and regions of the world are developing fast, and this is threatening the positions of Sweden and Europe. Such problems must be handled. It is argued that there are people who do not have the prerequisites to learn, and thus they risk being marginalised. For the welfare of society and of each individual, everyone needs to become lifelong learners. By being in a state of constant learning, the citizens will become flexible and adaptable to the constantly changing future. The solution put forward is education and systems of lifelong learning, which will enable the citizens of these spaces to contribute to the continuing prosperity of a country/region (Ministry of Education, 1998; European commission, 2001). Thus, the telos of government constructed is a prosperous welfare society, which can compete with the surrounding world. Sweden and Europe should be at the forefront of economic and educational development. As a way of reaching such a future, the citizens need to become lifelong learners. Such construction is made possible through enabling the citizens to exercise their freedom, i.e. governing is to take place through the regulated choices of each citizen (Rose 1996).

The lifelong learner is a contemporary construct which becomes clear when we turn our attention to texts from the mid 20th century. In those texts another subjectivity is being shaped. It is stated that Sweden needs a highly educated population to be able to maintain good living standards. The needs of the labour market have to be met. Thus, the adult who did not have the chance to study as a youth, but who has the ability to study, should be encouraged to do so (Ministry of Education, 1952). The texts state that everyone is born with a certain potential, which should be developed in life as a way of achieving happiness, which can be seen in the following quotation.

> The individual, who finds a place in life where he best can use his talent and other resources, will achieve a sense of satisfaction. This is also in the interest of society since the individual can then be expected to make a greater effort in his work (Ministry of Education 1952, p. 14).

Further, a person's ability can be measured using different tests, and in this way persons with an aptitude for studies can be recruited to adult education (Ministry of Education, 1952). Instead of transforming everyone into constant learners, as is the case today, everyone should work on the desire to find the 'correct' position in the world according to one's potential. Another difference from today is that references to competition with the surrounding world is not as emphasised as in the documents from the present time, even if there is a desire for good living standards emphasised during both times. Thus, today and in the mid 20th Century a prosperous future should be created where Sweden has a good living standard. But today, a telos is related to a construction of a more competitive environment than previously. One could say that the definition of good living standards has changed. Further, in the mid 20th Century adult education participates in the construction of such a future through the recruitment and construction of talented adults, while today this is done through the construction of the lifelong learners.

In texts from the early 20th century, the problematisation of government, a situation in which governance is put into question and problematised, is focused on how the citizens will be able to make good political decisions in relation to the introduction of everyone's right to vote. The good of the nation is dependent on a stable political life where everyone is educated to become good political citizens. Lecturers travelling around the countryside need to complement their lectures with suggestions of literature to read afterwards, otherwise there is a risk of superficial education.

> The condition of literature instructions, accompanying lectures, should be one of the conditions for acquiring state funding of any lecture activity. An educational activity that only results in arousing interest in a certain subject matter, without the opportunity for a deeper study of this subject, will lead to shallowness and superficial education (Ministry of Education, 1924, p. 79).

The problematisation of government of the adult is not related to the labour market as in the texts from the mid 20th century and today, nor is it problematised in relation to 'threats' from the surrounding world. Instead, governing is related to 'threats' from within the nation (the superficially educated citizens). Thus, the international character of threats is absent. If everyone is properly educated, they can make good political decisions, which will make the society stable and prosperous. Popular adult education is proposed as a solution for making such a future a reality. Through it, the adult is constructed as a learner in the sense that everyone is seen as having the possibility to participate in popular adult education. But it is a specific group, those without the prerequisites to make good political decisions, that is the target of popular adult education. Work should be done to make the population's desire to become good political citizens which is quite another construct than fabricating a flexible lifelong learner in contemporary time.

Thus, we can conclude that the lifelong learner and the focus on fostering the will to learn is a contemporary construction related to specific ideas of why governing should be practised. To continue the argument, the next question concerns how governing should be conducted.

THE 'HOW' OF GOVERNING

In this section, I ask the question: What techniques shape the ethical substance of the lifelong learner? More precisely, I will discuss how the techniques of educational guidance, risk and recognition of prior learning operate as a way of shaping our will to learn.

Educational guidance and interaction

Educational guidance is a central part of the discourse of adult education in Sweden today. There are ideas about the adult as an entrepreneur who should choose education by him/herself. Not only what to study but also when to study, where to study, how to study, etc. To make such a position possible, guidance is proposed as support for the adult (Ministry of Education, 1998, 2003; Fejes, 2005). In the relation between the adult learner and the educational counsellor, several techniques operate to shape the ethical substance of the adult, which can be seen in the following quotation.

> If the adult education initiative and lifelong learning are to be realized, adult education will have to satisfy the individual needs and be adjusted according to the individual's capabilities. Not least from a motivational point of view, it is important that the individual participates in the planning of his/hers own education and is supported in taking responsibility for his/her own study planning. A dialogue concerning their educational profile, possible opportunities for development and alterative educational organizers is an important service that the municipalities should give the citizens during the different stages of life. An individual study plan should also be a requirement for participating in the adult education initiative (Ministry of Education, 1998, pp. 31–32).

First of all, we have the two-sided relation where the counsellor should give advice, and the adult should choose. This is a two-sided relation based on a specific pedagogy (the dialogue pedagogy). Secondly, such a two-sided relation is also embedded in the idea of an individual study plan. The plan should be created in a dialogue between the adult learner and the counsellor. Such a relation produces a lifelong learner who should work on his/her desires in life by being active and responsible. You have the freedom to choose, but not the freedom not to choose.

We can see such a relation as a practice of confession. We have the one making the confession (the lifelong learner) and the confessor (the educational counsellor). Confession emerged in the Christian faith as a path to salvation through the control of ones desires (Foucault, 1990, 2003b). Previously, one had to renounce one's self so as to be able to take care of the self. Today, such renunciation of the self is not necessary. Instead, we construct knowledge about ourselves through verbalization of our self. Such a practice has spread in society and we make confessions in many different practices. Not as a way of achieving salvation but as a way of achieving our desires in life through verbalising these desires and imposing self-regulation, e.g. in the practice of guidance, in relation to one's love, to one's friends, to one's doctor, lawyer, teacher, etc. Such reasoning can be related to Foucault's discussion on the shift from disciplinary power to one of pastoral power and self-discipline. There is a change from one situation of making changes to a mute and 'docile' body to a situation where the subject makes changes to him/herself through technologies of the self. In the confessional relation, the one making the confession is enfolded in power as he/she becomes subject to the authoritative discourse of the confessor. Through such a relation, knowledge about the lifelong learner is created at the same time as the lifelong learner is fabricated on the basis of such knowledge. Acknowledging the confessional practices means that you also acknowledge the legitimacy of such a practice (Usher & Edwards, 2005), i.e. such practice construct verbalization of ones desires as a 'natural' part of life. Thus, the learner making the confession has accepted being positioned as a specific kind of learner – one who constantly learns and whose learning is never finished (Edwards, 2008).

Guidance and the dialogue-pedagogy can also be seen as an expression of a more general trend in the changes in rationalities of governing. Today, interaction is presented as something central in the discourse of adult education, i.e. active relations to others. You need to actively interact with others in order to be presented with choices possible to make and as a way to take responsibility for your own future – activity is here both the prerequisite and the outcome of governing. Guidance is one governing practice where this can be seen (others could be group work, the use of problem-based learning, etc.). If we turn our attention to the mid 20th century, we can see how active interaction is not part of the relation between the educational counsellor and the presumptive student. Instead, there is a one-sided relation where the counsellor evaluates the adult's potential and then advises the person about what path is suitable in relation to his/her potential (Ministry of Education, 1952).

> In the proclamation of 30th September, 1947, concerning the public employment office (no. 983), it is stated that vocational guidance should be available at the public employment office, with the task of giving the general public advice and information on choice of profession and educational issues and in other ways [offering] suitable measures for promoting the individual's vocational training and adaptation to a profession. (Ministry of Education, 1952, 136)

Here, guidance is defined as providing advice and information on study opportunities and vocational career paths. If we relate this to then analysis in the previous section, where the adult is constructed as talented/not talented, guidance is part of the process in which such subjectivity is fostered. Through a board of exemption and its associated tests, and through the process of guidance, the aim and hope is to get the individual to find the place in life which corresponds to her/his potential. Further, such a definition of guidance discursively constructs a passive subject. Firstly, the adult is defined as talented/not talented through different tests and secondly, she/he is provided with information on what is a suitable path to choose in life based on the results of these tests. Thirdly, the adult not defined as talented is excluded from studying. Here, guidance seems to represent more of a one-way communication than a two-way communication. The subject is not fostered as an active subject who governs her/himself. What we see is a 'visible' kind of governing operating in the discourse, where the counsellor and the board of exemption are construed as the 'state's' representatives in the local practice. They participate in the construction of the desirable subject by carrying out the tests and, based on these, deciding who should study or not.

Thus, there seem to be a shift from the more visible and less interactive governing in the mid 20th Century, to a more active interaction part of governing in contemporary time. What we see is the emergence of a new order of responsibility where there is a shift from a centralised and hierarchical form of governing to a decentralised and horizontal one (Petersson, 2003). Through such a form of governing, the individual is constructed as an autonomous, active person who takes responsibility for his/her life. Such a subject construction is related, as discussed

361

above, to a change in the rationalities of governing where the constantly changing future needs to be handled by constructing a flexible, adaptable population.

Risk

Another technique of governing is the idea of risk. Risk has always been part of our society, but it is not a pre-existing reality (Hultqvist et al., 2003). We can see how risk is part of the relation between the lifelong learner and the educational counsellor.

> Here, the employment office has an important task to handle. It involves providing the unemployed and other people applying for jobs with information about the prospects on the labour market in relation to different educational levels and differing education. What the risks are when ending up in and retaining an unqualified job. This is not only an assignment for the employment office but also for the study and vocational counsellors and the different agencies and authorities that supply them with information about developments in society and about labour market developments (Ministry of Education, 1998, pp. 79–80).

The counsellor should give a presentation of what the labour market looks like to provide the adult with a basis on which to make a decision about what to study. Here, the lifelong learner needs to uncover his/her inner desires once again and relate them to the risks he/she calculates in relation to the presentation given by the counsellor. Thus, based on the calculation of risks and guidance the adult is fabricated as an acting, choosing individual, who plans his/hers own future.

Further, we can also see how risk is part of the idea of a constantly changing future, which can be seen in the different documents. It is stated that we live in a society where the future is not possible to foresee, other than knowing that it will change. In such a future, there are risks which need to be avoided such as low economic development, unemployment etc. Thus, people need to become constant learners who are flexible and mobile as a way of facing such an uncertain future and as a way of minimizing risks (Ministry of Education, 1998; European Commission, 2001).

At first glance, one could view such an idea of risk as an external risk, something that comes from the outside, i.e. risk as something inherited in society and the world. But, as Giddens (2000) argues, today, risk is manufactured based on the knowledge we create concerning ourselves and our world. Thus, the production of 'bad' visions (risks) of the future, which is said to have to be avoided, doesn't come from the outside. Instead, it is a manufactured risk made into a fact through the production of, for example, policy documents. Within these documents, statements about the future, and the future risks, are produced as facts and truth. So are the required actions suggested as to face and minimize these risks. Therefore, each individual is thus made into active subjects (lifelong learners) who have to address these risks based on knowledge produced about them (knowledge about what they know, and what they need to know to become flexible and adaptable to changes). Risk has not become more dangerous than before, instead it has taken on new shapes and today we create our own risks (Giddens, 2000). I argue that such a way of reasoning about risk is part of the construction of a specific rationality of governing. It acts as an argument for why certain measures should be taken and it constructs specific subjects, the one who needs to work upon his/her will to learn.

Recognition of prior learning

Recognition of prior learning (RPL) also operates in the discourse of lifelong learning as to shape constantly learning subjectivities. Through the construction of systems of measurement of ones prior learning, the subject is made into a calculable self who is open to comparisons and interventions. Ones knowledge is measured and compared to the curriculum within the area of which the recognitions is taking place, thus there is also a comparison in relation to others through a normalizing judgement. Foucault (1991) refers to examination as a disciplining technique in which the 'docile' body is shaped by the gaze of examination. A dividing practice is created in which the adult is made into an object of knowledge production followed by a process of subjectification in which the lifelong learner is constructed. Thus, the normal and abnormal is created. In the case of RPL, not only formal knowledge and competencies should be assessed, but also informal knowledge.

> Validating, that is, utilising all the knowledge and competence a person has acquired through lifelong and lifewide learning, results, of course, in a variety of different gains…They do not have to study in areas where they already have knowledge and skills. They enter the labour market faster, can earn their living and contribute to the welfare system. Validation also means that people in lifelong learning can complete formal education programmes in less time. Their real competence is put to good use. They can take on more advanced work tasks or, alternatively, study at higher levels than their previous formal level of knowledge would allow for. They contribute to higher economic growth and are paid higher wages (Ministry of Education, 2001, p. 146).

What we now see is a trend where the informal and non-formal competence/ knowledge should be transformed into formal knowledge. Thus, a greater part of life will be placed under the gaze of examination (Andersson & Fejes, 2005). Here, I would argue that RPL cannot only be seen as a disciplining technique, but also as a technology of the self in which the adult is making changes to him/herself (Foucault, 1991). Since the adult subject knows that everything he/she does might be valuable in a formal sense (the person can have the informal knowledge transformed into a formal document), specific planning of everyday activities can be a way of attaining the desires in life. Through RPL the adult is made to reflect on his/her desires in life and how they can best be attained. Thus, the subject positions him/herself as a learner who constantly learns, in all settings throughout his/her life. RPL becomes a technology of the self where one should work on one's desire and will to learn.

A NEOLIBERAL GOVERNMENTALITY

My main argument drawing on the analysis above is that different texts and techniques produced in the present time concerning adult, higher and popular adult education are constructed by, and construct, a neoliberal governmentality, which has specific effects as regards who the lifelong learner should become. He/she should become an autonomous, self-choosing and self-regulating self who should take responsibility for his/her own life. In a governmentality perspective, the 'state' is not an actor who governs. Instead the state is seen as a changing epistemological pattern of assumptions about government (Hultqvist, 2004) which change over time and space. Today, the 'state' is constructed as the 'enabling state' (Rose, 1999a), which should make it possible for the citizens to make their own choices and it is in the regulated choices of each and every citizen that the state is inscribed. To govern is to get the subjects to govern themselves – the conduct of conduct. But this does not mean that the 'state' is governing less than before or that it is absent from the governing process. Instead, the art of governing has changed and assumed new forms where the 'state' has become more distant from the governing practice.

Thus, a neoliberal governmentality is a particular conduct which enables the construction of the lifelong learner as one who governs and one who is being governed. Such an argument is supported by the historicizing analysis made in this article where I have illustrated how other subjectivities and other ways of governing has been present in other historical practices. It has enabled me to perspectivise the neoliberal rationality of governing constructed today with rationalities constructed earlier on. For example, when analysing texts from the early 20th century, there are ideas that the future can be planned through institutional legislation. The population is to be made into political responsible citizens. To become such a citizen one must participate in popular adult education where one listens to lectures and reads books, which are approved and decided on by the 'state'. I argue, in line with Nikolas Rose (1999a), that there is a 'social state' constructed by the discourses of the early 20th century – a state that plans the future which can be contrasted to the enabling state constructed today.

In the analysis, we can see that there has been a shift in the relation between public and private. In the early 20th century, the future was seen as being possible to plan. Each individual had a responsibility to contribute to the good of the entire population. The expertise of the 'state' intervened in private life, e.g. those not mature enough would be denied certain literature. They would be dangerous to the welfare of society if they did not become educated (Ministry of Education, 1924; Fejes, 2006). A similar construction of the relation between public and private is present in the mid 20th century. Through processes in the form of statistics and intelligence tests, the population could be measured and the future could be planned. Experts, such as a board of exemption, directly intervened in the private life of individuals to define who should and should not study in adult life (Ministry of Education, 1952; Fejes, 2006).

Today, we can see how the division between public and private seem to have vanished. Learning is constructed as a norm, and you as an adult are responsible for always learning, in all settings, throughout your life as a way of creating a good future. You must realize that you are a learner whose learning is never complete. Thus, you should be the producer of knowledge and competencies. Everyone needs to become the 'experts of themselves' (Rose, 1996) where they become educated and knowledgeable in relation to their selves. The ones who do not take responsibility for themselves will become 'the other', the one who does not have the prerequisites to learn. In such a case, they will need to be placed in programs where they participate in an ethical re-programming where the will to learn is shaped, for example in adult education. Thus, they are transformed into active citizens with the prerequisites to make their own choices in order to reach self-fulfilment (Rose, 1996).

We can see such a construct in the discourse of lifelong learning where those at risk, such as the long-term unemployed, social-security dependent, immigrants, etc., need to acquire the prerequisites to participate in lifelong learning through participation in adult education (Ministry of Education, 1998). Without those prerequisites, they are categorised as 'the other', and thus they should be the focus of social policy where work should be carried out on their will to learn. If we compare this to the earlier part of the 20th century, 'the other' was the one who was the target of interventions by experts (Ministry of Education, 1952). The talented one who did not do what his/her inner potential predicted was defined and encouraged to enter adult education. Such a change in relations does not mean that no governing is practised. Instead, it has assumed new forms. Governing techniques have been detached from the political apparatuses and have been reconceptualised in a market of choices. For example, the educational counsellor no longer tells the adult what to do. Instead, he/she presents possible choices in a dialogue with the adult based on risk calculations. Another example is the idea of recognition of prior learning. The adult is presented with the option to have all kinds of knowledge recognised formally, thus he/she know that everything he/she does counts. Through the choice of becoming a constant learner who wants to have his/her knowledge recognised, the adult will become happy and reach self-fulfilment, at the same time as the telos of government will be achieved. One's desires merge with the telos of government. Government has changed where the state is now governing at a distance through practices of self-government.

DISCUSSION

A central question in this chapter has concerned the relation constructed between the citizen of today and learning. When analyzing official documents, when reading newspapers, or when speaking with students, the idea of lifelong learning is often mentioned in relation to an idea that everyone should always have the possibility to enter education at any time in his/her life, at the same time as the idea is that people learn all that time. Further, you should also be keen on learning new things as a way of being able to acquire a job and being able to move between different jobs. What I think is striking is the emphasis on learning as a way of handling oneself in the world. Such ideas seem to be taken for granted, an argument I have pursued in this chapter. What I have wanted to do is to question such reasoning by re-reading policy texts based on a Foucauldian inspired framework. Through the analysis I show how our way of arguing is specific to time and space, and how it is related to the current relations of power, which are produced by and produce discourse. What we can see in the present is how lifelong learning is being inscribed in society as a whole. Society is constructed as a learning society where the notion of "school as Society" has turned into "Society as a school" (Olsson & Petersson, 2005). No longer is learning mostly related to school settings but to 'life'. Nowadays learning is put at stake in the political ambition to govern, thus making lifelong learning important to analyse and problematised.

Such dominating discourse on lifelong learning can be seen in relation to how the aim of adult education is constructed differently today than before. If popular adult education was to make the population into politically responsible citizens during the early 20th century, and adult education was to make the talented adult become what their inner potential predicted in the mid 20th century, adult education today should transform the citizen into a constant learner. However, institutional education does not stand by itself as a promoter of the learning subject. We can see how the discourse of lifelong learning permeates many different practices in society.

Let us take the example of TV shows where we can follow the work of a nanny expert, fitness expert or an expert on sex life. These programs are offered to anyone who wants to learn more about specific issues. Their design invites us to become learners. They shape our desires to be a good father or mother, or our desire to be a healthy person with a good sex life. Similar topics are a major part of the content of newspapers today. There are innumerable places where we can get advice on how to fulfil our desires, and this advice works upon our will to learn – we want to learn how to have a good life. There are many other examples one might take. But my point is to show how the will to learn is emphasised in many different practices, which are not only related to school. It seems as if we are never free from learning. There are always practices that try to foster our will to learn.

CONCLUSION – RE-READING POLICIES ON LIFELONG LEARNING

A central aim of this chapter has been to re-read policies on lifelong learning drawing on some concepts from Foucault. Through my re-reading, it has been possible to destabilise the truths produced in policy documents on lifelong learning – to show how the lifelong learner is a contemporary construct enfolded in relations of power with exclusionary effects. The policy ambitions throughout the 20th century to be inclusive, thus also have the effect of exclusion. However, such exclusionary practices are not mentioned in the policy documents. In one way, the approach I have adopted is a way of making possible a:

revaluation of those values by which we are ruled or governed, showing the humble and mundane origins of the supposedly pure and transcendent, revealing the lies, falsehoods, deceptions and self-deceptions which are inherent within these attempts to govern us for our own good (Rose, 1999a, p. 282).

My hope is that such an analysis has contributed to perspectivising the lifelong learner in a new way as a contribution to a critical discussion on our present. Where are we today and what has made such a position possible? Thus, a space of reflection might be created in which we can bring out how lifelong learning comes to be persuasive and powerful, and how the narrations of it that we come to take as truthful might be made to stutter.

REFERENCES

Andersson, p. , & Fejes, A. (2005). Recognition of prior learning as a technique for fabricating the adult learner: A genealogical analysis of Swedish adult education policy. *Journal of Education Policy, 20*(5), 595–613.

Burchell, G. (1996). Liberal government and techniques of the self. In A. Barry, T. Osborne, & N. Rose (Eds.), *Foucault and political reason: Liberalism, neo-liberalism and rationalities of government.* Chicago: The University of Chicago Press.

Dean, M. (1999). *Governmentality: Power and rule in modern society.* London: Sage publications.

Edwards, R. (2008). Actively seeking subjects? In A. Fejes & K. Nicoll (Eds.), *Foucault and lifelong learning: Governing the subject.* London: Routledge.

European Commission. (2001). *Communication from the commission: Making a European area of lifelong learning a reality.* Brussels: European commission, Directorate – general for Education and Culture and Directorate – general for Employment and Social Affairs.

Fejes, A. (2005). New wine in old skins: Changing patterns in the governing of the adult learner in Sweden. *International Journal of Lifelong Education, 24*(1), 71–86.

Fejes, A. (2006). The planetspeak discourse of lifelong learning in Sweden: What is an educable adult? *Journal of education Policy, 21*(6), 697–716.

Fejes, A., & Nicoll, K. (Eds.). (2008). *Foucault and lifelong learning: Governing the subject.* London: Routledge.

Foucault, M. (1977). Nietzsche, genealogy, history. In F. F. Bouchard (Ed.), *Michel Foucault: Language, counter-memory, practice: Selected essays and interviews.* Oxford: Bacil Blackwell.

Foucault, M. (1980). *Power/knowledge: Selected interviews and other writings 1972–1977.* New York: Pantheon.

Foucault, M. (1983). On the genealogy of ethics: An overview of work in progress. In H. L. Dreyfus & p. Rabinow (Eds.), *Michel Foucault: Beyond structuralism and hermeneutics.* Chicago: The University of Chicago press.

Foucault, M. (1991). *Discipline and punish: The birth of the prison.* Harmondsworth: Penguin.

Foucault, M. (2003a). Governmentality. In p. Rabinow & N. Rose (Eds.), *The essential Foucault: Selections from the essential works of Foucault 1954–1984.* New York: The new press.

Foucault, M. (2003b). The subject and power. In p. Rabinow & N. Rose (Eds.), *The essential Foucault: Selections from the essential works of Foucault 1954–1984.* New York: The new press.

Giddens, A. (2000). *Runaway world: How globalization is reshapening our lives.* Routledge: New York.

Hultqvist, K. (2004). The travelling state: The nation, and the subject of education'. In B. M. Baker & K. E. Heyning (Eds.), *Dangerous coagulations? The uses of Foucault in the study of education*. New York: Peter Lang.

Hultqvist, K., Olsson, U., Petersson, K., Popkewitz, T., & Andersson, D. (2003). *Deciphering educational thought in Sweden in the early 2000: Fabricating subjects in the name of history and the future*. Paper presented at Philosophy and History of the Discipline of Education: Evaluation and Evolution of the Criteria for Educational Research, Leuven, Belgium.

Ministry of education. (1924). *SOU 1924: 5. Betänkande med utredning och förslag angående det fria och frivilliga folkbildningsarbetet*. Stockholm: Ecklesiastikdepartementet.

Ministry of Education. (1952). *SOU 1952: 29. Vidgat tillträde till högre studier*. Stockholm: Ecklesiastikdepartementet.

Ministry of Education. (1998). *SOU 1998: 51. Vuxenutbildning och livslångt lärande. Situationen inför och under första året med Kunskapslyftet*. Stockholm: Utbildningsdepartementet.

Ministry of Education. (1999). *SOU 1999: 141. Från Kunskapslyft till en strategi för livslångt lärande*. Stockholm: Utbildningsdepartementet.

Ministry of Education. (2001). *SOU 2001: 78. Validering av vuxnas kunskap och kompetens*. Stockholm: Utbildningsdepartementet.

Ministry of Education. (2003). *Ds 2003: 23. Validering m.m. – fortsatt utveckling av vuxnas lärande*. Stockholm: Ministry of education.

Olsson, U., & Petersson, K. (2005). Dewey as an epistemic figure in the Swedish discourse on governing the self. In T. S. Popkewitz (Ed.), *Inventing the modern self and John Dewey: Modernities and the travelling of pragmatism in education*. New York: Palgrave Macmillan.

Petersson, K. (2003). *Fängelset och den liberala fantasin: En studie om rekonstruktionen av det moraliska subjektet inom svensk kriminalvård*. Norrköping: Kriminalvårdsstyrelsen.

Rose, N. (1996). Governing "advanced" liberal democracies. In A. Barry, T. Osborne, & N. Rose (Eds.), *Foucault and political reason: Liberalism, neo-liberalism and rationalities of government*. Chicago: The University of Chicago Press.

Rose, N. (1999a). *Powers of freedom: Reframing political thought*. Cambridge: Cambridge University Press.

Rose, N. (1999b). *Governing the soul: The shaping of the private self*. London: Free association books.

Usher, U., & Edwards, R. (2005). Subjects, networks and positions: Thinking educational guidance differently. *British Journal of Guidance & Counselling, 33*(3), 397–410.

FURTHER READINGS

Dean, M. (1999). *Governmentality: Power and rule in modern society*. London: Sage publications.

Fejes, A., & Nicoll, K. (Eds.). (2008). *Foucault and lifelong learning: Governing the subject*. London: Routledge.

Masschelein, J., Somins, M., Bröckling, U., & Pongratz, L. (Eds.). (2007). *The learning society from the perspective of governmentality*. London: Blackwell.

Nicoll, K. (2006). *Flexibility and lifelong learning: Policy, discourse and politics*. London: Routledge.

Rose, N. (1999a). *Powers of freedom: Reframing political thought*. Cambridge: Cambridge University Press.

Andreas Fejes
Department of Behavioural Sciences and Learning
Linköping University, Sweden

ROGER DALE

CONSTRUCTING EUROPE THROUGH
CONSTRUCTING A EUROPEAN EDUCATION SPACE

INTRODUCTION

There has been considerable interest in the possibility and nature of European education policy. While there have been a range of discussions around this issue, interest is piqued by two fundamental, and apparently opposing, factors in particular: the status of education as the most 'national' and most comprehensive, in terms of its coverage of populations, of publicly provided services, and the apparent desire, despite a lack of formal capacity, of the EU, the most fully developed organisation of transnational governance that we have seen, to establish a presence in the area of education. Many of those discussions, however, have had rather parochial foci, often assuming that an EU education policy could be taken as a scaled up version of national education policies, and limiting consideration of the nature of the relationship to studies of the 'effects' of 'EU policy' on national policy. At the same time, the wider contexts of the changes, such as the relationship between globalisation and Europeanisation, seem also to have been taken for granted.

Methodologically, as will be pointed out below, these approaches have assumed and reinforced the continuing centrality of the national as the appropriate level of analysis, and the social democratic state as the model for the governance of education. These not only lead to serious problems of methodological nationalism and methodological statism (see Dale 2005), but they leave a considerable gap in our understanding of European education policy – in the form of an understanding of 'Europe' – which this paper seeks to address. So, while it looks at changes in the use and nature of mechanisms, especially of 'soft governance', such as indicators and benchmarks, in the construction of a European Education Space (EES), it differs from most forays into this area in that its focus is not on how far this construction can be inferred from, or seen through, its effects on Member State education systems, but on its consequences for the idea of, and the nature of, the 'Europe' that informs and gives shape to the posited EES. So, rather than seeking to marshal and appraise the evidence for the existence of such a space from its attributable and/or perceived effects at national level, I will seek to address the questions of how, how far, and under what circumstances 'education policy' moves promoted by the EU have generated a specific 'Europe' of education. I will argue that it is possible to discern three distinct stages in this process over the past decade, and that these changes may be seen as responses to shifts in both global contexts and their interpretation at the European level, and the recursive processes

M. Simons, M. Olssen and M.A. Peters (eds.), Re-Reading Education Policies: A Handbook Studying the Policy Agenda of the 21st Century, 369–386.

of response themselves. I will then briefly describe the processes at work in the three stages and attempt to come to a judgment on the nature and extent of the 'Europe' that frames the Education Space that they have constructed.

CHANGING GLOBAL CONTEXTS OF THE EUROPEAN PROJECT AND THEIR
IMPLICATIONS FOR EDUCATION.

In this section I will consider, extremely briefly, the effects of four significant changes to the external context of the construction of a European Education Space over the past ten years that have profoundly shaped both the nature of the challenges faced by education systems and the possibility of constructing a 'European' response to them. These are: changes in the wider political economic context; changes in the 'architecture' of education systems, including their relationships with capitalism and modernity, and their relationship to each other; changes in the 'capacity' (conceptions of what is feasible) and the 'mandate' (conceptions of what is desirable) of education systems; and changes in the appraisal of the contribution of education systems to the demands created by these changes in context.

Changes in the wider political economic context

The key issues arising from the intensification of neoliberalism are nicely caught in this quotation from Boaventura de Sousa Santos: "The state ceased to be the controlling agency over the articulations among the three pillars of modern regulation (State, market and community) to become the servant of the market and redesign the community to become the same" (de Sousa Santos, 2004, p. 154). Put very simply, neoliberalism swept away some of the key bases of modernity with which it had lived for so long, but which it now found to be an obstacle.

The most effective way of mapping the nature of these changes is to be found in Bob Jessop's (1999) account of the dimensions of change from 1975-2000, which is taken as a framework.

These dimensions are
– A shift in the relationship between the state and the economy from state planning and intervention to minimal state involvement in the economy (though as neoliberalism advances, this changes to a relationship where the state becomes an active enabler of free trade rather than merely not being an obstacle to it). For education this erodes the national economic basis on which the resourcing of education was premised.
– A shift from state to individual responsibility for security and risk, especially in the area of employment. For education, this shifts the relationship between its social and economic functions, from one where the latter supported the former, to its opposite, to the point where we arrive at the concept of 'productive social policy', where social policy's role is to furnish the necessary infrastructure for economic expansion rather than being seen as a beneficiary of economic expansion.

– A shift from a national to a postnational focus, reflecting the decreasing level of 'national' ownership of the economy and the declining influence of borders, as well as the growth of international organisations that carry out many of what were formerly regarded as 'national' prerogatives and responsibilities. For education, this means that the state is no longer necessarily the only party involved in the governance of education. Note that this also requires a rethinking of the methodological nationalist assumption that nation states and their boundaries are the 'natural' containers of societies and hence the appropriate unit of analysis for sociology (see Dale, 2005).

– Changes in the nature and sources of governance, especially of the public sector, which involve a shift from 'state does it all' to a variety of form and agents of governing activities, and from the assumption that the state is the source and means of all governing activity. For education, this means that the national is no longer the only level at which education systems are to be found, and their activities governed.

The architecture of education systems

We might see four components, which are fundamentally grounded in education's links with modernity on the one hand and capitalism on the other, making up this architecture. They are: modernity; the core problems of capitalism; the 'grammar of schooling'; and education's relationship with national societies. These four elements combine, in different and changing ways, to provide the architecture through which 'education' takes place in contemporary societies. They comprise the means of defining education and its purposes, and the means through which it will be delivered. I will now briefly discuss each element in a little more detail.

Modernity and education

The link between modernity and education has been the focus of a group of theorists who advance the argument for a standardised world model of education, based on the principles of the enlightenment, that applies equally to all nation states. First, as John Meyer, who may be seen as the intellectual inspiration of this group, puts it, "the two main goals of the proper modern national state – individual equality and collective progress – come together in an extraordinary worldwide wave of astonishingly homogeneous educational expansion" (Meyer, 2001, p. 6). Elsewhere, Meyer and his colleagues have supplied compelling evidence of this homogeneous expansion, that has come to include effectively all the countries of the world, certainly at a formal level (see Meyer et al., 1992). The spread of the model, however, is not as 'spontaneous' as may sometimes be implied. Indeed the recognition that relationship between the model and its sponsors is not confined to 'diffusion between experts' but is driven by the agendas of leading international organisations such as the World Bank and the OECD points us very clearly to the need not to consider modernity in isolation from the nature of the links with capitalism (see Dale, 2000). Third, the world polity theorists emphasise the importance of science, and the rationalisation, 'scientisation' and professionalisation of an ever increasing range of social issues and problems. These either cease to be subject to, or to be seen as beyond the capacities of, 'local' interpretations and remedies.

The core problems for education

I have argued elsewhere (see Dale, 1989) that the fundamental key to understanding education systems lies in recognising their relationship to the core problems of capitalism, that it cannot itself provide and that it needs an institution like the state to provide. These core problems are: ensuring an infrastructure for continuing accumulation and economic development, such as the *provision* of a diversely skilled labour force; *ensuring* a level of social order and social cohesion; and *legitimating* the inherent inequalities of the system. I suggested that the solutions to these problems were as likely to be mutually contradictory as mutually complementary. Streaming is a good example here; it is claimed to enhance the identification and development of academic strength, thus serving the accumulation purpose, but at the same time it is widely regarded as unfair, thus threatening the legitimation purpose. Attempts to resolve these contradictions lay at the heart of education policy. Essentially, these problems may be seen to set the limits of the possible for education systems, not in the sense that they require particular curricula, for instance – capitalism has shown itself capable of living quite comfortably with a range of different social preferences and movements, for instance, feminism, and has successfully lived with a wide range of different education systems – but in the sense that they lay down what is not in the interests of capital. Such limits are difficult to predict, and may only be recognised when they are breached, but their reality is reinforced by the increasing mobility of capital, which permits rapid shifts from educational regimes deemed to be insufficiently supportive.

The grammar of schooling

This term (see Tyack and Tobin, 1994) is used to refer to the set of organisational assumptions and practices that have grown up around the development of mass schooling and have come to be seen as defining it, to become, in effect, education as practised. The existence of these conventions and of the practices associated with them may become apparent only when breached or threatened. Thus, the spatial separation of 'the school' becomes 'strange' or problematic only when challenged, for instance by current calls for 'any time, any place' learning to replace the current spatially and temporally restricted forms of education. The temporal basis of education is particularly deeply embedded into the fabric, rhythms and even the calendar of contemporary societies, through the conception of the 'school (or academic) year', with its effects on such unconnected items as the cost of holidays, for instance. Schooling is universalist in a number of ways. Universal Primary Education is considered a key step towards eliminating poverty through the *Millenium Development Goals* (see Robertson et al., 2007). Participation in education is the only compulsory requirement of citizens, and the expectation that all will be treated at least formally equally is deeply embedded in the institutional forms of schooling. Finally, education is typically seen as a job for professional experts, with a dedicated teaching force – and this in itself has major consequences for the provision and experiences of education, in terms of implications for funding, access, control and accountability, as well as outcomes. It means that education is assumed to be based on professional norms, rather than those of the state or the market (see Robertson, 2000).

Education as the repository of national tradition and identity

Finally, national education systems are the major means by which societies seek: to define, replicate and ensure their national distinctiveness; to strengthen their national economies; to address their social problems; to influence the distribution of individual life chances. It is this image of 'Education' that most people have in mind when they think about the issue. It provides the grist for national education politics. These national traditions and issues grow from nationally specific path dependencies (policies and practices that take their form from what has gone before); one especially interesting path dependency derives from whether a national education system preceded or followed industrialisation, for instance. Another important area where national path dependencies are significant is in the definition of a national education 'sector'; the set of responsibilities attributed to 'Education' as a sector, or a Ministry, varies greatly, albeit around a common core, which means that they cannot be automatically assumed to be comparable or commensurable on the basis of their common title alone.

The precise forms taken by these elements, and the relationships between them, may vary, but they essentially lay down the parameters of what is to count as education. Each of the elements separately, and their mutual relationships, permit broad interpretation within the limits they set.

Changes in conceptions of the mandate and capacity of education systems

As we saw in the last section, the demands on education systems have always been multiple, and national education systems have attempted to incorporate them in different ways, with different priorities and different degrees of success. The implications of these changes for the governance of education systems have been clearly realised and have begun to be addressed, as discussed above. However, their implications for the mandate and capacity of education systems have been rather neglected by comparison. While there have been repeated calls for education to contribute more to the competitiveness agenda and suggestions that the capacity required to achieve this mandate cannot be achieved at the national level, or by public sector activity alone, but only at European level and with the contribution of the private sector, what these discussions have revealed most starkly is that, as pointed out by John Meyer some 20 years ago (Meyer, 1986), there is not only no agreement over the ends of education, but nor is there any recognised and agreed best way of meeting any such ends should they be identified. This means that though they subscribe to a common set of curriculum categories there are no shared assumptions about what those categories mean, how they are prioritised, or how they are delivered – in short, no common conception of the proper content of education. Neither is there any shared concept of what makes for efficacious education systems. The key point that flows from this in the present context is that one major consequence of the combination of the changing architecture of education systems and the changing demands made of them, on the one hand, and the unchanging technical base from which they might be addressed, has been a proliferation of the search for effective proxies of 'education' and its efficaciousness. Indeed, one major and troubling concerns how far 'education' has come to be identified with its proxies in the form of indicators etc., and the 'best' ways of doing it inferred from their success, defined according to 'scores' on those proxy items.

Changes in the appraisal of the contribution of education systems

One major and relevant consequence of the issues discussed in the last three sections is that education systems have been found wanting in terms of their contribution to the competitiveness and 'Knowledge Economy/Lifelong Learning' [KnELL] agendas. This has produced a steady flow of reports from not just the EU, but OECD and international think tanks both elaborating these shortcomings – often seen to be associated with the architecture of education systems – and emphasising that they cannot be remedied on the basis of existing education systems. Existing national sectors are seen to be framed by and set up to serve much wider sets of interests and issues than is required by Lisbon, and not up to the job of serving Lisbon goals. This is one consequence of seeing the 'European' level of education as a scaled up version of national education systems, and of seeing 'Europe' as having identical political/economic needs as those of its Member States. If Europe is to meet the Lisbon goals, it is argued, those systems require not reform, but transformation, both in ends and means. A similar example of this is to be found in the OECD's 'education scenarios' exercise (OECD, 2001a).

Six scenarios for future schooling are proposed for consideration. The first two of these, 'Bureaucratic School Systems Continue', and 'Teacher Exodus: The Meltdown Scenario' come under the heading of 'Maintaining the Status Quo' and are presented as being inadequate, or even obstructive, to the attainment of the new demands. They are followed by two further sets of two possibilities under the headings 'Reschooling' and 'Deschooling'. If these scenarios focus on the need to change the means of delivery of education more than the means, there are also powerful discourses stressing the need for new kinds of educational ends and the conditions necessary to deliver them. Prominent here are the calls for education to be 'personalised', or customised, if the rapidly changing demands of the KnELL are to be met. We see this expressed in one OECD document as involving the need to move beyond "just in case" and even "just in time" models for education, to one that is aimed at delivering education "just for me" (OECD 2001b, p. 7). Further, a "main political orientation" driving the Lisbon agenda after the Mid Term Review of it progress, which narrowed its focus to one on 'Growth and Jobs' is for; "new priorities defined for national education policies, i.e., turning schools into open learning centres, providing support to (all) population groups, using the Internet and multimedia." (Rodrigues, 2005, p. 6)

In summary, then, these wider changes frame the challenges and opportunities for a European Education Space where the scale and nature of educational governance are changing, where the purposes and contributions of education are under challenge, where there is no strong and shared core content of education, but where its architecture, and particularly the grammar of schooling and its national responsibilities, though under considerable pressure, is still a powerful element of continuity.

CHANGING RESPONSES AT EU LEVEL

In this section I will discuss how existing attempts at EU level to address the kinds of changes just outlined have themselves shaped the possibilities for the construction of a EES.

The fundamental basis for these attempts is the Treaty status of education. As laid out in the Maastricht and Amsterdam Treaties that frame the EU's operations and limitations, compulsory education is a national responsibility, and fully subject to subsidiarity, which means roughly that it is to be carried out at the 'lowest' possible level of governance. In particular the Community has to respect fully the responsibility of the Member States for the content of teaching and the organisation of education systems and their cultural and linguistic diversity. However, there is one significant loophole in the Treaty; Article 149.1 states that "The Community shall contribute to the development of quality education by encouraging cooperation between Member States and, if necessary, by supporting and supplementing their actions, while fully respecting the responsibility of Member States for the content of teaching and the organisation of education systems and their linguistic and cultural diversity" (see OJEC, 2002). Article 149 has been the vehicle of considerable agenda amplification by the Commission in the area of education, while what has been admitted through the 'quality' gateway it offered has moved from being a shared tool for the evaluation of the efficiency of national systems to the means for the delivery of a European education policy that is explicit, political, supranational, based on political coordination rather than technical cooperation, and that has largely replaced common indicators of national efficiency with shared targets, content and criteria for effectiveness.

However, the Lisbon declaration of 2000 brought about fundamental changes in the nature and scope of EU involvement in education policy. Those changes have been well canvassed, but I want to suggest that more broadly, (a) while respecting the functional and scalar division of formal competences represented in Article 149 and the principle of subsidiarity, Lisbon involved effectively a new understanding of subsidiarity in education and (b) at the same time it led to the creation of a new

EES based on a functional and scalar division of the labour of educational governance (see Dale, 2002), that co-existed with subsidiarity without superseding it.

In terms of the first, the Lisbon conclusions, for instance, not only detailed a set of 'Concrete Future Objectives for Education Systems' but specified that they could only be met at the Community and not MS level. This might, indeed, be seen as either replacing subsidiarity with 'supersidiarity', or as interpreting the nature and seriousness of the Lisbon agenda to mean that the Community itself was the lowest possible effective administrative level. In terms of the second, Lisbon essentially both announced 'Europe' as a space of educational governance that creates the conditions for, and asserts the necessity of, a functional and scalar division of the labour of educational governance that cross-cuts Article 149, and provided the crucial mechanism that makes this possible in the form of the Open Method of Coordination. As we shall see, the experience of attempting to construct an EES through the vehicle of the OMC, and the explicit encouragement of 'common goals, multiple routes', has been crucial to its formation.

The conditions of framing an EES, then, must not infringe the set of obstacles just outlined. They must comply with subsidiarity, or be based on particular emphases that are not subject to subsidiarity. As we shall see, one significant way around this problem has been to avoid any suspicion of challenge to national competence, by focussing on areas outside the compulsory sector, such as lifelong learning and activities that are not intrinsic to, or 'property rights' of, any national education system; a key example here is 'competencies', which can be seen to 'cross-cut' curricula and thus offer little threat to national authority since they can in principle be accommodated to any national policy. And finally, such an approach sits very well with the substantive desire to transform existing education systems, and to make use of 'productive social policy' as the key means of resolving the contradictions of Lisbon, which, it should in any case be noted, did not acknowledge education as a "teleological" policy area, an area in itself, but rather it is part of social policy, labour market and overall economic policy (Gornitzka, 2005, p. 17).

I shall suggest below that 'Lifelong Learning' meets both the political economic and the EU specific conditions to provide the basis for a EES, but first I will go through the three stages of development of the EES that are summarised in Table 1.

Phase 1 – Establishing 'quality' as a basis for comparison

As I pointed out above, the absence of any agreed assumptions about what constituted the content of education and what made education systems efficacious opened the door for the creation of proxies, and we see a very good example of how this enabled what might be seen as the problem of the diversity of European education systems to be converted into an opportunity for the creation of the basis of a distinct EES.

Table 1. Phases in the development of a European Education Space

	GOVERNANCE	MECHANISMS	PURPOSE	'EUROPE'
PHASE 1 - PRE-LISBON	Working Party of MS	Indicators	Common conception of 'Education'	Coordinator of National experiences/definer of 'Quality'
PHASE 2- LISBON 2000-05	OMC	Benchmarks; Best practice	Common problem identification and policy coordination, diverse means	Orchestrator of Functional and Scalar Division of Labour of Educational Governance
PHASE 3 - LISBON POST MID TERM REVIEW	Single (LLL) Organising Framework	Targets (e.g. Investment)	Common objectives, common route	Creator of new European 'Social policy' and 'Knowledge policy' sectors

Article 149 expressly permitted intervention in the 'quality' of education systems and 'quality' is an ideal basis for providing an entrée, or a plank of intervention, for the EU in education policy, indeed, for the construction of a European education policy. It is an ideal choice because of two, associated, features. On the one hand, it is vague, flexible and imprecise; it can most usefully be seen as a 'tofu' concept, one that has no meaning of its own but takes its meaning from what surrounds it, which it is then well-equipped to absorb and carry forward. On the other hand, it is neutral, a-political (even seen as being 'above' politics) and a-national; the technical language (and often numbers) through which its presence is detected or inferred stands outside, above and across existing national discourses. It thus represents no threat to existing interests and offers possibilities of 'painless', a-political improvement, the essential negative and positive conditions of acceptable European intervention in education.

The EU's interest in quality indicators emerged in a pilot project on evaluating quality in school education which ran between 1997-8 (see Macbeath et al., 1999), which was followed up by an agreement (at the Prague Ministers of Education meeting in 1998) to establish a working committee of national experts who would produce "a limited number of indicators or benchmarks for school standards to assist national evaluation of systems (...) (with) the objective of (...) identify(ing) areas (supported by indicators) within which comparisons between countries can be made in order to identify good practice, exchange experience and define main policy changes" (Hingel, 2001, p. 13). This eventually emerged in May 2000 as the *European Report on Quality of School Education: Sixteen Quality Indicators* (EU, 2000) – but as we shall see, what emerged departed considerably and very significantly from its remit. This does not mean that the original 'national/technical/efficiency/ indicators' project had been abandoned altogether, but the effectiveness and targets agenda had become dominant, especially after the Lisbon summit. The concern of the 'evaluation/efficiency' agenda was precisely that; evaluating the efficiency of national systems at a national level. The post-Lisbon concern is with enhancing MS ability (i.e. their effectiveness) to identify and attain objectives cooperatively.

By the time of the publication of the document *Sixteen Quality Indicators for Education Systems* (EU, 2000) in May 2000, the 'quality evaluation' programme had undergone a set of rather significant changes. It was certainly no longer centrally concerned exclusively or even predominantly with the quality of school education as it had been construed in the earlier phase. Indeed, 'quality' appears to be interpreted with all the flexibility it inherently possesses. However, when we look at the report, we find a number of difficulties and differences in the ways that it is used. First of all, it contains no definition at all of quality. Indeed, there is substantial slippage, or flexibility, in the uses of the term. For instance, while Article 149 talks about 'quality education', that term never appears in the Report except when the Article is being quoted. In its first page the Report moves to discuss 'quality of education' as a priority issue, and then moves on to talk about 'quality evaluation'. Such differences are particularly important when, 'quality' – at all levels of the education system – is defined by what is 'evaluated' and why, which makes it very much a political issue.

Further, the stated purpose of the indicators, to "allow countries to learn from one another through comparison of common interests and shared differences", while "benchmarks are to provide policy makers with reference points", does suggest at least a move away from evaluating efficiency in the direction of cooperating towards common objectives (OJCE, op cit.). And this move is strongly reinforced when after the introduction there is a sharp, unannounced and unexplained jump in the document to allow the indicators to lead us to identify "five key challenges for the future" – knowledge, decentralisation, resource, social inclusion and data and comparability. This distinct shift of emphasis from indicators and benchmarks to "challenges", from "common interest approaches" and "learning from each other" to "common challenges/agendas", clearly underlines the nature of the shift that has taken place in the approach and purpose of the programme. It seems plausible to infer that the "Five Challenges" section was written after the rest of the paper, and after the publication of the Lisbon agenda.[1] The Introduction to the *Sixteen Quality Indicators for Education Systems* report says that it "represents the Commission's first response to the Lisbon conclusions." However, as we have seen, the programme it reported on was not and could not have been originally conceived in those terms.

Phase 2 – Constructing a European Education Space through the Open Method of Coordination

The means by which the unprecedented shift in the nature of education policy at the European level called for by Lisbon were to be achieved were also specified in the Lisbon Council. The means selected was the Open Method of Coordination (OMC). Its main appeal was that it offered the possibility of overcoming the impasse in European policy caused by the limitations of the two main routes – 'hard law' and 'harmonisation' – to integration, regulation and consensus. It promised to achieve this pre-eminently through the prospect it offered of being able to bring about regional convergence with national diversity

As stated in the Bulletin on the *Conclusions of the Portuguese Presidency*, "the open method of coordination, which is designed to help the Member States to progressively develop their own policies, involves:

- fixing guidelines for the Union combined with specific timetables for achieving the goals which they set in the short, medium and long terms;
- establishing, where appropriate, quantitative and qualitative indicators and benchmarks against the best in the world and tailored to the needs of different Member States and sectors as a means of comparing best practice;
- translating these European guidelines into national and regional policies by setting specific targets and adopting measures, taking into account national and regional differences;
- periodic monitoring, evaluation and peer review as mutual learning processes. (emphases added)." (European Union, 2000, §37)

The attraction and value of the OMC in areas like education is rather obvious. As Mario Telo (2001, p. 2) points out, it is only possible to move towards convergence in the areas most important for the modernisation project, including education, which paradoxically are nationally the most important and sensitive, by means of methods that do not rely on the extension of regulation. It is also important to note that as Caroline de la Porte points out, "the areas dealt with under the auspices of the OMC are politically linked to the overall strategic objective of the EU as defined at Lisbon. Therefore, although the social dimension of the Union has been boosted, it continues to be linked to the economic project of the Union. Indeed, it appears there is a tension between the top-down objectives agreed during the successive sessions of the European Council, and the need for the OMC to take on a life of its own in their individual spheres" (de la Porte, 2001, p. 360).

A range of contributors have suggested how the OMC works to construct a European entity and policy presence, some of them referring directly to the EES, and we will consider some of them now.

The contribution most directly linked to the EES has been made by Ase Gornitzka (2005). She argues that the European level in areas like education is essentially brought into being by the activities promoted by the OMC; without the OMC, 'Europe' would not exist in the form(s) that it does. Similarly, the same devices of benchmarking, sharing of best practice etc., are not only the means through which the national and European 'universes' are constructed, but also the means through which they are linked to each other; the OMC provides the means of both constructing (European) 'unity' and enabling (national) 'diversity' in subscribing to that unity.

Gornitzka's paper also provides detailed evidence of how the European level is constructed in education through the OMC. She points out, for instance, that the five benchmarks for the improvement of education and training in Europe up to 2010 (reducing rates of early school leaving; reducing rates of poor academic performance; increasing the numbers of graduates in Mathematics, Science and Technology; increasing of the proportion of the population completing upper secondary education; and increasing of rates of participation in Lifelong Learning), "are not concrete targets for *individual* countries to be reached by 2010. They are defined by the Council as 'reference levels for the European *average* performance'" (Gornitzka, 2005, p. 17, emphases in original).

Claus Offe (2003) places the OMC at the centre of pressure from the EC to see existing social policy arrangements as potentially obsolete and in need of revision, experimentation and innovation. We might see this pressure deriving from the increasingly competitive global environment identified by, and central to the achievement of, the Lisbon goals. One focus of his paper is the idea of 'best practice' as a feature of the OMC, and he argues that a requirement for all countries to imitate an agreed form of 'best practice' would not just mean adopting these practices, but the "unlearning and partial demolition' of (nationally) entrenched institutional patterns." He goes so far as to suggest that this unlearning "may be the main purpose, or hidden curriculum of the OMC", that it "(brings) home to member states' political elites and constituencies the need for 'modernisation' and 'recalibration' of their hitherto adopted (social) policies." (Offe, 2003, pp. 463–464). He suggests that

> Th(e) functionalist and productivist view of these arrangements also implies that what used to be, in the framework of welfare states as relatively self-contained nation-states, *exogenously* established and enforced social policy institutions is now *endogenised* into the game itself: status, security and solidarity does itself become contingent upon contractual voluntarism. Accordingly, the game is no longer a game *under* rules, but increasingly one *about* rules. (ibid., p. 463, emphases in original)

Colin Scott suggests that benchmarks can be used to enhance quality and performance (the original sense in which the concept was used in industry), or applied to adherence to policies as opposed to operational standards (which he suggest is how benchmarking has been used in some domains of EU governance), where "the target of the intervention is to align policies rather than performance per se. In this manner (benchmarking) is likely to come to resemble the OMC (…) in the sense that it is likely to have to address divergence not only or mainly of performance, but rather divergence in policy views" (Scott, 2002, pp. 72–73). This is a very significant element of flexibility. It means, for instance, that *performance* benchmarks (or 'good practice') could be used inter-nationally, to lay down proscriptive/exclusive limits within which MS may operate, and *benchmarks* as *policy tools* could be used to align MS policy supranationally.

Fundamentally the OMC makes policy decisions into 'technical' matters for long term negotiation between 'de-nationalised' experts, rather than for national preferences that have to be defended nationally. Indicators and benchmarks may be seen as simple, transparent, flexible, non-directive, quantitative mechanisms that allow for considerable latitude in involvement and interpretation – all of which make them politically very attractive mechanisms of rule, nationally or supranationally.

But at the same time, they displace immediate problems, both temporally and spatially; their use extends the time horizon over which problems are to be addressed and removes the locus of decision to another place. This also makes education policy making at the EU level a matter for *technical problem solving* between *stakeholders* within the system, rather than the result of the political resolution of political conflicts between different *interests*. Finally the OMC operates on the basis of *proscription* rather than *prescription*; that is to say, it tends to patrol the boundaries of the possible rather than defining precisely what the territory thus defined should contain. Or, to put it another way, we should not look to explain the OMC on the basis of what it includes, but on what it excludes

Overall, we may see the OMC in education both constructing a EES and providing the basis of a functional and scalar division of labour between that regional space and national policy spaces.

Phase 3 – Lifelong learning as a single integrated programme

The Mid Term Review of the progress of the Lisbon agenda was generally uncomplimentary about the achievements of the first five years of the programme. It called for tighter targeting of economic development objectives and for alternative methods of delivering and implementing EU programmes in view of the perceived shortcomings of the OMC. The 2004 Council/Commission Interim report on the implementation of the education work programme (significantly titled) was similarly lukewarm about what had been achieved, and the 2005 Spring European Council also sought to redirect both the goals of the work programme for education, and the means of attaining them. The basis of the redirection of goals was to be an "integrated action programme in the field of lifelong learning" that would form the basis of the new generation of EU programmes in education from 2007-2013 (Council, 2004). The Commission's 2006 report on progress with the implementation of *Education and Training 2010* continued the emphasis on the need to accelerate the pace of reform, especially in the area of lifelong learning, which is seen as "a sine qua non of achieving the Lisbon goals while strengthening the European social model" (CEC, 2005a, p. 10). A further significant emphasis in the report is on the efficiency and targeting of investments in education. It also points to the need to improve the governance of the programme. While pointing out that over 2004-5 the Education Council had "adopted a number of common tools, principles and frameworks, for example related to mobility, quality assurance, non-formal learning and guidance", it also drew attention to two new means that have been introduce to improve governance (ibid., p. 9). These are the creation of an "Education and Training 2010 Coordination" group, made up of ministerial representatives and social partners, and the introduction of new working methods, replacing the existing (OMC-related) working groups with 'clusters' of countries focussing on key issues.

In the remainder of this section I will briefly outline and discuss these focus and process changes. The position accorded to lifelong learning in recent education EU education publications is quite remarkable. The apogee of its importance is its designation as the organising basis of the new integrated framework for all the EU's whole work programme in education and training, which establishes it as the carrier of the EU education and training flag. This is remarkable for at least two reasons. First, it is not at all clear what lifelong learning denotes or connotes, and second, member states' embrace and delivery of the idea has been, according to all the evidence, extremely poor. In considering what these two factors may reveal about the reasons for and consequences of this rapid rise, it is useful to try to trace lifelong learning's road to prominence. It actually has quite a long history in the EU, with a string of official documents promoting it over the last decade. Lifelong learning – or rather lifelong, or recurrent, education – was a prominent strand in progressive education reform after World War II, when it was promoted enthusiastically by UNESCO. The more recent versions of lifelong learning, especially as promoted by the EU, have had a rather different tone, that consistently identifies it as a crucial weapon in the response to the challenges presented by globalisation. The first promotional project for lifelong learning set up by the EU was the designation of 1996 as the *European Year of Lifelong Learning*, and as Dehmel points out in her account of the development of EU lifelong learning policies, it prominence and profile have continued to increase since that time (Dehmel, 2006). It was closely linked to the Lisbon agenda, with the Commission presenting a *Memorandum on Lifelong Learning* in October 2000 that emphasised that "*lifelong learning* is no longer just one aspect of education and training; it *must become the guiding principle* for participation across the full continuum of learning contexts" (quoted in Dehmel, 2006, p. 54, emphases in original). The consultation on the *Memorandum on Lifelong Learning* led to the Commission publication in 2001 of *Making a European Area of Lifelong Learning a Reality* (CEC, 2001), and lifelong learning was similarly, and not accidentally, the guiding principle of *Education and Training 2010*; it was also one educational project selected for development under the OMC.

Despite this prominence, however, there is no clear understanding of what lifelong learning is. Dehmel traces the changes in its use, and suggests that its primary focus is that associated with employment. She also speculates about the value of its flexible, slogan-like qualities, "a catchphrase that seems to fit perfectly almost anywhere without further explanation" (Dehmel, 2006, p. 56).

While these qualities are necessary to the understanding of what might be seen as the 'rise without trace' of lifelong learning, they are not sufficient. Three other factors are crucial in understanding lifelong learning's role as a key element of a EES.

– Formally, it does not infringe the rules of subsidiarity or trespass on national prerogatives, because most MS have fairly rudimentary LLL policies and there is considerable national variation over its meaning. Similarly, what it promotes is the development of competences, which again does not impinge on national turf in the same way that proposing new content would.

– The focus on employment and particularly the implicit and often explicit promises to solve the contradictions between the Lisbon goals by contributing to 'productive social policy' have had a clear impact on its prominence. This, in essence represents the basis of new European level sectors, that overlap with existing national sectors but do not replicate them; such a 'social policy' sector was referred to by Gornitzka (in the quotation above) for instance, and the 2006 progress report on the implementation of *Education and Training 2010* calls for "effective inter-ministerial synergy between 'knowledge policies' (education, training, employment/social affairs, research, etc)" (CEC, 2005a). This 'resectoralisation (see Dale, 2006) both takes distance from 'Education' as conventionally perceived and is consequently not regarded as threatening, and provides a basis for the development of European level sectors and policies.

– These same qualities also enable LLL to be used as the basis of a critique of the existing architecture of education systems, and especially the grammar of schooling. It explicitly breaks with the conventional temporal, spatial and professional assumptions, for instance with the 'learning anywhere, any time, from any provider' slogan. It also directly addresses the core of the conventional system in its promotion of learning rather than teaching at the heart of education systems.

Finally, it is important to note that a new means of coordinating the implementation of Education and Training 2010 has been introduced, in the shape of the Education and Training Coordination Group (ETCG), which will fill the need for an interface between the national level and the European work programme, and "will support the operational management and efficient implementation, in an integrated way and in a lifelong learning perspective, of the programme (...). It would focus on issues related (...) to the coordination and planning of activities, and stocktaking of results, whereas overall political and strategy issues will be dealt with at Council level" (EC, 2005a; see also CEC, 2005b). This appears to confirm a functional and scalar division of labour between European level and member states, and to aim to place 'Europe' in the driving seat of the EES.

CONCLUSION

I have argued in this paper that the EU is moving towards establishing a European Education Space over which it has some control, and that in the process of this attempt it has established a new version of 'Europe' within education and possibly beyond. I have done this by setting out in the first half of the paper the nature of the challenges, obstacles and opportunities to which these projects have to respond, and which shape it in important ways. In the second half of the paper I have offered a brief chronology of the developments that have been aimed at bringing about a EES, and their implications for 'Europe'.

The wider aims of the paper have been, in attempting to indicate the new, and *sui generis*, nature of the EU as a polity, economy and education space, to demonstrate the need to move beyond methodological nationalism and methodological statism, not just in this case, but more generally, in an era when, if it means anything, the idea of globalisation requires us to rethink not just geographical, but also theoretical and methodological boundaries and tools. Much work remains to be done, especially around the relationships between globalisation and 'Europe', and central to that work will be an appreciation of the importance of not stretching the conceptual tools through which we made sense of the second half of the twentieth century. This means not overestimating the degree of 'horizontal' change – for instance through assuming the globalisation of everything, or accelerating convergence – nor underestimating the 'vertical' dimension, the degree to which the 'global' is to be found in the regional, national and local. This case of 'European education policy' offers an opportunity to bring these tendencies into a better balance.

NOTES

[1] For instance, the Five Challenges section points out that "a new term has entered the policy discourse –benchmarking." And it goes on to explain that "Benchmarks bring a new way of thinking, about national performance, about local and regional effectiveness, and performance at the level of individual schools" (EU, 2000, p.7). All this may seem quite unexceptionable except that in the preceding "Introduction section" of the report, the term has been used several times without any apparent need to have its novelty or its meaning explained. The nearest approach to a definition of benchmarks in the Introduction suggests that their aim "is not to set standards or targets, but rather to provide policy makers with reference points" (ibid., p. 3). This in itself is significant, since setting targets is precisely what the "Five Challenges" section seems to have been set up to do.

REFERENCES

Commission of the European Communities. (2001, November 21). *Communication from the commission: Making a European area of lifelong learning a reality. COM(2001), 678.* Brussels: CEC.

Commission of the European Communities. (2005a, November 10). *Modernising education and training: A vital contribution to prosperity and social cohesion in Europe. Draft 2006 joint progress report of the Council and Commission on the implementation of the "Education and Training 2010 work programme". SEC(2005), 1415.* Brussels: CEC.

Commission of the European Communities. (2005b, October 10). *Commission staff working document. Annex to the: Communication from the commission modernising education and training: A vital contribution to prosperity and social cohesion in Europe draft 2006 joint progress report of the council and commission on the implementation of the "Education and training 2010 work programme". COM(2005), 549 final.* Brussels: CEC.

Council of the European Union. (2004, March 3). *'Education and Training 2010': The success of the Lisbon strategy hinges on urgent reforms. Joint interim report of the council and commission on the detailed work programme on the follow-up of the objectives of education and training systems in Europe. EDUC 43, 6905/04.* Brussels: CEC.

Dale, R. (1989). *The state and education policy.* Milton Keynes: Open University Press.

Dale, R. (2000). Globalisation and education: Demonstrating a "Common world education culture" or locating a "Globally structured Agenda for education"? *Education Theory, 50*(4), 427–448.

Dale, R. (2002). *The construction of a European education space and education policy.* Paper presented to European Social Fund Exploratory Workshop on Globalisation, Educational Restructuring and Social Cohesion in Europe, Barcelona, 3–5 October 2002.

Dale, R. (2005). Globalisation, knowledge economy and comparative education. *Comparative Education,* *41*(2), 117–149.

Dale, R. (2006). *The nature of European statehood and the construction of a European education space.* Paper presented to Worldwide Universities Network Workshop on New State Spaces, New Knowledge Spaces, Bristol.

Dehmel, A. (2006). Making a European area of lifelong learning a reality? Some critical reflections on the European union's lifelong learning policies. *Comparative Education, 42*(1), 49–62.

De La Porte, C. (2001). *The soft open method of co-ordination in social protection European trade union yearbook 2001.* Brussels: European Trade Union Institute.

European Commission, Directorate-General for Education and Culture. (2000). *European report on quality of school education: Sixteen quality indicators.* Luxembourg: EC.

European Commission, Directorate-General for Education and Culture. (2005, May 18). *Information note on the implementation of the "Education and Training 2010" work programme in 2005/6.* Advisory Committee for Vocational Training (16–17 June 2005). *EAC/A1/LP D(2005),* Brussels.

European Union. (2000). *Presidency conclusion Lisbon European council,* 23–24 March, Lisbon.

Gornitzka, A. (2005, March). *Coordinating policies for a "Europe of knowledge". Emerging practices of the "Open method of coordination" in education and research.* Arena Working Paper No. 16. Centre for European Studies, University of Oslo.

Hingel, A. (2001). *Education policies and European governance: Contribution to interservice groups on European governance.* Brussels: European Commission Directorate for Education and Culture.

Jessop, B. (1999). The changing government of welfare: Recent trends in its primary functions, scale and modes of coordination. *Social Policy and Administration, 33*(4), 348–359.

Macbeath, J., Schwartz, M., Meuret, M., & Jakobsen, L. B. (1999). *Self-evaluation in schools - a story of change.* London: Routledge.

Meyer, J. W. (1986). Types of explanation in the sociology of education. In J. Richardson (Ed.), *Handbook for theory and research in the sociology of education* (pp. 341–359). New York: Greenwood Press.

Meyer, J. W, Benavot, A., & Kamens, D. (1992). *School knowledge for the masses: World models and national primary curricular categories in the twentieth century.* Brighton: Falmer.

Meyer, J. (2001, November 28). *Globalisation, national culture and the future of the world polity.* Wei Lun Lecture, The Chinese University of Hong Kong.

OECD. (2001a). *Schooling for tomorrow: OECD scenarios.* Paris: Author.

OECD. (2001b). *E-learning: The partnership challenge.* Paris: Author.

Offe, C. (2003). The European model of "Social capitalism": Can it survive EuropeanIntegration? *Journal of Political Philosophy, 11*(4), 437–469.

Official Journal of the European Communities. (2002). *Consolidated version of the treaty establishing the European community.* Brussels, 24/12.

Robertson, S. (2000). *A class act: Changing teachers' work, the state and globalisation.* London: Routledge.

Robertson, S., Novelli, M., Dale, R., Tikly, L., Dachi, H., & Alphonce, N. (2007). *Globalisation education and development: Ideas, actors and dynamics.* London: DfID.

Rodrigues, M. J. (2005). *An overview of the Lisbon strategy - the European agenda for competitiveness, employment and social cohesion.* Background paper for Konfernz des Komptetnzteams Wirtschaft: So profiteeit, Osterreich 17 September, Vienna.

Sanotos, Boaventura de Sousa. (2004). *Towards a new legal common sense.* London: Buterworth.

Scott, C. (2002). The governance of the European union: The potential for multi-level control. *European Law Review, 8*(1), 59–79.

Telo, M. (2001). *Combiner les instruments politiques en vue d'un gestion dynamique des diversites nationals.* Contribution to Jean Monnet Working Paper 6/01 (Symposium: Mountain or Molehill? A Critical Appraisal of the Commission White Paper on Governance). New York School of Law: Jean Monnet Center.

Tyack, D., & Tobin, W. (1994). The grammar of schooling: Why has it been so hard to change? *American Educational Research Journal, 31*(3), 453–479.

FURTHER READINGS

Chernilo, D. (2007). *A social theory of the nation-state*. London: Routledge.

Dale, R. (2005). Globalisation, knowledge economy and comparative education. *Comparative Education, 41*(2), 117–149.

Jessop, B. (1999). The changing government of welfare: Recent trends in its primary functions, scale and modes of coordination. *Social Policy and Administration, 33*(4), 348–359.

Jones, P. D. (2008). 'Requisite Irony', 'Critical Discourse Analysis' and 'The Knowledge Based Economy'. The drafting of education policy in the European Union. In N. Fairclough, B. Jessop, & R. Wodak (Eds.), *Higher education and the knowledge based economy*. London: Falmer Press.

Karagiannis, N., & Wagner, P. (2007). *Varieties of world-making: Beyond globalisation*. Liverpool: Liverpool University Press.

Roger Dale
Graduate School of Education
University of Bristol, UK

KATHERINE NICOLL

A POLITICS OF SPIN

Lifelong Learning Policy as Persuasion?[1]

INTRODUCTION

A globalization of formal policy discourses has been identified as a feature of the contemporary world by many policy writers (Taylor et al., 1997; Edwards, 1997; Lingard & Rizvi, 1998). Within and across these discourses there have emerged various relatively stable descriptions of the global environment and 'lifelong learning'. Lifelong learning is commonly articulated as necessary for our futures if we are to prosper and our communities cohere (cf. UNESCO, 1997; OECD, 1996). Changes in the world economy as a result of new technology and the speed of economic globalization are identified as the underlying reason for this. I argue here that policy analysts have tended to take this kind of policy description of lifelong learning as their starting point for analysis. They have taken lifelong learning and its globalization as a policy theme as some 'thing' for scrutiny in a variety of ways. For example, they have asked questions over the effectiveness/performativity of lifelong learning or the important issue of redress. They have identified ways in which policy descriptions such as lifelong learning travel globally in various material ways, through, for example, supra-national conferences held for national policy makers and politicians (Taylor et al., 1997). These kinds of analyses are obviously important.

However, a discursive and linguistic view of policy description draws our attention to quite another way of exploring the globalization of lifelong learning. Here by 'policy description' I mean those descriptions found within formal policy texts *and* those produced by those who study policy (such as is this one). With this view it is possible to examine *the persuasive and rhetorical work* of descriptions of lifelong learning whereby lifelong learning and particular associated descriptions of the world become mobilised across policy contexts. As policy narrations become globalised, their work in the *construction of* social actors (albeit different ones), their relationships and the 'we' that is required to act can be highlighted (Fairclough, 2000; Nicoll & Edwards, 2004). Here representations in descriptions – whether those of formal policy texts or more widely – such as of the 'global economy', 'knowledge society' and 'lifelong learning' can be examined for their active work as discourse. In this chapter the focus is on a rhetorical analysis of lifelong learning as it is represented within formal policy texts from the European Commission (EC). Of course implicated through this analysis are other similar representations in other descriptions elsewhere, as they are picked up and reproduced globally. I want to point out some of the rhetorical strategies that are

M. Simons, M. Olssen and M.A. Peters (eds.), Re-Reading Education Policies: A Handbook Studying the Policy Agenda of the 21st Century, 387–403.

drawn upon in making the EC description of lifelong learning *work as a factual description*, and thus encouraging us to take lifelong learning for critique in a variety of ways. For as long as policy analysts act to critique lifelong learning as if it were achievable or potentially achievable, or consider whether it could or should be achieved or achievable, they help constitute communities that act.

In itself, that policies and policy analysis act to persuade is not a new insight. For instance, when we examine the stories told by the analysts and practitioners of social policy it becomes apparent that the framing of problems and thus their solutions often depends upon metaphors underlying them. Problems generate problem-setting and set the directions of problem solving (Schön, 1979, p. 255). In this way metaphors can be powerful in their steering capacity. Schön points to the pervasiveness of metaphors of fragmentation and coordination in policy discourse. More recently, Straehle *et al.* (1999, p. 68) argued for the centrality of the metaphor of struggle in European Union discourses on unemployment, where "using metaphor to manage meaning is an expression of power through which reality is defined for others." Metaphors and the systems of metaphor from which they draw are powerful in the extent to which they are "figurable" to an audience (Shapiro 1989). This is the extent to which they persuade through their intertextuality of form. Where a familiar representational form is drawn upon in an unfamiliar setting this can be persuasive. Shapiro talks of this in the use of sports metaphors by politicians in arguments for war in North America. However, figurability does not suggest in any simple way that control is guaranteed. They can provoke strong emotive and oppositional responses. They can also raise expectations, were meaning governing one context can become expected within others. As with lifelong learning as metaphor within a system of such, they also provide opportunity for various forms of critique that take them literally.

The work of metaphor is one part of the persuasive work of policy discourse. A metaphor is commonly taken to be a figure of speech in which a term is transferred to an object to which it is not properly applicable. But metaphors are more intrinsic within language than common understandings of them might imply. Indeed, according to some our fundamental relation to language is metaphoric (Parker 1997) and this, as I have been attempting to say here, has huge implications for our reading of policy. However, the work of metaphor is only one aspect – one strategy – of persuasive work in such discourses. There are many others. In earlier writings (Nicoll & Edwards, 2000 & 2004; Edwards & Nicoll, 2001; Nicoll, 2006) we began to address questions of the rhetorical work of policy and identified a range of strategies which, although common within all language, do quite specific and persuasive work within policy.

The notion of 'spin', for example, has been deployed noisily by the media in UK politics, by politicians on both the left and right and some policy analysts against those whose views were being opposed. By accusing others of 'spin' were suggesting that a 'tall tale' was being told or a good 'yarn spun', with the implication that the story was fiction. Quite commonly then the charge of spin is read as one of being economic with or failing to tell the truth; 'truth' and 'spin' are quite generally considered in terms of the binary truth/rhetoric. A description either tells the truth, or it is empty rhetoric or spin. However, the notion of spin when deployed in this way is a rhetorical strategy. It is drawn upon in an act to counter and undermine an otherwise potentially persuasive description. As it has been used in the UK so commonly, it is then in danger of undermining policy processes altogether. Cynicism can result in a debilitated polity, as possibly evidenced by falling participation in elections in many countries. Our argument, therefore, has been that such a strategy fails to deliver a productive politics through which to engage in and counter policy processes.

By contrast a rhetorical analysis we have felt helps to bring forth such possibilities. The legitimacy of rhetorical acts in policy processes we have suggested needs to be recognised and (en)countered, as "to be truly persuasive one has to *imagine* the other view, and be able to 'play at' addressing it. Such as an act of playful imagination continues to be necessary even in the act of addressing someone with another view" (Leith & Myerson, 1989, p. 100, emphasis in original). This is a distinction then between approaching the rhetoric of language in terms of the binary truth/rhetoric or through an analytics of language. Through the former the charge of spin is a strategy that may be deployed to point to falsehood and so undermine an opponents argument. Through the latter, questions of truth are put to one side so as to explore the rhetorical strategies that are intrinsic within *all* policy language; in which the charge of 'spin' is but one possible rhetorical strategy within a whole set of these. Of course, the problem for some may be that this latter would appear to involve participating in the very processes of spin that are held in such contempt. Imaginings, though, are part of what I am involved in with this text and feel is lacking in analysis of educational policy. Who is mobilised and persuaded by such discourses and how is a serious question in its own right.

Here, then, I wish to pursue my interest in rhetoric further, both in terms of drawing upon the resources of rhetoric but also in exploring the rhetorical strategies drawn upon in the representations of the need for lifelong learning in policy texts of the European Union. The chapter is in two sections. First, I repeat some of our previous discussion of the question of spin and rhetoric in policy in general and lifelong learning policy in particular (Nicoll & Edwards, 2004). Second, I offer some rhetorical analysis of lifelong learning, expanding the frame and argument of our previous work. This is followed by a brief summary of the argument for the importance of rhetorical analysis to policy analysis more generally.

THE POLITICS OF SPIN

To assert the need for "a European area of lifelong learning" within policy discourse, as does the European Commission communication on making a European area of lifelong learning a reality (EC, 2001) is to attempt to configure a description of the world that is persuasive to an audience. It is an attempt to mobilise an audience, translating the concerns of different individuals and groups into a single narrative of change and adaptation. We may accept the assertion as a literal description of the required future state of the world, as if the European area could exist and would be unproblematic. We may also argue that the notion is merely 'spin', hyperbole, designed to deceive, and, thus, search for the meanings behind this deception. However, to respond in either such way is to fail to recognise that rhetoric is involved in all descriptions of reality, and always has been, including those of policy. It is also to miss the opportunity precisely to examine the work that rhetoric does in fabricating and mobilizing a European area of lifelong learning. What rhetorical strategies are involved in representing it as a requirement? With what effects? If we can go some way to answering such questions then we may begin to understand how policy works as persuasion and become more discerning as to the way in which problems and possibilities are framed and fabricated. We may also be able to reconfigure our responses to policy.

To put forward the view of policy as spin that is concerned only with distorting truth through particular representations of it in some ways misses the point, as acts of persuasion are inherent in all policy and political processes, just as they are within all communications. To suggest that a policy discourse is 'simply' spin or 'empty' rhetoric implies that there is a more truthful or honest political discourse. Views of policy as spin or governance as discourse management take us back to earlier critiques of rhetoric as appealing to the emotions and lacking evidence or substance, politics as manipulation, rhetoric as propaganda. Politicians who are said to spin are positioned as those who are interested in representation alone. Perhaps in a more sinister way it is suggested that they are prepared to mask a truth that it is then up to others to uncover. The latter is an argument much favoured by those in the media, thereby ignoring their own rhetorical work while positioning themselves as having a certain ethos in their own reporting of politics. This then involves a politics of spin. While having some sympathy with this view, as we have suggested elsewhere it is rhetorically powerful, I will again take a slightly different tack (Nicoll & Edwards, 2004; Edwards et al., 2004). As we have felt, the type of ideology critique that often underpins such an approach overlooks important issues about what is going on and what our responses might be. Similarly, we have suggested that some of the discursive analysis of policy, drawing on understandings of rhetoric (Fairclough, 2000), although valuable, pays too little attention to the work of rhetoric in its own formulations. Fairclough (2000) in his analysis of the language of the 1997 New Labour government in the UK suggests that language has become more important, that "New Labour is involved in a 'reinvention of government' which in itself entails a greater salience for language" (Fairclough, 2000, p. 5). He suggests that the language of new and old labour reflect different ideological positions. Our view has been that in both cases he is falling into the trap that haunts the discussion of rhetoric and leaves space for the reinforcement of a reading of spin. In attempting to make a literal description this only points to the rhetorical work being done.

While studies that point to a lack of substance in lifelong learning policy are important, they devalue and misunderstand the role and work of rhetoric. This is despite the importance of rhetoric and rhetorical analysis to be found in areas such as deconstruction (Parker, 1997), genre studies (Freedman & Medway, 1994) and the representation of research (Nelson et al., 1987; Atkinson, 1996). The argument made here is that the study of policy in general and lifelong learning policy in particular precisely as rhetoric, can illuminate our understanding in slightly different ways that point to the very real and powerful practices that are in play. Here, the significance of the work is because "part of the job of the rhetorical analyst is to determine how constructions of 'the real' are made persuasive" (Simons, 1990, p. 11). The question is not about whether reality matches rhetoric or not, but which rhetorical performance is persuasive, how and why. Here presentation and representation are taken to be substantial actions in their own right.

In this chapter then I explore a particular example of a policy notion that has become popular in recent years in many nations and among certain international organizations, such as the European Union (EU) and the Organization of Economic Co-operation and Development (OECD). This is the notion of lifelong learning, supported by a narrative of the need to construct Europe as a knowledge society and economy. The importance here is to find some tools for analysis that can get to the detail of the rhetorical work done within policy discourses and texts.

> Potentially, there are a huge number of ways in which the production of descriptions is involved with actions. Descriptions are closely bound up with the idiosyncratic particulars of settings ... The point, then, is that, although the details of what is talked about may be endlessly varied, the sorts of procedures for constructing and managing description may be much more regular, and, therefore, tractable in analysis (Potter, 1996, pp. 111–112).

For those, like myself, who are interested in identifying and analysing these more or less regularities in procedure, in and across policy discourses of lifelong learning, it is the details of these procedures or strategies that I want to focus on, to look at what they do. I work in this chapter with notions of "offensive" and "defensive" rhetoric from Potter (1996) and some rhetorical strategies identified by him from conversation analysis as common within descriptions. I also work lightly with some resources from Fairclough (2000) and Foucault (1996). In some parts of the chapter I begin to suggest that some strategies might do work specific in policy descriptions.

Rhetoric can be taken to work offensively to 'reify' and defensively to 'ironise' positions:

> Reifying means to turn something abstract into a material thing ... These are accounts which are producing something as an object, be it an event, a thought or a set of circumstances. In contrast, we will refer to discourse which is undermining versions as ironizing (Potter, 1996, p. 107, emphasis in original).

Reification is done through strategies to put some position, objects, or narrations of the world beyond question, to naturalise or ontologically gerrymander them. Ironizing attempts to undermine a potential alternative narration or position, in advance or in retrospect, by, for instance, positioning it as spin, or, as we will see by incorporating aspects of one argument into another. These are useful notions, as they emphasise the struggle that goes on within policy discourses, the struggle to produce descriptions that can be taken as literal and the ways in which they work defensively to counter alternative possibilities. The important point here is that policy facts and narrations of the way in which the world is and should be are represented as such in order to *do something*, and such representation is itself action. Discourses of lifelong learning are then represented, and in so doing are action-orientated, just as is this chapter. Let me now turn to a few examples of the procedures – strategies – used to construct and manage policy descriptions of the need for lifelong learning.

THE RHETORIC OF LIFELONG LEARNING FOR EUROPE

There was an agreement by heads of European Union (EU) member states and governments at the Lisbon meeting of the Lisbon European Council, March 2000, to make the EU "the most competitive and dynamic knowledge-driven society in the world" (EC, 2000). A communication from the European Commission (2001) on making a European area of lifelong learning a reality, described the need for lifelong learning in terms of its capacity to support the transition to this knowledge-based society, and with reference to the Lisbon Strategy from the Feira and Lisbon Council meetings:

> The Feira European Council in June 2000 asked the Member States, the Council and the Commission, within their areas of competence, to "identify coherent strategies and practical measures with a view to fostering lifelong learning for all." This mandate confirms lifelong learning as a key element of the strategy, devised at Lisbon, to make Europe the most competitive and dynamic knowledge-based society in the world (EC, 2001, Executive Summary).

The EUROPA portal website of the European Union (http://europa.eu) offers the following introduction to the European area of lifelong learning:

> To facilitate the transition to a knowledge-based society, the Commission is promoting the establishing of strategies for lifelong learning, together with specific activities, with a view to achieving a European area of lifelong learning. This objective is at the heart of the Lisbon Strategy, in particular the "Education and Training 2010" programme. The Member States have undertaken to develop appropriate strategies by 2006 (EUROPA, 2007a, p. 1).

This site is designed to inform the public as to the activities of the various bodies of the European Union, and it is this site and various European Commission policy texts that I draw upon for the ensuing analysis.

Narrative start and structure

It is helpful to begin this analysis by identifying the rhetorical strategies of 'narrative start' and 'narrative structure'. The point at which a description starts and the way it is organised is very important for the work that it is then capable of. We see, for example, their significance as strategies in the legal profession in courtrooms (Potter, 1996). Here Potter's (1996) explication is helpful to elaborate. A nuanced description offered by a defendant can help ensure that the focus of subsequent discussion is advantageous to that party and that what can count as a complete answer is managed. Narrative organization is important also. By ordering events and identifying what is to be included within a description and what is to be left out, very different descriptions of reality can be forthcoming. We have only to consider the variety found in witness accounts to see how this happens. People tend to notice different things and in part construct what they have seen through the later organization of their descriptions. Narrative organization of this sort is not only isolated to these sorts of extreme cases. Indeed, we cannot really give any kind of description without such organization even though we may not think explicitly of what we are doing. The way a narrative starts and the subsequent structuring of it is therefore fundamental to the rhetorical work of policy.

The start of the narrative as constructed through these selected quotes (above) and within other policy documents of the European Union is that of "the transition to a knowledge-based society" (EUROPA 2007a) with the aim to "make Europe the most competitive and dynamic knowledge-based society in the world" (EC, 2001). Lifelong learning is identified as needed to facilitate this transition. And with this assertion what is to count as a complete answer to a problem – the achievement of a knowledge-based society – is proscribed. The problem is the potential future lack of a knowledge-based society, even though this is not explicitly asserted. The narrative thus starts at a point that clearly manages a specific description of the problem, detail or rationale for the need of a knowledge society right out of discussion. We can see this kind of management in the EUROPA site in that the narrative is started with reference to a quote from the Lisbon meeting for, not a society, but a knowledge-based *economy*. All that is said about the knowledge-based economy is an assertion of our society as both an information and knowledge-based society: "Our society is now defined as the 'Information Society', a society in which low-cost information and ICT are in general use, or as the 'Knowledge(-based) Society', to stress the fact that the most valuable asset is investment in intangible, human and social capital and that the key factors are knowledge and creativity" (EUROPA, 2007b). It is interesting to note that more widely key texts subsequent to the Lisbon meeting appear to have dropped the notion of making Europe a knowledge-based economy, and some suggest that we are already in a knowledge-based society. I will pick up on these points later on in the chapter.

The structure of the narrative for lifelong learning can be considered from the following narration of a European area of lifelong learning. This is a quote from the Communication from the European Commission on making a European area of lifelong learning a reality (EC, 2001, The Context) and has the following to say about the need for lifelong learning:

> Lifelong learning has been the subject of policy discussion and development for many years now. Yet today there is a greater need than ever for citizens to acquire the knowledge and competences necessary both to tap into the benefits, and to meet the challenges of the knowledge-based society. This is why the Lisbon European Council confirmed lifelong learning as a basic component of the European social model.
>
> In economic terms, the employability and adaptability of citizens is vital for Europe to maintain its commitment to becoming the most competitive and dynamic knowledge-based society in the world. Labour shortages and competence gaps risk limiting the capacity of the European Union for further growth, at any point in the economic cycle. Lifelong learning, therefore, has a key role to play in developing a coordinated strategy for employment and particularly for promoting a skilled, trained and adaptable workforce. This means removing the barriers that prevent people from entering the labour market and limit progression within it. Tackling inequality and social exclusion is part of this.
>
> Lifelong learning is, however, about much more than economics. It also promotes the goals and ambitions of European countries to become more inclusive, tolerant and democratic. And it promises a Europe in which citizens have the opportunity and ability to realise their ambitions and to participate in building a better society. Indeed, a recent OECD report refers to the growing evidence that learning and investment in human capital is associated not just with increased GDP, but also with greater civic participation, higher reported well-being and lower criminality.

We have already seen from the previous quotes that lifelong learning is represented by the Commission as a required response in the construction of Europe as a knowledge-based society. Here is an elaboration that it is needed *in order that* European citizens can "acquire the knowledge and competences necessary both to tap into the benefits, and to meet the challenges of the knowledge-based society" (EC, 2001, The Context). It is also needed in order that citizens are continually employable and adaptable in order that the economy can continue to grow: "In economic terms, the employability and adaptability of citizens is vital" (EC, 2001, The Context). In addition, it is necessary in that it can promote "the goals and ambitions of European countries to become more inclusive, tolerant and democratic" (EC, 2001, The Context). Lifelong learning carries with it promises; "of greater civic participation, higher reported well-being and lower criminality" (EC, 2001, The Context). This then can be seen as an elaboration of the terrain and structure of the narrative that is being built – the objects, characters, the order of relationships and events and so forth.

Correspondence and coherence

In part, this narrative terrain and structure is rhetorically persuasive in that it resonates with descriptions of the need for lifelong learning that are accepted elsewhere, and not only within policy discourses. It 'corresponds' with other descriptions, and correspondence is a rhetorical strategy that can be deployed to increase the likelihood of a description being commonly accepted. It is also persuasive in that it appears 'coherent'. Narrative descriptions of this sort are commonly expected to meet up with standards of coherence and correspondence with prior descriptions if they are to pass as real. Indeed, it would be quite strange if every description of the world within policy differed from every other. We expect similarity because plausible accounts are commonly taken to be produced by putting facts, which correspond with reality, within a coherent narrative structure. However, research does not confirm a simple relationship between narrative structures and the "plot structures" that are drawn upon in particular cultural settings (Potter, 1996, p. 170). Narratives are not just about selecting facts and putting them into an order that an audience may find persuasive, but there are particular configurations – narrative forms or plot structures – that are part of our "cultural endowment" (White, in Potter, 1996, p. 170). They are persuasive within those cultures that use them. Although such research has not been specifically focused in the policy domain it indicates that regularities within the narratives of policy discourses may be related to their plot structure and activity orientation. Thus, narrative structure may be conditioned by the forms of narrative that are part of the cultural endowment of the policy domain, and indeed by the many ways in which the authors wish the text to act. This is one of the issues that I am examining here.

The narratives within the EC 2001 document and associated public website act not only in terms of their correspondence and coherence in the above sense, but in that they delineate a discursive terrain from which further discussion then departs. Narratives act in this way to control and manage ensuing debate and activity for the future and can also be constructed retrospectively to act as explanation or give account. From the time of the above EC 2001 quote we might expect that policy debate was largely concerned to explore the merits, demerits and so forth of lifelong learning in terms of this terrain and structure (the knowledge and competencies necessary for the knowledge society, employability, adaptability, the amounts of civic participation, well-being and criminality, and so on), and not in other terms (and indeed one could to examine if this has been the case). The structure of a policy narrative is particularly important in the control and management of discussion in this sense, as arranging a narrative with certain props already on the stage takes our attention away from anything that might alternatively have been there. We saw in the example of the courtroom discourse that we would expect any well formed exegesis to delineate the main structure of a narrative at the outset, and indeed we are quite familiar with this requirement within our own writing. This kind of structured narration within policy then offers potential for a form of policy endowment, targeted rhetorically at the mobilization of specific people and organizations. It has potential to operate quite without the explicit provision of a root cause for the requirement for action. A familiar structure and set of actors, aspirations, reasons for acting and indicators for the success of that action may be sufficient.

This kind of narrative structure in policy acts defensively in a way that is quite specific to the policy context and which may well help preclude its subsequent undermining. In this is a potential ironizing strategy, built into the narrative by the way in which it crosses disciplinary divides in its concern with the economy, society and education, which helps make subsequent critical scholarly engagement difficult. For, if policy analysts are to engage in critique in realist terms they are positioned to need to work authoritatively across disciplinary divides. And how many education policy analysts could easily do this? In this sense then, it may be that policy narrations that cross academic disciplinary boundaries may be less easy to engage with than would otherwise be the case.

Nominalization

It is also in part through the reifying strategy of the nominalization of objects that policy narrations do effective, persuasive, work. Reifying certain concepts as objects rather than the outcome of human activity is central to the work of policy language, and this is so in the above quotes. The props of policy discourse are brought on the stage as real objects—a chair and table—rather than as things that are being done by actors; the 'knowledge-based society', 'labour market', 'competitive economy', 'workforce'. Fairclough (2000, p. 27) points to the significance of this kind of nominalization in policy discourse, where words are used as nouns instead of verbs. For example, instead of representing economic processes as people applying means to materials to produce things, the actual processes and people and things involved are backgrounded and we have instead 'the economy' as an entity. The 'knowledge-based society' and 'the economy' presuppose that there is such a society and economy, that is, they are taken for granted as some things that we all know exist. As Fairclough points out, it is through this kind of action that the economy as the work of many specific actors with more or less power is lost (in particular, perhaps, the work of multi-national companies). Global competition, the age of information, the knowledge economy and change are commonly represented as nominalizations within policy discourse. What this does is to set up and reify a range of objects that appear to exist externally to our action, they become the 'natural' background in terms of which we must act. At the same time nominalization allows the writers to avoid attributing the set of activities, or the activity of their nominalization, to any particular population, group or author. As Fairclough indicates, there are important omissions in this, and nominalizations that become taken-for-granted within policy language are commonly replicated in the subsequent work of policy analysis and wider debate.

It is interesting to look at the detail of nominalization and action that is represented in and around 'lifelong learning' in the description "Lifelong learning, therefore, has a key role to play in developing a coordinated strategy for employment and particularly for promoting a skilled, trained and adaptable workforce" (EC, 2001). Here we see that, rather than the people who are learning doing the action, it is either lifelong learning that acts in developing a strategy, or invisible people who are developing a strategy. By combining nominalization with the use of the passive voice the people who act are hidden. The passive voice is a rhetorical strategy, which works to increase the authority of what is said, in part by making it unnecessary to that a person be visible as speaking or acting. No people are identified here, and this serves to reify lifelong learning as *both* nominalised and (potentially and ambiguously) agentic. This helps to lever up the facticity of the key role that is to be played by it. Consider how much weaker the following alternative construction would have been: "*People learning through their lives, therefore, are key to our development* of a coordinated strategy for employment (...).*" Naming the people who are acting makes the reader much more aware that some people are making decisions as to how other people should be mobilised and to what ends.

'The labour market' is also nominalised within the above description. However, people *are* attributed to *certain* activities in relation to it, but only in a limited way: "[t]his means removing the barriers that prevent people from entering the labour market and limit progression within it" (EC, 2001). They can act either to 'enter' the labour market, 'progress' within it, or fail to so enter or progress. That these activities have been picked out is rhetorically significant. They have been foregrounded in relation to all other potential activities. That they have been picked out in this way, as we saw earlier, enters these activities into the narrative terrain in a similar way that props are placed on a stage before the curtain rises. Props placed in this way are made available for later use onstage. If they were not so positioned at the outset, bringing them onstage at a later time would have focused audience attention on them and this might be disadvantageous. Audiences tend to notice props that are brought in during action more than those that are always there. This is then rhetorically significant, for these objects 'strategy for employment', 'promotion of a workforce', barriers' for 'entry' and 'progression' are positioned *a priori* as objects easily available to be taken up and deployed at a later point within the narrative. This is a feature of the structuring of the narrative that we saw earlier.

Ontological gerrymandering

Here I want to turn to another rhetorical strategy that has been much discussed as one suffusing social scientific discourse. This is that of ontological gerrymandering (Woolgar & Pawluch, 1985; Potter, 1996). As we have seen, the *achievement* of a competitive and knowledge-based society has become a focus of policy narratives within the EU and Member States (EC, 2000). This involves a nominalization of the object that acts to reify it and avoid the need to identify the differential actors, activities and power relations involved. It allows certain activity to be represented in a way that is therefore depoliticised. This achievement is identified within the Presidency conclusions to the Lisbon meeting as the "new challenge" that must be met by the European Union (EC, 2000b, p. 1). Here the logos of this exigence for change is articulated as "a quantum shift resulting from globalization and the challenges of a new knowledge-driven economy (…) affecting every aspect of people's lives" and as "the rapid and accelerating pace of change" (EC, 2000b, p. 1). Thus, the activity involved in the shift is positioned as *a result of* globalization and the challenges of a knowledge-driven economy. The knowledge-driven economy is thus positioned as with us now, rather than remaining to be achieved in the future. The globalizing tendencies and the knowledge economy that 'we know' are thus variously positioned within policy description as both reasons for and oft stated aims of policies of lifelong learning. They become positioned as the precursors for further policy in a 'virtuous' circle of discourse. Globalization and a knowledge-driven economy are positioned in this as 'natural' changes to which 'we', within the European Union, must respond, rather than as socially constructed. Education and training systems were argued within the Memorandum on Lifelong Learning (EC, 2000a) and again within the Presidency conclusions to the Lisbon meeting (EC, 2000b) as needed for us to *adapt* for the demands of a knowledge society or economy.

The knowledge-driven society and economy are then quite contradictorily represented within descriptions even from within the same policy text. They are both represented as constructed by social action, *and* as objects that are already on (or at least entering) the stage of policy, as a current or future problem to which we must respond. This, then, is to play rhetorically on the polyvalent attributes of the metaphors. They are used interchangeably, and gerrymandered either side of a divide between that which is natural and socially constructed and that which is already in existence and will be in the future. Their ontological and temporal status is confused and confusing. In part, this affords them their rhetorical utility, as they can be positioned multiply and ambiguously within descriptions as long as their detail is not spelt out. This tendency for a blurring of the ontological and temporal identities of objects key within policy narrations of the logos for lifelong learning is quite striking. Although, these may tend to become relatively fixed or stabilised within narrations in discourses that target different groups in different ways. For example, economic narrations may favour the positioning of the knowledge economy as that which is being built through activity, such as is the case within the Lisbon Agenda. Within narrations of lifelong learning, the knowledge economy or society appears to be positioned quite often as the *reason* for its requirement. Consider, for example, the statement made at the beginning of the official lifelong learning website for the European Commission (EUROPA, 2007a, p. 1) "On 21 November 2001, the Commission adopted a Communication on Making a European Area of Lifelong Learning a Reality (…) In doing so, it makes an important contribution to achieving the strategic goal set at Lisbon for Europe *to become the most competitive and dynamic knowledge-based society in the world*" and, in comparison, that made at the end of the text of that same site "The Communication makes proposals that contribute to *the realization of a European area of lifelong learning*, the objectives of which are both to empower citizens to *meet the challenges of the knowledge-based society* (…)" (EUROPA, 2007a, p. 2). Within the first statement, and the first part of the second, activity will *realize* a knowledge-based society. Within the second part of the second statement, lifelong learning (the activity) will empower us to *respond appropriately to* a knowledge-based society. The ontological and temporal status of the knowledge-based society is confusing.

Managing polyvalence

There are potential dangers to be seen for policy makers in particular stabilizations on one side or other of this divide between that which is naturally occurring and socially constructed within descriptions. Onman (1996) an economic advisor to the OECD was keen, for example, that 'globalization' should not be positioned within them as a part of the problem of the current environment to which we must then respond. Onman was pointing to the persuasive work of policy and how it can 'mislead' by providing rhetorical ammunition for oppositional groups. He argued that policy makers should avoid talking about globalization as an aspect of the problem that required increasing flexibility as a response. This was because he saw globalization being used increasingly by some groups as a 'scapegoat' for lack of action towards increased flexibility and as a means to articulate and support resistance to change. What is of interest here is the suggestion of the construction of exigencies that will rhetorically manage the allegiance of different groups. It may be that the potential positioning of nominalizations within descriptions is quite useful. The quality of polyvalence in nominalizations may help in the constitution and management of a "doctrine" (Foucault, 1996). This is through descriptions to which diverse groups with quite different aspirations can be productively subjected. To construct a doctrine is at the same time to construct a system of exchange and communication that operates across its boundaries. Here polyvalences internal to a doctrinal description support the assimilation of a wide range of discourses, and thus operate to manage allegiance effectively within and across them.

The Communication (EC 2001) rhetorically guards against the future possible undermining of this narration by a further *ironizing* strategy. Counter-arguments to the construction of a knowledge economy had been pointed out by respondents to the large policy consultation process that followed the Lisbon Meeting. These were based on arguments that the consequences of the knowledge economy would be greater inequality and social exclusion. In the Communication these consequences are generalised as 'risks'. In other words, such consequences are only possibilities – there is no necessity that they will occur. In this they are not positioned in the same way as the future goals, which are similarly only possibilities of the outcomes of the same action.

This suggests perhaps that the identification and constitution of successful ironizing and reification strategies may be a rhetorical function of the consultation process itself; as to label counterarguments of consequence as risks is to play down their possible significance. As in contemporary discourses for war they are positioned as the collateral damage of what is occurring rather than as integral to it. They are not only positioned within the Communication (EC, 2001, The Context) as the potential consequence of action towards a knowledge-based society, but also as one that needs to be dealt with through activities towards lifelong learning.

Lifelong learning becomes the strategy to address risks. Given its contextualization as integral to the knowledge economy and society, to then position lifelong learning as that which will ameliorate the risks associated with this economy and society appears strange. Risks become a support for the *exigence* for lifelong learning. Requiring precisely "a radical new approach to education and training", "renewed emphasis and importance on lifelong learning", and new policies and institutions that will equip individuals in dealing with the consequences of change (EC, 2001, p. 3). In other words a reworked definition arises from the consultation process, acting to amplify the centrality of the discourse of lifelong learning with the EU.

POLICY AS PERSUASION?

"Political differences have always been constituted as differences in language, political struggles have always been partly struggles over the dominant language, and both the theory and practice of political rhetoric go back to ancient times" (Fairclough, 2000, p. 3). It is commonly suggested that policy rhetoric in general and in relation to lifelong learning in particular is grandiose. Such suggestions tend to assume that the goals of policy are achievable, something to be striven for and that it can produce. There is often an implicit suggestion that, if only the government got it right and put in more resources lifelong learning would be both possible and achievable. Lifelong learning could play a role in achieving all those goals of personal fulfilment, social inclusion, and economic competitiveness that are to be found in policy rhetoric.

I have not adopted that approach here. I have sought once again to argue and maybe persuade that there is a need to explore the rhetorical work of policy discourses. Where policies present particular descriptions of the world as literal, analysts, such as ourselves are strongly positioned to do work to support, critique, or undermine the facticity of *these descriptions*. We have only a limited number of approaches that operate persuasively for this, and all have their particular productivities and constraints. What they have in common is, however, pursuit of the question of truth.

What a rhetorical analysis makes possible is a different kind of approach. It refuses to focus on whether or not descriptions of the world that are represented to us as factual and possible, are or are not factual or possible. By contrast, it examines how rhetorical strategies are deployed in order to make descriptions persuasive, and the work that these do in the mobilization of audiences. As I have said, this idea is of course not new. We have known for a long time that different narratives of the world operate powerfully at particular times, and that the analytic resources that we deploy, both to contribute to and to engage with these, are finite and limited. What a rhetorical analysis appears to offer is the possibility of a fine grain examination of some aspects of what is going on within our time. Lifelong learning is a policy discourse that is mobilised in part as part of governing, as one of those intellectual technologies acting at a distance in the administration of populations (Miller & Rose, 1993; Edwards, 2002; Nicoll 2006; Fejes & Nicoll,

2008). As I have argued here, governing is performed in part through the stabilization of particular narratives of the world – such as that of lifelong learning as we have examined. We may find this acceptable, argue against it, or might adopt different understandings of it, depending upon the recontextualizations to which it is subject (Edwards & Boreham, 2003). In all cases, we all end up working up its facticity through our constant repetition and commentary. Thus, even as we contribute to the analysis of lifelong learning policy, commenting upon it, we help to fabricate its facticity and ontological position. In this sense, as scholars and researchers, we are as much involved in the spin of policy as those politicians and policy makers who are positioned as the darker forces of the art. To argue that lifelong learning policy is spin is to undermine the status of the policy makers involved in promoting it, and reinforce the truth/falsehood binary that keeps us focused on our search for better truths. While this may be productive, it takes attention from its/our rhetorical work and the productivity of forms of analysis that identify how particular truths become fabricated and act and the possibilities for alternatives.

NOTES

[1] This chapter is a revised and amended version of a chapter in R. Edwards, K. Nicoll, N. Solomon & R. Usher, *Rhetoric and Educational Discourse Persuasive Texts?* London, Routledge, 2004, and an article Nicoll K. and Edwards R., Sultans of spin: policy as persuasion. *Journal of Education Policy*, 2004, 19, 1: 43-55.

REFERENCES

Atkinson, P. (1996). *Sociological readings and re-readings.* Aldershot: Avebury Press.

Barry, A. (2002). In the middle of the network. In J. Law & A. Mol (Eds.), *Complexities: Social studies of knowledge practices* (pp. 142–165). Durham, NC: Duke University Press.

Coffield, F. (2002). Breaking the consensus: Lifelong learning as social control. In R. Edwards, N. Miller, N. Small, & A. Tait (Eds.), *Supporting lifelong learning, volume 3: Making policy work.* London: RoutlegeFalmer.

Department for Education and Employment. (1998). *The learning age: A renaissance for a new Britain.* London: Stationery Office.

Department for Education and Employment. (1999). *Learning to succeed: A new framework for post-16 Learning.* London: Stationery Office.

Edwards, R. (1997). *Changing places? Flexibility, lifelong learning and a learning society.* London: Routledge.

Edwards, R., & Boreham, N. (2003). The centre cannot hold: Complexity and difference in European union policy towards a learning society. *Journal of Education Policy, 18*(3), 429–443.

Edwards, R., & Nicoll, K. (2001). Researching the rhetoric of lifelong learning. *Journal of Education Policy, 16*(2), 103–112.

Edwards, R. (2002). Mobilizing lifelong learning: Governmentality in educational practices. *Journal of Education Policy, 17*(3), 353–365.

Edwards, R., Nicoll, K., Solomon, N., & Usher, R. (2004). *Rhetoric and educational discourse: Persuasive texts.* London: RoutledgeFalmer.

European Commission (2000a). *A Memorandum on Lifelong Learning*. Commission Staff Working Paper, Brussels 30.10.2000. Retrieved March 2008, from HTTP http://www.bologna-berlin2003.de/pdf/MemorandumEng.pdf

European Commission. (2000a). *Presidency conclusions, Lisbon European Council, European Commission*. Retrieved October 14, 2005, from HTTP http://ue.eu.int/ueDocs/cms_Data/docs/pressData/en/ec/00100-rl.en0.htm

European Commission. (2001). *Communication from the commission of 21 November 2001 on making a European area of lifelong learning a reality* [COM(2001) 678 final – Not published in the Official Journal]. Retrieved from HTTP <http://eur-lex.europa.eu/smartapi /cgi/sga_doc?smartapi! celexplus!prod!DocNumber&lg=en&type_doc=COMfinal&an_doc=200&n u_doc=678>

EUROPA. (2007a). *The European area of lifelong learning*. Retrieved July 12, 2007, from HTTP <http://ec. europa.eu/education/policies/lll/life/index_en.html >

EUROPA. (2007b). *Knowledge society - homepage*. Retrieved July 12, 2007, from HTTP http://ec.eur opa.eu/employment_social/knowledge_society/index_en.html

Fairclough, N. (2000). *New labour, new language?* London: Routledge.

Fejes, A., & Nicoll, K. (2008). *Foucault and lifelong learning: Governing the subject*. London: RoutledgeFalmer.

Foucault, M. (1996). The discourse on language. In R. Kearny & M. Rainwater (Eds.), *The continental philosophy reader*. London: Routledge.

Freedman, A., & Medway, P. (Eds.). (1994). *Genre and the new rhetoric*. London: Taylor & Francis.

Latour, B., & Wolgar, S. (1979). *Laboratory life: The construction of scientific facts*. Beverley Hills, CA.

Leach, J. (2000). Rhetorical analysis. In M. Bauer & G. Gaskell (Eds.), *Qualitative researching with text, image and sound*. London: Sage.

Leith, D., & Myerson, G. (1989). *The power of address: Explorations in rhetoric*. London: Routledge.

Lingard, B., & Rizvi, F. (1998). Globalisation and the fear of homogenisation in education. *Change: Transformations in education, 1*(1), 62–71.

MacLure, M. (2003). *Discourse in educational and social research*. London: Sage.

MacMillan, K. (2002). Narratives of social disruption: Education news in the British tabloid press. *Discourse, 23*(1), 27–38.

Miller, P., & Rose, N. (1993). Governing economic life. In M. Gane & T. Johnson (Eds.), *Foucault's new domains*. London: Routledge.

Nelson, J., Megill, A., & McCloskey, D. (Eds.). (1987). *The rhetoric of the human sciences: Language and argument in scholarship and public affairs*. Madison, WI: University of Wisconsin Press.

Nicoll, K. (2006). *Flexibility and lifelong learning: Policy, discourse and politics*. London: RoutledgeFalmer.

Nicoll, K., & Edwards, R. (2004). Sultans of spin: Policy as persuasion. *Journal of Education Policy, 19*(1), 43–55.

Nicoll, K., & Edwards, R. (2000). Reading policy texts: Lifelong learning as metaphor. *International Journal of Lifelong Education, 19*(5), 459–469.

Parker, S. (1997). *Reflective teaching in the postmodern world: A manifesto for education in postmodernity*. Buckingham: Open University Press.

Potter, J. (1996). *Representing reality: Discourse, rhetoric and social construction*. London: Sage.

Rose, N. (1999). *Powers of freedom: Reframing political thought*. Cambridge: Polity Press.

Shapiro, M. (1989). Representing world politics: The sport/war intertext. In J. Der Derian & M. Shapiro (Eds.), *International/intertextual relations*. Lexington, MA: Lexington Books.

Schön, D. (1979). Generative metaphor: A perspective on problem-setting in metaphor. In A. Ortony (Ed.), *Metaphor and thought*. Cambridge: Cambridge University Press.

Simons, H. (1990). Introduction: The rhetoric of inquiry as an intellectual movement. In H. Simons (Ed.), *The rhetorical turn: Invention and persuasion in the conduct of inquiry*. Chicago: University of Chicago Press.

Straehle, C., Weiss, G., Wodak, R., Muntigl, P., & Sedlak, M. (1999). Struggle as metaphor in European Union discourses on unemployment. *Discourse and Society, 10*(1), 67–99.

Stronach, I., & MacLure, M. (1997). *Educational research undone: The postmodern embrace.* Buckingham: Open University Press.

Taylor, S., Rizvi, F., Lingard, B., & Henry, M. (1997). *Educational policy and the politics of change.* London: Routledge.

Woolgar, S., & Pawluch, D. (1985). Ontological gerrymandering: The anatomy of social problems explanations. *Social Problems, 32*(3), 214–27.

FURTHER READINGS

Edwards, R., Nicoll, K., Solomon, N., & Usher, R., (2004). *Rhetoric and educational discourse: Persuasive texts.* London: RoutledgeFalmer.

Nicoll K. (2006). *Flexibility and lifelong learning: Policy, discourse and politics.* London: RoutledgeFalmer.

Nicoll K., & Edwards R. (2004). Sultans of spin: policy as persuasion. *Journal of Education Policy, 19*(1), 43–55.

Potter, J. (1996). *Representing reality: Discourse, rhetoric and social construction.* London: Sage.

Shapiro. (1989). Representing world politics: The sport/war intertext. In J. Der Derian & M. Shapiro (Eds.), *International/Intertextual relations.* Lexington, MA: Lexington Books.

Straehle, C., Weiss, G., Wodak, R., Muntigl, P., & Sedlak, M. (1999). Struggle as metaphor in European Union discourses on unemployment. *Discourse and Society, 10*(1), 67–99.

Katherine Nicoll
Senior Lecturer in Education at the Stirling Institute of Education,
University of Stirling, Scotland

LUDWIG PONGRATZ

TANTALUS' TORMENT

Notes on the Regime of Lifelong Learning

INTRODUCTION

Lifelong learning has long been a mega-theme in European and international education policy. The significance attached to it is a product, on the one hand, of the high economic and political expectations bound up with lifelong learning, and on the other hand of the extensive obligations which result for each individual. Lifelong learning comes to be declared the motor of social progress, from which no-one is either able or permitted to escape. However the question which then arises concerns the price to be paid for this progress, and if the benefits are worth the price. The analysis which follows remains sceptical in relation to the great expectations attached to lifelong learning, and proposes a counter-response: it shows that today lifelong learning has developed into a very particular sort of comprehensive 'regime'. In order to analysis how this regime functions, which purposes it serves and which conceptions of human beings and society it mobilises, the discussion will engage both with the arguments of critical social theory and critical pedagogy (Pongratz, 2005a), and with the 'studies of governmentality' inspired by Michel Foucault (Pongratz, 2006; Masschelein, Simons, Bröckling & Pongratz, 2006; Fejes & Nicoll, 2008).

EUROPEAN LANGUAGE RULES

Anyone who goes shopping these days in one of the big department stores or supermarkets can count on the cashier asking an oft-repeated question: 'do you save points?' The official representation is that such points constitute customer 'loyalty', but there is more going on under the surface. They are a way to establish customer profiles, develop corresponding marketing strategies and bind customers to the retailer over the long term. This bond arises when customer learns to understand their purchases as a sort of investment, in a favoured customer relationship with a rewards card. This quietly presupposes that people have internalised the basic lessons of modern exchange society; above all, to understand themselves as self-entrepreneurs and self-marketers, in which every enterprise in life – whether it is an office appointment, a rendezvous or a supermarket purchase – constitutes an investment. Being entrepreneurial means, then, making a choice among scarce resources (such as time, goods, services, relationships, etc), in order to maximise the satisfaction of one's own preferences and needs.

M. Simons, M. Olssen and M.A. Peters (eds.), Re-Reading Education Policies: A Handbook Studying the Policy Agenda of the 21st Century, 404–417.

Once the "capitalisation of (social) life" (Masschelein & Simons, 2005, p. 22 ff.)[1] has been established as the foundation of social interaction, social relationships then also take on the character of exchange and service relations, and pedagogic relations between teachers and learners are no exception. They become a means of making everything calculable, in short: they turn into investment in human capital. Certainly such investments, despite the cool calculation of costs and benefits, carry their own risks. The marketplace of life becomes a contingency arena *par excellence*, in which every investment decision encompasses the horizon of survival, which,

> (...) implies leading a mobile life in a market setting, a life which consists of taking chances and the deployment of human capital, and this before others do it, and doing it better than them. Further existence (the right to existence) is constantly at stake (...). More than this, whoever is not prepared to engage in the struggle (or play the game) has already lost (Bauman, in Knobloch 2004, p. 26).

The market presents itself as an opportunity with no alternative, as an "offer which cannot be refused" (ibid., p. 26). This is why the operation of the self-entrepreneur in the (educational) market takes on the more or less subtle character of compulsion. People are called upon to endlessly identify their needs, to constantly develop their learning capacities, to learn their whole life long.

The concept of lifelong learning, which in the European context has gained renewed salience since the middle of the 1990s, did not simply fall from the sky. It refers to a particular type of action, a specific configuration of identity, a particular form of self-mobilisation within a marketised educational arena. And this arena is surrounded by European programs and projects which, without any doubt, have dispensed with the traditional idea of voluntary adult education. They consistently demand of people that they ultimately *want* to do what they *have* to do: namely, comply their whole life long with the social pressure to conform. In the language of the Lisbon Memorandum it reads as follows: "Everyone living in Europe – without exception – shall have the opportunity to adapt to social change" (Europäische Kommission, 2000, p. 3). And further: "With lifelong learning, the totality of learning activities are seen as a seamless, from the cradle to the grave continuum" (p. 9). This comprehensive perspective (the ironic version is 'from sperm to urn') fits neatly within a political agenda aiming to make Europe the world's most competitive and dynamic knowledge-based economic arena by the year 2010. To this extent, it is not surprising that the concept of lifelong learning finds a home "in the context of the European employment strategy" (p. 3). Lifelong learning, according to the Europe-wide language rule, encompasses "all learning during one's whole life, which serves the improvement of knowledge, qualifications and competencies, and which takes place in the framework of a perspective of engagement with personal, social and citizenship concerns" (Bechtel et al., 2005, p. 134). It includes formal, non-formal and informal learning (ibid., p. 134)

The political objectives which this approach to adult education is being aligned with are clear enough. They demonstrate the definitional power of European institutions, to which even adult educational theory seems to have resigned itself. However, it is not only the origins of lifelong learning that deserve comment, but also its conceptual context: key concepts like 'capacity for engagement', 'entrepreneurial spirit' or 'adaptive capacity' reveal a pragmatic – more precisely, functionalist – conceptual background. It has long been part of the theoretical mainstream of adult education (Pongratz, 2005b), but it still does not characterise the whole discursive field. The current demand to learn one's whole life long is very different from similar pleas in the 1970s. Beneath the superficial thematic continuity which appears to characterise roughly 40 years of continuous discussion of lifelong learning, there are in fact important shifts and breaks. If one were to formulate the development of the concept of lifelong learning as briefly as possible, it would read "Being allowed, able, expected, required, and finally wanting to learn lifelong" (adapted from Conein & Nuissl, 2001, p. 71).

BEING ALLOWED TO LEARN LIFELONG

The first boom phase of lifelong learning started in 1970, identified by UNESCO as the *International Year of Education*. Such appeals in educational policy normally have their preludes, in this case: the prognosis of a world education crisis which Coombs (1969) saw looming at the end of the 1960s. His crisis scenario was very similar to Picht's (1964) "education catastrophe." Picht had already outlined West Germany's educational emergency a few years earlier, and Coombs moved this crisis scenario to the international level. He showed that education systems in the industrial societies were outdated, inflexible and no longer met the complex demands of a 'dynamic lifeworld'. In addition, the separate fields of education – from pre-school to technical and further education – were inadequately coordinated with each other. In this way Coombs provided the crucial catchphrases for UNESCO's 1972 Faure Report (Faure, 1973). Under the programmatic title *Learning to be* (*Apprendre à etre*), the UNESCO Education Commission began with developing a program "which summarises, in an overarching understanding of lifelong learning, all of the educational processes and learning phases in human life as an inter-dependent whole" (Gerlach, 2000, p. 160). Only one year later, the OECD published its report *Recurrent education – A strategy for lifelong education* (OECD 1973). Thus were born both of the trend terms which would determine the discussion in the 1970s: 'lifelong education' or '*education permanente*' on the one hand, and 'recurrent education' on the other. "Everyone must have the opportunity," said the Faure Report, "to learn over the course of their whole life. The idea of permanent education is a cornerstone of the learning society" (Faure, 1973, p. 246). Formulations like this express a central concept in educational policy, in which education is under-stood (if not as a citizenship right) as a legitimate claim by all members of society.

The UNESCO proposals of the 1970s were based on the humanist idea of a comprehensive development of the 'complete man', the improvement of human living conditions, and the democratization of society. The 1973 OECD report, in contrast, pursued primarily economic goals. Its most important plea was to bind three, hitherto loosely connected, sectors – traditional education, the training sector in private enterprise and adult education – more closely to each other. At the centre of 'recurrent education' there are various phases of working life and training and further education for adults. This 'interval learning' demands a stronger synchronisation and systematisation of education phases. Adult education clearly profited from this: it gained increasing significance as an integral part of the education system – which then also contributed to lifelong learning being misunderstood as a "simplified substitution for adult education" (Knoll 1998, p. 36). In reality the concept of lifelong learning is today understood in a more comprehensive sense, encompassing all forms of living and learning, moving away from the focus on fixed life phases or educational institutions.

In order better to understand the terminological shift from 'lifelong education' to 'lifelong learning', it is useful to take a closer look at the various understandings of a 'learning society' which underpin the different terms. The concepts 'lifelong education' or *'education permanente'* refer to an egalitarian, participatory model of society (which was primarily characteristic of the late 1960s and 1970s), while 'lifelong learning' corresponds to a market model aiming at well-educated, adaptable and 'flexible' workers, in order to be internationally competitive (Wiesner & Wolter, 2005, p. 12 ff.; Schuetze, 2005, p. 232 ff.). For a little while it looked as though the two conceptions could be combined. The investment in the education system at the end of the 1960s and beginning of the 1970s was not only to promote economic growth and employment, but also at the same time to contribute to educational and social participation. So the concepts of lifelong learning and human capital shared the policy stage. But as the reform phase came to an end, the participatory claim that lifelong learning was a citizenship right was gradually retracted. Since the second boom period of lifelong learning, which began in the 1990s, it has firmed up as a strategic element in a global process of the regulation of the markets in goods and services. It is hard to avoid the impression that "lifelong learning has been hijacked and transformed from an emancipatory and democratic concept to one that is dictated by a 'corporatist agenda'" (Schuetze, Sawano & Fraiz, 2004, cited in Wiesner & Wolter, 2005, p. 21). Lifelong learning ultimately becomes a strategy for the production of employable human resources. Its primary goal is to unleash individual powers and to make them as productive as possible.

BEING ABLE TO LEARN LIFELONG

However, this unleashing process cannot work with a static understanding of aptitude and home-baked models of life-course phases. So the demand that everyone should *be allowed* to learn lifelong, gets linked with the conviction that everyone *can* in fact learn lifelong. For the "flexible person" of industrial capitalism (Sennett, 1998), we get the notion that individuals go through a particular succession of developmental phases, to ultimately reach their most mature form, like a relic pulled down from the educational attic. If the 1950s characterised adults in terms of their 'seclusion' and 'maturity', the concepts in the 1960s and 70s, derived from anthropology, developmental psychology and socialisation theory, drew another picture: the traditional concept of talent was replaced with a dynamic, processual category: the process of 'becoming talented'. Instead of a generalised, step-by-step development model of the life-course, there came the presumption of the continuity of life, that is, previous experiences, surrounding social conditions and individual life situations all took on their own significance. Correspondingly, the permanence of learning and developmental processes (including the risks of various discontinuities) moved to the centre of attention. Studies of socialisation similarly thematised human plasticity and changeability. The idea of a transhistorical, stable human 'nature' noticeably lost ground. Anthropological reflection turned away from normative conceptions, and instead thematised human beings as open, expansive and uncontainable questions.

The theoretical shifts sketched very briefly here took place virtually simultaneously and within only a few years. They approximate the concept of lifelong learning, give it empirical content and legitimacy. On the other hand, the notion that mental development reaches its highest point in adolescence and declines thereafter was theoretically delegitimated and finally put out of action. Adulthood was no longer a period of peace and stability. Being adult means being constantly confronted with changes and having to deal with new life situations. All of this had to unleash uncertainties. But a certain pedagogic claim attached itself to this societal irritation: the idea, namely, that growing uncertainty can be managed with lifelong learning (Kade, 1997, p. 115). What little Hans did not learn, adult Hans can still learn – he accepts the restless expansion and intensification of learning demands, and responds with "permanent renewal, adaptation and redesign" (Seitter, 1997, 323). This conception constitutes an anthropology in which the person is as undetermined and content-free as they are endlessly plastic. This progressive process of unbinding puts lifelong learning into an ambivalent light: certainly the increase in learning demands will be subjectively experienced as an expanded realm of opportunity, but behind the happy message that one *can* learn lifelong lies a new directive: an expectation that one *should* learn lifelong.

BEING EXPECTED TO LEARN LIFELONG

In this way, the emancipatory intent of the 1970s quietly turned, through the confrontation of participatory processes of social development with 'lifelong learning', into every individual's responsibility constantly to 'update' their 'potential' and keep it permanently on the move. In a didactic sense, this is most clearly expressed in the shift in emphasis from 'teaching' to 'learning'. 'Learners' now have the responsibility to take the initiative and to concern themselves with the acquisition of knowledge. The "autodidactic turn" (Arnold, 1999) mobilises a range of new concepts and keywords which begin to play their own role on the stage of lifelong learning, such as 'learning to learn', 'self-directed learning', 'acquisition orientation' or 'key competencies'.

Such concepts define the horizon with which the transition, since the 1980s, to the 'learning society' has taken place. Often they turn into empty formulas with the character of self-fulfilling prophecies. Key competencies, for example, are meant to contribute to unlocking a broad spectrum of diverse work terrains alongside a set of 'general attributes'. Such competencies are thus not meant to have any specific content, they have to be conceived in abstract terms. Key competencies were defined by Mertens (one of the German originators of the concept) as contributing to "an enumerative- additive understanding of knowledge (knowledge of facts, instruments and methods) through the acquisition of an instrumental understanding of knowledge (know how to know) (…). Mental capacity should no longer be used for the storage of facts, but as an exchange for intelligent reactions" (Mertens, 1974, p. 40). 'Storage', 'exchange, 'intelligent reactions': the terms used indicate the unashamed triumph of the human as machine. The human being as a highly flexible robot, as hardware, which with modified software can develop constantly renewed capacities for problem-solving – these conceptions are all part of the inner logic of the 'qualification offensive' of the 1980s.

Since then, it has become increasingly clear that learning is not a free decision for a free-thinking individual. More often it reveals its compulsory character. Whoever fails to respond to this coercion finds themselves from the outset among the ranks of the losers in social upheaval. And those who do respond still get no guarantee that they will end up on the winning side. The 'qualification offensive' thus links, in a cynical way, possibility and coercion: it couples the promise of 'positive' achievement of opportunity with the threat of sanctions imposed on 'negative' life and occupational decisions. The compulsion towards permanent further qualification is too readily reinterpreted as underpinning limitless individual potential. But nobody is completely in charge of their own situation. Everyone understands themselves in terms of their deficits, what they still cannot do, what they still have to learn. Lifelong learning thus also means: lifelong 'student' status, lifelong transition. It is decreasingly possible to find a fixed position, a biographical home. We live at best as learning nomads, in the worst case we become an eternally wandering construction site. One's whole life becomes a preparation for life.

Since the 1980s, more and more providers have stepped into this market for 'preparation'. They operate with the impossible promise that one's life will be fulfilled with advanced qualifications. Hence also the yearning for exclusiveness, including costs, for glossy education in grand hotels. Even if the demand that one should learn lifelong is directed at everyone, it is by no means possible for everyone to respond to the same extent. On the contrary: further education programs are highly selective; they advantage all those who have already developed the appropriate disposition as well as their own learning techniques and styles, not to mention the increasing importance of financial resources. "The secular trend towards a learning society by no means encompasses, according to an egalitarian framework, the whole population, but is determined to a large extent by social imbalances and disparities (...)" (Wiesner & Wolter, 2005, p. 16)

This contributes to a growing risk of social tensions and crises. And it increases the concern about wasted human resources and the negative effects on the domestic economy. Precautions can be taken: the claim and the demand that one has to learn ones life long has to be anchored comprehensively (in the whole education system) and intensively (in each individual). A simple appeal to participation in further education is insufficient. Lifelong learning has become the dumb compulsion of a system which, with diverse techniques of observation and control, implants the "will to knowledge", the "will to learn", the "will to quality" in every individual (Simons, 2002). From the 1990s onwards, the call that one *should* learn lifelong is increasingly transformed into the structural compulsion towards *having to* learn lifelong. This structural compulsion is ultimately internalised as a *habitus* of *wanting to* learn lifelong.

BEING REQUIRED TO LEARN LIFELONG

In order to produce this 'learning compulsion' (as structural effect), during the second boom period of lifelong learning (from the middle of the 1990s), all European education systems were taken back to the drawing board and reorganised. The reference points of all learning are no longer school-based forms of organisation, no longer specific institutions for distinct age groups, but the unpredictable and changeable learning biographies of all members of society. Correspondingly, the term 'lifelong' acquires a comprehensive significance, it gets equated in meaning with 'life encompassing', 'life-wide' or 'life-broad' (Schuetze, 2005, p. 231). The concept of learning thus experiences a violent uprooting; it relates to organised as well as non-organised, institutional as well as non-institutional, formal as well as informal learning; it is directed without exception at one and all; it not only requests individuals to learn lifelong, but aims at bringing about the 'learning society' (Jarvis, 2008).

However, this is only possible with the corresponding infrastructure. This is why educational agencies have to develop the willingness and the capacity to react in the short term to the changing needs of a shifting clientele. For the 'learning society' requires flexible, adaptable and at the same time internationally competitive 'educational service providers'. Their services are oriented towards the (international) further education markets and an individualised clientele which is difficult to attract with traditional educational forms and learning experiences. In the place of the former curricula there appears a fragmented set of offerings: modulised, atomised components which can be linked together or exchanged as required.

Their interconnections underpin no critical conception of education (as encompassed, for example by the German concept of *Bildung*), but rather a desired pragmatic effect, that is, the capacity usefully to cobble together the debris of knowledge and life in ever-renewable forms. This is how the concept of competence enters the stage: labelled "disposition to self-organisation" (Erpenbeck & Weinberg, 1999), it appears as lifelong learning's twin brother. Its empty formulaic character makes it labile as well as diffuse. For confused learners, the same advice is always given: "look for the next connection operation (*Anschlussoperation*)", so that the process can continue. In order to find it, education service providers are ready with the appropriate offerings: advice, coaching and supervision are the trademarks of a new learning culture.

The forced 'unbinding' (*Entgrenzung*) of lifelong learning leads not just to the appearance of new educational service providers, but also to the dismantling of the existing education system. "One does not need so much education, so much intellect, so much knowledge, to keep the social enterprise operating" (Schirlbauer, 2005, p. 63). On the one hand this led to a new elite discourse, and on the other hand a new, reinvigorated search begins for the possibilities of social inclusion for those endangered by the system because it threatens to exclude them. Such threats are no longer responded to with an expansion of the education system, but with a shortening of formal education pathways alongside a simultaneous expansion of the possibilities for choice and linkage. Increased permeability and intensified selectivity come to the rescue; their combination enables "a flexible movement between education and training and work" (OECD, 1996, p. 89). The expansion of flexible learning pathways and individualised learning offerings has a dual consequence: first, with the deconstruction of the education system and the introduction of market mechanisms, there is increasing pressure to privatise the responsibilities and costs of education. At the same time, however, new steering and control instruments have to be implemented for the diverse transitions and degrees. Securing the certifiability and comparability of fragmented learning provision requires a comprehensive assessment of competencies, ongoing quality control, endless evaluation. Along with accreditation and standardisation, lifelong learning grows into a regime aiming "to plan, to document and to render comparable" (Tuschling, 2004, p. 155) the learning biographies occupying a huge educational terrain. As always, the new forms of domination appear with flags waving, proclaiming 'continuity', 'diversity, 'equity' and 'efficiency' (Knoll, 1998, p. 50). Everywhere accounts are settled with the input-oriented 'old' education system. The complaints revolve around: its unequal educational participation rates, its low retention rate, its too-strict separation of general from vocational education, its outdated orientation to the curriculum, etc. At the same time the international actors in the new boom are amazingly united in their proposed solutions: output-steering of the system through new forms of control and monitoring, knowledge-transfer through lifelong learning, vocational preparation through application-oriented training programs, development of an activating *habitus*, and finally the incorporation of all learners into a dynamic culture of testing and competition (Aspin, Chapman, Hatton & Sawano, 2001; Jarvis, 2004).

This "new educational order" (Field, 2002) was put into the spotlight with loud fanfare around the mid 1990s, by macro-actors like the OECD, UNESCO and the EU. The European Commission declared 1996 the "European Year of Lifelong Learning."[2] In the same year, UNESCO published the Delors Report *Learning: the treasure within* (Delors et al., 1996) and the OECD its comprehensive plan for lifelong learning *Lifelong learning for all* (OECD, 1996). The European Commission was also active: it published its *Teaching and learning – Towards the learning society* in 1996. Drawing on human capital approaches, it essentially committed lifelong learning to securing Europe's overall competitiveness. All the components of what had hitherto characterised a humanistic and critical understanding of education were now put into service for the purposes of securing Europe's position in a globalising world.

It seems that the watershed year 1996 started a particular ball rolling, which is now virtually unstoppable. Most recently, with the decisions of the European

Council in March 2000 in Lisbon and, published in the same year, the European Commission's (2000) Memorandum, the European economic and educational arenas are tied together more closely than ever. In order actually to realise the "global policy consensus" (Field, 2002, p. 3) concerning educational reform which has emerged between the EU and other international organisations (such as, for example, the OECD, the World Bank, and the International Monetary Fund), enormous financial resources have been mobilised at international as well as national levels. Germany, for example, established a five-year BLK (*Bund-Länder Kommission* = National-Regional Commission) model program for lifelong learning (2000-2005). In 2001, the Federal Ministry for Education and Research (BMBF = *Bundesministerium für Bildung und Forschung*) started a "Competency development learning culture" program. The Federal and State governments established the "Education Forum" (1999-2002), which developed its own recommendations concerning *Learning – a life long* (Forum Bildung, 2001). All these programs share the basic conviction of the "new educational order": individual responsibility for the steering of their lifelong learning activities; intensive dove-tailing of work and learning; orientating learning outcomes to utility and value; mobilisation of non-formal and informal learning processes; retreat of the state, which is merely to guarantee a legal framework and overall education and quality standards.

At the same time all the projects launched since then have a dissemination strategy, that is, the resources provided serve not only the project's organisation, but also the *promotion of the underlying key concepts and programs*. The central messages of the European educational arena and its reorganisation according to market principles have been spread through countless publications and announcements, public interviews and speeches. This creates the impression that the reforms are based on evidence and consensus (Drexel, 2001, p. 3). More than this: the internal dynamic characterising the reform instruments (testing, ranking, controlling) creates the impression of virtually natural processes. People are to want what is required of them. They are to internalise the compulsion towards lifelong learning to such an extent that it becomes second nature to them. The regime of lifelong learning constitutes a totalising demand. It aims to anchor "lifelong learning as an attitude" (OECD 1996, p. 90) firmly in every individual. "What was compulsion, becomes need" (Beck, 1999, p. 5). This is the new anthropology of self-learners, which no longer draws its inspiration from organic (growth, maturity) or informational (storage, exchange centre, software) sources, but inherits concepts from systems theory (autopoesis, functional differentiation) and economics (cost-benefit calculation, profit maximisation). Having to learn becomes the learning system's all-encompassing organisational principle. One wants what is required, and gives this compulsion a liberal gloss. In this respect the EU announcements have an unambiguous tone, which Holzer summarises as follows: "First lifelong learning is a 'duty' for everyone, which we all have to fulfil. Second, everyone's further education is to be adapted to economic developments" (Holzer, 2004, p. 95). These demands are finally mixed together with the demand for a diffuse loyalty, a "certain irrational attachment to the political enterprise called 'active citizenship' and which manifests itself as community engagement" (ibidem).

If one sets to one side the well-meaning declarations, behind the last decade's educational policy documents concerning lifelong learning, there lies a new social configuration, which Deleuze has tried to capture with the concept of the "control society" (Deleuze, 1992). It identifies a new 'initiating' type of person, self-motivating, self-steering, organised their own learning processes, a 'entrepreneur of the self' who constitutes a flesh-and-blood incarnation of the new techniques of governance and self-governance – from assessment centres to quality audits, from competency indicators to a European life-course.

Nonetheless, this type of self-learner does not yet actually describe the dominant empirical reality. It is more the case that it has to be proposed and made familiar to the majority of the population. People still have to become what the meta-educational programmes of the international and national actors already presume them to be. The programmes function as generative political strategies. They propagate governmental techniques of governance, "with which individuals are steered though practices of individualisation" (Forneck, 2001, p. 162). This steering is part of a specific "political technology" characterised by Foucault as the "conduct of conduct." "Lifelong learning constitutes a technique of self-governance with the *telos* of a comprehensive capacity for transformation and adaptation" (Tuschling, 2004, p. 157)

So that people resign themselves to the dumb compulsion of these relations without resisting them, they are lured with a promise that lifelong learning will be an adequate road to success and personal happiness. It does fulfil the grim expectation of gaining some advantage over one's competitors through the pursuit of achievement and lifelong learning, for a minority at least. The market model of lifelong learning systematically produces losers. For them, what the official pronouncements portray as 'exclusion' can subjectively appear as quite meaningful: withdrawing from submission to "lifelong cluelessness" (Illich, 1999, p. 12).

RESISTANCE AGAINST LIFELONG LEARNING?

With the victory of lifelong learning as a total program of flexible learning activity no retreat seems possible. In a reversal of his original insight, Illich's alternative to lifelong schooling – namely, the deschooling of society (Illich, 1971) in the form of an open education arena with informal learning possibilities and educational credits – has finally been fulfilled. However, the compulsion to permanent learning will not make relationships more human, but humans more 'relational'. "With an overexertion of their limited powers, the majority of permanent learners seek to reach their learning goal. Only a few will succeed in time, the majority will remain hanging, the prize dangling in front of them. But it stays attached to the branch. It is the torment of Tantalus – no longer that of Sisyphus – that afflicts our contemporaries" (Beck, 1999, p. 6).

Certainly there are limits to resilience, willingness to adapt, to self-subjection. There are well-founded reasons for opposition to the regime of lifelong learning.

This is why the regime exerts itself to integrate resistance (Holzer, 2004). From its perspective, all forms of disintegration constitute a stimulus to leave no one undisturbed and in peace: every non-participant is a potential participant – they just don't know it yet. "Non-participation in lifelong learning processes sets activities in motion which turn the non-participant into a participant, or at least to a not-yet-participant" (Geißler & Kutscha, 1992, p. 17). In this way resistance takes on paradoxical and many-sided forms. It occurs for example as silent withdrawal from pedagogically-occupied terrain, as disappearance. In some senses this passive resistance takes Foucault's analysis of power at its word: if, as Foucault writes, "visibility is a trap" (Foucault, 1977, p. 200), such opacity takes on its own particular quality, helping to escape the compulsion towards permanent observation and self-observation accompanying the regime of lifelong learning.

No doubt this figure of resistance is deeply ambivalent (Axmacher, 1990, p. 212 ff.). It is certainly not suited to be a general formula or a generalisable strategy. But this is also not what it wants to be. It is only one aspect of relating to a learning regime which opens up thoroughly contradictory possibilities for action. Instead of withdrawal, there could also be a takeover strategy of attempting to redefine the concepts and programs of lifelong learning, to confront it with the claim to freedom which now only serves those programs rhetorically. Both may be possible: refusing to play the game, and playing it differently. Whoever chooses the second option has to pay attention to contradictions: With its claim to autonomy, the learning regime constantly produces new dependence; it promises everyone expanded educational opportunities and systematically denies them to large parts of the population. This inconsistency could serve to ignite the critique of the current regime of lifelong learning (Pongratz, 2008). In practice, Tantalus' torment will ensure that such critique will not be silenced.

Looking back over these considerations, it is clear that in practically all advanced industrial societies today there are new educational regimes being established which spread the comprehensive and insistent demand to learn lifelong into every last corner of society. When this claim is linked the promise of freedom, lifelong learning nonetheless follows another logic: people are appealed to as 'lifelong learning competence machines', and are meant to incorporate this ascription into their self-understanding. The regime of lifelong learning does, however, remain fragile, because its inner contradictions constantly generate new critique and resistance. For this critique to become effective and capable of action, it needs the outline of an approach, a perspective, which allows for the possibility that people can also learn, work and live in radically different ways.

NOTES

[1] Concepts and quotations not previously translated into English are translated by the author.
[2] Just as an aside, the term 'life accompanying' wisely avoids the proximity to the term 'lifelong', which critics of the concept of lifelong learning are keen to focus on. But in its place there comes the unmistakable resonance with the modern figure of 'pastoral power' (Foucault, 2000, p.332 ff.)

REFERENCES

Arnold, R. (1999). Vom autodidactic zum facilitative turn – Weiterbildung auf dem Weg ins 21. Jahrhundert. In R. Arnold & W. Gieseke (Eds.), *Die Weiterbildungsgesellschaft, Bd. 1* (pp. 3–14). Neuwied: Luchterhand.

Aspin, D. N., Chapman, J., Hatton, M., & Sawano, Y. (Eds.). (2001). *International handbook of lifelong learning*. Dordrecht, Boston & London.

Axmacher, D. (1990). *Widerstand gegen Bildung*. Weinheim: Deutscher Studien Verlag.

Bechtel, M., Lattke, S., & Nuissl, E. (2005). *Portrait Weiterbildung Europäische Union*. Frankfurt/M.: Deutsches Institut für Erwachsenenbildung.

Beck, J. (1999). *Der verhältnismäßige Mensch, "Lifelong Learning – Inside and Outside Schools"* (pp. 2–7). Vortrag. 25–27 February 1999, University of Bremen.

Conein, S., & Nuissl, E. (2001). "Lernen wollen, können, müssen!" Lernmotivation und Lernkompetenz als Voraussetzung lebenslangen Lernens. In Forum Bildung (Ed.), *Lernen – ein Leben lang. Vorläufige Empfehlung und Expertenbericht* (pp. 71–85). Bonn: Forum Bildung.

Coombs, P. H., & Schmitz, E. (1969). *Die Weltbildungskrise*. Stuttgart: Klett.

Deleuze, G. (1992). Postscript on the societies of control. *October, 59*, 3–7.

Delors, J., & International Commission on Education for the Twenty-first Century. (1996). *Learning, the treasure within: Report to UNESCO of the international commission on education for the twenty-first century*. Paris: UNESCO.

Dohmen, G. (2001). Lebenslanges lernen. In R. Arnold, S. Nolda, & E. Nuissl (Eds.), *Wörterbuch Erwachsenenpädagogik* (pp. 186–187). Bad Heilbrunn: Klinkhardt.

Drexel, I. (2001). Neue Konzepte des Lernens in und für den Betrieb – Diskurse, betriebliche Realitäten und gesellschaftliche Perspektiven. In Gewerkschaft Erziehung und Wissenschaft (Ed.), *GEW-Herbstakademie Weiterbildung, Dok. 88* (pp. 1–15). Frankfurt am Main: GEW.

Erpenbeck, J., & Weinberg, J. (1999). Lernen in der Leonardo-Welt – Von der Weiterbildung zur Kompetenzentwicklung in offenen und selbstorganisierten Lernarrangements. In R. Arnold & W. Gieseke (Eds.), *Die Weiterbildungsgesellschaft, Bd. 1* (pp. 144–160). Neuwied: Luchterhand.

Europäische Kommission. (2000). *Memorandum über Lebenslanges Lernen*. Brüssel: Europäische Kommission.

Faure, E. (1973). *Wie wir leben lernen: der Unesco-Bericht über Ziele und Zukunft unserer Erziehungsprogramme*. Reinbek: Rowohlt.

Fejes, A., & Nicoll, K. (Eds.). (2008). *Foucault and lifelong learning: Governing the subject*. London: Rootledge.

Field, J. (2002). *Lifelong learning and the new educational order*. Stoke on Trent: Trentham.

Forneck, H. J. (2001). Die große Aspiration. *Erwachsenenbildung, 4*, 158–163.

Forum Bildung. (Ed.). (2001). *Lernen – ein Leben lang. Vorläufige Empfehlung und Expertenbericht*. Bonn: Forum Bildung.

Foucault, M. (1977). *Discipline and punish*. London: Allen & Unwin.

Foucault, M. (2000). The subject and power. In J. D. Faubion (Ed.), *The essential works of foucault 1954–1984, Vol. 3: Power* (pp. 326–348). New York: New Press.

Geißler, K. A., & Kutscha, S. (1992). Modernisierung der Berufsbildung – Paradoxien und Parodontosen. In M. Kipp, R. Czycholl, M. Dikau, & E. Meueler (Eds.), *Paradoxien in der beruflichen Aus- und Weiterbildung - zur Kritik ihrer Modernitaïskrise: Dirk Axmacher zum Gedenken* (pp. 13–23). Frankfurt/M.: Verlag der Gesellschaft zur Förderung arbeitsorientierter Forschung und Bildung.

Gerlach, C. (2000). *Lebenslanges Lernen – Konzepte und Entwicklungen 1972 bis 1997*. Köln: Böhlau Verlag.

Holzer, D. (2004). *Widerstand gegen Weiterbildung – Weiterbildungsabstinenz und die Forderung nach lebenslangem Lernen*. Vienna: Lit.

Illich, I. (1971). *Deschooling Society*. New York: Harper & Row.

Illich, I. (1999). *Lebenslängliche Verratlosung, Lifelong Learning – Inside and Outside Schools.* Vortrag. 25–27 February 1999, University of Bremen.

Jarvis, P. (2004). *Adult education and lifelong learning: Theory and practice.* London: Routledge.

Jarvis, P. (2008). *Democracy, lifelong learning and the learning society : A critical assessment of policies and ethics in lifelong education.* London: Routledge.

Kade, J. (1997). Riskante Biographien und die Risiken lebenslangen Lernens. In H. Faulstich-Wieland, E. Nuissl, H. Siebert, & J. Weinberg (Eds.), *Literatur- und Forschungsreport Weiterbildung, Thema: Lebenslanges Lernen – selbstorganisiert?* (pp. 112–124). Frankfurt/ M.: Deutsches Institut für Erwachsenenbildung.

Knobloch, C. (2004). Eine neoliberale Transformationsgeschichte: Vom Bildungsprivileg zur Selbstoptimierungspflicht. *SoWi 2004, 2,* 23–26.

Knoll, J. H. (1998). Lebenslanges Lernen und internationale Bildungspolitik: Zur Genese eines Begriffs und dessen nationalen Operationalisierungen. In R. Brödel (Ed.), *Lebenslanges Lernen – lebensbegleitende Bildung* (pp. 35–50). Neuwied: Luchterhand.

Masschelein, J., & Simons, M. (2005). *Globale Immunität- oder: Eine kleine Kartographie der europäischen Bildungsraums.* Zürich/Berlin: Diaphanes.

Masschelein, J., Simons, M., Bröckling, U., & Pongratz, L. (Eds.). (2006). *The learning society from the perspective of governmentality.* Oxford: Blackwell.

Mertens, D. (1974). Schlüsselqualifikationen. Thesen zur Schulung für eine moderne Gesellschaft. *Mitteilungen aus der Arbeitsmarkt- und Berufsforschung 1974, 7,* 36–43.

OECD. (1973). *Recurrent education – A strategy for lifelong education.* Paris: Author.

OECD. (1996). *Lifelong learning for all.* Paris: Author.

Picht, G. (1964). *Die deutsche Bildungskatastrophe: Analyse und Dokumentation.* Olten: Walter-Verlag.

Pongratz, L. A. (2003). *Zeitgeistsurfer: Beiträge zur Kritik der Erwachsenbildung.* Weinheim: Beltz.

Pongratz, L. A. (2005a). Critical theory and pedagogy: Adorno und Horkheimer's contemporary significance for a critical pedagogy. In G. Fishman, P. McLaren, H. Sünker, & C. Lankshear (Eds.), *Critical theories, critical pedagogies and global conflicts* (pp. 154–163). Boulder, CO: Rowman & Littlefield.

Pongratz, L. A. (2005b). *Untiefen im Mainstream – Zur Kritik konstruktivistisch- systemtheoretischer Pädagogik.* Wetzlar: Büchse d. Pandora.

Pongratz, L. A. (2006). Voluntary self-control – education reform as governmental strategy. *Educational Philosophy and Theory, 4,* 471–482.

Pongratz, L. A. (2008). Freedom and the society of control – notes on educational reform. *Tertium comparationis, 13(2).*

Schirlbauer, A. (2005). *Die Moralpredigt – Destruktive Beiträge zur Pädagogik und Bildungspolitik.* Vienna: Sonderzahl.

Schuetze, G. (2005). Modelle und Begründungen lebenslangen Lernens und die Rolle der Hochschule – Internationale Perspektiven. In G. Wiesner & A. Wolter (Eds.), *Die lernende Gesellschaft – Lernkulturen und Kompetenzentwicklung in der Wissensgesellschaft* (pp. 225–260). Weinheim/Munich: Juventa Verlag.

Seitter, W. (1997). Geschichte der Erwachsenenbildung. In K. Harney & H.-H. Krüger (Eds.), *Einführung in die Geschichte von Erziehungswissenschaft und Erziehungswirklichkeit* (pp. 311–329). Opladen: Leske & Budrich.

Sennett, R. (1998). *The corrosion of character: The personal consequences of work in the new capitalism.* New York: Norton.

Simons, M. (2002). Governmentality, education and quality management. *Zeitschrift für Erziehungswissenschaft, 5(4),* 617–633.

Tuschling, A. (2004). Lebenslanges lernen. In U. Bröckling, S. Krasmann, & T. Lemke (Eds.), *Glossar der Gegenwart* (pp. 152–158). Frankfurt/Main: Suhrkamp.

UNESCO. (1996). *Learning: The treasure within.* Paris: Author.

Wiesner, G., & Wolter, A. (Eds.). (2005). *Die lernende Gesellschaft – Lernkulturen und Kompetenzentwicklung in der Wissensgesellschaft.* Weinheim/München: Juventa Verlag.

FURTHER READINGS

Aspin, D., Chapman, J., Hatton, M., & Sawano, Y. (Eds.) (2001). *International Handbook of Lifelong Learning*. Dordrecht, Boston & London.

Field, J. (2002). *Lifelong learning and the new educational order*. Stoke on Trent: Trentham.

Tuschling, A. (2004). Lebenslanges Lernen. In U. Bröckling, S. Krasmann, & T. Lemke (Eds.), *Glossar der Gegenwart* (pp. 152–158). Frankfurt/Main: Suhrkamp.

Jarvis, P. (2004). *Adult education and lifelong learning: Theory and practice*. London: Routledge.

Masschelein, J., Simons, M., Bröckling, U., & Pongratz, L. (Eds.). (2006). *The learning society from the perspective of governmentality*. Oxford: Blackwell.

Fejes, A., & Nicoll, K. (Eds.). (2008). *Foucault and lifelong learning: Governing the subject*. London: Routledge.

Jarvis, P. (2008). *Democracy, lifelong learning and the learning society: A critical assessment of policies and ethics in lifelong education*. London: Routledge.

Ludwig Pongratz
Institute for General and Vocational Education
Darmstadt Technical University, Germany

RICHARD EDWARDS

RE-WRITING EDUCATION POLICY

Scribbling in the Margins of
Lifelong Learning

Comment:
"(...) there might
be something
even in my
scribblings
which, for the
mere sake of
scribbling, would
have interest for
others" (Poe,
1984, p. 1310,
emphasis in
original)

INTRODUCTION

This is an act of reading. For you at least. But for me, it is
an act of writing. And what happens in the act of reading?
You focus on the text, follow its traces across the page,
squeeze it for meaning, perhaps even attempt to discern
the intended meaning of the author(s), despite their alleged death. In relation to
reading policy texts, intended and unintended meanings are sought in the spaces
between the words, in the silences in the texts, often in order to bring forth its true
significance. This significance is often stated to be ideological, hiding what is
really going on or really intended. And there we have an aporia of course for the
truth of the text being ideological, when ideology is often positioned as an
antithesis to truth itself starts to trouble the notion of reading as a way of getting to
true meaning, for the truth of the text is a rhetorical achievement (Edwards et al.,
2004). In other words, the persuasiveness of texts does not simply rely on their
truthfulness, but on the rhetorical practices through which they become
convincing and are taken up as true. And there is a second troubling. For to read is
also to write, for to make more of a text requires further writing and often the
production of new texts. So texts start to pile up on each other like bricks in a
wall.

And what are you making of what you are reading here? You are following the
words on the page that I am leading you through in the very act of writing. But
what do we miss by focusing solely on what is written? What happens in those
white spaces that surround these words, sentences, paragraphs? These margins,
they appear empty and devoid of anything to be read. But it is the margins that are
the focus of this chapter and the notion that they can be read/written in ways
which supplement the text rather than simply adding another text to the existing
pile. The aim then is to explore an engagement with policy texts, in this case those
of lifelong learning, that involves writing in the margins as an act of reading, of
making and taking meaning. However, this writing is not simply another set of
sentences nor paragraphs, because what I also want to suggest is that the margins

M. Simons, M. Olsen and M.A. Peters (eds.), Re-Reading Education Policies: A Handbook Studying
the Policy Agenda of the 21ˢᵗ Century, 418–432.
© *2009 Sense Publishers. All rights reserved.*

of the text, without which there can be no centre, offer a space for more playful writing, what here I refer to as scribbling.

Now of course, there is something wrong here already, for I am writing about scribbling in the margins, but am not modelling this in the writing of this text. However, without a text there can be no margin to scribble in as the one requires the other. Thus the necessity to write about scribbling in margins as the centred focus of the text, in order to provide margins for you to scribble in.

> Comment:
> Thus my invitation to you as reader of this text is to scribble in its margins as part of your act of reading as deconstruction – to highlight, to erase, to underline, to comment.

Education policy does not exist but is inscribed. It is inscribed in texts that mediate the practices of politics. These inscriptions or re-writings are part of the work of politics through which meaning is, taken, made and translated. This chapter explores the ways in which aspects of education policy in many countries have been re-inscribed through the discourses of lifelong learning and argues that to engage in the politics of such practices entails itself alternative writings. These are what I refer to as scribblings in the margin. This chapter is about scribbling, but it is not itself purely an act of scribbling, of writing unconstrained by the disciplines of grammar, layout, genre, text. Scribbling is the result of trying to approach a topic through a different writing strategy, which both ties certain concepts together while untying others to supplement possible further writings of lifelong learning policy, what Derrida (1988) refers to as "grafting". And in this writing I want to argue that lifelong

If, as Freud suggested, education is an impossible profession, then what plight the educational researcher, attempting to understand the impossible. Is such a stance possible? Or is impossibility the only possibility open to us? Similar questions have been posed by John Law in his 2004 book on mess in social science research. If the world is messy, then how can we understand it through tidy methods? It is through such methods that the social world itself is partly tidied, organised, ordered, its complexity reduced. Rather than finding order in the world, we engage in ordering practices. Both in our methods and in our representations of the world then, there is an ordering in play. Similarly, we might say that it is through ordering practices that the impossible is also made possible. It is the nature of that possibility that becomes the question.

Freud of course noted education was impossible in the sense of producing predictable outcomes, of being able to mandate and thereby learning itself has become a reflexive enactment of a potential changed focus in doing educational policy and doing educational policy research. Thus its importance as a site for doing policy research, as it signifies different forms of policy and governing (Edwards, 2002).

But my argument is marginal to this overall text, as in scribbling I want to suggest that re-reading policy entails a re-writing of policy and that one strategy in that re-writing is to scribble in the margins, where the marginal is not taken to be simply at the edges of the text but to be part of and within the text (Parker 1997). Thus the white space created in writing a text of the sort you are reading here is not an external context for that text, but is part of it, integral to its existence as a text. In this endeavour, I am drawing not upon the canon of existing policy research alone, but on the work of the American author, Edgar Allan Poe (1984, p.1309, emphasis in original) who is well known for his dark interest in marginalia:

I have been always solicitous of an ample margin; this not so much through any love of the thing in itself, however agreeable, as for the faculty it affords me of pencilling suggested thoughts, agreements and differences of opinion, or brief critical comments in general... the *marginalia* are deliberately pencilled, because the mind of the reader wishes to unburden itself of a *thought* – however flippant – however

master the future. At one level, this is trivial and trite. There may be educational trajectories framed by class, gender, race, etc, but they are not mandated. And yet, the desire to mandate the future continues to infuse the practices of education, not least in the realms of education policy. Education is constantly invoked as the way to address this or that economic or social condition. Competitiveness, productivity, equity, inclusion all vie for space as central to the policy purpose of education. And this entails a form of mastery. To mandate is to attempt to master. Thus the frustration of those doing the invoking at the impossibility of that which they attempt and their continuing efforts to master through accountability and audit (Strathern, 2000).

Mastery is also a form of centring. It is common place in the study of educational policy to place policy making at the centre of events and focus on only certain of the actors in the policy process. Policy, policy makers and policy making become the central characters in narratives of change and the exercise of power in society, usually, but not always, looking to constrain. They are in many cases the pantomime villains that attempt to stop people doing what they should be allowed to do or make people do things that they should not have to do. Reading policy texts is often attempted to discern the real intentions of the policy and governing community, to re-centre policy by placing neo-liberalism, capitalism or globalisation as that to be attended to.

silly – however trivial... In the marginalia ... we therefore talk freshly – boldly – originally – with *abandonment*.

And here I am positioning myself as marginal, as the norm for policy analysis is to seek to explain. Yet to explain is to attempt to master, which, as we will see, lifelong learning itself signifies as a flawed approach. As Spivak (1988, p.105) has argued, "the possibility of explanation carries the presupposition of an explainable (even if not fully) universe and an explaining (even if imperfectly) subject". It is that desire to have a binary logic and its separation of subject and object that results in the dominance of explanation as a way of engaging with the world. Marginal abandonment offers an alternative, but not in an either-or sense, but in the sense of both-and, a supplement.

Of course, it is not simply that policy is positioned at the centre. It is also the case that policy inscribes certain issues as central, to be mastered, as well as how they are to be addressed and by whom. And insofar as certain issues and solutions are positioned as central, others are positioned as at the margin. The margin then, often represented as a white space around the text on the page, like this one, might then be read as full of possible inscriptions, perhaps written in invisible ink. Or perhaps one can envision beyond the page, all those possibilities attempting to get purchase on the edge in order to migrate from the margin to the centre and the inbetweenness that makes both centres and margins possible. As without the margins, the text itself cannot exist. Decentring policy therefore entails a writing that performs a double act. First it is to perform an act of decentring policy per se. Second, it is to decentre the content of policy. This involves what I am terming scribbling in the margins, abandoning oneself to forms of writing that may lead in many different directions

Comment:
It is in this spirit of writing as abandonment, that I scribble some thoughts on lifelong learning

This chapter therefore attempts to do two things. First, it explores the impossibility of educational policy as a form of mastery and how this is signified through the uptake of lifelong learning as part of a policy discourse. Here it will draw upon arguments derived in part from Lyotard's (1984) view of the postmodern condition. This suggests that rather than seeking mastery, policy making can be considered a form of apprenticeship, marked by fallibility and conditionality. This in my view is what Biesta (1998) has referred to in another context as an aspect of "emancipatory ignorance". Second it will consider the decentring of educational policy as evidenced though the uptake of lifelong learning, for there is an impossibility in mandating learning. As an act of writing, this chapter inscribes and performs this task through textual mediation. And it is the consideration of policy making as an act of inscription and communicating more broadly that this decentring becomes possible. This may seem like a task without purpose, and indeed it may be if there is no uptake of the writing herein. However, it is purposeful, in the sense that this decentring suggests an alternative politics to that which we are conventionally subject. This is a politics based upon interpretation and fallibility rather than one based on explanation and mastery. Rather than simply re-reading policy therefore, I am seeking to re-write it through the act of scribbling. For me, lifelong learning itself reflexively inscribes the very possibilities for scribbling that I am suggesting, as it signifies a decentring of education in education policy texts.

MASTERING SUBJECTS

Since the publication of *The Postmodern Condition of Knowledge* (Lyotard, 1984), there has been much debate about the significance of postmodern framings for education. These framings have taken a variety of forms across a spectrum ranging from enthusiastic support to outright hostility. At the very least, the postmodern has provided a space for the development of social imaginaries productive of a multiplicity and diversity of meanings and possibilities, through which to make sense of and engage with contemporary trends and processes. Lyotard (1984) argued that the grand narratives of modernity no longer have the ability to compel consensus in quite the same ways as in earlier times. These grand narratives frame actions as in the service of progress, truth and the mastery of the world. They are increasingly greeted with incredulity and understood as masterful narratives and narratives of mastery. Their relative decline in influence and power has also thrown into doubt the subaltern narratives they have helped to shape, including the narratives that frame the modernist educational project. This project positions education as the route to enlightenment and emancipation, as captured in the saying, 'the truth will make you free'. Modernist master signifiers then are generally seen as no longer quite as masterful, even if they remain powerful, as the effects they produce are seen not to have produced the progress and emancipation promised, or at least, to some, too often have come at an unacceptable cost.

Incredulity and doubt are widespread, encompassing a questioning of foundations or authorising centres and thus scepticism that certain kinds of knowledge have canonical status - that some knowledge is *intrinsically* worthwhile – whether this knowledge be conservative or critical. The authority invested in certain groupings

– the universities, scientific communities, professional bodies, government – is often treated with suspicion and scepticism. There is a diversification of modes, centres and sources of knowledge production and of social actor positions. The result is less certainty as to what constitutes authoritative discourse and who can speak authoritatively on and as a subject. Even then as some governments look to the education research community to provide them with evidence to inform policy and practice, those communities are less capable of giving clear messages or directions. The truth-tellers and truth-telling are neither clear nor straight-forward, the struggle over which has a long history (Foucault, 2001). It is a struggle to which the postmodern may push us further into consideration of, as "how can we distinguish the good, truth-telling teachers from the bad or inessential ones?" (Foucault, 2001, p.93). This is a crucial educational question, as education is in principle not simply about learning, but about learning *something worthwhile*.

The uncertainty of the markers for knowledge that characterise a postmodern condition can be argued to signify a loss of mastery as a goal of education. Yet mastery is inscribed in modernist educational policy making and its desires to mandate the future. Modernist education provides a training in certain forms of rationality, sensibilities, values and subjectivities. Through this comes a disembodying of learners with a consequent formation of bodies that inscribes a mind/body dualism in its place. Here the more educated you are, the more rational and the more 'civilised'. The focus is on the development of the mind, the denial of emotion, and the body as a site of learning is separated out to be trained through sport. The extension of education and educational opportunities is both a symbol of progress in a modern nation state – inscribed in league tables - and contributes to progress through the education provided. There is a mastering of the self in the mastering of knowledge and of others.

Mastery of the subject is a key educational goal. Mastery represents a form of completion, an end to learning. However, even as it points to a position of finality and closure, we can point to the oppositions to and incompleteness to which it is subject. Mastery of the subject and subjects and self-mastery themselves become subject to incredulity. There is an incredulity as to the possibility of mastering and mandating the modernist project, even as ever greater attempts are made to legislate, regulate, discipline and administer. Thus, the attempts at mastery – increasingly inscribed in discourses of standards and targets, and the accounts of accountability - only point to the inability to master. This points to the deconstructive logic within policy making, the impossibility of mandating the future to which I have already referred. For me, this is highlighted in the uptake of lifelong learning within policy.

At the heart of much educational policy making in recent years are attempts at mastery of uncertainly, incredulity, risk, with lifelong learning as the means to achieve this. Lifelong learning is placed in the centre of policy texts. Yet this search for mastery has within its margins a lack of mastery. For lifelong learning, an unavoidable human activity, does not remedy this lack, but actually accentuates it further. So the lack of mastery creates the conditions for the endlessness for lifelong learning. Thus, rather than being a solution to the problem of change and uncertainty – a condition for mastery – lifelong learning can be therefore understood differently – as actually fuelling the uncertainty to which it is the supposed response. Rather than a route to mastery, lifelong learning might be better considered a condition of constant apprenticeship (Rikowski, 1999). This may well still involve the attempt to master, but it is never fully achieved or achievable. This is marginal to the meanings of lifelong learning policy texts, but is central to its significance. We are abandoned to lifelong learning.

Lifelong learning as a policy goal therefore deconstructs the mastery of policy making through which it is invoked. It is in educational terms an expression of the impossibility of mastery, of mandating the future, even as it is invoked as the basis for continuing to master. Similarly, policy itself can be re-written, scribbled, in relation to its own lack of mastery, where policy making is a practice of constant apprenticeship in the ordering of the world.

Biesta (2004, p.71) argues that "something has been lost in the shift from the language of education to the language of learning". He views this shift as arising from a range of contradictory trends. The four he identifies are new theories of learning, postmodernism, the rise of the consumer market and the decline of the welfare state. Biesta suggests that questions of learning are educational questions and that there is a requirement to revitalise a language *for* education, and the *for* is significant as he is positioning this discourse as a aspect of action, an ordering. He bases his argument on three interlocking principles: "trust without ground, transcendental violence and responsibility without knowledge" (Biesta, 2004, p.76). With regard to the first, his suggestion is that learning involves the unexpected and that this entails trust because there is risk involved. His second principle involves challenging and confronting students – and note he does not use the notion of learners – with otherness and difference, what he refers to as coming into presence. This entails transcendental violence as it creates difficult situations, but it is only through these that coming into presence is possible. This is a form of challenge that enables people to move into other spaces. The third principle, responsibility without knowledge, is based on the notion that educators have unlimited responsibility for the subjectivities of students, but this is not based on calculation as we have no knowledge of what we take responsibility for.

> Comment:
> Risk, trust, responsibility, otherness, difference, pleasure…

These signify notions that are a far cry from any modernist certainty about the teleological goals of education. They are based upon processes rather than ultimate purposes as ends. And perhaps this is as it needs to be. In his critique of critical pedagogy's desire for a language of possibility, Biesta (1998) also draws upon the comment by Freud to which I have referred above. He extends this idea of the impossibility of mandating the future to all human interactions and suggests, drawing on Derrida and Foucault, that practices need to be developed around an "emancipatory ignorance". Here

It just is an ignorance that does not claim to know how the future will be or will have to be. It is an ignorance that does not show the way, but only issues an invitation to set out on the journey. It is an ignorance that does not say what to think of it, but only asks, 'What do you think about it?' In short it is an ignorance that makes room for the possibility of disclosure (Biesta, 1998, p. 505).

Biesta's argument is related specifically to critical pedagogy, but it is relevant also to the reformulation of a discourse of educational policy making.

Formulating an education policy making discourse around apprenticeship, impossibility and ignorance may seem absurd in these performative times. When outcomes and outputs are to the fore, what spaces are there for educational discourses around unending process? But it is here that I find the concepts of fallibility and conditionality helpful. Fallibility because, unlike its sister probability, it points to the notion that, even if we practice upon the basis of the best available evidence we have, we know full well it is not perfect. This is turn results in and from a position of conditionality, that is, we could do something rather than we should do something. Our policy making efforts then are only as good as we currently can establish and they are a learning process rather than an exercise in mandating and mastery. This is precisely signalled through the discourses of lifelong learning. In scribbling in the margins of lifelong learning therefore we start to point to it as a condition of as much as a response to the contemporary order. This is the logic of supplementarity at play. Here "the text weaves for itself the ghost of a context, a virtual space within which it tells its story" (Parker, 1997, p.88).

> Comment: "Supplementarity is the highlighting of something otherwise suppressed or forgotten by the text – its contextual margins'" (Parker 1997: 88).

MARGINALISING POLICY

To position policy making as a practice of apprenticeship learning, working on the basis of ignorance, fallibility and conditionality may seem perverse. But policy on lifelong learning is precisely that, a sign of the state of policy as well as a sign of policy intent. It is a sign of the lack of ability to master and mandate in and through policy in its very inscription as central to education policy. It is itself an abandonment. Scribbling in this way might be said to miss the point of course. But it is precisely such missing that is the point of this exercise, as the scribblings decentre certain notions of policy making, which precisely rest upon seeing it as a practice of (flawed) mastery. I am therefore attempting to engage in education policy research as a form of emancipatory ignorance based upon abandonment, a writing of interpretation rather than explanation.

As I have indicated, education policy like all policy centres certain issues to be addressed, literally on the page, but also through reference to that which it is writing about. Issues are centred and plans for action put forward in order that mastery of the situation will be possible. Here education, as has often been written, is positioned at the centre of efforts to cure the ills of society and the economy. It does not take a genius to realise that in this process policy, like curriculum, is selective and thus marginalises other issues, other ways of framing issues and other possible courses of action to address issues. In centring certain inscriptions, others are marginalised.

Much educational policy research engages in critique that attempts to reveal what lies behind the veils of policy, the true significance, the real intent, the interests, etc. Such unveilings and revelations are persistent in the literature. But perhaps ironically they also engage in acts of mastery and centring in their attempts to explain. They attempt to master the true meaning of policy, to wrestle with its real significance, in order that truth is revealed. They echo the modernist imperative but from a different position. And in the process, they tend to centre national policy making and sometimes international policy making as the locus of policy. In others words, they tend to centre the state as both that which seeks mastery and that which is to be mastered. Other actors in the overall practices of policy are themselves marginalised. In the texts of educational policy analysis we therefore witness a similarly centring logic both on the page but also in that to which reference is made (Nicoll, 2006). And once again in centring certain inscriptions, others are marginalised.

But there is always seepage and supplementarity, because centring takes a lot of work, but also because we might consider there to be plural contending centrings or graftings, such as I have very simplistically outlined above. Here one set of inscriptions comes into conflict with another, each centring pre-existing the point of engagement. And both are relatively untouched by each other's (en)counters. And both for different reasons bemoan the lack of influence.

So what I am suggesting is that another strategy is also possible – there are of course many such strategies. This entails an approach that rather than a process of centring and marginalising and of writing about the margins in order to centre them, we can engage in forms of policy analysis based on scribbling in the margins. This scribbling unfolds supplementarity:

> Supplementarity is the strategy of seizing upon the peripheral in the text to show its absolute necessity to the text's purpose. Supplementarity approaches the subversion of the text's hierarchies from the opposite strategy of strong mis-reading, where overtly external intertextual strategies are employed to erode the inside/outside impermeability of the text (Parker, 1997, p.87).

In the process, rather than policy positioning itself and being positioned as central, I am pointing to the ongoing interplay between centre and margins, which means that all such writing is a folding.

This of course may seem highly dubious. Surely lifelong learning is centred by state and international organisations as the way to master the future. Behind it, revealed through analysis, lie neo-liberalism, globalisation, capitalism.... But of course it is a marginal policy, and as I have already argued, it deconstructs as mastery, accelerating precisely the conditions of decontrol that it is meant to master. In centring lifelong learning as an inscription in education policy then, one is decentring the conditions of policy as mastery, as it can produce the conditions to which it is meant to be a response.

> Comment:
> Uncertainty, risk…

And here ironically it is the critique of lifelong learning policy that is often trying to keep it centred, to explain and master it, contributing to the relations through which lifelong learning and policy making can be black boxed as the centre of attention. Here policy critique adds to the materiality of policy even as it critiques it (Nicoll, 2006), adding another brick in the wall. But lifelong learning is itself disappearing off the page even as it is placed there for learning cannot be mandated, so policy is setting itself an impossible task.

But what we might ask has this to do with lifelong learning policy? Not much, one might say, as it is more about writing and policy. And indeed that is the case. However, I want to use the inscription of lifelong learning into education policy as a case upon which to engage in an act of decentring. Insofar as one moves away from policy as the centre and as a centring practice, which one can challenge, as in a war of position, then alternative engagements become possible. These represent less of the barricades associated with assaulting the centres of power and more the war of manoeuvre. Here is a strategy that is framed to engage with governmental power more than sovereign power, given the capillary action of the former.

> Comment:
> "In addition to disciplinary power invested in nation states, which has as its object the regulation of individuals within a territory, there is also sovereign power invested in the monarch; and *biopower* which involves a governmentality that regulates populations as resources to be used and optimized" (Edwards, 2008).

> Comment:

A Scottish Case

> Comment :
> What margins of debate are included

> Comment:
> Don't we need to forget sometimes too?

[Why] do we need lifelong learning?

The key challenges facing us are:

> Comment:
> Who is 'us' – the alignment of author and readership?

the increasing pace of technological change in the knowledge economy, which means we need a flexible and adaptable workforce that is ready to reskill and retrain to keep pace with the economy's skills needs.

> Comment:
> What makes this a need rather than a constraint or desire?

> Comment:
> Who is this 'we'?

> Comment:
> For which, read exploited and overworked…

> Comment:
> Partly being fuelled by lifelong learning itself. If we didn't have the capacities then we wouldn't need to learn more.

> Comment:
> This assumes we have a knowledge economy. Even if we know what it is, do we have it?

427

Scotland's changing population, which means we will have fewer young people entering the workforce in the future: by 2022, 42% of the population of Scotland will be aged over 50

> Comment:
> Not if migration continues at the pace it is…

closing the opportunity gap - learning plays an important role in providing a route out of poverty. It also enables people to take an active part in society

> Comment:
> Learning – the cure for the ills of society. Oh yeah!

In a modern, forward-looking, prosperous Scotland we cannot accept:

the **opportunity** between people who achieve their full potential and those who do not

the **skills** between people in work and those who are not - 35% of people not in work do not have any qualifications
the **productivity**

> Comment:
> Eliding skills and qualifications here

between Scotland and the leading economies of the world

> Comment:
> Interesting comparison given the size and history of Scotland by comparison with the leading economies...

Bridging   these   gaps

Bridging The Gap

... personalized assistance in providing healthcare options for older adults and their families ...

> Comment:
> Having established gaps as a key metaphor, then what alternative but to use a bridge to span them???

is vital if we are to make social justice a reality, if Scottish businesses are to grow and prosper and if we are to help the people of Scotland to help themselves.

> Comment:
> The logos for lifelong learning is established, but how well is pathos established in this mode of discourse? Exigence and kairos is attempted.

What is lifelong learning?
Our lifelong learning policy for Scotland is about personal fulfilment and enterprise, employability and adaptability, active citizenship and social inclusion.

Lifelong learning is mainly about the training and learning that people can achieve after they leave school. We want to make it possible for more young people to stay on at school or college. And we want all pupils and students over 14 to gain work-based vocational learning and enterprise experience.

> Comment:
> We don't start life until we leave school!

Lifelong learning covers the whole range of learning. That includes formal and informal learning and workplace learning. It also includes the skills, knowledge, attitudes and behaviours that people acquire in their day-to-day experiences.

> Comment:
> Including criminal behaviours no doubt too...

Why are we investing in lifelong learning?

We believe in investing public money in lifelong learning because investment in knowledge and skills brings direct economic benefits both to individuals and to society as a whole.

But people are not only interested in learning to increase their earnings. Lifelong learning helps people to achieve other goals, such as taking an active part in civic life, leading a more sustainable lifestyle, and improving their health and wellbeing. It also benefits society, by reducing crime and encouraging community activities.

(Scottish Government 2003)

MARGINALIA

This approach to policy raises a reflexive question about the role of research in mobilising certain concepts rather than others and in engaging with concepts as though they simply represent an existent reality 'out there'. Research can be considered "an 'intellectual technology', a way of making visible and intelligible certain features of persons, their conducts, and their relations with one another" (Rose, 1998, pp.10-11). To name is to make visible, to be visible is to be named. How does lifelong learning come to be named and made visible? This concept tends to be taken to be pre-existing in a social reality to be explored rather than being considered as mobilised through discursive practices. However, as Miller and Rose (1993, p.80) point out in relation to the economy, "before one can seek to manage a domain such as an economy it is first necessary to conceptualise a set of processes and

relations as an economy which is amenable to management". In other words, while objects of research are "an effect of stable arrays or networks of relations" (Law, 2002, p. 91), they are usually treated as naturalistic objects, pre-existing in the social world. The same might be argued of lifelong learning. I have therefore been following Pels *et al.* (2002, p.11) in the view that "objects need symbolic framings, storylines and human spokespersons in order to acquire social lives; social relationships and practices in turn need to be materially grounded in order to gain spatial and temporal endurance". In other words, they need ordering and mobilising, part of which is provided through the circulation of discourses and scribblings: "Different modes of ordering produce certain forms of organisation. They produce certain material arrangements. They produce certain subject positions. And they produce certain forms of knowledge." (Law, 2001, p.3) What I am suggesting is that this symbolic ordering is not being addressed in policy research to any great extent, as the latter is held to provide a secure footing of explanation upon which to develop further practices. The performative aspects of research on specifically *policy* as such are thereby left reflexively unquestioned. Indeed even the critiques of discourses of lifelong learning may increase the apparent reality of the concepts through their discursive repetition – lifelong learning policy becomes a truism, trite, taken for granted, not worth considering... dare I say, even marginal.

Comment:
'No matter how assiduous one is in scribbling, one can never cover all the blank space. It always surprises me, but scribbling of a certain type is blank itself.' (Abe 1974: 177-8)

To return to the ample margin... My suggestion is that scribbling, writing as abandonment, is both a manifestation of and contributes to policy making as fallible and conditional, based upon an emancipatory ignorance associated with learning and policy making as apprenticeship. This possibility for policy and for policy research is signified in the texts of lifelong learning and by the notions of lifelong learning itself. This is not about making the margins the centre, but of being constantly edgy in what we write and represent and of foldin g, supplementing and grafting. And re-writing education policy in the process perhaps.

Comment:
What do you think of it?

Notes

1. All images are courtesy of Google.
2. My original scribblings in the margins had to become part of the text because of book publishing conventions, thereby increasing the marginal space for you the reader to become writer through scribbling.

REFERENCES

Abe, K. (1974). *The box man*. New York: Vintage.

Biesta, G. (1998). Say you want a revolution.... Suggestions for the impossible future of critical pedagogy. *Educational Theory, 48*(4), 499-510.

Biesta, G. (2004). Against learning: Reclaiming a language for education in an age of learning. *Nordisk Pedogogik,* 24(1), 70-82.

Derrida, J. (1988). *Limited inc.* Evanston, IL: Northwestern University Press.

Edwards, R. (2002). Mobilising lifelong learning: Governmentality and educational practices. *Journal of Education Policy,* 17(3), 353-365.

Edwards, R. (2008) Ordering subjects: Governmentality and lifelong learning. Paper presented at the AERA, New York, March.

Edwards, R., Nicoll, K., Solomon, N., & Usher, R. (2004). *Rhetoric and educational discourse.* London: Routledge.

Foucault, M. (2001). *Fearless speech.* Los Angeles: Semiotext(e).

Law, J. (2001). Ordering and obduracy, published by the Centre for Science Studies and the Department of Sociology, Lancaster University at http://www.comp.lancs.ac.uk/ sociology/soc068jl.html (accessed 27 March 2003).

Law, J. (2002). Objects and spaces. *Theory, Culture & Society,* 19(5/6), 91-105.

Law, J. (2004). *After method: Mess in social science research.* London: Routledge.

Lyotard, J-F. (1984). *The postmodern condition: A report on knowledge.* Manchester: Manchester University Press.

Miller, P. & Rose, N. (1993). Governing economic life. In: M. Gane & T. Johnson (eds.), *Foucault's new domains.* London: Routledge.

Nicoll. K. (2006). *Flexibility and lifelong learning.* London: Routledge.

Parker, S. (1997). *Reflective teaching in the postmodern world.* Buckingham: Open University Press.

Pels, D., Hetherington, K. & Vandenberghe, F. (2002). The status of the object: performances, mediations, and techniques. *Theory, Culture & Society,* 19(5/6), 1-21.

Poe, E. (1984). *Marginalia, essays and reviews.* Cambridge: Cambridge University Press.

Rikowski, G. (1999). Nietzsche, Marx and mastery: The learning unto death. In: P. Ainley and H. Rainbird (Eds.), *Apprenticeship: Towards a new paradigm for learning.* London: Kogan Page.

Rose, N. (1998). *Inventing ourselves.* Cambridge: Policy Press.

Scottish Government (2003) Summary of Lifelong Learning Strategy for Scotland. Available at: http://www.scotland.gov.uk/Publications/2003/02/16309/17778 (accessed 29 January 2007).

Spivak, G. (1988). *In other worlds: Essays in cultural politics.* New York: Routledge.

Strathern, M. (ed.) (2000). *Audit cultures: Anthropological studies in accountability, ethics and the academy.* London: Routledge.

FURTHER READINGS

Biesta, G. (2004). Against learning: Reclaiming a language for education in an age of learning. *Nordisk Pedogogik,, 24*(1), 70-82.

Edwards, R., Nicoll, K., Solomon, N., & Usher, R. (2004). *Rhetoric and educational discourse.* London: Routledge.

Nicoll. K. (2006). *Flexibility and lifelong learning.* London: Routledge.

Rose, N. (1998). *Inventing ourselves..* Cambridge: Policy Press.

Usher, R. & Edwards, R. (2007). *Lifelong Learning – Signs, Discourses, Practices.* Dordrecht: Springer.

Richard Edwards
The Stirling Institute of Education
University of Stirling, UK

EQUALITY, SOCIAL INCLUSION AND DEMOCRACY*

MARK OLSSEN

NEOLIBERALISM, EDUCATION, AND THE RISE OF A GLOBAL COMMON GOOD

INTRODUCTION

The ascendancy of neoliberalism and the associated discourses of 'new public management', which came to prominence during the latter part of the twentieth century, have produced a fundamental shift in the way educators have defined and justified their institutional existence. Neoliberalism in this chapter is viewed as an emergent discourse of the early and mid twentieth century which did battle with, and eventually eclipsed, the dominant and effective theories of social democratic thought that were born in the late nineteenth and early twentieth centuries, and which prevailed as guiding paradigms of social and political thought throughout most of the twentieth century in many countries of the western world. This chapter traces the assumptions and consequences of neoliberal theories of restructuring, and seeks to document how their individualistic assumptions are in tension with current conceptions of the common good, as well as with the core values of liberal societies, based on notions of professional autonomy and academic freedom, and of a general entitlement to education defined as a public good available to all. It will attempt to document the operating assumptions of the theories at the level of both political philosophy and economic theory. By so doing, the chapter will aim to present a kind of hermeneutics or critical reading of neoliberal theories. It will examine their assumptions and consequences, as they served to reconfigure the worlds of economics, education, and politics, in the early twentieth century. It will look also at the way they replaced social-democratic models of the provision of education, associated with Keynesian demand management, based on universal and free entitlement in line with ideas of the public good, with the more competitive individualistic gearing of education as a marketable commodity operating in an arena of free competition. Finally, it will argue that, just as the neoliberal revolution was itself an historically contingent response to particular political and economic material conditions, the ascendancy of neoliberalism is itself now being modified and adapted in line with a newly emerging global common good.

---

*Some sections of this chapter are from my book *Liberalism, Neoliberalism, Social Democracy: Thin Communitarian Perspectives on Political Philosophy and Education*, (Routledge, New York, 2010). I would like to thank the publishers for reproducing it here.

M. Simons, M. Olssen and M.A. Peters (eds.), Re-Reading Education Policies: A Handbook Studying the Policy Agenda of the 21ˢᵗ Century, 433–457.

NEOLIBERALISM AS A DIMENSION OF GLOBALISATION

At an economic level, neoliberalism is linked to globalisation, especially as it relates to the 'freedom of commerce', or to 'free trade'. In this sense, neoliberalism is a particular element of globalisation in that it constitutes the form through which domestic and global economic relations are structured. Yet, neoliberalism is only one dimension of globalisation, which is to say, it is not to be seen as identical to the phenomenon of globalisation as such. Globalisation is a much broader phenomenon in that should neoliberalism not have replaced Keynesianism as the dominant economic discourse of western nations, it would still constitute a significant process. This is the sense that it has partly occurred as a consequence of changes in technology and science which have brought many parts of the world closer together through developments in forms of technology as they have influenced information, communications, and travel.

The advent of neoliberalism would not have prevented this process from occurring, and thus, it must not be confused with globalisation as such. Rather it must be seen as a specific economic discourse or philosophy which has become dominant and effective in world economic relations as a consequence of superpower sponsorship. Neoliberalism is a politically imposed discourse, which is to say that it constitutes the hegemonic discourse of western nation states. As such it is conceptually independent of the more general and older forms of globalisation based simply on changes in technology and science. In addition, it can not be seen as part of the effects of these more general changes, although this is not to say that there is no relationship at all. Its major characteristics emerged in the USA in the 1970s as a forced response to stagflation and the collapse of the Bretton Woods system of international trade and exchange, leading to the abolition of capital controls, in 1974 in America and 1979 in Britain (Mishra, 1999; Stiglitz, 2002). This made it extremely difficult to sustain Keynesian demand management. Financial globalisation made giant strides. Exchange rates were floated and capital controls abolished, giving money and capital the freedom to move across national boundaries. The changes in technology did certainly facilitate these changes, for developments in microelectronics and computers made it possible to shift financial reserves within seconds.

NEOLIBERALISM, WELFARE LIBERALISM AND CLASSICAL LIBERALISM

Within western nation-states neoliberalism has introduced a new mode of regulation or form of governmentality. In order to understand this it is necessary to understand that both the welfare liberal and classical liberal models it replaced maintained fundamentally different premises at the level of political and economic theory, as well as at the level of philosophical assumption. The central defining characteristic of this new brand of neoliberalism can be understood at one level as a revival of many of the central tenets of classical liberalism, particularly classical economic liberalism. The central presuppositions shared include:

- the self-interested individual: a view of individuals as economically self-interested subjects. In this perspective the individual was represented as a rational optimiser and the best judge of his/her own interests and needs.
- free market economics: the best way to allocate resources and opportunities is through the market. The market is both a more efficient mechanism and a morally superior mechanism.
- a distrust of government: because the free market is a self-regulating order it regulates itself better than the government or any other outside force. In this, neoliberals show a distinct distrust of governmental power and seek to limit state power within a negative conception, limiting its role to the protection of individual rights.
- a commitment to free trade: involving the abolition of tariffs or subsidies, or any form of state-imposed protection or support, as well as the maintenance of floating exchange rates and 'open' economies.

Notwithstanding a clear similarity between neo and classical liberal discourse, the two cannot be seen as identical, and an understanding of the differences between them provides an important key to understanding the distinctive nature of the neo-liberal revolution as it has impacted on OECD countries over the last fifty years.

Whereas classical liberalism represents a negative conception of state power in that the individual was taken as an object to be freed from the interventions of the state, neoliberalism has come to represent a positive conception of the state's role in creating the appropriate market by providing the conditions, laws and institutions necessary for its operation. In classical liberalism the individual is characterised as having an autonomous human nature and can practise freedom. In neoliberalism the state seeks to create an individual that is an enterprising and competitive entrepreneur. As Graham Burchell (1996, pp. 23–24) puts this point, while for classical liberalism the basis of government conduct is in terms of "natural, private-interest-motivated conduct of free, market exchanging individuals", for neoliberalism "the rational principle for regulating and limiting governmental activity must be determined by reference to *artificially* arranged or contrived forms of free, *entrepreneurial* and *competitive* conduct of economic-rational individuals." This means that for neoliberal perspectives, the end goals of freedom, choice, consumer sovereignty, competition and individual initiative, as well as those of compliance and obedience, must be constructions of the state acting now in its positive role through the development of the techniques of *auditing, accounting* and *management*. It is these techniques, as Barry, Osborne and Rose (1996, p. 14) put it:

> [that] enable the marketplace for services to be established as 'autonomous' from central control. Neo-liberalism, in these terms, involves less a retreat from governmental "intervention" than a re-inscription of the techniques and forms of expertise required for the exercise of government.

In his own analysis, Burchell is commenting on and articulating Foucault's perspective on liberalism as a form of state reason or 'governmentality'. For Foucault (1991), neoliberalism represents an art of government or form of political reason. A political rationality is not simply an ideology but a worked-out discourse containing theories and ideas that emerge in response to concrete problems within a determinate historical period. For Foucault, like Weber, political reason constituted a form of disciplinary power containing forms and systems of expertise and technology utilisable for the purposes of political control. Liberalism, rather than being the discovery of freedom as a natural condition, is thus a prescription for rule, which becomes both the *ēthos* and *technē* of government. In this sense, as Barry, Osborne and Rose (1996, p. 8) put it:

> Liberalism is understood not so much as a substantive doctrine or practice of government in itself, but as a restless and dissatisfied ethos of recurrent critique of State reason and politics. Hence, the advent of liberalism coincides with discovering that political government could be its own undoing, that by governing over-much, rulers thwarted the very ends of government.

For Foucault (1991), liberalism represented a constructed political space, or a political reconstruction of the spaces in terms of which market exchanges could take place and in terms of which a domain of individual freedom could be secured. As such a constructed space, liberalism, says Foucault, enabled the domain of "society" to emerge in that it stood opposed to the *Polizeiwissenschaften* of the state which constituted a formula of rule that sought total control. In this sense liberalism is a form of permanent critique of state reason, a form of rationality which is, as Thomas Osborne (1993, p. 346) puts it, "always suspicious of governing overmuch, a form of government always critical of itself."

MARKETS AS A NEW DISCIPLINARY TECHNOLOGY IN THE PUBLIC SECTOR

Ron Barnett (2000) utilises Lyotard's concept of 'performativity' to argue that marketisation has become a new universal theme manifested in the trends towards the commodification of teaching and research and the various ways in which universities meet the new performative criteria, both locally and globally in the emphasis upon measurable outputs. The ascendancy of neoliberalism and the associated discourses of 'new public management', during the 1980s and 1990s, have produced a fundamental shift in the way universities and other institutions of higher education have defined and justified their institutional existence. The traditional professional culture of open intellectual enquiry and debate has been replaced with an institutional stress on performativity, as evidenced by the emergence of an emphasis on measured outputs: on strategic planning, performance indicators, quality assurance measures, and academic audits.

Markets were of course traditionally important in classical economics, and formed an essential part of the welfare state, for regulating private entrepreneurial conduct in the public sphere of society. Under neoliberalism, markets have become a new technology by which control can be managed and performance can be enhanced in the public sector. As a technique by which government can manage control, its development for non-private institutional contexts depended upon developments in knowledge and research from the 1930s. These included the writings of Friedrich A. Hayek; the development of monetarist economics by

Milton Friedman; the development of Public Choice Theory by James Buchanan and his collaborators at Chicago, as well as the later development of institutional theories of internal organisational functioning, such as Agency Theory and Cost-Transaction Economics.

Although Friedrich Hayek (1899-1992) must in many senses be considered a classical liberal, his writings from the 1930s onwards contribute to neoliberalism in that he shares many of the themes of neoliberalism and, in addition, he deeply influenced later forms of the doctrine. Hayek can be considered a part of, and having major debts to, the Austrian School of Economics founded by Menger (1840-1921) and carried on by von Wieser (1851-1926) and von Mises (1881-1973). One of the major ways that Hayek departs from classical economic theory relates to his acceptance of the Austrian School's subjective theory of value, the theory that value is conferred on resources by the subjective preferences of agents. As John Gray (1984, p. 16) puts it, it was this "profound insight which spelt the end of the tradition of classical economic theory", marking a departure from economic theorists such as Adam Smith, David Ricardo, J. S. Mill and Karl Marx who had all analysed value in objective terms as deriving from the labour content of the asset or resource under consideration. Like von Mises, Hayek defends subjectivism in economic theory regarding value, but goes further, noting that the data of the social sciences are themselves subjective phenomena and that social objects like money or tools are constituted by human beliefs.[1]

Amongst the major themes of his economic and social philosophy are his argument that "local knowledge", as is found in markets, is always more valid and effective than the forms of codified text-book-type knowledge that it is possible to introduce through planning. For this reason, markets have distinct advantages over state regulation or planning. The laws of supply and demand operate, via the price mechanism, as indicators of under- and over-supply as well as incentives for producers to produce high-quality, competitively priced goods for which there is an established demand. In a multitude of ways, markets provide fast and efficient methods of supplying information on consumer demand, and a sure way of making sure that producers and providers will respond (see Hayek, 1945 especially).

Consequently, Hayek (1944, 1948, 1952, 1960, 1976) maintains that the proper functioning of markets is incompatible with state planning of any sort, either full-scale socialism or the more limited conception of the welfare state. A full-scale rational socialism is impossible because it would have no markets to guide resource allocation. In addition, central planning of any form, he claims, is not practical because of the scale of centralised calculation any effective attempt at allocation would require. On this basis Hayek contends that all forms of state action beyond the *minimal* functions of the defence of the realm and the protection of basic rights to life and property are dangerous threats to liberty which are likely to lead down the "road to serfdom."

His main arguments against central planning are based on two claims: (1) on its inefficiency, and (2) on the threat to freedom of the individual. It would be inefficient, in Hayek's view, because real knowledge is gained and true economic progress made as a consequence of locally generated knowledge derived from "particular circumstances of time and place" and the state is not privy to such knowledge (Hayek, 1945, p. 521). The market then is the mechanism which best allocates resources in society. Planning ignores this localistic character of knowledge and interferes with the self-regulating mechanism of the market. It would threaten the freedom of the individual in Hayek's view because it would interfere with his or her own decision-making capacity by imposing a politically defined and implemented conception of the good.

BUCHANAN AND PUBLIC CHOICE THEORY

Inasmuch as the economy was a central object of neoliberal analysis and restructuring from the 1970s, the analysis and redesign of public-sector institutions was also to receive attention. Unlike markets, the public sector, in the neoliberal view, lacked a comparable mechanism of economic efficiency to guide the utilisation or allocation of resources. In addition, neoliberals' claimed that the self-interested opportunism of bureaucrats and government officials would create conflicting loyalties and interests which would interfere with the implementation of policies in the genuine pursuit of the public interest. The school of Public Choice Theory (PCT) advocated the application of economic theories to public-sector institutions in the interest of making public organisations subject to the similar costs and benefits as operate in the private sector. In this, PCT represents an application of economic models and theories to politics on the assumption that economic behaviour (*homo economicus*) describes the true state of human nature and thus is applicable to all aspects of life.

The central figure in the 'economics of politics' is James Buchanan who since 1969 was Professor of Economics and Director of the Center for Study of Public Choice at the Virginia Polytechnic Institute, Blacksburg, Virginia. A member of the Mont Pelerin Society and of the Institute of Economic Affairs advisory council, Buchanan describes PCT as "the application and extension of economic theory to the realm of political or governmental choices" (1978, p. 3). Amongst his central books are included *Fiscal Theory and Political Economy* (1960), *Cost and Choice* (1969), *The Limits of Liberty* (1975) and, with Gordon Tullock, *The Calculus of Consent* (1962), which gave a lead to a group of economists at the Virginia Polytechnic Institute in America in the 1960s and 1970s. Buchanan claims to have come to PCT out of intellectual frustration with orthodox Pre-World War II Public Finance Theory, as enunciated by the likes of A. C. Pigou, Hugh Dalton in the UK and Harold Groves and Henry Simons in the US. Public finance and economics could not be independent of a theory of institutional politics, said Buchanan (1978), as those who adhered to the earlier Public Finance Theory argued. By this was meant that economics must also take on board the institutional framework of rules and procedures that are responsible for the governance of human relationships and formulate theories as to how these should operate. A major influence on Buchanan's distinctively institutional approach to economics and politics, and especially his dissatisfaction with Public Finance theory, was the 19th century Swedish economist, Knut Wicksell. In addition he was influenced by the political theories on voting behaviour of Duncan Black (especially his work on committees), and Kenneth Arrow (on social welfare). Impressed by Arrow's argument that a consistent social welfare function for a society could not be derived from individual preferences, Buchanan came to accept his view that any coherent social welfare approach must inevitably entail the imposition of will of some members or groups over others. Hence, he effectively denied the efficacy or utility of the concept of the 'public interest.' In analysing how public goods were supposed to emerge from individual self-interested behaviour, Buchanan's achievement was to abolish any notion of the public interest altogether, claiming it could not be derived from the aggregate self-interests of individuals.[2]

Central to PCT's abolition of notions of the public interest or common good are several interrelated arguments and ideas concerning the relationship between economics and politics. At the most general level, is the application of neo-classical analysis to non-market situations (Riesman, 1990, p. 136). In this view, politics was redescribed as an economic market. As Buchanan and Tullock (1962, p. 250) explain:

> One of the great advantages of an essentially economic approach to collective action lies in the implicit recognition that political exchange, at all levels, is basically equivalent to economic exchange.

With Hayek and Friedman, Buchanan characterises economics as a process of "catallaxy"; that is, of the voluntary exchange of goods and services between competing individuals. Lying behind such an analysis is a strong normative commitment to free-market individualism which for Buchanan provides a common rationality linking the economic and political worlds. Political action is represented as being governed by the same interests and motivation that govern the market. This libertarian quality of Buchanan's work is reflected also in his deeply individualist approach to public affairs. As far as political prospects were concerned, only those that resulted from the subjective choices of individuals were acceptable. Collective entities such as a 'society' or 'the public interest' were held not to exist because they were reducible to individual experiences. This 'methodological individualism' was fundamental to Buchanan's approach. As he acknowledged in *The Calculus of Consent*, "the whole calculus has meaning only if methodological individualism is accepted" (Buchanan & Tullock, 1962, p. 265). PCT is ruled by the imperative of a strict methodological individualism in which "all theorising, all analysis, is resolved finally into considerations faced by the individual person as decision-maker" (Buchanan, 1975, p. ix).

It is on this basis that PCT attacks as 'myth' the idea that government or public service is able to serve the public good. Influenced by William Niskanen's work on "bureaucratic growth", Anthony Downs' pioneering work on "political parties", Mancur Olson's work on "interest groups", and Gordon Tullock's writing on "rent-seeking" behaviour, it asserts the view that the notion of the public good is a fiction which cloaks the opportunistic behaviour of bureaucrats and politicians as they seek to expand their bureaus, increase their expenditures, and maximise their own personal advantages. In *The Limits of Liberty* (1975), Buchanan maintains that a coincidence of interests between the civil servant's private interests and their conception of the public interest ensues, such that "within the constraints that he faces the bureaucrat tends to maximise his own utility" (Buchanan, 1975, p. 161). If preferences are inherently subjective then they cannot be known and transferred into a collective value judgement, such as a public good, for such a notion neglects the rights of consumers whose interests the public service and politicians are meant to serve, but do not.

As a further part of the argument against collective politics, or any notion of a public good, PCT suggests redesigning public institutions to make them reflect more accurately the preferences of individuals. This involves counteracting the possible forms of 'capture' which serve to deflect the interests of public officials from the public's real needs. To do this, PCT advocates a variety of quasi-market strategies, such as contracting out services to the private sector, increasing competition between units within the public sector, placing all potentially conflicting responsibilities into separate institutions, separating the commercial and non-commercial functions of the state, separating the advisory, regulatory and delivery functions into different agencies, as well as introducing an assortment of accountability and monitoring techniques and strategies aimed to overcome all possible sources of corruption and bias, particularly those arising from the pursuit of self-interest. It is on this basis, too, that public sector reforms relating to health, security, or education, have sought to restructure the basis of accountability through notions tied to individually attached incentives and targets, and through periodic monitoring and assessment through audits.

One other aspect of PCT deserves attention. Although the classical liberal tradition had stressed the role of markets as 'self-regulating' and as supported by arguments based on the freedom of the individual from the state, Buchanan distrusted that the required efficiency gains would emerge through automatic mechanisms of the market, and supported efficiency achievements through a tightening of state control. In this, Buchanan introduced a major shift from liberal to neoliberal governmentality. For markets, rather than being seen, as they were for Hayek, and for classical political economy, as a natural, self-regulating reserve, where the hand of nature would produce an optimal social and economic equilibrium, would now become a technique of government's 'positive' power, acting deliberately through the vehicle of the state to engineer the conditions for efficient economic production.

The difference between Hayek and Buchanan on this point has not been sufficiently stressed in the literature on markets. While for Hayek, and the classical liberal tradition, economies are the outcome of spontaneous evolution which demonstrate the superiority of unregulated markets for creativity and progress, Buchanan had little faith in the 'spontaneous' ordering of the market or in the efficacy of the social evolutionary process. For him, evolution may produce social chaos and dysfunctional patterns as readily as it may social harmony and equilibrium. Significantly, it is on this point that Buchanan criticises Hayek:

> My basic criticism of F. A. Hayek's profound interpretation of modern history and his diagnosis for improvement is directed at his apparent belief or

faith that social evolution will, in fact, ensure the survival of efficient institutional forms. Hayek is so distrustful of man's explicit attempts of reforming institutions that he accepts uncritically the evolutionary alternative (Buchanan, 1975, 194n).

Rejecting all talk of *automaticity* and *evolution*, Buchanan expresses a much greater faith in *conscious political action* to legitimate the "long over-due task of institutional over-haul" that many commentators were calling for (Reisman, 1990, p. 74). In Buchanan's view, then, the state should tighten the screws on individuals and encourage supply-side monitoring in the interests of promoting efficiency in market terms.

NEOLIBERAL THEORIES OF INSTITUTIONAL REDESIGN: AGENCY THEORY AND COST-TRANSACTION ECONOMICS

It is with PCT that market techniques were systematically developed and first became a technology for institutional governance. Centrally PCT constituted a supply-side process of 'governing without governing', a process by which compliance is extracted through systems that measure performance according to both externally imposed levers, and internally reinforced targets. Influenced and building upon PCT, a number of internal theories of organisation through which efficiency and effectiveness are rendered operative in public sector institutions became prominent from the 1950s. Foremost amongst these were Agency Theory and Transaction Cost Economics.

Agency theory (AT) has been widely used in the economic and social restructuring programmes in OECD countries, including Britain, America, Australia and New Zealand.[3] As a theoretical orientation, it represents work relations hierarchically as a series of contracts between one party referred to as the principal and another referred to as the agent. The theory is concerned with problems of compliance and control in the division of labour between work relationships. Although initially developed in relation to business firms, it became adapted and extended to public sector work relationships as a means of exacting the accountability and performance of employees where market incentives and sanctions did not operate. AT theorises work relations hierarchically in terms of chains of authority and command which can be used to characterise authority relations at all levels of the management hierarchy. Hence, a single person will be principal to those further down the chain of command and agent to those further up. Central to its focus is how one gets an agent to act in accordance with the interests of the principal. Rather than specify a broad job specification based on a conception of professional autonomy and responsibility, it specifies chains of principal-agent relationships as a series of contracts as a means of rendering the management function clear and accountable. AT theorises hierarchical work relationships as contracts where a principal becomes a commissioning party to specify or delegate work to an agent to perform in return for some specified sanction or reward. As such, it is concerned with how to extract compliance from a voluntary exchange relationship based on dependency. Hence, it speaks to the relationship between employer and employee in all types of work contexts – schools, government agencies, universities and businesses.

In order to minimise risks and enable control in the employment situation, AT specifies a range of monitoring, information eliciting, and performance appraisal techniques which include the following:

- determining the best form of contract;
- determining the best way of motivating agents;
- determining the best way of spurring performance (via targets, rewards and sanctions);
- finding the best way of monitoring and specifying contracts to guard against excesses and dangers produced by opportunism on part of agent, due to 'shirking' deception, cheating, or collusion.

Agency costs are effectively the subject of Transaction Cost Economics (TCE), which is another form of economic theory linked closely to AT, PCT and Property Rights Theory.[4] Principally espoused in the work of Oliver Williamson (1975, 1983, 1985, 1991, 1992, 1994), it seeks to analyse and account for the efficiency costs of transacting business and the effect these have on organisational form. In this respect, as Charles Perrow (1986a, p. 18) puts it, TCE is "relentlessly and explicitly an efficiency argument." TCE is used to evaluate the efficiency of alternative governance structures or sets of institutional arrangements for various kinds of transactions, especially those generated by the market. Like other neo-liberal theories, it assumes a social-ontological context of 'uncertainty', 'bounded rationality', 'limited' and 'asymmetrical' information, and of the 'opportunism' of the 'self-interested' subject. While opportunism expresses the 'self-interested' nature of individual actions, bounded rationality attests to the absence of perfect information, or to the asymmetrical nature of information between two or more parties in any exchange relation. It is due to the absence of perfect information that the market equilibrium becomes unstable, introducing 'uncertainty', which in turn allows agents to act 'opportunistically'. For instance, where it is possible, a party to a contract may exhibit dishonest or unreliable behaviour in order to secure a market advantage. However, the ability to do so will depend upon the nature of the context, the degree of uncertainty in the environment and the extent to which information between the parties is 'asymmetrical'.

Using theory-specific concepts such as 'small numbers bargaining' and 'asset specificity', TCE endeavours to show why various sorts of organisational forms (involving mergers or takeovers or various forms of organisational integration) may be preferred to a pure market form. In accounting for the increasing size of business organisations over the century, Williamson (1983, p. 125) argues "that efficiency is the main and only systematic factor responsible for the organisational changes that have occurred." In essence, then, TCE is about the most efficient method of organisation given a particular market context. Also the other concepts introduced by Williamson attest to the bilateral nature of exchange and the distortions that are introduced and which need to be overcome when real-life interactions fail to match the precise model of the classical market. 'Small numbers bargaining' gives the parties to an initial contract an advantage over parties not so included in the contract and tends to constitute a conservative pressure for firms not to change or not to be responsive to actual market signals. In this sense, the convenience of preserving an existing arrangement, or of continuing to hire existing staff, may override the fact that more competitive tenders exist, or that 'better' or less disruptive staff could be employed. The concept of 'asset specificity' is related, for long term parties to a contract tend to have specific assets which become a form of bargaining power and, again, militate against change in line with the expectations generated by the classical model of the market order.

In the context of these potentially disruptive influences, TCE proposes that forms of administrative and governance structures can be instituted which counteract these adverse effects and which render transaction costs efficient relative to a specific form of market competition. Hence, while opportunism and bounded rationality produce different kinds of costs, these must be in turn offset by the types of governance structures in place. AT becomes relevant here in specifying a formalised structure of contracts between principals and agents to counter the possible distortions or costs associated with opportunism and bounded rationality. Forms of monitoring and performance appraisal also operate in this regard. In his later works, Williamson (1991, 1992, 1994) focuses attention on public-sector governance issues and specifically with the problem of selecting governance structures which are most efficient i.e., which minimise the costs of the different organisational transactions involved.

Both AT and TCE, as well as the other neoliberal theories (such as PCT, Property Rights Theory), are relevant to understanding the unprecedented disaggregation of the public sector that has occurred in Britain and other OECD countries since the 1980s. As Catherine Althaus (1997, p. 138) observes, AT has been central to the dramatic scale of the restructuring that has occurred in these countries. It has underpinned funder/provider and policy/delivery splits (the 'decoupling' strategies) both within the public-sector bureaucracy as well as between the bureaucracy and the state, and resulted in policies of deregulation, corporatisation, and privatisation. In addition, notes Althaus (1997, p. 137), "New Zealand and the United Kingdom have engaged in a unique application of agency theory which places them at the forefront of its application to the public sector." Indeed, "the striking aspect of an analysis of [the neoliberal] reform programme is its use of theory" notwithstanding the fact that "the agency model has serious deficiencies if applied uncritically to public sector management" (1997, p. 138). Such a model increases accountability and efficiency, rendering pubic non-private institutions analogous to private companies. As such, AT is a

> means of conceptualising and rationalising human behaviour and organisational forms (...). [I]t is a scrutiny of the interaction between a distinct relationship between two parties – the principal and agent – within a context assuming individual self-interest maximisation, bounded rationality, risk-aversion, goal conflict among members and the treatment of information as a commodity which can be purchased (Althaus, 1997, p. 141).

Underpinning TCE as well as AT is Property Rights Theory (PRT), which is the fundamental grounding theory for the conception of self-interested human behaviour assumed in neoliberal theories. As such, the incentives structure of agents and principals in AT is assumed using PRT which is essentially a theory of 'ownership' of property as it inheres in the individual. As such PRT reveals its fundamentally Lockean premises for property to be represented as an inalienable God-given right. Hence, central to PRT is the entitlement to scarce commodities and a conception of the system of exchange rules in terms of which such commodities may be transferred. As McKean (1974, p. 175) states, property rights are essentially "one's effective rights to do things and effective claims to reward (positive or negative) as a result of one's action." Such a theory assists in conceptualising the structuring of incentives in relation to the management of institutions.

TCE with AT, PRT, and PCT are collectively represented as part and parcel of the New Institutional Economics (NIE) or of New Public Management (NPM). The common language of such approaches stresses concepts such as 'outputs', 'outcomes', 'accountability', 'purchase', 'ownership', 'specification', contracts', 'purchase agreements', etc. Central to such an approach is an emphasis on contract which ostensibly replaces central regulation by a new system of public administration which introduces such concepts as clarification of purpose, role clarification, task specification, reliable reporting procedures and the freedom to manage. According to Matheson (1997), contractualism includes relations where (1) parties have some autonomy to their role, (2) where there are distinctions between roles and therefore where a clarification of roles is obtainable, (3) where the specific role components are specifiable and where as a consequence individuals can be held accountable, (4) where responsibility flows downwards, rather than upwards, i.e., responsibility can be identified as fixed in terms of a specific role, (5) where the assignment of work is by agreement, (6) where there is an objective basis for judging performance, (7) where transparency is a feature of the agreement process, and (8) where there are explicit consequences (sanctions or rewards) for fulfilment or non-fulfilment.

The consequence of such a contractualism was to view all work relations as principal-agent hierarchies, thereby redefining the appropriate process in terms of outputs, and where services are viewed in terms of cost and quality. Such a system gave rise to new patterns of employment (fixed-term contracts) and new forms of accountability whereby relationships were more directly clarified and services more clearly described. Such an approach has low transaction costs, few legal fees, and few direct compliance costs.

The New Institutional Economics, especially AT, constituted a strategy that appeared promising as neoliberal techniques of governmentality in terms of its commitments to (1) strategic management, (2) divestment of non-core activities, (3) re-engineering to create customer focus, (4) delayering/de-coupling, (5) total quality management, (6) use of modern information technology for management information systems, (7) improved accountability systems, and (8) establishing appropriate cultural values, teamwork and leadership. Not only was the NIE important for the selection and modification of governance structures, but it enabled a much tighter and clearer specification of roles, as well as greatly increased accountability. The key concerns of the NIE were a concern with transaction costs, concepts and principles for analysing them through enhanced specification of tasks and goals, increased transparency, clear allocation of responsibilities and duties, the imposition of a heightened incentive structure, a greater ability to monitor the contracts linked to a greatly increased accountability system. The following principles, derived from NIE, have been of central importance:

- separation of ownership and purchase responsibilities;
- separation of policy from operations;
- separation of funding, purchasing and provision of services;
- competition between service providers;
- reallocation of functions for focus, synergy and information (Scott, 1997, p. 158).

All of these neoliberal theories assume that individuals are rational utility maximisers and, because of this, the interests of principals and agents will inevitably diverge. In any management context, the problems that the principal will have amount to a range of uncertainties and difficulties in obtaining information. In many senses, both principals and agents have access to information that the other party does not. In addition, agents will have an incentive to exploit their situation to their own advantage. They may, for instance, withhold information that would be to their disadvantage.

What were not noted by the political reformers, however, were the negative consequences of such disaggretative theories. In Britain Hede (1991, p. 38), Greer (1992, p. 223) and Trosa (1994) note negative effects (increased tensions, rivalry, unnecessary duplication of services and resources, etc.) of disaggretative models. They maintain that when policy advice is separated from operations, the emergence of destructive sub-cultures can result, which can in turn lead to the duplication of advice as well as increased distrust and disruption instead of the theorised would-be benefits of greater contestability.

What neoliberal technologies also effect, further, is a new form of power which systematically undoes and reconstructs the spaces of classical and welfare liberalism. Because the institutionalisation of models of principal-agent chains of line management inserts a hierarchical mode of authority by which competitive market and state pressures for accountability are instituted, the consequences for academia constitute contributing factors for *deprofessionalisation.*[5] This involves a shift from collegial or democratic governance in flat structures, to hierarchical models based on dictated management *specifications* of job performance in principal-agent chains of command.

The essence of contractual models involves a *specification*, which is fundamentally at odds with the traditional notion of *professionalism* as it was defined in liberalism. In its traditional conception, professionalism conveys the idea of self-managed, subject-directed work based upon the liberal conceptions of rights, freedom and autonomy. It conveys the idea of a power given to the subject,

445

and of the subject's ability to make decisions in the workplace, involving an ability to regulate both the pace and time of their work. No professional, whether doctor, lawyer or teacher, has traditionally wanted to have the terms of their practice and conduct dictated by anyone else but their peers, or determined by groups or structural levers that are outside of their control. As a particular patterning of power, then, professionalism is systematically at odds with neo-liberalism, for neo-liberals see the professions as self-interested groups who indulge in *rent-seeking* behaviour. In neoliberalism the patterning of power is established on contract, which in turn is premised upon a need for compliance, monitoring, and accountability organised in a management line and established through a purchase contract based upon measurable outputs based upon market criteria.

Such neoliberal contractual accountabilities now run life in public institutions many western countries, although it is also pertinent to note, they do so *to varying extents* both between countries, and even between institutions. Generally, throughout the western world, and increasingly in the third world, too, universities are forced to operate in the context of a competitive market, and both research and teaching have been increasingly subject to external levers and outside pressures in the interests of accountability and measurement. While arguably, neoliberal accountability and performance criteria may exact a measure of both fairness and efficiency in relation to some traditional functions of universities, the demands for constant demonstrations of academic production, in relation to both teaching and research, seriously risk undermining the manner in which significant research achievements have been produced in the past.[6] Increasingly, too, public sector organisations are organised according to individually-assigned, market-driven, performance incentives, through chains of accountability, involving contractual relationships between principals and agents, where a purchase contract specifies outputs, where the principal is the purchaser of outputs and enforcer of the contract, and where monitoring and reporting procedures are attached to every purchase agreement, and given significance in market terms.

NEOLIBERALISM AS A MODE OF CONTROL AND THE EMERGENCE OF A NEW COMMON GOOD

Of pertinence here, in addition to a common priority concerning the scope of the market, both classical liberalism and neoliberalism share common views concerning the nature of the individual, as rational self-interested subjects. In this perspective the individual is presented as a rational optimiser and the best judge of his/her own interests and needs. Being rational was to follow a systematic programme of action underpinned and structured according to rules. The rules were rendered coherent and permissible in relation to the 'interests' of the individual. Such a notion is located both within classical liberalism and classical political economy. It is epitomised in the writings of Thomas Hobbes, John Locke, Adam Smith, Jeremy Bentham and John Stuart Mill amongst many others. Twentieth century neoliberals endorse this view.

Neo- and classical liberals also endorse a strong commitment to free trade. Consistent with the faith in market economics, in the international sphere classical economic liberals favoured 'free trade', involving the abolition of tariffs or subsidies, or any form of state-imposed protection or support, as well as the maintenance of floating exchange rates and 'open' economies. These commitments are today central to the philosophies of neoliberalism, and constitute central planks in the economic policies of global agencies such as the World Bank and the International Monetary Fund.

With regard to the nature of the relations between individuals and society or the role of the state there are some major differences however, as we have noted above. The theory in terms of which individual-society relations were structured in classical liberalism can be termed 'invisible hand theory'. This essentially is the view that the uncoordinated self-interest of individuals correlates with the interests and harmony or good of the whole society. Although it was no means a novel theory in the seventeenth and eighteenth centuries, it is most often associated with Adam Smith's writings on the harmonisation of the private determinations of individual interests with the interests or good of society as a whole. In considering the choices of individuals, Smith (1976, p. 456) writes that "he intends only his own gain, and he is in this, as in many other cases, led by an invisible hand to promote an end which was no part of his intention." Smith makes it clear that the workings of the hand have benefit only because it is invisible. There would be little good resulting from any attempt to direct the hand for the public good. Such a conception thus counters the heavily programmed conception as put forward by Hobbes in his book *Leviathan* as well as the more indirect conceptions of state control as advanced by Quesnay in his economic 'Table', a device intended to allow the sovereign to monitor the general order and health of the economy within the state. The notion of an 'invisible hand' thus constituted a counter to more 'interventionist' Physiocratic conceptions of the role of the state.[7]

Neoliberalism cannot be rendered compatible with these conceptions, for amongst those such as the *Ordoliberalen*, Human Capital theorists and Public Choice theorists, the state actively constructs the market. Far from existing within a protected and limited space, market relations now extend to cover all forms of voluntary behaviour amongst individuals. Rather than absenting itself from interfering in the private or market spheres of society, in the global economic era neoliberalism becomes a new authoritarian discourse of state management and control. Rather than being a form of political bureaucracy, which Weber (1921) saw as the supreme form of modernist rationality, neoliberalism constitutes a new and more advanced technology of control. It is both a substantive political doctrine of control and a self-driving technology of operations. It incorporates both more flexible and more devolved steering mechanisms than does bureaucracy. If, for Weber, bureaucracy constituted large scale organisation comprising a hierarchy of offices and lines of control, enabling efficiency, predictability, calculability and technical control, then neoliberalism, while incorporating these factors, goes beyond them to enable an extension of control in more devolved forms and in more flexible systems. This enables the function of control to be differentiated from the function of operations, or to use Osborne and Gaebler's (1992) metaphor, "steering" from "rowing." It points to a more effective means of social engineering and control than classical bureaucracy, scientific management, or the Fordist assembly line. Its overall rationale is to measure the costs of, and place a value on, all forms of human activity. It extends the market mechanism from the economic to the political to the social. Market exchanges now encapsulate all forms of voluntary behaviour amongst individuals.[8]

Thus, while subscribing to the doctrine of the *minimal* state, neoliberalism has promoted the development of the *strong* state. While advocating privatisation of resourcing and decentralisation of provision of social services, neoliberal governments have built stronger state structures and introduced more robust modes of centralised control and regulation. These discourses are clearly evident in the educational policy agendas of the various nation-states that have embraced neoliberalism since the 1970s and 1980s.

Neoliberalism also departed from the welfare state tradition in attacking the notion of the public interest which had underpinned western models of bureaucracy and government from the inception of the welfare state earlier in the twentieth century. In political terms in America it constituted a more free market response to Roosevelt and the New Deal, and to the more welfare-minded administrations of post-war reconstruction, namely those of Truman, Kennedy and Johnson. In disputing that civil servants, bureaucrats and public employees served the public good, or interest, Buchanan sought to develop quasi-market procedures to render such institutions efficient based on the classical economic model of individuals as 'self-interested appropriators.' Essentially, this meant structuring incentives and targets to appeal to their selfishness. This denial of the notion of the public good, or common good, and his appeal to the models of classical economics to structure public institutions, and politics, is perhaps the most contentious aspect of his theory.

Buchanan (1954a, 1954b, 1975, 1978, 1986; Buchanan and Tulloch 1962) had been influenced by the work of Kenneth Arrow (1950, 1951) on Social Choice theory, in developing this approach. As Amartya Sen (2002, p. 330) reports, Arrow had been asked by Olaf Helmer, a logician at the Rand Corporation, who was interested in applying game theory to international relations, and asked Arrow, who was a PhD student at the time, "In what sense could collectivities be said to have utility functions?" Arrow determined that no satisfactory method for aggregating a multiplicity of orderings into one single ordering existed. Hence, there was "a difficulty in the concept of social welfare" (Arrow, 1950, the title of the article). The outcome was a PhD that formulated the General Possibility Theorem, which was a modification of the old paradox of voting. As Sen (2002, p. 262) notes, this theorem was "an oddly optimistic name for what is more commonly – and more revealingly – called Arrow's 'impossibility theorem,'" in that it describes "that it is impossible to devise an integrated social preference for diverse individual preferences." Arrow's claim, essentially, was that a unified coherent social welfare function, expressing a single value, such as a public interest, could not be expressed from the disaggregated preferences of individuals, without dictatorially discounting some at the expense of others. As Arrow (1951, p. 24) states it:

If we exclude the possibility of interpersonal comparisons of utility, then the only method of passing from individual tastes to social preferences which will be satisfactory and which will be defined for a wide range of sets of individual orderings are either imposed or dictatorial.

In Sen's account, Arrow's work was central to developments in welfare economics and "fits solidly into a program of making the analysis of social aggregation more systematic" (Sen, 2002, p. 343). Such work has relevance, says Sen (p. 343), "in the context of political thought in which aggregative notions are used, such as the 'general will' or the 'common good' or the 'social imperative.'" What became clearly 'apparent' to writers like Buchanan, and others at the time, is that "these political ideas require[d] re-examination in the light of Arrow's results" (p. 343). For most economists at the time, as Sen (2002, p. 343) expresses it, "the economic policies of governments are rarely justified in terms of aggregation of individual preferences." Under conditions of optimal social choice, which included all, individual rankings of states of affairs, or preferences, could not be calculated in terms of a single value, like stability, or be Pareto optimal, unless conditions of dictatorship were presumed to operate. In theoretical terms, this makes effective government in any positive sense, for example, implementing or administrating welfare, creating systematic opportunities, or even collective action for pure individual convenience (like minting money, or taking action against pollution) difficult to justify. It indirectly supports, then, a minimal role for the state as an institution that simply keeps the peace.

Arrow's seminal work, *Social Choice and Individual Values*, was published in 1951. It was a time when developments in Game Theory at the Rand Corporation, were having a major effect on academic disciplines in various fields, notably economics, international relations, psychiatry and psychology, and criminology. Game theory came into existence in 1944 with the publication of John von Neumann's and Oskar Morgenstern's *Theory of Games and Economic Behaviour*. The Rand Corporation, a US military think tank, became the major centre for its development and application to different fields. Although initially developed as an arm of Cold War conflict with Russia, Helmer's interest was to have Arrow develop a model relevant to politics and institutional behaviour in general. Utilising mathematical models, and premised on conceptions of self-interested subjects, it eschewed existing theories of collective behaviour which postulated common interests, and prioritised a consistently individualistic and competitive model of human behaviour. The model of the Prisoner's dilemma, also developed at the Rand Corporation, similarly sought to explain individual behaviour based on biologically fixed, self-interested axioms in human nature. Expressing the logic of the Cold War, it advanced the thesis that selfishness is always the safest outcome, and can serve as the basis for social stability. Central to this, as to other neoliberal theories, was a profound distrust of all traditional models of collective politics premised on a conception of the public good. It received an important theoretical inspiration, of especial relevance to the development of institutional theories of neoliberalism, by John Nash (1950), made famous in the film *A Beautiful Mind*, whose development of the Nash Equilibrium postulated a game-theoretic conception of optimal strategies for individuals to pursue in response to other rational egoists also pursuing self-interested aims. According to Nash, a system driven by self-interest did not have to lead to chaos but could reach a point of equilibrium where everyone's self-interest was balanced against everyone else's.[9] Such a conception reinforced the model of the market as the system best geared to balance individual desires; as the superior information processor; and as the 'fairest' system of for representing individual aspirations. In this model, markets are the only true voting machines; they give consumers what they want; and are therefore fair and good.[10]

What both Arrow and the game theory approaches failed to see in an important theoretical sense was how both the existence, and importance of the public interest, or common good, does *not* disappear simply because of logical difficulties in aggregating individual preferences to become group values. Although Arrow's theorem testifies to the impossibility of any immediate or direct translation from individual to collective, group values, and means that democracy cannot directly express individuals' wills, what it points to is the necessity of an objective ethic and political-institutional model in order to express humanity's goals and values, and one which is itself theoretically adequate to the principles of democracy, justice, inclusion, and freedom. What this problem suggests is the question, how can the basis of representation or democratic expression be rendered adequate to the multiplicity of legitimate values in existence? And how can it be rendered more and more adequate? In other words, how can democracy be improved, or deepened?

What the game models also failed to adequately take into account was how the responses of individuals to their own interests depended to a large measure on the structuring of the external environment, and how some impending threat in the future, such as the prospect of a nuclear catastrophe, for instance, could significantly alter the calculus of individual versus group interests in terms of which decisions were taken. As Adam Curtis shows in his film *The Trap*, when Nash's games were tested on secretaries, they invariably defied the predictions of the model in that they invariably opted for cooperative strategies.[11] Ultimately, the failure of game theory approaches was to misidentify the cause of self-interested behaviour, mistakenly locating the source in human nature itself, rather than in the complex interplay in the relationship between the self and the organisation of the material environment. I have developed this materialist insight consistently in my work on neoliberalism over the last decade. It is also an insight which lies behind Robert Axelrod's (1990) explanation for the "evolution of cooperation."

What is overlooked by the neoliberal assault on the notion of a public good, in other words, relates to the ontology underpinning their alternative individualistic formulation. This relates to the important issue as to what is being talked about when we speak of a 'shared interest', or 'individual self interests'. In my view the calculus of the relative importance of these notions varies according to the organisation of the material environment at different locations and phases of history, and can not be related exclusively to human nature as all of the neoliberal thinkers were to do. The emergence of new problems around climate change, ecology and population, make it clear how the notion of a common interest is becoming increasingly significant, not just for national groups or territories, but for humanity as a whole, at this very period at the start of the twenty-first century.

We could say, indeed, that the greater the problems of security and danger facing communities, or humanity as a whole, the greater the level of *shared* relative to *individual* interests, and the greater the shadow of the future over contemporary events. In relation to climate change, indeed, we can speak of the emergence of a whole assortment of new shared concerns. To some extent, it is understandable how, in a period of relative affluence - as America was in the middle of the twentieth century - whole groups of academics, and others, could attribute human motivations as ontologically tied to human nature, thereby accepting the background environment as a neutral, passive, largely non-intrusive, secondary variable. Yet, as danger in the outside world increases, such as those dangers unleashed by climatic alterations, global warming, the frequency of tornadoes, or hurricanes, or associated with the possibility of nuclear terror, or nuclear accident, the calculus of what constitutes self-interest (for an individual or group), and what constitutes the 'common interest' (of a group, or a nation, or humanity) also changes. A nuclear accident, on the scale of Chernobyl, for example, generates a whole raft of new common concerns; concerns which can only be addressed collectively, on behalf of individuals, that is, in *their* interests, and where their individual as opposed to their common interests assume a different quantitative proportion and social significance. What constitutes 'interests', shifts in this scenario, from being of concern exclusively or primarily to *individuals,* to being of *common* concern to all. Similarly, due to growing interconnectedness, related to communication and technology, many structures which facilitate individual aspirations, are now of *common* concern. In general terms, then, we can say that an escalation of unpredictability, uncertainty, and danger in the environment will alter the nature of the calculus between what is *self* interest, and what is *common* interest. Such contingency was single-mindedly not taken into account by the neoliberals' of the post-war era. Hence, they were unable to theorise their own theories as the transitory, historically relative phenomenon that they clearly have been.

CONCLUSION

That such a purely individualist tradition eclipsed most of what was essential to models of social democracy under the welfare state could only be sustained for a time, of course. It led eventually to accommodations between a rigorous neoliberalism and notions of social justice, under such political labels as the 'third way', developed by Democrats in America, and New Labour in Britain. These were designed to steer a 'middle' course, where neoliberal economics advocated that the poor could be 'cushioned' by the public provision of a 'minimal safety net.' Notwithstanding this, the abolition of ideas of public duty for individually-structured incentive targets and performance incentives has become a normal feature of most people's lives in the public sector. Such a reality now structures employees' existence in relation to health, amongst the police and security forces, and in education, at every level. In higher education this has been especially true, with the consequent de-professionalisation of academics, as a consequence of the rapid expansion of the higher education sector as well as policies of widening participation from the 1990s. There is a need today for academics to seek to reassert their professionalism, and argue their own case for salaries and rewards, through increasing fees for external examining, journal reviewing, and undertaking doctorial viva voce examinations. There is a need also to articulate the specificities of the new shared concerns that face humanity, and imaginatively reconstruct educational and governance structures to adequately represent the diverse interests and values that constitute life's varied forms and types. Such a quest will lead inevitably, too, to a new understanding of global education and global curricula that can serve as a critical grounding for living in an unpredictable and uncertain world.

NOTES

[1] Hayek's earliest statement is in *The Counter-Revolution of Science: Studies in the Abuse of Reason* (1952b) where he defends a qualitative discontinuity between methods of natural and social sciences. There were also Kantian influences on Hayek's subjectivism in that, following Kant, he rejected the idea that knowledge could be constructed from a basis of raw sensory data, seeing order that we find in the world as a product of the creative activity of the human mind but suspecting that there are inherent limitations to the possibility of full explicit knowledge, and, in particular, an impossibility of ever fully explaining a mind as complex as our own (see *New Studies in Philosophy, Politics, Economics and the Study of Ideas*, London: Routledge, 1978, p. 45, note 14). In addition, relatedly, Hayek denies the ontological independence of mind *à la* Descartes, denies the possibility of complete intellectual self-understanding, and denies any foundationalism, seeing all criticism of social life as immanent criticism, and social order itself as spontaneous creation rather than as a rational construction.

[2] Buchanan develops these themes in all his writings, but see 1954a and 1954b for his early enthusiasm for Arrow's insights.

[3] There is an extensive literature on Agency Theory including Althaus (1997); Bendor (1988); Bergman and Lane (1990); Braun (1993); Boston (1991, 1996a, 1996b); Chan and Rosenbloom (1994); Deane (1989); Eisenhardt (1989); Heymann (1988); Jennings and Cameron (1987); Jensen and Meckling (1976); Kay (1992); Levinthal (1988); Moe (1984, 1990, 1991); Palmer (1993); Perrow (1986a, 1986b); Petersen (1993); Pratt and Zeckhauser (1985); Rees (1985a, 1985b); Scott and Gorringe (1989); Simon (1991); Thompson and Wright (1988); Treblicock (1995); Weingast (1984); Wistrich (1992).

[4] For an introduction to Transaction Cost Economics see, Boston (1994), Boston et al. (1996b), Bryson and Smith-Ring (1990), Dow (1987), Perrow (1986a, 1986b), Vining and Weimer (1990), Williamson (1975, 1983, 1985, 1991, 1992).

[5] In different countries other factors have also contributed to deprofessionalisation. Hence, in Britain, the expansion of the higher education sector in the 1990s, and widening participation policies also can be seen as factors.

[6] Many great works, by great scholars, for instance, have taken a decade or longer to produce and it can be argued that the ability of the scholar to work at their own pace, and on research that is not funded by external providers, is seriously challenged in terms of the competitive market model that

increasingly applies under neoliberalism. On the other hand, notions of 'capture' or 'rent-seeking' could be argued to offer some positive value which has encouraged greater transparency, and accountability in relation to many processes in higher education and in the public sector generally, in that such theories assisted in addressing criticisms relating to old boy networks, feather-nesting, and various forms of prejudice or corruption. In higher education, they could also be seen as useful in relation to improving fairness in relation to assessment in teaching and learning (e.g., even on such matters as the appointment of 'independent chairs' and removal of 'supervisors' from the process in viva voce oral examinations for students). While some of the theories may well be useful and result in greater transparency and fairness in relation to specific processes in higher education, when exalted as a societal policy which subordinates the political and social to the market, then it can be argued that the nature of higher education is transformed accordingly.

[7] In addition to Smith, Hirschman (1977, p. 10) recounts how Montesquieu had developed a similar argument as did Giambattista Vico in his *Scienza Nuovo* (especially pars. 132-133) and Bernard Mandeville in *The Fable of the Bees* (see also, Rosenberg 1963).

[8] This is the process which Ritzer (2000) describes as the "McDonaldisation of Society."

[9] A set of strategies is deemed to be a Nash Equilibrium so long as it constitutes the best set of responses in relation to all other strategies. 'Best' in this sense is defined as those strategies that succeed in competitive market terms. Nash won a Nobel Prize for his contributions in economic theory. He developed various cruel games, the most famous which he called, "Fuck You Buddy," where the only way to win was to betray your opponent, and which reinforced the priority of competition and the irrelevance of cooperation as either personal or group strategies. He later acknowledged that his paranoid schizophrenia was a major cause of his excessively individualistic and competitive approach to social relations (see Curtis, 2007, footnote 11 below).

[10] I am not intending here to document all of the failures of free market theory, simply to state that Keynes documented the various ways in which dysfunctional market patterns, and imperfect equilibriums, could survive for long period of time. Markets also do not guarantee inclusion, and constantly reject players; indeed they are self-diminishing in terms of the number of players in any game, and generate well-known problems in relation to monopoly and concentration (the big fish eat the little fish), which makes any association between markets as mechanisms of democracy or justice highly questionable. I believe, as Keynes believed, that while markets have an important role to play, it is only as subordinate to, not instead of, political direction.

[11] Adam Curtis (2007) *The Trap: What happened to our dream of freedom*, BBC documentary, 11th March, BBC 2. Also see: http://en.wikipedia.org/wiki/The_Trap_(television_documentary_series)

REFERENCES

Althaus, C. (1997). The application of agency theory to public sector management. In G. Davis, B. Sullivan, & A. Yeatman (Eds.), *The new contractualism?* (pp. 137–153). Melbourne: MacMillan Education.

Arrow, K. J. (1950). A difficulty in the concept of social welfare. *The Journal of Political Economy*, 58(4), 328–346.

Arrow, K. J. (1951). *Social choice and individual values*. New York: Wiley.

Axelrod, R. (1990). *The evolution of cooperation*. Harmondsworth: Penguin Books.

Barry, A., Osborne, T., & Rose, N. (Eds.). (1996). *Foucault and political reason: Liberalism, neo-liberalism and rationalities of government*. Chicago: University of Chicago Press.

Bendor, J. (1988). Review article: Formal models of bureaucracy. *British Journal of Political Science*, 18(3), 353–395.

Bergman, M., & Lane, J. (1990). Public policy in a principal-agent framework. *Journal of Theoretical Politics*, 2, 339–352.

Boston, J. (1991). The theoretical underpinnings of public sector restructuring in New Zealand. In J. Boston, et al. (Eds.), *Reshaping the state: New Zealand's bureaucratic revolution*. Auckland: Oxford University Press.

Boston, J. (1994). Purchasing policy advice: The limits to contracting out. *Governance, 6*(1), 1–30.

Boston, J. (1996a). Origins and destinations: New Zealand's model of public management and the international transfer of ideas. In G. Davis & P. Weller (Eds.), *New ideas, better government*. Sydney: Allen and Unwin.

Boston, J., Martin, J., Pallot, J., & Walsh, P. (1996b). *Public management: The New Zealand model*. New York: Oxford.

Braun, D. (1993). Who governs intermediary agencies? Principal-agents relations in research policy making. *Journal of Public Policy, 13*(2), 135–162.

Bryson, J., & Smith-Ring, P. (1990). A transaction-based approach to policy intervention. *Policy Studies, 23*, 205–229.

Buchanan, J. M. (1954a). Social choice, democracy, and free markets. *Journal of Political Economy, 62*(2), 114–123.

Buchanan, J. M. (1954b). Individual choice in voting and the market. *Journal of Political Economy, 62*(3), 334–343.

Buchanan, J., & Tullock, G. (1962). *The calculus of concent: Logical foundations of constitutional democracy*. Ann Arbor, MI: University of Michigan Press.

Buchanan, J. (1975). *The limits of liberty: Between anarchy and leviathan*. Chicago: University of Chicago Press.

Buchanan, J. (1978). From private preferences to public philosophy: The development of public choice. In J. Buchanan (Ed.), *The economics of politics*. London: The Institute of Economic Affairs.

Buchanan, J. (1986). *Liberty, market and state*. Brighton: Wheatsheaf.

Burchell, G. (1996). Liberal government and techniques of the self. In A. Barry, T. Osborne, & N. Rose (Eds.), *Foucault and political reason* (pp. 19–36). Chicago: Chicago University Press.

Chan, S., & Rosenbloom, D. (1994). Legal control of public administration: A principle agent perspective international. *Review of Administrative Sciences, 60*, 559–74.

Deane, R. S. (1989). Reforming the public sector. In S. Walker (Ed.), *Rogernomics: Reshaping New Zealand's economy*. Auckland: GP Books.

Denison, E. F. (1962). *The sources of economic growth in the United States and the alternatives before us*. New York: Committee for Economic Development.

Dow, G. (1987). The function of authority in transaction-cost economics. *Journal of Economic Behaviour and Organization, 8*, 13–38.

Eisenhardt, K. M. (1989). Agency theory: An assessment and review. *Academy of Management Review, 14*(1), 57–74.

Foucault, M. (1991). Governmentality. In G. Burchell, C. Gordon, & P. Miller (Eds.), *The foucault effect: Studies in governmentality* (pp. 87–104). Chicago: University of Chicago Press.

Friedman, M. (1970). *The counter-revolution in monetary theory*. London: Institute of Economic Affairs.

Gray, J. (1984). *Hayek on liberty*. Oxford: Blackwell.

Greer, P. (1992). The next steps initiative: The transformation of Britain's civil service. *The Political Quarterly, 63*(April/June), 222–227.

Hayek, F. A. (1944). *The road to serfdom*. London: Routledge & Kegan Paul.

Hayek, F. A. (1945). The use of knowledge in society. *American Economic Review, 35*(4), 519–530.

Hayek, F. A. (1948). *Individualism and economic order*. Chicago: University of Chicago Press.

Hayek, F. A. (1952a). *The sensory order*. London: Routledge & Kegan Paul.

Hayek, F. A. (1952b). *The counter-revolution of science: Studies in the abuse of reason*. London: Routledge & Kegan Paul.

Hayek, F. A. (1960). *The constitution of liberty*. London: Routledge & Kegan Paul.

Hayek, F. A. (1967). *Studies in philosophy, politics and economics*. London: Routledge & Kegan Paul.

Hayek, F. A. (1973). *Law, legislation & liberty* (Vol. 1). London: Routledge & Kegan Paul.

Hayek, F. A. (1976). *Law, legislation and liberty, Vol. II: The mirage of social justice.* London: Routledge & Kegan Paul.

Hayek, F. A. (1978). *New studies in philosophy, politics, economics and the history of ideas.* Chicago: University of Chicago Press.

Hayek, F. A. (1979). *Law, legislation and liberty, Vol. 3: The political order of a free people.* London: Routledge & Kegan Paul.

Hede, A. (1991). The next steps initiative for civil service reform in Britain: The emergence of managerialism in whitehall? *Canberra Bulletin of Public Administration, 65,* 32–40.

Heymann, D. (1988). *Input controls and the public sector: What does economic theory offer?* Paper prepared for the Fiscal Affairs Department, International Monetary Fund, Washington.

Hirschman, A. O. (1977). *The passions and the interests: Political arguments for capitalism before its triumph.* Princeton, NJ: Princeton University Press.

Jennings, S., & Cameron, R. (1987). State owned enterprise reform in New Zealand. In A. Bollard & R. Buckle (Eds.), *Economic liberalisation in New Zealand.* Auckland: Allen and Unwin.

Jensen, M., & Meckling, W. (1976). Theory of the firm: Managerial behaviour, agency costs and ownership structure. *Journal of Financial Economics, 3,* 305–360.

Kay, N. (1992). Markets, false hierarchies and the evolution of the modern corporation. *Journal of Economic Behaviour and Organization, 17,* 315–334.

Levinthal, D. (1988). A survey of agency models of organisation. *Journal of Economic Behaviour and Organisation, 9,* 153–185.

Matheson, A. (1997). The impact of contracts on public management. In G. Davis, B. Sullivan, & A. Yeatman (Eds.), *The new contractualism?* Melbourne: Macmillan.

McKean, R. (1974). Property rights within government, and devices to increase governmental efficiency. In E. G. Furubotn & S. Pejovich (Eds.), *The economics of property rights.* Massachusetts, MA: Ballinger.

Mishra, R. (1999). *Globalisation and the welfare state.* Cheltenham: Edward Elgar.

Moe, T. (1984). The new economics of organisations. *American Journal of Political Science, 28,* 739–775.

Moe, T. (1990). Political institutions: The neglected side of the story. *Journal of Law, Economics and Organization, 6,* 213–253.

Moe, T. (1991). Politics and the theory of organization. *Journal of Law, Economics and Organization, 7,* 106–129.

Nash, J. (1950). Equilibrium points in n-person games. *Proceedings of the National Academy of the USA, 36*(1), 48–49.

Olssen, M. (1999, July). *Academic freedom and tenure in New Zealand universities.* Paper presented at the AUS Managerialism and Restructuring conference, Wellington.

Olssen, M. (2006, July). Neoliberalism, globalization, democracy: Challenges for education. In A. H Halsey, H. Lauder, P. Brown, & A. S. Wells (Eds.), *Education, culture, economy, society* (Rev. ed.). Oxford: Oxford University Press.

Olssen, M. (2007). Education policy. In Gary McCulloch (Ed.), *International encyclopedia of education.* London and New York: Routledge.

Olssen, M. (2007). Critical theory. In Gary McCulloch (Ed.), *International encyclopedia of education.* London and New York: Routledge.

Olssen, M., & Peters, M. (2005). Neoliberalism, higher education and the knowledge economy: From the free market to knowledge capitalism. *Journal of Education Policy, 20*(3), 313–347.

Olssen, M. (2004). Globalization, the third way and education post 9/11: Building democratic citizenship. In M. Peters (Ed.), *Education, globalization and the state in the age of terrorism.* Boulder, CO: Paradigm Publishers.

Olssen, M., Codd, J., & O'Neill, A.-M. (2004). *Education policy: Globalisation, citizenship, democracy.* London: Sage.

Osborne, T. (1993). On liberalism, neo-liberalism and the 'liberal profession' of medicine. *Economy and Society, 22*(3), 345–356.

Osborne, D., & Gaebler, T. (1992). *Reinventing government: How the entrepreneurial spirit is transforming the public sector, from schoolhouse to statehouse, city hall to the Pentagon.* Reading, MA: Addison-Wesley.

Palmer, K. (1993). *Local government law in New Zealand* (2nd ed.). Sydney: Law Books.

Perrow, C. (1986a). Economic theories of organisation. *Theory and Society, 15*(6), 11–45.

Perrow, C. (1986b). *Complex organisations: A critical essay.* New York:Random House.

Petersen, J. (1993). The economics of organization: The principal-agent relationship. *Acta Sociologica, 36,* 277–293.

Pratt, J., & Zeckhauser, R. (Eds.). (1985). *Principals and agents: The structure of business.* Boston: Harvard Business School Press.

Rees, R. (1985a). The theory of principal and agent: Part 1. *Bulletin of Economic Research, 37*(1), 1–26.

Rees, R. (1985b). The theory of principal and agent: Part 2. *Bulletin of Economic Research, 37*(2), 75–95.

Reisman, D. (1990). *The political economy of james buchanan.* College Station, TX: Texas A&M University Press.

Ritzer, G. (2000). *The McDonaldization of society.* Thousand Oaks, CA: Pine Forge Press.

Rosenberg, N. (1963). Mandeville and laissez-faire. *Journal of the History of Ideas, 24,* 183–196.

Scott, G., & Gorringe, P. (1989). Reform of the core public sector: New Zealand experience. *Australian Journal of Public Administration, 48*(1), 81–92.

Scott, G. (1997). The new institutional economics and the shaping of the state in New Zealand. In G. Davis, B. Sullivan, & A. Yeatman (Eds.), *The new contractualism?* (pp. 154–163). Melbourne: MacMillan Education.

Self, P. (1989). What's wrong with government: The problem of public choice. *Political Quarterly, 6,* 317–344.

Sen, A. (2002). *Rationality and freedom.* Cambridge, MA: The Belknap Press.

Simon, H. (1991). Organizations and markets. *Journal of Economic Perspectives, 5*(2), 25–44.

Smith, A. (1976). *An inquiry into the nature and causes of the wealth of nations* (R. H. Campell & A. S. Skinner, Eds.). Oxford: Clarendon Press [originally published 1776].

Stiglitz, J. (2002). *Globalization and its discontents.* London: Penguin.

Thompson, S., & Wright, M. (Eds.). (1988). *Internal organisation, efficiency and profit.* Oxford: Philip Allan.

Treblicock, M. (1995). Can government be reinvented? In J. Boston (Ed.), *The state under contract.* Wellington: Bridget Williams Books.

Trosa, S. (1994). *Next steps: Moving on.* London: HMSO.

Vining, A., & Weimer, D. (1990). Government supply and government production failure: A framework based on contestability. *Journal of Public Policy, 10,* 1–22.

Weber, M. (1921). *Economy and society.* Totowa, NJ: Bedminster.

Williamson, O. E. (1975). *Markets and hierarchies.* New York: The Free Press.

Williamson, O. E. (1983). Organisational innovation: The transaction-cost approach. In J. Ronen (Ed.), *Entrepreneurship* (pp. 101–34). Lexington, MA: Heath Lexington.

Williamson, O. E. (1985). *The economic institutions of capitalism: Firms, markets, relational contracting.* New York: The Free Press.

Williamson, O. E. (1991). Comparative economic organization: The analysis of discrete structural alternatives. *Administrative Science Quarterly, 36,* 269–296.

Williamson, O. E. (1992). Markets, hierarchies and the modern corporation: An unfolding perspective. *Journal of Economic Behaviour and Organisation, 17,* 335–52.

Williamson, O. E. (1994). *Institutions and economic organization: The governance perspective.* Paper prepared for the World Bank's annual conference on Development Economics, April 28–29, 1994, Washington, DC.

Weingast, B. (1984). The congressional-bureaucratic system: A principal agent perspective. *Public Choice, 4,* 147–191.

Wistrich, E. (1992). Restructuring government New Zealand style. *Public Administration, 70*(1), 119–135.

FURTHER READINGS

Arrow, K. J. (1951). *Social choice and individual values.* New York: Wiley.

Buchanan, J., & Tullock, G. (1962). *The calculus of concent: Logical foundations of constitutional democracy.* Ann Arbor, MI: University of Michigan Press.

Buchanan, J. (1978). From private preferences to public philosophy: The development of public choice. In J. Buchanan (Ed.), *The economics of politics.* London: The Institute of Economic Affairs.

Reisman, D. (1990). *The political economy of James Buchanan.* College Station, TX: Texas A&M University Press.

Perrow, C. (1986). *Complex organisations: A critical essay.* New York: Random House.

Olssen, M., Codd, J., & O'Neill, A.-M. (2004). *Education policy: Globalisation, citizenship, democracy.* London: Sage.

Mark Olssen
Department of Political, International and Policy Studies
University of Surrey, UK

HENRY A. GIROUX

BEYOND THE CORPORATE TAKEOVER OF HIGHER EDUCATION

Rethinking Educational Theory, Pedagogy, and Policy

INTRODUCTION

Under governments that seem increasingly intent on corporatising the public sphere and shifting wealth from the working poor and middle class to the rich, too little attention has been given to the conditions of higher education and its professors. Usually considered an elite class due to their educational status and the practice of tenure, professors and their work within universities have largely been ignored. However, given the university's key role in public life as the protector and promoter of democratic values, it is worthwhile to take a look at how public policy is changing the conduct of higher education. This paper focuses in particular on the changed conditions of universities and professors in the US and under the George W. Bush administration (2001-2009). The critical analysis draws on a wide range of official documents and commentaries articulating ongoing processes of corporatisation in order to reveal the effects on academic values, the role of professors and the democratic dimensions of higher education. In an attempt to go beyond the corporate university the paper will focus as well on current struggles against corporatisation and in defence of democracy. Notwithstanding the focus of this critical re-reading is the US context, the study attempts to come to describe public policies and changed conditions similar to other parts of the world.

In a country in which corporations such as Halliburton and Bechtel rapaciously profit from the war in Iraq, the Food and Drug Administration appears more concerned about the financial well-being of the pharmaceutical industry than the health of the general public, and the Bush administration extends massive tax cuts to the rich amidst increasing poverty, hunger, and job losses, the university offers no escape and little resistance. Instead, the humanistic knowledge and values of the university are being excised as higher education becomes increasingly corporatised. The corporate university, according to Richard Ohmann, acts like a profit-making business rather than a public or philanthropic trust. Thus, we hear of universities applying productivity and performance measures to teaching (Illinois); of plans to put departments in competition with one another for resources (Florida); of cutting faculty costs not only by replacing full-timers with part-timers and temps and by subcontracting for everything from food services to the total management of physical plants, but also by substituting various schemes of computerised instruction; and so on (Ohmann, 2002).

M. Simons, M. Olssen and M.A. Peters (eds.), Re-Reading Education Policies: A Handbook Studying the Policy Agenda of the 21ˢᵗ Century, 458–477.

Such corporatisation affects not only the culture of the campus but also the very content delivered by the university, as academic labor is increasingly based on corporate needs, rather than either the demands of research for the public good or education designed to improve public life. In the corporate university, academics are now expected to be "academic entrepreneurs," valuable only for the money and prestige they bring, and not for the education they can offer. Sacrificed in this transformation is any notion of higher education as a crucial public sphere in which critical citizens and democratic agents are formed and become capable of addressing the anti-democratic forces that threatened democracy in the United States under the former Bush administration.

While the university should equip people to enter the workplace, it should also educate them to contest workplace inequalities, imagine democratically organised forms of work, and identify and challenge those injustices that contradict and undercut the most fundamental principles of freedom, equality, and respect for all people who constitute the global public sphere. Higher education is about more than job preparation and consciousness-raising; it is also about imagining different futures and politics as a form of intervention into public life. In contrast to the cynicism and political withdrawal that media culture fosters, education demands that citizens be able to negotiate the interface of private considerations and public issues; be able to recognise those undemocratic forces that deny social, economic, and political justice; and be willing to give some thought to the nature and meaning of their experiences in struggling for a better world. In view of these substantially democratic concerns, and the importance of the university as a public sphere, my re-reading of US education policy and the changed conditions of universities, professors and students has a clear and straightforward critical scope.

THE UNIVERSITY AS BRAND-NAME CORPORATION

Anyone who spends any time on a college campus in the United States these days cannot miss how higher education is changing. Strapped for money and increasingly defined through the language of corporate culture, many universities seem less interested in higher learning than in becoming licensed storefronts for brand-name corporations – selling off space, buildings, and endowed chairs to rich corporate donors. University bookstores are now managed by big corporate conglomerates such as Barnes & Noble, while companies such as Sodexho-Marriott (also a large investor in the U.S. private prison industry) run a large percentage of college dining halls, and McDonald's and Starbucks occupy prominent locations on the student commons. Student IDs are now adorned with MasterCard and Visa logos, providing students who may have few assets with an instant line of credit and an identity as full-time consumers.

In addition, housing, alumni relations, health care, and a vast array of other services are now being leased out to private interests to manage and run. One consequence is that spaces on university campuses once marked as public and non-commodified – places for quiet study or student gatherings – now have the appearance of a shopping mall. Commercial logos, billboards, and advertisements plaster the walls of student centres, dining halls, cafeterias, and bookstores. Everywhere students turn outside of the university classroom, they are confronted with vendors and commercial sponsors who are hawking credit cards, athletic goods, soft drinks, and other commodities that one associates with the local shopping mall. Universities and colleges compound this marriage of commercial and educational values by signing exclusive contracts with Pepsi, Nike, and other contractors, further blurring the distinction between student and consumer. The message to students is clear: customer satisfaction is offered as a surrogate for learning, "to be a citizen is to be a consumer, and nothing more. Freedom means freedom to purchase" (Croissant, 2001).

Why should we care? Colleges and universities do not simply produce knowledge and values for students; they also play an influential role in shaping their identities, values, and sense of what it means to become citizens of the world. If colleges and universities are to define themselves as centres of teaching and learning vital to the democratic life of the nation and globe, they must acknowledge the real danger of becoming mere adjuncts to big business, or corporate entities in themselves. As Robert Zemsky warns, "When the market interests totally dominate colleges and universities, their role as public agencies significantly diminishes – as does their capacity to provide venues for the testing of new ideas and the agendas for public action" (Zemsky, 2003).

And the threat is real. Commercial deals are no longer just a way for universities to make money. Corporate branding drives the administrative structure of the university. A growing number of college presidents are now hired because of their business connections and ability as fundraisers. Many have no previous experience in higher education and are hired, less for their intellectual leadership, than for their experience in the world of business. For example, Franklin & Marshall College in Pennsylvania hired a college president who did not earn a doctorate, did not teach, or publish research. But, he did have a successful career in marketing and finance, especially in neighbourhood development (Finder, 2005, p. A9). Gone are the days when university presidents were hired for their intellectual status and public roles. Venture capitalists now scour colleges and universities in search of big profits to be made through licensing agreements, the control of intellectual property rights, and investing in university spin-off companies. Deans are often hired from the ranks of the business community, and evaluated on the basis of their ability to attract external funding and impose business models of leadership and accountability. As Stanley Aronowitz points out, "Today (...) leaders of higher education wear the badge of corporate servants proudly" (Aronowitz, 1998, p. 32). The dean at my former university completely collapsed the distinction between scholarship and grant-getting by handing out distinguished professorships to academics who secured large grants but did very little in the way of either making important theoretical contributions or publishing widely recognised scholarly work. What is missing from the space of the corporate university is any perspective suggesting that, at the very least, university administrators, academics, students, and others exercise the political, civic, and ethical courage needed to refuse the commercial rewards that would reduce them to becoming simply another brand name, corporate logo, or adjunct to corporate interests.

PUBLIC POLICY AND CORPORATE EDUCATION

In the U.S., the Bush administration willingly supported the corporatisation of higher education, both through overt statements and by reinforcing the conditions that make such corporatisation possible. Reductions in grants for students, pressure on students to use their education as job-training, and the replacement of government grants with corporate funding are all speeding the process. As the Bush administration cuts student aid, plunders public services, and pushes states to the brink of financial disaster, higher education increasingly becomes a privilege rather than a right. Many middle- and working-class students either find it financially impossible to enter college or, because of increased costs, have to drop out. As the *Chronicle of Higher Education* recently reported, young people from poor and disadvantaged families face even more difficult hurdles in trying to attain a college education because the Bush administration has decided to cut Pell Grants, the nation's largest federal student aid program (Field, 2006). In addition, because Congress changed the federal needs-analysis formula, more than 90,000 disadvantaged students have been disqualified in 2005 from receiving not only Pell Grants but also state financial aid. As all levels of government reduce their funding to higher education, not only will tuition increase, but student loans will increasingly replace grants and scholarships. Lacking adequate financial aid, students, especially poor students, will have to finance the high costs of their education through private corporations such as Citibank, Chase Manhattan, Marine Midland, and other lenders. According to the U.S. Public Interest Group, student loans accounted for 20 percent of federal education assistance in 1976 but now have become the largest source of aid. The average student now graduates with a debt of more than $16,000, and one in three seniors have debts of more than $20,000.[1] As Jeff Williams points out, such loans "effectively indenture students for ten to twenty years after graduation and intractably [reduce] their career choices, funnelling them into the corporate workforce in order to pay their loans" (Williams, 1999, p. 740).

For many young people caught in the margins of poverty, low-paying jobs, recession, and "jobless recovery," the potential costs of higher education, regardless of its status or availability, will dissuade them from even thinking about attending college. Unfortunately, as state and federal agencies and university systems direct more and more of their resources (such as state tax credits and scholarship programs) toward middle- and upper-income students and away from need-based aid, the growing gap in college enrolments between high-income students (95 percent enrolment rate) and low-income students (75 percent enrolment rate) with comparable academic abilities will widen even further.[2] In fact, a report by a federal advisory committee claimed that nearly 48 percent of qualified students from low-income families would not be attending college in the fall of 2002 because of rising tuition charges and a shortfall in federal and state grants. The report claimed that "Nearly 170,000 of the top high-school graduates from low- and moderate-income families are not enrolling in college this year because they cannot afford to do so" (Burd, 2002, p. 1). It also predicted that if the financial barriers that low- and moderate-income students face are not addressed, more than 2 million students by the end of the decade will not attend any form of higher education (Reed, 2002). The current financial crisis has greatly intensified this problem.

The right-wing assault on youth, increasingly evident in the policy decisions of university administrations and the Bush government, can be understood more generally in terms of the practices of a rapacious, neoliberal capitalism. For many people today, the private sphere has become the only space in which to imagine any sense of hope, pleasure, or possibility. Culture as an activity in which people actually produce the conditions of their own agency through dialogue, community participation, resistance, and political struggle is being replaced by a "climate of cultural and linguistic privatisation," (Klein, 1999, p. 177) in which culture becomes something to consume, and the only kind of acceptable speech is that of the savvy shopper. Neoliberalism, with its emphasis on market forces and profit margins, narrows the legitimacy of the public sphere by redressing social concerns through privatisation, deregulation, consumption, and safety. Ardent consumers and disengaged citizens provide fodder for a growing cynicism and depoliticisation of public life at a time when there is an increasing awareness of corporate corruption, financial mismanagement, and systemic greed, as well as the recognition that a democracy of critical citizens is being replaced quickly by an ersatz democracy of consumers. In the vocabulary of neoliberalism, the public collapses into the personal, and the personal becomes "the only politics there is, the only politics with a tangible referent or emotional valence" (Comaroff & Comaroff, 2000, pp. 305–306). As a result, hope disappears or is diminished as the public sphere atrophies, and, as Peter Beilharz argues, "politics becomes banal, for there is not only an absence of citizenship but a striking absence of agency" (Beilharz, 2000, p. 160). As power is increasingly separated from traditional politics and public obligations, corporations are less subject to the control of the state, and "there is a strong impulse to displace political sovereignty with the sovereignty of the market, as if the latter has a mind and morality of its own" (Comaroff & Comaroff, 2000, p. 332). Samuel Weber suggested that what seems to be involved in this process of displacement is "a fundamental and political redefinition of the social value of public services in general, and of universities and education in particular" (Weber cited in Simon, 2001, pp. 47–48). Since September 11, 2001, the US desire to protect market freedoms and wage a war against terrorism at home and abroad in the name of national security has, ironically, not only ushered in a culture of fear but also dealt a lethal blow to civil freedoms. Resting in the balance of this contradiction are both the fate of democracy and the civic health and future of generations of young adults.

When universities can no longer balance their budget through tuition increases or federal grants, they turn to corporate money and self-branding to balance their budgets. Students become "customers," both of the university's own brand and of corporations who sell to them directly through university deals. Although higher education has never been free of the market, there is a new intimacy between higher education and corporate culture, characterised by what Larry Hanley (2001, p. 103) has called a "new, quickened symbiosis." The result is "not a fundamental or abrupt change perhaps, but still an unmistakable radical reduction of [higher education's] public and critical role" (Miyoshi, 1998, p. 263). What was once the hidden curriculum of many universities – the subordination of higher education to capital – has now become an open and much celebrated policy of both public and private higher education. As the line between for-profit and not-for-profit institutions of higher education blurs, the distinctions between democratic values and market interests, between education and job training, collapses. If right-wing reforms in higher education continue unchallenged, the consequences will result in a highly undemocratic, bifurcated civic body. In other words, we will have a society in which a highly trained, largely white elite will be allowed to command the techno-information revolution while a low-skilled majority of poor and minority workers will be relegated to filling the McJobs proliferating in the service sector.

An even closer symbiosis of corporate and university culture takes place among faculty who traditionally have sought outside support for research. As government grant money dries up, such researchers increasingly must turn for support to corporate funders. Higher education's need for new sources of funding neatly dovetails with the inexhaustible need on the part of corporations for new products. Within this symbiotic relationship, knowledge is directly linked to its application in the market, resulting in a collapse of the distinction between knowledge and the commodity. At the same time, as universities increasingly begin to pattern themselves after multinational businesses, they are more willing to allow corporations that sponsor research to influence the outcome or place questionable restrictions on what can be published. Collaborative relationships among faculty suffer as some firms insist that the results of corporate-sponsored research be kept secret. In other cases, researchers funded by corporations have been prohibited from speaking about their research at conferences, talking on the phone with colleagues, or making their labs available to faculty and students not directly involved in the research. Derek Bok reports that "Nearly one in five life-science professors admitted that they had delayed publication by more than six months for commercial reasons" (Bok, 2003, p. 65). Equally disturbing are both the growing number of academics who either hold company stocks or have financial connections to the company sponsoring their research and the refusals on the part of many universities to institute disclosure policies that would reveal such conflicts of interest (ibid., pp. 200–201). Moreover, as the boundaries between public and commercial values become blurred, many academics appear less as disinterested truth seekers than as apologists for corporate profiteering. This becomes particularly startling with respect to corporate-funded medical research.

The *New England Journal of Medicine* reported that "medical schools that conduct research sponsored by drug companies routinely disregard guidelines intended to ensure that the studies are unbiased and that the results are shared with the public" (cited in Mangan, 2002). The *Journal of the American Medical Association* has also reported that "one fourth of biomedical scientists have financial affiliations with industry (...) and that research financed by industry is more likely to draw commercially favourable conclusions" (cited in Guterman, 2003). Corporate power and influence also shape the outcome of the research and the design of clinical trials. Hence, it is not surprising to find, as the journal stated, that "studies reported by the tobacco industry reported pro-industry results [and that] studies on pharmaceuticals were affected by their source of funds as well" (Ibidem). In some instances, corporations place pressure on universities to suppress the publication of those studies whose data questions the effectiveness of the wares, threatening not only academic integrity but also public health and safety. For example, Canada's largest pharmaceutical company, Apotex, attempted to suppress the findings of a University of Toronto researcher, Dr. Nancy Olivieri, when she argued that the "drug the company was manufacturing was ineffective, and could even be toxic" (cited in Mangan, 2002). The University of Toronto not only refused to provide support for Dr. Olivieri, they also suspended her from her administrative role as program director, and warned her and her staff not to talk publicly about the case. It was later disclosed that "the university and Apotex had been for some years in discussions about a multimillion-dollar gift to the university and its teaching hospitals" (Bok, 2003, p. 75).

Turning higher education into the handmaiden of corporate culture works against the critical social imperative of educating citizens who can sustain and develop inclusive democratic public spheres. Lost in the merging of corporate culture and higher education is a historic and honourable democratic tradition that extends from John Adams to W.E.B. DuBois to John Dewey and that extols the importance of education as essential for a democratic public life (Colby et al., 2003). Education within this tradition integrated individual autonomy with the principles of social responsibility. Moreover, it cast a critical eye on the worst temptations of profit-making and market-driven values. For example, Sheila Slaughter has argued persuasively that at the close of the nineteenth century, "professors made it clear that they did not want to be part of a cutthroat capitalism (...). Instead, they tried to create a space between capital and labour where [they] could support a common intellectual project directed toward the public good" (Slaughter, 2001, p. 1). Amherst College President Alexander Meiklejohn echoed this sentiment in 1916 when he suggested:

> Insofar as a society is dominated by the attitudes of competitive business enterprise, freedom in its proper American meaning cannot be known, and hence, cannot be taught. That is the basic reason why the schools and colleges, which are presumably commissioned to study and promote the ways of freedom, are so weak, so confused, so ineffectual (cited in Huber, s.d.).

As the line between for-profit and not-for-profit institutions of higher education collapses, educator John Palattela observes, many "schools now serve as personnel offices for corporations" and quickly dispense with the historically burdened though important promise of creating democratic mandates for higher education (Palattela, 2001, p. 73).

Of all groups, university and college educators should be the most vocal and militant in challenging the corporatisation of education by making clear that at the heart of any form of inclusive democracy is the assumption that learning should be used to expand the public good, create a culture of questioning, and promote democratic social change. Individual and social agency become meaningful as part of the willingness to imagine otherwise, "in order to help us find our way to a more human future" (Chomsky, 2000, p. 34). Under such circumstances, knowledge can be used for amplifying human freedom and promoting social justice, and not simply for creating profits.

THE ACADEMIC ENTREPRENEUR

As corporate culture and values shape university life, academic labor is increasingly being transformed into the image of a multinational conglomerate workforce. While corporate values such as efficiency and downsizing in higher education appear to have caught the public's imagination at the moment, this belies the fact that such "reorganisation" has been going on for some time. What is new is that the ever growing and "steady corporatisation of American higher education has threatened to relegate faculty governance to the historical archive" (Aronowitz, 2006). The modern university was once governed, however weakly, by faculty, with the faculty senate naming the university president. That era of faculty control is long gone, with presidents now being named by boards of trustees, and governing through hand-picked (and well-paid) bureaucrats rather than through faculty committees. John Silber, the former president of Boston University from 1971 to 1996, best exemplifies this trend. As a number of notable academics and public figures have pointed out, Silber often used his administrative power to weaken faculty governance, "punish his critics – sometimes by denial of tenure (against faculty recommendation), sometimes by refusing merit raises and leaves, sometimes by personal abuse (including a false charge of arson, later withdrawn, against a member of the faculty)," engage in "repeated violations of civil liberties," and promote educational theories that by any progressive standard would have to be judged as reactionary (Piven, 1980).[3] Faculty power once rested in the fact that most faculty were full-time and a large percentage of them had tenure, so they could confront administration without fear of losing their jobs. One of the first steps taken by the newly corporatised university in the 1980s was to limit faculty power by hiring fewer full-time faculty, promoting fewer faculty to tenure, and instituting "post-tenure" reviews that threaten to take tenure away.

When full-time academic labour is outsourced to temporary or contract labour, the intellectual culture of the university declines as overworked graduate students and part-time faculty assume the role of undergraduate teaching with little or no portion of their pay allotted for research. Moreover, these contingent faculty are granted no role in the university governance process, are detached from the intellectual life of the university, rarely have time to engage in sustained scholarship, and appear largely as interchangeable instructors acting more like temporary visitors. In short, the hiring of part-time faculty to minimise costs simultaneously maximises managerial control over faculty and the educational process itself. Power now resides in the hands of a new cadre of corporate-oriented trustees and administrators who proudly define themselves as *entrepreneurs* rather than as educational leaders.

One possibility of what the future holds for the corporatising of higher education can be seen in the example of Rio Salado College in Tempe, Arizona. The college is the second largest in the Maricopa County Community College District and has a total of 13,314 students (Ashburn, 2006, p. A12). And, yet it has "only 33 permanent faculty members, 27 of whom are full-time" (ibid, p. A10). Its classes are almost entirely virtual, and it hires close to a 1000 part-time instructors scattered across the state. The part-time faculty carry the bulk of the teaching and are paid about $2200 a course. Teaching eight courses, four each semester, calculates to slightly less than $18,000 a year, which amounts to poverty level wages. The few, privileged full-time faculty earn between $40,000 to $88,000 a year (ibid., p. A11). The academic labour force at Rio Salado College in this instance has been, for the most part, entirely casualised with almost no possibility for any of its 1000 members landing a full-time position. Linda Thor, the president of the Rio Salado College often quotes from best-selling business books and "embraces the idea of students as customers" (ibid., p. A12). Moreover, consistent with Thor's embrace of corporate principles and efficiency-minded management style, the day-to-day duties of instructors at the college are "simplified by RioLearn, a course-management system designed specifically for the college through a partnership with Dell Inc. and the Microsoft Corporation" (ibid., p. A12). Most importantly, this utterly privatised, fragmented, exploitative, and commercialised vision of higher education should not be dismissed as a quirky approach to university administration. In this view, power, time, and decision-making are completely controlled by administrators who view faculty subordination to corporate control either "a thing of nature, and, more to the point, the royal road to academic and financial reward" (Aronowitz, 2005, p. 117). The latter is obvious in the ways in which non-profit institutions are emulating this model.

For instance, the University of Illinois, which has three land-grant non-profit campuses, plans to launch a whole new college, which would be completely online, operate as a for-profit entity, and consist almost entirely of part-time faculty with no tenured faculty at all. Issues central to university culture such as tenure, academic freedom, and intellectual integrity are dispensed with as faculty governance is now put largely in the hands of administrators, and faculty are reduced to outsourced, casual labour. Allegedly, the rationale for this utterly corporatised approach to education is to make the University of Illinois more competitive, while providing "access to high quality education first and foremost to the people of Illinois" (Jashik, 2006). In my view, this educational model with its stripped down version of teaching, its cost-efficiency model of management, and its views of students as customers and faculty as source of cheap labour is exactly what informs the current corporate understanding of the future of higher education. This model represents the face of higher education in the age of global capital and market fundamentalism and is less about education than about training, less about educating students to be informed and responsible citizens of the world than about short-term returns on revenue, all the time providing a pseudo-academic warrant to reduce education to an extension of the corporate world. Clearly, this is a view that needs to be resisted if higher education is to retain any democratic value at all.

The American Council of Education reported in 2002 that "The number of part-time faculty members increased by 79 percent from 1981 to 1999, to more than 400,000 out of a total of one million instructors over all," and that the "biggest growth spurt occurred between 1987 and 1993, when 82 percent of the 120,000 new faculty members hired during that period were for part-time positions" (Walsh, 2002). In fact, more professors are working part-time and at two-year community colleges now than at any other time in the country's recent history. The American Association of University Professors reported in 2007 that both part-timers and full-time faculty not on a tenure track now account for nearly "70 percent of professors at colleges and universities, both public and private" (Finder, 2006, p. A16). Creating a permanent underclass of part-time professional workers in higher education is not only demoralising and exploitative for many faculty who have such jobs but also deskills both part- and full-time faculty by increasing the amount of work they have to do. Many part timers have not earned doctoral degrees and have less time to meet with students. Moreover, with less time to prepare, larger class loads, almost no time for research, and excessive grading demands, many adjuncts run the risk of becoming demoralised and ineffective.

Any analysis concerning the deskilling and disempowering of faculty points to a politics of temporality, and how time is controlled and for whom at all levels of higher education. Time is crucial to how a university structures its public mission, shapes governance with faculty, controls the use of space, and limits or expands student access, as well as how it is organised in the legitimation and organisation of particular forms of knowledge, research, and pedagogy. For the past twenty years, time as a value and the value of time have been redefined through the dictates of neoliberal economics, which have largely undermined any notion of public time guided by the non-commodified values central to a political and social democracy. In higher education, corporate time maps faculty relationships through self-promoting market agendas and narrow definitions of self-interest. Caught on the treadmill of getting more grants, teaching larger classes, and producing revenue for the university, faculty become another casualty of a business ideology that attempts to "extract labour from campus workers at the lowest possible cost, one willing to sacrifice research independence and integrity for profit" (Nelson, 2002, p. 709). Time in this context is less about providing opportunities for faculty dialogue, shared responsibilities, class preparation, and rigorous scholarship than it is about a notion of *corporate time,* which is sped up, accelerated, and compressed. Time in its corporate versions becomes a deprivation rather than a resource, a temporality designed to excise any notion of self-development, an expansive sense of agency, and critical thought itself.

Grounded in the culture of hierarchical power relations, post-Fordist managerial principles, competitiveness, and bottom-line interests, corporate time reworks faculty loyalties, transforming educators into dispensable labour with little or no power over the basic decisions that structure academic labour (Watkins, 1993). Faculty interaction is structured less around collective solidarities built upon practices that offer a particular relationship to public life than through corporate-imposed rituals of competition and production that conform to the "narrowly focused idea of the university as a support to the economy" (Sharp, 2002, p. 280). But more is reproduced than structural dislocations among faculty: there is also an alarming preponderance of crippling fear, insecurity, and resentment that makes it difficult for faculty to take risks, forge bonds of solidarity, engage in social criticism, and perform as public intellectuals rather than as technicians in the service of corporate largesse. These structural and ideological factors threaten to undermine the collective power faculty need to challenge the increasing corporate-based, top-down administrative structures that are becoming commonplace in many colleges and universities. Powerlessness breeds resentment and anger among part-time faculty, and fear and despair among full-time faculty, who feel their tenure is no longer secure. The ease with which tenured faculty can now be replaced in the US has been demonstrated in recent years by major universities such as Penn State, which fired lesbian, feminist, drama professor Nona Gerad for writing derogatory email messages in which she complained about the lack of resources for her program, criticised the performance of some of her colleagues, and staged a play that a right-wing donor found offensive because of its partial nudity and sexually explicit language (Ward, 2004).

DOWNSIZING, DESKILLING, COMMODIFICATION

Academic downsizing has been legitimised through a particularly debased notion of professionalism that bears little resemblance to its once stated emphasis on quality teaching, creative research, and public service. The new corporate professionalism now positions and rewards educators as narrow specialists, unencumbered by matters of ethics, power, and ideology. No longer concerned with important social issues, democratic values, or the crucial task of educating students about important historical, cultural, social, and theoretical traditions, corporate-inspired notions of professionalism now shift the emphasis from the quality of academic work to a crude emphasis on quantity, from creativity and critical dialogue in the classroom to standardisation and rote learning, from supporting full-time tenured positions to constructing an increasing army of contract workers, and from emphasising rigorous scholarship and engagement with public issues to the push for grant writing and external funding.

The turn to downsizing and deskilling faculty is also exacerbated by the attempts on the part of many universities to expand into the profitable market of distance education, whose online courses reach thousands of students. David Noble has written extensively on the restructuring of higher education under the imperatives of the new digital technologies and the move into distance education. If he is correct, the news is not good. Distance education fuels the rise in the use of part-time faculty, who will be "perfectly suited to the investor-imagined university of the future" (Noble, 2001, p. 31; see Noble, 2002). According to Noble, online learning largely functions through pedagogical models and methods of delivery that not only rely on standardised, pre-packaged curricula and methodological efficiency; they also reinforce the commercial penchant toward training students and further deskilling the professoriate. The former president of Teachers College at Columbia University, Arthur Levine, has predicted that the new information technology may soon make the traditional college and university obsolete, and he is not alone (cited in Press & Washburn, 2001, p. 1). More than half of the nation's colleges and universities deliver courses online or over the Internet (ibid., p. 2). Mass-marketed degrees and courses are not only being offered by prestigious universities such as Seton Hall, Stanford, Harvard, The New School, and the University of Chicago; they are also giving rise to cyber-backed colleges such as the Western Governors University and for-profit, stand-alone, publicly traded institutions such as the University of Phoenix. The marriage of corporate culture, higher education, and the new high-speed technologies also offers universities big opportunities to cut back on maintenance expenses, eliminate entire buildings such as libraries and classroom facilities, and trim labour costs (Washburn, 2005).

This does not mean that technologies such as email, online discussion groups, and the Internet cannot improve classroom instruction by ameliorating existing modes of communication, or by simply making academic work more interesting. The real issue is whether such technology in its various pedagogical uses in higher education is governed by a technocratic rationality that undermines human freedom and democratic values. As Herbert Marcuse has argued, when the rationality that drives technology is instrumentalised and "transformed into standardised efficiency (...) liberty is confined to the selection of the most adequate means for reaching a goal which [the individual] did not set" (Marcuse, 1998, p. 45). The consequence of the substitution of technology for pedagogy is that instrumental goals replace ethical and political considerations, diminishing classroom control by teachers and dehumanising pedagogy for students.

Increasingly, academics find themselves pressured to teach more service-oriented and market-based courses. The processes of vocationalisation – fuelled by corporate values that mimic "flexibility," "competition," or "lean production," and rationalised through the application of accounting principles – threaten to gut many academic departments and programs that cannot translate their subject matter into commercial gains. As Michael Peters observes, entire disciplines and bodies of knowledge are now either valued or devalued on the basis of their "ability to attract global capital and (...) potential for serving transnational corporations. Knowledge is valued for its strict utility rather than as an end in itself or for its emancipatory effects (Peters, 2002, p. 148)." Good value for students means taking courses labelled as "relevant" in market terms, which are often counterposed to courses in the social sciences, humanities, and the fine arts that are concerned with forms of learning that do not readily translate into either private gain or commercial value. Similarly, many universities are finding that their remedial programs, affirmative action programs, and other crucial pedagogical resources are under massive assault, often by conservative trustees who want to eliminate from the university any attempt to address the deep inequities in society, while simultaneously denying a decent education to minorities of colour and class. For example, City University of New York, as a result of a decision made by its board of trustees, decided to end "its commitment to provide remedial courses for unprepared students, many of whom are immigrants requiring language training before or concurrent with entering the ordinary academic discipline. (...) Consequently (...) a growing number of prospective college students are forced on an already overburdened job market" (Aronowitz, 2000, pp. 63, 109–110). Both professors and students increasingly bear the burden of overcrowded classes, limited resources, and hostile legislators.

At the same time, while compassion and concern for students and teachers wane, universities are eagerly courting big business: "In recent years academic institutions and a growing number of Internet companies have been racing to tap into the booming market in virtual learning" (Press & Washburn, 2001, p. 2). As colleges and corporations collaborate over the content of degree programs, particularly with regard to online graduate degree programs, college curricula run the risk of being narrowly tailored to the needs of specific businesses. For example, Babson College developed a master's degree program in business administration specifically for Intel workers. Similarly, the University of Texas at Austin developed an online Masters of Science degree in science, technology, and commercialisation that caters only to students who work at IBM. Moreover, the program will orient its knowledge, skills, and research to focus exclusively on IBM projects.[4] Not only do such courses come dangerously close to becoming company training workshops; they also open up higher education to powerful corporate interests that have little regard for the more time-honoured educational mandate to cultivate an informed, critical citizenry.

Online courses also raise important issues about intellectual property – who owns the rights for course materials developed for online use. Because of the market potential of online lectures and course materials, various universities have attempted to lay ownership claims to such knowledge. For example, at the University of California at Los Angeles, an agreement was signed in 1994 that allowed an outside vender, OnlineLearning.net, to create and copyright online versions of UCLA courses. The agreement was eventually "amended in 1999 to allow professors' rights to the basic content of their courses (...) [but] under the amended contract, OnlineLearning retain[ed] their right to market and distribute those courses online, which is the crux of the copyright dispute" (Press & Washburn, 2001, p. 8). As universities make more and more claims on owning the content of faculty notes, lectures, books, computer files, and media for classroom use, the first casualty is, as Ed Condren, a UCLA professor, points out, "the legal protection that enables faculty to freely express their views without fear of censorship or appropriation of their ideas" (Condren cited in Press & Washburn, 2001, p. 8). At the same time, by selling course property rights for a fee, universities infringe on the ownership rights of faculty members by taking from them any control over how their courses might be used in the public domain.

Corporate interests are also exerting their influence over major aspects of university decision-making in and out of the classroom in a number of other ways. No longer content to make their presence felt on college campuses through the funding of endowed chairs, academic centres, or research about business issues that eventually are used as case studies, companies such as BMW and IBM are taking their involvement with higher education to a new level. When the German automaker BMW contributed $10 million to Clemson University in 2002 to help develop a $1.5 billion automotive and research center, Clemson gave BMW an extraordinary amount of control over curriculum and hiring procedures. Not only did BMW play a role in developing the curriculum for the automotive graduate engineering school, but it also "drew up profiles of its ideal students; [provided] a list of professors and specialists to interview, and even had approval rights over the school's architectural look" (Browning, 2006, p. C6). In addition, BMW gave Clemson's president a BMW X5 to drive. In spite of Clemson's claims that it retains its independence as a public university despite its close ties with BMW, candidates for the endowed chairs were interviewed by BMW executives and "a network council composed of BMW managers meets monthly to advise Clemson on the curriculum" (ibid., p. C6). Thomas Kurfess, the first person hired to fill a BMW endowed professorship, has no reservations about the growing corporatisation of higher education, noting that "This is a different model. It is nice to be able to show that it's not just the name beyond the chair (...) [and have] real ties to industry" (Jaschik, 2006, p. C1). A lawsuit contesting the contract between BMW and Clemson made public a letter written by a BMW official who stated that "BMW is going to drive the entire campus" (Browning, 2006, p. C6). At least BMW is honest about its intentions and the role it wants to play in shaping Clemson's relationship with industry.

Another indication of the growing symbiosis between higher education and the corporate world is exemplified in IBM's relationship with North Carolina State University. In return for a number of grants, IBM created a new academic discipline called "Service Sciences, Management and Engineering," along with a curriculum whose aim is to produce "graduates better prepared to work for IBM." In effect, IBM has created a specific program that is designed to serve its labor needs and is "tailored for potential employers." According to IBM, "the curriculum offers an academic way of understanding interaction between client and provider (...) using a mix of scientific and business concepts to focus on areas that might not be core in either a Masters of Business Administration or computer-science program" (Chaker, 2006, p. D1). As should be clear, a number of universities are now working with IBM along with an increasing number of faculty. At UC-Berkeley, one professor teaching at the School of Information met with "IBM executives at the company's Silicon Valley research centre to seek their advice on his syllabus" (ibidem). The result is that his students are now required to read "selections from the IBM Systems Journal" (ibidem). Such partnerships violate the academic integrity of the university and bode badly for the future of higher education in that they subordinate democratic values to corporate values and undercut the power of faculty and administration to define the meaning and purpose of the university and its relationship to the larger society.

While the cult of professionalism inspires fear and insecurity in academics terrified about maintaining tenure, getting it, or for that matter simply securing a part-time position, university educators also face the harsh lessons of financial deprivation, overburdened work loads, and the loss of power in shaping the governance process. They devote less time to their roles either as well-informed public intellectuals or as "cosmopolitan intellectuals situated in the public sphere" (Agger, 2002, p. 444). Many faculty live under the constant threat of either being downsized, punished, or fired and are less concerned about quality research and teaching than about accepting the new rules of corporate-based professionalism in order to simply survive in the new corporatised academy. Against the current drive to corporatise higher education, commodify curricula, treat students as customers and trainees, and relegate faculty to the status of contract employees, higher education needs to be defended as a public good. Central to such a task is the challenge to resist the university becoming what literary theorist Bill Readings has called a consumer-oriented corporation more concerned about accounting than accountability, and whose mission, defined largely through an appeal to excellence, is comprehended almost exclusively in terms of instrumental efficiency (Readings, 1996).

RETHINKING THE UNIVERSITY AS A DEMOCRATIC PUBLIC SPHERE

As the power of higher education is reduced in its ability to make corporate power accountable, it becomes more difficult within the logic of the bottom line for faculty, students, and administrators to address pressing social and ethical issues. This suggests a perilous turn in American society, and clearly in line with policy changes in other parts of the world. It is this turn that threatens both our understanding of democracy as fundamental to our basic rights and freedoms, as well as the ways in which we can rethink and re-appropriate the meaning, purpose, and future of higher education. Situated within a broader context of issues concerned with social responsibility, politics, and the dignity of human life, higher education should be engaged as a public sphere that offers students the opportunity to involve themselves in the deepest problems of society, to acquire the knowledge, skills, and ethical vocabulary necessary for modes of critical dialogue and forms of broadened civic participation. This suggests developing educational conditions for students to come to terms with their own sense of power and public voice as individual and social agents by enabling them to examine and frame critically what they learn in the classroom as part of a broader understanding of what it means to live in a global democracy. At the very least, students need to learn how to take responsibility for their own ideas, take intellectual risks, develop a sense of respect for others different than themselves, and learn how to think critically in order to shape the conditions that influence how they function in a wider democratic culture. The diverse but connected fields of cultural studies and critical pedagogy offer some insights for addressing these issues, and educators can learn from them in order to expand the meaning of the political and revitalise the pedagogical possibilities of cultural politics.

But more is needed than defending higher education as a vital sphere in which to develop and nourish the proper balance between democratic values and market fundamentalism, between identities founded on democratic principles and identities steeped in a form of competitive, self-interested individualism that celebrates its own material and ideological advantages. Given the current assault in the US on critical educators in light of the tragic events of September 11, 2001, and the conservative backlash against higher education being waged by the Bush administration, it is politically crucial that educators at all levels of involvement in the academy be defended as public intellectuals who provide an indispensable service to the nation. Such an appeal cannot be made in the name of professionalism but in terms of the civic benefits such intellectuals provide. The late Pierre Bourdieu argued that intellectuals need to create new ways for doing politics by investing in political struggles through a relentless critique of the abuses of authority and power. Bourdieu wanted scholars to use their skills and knowledge to break out of the microcosm of academia, combine scholarship with commitment, and "enter into sustained and vigorous exchange with the outside world (especially with unions, grassroots organisations, and issue-oriented activist groups) instead of being content with waging the 'political' battles, at once intimate and ultimate, and always a bit unreal, of the scholastic universe" (Bourdieu, 2000, p. 44).

Organising against the corporate takeover of higher education suggests fighting to protect the jobs of full-time faculty, turning adjunct jobs into full-time positions, expanding benefits to part-time workers, and putting power into the hands of faculty and students. Protecting the jobs of full-time faculty means insuring that they have the right to academic freedom, are paid a decent wage, and play an important role in governing the university. A weak faculty translates into a faculty without rights or power, one that is governed by fear rather than shared responsibilities and is susceptible to labour-bashing tactics such as increased work loads, contract labour, and the suppression of dissent. Adjunct or part-time labour must be given the opportunity to break the cycle of exploitative labour and within a short period of time be considered for full-time positions with full benefits and the power to influence governance policies. Within the universities and colleges today, power is top-heavy, largely controlled by trustees and administrators and removed from those who actually do the work of the university, namely the faculty, staff, and students. Moreover such struggles against corporations must consider addressing the exploitative conditions under which many graduate students work, constituting a de facto army of service workers who are underpaid, overworked, and shorn of any real power or benefits.

The challenge for faculty in higher education is both structural and ideological. On the structural side, faculty, students, and staff need to organise labour movements and unions to challenge the corporatisation of the university. Universities have enormous resources that can be mobilised to oppress faculty, exploit staff, and deny the rights of students to a decent education. To fight against such power demands a labour and student movement capable of collectively exercising enormous influence in both influencing and shaping academic policies. Such movements must connect to local communities, reach out to national and international organisations, and develop multiple strategies in taking back the universities from the corporations. I want to stress here the need for multiple interventions extending from anti-sweat shop movements to taking control of academic departments to organising larger faculty structures and organisations. At best, faculty and students must unionise whenever they can in order to speak with a collective voice and the power of collective opposition.

Ideologically, faculty must find ways to contribute their knowledge and skills to an understanding of how corporate values, identities, and practices create the conditions for devaluing critical learning and undermining viable forms of political agency. Academics, as Imre Szeman puts it, need to figure out how corporate power, culture, and values "constitute a problem of and for pedagogy" (Szeman, 2002, p. 4). Academics need to be attentive to the oppositional pedagogies put into place by various student movements in order to judge their "significance (...) for the shape and function of the university curricula today" as well as their rhetorical and material impact on public spheres (ibid., p. 5). Within the last few years in the US for instance, protests on and off campuses have picked up and spawned a number of student protest groups, including the United Students Against Sweatshops, with chapters in over 200 schools, the nationwide 180/Movement for Democracy and Education, and a multitude of groups protesting the policies of the World Trade Organisation and the International Monetary Fund. Such movements offer instances of collective resistance to the glaring material inequities and the growing cynical belief that today's culture of investment and finance makes it impossible to address many of the social problems facing both the United States and the world. The challenge here is for faculty to learn as much as possible from these student movements about what it means to deepen and expand the struggle for establishing pedagogical approaches and labour movements that can be used to mediate the fundamental tension between the public values of higher education and the commercial values of corporate culture, on the one hand, and fight against the more crucial assaults waged against the welfare state and public goods, on the other hand. If the forces of corporate culture are to be challenged, educators must consider enlisting the help of diverse communities, interests, foundations, social movements, and other forces to insure that public institutions of higher learning are adequately funded so that they will not have to rely on corporate sponsorship and advertising revenues.

As public intellectuals, academics can learn from such struggles by turning the university into a vibrant critical site of learning and an unconditional site of pedagogical and political resistance. The power of the dominant order does not merely reside in the economic realm or in the material relations of power, but also in the realm of ideas and culture. This is why intellectuals must take sides, speak out, and engage in the hard work of debunking corporate culture's assault on teaching and learning. They must orient their teaching toward social change, connect learning to public life, link knowledge to the operations of power, and allow issues of human rights and crimes against humanity in their diverse forms to occupy a space of critical and open discussion in the classroom. It also means stepping out of the classroom and working with others to create public spaces where it becomes possible not only to "shift the way people think about the moment, but potentially to energise them to do something differently in that moment," to link one's critical imagination with the possibility of activism in the public sphere (Guinier & Smith, 2002, pp. 34–35).

The language of the emerging corporate university radically alters the vocabulary available for appraising the meaning of citizenship, agency, and civic virtue. Within this discourse everything is for sale, and what is not has no value as a public good or practice. It is in the spirit of such a critique and act of resistance that educators need to break with what Pierre Bourdieu has described as a "new faith in the historical inevitability professed by the theorists of [neo] liberalism [in order] to invent new forms of collective political work" capable of confronting the march of corporate power (Bourdieu, 1999, p. 26). This will not be an easy task, but it is a necessary one if democracy is to be won back from the reign of financial markets and the Darwinian values of an unbridled capitalism. Academics can contribute to such a struggle by, among other things, defending higher education for its contribution to the quality of public life, fighting through organised resistance for the crucial role higher education can exercise pedagogically in asserting the primacy of democratic values over commercial interests, and struggling collectively through a powerful union movement to preserve the institutional and ideological conditions necessary to provide both faculty and students with the capacities they need for civic courage and engaged critical citizenship.

NOTES

[1] Cited in Action Alert, *Rock the Vote Issues in Education* (July 12, 2003). Available online at: http://www.rockthevote.org.
[2] This information is taken from Editorial, "Pricing the Poor Out of College," *New York Times* (March 27, 2002), p. A27. See also, Williams, 2006.
[3] For a devastating critique of Silber's presidency at Boston University, see "A Report on Academic Freedom at Boston University," *Boston University Faculty Bulletin* (February 1996), 50 pp. For some insightful criticisms of Silber, see Gross (1995); Zinn (1995). On my particular tenure case, see Jacoby (2000).
[4] For more details on the creation of online degrees for corporations, see Carnevale (2002).

REFERENCES

Agger, B. (2002). Sociological writing in the wake of postmodernism. *Cultural Studies/Cultural Methodologies, 2*(4), 427–459.
Aronowitz, S. (1998). The new corporate university. *Dollars and Sense, 21*(6), 32–35.
Aronowitz, S. (2000). *The knowledge factory. Dismantling the corporate university and creating true higher learning.* Boston: Beacon Press.
Aronowitz, S. (2005). Higher education in everyday life. In P. P. Trifonas & M. A. Peters (Eds.), *Deconstructing derrida: Tasks for the new humanities.* New York: Palgrave MacMillan.
Aronowitz, S. (2006, Fall). Should academic unions get involved in governance? *Liberal Education.* Retrieved from http://www.aacu.org/liberaleducation/le-fa06/le-fa06_feature3.cfm
Ashburn, E. (2006, October 6). The few, the proud, the professors. *Chronicle of Higher Education.*
Beilharz, P. (2000). *Zygmunt Bauman: Dialectic of modernity.* London: Sage.
Bok, D. (2003). *Universities in the marketplace.* Princeton, NJ: Princeton University Press.
Bourdieu, P. (1999). *Acts of resistance.* New York: New Press.

Bourdieu, P. (2000). For a scholarship with commitment. *Profession*, 40–45.

Browning, L. (2006, August 29). BMW's custom-made university. *New York Times*.

Burd, S. (2002, June 27). Lack of aid will keep 170,000 qualified, needy students out of college this year, report warns. *Chronicle of Higher Education*. Retrieved from http://chronicle.com/daily/2002/06/2002062701n.html

Carnevale, D. (2002, January 28). Colleges tailor online degrees for individual companies. *Chronicle of Higher Education*. Retrieved from http://chronicle.com/cgi2-bin/printable.cgi

Chaker, A. M. (2006, September 12). Majoring in IBM. *Wall Street Journal*, p. D1.

Chomsky, N. (2000). Paths taken, tasks ahead. *Profession*, 32–39.

Colby, A., Ehrlick, T., Baumont, E., & Stephens, J. (2003). *Educating citizens*. San Francisco: Jossey-Bass.

Comaroff, J., & Comaroff, J. L. (2000). Millennial capitalism: First thoughts on a second coming. *Public Culture, 12*(2), 291–343.

Croissant, J. L. (2001). Can this campus be bought. *Academe*. Retrieved from http://www.aaup.org/publications/Academe01SO/so01cro.html

Field, K. (2006, July 6). Congress cuts $12.7 billion from student loan programs. *The Chronicle of Higher Education, 52*(18).

Finder, A. (2005, March 5). A college President whose credentials stress taking care of business. *The New York Times*.

Finder, A. (2007, November 20). Decline of tenure track raises concerns. *The New York Times*.

Gross, D. (1995). Under the Volcano: Boston University in the silber age. *Lingua Franca*, 44–53.

Guinier, L., & Smith, A. D. (2002). A conversation between lani guinier and anna deavere smith, 'Rethinking power,rRethinking theatre'. *Theater, 31*(3), 34–35.

Guterman, L. (2003, January 22). Conflict of interest is widespread in biomedical research, study finds. *Chronicle of Higher Education*. Retrieved from http://chronicle.com /daily/2003/01/2003012202n.htm

Hanley, L. (2001). Conference roundtable. *Found Object, 10*.

Huber, B. (s.d.). Homogenizing the curriculum: Manufacturing the standardized student. *Features*. Retrieved date, from http://www.louisville.edu/journal/workplace/huber.html

Jacoby, R. (2000). *The last intellectuals*. New York: Basic Books.

Jaschik, S. (2006, August 25). BMW professors. *Inside Higher Ed*. Retrieved from http://insidehighered.com/news/2006/08/25/clemson

Jashik, S. (2006, August 31). The new state U. *Inside Higher Ed*. Retrieved from http://insidehighered.com/news/2006/08/31/illinois

Klein, N. (1999). *No logo*. New York: Picador.

Mangan, K. S. (2002, October 25). Medical schools routinely ignore guidelines on company-sponsored research, study finds. *Chronicle of Higher Education*. Retrieved from http://chronicle.com/daily/2002/10/200210250ln.htm

Marcuse, H. (1998). Some social implications of modern technology. In D. Kellner (Ed.), *Technology, war, and fascism*. New York: Routledge.

Miyoshi, M. (1998). 'Globalization', culture, and the University. In F. Jameson & M. Miyoshi (Eds.), *The cultures of globalization*. Durham, NC: Duke University Press.

Nelson, C. (2002). Between anonymity and celebrity: The zero degrees of professional identity. *College English, 64*(6), 696–709.

Noble, D. F. (2001). The future of the digital diploma mill. *Academe, 87*(5).

Noble, D. F. (2002). *Digital diploma mills: The automation of higher education*. New York: Monthly Review Press.

Ohmann, R. (2002). Citizenship and literacy work: Thoughts without a conclusion. *Workplace*. Retrieved from http://www.louisville.edu/journal/workplace/issue7/ohmann.html

Palattela, J. (2001). Ivory towers in the marketplace. *Dissent, 48*(3), 70–73.

Peters, M. (2002). The university in the knowledge economy. In S. Cooper, J. Hinkson, & G. Sharp (Eds.), *Scholars and entrepreneurs* (pp. 137–152). Melbourne: Arena Publications.

Piven, F., Rebelsky, F., Vendler, H., Zinn, H., Miller, S. M., & Hunt, S. (1980). Letter-academic freedom at B.U. *New York Review of Books*. Retrieved from http://www.nybooks.com/articles/7376

Press, E., & Washburn, J. (2001, January-February). Digital diplomas. *Mother Jones*. Retrieved from http://www.motherjones.com

Readings, B. (1996). *The university in ruins*. Cambridge, MA: Harvard University Press.

Reed, A. L., Jr. (2002, April). Free college for all. *The Progressive, 66*(4), 12–15.

Sharp, G. (2002). The idea of the intellectual and after. In S. Cooper, J. Hinkson, & G. Sharp (Eds.), *Scholars and entrepreneurs: The university in crisis* (pp. 269–316). Melbourne, Australia: Arena Publications.

Simon, R. (2001). The university: A place to think? In H. A. Giroux & K. Myrsiades (Eds.), *Beyond the corporate university* (pp. 43–56). Lanham, MD: Rowman and Littlefield.

Slaughter, S. (2001, September–October). Professional values and the allure of the market. *Academe*.

Szeman, I. (2002). Introduction: Learning to learn from seattle. *Review of Education, Pedagogy, and Cultural Studies, 24*(1–2), 1–12.

Walsh, S. (2002, October 29). Study finds significant increase in number of part-time and non-tenure-track professors. *Chronicle of Higher Education*. Retrieved from http://chronicle.com/daily/2002/10/2002102904n.htm

Ward, P. (2004, March 2). PSU fires tenured theater professor. *Post-Gasette.Com*. Retrieved from http://www.post-gazette.com/[g/04062/279825

Washburn, J. (2005). *University Inc.: The corporate corruption of American higher education*. New York: Basic Books.

Watkins, E. (1993). *Throwaways: Work culture and consumer education*. Stanford, CA: Stanford University Press.

Williams, J. (1999). Brave new university. *College English, 61*(6), 740–751.

Williams, J. (2006). Students in debt. *Dissent*, 53–59.

Zemsky, R. (2003, May 30). Have we lost the 'Public' in higher education? *The Chronicle of Higher Education*.

Zinn, H. (1995). *You can't be neutral on a moving train*. New York: Fitzhenry and Whiteside.

FURTHER READINGS

Bok, D. (2003). *Universities in the marketplace*. Princeton, NJ: Princeton University Press.

Bourdieu, P. (2000). For a scholarship with commitment. *Profession*, 40–45.

Cooper, S., Hinkson, J., & Sharp, G. (Eds.). (2002). *Scholars and entrepreneurs: The University in crisis*. Melbourne, Australia: Arena Publications.

Giroux, H. A., & Myrsiades, K. (Eds.). (2001). *Beyond the corporate university*. Lanham, MD: Rowman and Littlefield.

Giroux, H. A. (2007). *The University in chains: Confronting the military-industrial-academic complex*. Boulder, CO: Paradigm Publishers.

Giroux, H. A., & Giroux, S. (2006). *Take back higher education*. New York: Palgrave.

Washburn, J. (2005). *University Inc.: The corporate corruption of American higher education*. New York: Basic Books.

Henri Giroux
McMaster University, Canada

AGNES VAN ZANTEN

NEW POSITIVE DISCRIMINATION POLICIES IN BASIC AND HIGHER EDUCATION

From the Quest for Social Justice to Optimal Mobilisation of Human Resources

INTRODUCTION

This chapter is concerned with changes in the ways in which a central topic in education, equality, has been addressed by policy-makers in the last thirty years, and, more precisely, with recent thinking and action on equality of results through 'positive discrimination', that is through an unequal distribution of educational resources favouring disadvantaged groups in order to improve their educational achievement. The research perspective is based on an original combination of two main approaches to the study of policy: a focus on policy technologies and actors and a focus on ideas and values, that is an instrumental and a cognitive perspective (van Zanten, 2004a). The underlying hypotheses are that "policy ruptures" take place when there are observable changes in these two dimensions and that these "policy ruptures" in educational debates and practices reflect and relay broader social shifts (Ball, 2008). Although the chapter's focus is on changes linked to positive discrimination policies in France, another underlying assumption, briefly addressed in the conclusion of the chapter, is that there are similar changes in educational policy in other European countries although they take different forms according to specific national educational, social and political configurations.

Equality became a major issue in French educational policy after World War I. Up to the World War II the main focus was on equality of opportunity and on the elimination of institutional and economic barriers to universal access to the first level of secondary education. In the 1960s a new focus was put on equality of results by means of standardised provision of middle secondary schools (*colleges*). However, the educational failure of disadvantaged children in these schools started a new reflection on the need for differential treatment according to pupils' needs in the 1970s that ended up with the development, in the early 1980s, of 'positive discrimination' policies through 'priority education zones' (*zones d'éducation prioritaires – ZEPs*) which addressed the problems of primary schools and *collèges* in disadvantaged urban areas. ZEPs were based on the principle of giving more resources (which consisted mainly in the reduction of the number of children per class and in the allocation of an additional bonus to teachers) to disadvantaged schools selected on the basis of pupils' characteristics (socio-economic status and

M. Simons, M. Olssen and M.A. Peters (eds.), Re-Reading Education Policies: A Handbook Studying the Policy Agenda of the 21ˢᵗ Century, 478–494.

nationality) and educational performance. They encouraged the development of educational projects adapted to the specific problems of local schools and collaboration with other local educational actors.

Although the ZEP policy has been maintained up to the present, the term 'positive discrimination' was gradually abandoned in the 1990s by most policy-makers and the national educational administration. A new period has nevertheless started in 2000. Although there are, as usual, significant continuities due to the weight of tradition both concerning the content of educational debates and decisions and the form taken by educational technologies and devices, there have been important changes in policies aimed at providing preferential treatment for disadvantaged pupils and new terms have been invented or re-invented for them. Thus, in basic education, 'priority education zones' have been replaced in official texts and discourses by 'networks targeted for success' (*réseaux ambition réussite – RAR*) and 'personalised programmes for educational success' (*programmes personnalisés de réussite educative – PPRE*). At the same time, new policies for 'socially opening up' higher education (*politiques d'ouverture sociale*) have been introduced. These policies have not been launched by the same educational actors but, in addition to their simultaneity, they share enough features in common to suggest that they represent a major turn in the conception and enactment of positive discrimination.

In the first two sections of this chapter, I argue that these new policies reflect important transformations with regard to two procedural dimensions. The first concerns policy instruments (Lascoumes & Le Galès, 2004) and targets and involves a gradual transition from place-based to people-place-based and people-based policies, that is, a move from collective territorial policy action to selective territorial policy action for disadvantaged areas and schools and to personalised action in the direction of disadvantaged students (Donzelot, Mevel & Wyvekens, 2003). The second transformation concerns the actors involved in launching and implementing these policies, and here we observe a gradual shift from an actor network made up exclusively of educational policy-makers, administrative officials, head teachers and teachers to a variety of other educational decision-makers including local political authorities, higher education institutions and private firms as well as a variety of educational specialists ranging from counsellors, psychologists and social workers to new student tutors.

In the last section of the chapter, I argue that these new policy dimensions not only lead to relative transformation of educational policy procedures but also to a crucial transformation of educational policy aims and normative and intellectual foundations (Muller, 2000). The initial educational priority zones were created for purposes of social justice and were designed from an axiological and cognitive point of view to act on external structural barriers to equality and inclusion. The new policies are much more concerned about optimising human resources – of recipients as well as policy providers. From a normative and cognitive point of view they give much more importance to individual responsibility, effectiveness and the idea of following in public policy a 'a reward proportionate to contribution' fairness principle.

FROM PLACE-BASED TO PEOPLE-PLACE BASED POSITIVE DISCRIMINATION POLICIES IN EDUCATION

The rise and fall of territorial educational action

Alongside abolition of the death penalty, the creation of 'educational priority zones' (hereafter called ZEPs) by a short official decree in June 1981 was one of the first political decisions made by the Socialist-Communist coalition winners of the May 1981 French elections. It was a strong symbolic policy meant to signal a leftward turn towards a more humanistic, egalitarian perspective on society. It was also a central ideological and procedural move from equality of opportunity to equality of results, and from a legal perspective in which equality was to be attained through equality of treatment to a sociological perspective where observed inequalities led to concluding there was a need for preferential treatment of disadvantaged groups. However, this is only one of the "policy streams" (Kingdon, 1984) that led to the ZEP idea and determined its dominant features. In order to understand the whole picture it is necessary to take into account that ZEPs were also seen as a means of introducing pedagogical experimentation and new forms of teaching in schools. A third stream, of secondary importance at the outset but gradually coming to the fore, was including ZEPs in a wide array of similar policies and implicating them in a major process of political decentralisation (Henriot-van Zanten, 1990).

The territory – i.e., place, locale – was chosen as the main instrument for designating the educational targets of ZEP policy, first and foremost because of the strong political opposition in the French system to procedures that officially designate specific social groups, especially immigrants; such procedures are traditionally seen as promoting negative 'communitarian' processes. Setting up 'educational priority zones' was thus clearly a way of taking into account patterns of spatial segregation in such a way as to target specific social and ethnic groups without publicly acknowledging it. Nevertheless, in relation to the other policy streams, that is pedagogical experimentation and political decentralisation, it was also a way of introducing the possibility of collaborative teaching around specific local projects within and among schools, and of encouraging local echelon funding of public policies. Because of its multiple goals, this territorial approach proved extremely resistant to changes in political majorities, presidents and ministers of education throughout the 1980s and 1990s and was extended to other policies in the educational, urban and even economic domains.

But in spite of its sustainability and quantitative success – or perhaps partly because of that – territorial educational policy action has become since the early 2000s a target of growing criticism from educational officials, researchers and the media. The criticism appeared quite late in the policy process because of a limited interest in the effectiveness of the ZEP policy. In fact, the initial purpose of this policy was to develop a strong social justice rhetoric rather than to choose the best pedagogical practices or organisational arrangements for reducing inequality, so there was almost no political or scientific discussion of the choices made. For instance, unlike England, where scientific and political observers began pointing out as soon as the policy was first implemented that despite high levels of academic segregation, there would still be more pupils with learning difficulties outside than inside the Educational Priority Areas (EPAs) set up at the end of the 1960s with a similar background and purpose than the French ZEPs, and that this meant that individual-focused action would probably be more effective, in France there was never any such debate (van Zanten & Ball, 2000). In addition, there has been very little official assessment of the ZEP policy until recently.

There are several reasons for this. One reason is that French researchers, again unlike their counterparts in England, were not associated to the conception, implementation and evaluation of this policy. This is a more general phenomenon in France and is the result both of a conception of policy as a political activity whose main aims are to ensure consensus and legitimation rather than as a problem-solving process aiming for greater effectiveness, and of the existence of a long-standing and large educational administration that uses a specific kind of "state knowledge" as opposed to "research knowledge" in the design and enactment of policy (van Zanten, 2006) Another is that whereas during its first years the ZEP policy was actively promoted by the government and educational officials and enacted by teachers as a form of political engagement, little by little, and especially due to its growing links with other urban and decentralised policies, it became at once a kind of formal procedure, a label giving access to a larger share of resources, and a policy oriented more towards "pacifying" urban areas than reducing inequalities in learning and school careers (Bouveau & Rochex, 1997).

The present wave of criticism was in fact fostered by recurrent problems of violence in disadvantaged *banlieues*, especially the riots that took place in 2005 in the Parisian periphery, which showed the existence of strong divisions between urban disadvantaged youngsters and mainstream social groups, institutional representatives and politicians. This social movement led political actors to focus on the causes of segregation and inequality, particularly on how these phenomena affect minority youth. One of the main factors that came to the forefront was the role of schools and the fact that territorial positive discrimination policies had not enabled youth to move out of the *banlieues* and move up in the economic and social system and become integrated. Although this was not stated explicitly and did not become a topic of public debate, a link was made by educational actors between the eruption of violence and what were then the latest assessments of the ZEP policy (Caille, 2001) showing that there had not been considerable improvement in educational achievement among pupils from low socio-economic status (SES) and immigrant backgrounds in ZEP schools. Although these pupils' school careers are slightly better than those of similar students in non-ZEP schools – they are less likely to be held back a year to catch up and less likely to be oriented to the less prestigious technical and vocational tracks in secondary schools – tests show that their actual results are actually worse, that is that their educational performance has not improved and might even have deteriorated leading to the interpretation that the observed amelioration is only the consequence of greater indulgence on the part of teachers and educational professionals when making decisions about careers.

Although this interpretation is unilateral and simplistic, the existence of "contextual adaptation" processes and their effects on school functioning and pupils' results has been documented in qualitative studies (van Zanten, 2001). These studies have shown that in ZEP schools, teachers adapt their expectations, teaching content, methods and student evaluation to the supposed capacities and tastes of lower-class and immigrant students. They have also shown that these practices lead to poor examination results, lowered ambitions, stigmatised identities, absenteeism, bullying and inter-racial tensions. Moreover, the social and ethnic composition of these schools as well as their internal functioning encourage a continuous process of 'white flight', that is, avoidance by middle-class parents, who choose another public school or a private school or move to another neighbourhood, thus creating a vicious segregation circle. Despite their number and variety, place-based policies such as the ZEP have not been able to change this. At best they have 'pacified' potentially conflictual local situations and developed some forms of local integration that does not encourage geographical and social mobility. More frequently however, they have intensified the stigmatisation and marginalisation of youth in disadvantaged areas.

Saving individual students from the 'geographic trap'

Prestigious higher education institutions that launched new programmes targeting disadvantaged pupils in the early 2000 – namely, Sciences Po and ESSEC, a renowned management school, and more recently, the *Lycée Henri IV* – tended to conceptualise the educational and more general social problems of youth in the *banlieues* as related to the existence of a 'geographic trap'. The poor school careers and results of lower-class and immigrant young people were attributed mostly to the poverty and closure of their family, urban and school environments. These restricted environments were understood to severely limit young people's access to the cultural activities of middle-class youth and to leave them completely uninformed about higher education tracks, on the one hand, and on the other hand, to fail to develop the social codes and social relations necessary for moving up the educational and social ladder. Although the ZEP policy and other territorial policies were not directly criticised, the main arguments developed by these institutions clearly tended to underline that Ministry of Education action to assist disadvantaged urban youth had not been effective in these areas and should be supplemented if not altogether abandoned.

This double perspective, very critical of disadvantaged schools and very self-confident on their capacity to be a role model for secondary schools is linked to the specific position of these elite institutions. On the one hand, these institutions form a specific system of higher education which starts with preparatory classes located in well-ranked *lycées* (upper-secondary schools) and attended by students after the *baccalauréat* to prepare the competitive examinations required for admission at the *Grandes Écoles*. These *Grandes Écoles* are very selective higher education institutions that have until recently functioned totally apart from universities which do not select students on the basis of school results. Because of their focus on academic excellence elite institutions tend to hold very negative views on pupils' results in disadvantaged schools and to set strong cultural frontiers between elite students and the rest of the student body. On the other hand, because these preparatory classes and *Grandes Écoles* enjoy considerable prestige, they are considered as possessing a unique kind of educational expertise and therefore as legitimate educational actors.

It is important to note, however, that in proposing these new programmes, these elite education institutions were also trying to counteract another line of criticism about their functioning. Four strands of criticism can be distinguished. The first consists in denouncing the weaknesses of the French higher education system when situated in a context of international competition. The *Grandes Écoles* are accused of being unable to hold their own in this competition because of their size and the low priority given to research but also because of their socially biased selection procedures (Veltz, 2007). The second strand of criticism is to be found in research studies such as the one conducted by Euriat et Thélot (1995), that have shown a decrease in the percentage of students from working-class and small employee background in the last forty years (from 29% in the early 1950s to 9% in the early 1990s) in the most prestigious *Grandes Écoles*. The third strand is less audible and involves more fragmented evidence on an increase of 'geographic closure'. Although the Parisian character of French elite education has frequently been denounced, it is only recently that the Ministry of Education has become interested in the number of *lycées*, especially outside Paris, that never send any students to the *classes préparatoires* and *Grandes Écoles*. Last but not least is criticism coming from a small number of businessmen and politicians, frequently of foreign background, who have started to denounce the ethnic and racial barriers not only to jobs but also to elite educational institutions (Sabeg & Méhaignerie, 2006).

The responses provided by the above-named elite institutions were designed to enable them to show that they were simultaneously fighting back against segregation and renewing elite education by admitting and thereby 'saving' a limited number of deserving students and increasing diversity in elite schools. They need to be analysed carefully for despite the limited scope of the programmes, they represent an important shift from place-based policies to people-place-based policies and people-based policies. On the one hand, most of these policies have maintained a territorial dimension, in order to be integrated into the present policy landscape and also to have easier access to students. Both Sciences-Po and ESSEC have developed outreach policies towards disadvantaged *lycées* rather than directly towards disadvantaged students, but the policies of the two institutions differ in one important dimension. Whereas Sciences Po has developed 'educational priority contracts' (*conventions education prioritaire – CEP*) with *lycées* scattered throughout France, the ESSEC programme called *Une Grande École, Pourquoi pas moi?* (PQPM) has also developed a formal relationship with a limited number of secondary schools but on a local basis, thereby reinforcing the territorial dimension. However, both these programmes, as well as the third most important programme, the *Classe Préparatoire aux Etudes Supérieures* (CPES) launched by the *lycée* Henri IV, which does not have a territorial dimension, imply selection of a limited number of already successful students, who are then 'extracted' for short or long periods (several times a year in the Sciences Po programme, 3 hours a week in the ESSEC programme, the whole year at the *lycée* Henri IV) from their family, urban and school environments and given more intensive preferential treatment than in the ZEP programmes. The main purpose is to provide them with the cultural and social capital that students from privileged backgrounds have and use to strengthen their school careers.

The shift from an exclusively place-based positive discrimination approach to a people-place-based one is also observable in the ZEP policy. Important revisions of 'priority education' in secondary and primary schools were introduced by two official decrees in 2005 and 2006. The new policy is presented as a follow-up of the ZEP policy and maintains the idea of 'educational networks'. This concept was already being introduced in the late 1980s to extend the number of 'educational zones' but the financial resources allotted were lower then, since 'networks' were understood to be less disadvantaged than 'zones'. The present orientation is quite the opposite: the 249 chosen *ambition réussite* networks are supposed to correspond to groups of feeder primary schools with their middle secondary school, with high concentrations of students from disadvantaged backgrounds and with learning difficulties, while level 2 'educational priority zones' and level 3 'educational priority networks' cater to less problematic areas. This territorial hierarchy goes along with a more individualist perspective. The initial argument for the policy in the official 2006 document holds that while all pupils in both networks and zones must acquire the same core skills, there is also a need for more ambitious and positive orienting of successful pupils toward higher education. And the 2005 text introduced a new policy instrument, 'personalised programs for education success,' which involves individual treatment, outside the classroom, of pupils who score particularly low on tests and examinations.

FROM TEACHERS' WORK TO THE EDUCATIONAL PROFESSIONALISATION OF EVERYONE?

The failure of local coordination of educational work

Parallel to the change in type of positive discrimination policy, there have been changes in connection with the actors involved in developing, coordinating and implementing educational projects. The ZEP introduced another important change in educational policy by giving a role to any and everyone wishing to work to improve schools in a given local space. The idea was that these new 'educational helpers' could be parents, social workers and local political officials. This virtually communitarian call for participation, quite unusual in the centralised French educational system, gradually evolved into a new formal compulsory procedure for establishing local partnerships. It became an integral part of a whole set of new post-bureaucratic procedures, such as projects and contracts used to increase local actor initiatives and autonomy, develop less hierarchical relationships and increase professional accountability with respect to a common defined goal (van Zanten, 2004b).

Two main kinds of local partnerships were and still are aimed at sustaining territorial educational policies: formal partnerships among decision-makers and informal partnerships among professionals. However, although the terms 'partnerships' and 'partners' have become part of the official terminology in policy texts and discourses, neither of these two types of partnerships have worked well (though there are local exceptions) (Lorcerie, 1991; Glasman, 1992). This is so for historical reasons similar to those cited above, that is, the very strong closure of the educational system, which was conceived by Napoleon and has remained a kind of 'moral magistracy' protected from political pressures and changes and autonomous from others administrations. Resistance to partnering is also linked to teachers' and educational administrators' fears of losing professional autonomy and authority in a context where the disappearance of many national bureaucratic regulations has been increasing the risk of external interventions to gain control of the educational system, and of losing their professional identity by being forced to focus less on the transmission of knowledge and more on cultural and social projects linked to the varied interests of external partners such as local political authorities, local museums, libraries, cultural centres or social workers.

Formal decision-making partnerships have been extensively developed but mostly for economic reasons, as most of them involve financial contributions from other ministries or local political authorities. The relationships between these 'educational partners' and members of local educational administrations is frequently tense if not overtly conflictual: the latter do not see their supposed partners as apt to help define educational goals or design educational projects. Local educational administrators think of anyone who is not part of the education system – which, it should be noted, is an almost totally closed job market; most head teachers, inspectors and high administration officials started their careers as teachers – as incompetent and illegitimate in educational matters. They have succeeded in maintaining a formally neat but in reality blurred dividing line between pedagogical actions within schools, actions that remain under their control, and educational actions taking place outside the classroom or outside the school, which can be launched and coordinated by other local groups (van Zanten, 2004b). They have also put up strong resistance to assessment of the overall effects of these partnerships on pupils' results, satisfaction and behaviour. Members of local political entities or private firms that participate in these partnerships have tolerated this situation but are growing increasingly dissatisfied with it.

Working partnerships between teachers and other educational specialists outside schools – social workers, for instance and members of associations who help pupils with their homework and the organisation of their learning activities after school – are even less successful. The great majority of teachers do not think it is their responsibility to coordinate their activities with those of specialists working outside the school, and they are critical of work that they do not see as 'professional.' This means that disadvantaged children and youngsters who participate in these extracurricular activities experience strong learning discontinuities. Even inside schools, the level and quality of coordination between teachers and other professional groups such as educational counsellors and helpers, school social workers or nurses is quite low and characterised by a refusal to share information, competing definitions of professional domains, and delegation of "dirty work" (Hughes, 1958) – that is, repressive or routine control tasks – to newcomers, the youngest and least qualified (Payet, 1997; van Zanten, 2001). Teamwork among teachers, although strongly recommended in official discourse, is also limited, as teachers tend to see it as a way of more closely and tightly overseeing their work. They therefore tend to reject formal coordination and to choose their teaching partners mainly by personal affinities (Barrère, 2002).

New specialists for a new era of positive discrimination?

By criticising educational professionals (in most cases indirectly) for being unable to set up collective dynamics in disadvantaged schools and areas, Sciences-Po, ESSEC and Henri IV, along with other selective higher education institutions, have worked to legitimise the use in their own programs of a new group of educational specialists, 'tutors,' who are either students from these institutions, specialised teachers or counsellors, or professionals from private firms. 'Tutoring' has in fact become the main compensatory device in all of these programmes and is strongly linked to individualisation of positive discrimination in that the idea is to offer a select number of students 'customised' support to improve their learning, broaden their cultural capital, improve their social manners, increase their social networks and gain larger access to all kinds of useful information about higher education institutions and professional careers.

Student tutors are the most important support group, both numerically and in terms of their degree of commitment. They are expected to play two central roles whose importance varies by programme. In the *Classe Préparatoire aux Etudes Supérieures* created at the *Lycée* Henri IV in September 2006 to provide a year of foundation courses for good students from disadvantaged *lycées* wanting to enter the selective *classes préparatoires* in the same school, two kinds of student tutors were recruited from a limited number of *Grandes Écoles* (*École Normale Supérieure de Paris, Polytechnique, Sciences Po*). The first group was assigned to help students organise their work and prepare their lessons, while the second, smaller group was assigned to counsel those students on their future educational careers and provide a kind of 'social guidance' with regard to elite education and the elite world. In the ESSEC programme, which started in 2002, student tutors are mostly expected to provide this kind of 'social guidance' and counselling although during collective tutoring sessions some of them assume a role closer to teaching. Elsewhere tutors assume all of these roles to various degrees. Tutors are supposed to provide social and educational support based not on any specific learned skill but on who they are. They are supposed to provide models of academic success and social integration that are expected to be better accepted by disadvantaged students than those coming from teachers and educational professionals because of the role of generational closeness in identification processes (Allouch & van Zanten, 2008).

The *Grandes Ecoles* and the *lycées* that have set up these programmes have also called on other specialists to provide students with social skills not taught directly in subject courses. For instance, at the *Lycée* Henri IV a professor who teaches

French in other *Classes Préparatoires* gives CPES students a specific course on how to speak in public, and a university sociology professor teaches a course on 'social codes' to students of the PQPM program. All the programmes, including that of Sciences Po, have also brought in tutors from the business world. These tutors come from the firms that partly sponsor the programs – all programs are funded partly by the state or the institutions themselves and partly by private companies – and are supposed to act as 'godfathers' or 'godmothers' for the students, taking them out to concerts, theatres or museums or inviting them to discover different aspects of the business world. These two groups, in addition to the student tutors, are supposed to give disadvantaged students what their local schools do not give them, that is, an insight into different dimensions of elite education, work and life and some skills to be able to get admitted for elite training, survive and, hopefully, become an elite member.

Although these new educational figures are not professional in the usual sense of the word (they have not received specific training; their involvement in these educational activities is limited and temporary, and most of them do not get a real salary for it), they are seen as credible educators because they are part of an elite higher education model. In this model, transmission of knowledge through a professor-student relationship is conceived as only one aspect of an all-encompassing education that implies access to other, more varied sources of cultural and social knowledge. And although these educational figures could be seen to be competing with teachers and educational counsellors, introducing them into the educational system and into the schools themselves has not engendered strong negative reactions, for several reasons. First, there is the great fascination for elites and elite education. Second, as opposed to local political authorities who, as underlined above, are perceived as incompetent in the field of education, directors and personnel of higher education institutions and *lycées* are seen as educational experts. Third – and here individualisation again plays a central role – because these programmes only address the problems of a limited number of disadvantaged students, and in fact only students with minor learning problems, they are perceived as both particularly successful and non-threatening to the system as a whole.

It is important to note that there have also been some changes in ZEP policy as concerns the intervention of new educational specialists. In direct opposition to the policies developed by the *Grandes Écoles* and prestigious *lycées*, however, individuals 'extracted' from ZEP classrooms are those with the greatest learning problems. In this case, the individual treatment is provided by speech therapists or psychologists and it is not supposed to add more to the students' curriculum but rather to get back to and treat fundamental problems and their causes. However, these specialists are not well regarded by teachers in general, who do not collaborate with them and may be tempted to use them to get rid of children who are disruptive in the classroom. Also, as shown by different research studies, since individual treatment in ZEPs is provided while the other children are following their normal courses and since that treatment is limited in time and scope, it is rarely effective and may actually aggravate the initial deficit and stigmatise the children selected for it (Bouche, 2008). Moreover, each new *'ambition réussite'* network can bring in four additional, supposedly more experienced, teachers and pedagogical assistants. The problem again, as with the previous ZEP policy, is that all these additional specialists are sent to schools without those schools having any specific project as to how to benefit from their presence and coordinate their action.

SOCIAL JUSTICE OR OPTIMAL MOBILISATION OF HUMAN RESOURCES?

Choosing deserving recipients

These changes are important not only because they have introduced new policy instruments and new policy agents, but because they represent crucial 'normative turns' in educational policy. The initial 'turn' was the creation of the ZEPs in the first place, which was a major change not only in educational resource distribution mode but also in the conception of equality. It represented a fundamental shift from the prevailing model of equality of opportunity to a model of equality of results. The equality of opportunity model became dominant in the 1920s but it was fully applied only after the Second World War, when major educational reforms were undertaken in a relatively consensual climate between opposed political factions that culminated in the creation of the *collège unique*, that is, the comprehensive middle secondary school. However, even before the shift was completed, it became clear that putting pupils together in similar schools and classrooms was not all that was required for them to succeed. School failure emerged indeed as a collective phenomenon in schools with large numbers of disadvantaged pupils and the same official texts that created the *collège unique* in 1975 also introduced the idea that specific forms of school support had to be set up to reduce the learning problems of a large fraction of the newcomers (Isambert-Jamati, 1984).

This initial introduction of a limited form of positive discrimination by a Minister of Education who was part of a conservative government took a more radical turn with the arrival of the left and the launching of the ZEP policy in 1981. However, there was a form of policy continuity. For this reason, and because the focus at the time was more on limited changes in the resource distribution modes than on changes in the political model, the ZEP did not become a major point of conflict between left and right. What was under way in fact was a long process of disenchantment with the promises of social justice. The limited success of the ZEP policy in improving examination scores and school careers of disadvantaged pupils gave rise to strong scepticism and the development of the three rhetorical strands of reaction (inanity, unattended consequences and jeopardy) evoked by Hirschman (1991). On the one hand, especially within the left, the limited success of the ZEP policy encouraged strongly deterministic interpretations presenting equality of results as a utopia given the structural character of social divisions, poverty and inequality. It reinforced the idea, already encouraged by the sociological works of Bourdieu & Passeron (1970) and Baudelot & Establet (1971) that any kind of pedagogical innovation was powerless with regard to social inequalities embedded in family socialisation and in school processes. On the other hand, the continuous development of positive discrimination policies, without any serious assessment of their benefits and limitations or of the new coordination problems they had created, has also reinforced the perception of the frequent unexpected consequences of policies and thus of their limited ability to contribute to reduce inequality. This line of argument is more readily encountered within the right (Boudon, 1977). Moreover, especially among teachers, the general perception of the relative failure of these policies, coupled with the fear that any kind of reform will now take an explicit or implicit neo-liberal 'turn', has created a strong defensive position against all reform, the general feeling being that anything new can only further jeopardise the present professional autonomy of educational professionals and the situation of disadvantaged pupils (Rayou & van Zanten, 2004).

It was in this general climate of opinion that the new 'normative turn' took place, with the launching of the Sciences Po programme in 2001, exactly twenty years after the ZEP policy was launched. The *Grandes Écoles* and prestigious *lycées* and later and to a lesser extent the Ministry of Education have not only moved from a territorial to an individual approach and introduced new educational actors in the educational field but have also changed the goals of positive discrimination and its value framework from the search for equality of results to the search for equity, considered as a good fit between talent and potential on one hand and distribution of educational resources on the other. Discourses have been developed similar to those popular in the 1950s, influenced by human capital theory, pleading in favour of the search for "untapped talents" among disadvantaged groups (Forquin, 1979). However, a new factor in this search for new talents is that although most *Grandes Écoles* still conceive of talent as reflected in grades and credentials, some, especially Sciences Po, are going strictly meritocratic educational criteria to encompass a wider definition of talent, less linked to school success and more to students' capacity to adapt to new employer demands, given that in a context of increasing competition among university graduates, employers are now using various personal criteria as a basis for recruitment, in addition to educational credentials (Brown & Hesketh, 2004). These new categories of students are not admitted to Sciences Po through the traditional competitive examinations; admission is determined on the basis of an oral examination consisting of students' presentation of a review of press and media coverage of a topic that they are totally free to choose. The applicants' presentations allow members of the jury (composed of university professors, top managers and high administrative officials) to evaluate not only the knowledge and cultural capital of the candidates but their curiosity, variety of interests and ability to express themselves. In organising admission this way, Sciences Po wants both to show its ability to help disadvantaged students move out of the *banlieues* and to increase the social and ethnic diversity of elite higher education institutions.

However, the procedure chosen by Sciences Po has been perceived as an excessively radical turn, opening the way to what is presented as demagogic erosion of meritocratic educational barriers and to what are considered illegitimate claims from disadvantaged students for places in elite institutions. The majority of other institutions plead for a 'softer' individual turn founded on the idea of keeping the present barriers while giving additional resources to disadvantaged students who show high potential and strong motivation. The focus both on a more efficient use of economic resources and on individual choices and responsibility as opposed to general welfare to all has led policy beneficiaries' motivation and commitment to become key concepts that binds together all the new policies, including those determined by the Ministry of Education for primary and secondary schools. It entails a clear separation between 'deserving' and 'non-deserving' students, either on the basis of good results linked with a will to volunteer for the new programmes in higher education and the ability to show initiative and commitment in different ways or, as in the PPRE programme in primary and secondary schools, on the basis of perceived needs, although teachers frequently select the most motivated pupils among those with special needs (Bouche, 2008). The central idea from the perspective of policy-makers is to target a limited number of individuals for positive discrimination in order to optimise resource allocation in terms of both efficiency-and-cost-reduction and effectiveness and success.

Combining pragmatism and a fair social deal

There is a second moral and political dimension to these changes, related to the promotion of an ideal of effectiveness and fairness. This entails first a combination of the social principle of positive discrimination with a constrictive goal of short-term success: every public choice must be effective in a short-time span and in visible, measurable ways (van Zanten, 1997; Thrupp, 2001). This insistence on effectiveness, although it is still mostly rhetorical given the lack of official evaluation procedures, seems indeed necessary given the fact that previous positive discrimination policy implementation relied to a large extent on the motivation and methods and procedures set by teachers and schools that did not have a clear sense of direction; it included little monitoring or external support and almost no assessment or research that would have enabled teachers and schools to analyse the consequences of their choices. The responsibility for the lack of focus or emphasis on effectiveness lied mostly with policy-makers and the education administration, but also partly on teachers, who have resisted efforts to increase that emphasis because they have come to equate 'effectiveness' with government cuts and what are seen as 'cosmetic changes' in management.

However, the 'effectiveness' model provided by the new programmes, especially those launched by the *Grandes Écoles*, has certain characteristics that have limited negative criticism of it from educational professionals and administration members. First, there is a great deal of money involved, a major part of it coming from private firms, which makes these programmes look much more ambitious than previous positive discrimination policies and brings additional prestige and resources to the schools involved. There is also a much less authoritarian approach to management, with efforts to build more horizontal relationships between *Grandes Écoles'* directors and managers and head teachers and teachers and to take into account their points of view and their proposals, and with close monitoring of programme needs and unexpected effects. Another important factor is that the sporadic presence of 'business tutors' and the more intensive activity of 'student tutors' for reasons that have to do in both cases with their lack of any claim to professional expertise in education do not represent a threat to teachers' professional identity unlike for instance the new category of 'referent professors' in the 'networks targeted for success' who were initially strongly resisted to in many schools because of their supposedly superior pedagogical expertise. Finally, the *Grandes Écoles* are seen as decisions-makers with superior educational expertise due to their role in the training of elites.

Nevertheless, what is seen as a more ambitious, original and pragmatic approach is also one in which there is deliberate confusion between presentation and promotion, assessment and marketing (Ball, 1997). Presentations by persons recruited to coordinate the programmes and communicate about them emphasise numbers (increases in numbers of recipients and schools involved and financial and human resources devoted to various actions), the positive qualitative results for some students (here they frequently cite students' own remarks and personal anecdotes) and the potential benefits for many other students (Delhay, 2006). It is important to note, however, that up to now, there has been little assessment of or research on these programmes and that assessments and studies that exist or are in progress have been conducted by persons either hired by the programme leaders or closely linked to them. The results of these assessments are used more to market the programmes in leaflets, websites and oral presentations than to critically examine their advantages or potential problems. The focus in the *Grandes École's* positive discrimination programmes is clearly much more on 'what works' and on experimenting and adapting to complex situations and unique individuals, than in the previous programmes. For that reason, their general effectiveness, even within their limited scope, is compromised by their being part of a strategy to improve their image and legitimise their position. These programmes are in fact torn between their instrumental goals and their symbolic ones.

However, the institutions themselves do not necessarily see these as two conflicting perspectives, as the programmes have also introduced the idea of a new social deal, while programmes are understood to be 'fair' if they not only bring benefits to the recipients but also to those involved in the launching and implementation of the programs, thus optimally mobilising policy providers and mediators. This 'win-win' or 'give-give' principle in public policy was popularised during the last presidential campaign in 2006 not only by French President Nicolas Sarkozy and some of his close advisers, but also by the Socialist candidate. A concrete application of this principle may be seen, for instance, in the fact that while disadvantaged students are supposed to benefit from their involvement in the programme, so are student tutors, not necessarily on a financial basis (some are paid but not much, and others are not paid anything) but because their involvement helps them acquire specific skills and is something that can be a valuable, distinctive item on the CV they will present to prospective employers. It is also presented as 'fair' that the *Grandes Écoles* as well as the private companies involved use the programmes not only to improve their image, as mentioned before, but also to extend their social networks and even to obtain material benefits by appearing more competitive in the international market.

CONCLUSION

Changes in positive discrimination are not just local changes in the educational sector. They reflect wider changes in French society and its welfare model. The importance of the state, the central importance given to solidarity as a social value and the expanding economy in the first decades following World War II explain the previous social consensus on equality (Esping-Andersen, 1990) as well as on limited forms of positive discrimination that did not threaten established forms of State control and existing class relationships The present situation is quite different. On one hand, the central national state has been weakened both by globalisation processes and supranational decisions and by the devolution of resources and power to local entities. On the other hand, an economy that has been shrinking lately and the expansion of the educational system have worked to reduce middle class solidarity towards the working class and towards immigrants because of fear of losing their positional advantages (Chauvel, 1998, Ball & Vincent 2001; van Zanten, 2008) and to reduce teachers' engagement in reform, because of fear of losing their professional autonomy (Rayou & van Zanten, 2004).

This has opened the way for the emergence of new policies that make use of new procedures and agents. These policies might introduce some needed changes in the functioning of the educational system, especially in light of the shortcomings of territorial policies and teacher action in disadvantaged areas. However, their limited scope in terms of the number of schools and individuals concerned not only considerably reduces their overall impact but creates new problems. These policies are indeed part of a 'normative individualistic turn' based on the principle of providing social support to a small number of deserving individuals from disadvantaged groups, and leaving all others physically more vulnerable to market forces and morally more open to criticism if they fail because of the devolution of responsibility from the state to the individual (Martucelli, 2001; Castel, 2003). Among the disadvantaged, these policies create stronger social splits between the highly motivated and the less motivated, the truly needy and the less needy. These processes undermine solidarity and will probably erode rather than strengthen social cohesion, without significantly reducing educational inequalities.

These processes are not only visible in the French context. Policy periods are not exactly the same from one country to the other according to specific national political and educational agendas and complex processes of international policy borrowing. However, the trends that we have documented in this chapter are based on the introduction of a repertoire of tools, such as public-private partnerships and managerial techniques, and of ideas, notably the combination of individualism with moral authoritarianism leading to an emphasis on responsibility and reciprocity, very similar to those introduced by Labour Third Way governments in England (Gewirtz, 2001; Ball, 2008). Some of them are also visible in other European countries where the private sector has also come to play a more significant role in education, including in the development of new forms of positive discrimination as in Hungary and other Eastern European countries (Maroy, 2006). It is difficult however at this stage to evaluate the extent to which these convergent processes could be mostly rhetorical and superficial and the extent to which they might signal a strong international turn in the way educational inequality and inequality in general is integrated into the policy debate and in policy decisions.

REFERENCES

Allouch, A., & van Zanten, A. (in press, 2008). Formateurs ou 'grands frères?' Les tuteurs des programmes d'ouverture sociale des Grandes Ecoles et des classes préparatoires. *Education et sociétés, 21.*

Ball, S. J. (1997). Good school/bad school: Paradox and fabrication. *British Journal of Sociology of Education, 18*(3), 317–336.

Ball, S. J. (2008). *The education debate*. London: The Policy Press.

Ball, S. J., & Vincent, C. (2001). New class relations in education: The strategies of the 'fearful' middle classes. In Demaine (Ed.), *Sociology of education today*. London: Palgrave.

Barrère, A. (2002). *Les enseignants au travail: Routines incertaines*. Paris: L'Harmattan.

Baudelot, C., & Establet, R. (1971). *L'école capitaliste en France*. Paris: Maspéro.

Bouche, G. (in press 2008). Soutien pédagogique. In A. van Zanten (Ed.), *Dictionnaire de l'éducation*. Paris: Presses Universitaires de France.

Boudon, R. (1977). *Effets pervers et ordre social*. Paris: PUF.

Bourdieu, p. , & Passeron, J. C. (1970). *La reproduction: éléments pour une théorie du système d'enseignement*. Paris: Éditions de Minuit.

Bouveau, p. , & Rochex, J. Y. (1997). *Les ZEP, entre école et société*. Paris: CNDP-Hachette.

Brown, Ph. & Hesketh, A. (2004). *The mismanagement of talent. Employability and jobs in the knowledge economy*. Oxford: Oxford University Press.

Caille, J.-P. (2001). Les collégiens de ZEP à la fin des années 90: caractéristiques des élèves et impact de la scolarisation en ZEP sur la réussite. *Éducation et Formations, 61*, 111–140.

Castel, R. (2003). *L'insécurité sociale. Qu'est-ce qu'être protégé?* Paris: Seuil, La République des Idées.

Chauvel, L. (1998). *Le destin des générations*. Paris: Presses Universitaires de France.

Delhay, C. (2006). *Promotion ZEP. Des quartiers à Sciences Po*. Paris: Hachette Litteratures.

Donzelot, J., Mevel, C., & Wyvekens, A. (2003). *Faire société. La politique de la ville aux Etats-Unis et en France*. Paris: Le Seuil.

Esping-Andersen, G. (1990). *The three worlds of welfare capitalism*. Princeton, NJ: Princeton University Press.

Euriat, M., & Thélot, C. (1995). Le recrutement social de l'élite scolaire depuis 40 ans. *Éducation et Formations, 41*, 3–21.

Forquin, J. C. (1979). La sociologie des inégalités d'éducation: principales orientations, principaux résultats depuis 1965. *Revue Française de Pédagogie, 48* (Reprinted in *Sociologie de l'éducation. Dix ans de recherches*. Paris: INRP/L'Harmattan).

Gewirtz, S. (2001). *The managerial school. Post-welfarism and social justice in education*. Buckingham: Open University Press.

Glasman, D. (1992). *L'école réinventée? Le partenariat dans les zones d'éducation prioritaires*. Paris: L'Harmattan.

Henriot-van Zanten, A. (1990). *L'Ecole et l'espace local. Les enjeux des zones d'éducation prioritaires*. Lyon: Presses Universitaires de Lyon.

Hirschman, A. O. (1991). *The rhetoric of reaction. Perversity, futility, jeopardy*. Cambridge, MMA: Harvard University Press.

Hughes, E. C. (1958). *Men and their work*. Glencoe: The Free Press.

Isambert-Jamati, V. (1984). Quelques rappels de l'émergence de l'échec scolaire comme problème social dans les milieux pédagogiques français. In E. Plaisance (Ed.), *L'échec scolaire. Nouveaux débats, nouvelles approches sociologiques*. Paris: Editions du Centre national de la recherche scientifique.

Kingdon, J. (1984). *Agendas, alternatives and public policies*. New York: Harper Collins.

Lascoumes, p. , & Le Galès, p. (2004). *Gouverner par les instruments*. Paris: Presses de Sciences-Po.

Lorcerie, F. (1991). La 'modernisation' de l'Education nationale et 'le partenariat'. *Migrants-formation, 85*, 49–67.

Martucelli, D. (2001). *Dominations ordinaires. Explorations de la condition moderne*. Paris: Balland.

Maroy, C. (2006). *Ecole, regulation et marché. Une comparaison de six espaces scolaires en Europe*. Paris: Presses universitaires de France.

Muller, p. (2000). L'analyse cognitive des politiques publiques: vers une sociologie politique de l'action publique. *Revue française de science politique, 50*(2), 89–207.

Payet, J. p. (1997). 'Le sale boulot': Division morale du travail dans un collège de banlieue. *Annales de la Recherche Urbaine, 75*, 19–31.

Rayou, p. , & van Zanten, A. (2004). *Enquête sur les Nouveaux enseignants: changeront-ils l'école?* Paris: Bayard.

Sabeg, Y., & Méhaignerie, L. (2006). *Les oubliés de l'égalité des chances*. Paris: Hachette Littératures.

Thrupp, M. (2001). Sociological and political concerns about school effectiveness research: Time for a new research Agenda. *School Effectiveness and School Improvement, 12*(1), 7–40.

Veltz, p. (2007). *Faut-il sauver les grandes écoles?* Paris: Les Presses de Sciences-Po.

van Zanten, A. (1997). L'action éducative à l'échelon municipal: rapport aux valeurs, orientations et outils. In F. Cardi & A. Chambon (Eds.), *Les métamorphoses de la formation: alternance, partenariat, développement local*. Paris: L'Harmattan.

van Zanten, A. (2001). *L'école de la périphérie: scolarité et ségrégation en banlieue*. Paris: Presses Universitaires de France.

van Zanten, A. (2004a). *Les Politiques d'éducation*. Paris: Presses Universitaires de France.

van Zanten, A. (2004b). Vers une régulation territoriale des établissements d'enseignement en France ? Le cas de deux départements de la région parisienne. *Recherches Sociologiques, 35*(2), 47–64.

van Zanten, A. (2006). Competition and interaction between research knowledge and state knowledge in policy steering in France. In J. Ozga, T. Seddon, T. S. Popkewitz (Eds.), *Education, research and policy. Steering the knowledge-based economy. World yearbook of education 2006*. London: Routledge.

van Zanten, A. (in press, 2009). *Choisir son école. Les strategies éducatives des classes moyennes*. Paris: Presses Universiraires de France.

van Zanten, A., & Ball S. J. (2000). Comparer pour comprendre: Globalisation, réinterprétations nationales et recontextualisations locales. *Revue de L'institut de sociologie, 1*(4), 112–131.

FURTHER READINGS

Ball, S. J. (2008). *The education debate*. London: The Policy Press.

Gewirtz, S. (2001). *The managerial school. Post-welfarism and social justice in education*. Buckingham: Open University Press.

Maroy, C. (2006). *École, regulation et marché. Une comparaison de sis espaces scolaires en Europe*. Paris: Presses univesitaires de France.

Ozga, J., T. Seddon, T. S. Popkewitz (Eds.), *Education, research and policy. Steering the knowledge-based economy. World yearbook of education 2006*. London: Routledge.

van Zanten, A. (2004). *Les Politiques d'éducation*. Paris: Presses Universitaires de France.

Agnès van Zanten
Observatoire Sociologique du Changement
Centre National de la Recherche Scientifique
Sciences Po, Paris, France

YUSEF WAGHID

HIGHER EDUCATION POLICY DISCOURSE(S) IN SOUTH AFRICA

Procedural or Substantive Democracy?

INTRODUCTION

Prior to South Africa's first democratic elections in 1994, the political and educational systems in the country were racially determined. The tricameral parliament, comprising of the House of Assembly (representing the White population), House of Representatives (representing the Coloured population) and House of Delegates (representing the Indian population), which was instituted in 1983 divided the education system into 19 separately controlled departments, with Whites, Coloureds, Indians and Blacks being controlled by mutually exclusive education departments with their own budgets. In general, the segregated education departments were designed to favour the minority White population. Basically, Blacks were denied the franchise, whereas the other racial groups had representation in government, but on the basis of inequality and discrimination. The terms 'Blacks', 'Coloureds' and 'Indians' are used for those racial groups in South African society that are other than 'White'. These terms are still being used today to distinguish between 'Whites' favoured by the racist apartheid system and those 'Coloureds', 'Indians' and 'Blacks' discriminated against. Over the past decade higher education in South Africa has undergone a significant shift from an apartheid-dominated system to one which incorporates principles of liberal democracy and social justice. This essay attempts to map some of the pertinent conceptual and structural changes which occurred during this period in relation to frameworks of deliberative democracy as articulated by Seyla Benhabib (1996) and Eamonn Callan (1997). I shall firstly show how the Education White Paper 3 (1997) and the National Plan for Higher Education (2001) emerged; secondly, I shall explain how the South African Qualifications Authority (SAQA) and the National Qualifications Framework (NQF) were established; and thirdly, I shall describe how the Higher Education Quality Committee (HEQC) and the National Review of Teacher Education were constituted – all salient moments in the higher education policy discourse as the government endeavoured to break with the apartheid past and move towards the achievement of substantive democracy.

In 1994 the higher education sector consisted of 36 public higher education institutions. The size and shape of the higher education system posed significant challenges to the state in 1994 and debates on the appropriate configuration of the higher education system for South Africa ensued. The period 1999-2002 was

M. Simons, M. Olssen and M.A. Peters (eds.), Re-Reading Education Policies: A Handbook Studying the Policy Agenda of the 21st Century, 495–514.

dominated by intense debate on mergers, incorporations and closures of higher education institutions. By 2002 the Minister gazetted the newly configured landscape, which would reduce the number of institutions from 36 to 22 over a three-year period from 2002-2005. Higher education policy transformation in South Africa can be demarcated into three pertinent phases: 1990-1994 – symbolic policy making with an agreement on values, goals and principles (this was the period just before the first democratic elections in 1994, when the African National Congress was still the government in the making and already beginning a process of national policy investigation); 1995-1998 – formalisation of the legislative and policy framework with the establishment of appropriate governance structures for higher education (during this period the newly elected government instituted major policy changes); and 1999 to the present – accelerated policy making of a distributive, redistributive and material nature (this period was characterised by the implementation of the policy changes in the country) (Badat, 2005, pp.18-20). Kraak (2001, pp.86-87) offers a similar account of higher education policy transformation according to five overlapping phases: 1989-1994: the phase prior to taking of power; 1994-1997: the legislative era; 1997-1998: the policy implementation phase; 1999-2000: a vacillating state, the era of doubt and retraction; and 2001: the National Plan. For purposes of this essay I shall firstly describe the events leading up to the formulation and implementation of both the Education White Paper 3 (1997) and the National Plan for Higher Education (2001).

HIGHER EDUCATION POLICY TRANSFORMATION AS A DELIBERATIVE DEMOCRATIC DISCOURSE: FROM THE EDUCATION WHITE PAPER 3 TO THE NATIONAL PLAN FOR HIGHER EDUCATION

Radical education policy changes

South Africa's higher education policy discourse took its first substantive steps with the appointment of the National Commission of Higher Education (NCHE) in 1995 after the publication of the first White Paper on Education and Training (WPET, 1995). The Centre for Education Policy Development (CEPD), aligned with the ruling African National Congress (ANC), produced the NCHE's policy brief to come up with a document that satisfied a plurality of competing interests, including those of apartheid bureaucrats whose jobs had been secured as part of the negotiated political settlement and who arguably represented White minority interests (Moja & Hayward, 2000, p. 338). Prior to 1994 the government favoured the position of Whites and one of the decisions taken at the Kempton Park negotiations between the ANC and the then ruling National Party was that Whites' economic interests, including capital, would be protected under a new government. The substantive NCHE process – constituted by representatives from varying political, cultural, academic and economic spheres, who had the self-determining, conscious and political will-formation – was characterised by argumentation and deliberative consensus-seeking, drawing considerably from international expertise and practical experience in higher education restructuring.

Despite so many diverse and competing interests at stake, the NCHE was able to produce a report which called for increased participation, greater responsiveness and relevance, and increased co-operation and partnerships in the higher education sector (NCHE, 1996, pp. 6–8). Central to the deliberative efforts of the NCHE was their conscious and political will-formation to achieve equity in the development of a single co-ordinated higher education system characterised by participation, responsiveness and relevance as the primary driving force of the report equity in the allocation of resources, redress (that is rectifying the past injustices) of historical inequalities with a new funding formula for historically disadvantaged institutions (HDIs), co-operative governance at institutional and national levels, a balanced approach to material and human resources, and high standards of quality, particularly in the domains of curriculum provision. Let me discuss these in more detail.

State funding was skewed because higher education institutions designated for Black, Coloured and Indian students received less funding than those institutions meant for Whites. For instance, the University of Cape Town (an historically White university) received more funding from the state than the University of the Western Cape (a historically Coloured university). Also, the University of Fort Hare (a former Black university) received fewer material resources than a former White university such as Stellenbosch. Education was heavily censored, meaning that universities were not supposed to encourage a critical pedagogy which could potentially result in student uprisings at campuses. Consequently, the quality of the curriculum was severely compromised at all institutions.

First, on the issue of increasing the participation of students in the higher education sector, the NCHE envisaged that an increase in the number of students who had been denied access to higher education in the past would invariably improve students' chances to become better practical 'reasoners', or produce students who have developed the capacities to be responsive to reasons and to engage as democratic citizens in the new South African society. Unfortunately, as a result of problems related to epistemological access (that is, students who have the competence to pursue graduate studies as a consequence of their credible level of education) and funding, only 580 000 students enrolled for the higher education sector in 2000 compared with 608 000 in 1998 – a significant decline in the student intake. In other words, although students might qualify procedurally to enter the higher education sector, because of their impoverished learning environment, many students were already excluded from the point of view of knowledge base, that is, epistemologically (and substantively). For example, students who attended historically disadvantaged schools might qualify to enter universities. However, in some cases many of these students perform inadequately at school, which leads to these students not being sufficiently equipped to cope with university studies. By implication equitable access to higher education did not (as) yet have the desired effect of producing a critical mass of students whose quality of life chances, according to the NCHE, could improve, particularly those Blacks denied access to higher education in the past and who had (and arguably continue to have) limited employment opportunities as white-collar workers.

Second, the NCHE's announcement striving for achieving greater responsiveness and relevance through restructured programmes underscored by 'effective quality assurance' can be seen as an attempt to cultivate in students the capacity of 'self-realisation' to become skilled people who can contribute towards addressing the country's urgent need for social reconstruction and national development (NCHE, 1996, p. 127) – clearly an indication that equitable redress (that is, redistributing the country's material and human resources on the basis of equality) had been considered as a priority for the higher education policy discourse.

Third, on the question of increased co-operation and partnerships among White historically advantaged institutions (HAIs) and Black historically disadvantaged institutions (HDIs),[1] the NCHE envisaged that, through co-operative relationships and partnerships among HAIs and HDIs, the higher education student base would hopefully become deracialised. Instead, the deracialisation of the new post-1994 higher education landscape resulted in many Black students leaving several HDIs (out of a total of 21 universities and 15 technikons or polytechnics, that is, institutions which focus on both academic/professional training and experiential/on-site learning in the country) where deficits caused by non-paying poor students, financial mismanagement, student unrest (leading to campus occupations by police and private security firms) and poor educational quality were increasing. Yet there can be no doubt that the 'fallible' report of the NCHE for a while enjoyed what Habermas (1996, p. 24) refers to as "the presumption of rationality" within the deliberative discourse of collaborating stakeholders. This "presumption of rationality" means that higher education had merely a technical interest in preparing students for the world of work without considering that these students should also be critical about what they learn. In other words, the NCHE rationally defended the idea that equity and redress as the primary driving forces of the higher education policy agenda could lead to the reconstruction and development of South African society after decades of apartheid rule.

Learning for global competitiveness

This "presumption of rationality" also prevailed among the authors of the Education White Paper 3, *A Programme for the Transformation of Higher Education* (EWP, 1997), which outlined the country's higher education policy framework by taking up most of the NCHE's recommendations. The EWP (1997) stems from a Green Paper published by the Ministry of Education in December 1996, which gave firmer rhetorical commitment to the principles of equity, redress (specifically institutional redress), justice and democratisation. Although the Green Paper endorsed the NCHE's recommendations on accountability, efficiency and a national qualifications structure, it assigned a greater role to national development through global competitiveness, thus for the first time ostensibly minimising demands for substantive equity and redress in the higher education sector. In fact, the authors of the Green Paper and later the EWP (1997) reduced the emphasis on substantive equitable redress discourse in favour of human capacity enhancement for national development and economic global competitiveness.

The point I am making is that, although the EWP did not entirely dismiss the equitable redress agenda, it was certainly minimised and reconceptualised through a renewed emphasis on increasing the human potential of students to meet national development needs (as proposed by the NCHE), including high-skilled employment needs presented by a growing economy operating in a global, neoliberal environment. Put differently, the EWP contends that equity of access and a fair chance of success for all, together with the eradication of all forms of unfair discrimination and past inequalities, can no longer solely be seen as revolving around the provision of institutional redress funding, and that funding solely for eradicating institutional inequalities should be given by the state to these institutions (EWP, 1997, pp. 1–14). The higher education policy discourse around redress funding was criticised as highly inefficient in terms of achieving successful student throughputs, since it was merely used as a means to alleviate the debt burden at most HDIs (Habib, 2001, p. 4). In a different way, the expectation of redress led many HDIs linking the resolution of their institutional crises to receiving additional earmarked government funding. Institutions should not just be seen as being in need of funding to eradicate inequalities. Rather they should also be funded to promote and advance research, teaching and learning. What the EWP purports is that the attainment of equitable redress is conditional upon cultivating a democratic ethos (humaneness, non-racism, non-sexism and tolerance), a culture of human rights and citizenship, and the development of a critical discourse (creativity and imagination) in students in order to address the diverse problems and demands of the local, national, Southern African and African contexts (EWP, 1997, p. 14) – a tentative shift towards becoming globally responsive and competitive.

The processes which led to the finalisation of the NCHE report and the EWP policy document indicate that a conditional consensus had been attained among deliberative stakeholders, and that deliberation about the evolving higher education discourse remained free and unconstrained – this means that what higher education would become was determined by the manner in which stakeholders agreed and/or disagreed about higher education policy. This is borne out by the fact that the vision to redress the inequities of apartheid, and simultaneously to move away from these equity objectives to develop the socio-political and economic needs of the country, has changed to one that Kraak (2001) describes as entailing a preponderance of "economic rationalism" – a significant moment in the higher education policy discourse in South Africa. This brings me to a discussion of the higher education policy discourse in relation to Seyla Benhabib's account of deliberative (substantive) democracy – that is, discursive-reflexive democracy.

Discursive-reflexive democracy and the market economy

Benhabib's notion of discursive-reflexive democracy does not separate the personal from the political, because "politics and public reason are always seen to emerge out of a cultural and social context" (Benhabib, 1996, p. 76). In a different way, for Benhabib reason is always situated in a context, which means that it can never render transparent all the cultural and social conditions that give rise to it. Hence, for Benhabib deliberative democracy does not restrict the agenda of public conversation, but rather encourages discourse which integrates the public and the private, as well as being more interested in the ways in which political processes interact with cultural and social contexts. Moreover, Benhabib posits that political processes involve more than self-interested competition governed by bargaining and an aggregative mechanism of voting. Rather, participants (say, at parliamentary level) could temporarily come to an agreement based on majoritarian decision-making, but should also procedurally build into the deliberative process a reflexivity principle which allows for the public re-examination of majoritarian decisions—what Benhabib (1996, p. 72) refers to as that reflexivity condition which allows abuses and misapplications at the first level (say, parliamentary level) to be challenged at a second meta-level of discourse (say, in public forums). Considering Benhabib's notion of a discursive practice, I intend to show that higher education cannot just be about what the state decides higher education to be like, but also how local conditions ought to integrate with global, market-driven concerns. Likewise, following Benhabib's idea of reflexivity, I shall show that higher education policy changes cannot be a matter of simply voting about its political correctness, but more importantly allowing stakeholders sufficient time and thinking to conclude policy decisions.

Could the higher education policy discourse which led to the promulgation of the National Plan for Higher Education (NPHE, 2001) be explained in relation to discursiveness and reflexivity – that is substantive and/or procedural democracy? In the first instance, the strategic policy goals of the NPHE are based on the policy framework outlined in the EWP (1997). These key goals include the following:

- To provide increased access to higher education to all, irrespective of race, gender, age, creed, class or disability, and to produce graduates with the skills and competencies necessary to meet the human resource needs of the country;
- To promote equity of access and to redress past inequalities through ensuring that the staff and student profiles in higher education progressively reflect the demographic realities of South African society;
- To ensure diversity in the organisational form and institutional landscape of the higher education system through mission and programme differentiation, thus enabling the addressing of regional and national needs in social and economic development;
- To build high-level research capacity to address the research and knowledge needs of South Africa; and
- To build new institutional and organisational forms and new institutional identities through regional collaboration between institutions (NPHE, 2001, pp. 16–17).

The way that the NPHE outlines how the higher education policy framework of the EWP should be implemented corroborates the view that its authors extended the legacy of intersubjective deliberation (creating opportunities for stakeholder participation and engagement) used in the earlier period of policy formulation – they did not simply dismiss what had been deliberated upon earlier. Whereas in the earlier period of the higher education policy discourse there was much wider and exhaustive stakeholder participation and consultation, the Minister of Education intervened by appointing the Council on Higher Education (CHE), comprised of a small group of intellectuals, politicians and business people to advise him on a National Plan for Higher Education through a process of "free and unconstrained deliberation." In 2000 the CHE produced a report entitled *Towards a Higher Education Landscape: Meeting the Equity, Quality and Social Development Imperatives of South Africa in the 21st century* (2000). In this report the CHE proposed a differentiated system of three types of higher education institutions: (1) exclusive postgraduate and research institutions; (2) extensive Masters and selective PhD institutions; and (3) bedrock institutions for undergraduate programmes and limited postgraduate programmes up to Masters level. These proposals were met with vehement opposition from higher education stakeholders, in particular, universities; they were accused of reproducing apartheid structures, as it was expected that historically disadvantaged institutions (HDIs) would be assigned bedrock status. In response, the CHE proposed that the Minister of Education should appoint a National Working Group (NWG) to advise him on the restructuring of the higher education landscape. Eventually the NPHE was released in 2001. As can be deduced from the aforementioned strategic goals of the NPHE, a clear economic-rationalist discourse had come to characterise the terrain of higher education discourse, which favoured a stronger link between higher education and its neoliberal export-led growth orientation. Higher education was considered a public good serving the interests of capital with the intent to produce a competitive workforce. Higher education policy discourse has increasingly minimised its initial strong thrust towards equity and redress, and instead substantively emphasised the need for efficient human resource development commensurate with regional and national needs, as well as global economic imperatives. The achievement of equity and redress, which had been so prominent in earlier higher education policy discourse, became secondary to the primary objective of making higher education more responsive to attending to economic labour market imperatives and concomitant neoliberal requirements for skilled and innovative knowledge workers and producers who, in the words of Bourdieu (1998, p. 2), can ensure "an unprecedented mobility of capital."

The question arises: why can the economic-rationalist agenda of the NPHE be explained within a discursive-reflexive paradigm? Firstly, Benhabib's notion of discursive-reflexive democracy recognises discourse that integrates the public and private spheres. Certainly the growth in private higher education provision (announced as an outcome to be achieved in the NPHE), established mainly through partnerships with public institutions, reflects the impact of economic market forces on higher education discourse. On the one hand, it is claimed that this integration between the private and public sectors of the higher education terrain is primarily geared towards providing vocational educational programmes that would result in employment for previously unskilled and poorly prepared Black students, whereas on the other hand, it is seen as a response to economic labour market imperatives (Subotzky, 2002).

Secondly, the discursive-reflexive idea that justifiable ways should be found in which political processes interact with cultural and social contexts– in this instance higher education restructuring – can be linked to the specific low-skills labour base of the country. As a corollary of the skills shortage in the country, it has become imperative for the NPHE to link higher education provision to skills development and economic growth (Kraak, 2001, pp. 90–94). More specifically, the NPHE announces as an outcome that all graduates should be equipped with skills and qualities required for participation as citizens in a democratic society and as workers and professionals in the economy (NPHE, 2001, p. 76).

Thirdly, establishing new institutional and organisational forms (which have now become known as mergers) seems to be in line with Benhabib's reflexivity principle, which challenges 'self-interested competition' amongst higher education institutions. In May 2002 the Cabinet or the Executive of Parliament accepted the Ministry of Education's proposals for mergers and their recommendation that the higher education landscape be reconfigured by reducing the institutions from 36 (21 universities and 15 technikons) to 23. The government proposed the closure of some HDIs and the merging of others with either HDIs or former HAIs (universities and technikons) (Asmal, 2002). Kraak (2001, p. 115) posits that mergers should be understood in the context of unanticipated developments that emerged in the higher education sector, such as competition among institutions related to programmes, human capacity problems in national and institutional planning processes, declining student enrolments and the proliferation of private higher education. The NPHE (2001, p. 8) states that the aforementioned unanticipated and unintended cones-quences, if left unchecked, threaten the development of a single, national, co-ordinated but diverse higher education sector. Higher education would have been subjected to 'abuse and misapplications', which would further have entrenched existing systemic fragmentation, throughput and graduation rate inefficiencies, skewed student distribution between science, commerce and humanities, low research output and poor staff equity. For instance, if HAIs (White universities) were not subjected to mergers, they would retain their material and human resources (which they in any case acquired through apartheid legislation), and the chances of redistributing resources among unequal institutions would be minimised.

So mergers are seen as major restructuring efforts to address problems of institutional fragmentation, lack of financial and academic viability in relation to declining student demand and competition amongst institutions. Harman and Harman (2003, p. 41) assert that mergers invariably involve additional costs, especially in the planning and restructuring of academic and administrative departments, which in turn lead to staff redundancy packages. Yet, according to them, "sensibly conceived and well-managed mergers, with due sensitivity paid to cultural and human issues, can produce substantial long-term benefits, both for individual institutions and higher education systems" (Harman & Harman, 2003, p. 42). Certainly in South Africa mergers could lead to substantial increases in student access and greater differentiation in course offerings to cater for diverse student masses, thus counteracting 'self-interested' competition among institutions. But then such a view is based on an understanding that in an era of corporatisation mergers would not result in competition. Slaughter and Leslie (1997, pp. 129–132) argue that, on the contrary, corporatisation creates a sense of competition among higher education institutions when they confront the marketplace, which could lead to problems of conformity and a lack of creativity in basic research, because of the confidentiality of research results encouraged by governing bodies of higher education institutions. I have a suspicion that in South Africa mergers have the potential to encourage competition which would invariably favour the already advantaged institutions (some advantaged institutions merged) as far as research output is concerned. This would further entrench existing inequalities, since inadequately trained academic staff work mostly at HDIs (some historically disadvantaged institutions merged).

In essence, the higher education discourse in South Africa, which culminated in the promulgation of the National Plan for Higher Education 2001, has mainly been characterised by forms of both procedural and substantive democracy. It is procedural in the sense that education policies were developed on the basis of an agreed-upon consensus, whereas the deliberations of participants about the legitimacy and authenticity of such policies can arguably lay claim to have been achieved on the grounds of a discursiveness and reflexivity which require that participants/ policy makers attend to the different and at times conflicting opinions of others as they endeavoured to come up with defensible and justifiable education policies.

This brings me to a discussion of the establishment of the South African Qualifications Authority (SAQA) and the National Qualifications Framework (NQF) in relation to a lack of deliberative (substantive) democracy.

THE SOUTH AFRICAN QUALIFICATIONS AUTHORITY, THE NATIONAL QUALIFICATIONS FRAMEWORK AND A LACK OF SUBSTANTIVE DEMOCRACY?

The South African Qualifications Framework

Significantly, the SAQA Act was the first piece of education and training legislation approved by the new democratic government and formed a key reference point for the development of many government policies, regulations and acts. Notable examples include: the *Higher Education Act (1997)*, the *Further Education and Training Act (1998)*, the *Adult Basic Education and Training Act (2000)*, and the *General and Further Education and Training Act (2001)*. The SAQA Act was followed by numerous publications that announced the intentions of SAQA in its capacity as primary overseer of the development and imple-mentation of the National Qualifications Framework (NQF). By the end of 1998 the *National Standards Bodies (NSB) Regulations* and the *Education Training and*

Quality Assurance (ETQA) Regulations had been promulgated, twelve NSBs and four Standards Generating Bodies (SGBs) and a number of initial qualifications and unit standards had been registered (SAQA, 2004). In March 1997 the SAQA Executive Officer assumed duties with a small staff contingent. Government funding was limited and was supplemented with external donor funds, mainly from the Canadian International Development Agency (1995) and the European Union (2002). SAQA has managed to secure the support of the Department of Education, the Department of Labour, organised business and organised labour (Cosser, 2001, p. 163). SAQA's early dominance gradually receded to create space for the much greater prominence of ETQAs, particularly the Council on Higher Education's Higher Education Quality Committee (HEQC) and UMALUSI (the General and Further Education and Training Quality Assurance Council). The difference in capacity between the different bands of ETQAs, SAQA and other partners such as the Department of Education and the Department of Labour led to constant disparities and lack of coherence across the education and training system, despite claims by many that the NQF can be considered legitimately as a social construct (Kraak & Young, 2001, p. 30).

The South African National Qualifications Framework (NQF) was established through the promulgation of the South African Qualifications Authority (SAQA) Act in 1995. The aim of the framework is to create an integrated national framework for learning achievements; to facilitate access to and mobility and progression within education, training and career paths; to enhance the quality of education and training; to accelerate the redress of past unfair discrimination in education, training and employment opportunities; and to contribute to the personal development of each learner and the socio-development of the nation at large (SAQA, 1995, p. 1). Following David Miller's (1999, pp. 245–250) account of social justice, one finds three constitutive features: the institutional structure that must ensure that an adequate share of social resources is set aside for the distribution to individuals on the basis of (special) need(s); many social resources be allocated to individuals on the basis of their preferences; and people, in their capacity as citizens, must be treated as equals, which requires that they enjoy equal legal, political and social rights. In line with Miller's equality principle, it seems as if the SAQA Act succeeds in affording those in the education system equal legal and political rights – for instance, all students have the right to university access. Yet, it seems as if all students do not enjoy equal social rights with respect to their education, because not everyone who qualifies to enter university might be able to afford to pay the exorbitant fees. Secondly, the progression of students based on their performances and individual preferences is recognised by SAQA. For instance, students who wish to pursue a Masters qualification can do so on the grounds that their prior qualification is in line with SAQA criteria. Thirdly, SAQA does make provision for students to be treated equally, that is, no student can be discriminated against in pursuing a particular qualification, if that student meets the entry requirements. In some cases students are also allowed access to university programmes on the basis of lowering the access requirements, provided that such students come from historically disadvantaged schools.

This brings me back to a discussion of the National Qualifications Framework (NQF) as a social construct. The critical need to understand the NQF as a social construct finds expression in the views of Cosser *et al.* (1999), who claim that, because the NQF is characterised by processes of democratic participation, it should be considered as a social construct. Likewise, Cosser (2001, p. 157) corroborates this claim on the basis that the NQF is a consensus-oriented discourse – one underscored by negotiation (Kraak & Young, 2001, p. 30) and contestation (Isaacs, 2001, p. 124). On the face of it, there seems to be little wrong with considering the NQF processes as democratic and participatory, and premised on consensus, negotiation and contestation. However, such a notion of democratic participation seems to be procedural and, hence, restricted in the sense that people ('stakeholders' or participants) can participate and reach consensus through negotiation and contestation, but this does not necessarily mean that the consensus which has been achieved is necessarily defensible or reasonably justifiable – that is, substantive. An important case in point is, for instance, the consensus decision that was taken by the Inter-Departmental Task Team jointly appointed by the Department of Education (DoE) and Department of Labour (DoL) in 2002. This Task Team's purpose was to review and revise NQF legislation to the effect that the strategic leadership of the NQF be assumed by an Inter-Departmental NQF Strategic Team, which would exclude SAQA. This exclusion of SAQA seems to have been unjustifiable in the light of the agency of democratic participation. How could one exclude a body from such a strategic initiative, in particular when that same body was influential in shaping the initial NQF discourse and understood some of its hiccups? So, procedurally SAQA has been excluded from further deliberations and, hence, the practice of democratic participation can be claimed to have been unsubstantive. The point I am making is that democratic participation based on consensus, negotiation and contestation is not sufficient to ensure substantive democracy.

Instead, substantive democracy requires what Eamon Callan (1997, p. 215) refers to as a conception of public deliberation characterised by distress and belligerence. This kind of public deliberation is a rough process of struggle or confrontation that will naturally give way to conciliation pieced together from the insights of conflicting viewpoints. For him, the idea of public deliberation is not an attempt "to achieve dialogical victory over our adversaries but rather the attempt to find and enact terms of political coexistence that we and they can reasonably endorse as morally acceptable" (Callan, 1997, p. 215). Through public deliberation participants raise doubts about the correctness of their moral beliefs or about the importance of the differences between what they and others believe (a matter of arousing distress) accompanied by a rough process of struggle and ethical confrontation – that is, belligerence (Callan, 1997, p. 211). If this happens, belligerence and distress give way eventually to moments of ethical conciliation, when the truth and error in rival positions have been made clear and a fitting synthesis of factional viewpoints is achieved (Callan, 1997, p. 212). This is an idea of public deliberation – one with which I agree – where no one has the right to silence dissent and where participants can speak their minds. In the words of Callan (1997, pp. 201–202), "real moral dialogue" (as constitutive of substantive democracy), as opposed to carefully policed conversations about the meaning of some moral orthodoxy, cannot occur without the risk of offence. An offence-free school [I would say, the NQF process] would oblige us to eschew dialogue. On the one hand, it does seem that some participants in the NQF process (DoE and DoL) became culpable of steering the process in a way whereby preference is no longer given to the substantiveness of articulated views, considering that SAQA was excluded from the process. Rather, these participants (stakeholders) seem to focus on who their colleagues are (and might be) and not also on what they have to say substantively – small wonder Young (2003) calls for a more nuanced under-standing of "communities of trust." On the other hand, SAQA should not be affronted when criticised for being too technicist and bureaucratic (CHE, 2003). In any case, following Callan, public deliberation depends on critical scrutiny of one's viewpoints by others.

In addition, substantive democracy constituted by public deliberation also requires that we take into account people's linguistic, cultural and ethnic commonalities and differences (Benhabib, 2002, p. 162). The idea of finding a civil space for the sharing of different people's differences is based on the understanding that people need to learn to live with the otherness of others whose ways of being may be deeply threatening to our own (Benhabib, 2002, p. 130). And by creating a civil space, referred to by Benhabib (2002, p. 127) as "intercultural dialogue", whereby people can enact what they have in common and at the same time make public their competing narratives and significations, people might have a real opportunity to co-exist. In this way they would not only establish a community of conversation and interdependence (that is, they share commonalities), but also one of disagreement (that is, they do not share commonalities) without disrespecting others' life-worlds (Benhabib, 2002, pp. 35 & 41). Put differently, when people are engaged in a conversation underpinned by interdependence and disagreement, they engage in a legitimate dialogical process with a collective identity – they share commonalities and respect the differences of others. Its appears as if the NQF 'stakeholders' do not practise such a form of substantive democracy.

Thus, on the basis of Eamon Callan's and Seyla Benhabib's accounts of substantive (deliberative) democracy, it seems premature to refer, as an uncontested premise, to the NQF as being a justifiable social construct, because such a construct not only requires procedural democratic participation but also substantive deliberative engagement. Substantive democracy can be very helpful as the NQF stakeholders endeavour to make the NQF a justifiable social construct.

This brings me to a discussion of the National Review of Teacher Education in relation to the activities of the HEQC.

The Higher Education Quality Committee and the National Review of Teacher Education: Procedural or Substantive Democracy?

Quality Assurance (QA) gained currency in South Africa when, in 1995, the South African Universities' Vice-Chancellors' Association (now Higher Education South

Africa) agreed to establish a Quality Promotion Unit that would assist universities "to conduct productive institutional self-evaluation at different levels; and create a basis in the higher education system for accreditation of programmes for the purpose of articulation" (SAUVCA in Smout & Stephenson, 2002, p. 199). The Higher Education Act of 1997 established a statutory body known as the Higher Education Quality Committee (HEQC), which functions under the auspices of the Council on Higher Education. Some of the main tasks of the HEQC, fully constituted in 2001, are to conduct institutional audits and to accredit academic programmes. This brings me to a cursory glance at the national review of teacher education in South Africa, with a focus on the accreditation of academic programmes.[2] This process of review is an intensive one, based on a self-evaluation report supported by additional documentation or 'evidence'. Following receipt of the 23 institutions' self-evaluation reports, the HEQC appoints panels to critically peruse the documentation and to visit the institutions to conduct conversations and interviews with staff and students. A series of professional judgements are made, benchmarked against criteria or 'minimum standards' of good practice. Then reports, embodying judgements (conditional accreditation, provisional accreditation, full accreditation and withdrawal of accreditation) and a number of recommendations are made to the HEQC Board and the various institutions. What is very pertinent about accreditation is that it operates on the basis of peer review, which results in what is effectively a 'certificate of competence' for institutions. The accreditation process has just witnessed its first judgements in relation to the MBA (2004/2005) and MEd (2005/6) programmes, which have been endorsed by the HEQC Board and subsequently communicated to institutions. Institutions whose accreditation were withdrawn will now have to produce 'teach-out' plans; those with conditional or provisional accreditation were to submit action plans on improving their programmes; and the fully accredited programmes have been endorsed as complying with the HEQC's 'minimum standards' of best practice.

Undoubtedly, the HEQC's accreditation process began with the best of intentions: to contribute to the transformation of higher education in the country; to engender international best practice, while simultaneously being responsive to the specific needs of South African society; and to encourage academics to take teaching more seriously and demystify the link between quality and exclusivity (Stephenson, 2004). For the HEQC, academics ought to integrate their scholarship with the agenda of the accreditation process – that is, achieving a unified higher education system based on the principles of equity, democratisation, development, quality, academic freedom, institutional autonomy, effectiveness and efficiency (CHE, 2000). It seems as if the accreditation process has already made a difference in the academic lives of many university educators and perhaps their students, considering that many academic programmes have been revised on the recommendations of the HEQC.

Yet there is some indication that the current state of play on accreditation is not without its critics.[3] In some circles the accreditation process is branded as highly 'techno-bureaucratic' and the claim is that it has imposed extra work loads on university academics, who now have less time for research and teaching. Others claim that the process spawned a 'checklist' mentality characterised by window-dressing, external policing and over-zealous panel members, whose biases lead to negative evaluations instead of establishing opportunities for development. There is widespread concern that the accreditation process initially began with a developmental focus in mind, which gradually dissipated on the grounds that professional judgements have been made about academic programmes and that the onus is on institutions to improve their programmes. This is quite possible with programmes which have gained either a full or conditional and provisional accreditation, but not necessarily with those which have to be terminated. Such challenges are not unusual for the Quality Assurance process in South Africa, which is still in its embryonic phase and where there is so much more to learn and experience. In particular, institutions that feel aggrieved at the treatment they have received from the HEQC and they begin to ask more questions about the accountability of those whose judgements are being questioned. And, as in the United States and Britain, recourse to the legal process would become more prevalent, as Alderman and Brown (2005, p. 313) have warned.

A word of caution is that one should not leave these whispers of suspicion unattended, but actually cultivate a process of deliberation where ideas can be shared, critiques offered and engaged with, and new imaginaries be brought to bear on improving the QA process. I contend that QA processes should not involve merely manifesting procedural democracy as is currently the case, but should also reflect a substantiveness which would make the processes more authentic than is currently the case. For instance, during the HEQC Accreditation Committee meetings it seems as if members are more intent on ensuring that appropriate procedures are followed rather than on whether the judgements that are made about particular programmes are substantive or not. If this happens – that is, more substantive judgements are made during discussions – the QA in South Africa process has some chance of being sustained and more improvements to our higher education system can be anticipated. Failing to do so would undermine the integrity of the accreditation process and merely "deepen the suspicion that universities are being infiltrated by technocrats" (Stephenson, 2004, p. 66).

In addition, there seems to be another concern: "Who is guarding the guards?" (Strydom & Strydom, 2004, p. 111) or "Who accredits the HEQC?." Put differently, to whom is the accrediting committee accountable for its work? This seems to be a legitimate concern, because no one can pretend that accreditation is 'foolproof' – it can be manipulated and is open to abuse (Alderman & Stephenson, 2005, p. 326). Therefore more substantive ways have to be found to maintain the integrity of the accreditation process. In the final section of this essay I shall show, with reference to the MEd review at my institution, why using procedural processes only are limited and then put forward an argument for more substantive deliberations.

CONCLUSION: AN ANAYTICAL REFLECTION

The HEQC was instituted to ensure that higher education institutions 'deliver' (more than they had done before) in terms of their academic offerings, in particular producing a cadre of well-trained academics and students who would finally serve the interests of the broader, reconstructed democratic South African society. To guarantee (very optimistically one might assume) that universities in South Africa can produce such academics and students, the 'quality' of education that university teachers and students engage with has to comply with the 'minimum standards' recommended by the HEQC. The proposed 'minimum standards' include the following:

- Institutional organisational context – The programme is an integral part of offerings of the higher education institution at which it is located and it complies with all the national policies and regulations regarding the provision of higher education qualifications in South Africa. The unit offering the MEd has goals, objectives and forms of internal organisation to support the programme;
- Programme design and co-ordination – The learning programme has a clear structure leading to an MEd or to the designated areas of specialisation at MEd level. As a postgraduate degree, the MEd must correspond to the generally accepted minimum standards of an NQF level 8 Master's degree. The programme is effectively coordinated in a way that facilitates attainment of its intended purposes and outcomes;
- Student recruitment, admission and selection – Recruitment documentation informs potential students of the programme accurately and sufficiently, and admission adheres to current legislative requirements. Admission and selection of students are commensurate with the programme's academic requirements, within a framework of widened access and equity. The number of students selected takes into account the programme's intended learning outcomes, its capacity to offer good quality education, and the needs of the particular profession (in the case of professional programmes);
- Staffing – Academic staff responsible for the programme are suitably qualified, have sufficient relevant experience and teaching competence, and their assessment competence and research profiles are adequate for the nature and level of the programme. The institution and/or other recognised agencies contracted by the institution provide opportunities for academic staff to enhance their competences and to support their professional growth and development;
- Teaching and learning – The institution gives recognition to the importance of the promotion of student learning. The teaching and learning strategy is appropriate for the institutional type as reflected in its mission, modes of delivery and student composition, contains mechanisms to ensure the appropriateness of teaching and learning methods, and makes provision for staff to improve their teaching. Effective teaching and learning methods and suitable learning materials and learning opportunities facilitate the achievement of the purposes and outcomes of the programme. The programme ensures that each student displays an understanding of the areas of knowledge which are fundamental for an MEd, and acquires skills and competencies which are relevant to the academic and professional world of education;

- Research – The programme is actively based on research. Both staff and students contribute actively to the knowledge base in the fields of education through their research production;
- Supervision of research dissertation – Suitably qualified staff support students' independent work by offering guidance on all aspects of the research process and on keeping to an achievable time schedule for their projects. Supervisors are accessible within reason, keep records of decisions agreed upon, offer timeous feedback on student work, and support and encourage the student through completion;
- Student assessment – The different modes of delivery of the programme have appropriate policies and procedures for internal assessment, internal and external moderation, monitoring of student progress, explicitness, validity and reliability of assessment practices, recording of assessment results, settling of disputes, the rigour and security of the assessment system, RPL, and for the development of staff competence in assessment. The programme has effective assessment practices that include internal (or external) assessment, as well as internal and external moderation. The programme has taken measures to ensure the reliability, rigour and security of the assessment system;
- Infrastructure and library resources – Suitable and sufficient venues, IT infrastructure and library resources are available for students and staff in the programme. Policies ensure the proper management and maintenance of library resources, including support and access for students and staff. Staff development of library staff takes place on a regular basis;
- Student retention, throughput rates and programme impact – Student retention and throughput rates in the programme are monitored, especially in terms of race and gender equity, and remedial measures are taken, where necessary. The programme has taken steps to enhance the employability of students and to alleviate shortages of expertise in relevant fields, in cases where these are the desired outcomes of the programme; and
- Programme reviews – User surveys, reviews and impact studies on the effectiveness of the programme are undertaken at regular intervals.

Results are used to improve the programme's design, delivery and resourcing, and for staff development and student support, where necessary (HEQC, 2005). With reference to some of the 'minimum standards' recommended by the HEQC for MEd compliance, I shall now reflect on what is wrong with excessive proceduralism.

For the HEQC it seems as if a 'minimum standard' is associated with 'quality' education. And the assumption is that, unless universities' academic programmes meet at least the requirements of a 'minimum standard', their offerings cannot be of significant quality – or, should we say, they need some improvement to meet the quality criterion. This suggests that the HEQC, with its claim to have had input and responses on the development of the 'minimum standards' from academics – at least procedurally I would say – has some utopian idea of what constitutes good (quality) education. It seems as if the HEQC would be prepared to answer the question: what constitutes good education, or (what amounts to the same thing) what constitutes perfect, infallible knowledge (without errors) about 'good' education? And, in fact, it turns out that the HEQC knows exactly what constitutes good or quality education, since their recommended 'minimum standards' (and for purposes of this discussion I shall refer only to the 'minimum standards' of a structured MEd) give some indication of what the ultimate standards are which they expect universities to have in place when they conduct their audit. Today utopianism or perfectionism has developed into some kind of absolute, unquestioned rule, which instrumentally determines what is good for society. This kind of perfect knowledge seems unattainable. For me, such utopianism is not very helpful for the transformation of higher education in the country, since it seems as if utopianism has a tendency to prompt people to embark on 'witch-hunts' of institutions, which have to 'beware' of whatever consequences if the 'minimum standards' are not in place. While being questioned by HEQC panellists during the MEd audit, I got the sense that at times the types of questions already had some inappropriate judgmental undertones, which suggested that the HEQC came to search for information in the institution's self-evaluation which they thought would not comply with the 'minimum standards'. Of course, one can claim that this is their job; however, the demeaning ways in which staff were questioned and intimidated put a damper on the review. Some of the questions asked included the following: "Why are the research publications so unevenly spread in your department?"; "What would happen if academic X is no longer here?"; "Will your programme's intake exceed Y number of students?"; and "Your students say that they do not get enough research methodology?" In fact some of the questions which the students were asked border even more on a search for ultimate utopianism: "How frequently do you meet with your supervisors?"; and "Are they (supervisors) there when needed?". If responses from my colleagues were not 'favourable' (there seemed to have been many of these unfavourable responses), then the institution's programme was obviously lacking in certain respects. For instance, some of the apparently unsatisfactory responses were: "We cannot all publish like academic Z"; and "Our system of recording students' progress has not always been consistent with your 'minimum' expectations." This lack could potentially disqualify it, we assume, from meeting the ultimate 'minimum standards' recommended by the HEQC.

Now, what seems to be so pernicious about this demand for infallible and utopian 'minimum standards'? Critical rationalists such as Karl Popper were vociferous critics of utopianism. Popper (1962) argued that supposed infallibility undermines responsibility, the zeal for communication, good faith and the love of humanity, primarily because it (utopianism) rejects open-endedness – that is, substantive communication. In this regard, he claims "that we all take many things as self-evident, that we accept them uncritically and even with the naïve and cocksure belief that criticism is quite unnecessary" (Popper, 1962, p. 217). When a 'minimum standard' is there, it is 'closed', infallible and perfect on the basis that it has solid grounds – there seems to be no room left for doubts and disputes about the 'minimum standards', at least in a substantive way – and I have reason to believe that this could be the case with the HEQC's understanding of 'minimum standards'.

It is here that I want to proffer my argument commensurate with critical rationalism: critical rationalism does not ask what the utopian or good (quality) standard is, but rather suggests how we can possibly make our society – in this instance, our academic programmes – better or more just. Critical rationalists, being fallibilists, would respond that we could improve academic programmes by searching for mistakes or contradictions and trying to reduce or eliminate them. The method of trial and error would help us to discover errors and flaws, and by eliminating them we could potentially learn and improve. The problem is that predetermined standards have the potential to undermine a critical engagement with standards, because they have been determined as non-negotiable criteria for evaluation. Instead, 'trial and error' establishes opportunities to engage with standards which in any case should emanate from deliberations. Popper (1962, p. 215) makes the point that if contradictions (and mistakes) are avoided, then any criticism and any discussion become impossible, "since criticism always consists in pointing out contradictions." Critical rationalists dismiss alleged perfect or ultimate knowledge, but rather set about trying to improve problematic situations by critically examining their flaws and faults, for instance, those embedded in the 'minimum standards' – that is, by acting in a substantive way. Like Popper (1989, pp. 33–36), they advance by trial and error, by open debate of controversial questions, by conjectures and refutations, and by inviting and welcoming criticism, and considering ways as to how, in this instance, academic programmes can be improved. Popper (1962, p. 379) aptly makes the point: "Nothing is exempt from criticism, or should be held to be exempt from criticism – not even this principle of the critical method itself." The point I am making is that critical rationalists would not search for 'minimum standards' because that would imply a utopian and infallibilist quest for perfection – a matter of exercising proceduralism. Thus, following a Popperian critical and fallibilist method would entail that the HEQC panellists, in consultation and deliberation with the academics who offer a specific programme, would set about through trial and error, open debate, mutual criticism, conjectures and refutations (Popper, 1989) to construct an academically improved, more defensible programme. In this way mutual trust, good will and responsible action could possibly ensue. Popper (1994, p. 137) refers to good will as "the admission, to start with, that we may be wrong, and that we may learn something from the other fellow." Hence, through trial and error, open debate, mutual criticism, and brave conjectures and refutations between the HEQC and the institutions they audit, both parties can possibly come up with more justifiable and rigorous programmes.

Now my potential critic might argue that the 'minimum standards' are only a guiding framework according to which programmes should be evaluated (the word used is 'benchmarked'). The problem with using 'minimum standards' as a framework of reference is itself a valorisation of the 'standards' to a level immune to criticism and debate. So the guiding framework actually becomes the supreme, uncontestable truth. However, in order for debate to ensue, one has to start somewhere. But this does not mean that the starting point should be the 'minimum standards', for such a stance marks the closure of debate. What is there to debate about if the 'minimum standards' have already been decided in advance? In an open or democratic society, Popper would argue, there should be no 'minimum standards' – instead, what ought to emerge from the debates and deliberations are substantive practices (not standards and procedures alone) constitutive of what it means to do things in an open-ended way.

In essence, higher education policy discourse(s) in South Africa experienced both procedural and substantive moments. Yet it seems as if the procedural is gaining prominence over the substantive – a situation that the policy agenda has to contend with, in turn, if South Africa is to remain on course towards achieving deliberative democracy in its education policy processes.

NOTES

[1] White historically advantaged institutions, such as the University of Cape Town, Stellenbosch University, University of Pretoria, University of Johannesburg (formerly Rand Afrikaans University) and Rhodes University, have been privileged in terms of state funding and other resources. Black historically disadvantaged institutions such as the University of Fort Hare and University of Transkei (now Walter Sisulu University) received inadequate state support.

[2] The following programmes have been subjected to review: MEd (Master of Education), PGCE (Postgraduate Certificate in Education), BEd (Bachelor of Education) and ACE (Advanced Certificate in Education) from 2005-2007.

[3] Currently a research report on the HEQC is being compiled. The views expressed in the report have been raised with colleagues at different institutions as well as in the Accreditation Committee, of which I happen to be a member.

REFERENCES

Alderman, G., & Brown, R. (2005). Can quality assurance survive the market? Accreditation and audit at the crossroads. *Higher Education Quarterly, 59*(4), 313–328.

Badat, S. (2005). *Higher education change in South Africa: Achievements and critical issues and challenges of the next debate.* Unpublished paper presented at the National Assembly Education Portfolio Committee, Cape Town.

Benhabib, S. (2002). *The claims of culture: Equality and diversity in the global era.* Princeton, NJ: Princeton University Press.

Callan, E. (1997). *Creating citizens: Political education and liberal democracy.* Oxford: Oxford University Press.

Cosser, M., Isaacs, S. B. A., Mokhobo-Nomvete, S., & Gunthorp, J. (1999). *The higher education and training band and the NQF.* Unpublished paper, Pretoria: SAQA.

Cosser, M. (2001). The implementation of the national qualifications framework and the transformation of education and training in South Africa: A critique. In A. Kraak & M. Young (Eds.), *Education in retrospect: Policy and implementation since 1990* (pp. 153–167). Pretoria: Human Sciences Research Council.

Council on Higher Education (CHE). Shape and Size of Higher Education Task Team. (2000). *Towards a new higher education landscape: Meeting the equity, quality and social imperatives of South Africa in the 21st century.* Pretoria: CHE.

CHE. (2003). *Comments and advice to the Minister on the NQF consultative document: An interdependent national qualifications framework.* Pretoria: CHE.

Department of Education. (1997). *Education white paper 3: A programme for the transformation of higher education.* Pretoria: Government Printers.

Department of Education. (2001). *National plan for higher education in South Africa.* Pretoria: Government Printers.

Isaacs, S. (2001). Making the NQF road by walking reflectively, accountably and boldly. In Y. Sayed & J. Jansen (Eds.), *Implementing education policies: The South African experience* (pp. 124–139). Landsdowne: UCT Press.

Keevy, J. (2005). *A foucauldian critique of the development and implementation of the South African national qualifications framework.* Unpublished Doctoral Dissertation, University of South Africa, Pretoria.

Kraak, A., & Young, M. (Eds.). (2001). *Education in retrospect: Policy and implementation since 1990.* Pretoria: Human Sciences Research Council.

Miller, D. (1999). *Principles of social justice.* Cambridge, MA: Harvard University Press.

Popper, K. (1962). *The open society and its enemies: The high tide of prophecy: Hegel, Marx and the Aftermath.* London: Routledge & Kegan Paul.

Popper, K. (1989). *Conjectures and refutations: The growth of scientific knowledge.* London & New York: Routledge.

Popper, K. (1994). *Knowledge and the body-mind problem: In defence of interaction* (M. Notturno, Ed.). London & New York: Routledge.

Republic of South Africa. (1995). *SAQA Act No 58 of 1995.* Pretoria: Government Printers.

Smout, M., & Stephenson, S. (2002). Quality assurance in South African higher education: A new beginning. *Quality in Higher Education, 8*(2), 197–206.

South African Qualifications Authority (SAQA). (2004). *National qualifications framework impact study: Establishing the criteria against which to measure progress of the NQF.* Pretoria: SAQA.

Stephenson, S. (2004). Saving quality from quality assurance. *Perspective, 8*(3), 62–67.

Strydom, A., & Strydom, J. (2004). Establishing quality assurance in the South African context. *Quality in Higher Education, 10*(2), 101–113.

Young, M. (2003). *Report on an interdependent qualifications framework system.* Pretoria: Council on Higher Education.

FURTHER READINGS

Benhabib, S. (2002). *The claims of culture: Equality and diversity in the global era.* Princeton, NJ: Princeton University Press.

Callan, E. (1997). *Creating citizens: Political education and liberal democracy.* Oxford: Oxford University Press.

Popper, K. (1962). *The open society and its enemies: The high tide of prophecy: Hegel, Marx and the Aftermath.* London: Routledge & Kegan Paul.

Smout, M., & Stephenson, S. (2002). Quality assurance in South African higher education: A new beginning. *Quality in Higher Education, 8*(2), 197–206.

Strydom, A., & Strydom, J. (2004). Establishing quality assurance in the South African context. *Quality in Higher Education, 10*(2), 101–113.

Yusef Waghid
Faculty of Education
Stellenbosch University, South Africa

ALAN CRIBB & SHARON GEWIRTZ

IDENTITY, DIVERSITY AND EQUALITY IN EDUCATION

Mapping the Normative Terrain

INTRODUCTION

This chapter begins from the assumption that policy scholarship must involve evaluative as well as descriptive and explanatory agendas. Our particular interest is in developing an approach to policy sociology that is 'ethically reflexive' by which we mean an approach which is interested both in developing rich empirical descriptions and theoretically rigorous explanations of policy processes and effects *and* in being open to asking what form these policy processes and effects ought to take. This approach rests on the belief that sociological readings of policies need to be informed by a more rigorous and explicit engagement with values than is usual if those readings are going to be useful in helping to transform policy and practice. In this chapter we will undertake an ethically reflexive re-reading of policy responses to what Hall calls the multicultural question, that is:

> The question of how we are to envisage the futures of those many different societies now composed of peoples from very different histories, backgrounds, cultures, contexts, experiences and positions in the ranking order of the world, societies where difference refuses to disappear (Hall 2001).

To evaluate these policy responses we need to be able to characterise and explain the differentiated ways in which education policies and practices do or do not recognise, support or undermine diverse cultural identities and do or do not reproduce various kinds of educational and social inequality. But we also need to be able to think systematically about what ought to be going on. The latter involves confronting a number of important questions: Why does identity matter? What is ethically entailed in – and what are the limits to – recognising and supporting diverse cultural identities? In what ways are the various currents of what is sometimes referred to as multicultural education an adequate response to these complex normative questions? In this chapter, we will begin to respond to these questions by mapping out some of the dimensions and dilemmas involved in taking both identity and equality seriously. We start by briefly reviewing and unpacking the nature of identity. We then summarise the responses of multicultural education policies and practices to the question of identity and some of the principles and values underlying these policies. Finally, we identify and discuss some of the challenges arising from multicultural education that policymakers and practitioners

M. Simons, M. Olssen and M.A. Peters (eds.), Re-Reading Education Policies: A Handbook Studying the Policy Agenda of the 21ˢᵗ Century, 515–530.

committed to taking identity, diversity and equality seriously need to grapple with, highlighting in particular the tension between a politics of recognition and a politics of redistribution.

In the remainder of the chapter we do not make a sharp distinction between policymakers and practitioners because we are working with a conception of policy as a process - i.e. we see policies as being created and recreated at multiple levels from the global to the personal. Hence we are interested not only in the broad official policy frameworks, e.g. national curricula, through which 'multiculturalism' is attempted, but also in the micro-interactions between teachers and students through which such frameworks are lived, realised, inflected and/or interrupted. This view of policy is in line with much work in policy sociology which rejects a narrowly circumscribed version of policy as representing the authoritative and formal texts generated by governments or allied powerful agencies. Rather policy is seen as a field of struggle and contestation in which official policies are mediated, interrupted or recreated by individuals and groups at every level (Bowe et al., 2002).

We will begin with a short account of the nature of identity because this is critical both for understanding why identity matters in education, i.e. what is ethically at stake, and for understanding the various ways in which policy complexes may or may not support or recognise students' identities, i.e. what we described above as the descriptive and explanatory agenda.

WHAT IS IDENTITY?

In discussions around identity, there often appears to be a conflation between two uses of the term: the way in which people identify themselves and the way in which others identify them. For us, identity is first and foremost about the account that we give of ourselves rather than about the accounts that other people give of us. In other words, it is about who we think we are and who we want to be. Of course, this does not mean that other people's accounts are not relevant to our identities. As we go on to argue, this is far from being the case. In addition, it is important to distinguish, as Castells does, between roles and identities. Our identity is not *what* we are or what we want to become but *who* we think we are and want to become:

> Roles (for example, to be a worker, a mother, a neighbour, a socialist militant, a union member, a basketball player, a churchgoer, and a smoker, at the same time) are defined by norms structured by the institutions and organisations of society (...). Identities are sources of meaning for the actors themselves, and by themselves, constructed through a process of individuation. (...) [Roles] become identities only when and if social actors internalise them, and construct meaning around this internalisation (Castells, 2004, pp. 6–7).

The elements that make up our identity-accounts are drawn from those discursive representations that are available to us, including discourses that position us in particular ways, for example as a gifted student or a conscientious teacher or an irresponsible parent. However, this does not mean that we must uncritically adopt the subject positions that are made available to us by dominant discourses.[1]

In large part, individuals actively choose and negotiate their identities but these choices are limited by the discourses that are available to them. For some, these choices are far more limited than for others because processes of identity construction take place within networks of power and differential access to economic, social and cultural resources (Bauman, 2004, p. 38). In addition, the process of identity construction is not a neutral or innocent one but involves us strategically positioning ourselves in relation to others. For example, we may choose to position ourselves in relation to hierarchies as relatively powerful or powerless, and incorporate what we believe to be our powerfulness or powerlessness as an important part of our identity. Moreover, processes of identification necessarily involve the construction of boundaries and exclusions. In defining who we think we are, we are inevitably separating ourselves off from what and who we are not – a process Skeggs (1997) refers to as "dis-identification." For example, Walkerdine *et al.*, in their psychosocial study of girls' identities have written about how some of the families they researched used discourses of respectability to differentiate themselves from others – "the 'scruffs', the rough working class, the 'underclass', the poor the homeless or the hopeless" (Walkerdine et al., 2001, p. 40). Whilst Mac an Ghaill (2000, p. 94) has described how the dominant heterosexual males in his school-based ethnography of the cultural production of masculinities disparaged their male peers who focused on their schoolwork, "redefining them as gay and 'poncy'. Disidentification with them enabled the heterosexual males to establish their own identities."

Identities are neither fixed nor one-dimensional. Rather they are fluid, contingent, plural and hybrid. That is to say, in actively constructing our identities, we draw on a range of representations and the way that we combine these representations is different in different contexts and at different times. The hybrid nature of identity means that new identities are frequently created through the combination of different discursive elements, as in the example of Meera Syal's novels about daughters of Indian migrants growing up in the UK or Chaim Potok's novels about children of Eastern European Jewish migrants growing up in New York.[2]

It is also important to note that identities can have a collective aspect to them. The answer to the question 'who do I think I am?' may often point to some group with whom we think we are identified. Collective identities may revolve around a religious or ethnic affiliation or a political or territorial one or a combination of these (Castells, 2004). During the 1970s the notion of collective identity acquired a particular salience because of the rise of new social movements around social categories including those relating to ethnicity, gender, sexuality and disability.

Because identities are about the way we think and the people we want to be, they incorporate a set of beliefs, values and commitments, and in some cases a corresponding set of attitudes and dispositions. This might, for example, include political, religious and moral beliefs. But it could also include more materialist kinds of commitments, for example, to certain patterns of consumption or lifestyles and aesthetic preferences. However, the complex and constructed nature of identity means that we cannot read off from people's roles or surface features how people identify themselves or what they think or believe. Simply because a teenage girl spends a lot of time applying make-up and ensuring she has the latest designer accessories, it doesn't follow that this forms an important part of her identity or that she has the stereotypical values and beliefs that some might associate with these practices (e.g. materialistic or superficial). Or just because someone has the role of a woman or a mother or a teacher it does not mean that these characteristics are a key part of their identity. It is important to underline this feature as identity is an area where it is notoriously easy to slide into reductionist and essentialist assumptions.

The final aspect of identity we want to draw attention to here is that we have the capacity to be reflexive about our identities. A number of commentators have argued that this feature of identity is characteristic of late or post-modernity – an era characterised by rapid change, substantial global movements of people, the growth of instant communication and virtual relationships, hyper-consumerism and so on. All of these things change our relationships with other people and ourselves and require continual reassessment of who we are and who we want to be. As Giddens puts it:

> One of the distinctive features of modernity is an increasing interconnection between the two extremes of extensionality and intentionality: globalising influences on the one hand and personal dispositions on the other (...). The more tradition loses its hold, and the more daily life is reconstituted in terms of the dialectical interplay of the local and the global, the more individuals are forced to negotiate lifestyle choices among a diversity of options (...). Reflexively organised life-planning (...) becomes a central feature of the structuring of self-identity (Giddens, 1991, p. 1,5, cited in Castells, 2004, p. 11).

Even if such accounts are exaggerated, and even though they may underplay inequalities in the distribution of opportunities for reflexivity or for realising reflexively made choices (Adams, 2006), we nonetheless think that reflexivity has become an important feature of the world in which we live.

MULTICULTURAL EDUCATION AS A RESPONSE TO THE QUESTION OF IDENTITY

There are many different definitions of multicultural education but here we are using the term in its broadest sense to include anti-racist and critical multicultural approaches as well as narrower conceptions of multicultural education. What these approaches have in common is that they are predicated on a critique of more traditional ethnocentric and patriarchal forms of education which, for example, assume and perpetuate the myth that the values associated with dominant groups are shared by everyone else, and which thereby marginalise and fail to respect the identities associated with subordinate groups. Multicultural education policies are underpinned by a commitment to valuing and affirming the diverse identities of learners and therefore to eroding inequalities in the respect that is afforded to people who are deemed to belong to different cultural groups. Translated into practice, these policies – depending upon how radical they are – can penetrate more or less deeply into the structures and cultures of schooling. Shallower forms of multiculturalism might involve the incorporation of relatively superficial elements of the cultural heritage of learners in ways that are symbolic, or even tokenistic, sometimes referred to as the three S's approach (with the three S's standing for saris, samosas and steel bands) – that is clothes, food and music being used to represent minority ethnic cultures in a superficial, fragmented and essentialised way and as a substitute for more open ended and deeper engagement with cultural complexity and hybridity (Troyna & Carrington, 1990). More far-reaching forms involve rethinking components of what Bernstein called the three message systems of education – curriculum, pedagogy and assessment – so as to ensure that they don't operate in unnecessarily exclusionary ways. There seem to be three broad strategies that have been adopted here, either separately or in combination – what we might call the three R's: representation, relevance and responsive pedagogies.

A concern for *representation* entails ensuring that any people represented visually or textually in the curriculum are culturally diverse. This includes a concern with avoiding particularly pernicious use of imagery such as that illuminated by Monique Scott (2005) in her study of human origins museum exhibits which sometimes identify the primitive with 'African' and advanced with 'white Anglo-Saxon'. But, at a deeper level, representation can also include making visible the historical and contemporary contribution of different cultural groups to the construction of knowledge. For example, this would mean European or American pupils learning that systems of numbering and mathematical procedures derive from Asian and African cultural traditions. This marks a shift from an emphasis on providing equal access for diverse ethnic groups to dominant conceptions of knowledge towards the recognition that knowledge itself is culturally constituted and that what is important therefore is not just access to the canon. A concern for *relevance* involves using examples in curricula which reflect learners' everyday lives and existing enthusiasms, such as linking the teaching of sound to the technologies of urban music-making. More generally, this entails broadening conceptions of the curriculum, for example, expanding the notion of science education to include education about the social and cultural dimensions of science that might engage students' interest more successfully than an exclusive emphasis on the science content. The inclusion of such elements helps to dissolve perceived boundaries between science and everyday life. *Responsive pedagogies* provide a bridge between the everyday language that learners bring with them and the language of the subject discipline. This involves teachers starting from and engaging with the everyday language, culture and practices of the learners and using that as the medium to support learning and induct students into the languages and practices of the official curriculum.

Multicultural education policies can take on relatively naïve and relatively sophisticated forms. The problem of *naivety* arises when we assume that strategies of relevance, representation and responsive pedagogies enable us to affirm diverse identities in unproblematic ways that do not take into account the many complications surrounding identity that we have just reviewed. In particular, there are two kinds of risk that arise from this kind of apparently straightforward affirmation of diverse identities – stereotyping and relativism. Stereotyping is often linked to an essentialist position and occurs when we attempt to read off people's identities from superficial features or partial knowledge of individuals such as their names or physical appearance, or when we assume that people will only want to learn about 'their' own culture – as in the case of a young black South Londoner in Back's (1996) study who is quoted as saying that he would like to be reading Shakespeare but in his youth centre's library he can only find books about Rastafarianism (cited in Barry, 2001, p. 235). The risk of cultural relativism is the risk of assuming that all identities deserve equal affirmation. For not all identities are equally worth respecting, and indeed some may be seen as harmful. For example, learners may operate with identities based on beliefs and dispositions that are damaging or demeaning to others, such as racism or sexism, and which construct unjustifiable exclusions. Or they may operate with identities that could be seen as self-limiting – for example, identities that are based on an anti-school stance.

Those operating towards the more *sophisticated* end of the spectrum are concerned to overcome some of these risks. More sophisticated policies start from an anti-essentialist position and aim to support approaches to teaching that resist making assumptions about people's identities. An anti-essentialist approach demands that teachers actively and continuously engage with the identity projects of learners by talking with and listening to them. Underlying this position are the beliefs that: a) if we are interested in affirming people's actual identities – i.e. who *they* think they are – rather than in relating to them through our own categorisations and generalisations, then we have to treat them as individuals not categories and this involves being ready to listen to and learn from them; and b) the discerning of people's actual identities isn't something that can be done on a one-off basis because, as we have discussed, identities are not fixed but are fluid, hybrid and evolve and are negotiated over time.

In addition, more sophisticated versions of multiculturalism do not seek to affirm all the identities of learners equally. Rather they acknowledge that some identities may be harmful and need to be challenged, for instance, as we have just noted, identities which embody racist or sexist commitments. For example, "critical multiculturalism" (May, 1999; Kincheloe & Steinberg, 1997), arguably the most sophisticated version of multiculturalism, aims to continually challenge and reshape people's identities, beliefs, values and commitments and to provide a space in which learners are enabled – through the three message systems of schooling – continually to question their assumptions, including their assumptions about who they are and what does and could matter to them. As Connolly puts it:

The challenge is more than simply fostering a learning environment that is non-discriminatory, free from stereotypes and which is multicultural (...) , it is also about conceiving of appropriate means of engaging (...) children more critically in the ways they are encouraged to think about and experience identity, difference and diversity (Connolly, 2003, p. 180).

This involves formulating approaches that enable educators to capitalise on and foster the capacity of learners to be reflexive about their identities. Part of this task is to encourage learners to differentiate between the value of different identities – i.e. to encourage what Fraser calls a "more differentiated politics of difference" (Fraser, 1997, p. 204). In plain terms, this means differentiating between aspects of identity that could be harmful, those that ought to be encouraged and those which are neither particularly harmful nor beneficial but which can just be enjoyed as manifestations of difference. This kind of approach is reflected in Sewell's (1997) advocacy of teaching young people to critique the values of anti-school identities that revolve around consumerism, materialism and gangster rap by, for example, using role models from the rap community who are ready to advocate for the importance of education.

Finally, more sophisticated multicultural policies arise from an acknowledgement that there is more to education than simply respecting people's identities and that an exclusive focus on identity can serve as a distraction from economic and political inequality and the politics of redistribution – and may even exacerbate these forms of inequality. From the critical multicultural perspective, what is needed is for educators to be enabled to facilitate the understanding and skills needed to challenge existing inequalities including those that operate around the social axes of class, race and gender. However, combining a respect for students' identities with a concern to promote greater equality is a major dilemma for educators and education policymakers committed to social justice – and it is one that we will return to below.

DILEMMAS

Whilst our summary of the more sophisticated versions of multiculturalism shows how these might overcome the limitations of more naïve versions, it also points to some of the tensions and dilemmas that arise from trying to put multicultural policies into practice. There are many tensions and dilemmas that we could consider here but due to space constraints we will focus on what we see as three key, interlocking dilemmas relating to pedagogy but which also have implications for curriculum and assessment: engaging with the full complexity of learners' identities vs. categorising them; recognising identities vs. problematising and disrupting them; and living with vs. challenging hierarchy.

Engaging with the full complexity of learner's identities vs. categorising them

In the preceding section we have talked about the risks of stereotyping – that is, where we make assumptions about people's identities on the basis of superficial facts about them – and we have suggested that this needs to be avoided through closer attention to the complexities of people's actual identities. In practice, however, should policymakers assume that such a stance is either possible or altogether desirable? One reason such a stance may be practically impossible arises from the complexities of identity rehearsed above. That is, given that identity is hybrid, plural and fluid, there is a fundamental problem for educators in determining the nature of an individual learner's identity, and the investment of time and energy needed to try to understand the identity of any individual learner should not be underestimated.

In addition, there are circumstances in which it makes some sense to rely on broad generalisations. For example, in preparing curriculum proposals or resources, we might reasonably ask whether the age of the audience was going to be 7 or 12. Lying behind this question would be certain generalisations about the interests and frames of reference of people of different ages. In making these generalisations the curriculum content will no doubt fail to please everyone. For instance, choosing to use examples from children's television programmes for teaching themes in citizenship education to 7 year olds, but not for teaching the 12 year olds, may in fact disappoint a number of participants. However, this doesn't undermine the value of using statistical generalisations, such as the ones we have just referred to (e.g. children of 7 are more likely to engage with television programme x whereas children of 12 are more likely to engage with television programme y) when trying to be sensitive to the needs of particular audiences. There are countless ways in which generalisations about age and gender or cultural and religious identities might be made by educators who are being conscientious and interested both in being effective and equitable in the way they plan and deliver their classes. The difficulty is that making cautious generalisations about your audience and stereotyping them often amount to the same thing. We can only strive therefore to limit the amount of stereotyping we do, as we cannot avoid it altogether if we want to develop forms of education which are relevant and responsive to learners.

Not only is generalising about identity unavoidable or sometimes useful, but it can be argued that it is also politically necessary as a means of challenging oppressive practices. For example, in order to challenge racism it is necessary to acknowledge and work with the different ways in which racism is perpetrated and experienced. This, in turn, demands that we use racialised categories and some of the generalisations associated with them, for example statistical generalisations that show the under-representation of black people in higher education or high status careers. Controversies about the use of ethnic monitoring for affirmative action represent a high profile example of this dilemma. On the one hand, the drive towards ethnic monitoring has in large part emerged from the demands of anti-racist campaigners and it is in this respect one expression of the importance and strategic role of mobilisation and solidarity around collective identities. On the other hand, ethnic monitoring necessarily involves oversimplifying in ways that do not reflect the complexity of people's actual identities. Policies that depend on ethnic monitoring, therefore, can constantly produce frustrations and frictions in the life worlds of the people they are supposed to benefit (Bonnett & Carrington, 2000) by making essentialist or reductionist assumptions and thereby 'fixing' people's identities. In other words, people do not necessarily identify with the groups they are classified by others as belonging to, and even when such group identity is a part of someone's self-identity, it may only be one small aspect of that identity. Gunaratnam makes a very closely related point in writing about what she calls the "treacherous bind" of racial categorisation:

> Naming and examining 'race' and ethnicity (often in order to uncover oppressive relations of power), always runs the risk of reproducing 'race' and ethnicity as essentialised and deterministic categories that can (re)constitute these very power relations. (Gunaratnam, 2003, pp. 32–33)

Recognising identities vs. problematising and disrupting them

In formulating policies it is also important be aware of the ways in which the pedagogies that are supported or discouraged by these policies impact on the identities of students. There are compelling reasons for developing pedagogic approaches that both recognise and challenge identities. Recognition is important, of course, on its own terms as well as for pedagogical reasons. Recognising a person's identity is to see them and treat them in the way they want to be seen and treated. It is what is entailed in treating everyone with equal respect. In addition, to fail to recognise people's identities can be damaging to their self-esteem and sense of dignity. As well as some of these intrinsic reasons, recognition makes good pedagogic sense as it increases the chance of learners feeling engaged, involved and interested.

On the other hand, as we have argued, all aspects of identity may not be equally deserving of respect and an important goal of education is to encourage people to continually question the beliefs, values and commitments that make up their identities. There are two broad sets of reasons to challenge aspects of individuals' identities. The first we have summarised above, namely that some aspects of identity can be seen as harmful to individuals because they are either needlessly self-limiting, or harmful to others (e.g. because they embody racist or sexist assumptions). The second reason is that certain identities can be harmful at a wider level because they reinforce structures of oppression. For example, we would argue that identities that revolve around a sense of marginalisation can paradoxically contribute to the production of the very marginalisation that is of concern. This is a contentious thing to argue and some would accuse us of adopting a victim-blaming stance but we believe the opposite danger is equally important, that is the danger of educators colluding with learners' acceptance of structures of oppression rather than helping learners find strategies to resist them individually and collectively.

These are some of the reasons why educators need to be encouraged to move beyond the mere recognition of identities. Indeed, as we have argued, education cannot simply focus on the recognition of identities because it is centrally concerned with the construction and co-construction of identities. People's identities evolve over time and at any one point in time contain elements that are backward looking and forward looking. To borrow Williams's (1981) formulation, we might say that any individual's identity is composed of dominant, residual and emergent strands. Educators, therefore, need to make choices about which strands of learners' identities to focus on and work with and making these choices is part of their responsibility for the co-construction of identity with learners. Hence, working with identity necessarily involves a series of balancing acts in which educators have to attach weight both to who learners think they are (i.e. to their dominant and residual identities) and who they might become (i.e. their emergent identities). This entails problematising and disrupting identities as well as recognising them. The dilemma here is how to problematise and disrupt identities without damaging learners' self-esteem and dignity which is in some measure dependent upon recognition.

Living with hierarchy vs. challenging hierarchy

As we have seen, multicultural education aims to disrupt existing hierarchies of value so that the perspectives of dominant groups are not valued more highly than those of subordinate groups. However, the business of disrupting hierarchies generates dilemmas.

In writing on social justice it is frequently implied that all hierarchies are bad. However, anyone not adopting an extreme relativist position needs to accept that some hierarchies are both inevitable and defensible. In accepting, for example, that some people are better than others at football, music or physics, we are subscribing to a hierarchy of standards. And if we are interested in promoting high quality football, music or physics, then we are committed to working with and seeing the value of some kinds of hierarchy. Similarly, if we think it matters that people working in particular occupations – for example, plumbers, doctors or teachers – have the necessary skills, then we have to subscribe to a hierarchy of standards in which not everyone will make the grade. However, often closely linked to this kind of standards hierarchy are other much more contentious hierarchies – for example, a hierarchy of esteem in which a person's performance in a narrow area is valued more highly than their personal qualities seen more holistically. Whilst it is reasonable for anyone with a concern for education to subscribe to hierarchies of standards, many would want to resist their elision with hierarchies of esteem. This example illustrates why it is important for policymakers to be reflexive about hierarchy. There are two issues we have in mind here. First, policymakers and practitioners need to find ways of supporting and working with hierarchies they feel are valuable whilst not reinforcing hierarchies that they believe should be challenged. Second, they need to decide how far they should accommodate themselves to existing hierarchies even where these are of a kind that they believe should be challenged.

The first issue arises when two kinds of hierarchy are closely allied – one that is deemed to be benign and one that is deemed malign – as set out above. In practical terms this arises at the classroom level, for example, when teachers try to give feedback to someone in a way that indicates the deficiencies in their work without suggesting that they are somehow themselves deficient. Anyone who has ever taught will recognise that this is one of the dilemmas at the heart of education. Educators constantly have to make choices between privileging a concern for the development of a learner's knowledge and understanding and privileging a concern for their feelings. Analogous dilemmas arise for policymakers because they too have to take an interest in devising systems that are based on recognising and organising education around differential standards but they also need to be conscious of the effects such systems can have both for individuals' sense of self worth and wellbeing and for the equality of respect afforded to people achieving different levels and kinds of success. Notorious examples of controversies in this area are policies around selection and streaming. Whilst the examples we have already mentioned of plumbing, teaching and medicine, seem to us to necessitate some form of selection at some point, more generally there are very difficult balancing acts built into designing forms of organisation that reflect and support the different strengths and interests of learners without at the same time generating hierarchies of esteem or status.

The second issue can be approached by asking how those committed to changing the world can support learners who are living in the world as it is. At the classroom level, many teachers may want to resist the hierarchies inherent in formalised systems of assessment. They may regard them as essentially measuring the wrong things, as giving a misleading picture of the full range of capabilities of students and as not reflecting the things that learners value about themselves. We could imagine, for example, that if they were in charge of the education system they would want to abolish them and put in place more formative and holistic models of assessment. Nonetheless, they are not in charge of the education system and need to decide how best to prepare their students. In effect, they have to choose between, on the one hand, compromising their educational philosophy in order to ensure the students get the credentials they need to progress on to further and higher education or to valued occupations and, on the other, potentially disadvantaging the students by refusing to be reigned in by the demands of the examination. However, there are different degrees of compromise between these two poles that are possible and teachers have to decide where to place their centre of gravity.

Things do not necessarily get easier even for those who are 'in charge of the education system'. A Minister of Education, for instance, may also be personally sympathetic to more formative and holistic models of assessment but he or she does not operate in a vacuum. Until employers and other powerful lobbies and stakeholders in society are also convinced of the superiority of such assessment models, any reforms in this direction are unlikely to gain legitimacy and therefore be successfully implemented. Under these circumstances, the Minister is effectively in the same situation as the classroom teacher in having to compromise between his or her own conception of what ought to be in students' best interests and what in practical terms is deemed to be in students' best interests by powerful interests in society. In effect, policymakers and practitioners sometimes have to choose between adhering to their ideals and conforming to dominant approaches which may, however wrongly, be of significantly more instrumental value (in terms of cultural and economic capital) to students.

IDENTITY AND EQUALITY

Cutting across, and in some ways underpinning, these three dilemmas is arguably a more fundamental dilemma which Fraser (1997) calls the redistribution-recognition dilemma (RRD). In essence this refers to the tension between two different kinds of equality. The first kind relates to the distribution of opportunities and material resources and the second to the equal recognition of people's identities.[3] Before concluding, we want to reflect back on the three dilemmas we have rehearsed above, try to illustrate their relevance to the RRD and underline the central significance of the RRD for education policy and practice in a multi-cultural society.

The tension between, on the one hand, using ethnic monitoring to combat the racism that leads to an unequal distribution of valued social and economic goods and, on the other hand, its tendency to contribute to essentialist and reductionist thinking and practice is a clear example of the RRD. In relation to our second dilemma – i.e. how far to recognise or problematise identities – we have argued that some identities have harmful consequences in that they have the potential to reinforce wider structures of oppression. One example of this is the anti-school identities we mentioned earlier. Placing emphasis on recognising and valuing anti-school identities could reinforce processes of marginalisation from school and the differentiated patterns of attainment and economic wellbeing consequent upon such marginalisation. A comparable example, discussed by Barry, relates to policies for how language is taught in schools. Although it is important for schools to recognise and value non-standard variants of the dominant language if they are to treat all students with respect, there are limits to how far it is responsible for schools to place equal value on standard and non-standard variants. As Barry (2001, p. 324) has argued:

> There is no escaping the conclusion that, if they are not to short change their pupils, the schools should try to ensure that by the time they leave they are equipped with a command of the standard form of the language.

The third dilemma concerns the tension between living with and challenging hierarchy. Whilst accepting that policymakers and practitioners – and indeed students – might usefully contest and disrupt many of the hierarchies that are embedded in educational processes, we have argued that there are limits to the desirability of challenging hierarchies for both instrumental and intrinsic reasons. Looking at the question purely instrumentally, education provides forms of cultural capital that create life chances for students. This means that anyone concerned with distributive justice has some obligation to ensure that all students gain the knowledge that is valued by dominant groups in society and which provides access to socially valued opportunities, positions and goods. However, in many instances this knowledge and the goods associated with it are not merely of instrumental value but have intrinsic value in that they can enable people to live richer, more fulfilling lives and enable people to participate in a broader range of social and cultural activities.

For both instrumental and intrinsic reasons, therefore, we would argue that there are limits to how far education systems should compromise on transmitting and inducting children into official knowledges for the sake of showing respect for the 'street knowledge' that children bring to school. However, as we have made clear, we don't see this as an either-or choice, but rather a question of operating with both official and unofficial knowledges at the same time. In practice, this would mean classroom teachers being continuously engaged in working with students to make complex discriminations, neither assuming that unofficial knowledge is less worthy than the contents of the formal curriculum, nor assuming that these things are necessarily of equal value. Part of the job of education is to give learners the resources to make such discriminations on a case-by-case basis informed by an in-depth understanding of a broad range of examples. This, of course, gives scope for students to construct evaluative hierarchies that are different from those of the system in which they are educated. The crucial point that needs to be made here, however, is that some hierarchies are not only inevitable but in some key respects desirable.

These considerations thus highlight the impossibility of achieving wholesale educational equality in every respect. This impossibility arises from the fact that there are different dimensions of equality and it is this insight that is expressed in Fraser's phrase the RRD. As Fraser argues, in many cases the remedies for distributive inequality are incompatible with those for recognitional inequality. In addition, eliding the two kinds of inequality can be harmful. Specifically, turning too quickly to a presumed misrecognition of minority cultures as an explanation for social or educational inequalities (such as differences in academic attainment) risks both a) reinforcing pathological readings and b) obscuring real economic injustices that may be responsible for the inequalities. Likewise, strategies such as affirmative action, which rest upon the use of cultural labels to seek to rectify inequalities of access to high status goods, can serve to disguise underlying structural inequalities by superficially "changing the color of inequality" (Gitlin, 1995, cited in Barry, 2001, p. 326) rather than dismantling the structures themselves. In both of these cases, the 'cultural group' is being used as a proxy for need, thereby distorting perceptions both of 'cultural groups', by pathologising them, and of the real basis of need, i.e. material disadvantage.

CONCLUSION

In this chapter we have set out some of the complexities associated with the nature of identity and some of the complexities related to educational responses to identity. One consequence of our argument is the need to rule out two extremes. First, it is untenable to ask educators to ignore the identities of learners and to strive to teach in an identity-blind way. It is arguable that educators have to operate with some constructions of learners' identities whether or not these are soundly based. However, at the other extreme it does not make sense for education to be defined around an unqualified affirmation of learners' identities. This is not only because of the practical difficulties of so doing but also because of the harms that such a stance might produce. One important facet of this tension between recognising and challenging learners' identities that we have sought to highlight here are the competing values of distributive and recognitional forms of equality. That is, as we have argued, one of the justifiable constraints on stressing the recognition of identities is the potential for this to undermine the necessary conditions for other forms of equality. This is especially important because there is a danger, as a number of commentators have stressed (e.g. Barry, 2001; Fraser, 1997), of recognitional justice undermining what many see as more basic forms of social injustice relating in particular to structural and material disadvantage. So, according to this account, what policymakers and practitioners are left with is the task of continuously navigating a route through this difficult terrain. This will necessarily involve grappling with the many moral and political dilemmas, such as the ones discussed in this paper, that arise from taking seriously both the value of identity and the value of other educational and political goals which can sometimes conflict with valuing identity.

Policymakers, with support from policy scholars and others, need to be reflexive about such conflicts inherent in working with diverse student identities and to be aware that policies which tackle certain forms of inequality or misrecognition may lead to other forms. The role for policymakers here, as elsewhere, is neither to evade the dilemmas surrounding identity by conceiving of their work in technicist terms, nor to operate with a simple template or vision of what is for the best but rather to make explicit the range of competing value sets that are relevant to evaluating policy effects and to try and self-consciously and self-critically steer the least worst course through the dilemmas we have rehearsed in this chapter. In calling for policy sociologists to be more ethically reflexive, we are essentially saying that we think they should be prepared to lend a hand here. We hope that, by helping to set out and articulate the three dilemmas reviewed above along with the underlying tensions between identity and equality, we have contributed to building an analytical framework that might help in this difficult task.

NOTES

[1] In drawing attention to the role of discourse in the construction of identities, we are not adopting a strong social constructionist stance. Specifically, we are not claiming that there is no objective reality that is being represented by these discourses, but only that it is through discourse that certain features of the objective reality are made significant. For example, in our society it is common for people to identify themselves in terms of their ethnicity, but it is rare for people to identify themselves in terms of eye colour or foot size even though these are equally part of the objective reality.

[2]   For example, see Syal's (1997) *Anita and Me* and Potok's (1970) *The Chosen.*
[3]   It is important to note that there has been a critique of this distinction (see, for example, Bulter, 1997) and although there is insufficient space to go into these debates here, we should note that in making use of this distinction we are essentially drawing a conceptual distinction between two different facets of justice and are not wanting to imply that in practice redistribution and recognition are not inextricably bound together in various ways.

REFERENCES

Adams, M. (2006). Hybridising habitus and reflexivity: Towards an understanding of contemporary identity? *Sociology, 40*(3), 511–528.

Back, L. (1996). *New ethnicities and urban culture: Racisms and multiculture in young lives.* London: UCL Press.

Barry, B. (2001). *Culture and equality.* Cambridge: Polity.

Bowe, R., & Ball, S. J. with Gold, A. (1992). *Reforming education and changing schools: Case studies in policy sociology.* London: Routledge.

Bauman, Z. (2004). *Identity.* Cambridge: Polity.

Bonnett, A., & Carrington, B. (2000). Fitting into the categories or falling between them? Rethinking ethnic classification. *British Journal of Sociology of Education, 21*(4), 487–500.

Butler, J. (1997). Merely cultural. *Social Text, Queer Transexions of Race, Nation and Gender,* (52/53), 265–277.

Castells, M. (2004). *The power of identity: The information age - economy, society and culture* (Vol. 2, 2nd ed.). Oxford: Blackwell.

Connolly, P. (2003). The development of young children's ethnic identities. In C. Vincent (Ed.), *Social justice, education and identity.* London: RoutledgeFalmer.

Fraser, N. (1997). *Justice interruptus.* New York: Routledge.

Giddens, A. (1991). *Modernity and self-identity: Self and society in the late modern age.* Cambridge: Polity Press.

Gitlin, T. (1995). *The twilight of common dreams: Why America is wracked by culture wars.* New York: Henry Holt.

Hall, S. (2001). *The multicultural question.* Milton Keynes: Open University.

Kincheloe, J., & Steinberg, S. (1997). *Changing multiculturalism.* Buckingham: Open University Press.

Mac an Ghaill, M. (2000). The cultural production of English masculinities in late modernity. *Canadian Journal of Education, 23*(2), 88–101.

May, S. (Ed.). (1999). *Critical multiculturalism: Rethinking multicultural and anti-racist education.* London: Falmer Press.

Potok, C. (1970). *The chosen.* London: Penguin.

Scott, M. (2005). Writing the history of humanity: The role of museums in defining origins and ancestors in a transnational world. *Curator, 48*(1), 74–85.

Sewell, T. (1997). *Black masculinities and schooling.* Stoke on Trent: Trentham.

Skeggs, B. (1997). *Formations of class and gender.* London: Sage.

Syal, M. (1997). *Anita and me.* London: Flamingo.

Troyna, B., & Carrington, B. (1990). *Education, racism and reform.* London & New York: Routledge.

Walkerdine, V., Lucey, H., & Melody, J. (2001). *Growing up girl.* Basingstoke: Palgrave.

Williams, R. (1981). *The sociology of culture.* Chicago: University of Chicago Press.

Gunaratnam, Y. (2003). *Researching 'race' and ethnicity: Methods, knowledge and power.* London: Sage.

FURTHER READINGS

Barry, B. (2001). *Culture and equality*. Cambridge: Polity.
Fraser, N. (1997). *Justice interruptus*. New York: Routledge.
Hall, S. (2001). *The multicultural question*. Milton Keynes: Open University.
May, S. (Ed.). (1999). *Critical multiculturalism: Rethinking multicultural and anti-racist education*. London: Falmer Press.
Vincent, C. (Ed.). (2003). *Social justice, education and identity*. London: RoutledgeFalmer.

Alan Cribb
Centre for Public Policy Research
King's College London

Sharon Gewirtz
Centre for Public Policy Research
King's College London

THOMAS S. POPKEWITZ

INCLUSION AND EXCLUSION AS DOUBLE
GESTURES IN POLICY AND EDUCATION SCIENCES

INTRODUCTION

The chapter gives attention to the systems of reason that govern policy (Popkewitz, 1991, 2008).[1] At first glance it might seem odd to place the word "govern" as a verb that acts on the noun "policy"; one might say putting the cart before the horse. Policy is supposed to govern and not be governed! My reversal of the word order is to focus on the (re)reading of policy by directing attention to the principles (system of reason) that order and classify what is "seen", talked about, and acted upon. That is, the "thought" about schooling is not merely a thing of logic, or pure operations of the mind and "thought" that secure desired outcomes. The objects of teaching and learning in schooling are assembled through historical processes that shape and fashion what can be thought, done, and hoped for. Contemporary policy about equity and democracy, for example, are not merely commitments about what should occur. The policy discourses are made "reasonable" in grid or the weaving of different practices in which equity is connected with and acted on as children's capabilities and qualities of learning and problem solving; and through psych-social theories about classroom communication, participation in 'communities', and cultural diversity, among others. Re-reading policy is to focus on how the objects of schooling are given intelligibility and "reasonableness" through the historically produced rules and standards (the reason) that govern policy.

The political of schooling is embodied in this governing through "reason." Foucault's (1979) "governmentality" and Rancière's (2004) "partitioning of sensibilities", for example, direct attention to how systems of "reason" function to constitute the problems addressed in social practices, as well as enunciating principles to order solutions and plans for action, thus interning and enclosing what is (im)possible. But the political is not only in ordering conduct; the very principles generated about the child and teaching embody a particular modern comparative style of thought (Popkewitz, 2008). If I take the notion of lifelong learner in contemporary pedagogy, it embodies the cultural thesis about life as a continuous problem solving and learning activity. The characteristics of the lifelong learner, however, do not stand alone. The qualities and characteristics of the lifelong learner are inscribed comparatively with those capabilities that reside outside its spaces about normalcy and growth to abject and exclude.

This chapter explores the "reason" of policy as simultaneous gestures of inclusion, abjection, and exclusion. The first section outlines principles of inclusion

M. Simons, M. Olssen and M.A. Peters (eds.), Re-Reading Education Policies: A Handbook Studying the Policy Agenda of the 21ˢᵗ Century, 531–548.

and exclusion in the central policy research approach, what can be called 'the equity problematic' (Popkewitz & Lindblad, 2000). I use problematic to consider how particular rules and standards order and overlap in the methods of science, concepts and 'theories' of schooling and research. The equity problematic entails the concern with increasing the representation of marginalized groups; yet its style of thought ironically generates comparative cultural theses that excludes in the impulse to include. The second section gives attention to the sciences of education. The education sciences are technologies historically designed to change society by changing people. That design brings forth double gestures that differentiates and divides populations. The third and fourth sections explore the inscription of difference in pedagogy and its sciences. Pedagogy is likened to the Puritan teaching as a 'converting ordinances' designed to save the soul. Science is to design that soul, spoken about today in the name of democratic progress. The designing, however, inscribes double gestures. There is the cultural thesis of the lifelong learner, a cosmopolitan individual whose participation enables community, progress and human emancipation. And in the designing of the cosmopolitanism of the child are fears of 'Others', the dangerous populations who threaten the envisioned emancipatory future. The comparative designing "reason" of policy and pedagogy, I conclude, naturalizes the unequal status quo in the search for equality.

The (re)reading of policy critically examines "what is accepted as authority through a critique of the conditions of what is known, what must be done, what may be hoped" (Foucault, 1984, p. 38). This (re)reading of policy can be contrasted to studies of Neoliberalism[2], a topoi of contemporary policy analysis that takes conservative economics of the 1970s and the policies of the World Bank, Reaganism and Thatcherism of the 1980s, as a marker of an epoch that explains the 'cause' of inequalities and lack of democratization. The policy analysis undertaken in this chapter is, at one level, about 'the reason' through which the theories, programs and debates about Neoliberalism are framed and given a 'reasonableness'. The concern is succinctly expressed in Hultqvist (1998) study of contemporary Swedish school reforms. He argued that to understand adequately policies of decentralization and privatization of the 1990s considered as Neoliberal requires inquiring genealogically into the uneven historical processes that makes possible such "reasoning", with Hultqvist finding its genealogy in the 'decentered' child in the pedagogical reforms of the 1970s.

EQUITY IN SCHOOL: ITS STUDY AND THE PRACTICES OF 'THOUGHT' IN SCHOOL REFORM

A few years ago, a colleague of mine, Sverker Lindblad and I (2000) did a review of research on educational governance and social exclusion. The review sought to consider how broader commitments to equity and democratization were given expression through research practices. I will quickly summarize this review to consider its limits and to suggest a different 'reading' of the problem of social inclusion and exclusion.

The equity problematic entails research directed toward interventions to increase social participation through changes in schooling. The basic premise is that research identifies the factors that increase or hinder who benefits or is handicapped through existing school programs. The assumption of research is that once the factors and the mechanism of inequity are made apparent, more efficient policies and programs are possible to bring forth progress related to a more democratic society. Four principles of that orders the equity problematic are discussed to consider the rules and standards by which research 'problems', conceptualizations, and the practices of finding solutions for a more participatory society are constituted.

First is *the politics of representation*. Policy and research embody categories of populational groups that are identified as excluded and in need of programs of intervention. The assumption underlying the research is that measures, correlations and patterns of practices can indicate where intervention programs are necessary to create greater representation. The increase in representation is taken as the indicator of a more equitable and just society; hence the term 'politics of representation'.

Populations of groups margined in society are formed as the categories of subjects for determining equity, such as those of immigrants, the poor, ethnic, and disadvantaged. The population categories entail overlapping distinctions. For example, 'immigrants' might include different groups of Asians, religious groups and/or African. Further, the category of immigrant is connected with other social, psychological and school distinctions to form particular determinant classifications that overlap with intervention policies and programs. Statistical reporting in cross-national reports of education, for example, compare different characteristics of populations to school performance indicators; comparing ethnic, racial groups and gender populations to norms about school attendance, achievement levels, and graduation rates, and participation in curriculum areas given high priority, such as mathematics and sciences. Qualitative research provides narratives of the interactions, communications and cultures of classrooms to understand how bias is mobilized to prevent inclusive principles.

Second, change is finding *the right mixture of policies to produce an inclusionary institution and thus eliminate (at least theoretically) exclusion and inequities*. The sciences of schooling, as were the reform projects in early 20th century, are to identify the correct design to plan school reform (Popkewitz, 2008). In the past and today, research programs in North American and Northern Europe align with state initiatives to identify the most effective programs to deal with questions of poverty and the perceived moral disorder produced by urban conditions. The watchword of U.S. reform policies and research is identifying programs about 'what work' in achieving a more equitable school and thus society. The U.S. governmental website called "What Works" cites research of 'proven' reform programs that can be 'replicated' to all schools (http://www.whatworks. ed.gov/). Other researchers draw on communication theories and constructivist psychologies to design a continuous system of monitoring and evaluating reforms so the future child can be more humane and the world more progressive. That research re-visions concepts of early 20th-century Russian Marxist psychologist Lev Vygotsky and the American liberal philosopher-psychologist John Dewey into constructivist psychologies about individual problem solving and 'community' collaboration goals (Popkewitz, 1998a). U. S. reforms express the democratic ideal of schooling as 'all' children, parents, and stakeholders participating. The measure of this equity is said to be closing achievement gaps or school university partnerships to enable participation of groups previously excluded.

Science is said to be service of democratic ideals, a phrase that emerges in American Progressivism at the turn of the last century. The equity problematics overlaps with policy to provide 'useful' knowledge for that goal. Research about What Works captures the more general principle that scientific knowledge is to be useful to achieving the purposes and intentions of policy.

The term 'useful' implies that there is a consensus about what type of action is necessary to produce a more progressive society. There are different dimensions given to the term 'useful'. The premise of 'use' is embodied in the teacher asking 'What does this research tell us for improving classroom teaching?' The university researcher is heard to say 'How can this research be made relevant to what teachers do in the classroom?' The political activist implores that research serves as an agent of change and social reconstruction. The unspoken principle of this search for 'use' is that knowledge is the servant of democracy by giving agency and enabling progress. Historically a contentious assumptions but 'facts' do not intrude into these practices.

Third, inclusion and exclusion are *separate categories in planning.* The game is sum-zero; to create inclusion eliminates exclusion. This unspoken assumption is in US legislation entitled "No Children Left Behind." The phrase symbolizes the goal of an equal unified whole as all children succeed. If we take the phrase that 'all children learn' in school reforms, the phrase 'all' implies this hope of future unity and harmony. Simultaneously, I argue later, the 'all' erases differences as the proper application of procedures and planning produces sameness as there is only one 'all children'. Diversity is difference within the sameness, and the problem of research is to produce the unity implied in the phrasing of 'all children'.

Fourth, there is a premise that pedagogical change and research is *to change people in order to change society.* Although there are different notions of the qualities of people to be changed among conservatives and critical pedagogies, they overlap in the framework of reason about planning. I approach this notion of planning through out this discussion through examining its inscription of shepherds and as the fear of democracy.

The following sections explores the principles of the equity problematic as it circulates, first historically to connect policy and research in designing society through designing the child; and as inscriptions of exclusions in efforts for equity and democracy. The chapter then explores contemporary policy and research to examine concretely the cultural theses through which inclusive impulses embody dividing practices in pedagogy.

EDUCATION SCIENCES AND THE MAKING OF SOCIETY BY MAKING THE CHILD

How can the equity problematic be understood historically? How are its different proposals, plans, and solutions given intelligibility and plausibility even in its critiques? To consider these questions, this section first considers that the planning to change people and social conditions was not planned but an effect of power. Second, policy and research are discussed as inscribing comparative cultural theses. Efforts to produce equity through greater participation of different populations, I will argue, inscribes difference in its impulse for inclusion. Differences are embodied in the distinctions and divisions generated about who the child is and should be.

Schooling, the Citizen, and the Double Qualities of Science

Let me start with a simple historical claim. Modern schooling is a practice to *make society by making the child*. The founding figures of the American and French Republics recognized this transformation in the politics of the new nations. Democratic participation was 'something that had to be solicited, encouraged, guided, and directed' (Cruikshank, 1999, p. 97). The maintenance of the nation was dependent on making the citizen who was self-governing and participating in social affairs.

One might say that the problem of social (re)construction of society through schooling was placed at the foot of the child. Thomas Jefferson, a founder of the American republic and the third president, spoke of Enlightenment cosmopolitan principles of a society guided by the reason and science as providing a transcendent ethic of human rights and hospitality to others. But this citizen of the nation was ironic. The universal characteristics of the cosmopolitan citizen who acted for the progress for the whole of humanity paradoxically reinserted the provincialism and localism that the enlightenments were to replace. The cosmopolitanism was instantiated in national narratives of civic virtue and individual responsibility (Popkewitz, 2008).

The sciences of schooling had a central place in planning for the orderly development of society at the turn of the 20th century. Science had *polysemic qualities*. It was to master the principles that structured social conditions so that they could be designed through reforms. Theories and methodologies of investigation in the formation of the social sciences were to enable policy and programs for the administration of change. With the inventions of the modern sciences of psychology and sociology, for example, northern European and U.S. Protestant social reformers sought to understand the conditions of the city in order to rectify the debilitating effects of urbanization and industrialization on the new poor and immigrants. In effect, the cosmopolitan urbane of the city was to rationalize and civilize the life of the urban populations.[3]

The planning of the social and education sciences embodied the belief in the self-endowed reason of individuals. That reason, however, could not be left to chance. It needed to be specifically constructed through devices of a regulated society. The faith in human sciences crossed the North Atlantic, from the *Fabian*

Society to the *German Evangelical Social Congress*, the *French Musée Social*, and the *Settlement House* movements in many northern European and North American countries. Internationally, the new heterogeneous school reform movements, variously called the 'New Education Fellowship,' 'Active Pedagogy,' 'The New School,' and 'Progressive Education' that promoted school reforms at the turn of the 20th century made the sciences of pedagogy as central to future progress.

Science was not only practice of research. A general notion of science was brought into cultural theses to order how individuals plan everyday life and act on their experiences. John Dewey's problem solving, Hall's child development, and Thorndike's connectionist are different examples of the more insertion of scientific 'methods' in ordering thought, behaviors and individual actions. Pragmatism, for example, brought elite notions of science into pedagogy as strategies for children to observe and interpret experiences as problem solving activities directed to the future. The ordered life was to be rational and disciplined.

The notions of science in pedagogy had less to do with actual practices of the physics or history. School subjects formed around pedagogical problems of governing the child. The rationalizing processes were administrative practices related to cultural theses that linked the liberty and freedom of cosmopolitan child with collective norms and values of the nation (Popkewitz, 2008). Today that inscription of science in pedagogy is talked about as the Learning Society and Information Society with different 'constructivists' pedagogical theories and concepts about motivation, learning, achievement, problem solving, and community. The rules and standards of 'reason' go unscrutinized in pedagogical designs.

Inclusion, Difference and Threats to the Stability of the Future

The polysemic qualities of science bring us closer to thinking about policy, pedagogy and research.

First, the pedagogical sciences are responses to things of the world of schooling; yet the intelligibility given to talk about and "see" the child of schooling are assembled in cultural theses about 'reason' and 'reasonable people'. G.Stanley Hall at the turn of the century, for example, posed the notion of adolescence to think about the difficulties posed to the school by its new urban and immigrant populations. Adolescence, however, was more than finding a way to interpret and classify events. Thinking about the child's development and growth gave expression to a cultural thesis about modes of living. Further, the notion of adolescent had a looping effect as the category made things (Hacking, 1995, 2006). Adolescent became a classificatory scheme that ordered and classified who children are and will be through various theories, programs, and narratives.

Second, the pedagogical theories and its empirical substantiations are posited as universal in the sense that concepts and human qualities seems to have no particular historical space. Learning theories, for example, are imagined as if they apply everywhere there is a child. Nationality, ethnicity, gender, for example, matter only as they relate to some points of correspondence to the theory itself.

But the rules and standards were not universal. They are historically particular: to talk about child's learning through problem solving and 'constructing knowledge' embodies a particular way to organize one's biography and the planning of the self in a logic of time (Popkewitz, 2008).

Third, the sciences of pedagogy inscribe salvation themes of progress and redemption. In northern European and North American schools, redemption is of the soul. Comte expressed this when he spoke of positivist science as the new religion of society. The salvation themes were brought into the planning of late 19th century human sciences through the formation of the modern welfare state. The planning of science are to find solutions that remove obstacles to progress and enables 'better' people and society. This function of science can be said as planning to change society through changing people.

But life and human intentions are never that easy. Nor are the complexities of the human sciences just about discovering the 'right' knowledge. The very concepts of the citizen presuppose in theories of human development and social progress entails double gestures of inclusion and exclusion. Pedagogy, I discuss below, is to make the cosmopolitanism of the child who problem solves as lifelong learning; that cultural thesis differentiates the child who is disadvantaged and 'left behind' as threatening the future possibilities of progress.

The comparative instantiation in policy and research entails a particular system of reason of Northern American and European Enlightenments which mutated in schooling and its sciences. The rules and standards of the system of reason entailed a particular analytical consciousness that could see things in its parts that relate to some unity of the whole. That analytic, the way of ordering and classifying, made modern science possible. Its practices hierarchized things of nature into related and comparable parts from which to think of functions as they relate to the whole. The classification and differentiation were not only about understanding 'nature'. People were placed into a continuum of value and hierarchy that compared, for example, civilizations from those advanced to less advanced and uncivilized.

This comparativeness entailed the finitude in which qualities and characteristics of people are placed in an ordered temporality. Time was no longer the province of God but given a secular place. Modern historicism appears, for example, to enable thinking about the change and progress of the human life and things of the world. Historicism involved notions of progress that placed people and societies in a sequence of developments of 'civilizations' that started in Ancient Greece or Rome and arrived at the present. Time is also brought into ordering and classifying the inner qualities of the child. Studies about child development, readiness and measurements of achievement places children in continua of values related to time.

The comparative distinctions embody hopes and fears that order life in temporal sequences. The early school reformers talked about barbarians, backward children, and savages. Contemporary school policy and research have different comparative distinctions to express difference, such as the disadvantaged, the at-risk, and the immigrant, the poor, among others. The recognition of the excluded child to be included inscribed processes of abjection through generating principles of difference.

The gestures of recognition, difference, and the abjection are part of the same phenomenon in inclusion and exclusion overlap in policy, research and schooling.

I use the notion of abjection as a concept to describe the complexity of what is both inside and outside, both rescued and cast out as threats to cosmopolitanism, and thus as the unlivable spaces classified as moral disorder and deviance (see Shimakawa, 2002; also Kowalczyk & Popkewitz, 2006; Popkewitz, 2008). Abjection entails producing kinds of people whose differences are formed through overlapping distinctions that come together to form determinate categories about kinds of people (Hacking, 1986). The disadvantaged and urban child, for examples, are human kinds as different categories of difference are connected; such as psychological terms about the child's lack of esteem, attention deficit disorder, poor study habits, and impulse-related disorders; and sociological/cultural terms about juvenile delinquency, 'dysfunctional' families and communities.

The abjections embody different layers of fear. There are fears that if the right mixture of strategies and programs are not found, then the people and society will not be rescued. These fears travel in policy statements related to the equity problematic. And fears circulate about the qualities of those to be rescued as threatening the stability and harmony of the unity of society. The (re)reading of policy, if I summarize at this point, is not merely reading policy. The principles generated to order reflection and action about the child circulate in multiple practices to provide intelligibility to what is said and acted on. The previous sections about the equity problematic, for example, argued that particular assumptions about policy and research shaped and fashioned comparative cultural theses. In the following sections, I pursue this reading in pedagogy through first considering the relation of pedagogical policy and research as 'converting ordnances' in the making of the child. I then focus on contemporary reforms as differentiating and dividing cultural theses – the lifelong learner who embodies a particular cosmopolitanism and its Others, the disadvantaged, immigrant, and urban child 'left behind'.

PEDAGOGY AND SCIENCE: CONVERTING ORDINANCES/COMPARATIVE INSCRIPTIONS

The comparative quality of (the) reason of policy can be explore through thinking about pedagogy as a 'converting ordinance', drawing the Puritan phrase about the reading as the evangelizing and calculated design on the souls of their readers. Drawing on John Calvin's notion of curriculum vitæ or 'a course of life,' Puritan education was the persistent preparation for a conversion experience that gave the individual moral behavior (McKnight, 2003). That preparation in U.S. schools in the 19th century was linked to the Puritan's mission of creating the greater corporate mission in the 'New Israel'. The method of reason was to build revelatory, spiritual fulfilment. Community was part of this course of life or one's curriculum vitæ. The individual's freedom was indivisible from the shared cultural world that gave unity to all of human kind (ibid., p. 44).

The converting ordinances of pedagogy did not leave the ordered life to mere chance. The problem of pedagogy was one of design. Whereas design was a word that spoke of what God gave to human affairs in the First Coming of Puritan theology, design in pedagogy was to intervene and change the child as if it was divinely ordained. One can compare the Calvinist themes of salvation in pedagogy in Switzerland and the U.S. with those in Lutheran traditions in Germany to consider differences in the 'converting ordinances' that pedagogy embodies. The German *Geist* or spirit of the nation and *Bildung* placed the individual in a different relationship that links the spirituality of the nation with the upbringing and moral character of the individual (Tröhler, 2006).

Pedagogy is not longer spoken of directly as converting ordinances but are strategies and practices directed to the 'soul'. That soul is embodied in theories of the actor and agency. Horace Mann (1867), an early 19th century leader in the American school movements, talked about 'the promise of the future' by invoking the pact of the republican government to promote the public good as children acquire knowledge. This pact was embodied in pedagogy. The cosmology of a religious soul was replaced with teaching to instantiate the spiritual/moral life of the republic, shaped and fashioned through the principles generated about the rational, active child. Contemporary research about teaching and teacher education talks about the soul in reform projects to change the attitudes, dispositions and sensitivities of teachers in the fulfilment of school reforms. The soul in conception if not name!

Psychology is central to the converting ordinances. If I focus on Europe and North America, psychology opened up the interior of the child as the site of calculation and intervention in pedagogy. Speculative and analytical psychologies were replaced with experimental psychologies in sites as diverse as Russia, Germany and the U.S. From the beginning of modern schooling, pedagogy and its sciences of education, *Ó* (2003) argues, was designed to act on the spirit and the body of children and the young. Examining French and Portuguese pedagogy at the turn of the 20th century, *Ó* explores the method of the pedagogical sciences as observing and making visible the inner physical and moral life in order to map the spirituality of the educated subject ('the human soul'). The French pedagogue, Gabriel Compayré in 1885 asserted that pedagogy is an applied psychology and the sources of all the sciences "that are related to the moral faculties of man; pedagogy contains all the parts of the soul and must use always psychology" (cited in *Ó*, 2003, p. 106). The purpose was, however, not to find God but to provide knowledge that helps to free man through the path of reason.

The social sciences were to bring a moral order life through its two overlapping projects. One was the studying of behaviour, the mind, and social interaction to render the characteristics of the child and teacher visible and amenable to government. The other characteristic of science concerned its theories and methods that generated cultural theses of modes of living. Learning was not only about what was known but how that knowing is to be effected as principles in daily life. The agentive individual was to live as a planned biography ordered by the calculated rules and standards of reflection and action.[4]

CULTURAL THESES AND ABJECTIONS IN POLICY AND RESEARCH

If pedagogy and its sciences are considered as converting ordinances, it is possible to historically explore the comparative qualities of the practices of 'reason' in school reform. The converting ordinances of pedagogy, first, help to direct attention to the salvation narratives of schooling in classifying the capabilities and qualities of the child. Pedagogy, for example, gives expression to the hope of the future that is today expressed through the cultural thesis of the lifelong learner. That thesis, however, simultaneously engenders registers of fears about threats to the envisioned future, - *disadvantaged and immigrant child* who is 'left behind' in the race for the cosmopolitan's success, happiness, and self-realization. The generating of difference and fears are not the intention of reforms or the sciences but are embodied in the "reason" that orders what is said, talked about, and acted on. The two cultural theses of hope and danger, I argue in this section, are part of the same phenomenon. Thus, the reading of policy is to explore the ways in which recognition, difference, and abjection is produced in schooling. This rereading of policy is alters what is studied and sought from what I previously discussed as the equity problematic. The latter differentiates inclusion and exclusion as if it is a sum-zero game – policy can eliminate exclusion through the right mixtures of policies and practices.

The Hope of the Future: The Unfinished Cosmopolitan as the Lifelong Learner

The term 'lifelong learner' appears in worldwide reforms about the new conditions of the Knowledge Society that the school must respond to (Popkewitz, 2008; also see Fejes & Nicoll, 2008). A Google search entails an enormous number of pages and again appears as a category in Wikipedia. The phrase crosses broad social and political arenas and geographical locations. European, U.S, Mexican, and Taiwanese school and teacher education reforms, for example, evoke the term *lifelong learner* as the embodiment of who a person is and should be.

What is the cultural thesis about lifelong learners as a mode of life? Its converting ordinance directs attention to a life that never finishes in the pursuit of knowledge and innovation. Choice and flexibility are the goal of life. The project of life is to design one's biography as a continuous movement from one social sphere to another, as if life were a planning workshop that had a value in and of itself. This movement of continuous innovation, flexibility and choice produced a cosmopolitanism that is never finished.

The seduction of this mode of living is its political register of salvation that talks about giving 'voice' and empowerment by working continuously on self improvement and self-actualization. Problem solving and working collaboratively in communities are the modes of living through which personal fulfilment is achieved. Stories of the problem solving child, for example, are about life faced with constant changes. The child acts autonomously (seemingly) and responsibly (hopefully) in continuous decision making.

The cultural thesis can be thought of as an unfinished cosmopolitanism. It brings to bear Enlightenment images and narratives about the universal ethic of reason and rationality in the pursuit of progress and freedom. That thesis is not about transcendental quality but entails particular historical assemblies and connections as it moves along different ideological axes. It is spoken of as an entrepreneurial individual that seems to capture Neo-liberalism and its emphasis on individual interests as forming the social good. The lifelong learner is also spoken about in a practice of social reconstruction. Hargreaves (2003), for example, rejects the materialism and marketization of contemporary neo-liberal reform in favor of school reforms to prepare for the future of a knowledge society that "is really a learning society [that] process(es) information and knowledge in ways that maximize learning, stimulate ingenuity and invention and develop the capacity to initiate and cope with change" (Hargreaves, 2003, p. xviii). The child inhabits the Learning Society with "a cosmopolitan identity which shows tolerance of race and gender differences, genuine curiosity toward and willingness to learn from other cultures, and responsibility toward excluded groups within and beyond one's society" (ibid., p. xix).

The narrative of the unfinished cosmopolitan is not about the individual who acts alone. The lifelong learner is a thesis that connects the scope and aspirations of public powers with the personal and subjective capacities of individuals. Community participation and collaboration link problem solving and choices to collective norms of belonging and 'home'. The location of individual responsibility, however, is no longer traversed through the range of social practices directed toward a single public sphere – the social. Responsibility is located today in diverse, autonomous and plural communities perpetually constituted through one's own practice in 'communities' of learning. Research focuses on how children solve and interact in 'participatory structures' and 'discourse communities' of the classroom to chase desire in the infinite choices one makes in the pursuit of continuous innovation. The only thing that is not a choice is the choice of choosing.

The fears and hopes about who is and who is not changeable

The redemptive hopes of the unfinished cosmopolitan are double narrative that embody the fears of the individual who will prevent and destroy that future and its notions of the civilized. The hope and fears are not merely about the division of inclusion and exclusion, but about the particular qualities of the individuality that exist both inside and out the spaces of normalcy. The category of 'immigrant' is illustrative. The recognition given to include 'immigrants' radically differentiates and circumscribes something else that is both repulsive and fundamentally undifferentiated from the whole as processes of *abjection*. The immigrant is a category of a group and individuals whose status is somewhere not quite 'in' – worthy for inclusion but excluded. The immigrant lives in the in-between space. That space requires special intervention programs to access the equity of society and at the same time positions individuals as different and outside by virtue of the child's or parent's modes of life. To consider the notion of immigrant as a particular cultural space of difference, British and Scandinavians who come to the U.S. are not thought of or classified as immigrant in reform programs.

If I look at the Swedish reforms concerned with crime prevention, public health and education, they entail fears of the child who does not embrace the cosmopolitan 'lifelong learner' mode of living (Popkewitz, Olsson & Petersson, 2006). The anxiety of Public Health is about citizens only grasping a partial understanding of what life-long learning is and refusing to learn that health is not only about health. The anxiety is not directed to the sick but where the autonomous subject does not accept community responsibility by quitting smoking or drinking. The healthy citizen in governmental policies is an individual who feels and acts with responsibility for their immediate and broader community as a personal obligation for the future and the society as a whole. Each are seen as unhealthy moral dispositions that overlap with physical degenerations that impact others as well as one's self.

The assemblage of characteristics produces a determinate classification about a kind of person abjected in criminal prevention, schooling, and health education. This human kind brings forth fears of moral disintegration and social instability. Programs for intervention and remediation are placed into psychological qualities of the child who does not learn, problem solve and lacks self-esteem. The reclaiming of one's self is through the redemptive treks of lifelong learning. For the criminal this requires a correctional system that deals with the intimate social and psychological relations of the criminal being reclaimed.

The processes of abjection is generated within a discourse of inclusion and equity. Mathematics education reform research, for example, assert that instruction is to enable 'all children' to learn, but the research quickly morph into the qualities of the child who needs remediation and rescue – children categorized as minorities, ethnic groups, immigrants, sometimes girls; children from single parent families and who are poor, the socially disadvantaged, the at-risk child, the child with low self-worth, and so on. That latter child exists in a social space of social disintegration (the loss of 'civilization') and of moral degeneration that coexists with the hope of rescue and redemption through the proper planning.

While programs are to rescue that the individual through better management and self-management, the individual is one who never achieves the norms of 'the average.' The psychological qualities overlap with social narratives about the moral disintegration of the community, family and environment, such as single parents and teenage mothers, and 'recidivists.' The psychological qualities are assembled with social categories about, for example, dysfunctional families, single parent households, juvenile delinquency, and homes without books to read. A determinate category is formed about the child "who live in poverty, students who are not native speakers of English, students with disabilities, females, and many nonwhite students [who] have traditionally been far more likely than their counterparts in other demographic groups to be victims of low expectations" (National Council of Teachers of Mathematics, 2000, p. 13).

The fears of the unmotivated child also are of abjected family. The errant family is both inside and outside of the normalcy ascribed in the category of 'all children'.

The dangers and dangerous family are recalibrations of the cultural theses of cosmopolitanism and its others. Research on the family and children's school failure, for example, classifies the child as living in a "fragile" and "vulnerable" family (Hildago et al., 1995, p. 500). The parents are differentiated as having a lower level of education and socioeconomic status, as immigrants (the length of time living in country), and through categories of ethnically (living or not living in ethnic enclaves), among others (ibid., p. 501). Social and economic classifications of the child and family link to the life of the mother, such as whether she is a single or teen parent (ibid., p. 501). The aggregate of the "fragile" and "vulnerable" family acquires the abstraction of the sciences for the seemingly impersonal management of the reason that defines personal capabilities and the capacities of people.

As is evident in the examples above, the hopes and fears are expressed as part of the practices of schooling. The hopes of the future and optimism of participation 'needs' the fears about differentiating the qualities of reflection and action from the child. The inclusionary practices, are embedded in a comparative style of thought that continually produces a continuum of value that excludes and inscribes in-between spaces where different and an outside established.

FEARS OF DEMOCRACY: ENCLOSURES AND INTERNMENTS IN THE ORDERING OF THE PRESENT

The comparative style in the salvation narratives are inscribed in calls for democratization and empowerment. The emancipatory hope of democracy are to be realized in design projects of schooling and its children. Participation of various groups stands as the goal of schooling and the purpose of reform. The concrete practices of participation, however, embody a particular set of distinctions that police what is (im)possible. Research that is to design of classroom and children, for example, 'acts' as if there is the consensus of rules and standards applied to order reflection and action. That assertion of consensus makes possible notions of research providing 'useful' knowledge for policy makers and teachers alike. There is talk about making reforms and research practical, relevant to what occurs in the real world of teachers and parents' experiences. Each inserts a consensus and harmony that naturalize experience. This notion of consensus, ironically as the discussion below illustrates, is ordered through epistemological rules which inscribe fears of democracy itself.

The imagined consensus and harmony of the social whole is expressed in the policy directed to professional education. The *National Commission on Teaching and America's Future*. The policy report asserts, for example, the nation in the new global economy demands a new teacher.

> In this knowledge-based society, the United States urgently needs to reaffirm a consensus about the role and purposes of public education in a democracy (...) the challenge extends far beyond preparing students for the world of work. It includes building an American future that is just and humane as well as productive, that is as socially vibrant and civil in its pluralism as it is

competitive (National Commission on Teaching and America's Future, 1996, p. 11).

The consensus of future assumes the unfinished cosmopolitan as the principles of participating in the democracy. The 'socially vibrant' and 'pluralism' of that future in the policy text is dependent on the building of the world through the calculation and administration of the reason of the child. The teacher is the central agent in this planning.

> If every citizen is to be prepared for a democratic society whose major product is knowledge, every teacher must know how to teach students in ways that help them reach high levels of intellectual and social competence (National Commission on Teaching and America's Future, 1996, p. 3).

The report continues that national survival requires a school that entails collaboration with colleagues to create "rich learning environments" and "well-focused learning communities." That collaboration is to identify "major stakeholders" in school processes: state officials, researchers, parents, school officials, and so on. The notion of stakeholders is itself an interesting term. It assumes a consensus about who can and cannot be identified as 'decision-makers' and worthy of participation. That consensus is itself built upon organizational theories that regularizes and standardizes the agents and their mutual interests in organizing the future.

The collaboration, however, is not merely about the institutional actors and recognized institutional roles. The notion of stakeholders immediately abject those not recognized in the consensus that organized its presence.

The consensus embodied in collaboration reaches into the very planning of classrooms. The successful school is one that creates "a culture of continuous learning" for teachers. That learning is tied to a "learner centered" pedagogy and curriculum and collaborative "learning communities" in which "competent, caring, qualified teachers organized for success" in academic achievement (National Commission on Teaching and America's Future, 2003, p. 9).

One can read the defining of people as groups of 'stakeholders' and the 'learning communities' as naturalizing experience. There is an assumption that (a) what people say, do, and feel occurs through their lived familiarity and understanding; and (b) that the categories that organize how people experience their world and self are unproblematic. That is, it seems natural and commonsense to think about and act as if people are stakeholders whose participation ensures that democracy is working.

What the inscription of the subject elides is how the categories of the subject are historically produced to give stability and consensus to practices. The experiences that separate groups are premised on a consensus of the categories of the groups that make a difference and thus what sensibilities are necessary for inclusion.

This inscription of the experience becomes the metaphysics of democracy, the origin of explanation, and the grounds of what is known. There is the assumption that democracy is the participation of groups named and given 'voice' to speak through the consensus about which actors are to be 'heard'. Democracy is judged by the boundaries of the subject (and subjectivities) consecrated in the collaboration and community. The politics of representation discussed earlier in the equity problematic embodies this metaphysics of democracy. While important in policy for making apparent institutional patterns of inclusion, it naturalizes experience and thus ignores how experiences are not merely the autobiographical 'I' speaking. There is a double "I" in which what is (im)possible to speak is historically produced. That historical "I" entails the distinctions, oppositions, and differentiations through which the world is catalogued prior to our participation. This historical "I" that classifies experience itself is what is in need to be explained rather than deferred to the givenness of divisions that mark out its difference.

The naturalizing of experience is embedded in the rise of the phenomenological versions of qualitative research that emerged in the 1970s which continue as the preferred mode of inquiry in classroom and curriculum studies. Statistics was considered as dehumanizing. What was (and is) needed, it was said, was to capture the natural utterances and experiences of people. That data is seen as closer to the 'real' of schooling and part of a 'grounded theory' that assumes to provide for the naturalness of life in schooling. This phenomenology mixes with a hermeneutics that calls for the collaboration and participation that 'gives' the subject voice and autonomy that stands outside of history. The naturalness given to the experiences of schooling is to expel 'theories' so as to enable the researcher to find the experience lying in wait for discovery. The grid of institutions, ideas, and technologies through with experience is given intelligibility are elided.

This naturalizing of the experience is embedded in the notion of 'useful' knowledge. The idea of 'useful' assumes that there is a consensus and stability about the situation that enables the determination of what is of 'use'. This principles of harmony is carried in reform policy and research that direct attention to 'knowledge' that is valuable for practitioners, distinction between 'theory' and practice, and research about 'the lived experiences of the classroom' and teacher expert knowledge. A different version of this democratization is 'hearing' particular relevancies of teachers, communities, and the child as the base or starting point of reform.

This redemptive thesis of democracy embodies fears of the people from which democracy needs to be protected. If I return to the deployment of 'all children', it is the inscription of unity and difference that establishes consensus through which each is to be allotted comparable shares, and in that allotment is the casting out of those not represented and thus surplus.

> Consensus is more than the reasonable idea and practice of settling political conflicts by forms of negotiation and agreement, and by allotting to each party the best share compatible with the interests of other parties. It is a means to get rid of politics by ousting the surplus subjects and replacing them with real partners, social groups, identity groups, and so on. Correspondingly, conflicts are turned into problems that have to be sorted out by learned expertise and a negotiated adjustment of interests (Rancière, 2006, p. 306).

The fear of democracy requires the shepherds to plan the mediation of participation. The shepherding brings into the very processes of participation processes of abjection. The "ousting the surplus subjects" that Rancière speaks about creates an undifferentiated unity from which others are placed in unequal situations that installs difference. If I use current discussion about collaboration of 'stakeholders' in school and university reforms in current American policies and research, the categories of what constitutes the reflection and action are shepherded by the distinctions assembled and connected to constitute reason and 'reasonable people'. There is the radical differentiation that casts out others that paradoxically is to include an undifferentiated part of the whole.

SCHOOLING AS CHANGING SOCIETY BY CHANGING PEOPLE: MAKING EXCLUSION IN THE MAKING OF INCLUSION

This discussion is to outline a strategy for thinking about research about change that accepts general commitments for a more equitable and democratic society. The method of study, however, is a form of resistance and a counter-praxis (Lather, 2007) by examining the precariousness of what seems self-evidence and commonsense, thus making possible other alternatives other than those currently existing.

The 're-reading' of policy as systems of reasons treats the knowledge of schooling as not merely texts but simultaneously material in making of 'things'. I argued that the systems of reason in school reforms and research are to change the condition of people by changing people. That changing of people embodies comparative distinctions and a continuum of values. The impulse to democratize embodied, I argued, the hope of the child as the future cosmopolitan citizen, a mode of live ordered as one of problem solving and lifelong learning. Embedded in the salvation themes about the lifelong learner, I continued, was recognition of those excluded from that progress. The strategies of remediation and rescue, however, were processes of abjection. While the narratives of reforms were to include the excluded child, the practices of inclusion are continually placed against the background of something simultaneously excluded. The gestures of inclusion and exclusion were explored in the reform phrase about equity – schooling is for 'all children to learn'. The concrete strategies to search for a unified society, however, bring to the fore comparative distinctions of recognition of and differentiation from the imagined unified whole.

The (re)reading of policy raised questions about the particular principles generated to shape and fashion participation and collaboration. These principles are not merely about texts as they leach into programs and practices of schooling to create a materiality to the "reason" of schooling. With the comparative principles that separated and divided was the insertion of shepherds in the very theorizing of harmony and consensus. The inscription of consensus elides politics by placing outside of its grid of social groups that do not 'fit' into the categories of identity.

This brings me back to the instantiations of Neoliberalism as an epoch and cause of enabling or limiting participation. Studies of Neoliberalism assumed the rules and standards related to the equity problematic and the politics of representation. The politics of representation is important to considering what groups are excluded; but leaves unscrutinized the politics of how sensibilities are partitioned through the systems of reason of schooling, and with that, the processes of abjection. The issue at hand, then, is not to view policy as something brought by the state to schools or as a separate line of inquiry from the grid through which it is given intelligibility. The stance taken is neither realist nor nominalist but their interplay in the making of (im) possibilities of the present.

NOTES

[1] Foucault (1979) gives attention to the notion of 'reason' in his discussion of *governmentality*.
[2] I have not cited the broad corpus of literature in which this term is used. A google search would suffice for that. I capitalize Neoliberalism to emphasize a term that is named as an epoch and assigned an origin for locating "cause."
[3] The distinction of "urban" as embodying a system of reason is discussed in Popkewitz, 1998b.
[4] Notions of agency are so much a part of the modern orthodoxy that a theory of childhood, schooling, and society that is often not recognized that the autonomous agent who acts to improve the self and world is historically related to European enlightenments that becomes *doxa* in modernity. And with the idea of actors in the sense of having capacities to act on others is the notion of planning and the administration of that freedom (see, e.g., Wagner, 1994; Popkewitz, 2008).

REFERENCES

Cruikshank, B. (1999). *The will to empower: Democratic citizens and the other subjects.* Ithaca, NY: Cornell University.
Do Ó, J. R. (2003). The disciplinary terrains of soul and self-government in the first map of the Educational Sciences (1879–1911). In P. Smeyers & M. Depaepe (Eds.), *Beyond empiricism: On criteria for educational research. Studia Paedoagogica 34* (pp. 105–116). Leuven, Belgium: Leuven University Press.
Fejes, A., & Nicoll, K. (2008). *Foucault and lifelong learning: Governing the subject.* London: Routledge.
Foucault, M. (1984). What is the enlightenment? Was ist Auflärlung? In P. Rabinow (Ed.), *The Foucault reader* (pp. 32–51). New York: Pantheon Books.
Foucault, M. (1979). Governmentality. *Ideology and Consciousness, 6,* 5–22.
Hacking, I. (1986). Making up people. In T. C. Heller, M. Sosna & D. E. Wellbery (Eds.), *Reconstructing individualism: Autonomy, individuality, and the self in Western thought* (pp. 222-236 & 347-348). Stanford, CA: Stanford University Press.
Hacking, I. (1995). The looping effects of human kinds. In D. Sperber, D. Premack & A. J. Premack (Eds.), *Causal cognition: A multidisciplinary debate* (pp. 351-394). Oxford: Clarendon Press.
Hacking, I. (2006). *Kinds of people: Moving targets. The Tenth British Academy Lecture.* London: The British Academy.
Hargreaves, A. (2003). *Teaching in the knowledge society: Education in the age of insecurity.* Maindenhead, England: Open University Press.
Hidalgo, N., Siu, S., Bright, J., Swap, S., & Epstein, J. (1995). Research on families, schools, and communities: A multicultural perspective. In J. Banks (Ed.), *Handbook of research on multicultural education* (pp. 498–524). New York: Macmillan.
Hultqvist, K. (1998). A history of the present on children's welfare in Sweden. In T. Popkewitz & M. Brennan (Eds.), *Foucault's challenge: Discourse, knowledge, and power in education* (pp. 91–117). New York: Teachers College Press.

Kowalczyk, J., & Popkewitz, T. S. (2006). Multiculturalism, recognition, and abjection: (Re)mapping Italian identity. *Policy Futures in Education, 3*(4), 432–435.

Lather, P. (2007). *Getting lost: Feminist efforts toward a double(d) science.* Albany, NY: The State University of New York.

Mann, H. (1867). *Lectures and annual reports on education.* Cambridge, MA: Fuller.

McKnight, D. (2003). *Schooling, the Puritan imperative, and the molding of an American national identity. Education's "errand into the wilderness".* Mahwah, NJ: Lawrence Erlbaum Associates.

Popkewitz, T. (2008). *Cosmopolitanism and the age of school reform: Science, education, and making society by making the child.* New York: Routledge.

Popkewitz, T. (1998a). Dewey, Vygotsky, and the social administration of the individual: Constructivist pedagogy as systems of ideas in historical spaces. *American Educational Research Journal, 35*(4), 535–570.

Popkewitz, T. (1998b). *Struggling for the soul: The politics of education and the construction of the teacher.* New York: Teachers College Press.

Popkewitz, T. S., & Lindblad, S. (2000). Educational governance and social inclusion and exclusion: Some conceptual difficulties and problematics in policy and research. *Discourse, 21*(1), 5–54.

Popkewitz, T. (1991). *A political sociology of educational reform: Power/Knowledge in teaching, teacher education, and research.* New York: Teachers College Press.

Popkewitz, T., Olsson, U., & Petersson, K. (2006). The learning society, the unfinished cosmopolitan, and governing education, public health and crime prevention at the beginning of the twenty-first century. *Educational Philosophy and Theory, 37*(4), 431–449.

Rancière, J. (2004). *The politics of aesthetics.* Retrieved May 1, 2007, from http://theater.kein.org/node/99

Rancière, J. (2006). *Hatred of democracy* (S. Cororan, Trans.). London: Verso.

National Commission on Teaching and America's Future. (1996). *What matters most: Teaching for America's future.* Washington, DC: Author.

National Council of Teachers of Mathematics. (2000). *Principles and standards for school mathematics.* Reston, VA: Author.

National Commission on Teaching and America's Future. (2003). *No dream denied: A pledge to America's children.* Washington, DC: Author.

Shimakawa, K. (2002). *National abjection: The Asian American body onstage.* Durham, NC: Duke University.

Tröhler, D. (2006). *Max Weber and the protestant ethic in America* (unpublished paper). Zurich, Switzerland: Pestalozzianum Research Institute for the History of Education, University of Zurich.

Wagner, P. (1994). *The sociology of modernity.* New York: Routledge.

FURTHER READINGS

Cruikshank, B. (1999). *The will to empower: Democratic citizens and the other subjects.* Ithaca, NY: Cornell University.

Popkewitz, T. (2008). *Cosmopolitanism and the age of school reform: Science, education, and making society by making the child.* New York: Routledge.

Wagner, P. (1994). *The sociology of modernity.* New York: Routledge.

Wagner, P., Weiss, C., Wittrock, B., & Wollmann, H. (Eds.). (1991). *Social sciences and modern states. National experiences and theoretical crossroads* (pp. 2–27). Cambridge, UK: Cambridge University Press.

Thomas S. Popkewitz
Department of Curriculum and Instruction
University of Wisconsin-Madison, USA

QUALITY, ACCOUNTABILITY, CONTROL

LESLEY VIDOVICH

'YOU DON'T FATTEN THE PIG BY WEIGHTING IT'

Contradictory Tensions in the 'Policy Pandemic' of Accountability Infecting Education.

INTRODUCTION

This chapter brings critical perspectives to an analysis of contemporary policy on accountability in education. It argues that prevailing neo-liberal forms of account-ability – which constitute a 'policy pandemic' infecting education across the globe – are characterised by a series of contradictory tensions which significantly reduce the transparency of increasingly complex accountability relationships and distort 'authentic' education practices, as well as undermine diversity, social justice and democracy in education. The chapter offers a re-reading based on original empirical research, literature which develops finer nuances of the construct of accountability and critiques by leading policy scholars. From an analysis of all of these sources, an alternative conceptualisation, labelled here as *democratic network accountability*, is proposed.

The foundation for this chapter is empirical research on accountability policies and practices in the higher education sectors of a number of different countries over the last decade. This includes research conducted in Australia (Vidovich & Porter,1999; Vidovich, 2004), South Africa (Vidovich, Fourie, Van der Westhuizen, Alt & Holtzhausen, 2000), England (Vidovich & Slee, 2001), and recently as part of an Australian Research Council study in mainland China, Hong Kong Special Administrative Region and Singapore (Vidovich, Yang & Currie, 2007; Currie, Vidovich & Yang, 2008). The study in the 'Asian'[1] region will be used as illustrative of the empirical data which generated the broader conceptual themes developed in the chapter. However, although the meta analysis and conceptual themes presented here move beyond specific empirical findings in particular national and institutional settings, it must be emphasised that it is certainly not the intention to homogenise the way 'globalised' policy trends play out in *situ*; the focus is on local-global dynamics.

In the sections of this chapter to follow, the concepts of 'policy pandemic' and accountability are explicated. Then, a selection of findings from empirical research in the Asian region is presented to ground the more conceptual discussion in data derived from specific contexts, in the voices of interview participants at the grassroots of accountability policy trajectories. From a meta analysis of empirical research, the subsequent section extracts a series of contradictory tensions embedded within accountability policies and practices. The concluding discussion conceptualises a

M. Simons, M. Olssen and M.A. Peters (eds.), Re-Reading Education Policies: A Handbook Studying the Policy Agenda of the 21ˢᵗ Century, 549–567.

democratic network accountability as a possible contribution to re-thinking and dislodging the hegemony of prevailing neo-liberal accountabilities.

A 'POLICY PANDEMIC' OF EDUCATIONAL ACCOUNTABILITY?

Policy pandemic moves Levin's (1998) disease analogy of 'policy epidemic' one step further, as the terrain for policy borrowing expands across continents and countries with very different historical, cultural, political and economic traditions and circumstances. As such, the notion of a 'policy pandemic' parallels the phenomenon of globalisation, and integral to both has been a set of neo-liberal economistic discourses framing public policy across different jurisdictions. Thus, whilst globalisation has involved a greater interconnectedness and interdependence of the world, as Bottery (2006) has highlighted, it is economic globalisation which 'captures the discourses' of other forms such as cultural, political, managerial and environmental globalisation.

While there is growing evidence of convergence of education policies across different national settings with globalisation (Rizvi, 2006), care should be exercised in conceiving globalisation as a deterministic, top-down, omnipotent force. Such reification of globalisation can become a self fulfilling prescription and exclude the possibility of more localised agency. Gradually, more finely nuanced conceptualisations of globalisation, which highlight the two way interactions between policy actors at the different levels from global to local are being offered (e.g. Marginson & Rhoades, 2002). Furthermore, calls for more empirical research which highlights such dynamic interactions between 'the local' and 'the global' are becoming louder. For example, Rizvi (2006, p. 203) emphasises the importance of "sound empirical research designed to locate local and national education policy developments within a broader framework of the global system of communication and power relations." In the field of higher education, Marginson (2007, p. 7) points to the value of 'situated case studies' of national systems and individual institutions to more fully understand the dynamics of globalisation. Further, he criticises analyses which are only conducted through an Anglo-American cultural lens because they fail to recognise the global hegemonic position of this axis: "flows between the global and the local/national are two-way but this very reciprocity is unevenly distributed... some universities and national systems are not only shaped by global factors, but they also share the shaping of those global factors themselves." Consistent with these positions (above), the various empirical studies used as the basis for a meta analysis of higher education accountability policies and practices in this chapter have all been designed to capture dynamic interactions between 'the local' and 'the global'. Further, the empirical examples are drawn from the Asian region rather than the West where there is a larger volume of literature about accountability policies in education. Before turning to the specifics of this empirical research, the concept of accountability is explored in more detail to highlight its changing complexity and contestability.

Accountability in education has exploded to the foreground in an era where the discourses of a 'global knowledge economy' permeate public policy. Such economistic discourses are fuelling a scramble to create 'world class' educational institutions which are increasingly importing corporate structures and cultures in the drive to enhance efficiency and effectiveness and to thereby gain a competitive edge. With this corporatisation, two apparently contradictory processes are occurring simultaneously: increasing devolution and increasing accountability. On the one hand policy discourses highlight devolution of power for enhanced autonomy of localised decision making (or is it more responsibility than power?), but on the other hand this autonomy is strictly circumscribed by a requirement for enhanced accountability to central authorities who prescribe the outcomes to be achieved. As such, accountability policies have been significant in repositioning education to serve the economy. Accountability has been variously defined as "answerability for performance" (Romzek, 2000. p. 22); as "a *social practice* pursuing particular purposes, defined by distinctive relationships and evaluative procedures" (Ranson, 2003, p. 462); and as "the legal obligation to be responsive to the legitimate interests of those affected by decisions, programmes and interventions" (Considine, 2005, p. 207). Such definitions appear to be relatively unproblematic, but contestation arises with questions of accountability 'to whom?', 'for what?' and 'in what ways?'. Typologies, like those outlined in the following paragraphs, have arisen in response to such questions.

Corbett (1992) has employed a four-way directional typology of accountability where 'upwards' is legally and constitutionally-based, and 'outwards' focuses on responsiveness to clients and other stakeholders in the community. Upwards and outwards accountabilities together constitute political accountability, according to Corbett. To these he added more contentious and less frequently articulated 'downwards' accountability, where managers are answerable to subordinates, and 'inwards' accountability, where one's own personal conscience in relation to moral standards is foregrounded. Considine (2005), too, has recognised distinctions between traditional vertical ('upwards') and more recent horizontal ('outwards') accountabilities. He described a vertical form of accountability in terms of hierarchical uni-dimensional power relationships between policy actors where the "line of authority becomes the line of accountability; making a unified chain of command" (p. 215), such that the accountability of each actor is upwards to a superior and ultimately to an executive. In contrast, horizontal accountability is characterised by multi-dimensional power relationships where different actors share responsibility for policy outcomes to create a "culture of responsibility" (p. 214).

As with many other writers, Keohane (2003, p. 141) has differentiated between internal accountability where "the principal and agent are institutionally linked to one another" and external accountability "to people outside the acting entity whose lives are affected by it." He employed some different nomenclature for his typology, although vertical ('upwards') and horizontal ('outwards') directions are still key features. He identified three main types of accountability: hierarchic (where subordinates are accountable to superiors); pluralistic (where the relationships are more horizontal); and democratic (where accountability is to broad publics). Keohane also points to a more generalised notion of reputational accountability as a form of external accountability and he notes, for example, that "reputation is the only form of external accountability that appears to constrain the United States with respect to its political-military activities" (2003, p. 150). He adds, however, that the absence of institutionalisation of reputation renders it relatively unreliable as a form of constraint. Although he identified reputational accountability as relatively weak, he argues that it can still be potentially significant because reputations are often important for other activities, beyond accountability. Finally, in this brief look at typologies, Ranson (2003) differentiated traditional professional accountability which serves the client's needs from types of neo-liberal accountability which he identified as consumer (for consumer responsiveness), contract (for service efficiency), performative (for product quality) and corporate (for controlling infrastructure).

Thus, neither accountability nor globalisation is a single phenomenon. Both are characterised by a multiplicity of forms operating at many levels and involving complex and contested relationships pushing and pulling in different directions. With the acceleration of neo-liberal globalisation new forms of accountability policies have emerged across public and private sectors, including education, since the 1980s. We hear much talk of key performance indicators, standards and quality (with all of its variants including quality assurance or QA and quality improvement or QI). Such policies represent significant subsets of the accountability policy ensemble, but they are far from discrete policy domains, and there is extensive slippage between these various accountability discourses. Arguably, policies about 'quality' represent a 'clever' strategy by the policy elite to forge enhanced educational accountability as it neatly elides with a more traditional notion of 'excellence' to which most professional educators would readily subscribe.

Altogether, we have been witnessing a 'policy pandemic' of an increasingly diverse array of educational accountability regimes sweeping the globe. In Ozga and Jones' (2006) terms, this would be an example, *par excellence*, of 'travelling' policy. However, the interaction between 'travelling' and 'embedded' policies "where global policy agendas come up against the existing priorities and practices" in context-specific localized sites is worthy of much closer investigation (Ozga & Jones, 2006, p. 2).

EMPIRICAL RESEARCH ON ACCOUNTABILITY POLICIES AND PRACTICES

All studies forming the basis for this analysis (cited in the introduction) were framed around a similar research design, allowing ultimately for meta analysis. Based on the work of Stephen Ball (1994; 2006) and others, this suite of research projects defined policy broadly as a process which incorporates the contexts of influence, policy text production and practices. The context of influence involves identifying factors which drive the policy, the prevailing conditions leading to changes and the interest groups involved in stimulating the new policy agenda. The context of policy text production focuses on the policy statement itself, interrogating the policy discourses with questions about 'who, what, why, when, where and how?', with particular attention directed to exposing the dominant ideology underpinning the policy and the embedded power relations. The context of practices/effects refers to the enactment of the policy; the interpretation by actors at localised sites and the way the policy is potentially resisted, negotiated and transformed from its original intentions. Ball (1994; 2006) also identified contexts of outcomes and political strategies which re-focus on 'bigger picture' patterns of social justice ensuing from a policy. The research questions guiding each of the empirical studies about accountability referred to in the introduction were structured around these five contexts of a policy process, with more explicit attention to the first three: what were the influences operating to create the accountability policies in each jurisdiction?; what was the nature of the discourses in the national accountability policy texts in each country; and what were the practices and effects stemming from the accountability policies within higher education institutions? Later consideration was given to issues of social justice in the concluding discussion. Thus, each study tracked accountability policy processes in higher education through a trajectory from global/international influences (defined as macro) to national level policy texts (defined as meso) to practices and effects within individual higher education institutions (defined as the micro level). Qualitative methodologies for both data collection and analysis were employed, as outlined in Punch (1998), and in some cases where participant numbers were larger, the investigation was assisted by NUDIST software for qualitative analysis.

In bringing together an analysis of macro through to micro levels of policy processes, both critical and post-structural theoretical perspectives were employed to offer a more 'complete picture' of the entire policy process (Vidovich, 2007). While both theoretical orientations focus on power relationships as central to policy processes they conceive of power in different ways.[2] On the one hand, critical theory highlights hegemonic power which, in policy terms, points to the dominance of macro level policy elite and strong state control of policy. On the other hand, post-structural perspectives focus more on the circulation of power at micro levels and the potential for both repressive and productive effects of power relationships. In this, critical perspectives assume that constraints imposed by macro level policy elite severely limit the agency of policy actors at the micro level whereas post-structural perspectives highlight agency by policy players at the micro level.

The most recent in the suite of accountability studies which form the empirical basis for this chapter were conducted in Mainland China, Hong Kong Special Administrative Region (hereafter referred to as HK) and Singapore, and it is this Asian arena which will be used here to illustrate the emergence of some broader conceptual themes.

Sampling and data collection in the Asian region

Singapore, China and HK were purposively selected as sites because all three were experiencing rapid economic and social changes, with Singapore striving to establish itself as a global 'education hub' in a knowledge economy; China opening its doors and moving quickly to establish itself as a new centre of global power; and HK adjusting to handing back to China (although remaining as an administratively separate region), yet still holding many strong British traditions. Within each country/region, two case study institutions were purposively selected to represent an older, more traditional, comprehensive and research-intensive university which enjoys an elite status both nationally and internationally on the one hand and a newer, more technologically-oriented university of more moderate status on the other. Within each university, snowball sampling was then used to identify approximately 20-25 participants (125 in total across the six institutions) who were ultimately recruited from different faculties (sciences, social sciences and professional), and from a range of status positions (senior managers, department heads, professors and lecturers). Data was collected in the form of documents at both national and institutional levels as well as semi-structured interviews with participants within universities conducted in English in Singapore and HK, and in Chinese in mainland China. Data collection extended over the time period from 2003 to 2007, with pilots in 2003, the main body of interviews in 2004 and follow-ups in 2006/07.

Reported below is a small sample of perspectives from interview participants on accountability policies in research and teaching in their country/region and university. While influences and policy texts are only briefly highlighted here, the main focus is on the effects, as perceived by the participants. Although the majority of participants at each site in the Asian region could identify positive effects of the significant increase in accountability in research and teaching, most also pointed to issues of contradiction, confusion, concern and contestation in the policy processes. It is these issues, which were strikingly common across the three countries/regions and six case study universities, which are exemplified here, in the voices of participants. Participant quotes are identified only by country/region, university (old or new) and number to protect anonymity. Key themes are identified with the use of italics within quotes.

Influences

Participants were asked to identify the factors influencing the exponential growth in accountability policies witnessed in their higher education sectors. There was a total consensus across all participants in each region that the most significant influences stemmed from global markets. The effects of globalisation were seen variously in positive, neutral and negative terms, but often as a taken-for-granted feature of new times, or as a game to be played. For example, "if you want to be an international player, then you have to play by the international *rules*" (HK:old,100) and "the local [Singapore] government thinks that education is becoming a global industry, and in order to be a hub for education you have to play the global *game*" (Singapore:old,109). In China, "globalisation means being open and facing the world. It brings lots of changes in research and teaching to universities" (China:old,2). The significant impact of international rankings (league tables) was frequently highlighted by participants in all regions, along with the unrelenting pressure to improve their university's position in such rankings to claim 'world class' status. Thus, in the global field of higher education market competition in conjunction with leagues tables where universities are publicly compared and ranked on a single vertical hierarchy have proven to be powerful 'bedfellows' in driving national and institutional accountability policy agendas.

Policy text production

Analysis of national accountability policy texts in the three regions (not included here due to limits of space) revealed similarities in the tenor of the discourses, albeit with variations in structural and procedural detail. In research, HK had a national *Research Assessment Exercise* (RAE) with external (often international) assessors, paralleling the process in the UK (its former colonial master). China was moving from a system of significant personal financial rewards for academics publishing in top international (English speaking) journals to a system of 'position allowances' where a performance contract included a certain number of publications a year and a threat of a salary drop as a sanction if targets were not met. Singapore had only recently adopted a *Quality Assurance Framework* for Universities to combine institutional self assessment (against a selection of national goals) with an external review for validation. Accountability for research was directly linked to financial rewards for institutions and individual academics in HK and China, but not in Singapore, although the move to short term academic contracts in Singapore was creating similar pressures for research productivity. In teaching, all case study universities were developing more formalized teaching assessments by both students and academic peers, and teaching awards were becoming prominent. In all three countries/regions, rewards and sanctions for teaching were much less explicit and less 'high stakes' than for research. Therefore, despite variations in detail and timing, the direction of university accountability policy changes was very similar in each country/region, with a notable increase in contractual forms of account-ability for academics.

Effects

A majority of participants in the Asian region believed that accountability policies had been effective in enhancing research productivity; racking up a greater quantity of publications. Most also believed that accountability policies in teaching had enhanced its recognition relative to research (albeit marginally) within their institution. However, the significant costs of accountability were also recognized. The quotes below focus on issues raised by participants, whether they were overall positive or negative about the effects of the new policies. Quotes are grouped according to six major themes which emerged from the data when participants were asked a general question about the impact of the accountability measures in place in each country and university.

External accountability pressures impacting on internal wellbeing:

> They lead to a kind of *pressure-cooker* phenomenon, driven by competition. (HK:new,105)

If you look at *staff relations*, it has had a great *devastating* effect. (HK:new,101)

There's *no trust*, there's no discretion and there's no willingness to think outside the box... If you don't have that trust, you end up with a system that is *policed* from top to bottom, academically and administratively. We have become far *less collegial*. (HK:old,100)

I think it [teaching accountability] is more intrinsic. All these extrinsic measures, *I do not see them as a motivator.* ... It is more the day to day, your relationship with your students, you hope to see them do well. (Singapore:new,114)

The [teaching evaluation] scores given by students will be released in public every year, therefore *teachers feel more pressure.* (China:new,6)

Validity of research assessment mechanisms:
(accountability for quantity or quality of publications)

You have to prove your merit to a bureaucracy that can only credit *countable items*. But the fact is that if you are just *publishing crap*, and publish a lot of it, then more quantity harms your *reputation* rather than helping it. (HK:old,105)

Too much emphasis on the publications. How long is the publication list? *Research should be making an impact on the community* but we really don't make an assessment of that. (Singapore:new,117)

Well there is research productivity and there is research quality. I worry about the danger of *bean counting* without the proper instrument in place to ascertain rather than measure quality. (Singapore:old,119)

The measure for evaluating research outcomes is quantification. ...The advantage is that it is easy for leaders to do assessments. The disadvantage is that it is easy to *ignore the quality* of outcomes. (China:old,11)

Validity of teaching assessment mechanisms:
(accountability to students or academic peers; accountability for outcomes or processes)

The documentation of actual learning *outcomes is extremely difficult* and that's what we are moving towards. I can say with some pride that our *processes are quite robust*, but now we have to show that those outcomes are indeed accomplished. (HK:new,111)

I find that *students are not in a position to judge*, especially for those who get a below average grade. Are you willing to *trust* those people with a significant evaluation? (Singapore:old,106)

We know that sometimes *colleagues can be rather nice to their own friends*. (Singapore:old,116)

The university asks students to tick the boxes. ... Some of them are very impatient and do it carelessly. It is *hard to see the extent of credibility* it has. ... We [teachers] observe each other. Some teachers are very busy and they have no time [to observe their colleagues in the classroom and complete a formal evaluation of their teaching]; what they do is ticking [the boxes on the evaluation form] without observation and hand it in. (China:new,8)

Lack of transparency in accountability mechanisms:

We have the impression, right or wrong, that the reviewers don't read the publications but simply peruse them at best and are much more likely to be impressed by quantity than quality. But that's only an impression. *We don't know exactly what happens.* (HK:old,112)

The problem is that the evaluation criteria [for teaching] are *unclear and ambiguous*. (HK:old,110)

The phenomenon of papers being published because of *guanxi* [personal sponsorship relationships] *is very serious*. In domestic publications if you do not know the editors, they will not even take a look. The process of sending a paper to several authorities in the field [peer review] is just beginning in China. It will be lamentable if the human relations factor [guanxi] also mixes into it and has a dominant position. (China:old,7)

Accountability mechanisms undermining contributions to local communities:

You want to encourage *scholarship that is relevant to the community* you are living and working in. Yet this RAE exercise in the eyes of our colleagues is too much of a paper exercise, more for administrative purposes, rather than really enhancing scholarship. (HK:new,104)

The real internationalisation should be to *answer China's needs first.* (China:old,10)

We have to say that this is *not a money-making business*. We have to make sure that we create an environment for the intellectual development of the people in Singapore and in the region. (Singapore:old,109)

Western bias exacerbating inequalities:
(In the Asian region, the effect of 'global' accountability mechanisms in undermining local communities was a major concern for participants, many of whom expressed this impact as 'western bias', as highlighted below.)

I see them [influences] as *UK, Australasia, US, and Canada*. I do not see them as coming from China, Vietnam, Mongolia, Russia, or these other places. (HK:old,102)

We have inherited the *worst of both worlds; US and UK*. We have developed a complex bureaucracy to deal with all of these quality measures. From the USA we've inherited the mindless pursuit of excellence, *trying to have 'world class' universities* and the USA obsession with *ranking*. From the UK, we've inherited the *worst form of 'new public management'*. (HK:new,105)

They made a decision a few years ago to *move from an English model of higher education to an American one*. ... They are always looking at benchmarks or *best international practice*. (Singapore:old,100)

It has other repercussions like people ignoring small presses or local audiences in favour of *Western presses* and adding on to the generally Eurocentric nature of the field and *Western bias*. (Singapore:new,120)

If ['old' university] wants to be *world class it should not totally think of Harvard and MIT* as its reference; its sights should be further. (China: old,10).

Development of Chinese universities is quick indeed, but *we cannot compare with the world well-known universities*. There is no way to catch up within several decades. The key is investment, and currently the investment is not good. (China:new,5)

It is pertinent here to link this last theme of 'western bias' to the issue of international league tables raised under the 'influences' section earlier. Such rankings reveal that it is American universities (and to a lesser extent British universities) which significantly outnumber others in the 'top 100' (Marginson, 2007). Rankings create pressure on other universities wanting to ascend the league tables to emulate those at the top. This 'Western' hegemony has significantly impacted on universities in the 'Asian' region aspiring to 'world class' status and many have responded by attempting to copy 'Western' models of university, and their accountability regimes, with all of the associated costs. As Lingard (2006, p. 293), drawing on Bourdieu, has articulated "national capital can be seen to mediate the extent to which nations are able to be context generative in respect of the global field", suggesting that the 'global south' are more restricted in their autonomy to develop policies adapted to their own localised circumstances if they aspire to successfully compete in the global marketplace.

Within each country/region in this study, the only significant difference between participants' views from old and new universities was the frustration within the newer institutions as they tried to compete in the so-called global game for world class status from lower positions in national and international hierarchies. For example, participants' views from old and new universities in China, where a small handful of elite universities are singled out for extra funding to support their drive for world class status, can be contrasted: "[Old] university should and can become the best university in China and compete as a world class university" (China:old,5), whereas "This [new] university wants to be well known in the world, but this is ridiculous, extraordinarily inane and meaningless" (China:new,8).

There is a need to comment briefly here on the relative degree of positive responses from Asian participants about the effect of accountability policies (e.g. Vidovich, Yang & Currie, 2007; Currie, Vidovich & Yang, 2008), compared to the more negative findings from similar studies in the West (e.g. Vidovich, 2004; Vidovich & Slee, 2001). This might be understood, for the Asian countries, in terms of a higher level of acceptance of (or at least compliance with) government policy aimed at enhancing national economic sustainability through successful competition in the global marketplace. Considerable pride was expressed by many Asian participants in the capacity-building of universities in the region, as reflected in their ascension in league tables, and new forms of accountability policies were seen to play a central role in this status elevation. The relatively higher level of positive response to accountability policies from Asian participants compared to those in the West might also be understood in terms of more restricted freedom to express critique, especially in Singapore and China where potentially severe sanctions for criticism of government policy have been evident. Many participants in these regions needed constant reassurances that they would remain totally anonymous before speaking. In contrast, in HK, with its recent British traditions of greater academic freedom, participants were more forthcoming with their critique of accountability policies.

A META ANALYSIS OF CONTRADICTORY TENSIONS IN ACCOUNTABILITY POLICIES

At this point a meta analysis of findings across different sites steps back from empirical research in particular national and institutional contexts (as cited in the introduction and exemplified in the previous section) to highlight some common tensions characteristic of accountability policies and practices over the last decade. The following contradictory tensions were the most striking feature of the empirical data from this earlier research: between internal and external accountabilities; horizontal and vertical accountabilities; assessments of processes and outcomes; and assessments of a qualitative and quantitative nature. They are represented in Figure 1 as a series of continua between polar positions (not as dichotomies).

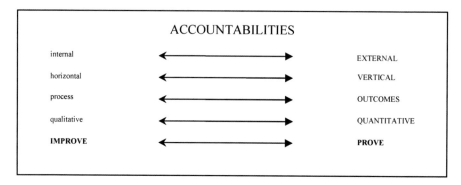

Figure 1. Contradictory tensions in accountability policies and practices

The majority of university participants reported tensions between more traditional *internal* accountability relationships amongst professional peers on the one hand, and an increasing emphasis on *external* accountability on the other. For example, representatives of external groups are now frequently formally co-opted into national university quality auditing panels. Although such auditing often consists of a two stage process (internal self assessment followed by an external audit), many university participants emphasised that it is the external component and associated public reporting, often with financial implications, which carries the most weight. In particular, international league tables were seen to constitute a growing publicly visible accountability mechanism directed towards external stakeholders.

Within this expanding domain of external accountabilities, many participants reported tensions between *horizontal* and *vertical* forms. Traditional horizontal answerability relationships with the community (democratic accountability) have been relatively silenced by a complex combination of attenuated vertical accountability to governments along with newer market accountabilities which increasingly operate in a global arena (beyond local, national or even regional communities). These newer market accountabilities – which foreground students as fee-paying customers and businesses/industries as employers of graduating 'human capital' as well as purchasers of research outcomes – are characterised by a more acutely felt vertical (global) component (e.g. international rankings), and participants frequently articulated the pressures of competing in global markets so far 'above' their localised contexts. The role that governments have assumed, as 'market managers' attempting to steer national positioning in this global marketplace, has then significantly augmented vertical accountabilities. The financial implications for universities are perceived as potentially 'life-threatening', especially where government funding is reducing in real terms.

Participants also frequently reported tensions between accountability for the *processes* and/or *outcomes* of higher education. The general trend has been to move from a focus on processes to outcomes. Publication counts as measures of the outcomes of research, while still contested, seem to have been more readily accepted in universities than moves to assess the outcomes of teaching. Although policy discourses now focus more on outcomes, participants often criticized accountability audits for a continued focus on the minutiae of processes (micro-management) and they reported considerable confusion about just what they were accountable for. Importantly, the push towards quantitative assessments of outcomes in both teaching and research raises social justice issues across the field of higher education given the differential levels of financial and human capital 'inputs' in different national and institutional contexts.

The majority of participants expressed particularly strong views about tensions between more *qualitative* assessments aligned with professional judgments and more 'hard-nosed' *quantitative* assessments in both research and teaching. The trend has been to increasingly rely on quantitative measures, yet serious questions remained for participants about the validity of these mechanisms and the effect of ignoring qualitative judgments in such a complex arena as higher education where the most desirable outcomes are difficult to measure and are unlikely to fully reveal themselves in the short term. A narrowing of research and teaching activities to fit with government prescribed quantifiable parameters was a repeated concern.

Overall, contemporary accountability policies and practices reveal a trend from left to right on each of the separate continua in Figure 1 above; that is, towards external and vertical accountabilities, and a focus on assessment of outcomes in quantitative terms. Arguably, together this represents an increasing emphasis on the *prove* (quality assurance) dimension of accountability at the expense of an *improve* (quality improvement or enhancement) dimension. While the former is more about maintaining control, the latter is more oriented towards critical reflection for development.

Altogether, across the different national contexts identified in the introduction, there was a disturbing level of convergence in the policy pandemic of accountability. Despite the design of the research allowing for localised variation to emerge within an umbrella of globalisation, 'the global' ('travelling' policy) has significantly overshadowed 'the local' ('embedded policy') in the domain of accountability. Context-specific differences were usually more a matter of finer detail, degree and timing in each country/region and sector. Green's (1999) study of education policy in European and Asian countries aimed to examine the claim that globalisation was leading to increasing convergence of education systems across different jurisdictions. His analysis revealed that although there was a significant convergence of general education policy discourses and objectives, specific structures and processes remained quite distinct across different national contexts and therefore "national education systems, though more international, are far from disappearing" (Green, 1999, p. 55) under the impact of globalisation. Thus, at that time Green was not of the view that globalisation was wiping out context-specific differences in education, although he did emphasise the importance of further research to conduct comparative analysis of trends in specific structures and processes – as the research agenda reported in this chapter has attempted to do. Also of relevance to the topic addressed in this chapter, Green did make special note that in higher education, policy convergence was particularly strong in the areas of quality control and performance evaluation – two major arms of accountability policy. A decade after Green's research, I would suggest that there has been an acceleration of convergence of accountability policy processes across different contexts in the quest to achieve 'world class' universities in an increasingly competitive global marketplace. Such convergence is at the expense of both diversity and social justice throughout the field of higher education.

CONCLUDING DISCUSSION

The themes highlighted in this concluding discussion are raised, tentatively, for critical reflection. While the empirical research reported earlier was located in particular contexts, the meta themes to emerge may also provide 'food for thought' in other educational settings, as *all* sectors of education have been harnessed by governments to serve the economy in the 'national interest', and in this, accountability policies have been central.

Where are we now?

A 'policy pandemic' of educational accountability accompanying neo-liberal globalisation has meant a significant shift in the balance of power within Burke's (2005) 'accountability triangle' (following Burton Clarke's model).[3] This triangle has been modified in Figure 2 below, to depict the relative strength of influences amongst the trilogy of markets, governments and educators at global, national and local levels. Educators are assigned a lower positioning, with the size of arrows (albeit signalling two way interactions) indicating that the most powerful influences are exerted downwards as governments and markets have tightened their controls over educators. Markets, which increasingly operate at global levels, are positioned above both educators and governments, to reflect the dominating discourses of a *global* market economy. The two-way bolded arrows between governments and markets depict their symbiotic relationship as they often operate in concert, with governments assuming the role of 'market managers'. That is, governments and markets mutually reinforce each other's claims to legitimacy in harnessing education to serve the economy, and educators are disempowered in the process as they are simultaneously pushed and pulled by new accountability mechanisms which are generated external to the education sector.

In Figure 2, the principal power base from which each of the three groups in the triangle exerts their influence is at a different level. That is, the main arena from which markets draw their power is global, for governments it is national and for educators, their power base is largely confined to localised contexts. What have been rendered invisible and silent by dominant neo-liberal ideologies – and are notable for their absence from Figure 2 – are professional and democratic forms of accountability where professional peers and broader communities play important – even primary – roles in 'authentic' accountability which is connected to 'grassroots' educational values and practices. Instead, the hegemony of neo-liberal accountability has produced a 'sophisticated network of surveillance' (Webb, 2005) by governments and markets, which feature strong controls and punitive sanctions, bearing down on educators. Further, powerful financial levers attached to accountability mechanisms have been systematically applied to both institutions and individuals, creating significant drivers to rapidly embed a culture of 'performativity' (Ball, 2006) deep within the education sphere.

Despite this disempowerment of educators, as depicted in Figure 2, the hegemony of neo-liberal accountability is not utterly complete. Empirical evidence from the suite of accountability studies cited earlier indicates that pockets of resistance and resilience in certain structures, processes and people remain at the micro (institutional) level to (partially) protect a whisper of professional and democratic accountabilities. However, educational practitioners are experiencing a dissonance over competing forms of accountability. The (often hidden) costs of new accountability regimes – in money, time, stress and morale – are unacceptably high. Further, given the empirical evidence presented earlier of the distortion of educational activities through the establishment of a narrow range of prescribed, instrumental performance indicators measured within short time frames, there are also significant costs for the longer term contributions of education to societal well-being. Arguably, social sustainability has been marginalised by the presage for economic sustainability.

Where could/should we be?

We should be challenging the imbalanced power relationships embedded in contemporary neo-liberal accountability policies. To offer an alternative, I briefly refer back to the accountability typologies explored earlier in the chapter. Such

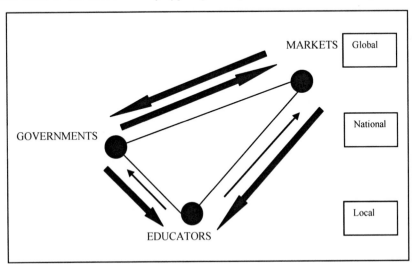

Figure 2. New power relationships with neo-liberal accountabilities
(adapted from Burke, 2005)

typologies are most often structured as dichotomies – internal/external and vertical/ horizontal – which are assumed to be enduring static categories. However, in globalising new times, rigid dichotomies no longer have the same analytic value in clarifying accountability relationships. Neo-liberal globalisation has blurred boundaries. For example, the internal-external divide is less clear with public-private partnerships and contracting out of public services. Also, horizontal forms of external accountability to the general community (democratic accountability) have blurred with market accountability such that community is often conflated with customer and contract. Thus, neo-liberal blurring of boundaries renders accountability relationships much less transparent; the accountability 'waters' have been 'muddied', and what we now have is more like an 'accountability swamp'.

We need some new ways of thinking about productive rather than destructive accountability relationships, but I am not suggesting that we need to 'throw the baby out with the bathwater'. Typologies such as those overviewed earlier in the chapter have offered insights about individual accountability relationships although, arguably, with the explosion in the number of specific incarnations of neo-liberal accountabilities, these typologies fall short when it comes to understanding how the different types (often in tension) interact with each other. That is, insufficient attention has been paid to the *dynamics* of accountability relationships. However, accountability envisaged in terms of network relationships might be a useful way to begin to capture these dynamics which operate at multiple levels and in multiple directions, simultaneously. An 'ideal type' network of accountability would be characterised by hybrid forms negotiated between interested parties (or stakeholders in the economic jargon) which foreground democratic processes, and where the 'public' is conceived more as a whole than as fragmented parts in competition. Thus, a concept of *democratic network accountability* might offer heuristic value as a 'thinking tool'. The particular hybrid forms of accountability best suited to particular circumstances could be negotiated separately in the different policy spaces within networks (which might extend between local and global levels). Accountability policies and practices may well play out differently in different policy spaces – one size does *not* fit all – and for this reason 'democratic network accountability' cannot be represented as a static model. Negotiations within such networks might raise questions of accountability 'for what?' and 'in what ways?', as current typologies usually only address the 'to whom?' question. For example, the issue of balance between accountability for processes and/or for outcomes would constitute part of the 'for what?' question, and the issue of the balance between qualitative judgments and quantitative measurements would constitute part of the 'in what ways?' question. After all, not everything of value in education can be reduced to readily measurable and quantifiable outcomes. Thus, the current imbalance between 'prove' and 'improve' forms of accountability (see Figure 1) requires the negotiation of new settlements. Governments have a role, a responsibility, here to support democratic negotiations; rather than being 'market managers' they could/should become custodians of a 'democratic network accountability'.

The main difference between what is being proposed here and current neo-liberal practices is that accountability should be openly negotiated, transparent, and dynamic, not imposed, opaque and static. The essential ingredient is democratic negotiations, and in this, the trust which has been eroded by the constant surveillance of neo-liberal accountabilities must be re-established (see also Ranson, 2003; Olssen, Codd & O'Neill, 2004). It is readily acknowledged, however, that such negotiation is not likely to be straight forward. For a start, it will be time consuming, although for educators this time will be better spent on constructive negotiation than wasted on compliance with separate and often conflicting accountability regimes in which they have no sense of ownership.

Considine (2005) also highlights the existence of multiple accountability relation-ships and argues that in contemporary contexts, in order to establish 'real respon-siveness' it is no longer sufficient to simply follow a set of rules or be answerable to superiors. Instead, he highlights the need for 'navigational competence' or "the proper use of authority to range freely across a multi-relationship terrain (…) this so-called steering mandate involves different relationships and trade-offs from those defined by constitutional convention and classical organisational theory" (Considine, 2005, p. 213). However, I suggest that rather than Considine's term of 'navigation', the term 'negotiation' (as I have used in this chapter) might be more appropriate, as the former implies movement around fixed obstacles, whereas negotiation offers the more active potential of transforming such obstacles. While Considine's work reveals useful insights into contemporary approaches to account-ability, it must be challenged in relation to his concept of horizontal accountability and the need to develop a 'culture of responsibility' or shared accountability, which requires cultural processes to be made visible and measurable. This is the weak point in Considine's position, in my view, as a culture of shared accountability too easily degenerates into a tokenistic gesture towards the friendly, familiar concept of 'community' as caring and sharing. Differential power relations and contestation between interested parties must be foregrounded. I have argued elsewhere (e.g. Vidovich, 2007) that insufficient attention to power relationships is a weakness of contemporary network theory generally, and therefore in the 'democratic network accountability' proposed here, attention to power relations is paramount, and both contestation and active negotiation are the keys.

The argument, then, is to envisage 'democratic network accountability' which features negotiation between interested parties and well conceived hybridisation of different types of accountability. However, Webb's caution should be noted that early evidence of hybrid systems of accountability points to "an escalation of accountability politics" (Webb's, 2005, p. 191) as the professional power of educators is eroded by a combination of governments and the corporate community. I would counter, though, that the power of educators has already been eroded, and therefore they need to re-establish a position at the 'bargaining table', and be *actively* involved in negotiating the form and function of hybridised accountability.

To imagine alternatives to neo-liberal accountabilities, there is a need to dislodge the hegemony of economistic discourses, and we might begin by putting 'education' back into 'educational accountability'. With the proposed 'democratic network accountability', where hybrid forms are negotiated in particular policy spaces, there is an opportunity for critical and active policy *learning* rather than uncritical policy *borrowing* across jurisdictions. Both globalisation and accountability are characterised by multidimensional networks, and both need to be problematised, especially in relation to the unequal power relations they are sustaining. A re-reading of contemporary global or 'travelling' accountability regimes points to the need to address the weaknesses of neo-liberal forms; that is, their complexity and instability; lack of transparency; static nature without suitable adaptation to different contexts; distortion of 'authentic' educational quality due to disconnection from 'grassroots' educational values and practices; and, of vital importance, their serious threat to diversity, social justice and democracy.

Therefore, it seems somewhat appropriate that in the year in which this chapter was written, the Chinese Year of the Pig (2007), the policy elite driving the accountability policy pandemic infecting education be reminded of the adage that 'you don't fatten the pig by weighing it'!

NOTES

[1] 'Asian' is not intended to homogenise different countries, but refers to a general geographic location.
[2] For an excellent overview of the application of critical and post-structural approaches to policy analysis, and the tensions between them, see the special edition of *Journal of Education Policy* 18(2), 2003.
[3] Although Burke's (2005) 'accountability triangle' (and Burton Clarke's model on which it is based) specifically relate to the higher education sector, arguably the impact of neo-liberal accountability policies have been similar across *all* education sectors as governments and markets together enhance their control over education to serve economic interests.

LITERATURE

Ball, S. (1994). *Education policy: A critical and post-structural approach*. London: Routledge.
Ball, S. (2006). *Education policy and social class: The selected works of Stephen J. Ball*. London: Routledge.
Bottery, M. (2006). Education and globalisation: Redefining the role of the educational professional. *Educational Review, 58*(1), 95–113.
Burke, J. (2005). *Achieving accountability in higher education*. San Francisco: John Wiley & Sons.
Considine, M. (2005). *Making public policy*. Cambridge: Polity.
Corbett, D. (1992). *Australian public sector management*. St Leonards, NSW: Allen & Unwin.
Currie, J., Vidovich, L., & Yang, R. (2008). Embedding performance cultures in Hong Kong and Singaporean higher education. *Asia-Pacific Journal of Education, 28*(1), 67–85.
Green, A. (1999). Education and globalisation in Europe and East Asia: Convergent and divergent trends. *Journal of Education Policy, 14*(1), 55–71.
Keohane, R. (2003). Global governance and democratic accountability. In D. Held & M. Koenig-Archibugi (Eds.), *Taming globalisation*. Cambridge: Polity.
Levin, B. (1998). An epidemic of education policy: What we can learn from each other? *Comparative Education, 34*(2), 131–141.
Lingard, B. (2006). Globalisation, the research imagination and deparochialising the study of education. *Globalisation, Societies and Education, 4*(2), 287–302.
Marginson, S. (2007). Global position and position taking: The case of Australia. *Journal of Studies in International Education, 11*(1), 5–32.
Marginson, S., & Rhoades, G. (2002). Beyond national states, markets and systems of higher education: A glonacal agency heuristic. *Higher Education, 43*(3), 281–309.
Olssen, M., Codd, J., & O'Neil, A. (2004). *Education policy*. London: Sage.

Ozga, J., & Jones, R. (2006). Travelling and embedded policy: The case of knowledge transfer. *Journal of Education Policy, 21*(1), 1–17.

Punch, K. (1998). *Introduction to social research*. London: Sage.

Ranson, S. (2003). Public accountability in the age of neo-liberal governance. *Journal of Education Policy, 18*(5), 459–480.

Romzek, B. (2000). Dynamics of public accountability in an era of reform. *International Review of Administrative Sciences, 66*(1), 21–44.

Rizvi, F. (2006). Imagination and the globalisation of educational policy research. *Globalisation, Societies and Education, 4*(2), 167–177.

Vidovich, L. (2004). Global-national-local dynamics in policy processes: A case study of 'quality' policy in higher education. *British Journal of Sociology of Education, 25*(3), 341–354.

Vidovich, L. (2007). Removing policy from its pedestal: Some theoretical framing and practical possibilities. *Educational Review, 59*(3), 285–298.

Vidovich, L., & Porter, P. (1999). Quality policy in Australian higher education of the 1990s: University perspectives. *Journal of Education Policy, 14*(6), 567–586.

Vidovich, L., Fourie, M., Van der Westhuizen, L., Alt, H., & Holtzhausen, S. (2000). Quality teaching and learning in Australian and South African universities: Comparing policies and practices. *Compare, 30*(2), 193–209.

Vidovich, L., & Slee, R. (2001). Bringing universities to account? Exploring some global and local policy tensions. *Journal of Education Policy, 16*(5), 431–453.

Vidovich, L., Yang, R., & Currie, J. (2007). Changing accountabilities in higher education as China 'opens up' to globalisation. *Globalisation, Societies and Education, 5*(1), 89–107.

Webb, T. P. (2005). The anatomy of accountability. *Journal of Education Policy, 20*(2), 189–208.

FURTHER READINGS

Considine, M. (2005). *Making public policy*. Cambridge: Polity.

Currie, J., Vidovich, L., & Yang, R. (2008). Embedding performance cultures in Hong Kong and Singaporean higher education. *Asia-Pacific Journal of Education, 28*(1), 67–85.

Keohane, R. (2003). Global governance and democratic accountability. In D. Held & M. Koenig-Archibugi (Eds.), *Taming Globalisation*. Cambridge: Polity.

Ranson, S. (2003). Public accountability in the age of neo-liberal governance. *Journal of Education Policy, 18*(5), 459–480.

Vidovich, L., Yang, R., & Currie, J. (2007). Changing accountabilities in higher education as China 'opens up' to globalisation. *Globalisation, Societies and Education, 5*(1), 89–107.

Webb, T. P. (2005). The anatomy of accountability. *Journal of Education Policy, 20*(2), 189–208.

Lesley Vidovich
Graduate School of Education
The University of Western Australia

MARTIN LAWN & SOTIRIA GREK

FIGURES IN THE (LAND) SCAPE

Hybridity and Transformation in Education Governance in England

INTRODUCTION

The central hypothesis of the research project this chapter builds on, "Governing by Numbers" takes as its focal supposition that UK education policy-making is shaped by an increased emphasis on the close monitoring and analysis of education data. [1] By data we mean all elements of quality assurance processes in schools, such as education statistics, tables and figures; every possible school reality categorised, measured and inspected through numbers. We explore how this 'data dream' works in conjunction with the new ideas about governance and accountability at the local education authority level in England. Indeed, as we will show, the notion of the *figure* in the education 'policy-scape' has changed meaning considerably over the recent years. School figures in the past were usually people (and not data); they were headteachers, inspectors, teachers and pupils, who were significant in their landscape and in the narratives, reports and texts of their education service. They produced education through their character, stories and daily interactions, and were known for this. They personified the service.

Today the figures have changed, the landscape has been reconfigured. For example, now it is composed of the London school league tables; the European indicators of research outputs; the OECD PISA results; the European Commission's indicators and benchmarks. Numbers have become increasingly significant in the governance of education in the globalised, knowledge-based world. This paper examines the ways in which numerical data have changed education governance in England in particular, through the application of Thomas Hughes's thesis on the transformation of governing systems in, what he calls, the "second industrial revolution" (2004). According to him, the hierarchies and centralisation of the first industrial revolution (the Fordist model) have given way to the 'flatness' and 'heterogeneity' of the 'second' industrial revolution or 'the systems world'. The paper tests this hypothesis on the basis of the English experience at the local authority level and the contradictions of governing education by numerical calculations.

Our own evidence stems from the "Governing by Numbers" project, which comparatively examines quality assurance and evaluation in Scotland and England, as well as within a wider European context. In this paper, we discuss the heaviness and complexity of these new processes of data work, and the role of the local education authorities, the central government and private contractors in governing

M. Simons, M. Olssen and M.A. Peters (eds.), Re-Reading Education Policies: A Handbook Studying the Policy Agenda of the 21st Century, 568–583.

education: we examine the decline of judgement and the rise of measurement in the governing of education systems, and the emergence of a hybrid system in education, neither fully hierarchical nor entirely decentralised.[2] In order to do that, we make comparisons of the development of quality assurance as a governing tool in England and the US and conclude by examining the ways this new governance turn has had an impact on the work of a large local education authority in England. For the purpose of this paper, we have extracted elements from case study interviews conducted as part of the larger project; this case study was one of eight local education authority case studies in Scotland and England.

TO KNOW AND TO RULE: DATA AND THE KNOWLEDGE ECONOMY

Over the last couple of decades the growth and sophistication of ICT has either led to or is led by the requirement to *know* more about the agencies and departments of the state. This is not as a new development as it might seem: the collection of statistical data about state functions, particularly on the resources of the state and people in society, has been part of governing as the state formed itself. Hacking (1975; 1990), Porter (1995) and Desrosieres (1998) have written persuasively about the intimate and interwoven relationships between the development of state administrative structures -what Bruno Latour (1987) calls a "centre of calculation"- and the development of standardisation, methodologies, technologies and related cognitive schemes of statistics and scientific thinking.

However, the speed of change to the economy, and to public services, means that data collection and analysis is behind what some private companies can do across their operations, in the commercial and production sectors. For example, through its Clubcard scheme, the accumulation of customer data about its 12 million customers, allows Tesco (the UK based supermarket group), to understand their lifestyle and food buying behaviour; this information continues to reshape the firm and its suppliers. In the last ten years, the UK government has used this capacity in the private sector as a model for its own operations. However, government information systems still lag behind the rapid transformation of ever-new social realities. Their formalised and top-down functions cannot compete with the interoperability of the information management systems that some private companies have. Nigel Thrift (2005) calls this "Knowing Capitalism": by this he means a form of capitalism that is self-knowing or reflexive. It is capitalism with a brain, actively seeking new knowledge for competitive advantage, steering and reshaping itself by research -or at least, by analysing data flows.

Yet in the same spirit, the UK government has also been trying to find ways of collecting data about service industries, which now account for almost three-quarters of the economy. Measuring them provided a range of problems as it had always been easier to produce data about simple outputs (manufacturing, for example) than it was about local authority housing or schools. It was also easier to manage and analyse simple production data than, for example, patterns of service use. Data used for governing is intended to be used as a basis for action, on resource, use or policy implementation. The issue here is about the speed, scale and range of the data acquired today, and its use in managing the system at all levels. Quality assurance is a justification not just for standardisation but also for target-setting, often closely tied with restructuring, budget cutting, steering for national outcomes, reshaping local services and encouraging self regulation.

Knowledge production was thus brought into close relationship with economic policy – what matters is what works for the economy and its efficient management. We experience the promotion of a new ethics and politics of governance in which "a particular style of formalised accountability" has become a ruling principle (Power, 1997, p. 4). The change of behaviours demanded of sectors, organisations and individuals is closely tied to the creation of new sources of data because "political judgments are implicit in the choice of what to measure, how to measure it, how often to measure it and how to present and interpret the results" (Power 1997, p. 3). In education, governing knowledge, produced and analysed by both international organisations (like the EU and the OECD) and government agencies, mobilised by actors taking that knowledge and 'drilling down' -as they themselves often put it- to the individual school, classroom and pupil provides a resource through which surveillance can be exercised. While experts promote "calculative rationality" (Bauman, 1992), political technologies disguise how power works:

> Political technologies advance by taking what is essentially a political problem, removing it from the realm of the political, and recasting it in the neutral language of science (Dreyfus & Rabinow, 1982, p. 196).

These 'political technologies' seek to bring persons, organisations and objectives into alignment. In a sense, this is the significance of the governance turn: in brief, first, a shift from centralised and vertical hierarchical forms of regulation to decentralised, horizontal and networked forms and, second, a centring on the subject and a disciplining of them. Governing has been associated with data (as well as judgement), however we are signalling a shift from a recording of the past to a shaping of the future, and especially into the development of self- governing subjects. The key to this system of governmentality lies in inculcating new norms and values by which external regulatory mechanisms transform the conduct of organisations and individuals in their capacity as "self-actualising" agents, so as to achieve political objectives through "action at a distance" (Miller and Rose, 1990, p. 1).

So, how do developments in the English education system over the last ten years fit in this new context? And how does history justify new governing choices and trends? The next section will attempt a brief overview of the shift from judgement to measurement in the quality assurance processes in England (coming closer to the US) in the 20th century, while keeping Hughes' thesis in mind and testing it in the relevant contexts.

HYBRIDITY AND TRANSFORMATION: THE CHANGING FACE OF EDUCATION GOVERNANCE IN ENGLAND

Traditionally, education systems varied in the way they were administrated or managed but in each case, there was distance through most of the 20th century between production system management and public service management. Each felt itself to be, or was managed as if, there was a distance between production and service, and even between private and public. Yet there were parallels. Hierarchy, standardisation, centralisation, expertise and bureaucracy signified the first industrial revolution (Hughes, 2004, p. 100) and while Fordism is associated with advanced and concentrated sites of production, there were elements of this first wave industrial revolution in education systems as well. Schools operated within hierarchies of control, often replicated within local authorities; while bureaucrats were few in number, systems and rule bound behaviour were managed by them; key elements of building design or examinations or intelligence testing were standardised; and expertise was associated with the inspectorate of schools. This was the British and Commonwealth systems of education. Centralisation was sometimes more indistinct, operating through examination boards, grant formulas or inspector reports. This system worked reasonably, coping with stability and rationing, but found expansion and massification much more complex:

> A hierarchical management structure feeding information up to a few executives who pass orders down, is not (...) sufficiently informed and flexible to respond to the complexity of present day organic systems (Hughes, 2004, p. 79).

Information systems were crude and needed intensive human involvement in collation and analysis. In the UK, the quantitative dimension of education was limited and simply categorised and collected. Indeed, it was recognised early on, in a standard guide of the 1920s, that there were limits on the "demands which the Board of Education (could) prudently make on Local Education Authorities for statistical information (and that) the resources of the Board for the extraction and appropriate tabulation of administrative data are not unlimited" (Selby Bigge, 1927, p. 220). Instead, inspection and examination were used as the means to judge the efficiency of schooling (however it was defined at the time). Uniformity of judgement and practice in the inspection process was to become a central question in the 'measurement' of education. Experience and advice were the core skills of inspection (Selby Bigge, 1927, p. 154). In the absence of standardisation of judgements about the meaning of efficiency, a key term in the administration of education, it was argued that the central authority was able to make solid judgments about it nevertheless:

> This process is one of comparison of school with school, of area with area, of branch of education at any one period with the same branch of another. Any conclusions must in the last resort rest on what is found in individual schools and become more precarious and disputable as they become more general and cover more ground (Selby Bigge, 1927, p. 47).

In the same early decades of the 20th century, the US was less beguiled by judgement and focused instead on measurement:

> To have in education the real benefits of quantitative science, we must spend arduous years in devising, testing and standardising units of measurement (Thorndike, 1904 quoted in Lagemann, 2000).

Measuring makes systems transparent. In Lagemann's analysis of Thorndike, it created a new relation in education between the measurers, the managers and the teachers. Managers would come to define education, using statistical data and expertise, and teachers would be responsible for achieving what was asked of them. School data was to become the main preoccupation and definition of the new professional expert, the newly defined school administrator. Measuring, the main element of the contemporary definition of education research, would be undertaken by managers. They would not manage the day to day processes of schooling but act as a new body of people, the scientific experts of the new administration. Their tools of trade were borrowed from the business domain and the professors of education – tests and statistics. Written within the context of the American efficiency movement in education, Sears places the "measurement movement" as a study across mental measurement and school management;

> so completely has the idea of measurement permeated every aspect of educational theory and measurement (...) [broadly] the movement represents virtually a new philosophy of education [and in a narrower sense] a new technique, a new set of devices for use in the study of education (Sears, 1924, p. 117).

To measure efficiency of action, resource or taxes, measures were needed which could produce standards applicable across contexts and spaces. These measures had to make comparable the management of education systems in different cities, or schools in the same city, or the teaching of a subject within the same school and city and between them. While accounting measures or work time measurements were developed to standardise elements of the system, measuring improvements or quality or efficiency in the school (sometimes called child accounting) were more difficult. In this situation, the production of school tests was important. The tests could enable progress or efficiency to be measured and compared; they rendered schooling processes transparent and so manageable. Manageable meant they could be planned and ordered through effective standards rather than a series of negotiations with or haphazard acts over human processes in the workplace.

Until the 1950s, this was the difference between the US and UK influenced systems of education; the former was based upon quantitative measurements, and the latter on professional judgement; the former saw the rise of measurement expertise, and the latter, inspection knowledge.

This changed from the late 1980s as the education systems of the UK generally moved towards local financial management and the decentralisation of decision making. Performance targets, including staffing targets, agreed with the Local Education Authorities (LEAs), meant that information needed for strategic and operation planning was in demand. Information flowed through the school office to the local authority, through new commercial software systems, at more and more frequent intervals. This information began to be used for more sophisticated purposes, for example, across secondary and further education, including course unit costs and student production costs. The local education authorities had to develop a new role; no longer disbursing resource and information in a piecemeal system, it had to establish clear guidelines -and soon performance indicators- about schooling outcomes and value for money procedures. New accounting software in schools such as the *School Information Management System*[3] (SIMS), the commercial software which was used by LEAs and schools in England automated many aspects of teacher workload and its information duties. It was even advertised as able to "predict individual pupils' future achievement", and able to raise standards in teaching and learning – by tracking the performance of individuals or groups in the school and comparing their achievement with national or school guidelines. While inspection played a strong role as well, both inspection and quality assurance systems were to be based on performance data. The leading late 1990s promoter of this approach argued that,

> we are among the world leaders – in part, this is a factor of our constitution which gives central government extensive power to implement change – a risk of course as well as an opportunity, but it is also a result of the quality of performance data and the capacity developed at LEA and school level over the last decade since the Education Reform Act, to manage change successfully (...). [To be] world-class in five or ten years time we need to study trends (...). Here in this country we are hugely advantaged in this respect since in terms of the data our system produces and the quality of research with which we analyse that data, we are truly world-class already (Barber, 1998).

Under the Labour government (from 1996 onwards) the collection and analysis of increasing amounts of assessment data, particularly performance data, by schools has been viewed as crucial to monitoring and promoting pupil achievement and in progressing towards government attainment targets. The ability of private companies to manage information flow, and to create systems which deliver information about the goods or services produced, appears to be the model upon which new governance in public services works. Companies who work, merge or compete with each other may become isomorphic or develop identical qualities, through the actions of mobile professionals or through mimetic response to other successful companies (Rhoades & Spron, 2002, p. 3). Not only are private companies an exemplar in the system, for their use of data to steer their organisations, but they are increasingly partners in the development of this intensive data based system of production.

In the description of the education system in England, some common features can be seen with other forms of production and service. They are built on data collection within large quality assurance systems and dependent on a range of information and communication technologies. Data is produced, reviewed and circulated constantly to steer the system. Data provides shape and direction as it used to compare and predict. Metaphorically, it is viewed as a single but complex, reflexive system, responding to feedback (Hughes, 2004, p. 95/6). This is not just a description of England, of course, since the system of comparison, the projection into an imagined space of global competition, is borderless. Knowledge is to be mined wherever it can be found as long as new experts can guarantee its value.

So, returning to our examination of Hughes' thesis, the Fordist model of organisation, with its emphasis on hierarchy, standardisation and centralisation, was not entirely congruent with the UK education systems, but there were overlaps. Hierarchy and bureaucracy were built into the professional and administrative relations of education although standardisation of processes, especially in assessment, were rarer, except in IQ testing. Unlike the US, the system depended upon judgement not data or experts, and upon comparison and experience and not measurement and standardisation. Yet this is not the case today. The systems are much nearer together, with a similar impetus even though uneven or different time/space positions. The impact of private company models has probably been greater in the UK (particularly in England), starting as it did from its public (state) model of education and from its suspicion of data in education systems (for most of the 20th century):

Hypercritical Europeans found simplistic quantification to be the hallmark of the mechanised Americans, who believed that bigger is better. They measured achievement numerically in the workplace, professional life and sports (...) [they] spoke and wrote mesmerised by the spell of the quantitative. They could not penetrate qualitatively the profundity of life (Hughes, 2004, p. 78).

The global policy space is envisaged, or recognised, as a space of numbers; no longer American, it is international.

Hughes argues that the second industrial revolution has moved away from hierarchy, centralisation, expertise and bureaucracy and towards flatness, inter-disciplinarity, heterogeneity, distributed control, meritocracy and nimble flexibility. There are mixed messages here from UK education (or more particularly in this case, English education). Technology driven features of this revolution are recognisable in education. Data flows around the system, connecting together small and large schools, towns and cities, and local and national authorities, often aided by the software of private companies. Heterogeneous elements allow this process to speed and extend. Data software, management consultants, assessment offices, local and national inspections, private companies, bands of data input assistants, reams of documents and web based files ports, are all part of this system. Distributed control makes questions about control more difficult; control is now hidden among a range of partners, standards and procedures but the centre still holds:

In fact actually we've been developing a concept here in the Department which we've called 'the bridge' where we corral all of this data and information and at a glance now across all local authorities in England you can go downstairs and look at a big screen and you can look across all the key performance areas and that's actually across all the social care areas as well as education. So at that level we're doing quite active performance management of the system and that's quite a powerful tool (UK DCSF [4]– official).

Agents freed from older bureaucracies and their hierarchies have been made responsible for themselves; self governing means governed or steered at a distance. This happens through data based performance systems: the regular, sometimes even continuous audit of indicators, benchmarks, and targets. The devices of performance produce data which, in electronic form, flows from the classroom, school, authority or company and into vast metaphorical vats where it is cleaned, filtered, sorted, and the calculative rationality proceeds. Control through performance has moved from the application of external judgement and organisational or professional rules and into fast data and 'self government'.

What we want to do next is show how data has become a crucial element of education. Data and its advantages and problems are at the core of this governance shift. We ask questions about Hughes's (2004) ideas – the situation seems to be trapped between his two revolutions: it appears as centralised *and* flexible; closely monitored *and* de-regulated; self-evaluated *and* performance driven; locally decided *and* centrally controlled. In order to do that, we explore sites of data work that act as mediators, receivers and diffusers of governing mechanisms and controls. This is the meso-level between government and school –the local education authority level. Through interview data, we present and analyse the case of ECS1 – a large LEA in England. [5]

NODES AND PARTS: THE ROLE OF THE LOCAL EDUCATION AUTHORITIES IN EDUCATION GOVERNANCE IN ENGLAND

In the city [ECS1], the Assessment and Statistics Units have been based together, for several years now, in an old secondary school campus on the edge of the city in a post war suburb. Both are concerned with performance data. In one of the larger rooms – cluttered with several large desks, shelves with files, wall production charts and computers- many of the main tasks of the city's education data management are carried out. It is a very busy hub of activity as inquiries are received, pupils are being tracked, attainment levels are clarified and schools consulted and advised. The email, the post and the telephone are the office's main connections with the outside world and are constantly used. Data appears to have both a physical and a virtual form:

> The Assessment Unit was set up in 1991 when I joined, just to deal with the National Curriculum (…). Traditional data has got more and more sophisticated and more and more (…) collected – this year they are collecting children's height and weight (…) there are always new things being added on [P1 (senior manager)].

Together the two Units provide information and advice on school and pupil performance data analysis and interpretation; school context data (e.g. deprivation indices); statutory target setting; school census and other school data collections and ESC1's central database of children. They undertake research and evaluation, obtain feedback from parents and pupils and provide guidance and training for staff on the interpretation and use of performance data for setting targets, tracking pupil progress and evaluating outcomes. Data is provided for the individual school, for school clusters or networks, and by geographic areas. For example, the Individual School Data includes performance trends for each Key Stage (of the Curriculum), pupil level 'forecasts' to support target setting, school and pupil level value-added[6] analysis and school attendance and exclusion trends. Comparative data works with software that includes attainment and value-added analysis for each school and for groups of schools, and produces analysis by gender, ethnic group, pupils with special educational needs, looked after children, pupils eligible for free school meals etc. Since 2007, the School census is to be carried out three times a year (January, May and September). Finally, the creation of the Children's Database follows the Children Act of 2004 which asked local authorities and partner organisations to maintain an accurate and up-to-date database of children.

> Datasets are now coming from a lot of different sources, including schools. (...). From 2008 there will be a National Chart Index for England which means that every kid in the country will be in a central database and the management of that data is a responsibility of local authorities....So the idea of this central database was (...) that you know where all the kids are and so if some of the children in the database don't have a school record then you know you have to check that up. But the main use is for different children's services to use this database to see who else is working with that child. So if you are a teacher that is concerned about the safety of a child you can check if that child is already known to social care and if it has a social worker, it gives you the contact details of the social worker [P2 (senior statistician)].

The task of managing data includes their constant organising, brokering and cleaning in order to flow. The phone constantly rings. It could be fairly straightforward, progress chasing, or it becomes a telephone-based hunt around the city for clean data. At times of the year, the atmosphere in the office, and in school offices dealing with data, is hurried, furious and confused. Confidentiality is also a problem:

> The first thing you have to ascertain is who are they? Are they a bonafide person who can [have] access to this data and what do they actually want it for? [P1]

The city is linked in a series of work relations with the local schools and the government. It works with schools directly, drawing data about the pupils. It works with the centre, either the DCSF or its agencies or contractors, cleaning the schools' data it sends to them and sometimes receiving dirty data back: as we shall see, in this relation, it is an outsider, excluded by structures over time but practically essential because of its expertise, trustworthiness locally and supporting processes. The office represents a significant actor, because of tradition and expertise.

In the early1990s, these city schools tended to be described in broad spatial and class terms, where district and area were seen as synonyms for deprivation, poor schools or low achievement. The production of local comparative data meant that these older and often politically and educationally useful terms were not easily usable anymore. Schools could be clustered together, not by geography, but in various useful ways, for example, their similar social profile but dissimilar examination results. Comparator schools, using new data, could work together on science curriculum processes and results, even though they were across the city from each other. Within a few years, simple data, like free school meal provision, a standard indicator of school achievement, was being replaced by new sources of data and new ways of analysing data. Within the city, the driver of this change was the new Director (using the political capital available locally) but the engine of improvement was the city professionals – the advisers, head teachers, teachers and specialists. The city's pride, faced with failure in the rankings, and a contemporary social justice argument, focused on the multicultural city, were utilised in this process of transformation. In addition, during the 1990s, the creation of data based governing of the city schools, replacing more paternal, random or inefficient decision making, was welcomed by many headteachers. It seemed to fit with either the competitive agendas of suburban schools or the strong social justice agendas of the urban areas. The city developed an identity as a successful (or improving) city in education, after a long period of neglect. As a city which was losing a lot of its industrial base and not acquiring the capacity to attract service based companies, this identity was important. It was helped by a residual strength and sense of place in the city, which was used to change itself.

However, as the local authorities in England developed their own systems and vernacular practices, at the turn of the century, new Labour began to overlay and then supersede their efforts with national measures:

It was probably 5 years ago [2001] when the DfES with OFSTED [7] started to look at common systems for assessing the performance of schools that would be available in electronic format where you can drill down not only to the level of school performance but also in terms of groups of students (…). So [in 2001] they were looking at how they may do this and three years ago they produced their first version which they call 'pupil achievement tracker' which was of mixed… it wasn't a perfect system by any means and there were some problems with actually running the software. A lot of the data had to be put in locally which put a lot of schools off in the first place but that was the first time that there was any national system for analysing data which was more than just having school league tables. Basically what we were doing in [City]could be done nationally [P2].

They are attempting to get every single school in England, primary and secondary, thousands of schools, all the data at an individual pupil level in a massive database held on a server somewhere in London which then is accessed by all the schools in the country and OFSTED inspectors, and school advisors and other people, in order to analyse the data [P2].

An incentive in the system was that schools could make a clear link between data returns and income; being clear about the data returned is essential if money is attached to the data. Every extra child meant an additional funding point -data had to be kept up to date. Perhaps the key to compliance is the strong system of external accountability in which it is embedded:

> If you removed inspection and performance tables out of the equation, the level of interest in this would be significantly lower. There would still be some schools that would still be interested in doing it but a lot of schools wouldn't (...) partly because of the effort needed, partly because of the arcane nature of the way the data is provided [P2].

However, problems with the interoperability of national systems means that the city policy is to continue with local support on data:

> What's happening so far is that because the national systems aren't yet robust enough and reliable enough we are still supporting our schools in the same way and the schools say they want that [P2].

As well as the complexity and scope of the data they are now dealing with, and the training and techniques needed to produce operational value in schools, there is the question of the speed at which this data is now flowing between schools and the local authority. While once there was a winter pupil census, managed by a paper-based process, now there was a constant flow of data:

> In effect it is constantly on-line, it works as a weekly up-dating process. Automatically. So each week the computer asks for this data, the school gives it and then sticks it in a central database and then we find that it does not match properly ! (...) Now we are talking about on-going electronic systems that operate all the time, so when an event happens it is recorded. So if a child loses school tomorrow we don't wait until the end of the term, we know it real-time on a weekly basis [P2].

In the past, assessment data gushed through the school and into the office in the summer term, and the census return flowed hard in winter. This was the early rhythm of the year, intensive cyclically with periods of calm preparation in between.

> From January to May, there was more of a chance to reflect upon the data in the past (...) whereas we used to have a quietish period it doesn't really exist anymore I'm afraid. We are doing all sorts of reports to go up on the web (...) it seems as if we are constantly disseminating information for various things and answering queries on it really (...) there is all these initiatives going on [P1].

Both the assessment and statistics Units are trying to manage the space between the central government and the LEA. Generally, with a lot of effort, they can resolve most problems within their boundaries; this is done through personal relationships, helpful support, clear documentation, tailored city systems. The 'known' is all the data that they hold – the unknown is,

> what on earth is the government up to this year and how're the schools going to get the stuff to me (…) so I am sort of the broker in the middle I suppose [P1].

The 'unknown' is the centre. The office and the schools work in an arena that they don't control. However, where is the centre? In reality, it seems as if there is no centre, but a series of contracted arrangements with private data companies, working with DCSF. In order to manage this complex and demanding work process, DCSF created a regular series of meetings with the LEA data officers. In these meetings, brokering takes place but within its asymmetric relations:

> Back in 1997, when things were starting up, they were sloppy and difficult, there were problems, (…) moaning to DfES (…) we began to get RIG meetings [and you have to laugh] rapid integration something or other meetings at the DfES – and rapid has to make you laugh because everything always took ages but never mind…we said why don't you have a [city] area, we would loan you a room with computers, you could give the stuff straight to the LEA, and we would send it to schools on your behalf? They didn't want us to do that. They wanted to control it but they couldn't, it was too big a job [P1].

Brokering operates to manage the workflow problems which stop the city achieving its own aims; to service its teachers and help them improve education. Given the constant push from the centre, these meetings offer a space in which to influence the central technocrats and haggle:

> That's where these meetings are useful because you do go up and chat with these powerful (…) and to be honest (…) even if you don't say it in the main forum, you catch them over lunch and you say there is a particular problem and they will say email me and because [city] is so big, they are often waiting for our data feeds (…) to give them an idea about how things are going to go nationally – they want to know if things are getting better [P1].

The LEA has a history of development responsibility for its schools, and long standing deep relations with them. The new direct relation between the centre and the school, envisaged in this construction of data production and flow, denies the role of the LEA. The LEA represents the old relation of the centre and the local. While this is the new discourse of education and its governance, local government does not intend to be excluded. Its arguments are not the old ones – 'these are our schools' – but the new one – 'our responsibility for improvement':

So if something does go wrong even though we are not supposed to be involved , we get the phone call and we don't say its not our problem, we sort it out [P1].

Regulation and technology have not created a new governance relation, only attempted to. Helpline culture and contract workers have not, in this case, substituted for a direct and supportive local relation. Questions arise about trusting data, and whose data to trust. Schools are becoming better at managing data and the political space around it. There is a rise in expert conversations in the city. Headteachers, school assistants, governors and teachers are able to talk about the problems of data and its manipulation. They have become much more expert:

It is also the case that if enough LAs feel that there are new questions to be asked about data and its use in governing education, and on behalf of schools, then presumably we get together and say to the DfES that 'sorry, you have to look at something because what's on the ground, that we know (...) your model needs tweaking a bit' [P1].

However, the processes that data undergo at central level are becoming more opaque for the LEA, and what was once possible is becoming impossible. While data flows more easily, as it becomes more refined, through complex procedures which few understand, then it begins to lose persuasive power and is interpreted as at least unhelpful, even arbitrary.

CONCLUSIONS: A PARADOXICAL POSITIONING – THE EXCLUDED CENTRE

This paper has examined the growth of the dream and the practice of new governance, and its heightened delusions of seamless control through transparent system data. We have argued that the shift of control mechanisms from hierarchies of officers and rules to data based systems and software has changed education governance. Judgement has been replaced by calculation, and bureaucracy by heterogeneous relations.

The paper tries to show how the education system has been reconfigured. The narratives of the past have been replaced by the imaginaries of the future. A data production process has been designed to exclude firstly, one of the old core partners in the education service, the local government, and secondly, intuition, experience and judgement, the skills of its inspectors and officers. Contracted companies and direct school connections, linked together by transparent webs of data and a centre of calculation, appear to be the goal of this reconfiguration. Yet the schools, particularly the primary in the city, and the secondary as well in the country, may still see the LEA as the legitimate and helpful local guardian of education. The companies, and through them, the central government agency and department, appear to have no view of the LEA, neither historical nor democratic or even as a knowledge broker. It exists as an organisation which may help to sort some data flow and validity problems – when absolutely necessary.

Hughes regarded the hierarchy, centralisation, expertise and bureaucracy of the first industrial revolution to have given way to the 'flatness', 'distributed control' and 'heterogeneity' of the 'second' industrial revolution or 'the systems world'. Technically, it is possible to view the new system of governance as representing this second industrial revolution. It is heavily dependent on advanced systems software, computing power and data specialists. Indeed, it is the same set of skills and resources which enable commercial companies to sift, shape and construct relations with consumers and their buying power. These companies are both exemplars of the possible and often, through their expertise, agents of this governance step. Political visions of the future society have been driven down into contracted relations of performance and production. Self governed behaviour is the object. In this, technical support has also metamorphosed; it is both technically capable and politically involved. It creates the data flows and analyses and the shaping of future behaviours by indicators and innovatory schemes. The understanding of the present is seamlessly turned into the construction of the future. As the future has no shape, behaviours are determined to be flexible. Education data passes through a series of constructed nodes as it flows through the system; it is coded to enable smooth passage; it is drilled and mined; and it is constantly re-imagined. New hybrid technicians re-engineer its flow paths, its constituent objects, its protocols and its manuals. They operate on the basis of problems (policy and material problems of flow] and technical imagination (the capabilities and potential of data and systems].

In this way, Hughes' analysis appears to fit the new governance of education. However if the perspective is shifted from the technical (although, as we have shown, even that has hybrid features), and onto the political, then it is not just flexibility, distributed control and flatness which are present. Local authorities still represent a locality, a political entity in education, with its own history, strategy and resources which have been politically excluded from many elements of the national data management systems and yet they are essential to the effective working of that same system. They are both necessary and not in partnership. In some cases, the demands of the new system will have enabled some local authorities to upskill themselves but it is more likely that they will have been turned into rule followers, managing the wide range of tasks, seasonal and continual, demanded by the centre, or even processing centres, checking software problems. Yet although data flows, there are physical, expert and contextual processes which enable it to do this; without them, flow is halted and data sticks. Our case extracts suggest the crucial role of the local authority in helping the flow, without which it would soon solidify the fluid conduits it uses. Also, data demands sophistication of use and people to learn to process it. However, data in such force exists because of the governing demands (and redesign) in the system and data cannot be divorced from this – people manage data, and argue about it, to widen their space of manoeuvre. Seen in this way, it is not flatness or distributed control which is visible but a hybrid in which standardisation, centralisation and expertise (key elements of the first industrial revolution) are still prominent in education in England as well. The language of the technical imaginary has been merged into a new governance model for education. Unable to renew itself, the education system has been turned into a hybrid of constant readjustment, micro control and centralisation. Transparency of data has replaced hierarchical judgement but only as a means of effective control. Private companies, managing data processing services, and using their consultancy and strategic divisions, have produced system heterogeneity and distributed production. Centralisation is untouched, possibly more effective and certainly dominant. Education is not located in the first or second industrial revolution but in a hybrid of both.

Not many years ago, it was possible to describe the English education system in common explanatory phrases; it was a 'central system, locally administered' or it was a 'partnership between central and local government, and the teaching profession'. Not only are these phrases redundant now, but they cannot be replaced by new ones. The effect of the quasi-market, micro-management, performance delivery systems, and powerful regulatory bodies (like OfSted), combined with rapid and short-lived innovations and almost no system memory, is that there appears to be a 'systemless system' in operation. Studying closely the working of standards, targets, data flow, and actual work within it is vital now, in the absence of core myths and the omnipresence of normative discourses of improvement. Data flow and governance is a fruitful source of study, and may even be the only place in which the 'English education system' can be viewed today.

NOTES

[1] This paper draws on research in progress on the ESRC funded project 'Governing by Numbers: Data and education governance in Scotland and England' RES—00-23-1385, which is part of the Eurocores 'Fabricating Quality in European Education' project of the European Science Foundation.

[2] England and Scotland have two different education systems and means of governing them. The main part of this paper uses a case study from an English city and its arguments work relate more to England .

[3] This is management information software purchased by Capita Children Services, "the UK's leading supplier of Management Information Systems to the Education Sector and Children's Services Divisions within Local Authorities." According to the company's website, "SIMS .net is a Management Information System (MIS) designed specifically for schools to tackle the issues that really matter to them, such as reducing workload, raising pupil performance and being ready to support the latest government initiative" (online, Capita, 2008).

[4] In England, the Ministry of Education has had several changes of name; it was known as the DES (Department of Education and Science], the DfES (Department for Education and Skills] and today, as the Department of Children, Schools and Families (DCSF].

[5] Code name for English Case Study 1.

[6] Value-added analysis means that each pupil's performance in a set of tests is compared with the middle performance of all pupils nationally who had a similar performance at the previous test level. The result does not depend on how well pupils do in outright terms, but how much they have improved, whatever their ability.

[7] The Inspection Agency was known as OfSted, the Office for Standards in Education, and now as the Office for Standards in Education, Children's Services and Skills.

REFERENCES

Barber, M. (1998). *Creating a world class education service.* The North of England Education conference proceedings, Bradford, 5–7th January.

Bauman, Z. (1992). *Intimations of postmodernity.* London: Routledge.

Desrosieres, A. (1998). *The politics of large numbers.* Harvard: Harvard University Press.

Dreyfus, H. L., & Rabinow, P. (Eds.). (1982). *Michel Foucault: Beyond structuralism and hermeneutics.* Chicago: University of Chicago Press.

Hacking, I. (1975). *The emergence of probability.* Cambridge: Cambridge University Press.

Hacking, I. (1990). *The taming of chance.* Cambridge: Cambridge University Press.

Hughes, T. (2004). *Human-built world.* Chicago: University of Chicago Press.

Lagemann, E. C. (2000). *The elusive science – the troubling history of education research.* Chicago: Chicago University Press.

Latour, B. (1987). *Science in action: How to follow scientists and engineers through society.* Milton Keynes: Open University Press.

Miller, P., & Rose, N. (1990). Governing economic life. *Economy and Society, 19,* 1–31.

Porter, T. (1995). *Trust in numbers: The pursuit of objectivity in science and public life.* Princeton: Princeton University Press.

Power, M. (1997). *The audit society: Rituals of verification.* Oxford: Oxford University Press.

Rhoades, G., & Spron, B. (2002). Quality assurance in Europe and the US: Professional and political economic framing of higher education policy. *Higher Education, 43*(3), 355–390.

Sears, J. S. (1924). Development of tests and measurements. In I. L. Kandel (Ed.), *Twenty five years of American education* (pp. 117–139). New York: Macmillan.

Selby Bigge, Sir L. A. (1927). *The board of education.* London: Putnam and Sons.

Thompson, G. (2007). *Are we all neo-liberals now?* Online material: Soundings Debate 2007. Retrieved from http://www.soundings.org.uk/

Thrift, N. (2005). *Knowing capitalism.* London: Sage.

FURTHER READINGS

Lascoumes, P., & Le Galès, P. (2007). Understanding Public Policy through its instruments-from the nature of instruments to the sociology of public policy instrumentation. *Governance, 20*(1), 1–21.

Lawn, M. (2006). Soft Governance and the Learning Spaces of Europe. *Comparative European Politics, 4*(2-3), 272-288.

Ozga, J. (2009). Governing education through data in England: From regulation to self-evaluation. *Journal of Education Policy, 24*(2), 149-162.

Porter, T. (1995). *Trust in numbers: The pursuit of objectivity in science and public life.* Princeton, NJ: Princeton University Press.

Power, M. (1997). *The audit society: Rituals of verification.* Oxford: Oxford University Press.

Rhodes, R. A. W. (1997). *Understanding governance policy networks, governance, reflexivity and accountability.* Buckingham: Open University Press.

Martin Lawn
Centre for Educational Sociology
University of Edinburgh

Sotiria Grek
Centre for Educational Sociology
University of Edinburgh

SIMON MARGINSON

UNIVERSITY RANKINGS, GOVERNMENT
AND SOCIAL ORDER

*Managing the Field of Higher Education according to the Logic
of the Performative Present-as-Future*

INTRODUCTION: RE-READING GLOBAL UNIVERSITY RANKINGS

The past half decade has seen the emergence of new systems for ranking individual universities against each other on a worldwide scale, of which the most prominent and authoritative is the ordering of university research performance by the Shanghai Jiao Tong University Institute for Higher Education (SJTUIHE, 2007). In many nations, these rankings are widely cited in the media, and in advertising and other communications by universities. In some nations the rankings appear to influence government thinking concerning the ordering of higher education systems, particularly by encouraging policies of concentration of funding and other resources designed to boost the global standing of selected research universities.

As a set of techniques for measuring university performance and ordering universities in relation to each other, global university ranking have roots in longer-standing systems of national university ranking, particularly the annual rankings by the US News and World Report in the United States (USNWR, 2007). At the same time global ranking has gained its sudden importance from the coincidence of two larger policy developments. First, the development of the techniques of the New Public Management (NPM) in the administration of educational systems and institutions, in a period in which neo-liberal perspectives are dominant in government; and in particular the NPM's imagining of higher education as a kind of quasi-economy in which universities compete with each other on the basis of measurable outputs, so that comparative performance can be assessed and used to guide the reform of organisation and the allocation of funds for future activity. Second, the globalisation of higher education; the growing role played by cross-border movements of research, ideas and people in higher education and in particular the growing reliance by national policy makers on international comparisons as a means of judging performance; that is, global referencing.

This paper uses a critical perspective to summarise, examine and explain the main systems of global university rankings that have emerged. It focuses on the utilities of rankings as a technique of government that is informed by the perspectives of neo-liberalism and the methods of the NPM. The argument is grounded in the author's scepticism about the desirability and feasibility of the

M. Simons, M. Olssen and M.A. Peters (eds.), Re-Reading Education Policies: A Handbook Studying the Policy Agenda of the 21ˢᵗ Century, 584–604.

ambitious neo-liberal project to 'economise' education (Marginson, 1997). In its discussion of the policy space, the paper draws in part on the theorisations of Pierre Bourdieu, in particular his imagining of a competitive university "field" that is structured by a polar opposition between elite research universities and vocational mass institutions (for further discussion of Bourdieu's conception of field see immediately below).

At the same time the paper does not adopt a full blown 'Bourdieu-ian' perspective. It can be argued that Bourdieu's summation of human identity and behaviour under the label of acquired "habitus" (Bourdieu, 1984), while again suggestive, underestimates the scope of human agency in imagining alternatives and transforming social structures: for more of this kind of critique of Bourdieu's 'structuralist' bias see Marginson (2008a); and also the work of Arjun Appadurai (1996) on global agency. Arguably Bourdieu is at his best when describing the endogenous dynamics of structures, to the extent that these dynamics are independent of human agency; and his insights there are helpful in exploring the structure-building neo-liberal project, for example the manner in which constructed markets work. Nevertheless neo-liberalism and the NPM are also designed to change objectives, values and practices. To more fully understand the effects of university rankings in human and governmental behaviour, as well as more on the scope for resistances and alternatives to the dominant neo-liberal practices in higher education, we need to look also beyond Bourdieu to many others: for example Rose (1999) and other post-Foucaultian social theorists; and various critiques 'from below' of globalisation in higher education, for example the collections by Burbules & Torres (2000), and Rhoads & Torres (2006). This larger zone of criticism and discussion will not be explored in detail in this paper which for reasons of length and focus concentrates on global university rankings.

MODELLING UNIVERSITY PERFORMANCE

Bourdieu's theorisation of the "field" of higher education.

In the last half century the only major social theorist who has conducted a sustained investigation into the dynamics of higher education is Pierre Bourdieu (1984; 1988; 1993; 1996). Bourdieu develops the notion of a field of power, such as the university field or field of higher education, "understood as a space, that is, an ensemble of positions in a relationship of mutual exclusion" (1996, p. 232). A field of power is a social universe with its own laws of functioning. The field enjoys a degree of autonomy, to the extent that it holds off external determinants and is driven by its own internal logic. Within the field of power, agents (in higher education both institutions and individuals are agents) are locked into competition for resources, status or other objects. In this competition there is inter-dependency between the prior positions of agents within the hierarchy – their starting positions in the competition, the resources and networks at their command, and so on – and the 'position-taking' strategies they select. Bourdieu describes the position-taking activities of agents as the "space of creative works" (p. 39) but this is not an open-ended free-wheeling creativity. "Every position-taking is defined in relation to the space of possibles which is objectively realised as a problematic in the form of the actual or potential position-takings corresponding to the different positions" (Bourdieu, 1993, p. 30). In other words, only some position-takings are possible; and the moves of agents tend to correspond to their starting positions; so that within a social order people tend to make moves that fit with their own expectations, their identity and their senses of possible is possible and likely. The possible positions that agents can adopt are identified by them as they respond to changes in the settings of the competition game, and also to the moves of others within that game. Agents have a number of possible 'trajectories', that is, the succession of positions occupied by the same agent over time; and employ semi-instinctual 'strategies' to achieve those trajectories. In doing so agents respond in terms of their 'habitus' which is the mix of beliefs and capabilities they have acquired through their upbringing and their past experiences of social competition (pp. 61–73). For example both the habitus and the prior position in the hierarchy of universities tend to shape the degree to which individual university leaders use strategies that are characteristic of elite research universities.

For Bourdieu the field of higher education is structured by a polar opposition. At one end there is the sub-field of restricted elite production. At the other end is the sub-field of mass production tending to commercial production. Each sub-field has its own distinct principle of hierarchization. In the aristocratic elite universities, where the high value products are immersed in knowledge and power and shaped as tools of advantage, the principle of hierarchization is that of cultural status and is autonomous and specific to the field. In the mass or popular institutions, hierarchy is shaped by economic capital and market demand, and the institutions are heteronomous; though from time to time mass institutions renew themselves by adapting ideas from the elite sector. Between these two sub-fields lie a range of intermediate institutions combining the two opposing principles in varying degrees.

As noted, Bourdieu's theorisation has been criticised for his failure to overcome, despite his own strenuous efforts, especially in *Distinction* (1984), the dualism he creates between structure and agency and the manner in which his notion of agency becomes trapped on the structure side. More specifically, the picture of higher education governed by universal relations of competition is open to criticism, as it neglects the prevalence also of gift relations and public goods, for example in scholarship and research (Kenway, et al., 2006; Marginson, 2007a, Marginson, 2007c). Much of Bourdieu's underlying research took place in pre-1968 French institutions, prior to the fuller growth of mass higher education, and prior to policy neo-liberalism and contemporary globalisation. Yet despite these limitations, Bourdieu's idea of the field of higher education, if not a satisfactory general theory of higher education, is in some respects powerfully explanatory of the contemporary dynamics of competition in that sector. It seems that in a period in which inter-university competition has taken a more powerful, pervasive and more specifically economic form, Bourdieu's notion of the field of higher education, which like all his theorisations tends to universalise social relations instrumental to capitalist society, comes into its own. The Bourdieuian polarity between the sub-field of elite institutions and the sub-field of mass-commercial institutions can readily observed in national higher education systems (Naidoo, 2004) where it helps to explain inter-institutional tension and differentiation. More remarkably, perhaps, Bourdieu's 1960s polarity and his principles of hierarchization, especially in the elite sub-field, also illuminate the emerging global competition.

Neo-liberal ordering of the field

If competition in higher education has long-standing social roots as Bourdieu argues, its contemporary form as a market derives primarily from the evolution of government. Most of the world's higher education systems have been affected by neo-liberal policy and its financial and administrative technologies collated in the New Public Management (NPM). The passage of those policy ideas between countries has moved faster in the present more global era which is characterised by instantaneous communications and complex data transfer, cheaper air travel and more intensive people movement between national governments and between universities in different countries. There has been a perceptible increase in the tendency for national policies and the practices of institutional management to converge (Marginson & van der Wende, 2007); and numerous studies, supportive and critical, attest to the impact of the New Public Management in system organisation and institutional culture (e.g. Clark, 1998; Rose, 1999; Marginson & Considine, 2000; Musselin, 2005; Henkel, 2005; Rhoads & Torres, 2006). As is now well known the NPM imagines national systems as economic markets and universities and other higher education institutions as firms driven by desires for economic revenues and market share, not by teaching, research and service as ends in themselves. The NPM norms higher education as a state-steered competition, national systems as a mixture of public and private institutions, and institutions as an executive-steered competition between academic units and personnel. Social demand is meant to be regulated by tuition prices, and institutions engaged in marketing, customer focus, entrepreneurship and research programs advocated by policy researchers who argue that research is or should be driven by industry requirements and government-determined research priorities rather than the curiosity of researchers themselves (Gibbons et al., 1994; Nowotny, et al., 2001). At the same time the neo-liberal era in higher education is an era of utilitarian performativity as Lyotard (1984) remarks, in which competition is serviced by performance measures, output-based funding, measures of economic value, tests of relevance and impact, and relations with funding agencies based on contracts, accountability and audit.

NPM reforms drive towards fiscal efficiency, global trade and competitiveness and more effective systems of nation-state control of universities and their work. The double move, the deregulation of the university-as-firm and over-regulation of academic output as performance, creates a complex mix of tendencies to autonomy and heteronomy in which the older freedoms of basic research and scholarly agency are not so much abolished as reworked, becoming more mobile, multiple, fragmented, fragile and contested (Henkel, 2005; Marginson, 2008b).

This historical project of neo-liberalism and the NPM, that of recasting the field of higher education as a performative market of competing universities-as-firms, in turn generates the need for two innovations in policy technology site-specific to higher education. The first innovation is a plausible and coherent model or models of the ideal university-as-firm. The second innovation is a plausible mapping of the higher education field in the form of a hierarchy of institutional performance, that can be represented as the outcome of market competition. These two policy innovations are inter-dependent. The ideal model functions as a template against which institutions of higher education are measured and ranked.

Idealised models. Across world-wide higher education there are many different combinations of mission, structure and organisational culture, each set associated with distinctive traditions and models nested in national contexts, historical identities and conditions. In the 'Westminster' countries (UK, Australia, New Zealand) systems combine university autonomy and public/private investment with explicit national steering. The Scandinavian university combines high and socially equitable participation, research culture and university autonomy with state investment (Valimaa, 2004; 2005). The German-style university opts for elite participation, research culture and state administration. The classical Latin American public university as at the University of Buenos Aires combines high participation, scholarly culture and a central social and political role in building the nation-state. The emerging science universities of East and Southeast Asia, including China, Taiwan, Korea and Singapore are fostered by state investment and in Singapore are explicitly designed to secure global competitiveness. India has developed a unique model of technological and business-focused institutions combining high quality with commercialism. Beyond the research university are strong vocational sectors in Finland, Germany (the *Fachhochschulen*), France; other vocational and community-based programs; and a wide range of for-profit providers, online institutions and institutions with single-specialisms.

Nevertheless, in the generic policies of the NPM, exemplified by the checklists used by the World Bank in its lending programs in the developing world, there are two favoured models against which institutions around the world are readily judged. These models are quite different, but one (that of the ideal research university) enjoys greater status in most circles than does the other. Given the weight of the United States in the global political economy and culture, and in the higher education sector itself, it is unsurprising that both of these models have been derived primarily from the American experience. The models are:

– The idealised research university. Emphasises research and graduate studies, excellence and prestige. Entrepreneurial (Clark, 1998). Tied to business and the knowledge economy. Competes for students and funds. Internationally oriented. Achieving a growing autonomy via financial diversity, including tuition and philanthropy. The US Ivy League private universities are closest to this model in the real world. In some respects the practices of these institutions diverge from the model – for example their funding (especially in research) is more state-dependent than the NPM ideal would suggest; they do not evidence a strong dynamic of responding to the preferences of the student consumer; and their support and prestige rest to a surprising extent on lobbying politics in Washington, rather than market demand pure and simple. Nevertheless, the real life Ivy League universities, which are powerful institutions, are close enough to the idealised research university in the model to confer on that model exceptional prestige and therefore a tremendous potency in shaping notions of good practice across the world.

– The idealised institution of mass vocational higher education. Focused on training for business, computing, and mass professions such as health and education. Accountable for immediate vocational relevance. Expansionary of student numbers, sites and market share; and in the case of fully commercial institutions driven by profit. Marketing-driven. Spare and efficient with no 'frills' such as research, libraries or academic freedoms. 'Customer'-focused using performance management of staff and quality assurance. Mass vocational higher education, tending to commercialisation, has a mixed record around the world but in the US has become embodied in corporations raising significant equity funds, including the Apollo Group, parent company of the University of Phoenix. Phoenix is the largest private university in the USA and has spread to a dozen countries.

These two models are idealised manifestations of each of the two sub-fields identified by Bourdieu, confirming the relevance of his notion of the field.

The mass vocational higher education model is also not very far from the practices of commercial cross-border education in the UK and Australia, where mostly non-profit universities provide for-profit education of foreign students at home or in transnational campuses abroad. We find this kind of commercial international education even in certain research-intensive universities. While on one hand those institutions position themselves as elite providers in relation to domestic students; on the other hand, in the global market they position themselves as mass providers engaged in an expansionary form of education designed to maximise revenues in true capitalist fashion. Typically, the dominant form of cross-border program is the standardised high volume production of programs of medium quality business education (for more discussion see Marginson, 2007b).

Of course there are other possible 'American models' in a national system that is a by-word for structured diversity: the liberal arts college, the state universities and four year institutions, and the community colleges. Most US enrolments are in the public sector, including the University of California system and the land grant and other public flagship universities. But the Ivy League private institutions have the highest status; while in neo-liberal circles the US public institutions are seen as ambiguous institutions, inferior to the commercial sector as vehicles for expanding mass education; subsidy-heavy, often research-thick, supply driven and inflexible.

Rank ordering the field on the basis of performance. National rankings of universities date back to the 1920s and a long established method of creating a status hierarchy, apparently based on merit, which can be deployed for the purposes of annual 'consumer guides' to student choice; a practice that has become entrenched more in some countries more than others. Now we have global rankings, the listing of a university hierarchy on a world-wide scale, which began in 2003. University rankings have proven an effective means of normalising higher education as a market of competing institutions, in which 'quality' is grounded in 'performance' and equated with market power. Global university rankings translate that notion of competitive market onto the global plane, while quietly hustling from the stage the more cooperative elements in inter-institutional relations, for example the free exchange of research information. Rankings create a compelling picture. Apparently, they summarise the whole university world in a single table. Everyone wants to know which universities and which nations are regarded as 'better' or 'worse' and whether their institutions/systems are rising or falling. Rankings give such judgments a telling kind of authority. At the popular level this authority is sustained regardless of the many technical and methodological issues, and the omissions and biases, inherent in any and every ranking system. Thus the ranking process combines the neo-liberal imaginary of education as a market, and the practices of competition and performance measurement established by the NPM, with a compelling simplification that explains a lot by means of a little.

In global rankings systems the leading institutions are normally those US and UK (principally American) research universities that operate in the elite sub-field of the global market and congruent with the first idealised model listed above. The idealised mass vocational university also plays a role in some rankings systems, albeit a subordinate role. Let's look more closely at the conditions that made global ranking of universities possible and perhaps (in the eyes of some) necessary.

Hierarchical global comparison of universities has been made possible by a particular conjunction of discursive conditions. The development of a global performative hierarchy was foreshadowed in the practices of hierarchical ordering and exclusion traditional to higher education, in credentialing and knowledge cultures: informal status ranking has long been part of thinking in many countries. As noted some of the groundwork was laid by global communications, trade in education and the NPM; and also by the world-wide organisation of science and research and the growing dominance of English as the one global language of research. Comparisons of national performance in education have been legitimated by the widespread use of cross-country comparisons in economic policy, in which the nation-state is understood as a competition state and government performance is according to whether the nation is seen to be rising or falling on the global plane. More specifically, university rankings have roots in the normative methods of comparative education and development education, particularly the pervasive comparisons of national policy performance by the OECD (2006) and World Bank.

Global university rankings have gripped the attention of higher education institutions, governments, media and public throughout the world. They have quickly secured a major influence in the definition of the field of higher education.

University rankings seem to tap into strong desires for rank ordering as an end in itself, without much regard as to what the rankings measure, which objectives or activities of higher education they incorporate and which models of institution they embody, whether they are well grounded in observation and logic, whether their use has constructive effects. Strikingly, institutions are often rank ordered even where differences in the data are not statistically significant. League tables rule.

Rankings more precisely identify a global hierarchy of leading universities, a hierarchy which varies according to ranking system, but not much at the very top; and hence enable league tables of national system performance, for example the proportion of universities from each nation in the top group of universities. Rankings always pose the question: 'How can our university/nation perform better?' University rankings entrench understandings of the field of higher education in 'Bourdieuian' terms – as competitive, a site of struggles for position, in which the strategic options are shaped by prior position – while more deeply legitimating cross-border comparison. University rankings also entrench understandings of the field in 'Lyotardian' terms, as a contest in performativity in which performance is measurable and visible and its utilities are determinant.

Here the definition of 'performance' is all important. Rankings systems appear to 'evaluate universities as a whole' (van Dyke 2005, p. 106). But of course no rankings system can cover all purposes of higher education from the point of view of all actual or potential stakeholders: the outputs are multiple and complex, some are potentially in tension with others, not all are open to numerical measurement; and one key area, the quality of teaching and learning and the 'value added' during the educational process, eludes comparative measurement (Dill & Soo, 2005). In composite ranking systems across multiple domains, or more than one numerical measure within a domain, the weightings are both largely hidden and essentially arbitrary. All ranking systems encompass the needs of some stakeholders better than others. Usher & Savino (2006) examine 19 league tables and university rankings, noting they are driven by varied purposes and definitions of quality. The point is not that this heterogeneity allows rankings to be dismissed as relative. The composition of each ranking system matters, because it generates specific effects.

The remainder of the chapter will discuss national rankings in the United States; the principal global rankings systems now in use, those prepared by Shanghai Jiao Tong University Institute of Higher Education (SJTUIHE, 2007) and the Times Higher Education Supplement (THES, 2006) review the policy responses to rankings; and consider their effects in a little more detail; before concluding.

RANKINGS SYSTEMS

National Rankings

National rankings date back to the 1920s in the United States. Most countries with large higher education systems have rankings of one kind or another. Countries with rankings devised by newspapers and magazines include China and Hong Kong China, Japan, India, the Ukraine, Romania, Poland, Portugal, Italy, Spain, Germany,

Sweden, Switzerland, France, UK, USA and Canada. In China, Japan, Australia, Kazakhstan, Slovakia, Romania, Russia, the Ukraine, Germany, Spain, Switzerland, the UK and Canada rankings have been initiated by universities, professional associations or other organisations. In Thailand, Malaysia, Pakistan, India, Kazakhstan, Korea, Tunisia, Nigeria, the Netherlands, the UK, Brazil and Argentina rankings have been instigated by ministries of education, grants councils or accreditation agencies (Salmi & Saroyan, 2006). Usher and Savino (2006) review rankings complied in Australia (Williams & van Dyke, 2006); Canada; China, with several rankings systems (Liu &d Liu, 2005), and Hong Kong; Germany; Italy; Poland; Spain; the UK with its four newspaper systems, and USA.

US News and World Report rankings. The annual *US News and World Report* rankings are worth noting here, given the world-wide importance of higher education in the United States. The USNWR exercise has played a key role in legitimating global rankings; and given the global leadership exercised by the American sector this ranking also acts as a de facto global ranking of sorts. Most part national rankings consist of a single table but in the USA and Canada higher education institutions are divided into groups according to mission and characteristics, creating a set of mini league-tables. The *US News and World Report* survey focuses principally on aspects of institutions seen to contribute to the quality of teaching and the student experience, servicing the national student market which is underpinned by government-backed loans and university tuition scholarships. The categories are drawn from the 2000 classification by the *Carnegie Foundation for the Advancement of Teaching* (USNWR, 2006, p. 81ff). The leading grouping is the 'national Universities', 248 universities (162 public and 86 private) with a range of fields of study, degrees to doctoral level and mostly research intensive.

In the category of National Universities 25 per cent of the index is comprised by a survey of 'undergraduate academic excellence' sent to university presidents, provosts and deans of admissions. Two items each constitute 20 per cent: student retention and graduation rates; and 'faculty resources' which rewards small classes, high academic salaries, high academic qualifications and a high proportion of staff full-time. Student selectivity at entry, a proxy for positional status, is 15 per cent. The lesser items are spending per student (10 per cent), the proportion of alumni who donate to the institution (5 per cent), and the graduation rate after controlling for spending and student aptitude (5 per cent) (USNWR, 2006, pp. 77–79). These details have become very significant. Over the years institutions have learned to modify and target their behaviour so as to maximise their *US News* position. This has also had specific effects perverse from the viewpoint of the public good. For example, in order to maximise their USNWR score, institutions manipulate the administration of student entry so as to pluralise entry methods and reduce the number of students following what is seen as the 'normal' route of entry. This allows the institutions to raise the (apparent) lowest score that a student needs to enter so it appears as more selective. More generally, institutions seek to compose their student body as selectively as possible, not just in appearance but in reality – maximising both student scores and also application refusal rates, each of which comes into play in the USNWR tables. This is despite the fact that student entry scores tend to be correlated with social advantage, so that the more academically selective the student body, and more it is also socially selective and tends to under-represent students from poorer backgrounds. A study of American 'enrolment management' by David Kirp also notes the growth of merit-based student aid at the expense of needs-based student aid. Again, the purpose is to attract an academic elite rather than a socially representative cohort so as to lift the UNSWR performance on the indicators of student selectivity, student retention and graduation rate indicators (Kirp, 2004). These are telling examples that point to the tendency of competitive rankings to install socially regressive behaviours at the level of the individual university, that subtract from the common social good.

The Jiao Tong World University Ranking

The world-wide university ranking first issued by the *Shanghai Jiao Tong University Institute of Higher Education* (SJTUIHE) in 2003 was supported by the Chinese government, which wanted to assess the research performance of Chinese universities according to international standards in order to inform strategies designed to lift the competitive position of science and technology in China.

Institutional rankings are issued annually and in February 2007 rankings in five broad disciplinary fields were released. The *Jiao Tong* group argues that the only data sufficiently reliable for ranking purposes are broadly available and inter-nationally comparable data of measurable research performance (Liu & Cheng, 2005, p. 133) and this is the sole focus. Research performance is measured using a composite index with weights given to the different criteria. The index is primarily driven by academic publication and citation, mostly in science-based disciplines with some attention to social sciences and humanities: 20 per cent citation in leading journals as listed by publisher *Thomson*; 20 per cent articles in *Science* and *Nature*; and 20 per cent the number of Thomson/ISI 'HiCi' researchers in the top 250-300 in their fields on the basis of citation (ISI-Thomson, 2006). Another 30 per cent is determined by the winners of Nobel Prizes in the sciences and economics and Fields Medals in mathematics, based on the location of training (10 per cent) and current employment (20 per cent). The remaining 10 per cent is determined by dividing the above total by the number of academic staff. The separate discipline rankings fall into five categories: natural sciences and mathematics, engineering/technologies and computer sciences, life and agricultural sciences, clinical medicine and pharmacy, and social sciences. While the same broad schema is followed in the determination and weighting of criteria, there is some variation by discipline due to publishing conventions (SJTUIHE, 2007). The Jiao Tong index focuses on real outputs not subjective assessments of performance or reputation, except that decisions on Nobel Prizes/Fields Medals are submission based, so that science and scholarship are not the only determining factors.

The SJTUIHE rankings value large comprehensive universities with strong research performance over a broad range of science and few research inactive staff. The rankings favour universities from English language nations because English is the language of research, non English language work is published less and cited less in journals distributed on a world-wide basis; and favour universities from the USA because Americans tend to cite Americans (Altbach, 2006). Jiao Tong research performance is dominated by English speaking nations, with 71 per cent of the world's top 100 research universities in 2006. The United States has 17 of the Jiao Tong world top 20, led by Harvard, and 54 of the top 100. A university's number of Thomson/ISI 'HighCi' researchers directly and indirectly drives performance across much of the index. HiCi researchers are overwhelmingly concentrated in the USA, with 3835 in June 2007 compared to the next best, the UK with 443 (Thomson-ISI, 2007). On the world scale the distribution of mainstream research capacity is overwhelmingly lop-sided. In 2001 US scientists and social scientists published 200,870 papers in major journals. Indonesia with two thirds the U.S. population created 207 papers (NSB, 2006).

In the Jiao Tong rankings the principle of hierarchization at work is essentially that of Bourdieu's sub-field of elite institutions. That is, the criteria for success are the volume and quality of research knowledge, cultural values that are autonomous to the field of higher education itself and defined and controlled by its practitioners. The doubt is where the boundary of the sub-field falls, which institutions lie within the global elite. This is impossible to resolve in technical terms using Jiao Tong style calculations. When institutions are ordered according to a single set of numerical indicators, differences are expressed in degree not in kind. Nevertheless, by naming a top 100 with place-by-place rankings and an overall top 500 the SJTUIHE provides a two tier descriptor of the global hierarchy based on arbitrary place-divisions. Further, given that it is as significant to be excluded from the Jiao Tong top 500 as to be ranked within it, the SJTUIHE has constructed a de facto hierarchy across the entire sector.

The SJTUIHE group (2007) emphasises that this is not a holistic ranking of all aspects of universities, for example teaching quality, only elements of research. But by arranging universities according to research status, the Jiao Tong rankings construct what becomes a reputational hierarchy. Harvard becomes understood not as leading research site but leading university. Market research and anecdotal evidence from educational agents indicate that the rankings feed into student choice-making, not just of doctoral programs, where research capacity is instrumental, but first degree and Masters programs as well. And Jiao Tong performance has quickly become an indicator of national status. At this point the Jiao Tong rankings, however soundly based in recognised metrics, start to function just like all reputational rankings. A hierarchy based on reputation, once established, recycles its own conditions of possibility. Known university brands generate 'halo' effects. They attract ever more money and talent so that their measured performance continues to climb and their stellar reputation is continually reproduced. Newcomer institutions tend to be blocked, regardless of talent or effort unless, like research universities in Singapore and China at present, they are the subject of strategies of state investment on a spectacular scale.

The Times Higher Global Ranking

The first *Times Higher Education Supplement* 'World University Rankings' were published in 2004. The aim is a summative, holistic ranking of university 'quality'. In entering the rankings game the ultimate purpose of the *Times* was to sell publications and data though a secondary purpose might be inferred from the manner of the exercise, to elevate the global position of British universities.

The *Times Higher* also uses a composite index, one that is more heterogeneous than the Jiao Tong. Half of the index is grounded in present reputation, 40 per cent comprised by a survey of academics ('peer review') and 10 per cent by a survey of 'global employers'. There are two internationalisation indicators: the proportion of students who are international (5 per cent) and the proportion of staff (5 per cent). Another 20 per cent is fixed by the student-staff ratio, a quantity measure intended as a proxy for teaching 'quality'. The other 20 per cent is comprised by research citation performance per academic staff. The Times issues an annual list of the top 200 universities in order of merit, plus rankings by institution in natural sciences, engineering and IT, biomedicine, social science and arts/humanities (THES, 2006). The 'Times tables' are open to methodological criticism in relation to most parts of the index. For example, in 2006 the survey of academic 'peers' gathered a response of just 1 per cent from 200,000 e-mails sent worldwide, and the pool of responses was weighted towards the UK and Australia. Teaching quality cannot be assessed using student-staff ratios. The student internationalisation indicator rewards student volume without accounting for the quality or quantity of applications.

In composing a global market the Times Higher is more ambiguous than the Jiao Tong. Leaving aside composition bias, the 50 per cent of the index measuring comparative reputation reproduces the established global hierarchy. Much the same research intensive universities lead the Times Higher as lead the Jiao Tong, though below Harvard the order is somewhat eclectic. The effects of elite reputation are reinforced by the 20 per cent based on research performance. At the same time, reputation is affected by more than just research performance. Compared to the Jiao Tong, the Times Higher elevates well known institutions in national systems especially those in national capitals, so that the leading Chinese universities do very well in the Times Higher. It is likely its reputational indicators are also influenced by the heavy marketing by some Australian and UK universities in the cross-border student market. Likewise the internationalisation of students indicator rewards institutions active in the cross-border student market; and because it is a quantity indicator, it unambiguously rewards a mass orientation within that market. Strictly speaking, the Times Higher rankings reward a university's marketing division as well as its researchers. The Times Higher combines, in ,a more erratic fashion than the Jiao Tong, both of Bourdieu's principles of hierarchization. Universities that lead the elite sub-field are in a dominant position, and these are accompanied also by certain institutions that draw strength from a role in the cross-border mass education sub-field, and a handful that have particularly strong vocational reputations. The mass/vocational subfield is less prominent than the elite research subfield. The result is a less coherent order in which the hierarchy of research universities is under-determined by the hierarchy of universities that provide mass cross-border education or emphasise vocational mission.

Below the top 40 places the Times Higher is also a volatile hierarchy. Many institutions experience sharp rises and/or falls. For example between 2004 and 2006 the University of Geneva in Switserland moved from outside the top 200 to 39, Fudan University in China was placed successively at 195, 72 and 116, the University of Seoul in Korea jumped from 118 to 63, and RMIT University in Australia moved down from 55 to 146. Many other examples can be cited. These fluctuations do not appear to be performance related, being largely random effects consequent on weaknesses in data gathering and changes in data collation methods.

The Times Higher ranking also generates more particular effects arising from uncorrected composition bias. The UK and Australia do too well. The UK has 15 per cent of the GDP of the USA but half as many universities in the Times top 100 in 2006: UK 15, USA 33. (The USA had 54 research universities in the Jiao Tong top 100). In 2006 the UK had two of the Times Higher top three and Cambridge UK almost closed the gap on Harvard. Yet the Harvard faculty is cited at three and a half times the rate of Cambridge and has greater world-wide prestige. Australian universities perform exceptionally in the peer survey of academic staff and student internationalisation indicator, thereby benefiting from both Bourdieuian principles of hierarchization. In 2006 the Australian National University was ranked by the 'academic peers' as ahead of Yale, Princeton, Caltech, Chicago, Penn and UCLA. Despite a relatively poor citation rate and moderate staffing ratios Australia had 13 of the Times top 200, making it the third strongest national system, ahead of Japan, Canada, Germany and France. The prominence accorded to the Australian institutions by the Times is consistent with their leading role in international marketing – where Australia is a successful exporter – but is inconsistent with their weaker role in research and hence in the elite subfield. Thus the Times exaggerates also the overall reputation of the Australian institutions. The Times tables have been much criticised, particularly in Western Europe. Nevertheless, with the Jiao Tong, though less effectively, the Times Higher shares the ordering of the global market.

POLICY EFFECTS OF GLOBAL RANKINGS

General policy effects

Outside the USA (where only the US News ranking is important) Jiao Tong and the Times Higher have already secured visible effects in behaviours and policies. Rankings function as a meta-performance indicator. The criteria used to determine each institution's position in the ranking system become meta-outputs that each institution places on priority, so that rankings begin to define 'quality'. In the world of the Jiao Tong rankings, 'quality' means scientific research and Nobel Prizes, not teaching or community building or solving local or global problems. In the world of the Times Higher, 'quality' is reputation, larger staff-student ratios, research, and international staff and students; and is partly fostered by marketing. It seems that institutional leaders, and governments, have been given their marching orders. By shaping university and system behaviours, while standardising the definitions of outcome and output, rankings begin to decide university mission and the balance of activity, externalising part of university identity. This shift from autonomy to heteronomy is important, carrying with it serious problems for the trajectory of higher education in many countries, but is not universal. Heteronomy scarcely touches institutions at the very top which remain masters of their own identity. The elite sub-field if anything cuts a stronger figure in the world, though it has become a smaller group: outside the USA and UK the status of elite institutions at the national level has now been partly displaced by that of the global super-league.

The two rankings systems have triggered a flurry of marketing by the successful institutions, and the common desire to lift performance, either by changing what is measured or changing how it is interpreted. Within universities they encourage the concentration of internal resources in the principal science-based fields, greater separation of teaching and research, and the refashioning of research programs in terms of specific indicators such as ISI journal publication. Rankings encourage those strategic initiatives within institutions that lift measured performance in the short term and medium term; and they tend to discourage initiatives in mission and organisation, curriculum, pedagogy and research without implications for rankings performance (the opportunity cost is increased). In inculcating the model of ideal performance that underlies them, rankings standardise the sector over time and reducing the diversity of mission and outputs. The normalising effects are maximised when there is only one or a very small number of rankings systems. The more diverse and multiple the measures, the less potent the effects of each.

At government level, ranking has triggered the desire to see more universities in the upper echelons of the tables, as a signifier of national success and potential in the policy context of a global knowledge economy. In turn this has created or further encouraged policies to concentrate a higher proportion of research activity and resources in a selected group of leading universities and to attract and hold top flight researchers. Singapore has set out to attract high quality academic expatriates with US-level salaries. China and Germany (van der Wende, 2007a) have selected groups of universities given special additional research status and others, such as Australia and the UK, are talking about it. Everywhere the goal is to replicate the global attractiveness and impact of the American doctoral sector, though this is difficult to do without American economic, technological, and cultural power.

The intensified competitiveness consequent on rankings has the potential to trigger an increase in levels of national investment in research and is likely to boost science-strong institutions. But it contains negative potentials for many others. On the whole vocational education is downgraded, as it is largely unable to contribute to performative global competitiveness, though some research universities with a vocational twist, for example in India and the Netherlands, have prospered in the

Times Higher ranking. Research universities outside the Anglo-American norm, such as the high participation national universities of Latin America, are placed under increasing pressure to remake themselves. All universities have stronger incentives to put performance ahead of social access. More generally, a rankings-based reputational race is a race that few can win, even research universities. When positional competition is intensified and everyone stands on tip-toe, no one can see better. "The race gets longer for the same prize" (Hirsch, 1976, p. 67).

A principal concern in many countries is the bias in favour of knowledge in English. Although English is the only global language of research publication it is not the only language of thought. The exclusion of work in other languages is most problematic in the humanistic social sciences and humanities/arts. This problem have generated a range of responses in the non English-speaking world, from lobbying for the inclusion of non-English publications in rankings systems, to the creation of separate language-based rankings lists, to a rejection of rankings.

European Policy Responses

In Europe the accelerated research race has generated not just national but multilateral actions. Leiden University in the Netherlands has led the formation of a League of European Research Universities. The European Union plans a combined European Institute of Technology (van der Wende, 2007a; 2007b). There has also been a range of responses centred on comparison itself: development of a comprehensive comparison of teaching and research based on survey data, by the Centre for Higher Education Development (CHE) in Germany; construction of publication and citation metrics by a Leiden University group; and negotiation of a typology of European institutions enabling a more diverse set of comparisons.

The Centre for Higher Education Development (CHE) comparisons. The Centre for Higher Education Development (CHE), located in Gutersloh in North Rhine-Westphalia in Germany, compares the programs of universities, in conjunction with the German Academic Exchange Service and the publisher Die Zeit. CHE surveys 130,000 students and 16,000 staff in almost 250 institutions, collecting data on student experiences and satisfaction, and academic recommendations on the best locations in each field. It focuses on 36 academic subjects each offered by a substantial number of institutions. It supplements the surveys with independent sources comprising one third of the data base. No data are taken from institutions. CHE ranks departments according to each separate indicator of academic and service quality, assigning them to top third, middle third or bottom third of all institutions. It refuses to integrate the indicators into a single weighted indicator either for each subject or each institution. It states that there is no "one best university" across all areas, and "minimal differences produced by random fluctuations may be misinterpreted as real differences" (CHE, 2006).

CHE notes also that students have heterogeneous preferences as to mission and purpose. Accordingly, the CHE data are made available to prospective students and the public free of charge via an interactive web-enabled database. Any person can interrogate this data base by investigating the comparisons in their own chosen disciplines and services, thereby creating the weightings and rankings themselves.

Thus CHE dispenses with holistic rank ordering of institutions in league tables, avoided problems of arbitrary weighting and composite indicators and admits multiple purposes into the comparison, and has shifted the normative power of the comparison process from the ranking agency to the user of higher education. Its approach lacks the discursive potency of a single league table but the data are more useful to more people. Significantly, the approach has proven highly successful with public and students, governments, and academic experts on rankings systems (van Dyke, 2005; Salmi & Saroyan, 2006; Usher & Savino, 2007). The CHE data collection has been extended to Switzerland, Austria, the Netherlands and Flanders, the Dutch-speaking portion of Belgium. "The CHE ranking system is thus well positioned to develop into a European-wide system" (van der Wende, 2007b).

Other developments. The Centre for Science and Technology Studies (CWTS) at Leiden University in the Netherlands is preparing a new ranking system based solely on bibliometric indicators that it has developed (CWTS, 2007). This takes in the 400 universities with the largest number of academic publications, covering the output of at least 600 active researchers in each of those universities. The CWTS has developed range of indicators. Its favoured approach is ranking by average impact as measured by citations per publication, modified by normalisation for academic field, and controlled also for institution size, thereby addressing two weaknesses in the Jiao Tong approach. The Leiden group has also dispensed with the Nobel indicators used by Jiao Tong. The result is an arguably more accurate comparison which like the Jiao Tong, entrenches the research university market.

A comprehensive typology of European institutions is also being developed (van Vught, et al., 2005; van der Wende, 2007b). This typology is made up of a number of parallel schemes each based on a different characteristic: size of institution, legal status, type of education (degrees offered, range of disciplines), student and staff profiles, activities in research and innovation. The areas of teaching, lifelong learning, innovation, knowledge transfer and local and regional engagement all require further work (van der Wende, 2007b). Europe institutions are being asked to specify their own missions, consistent with autonomy. It is unclear whether once the typology is established institutions will be free to redefine their category.

CONCLUSION: THE PERFORMATIVE PRESENT-AS-FUTURE

It is likely that a more plural set of indicators and of rankings will develop; with greater specialisation in relation to mission and function, as indicated by emerging discipline indicators and citation metrics, especially in Europe. However it is by no means clear that the normative function of indicators focused on the elite Anglo-American science university will be displaced. There are distinctive beneficiaries and powerful support for the single league table approach, despite its flaws.

University rankings are marred by limiting, reductive and reifying qualities. These rankings are by most reasonable definitions 'unfair'. This is not a pathology of the techniques of ranking but of their social uses; whereby the processes of reduction and comparison, the creation of winners and losers, and the over-simplification of problems of complex judgement that are entailed, are the very rationales for the ranking process. Rankings reflect prestige and power; and rankings confirm, entrench and reproduce prestige and power. The particular systems in use tend to further the particular interests that do well within them. University rankings not only imagine and describe higher education in terms of Bourdieu's universal positional competition, they themselves are the outcome of the kind of struggle he describes over the terms in which social positionality is understood, described and fixed. Many institutions attempt to influence the system of classification and the contents of the data input in the rankings systems. In this some are more effective than others. As Bourdieu states in *Distinction* (1984):

> Principles of division, inextricably logical and sociological, function within and for the purposes of the struggle between social groups; in producing concepts, they produce groups, the very groups which produce the principles and the groups against which they are produced (Bourdieu, 1984, p. 479).

In other words, there is a technical/social circularity about the rankings project; as in other such policy technologies that are designed to order and control the educational world, such as standardised testing in school systems. Categories such as university rank, as with the indicators that compose it, help to shape the world of institutional hierarchy and social preference. Powerful social interests are assisted by these categories, and those interests return the favour, helping to shape or at least legitimate the categories in use. Those social interests are also shaped in the process of the use of ranking. And all this is now taking place on an international scale. Rankings provide a powerful support for the English-language university systems already leading higher education, perpetuating their global dominance, while also setting the objectives that those nations along with others must meet.

Global university rankings are tools of the imagination, discursive technologies and data sets whose time, it seems, has come. But rankings also frame imaginings and make the time. University rankings recall Foucault's famous words in *The archaeology of knowledge* (1972), where he describes discourses, with Mozartian simplicity, as "practices that systematically form the objects of which they speak" (Foucault, 1972, p. 49). Rankings inculcate the idealised model of institution as a norm to be achieved and generalise the failure to achieve it. By installing at their apex a particular kind of elite institution (particular to mission and activity profile, to resources, to language of use and even, because of the preceding elements, to nation), in the university sector in which a status hierarchy once established sustains itself in the manner Bourdieu describes, rankings entrench the potency of the existing hierarchy. Global university rankings, appearing to all the world as a bold, open competitive struggle akin to a football championship, are a simple and brilliant device for reproducing the performative present into the future.

Discourses of social status are primary in the sustaining of status and are all the more powerful when joined to the force of calculation. Winner-take-all markets in all sectors, not just universities, tend over time to concentrate power and resources at the top and become more steeply hierarchical (Frank & Cook, 1995; Frank 2001). In ordering university performance as status, while shaping the distribution of resources (money, research concentrations) which are the means of competitive performance according to the status order, rankings help to ensure a continuous reinvestment in that order. Equally important is the function of rankings as a device of legitimation. University rankings install in the common mind the notion of competition in higher education as a level playing field, despite the lop-sided system settings, despite the rigged nature of the game, despite the relentless reproduction of the global university hierarchy. Rankings explain the failure of institutions to move up the league table in the manner of a football team, as their own failure of talent or volition, not as a failure of government policy or the outcome of gross world-wide inequalities in political economy and cultural clout.

Rankings originate in publishing of universities more often than state agencies but are near perfect tools for government in higher education. The routine of state management is to quell avoidable social tensions and reproduce the status quo while sustaining a thin sliver of space for changes of order within the elite, and a thinner space for upward mobility. Following the arguments of Hayek, and in response to the cultural disorders of the 1960s, neo-liberalism in education is less concerned about profitability than about social control. It wants to create the forms of economic competition without the openness and uncertainty, even anarchy, that would have accompanied a purer, less ordered market framework; and it seeks to do so on not just a national scale but a global scale. If neo-liberal government had not been given global university rankings, it would have had to invent them.

This paper has used the critique of neo-liberal government and the NPM as a system of relations of power, in order to interpret the purposes and outcomes of global university rankings, and to situate the rankings process within contemporary government and the patterns of global hegemony. Pierre Bourdieu is one of a number of theorists who provide useful resources for such an exercise. The chapter has sought to develop its critique while acknowledging salient features of the contemporary environment in higher education, including the accelerating moving of people, knowledge and ideas across borders; the growth in the role of market forces, especially in cross-border degrees; the prestige enjoyed by leading universities from the U.S.A. and (to a lesser extent) the U.K; and the openness and ambiguity of global relations. However, despite the efforts of global rankings systems to define a competitive educational order, the hierarchy is more open and relations are more unstable than is the case at the national level.

The production of global public goods such as knowledge, where exchange is free and takes place outside market relations, is at least as materially formative as is the production of global private goods such as status and earnings benefits. In taking the analysis further, it would be useful to conduct situated case studies (Deem, 2001) mapping the effects of rankings (and international competition more generally) in national systems and individual institutional strategies; and in supplementing the fashionable emphasis on competitive markets, to draw out the effects of contemporary practices of cooperation and collective production, within and between national borders, in structuring higher education (Marginson, 2007a).

REFERENCES

Altbach, p. (2006). The dilemmas of ranking. *International Higher Education, 42.*

Appadurai, A. (1996). *Modernity at large: Cultural dimensions of globalisation.* Minneapolis, MN: University of Minnesota Press.

Bourdieu, p. (1984). *Distinction: A social critique of the judgment of taste* (R. Nice, Trans.). London: Routledge & Kegan Paul.

Bourdieu, p. (1988). *Homo Academicus* (P. Collier, Trans.). Cambridge: Polity.

Bourdieu, p. (1993). *The field of cultural production* (R. Johnson, Ed.). New York: Columbia University Press.

Bourdieu, p. (1996). *The state nobility: Elite schools in the field of power* (L. Clough, Trans.). Oxford: Polity.

Burbules, N., & Torres, C. (Eds.). *Globalisation and education: Critical perspectives.* New York: Routledge.

Centre for Higher Education Development, CHE. (2006). *Study and research in Germany.* University rankings, published in association with Die Zeit. Retrieved December 16, 2006, from http://www.daad.de/deutschland/studium/hochschulranking/04708.en.html

Centre for Science and Technology Studies, Leiden University, (CWTS). (2007). The Leidien ranking. Retrieved June 20, 2007, from http://www.cwts.nl/cwts/LeidenRankingWebSite.html

Clark, B. (1998). *Creating entrepreneurial universities: Organisational pathways of transformation.* Oxford: Pergamon Press.

Deem, R. (2001). Globalisation, new managerialism, academic capitalism and entrepreneurialism in universities: Is the local dimension still important? *Comparative Education, 37*(1), 7–20.

Dill, D., & Soo, M. (2005). Academic quality, league tables, and public policy: A cross-national analysis of university rankings. *Higher Education, 49,* 495–533.

Foucault, M. (1972). *The archaeology of knowledge* (A. M. Sheridan Smith, Trans.). London: Tavistock.

Frank, R. (2001). Higher education: The ultimate winner-take-all market? In M. Devlin & J. Meyerson (Eds.), *Forum futures: Exploring the future of higher education.* San Francisco: Jossey-Bass.

Frank, R., & Cook, p. (1995). *The winner-take-all society.* New York: The Free Press.

Gibbons, M., Limoges, C., Nowotny, H., Schwartzman, S., Scott, p. , & Trow, M. (1994). *The new production of knowledge: The dynamics of science and research in contemporary societies.* London: Sage.

Henkel, M. (2005). Academic identity and autonomy in a changing policy environment. *Higher Education, 49,* 155–176.

Hirsch, F. (1976). *Social limits to growth.* Cambridge: Harvard University Press.

Institute for Scientific Information, ISI-Thomson. (2006). Data on highly cited researchers, ISIHighlyCited.com. Retrieved August 15, 2006, from http://isihighlycited.com/

Kenway, J., Bullen, E., Fahey, J., with Robb, S. (2006). *Haunting the knowledge economy.* London: Routledge.

Kirp, D. (2004). *Shakespeare, Einstein and the bottom-line: The marketing of higher education.* Cambridge, MA: Harvard University Press.

Liu, N., & Cheng, Y. (2005). The academic ranking of world universities. *Higher Education in Europe, 30*(2), 127–136.

Liu, N., & Liu, L. (2005). University rankings in China. *Higher Education in Europe, 30*(2), 217–227.

Lyotard, J. F. (1984). *The post-modern condition: A report on Knowledge* (G. Bennington & B. Massumi, Trans.). Minneapolis, MN: University of Minnesota Press.

Marginson, S. (1997). *Markets in education.* Sydney: Allen and Unwin.

Marginson, S. (2007a). The public/private division in higher education: A global revision. *Higher Education, 53*, 307–333.

Marginson, S. (2007b). Global position and position-taking: the case of Australia. *Journal of Studies in International Education, 11*(1), 5–32.

Marginson, S. (2007c). *Prospects of higher education. Globalisation, market competition, public goods and the future of the university.* Rotterdam: Sense Publishers.

Marginson, S. (2008a). Global field and global imagining: Bourdieu and relations of power in worldwide higher education. *British Journal of Sociology of Education, 29*(3), 303-316.

Marginson, S. (2008b). Hayekian neo-liberalism and academic self-determination. *Educational Theory, 58*(3), 269-287.

Marginson, S., & Considine, M. (2000). *The enterprise university: Power, governance and reinvention in Australia.* Cambridge: Cambridge University Press.

Marginson, S., & Mollis, M. (2001). "The door opens and the tiger leaps": Theories and reflexivities of comparative education for a global millennium. *Comparative Education Review, 45*(4), 581–615.

Marginson, S., & van der Wende, M. (2007). *Globalisation and higher education.* Education Working Paper No. 8, Directorate of Education, OECD. Paris: OECD. Retrieved July 31, 2007, from http://www.cshe.unimelb.edu.au/people/staff_pages/Marginson/OECD-Globalisation&HigherEd.pdf

McCormick, A. C., & Zhao, C. (2005). Rethinking and reframing the Carnegie classification. *Change, 37*(5), 51–57.

Musselin, C. (2005). European academic labour markets in transition. *Higher Education, 49*, 135–154.

Naidoo, R. (2004). Fields and institutional strategy: Bourdieu on the relationship between higher education, inequality and society. *British Journal of Sociology of Education, 25*(4), 446–472.

National Science Board, NSB. (2006). *Science and engineering indicators 2004.* Retrieved April 9, 2006, from http://www.nsf.gov/statistics/seind04/

Nowotny, H., Scott, p. , & Gibbons, M. (2001). *Rethinking science: Knowledge and the public in an age of uncertainty.* Cambridge: Polity.

Organisation for Economic Cooperation and Development, OECD. (2006). *Education at a glance.* Paris: Author.

Rhoads, R., & Torres, C. (2006). *The university, state, and market: The political economy of globalisation in the Americas.* Stanford, CA: Stanford University Press.

Rose, N. (1999). *Powers of freedom.* Cambridge: Cambridge University Press.

Salmi, J., & Saroyan, A. (2006). *League tables as policy instruments: Uses and misuses.* OECD/IMHE & Hochschulrektorenkonferenz, Germany, Workshop 4-5 December, Bonn. See Organisation for Economic Cooperation and Development, Institutional Management in Higher Education program, Retrieved March 10, 2007, from http://www.oecd.org

Shanghai Jiao Tong University Institute of Higher Education, SJTUIHE. (2007). *Academic ranking of world universities.* Retrieved June 20, 2007, from http://ed.sjtu.edu.cn/ranking.htm

The Times Higher. (2006). World university rankings. *The Times Higher Education Supplement.* Retrieved November 30, 2006, from www.thes.co.uk [subscription required]

Usher, A., & Savino, M. (2006). *A world of difference: A global survey of university league tables.* Retrieved April 2, 2006, from http://www.educationalpolicy.org

U.S. News and World Report. (2006). *America's best colleges, 2007 edition.* Washington: USNWR.

Valimaa, J. (2004). Nationalisation, localisation and globalisation in Finnish higher education. *Higher Education, 48*, 27–54.

Valimaa, J. (2005). Globalisation in the concept of Nordic Higher Education. In A. Arimoto, F. Huang, & K. Yokoyama (Eds.), *Globalisation and higher education.* International Publications Series 9, Research Institute for Higher Education, Hiroshima University. Retrieved February 10, 2006, from http://en.rihe.hiroshima-u.ac.jp/pl_default_2.php?bid=63653

Van der Wende. (2007a). *European responses to global competition in higher education.* Symposium 'Crisis of the publics', Centre for Studies in Higher Education, UC Berkeley, 26-27 March. Retrieved June 1, 2007, from http://cshe.berkeley.edu/events/crisis/docs/ [password required]

Van der Wende. (2007b). *Rankings and classifications in higher education: A European perspective.* 2nd Leiden University International Symposium on Ranking, 2 & 3 February.

Van Dyke, N. (2005). Twenty years of university report cards. *Higher Educatiton in Europe, 30*(2), 103–125.

Van Vught, F., Batelse, J., Bohmert, D., Burquel, N., Divis, J., Huisman, J., et al. (2005). *Institutional profiles. Towards a typology of higher education institutions in Europe.* Report to the European Commission. Retrieved March 31, 2007, from http://www.utwente.nl/cheps/documenten/engreport05institutionalprofiles.pdf

Williams, R., & Van Dyke, N. (2006). *Rating major disciplines in Australian universities: Perceptions and reality.* Melbourne: Melbourne Institute of Applied Economic and Social Research.

FURTHER READINGS

Altbach, p. (2006). The dilemmas of ranking. *International Higher Education,* 42.

Bourdieu, p. (1993). *The field of cultural production* (R. Johnson, Ed.). New York: Columbia University Press.

Centre for Higher Education Development, CHE. (2006). *Study and research in Germany.* University rankings, published in association with Die Zeit. Retrieved December 16, 2006, from http://www.daad.de/deutschland/studium/hochschulranking/04708.en.html

Kirp, D. (2004). *Shakespeare, Einstein and the bottom-line: The marketing of higher education.* Cambridge, MA: Harvard University Press.

Marginson, S. (2007a). The public/private division in higher education: A global revision. *Higher Education, 53,* 307–333.

Shanghai Jiao Tong University Institute of Higher Education, SJTUIHE. (2007). *Academic ranking of world universities.* Retrieved June 20, 2007, from http://ed.sjtu.edu.cn/ranking.htm

Simon Marginson
Centre for the Study of Higher Education
University of Melbourne, Australia

SIMON BRADFORD & VALERIE HEY

SUCCESSFUL SUBJECTIVITIES?

The Successification of Class, Ethnic and Gender Positions [1]

INTRODUCTION

In New Labour's Britain it seems impermissible for the citizen to be anything other than successful. In education there has been an unrelenting focus on successful pupils and students, successful teachers and, of course, successful schools. New Labour's 'Beacon schools', identified "as amongst the best performing in the country and represent examples of successful practice" (DfES, 2004a), were established in 1998. Beacon schools were phased out in 2005 becoming incorporated into the 'Leading Edge partnership programme', designed to be at "the forefront of the drive to reform secondary education" (DfES, 2004b). High-performing schools were recruited to these programmes to collaborate with less successful schools in furthering New Labour's approach to school improvement and raising standards.

This article explores the understanding of success of a small group of students in two secondary schools in west London (originally Beacon schools, one now a specialist humanities college and the other a Leading Edge 'lead school'). It discusses preliminary findings from a small pilot investigation into how young men and young women imagine their futures in the context of an incessant exhortation to "become (a successful) somebody" (Wexler, 1992). We briefly explore the discursive and policy context in which success discourses emerged and, through the voices of the young people interviewed, the ways in which social difference (class, ethnicity and gender) have become key elements in the constitution of success on New Labour's educational landscape.

We suggest that New Labour's education agenda is designed, in part, to keep 'middle England' psychologically and psychically 'on side' in respect of its children's pathways into and through state schooling. Contemporary appeals to middle-class priorities, unashamedly expressed through the 'standards and excellence' agenda, can be seen as an attempt to retain middle-class support for state education. Initiatives such as 'gifted and talented', 'excellence in cities', 'Beacon schools' and 'Leading Edge partnership schools', all forming a complex of policy and governance designed to 'raise standards', have been designed to demonstrate the capacity of the state system to both maintain and reproduce middle-class advantage *as well as* advance the promise that other young people (the 'socially excluded', for example) can achieve some educational and social mobility. This should be understood in the context of recurrent moral panic over

M. Simons, M. Olssen and M.A. Peters (eds.), *Re-Reading Education Policies: A Handbook Studying the Policy Agenda of the 21ˢᵗ Century*, 605–624.

the condition and performance of state education in England and young people whose educational outcomes are not deemed successful.

The article explores the processes of articulation (in both senses of the word; see Hall, 1996)[2] of subjects to the project of 'successification' whose appeal lies in its promise to offer pathways from recognisably disadvantaged spaces to more desirable ones. More specifically, we consider how some young people (defined variously by their teachers as 'successful') come to understand themselves and their futures in schools that have acquired the accolade 'successful school'. What does being a successful school imply for these young people? How do young men and young women from different backgrounds (class and ethnicity) come to recognise themselves in the success discourses that our two schools promote?

RE-INVENTING EDUCATION: NEW LABOUR AND THE GOVERNANCE OF AMBITION

The collapse of the post-war settlements that constituted the welfare state (Clarke & Newman, 1997) irrevocably altered the landscape of education that New Labour inherited in 1997. Since then, New Labour social policy has evolved through a commitment to the developing narrative of the so-called 'Third Way'. This is a response to perceived "globalisation(s)", the rapid emergence of "knowledge economies" and the development of a "reflexive modernity" (Giddens, 1998, 2000). Third way politics circumscribe a new 'ethics' and seek to emphasise a duality of freedom and responsibility appropriate to a radically altered world. As such, the third way is essentially a normative ethical framework situating welfare policy including education. Choices for the welfare state in the global economy are, apparently, stark:

> A privatised future, with the welfare state becoming a residualised safety net for the poorest and most marginalised; the *status quo (...)* or the Government's third way – promoting opportunity instead of dependence, with a welfare state providing for the mass of the people, but in new ways to fit the modern world (DSS, 1998, p. 19).

Gewirtz (2002) points to a corpus of retained 'New Right' ideas that form the third way and which have shaped New Labour education policy (marketisation, privatisation, managerialism, the promotion of work and central control of schools and curriculum). 'Social inclusion' (generally defined through the prism of labour market participation), 'social cohesion' and 'equality of opportunity'[3] are also elements in a constellation of concepts shaping education policy and practice. As the aptly named White Paper on lifelong learning, 'Learning to Succeed', puts it, "Our vision is to build a new culture of learning which will underpin national competitiveness and personal prosperity, encourage creativity and innovation and help to build a cohesive society" (DfEE, 1999, p. 13).

This is an attempt to reconcile ideologies of competitiveness with discourses of personal fulfilment. As such, education and learning have become the means, *par excellence*, of achieving a range of governmental objectives by aligning outcomes for the nation in a global economy ('national competitiveness'), goals for the domain of the social ('social cohesion') with the desires and aspirations of individual subjects ('creativity' and 'personal prosperity', for example). Implicit in this configuration is the 'responsible citizen', maximising their own human capital in constructing a viable and rational identity that incorporates ambition and aspiration as principal elements of self. Schools and other educational institutions are enjoined to encourage their students to think of themselves as ambitious and aspirational subjects, in charge of their own futures. Beacon schools in particular exemplified these policy objectives of excellence, achievement and success and these have been absorbed into the diversity of schools that has grown under New Labour.

SUCCESSFUL SCHOOLS: "UNLEASHING ASPIRATION" [4]

Beacon and Leading Edge schools have embodied the objectives of "spreading excellence", "sharing success" and "working collaboratively" (DfES, 2001, p. 38) within the 'mixed economy' of provision that has become so familiar in the re-invented welfare state of the last 20 years. Beacons attempted to 'bridge' social democratic commitments (collaboration and networking, for example) to values associated with 'modernisation': standards, achievement and excellence (Fergusson, 2000). By embodying these, such schools have become powerful symbols of New Labour education policy reflecting the essentially communitarian position taken up by New Labour in its critique and re-moralisation of competitive individualism. Communitarians argue that the market cannot provide a rational foundation for ethics because 'the good' can only be understood in the context of *collective*, rather than *individual*, identities (Frazer, 2000). This critique is mirrored in three elements of Beacon and Leading Edge philosophy that have become established in a normative model of the successful school. First, it challenges the idea of the 'atomised' and autonomous school (reflecting the rejection of strong individualism) in preference for connectedness and collaboration. Second, it advances a notion of rights that entail corresponding duties, countering the tendency of rights discourses to separate and disconnect. Thus, successful schools are required to engage in supporting less effective or developed schools. Third, the critique implies that competitive individualism diminishes the stock of 'social capital' (trust, reciprocity and honesty, for example) and the (often informal) social goods and social control mechanisms that these generate (care and mutual aid, for example). By sharing their resources (experience and expertise), successful schools are expected to generate and contribute to a form of solidarity within a diverse educational community. However, it is clear that competition continues to play a central role in current education policy and in the workings of Leading Edge schools particularly. By being part of an educational elite (determined by their performance against other schools) whilst simultaneously located on the ground of 'collaboration', these schools signal one of the principal contradictions of New Labour education policy.[5]

Failure and mediocrity provide the comparators against which successful schools can be judged (Webster, 2001). However, success, like excellence, is a relational and dynamic concept and can only be understood as coming from the shadow of its 'other': *failure*. Education policy in England superficially appears to focus on the eradication of failure and mediocrity, but simultaneously entails a perverse need to maintain their visibility against which success can be affirmed (Lucey & Reay, 2002). Bauman (1997), drawing on Mary Douglas, points out that each "scheme of purity" (and the Beacon school discourse can be seen as such: *pure* excellence, *pure* success) "generates its own dirt and each order generates its own strangers" (p. 13). Seeking to purge or purify the system by expelling failure - the stranger - the ideal of purity itself raises (and requires) the spectre of its counter. Thus, ironically, the existence of elite schools (like Beacon or Leading Edge schools) both confirms and sustains failure in other schools, as one of our interviewees (a young Sikh man in Year 10) suggests in this knowing reference to his own school:

R   I think it's an excellent school ... we've got Beacon status and it makes us stand out.

SB   Does that make you better than other schools?

R   It gives you something to be proud about, not many schools in the borough have got Beacon status.

Importantly, we think, the binary 'other' of failure not only assumes institutional form as 'failing school'. It is also constructed *internally* and *within* the self as the 'other' - the stranger within - against which some of these young people police their own narratives of success. We do not claim that there is any direct 'transfer' between policy and the views of individuals, but the message that successful schools seek to recruit and legitimate aspiration appears to resonate for this young man.

THE PILOT STUDY

We completed 12 interviews with young people and two interviews with heads of year in two schools in the west London borough of Chelvey. One school was mixed and the other was a single-sex girls' school. Both had earlier acquired Beacon status and had high reputations amongst parents and students alike. Chelvey is characterised by its location fringing one of the main arterial roads to the airport, a central hub of the local economy and accounting for a significant number of distribution jobs and other low-skill employment opportunities in the borough. The 2001 Census showed that 35% of the population was from an ethnic minority group, the largest of which was Indian (17.33% of residents), followed by Pakistani (4.2%) and Black African (2.6%). However, it is significant that like many local educational markets there is an outflow of white pupils. Fifty-nine per cent of pupils were from an ethnic minority, the largest groups being Indian (21%) and Pakistani (8%). A 2003 survey showed that Chelvey's pupils speak, as a first language, an estimated 133 languages, the highest percentage being English (56.5%), then Punjabi (13.9%), Urdu (6.6%), Gujarati (3.9%), Somali (2.2%), Arabic (2.2%) and Hindi (1.7%). Of course, some pupils are bi- and trilingual.

We were primarily interested to explore how discourses of aspiration and success work in 'speaking subjects' and decided to interview young people in Year 10. We met with two supportive heads of year, and asked them to arrange opportunities for us to interview 'successful' young people in 'friendship pairs'. This was done in order for the young people to feel supported and we were also interested to gather 'pair talk data' as examples of young people 'working out' their views and understandings of success. Interviews were undertaken in quiet settings in school. We were not prescriptive about success (either with teachers or young people, inviting them to elaborate on their own ideas of what counted as success for them), and encouraged the teachers to choose young people who would be comfortable talking to unknown outsider adults. The interviews, all about an hour long, took the form of focused discussions around the idea of success in school and in life generally.

DATA ANALYSIS

Our analysis draws specifically on two of our interviews. These are selected as offering a rich theoretical yield. Given our methodological focus on the entwining of difference and power, any pair of interviewees (or, indeed, individual interviewee) would offer points of contradiction and comparison in tracing through the pressure points of identity work in the context of discursive complexity. Our data presentation offers the chance of holding some focus on the shifts staged in terms of gender, class, ethnicity, traditional, questioning or reflexive identities as these are construed in similar policy, institutional and shared community settings.

Stabilising success/ful identifications: the Beacon identity formation

Our analysis tracks the social constitution as well as the articulation and intersection of discourses of class, gender and race. We take this to require grounding in the spatial, cultural and material relations of institutions and communities. This allows us to consider how the national preoccupation with success becomes deposited in the ideological DNA of successful schools.[6] In order to locate the incorporation of policy in the micro-social we have taken Bourdieu's conceptualisation of the "social logics of the individual" as a starting point. He conceived the individual, contra neo-liberal and some sociological accounts as a thoroughly *social* subject inscribed by social dispositions that carry the force of the wider social hierarchies of power: "Contrary to the common preconception that associates sociology with the collective, it has to be pointed out that the collective is deposited in each individual in the form of durable dispositions such as mental structures" (Bourdieu, 1995, p. 18).

Bourdieu's conceptualisation of *sens practique* or social logic provides a platform for generating an account of how contrasting locales might shape the institutional culture within which subjects 'do' success. We are not suggesting that all subjects sign up to this position but that discourses of success are, almost by definition, normative and dominant in successful schools. As such they invariably require a response since they make up the dominant "discursive noise" (Fairclough, 2000) against which subjects are compelled to understand their social and subject position. Hey has argued recently (2002, 2003), in reviewing the trend for reading the contemporary world as reflexive modernity, that feminist work inflects how 'social logics' get put into place at a less abstract level of realisation because it provides for a *more* embodied (and embedded) reading of class and consciousness as the ideological sedimentation of everyday discourse.

Within this more localised but not anti-structuralist framework, social interactions between self and others are conceived as neither arbitrary nor innocent but are positional, positioning and produce discourses of self-positioning (Hey, 2002). Moreover, psychically these occurrences differentiate us *through* as well as add to, differential types (and amounts?) of capital (Reay, 2004/5; Skeggs, 2004) including psychological capital (Hey, 2003). Psychological capital is conceptualised here as an additional resource related to, but not identical with, cultural or social capital already specified as part of Bourdieu's theorisation of class and power (Bourdieu, 1986). Psychological capital inevitably intersects with these other forms and, like them, it is differentially distributed. It is constituted in practices of self-esteem, confidence and self-belief which are generated in a range of settings (the family, communities of various types, friendships and formal institutional settings like schools and youth projects) and can be transformed into resilience and the dispositions needed to cope with the exigencies of contemporary life (Bradford, 1999; Bradford *et al.*, 2004). Social experience produces memories, desires and emotions including rage, shame, resentment and pain as well as power and pleasure. This lived experience of the material, the psychological, and the comprehension of social difference that is so entailed is 'worked over' by success discourse's effective interpellation of the young people we interviewed. Yet there is a paradox here. By fostering psychological capital the potential reach of governmental power is also extended by increasing the capacity (and, potentially, desire) of the subject to work on self under the specific tutelage of the authority of success discourses. As we have suggested, these are aimed at keeping sections of the middle class 'on side' and thus with achieving political legitimacy. However, our data also indicate that they represent a new twist on redistribution in the sense that the discursive tactics entailed seek to inscribe young people from *disadvantaged* backgrounds with confidence and resilience in the face of psychological and social pressures. The idea of psychological capital is, inevitably, speculative and we have noted that it is a contradictory resource. It is a way of thinking about what might keep the ambivalent positioning of socially disadvantaged young people viable and safe from modes of self-sabotage. We suggest that is one of the ways in which young people 'resolve' the conflict of living originary loyalties to communities from which their success may alienate them. White working-class ethnicities seem to provide fewer opportunities in which such a resource may proliferate although we think further investigation of this is necessary.

We offer the following account of the role of successful schools in the construction of young people's psychological capital and their understandings of themselves as successful or otherwise. These narratives are, we argue, indicative of a working through of a successful self (a work, necessarily, in process and progress) structured by the entwined discourses of class, ethnicity, faith, gender and generation.

Building psychological capital in Sikh masculinities: Gandeep, Sandeep and 'staying focused'

After 'settling in' our interviewees (introducing ourselves, finding out something of them, their interests and their lives at school), we asked them about successful people they knew. This extract comes from an in-depth interview with Gandeep and Sandeep, two young Sikh men.

SB   Who would you say is really successful?
GI   think one of the new teachers here, Mr H. – he's still under 30 and he
        drives around in a Lexus. He's head of the whole science department
        … [he's] young, he's achieved so much at a young age.

When further prompted, the boys referred to members of their households in describing 'successful people' (Gandeep, for example, referred to his brother who had gone to university, and he acknowledged that his mum's work was 'hard' but didn't see her as specifically successful). However, the prime models of success for the boys were teachers. Both young men were articulate and aspirational and again cited the Muslim senior staff member as a successful person. The teacher's car may well signify as a particularly potent (masculine) symbol here, given that this is not the conventional type of teacher transport!

Existing alongside positive aspirations symbolised by teachers were worries on the boys' part about their own personal flaws that might deter success:

G   He's quite focused as well.
SB   What does that mean?
G   He gets to the point … he knows what he's doing.
SB   Focus… tell me a bit about that?
G   I suppose if you know what you want and lots of things distract you …
        Say girls and drugs and things like can get in your way and putting you
        off but if you are focused you get to the point.

Perhaps what is most interesting here is how the boys construct the 'discourse of distraction' as one major way to destabilise their *focus.*

The injunction against 'not being focused' is a core preoccupation in these young men's school. It appears to amplify, as well as respond to, aspects of the rationale of boys' underachievement, a complex construction articulating semi-biologistic and behaviourist notions about the historic male propensity for distraction. This formation has been persuasive in explaining boys' comparative lack of success vis-à-vis girls (Epstein *et al.*, 1998). This discourse resonated in the data and the boys pointed out how a senior male teacher recontextualised this through his own biography:

G   One day Mr W. spoke to us about not really being focused at school like he only got one O level but from then on he kept focused and everything … look at him now, he's like head of year at L School which I think is quite an achievement.

There is much of interest here in terms of the powerful use of the personal as a 'pedagogic text'. The young men repeat the story, suggesting an appreciation of its force. For Gandeep and Sandeep, the school had confirmed their own community values about respecting education, irrespective of social class (Abbas, 2003), and they also believed it had responded firmly to racism. By virtue of this both boys had a strong sense that the school was a safe learning space (in a sense, extending the capacity of community resources available to them) and they contrasted this with their experiences on the streets of west London. We are reluctant to move to any reductive view implying the existence of direct religious influence or faith crossover, especially as Sikhism is one of the least doctrinal of religious practices. Yet Sikhism's ideal subject is produced by a constellation of moral capacities that do, to some extent, overlap or articulate with those demanded by occupying a 'successful' school subject position. It is such articulations, we suggest, that open up spaces in which these young people become positioned and position themselves. Indeed, the two young men saw no contradiction between their Sikh masculinity and the model of successful *professional* masculinity with which they identify. Their main responsibility is to pay heed to the injunction of 'getting focused', governing themselves appropriately through the acquisition of the right kind of psychological capital in order to curb any potential impediment:

G   I'd have to set my goals now and go for the career I want and like G. said like if I achieved those goals in 10–15 years time I'd be quite happy…
SB   Goals?
G   Kind of but I have to focus 'cos I chat a bit so I just have to work a bit more and produce a good standard of work…

Here is the subject position of a well-defended boy (shielded from the temptations of the world) aiming to become the ideal self-regulating pupil. Three other boys in our pilot study shared this view of their task, which was to recognise and then police their 'unsound' formation. They sought to guard against biology (boys being prone to hormonal rushes and the temptation of girls) as well as quasi-sociological notions (their socialisation as disorganised workers). This 'flaky male subject' – their inner 'other' – was the subject some of them had to work on and work over. As we have suggested, the boys' *success* is perversely contingent upon the existence of the spectral stranger within, against whom discourses of success are ranged. Without this presence (either on the internal landscape of the self or as some other *external* representation) it is difficult to know how the boys' positioning practices would work out.

Future masculinities: cashing in on human capital?

In the context of discussing success in the interview with Gandeep and Sandeep, we asked about their imagined futures. As we show above, Sandeep saw that 'setting goals' was central to the process of becoming successful. His vocabulary of 'goals' is consonant with the notion of focus. It constructs a metaphor of a rational and end-oriented purposive worker. Interestingly, these young men are not the natural inheritors of hegemonic masculinity (Connell, 1995), a formation that is associated with instrumental rationality and technological competence, but can be seen to be acquiring (perhaps via the success discourses promoted through school as well as other spaces) the right contributory sort of psychological capital as part of their 'project of the self'.

SB   Would you be able to set goals for 10–15 years ahead?

S   No I can't really see that far… but it's like G. said… the base of the pyramid, if you complete that well then you can do what ever you want … say I've got all my GCSE and then my A levels, it just gives you a better job … I get married and have a couple of kids and stuff and I can say to them 'Look I done all my GCSEs and A levels'…

The metaphor of building organises the discourse as Sandeep articulates the ideal future. This is the responsible future subject secured through the acquisition of educational capital; the psychologically focused and robust, goal-oriented masculine self, capable of accumulating other forms of capital as a result which comes to embody for his own children (and, indeed, himself) an account of success.

G   I am not sure about the kids and family yet 'cos it's early days but I hope to have a family I can look after and keep running … so just try and aim and get good grade, finish school, get a degree, get a good career, stand on your own two feet.

Gandeep too may baulk at the abstract notion of being a family man but he identifies with the project of 'aiming higher' in which the self is able to 'stand on [its] own two feet'.

It is interesting that these Sikh boys construct a traditional masculine position, echoing the positions of their fathers as the head of a household. This aspiration holds in place a dynastic ambition offering the aspirant continuity of predestined family forms. As Sandeep says, "I see it as a challenge… a difficult one… if you can get it having grandchildren and seeing my kids grow up…." This traditional (patriarchal) role is valorised and viewed as a source of respect as well as difficulty. It is important to stress that we reflect here, not on observable realities - 'real' families – rather, the elicited views from two young Sikh males that *project* anticipated futures. However, recent work on the aspirations and understandings of

South Asian young women in Birmingham (Abbas, 2003) critically contextualises these "male-centric" comments, suggesting a more contested gendered future. This is so, even amongst young women other than Sikhs who may be subject to higher degrees of control through more restrictive religious practices associated with Islamic orthodoxies (for example, in the form of Pakistani and Bangladeshi Muslim exclusivity). Moreover, from a more abstract viewpoint, these young men's projected identities as *respected providers*, are at odds with some accounts of radical decentred individualisation, at least at the level of family forms (Giddens, 1993). What the boys speak to is a model that is, of course, structured through an ethnically specific masculine version of power, community values and aspirations.

But, significantly, this family and community formation (imagined or ideological) is highly valued by the school and against whose putative stability the white working-class community is seen as 'lack'. We do not have space here to explore the ways in which 'lack' in embedded white working-class communities is often code for the absence of male authority/figures (see Hey & Bradford, 2006). This remains a theme for future work. However, it *is* our view that in the context of successful schools extended family forms are equated with 'stability' and worked up as vibrant social capital that has utility for the school since it is claimed as support for educational projects of the male self. It may be that the "education extra" provided in the form of a network of adults within extended and complex families (see Abbas, 2003) may partly explain the synergies between certain ethnic minority communities and the values and aspirations of successful schools. This is not to argue a romantic, much less a homogenous, view of the non-white family form (Williams, 2004). Indeed, we have found it hard to hold to any notion of South Asian minority ethnic groups since, as recent work shows, there are large variations structured through class, geography, culture and religion that complicate such a designation (Weedon, 2004). Yet, we suggest, there are likely to be some common pro-education positions that can 'unite' South Asian minority students.

By way of contrast, we turn to consider the views of two young women from a companion and successful girls' school. They share accounts of a similar awareness about being prepared to 'take up' places within their families or within discursively organised educational and career aspirations, but not the uncontested responsibilities discussed by the boys.

Building psychological capital in Hindu femininities: Henara and Vita 'striving'

Henara was from a lower middle-class background and a marriage between a Sikh and a Hindu. Her family owned a dry cleaning franchise. Her best friend was a middle-class Hindu girl (Vita) whose father was an accountant. For these two South Asian girls, it is perhaps significant that their first nominations as 'successful people' were personal; Vita immediately nominated Henara, her 'best friend':

V   She (Henara) doesn't get upset that if she didn't get the part she keeps trying. I don't think success is all about winning. I think it's about trying and being able to do some things … She tries out for everything even if she doesn't want to do it. She's the perfect package. She's clever as well.

H   Most of the time…

VH   What does being clever mean?

V   She doesn't slack on her work. If she has something to do she will do it.

This nomination was not about identifying with public symbols of prestige such as material goods (cars, authority) but more local and personal, and may reflect girls' powerful emotional and social investments in their intimate friendships. The interview question may have induced a compliant response to signal 'a best friend', since not to do so may have been experienced as unethical (Hey, 1997). The girls we interviewed routinely cited other girls in their class and, unlike the boys we interviewed, teachers were not mentioned as examples of success.

The criteria for success were fortitude and determination, and were subtly different from those mentioned by the two Sikh boys. 'Trying' was valorised even with things you did not want to do and 'stick-ability' was seen as a particular virtue. Even cleverness was seen as the effect of effort and doing the work, rather than natural talent. As other work has noted, "effortless flair" (Cohen, 1998) is an attribute that is only recognised in the masculine. Moreover, within this 'discourse of application', there is evidence of a form of psychological capital (resilience) essential to coping with the demands of a competitive world. This allusion to anticipated disappointment is not apparent in the boys' narratives with their reference to 'inner flaws'. The theme of fortitude is also continuous in family narratives in which stories of struggle and forbearance emerge very strongly. When prompted further to think beyond their friends, they respectively designated family members: mother (Henara) and grandmother (Vita). Much of the girls' talk takes issue with the dominant gender regime of their households in which their fathers are presented as 'old-fashioned'. Henara and Vita offer a modest 'reflexive rebellion' against being positioned as subordinates in paternalistic households which normalise their role as 'serving' their brothers domestically. Our data suggest that daughters and mothers shared in a contestation of patriarchal values, with daughters following on from what they described as their own mothers' claims on independence and equality within their household. This 'sisterhood' casts light on the safe assumptions of male gender privilege outlined above.

Yet these two girls attach significance to a different tradition that inheres in female tales of fortitude and survival which are reflected in the virtues of striving and 'never giving up' demanded of them by their schooling. If these girls' psychological capital is accrued around the need to defend against disappointment, compared to the boys' need to avoid the self-sabotage of disruption, the girls see in their female family figures exemplary heroines who have battled and won through and who are deemed worthy of respect and recognition. What is constructed here is a very different model of the family, one that is far less abstract, in some ways more real and immediate, not least because the girls do not *consume* as much as *produce* the family through their own emotional and material labour (Reay, 2004/5). Theirs reflects a differently gendered dynastic inheritance, reflecting different discursive resources (closeness or intimacy in some families, for example) from which psychological capital may derive.

Strivers and survivors: 'im/migrant tales'

It was pertinent that the next nomination of a successful person generated by the girls was in terms of their immediate family:

VH   If you were to name someone you know as successful who would it be?
H   My mum…
V   My grandma.

Henara continues:

H   It's not like she's successful as in clever or bright or she's got a great job or anything. It's just that she has managed to look after all four of us. She's had quite a tough life … she's had loads of pregnancies 'cos in Indian tradition, it's like you want a boy and mum's having to go through loads of these girls and finally she's got this boy and … raising all of us. When my third sister came she had to hear the reactions of everyone saying 'Oh no! It's a girl again!' and try to keep herself and say 'No, this girl's special' and try to keep herself and instead of her like being 'er yes she is a bit of a waste' but now my mum supports us in everything we do. My dad's a bit more traditional … jobs like a doctor but I'm a bit whacky … the whacky one who wants to be an actress 'cos like so she says we'll take you here and there and all that … I think my mum's successful being a great mother and like being able to faze all of us we're like not very easy children to deal with … She's not been very well recently but she gives it her all, tries her best. My mum's like Superwoman …

This loving account positions Henara's – successful – mother through a discourse of recognition and respect. Not only is this set *against* how New Labour discourses routinely privilege paid employment as the primary maternal obligation (Levitas, 1998) but it also resists the over-determination of her mother's role by the biological and patriarchal imperatives of producing a male child. Henara reads her mother's oppression (and 'success') here through a narrative of resilience, redeeming her 'fate' as the positive capacity to cope to 'give it her all' and, like the value of dedication applied to her by Vita, she notes her own mother's tenacity in that she 'tries her best'. Moreover, her mother's consistent support is set against the comment about her father preferring a more traditional aspiration for his daughter (a doctor), but her mother backs her up in pursuit of her own 'whacky' idea of being an actress. This redescription of her mother's position is instructive. It simultaneously cites feminism (woman as victim) and post-feminism (personal fortitude) as repositioning female figures in the different ethical space of an idiosyncratic preference that celebrates individual psychology and survival. The explicit reference to 'whacky' also suggests the unique individualised self and is perhaps emblematic of how the vocabulary of new times captures the creativity and individuality that is so appealing to some aspirant young women. It is interesting that the figure of the 'striving survivor' resonates as 'storied narratives' (held within particular migrant communities and groups (Breckner, 2002)) and re-emerges so that it might articulate with ideologies of success to be further inflected by girls' stories of successful selves.

We turn next to another 'survival story' also offered in the same context. Here is Vita's echoing story about her grandmother.

> V   She's born in Uganda and [was] kicked out. She has four children and one of them's a deaf-mute who has two children and her husband left her. My grandma has to look after her. She doesn't get to live her own life. One of her sons doesn't speak to her and so she's got so many problems. She's just broken her leg and her mum's recently died as well. Like she's gone though a lot but she's not giving up like. She's still … she has traditions and she keeps them. She doesn't break them 'cos it'll be too much hassle … She doesn't give up, she still makes it … she cooks for us and it's just great.

Again the themes focus on severe duress but these are not seen as sufficient to daunt the indomitable spirit of this feminine figure, who is rendered as the heart of the family, someone who can be relied upon to centre traditional Hindu values. This is a very different version of living within a dynasty and is associated with the gendering of the private/public dialectic. Female senior roles in families are not seen as much as an inheritance with difficult responsibilities but as a relentless set of demands engendering forms of hard, complex emotional and practical labour (Reay, 2004/5).

One way to situate this narrative is to see it echoing as part of the discursive repertoire established by Henara previously. Another possibility is to appreciate its intertextual quality and note how redolent both these stories are of soap opera themes of female survival (Geraghty, 2001). But what is interesting is *how* these girls present their examples of successful people in terms of survival and relocation stories. This genre recontextualises the 'family romance' of struggle to move beyond the public front-stage account into backstage domestic citations to recognise a specifically feminine version of success.

Successful schools are built on the assumption that diversity means a weakened politics of rhetorical recognition as 'excellence for all'. Whilst New Labour values iterate the desired position of self-actualising employee, young women (especially from working-class and some non-Anglo minority ethnic groups), know that there are other contradictory demands placed on them that cannot be so easily set aside but require negotiation and attention since they involve important questions of power and identity that cannot be discounted

It might be the case that one way for girls to negotiate their positions within traditional relations expected by their fathers and post-traditional aspirations of their schooling is to valorise both the public aspiration of success and its unacknowledged 'other' (Mann, 1998). This might then also be seen as reflecting the need for the recognition of the psychological resilience required in being the right sort of successful girl living between the dreams of individualised choice and the more complex conditions of familial dramas (Gonick, 2005). It is possible that feminism's political presence, at times residual and at others more marked, may support young women's reflexive capacity for narrating stories of success and identity.

Stars in successful schools

In order to focus our questions on schooling more directly, we resorted to asking specific questions about school. The girls mentioned the public prestige markers only *after* their family accounts and in this there was no equivocation about how the school measured success.

VH   What does the school understand as success?
V   *A stars! If it's not A stars* it's high grades … [emphasis in the recording]
H   The best of your ability … it's success so that you can have a stable future …
V   … like trying out for everything and not being afraid of what other people might think…

Again the important notion of trying things and persistence, whilst disregarding what others might think emerges in the discussion. This resonates with the language of liberal feminism with its positive interventions of expanding the range of girls' options. However, it has a new twist linked to the claim that this success may secure a stable future, a future that does not assume the central role and responsibility of wife. Henara confirms this in the follow-up question:

VH   Tell me what a stable future means …
H   You come to school for a reason so that you can get a good job and make a lot of money eventually … and then you know… you are not out on the streets you're educated … education will get you somewhere …

She amplifies this in a comment on the need to have good qualifications in the context of her ambitions to be an actress; she needs something to 'fall back on', 'sensible qualifications'.

VH   How do you see your future?
H   I dream of seeing myself on TV … trying to get somewhere …

This 'dreamy' comment is quite typical of the girls we interviewed, as is the aspiration of 'trying to get somewhere'. When pressed further about the qualities needed, Vita responded:

VH   What qualities do you need to be successful?
V   Patience ... tolerance ... patience with yourself and tolerance of other people ...

And, perhaps, more interestingly:

V   Strength to keep on going and not giving up
VH   Where does that message come from?
V   You get pushed by other people but it's in yourself ...
H   You know yourself you will really get it ...

Here the intersection of traditional 'moral feminine' qualities ('going on', 'not giving up'), previously amplified in the girls' stories of female relatives, articulates with the newer imperatives of marketised self-actualisation and enterprise to suggest a new driven subject negotiating the fine lines of self and (competitive) 'other'. This is a story of personal psychological resources (patience, persistence, resilience), and of capacities that lie inside to be activated at appropriate times. Our data suggest that the successful school seeks to engage (with boys and girls, but in different ways) in practices that order, draw out and animate these inner resources which act as important potential capital.

To explore these ideas in more detail the girls were asked to imagine giving advice to new girls at school:

VH   What advice would you give to girls about success in starting this school?
H   Enjoy themselves.
V   Go for all the extracurricular activities.
V   Go for all the opportunities you can ...
H   It'll look great on your CV.

Again, the mix is enlightening. It reveals an eclectic vocabulary of liberal cliché about enjoyment, the school mantra about maximising opportunities and the bottom-line pragmatism of 'it'll look great on your CV'. This combination reproduces the late modern preoccupation of self-surveillance and self-monitoring as Bauman (2001) avers. In this, the girls were also clear about the nature of failure:

VH   What is failure?
H   It's not trying your best ...
V   Regret is waste ... look ahead and get more prepared next time [in the context of ill-preparedness for exams].

So the subject here takes on the project of success to herself. Its 'other' is construed as personal lack and the outcome of insufficient preparation and thus has the capacity to animate self. In this way, as Benjamin (2002) notes, the elision of New Labour's "educational other" is secured. There is no place in this account (and its policy imperative) for the inevitable consequences of a competitive exam system or the differential distribution of capitals (educational, symbolic, material and psychological); all can be winners, if not then the fault 'oft doth lie within'.

CONCLUSIONS

Although we draw on only four interviewees, we argue that these are suggestive of how discourses of success mesh within other discursive fields and sites of identity and belonging. We acknowledge the need for further work here but insist that potential new class/gender/ethnic formations situated on the New Labour policy landscape cannot be read without an appreciation of how private and public affiliations entail relations of power and emotion that entwine one with the other. Our data and discussion suggest the complex articulations between policies that valorise success and status, aspirations mapped by the discourses of success and the lived horizons of possibility realised within the family, community, class, gender and ethnic relations. The *actual* capacity of these to form support in building the competitive individualism demanded in contemporary times plays out variously for different young people and further work is needed to explore this.

Our research interests lie in the ways that political objectives – in this context the 'unleashing of aspiration' in schools where discourses of success are dominant – become articulated with subject positions and how social difference mediates subjects' lives in such settings. We looked at class, gender and race intersections in discourses of aspiration and success and this entailed exploring young people's 'vocabularies of success' and the ways in which young people were positioned (and how they positioned themselves) in relation to wider school practices designed to cultivate aspiration and success. Our own starting assumptions indicated that success is socially constructed and mediated through complex social networks: school, family, friendship groups, peer groups and communities of different kinds.

Our focus poses a potential critique to aspects of the "reflexive modernity" thesis *if* this is taken to signal a displacement of the social in favour of 'the individual' in young people's lives. We have, for some time, been unhappy with the work of those sociologists who seem to suggest that pathways to adulthood have become increasingly 'individualised' in recent times (Beck *et al.*, 1994; Furlong & Cartmel, 1997; Bye, 2001; Kelly, 2001). We do not accept that life decisions have become relatively *less* mediated by the social domain in which they are situated and our data suggest the fundamental significance of 'the social'. Our research suggests that this works in different ways for different young people, yet retains great significance through the institutions to which we refer above: friendship, peer groups, families and communities, for example (Hey, 2002). Class, gender and race (themselves constitutive elements of the social) powerfully mediate young people's lives. To suggest otherwise is to fly in the face of people's lived experiences. We are adamant that a thoroughgoing sociological account –

hence our adoption of Bourdieu's position on the nature of the social – is the means to understanding accounts such as those we present here.

If individualisation and responsibilisation are not unitary and unidirectional practices, the 'can do' and enterprising young person is inflected through modernising, retraditionalising and detraditionalising discourses. On the one hand, these discourses differentially interpellate young people in symbolising success and, on the other, they shape that which young people 'recognise' as successful (with which they may identify) or which others project onto them. Indeed, the power of ideology (as Althusser, 1971, showed) lies *precisely* in its capacity to speak to subjects, who are able to *actively* invest (or identify with) subject positions. In the case of success discourses, these articulations between ideology and subjects arise from young people's social locations within the spaces of home and community. In turn, these spaces impact upon how young people are able to locate (imagine) or identify themselves as successful (or otherwise) subjects. Such positional possibilities are socially, and differentially, distributed through religion, faith, class and gender and most convincingly, perhaps, manifested in the localised and mediated forms of family micro-politics in which gender is central.

We contend that discourses – discourses of success, for example – travel and, indeed, potentially unravel the border between the public and the private. What happens at the level of public discourse (and 'policy' particularly) reaches into the local and the personal where it is mediated by a range of factors (family, school or community, for example). We have argued this elsewhere (Hey & Bradford, 2004), suggesting that contemporary power modalities can be thought of as forms of compulsory reflexive self-invention that remain within as well as outside traditional gender regimes. For example, Henara and Vita "make themselves up" (Hacking, 1986) by citing and reciting their traditional values as valorisations of their grand/ mothers through feminist tropes of a heroic 'grand maternalism'. Both girls are mindful of how their domestic rebellion connects to the neo-liberal successful girl celebrated in their schools. Sandeep and Gandeep, on the other hand, reflect alternative practices of self-regulation, assiduously cultivated in their successful school. They display insight into their own capacity for 'self-distraction' (and potentially for self-destruction) – '... girls and drugs and things ...' – but the school, in conjunction with other forces, exercises its tutelage in enabling them to 'get focused' and to construct the '... base of the pyramid'. The boys seem to see this as an acceptable route to their dynastic future as potentially successful participants in the labour market as well as effective providers in the domestic sphere.

Girls stand differently in relation to the policy-led reconfiguration of the sexual division of labour. This has not so much been *dismantled* through new ideologies of work as more deeply inscribed for middle-class women as a successful career and, perhaps, for working-class women as a successful 'job'. These are now expected *in addition to* a 'performative maternity'. However, the point here is that New Labour's third way policies, with their centrality of labour market participation, are fundamental to the production of new forms of classed and gendered ethnicities (see Bullen *et al.*, 2000; McRobbie, 2004/5).

And what of the status of the successful school? Even if the 'badge' of Beacon or Leading Edge is seen (understandably) as positive, how young people *live* these discourses of success cannot be simply read off from it in any direct way. We do not claim that it becomes part of these young people's make-up by some veiled form of osmosis. Our data show that young people's lived circumstances are crucial in enabling (or, indeed, *dis*abling) their capacity to form successful identities. Young people's material location continues to shape their radically different futures. However, we are also impressed by the extent to which the two schools in which we collected our data have engaged with young people in ways that encourage some of them (through practices of the self that form 'psychological capital'), at least, to implicitly identify with New Labour's aspirational project. What are the messages here for feminism and social justice projects? What does or could this do to gender and class re- and decompositions? And do girls in other Beacon schools get or hear the same message? Do boys receive, let alone hear the same or a differently inflected message in their equivalent Beacon schools? Clearly, we cannot answer this on the basis of this pilot study, but such questions form the basis of ongoing work.

NOTES

[1] This chapter has been published earlier as: Bradford, S. &. Hey, V. (2007). Successful subjectivities. The successification of class, ethnic and gender positions. *Journal of Education Policy, 22*(6), 595-614. Reprinted with the much appreciated permission of the publisher.

[2] Hall argues that identity (successful identity, for example) entails the hailing or positioning of the subject *as well as* the specific forms in which subjects produce or perform subject positions. This positioning and performing constitutes an attachment, a dual *articulation* between subject and discourse, always incomplete, partial and contingent.

[3] There is a distinction is between a traditional labour 'redistributionist' ideology designed to increase equality (largely rejected by New Labour), and the strong policy commitment to 'equality of opportunity' in the labour market or in education.

[4] The words come from Alan Milburn in describing the government's fundamental objectives (Radio 4, 'Today', 11 November 2004).

[5] One of the authors of this paper was Chair of Governors of a Beacon school. On achieving Beacon status, some parents in that school expressed concern that the requirement to work with and support other schools would undermine their own school's capacity to sustain its position in the league tables.

[6] This could be called the capital that is institutionalised: the habituated expectation of success.

REFERENCES

Abbas, T. (2003). The impact of religio-cultural norms and values on the education of young South Asian women. *British Journal of Sociology of Education, 24*(4), 411–428.

Althusser, L. (1971). *Lenin and philosophy and other essays.* London: New Left Books.

Bauman, Z. (1997). The dream of purity. In: Z. Bauman (Ed.), *Postmodernity and its discontents* Cambridge: Polity Press.

Bauman, Z. (2001). *Community: seeking safety in an insecure world.* Cambridge: Polity Press.

Beck, U., Giddens, A. & Lash, S. (1994). *Reflexive modernization politics, tradition and aesthetics in the modern social order.* Cambridge: Polity Press.

Benjamin, S. (2002). *The micropolitics of inclusive education: an ethnography.* Buckingham: Open University Press.

Bourdieu, P. (1986). The forms of capital. In: J. G. Richardson (Ed.), *Handbook of theory and research for the sociology of education.* New York: Greenwood Press.

Bourdieu, P. (1995). *Sociology in question.* London: Sage.

Bradford, S. (1999). Youth work: young people and transitions to adulthood. In: M. Hill (Ed.), *Effective ways of working with children and their families.* London: Jessica Kingsley.

Bradford, S., Hey, V. & Cullen, F. (2004). *What works? An exploration of the value of informal education work with young people.* London, Clubs for Young People in association with Brunel University.

Breckner, R. (2002). 'Migrants': a target-category for social policy? Experiences of first-generation migration. In: P. Chamberlayne, M. Rustin & T. Wengraf (Eds.), *Biography and social exclusion in Europe: experiences and life journeys.* Bristol: Policy Press.

Bullen, E., Kenway, J. & Hey, V. (2000). New Labour, social exclusion and educational risk management: the case of 'gymslip mums'. *British Educational Research Journal,* 28(4), 441–456.

Bye, J. (2001). *Making pathways: young people and their informal vocational learning—a discussion paper.* Working Paper 00-01. Sydney, UTS Research Centre Vocational Education and Training.

Clarke, J. & Newman, J. (1997). *The managerial state.* London: Sage.

Cohen, M. (1998). *'A habit of healthy idleness'; boys' underachievement in historical perspective.* Buckingham: Open University Press.

Connell, R. W. (1995). *Masculinities.* Cambridge: Polity Press.

DfEE (1999). *Learning to succeed: a new framework for post-16 learning.* London: Stationery Office.

DfES (2001). *Schools - achieving success.* London: Stationery Office.

DfES (2004a). *Beacon schools in the UK.* Available online at: http://www.dfes.gov.uk/beacon/ (accessed 21 November 2006).

DfES (2004b). *Leading edge partnership programme.* Available online at: http://www.standards.dfes. gov.uk/beaconschools/general/535239 (accessed 21 November 2006).

DSS (1998). *New ambitions for our country: a new contract for welfare.* Cm 3805. London: Stationery Office.

Epstein, D., Ellwood, J., Hey, V. & Maw, J. (1998). *Failing boys? Issues in gender and achievement.* Buckingham: Open University Press.

Fairclough, N. (2000). *New Labour, new language.* London: Routledge.

Fergusson, R. (2000). Modernizing managerialism in education. In: J. Clarke, S. Gewirtz & E. McLaughlin (Eds.), *New managerialism, new welfare.* London: Sage.

Frazer, E. (2000). Communitarianism. In: G. Browning, A. Halcli & F. Webster (Eds.), *Understanding contemporary society: theories of the present.* London: Sage.

Furlong, A. & Cartmel, F. (1997). *Young people and social change: new perspectives* (2nd edn). Buckingham: Open University Press.

Geraghty, C. (2001). *Women and soap opera.* Cambridge: Polity Press.

Gewirtz, S. (2002). Achieving success? Critical reflections on New Labour's 'third way' agenda for education, keynote lecture to *International Meeting on Curriculum Politics,* Oporto, May.

Giddens, A. (1993). *The transformation of intimacy: sexuality, love and eroticism in modern societies.* Cambridge: Polity Press.

Giddens, A. (1998). *The third way: the renewal of social democracy.* Cambridge: Polity Press.

Giddens, A. (2000) *The third way and its critics.* Cambridge: Polity Press.

Gonick, M. (2005). Girl number twenty revisited: feminist pedagogies for new hard times, paper presented at *Gender and Education, 5th International Conference,* Cardiff, 29–31 March.

Hacking, I. (1986). Making up people. In: T. Heller (Ed.), *Reconstructing individualism: autonomy, individuality and self in western thought.* Stanford, CA: Stanford University Press.

Hall, S. (1996). Who needs identity? In: S. Hall & P. du Gay (Eds.), *Questions of cultural identity.* London: Sage.

Hey, V. (1997). *The company she keeps; an ethnography of girls' friendship.* London: Routledge.

Hey, V. (2002). Horizontal solidarities and molten capitalism; the subject, intersubjectivity, self and the other in late modernity. *Discourse,* 23(2), 227–241.

Hey, V. (2003). Joining the club? Academia and working class femininities. *Gender and Education,* 13(3), 319–335.

Hey, V. & Bradford, S. (2004). The return of the repressed? The gender politics of emergent forms of professionalism in education. *Journal of Education Policy,* 19(6), 691–713.

Hey, V. & Bradford, S. (2006). Re-engineering motherhood? Surestart in the Community. *Contemporary Issues in Early Childhood,* 7(1), 53–67.

Kelly, P. (2001). Youth at risk: processes of individualisation and responsibilisation in the risk society. *Discourse: studies in the cultural politics of education,* 22(1), 23–33.

Levitas, R. (1998). *The inclusive society? Social exclusion and New Labour.* Basingstoke: Macmillan.

Lucey, H. & Reay, D. (2002). Carrying the beacon of excellence: social class differentiation and anxiety at a time of transition. *Journal of Education Policy,* 17(3), 321–336.

Mann, C. (1998). The impact of working class mothers on the educational success of their adolescent daughters at a time of social change. *British Journal of the Sociology of Education,* 19(2), 211–226.

McRobbie, A. (2004/5). Notes on 'what not to wear' and post-feminist symbolic violence: feminism, Bourdieu and after. *The Sociological Review Monograph,* 2, 99–109.

Reay, D. (2004/5). Gendering Bourdieu's concept of capitals? Emotional capital, women and social class. *The Sociological Review Monograph,* 2, 57–74.

Skeggs, B. (2004). *Class, self, culture.* London: Routledge.

Webster, D. (2001). Beacon schools: New Labour education policy in a nutshell. *Forum,* 43(3), 127–130.

Weedon, C. (2004). *Identity and culture, narratives of difference and belonging.* Buckingham: Open University Press.

Wexler, P. (1992). *Becoming somebody; toward a social psychology of school.* London: Falmer Press.

Williams, F. (2004). *Rethinking families.* London: Calouste Gulbenkian Foundation.

FURTHER READINGS

Benjamin, S. (2002). *The micropolitics of inclusive education: an ethnography.* Buckingham: Open University Press.

Hey, V. & Bradford, S. (2004). The return of the repressed? The gender politics of emergent forms of professionalism in education. *Journal of Education Policy,* 19(6), 691–713.

Hey, V. & Bradford, S. (2006). Re-engineering motherhood? Surestart in the Community. *Contemporary Issues in Early Childhood,* 7(1), 53–67.

Reay, D. (2004/5). Gendering Bourdieu's concept of capitals? Emotional capital, women and social class. *The Sociological Review Monograph,* 2, 57–74.

Weedon, C. (2004). *Identity and culture, narratives of difference and belonging.* Buckingham, Open University Press.

Simon Bradford
School of Sport and Education
Brunel University, UK

Valerie Hey
Sussex School of Education
University of Sussex, UK

MICHAEL W. APPLE

PRODUCING DIFFERENCE

Neo-liberalism, Neo-conservatism and the Politics of Educational Reform[1]

INTRODUCTION

In this chapter, I raise serious questions about current educational 'reform' efforts now underway in a number of nations. I use research and arguments based on the English, US, New Zealand, and Scandinavian experience(s) to document some of the hidden differential effects of two connected strategies – neo-liberal inspired *market proposals* with their emphasis on what I will call 'thin democracy' based on individual consumer choice rather than 'thick democracy based on full collective participation and neo-liberal, neo-conservative, and middle class *managerial inspired regulatory proposals*.

In the process of critically examining a number of current reforms, I examine the inter-relations among class, gender, and race. All three must be taken up *together* since, for example, in the United States 70% of working class positions are held by women and persons of colour (Apple, 1996; see also Bourdieu, 1984). This is also occurring in other nations. Yet, this chapter has another agenda as well. I also suggest that the rhetorical flourishes of the discourses of critical pedagogy – a tradition that continues to play a role in challenging parts of neo-liberal and neo-conservative policies in education – need to come to grips with these changing material and ideological conditions. Critical pedagogy – the radical tradition(s) that seek to interrupt class, race, and gender dominance in policy and practice – can not and will not occur in a vacuum. Unless we honestly face these profound rightist transformations and think tactically about them, we will have little effect either on the creation of a counter-hegemonic common-sense or on the building of a counter-hegemonic alliance.

Thus, I examine the ways in which the social and cultural terrain of educational policy and discourse has been altered 'on the ground' so to speak. I argue that we need to make closer connections between our theoretical and critical discourses on the one hand and the real transformations that are currently shifting educational policies and practices in fundamentally rightist directions on the other. Part of my discussion will need to be conceptual; but part of it will appropriately need to be empirical in order for me to pull together what is known about the real and material effects of the shift to the right in education.

My focus on the 'gritty materialities' of these effects is not meant to dismiss the importance of theoretical interventions. Nor is it meant to suggest that dominant discourses should not be constantly interrupted by the creative gains that have

M. Simons, M. Olssen and M.A. Peters (eds.), Re-Reading Education Policies: A Handbook Studying the Policy Agenda of the 21ˢᵗ Century, 625–649.

emerged from the varied communities that make up critical educational studies. Indeed, critical educational research, policy, and practice *require* the fundamental interruption of common-sense. However, while the construction of new theories and utopian visions is important, it is equally crucial to base these theories and visions in an unromantic appraisal of the material and discursive terrain that now exists. Common-sense is already being radically altered, but not in directions that many critical educators would find comforting. Without an analysis of such transformations and of the balance of forces that have created such discomforting alterations, without an analysis of the tensions, differential relations of power, and contradictions within it, we are left with increasingly elegant new theoretical formulations, but with a less than elegant understanding of the field of social power on which they operate (Bourdieu 1984).

Hence, while much of the literature on 'critical pedagogies' has been politically and theoretically important and has helped us make a number of gains, it has a number of flaws. It too often has not been sufficiently connected to the ways in which the current movement toward what might best be called 'conservative modernization' – the combination of turning toward the 'new' of markets, accountability, and efficiency and the 'old' of traditional culture and discipline (Apple, 2006; Apple & Buras, 2006) – both has altered common-sense and has transformed the material and ideological conditions surrounding schooling. It, thereby, sometimes becomes a form of what might best be called 'romantic possibilitarian' rhetoric, in which the language of possibility substitutes for a consistent tactical analysis of what the balance of forces actually is and what is necessary to change it (Whitty, 1974). This is the task in which I engage in this chapter.

RIGHT TURN

In his influential history of curriculum debates, Herbert Kliebard has documented that educational issues have consistently involved major conflicts and compromises among groups with competing visions of 'legitimate' knowledge, what counts as 'good' teaching and learning, and what is a 'just' society (Kliebard, 1995). That such conflicts have deep roots in conflicting views of racial, class, and gender justice in education and the larger society is ratified in even more critical recent work as well (Rury & Mirel, 1997; Teitelbaum, 1996; Selden, 1999). These competing visions have never had equal holds on the imagination of educators or the general citizenry nor have they ever had equal power to effect their visions. Because of this, no analysis of education can be fully serious without placing at its very core a sensitivity to the ongoing struggles that constantly shape the terrain on which education operates.

Today is no different than in the past. A 'new' set of compromises, a new alliance and new power bloc has been formed that has increasing influence in education and all things social. This power bloc combines multiple fractions of capital who are committed to neo-liberal marketised solutions to educational problems (Brown, Green & Lauder, 2001), neo-conservative intellectuals who want a 'return' to higher standards and a 'common culture,' authoritarian populist religious conservatives who are deeply worried about secularity and the preservation of their own traditions, and particular fractions of the professionally oriented new middle class who are committed to the ideology and techniques of accountability, measurement, and 'management.' While there are clear tensions and conflicts within this alliance, in general its overall aims are in providing the educational conditions believed necessary both for increasing international competitiveness, profit, and discipline and for returning us to a romanticised past of the 'ideal' home, family, and school (Apple, 1996, 2000, 2006; Apple et al., 2003).

In essence, the new alliance has integrated education into a wider set of ideological commitments. The objectives in education are the same as those that guide its economic and social welfare goals. They include the dramatic expansion of that eloquent fiction, the free market; the drastic reduction of government responsibility for social needs; the reinforcement of intensely competitive structures of mobility both inside and outside the school; the lowering of people's expectations for economic security; the 'disciplining' of culture and the body; and the popularisation of what is clearly a form of Social Darwinist thinking, as the recent popularity of *The Bell Curve* so obviously and distressingly indicates (Herrnstein & Murray, 1994; see also Kincheloe, Steinberg & Greeson, 1997).

The seemingly contradictory discourse of competition, markets, and choice on the one hand and accountability, performance objectives, standards, national testing, and national curriculum have created such a din that it is hard to hear anything else. As I have shown in a number of recent books, these tendencies actually oddly reinforce each other and help cement conservative educational positions into our daily lives (Apple, 1996, 2000, 2006; Apple et al., 2003).

While lamentable, the changes that are occurring present an exceptional opportunity for serious critical reflection. In a time of radical social and educational change, it is crucial to document the processes and effects of the various and sometimes contradictory elements of the conservative restoration and of the ways in which they are mediated, compromised with, accepted, used in different ways by different groups for their own purposes, and/or struggled over in the policies and practices of people's daily educational lives (Ranson, 1995). I shall want to give a sense of how this might be happening in current 'reforms' such as marketisation and national curricula and national testing in this chapter. For those interested in critical educational policies and practices, not to do this means that we act without understanding the shifting relations of power that are constructing and reconstructing the social field of power. While Gramsci's saying, "Pessimism of the intellect, optimism of the will," has a powerful resonance to it and is useful for mobilisation and for not losing hope, it would be foolish to substitute rhetorical slogans for the fuller analysis that is undoubtedly required if we are to be successful.

NEW MARKETS, OLD TRADITIONS

Behind a good deal of the New Right's emerging discursive ensemble in a number of nations was a position that emphasised "a culturalist construction of the nation as a (threatened) haven for white (Christian) traditions and values" (Gillborn, 1997). This involved the construction of an imagined national past that is at least partly mythologised, and then employing it to castigate the present. Gary McCulloch argues that the nature of the historical images of schooling has changed. Dominant imagery of education as being "safe, domesticated, and progressive" (that is, as leading toward progress and social/personal improvement) has shifted to become "threatening, estranged, and regressive" (McCulloch, 1997, p. 80). The past is no longer the source of stability, but a mark of failure, disappointment, and loss. This is seen most vividly in the attacks on the "progressive orthodoxy" that supposedly now reigns supreme in classrooms in many nations (see Hirsch, 1996).

For example, in England – though much the same is echoed in the United States, Australia, and elsewhere – Michael Jones, the political editor of *The Sunday Times*, recalls the primary school of his day.

> Primary school was a happy time for me. About 40 of us sat at fixed wooden desks with ink wells and moved from them only with grudging permission. Teacher sat in a higher desk in front of us and moved only to the blackboard. She smelled of scent and inspired awe (quoted in McCulloch, 1997, p. 78).

The mix of metaphors invoking discipline, scent (visceral and almost 'natural'), and awe is fascinating. But he goes on, lamenting the past 30 years of 'reform' that transformed primary schools. Speaking of his own children's experience, Jones says:

> My children spent their primary years in a showplace school where they were allowed to wander around at will, develop their real individuality and dodge the 3Rs [Reading, Writing, Arithmetic]. It was all for the best, we were assured. But it was not (quoted in McCulloch, 1997, p. 78).

For Jones, the "dogmatic orthodoxy" of progressive education "had led directly to educational and social decline." Only the rightist reforms instituted in the 1980s and 1990s could halt and then reverse this decline (McCulloch, 1997, p. 78). Only then could the imagined past return.

Much the same is being said on United States' side of the Atlantic. These sentiments are echoed in the public pronouncements of such figures as William Bennett, E.D. Hirsch, Jr., Diane Ravitch, and others, all of whom seem to believe that progressivism is now in the dominant position in educational policy and practice and has destroyed a valued past (see., e.g., Ravitch, 2000; Ravitch, 2005; Apple, 2001). All of them believe that only by tightening control over curriculum and teaching (and students, of course), restoring 'our' lost traditions, making education more disciplined and competitive as they are certain it was in the past – only then can we have effective schools. These figures are joined by others who have similar criticisms, but who instead turn to a different past for a different future. Their past is less that of scent and awe and authority, but one of market 'freedom.' For them, nothing can be accomplished – even the restoration of awe and authority – without setting the market loose on schools so as to ensure that only 'good' ones survive.

We should understand that these policies are radical transformations. If they had come from the other side of the political spectrum, they would have been ridiculed in many ways, given the ideological tendencies in our nations. Further, not only are these policies based on a romanticised pastoral past, these reforms have not been notable for their grounding in research findings. Indeed, when research has been used to justify the policies associated with conservative modernisation, it has often either served as a rhetoric of justification for preconceived beliefs about the supposed efficacy of markets or regimes of tight accountability or they have been based – as in the case of Chubb and Moe's much publicised work on marketisation – on quite flawed research (Chubb & Moe, 1990; Whitty, 1997).

Yet, no matter how radical some of these proposed 'reforms' are and no matter how weak the empirical basis of their support, they have now redefined the terrain of debate of all things educational. After years of conservative attacks and mobilisations, it has become clear that "ideas that were once deemed fanciful, unworkable – or just plain extreme" are now increasingly being seen as common-sense (Gillborn, 1997, p. 357).

Tactically, the reconstruction of common-sense that has been accomplished has proven to be extremely effective. For example, there are clear discursive strategies being employed here, ones that are characterised by 'plain speaking' and speaking in a language that 'everyone can understand.' I do not wish to be wholly negative about this. The importance of these things is something many 'progressive' educators, including many writers on critical pedagogy, have yet to understand. (See Apple 1988; 1999). However, these strategies also involve not only presenting one's own position as 'common-sense,' but also usually tacitly implying that there is something of a conspiracy among one's opponents to deny the truth or to say only that which is "fashionable" (Gillborn, 1997b, p. 353). As Gillborn notes,

> This is a powerful technique. First, it assumes that there are no *genuine* arguments against the chosen position; any opposing views are thereby positioned as false, insincere or self-serving. Second, the technique presents the speaker as someone brave or honest enough to speak the (previously) unspeakable. Hence, the moral high ground is assumed and opponents are further denigrated (Gillborn, 1997b, p. 353).

It is hard to miss these characteristics in some of the conservative literature such as Herrnstein and Murray's (1994) publicising of the unthinkable 'truth' about genetics and intelligence or E.D. Hirsch's latest 'tough' discussion of the destruction of 'serious' schooling by progressive educators (Hirsch, 1996; Ravitch, 2005).

MARKETS AND PERFORMANCE

Let us take as an example of the ways in which all this operates one element of conservative modernisation – the neo-liberal claim that the invisible hand of the market will inexorably lead to better schools. As Roger Dale reminds us, 'the market' acts as a metaphor rather than an explicit guide for action. It is not denotative, but connotative. Thus, it must itself be "marketed" to those who will exist in it and live with its effects (quoted in Menter et al., 1997, p. 27). Markets are marketed, are made legitimate, by a depoliticising strategy. They are said to be natural and neutral, and governed by effort and merit. And those opposed to them are by definition, hence, also opposed to effort and merit. Markets, as well, are supposedly less subject to political interference and the weight of bureaucratic procedures. Plus, they are grounded in the rational choices of individual actors (Menter et al., p. 27; see also Witte, 2000). Thus, markets and the guarantee of rewards for effort and merit are to be coupled together to produce 'neutral,' yet positive, results. Mechanisms, hence, must be put into place that give evidence of entrepreneurial efficiency and effectiveness. This coupling of markets and mechanisms for the generation of evidence of performance is exactly what has occurred. Whether it works is open to question.

False hopes

In one of the most thoughtful critical reviews of much of the evidence on marketisation, Geoff Whitty cautions us not to mistake rhetoric for reality. After examining research from a number of countries, Whitty argues that while advocates of marketised 'choice' plans assume that competition will enhance the efficiency and responsiveness of schools, as well as give disadvantaged children opportunities that they currently do not have, this may be a false hope (Whitty, 1997, p. 58). These hopes are not now being realized and are unlikely to be realized in the future "in the context of broader policies that do nothing to challenge deeper social and cultural inequalities." As he goes on to say, "Atomised decision-making in a highly stratified society may appear to give everyone equal opportunities, but transforming responsibility for decision-making from the public to the private sphere can actually reduce the scope of collective action to improve the quality of education for all" (Whitty, 1997, p. 58). When this is connected to the fact that, as I shall show shortly, in practice neo-liberal policies involving market 'solutions' may actually serve to reproduce – not subvert – traditional hierarchies of class and race, this should give us reason to pause (Whitty,1997; see also Whitty, Edwards & Gewirtz, 1993; Apple, 1996, 2006).

Thus, rather than taking neo-liberal claims at face value, we should want to ask about their hidden effects that are too often invisible in the rhetoric and metaphors of their proponents. Given the limitations of what one can say in a chapter of this length, I shall select a few issues that have been given less attention than they deserve, but on which there is now significant research.

The English experience is apposite here, especially since proponents of the market such as Chubb and Moe (1990) rely so heavily on it and because that is where the tendencies I analyse are most advanced. In England, the 1993 Education Act documented the state's commitment to marketisation. Governing bodies of local educational authorities (LEAs) were mandated to formally consider "going GM [grant-maintained]" (that is, opting out of the local school system's control and entering into the competitive market) every year (Power, Halpin & Fitz, 1994, p. 27). Thus, the weight of the state stood behind the press towards neo-liberal reforms there. Yet, rather than leading to curriculum responsiveness and diversification, the competitive market has not created much that is different from the traditional models so firmly entrenched in schools today (Power, Halpin & Fitz, 1994). Nor has it radically altered the relations of inequality that characterise schooling.

In their own extensive analyses of the effects of marketised reforms 'on the ground,' Ball and his colleagues point to some of the reasons why we need to be quite cautious here. As they document, in these situations educational principles and values are often compromised such that commercial issues become more important in curriculum design and resource allocation (Ball, Bowe & Gewirtz, 1994, p. 39; see also Ball, 2007). For instance, the coupling of markets with the demand for and publication of performance indicators such as 'examination league tables' in England has meant that schools are increasingly looking for ways to attract 'motivated' parents with 'able' children. In this way, schools are able to enhance their relative position in local systems of competition. This represents a subtle, but crucial shift in emphasis – one that is not openly discussed as often as it should be – from student needs to student performance and from what the school does for the student to what the student does for the school. This is also accompanied too uncomfortably often by a shift of resources away from students who are labelled as having special needs or learning difficulties, with some of these needed resources now being shifted to marketing and public relations. 'Special needs' students are not only expensive, but deflate test scores on those all important league tables (Gillborn & Youdell 2000).

Not only does this make it difficult to 'manage public impressions' so that the public thinks that the school is good, but it also makes it difficult to attract the 'best' and most academically talented teachers (Ball, Bowe & Gewirtz, 1994, pp. 17–19). The entire enterprise does, however, establish a new metric and a new set of goals based on a constant striving to win the market game. What this means is of considerable importance, not only in terms of its effects on daily school life (Gewirtz, 2002), but in the ways all of this signifies a transformation of what counts as a good society and a responsible citizen. Let me say something about this generally.

I noted earlier that behind all educational proposals are visions of a just society and a good student. The neo-liberal reforms I have been discussing construct this in a particular way. While the defining characteristic of neo-liberalism is largely based on the central tenets of classical liberalism, in particular classic economic liberalism, there are crucial differences between classical liberalism and neo-liberalism. These differences are absolutely essential in understanding the politics of education and the transformations education is currently undergoing. Mark Olssen clearly details these differences in the following passage.

In neo-liberalism the state seeks to create an individual who is an enterprising and competitive entrepreneur (...) [The] shift from classical liberalism to neo-liberalism (...) involves a change in subject position from 'homo economicus,' who naturally behaves out of self-interest and is relatively detached from the state, to 'manipulatable man,' who is created by the state and who is continually encouraged to be 'perpetually responsive.' It is not that the conception of the self-interested subject is replaced or done away with by the new ideals of 'neo-liberalism,' but that in an age of universal welfare, the perceived possibilities of slothful indolence create necessities for new forms of vigilance, surveillance, 'performance appraisal' and of forms of control generally. In this model the state has taken it upon itself to keep us all up to the mark. The state will see to it that each one makes a 'continual enterprise of ourselves' (...) in what seems to be a process of 'governing without governing' (Olssen, 1996, p. 340).

The results of Ball and his colleagues' research document how the state does indeed do this, enhancing that odd combination of marketised individualism and control through constant and comparative public assessment. Widely publicised league tables determine one's relative value in the educational marketplace. Only those schools with rising performance indicators are worthy. And only those students who can 'make a continual enterprise of themselves' can keep such schools going in the 'correct' direction. Yet, while these issues are important, they fail to fully illuminate some of the other mechanisms through which *differential* effects are produced by neo-liberal reforms. Here, class issues come to the fore in ways that Ball, Bowe, and Gewirtz (1994) make clear.

Middle class parents are clearly the most advantaged in this kind of cultural assemblage, and not only as we saw because schools seek them out. Middle class parents have become quite skilled, in general, in exploiting market mechanisms in education and in bringing their social, economic, and cultural capital to bear on them. "Middle class parents are more likely to have the knowledge, skills and contacts to decode and manipulate what are increasingly complex and deregulated systems of choice and recruitment. The more deregulation, the more possibility of informal procedures being employed. The middle class also, on the whole, are more able to move their children around the system" (Ball, Bowe & Gewirtz, 1994, p. 19; see also Ball, 2003; Power, Edwards, Whitty & Wigfall 2003). That class and race intersect and interact in complex ways means that – even though we need to be clear that marketised systems in education often *expressly* have their conscious and unconscious *raison d'être* in a fear of 'the Other' and often are hidden expressions of a racialisation of educational policy – as I will show later in this chapter, the differential results will 'naturally' be decidedly raced as well as classed in many nations (Apple 2006; Omi & Winant, 1994; McCarthy & Crichlow, 1994; McCarthy, 1998; Gillborn & Youdell, 2000; Gillborn, 2008).

Economic and social capital can be converted into cultural capital in various ways. In marketised plans, more affluent parents often have more flexible hours and can visit multiple schools. They have cars – often more than one – and can *afford* driving their children across town to attend a 'better' school. They can as well provide the hidden cultural resources such as camps and after school programs (dance, music, computer classes, etc.) that give their children an 'ease,' a 'style,' that seems 'natural' and acts as a set of cultural resources. Their previous stock of social and cultural capital – who they know, their 'comfort' in social encounters with educational officials – is an unseen but powerful storehouse of resources. Thus, more affluent parents are more likely to have the informal knowledge and skill – what Bourdieu (1984) would call the "habitus" – to be able to decode and use marketised forms to their own benefit. This sense of what might be called 'confidence' – which is itself the result of past choices that tacitly but no less powerfully depend on the economic resources to actually have had the ability to make economic choices – is the unseen capital that underpins their ability to negotiate marketised forms and "work the system" through sets of informal cultural rules (Ball, Bowe & Gewirtz, 1994, pp. 20–22; Ball, 2003; Power, Edwards, Whitty & Wigfall, 2003). Given this, the match between the historically grounded habitus expected in schools and in its actors and those of more affluent parents, combined with the material resources available to more affluent parents, usually leads to a successful conversion of economic and social capital into cultural capital (Bourdieu, 1996; Swartz, 1997). And this is exactly what is happening in England (Power, Edwards, Whitty, & Wigfall 2003; Ball, 2003).

Connecting markets and testing

These claims both about what is happening inside of schools and about larger sets of power relations are supported by even more recent synthetic analyses of the overall results of marketised models. This research on the effects of the tense but still effective combination of neo-liberal and neo-conservative policies examines the tendencies internationally by comparing what has happened in a number of nations – for example, the United States, England and Wales, Australia, and New Zealand – where this combination has been increasingly powerful. The results confirm the arguments I have made here. Let me rehearse some of the most significant and disturbing findings of such research.

It is unfortunately all too usual that the most widely used measures of the 'success' of school reforms are the results of standardised achievement tests. This simply will not do. We need to constantly ask what reforms do to schools as a whole and to each of their participants, including teachers, students, administrators, community members, local activists, and so on. To take one set of examples, as marketised 'self-managing' schools grow in many nations, the role of the school principal is radically transformed. More, not less, power is actually consolidated within an administrative structure. More time and energy is spent on maintaining or enhancing a public image of a 'good school' and less time and energy is spent on pedagogic and curricular substance. At the same time, teachers seem to be experiencing not increased autonomy and professionalism, but intensification, a situation in which there is always so much more to do and often fewer financial, material, human, and emotional resources to do it (Apple, 1988, 2000, pp. 113–136; Gewirtz, 2002; Valenzuela, 2005). And, oddly, as noted before schools themselves become more *similar*, and more committed, to standard, traditional, whole class methods of teaching and a standard and traditional (and often mono-cultural) curriculum (Whitty, Power & Halpin, 1998, pp. 12–13). Only directing our attention to test scores would cause us to miss some truly profound transformations, many of which we may find disquieting.

One of the reasons these broader effects are so often produced is that in all too many countries, neo-liberal visions of quasi-markets are usually accompanied by neo-conservative pressure to regulate content and behaviour through such things as national curricula, national standards, and national systems of assessment. The combination is historically contingent; that is, it is not absolutely necessary that the two emphases are combined. But there are characteristics of neo-liberalism that make it more likely that an emphasis on the weak state and a faith in markets will cohere with an emphasis on the strong state and a commitment to regulating knowledge, values, and the body.

This is partly the case because of the increasing power of the "evaluative state" and the growth of the audit culture that accompanies it (Apple 2006). This signifies what initially may seem to be contradictory tendencies. At the same time as the state appears to be devolving power to individuals and autonomous institutions which are themselves increasingly competing in a market, the state remains strong in key areas (Whitty, Power & Halpin 1998, p. 36; Clarke & Newman, 1997). As I claimed earlier, one of the key differences between classical liberalism and its faith in 'enterprising individuals' in a market and current forms of neo-liberalism is the latter's commitment to a regulatory state. Neo-liberalism does indeed demand the constant production of evidence that one is in fact "making an enterprise of oneself" (Olssen, 1996). Thus, under these conditions not only does education become a marketable commodity like bread and cars in which the values, procedures, and metaphors of business dominate, but its results must be reducible to standardised 'performance indicators' (Whitty, Power & Halpin, 1998, pp. 37–38; Clarke & Newman, 1997). This is ideally suited to the task of providing a mechanism for the neo-conservative attempts to specify what knowledge, values, and behaviors should be standardised and officially defined as 'legitimate,' a point I shall expand upon in the next section of this chapter.

In essence, we are witnessing a process in which the state shifts the blame for the very evident inequalities in access and outcome it has promised to reduce, from itself onto individual schools, parents, and children. This is, of course, also part of a larger process in which dominant economic groups shift the blame for the massive and unequal effects of their own misguided decisions from themselves onto the state. The state is then faced with a very real crisis in legitimacy. Given this, we should not be at all surprised that the state will then seek to export this crisis outside itself (Apple, 1995).

Of course, the state is not only classed, but is inherently *sex/gendered* and *raced* as well (Apple et al., 2003; Omi & Winant, 1994; Epstein & Johnson, 1998; Middleton, 1998). The gendered nature is evident in Whitty, Power and Halpin's

(1998) arguments. They point to the gendered nature of the ways in which the management of schools is thought about, as 'masculinist' business models become increasingly dominant (ibid., pp. 60–62). While there is a danger of these claims degenerating into reductive and essentialising arguments, there is a good deal of insight here. They do cohere with the work of other scholars inside and outside of education who recognise that the ways in which our very definitions of public and private, of what knowledge is of most worth, and of how institutions should be thought about and run are fully implicated in the gendered nature of this society (Fraser, 1989, 1997). These broad ideological effects – e.g., enabling a coalition between neo-liberals and neo-conservatives to be formed, the masculinisation of theories, policies, and management talk – are of considerable import and make it harder to change common-sense in more critical directions. When these tendencies are combined with dominant and new middle class discourses associated with the new managerialism, the results can be very damaging.

Other, more proximate, effects inside schools are equally striking. Thus, even though principals seem to have more local power in these supposedly decentralised schools, because of the cementing in of neo-conservative policies principals "are increasingly forced into a position in which they have to demonstrate performance along centrally prescribed curricula in a context in which they have diminishing control" (Whitty, Power & Halpin, 1998, p. 63; Gewirtz, 2002). Because of the intensification that I mentioned before, both principals and teachers experience considerably heavier work loads and ever escalating demands for accountability, a never ending schedule of meetings, and in many cases a growing scarcity of resources both emotional and physical (Whitty, Power & Halpin, 1998, pp. 67–68; Gillborn & Youdell 2000).

Further, as in the research in England, in nearly all of the countries studied the market did *not* encourage diversity in curriculum, pedagogy, organisation, clientele, or even image. It instead consistently devalued alternatives and increased the power of dominant models. Of equal significance, it also consistently exacerbated differences in access and outcome based on race, ethnicity, and class (Gillborn &Youdell, 2000).

The return to 'traditionalism' led to a number of things. It *delegitimated* more critical models of teaching and learning, a point that is crucial to recognise in any attempt to think through the possibilities of cultural struggles and critical pedagogies in schools. It both reintroduced class and race re-stratification within the school and lessened the possibility that de-tracking would occur. More emphasis was given to 'gifted' children and 'fast track' classes, while students who were seen as less academically able were therefore 'less attractive.' In England, the extent of this was nowhere more visible than in the alarming rate of students being excluded from schools. Much of this was caused by the intense pressure to constantly demonstrate higher achievement rates. This was especially powerful in marketised contexts in which the "main driving force appeared to be *commercial* rather than *educational*" (Whitty, Power & Halpin, 1998, p. 80).

In their own analysis of these worrisome and more hidden results, Whitty, Power, and Halpin (1998) and others demonstrate that among the dangerous effects of quasi-markets are the ways in which schools that wish to maintain or enhance their market position engage in 'cream-skimming,' ensuring that *particular* kinds of students with particular characteristics are accepted and particular kinds of students are found wanting. For some schools, stereotypes were reproduced in that girls were seen a more valuable, as were students from some Asian communities. Afro-Caribbean children were often clear losers in this situation (Gillborn & Youdell, 2000; Gewirtz, Ball & Bowe, 1995).

Privileging privilege

So far I have focused largely on England. Yet, as I mentioned in my introductory points, these movements are truly global. Their logics have spread rapidly to many nations, with results that tend to mirror those I have discussed so far. The case of New Zealand is useful here, especially since a large percentage of the population of New Zealand is multi-ethnic and the nation has a history of racial tensions and class and race inequalities. Furthermore, the move toward New Right policies occurred faster there than elsewhere. In essence, New Zealand became the laboratory for many of the policies I am analyzing. In their exceptional study, based in large part on a conceptual apparatus influenced by Pierre Bourdieu, Lauder and Hughes (1999) document that educational markets seem to lead to an overall decline in educational standards. Paradoxically, they have a negative, not a positive, effect on the performance of schools with large working class and minority populations. In essence, they "trade off the opportunities of less privileged children to those already privileged" (Lauder & Hughes, 1999, p. 2). The combination of neo-liberal policies of marketisation and the neo-conservative emphasis on 'tougher standards,' about which I shall say more in the next section, creates an even more dangerous set of conditions. Their analysis confirms the conceptual and empirical arguments of Ball, Brown, and others that markets in education are not only responses by capital to reduce both the sphere of the state and of public control. They are also part of an attempt by the middle class to alter the rules of competition in education in light of the increased insecurities their children face. "By changing the process of selection to schools, middle class parents can raise the stakes in creating stronger mechanisms of exclusion for blue collar and post-colonial peoples in their struggle for equality of opportunity" (Lauder & Hughes, 1999, p. 29; see also Brown, 1997).

The results from New Zealand not only mirror what was found elsewhere, but demonstrate that the further one's practices follow the logics of action embodied in marketising principles the worse the situation tends to get. Markets *systematically* privilege higher socio-economic status [SES] families through their knowledge and material resources. These are the families who are most likely to exercise choice. Rather than giving large numbers of students who are working class, poor, or of colour the ability to exit, it is largely higher SES families who exit from public schools and schools with mixed populations. In a situation of increased competition, this in turn produces a spiral of decline in which schools populated by poorer students and students of colour are again systematically disadvantaged and schools with higher SES and higher white populations are able to insulate themselves from the effects of market competition (Lauder & Hughes, 1999, p. 101). 'White flight' then enhances the relative status of those schools already advantaged by larger economic forces; schooling for the 'Other' becomes even more polarised and continues a downward spiral (Lauder and Hughes, 1999, p. 132).

Having said this, however, we need to be cautious not to ignore historical specificities. Social movements, existing ideological formations, and institutions in civil society and the state may provide some support for countervailing logics. In some cases, in those nations with stronger and more extensive histories of social democratic policies and visions of collective positive freedoms, the neo-liberal emphasis on the market has been significantly mediated. Hence, as Petter Aasen has demonstrated in Norway and Sweden, for instance, privatising initiatives in education have had to cope with a greater collective commitment than in, say, the United States, England, and New Zealand (Aasen, 1998; see also Apple et al., 2003). However, these commitments partly rest on class relations. They are weakened when racial dynamics enter in. Thus, for example, the sense of 'everyone being the same' and hence being all subject to similar collective sensibilities is challenged by the growth of immigrant populations from Africa, Asia, and the Middle East. Greater sympathy for marketised forms may arise once the commonly understood assumptions of what it means to be, say, Norwegian or Swedish are interrupted by populations of colour who now claim the status of national citizenship. For this reason, it may be the case that the collective sensibilities that provide support for less market oriented policies are based on an unacknowledged *racial contract* (Mills, 1997) that underpins the ideological foundations of a national "imagined community" (Anderson, 1991). This, then, may also generate support for neo-conservative policies, not because of neo-liberalism's commitment to 'perpetual responsiveness,' but rather as a form of cultural restoration, as a way of re-establishing an imagined past when 'we were all one.' Because of this, it is important that any analysis of the current play of forces surrounding conservative modernisation is aware of the fact that not only are such movements in constant motion, but once again we need to remember that they have a multitude of intersecting and contradictory dynamics including not only class, but race and gender as well (Apple et al., 2003; Arnot, David & Weiner 1999; Epstein & Johnson, 1998).

Markets and class habitus

The overall conclusions are clear: "[In] current circumstances choice is as likely to reinforce hierarchies as to improve educational opportunities and the overall quality of schooling" (Whitty, Power & Halpin, 1998, p. 14). All of this gives us ample reason to agree with Henig's insightful argument that "the sad irony of the current education-reform movement is that, through over-identification with school-choice proposals rooted in market-based ideas, the healthy impulse to consider radical reforms to address social problems may be channelled into initiatives that further erode the potential for collective deliberation and collective response" (Henig, 1994, p. 222).

This is not to dismiss either the possibility or necessity of school reform. However, we need to take seriously the probability that only by focussing on the exogenous socio-economic features, not simply the organisational features, of 'successful' schools can all schools succeed. Eliminating poverty through greater income parity, establishing effective and much more equal health and housing programs, and positively refusing to continue the hidden and not so hidden politics of racial exclusion and degradation that so clearly still characterise daily life in many nations (and in which marketised plans need to be seen as partly a structure to avoid the body and culture of 'the Other') – only by tackling these issues together can substantive progress be made. Unless discussions of critical pedagogy are themselves grounded in a recognition of these realities, they too may fall into the trap of assuming that schools can do it alone.

These empirical findings are made more understandable in terms of Pierre Bourdieu's (1996) analysis of the relative weight given to cultural capital as part of mobility strategies today. The rise in importance of cultural capital infiltrates all institutions in such a way that there is a relative movement away from the *direct* reproduction of class privilege (where power is transmitted largely within families through economic property) to *school-mediated* forms of class privilege. Here, "the bequeathal of privilege is simultaneously effectuated and transfigured by the intercession of educational institutions" (Wacquant, 1996, p. iii). This is *not* a conspiracy; it is not 'conscious' in the ways we normally use that concept. Rather it is the result of a long chain of relatively autonomous connections between differentially accumulated economic, social, and cultural capital operating at the level of daily events as we make our respective ways in the world, including as we saw in the world of school choice.

Thus, while not taking an unyieldingly determinist position, Bourdieu argues that a class habitus tends to reproduce the conditions of its own reproduction 'unconsciously.' It does this by producing a relatively coherent and systematically *characteristic* set of seemingly natural and unconscious strategies – in essence, ways of understanding and acting on the world that act as forms of cultural capital that can be and are employed to protect and enhance one's status in a social field of power, and then having a habitus that enables one to work in multiple fields of economic, political, and cultural power. This very connection of habitus across fields of power – the ease of bringing one's economic, social, and cultural resources to bear on 'markets' – enables a comfort between markets and self that characterises the middle class actor here (Ball, 2003). This constantly *produces* differential effects. These effects are not neutral, no matter what the advocates of neo-liberalism suggest. Rather, they are themselves the results of a particular kind of morality. Unlike the conditions of what might best be called 'thick morality' where principles of the common good are the ethical basis for adjudicating policies and practices, markets are grounded in aggregative principles. They are constituted out of the sum of individual goods and choices. "Founded on individual and property rights that enable citizens to address problems of interdependence via exchange," they offer a prime example of 'thin morality' by generating both hierarchy and division based on competitive individualism (Ball, Bowe, & Gewirtz, 1994, p. 24). Although this does *not* mean that oppressed groups will not attempt to use such markets for their own strategic purposes (Apple & Pedroni, 2005), in this competition the general outline of the winners and losers *has* been identified empirically.

NATIONAL CURRICULUM AND NATIONAL TESTING

I showed in the previous section that there are connections between at least two dynamics operating in neo-liberal reforms, 'free' markets and increased surveillance. This can be seen in the fact that in many contexts, marketisation has been accompanied by a set of particular policies for 'producers,' for those professionals working within education. These policies have been strongly regulatory and have been quite instrumental in reconstituting common-sense. As in the case of the linkage between national tests and performance indicators published as league tables, they have been organised around a concern for external supervision, regulation, and external judgement of performance (Menter et al., 1997, p. 8) and have increasingly been colonised by parents who possess what is seen as 'appropriate' economic, social, and cultural capital (Ball 2003). This concern for external supervision and regulation is not only connected with a strong mistrust of 'producers' (e.g., teachers) and to the need for ensuring that people continually make enterprises out of themselves. It is also clearly linked both to the neo-conservative sense of a need to 'return' to a lost past of high standards, discipline, awe, and 'real' knowledge and to the professional middle class's own ability to carve out a sphere of authority within the state for its own commitment to management techniques and efficiency. The focus on efficient management plays a prime role here, one in which many neo-liberals and neo-conservatives alike find useful (Apple, 2006).

Managerialism and professionalism

There has been a shift in the relationship between the state and 'professionals.' In essence, the move toward a small strong state that is increasingly guided by market needs seems inevitably to bring with it reduced professional power and status (Menter et al., 1997, p. 57). Managerialism takes center stage here. Managerialism is largely charged with "bringing about the cultural transformation that shifts professional identities in order to make them more responsive to client demand and external judgement" (Menter et al., 1997, p. 91). It aims to justify and to have people internalise fundamental alterations in professional practices. It both harnesses energy and discourages dissent.

There is no necessary contradiction between a general set of marketising and deregulating interests and processes – such as voucher and choice plans – and a set of enhanced regulatory processes – such as plans for national curricula and national testing. "The regulatory form permits the state to maintain 'steerage' over the aims and processes of education from within the market mechanism" (Menter, et al., 1997, p. 27). Such steerage has often been vested in such things as national standards, national curricula, and national testing. Forms of all of these are being pushed for in the United States and elsewhere currently and are the subject of considerable controversy, some of which cuts across ideological lines and shows some of the tensions within the different elements contained under the umbrella of conservative modernisation.

I have argued that paradoxically a national curriculum and especially a national testing program are the first and most essential steps toward increased marketisation. They actually provide the mechanisms for comparative data that 'consumers' need to make markets work as markets (Apple, 2006). Absent these mechanisms, there is no comparative base of information for 'choice.' Yet, we do not have to argue about these regulatory forms in a vacuum. Like the neo-liberal markets I discussed in the previous section, they too have been instituted in England; and, once again, there is important research available that can and must make us duly cautious in going down this path.

One might want to claim that a set of national standards, national curricula, and national tests would provide the conditions for 'thick morality.' After all, such regulatory reforms are supposedly based on shared values and common sentiments that also create social spaces in which common issues of concern can be debated and made subject to moral interrogation (Ball, Bowe & Gewirtz, 1994, p. 23). Yet, what counts as the 'common,' and how and by whom it is actually determined, is rather more thin than thick, since the process by which the common has been decided did not arise from the full participation of those whose cultures have historically been marginalised (Apple, 1996, 2000, 2006).

It is the case that while the national curriculum now so solidly in place in England and Wales is clearly prescriptive, it has not always proven to be the kind of straight-jacket it has often been made out to be. As a number of researchers have documented, it is not only possible that policies and legislative mandates are interpreted and adapted, but it seems inevitable. Thus, the national curriculum is "not so much being 'implemented' in schools as being 'recreated,' not so much 'reproduced,' as 'produced'" (Power, Halpin & Fitz, 1994, p. 38; Ranson, 1995).

However, this general principle may be just a bit too romantic. None of this occurs on a level playing field. As with market plans, there are very real differences in power in one's ability to influence, mediate, transform, or reject a policy or a regulatory process. Granted, it is important to recognise that a 'state control model'- with its assumption of top-down linearity – is much too simplistic and that the possibility of human agency and influence is always there. However, having said this, this should not imply that such agency and influence will be powerful (Ranson, 1995, p. 437).

The case of national curriculum and national testing in England and Wales documents the tensions in these two accounts. It was the case that the national curriculum that was first legislated and then imposed there, was indeed struggled over. It was originally too detailed and too specific, and, hence, was subject to major transformations at the national, community, school, and then classroom levels. However, even though the national curriculum was subject to conflict, mediation, and some transformation of its content, organisation, and its invasive and immensely time consuming forms of evaluation, its utter power is demonstrated in its radical reconfiguration of the very process of knowledge selection, organisation, and assessment. It changed the entire terrain of education radically. Its subject divisions "provide more constraint than scope for discretion" (Ranson, 1995, p. 438). The 'standard attainment targets' that have been mandated cement these constraints in place. "The imposition of national testing locks the national curriculum in place as the dominant framework of teachers' work whatever opportunities teachers may take to evade or reshape it" (ibid., p. 438).

The national curricula and national tests *did* generate conflict about issues. They did partly lead to the creation of social spaces for moral questions to get asked. Thus, it was clear to many people that the creation of mandatory and reductive tests that emphasised memory and decontextualised abstraction pulled the national curriculum in a particular direction – that of encouraging a selective educational market in which elite students and elite schools with a wide range of resources would be well (if narrowly) served (O'Hear, 1994, p. 66). Diverse groups of people argued that such reductive, detailed, and simplistic paper and pencil tests "had the potential to do enormous damage," a situation that was made even worse because the tests were so onerous in terms of time and record keeping (O'Hear, 1994, pp. 55–57). Teachers had a good deal of support when as a group they decided to boycott the administration of the test in a remarkable act of public protest. This also led to serious questioning of the arbitrary, inflexible, and overly prescriptive national curriculum. While the curriculum is still inherently problematic and the assessment system does still contain numerous dangerous and onerous elements within it, organised activity against them did have an impact (ibid., pp. 55–57).

Yet, unfortunately, the story does not end there. By the mid-1990s, even with the government's partial retreat on such regulatory forms as its program of constant and reductive testing, it had become clearer by the year that the development of testing and the specification of content had been 'hijacked' by those who were ideologically committed to traditional pedagogies and to the idea of more rigorous selection (O'Hear, 1994, p. 68). The residual effects are both material and ideological. They include a continuing emphasis on trying to provide the "rigor [that is] missing in the practice of most teachers, (…) judging progress solely by what is testable in tests of this kind" and the development of a "very hostile view of the accountability of teachers" that was seen as "part of a wider thrust of policy to take away professional control of public services and establish so called consumer control through a market structure" (O'Hear, 1994, pp. 65–66; see also Gewirtz, 2002).

The authors of an extremely thorough review of recent assessment programs instituted in England and Wales provide a summary of what has happened. Gipps and Murphy argue that it has become increasingly obvious that the national assessment program attached to the national curriculum is more and more dominated by traditional models of testing and the assumptions about teaching and learning that lie behind them. At the same time, equity issues are becoming much less visible. In the calculus of values now in place in the regulatory state, efficiency, speed, and cost control replace more substantive concerns about social and educational justice. The pressure to get tests in place rapidly has meant that "the speed of test development is so great, and the curriculum and assessment changes so regular, that [there is] little time to carry out detailed analyses and trialing to ensure that the tests are as fair as possible to all groups" (Gipps & Murphy, 1994, p. 204; see also Apple, 2008). The conditions for 'thin morality' – in which the competitive individual of the market dominates and social justice will somehow take care of itself – are re-produced here. The combination of the neo-liberal market and the regulatory state, then, does indeed 'work.' However, it works in ways in which the metaphors of free market, merit, and effort hide the differential reality that is produced. While on the one hand this makes a socially and culturally critical pedagogy even more essential, it also makes it much more difficult to actually accomplish.

But, it is important not to leave our discussion at such an abstract level or at the level of curriculum planning. What has happened in schools themselves in England, the United States, and elsewhere when such 'pragmatic' standards, curricula, and tests are actually instituted?

CREATING EDUCATIONAL TRIAGE

There have been analyses in the United States that have begun to document similar kinds of effects (Linn, 2000; Oakes, 1992; Oakes, Wells, Jones & Datnow, 1997; Wells, Lopez, Scott & Holmes, 1999; Lipman, 2004; Valenzuela, 2005). However, unfortunately, the predominance of relatively unreflective and at times almost self-congratulatory policies around markets, standards, testing, and reductive forms of accountability is exactly that here–predominant. Even given the exceptional work that is being done on the hidden effects of some of these kinds of policies and practices, and even given the fact that there are numerous examples of extremely effective schools in our urban and rural areas that succeed through using much more democratic and critical models of curriculum, teaching, and evaluation (Apple & Beane, 2007; for other nations see Apple et al., 2003; Apple & Buras, 2006; Apple, in press), it still feels as if one has to constantly swim against the tide of conservative modernisation.

Given this state of affairs, it is now even more important that we pay attention to material that demonstrates what can happen in situations where the stress on higher standards and higher test scores hits both the realities of schools and the different populations they serve. David Gillborn and Deborah Yudell's volume *Rationing Education* (2000) is just such a book. It goes into even more detail about the powerful, and often damaging, effects on teachers and students of our seeming fascination with ever-rising standards, mandated curricula, and over-emphasis on testing.

The volume details the overt and hidden effects of policies that are currently being undertaken in many nations. These include such things as creating a situation where the tail of a high-stakes test 'wags the dog' of the teacher, pressuring schools to constantly show increased achievement scores on such standardised tests no matter what the level of support or the impoverished conditions in schools and local communities, to publicly display such results in a process of what might be realistically called shaming, and to threaten schools that do not show 'improvement' on these tests with severe sanctions or loss of control.

In many ways, *Rationing Education* provides what might be called a micro-economy of school life. It examines the ways in which certain valued commodities are accumulated by schools in a time of intense competition for scarce resources. In this case, the commodities are higher test scores and the resources are both numbers of students and public recognition of being a 'good' school. The authors' way of describing this is what they call the 'A-C economy.'

Like the United States, in England schools exist in what is really a hierarchical ordering, a market, in prestige and reputation. They are valued by the number of students that get passing scores on particular national tests. The national tests are made public as a form of 'league tables' in which schools are rank-ordered according to their relative results. Schools with large numbers of students getting grades A-C are more highly valued than those with students whose rates of passing are less – even though everyone tacitly knows that there is a very strong relationship between school results and poverty.

This is straightforward and not surprising. However, this situation creates an economy that has certain characteristics. Students with predicted higher test scores are even more valuable. Students with predicted lower test scores are seen as less useful to the school's place in the market. This too is not surprising. The results of such an economy, however, are powerful. There is another key group of students who are focused upon and on whom considerable resources, energy, and attention is devoted–students who are on the border between passing grades and failing grades. These students – often seen as middle class 'under-achievers' – become objects of great value in the school. After all, if this key group can be pulled across the border into the A-C column, the school's results will be that much more positive.

What could be wrong with an increased focus on students on the border? Here is one of the places where Gillborn and Youdell's results are ominous. In such an A-C economy, specific students are seen as moveable. Other students' abilities are seen as increasingly fixed and less worthy of attention. The class and race characteristics of these latter students are striking. Poor and working class students, students of African descent, and other ethnically 'different' children are not valued commodities on this kind of market. Even though gender divisions were less pronounced in the schools that Gillborn and Youdell studied, divisions strongly rooted in racializing and class based structures were not simply mirrored in the schools. They actually were *produced* in these institutions.

Thus, policies that were put in place to raise standards, to increase test scores, to guarantee public accountability, and to make schools more competitive had results that were more than a little damaging to those students who were already the least advantaged in these same schools. Yet, it was not only the students who witnessed these negative effects. The voices of teachers and administrators indicate what happens to them as well. They too begin to harden their sense of which students are 'able' and which students are not. Tracking returns in both overt and covert ways. And once again, black students and students in government subsidised lunch programs are the ones most likely to be placed in those tracks or given academic and career advice that nearly guarantees that they will not only have limited or no mobility but will confirm their status as students who are 'less worthy.'

Equally worth noting here is the specific way the A-C economy works to choose those students who are deemed to have worthiness. Often, students whose behavior and test results are quite similar have very different careers in the school. Thus, a black student and a white student may be, say, on the border of the A-C/failing divide, but the black student will not be the beneficiary of the added attention. These situations are all too often characterised by tacitly operating visions of ability, ones that have been hardened by years of discourse on the 'problem' of black student achievement and especially by the increased visibility once again of supposedly scientific (and ultimately racist and empirically problematic) 'research' on genetic differences in mean intelligence between blacks and whites.

Unfortunately, recent research on the effects of all of this in the United States confirms these worries (McNiel, 2000; Valenzuela, 2005; Wilson, 2000; Moses, 2000; Smith et al., 2004). These studies clearly show how such policies actually function as a form of 'symbolic politics' in which the unequal effects produced by such policies are largely hidden from public view. "Political spectacle" replaces substantive transformation and the real benefits of such policies usually favour those groups with economic, social, and political capital (Smith et al., 2004).

CONCLUSION

In this chapter, I have raised serious questions about current educational 'reform' efforts now underway in a number of nations. I have used research largely, but not solely, on the English experience(s) to document some of the hidden differential effects of two connected strategies – neo-liberal inspired *market proposals* and neo-liberal, neo-conservative, and middle class *managerial inspired regulatory proposals*. Taking a key from Herbert Kliebard's (1995) historical analysis, I have described how different interests with different educational and social visions compete for dominion in the social field of power surrounding educational policy and practice. In the process, I have documented some of the complexities and imbalances in this field of power. These complexities and imbalances result in 'thin' rather than 'thick' morality and tend toward the reproduction of both dominant pedagogical and curricular forms and ideologies and the social privileges that accompany them. I have suggested that the rhetorical flourishes of the discourses of critical pedagogy need to come to grips with these changing material and ideological conditions. Critical pedagogy can not and will not occur in a vacuum. Unless we honestly face these profound rightist transformations and think tactically about them, we will have little effect either on the creation of a counter-hegemonic common-sense or on the building of a counter-hegemonic alliance. The growth of that odd combination of marketisation and regulatory state, the move towards pedagogic similarity and 'traditional' academic curricula and teaching, the ability of dominant groups to exert leadership in the struggle over this, and the accompanying shifts in common-sense – all this cannot be wished away. Instead, they need to be confronted honestly, and self-critically.

Having said this, however, I want to point to a hidden paradox in what I have done. Even though much of my own and others' research recently has been on the processes and effects conservative modernisation, there are dangers in such a focus of which we should be aware. Research on the history, politics, and practices of rightist social and educational movements and 'reforms' has enabled us to show the contradictions and unequal effects of such policies and practices. It has enabled the re-articulation of claims to social justice on the basis of solid evidence. This is all to the good. However, in the process, one of the latent effects has been the gradual framing of educational issues largely in terms of the conservative agenda. The very categories themselves – markets, choice, national curricula, national testing, standards – bring the debate onto the terrain established by neo-liberals and neo-conservatives. The analysis of 'what is' has led to a neglect of 'what might be.' Thus, there has been a withering of substantive large scale discussions of feasible alternatives to neo-liberal and neo-conservative visions, policies, and practices, ones that would move well beyond them (Seddon, 1997, pp. 165–166).

Because of this, at least part of our task may be politically and conceptually complex, but it can be said simply. In the long term, we need to "develop a political project that is both local yet generalizable, systematic without making Eurocentric, masculinist claims to essential and universal truths about human subjects" (Luke, 1995, pp. vi–vii). Another part of our task, though, must be and is more proximate, more appropriately educational. Defensible, articulate, and fully fleshed out alternative critical and progressive policies and practices in curriculum, teaching, and evaluation need to be developed and made widely available (Apple & Beane, 2007). But this too must be done with due recognition of the changing nature of the social field of power and the importance of thinking tactically and strategically.

In *Educating the 'Right' Way* (Apple, 2006) and *The State and the Politics of Education* (Apple, et al., 2003), I have discussed in considerably more detail the kinds of strategic alliances, and the policies and practices that should accompany them, that might enable us to do this. I have suggested ways both to interrupt neo-liberal and neo-conservative tendencies and create a thicker version of democracy in education on the ground. At the same time that this is going on, however, we cannot ignore the importance of broadening the kinds of issues we raise and the questions we ask of the supposedly more 'democratic' policies that are current becoming increasingly global. This has been my task in this chapter. By drawing on a range of analyses taken from a number of nations, I have demonstrated why it is so crucial to do so.

Yet, while I have argued that the overall leadership in educational policy is exercised by a conservative alliance, I do not want to give the impression that this coalition of forces is uncontested or is always victorious. This is simply not the case. As a number of people have demonstrated, at the local level throughout the world there are scores of counter-hegemonic programs and possibilities. Many institutions of higher education, schools, and even entire school districts have shown remarkable resiliency in the face of the concerted ideological attacks and pressures from conservative restorational groups. And many teachers, academics, community activists, and others have created and defended educational programs that are both pedagogically and politically emancipatory (Apple, in press; Apple & Beane, 2007; Gutstein, 2006).

Indeed, in the face of a considerable number of structural, financial, and political dilemmas, the fact that so many groups of people have not been integrated under the alliance's hegemonic umbrella and have created scores of examples of the very possibility of difference, shows us in the most eloquent and lived ways that educational policies and practices do not go in any one unidimensional direction. Even more importantly, these multiple examples demonstrate that the success of conservative policies is never guaranteed. This is imperative in a time when it is easy to lose sight of what is necessary for an education worthy of its name.

NOTES

[1] This is an expanded version of a keynote address at the *Conference on Education and Social Inequality* at the University of Melbourne, and is based as well on a much larger discussion in Apple (2006).

REFERENCES

Aasen, P. (1998). *What happened to social democratic progressivism in Scandinavia?* Unpublished paper, Department of Education, Norwegian University of Science and Technology, Trondheim, Norway.

Anderson, B. (1991). *Imagined communities.* New York: Verso.

Apple, M. W. (1988). *Teachers and texts.* New York: Routledge.

Apple, M. W. (1995). *Education and power* (2nd ed.). New York: Routledge.

Apple, M. W. (1996). *Cultural politics and education.* New York: Teachers College Press.

Apple, M. W. (1999). *Power, meaning, and identity.* New York: Peter Lang.

Apple, M. W. (2000). *Official knowledge* (2nd ed.). New York: Routledge.

Apple, M. W. (2001). Standards, subject matter, and a romantic past. *Educational Policy, 15,* 323–333.

Apple, M. W. (2002). Does education have independent power. *British Journal of Sociology of Education, 23,* 607–616.

Apple, M. W. (2003). Strategic alliance or hegemonic strategy: Conservatism among the dispossessed. *London Review of Education, 1,* 47–60.

Apple, M. W. (2006). *Educating the "right" way: Markets, standards, god, and inequality* (2nd ed.). New York: Routledge.

Apple, M. W. (2008). Curriculum planning: Content, form, and the politics of accountability. In M. Connelly, et al. (Eds.), *Handbook of curriculum and instruction* (pp. 25–44). New York: Sage.

Apple, M. W. (Ed.). (in press). *Global crises, education, and social justice: What can education do?* New York: Routledge.

Apple, M. W., et al. (2003). *The state and the politics of knowledge.* New York: Routledge.

Apple, M. W., & Pedroni, T. (2005). Conservative alliance building and African American support for vouchers. *Teachers College Record, 107*, 2068–2105.

Apple, M. W., & Buras, K. L. (Eds.). (2006). *The subaltern speak: Curriculum, power, and educational struggles*. New York: Routledge.

Apple, M. W., & Beane, J. A. (Eds.). (2007). *Democratic schools: Lessons in powerful education* (2nd ed.). Portsmouth, NH: Heinemann.

Arnot, M., David, M., & Weiner, G. (1999). *Closing the gender gap*. Cambridge: Policy Press.

Ball, S., Bowe, R., & Gewirtz, S. (1994). Market forces and parental choice. In S. Tomlinson (Ed.), *Educational reform and its consequences* (pp. 13–25). London: IPPR/Rivers Oram Press.

Ball, S. (2003). *Class strategies and the education market*. London: Routledge.

Bernstein, B. (1990). *The structuring of pedagogic discourse*. New York: Routledge.

Bernstein, B. (1996). *Pedagogy, symbolic control, and identity*. Bristol, PA: Taylor and Francis.

Bourdieu, P. (1984). *Distinction*. Cambridge: Harvard University Press.

Bourdieu, P. (1996). *The state nobility*. Stanford, CA: Stanford University Press.

Brown, P. (1997). Cultural capital and social exclusion. In A. H. Halsey, H. Lauder, P. Brown, & A. S. Wells (Eds.), *Education, culture, economy, and society* (pp. 736–749). New York: Oxford University Press.

Brown, P., Green, A., & Lauder, H. (2001). *High skills*. New York: Oxford University Press.

Chubb, J., & Moe, T. (1990). *Politics, markets, and American schools*. Washington, DC: Brooking Institution.

Clarke, J., & Newman, J. (1997). *The managerial state*. Thousand Oaks, CA: Sage.

Epstein, D., & Johnson, R. (1998). *Schooling sexualities*. Philadelphia: Open University Press.

Fraser, N. (1989). *Unruly practices*. Minneapolis, MN: University of Minnesota Press.

Fraser, N. (1997). *Justice interruptus*. New York: Routledge.

Fuller, B. (Ed.). (2000). *Inside charter schools*. Cambridge: Harvard University Press.

Gewirtz, S. (2002). *The managerial school*. New York: Routledge.

Gewirtz, S., Ball, S., & Bowe, R. (1995). *Markets, choice, and equity in education*. Philadelphia: Open University Press.

Gillborn, D. (1997). Racism and reform. *British Educational Research Journal, 23*, 345–360.

Gillborn, D. (2008). *Racism and education*. London: Routledge.

Gillborn, D., & Youdell, D. (2000). *Rationing education*. Philadelphia: Open University Press.

Gipps, C., & Murphy, P. (1994). *A fair test?* Philadelphia: Open University Press.

Gould, S. J. (1981). *The mismeasure of man*. New York: Norton.

Gutstein, E. (2006). *Reading and writing the world with mathematics*. New York: Routledge.

Henig, J. (1994). *Rethinking school choice*. Princeton, NJ: Princeton University Press.

Herrnstein, R., & Murray, C. (1994). *The bell curve*. New York: Free Press.

Hirsch, E. D., Jr. (1996). *The schools we want and why we don't have them*. New York: Doubleday.

Kincheloe, J., Steinberg, S., & Greeson, A. (Eds.). (1997). *Measured lies*. New York: St. Martin's Press.

Kliebard, H. (1995). *The struggle for the American curriculum* (2nd ed.). New York: Routledge.

Lauder, H., & Hughes, D. (1999). *Trading in futures*. Philadelphia: Open University Press.

Linn, R. (2000). Assessment and accountability. *Educational Researcher, 29*, 4–16.

Lipman, P. (2004). *High stakes education*. New York: Routledge.

Luke, A. (1995). Series editor's introduction. In J. Lemke (Ed.), *Textual politics* (pp. i–viii). Bristol, PA: Taylor and Francis.

McCarthy, C. (1998). *The uses of culture*. New York: Routledge.

McCarthy, C., & Crichlow, W. (Eds.). (1994). *Race, identity, and representation in education*. New York: Routledge.

McCulloch, G. (1997). Privatising the past. *British Journal of Educational Studies, 45*, 69–82.

McNeil, L. (2000). *The contradictions of school reform*. New York: Routledge.

Menter, I., Muschamp, Y., Nicholls, P., Ozga, J., & Pollard, A. (1997). *Work and identity in the primary school*. Philadelphia: Open University Press.

Middleton, S. (1998). *Disciplining sexualities*. New York: Teachers College Press.

Mills, C. (1997). *The racial contract*. Ithaca, NY: Cornell University Press.

Moe, T. (2001). *Schools, vouchers, and the American public*. Washington, DC: Brookings Institution.

Moses, M. (2000). *The Arizona tax credit and hidden consequences of justice*. Paper presented at the American Educational Research Association annual meeting, New Orleans.

Oakes, J. (1992). Can tracking research inform practice? *Educational Researcher, 21*, 12–21.

Oakes, J., Wells, A. S., Jones, M., & Datnow, A. (1997). Detracking: The social construction of ability, cultural politics, and resistance to reform. *Teachers College Record, 98*, 482–510.

Oakes, J., Quartz, K., Ryan, S., & Lipton, M. (2000). *Becoming good American schools*. San Francisco: Jossey-Bass.

O'Hear, P. (1994). An alternative national curriculum. In S. Tomlinson (Ed.), *Educational reform and its consequences* (pp. 55–72). London: IPPR/Rivers Oram Press.

Olssen, M. (1996). In defence of the welfare state and of publicly provided education. *Journal of Education Policy, 11*, 337–362.

Omi, M., & Winant, H. (1994). *Racial formation in the United States*. New York: Routledge.

Power, S., Halpin, D., & Fitz, J. (1994). Underpinning choice and diversity. In S. Tomlinson (Ed.), *Educational reform and its consequences* (pp. 26–40). London: IPPR/Rivers Oram Press.

Power, S., Edwards, T., Whitty, G., & Wigfall, V. (2003). *Education and the middle class*. Philadelphia: Open University Press.

Ranson, S. (1995). Theorizing educational policy. *Journal of Education Policy, 10*, 427–448.

Ravitch, D. (2000). *Left back*. New York: Simon and Schuster.

Ravitch, D. (Ed.). (2005). *Brookings papers on education policy, 2005*. Washington, DC: Brookings Institution Press.

Rury, J., & Mirel, J. (1997). The political economy of urban education. In M. W. Apple (Ed.), *Review of research in education* (Vol. 22, pp. 49–110). Washington, DC: American Educational research Association.

Seddon, T. (1997). Markets and the English. *British Journal of Sociology of Education, 18*, 165–185.

Selden, S. (1999). *Inheriting shame*. New York: Teachers College Press.

Smith, M. L., et al. (2004). *Political spectacle and the fate of American schools*. New York: Routledge.

Steinberg, J. (2000, April 13). Blue books closed, students boycott standardised tests. *The New York Times*, p. A1, A22.

Swartz, D. (1997). *Culture and power*. Chicago: University of Chicago Press.

Teitelbaum, K. (1996). *Schooling for good rebels*. New York: Teachers College Press.

Valenzuela, A. (Ed.). (2005). *Leaving children behind*. Albany: State University of New York Press.

Wacquant, L. (1996). Foreword. In P. Bourdieu (Ed.), *The state nobility* (pp. ix–xxii). Stanford, CA: Stanford University Press.

Wells, A. S., et al. (1999). *Beyond the rhetoric of charter school reform*. Los Angeles: University of California at Los Angeles, Graduate School of Education and Information Studies.

Wells, A. S., Lopez, A., Scott, J., & Holme, J. (1999). Charter schools as postmodern paradox. *Harvard Educational Review, 69*, 172–204.

Whitty, G. (1974). Sociology and the problem of radical educational change. In M. Flude & J. Ahier (Eds.), *Educability, schools, and ideology* (pp. 112–137). London: Halstead Press.

Whitty, G. (1997). Creating quasi-markets in education. In M. W. Apple (Ed.), *Review of research in education* (Vol. 22, pp. 30–47). Washington, DC: American Educational Research Association.

Whitty, G., Edwards, T., & Gewirtz, S. (1993). *Specialisation and choice in urban education*. London: Routledge.

Wilson, G. (2000). *Effects on funding equity of Arizona tax credit law*. Paper presented at the American Educational research Association annual meeting, New Orleans.

Witte, J. (2000). *The market approach to education*. Princeton, NJ: Princeton University Press.

FURTHER READINGS

Apple, M. W. (2006). *Educating the "right" way: Markets, standards, god, and inequality* (2nd ed.). New York: Routledge.

Bernstein, B. (1996). *Pedagogy, symbolic control, and identity*. Bristol, PA: Taylor and Francis.

Bourdieu, P. (1996). *The state nobility*. Stanford, CA: Stanford University Press.

Power, S., Edwards, T., Whitty, G., & Wigfall, V. (2003). *Education and the middle class*. Philadelphia: Open University Press.

Smith, M. L., et al. (2004). *Political spectacle and the fate of American Schools*. New York: Routledge.

Whitty, G., Edwards, T., & Gewirtz, S. (1993). *Specialization and choice in urban education*. London: Routledge.

Michael Apple
Department of Educational Policy Studies
University of Wisconsin, USA

GERT BIESTA

EDUCATION BETWEEN ACCOUNTABILITY
AND RESPONSIBILITY [1]

INTRODUCTION

Accountability has become an integral part of the educational system and the day
to day practice of educators in many countries around the world. In England and
Wales a decisive step in the rise of the culture of accountability was the passage
of the 1988 Education Reform Act, which fundamentally transformed the
organisation of educational provision. As Gewirtz (2002, p. x) has shown, the 1988
Act "redefined parents as consumers who – at least in principle – were given the
right to choose a school for their child." At the same time, schools were
"effectively reconfigured as small businesses whose income was to become
dependent on their success in attracting customers within competitive local school
markets." However, the environment in which schools were to operate was not a
free market, but one highly regulated by the state. The Act gave government the
right "to specify precisely what was to be taught in schools and to monitor closely
the performance of schools, through the national curriculum, regular testing of
students, the publication of those results, and inspection" (ibid.). Although the
1988 Act was the product of a Conservative government, many authors have
argued that the educational policies of so-called 'New Labour' (in power from
1997 onwards) are effectively a continuation of what was set in motion by the
Conservatives (see, e.g., Ball, 1999; Tomlinson, 2001, pp. 85–111). While there
are particular reasons for the emergence of the culture of accountability in
education, the rise of accountability is part of a much wider social transformation
which has affected many, if not all spheres of modern life – something which has
been captured particularly well in Michael Power's notion of the "audit society"
(Power, 1997).

In this chapter I want to focus on the question of what kind of *relationships* are
promoted or produced by the culture of accountability. I wish to explore how the
culture of accountability affects the ways in which people relate, either as
individuals or as (organised) groups. The question that interests me is not only
what kind of relationships are made possible by the culture of accountability, but
also what kinds of relationships are made difficult or even impossible as a result of
the accountability regime. To answer this question, I will begin with a discussion
of the way in which the meaning of accountability has been transformed over the
past decades. I will then introduce a philosophical perspective, informed by
Zygmunt Bauman's postmodern moral philosophy in order to examine the

*M. Simons, M. Olsen and M.A. Peters (eds.), Re-Reading Education Policies: A Handbook Studying
the Policy Agenda of the 21ˢᵗ Century, 650–666.*

relationship between accountability and responsibility and to ascertain the extent to which responsibility is possible under conditions of accountability. My goal in this analysis is not to argue that any solution to the problem of accountability has to be strictly individual. The ultimate purpose of this chapter is to examine whether the democratic potential of accountability can be regained and, if so, how this might be achieved. Most of the examples in this chapter are taken from recent developments in England, This is not to suggest that accountability is only a problem for English education, but the English situation may well be one of the more 'ironic' examples of this problem, in that the excesses and antidemocratic tendencies of the accountability regime are as much the product of the New Labour government's interventions during the past decade as they are of the Thatcherism that was dominant in the 1980s and early 1990s.

THE RISE OF MANAGERIALISM IN EDUCATIONAL ACCOUNTABILITY

As Charlton (1999; 2002) has argued, accountability is a "slippery rhetorical term" with at least two largely distinct meanings: a technical-managerial meaning, and a looser, more general meaning. In general discourse, accountability has to do with responsibility and carries connotations of 'being answerable-to'. The technical meaning, on the other hand, refers narrowly to the duty to present auditable accounts. Charlton observes that originally 'accountability' only referred to financial documentation. The current *managerial* use of accountability is, however, a direct extension of this financial usage; an accountable organisation is one that has the duty to present auditable accounts of *all* of its activities. The link between the two meanings of accountability is weak. Charlton correctly argues that "(o)nly insofar as it is legitimate to assume that the provision of auditable documentation is synonymous with responsible behaviour" is there any overlap between the two meanings of accountability (see Charlton, 2002, p. 18). Yet, the rhetoric of accountability operates precisely on the basis of a "quick switch" between the two meanings, making it difficult to see an argument against accountability as anything other than a plea for irresponsible action

Charlton not only makes a helpful conceptual distinction between the two meanings of accountability; his account also shows that the *managerial* use of the idea of accountability has its history in a strictly financial context in which the purpose of auditing is "to detect and deter incompetence and dishonesty in the handling of money" (ibid., p. 24). He argues that the logic of financial auditing has simply been *transposed* to the managerial context, without much consideration for the question to what extent this logic is appropriate for managerial purposes. Rather than adapting the principles of the audit process to the specifics and requirements of a different context, Charlton demonstrates that the culture of accountability has led to a situation in which practices had to adapt to the principles of the auditing process. "Transparent organisations are auditable, and auditable organisations are manageable – and *vice versa*. Therefore, organisations *must be made auditable*" (ibid., p. 22).

Although Charlton seems to suggest that the two meanings of accountability currently exist together, it could be argued that the tradition which sees accountability as a system of (mutual) responsibility rather than as a system of governance, was the dominant tradition before the rise of the technical-managerial approach. There is clear evidence for this in education, where, as Poulson (1996; 1998) has argued, discussions about accountability in the late 1970s and early 1980s were strongly focused on a *professional* interpretation of accountability. Apart from a professional interpretation of accountability, there were also attempts to articulate a *democratic* approach to accountability, arguing that making schools accountable to parents, students and the wider citizenry would support the democratisation of education (see Epstein, 1993; Davis & White, 2001).

The shift from professional and democratic notions of accountability to the current hegemony of the technical-managerial approach should be read against the background of a wider societal transformation and transformation of the educational system. Gewirtz, in her study of educational reform in England, characterizes this transformation as a development from "welfarism"– the educational settlement in England before 1988 – to the "new managerialism" of "post-welfarism" (see Gewirtz, 2002). Welfarism is characterized by a public-service ethos, a commitment to professional standards and values such as equity, care, and social justice, and an emphasis on cooperation. The "new managerialism," on the other hand, is characterized by a customer-oriented ethos, decisions driven by efficiency and cost-effectiveness, and an emphasis on competition, especially free-market competition (see Gewirtz, 2002, p. 32). Accountability and its corollary quality assurance are the main instruments of the new managerialism. In her study Gewirtz shows in much detail the problematic impact of the new managerialism on the day to day practice in secondary schools in England (see Gewirtz, 2002, especially pp. 138–154).

THE CHANGING RELATIONSHIP BETWEEN THE STATE AND ITS CITIZENS

Besides the question how the history of accountability in education may best be described, there is, of course, also the question how the shift from a professional and democratic to a managerial approach to accountability can be understood. This has been a major question in educational policy research over the past decade, and continues to be a central topic for debate and research (see, e.g., Gewirtz, Ball & Bowe, 1995; Whitty, Power & Halpin, 1998). Most authors agree that the rise of accountability should be understood against the background of *ideological* transformations (the rise of neo-liberalism and neo-conservatism) and *economic* changes (most importantly the oil-crisis and the economic slowdown in the mid 1970s, and the subsequent rise of global capitalism) which, together, have resulted in the decline – if not demolition – of the welfare state and the rise – if not hegemony – of the neo-liberal/global capitalist logic of the market (for a comprehensive overview see Apple, 2000).[2]

One of the most significant changes that has been brought about as a result of this development – and recognizing this is crucial for understanding the current 'mode' of accountability in education – is the *reconfiguration of the relationship between the state and its citizens*. This relationship, so I wish to argue, has become less a *political* relationship – that, is, a relationship between government and citizens who, together, are concerned about the common good – and more an *economic* relationship – that is, a relationship between the state as provider and the tax-payer as consumer of public services.

The reconfiguration of the relationship between the state and its citizens should not be understood as simply a different way of relating. The new relationship has fundamentally changed the role and identity of the two parties and the terms on which they relate. Not only can it be argued that the relationship between the state and its citizens has been de-politicised. One could even argue that the sphere of the political itself has disappeared (see, e.g., Marquand, 2003; Biesta, 2005a). Crucially, the language that is used is an economic language which positions the government as provider and the citizen as consumer (see Biesta, 2004; 2006). *Choice* has become the keyword in this discourse. Yet 'choice' is about the behaviour of consumers in a market where their aim is to satisfy their needs, and should not be conflated with democracy, which is about public deliberation and contestation about the common good. If there is a trace of democracy left in the New Labour newspeak, it might be in the contention that public sector organisations "have to respond to the desire of communities to have a greater say in the design and delivery of their local services." But even here, the underlying logic is ultimately a market-logic, since there is no indication of the wider, political issue concerning the just and equitable (re)distribution of public resources.

According to the logic of the market the relationship between the state and its citizens is no longer a *substantial* relationship but has turned into a strictly *formal* relationship. This reconfiguration is closely connected to the rise of the culture of quality assurance, the corollary of accountability. Indeed, current quality assurance practices typically concentrate "upon *systems* and *processes* rather than outcomes" (Charlton, 2002, p. 20). Quality assurance is about efficiency and effectiveness of the process, not about what the process is supposed to bring about. This is why the constant emphasis of the British government on 'raising standards' in education and other public services, is rather vacuous since it lacks proper (democratic) discussion about which standards or 'outcomes' are most desirable. The same problem underlies much of the research of the "school effectiveness and improvement industry" (Gewirtz, 2002, p. 15), since these studies mainly focus on the effectiveness and efficiency of processes, without raising the far more difficult normative and political question about the desirability of what such processes should result in (see also Bogotch, Miron & Biesta, 2007).

CITIZENS AS CONSUMERS: FROM DIRECT TO INDIRECT ACCOUNTABILITY

Turning citizens into consumers was a central part of the 1988 Education Reform Act, which heralded the idea of school choice for all parents. Epstein (1993) has argued that the ideas of parental choice and of making schools accountable to parents represented a real democratic opportunity, but that progressive and radical educators did not seize this opportunity. As a result, the conservative interpretation of accountability became hegemonic. It is important to remember that parental choice in itself can hardly be called democratic if it is not a part of wider democratic deliberation about the aims and shape of education in society. If the latter dimension is lacking, parental choice simply leads to what Apple aptly describes as the "conversion of economic and social capital into cultural capital" (Apple, 2000, p. 237). In such a situation parental choice simply reproduces existing inequalities.

What also should not be forgotten is that the context in which parental choice was introduced in Britain was not classical liberalism but neo-liberalism.

> Whereas classical liberalism represents a negative conception of state power in that the individual was to be taken as an object to be freed from the interventions of the state, neoliberalism has come to represent a positive conception of the state's role in creating the appropriate market by providing the conditions, laws and institutions necessary for its operation. In classical liberalism, the individual is characterized as having an autonomous human nature and can practice freedom. In neoliberalism the state seeks to create an individual who is an enterprising and competitive entrepreneur (Olssen, 1996, p. 340).

This is the particular constellation under which accountability in education currently operates. What is most peculiar about this situation is the odd combination of marketized individualism and central control. This explains why professional and democratic models of accountability have become extinct. The reason for this is that education has been repositioned as a public service, provided by the government and paid for by taxpayers' money. In this constellation there is no *direct* accountability between parents (or for that matter: students) and schools. The accountability is *indirect*. Direct accountability takes place between schools and the state, and the rationale for this mode of accountability is mainly formal (i.e., financial or in terms of the quality of processes), although there is also a quasi-substantial concern (through the national curriculum and the agenda of 'raising standards').

The relationship between schools and parents (or, again, students) that is 'produced' through this system, is, as I have mentioned before, a purely economic one. The role of parents and students in the 'accountability loop' is only *indirect*, in that the government can ultimately be held accountability for the 'quality' of the public services they deliver. But the latter relationship is, itself, an a-political relationship, in that it positions citizens as consumers who can 'vote' about the quality of the services delivered by the government but don't have a democratic say in the overall direction or content of what is being delivered – if delivery is an appropriate concept in the first place.

While the government constantly refers to citizens as consumers, Poulson (1998) reports that research on parental views and choices in education conducted in the 1980s and early 1990s predominantly found that parents "neither saw themselves as consumers, not education as a product" (Poulson, 1998, p. 420). Yet research conducted by Hughes et al. (1994) revealed that "parents of children in primary schools in England increasingly began to identify themselves as consumers during the course of the study" (Poulson, 1998, p. 420). Similarly, Gewirtz (2002) documents how the discourse of accountability has been internalised by headteachers, radically changing their professional self-perception and identity. Both examples show that the culture of accountability is producing a particular kind of relationships and particular identities within these relationships.

ACCOUNTABILITY OR RESPONSIBILITY?

The foregoing reconstruction of the rise of the managerial approach to accountability shows that this rise is not an isolated phenomenon, but that it is part of a transformation of society in which political relationships and the sphere of the political itself seem to have been replaced by economic relationships. The ground for the current mode of accountability seems to be an economic one, in that the right to accountability that the government claims seems to arise from the financial investment it makes into public services like education. Although at first sight there seem to be opportunities for a more democratic 'face' of accountability, i.e., in the relationship between parents and students as 'consumers' of education and schools as 'providers,' I have argued that there is no direct relationship of accountability between these parties, but only an indirect one. The only role parents and students can play is that of consumers of educational provision, but there is no opportunity to participate in any public, democratic discourse about education. O'Neill describes the predicament as follows:

> *In theory* the new culture of accountability and audit makes professionals and institutions more accountable *to the public*. This is supposedly done by publishing targets and levels of attainment in league tables, and by establishing complaint procedures by which members of the public can seek redress for any professional or institutional failures. But underlying this ostensible aim of accountability *to the public* the real requirements are for accountability *to regulators, to departments of government, to funders, to legal standards*. The new forms of accountability impose forms of central control – quite often indeed a *range of different and mutually inconsistent* forms of central control (O'Neill, 2002, p. 4).

The problem is that while many would want the culture of accountability to do the first (i.e., to be accountable to the public), it actually does the second (i.e, being accountable to the regulators, etc.) and thereby takes the real stakeholders out of the 'accountability loop.' In this respect the current technical-managerial approach to accountability produces economic relationships between people and makes democratic relationships difficult if not impossible.

The impact of this on the day to day practice in schools and other institutions is that institutions seem to adapt themselves to the requirements of accountability and audit, rather than the other way around. To quote O'Neill once more:

> *In theory* again the new culture of accountability and audit makes professionals and institutions more accountable *for good performance*. This is manifest in the rhetoric of improvement and raising standards, of efficiency gains and best practice, of respect for patients and pupils and employees. But beneath this admirable rhetoric the real focus is on performance indicators chosen for ease of measurement and control rather than because they measure accurately what the quality of performance is (O'Neill, 2002, pp. 4–5).

O'Neill points out that the incentives of the culture of accountability are by no means unreal. Yet what they seem to elicit is behaviour that suits the accountability system – behaviour that suits the inspectors and those responsible for quality assurance – rather than that it acts as an incentive for professional and responsible action. This can easily lead to a situation that is detrimental for the consumers of public services. If, for example, schools are rewarded for high exam scores, they will increasingly try only to attract 'motivated' parents and 'able' children and will try to keep 'difficult students' out. Ultimately, this results in a situation where it is no longer the question what schools can do for their students, but what students can do for their school (see Apple, 2000, p. 235).

The conclusion of the foregoing analysis can only be that the current culture of accountability is deeply problematic. Accountability is an apolitical and antidemocratic strategy that redefines all significant relationships in economic terms, and hence conceives of them as formal rather than substantial relationships. This, as I have shown, is both the case with the relationship between government and citizens, and with the relationship between government and educational institutions. As a result, parents and students are also manoeuvred into an economic relationship – one in which they are the consumers of the provision called 'education' – without there being an opportunity for them to hold either the schools or the government directly accountable. In the end, we are left with a situation in which systems, institutions and individual people adapt themselves to the imperatives of the 'logic' of accountability, so that accountability becomes an end in itself, rather than a means for achieving other ends.

MIDDLE-CLASS ANXIETY

The conclusion that the current culture of accountability is problematic is, of course, not new, although I do hope to have shed some new light on why and how this is so. But while an adequate diagnosis is important, the real and most urgent question is whether there is a way out of this situation. Is there an alternative for the current regime of accountability? Are there ways to resist and intervene in the current culture of accountability? Answering these questions requires that we first consider how it has been possible for the culture of accountability to have become so prominent and pervasive. Why do people believe in the culture of accountability? Why do they actively invest in it?

One particular reason for the success of accountability in English education may have to do with a phenomenon that I suggest to call 'middle class anxiety.' In the English educational system there is a deep rift between so-called public schools (the fee-paying or independent schools) and state schools. From the outside, it seems as if public schools are more successful in that, on average, they 'produce' students with higher exam scores who, generally, have a better starting position on the job market and have access to higher status higher education. Many middle class parents aspire to the culture of public schools, which they perceive as the 'golden standard,' and they do not want their children to be disadvantaged or left out. For precisely this reason, they are willing to actively support a government agenda of 'raising standards' in state schools and the accompanying regime of inspection, central control and accountability. But they forget that the success of public schools has as much to do with the 'quality' of the school as with the social and culture capital of its students and their parents.

A further reason why the culture of accountability has become possible lies in the fact that parents and students may indeed believe that if they position themselves as consumers in relation to education, they will obtain real power over education. As I have tried to demonstrate, this is not the case in the current situation because there is no *direct* accountability between the 'consumers' and 'providers' of education. The state exerts central control over education, leaving parents and students out of the decision loop.

A third reason is associated with what Charlton calls the 'quick switch' between the two different meanings of accountability: the technical-managerial meaning and the more general idea of accountability as having to do with responsible action. As noted previously, because it is assumed that accountability has to do with responsibility, it has become difficult to argue *against* accountability, since this may look like an argument *for* irresponsible action. But what is the connection between accountability – or more precisely: the current culture of accountability – and responsibility? In the next section I want to take a closer look at Zygmunt Bauman's work, with particular emphasis on his ideas regarding responsibility, in order to consider the extent to which accountability and responsibility can be connected and how we might go about reconnecting them.

ZYGMUNT BAUMAN: BEING RESPONSIBLE FOR OUR RESPONSIBILITY

Bauman's work relies on a clear distinction between ethics and morality. *Morality* concerns "the aspect of human thought, feeling and action that pertains to the distinction between 'right and 'wrong'" (Bauman, 1993, p. 4). *Ethics*, on the other hand, refers to rules, codes and norms. It is the codification of what counts as moral action; a codification in terms of (universal) laws. Implied in the idea of *ethics* is not only the assumption that it is *possible* to articulate such laws. *Ethics* also expresses a particular belief as to what it is to lead a moral life, viz., the life of obedience to the moral law(s) (Bauman, 1998, p. 75). This view stands in sharp contrast to the view in which the moral life is conceived as a life of choice between right and wrong *without* the guidance of norms, codes and laws.

Bauman characterizes modernity as the era of *ethics*, i.e., the era in which it is/was assumed to be possible to articulate, define and codify what would count as moral behavior. The moral thought and practice of modernity, he writes, "was animated by the belief in the possibility of a *non-ambivalent, non-aporetic code*" (Bauman, 1993, p. 9). It is precisely the *disbelief* in this possibility, which is distinctly *post*modern. The 'post' here is not meant in a chronological sense, i.e., in the sense of displacing and replacing modernity at the moment when it ends or fades away. It rather is meant to imply "that the long and earnest efforts of modernity have been misguided, undertaken under false pretences" and that "it is modernity itself that will demonstrate (if it has not demonstrated yet) (...) its impossibility" (ibid., p. 10).

For Bauman, therefore, the postmodern implies the end of *ethics*. But it is important to see that this does not imply the end of all morality, but only the end of 'codified morality.' This does not mean that morality is 'saved.' Bauman only claims that the end of (modern) ethics opens up the *possibility* for (postmodern) morality. But there is no guarantee whatsoever that the postmodern era will actually be more moral than the modern one. It is only *a chance* and nothing more than that (see, e.g., Bauman, 1998, p. 109). "It remains to be seen," he writes, "whether the time of postmodernity will go down the history as the twilight, or the renaissance, of morality" (Bauman, 1993, p. 3).

TAKING RESPONSIBILITY SERIOUSLY

The central notion in Bauman's articulation of postmodern morality is the idea of *responsibility*. Bauman provides a range of arguments for supporting his claim that responsibility is what postmodern morality is about, yet the most convincing argument may well be found in the contention that following the rules, however scrupulously, does not and will never save us from responsibility. We can always ask ourselves and we can always be asked by others whether our following of some set of (ethical) rules is or was the right thing to do – and we will never have a conclusive answer to that question.

This is precisely what postmodernism shows us: that moral choices are indeed *choices*, and that moral dilemmas are indeed *dilemmas*, and not "the temporary and rectifiable effects of human weakness, ignorance or blunders" (Bauman, 1993, p. 32). The postmodern world, Bauman argues, is one "in which *mystery* is no more a barely tolerated alien awaiting a deportation order" (ibid., p. 33). It is a world in which we learn to live "with events and acts that are not only not-yet-explained, but (for all we know about what we will ever know) inexplicable" (ibid.).

Some would say – and this is a recurring theme in the writings of all critics of postmodernity and postmodernism (see Biesta, 2005b) – that the postmodern acceptance of contingency and ambiguity implies the end of morality and even poses a severe threat to the very possibility of human cohabitation as such. Bauman, however, clearly takes the opposite view. He argues that the postmodern re-enchantment of the world carries a chance of readmitting human moral capacity to that world. Not so that the world will as a consequence become necessarily better and more hospitable. "But it will stand a chance of coming to terms with the tough and resilient human proclivities it evidently failed to legislate away – and of starting from there" (Bauman, 1993, p. 34).

Bauman's account reveals, in sum, why responsibility is both possible and necessary under the postmodern 'condition'. It is *possible* because postmodernity leaves behind the belief in the possibility of a universal moral code, and more specifically the codified rational ethics of modernity. It is for this very reason, however, that responsibility becomes necessary. This raises the question how we should actually understand responsibility.

RESPONSIBILITY AND MORAL AUTONOMY

One way to approach Bauman's understanding of responsibility is to say that for him only an individual can be responsible. He argues that the problem with attempts to codify morality is that the moral 'I' is just being seen as "a singular form of the ethical 'us'" and that "within this ethical 'we', 'I' is exchangeable with 's/he'" (Bauman ,1993, p. 47). Yet in the moral relationship ""I and the Other are not exchangeable, and thus cannot be 'added up' to form a plural 'we'" (ibid., p. 50). To understand why this is so, we need to take a closer look at the moral relationship.

Following the work of Emmanuel Levinas, Bauman argues that a moral relationship *is* a relationship of *responsibility*. What distinguishes a moral relationship from a contractual relationship is that responsibility is *not* reciprocal. It is not, Bauman argues, that I am responsible for the other because the other is, will be, or has been responsible for me. Responsibility for the other – *real* responsibility, so we could say – is one-sided, non-reciprocal and non-reversible.

Bauman argues that my responsibility for the other is always already 'there'. It is *not* a responsibility which follows from my decision to be responsible or not. Bauman stresses that it rather is "the *impossibility* of not being responsible for this Other here and now that constitutes my moral capacity" (ibid., p. 53). This is not to say that everybody will actually *be* responsible. But the point is that in order *not* to be responsible we must 'forget' something.

> The condition of *not* being haunted by scruples is quite easy to obtain, to be sure. In fact we all obtain it and are in it, most of the time. But 'most of the time' we move outside the realm of moral action into the area where conventions and etiquette, going through the codified and thus easily learnable and readable motions, as well as the simple rule of respecting the other's privacy (...) will do. The rest of the time, though, we are in morally charged situations, and that means being on our own (ibid., pp. 53–54, n.19).

While rules can be universal, responsibility is by its very 'nature' non-universal, singular, unique. By the same token, morality is "endemically and irredeemably *non-rational* – in the sense of not being calculable" (ibid., p. 60). The 'moral call' rather is thoroughly personal, it appeals to *my* responsibility, which means that "I am moral *before* I think" (Bauman, 1993, p. 61). It is not, therefore, that one can choose to be responsible for the other or not. Bauman rather holds that being responsible for the other is our human condition: "moral responsibility – being *for* the Other before one can be *with* the Other – is the first reality of the self" (Bauman, 1993, p. 13).

MORALITY, PROXIMITY, AND MODERNITY

The preceding analysis provides an outline of a postmodern moral philosophy which tries to take responsibility seriously in its own terms, and which urges us to take responsibility for our responsibility. The interesting thing about Bauman's work, however, is that he not only develops this new understanding of our postmodern moral condition, but that he also raises the sociological issue of the extent to which responsibility is actually possible in our society. The central concept in this discussion is the Levinasian idea of *proximity*.

For Levinas morality concerns the relationship between two beings – and not more than two. Bauman aptly speaks of the "moral party of two." Levinas expresses the unique quality of the moral relationship with the idea of *proximity*. Proximity is not about physical closeness. It does not refer to a shortening of distance, but should be understood as a "suppression of distance" (Bauman, 1993, p. 87). This suppression is, however, not an act. Proximity is more like "attention" or "waiting." Seen in this way we could say that proximity describes the predicament of being in the moral situation and of being a moral self. It describes at the same time the specific *quality* of the moral situation, and something like the *condition* upon which morality might become possible, might 'happen'.

Since morality only exists in the moral party of two, the situation dramatically changes when a third person enters the scene. This is when 'society' appears. Now "the naive, un-ruled and unruly moral impulse – that both necessary and sufficient condition of the 'moral party' – does not suffice anymore" (ibid., p. 112). Society needs "norms, laws, ethical rules and course of justice" (ibid., p. 114). Bauman basically sees this necessity as a *loss*. "Objectivity, the gift of the Third, has delivered a mortal, and at least potentially terminal, blow to the affection which moved the moral partners." (ibid.) The 'Other' now dissolves in the 'Many', and the first thing to dissolve is what Levinas calls the 'Face', i.e., the otherness of the other, and hence morality, that is "the responsibility for that otherness" (ibid., p. 130). In this situation we need help and the name of that help, according Bauman, is 'society' (ibid., p. 116). Yet society offers its help in two different ways. Or, to put it differently, society 'consists' of two different processes – Bauman calls them *socialization* and *sociality* – which both, in a different way, offer 'help,' though quite ambivalent help, when morality is no longer possible.

SOCIALIZATION AND SOCIALITY

Socialization and *sociality* might best be understood as two different reactions of society to the 'fact' of the moral impulse; reactions, more specifically, to the spontaneity and unpredictability of this impulse. *Socialization* is the attempt to domesticate the moral impulse, to provide structure to society, or to see society as structure (Bauman, 1993, p. 123). Bauman discerns three ways in which "the disruptive and deregulating impact of moral impulse" *can* be neutralized by society and also actually *has* been neutralized by (modern) society.

The first of these is by "assuring that there is *distance*, not *proximity* between the two poles of action – the 'doing' and the 'suffering' one" (ibid., p. 125). It is, in other words, "the removal of effects of action beyond the reach of moral limits" (ibid.). In this situation actors become just one link in a long chain, and they see and have the ability to control only the next link; they can neither see nor control the ultimate and overall aims. In such a situation the moral capacity of the actor, now prevented from interfering with the overall aim and outcome, is deployed in the service of the *efficiency* of the process. The moral focus shifts, in other words, to the "loyalty to the mates" (ibid., p. 126) – a development which "reinforces discipline and willingness to cooperate" (ibid., p. 127) but at the same time stifles responsibility.

The second 'arrangement' consists of exempting some 'others' "from the class of potential objects of moral responsibility" (ibid., p. 125) – a process which Bauman calls *de-humanization*. What happens here is that those who are at 'the receiving end of action' are *denied* the capacity to be moral subjects and are "thus disallowed from mounting a moral challenge against the intentions and effects of the action" (ibid., p. 127). The third 'arrangement' involves disassembling the object of action into a set of 'traits', so that it no longer appears as a (potentially) moral self. In this case actions become targeted to specific traits but not to the person as a whole – as a result of which an encounter with that whole person is unlikely to happen.

Bauman stresses that these 'arrangements' are not simply strategies that have been or can be deployed in order to make morality more difficult or to make morality disappear – although they can be used as such. They are also simply the 'effects' of socialization, the 'effects' of society's attempt to become more structured, more organised and more ordered. While these arrangements do not promote immoral behaviour, and in that respect could be called 'neutral', they do not promote good behaviour either. They rather render social action morally "adiaphoric," i.e., morally indifferent. The overall effect of socialization is what Bauman describes as an 'out-rationalizing' of the moral impulse (ibid., p. 119).

The process of *sociality*, on the other hand, results in 'out-aesthetizing' of the moral impulse. Sociality is, in a sense, everything that socialization is not. Sociality "puts uniqueness above regularity and the sublime above the rational, being therefore generally inhospitable to rules" (ibid., p. 119). While this process presents no danger of out-rationalizing the moral impulse, sociality poses a different threat to proximity. The main point of sociality, of the 'celebration of spontaneity', is that it brings individuals together in what Bauman calls the 'crowd'. The 'crowd' is the situation where individuals simply 'do' and 'are'. It brings "the comfort of non-decision and non-uncertainty" (ibid., p. 132). It is for that reason that in the 'crowd' the question of responsibility will simply never arise. Bauman demonstrates that both processes result in much the same outcome – they both create a situation in which heteronomy – heteronomy of rules or heteronomy of crowds – taking the place of the autonomy of the moral self. "Neither (...) socialization of society nor the sociality of the crowd, tolerate moral independence. Both explore and obtain obedience – though one by design, the other by default"(ibid.).

In a sense we now have come full circle in that we can say that the major tendency of modernity with respect to morality has been that of socialization. For Bauman after all modernity is/was the era of *ethics*, the era of codified, structured, regulated morality. In this respect Bauman also offers a moral diagnosis of modernity – or a diagnosis of modern morality – in that he shows how the process of socialization (which is the more encompassing attempt of society to structure, order and control), makes proximity, and hence responsibility, more and more difficult. Although the emphasis in Bauman's analysis is on the effects of socialization, we can also deduce from Bauman's writings that we should not think of sociality as the process which can save morality from the iron grip of socialization. Sociality appears as the other dangerous extreme of social life, the other threat to morality.

Bauman's overall conclusion is, however, slightly optimistic. While he argues again and again that morality has become difficult under conditions of modern life, it has not become impossible. Bauman argues that fortunately "the moral conscience", that "ultimate prompt of moral impulse and root of moral responsibility – has only been *anaesthesized*, not amputated" (ibid., p. 249). He clearly puts his hope and faith in the possibility that moral conscience is only dormant and therefore, in principle, be awakened. It may strike the modern mind as 'preposterous' to suggest that conscience is "humanity's only warrant and hope" (ibid.). Yet it seems to be the only possibility we have to at least to be able to expose both the immorality of codified morality and the immorality of the norms of the majority. "(W)e have little choice but to place our bet on that conscience which, however wan, alone can instill the responsibility for disobeying the command to do evil" (ibid., p. 250).

DISCUSSION

I began this chapter by asking how the current culture of accountability has affected relationships. The first conclusion I want to draw is that the culture of accountability poses a threat to *political* relationships in that accountability redefines relationships in economic terms. As a result, the accountability relationship becomes a *formal* relationship where 'quality,' the most empty and abused word of the past decade, becomes confined to processes and procedures, rather than concerned with content and aims. The de-politicisation of relationships is at stake both in the relationship between the state and its citizens and between the state and educational institutions.

This change has also affected relationships between schools and teachers on the one hand and parents and students on the other. They have been manoeuvred into a position in which it is easier to think of their relationship in economic terms as well. In using the term 'easier' I am avoiding the suggestion that the 'providers' and 'consumers' have been pressed into this kind of thinking. The mechanisms at work are subtler and have more to do with falling into what turns out to be the most 'convenient,' most 'normal' way of thinking and acting. Going against the grain always requires more effort and conviction than choosing the path of least resistance.

One effect of this redefinition process has been the *de-politicisation* of the relationship between schools/teachers and parents/students, in that their interaction focuses primarily on questions about the 'quality' of the provision (e.g., compared to other providers; an effect of league tables) and *individual* value for money ('Is my child getting the best out of this school?'), rather than on questions about the common educational good ('What is it that we want to achieve as a community for the community?'). 'Middle class' anxiety, so I have suggested, may be one of the 'mechanisms' at stake in the de-politicisation of the relationship between schools/teachers and parents/students. All of this is unfortunate, since there are real democratic possibilities at the local level of schools and educational institutions, even opportunities for what one might call *democratic* accountability.

A further effect of this process has been the *de-professionalisation* of the relationship between schools/teachers and parents/students. Teachers and educational institutions have been manoeuvred into a position in which they have to go along with the customer and meet customers needs. As a result it has become more and more difficult for them to make use of their professional judgement if this goes against apparent 'needs' of 'the learner'. Similarly, parents and students have been manoeuvred into a consumer-position in which it becomes more difficult for them to rely upon and ultimately trust the professionality of educators and educational institutions.

The only democratic option that seems to be left in the wake of these changes is an *indirect* approach where parents and students can call the state to account. The problem is, however, that under the culture of accountability, the state only wants to be held accountable in terms of the 'quality' of its delivery of public services, and not in political, let alone democratic terms. The positions of teachers and educational institutions in all this is even more problematic, because they have become trapped on the provider-side of the equation. Parents and students can still raise their voice on the basis of the fact that they are the consumers of what the state 'provides.' Teachers and educational institutions do not possess such 'spending-power' and, as a result, don't seem to have any basis in the economic equation to raise their voice. The 'natural' option for them would, of course, be to raise their professional voice; but this voice has been made suspect under the culture of accountability.

The inevitable conclusion is that the culture of accountability has dramatically changed the relationships in the educational landscape and, by the very same process, it has changed the identities and, even more importantly, the self-perceptions of the parties involved. There are, as I have suggested, powerful psychological 'mechanisms' at work in all this. By taking on the role of the consumers of educational provision, parents and students may gain a feeling of power that may be difficult to resist. I am not suggesting, of course, that parents and students should simply be subjected to the judgments of educational professionals, and even less to the bureaucratic whims of educational institutions. But the culture of accountability has made it very difficult for the relations between parents/students and educators/institutions to develop into mutual, reciprocal and democratic relationships, relationships that are based upon a shared concern for the common educational good; relationships, in other words, characterized by a mutual responsibility. It is precisely here that I believe the work of Bauman is significant.

Bauman's work first of all demonstrated that postmodernism should not be seen as undermining responsibility. On the contrary, it is precisely the situation in which responsibility becomes an issue, a necessity, and a real possibility. The postmodern doubt about the possibility for ethical rules and systems is the beginning of responsibility, not its end. Secondly, Bauman urges us to take responsibility for our responsibility. He urges us to acknowledge that the possibility for responsibility depends upon each of us individually. Thirdly, I believe that Bauman's work is extremely helpful in understanding why it is so difficult for the moral impulse to manifest itself in our society. This is the main significance of his discussion about socialization and sociality. On the one hand he shows how socialization stifles the moral impulse. Yet at the very same time he argues that sociality is not the 'solution' for socialization, since it ultimately makes proximity impossible.

Against this background I am inclined to conclude that the culture of accountability ultimately makes relationships of responsibility impossible. Accountability is not simply another discourse about how we might understand responsibility, nor is it another definition or operationalisation of responsibility. The culture of accountability poses a serious threat to the possibility for proximity. Bauman's account of the three ways in which the moral impulse can be neutralized offers a surprisingly accurate account of the micro-relationships that are brought about by the culture of accountability. It reveals that the technical-managerial approach to accountability can in no way be reconciled with an approach in which responsibility is central.

Does any positive agenda follow from these deliberations? I am inclined to say that one of the most important lessons to be gained by viewing the culture of accountability through the lens of postmodern ethics is an understanding of how this culture poses a threat to the possibility for proximity and thus responsibility. It is important, at this point, to recognize that proximity is not a romantic notion. Bauman's argument is not that *Gesellschaft* (society) is the problem and that *Gemeinschaft* (community) is the solution. Proximity, to put it differently, is not 'sociality'. Proximity is not about physical closeness, it does not refer to a shortening of distance. Proximity is like attention or waiting. Proximity is something that has to be 'achieved' again and again and that crucially depends upon our own, individual efforts and commitments to be attentive, to wait, and so on. It articulates both the predicament of being a moral self and the quality of the moral situation qua moral situation, the condition upon which responsibility might 'happen.'

It want to emphasise that this is not only a personal task. It is also a professional task that is, if we are willing to see that responsibility is an essential component of what educational relationships are made of. Ultimately, redefining our relationship on the basis of responsibility might also be a way to regain and reclaim the political dimension of accountability, in that we can understand the political as taking responsibility for that which is of common concern (the *res publica*). After all, to take political responsibility is precisely to take responsibility for what is not directly of interest to us, and may not even be of interest to us at all.

NOTES

1 This chapter has been adapted from: Biesta, G. (2004). Education, Accountability, and the Ethical Demand: Can the Democratic Potential of Accountability Be Regained? *Educational Theory 54*(3), 233-250. Reprinted by permission of the University of Illinois.

2 One of the important questions in the discussion concerns the exact relationship between ideological and economic changes. Some would argue that they were relatively independent and have mutually reinforced each other. Faulks, in his excellent analysis of the political changes in post-war Britain, has suggested the Thatcherism was much more a response to the changing economic situation, than that it was an independent ideological factor (see Faulks, 1998).

REFERENCES

Apple, M. (2000). Can critical pedagogies interrupt rightist policies? *Educational Theory, 50*(2), 229–254.

Bauman, Z. (1993). *Postmodern ethics*. Oxford: Blackwell.

Bauman, Z. (1998). *Leven met veranderlijkheid, verscheidenheid en onderzekerheid*. Amsterdam: Boom.

Biesta, G. J. J. (2004). Against learning. Reclaiming a language for education in an age of learning. *Nordisk Pedagogik, 23*, 70–82.

Biesta, G. J. J. (2005a). The learning democracy? Adult learning and the condition of democratic citizenship. *British Journal of Sociology of Education, 26*(5), 693–709.

Biesta, G. J. J. (2005b). What can critical pedagogy learn from postmodernism? Further reflections on the impossible future of critical pedagogy. In Ilan Gur Ze'eve (Ed.), *Critical theory and critical pedagogy today. Toward a new critical language in education* (pp. 143–159). Haifa: Studies in Education (University of Haifa).

Biesta, G. J. J. (2006). *Beyond learning. Democratic education for a human future*. Boulder, CO: Paradigm Publishers.

Bogotch, I., Mirón, L., & Biesta, G. (2007). "Effective for what; Effective for whom?" Two questions SESI should not ignore. In T. Townsend (Ed.), *International handbook of school effectiveness and school improvement* (pp. 93–110). Dordrecht/Boston: Springer.

Charlton, B. G. (1999). The ideology of 'accountability'. *Journal of the Royal College of Physicians of London, 33*, 33–35.

Charlton, B. G. (2002). Audit, accountability, quality and all that: The growth of managerial technologies in UK universities. In S. Prickett & P. Erskine-Hill (Eds.), *Education! Education! Education! – Managerial ethics and the law of unintended consequences*. Exeter: Imprint Academic.

Davis, A., & White, J. (2001). Accountability and school inspection: In defence of audited self-review. *Journal of Philosophy of Education, 35*(4), 667–681.

Epstein, D. (1993). Defining accountability in education. *British Educational Research Journal, 19*(3), 243–257.

Faulks, K. (1998). *Citizenship in modern Britain.* Edinburgh: Edinburgh University Press.

Gewirtz, S. (2002). *The managerial school. Post-welfarism and social justice in education.* London/New York: Routledge.

Gewirtz, S., Ball, S., & Bowe, R. (1995). *Markets, choice and equity in education.* Buckingham: Open University Press.

Hughes, M., Wikely, F., & Nash, T. (1994). *Parents and their children's schools.* Oxford: Blackwell.

Marquand, D. (2003). *Decline of the public.* Cambridge: Polity Press.

O'Neill, O. (2002). *BBC Reith lectures 2002. A question of trust.* Retrieved from http://www.bbc.co.uk/radio4/reith2002

Olssen, M. (1996). In defence of the welfare state and of publicly provided education. *Journal of Education Policy, 11*, 337–367.

Poulson, L. (1996). Accountability: A key-word in the discourse of educational reform. *Journal of Education Policy, 11*, 580–592.

Poulson, L. (1998). Accountability, teacher professionalism and education reform in England. *Teacher Development, 2*(3), 419–432.

Power, M. (1994). *The audit explosion.* London: Demos.

Power, M. (1997). *The audit society: Rituals of verification.* Oxford: Oxford University Press.

Tomlinson, S. (2001). *Education in a post-welfare society.* Buckingham: Open University Press.

Whitty, G., Power, S., & Halpin, D. (1998). *Devolution and choice in education: The school, the state and the market.* Buckingham: Open University Press.

FURTHER READINGS

Ball, S. J. (2007). *Education Plc: Understanding private sector participation in public sector education.* London/New York: Routledge.

Deretchin, L., & Craig,. C. J. (Eds.). (2007). *International research on the impact of accountability systems: Teacher education yearbook XV.* Lanham, MD: Rowman & Littlefield.

Lieberman, M., & C.K. Haar (2003). *Public education as a business: Real costs and accountability.* Lanham, MD: Scarecrow Press.

Sleeter, C. E. (Ed.). (2007). *Facing accountability in education: Democracy and equity at risk.* New York/London: Teachers College Press.

Strathern, M. (Ed.). (2000). *Audit cultures: Anthropological studies in accountability, ethics and the academy.* London/New York: Routledge.

Gert Biesta
The Stirling Institute of Education
University of Stirling, UK

TEACHER PROFESSIONALISM

STEPHEN J. BALL

EDUCATION REFORM, TEACHER PROFESSIONALISM AND THE END OF AUTHENTICITY

> All these concepts have been ill-defined,
> so that one hardly knows what
> one is talking about
> (Foucault Live, 1996, p. 447)

INTRODUCTION

My concern here is with the consequences of recent educational reforms for what we commonly and imprecisely refer to as teacher professionalism. However, it is enormously difficult to speak sensibly about professionalism at the current point in time, given what Stronach and colleagues (2002, p. 110), quite rightly, refer to as the "methodological reduction, rhetorical inflation and universalist excess" within which the construct is embedded. I will 'own up' straight away to trading on and perpetuating parts of the "folk epistemology of professionalism" (Pels, 1999, p. 102) and I want to have my conceptual cake and eat it. I shall try to treat it as 'what it is', a form of situated practice, and make some claims for a normative version of a sort professionalism which is neither 'folk' nor 'post'. I also want to take professionalism as emblematic of something else, of certain general changes in the nature of, or possibilities of our lives within high modernism. My theoretical resources for this task are mainly post-structuralist – Foucault, Lyotard, Rose, Bauman etc. These writers in different ways offer ways of thinking about the production of new kinds of professional workers in new kinds of neo-liberal organisations.

I also want to acknowledge that I write here from personal experience, from within rather than simply *about* the practices of professionalism. This is one more contribution to the cacophony of voices which speak to, for and about teachers which are competing to be heard with more or less success.

I want to argue here that professionalism is coming to its end, is being dislodged from its "precarious, glittering existence" – that there is a profound shift underway in several of the "many independent forces which condition the formation of teachers' professional identities in practice" (Dillabough, 1999, p. 390). A shift so profound that within the 'post-welfare' regime of social service, professionalism as

M. Simons, M. Olssen and M.A. Peters (eds.), Re-Reading Education Policies: A Handbook Studying the Policy Agenda of the 21st Century, 667–682.

an ethical-cultural practice, appears to have no place, no future.[1] Mine then is a narrative of despair, of loss and pain and betrayal, though it should not necessarily be read as a story of tarnished glory – more like a fairy story about the struggle between the lesser of two, or more, evils.

I take it that professionalism, as a pre-reform or un-reformed category, rests, in part at least – because it also has important structural and organisational features – on a particular relationship between the practitioner and their work, a relationship of commitment that is located within communal and internal dialogues.[2] That is, within moral reflection – in the attempt to organise practice by making the 'right' decision, in a moral landscape that allows space for moral uncertainty, and the deployment of 'moral knowledge', knowledge which is as Lambek (2000, p. 316) puts it both 'practical' and 'indefinite'. Professionalism in these terms rests upon ambiguity and pluralism. As Bauman (1991, p. 51) puts it: "Only pluralism returns moral responsibility for action to its natural bearer: the acting individual." That is, professionalism is meaningful only within the framework of a *substantive* rationality, and that attempts to re-define professionalism within a framework dominated by *technical* rationality renders the term meaningless. With all the modernist dangers it forebodes I will refer to the pre-reform professional – as an *authentic professional.* Where authenticity rests on the value of reflection and the ever present possibility of indecision[3] – not that this was necessarily always realised in practice – but once the possibilities of moral reflection and dialogue and indecision are eradicated then the possibilities of professionalism are in effect eradicated.[4] I want to go on to argue that this eradication is achieved, brought out, by the combined effects of the technologies of *performativity* and *managerialism*, which together perfectly and terrifyingly represent the modernist quest for order, transparency and classification – "a consciousness prompted and moved by the premonition of inadequacy" (Bauman, 1991, p. 9). I shall locate this eradication, and its consequences, illustrated through some snippets of data, *within* persons.

One of the problems now involved in talking about professionalism is that in much of the current usage of the term, particularly in political and managerial texts, the just about comprehensible signifier and the vaguely recognisable signified have been rent asunder. What is variously called "new professionalism" (McNess, Broadfoot & Osborn, 2003, p. 248), "re -professionalism", "post-professionalism" or even "post-modern professionalism" are not professionalism at all (in the terms of my normativity). Indeed in their terms what I might call professionalism can even become "unprofessional" (Smyth et al., 2000, p. 85). Thus, if we are to be able to talk about professionalism, we must be sure we know what we mean by it – of course part of the re-signification of professionalism in managerial texts is based on the hope that we will not notice that what is meant and practised is different from what was meant and practised before. The key points of difference, or two of them at least, are *first,* that these re-workings, these 'post-professionalisms' are ultimately reducible to exogenously generated, rule-following, and *second*, that they render professionalism into a form of performance, that what counts as professional practice rests upon meeting fixed, externally imposed judgements. The criteria of quality or good practice here are closed and complete – as against "the need for moral reasoning and proper uncertainty" (Lambek, 2000) as definitive characteristics of professional practice. To put in another way, 'post-professionalism' stands over and against 'trust' and contingency. Effectiveness only exists when it is measured and demonstrated and local circumstances only exist as an unacceptable 'excuse' for failure to deliver or failure to conform.

In the text by Stronach and colleagues (2002) data are deployed and at one point they write about the teachers and nurses whom they quote as talking about "*their* professionalism as something they had lost" (p. 117, emphasis in original). It seems to me that the 'their' in this phrase, 'their professionalism', gets to the nub of many issues here. Post-professionalism is somebody else's professionalism, it is not the professionalism of the practitioner. The practitioner is left or held responsible for their performance, but not for the judgement as to whether that performance is 'right' or 'appropriate', but rather whether it meets audit criteria. They are "mere spectators" (Stronach, 2002, p. 115) or "disembedded subjects" (Weir, 1997) who are required to "extract themselves from their social experience" (Dillabough, 1999 p. 378) and strive for some kind of "disengaged instrumentalism" (Taylor, 1989). Within all this teachers have lost the possibility of claims to respect except in terms of performance. They have been subjects of a discourse of derision and can no longer 'speak for themselves' in the public debate *about* [5] their practice. The sense of loss referred to above is, according to Taylor (1991, p. 1) a significant feature of the malaise of modernity: "people feel that some important decline has occurred." A sense which again he relates to the "primacy of instrumental reason" (p. 6) and a concomitant "fading of moral horizons" (p. 10).

Now you may want to convince me that my characterisation on "new professionalism" is mis-guided, too English – but in anticipation of that I would want to say several things. First, my interpretation of reform here does not focus on single-policies related to teachers' status or conditions of work but rather the effects of policy ensembles, like the introduction of curriculum guidelines, and testing, and classroom monitoring, and forms of competition between schools for student enrolment based on parental choice, which can be observed to different degrees in many education systems. Second, I want to disconnect policy technologies from policy texts and focus on the effects of technologies in their own right. Third, while not wanting to dispense entirely with the significance of national variations my emphasis is on what Menter, Mahony et al. (2004) call "a global performative cultural formation" (p. 211). [6]

PERFORMATIVITY AND MANAGERIALISM

Having tried to be clear about the use of the term professionalism perhaps I should now do the same thing for my other key terms – performativity and managerialism. *Performativity* is a technology, a culture and a mode of regulation that employs judgements, comparisons and displays as means of control, attrition and change. The performances of individual subjects or organisations serve as measures of productivity or output, or displays of 'quality', or 'moments' of promotion or inspection. They stand for, encapsulate or represent the worth, quality or value of an individual or organisation within a field of judgement, making "silences audible" (Bauman, 1991 p. 5). The issue of who controls the field of judgement is crucial and one key aspect of the global educational reform movement are situated struggles over and shifts in the control of the field of judgement and its values. Performativity is what Lyotard (1984, p. xxiv) calls "the terrors" – soft and hard – of performance and efficiency – that is, "be operational (that is, commensurable) or disappear." This arises in good part from "the natural inclination of modern practice – intolerance" (Bauman, 1991, p. 8). For Lyotard performativity encapsulates the functionality and instrumentality of modernity and the commodification and exteriorisation of knowledge. It is achieved through the construction and publication of information, indicators and other institutional performances and promotional materials as mechanisms to animate, judge and compare professionals in terms of outcomes; the drive to name, differentiate and classify – as through for example the "excellence standard" (TES, 2004, p. 8). Performativity, or what Lyotard also calls "context control", is intimately intertwined with the seductive possibilities of a particular kind of economic (rather than moral) 'autonomy', what Edwards (2000, p. 154) calls "coercive autonomy", for both institutions and in some cases individuals – like principals – or should I say leaders; the 'autonomous' subjectivity of such productive individuals has become a central economic resource in the reformed, entrepreneurial public sector.

Alongside and in relation to this, *managerialism* has been the key mechanism in/for the political reform and cultural re-engineering of the public sector in northern countries over the past 20 years. Management works to instil performativity in the worker's soul. It has been the primary means "through which the structure and culture of public services are recast (...) [and] (...) in doing so it seeks to introduce new orientations, remodels existing relations of power and affects how and where social policy choices are made" (Clarke, Cochrane & McLaughlin, 1994 p. 4). It plays a key role of the wearing-away of professional-ethical regimes that have been dominant in schools and bringing about their replacement by entrepreneurial-competitive regimes. This involves "processes of institutionalisation and deinstitu-tionalisation" (Lowndes, 1997, p. 61) rather than a 'once and for all' change, it is an ongoing attrition, made up of incremental larger and smaller changes which are many and disparate. Overtime the workplace is "re-enchanted", using an instrumental emotionalism and revived pre-modern "charismatic" leadership (Hartley, 1999).

Performativity and management then are two of the primary policy technologies of education reform. Policy technologies involve the calculated deployment of techniques and artefacts to organise human forces and capabilities into functioning networks of power. Various disparate elements are inter-related within these technologies; involving architectural forms, relations of hierarchy, procedures of motivation and mechanisms of reformation or therapy.

When employed together these technologies offer a politically attractive and 'effective' alternative to the state-centred, public welfare tradition of educational provision. They are set over and against the older technologies of professionalism and bureaucracy. They combine to produce what the OECD (1995) calls "a devolved environment" which "requires a shift by central management bodies toward setting the overall framework rather than micromanaging (...) and changes in attitudes and behaviour on both sides" (p.74). The changing roles of the central management agencies in this new environment rests, as the OECD put it, on "monitoring systems" and the "production of information" (p. 75). Management and performativity are then the ugly sisters of reform – they dispense the twin disciplines of evidence and imperative in the effort towards order and clarity. These are restless and future-oriented technologies. Inherent in their dynamism is a continual de-valuing of the present – "which makes it ugly, abhorrent and unendurable" (Bauman, 1991, p. 11). They are defined by states of performance and perfection which can never be reached, by the illusion, which always recedes, of an end to change. They are bitter, unforgiving and tireless, and impossible to satisfy.

Significantly then the policy technologies of public sector reform are not simply vehicles for the technical and structural change of organisations but are also mechanisms for reforming public sector practitioners, like teachers, for changing what it means to be a teacher, social worker or nurse. That is, "the formation and reformation of the capacities and attributes of the [teacher's] self" (Dean, 1995 p. 567). Reform does not just change what we do. It also seeks to change who we are, who it is possible for us to become – our "social identity" (Bernstein, 1996 p. 73). That is, education reform is "about the powers that have come to bear upon the subjective existence of people and their relations one with another" (Rose, 1989 p. ix). Thus, my particular focus here is not primarily upon structures and practices, but upon the re-forming of relationships and subjectivities, and the forms of new or re-invented discipline to which this gives rise. Within the policy technologies of reform there are embedded and provided new identities, new forms of interaction and new values.

Throughout the installation of these technologies into public service organisations the use of new language to describe roles and relationships is important, the reformed educational organisations are now 'peopled' by human resources which need to be managed; learning is re-rendered as a 'cost-effective policy outcome'; achievement is a set of 'productivity targets' etc. To be relevant, up-to-date, we need to talk about ourselves and others, think about our actions and relationships in new ways. This is what Morley (2003) calls "ventriloquism." These languages speak us, make us up in a lexicon of order and clarity. New roles and subjectivities are produced as teachers and lecturers are re-worked as producers/providers, educational entrepreneurs, and managers and are subject to regular appraisal and review and performance comparisons. New forms of discipline are put in place by competition, efficiency and productivity. And new ethical systems are introduced based upon institutional self-interest, pragmatics and performative worth. In each case the technologies provide new modes of description for what we do and produce new constraints upon our possibilities for action. We are not determined but specifically enabled by them. This re-making can be enhancing and empowering for some but this has to be set over and against the potential for 'inauthenticity' (see below). What is happening here is that human complexity is reduced to the most simple possible form – a category or a number in a table.

However, within all of this, while we may be constantly tempted to speak about 'the professional', and indeed 'the manager' and 'the leader' – these are neither collectively nor individually unitary, nor coherent and fixed identities. Despite the ambitions of reform, the nature of commitment, purpose and role-definition varies and always has varied between individuals and is situationally dependent. Different settings offer different possibilities and limits to professionalism. And indeed, also, within the definition of professionalism with which I am working, authenticity depicts the professional as always "becoming", as "dynamic and ambivalent" (Stronach et al. 2002, p. 117), as a moral agent who is "always responsive to the situation" and "perpetually learning" (Dawson, 1994 p. 153), as managing dilemmas and not simply a promiscuous, 'empty' and pragmatic self.

Nonetheless, in emphasising the situational qualities of professionalism I do not intend to suggest that the new 'performative' institutions are 'of a piece' – as Lowndes (1997, p. 63) suggests the task of management is to build "a relatively stable configuration of different institutional elements." Configurations will differ between institutions even of the same type and their institutional elements may be experienced and responded to differently by practitioners. There still may be places to hide, places where the 'right' decision can still be made within "the complex and diverse purposes of public service organisations" (p. 62). We well might find some "principled principals" (Gold, Evans, Earley, Haplin & Collarbone, 2003) seeking to resist the imperatives of "bastard leadership" – as Wright (2001) calls it – "the capture of the leadership discourse by the 'managerialist' project" (Wright, 2003 p. 1). Or am I falling into the mire of hopefulness?

What I am suggesting here is that the combination of managerial and performative reforms bites deep into the practice of teaching and into the teacher's soul – into the 'classroom life' and world of the teacher imagination (Egan, 1994) – specific and diverse aspects of conduct are reworked and the locus of control over the selection of pedagogies and curricula is shifted. Classroom practice is increasingly 'made up' out of responses to changing external demands. Teachers are *thought of* and characterised in new ways; increasingly they are *thought of* as pedagogic technicians.

In essence performativity is a struggle over visibility. Information is collected continuously, recorded and published – often in the form of *League Tables*. Performance is also monitored eventfully by peer reviews, site visits and inspections. Within all this, "violence is done to the concreteness of" individual humanity and "particularity" (De Lissovoy & McLaren, 2003 p. 133) and "complex human and social processes are more and more flattened into crude representations that will conform to the logic of commodity production" (p. 133). We become "dividuals" (Deleuze, 1992) – a market statistic, an item in a data bank, part of a sample. It is the generalised effect of visibility and judgement entering into the ways that we think about our practice that does the work of performativity. Not infrequently the requirements of such systems bring into being unhelpful or indeed damaging practices, which nonetheless satisfy performance requirements. Within the matrix of judgement, comparisons and performance-related incentives individuals and organisations will do whatever is necessary to excel or to survive. In other words, these policy technologies have the "capacity to re-shape in their own image the organisations they monitor" (Shore & Wright, 1999 p. 570). Constant doubts about which judgements may be in play at any point mean that any and all comparisons and requirements to perform have to be attended to. Selection and prioritisation become impossible and work and its pressures intensify. And always just beyond the cold rationality of performativity is the public moral outrage, constructed on our behalf within the media, that is aimed at vilifying the 'worst school', and 'unsatisfactory teachers'. This is the "furious tenacity of the belief in personal responsibility" (De Lissovoy & McLaren, 2003, p. 134), which is deeply inscribed in modern consciousness, is revealed in what Adorno (1995) calls "idealism as rage."

Performativity then bites deeply into our sense of self and self worth. It calls up an emotional status dimension, despite the appearance of rationality and objectivity – it trades heavily upon guilt and responsibility. Here is Bronwyn, a year 4 teacher quoted in Woods, Jeffrey et al. (1997 p. 69) account of *Restructuring Schools, Reconstructing Teachers*, talking about a forthcoming Ofsted inspection.

> I will cope with it, I will take it on board, I will do all the things I'm meant to do and I'll scrape and bow and I will back the headteacher to the hilt and I will back the school to be hilt. I won't let anybody down. But secretly inside myself I'm very, very angry that we're being made to go through this but I'm not quite sure at whom I'm being angry. It is the Government? Is it the LEA? It must be the Government.

We also see the peculiar elusiveness of performativity. These judgements take on a life of their own. We are responsible for and to *them*. They are disembodied requirements which entangle and confuse us. And the anger, the dismay, the confusion and the dissonance which result are turned inward and must be struggled with internally. As a consequence "any resistance becomes that of the individual seeking personal integrity" (Edwards, 2000, p. 142) – but such internalised resistance can be immensely stressful and damaging.[7] Bronwyn takes on both the responsibility of doing what seems necessary to support her headteacher and her colleagues, while dealing with her anger 'secretly inside'. Much of the work that performativity does on us is done by us as we seek to be responsible to others.

THE VIOLENCE OF REFORM

Let me quote two more English primary school teachers, first Elizabeth (Woods, Jeffrey et al. 1997 p. 71) and then Cloe (Woods, Jeffrey et al., 1997, p. 66). Elizabeth is talking about her school's new maths policy and Cloe about teaching for SATs [Standard Attainment Tests].

> It's cloning us again. I've written the maths policy the same way as everybody else has done, but its not couched in the way that I speak or think or I believe.

> It is completely alien to my way of teaching – testing and teaching, teaching to test. However, my focus is on that really, and I don't give a monkey's uncle about anything else. If that's what they want....

Here then is what Casey (1995) calls "defensive selves", confused and alienated subjectivities.[8] Subjectivities, and a "new professionalism", which work from the *"outside in"* (Dawson, 1994) "where virtue is consequent upon following prior principles regarding belief and conduct" (Stronach et al., 2002, p. 113). What Bernstein (2000, p. 1942) calls "mechanisms of introjection" whereby "the identity finds its core in its place in an organisation of knowledge and practice" are here being threatened by or replaced by "mechanisms of *projection*", that is an "identity is a reflection of external contingencies" (Bernstein, 2000, p. 1942) – Elizabeth's 'cloning'. And in response to all this, as a way of coping, Cloe is giving up on authenticity, on belief and commitment, she is doing what is necessary, what is required, rather than what she feels is right.

For individual *pre-reform* or un-reformed teachers, struggling with authenticity, a kind of *values schizophrenia* is experienced when commitment and experience within practice have to be sacrificed for impression and performance. Here there is a potential 'splitting' between the teachers own judgements about 'good practice' and students 'needs' on the one hand, and the rigours of performance on the other. There is a "disjunction between policy and preferred practice" (NcNess, Broadfoot & Osborn, 2003, p. 255). These teachers experience a "bifurcated consciousness" (Smith, 1987) or "segmented self" (Miller, 1983) or struggle with "outlaw emotions" (Jaggar, 1989) as they try to live up to and manage "the contradictions of belief and expectation" (Acker & Feuerverger, 1997 quoted in Dillabough, 1999 p. 382) which are embedded in the subject positions of authenticity and reform. In Bauman's (1991, p. 197) terms this is "the privatisation of ambivalence" which, "cast on individual shoulders calls for a bone structure few individuals can boast" – stress, illness and burn out are often the result. To the extent to which they hold onto their 'outlaw emotions', teachers like those quoted above and below risk being "constructed outside this dominant view of the professional, despite the demands placed upon them to conform to it" (Dillabough, 1999 p. 382). Authenticity and performativity clash and grate – particularly perhaps, as McNess, Broadfoot & Osborn (2003, pp. 255–6) found, for teachers in England. And Frank (Woods, Jeffrey et al., 1997, p. 80) complains:

> I love the contact with the children and when I say paperwork, I'm not talking about marking or preparation. It is the interference, not from the head, but from the Government and outside bodies (…) So much of the pleasure is going from it (…) We are so busy assessing children that we're forgetting to teach them.

Frank is having real problems in thinking of herself as the kind of teacher who simply produces performances – of his own and by his children. His commitments to and pleasures from teaching, his reasons for becoming and being a teacher seem to have no place in the reformed classroom. He sees himself becoming "a teacher devoid of meaningful connections to those whom she is expected to educate" (Dillabough, 1999, p. 379). What Smyth, Dow et al. (2000, p. 140) call the "primacy of caring relations in work with pupils and colleagues", or what McNess, Broadfoot and Osborn (2003, p. 246) describe as "a sociocultural model which recognised and included the emotional and social aspects necessary for a more learner-centred approach" have no place in the productive world of performativity. The effective is compromising the affective (McNess, Broadfoot & Osborn, 2003). Frank's story is a not uncommon one in the UK as the regime of performativity drives increasing numbers of teachers out of the education system. It would appear that current concerns relating to the low morale of teachers, and in some contexts the problem of under-recruitment into teaching, have their basis, in some part at least, in teachers' sense of having to 'give-up' their authentic commitments to and beliefs about teaching in the face of reform (McNess, Broadfoot & Osborn, 2003, p. 255). Teachers like Frank and Cloe and Elizabeth are no longer encouraged to have a personal rationale for practice, an account of themselves in terms of a relationship to the meaningfulness of what they do, but rather they are required to produce measurable and 'improving' outputs and performances, what is important is *what works* in achieving these ends. This leads to what Acker and Feuerverger (1997) call "doing good and feeling bad", which may also be a version of what Moore et al. (2002, p. 554) call "contingent pragmatism" – "a sense, that is, of consciously being in a state of largely enforced *adjustment*" (my emphasis).

There are three versions of (in)authentic practice here; in relation to oneself, one's sense of what is right; in relations with one's students, when a commitment to learning is replaced by the goals of performance; and in relations with colleagues, when struggle and debate – what De Lissovoy and McLaren (2003, p. 134) in their version of authenticity refer to as "a true dialectical relationship (...) between individual and collective moments of being" – is replaced by compliance and silence. This structural and individual schizophrenia of values and purposes, and the potential for inauthenticity and meaninglessness is increasingly an everyday experience for us all. The activities of the new technical intelligentsia, of management, drive performativity into the day to day practices of teachers and into the social relations between teachers. They make management, ubiquitous, invisible, inescapable – part of and embedded in everything we do. Increasingly, we choose and judge our actions and they are judged by others on the basis of their contribution to organisational performance, rendered in terms of measurable outputs. Beliefs are no longer important – it is output that counts. Beliefs are part of an older, increasingly displaced discourse. Put another way, teachers like Frank and Elizabeth are seeking to hold onto knowledges about themselves and about their practice which diverge from prevailing categories. These are now seen, in Foucault's terms, as "knowledges inadequate to their task (...) naive knowledges (...) disqualified knowledges" (Foucault, 1980, pp. 81–82). A new kind of teacher and new kinds of knowledges are 'called up' by educational reform – a teacher who can maximise performance, who can set aside irrelevant principles, or outmoded social commitments, for whom excellence and improvement are the driving force of their practice. Under a regime of performativity "identity depends on the facility for projecting discursive organisation/practices themselves driven by external contingencies" (Bernstein, 2000, p. 1942). These new post-professional identities are very powerful but also very fragile and there are moments, as indicated above, when they become unsustainable. This kind of 'post-professionalism' is commonly articulated in terms of increased collegiality, but a collegiality realised by individuation and indeed competition, and fixed in relation to the visions of leadership and corporate goals – a contrived collegiality (Hargreaves, 1991).

Embedded in almost all of the examples I have quoted are a set of dualisms or tensions – and as such we might want to be rightly suspicious of them (MacLure, 2003 pp. 9–10). They are tensions between belief and representation. On the one hand, teachers are concerned that what they do will not be represented by or valued within the metrics of accountability and, on the other, that these metrics, if taken seriously, will distort or 'hollow out' their practice. Alongside this is a further tension, indicated already, between metric performances and authentic and purposeful relationships.[9] This goes to the heart of what it means to teach.

Crucially, as indicated already, these new forms of institutional and system regulation have both a social and interpersonal dimension. They penetrate our mundane day to day interactions in such a way that the interplay of their collegial and disciplinary aspects become very murky indeed. In this there is a real possibility that authentic social relations are replaced by performative relations wherein persons are valued for their productivity alone. Their value as a person is eradicated. An example of what De Lissovoy and McLaren call "the violence of erasure" (2003, p. 133). The same can occur in teacher-student relations, when student performances are viewed primarily in terms of their impact upon institutional standing – for example within what Gillborn and Youdell (2001, p. 74) call the "A-C economy" (that is, an economy that focuses on the production of A-C grades in the final school examination system for students aged 16, which are used to construct League Tables of school performance) which, they argue, "captures something of the de-personalised nature of the processes within which teachers and pupils feel caught." However, these are not simply things done to us, as in previous regimes of power. These are things that we do to ourselves and to others. What we see here is a particular set of "practices through which we act upon ourselves and one another in order to make us particular kinds of being" (Rose, 1992, p. 161). Mahony, Menter et al. (2004) take up these issues and the emotional impacts of reform on teachers in their account of performance-related pay and they quote this teacher:

> When I started teaching it was a very nice profession (...) you actually got to know the children you were teaching. But now, it's almost as if, because we're under this huge amount of stress and strain that we have now, we've become immune to it and that is being pushed down into the pupils. We're

producing children who are very stressed (…) I don't think it's healthy (Teacher 1/f, Seamill Secondary).

TWO DISCOURSES – AND THE POSSIBILITIES OF ESTABLISHING A DIFFERENT RELATION TO ONESELF

A complex of overlapping, agonistic and antagonistic discourses swarm and seethe around the would-be or erstwhile professional in this scenario of reform.[10] But these can be reduced, with some degree of simplification, to two. One dominant and one currently very much subordinate (see for example, Fullan & Hargreaves, 1992; Grimmett & Neufeld, 1994). The former encompasses the 'reformed or post-professional', or in Laughlin's (1991) terms the "colonised" professional, who is accountable, and generically and primarily oriented to performance indicators, competition, comparison and responsiveness etc. Here cold calculation and extrinsic values predominate. This is the archetypal 'post-modern' professional – defined by depthlessness, flexibility, transparency and represented within spectacle – within performances. Like the performative institution the 'post-professional' is conceived of as simply responsive to external requirements and specified targets, armed with formulaic methods suited to every eventuality – a "specialist without spirit" in Weber's words. Their 'professionalism' inheres in the willingness and ability to adapt to the necessities and vicissitudes of policy. This is a professional who is essentially inessential and insubstantial; who is "disembedded" (Weir 1997) and an "object of knowledge" (Dillabough, 1999, p. 387). A professional whose social action is rendered "adiaphoric" to use Bauman's term. Such social action is "neither good nor evil, measurable against technical (purpose-oriented or procedural), but not against moral criteria … it renders moral responsibility for the Other ineffective" (Bauman, 1993, p. 125).

The latter, the subordinate, is a very modernist discourse, an under-stated and under-valued discourse expressed in a very different register, which interpolates what I have called the "authentic professional" or (perhaps) "re-oriented" professional, who absorbs and learns from but is not fundamentally re-made by reform. Such a professional exists "in a space of concerns" (Taylor 1989 p. 51). The work of the "authentic teacher" involves "issues of moral purpose, emotional investment and political awareness, adeptness and acuity" (Hargreaves, 1994 p. 6). Authenticity is about teaching having an "emotional heart" (Woods, 1996) or as Hargreaves argues, teaching, in this sense, is about desire, because "without desire, teaching becomes arid and empty, it loses its meaning" (Hargreaves, 1994 p. 12). Meaning is founded upon both a personal commitment – motivation – and a shared moral language. According to Charles Taylor "authenticity (…) requires (i) openness to horizons of significance and (ii) a self definition in dialogue" (Taylor, 1991 p. 66). Here professional practice is "not solely determined by one's own narrative, but (…) also shaped by social and structural relations both within and beyond (…)" (Dillabough, 1999, p. 387). As Dillabough (p. 393) puts it "teachers, as authentic individuals, bring into the practice of teaching (history, narrative, subjectivity, positioning)." Authentic teachers know where they stand in relation to a metaphorical field of open, self-governing discipline but do not necessarily stand still. This field provides a basis of reflection, dialogue and debate, a public space for moral and critical discourse. It does not tell them what to do. It provides them with a language for thinking about what they do and reflecting upon their work and the work of others within a relationship of active subjects. They act within a set of situated dilemmas and messy confusions – to which there are often no satisfactory, simple, singular, solutions. They learn to live with ambivalence. Professionalism here is a matter as acting within uncertainty and learning from the consequences – a "learning profession" (Nixon et al., 1997). It is a matter of "grappling with how to act morally in an uncertain and constantly changing educational context" (Grimmett & Neufeld, 1994, p. 229). They struggle and compromise, plan and act spontaneously, and improvise within and across contradictory roles and expectations, creativity and imagination are important; "the teacher herself is a resource in managing the problems of educational practice" (Lampert, 1985, p. 194) [11] – this is a mix of artistry and intuition (Humphreys and Hyland 2002 p. 9). Clearly, such language and imagery grate against both the rational, calculability of reform and the fake, celebratory performances of excellence and quality.[12] All of this may be something like what Nixon et al. (1997, p. 25) call "emergent professionalism" which "can be defined around the values and practices of 'agreement' and 'agreement-making'."

'Authentic' and 'reformed' classrooms may well be very different places to be, for the learner as much as for the teacher.[13] I also want to be very clear here that the 'authentic' teacher is not simply the teacher as she was prior to reform. I am not simply trying to conjure up an 'imaginary antecedent'; although some of the teachers quoted refer back to 'better times' and clearly the critique of teachers which underpins 'post-professionalism' often trades heavily, certainly in the UK, upon a revisionist history of teaching which eradicates 'counter-memories' (Barber and Sebba, 1999 is a stunning example of such revisionism). Nonetheless, my point is that authenticity is a *different* discourse of professionalism, not simply an old one.

AFTERWORD

The point of performative systems is that we make ourselves calculable rather than memorable. Experience is nothing, productivity is everything. Deliberation and judgment are no longer of value here – except when applied to commercial well-being. Our contractual obligations, survival in the marketplace or achievement of targets are the new basis of 'professional' responsibility. We must keep up, meet the new and ever more diverse targets which we set for ourselves in appraisal meetings, confess and confront our weaknesses, undertake appropriate and value-enhancing professional development, and take up opportunities for making ourselves more productive. Within all of this more and more of the personality is rendered explicit and auditable. Performativity comes to be inscribed on our bodies as well as our minds making us anxious, tired and stressed and sometimes ill. We are only beginning to understand the damage that performative regimes do to us and there is an urgent need for more research and more resistance to the terrors of calculation.

NOTES

[1] I shall leave it to others to offer of more optimistic account of possibilities for reconstruction in this new world (Gold et al., 2003; Moore et al., 2002; Stronach et al., 2002). I want to take the position here that narratives of hope, and the ontology of 'not yet' (Jonas, 1984), of possibilities, are distractions from the immediacy, the 'real', of wretchedness and torment.

[2] I have to own up to my own ambivalences here – about professionalism. Professionals are both heroes and villains within modern sociology.

[3] Thus, I do not use authenticity here in quite the sense that Taylor (1991, p. 77) does - as "a more self-responsible form of life" – but I do not exclude this. Authenticity for me is the possibility and the validity of a relationship of reflection between the self and the collectivities of the social world. And this would certainly incorporate Taylor's view of "self-centred practices as the site of ineradicable tension" which comes from "the sense of an ideal that is not being fully met in reality" (p. 76), and as he goes on to say "this tension can turn into a struggle" (p. 77), and as in my definition of professionalism, this "will be bad news for anyone who hoped for a definitive solution" (p. 77).

[4] As part of what Foucault (1970, p. 342) calls "man's disappearance."

[5] Rather than 'for' or 'in' education.

[6] While as Menter et al (2004, p. 198) point out the McCrone approach [in the Scottish case] is characterised by concerns about professional development in contrast to the English Threshold Assessment's "heavy emphasis on 'performance management'", I wonder to what extent in practice 'professional development' is separated off from the 'pressures' (Macdonald, p. 424) of a classroom performance regime.

[7] See also Osborne's (1996) case studies of two primary teachers.

[8] Subjectivity is: patterns by which experiential and emotional contexts, feelings, images and memories are organised to form one's self image, one's sense of self and others, and our possibilities of existence (De Lauretis, 1986, p. 5).

[9] Although as various commentators have pointed out, it is not impossible to conceive of a system of benign or progressive metrics, related to reducing social inequalities for example. The question is whether the form and substance of performativity can be separated out. I have my doubts.

[10] And as I have suggested in practice some teachers as social subjects live both discourses and struggle to cope with their discordance.

[11] As with schools teachers will also be positioned differently to resist the pressures of reform, or 'retain' an 'authentic' perspective.

[12] The issue of language, and more generally of discourse, has probably never been more important in the field of education. Teacher educators and teachers themselves need to be very aware of the vocabularies in use when accounting for the act of teaching.

[13] This perhaps begs the question as to whether we might find 'authentic' teachers in 'reformed' classrooms.

REFERENCES

Adorno, T. (1995). *Negative dialectics*. New York: Continuum.

Acker, S., & Feuerverger, G. (1997). Doing good and feeling bad: The work of women university teachers. *Cambridge Journal of Education, 26*, 410–422.

Barber, M., & Sebba, J. (1999). Reflections on progress towards a world class education system. *Cambridge Journal of Education, 25*(3), 183–193.

Bauman, Z. (1991). *Modernity and ambivalence*. Oxford: Polity Press.

Bauman, Z. (1993). *Postmodern ethics*. Oxford: Blackwell.

Bernstein, B. (1996). *Pedagogy symbolic control and identity*. London: Taylor and Francis.

Bernstein, B. (2000). Official knowledge and pedagogic identities: The politics of recontextualising. In S. J. Ball (Ed.), *The sociology of education: Major themes*. London: RoutledgeFalmer.

Casey, C. (1995). *Work, self and society after industrialisation*. London: Routledge.

Clarke, J., Cochrane, A., & McLaughlin, E. (1994). *Managing social policy*. London: Sage.

Dawson, A. (1994). Professional codes of practices and ethical conduct. *Journal of Applied Philosophy, 11*(2), 145–153.

De Lauretis, T. (1986). *Feminist studies, critical studies*. Bloomington, IN: Indiana University.

Deleuze, G. (1992). Postscript on the societies of control. *October, 59*, 3–7.

De Lissovoy, N., & McLaren, P. (2003). Educational 'accountability' and the violence of capital: A Marxian reading of post-structuralist positions. *Journal of Education Policy, 18*(2), 131–144.

Dean, M. (1995). Governing the unemployed self in an active society. *Economy and Society, 24*(4), 559–583.

Dillabough, J.-A. (1999). Gender politics and conceptions of the modern teacher: Women, identity and professionalism. *British Journal of Sociology of Education, 20*(3), 373–394.

Edwards, P. (2000). Late twentieth century workplace relations: Class struggle without classes. In R. Crompton, F. Devine, M. Savage, & J. Scott (Eds.), *Renewing class analysis*. Oxford: Blackwell, The Sociological Review.

Egan, K. (1994). Tools for enhancing imagination in teaching. In P. P. Grimmett & J. Nuefeld (Eds.), *Teacher development and the struggle for authenticity*. New York: Teachers College Press.

Foucault, M. (1970). *The order of things: An archaeology of the human sciences*. London: Tavistock.

Foucault, M. (1980). Two lectures. *Power/Knowledge* (C. Gordon, Ed. & Trans.). London: Longman.

Foucault, M. (1996). *Foucault live: Collected interviews, 1961–84* (S. Lotringer, Ed.). New York: Semiotext(e).

Fullan, M., & Hargreaves, A. (1992). *Teacher development and educational change*. Lewes: Falmer.

Gillborn, D., & Youdell, D. (2001). Intelligence, 'ability' and the rationing of education. In J. Demaine (Ed.), *Sociology of education today*. London, Palgrave.

Gold, A., Evans, J., Earley, P., Halpin, D., & Collarbone, P. (2003). Principled Principals? Values driven leadership: Evidence from ten case studies of 'outstanding' school leaders. *Educational Management and Administration, 31*(2), 127–138.

Grimmett, P. P., & Neufeld, J. (Eds.). (1994). *Teacher development and the struggle for authenticity*. New York: Teachers College Press.

Hargreaves, A. (1991). Contrived collegiality: The micropolitics of teacher collaboration. In J. Blase (Ed.), *The politics of life in schools: Power conflict and cooperation*. London: Sage.

Hargreaves, A. (1994). *Changing teachers, changing times*. London: Cassell.

Hartley, D. (1999). Marketing and the 'Re-enchantment' of school management. *British Journal of Sociology of Education, 20*(3), 309–323.

Humphreys, M., & Hyland, T. (2002). Theory, practice and performance in teaching: Professionalism, intuition and jazz. *Educational Studies, 28*(1), 5–15.

Jaggar, A. (1989). Love and knowledge: Emotion in feminist epistemology. In A. Jaggar & S. Bordo (Eds.), *Gender/body/knowledge*. New Brunswick, NJ: Rutgers University Press.

Jeffrey, B., & Woods, P. (1998). *Testing teachers: The effect of school inspections on primary teachers*. London: Falmer Press.

Jonas, H. (1974). *Philosophical essays: From ancient creed to technological man*. Englewood Cliffs, NJ: Prentice-Hall.

Lambek, M. (2000). The anthropology of religion and the quarrel between poetry and philosophy. *Current Anthropology, 41*(3), 309–320.

Lampert, M. (1985). How do teachers manage to teacher? Perspectives on problems in practice. *Harvard Educational Review, 55*(2), 178–194.

Laughlin, R. (1991, Autumn). Can the information systems for the NHS internal market work? *Public Money and Management*, 37–41.

Lowndes, V. (1997). Change in public service management: New institutions and new managerial regimes. *Local Government Studies, 23*(2), 42–66.

Lyotard, J.-F. (1984). *The postmodern condition: A report on knowledge* (Vol. 10). Manchester: Manchester University Press.

MacDonald, A. (2004). Collegiate or compliant? Primary teachers in post-McCrone Scotland. *British Educational Research Journal, 30*(3), 413–433.

MacLure, M. (2003). *Discourse in educational and social research*. Buckingham: Open university Press.

McNess, E., Broadfoot, P., & Osborn, M. (2003). Is the effective compromising the affective? *British Educational Research Journal, 29*(2), 243–257.

Mahony, P., Menter, I., et al. (2004). The emotional impact of performance-related pay on teachers in England. *British Educational Research Journal, 30*(3), 435–456.

Menter, I., Mahony, P., et al. (2004). Ne'er the twain shall meet? modernizing the teaching profession in Scotland and England. *Journal of Education Policy, 19*(2), 195–214.

Miller, J. L. (1983). The resistance of women academics: an autobiographical account. *Journal of Educational Equity and Leadership, 3*, 101–109.

Moore, A., Edwards, G., Halpin, D., & George, R. (2002). Compliance, resistance and pragmatism: The (re)construction of schoolteacher identities in a period of intensive educational reform. *British Educational Research Journal, 28*(4), 551–665.

Morley, L. (2003). *Quality and power in higher education*. Buckingham: Society for Research into Higher Education and Open University Press.

Nixon, J., Martin, J., McKeown, P., & Ranson, S. (1997). Towards a learning profession: Changing codes of occupational practice within the new management of education. *British Journal of Sociology of Education, 18*(1), 5–29.

OECD. (1995). *Governance in transition: Public Management Reforms in OECD countries*. Paris: Author.

Osborne, M. (1996). Identity, career and change: A tale of two teachers. In P. Croll (Ed.), *Teachers, pupils and primary schooling: Continuity and change*. London: Cassell.

Pels, P. (1999). Professions of duplexity: A prehistory of ethical codes in anthropology. *Current Anthropology? 40*(2), 101–136.

Peters, T., & Waterman, R. (1982). *In search of excellence*. London: Harper Row.

Rose, N. (1989). *Governing the soul: The shaping of the private self*. London: Routledge.

Rose, N. (1992). Governing the enterprising self. In P. Heelas & P. Morris (Eds.), *The values of the enterprise culture*. London: Routledge.

Rose, N. (1996). Governing "advanced" liberal democracies. In A. Barry, T. Osborne, & N. Rose (Eds.), *Foucault and political reason: Liberalism, neo-liberalism and rationalities of government*. London: UCL Press.

Shore, C., & Wright, S. (1999). Audit culture and anthropology: Neo-liberalism in British higher education. *The Journal of the Royal Anthropological Institute, 5*(4), 557–575.

Smith, D. (1987). *The everyday world as problematic: A feminist sociology*. Boston: NorthEastern University Press.

Smyth, J., Dow, A., Hattam, R., Reid, A., & Shacklock, G. (2000). *Teachers' work in a globalising economy*. London: Falmer Press.

Stronach, I., Corbin, B., et al. (2002). Towards an uncertain politics of professionalism: Teacher and nurse identities in flux. *Journal of Education Policy, 17*(1), 109–138.

Taylor, C. (1989). *Sources of the self: The making of the modern identity*. Cambridge, MA: Harvard University Press.

Taylor, C. (1991). *The Malaise of modernity*. Toronto: Anansi.

Taylor, C. (1991). *The ethics of authenticity*. Cambridge, MA: Harvard University Press.

TES [Times Education Supplement]. (2004, November 9). *The standard of excellence is increasing.*.

Weir, A. (1997). *Sacrificial logics: Feminist theory and the critique of identity.* New York: Routledge.

Woods, P. (1996). *Researching the art of teaching: Ethnography for educational use.* London: Routledge.

Woods, P., Jeffrey, B., et al. (1997). *Restructuring schools, reconstructing teachers.* Buckingham: Open University Press.

Wright, N. (2001). Leadership, 'Bastard Leadership' and managerialism: Confronting twin paradoxes of the Blair education project. *Educational Management and Administration, 29*(3), 275–290.

Wright, N. (2003). *Principled 'Bastard' leadership?* A rejoinder to Gold, Evans, Earley, Halpin and Collarbone, Centre of Educational Studies, University of Hull.

FURTHER READINGS

Ball, S. J. (2008). *The education debate: Policy and politics in the 21st century.* Bristol: Policy Press.

Broadhead, L.-A., & Howard, S. (1998). The art of punishing: The research assessment exercise and the ritualisation of power in higher education. *Education Policy Analysis Archives, 6*(8).

Gee, J. (1999). New people in new worlds: Networks, the new capitalism and schools. In B. Cope & M. Kalantzis (Eds.), *Multiliteracies: Literacy learning and the design of social futures.* London: Routledge.

Perryman, J. (2007). Inspection and emotion. *Cambridge Journal of Education, 37,* 173–190.

Sparkes, A. C. (2007). Embodiment, academics and the audit culture: A story seeking consideration. *Qualitative Research, 7*(4), 521–550.

Stephen J. Ball
Institute of Education
University of London, UK

MIKE BOTTERY

CRITICAL PROFESSIONAL OR BRANDED TECHNICIAN?

Changing Conceptions of the Education Worker [1]

INTRODUCTION

This chapter uses a case study of five phases in the changing meaning of teacher professionalism in England to suggest that changes caused by current legislation there, notably to do with workforce reform and inclusion agendas, are probably reducing rather than facilitating teaching professions' ability to respond adequately to these challenges. It does not assume that precisely this path will be taken elsewhere, but it does argue that with the extent of global policy borrowing going on, educational professionals in other countries who have gone through much of the same process, need to reflect on whether they face similar kinds of challenges and changes to their practice, and whether their current position enables them to respond adequately to the challenges presented by a globalising world, from which educational practitioners are not exempt.

Indeed, across much of the western world, the role of educational practitioners over the last sixty years has changed from something like trusted experts, gatekeepers in a social democratic welfare state, to something nearer to employees in a competitive institution within a larger directed societal agenda. They have done so, as Levin (2002) has shown, within similar policy programmes of greater accountability, more targets and standards, more marketisation and consumer choice. They have moved from being trusted because they were of a profession whose values and practice were respected – a kind of 'role' trust, to something like a body of workers trusted – if that is the word – because close inspection of their work on a continual basis shows that they are performing in the manner demanded of them. This is a short-term, low-level trust. They have moved from what Pollitt (1992) called being "on top" to being "on tap", and a large part of this reason has been a shift in policy emphasis from nation-building and citizenship to a focus on the knowledge economy and the production of knowledge-based societies – something seen, as Codd (2005) and Fitzgerald (2007) argue in other countries as well as in England. This chapter will attempt to trace such changes, by telling five interlinked stories of different conceptions of the professional educator, and ask whether current directions are helpful in dealing with the problems raised by a globalising world (Bottery, 2004).

M. Simons, M. Olssen and M.A. Peters (eds.), Re-Reading Education Policies: A Handbook Studying the Policy Agenda of the 21st Century, 683–700.

STORY ONE – THE SOCIAL DEMOCRATIC PROFESSIONAL MODEL

The first three of these stories occurred in one time frame simultaneously, and for two to three decades co-existed uneasily together. The first story is that of benign professionals, which began before the foundation of the Welfare State at the end of the Second World War. It had a long history, going back to medieval times, when there were only a limited number of professions, destinations exclusively for upper-class children. Such occupations were then assigned high status, and their claims to autonomy, self-regulation, and expertise were hardly questioned. As the industrial age arrived, writers like Durkheim (1957) would boost professionals' status even further, by claiming that they were a bulwark against its socially destructive effects. It is therefore little wonder that other occupations – such as nursing, police, and teaching – would aspire to the title of professions, even if some (e.g. Etzioni, 1969) would never feel able to credit them with anything more than a 'semi-professional' status. The trustworthy image of professionals was also boosted by a professional literature largely concerned with the depiction of great individuals (e.g. Carr-Saunders & Wilson, 1933), and by a similar complimentary depiction on the new media of radio and television. It is perhaps not coincidental that a harder-edged approach to professionals would accompany a more critical literature in the early 1970s, which itself occurred at a time of economic crisis, when the very concept of a welfare state was being seriously questioned.

But we get ahead of ourselves slightly. At the end of the Second Word War, the UK Labour government, like the governments of many other countries (e.g. Codd, 2005), were intent on developing social democratic ideals, and furthering a collective responsibility and identity. In England, government was primarily concerned with rebuilding the nation's shattered physical infrastructure, and with creating universal provision in areas like health, education, and pensions, underpinned by the widely held belief in the need for strong and involved government. This was in part generated by memories of the effects of unrestricted markets in the depressions of the 1930s, in part borne of the citizens of a nation which had successfully pulled together through a World War, and in part through a belief that social engineering should and could create a more equitable society. Education (not for the first time) was seem as more than a matter of private benefit, more than a personal positional good, but rather part of a societal project, a moral good because it sought " (…) to develop in all citizens a moral sense of social and fraternal responsibility for others and a disposition to act in rational and cooperative ways (…)" (Grace, 1989, p. 214).

Given the government's need to focus on rebuilding structures, and with professionals viewed as altruistic individuals, it was perhaps little wonder that professionals would be largely trusted – because of their role and their reputation – to make the right decisions for their clients. A tripartite balance of power between central government, local education authorities, and individual schools then held uneasily for over twenty years. Yet there were already the seeds of the destruction of such an arrangement. Ministers of Education would have to accept, as David Eccles did in 1961, that the curriculum was the 'secret garden of the teachers', but without a well-articulated knowledge base for either the curriculum or the pedagogy used, this claim would be interrogated much more closely. If politicians were excluded from this garden, so were parents, and numerous were the schools where they remained on the far side of playgrounds until the teachers had finished with their children, the clear message being that they had nothing to contribute to the endeavour of education. Not only did this have a negative social message: it reinforced the assertion that professional expertise was founded upon a body of knowledge to which only the professional educator had access. This epistemological position would be increasingly challenged, in part by the suggestion that advanced economies didn't require individuals acquainted with blocks of knowledge but with how to access information relevant to a fast-changing set of problems. In addition, teachers failed to grasp the opportunity of forming a truly professional body, their concerns seemingly more about pay and conditions, and rather less about their larger educational, social and public roles. It was an opportunity missed, and when anti-professional propaganda and critique occurred in the 1970s, educators were not well placed to counter it.

STORY TWO – THE BUREAUCRATISED PROFESSIONAL MODEL

Yet running alongside this benign picture of the autonomous professional is another picture, but one which also has roots reaching back hundreds of years, the bureaucratisation of the professional. Such bureaucracy has many roots: perhaps the earliest being as a governmental strategy, first employed with the military, but then with other occupations, to more clearly control their work through increasing the number of rules and degree of surveillance (Dandeker, 1990). Its further development in the eighteenth and nineteenth centuries was a product not only of an industrial/capitalist system which saw it as needed for the systematising, coordination, control and planning of work for efficiency and effectiveness – the most efficient way of generating work and profits. It was also an unintended by-product of the intellectual enlightenment project, which saw reason and analysis as the means to liberate humanity, but which increasingly was used to control not just nature, but humanity itself (Bottery, 2000). So whilst during the supposed golden period of professionalism, there was much professional autonomy, there was also an extensive structure in place to ensure a degree of coordination and planning. Trust here takes a much more calculating, inspectoral-based form. In Handy's (1978) terms, an Apollian (bureaucratic) form of organisation functioned alongside a Dionysian (individual) one.

STORY THREE – THE PATRIARCHAL PROFESSIONAL MODEL

Given the historical nature of nineteenth century schools in England, in particular the patriarchal, class-based and moral nature of leadership of private schools, and its transference to the developing public sector in the twentieth century, there was a third addition to this post-war educational culture – what Handy (1978) called the Zeus type: the individual leader, who attempted to keep a 'feel' and control on all the strands of events happening in the organisation. Whilst a particular emphasis on moral patriarchy may be particularly English, the existence of similar independent minded principals is seen in many other countries as well. In England, however, all three of these stories managed to live in some kind of stability for a couple of decades, though the Dionysian professionals asserted their subject expertise in the secondary classroom, whilst in the primary classroom the child-centred philosophy of the late 1960s (Plowden, 1967) provided them with the intellectual argument that only those closest to the child could know what was really needed. These Patriarchal headteachers managed the school boundaries and provided the overall ethos of their schools, as well as championing educational ideas which reflected their own temperament and intellectual predilections. Both the classteacher and the headteacher then worked within a bureaucratised system which laid down standard conditions for many aspects of administration, recruitment, pay, and promotion, but left large areas of the curriculum, teaching, learning and management to their own choice. Schools were bastions of the profession, and external ideas were normally selected by them for their coherence with existing values.

Yet each of these three models in their own different ways would be threatened. The welfare state model would be challenged by the problems of individualism in an era which increasingly saw the need for greater collegiality, as well as by perceived problems of abuse of individual autonomy. The bureaucratic model would be challenged by charges of inflexibility in increasingly changeable times. The patriarchal professional leadership model would be challenged by the state's desire for a more managerial dominance over class teachers' thought and actions, but wanted this less subject to the idiosyncrasies of the local Zeus headteacher.

Some of the causes of these changes – particularly economic globalisation – resulted in nation states increasingly finding themselves unable to firewall their economies, resulting in an increasing inability or unwillingness to sustain previous levels of welfare state expenditure. They were also increasingly persuaded that not only should financial responsibilities, if little more power, be devolved to more local levels, but that the way to generate greater efficiencies and better academic results was to create a more competitive atmosphere. Part of *that* strategy involved, as Hayek (1944) had argued many years previously, the empowerment of other stakeholder groups, particularly the clients, by providing them with greater choice. Finally, an increasingly international outlook by governments led to the espousal of international comparisons of school standards. Even if there is real doubt about their validity (see Torrance, 2006), these were increasingly used by governments of a variety of persuasions around the world to argue that schools were under-achieving, and required external intervention in both the structuring of schools, and in the practices and values of those working within them. The result was that whilst Dionysian welfare state professionals underwent a gradual but terminal decline in their power, and Zeus headteachers found themselves increasingly steered with more centrally-determined responsibilities, Apollonian bureaucracy would curiously and paradoxically find itself alive and invigorated as it achieved a new life within the fourth story of professionalism, the Managed Market professional model.

STORY FOUR – THE MANAGED MARKET PROFESSIONAL MODEL

If Social Democratic models had economic and moral arguments to their existence, the changes which politicians like Margaret Thatcher brought in had very different bases. The former had embraced Keynesian economic ideas of states investing in their institutions and industries, in order to create both the demand and the employment which would allow purchase of goods so produced; it had also embraced a moral basis of creating a national fellow-feeling of cooperation, interdependence, and social responsibility. The new state however embraced the ideas of reducing the money supply, competitiveness and the market, and of not supporting 'lame duck' enterprises, whilst the virtues of personal responsibility and independence came to the fore. The Welfare State was then to be re-created to possess many of the features of the private sector, educational organisations being modelled on the notion of the private firm, with professionals as responsive, efficient entrepreneurs, engaged in competition with rival 'firms'. All of this could only work if 'consumers' were given the information and the choice upon which to make decisions, and thus came into being inspections, continual testing of students, the publication of results by which consumers could evaluate these rival 'firms'. In addition to this was added a financial incentive for schools to do well by means of the money following the child. If 'a quality education' had previously been essentially a judgement by professionals of their own work, now quality resembled more the consumerist 'conformance to requirements' espoused by the American business writer Philip Crosby (1979), with autonomy ultimately dependent on client perception and wishes. When I conducted research in the 1990s (Bottery, 1998), interviewing individuals in state and private schools and hospitals, I found a gradual culture change in the state institutions, from a 'public' orientation to a private one. Individuals in the public sector still held dear the idea of working within a service which was wedded to the building of a 'better', more equitable nation, and found it hard to countenance that they had to seek and maintain a competitive advantage against the school or hospital down the road, which essentially meant not sharing good practice. Yet they and their leaders were aware of the potential consequences of not viewing other institutions in that way, and there was a gradual move from a cooperative to a competitive, from a national to an institutional, and from a public to a private frame of mind.

In an Aristotelian way, practice would then create values, for as Fergusson (1994, p. 113) argued, as teachers and headteachers were made to make these things part of their daily routines, "they come gradually to live and be imbued with the logic of the new roles, new tasks, new functions, and in the end to absorb partial redefinition of their professional selves, first inhabiting them, eventually becoming them." This is not, however, just a one-nation picture. The 1988 Education Act in England, for instance, was very closely followed by New Zealand's *Tomorrow's Schools,* the legislative similarities between the two settings leading Gordon and Whitty to conclude that there are few places "where reforms have proceeded with such similarity of pace, approach, rhetoric and policy patterns" (Gordon & Whitty, 1997, p. 454).

Only this is not a one-theme story, because at the heart of English legislation was the massive bureaucracy of a National Curriculum and its attendant testing. The end result was clearly not a full market solution, for this would have asked each firm/school to devise their own product/curriculum and sell it to their consumers/parents, in competition with other firms/schools, on the basis of which firms/schools would grow/go bankrupt. Each school in fact was also prescribed a large rigid curriculum, and a panoply of inspections and testings was used and publicised to supposedly enable parents to make more informed, more market driven choices. What occurred then was not a true market situation, but one in which there was tight central control of much policy, but responsibility for the implementation was devolved to management at the periphery. In business terminology, schools would be selling much the same product, but judged on how well they sold it. On this model, teachers they would then be 'empowered' in implementing these highly specified packages, and they and their schools would be judged on how well they achieved results on these packages.

The result for professionals was a paradoxical combination of both more control/direction of their work (largely through the bureaucratic/Apollonian model), yet at the same time the greater flexibility/fragmentation of work, largely because of the market model. Both of these conditions reduce the kind of trust that is extended to such workers. And this paradoxical combination of increased control and increased flexibility of public sector professionals remained the hallmark of both the later Thatcher and Major governments, through to Blair and Brown.

CURRENT EDUCATIONAL TRENDS IN ENGLAND

When New Labour came to power in 1998, many thought that there would be a radical change of direction; some even believed that the 'golden' days of the Welfare State Professional were about to return. Reality is inevitably more complicated, and in England at least, a number of agendas are currently in play.

Command and Control

Some writers (e.g. Jenkins, 2007) have argued that all that has happened has been a continuation of Thatcherite traditions of control. There is clearly some truth in this argument, as there is a considerable history of early strategy by Blair, Brown, and Mandelson focussing upon control of the Labour party, and on managing the media to a degree not seen in that political party before. Moreover, Hennessy's (2001) book on Prime Ministers devoted a chapter to Blair with the title *Command and Control*, and suggested that whilst the closest parallel to Blair's style was Margaret Thatcher's, he has been even more centralising and controlling. This has manifested itself in a number of ways, and two will be mentioned here. One has been a belief in the superiority of central over peripheral decision making (Jenkins, 2007). For Blair, on coming to power, this periphery largely comprised public sector workers whom he saw as problems rather than solutions, people who had to be steered and directed rather than trusted:

> You try getting change in the public sector and the public services. I bear the scars on my back after two years in government and heaven knows what it will be like after a bit longer. People in the public sector [are] more rooted in the concept that 'if it has always been done this way, it must always be done this way' than any group of people I have come across (quoted approvingly in Barber, 2007, p. 46).

Good policy has then largely been seen as policy decided by the centre and implemented with as little mediation as possible by the periphery. Such policy has been increasingly defined in terms of targets and outcomes, though the actual process has also received considerable attention through the Literacy and Numeracy hours in primary schools, the governmental advice for which not only stipulated what should be taught but how they should be taught, and for how long. A second way has been the continuation of an Apollonian/bureaucratic belief, strong threads of which can be traced back to Taylorian beliefs in the merits of the analysis of professional work, in order to produce a more focused, and more efficient workforce. In the process, that work which does not require 'professional' expertise is dissected out, and passed on to para-professionals. Professionals are then increasingly focussed on the strategies and technicalities of teaching/learning, and managing others in the implementation of these. The vision is well expressed by Michael Barber, former head of the Prime Minister's Delivery Unit:

> Improving children's performance in schools is a question of how well teachers teach in their classroom. The task of everyone else in a school system – school principals, local administrators, teacher trainers, government and other stakeholders – it to align everything they do to ensure that each teacher walks into every lesson with the skills, knowledge, equipment and motivation to teach a great lesson – and find in their classroom pupils who are ready to learn (Barber, 2007, pp. 1–2).

This kind of focussing achieves a number of goals. It is a more efficient and a more economic use of resources. It also goes a considerable way to addressing the well-publicised concerns of teacher work overload, poor work-life balance, and projected workforce shortages, which were the official prompts for such policy direction in the first place. However, it also facilitates the kind of remodelling and worker 're-agenting' (Hatcher, 2006) which change not only the nature of the worker but what they perceive as their key purposes, both of which are seen as essential for culture change. If then control has been a dominant first theme, there are other potentially contradictory themes that need attention.

An espousal of 'third-way' policies with a heavy economic emphasis

Whilst in practice these policies were not as intellectually challenging as some might argue (Giddens, 1998), they did nail to the mast a series of beliefs about the nature of society and education's role within it. These centred around the belief that society couldn't afford to support its citizens without their reciprocal contribution. Responsibilities and rights were thus two sides of a healthy society; this meant that whilst society would provide education for its citizens, individuals had to repay this by being active and contributory members. Yet this agenda was heavily dominated by economics, and in practice meant that individuals had to become contributors to a society engaged in global economic competition. Thus Tony Blair described how "governments had to meet the aspirations of global capital – or suffer a response that is likely to be prejudicial to economic growth" (quoted in Wickham-Jones, 1997, p. 257). Such acceptance meant that education had to be geared towards such competition. David Blunkett, Secretary of State for Education, would then also write a foreword to the UK government's Green Paper, *The Learning Age*, arguing that "(…) learning is the key to prosperity – for each of us as individuals, as well as for the nation as a whole. Investment in human capital will be the foundation of success in the knowledge-based global economy of the twenty-first century." Education and the economy were to be even more tightly bound together, as terms like 'intellectual capital' and 'knowledge society' suggested a shift in the kind of learning that was required.

A rather belated belief in this agenda (first expressed in a White Paper *Excellence and Enjoyment* in 2002, but an increasingly repeated phrase not only here, but worldwide in educational policies) has been that global economic competition needs a workforce that is creative and dynamic in its thinking, and therefore needs a teaching force that is similarly creative and dynamic, but also much more heavily focussed upon the critical functions of teaching and learning, and less upon other traditional activities. This increased reduction of focus of teachers' work then becomes a key factor in the implementation of an economic agenda which has dominated much of New Labour's thinking about education.

A belief in the superiority of private sector over public sector practice

Such remodelling has another function, for as Gunter & Butt argue, "remodelling could become the way in which public education is to be dismantled" (Gunter & Butt, 2007, p. 235). It is then part of a position heavily influenced by a literature suggesting that the state's involvement in education should be reduced because of its inability to achieve high results (Chubb & Moe, 1990), by a critique of public providers' size and inefficiency (Osborne & Gaebler, 1992), and by the assertion of the necessary movement of the nation state to a 'market state', whose function will be merely to facilitate and umpire market decisions (Bobbitt, 2003). Some commentators, like Cuban (2004), argue that public education internationally has constantly been 'set up' by policy makers appealing to it to solve complex social, political and economic issues, and then criticising it when it struggles to deliver on these. The result overall has been a very negative discourse on public sector education, providing policy makers in many countries with the reason or excuse to adopt a diverse and complex experimentation in state activities, largely through private sector involvement. Such experimentation has been confusing and opaque to the observer, with the government financing of private education through its academies' and Trust Schools programmes, the outsourcing of public sector work to the private sector, the widespread use of private sector consultancies, and the development of public-private partnerships. It has led writers like Ball (2007) to suggest that because so much is going on without a formal appraisal of outcomes, and so much is developing in unforeseen directions, that it is very difficult if not impossible to predict the eventual destinations. The academies and trust schools' programmes are worthy of particular comment here, being continuations of Conservative governmental policies of greater parental choice, and of the gradual development of semi-private schools. The business, religious or voluntary sector sponsors of such schools determine who they hire and fire, can suspend the national curriculum, and choose what these schools teach (including creationism) (for a sustained critique of this, see Beckett, 2007) – all using taxpayers' money. Whilst Gordon Brown is currently Prime Minister, his own thoughts on the subject (Brown, 2003) leave little doubt that he is similarly impressed by the private sector, seeing markets as *the* way of managing the public sector. A change of government is hardly likely to alter such preferences.

A belief in a strong social inclusion agenda.

Yet whilst New Labour has adopted many of the policies of the former Conservative governments, there are also strong elements of a social democratic welfare agenda which have not been discarded, even if they may have been given strange bedfellows. Thus, a belief in the need for a globally competitive work force has been joined to a belief in a "(…) a fairer and more inclusive society" (p.7) by the strategy of "ensuring that everyone has the skills they need to become more employable and adaptable" (Skills Strategy, 2003, p. 12). In this way can "the cycle of deprivation, underachievement and worklessness that is often perpetuated from generation to generation" be broken (ibid., p. 106).

Academies and Trust Schools, then need to be seen as rather more nuanced in their creation than simply being routes for the privatisation of the education system. Indeed, Barber (2007) argues that Blair's education strategy has been based upon ensuring that public sector provision is good enough to dissuade the middle-classes from sending their children to private schools, and to ensure that the children at schools in lower socio-economic areas are provided with the choice and quality of education that middle-class children receive. Academies, for instance, when first proposed by David Blunkett in 2000, the then Secretary of State for Education and Employment, were described by him as "a radical new approach to promote greater diversity and break the cycle of failing schools in inner cities" (quoted in Becket, 2007, p. 10.). This then requires an 'entrepreneurialism', but not necessarily a business entrepreneurialism – for as Woods et al. (2007) point out, there are also social, public and cultural entrepreneurialisms – and it is through the creation of such schools that these different entrepreneurialisms are to be encouraged.

Thus, it would be incorrect to view the Blairite agenda as simply a privatisation agenda. It would seem emphatically that it has not been intended as such. Indeed, even robust critics like Hatcher (2006) agree that there is no evidence that the plan is, or that in the future sponsors intend to run schools for profit: as he succinctly states "it is explicitly prohibited by government policy; it isn't profitable enough; and employers don't want it" (Hatcher, 2006, p. 608). Moreover, he suggests that there is also no evidence that sponsors of such schools have such an interest themselves: the businessmen (and it is men) who are sponsoring such schools are doing it for varied personal motives, many of them of an altruistic nature, of giving something back to society. What is clear however, is that whilst there seems no intent, and very little interest in privatising the education system, part of the reason for this, as Hatcher points out, is because business influence is very nicely accommodated by these current forms of school organisation: in essence, they have their concerns met out of public money. However it must be said that with such private/business involvement, if wide-scale privatisation were to be contemplated by another government, the New Labour reforms would certainly have provided the Trojan Horse for such movement.

However, given the avowed social purposes of such schooling, and particularly with respect to tackling cycles of underachievement, it is unsurprising to find a linkage with two major policy drives of the Blair years. A first is a concern for the development of 'joined-up thinking', in which those professions impacting on childrens' well-being (such as education, health and social work) increasingly mesh their work together, with the much greater focus on teaching and learning. A second, originally described as a solution to teacher overwork, is the legislation on workforce remodelling, in which analyses of educational work suggest that teachers did not need to do many of the tasks which traditionally they had done, and that these could be delegated to those lower in an organisational hierarchy – a strategy already well developed in the health service and other areas of the public sector. In effect, the professional educator becomes more involved in the management of para-professionals with respect to teaching and learning, and less concerned with the actual physical activity itself.

STORY FIVE: THE FOCUSSED WORKER

What does all this meant in terms of conceptions of the educational professional? It would be surprising if such a mix of policies did not produce a mixed, even paradoxical conception of the educational professional. A vision of the educational professional seems to be emerging, however, embodying the following characteristics:

– highly focused on the management and technicalities of teaching and learning;

- highly trained to be delivery oriented;
- hierarchically situated, interacting with educational workers above and below them in such functional delivery;
- integrated in such delivery with other hierarchically ordered workers from other professional areas like health and social work;
- working within workforces and organisations increasingly located within or integrated with those from the private sector;
- working on implementing highly centralised policies.

Such an array of characteristics could develop into quite new configurations of what it means to be an educational professional. Whilst there may be a fair number, I want to suggest two here, which whilst overlapping in some respects, are sufficiently dissimilar to be worth differentiating. I don't believe it is yet possible to judge which of these is likely to be dominant. However, given the right conditions, either seems possible.

- The *Focused Craftsperson*. This version takes the current context of many English schools as its starting point, where QTS (Qualified Teacher Status) is no longer a requirement for becoming a Headteacher, and where workforce remodelling increasing blurs the boundaries between 'professional educators' and 'para-professionals'. It sees the teacher as a deliverer of high quality curricula with expert knowledge on issues of pedagogy, the management of those lower in a school hierarchy, and with considerable inter-personal skills for working in an inter-professional context. Given the great increase in policies, paperwork and legislation, a culture of 'distributed leadership' will be necessary for pragmatic purposes. Such educators will work out the best ways of implementing centrally constructed policies with relevance to local context, and do so in coordination with other professional bodies. This will ensure that their students achieve the highest possible standards in terms of learning specified areas and targets, in order in the long term for these students, whatever their disadvantages, to enjoy the privileges of living in such a society, and also by being employable, able to contribute to its prosperity and global competitiveness.
- The *Branded Technician*. This version takes the same scenario as above – Principals with no teaching qualifications, professional boundaries increasingly blurred, but adds to this an increasingly privatised context. It assumes that an increasing number of schools will be partly – or fully -privatised, in part because of the intention of creating a real 'market' of individual products, in part because of an assumption that privatisation and the extensive use of business practices and organisations produce the best 'products'. Professionals in this context would work for a company which had as one of its portfolio of activities a range of schools, which promised a particular set of values and skills, and therefore promised to deliver a particular brand of education to its customers. Teachers on this scenario would have many of the qualities of the focussed teacher, in that they would be deliverers of high quality curricula to pupils, in the manner specified by government and the company, though they would be

less likely to be asked to commit themselves to inter-professional work, unless this was a central aspect of its brand image, or enhanced its reputation by improving its results. Certainly, the business and mission statements of some academy schools suggest this is already a reality.

There are certainly things to commend in these two models. Such teachers are dedicated, focussed on their pupils and their learning, probably using the very latest pedagogies and technologies, and actively and collaboratively engaging with others similarly concerned with children's welfare so that as few as possible are deprived of their possibilities, whatever their initial disadvantages in life. As many as possible of these individuals will then be given the opportunity to experience the pride that comes from making an active contribution to their society.

Yet there are things lacking from these scenarios. As argued in greater detail elsewhere (see Bottery, 2004), the educational professional of the 21st century will need:

– a fair degree of accountable autonomy: because they will have to work in increasingly non-standard situations, but will still need to provide an account of what they are doing;
– an appreciation of the irony and ambiguity of much educational work: because the conflicting demands of the various stakeholders in the educational endeavour renders the belief that any single voice should be implemented in a single-minded manner impossible;
– the development of foresight and an 'ecological' perspective on their profession's direction: because so many forces beyond education are, and will increasingly, be important in determining its purpose and direction;
– a championing of the public nature of educational work: because so many of these forces require not individual, but collective, even global, responses.

To do all of these, the educational professional will also need the courage to be critically engaged. How far do either of the models described above meet these requirements?

In terms of autonomy, there does seem to be some movement within the proposals for workforce remodelling for the kind of restricted autonomy normally granted to people who are acknowledged experts in their focused task, in this case in terms of teaching and learning, and in terms of the management of a team of para-professionals within the school, as well as in working within a larger inter-professional team. Yet currently it would seem that a quantitative form of target-driven accountability will be a driving feature of such work. Moreover, whilst there is also little doubt that there will be greater autonomy for the organisations within which such individuals work, this is unlikely in many cases to be matched by an individual professional autonomy. Any autonomy granted is more likely to be the autonomy of implementation delivery. Professional work is likely to remain tightly focussed and defined, there being little of the kind of autonomy that comes from mediating and translating policy advice into particular contexts, and even less an input into the nature and direction of the education system's aims and purposes. The teaching profession will in no sense be a partner in this endeavour, but a deliverer of policies made elsewhere. Its accountability and autonomy will be defined in those terms. Trust is now a function of how closely behaviour conforms to demands. As Vidovich said of the Australian situation, "teachers have become the objects of policy rather than active participants in the process" (Vidovich, 2007, p. 199).

Given the limited nature of the role, and the view of policy described above, the individual teacher and leader will experience even more ambiguity in educational decision making, and particularly as they will now work in an even more complex inter-professional situations, with even more varied views and values on what should be done. However, the inevitability of some value conflict is unlikely to be acknowledged from above, and is more likely to be seen as a local issue, to be resolved at local level, in the course of policy implementation. This does not bode well for the morale of professional educators, nor ultimately for the intelligent application of good policy.

What of the increasingly need for the foresight of an 'ecological' perspective, which takes as critical to its professional standing and development an understanding, not just of the role it is being assigned, but a critical engagement with the nature of the forces, local, national and global, that surround it as a profession, and its critical understanding of its subsequent role within an educational system? Again, and worryingly, little of this seems to be addressed by current initiatives and legislation. The message from government seems to be: these are not your concerns; we will decide the role of a teaching profession, and how it is best deployed. Your job is simply to become the best in the areas in which you are deployed. This is a highly restricted view of professional work, and should be seen as an affront to professional educators, as the nature of professionalism, I suggest, precisely involves such critical engagement with the issues surrounding and attempting to steer the nature of the work. Professionals either engage in this way, or they cease to be 'professionals' in any real sense of the word. The counter view to such restricted professionalism, however, is not that professionals know best (a hallmark of the previous social democratic model), but that the best solutions are usually made when all the interested parties are critically engaged in making contributions to defining and then solving a problem. This involves more than consultation, but participation as well; yet in reality neither seem to be high on any policy agenda.

Finally, if both of these two models only seem to address these issues in very limited ways, there is some difference between the two with respect to the promotion of the public good nature of education, though both are highly problematic. The Branded Technician model, through its embrace of the superiority of private sector models, has largely dispensed with this notion: public sector education will be almost extinct, and so will the notion of education as a public good. Its only evidence will be in the schools with sponsors who see this as a critical mission statement of their particular 'brand'. The Focussed Teacher model seems to be a slightly better promoter of this ideal, through its apparently continued embrace of the public nature of education. However, it is still heavily incapacitated by its focus upon the techniques of teaching, and is thus focussed away from larger issues of educational purposes. It is then in no position to fight for a public conception of education, nor to be influential in the future direction of the profession. Both will be intent on pulling their curricular and pedagogic carts, with no view of the road ahead. Neither has a moral vision of the purposes of education.

CONCLUSIONS

Both Margaret Thatcher and Tony Blair have seen public sector workers as resistant to change, not only with respect to education, but also with respect to new directions for the public sector generally, and have attempted to engineer to reduce their autonomy and redirect their focus. Yet I doubt that the disempowering of public sector professionals has been any more than a means to an end in Blair's vision of the development of a variety entrepreneurial forms, some from the private sector, to actually safeguard public sector activity. The remodelling of public sector professionals – educators in particular – has then been seen as a necessary but secondary element of this. The irony is that these policies with respect to public sector workers are highly likely to damage rather than safeguard public sector activity, as they prevent its professional workforces from defending it against a creeping privatisation agenda. There will be many, however, who will disagree with me here, and argue that such privatisation has been the agenda all along. Whichever is true, the danger is there.

Of course, such dangers are not exclusive to public sector educators in England. The belief that a globally competitive workforce is needed to meet global economic challenges, and that therefore education systems and their workforces need to be re-engineered to meet this challenge, is not exclusive to the UK. In this process, the influence of global institutions like the World Bank, the IMF, and the World Trade Organisation, which have had over the last three decades very similar neo-liberal global agendas, have been extremely influential, and have undoubtedly produced a similarity of direction. In addition, and as Brundrett et al. (2006) point out, when private firms like the Hay Group are invited by UK, New Zealand and Australian (Victorian) governments to introduce their own model for the development of leadership training, it is unsurprising if there are strong similarities between the approaches adopted.

Yet, it would be a mistake to assume inevitability, even uniformity in response, for whilst there have been general policy trends internationally, and an increase in policy borrowing, particularly in terms of the adoption of negative attitudes towards professionals, and of neo-liberal privatising policies, much is not inevitable. Take for instance the observations made by Ozga (2005) with respect to policies in England and its neighbour Scotland. She argues that whilst the same global/international trends affect both countries, the very different attitudes towards welfare policy, and a respect for education as a good in itself, and for the role of teachers in its exercise, all produce a distinctively less strident agenda than in England. This may also explain that whilst Codd (2005) suggests that teachers in

New Zealand are "managed professionals" as part of a description of the strong similarities between English and New Zealand policies, this may again be a matter of degree. Thrupp (2001), for instance, despite being someone frequently cited as arguing for such similarities, argues that

> (...) when the apparent similarity of English and New Zealand education policy is subjected to closer scrutiny, it is clear that (...) contextual factors have long resulted in distinctive policies despite the neo-liberal politics which have been common to both settings (...) (Thrupp, 2001, p. 2)

He discusses a number of reasons for this, most notably the differing class structures of the two countries, especially the status and class-conscious nature of English society, and the "post-colonial egalitarianism", and the different reactions these provoke, the relative lack of neo-conservative dimensions in New Zealand society as opposed to English society, the influence in New Zealand of Maori issues, totally lacking in England, and the effects of neo-liberal policies being introduced in England by a Conservative party, whilst in New Zealand by a Labour party, which subsequently tried to reclaim its more traditional soul (ibid., p. 12)

Similarly, with respect to different national approaches to educational leadership policies, whilst Bush and Jackson argue that "the content of educational leadership programmes has considerable similarity internationally", they go on to say that "(...) the striking feature is that nations and states have developed very different models to address their common need for high quality leadership in schools" (Bush & Jackson, 2002, p. 427). Much of this is explained by the different cultural, historical, political and personality backgrounds of different nations. What one finds is a complex melange of influences which produce different national reactions and mediations, influences which as Stephen Ball said (1998) continue to change in their relationships with each other. For those then who are inclined to despair at the inevitability of economic global juggernauts of educational change, this needs to be combated – partly because it is not as simple as that, but also because if accepted, may become a self-fulfilling prophecy. There is then very little in the policy arena which is not ultimately challengeable and reversible, because as Ozga (2005) argues, "travelling policies" are always to some extent mediated by those "embedded" in local contexts.

Are there ways, then, of combating or avoiding such outcomes? The acknowledgement that nothing is inevitable is an important insight here. The (false) beliefs by politicians that global neo-liberal free market competition is inevitable, and that they have no option but to shape education systems in line with this, are large contributors to the present shaping of the teaching professions in many advanced western countries. There *are* other issues on political agendas which can and still do shape education systems. Just because social democratic concerns with redressing issues of equity, justice, democratic citizenship, and the generating of a public good have taken or been given a back seat in some countries over the last few decades does not mean that these cannot be forefronted again.

Second, if neo-liberal thought views parents as consumers, educators do not need to do the same: pursuing an ecological vision as a core definition of professionality would entail viewing a major part of citizenship education as a continuing and life-long education in such ecology. This means educating not just pupils, but cooperating with parents and communities in understanding the nature of current challenges. In any political system where the vote counts, this is one way of changing the minds of policy makers.

Third, Ozga's (2005) work in Scotland suggests that the teaching profession, if it takes its role seriously enough, can be part of a genuine counter-thrust to such macro-movements. Where, however, it seems embroiled in inter-union disputes, and where it adopts a restricted view as to the limits of its functioning, then it may be cooperating in its own deprofessionalisation (Bottery & Wright, 2000). Where this happens, the teaching profession needs to take a long hard look at itself, for limited visions and internecine squabbles will affect society's perceptions of its competence, and the degree of trust with which it will be credited.

Fourth, whilst trust needs to be earned, it needs to be given as well. A dialogue between educators and policy makers needs to be one where both try to find common ground, for it is only by both parties engaging in this way that a benign cycle of trust is generated. Malign cycles happen when individual or group makes it clear they distrust the other – and this feeling is normally reciprocated, which usually provides the evidence to the first party for their original suspicions (Bottery, 2004). The more people are not trusted, the more they will become untrustworthy. It is essential for education and society at large to reverse this process – for both sides to build relationships based on trust and partnership rather than on distrust and suspicion of the other.

Finally, and with respect to leadership, there are many models on offer, many of them resembling the "designer leadership" which Gronn (2003) describes, going down roads of being trained in desired competencies. This seems radically insufficient. Leaders need to have and use internal moral compasses; they need to believe in and to exemplify trust, judgement and accountable autonomy. They need to recognise the different levels and ecology of educational work, the numerous parties justifiably expressing their views, and need to work towards a dialectical solution which brings and synthesises these views together. In sum they need to use this internal moral compass in a dialectic with interested parties. This it seems to me is the essence of real professional leadership.

NOTES

[1] This chapter is an amended version of a keynote address at the NZEALS International Educational Leadership conference held in Auckland, New Zealand, 30th April-3rd May, 2008

REFERENCES

Ball, S. (1998). Big policies, small world: An introduction to international perspectives in education policy. *Comparative Education, 34*(2), 119–130.

Ball, S. (2007). *Education plc: Understanding private sector participation in public sector education.* London: Routledge.

Barber, M. (2007). *Instruction to deliver.* London: Politicos.

Beckett, F. (2007). *The great city academy fraud.* London: Cassell.

Bobbitt, P. (2003). *The shield of Achilles: War, peace and the course of history.* New York: Knopf.

Bottery, M. (1998). *Professionals and policy.* London: Cassell.

Bottery, M., & Wright, N. (2000). *Teachers and the state.* London: Routledge.

Bottery, M. (2004). *The challenges of educational leadership.* London: Paul Chapman.

Brown, G. (2003). *A modern agenda for prosperity and social reform.* Speech at the Social Market Foundation, 3rd February.

Brundrett, M., Fitzgerald, T., & Sommerfeldt, D. (2006). The creation of national programmes of school leadership development in England and New Zealand: A comparative study. *International Studies in Educational Administration, 34*(1), 89–105.

Bush, T., & Jackson, D. (2002). Leadership studies in education: Towards a map of the field. *Educational Management and Administration, 30*(2), 417–430.

Carr Saunders, E. M., & Wilson, P. A. (1933). *The professions.* Oxford: Clarendon Press.

Chubb, J., & Moe, T. (1990). *Politics, markets, and American schools.* Washington, DC: Brooking Institution.

Cuban, L. (2004). *The blackboard and the bottom line.* Cambridge, MA: Harvard University Press.

Codd, J. (2005). Teachers as 'managed professionals' in the global education industry: The New Zealand experience. *Educational Review, 57*(2), 193–206.

Crosby, P. (1979). *Quality is free.* New York: Mentor Books.

Dandeker, C. (1990). *Surveillance, power and modernity.* New York: St. Martin's Press.

Department for Children, Schools and Families. (2003). *21st century skills strategy, realising our potential.* The Stationery Office.

Durkheim, E. (1957). *Professional ethics and civic morals.* London: RKP.

Etzioni, A. (1969). *The semi-professionals and their organisations.* New York: Macmillan.

Fergusson, R. (1994). Managerialism in education. In J. Clarke, A. Cochrane, & E. McLaughlin (Eds.), *Managing social policy* (pp. 93–114). London: Sage.

Fitzgerald, T. (2007). Remodelling schools and schooling, teachers and teaching: A New Zealand perspective. In G. Butt & H. Gunter (Eds.), *Modernizing schools: People, learning, and organizations* (pp. 163–175). London: Continuum.

Giddens, A. (1998). *The third way.* Cambridge: Polity Press.

Gordon, L., & Whitty, G. (1997). Giving the 'hidden hand' a helping hand? The rhetoric and reality of neo-liberal educational reform in England and New Zealand. *Comparative Education, 33*, 435–467.

Grace, G. (1989). Education: Commodity or public good? *British Journal of Educational Studies, 37*, 207–221.

Gronn, P. (2003). Leadership: Who needs it? *School Leadership and Management, 23*(3), 267–291.

Gunter, H., & Butt, H. (2007). Conclusion: Whither modernization. In G. Butt & H. Gunter (Eds.), *Modernizing schools: People, learning, and organizations* (pp. 217–236). London: Continuum.

Handy, C. (1978). *Gods of management.* London: Pan.

Hatcher, R. (2006). Privatization and sponsorship: The re-agenting of the school system in England. *Journal of Education Policy, 21*(5), 599–619.

Hayek, F. (1944). *The road to serfdom.* London: RKP.

Jenkins, S. (2007). *Thatcher and sons. A revolution in three acts.* London: Penguin Books.

Levin, B. (2001). *Reforming education.* London: Routledge Falmer.

Osborne, D., & Gaebler, T. (1992). *Reinventing government: How the entrepreneurial spirit is transforming the public sector, from schoolhouse to statehouse, city hall to the Pentagon.* Reading, MA: Addison-Wesley.

Ozga, J. (2005). Modernizing the education workforce: A perspective from Scotland. *Educational Review, 57*(2), 207–219.

Plowden Report. (1967). *Children and their primary schools*. London: HMSO.

Pollitt, C. (1992). *Managerialism and the public services* (2nd ed.). Oxford: Basil Blackwell.

Thrupp, M. (2001). School-level education policy under New Labour and New Zealand labour: A comparative update. *British Journal of Educational Studies, 49*(2), 186–213.

Torrance, H. (2006). Globalizing empiricism: What, if anything, can be learned from international comparisons of educational achievement? In H. Lauder, P. Brown, J. Dillabough, & A. H. Halsey (Eds.), *Education, globalization and social change* (pp. 824–834). Oxford: Oxford University Press.

Vidovich, L. (2007). Navigating 'global' modernization policies in education: Responses from Australia. In G. Butt & H. Gunter (Eds.), *Moderninizing schools: People, learning, and organizations* (pp. 189–202). London: Continuum.

Wickham-Jones, M. (1997). Social democracy and structural dependency: The British case. *Politics and Society, 25*(2), 257–265.

Woods, A., Woods, G., & Gunter, H. (2007). Academy schools and entrepreneurialism in education. *Journal of Education Policy, 22*(2), 237–259.

FURTHER READINGS

Beckett, F. (2007). *The great City Academy fraud*. London: Cassell.

Bottery, M. (2004). *The Challenges of Educational Leadership*. London: Paul Chapman.

Brown, G. (2003). *A modern agenda for prosperity and social reform*. Speech at the Social Market Foundation, 3rd February.

Hatcher, R. (2006). Privatization and sponsorship: The re-agenting of the school system in England. *Journal of Education Policy, 21*(5), 599–619.

Ozga, J. (2005). Modernizing the education workforce: A perspective from Scotland. *Educational Review, 57*(2), 207–219.

Thrupp, M. (2001). School-level Education policy under New Labour and New Zealand Labour: A comparative update. *British Journal of Educational Studies, 49*(2), 186–213.

Mike Bottery
Institute for Learning,
University of Hull, UK

GEERT KELCHTERMANS

MACROPOLITICS CAUGHT UP IN MICROPOLITICS

The Case of the Policy on Quality Control in Flanders (Belgium) [1]

INTRODUCTION

Most often educational policy measures are both reactive or responsive and creative in character. On the one hand they respond to particular questions, needs and demands that stem either from the educational system or from other institutions or groups in society. The responses, on the other hand, at the same time aim at putting in place the conditions that enable or at least stimulate particular educational practices. Whether and to what degree those measures will be effective can only be judged by looking at their actual implementation. Research on educational innovation (see e.g. Fullan & Stiegelbauer, 1991; Hargreaves et al., 1998; Hopkins, 2001; Coburn, 2001, 2006) has shown that this implementation encompasses far more complex and unpredictable processes than a straightforward execution of policy prescriptions. The same has been argued in policy studies (see e.g. Ball, 1994b; Troman, 1999; Jephcote & Davies, 2004).

This is even more applicable to the context of the Belgian (Flemish) education system, with its long tradition of constitutional 'freedom of education'. This legal cornerstone implies that school boards of private schools have far-reaching autonomy in matters of curriculum and pedagogy. A same has been argued in policy studies (see e.g. Ball, 1994b; Troman, 1999; Jephcote & Davies, 2004). As long as the schools meet the legally defined minimum goals (core curriculum), they are state-subsidised. In Flanders, almost 60% of all primary schools are Catholic schools, organised by private school boards. They receive full funding for staff wages and are subsidised for teaching materials, infrastructure, and so forth. Given these facts, it becomes obvious that 'private' schools are actually used by the government as a "functional public service", even without them formally belonging to the public school system (Verstegen, 2004, p. 70). This does have as a consequence, however, that all private schools are subject to the state policy on education. The policy on quality control, for example, also fully applies to those private schools. Yet, following the constitutional freedom of education, inspectors are not allowed to judge and comment on teaching methods and pedagogy (see below).

In this article we argue that policy measures during their implementation get caught up in processes of interpretation and translation towards the particularities of the local context (see also Ball, 1994b). The schools – as receivers of the measures – are not simply passive executors of external instructions, but interpret what is imposed on them (even legally) and this interpretation is guided by their

M. Simons, M. Olssen and M.A. Peters (eds.), Re-Reading Education Policies: A Handbook Studying the Policy Agenda of the 21st Century, 701–721.

own agenda of goals and interests. Since our analysis focuses on these processes of sense-making, we opted for the more fine-grained approach of the micropolitical perspective on schools as organisations (Ball, 1987, 1994a; Blase, 1991). We thus argue that this perspective still provides a powerful conceptual lens to reconstruct and analyse processes of policy implementation (see also Troman et al., 2006), even though broader macro approaches have become more dominant in studies on the 'gap' between policy development and implementation (see e.g. Ball, 1994b; Jephcote & Davies, 2004).

In this article we present the case of the policy on quality control in schools (Decree of 17 July 1991).[2] First we briefly summarise the procedures on quality control as they were installed by the 1991 Decree, explaining the major differences with the situation before. Next we present the micropolitical perspective as we applied it in our analysis. Third, we provide the methodological information about the data collection and analysis. We then extensively discuss the results of our interpretative analysis and end with concluding comments.

QUALITY CONTROL IN PRIMARY SCHOOLS

As in other European countries, the issue of quality management and control has taken a very central position in the educational policy of the Flemish government, who – after the federalisation of the Belgian state (revision of the Constitution in 1989) – received (almost) full and exclusive authority in educational matters. The Decree on Inspectorate and Educational Consultants (17 July 1991) was a milestone in the policy on educational quality. On the one hand the Decree changed the organisation and modus operandi of the inspectorate, and on the other hand it installed a new professional body, the educational consultants (*pedagogisch begeleiders*). Instead of individual inspectors evaluating individual teachers through unannounced visits in the classroom, the re-organised inspectorate makes audits of the entire school. Schools are informed that such an external audit is planned on beforehand and need to engage in (self-) evaluation procedures in order to prepare for the external audit. A team of inspectors then visits the school for a week, using the internal evaluation outcomes as a starting point, checking its findings and complementing them if necessary. This is done through a systematic audit procedure, in which the legally defined minimum goals (*eindtermen/ ontwikkelingsdoelen*) operate as guiding criteria (Flanders has no system of national curriculum nor national exams or forms of high-stakes testing yet). The key task of the inspectorate thus can be defined as evaluating whether the state investment in schools is used effectively to provide quality education for all students. The audit eventually results in a report for the entire school, which contains the inspectorate's final judgement about the educational quality.[3]

Complementary to this quality control, but strictly separated from it, the body of educational consultants was created to support schools in their efforts to maintain or improve the quality of their education. Their task thus is to guide, support and help sustain educational quality in school, but they are in no way allowed to evaluate or control teachers or schools. Control and support of educational quality are thus supposed to be two separate tasks, to be taken care of by two separate bodies of professionals. This strict division between assessment and support was assumed to provide the best warranty for successful and effective improvement of the educational quality.

Through this Decree the Flemish government (and ultimately the Flemish Parliament) thus legally established the bodies (inspectorate and educational consultants) as well as the procedures to create the conditions for both controlling (evaluating) and supporting (improving) educational quality. These policy measures have a very clear and straightforward rationale and therefore an almost self-evidently accepted legitimacy: it is the government's duty – as a representative of society – to control whether the means (tax money) invested in schools do result in high quality education (as a public good). Because of this convergence of clear rationale, self-evident legitimacy and its legally binding nature, one would expect this measure to be very effective in its steering of practices in schools. Although the impact of this policy on schools is undeniable, we will argue below that the actual implementation practices are still more complex and surprising than one would have expected given the rationale and legitimacy of the measures. Even this strong type of steering policy measures does not operate as straightforwardly in its implementation as one would expect.

The research interest guiding our analysis thus was to describe and explain how schools actually deal with inspectorate and educational consultants, as instances of the policy on educational quality. As such, the analysis is a case study of policy implementation, with a central focus on the local processes of interpretation and translation that determine the actual impact of educational policy on practices in schools.

CONCEPTUAL FRAMEWORK

Although the analysis presented in this article focuses on the micropolitics of policy implementation (see below), we will start by briefly elaborating the more general theoretical principles that guided our approach.

Theoretical principles

The research interest already suggests that we focus on the meaningful interactions between the school and teachers on the one hand, and the external services for educational quality on the other. From this *interpretative and interactionist* point of view, we assume that the character and the degree of the changes in the school will have to be explained from the interplay between certain characteristics of the external services as well as characteristics of the client system – that is, the school and the teachers (see below).

We also take a *contextualised* stance. The way schools and teachers deal with the external quality services is to an important degree determined by specific, local conditions (e.g. the actual composition of the school staff; the student population;

the relation between the school and the local community, and so on). Local educational needs, but also the goals and beliefs of the school staff, affect the way the external services are dealt with. For that reason, our analysis of the determinants was first of all embedded in the local context. Only in a second step did the analysis move to more decontextualised, general conclusions.

Closely connected to this is the *constructivist principle*. The way teachers and schools deal with the external services is also dependent on the meaning these services get in the eyes of the people involved. From their perception of the external services, the staff members construct a reaction that is meaningful to them. In our approach, we thus give a central role to processes of sense-making by the local actors in order to develop an adequate understanding and valid explanation of their implementation practices.

These general theoretical principles were 'operationalised' through a series of educational concepts (stemming from our own and others' former research), constituting the *conceptual framework* that guided both the collection and the analysis of the data. The conceptual framework on the one hand thus contained a set of indicators on the characteristics of the educational quality services (the 'provider system') – for example, form, content, availability of follow up, procedure, duration of the interventions, and so on. On the other hand, we looked at the characteristics of the client system (both the individual teachers and the meso-level of the school [organisational working conditions]). This framework of sensitising concepts was used to construct procedures for data collection and analysis (see below). An overview of the sensitising concepts is as follows:

- at the level of the individual teachers:
  - o teachers' and principal's professional self-understanding (= representations of oneself as a teacher/principal) and their subjective educational theory (= personal system of knowledge and beliefs on teaching and schooling) (Kelchtermans, 1993, 1996, 2007).
- at the level of the school organisation:
  - o the leadership by the principal (see e.g. Blase & Anderson, 1995);
  - o school culture (Schein, 1985; Staessens, 1993; Hargreaves, 1994);
  - o collegial relations and collaboration (Little, 1990; Clement & Vandenberghe, 2000; Achinstein, 2002; Kelchtermans, 2006);
  - o organisational changes in the school's working conditions (Smylie, 1994).

The micropolitical perspective

The micropolitical perspective constituted the analytical lens in our study. This perspective "embraces those strategies by which individuals and groups in organisational contexts seek to use their resources of power and influence to further their interests" (Hoyle, 1982, p. 88). The micropolitical perspective was developed partly as a critique on the systems models of organisations which over-emphasised the structural elements in an organisation as well as their goal consensus, rational efficiency and effectiveness in processes of decision-making and problem solving (Ball, 1987, 1994a; Blase, 1991). Especially in schools, where the core processes of the organisation intrinsically reflect value-laden choices, the risk for differences in opinion or conflicts is higher. Therefore the conflicts and the attempts to proactively influence the situation by the organisation members cannot but be very central in any analysis of organisational processes (like policy implementation) (see also Malen, 1994; Altrichter & Salzgeber, 2000; Achinstein, 2002). "In essence, political theorists have argued that rational and systems models of organisations have failed to account for complexity, instability, and conflict in organisational settings. They contend that such models also ignore individual differences, for example, in values, ideologies, choices, goals, interests, expertise, history, motivation, and interpretation – factors central to the micropolitical perspective" (Blase, 1991, p. 3). Ball (1994a, p. 3822) stresses the same point: "Micropolitics is about relationships rather than structures, knowledge rather than information, skills rather than positions, verbal interaction rather than minutes and memos." Understanding the processes of influence, control and power thus implies a focus beyond the formal, structural characteristics of the school as an organisation (for example, formal leadership positions), by looking at the actual processes of sense-making.

A central assumption in the micropolitical perspective is that the behaviour of organisation members is to be understood as largely driven by interests (Ball, 1987, 1994a; Blase, 1991, 1997, 1998; Malen, 1994; Blase & Anderson, 1995, Altrichter & Salzgeber, 2000; Kelchtermans & Ballet, 2002). In line with our constructivist and interactionist stance, we conceive of those interests in terms of *desired working conditions*. Teachers and principals have – partly individual, partly shared – opinions about what working conditions are desirable or necessary to do a good job. 'Good' then means effective (in terms of pupils' academic achievement) as well as personally satisfying for both teachers and principal. These desired working conditions constitute professional interests for the teachers and principals. Micropolitical actions, then, are those interventions through which teachers and principals will strive to *establish those desirable working conditions, to safeguard them in case they are threatened, or to restore them when they have got lost* (see also Kelchtermans & Ballet, 2002).

RESEARCH DESIGN AND METHODOLOGY

Overview of the research project

This article draws on a series of studies on the implementation and effectiveness of the policy on educational quality control that was carried out between 1995 and 2002 at the Centre for Educational Innovation and Policy (Katholieke Universiteit Leuven). Although the scope of the studies was broader (see Table 1), we will limit our discussion in this article to the issue of policy implementation and the micropolitical processes that determine them.

Table 1. Overview of the studies

Main study on effectiveness of inspectorate, educational consultants and INSET in primary schools	Phase 1: 4 schools (= 4 case studies; prospective and retrospective)
	- questionnaires (principals + teachers) (n = 92)
	- interviews teachers (n = 88) and principals (n = 4)
(Kelchtermans & Vandenberghe, 1998; Kelchtermans et al., 2000):	- observations before and after audit
	- document analysis (e.g. audit report; educational project of the school; minutes of staff meetings)
- Phase 1 + Phase 2a: (Vandenberghe et al., 1997)	Phase 2a (retrospective): 9 schools (= 9 case studies):
	- 47 questionnaires (teachers and principals)
	- 44 interviews (teachers and principals)
- Phase 2b: (Devis, 1998)	Phase 2b (retrospective): 3 schools (= 3 cases):
	- 18 interviews (teachers, remedial teacher, principal)
	- 18 questionnaires (teachers, remedial teacher, principal)
Follow-up: Quality control by the inspectorate in primary schools (Geerts, 2002)	3 schools (= 3 retrospective case studies):
	- 14 questionnaires (teachers, remedial teacher, principal)
	- 14 interviews (teachers, remedial teacher, principal)
Follow-up: Quality control by the inspectorate in secondary schools (Daniëls & Kemps, 2001)	4 schools (= 4 retrospective case studies):
	- 24 questionnaires (teachers, head teacher, head subject department or vice-head teacher)
	- 24 interviews (teachers, head teacher, head subject department or vice-head teacher)
	- document analysis: audit reports

The extensive *main study* (Vandenberghe et al., 1997; Devis, 1998; Kelchtermans & Vandenberghe, 1998; Kelchtermans et al., 2000) was followed by two studies addressing the development of the policy impact on quality over time, one on primary schools and one on secondary schools (see Daniëls & Kemps, 2001; Daniëls et al., 2002; Geerts, 2002). Though there were minor differences in the specific procedures of data collection, all studies used the same conceptual framework, guiding both data collection and analysis. The findings presented in this article were developed in the main study and critically evaluated and modified in the follow-up studies. Most illustrative quotes therefore stem from the main study.

The main study

Because of the central place of sense-making processes in our study, we opted for a qualitative-interpretative approach and more in particular for the methodology of *case studies* (i.e. Merriam, 1988; Yin, 1989; Denzin & Lincoln, 1994; Miles & Huberman, 1994). Yin (1989, p. 20) argues that this research methodology is particularly relevant when "a 'how' or 'why' question is being asked about a contemporary set of events over which the investigator has little or no control." Case studies make it possible to ground the research in the experiences of the school members. By opting for a 'multiple case design', in which different case studies are developed from the same conceptual framework, a comparative analysis became possible that allowed for the identification of certain scenarios, processes or patterns, whose relevance goes beyond the specific local situation of the case.

The study encompassed *two research phases*, in each of which – although in different ways – case studies were developed in Flemish primary schools. Common to both phases was the collecting of data from different respondents in the same school, in order to develop an in-depth and contextualised understanding of the interplay between the external services on the one hand and teachers and principals on the other.

In the *first phase* we developed extensive case studies of four Flemish primary schools. The research period started just before the audit by the inspectorate, continued immediately after the audit and also included a follow-up about six months later. This design made it possible to collect data almost parallel in time with the audit, as well as to follow up the developments in the school in order to explore the possible long-term effects of the audit. Data were collected through *document analysis* (i.e. information brochures about the school; the school's educational project; minutes of staff meetings; and the final audit report), questionnaires, observations and interviews. The written *questionnaires* were aimed at getting formal information about the respondent, his/her career and position and perception of the audit process. The *interview* built on and elaborated the findings of the questionnaires. Specific guidelines were developed for interviews with the principal and the teachers about their experiences with the inspectors and the educational consultants. The interviews explored teachers' and principals' expectations towards the audit, as well as the eventual effects of the audit or of the collaboration with the consultants. In the four schools 92 interviews were collected.

The interviews were transcribed, coded and interpretatively analysed at the level of the individual respondent. In a next step, these data from the respondents of the same school were integrated with the other data (observations, document analysis) at school level. This resulted in an extensive case report per school (guided by the principle of developing 'thick descriptions'), structured by a fixed set of paragraphs, that organised and presented the data of each school level in the same format. In a final step these case-study reports at school level were submitted to a 'horizontal analysis', in which the cases were systematically compared for similarities and differences between schools (cross-site analysis; Miles & Huberman, 1994). The findings from Phase 1 provided working hypotheses that were further explored in a larger number of schools in Phase 2 (and later on in the follow-up studies).

In Phase 2, 12 primary schools were involved, that had been audited by the inspectorate about two years before the study. In this second phase we wanted to focus more on the possible long-term effects of the external services. For this purpose we adapted the procedure for data collection as used in Phase 1 so as to achieve a rich data set, but in a less time-consuming way. The data collection encompassed a questionnaire, a structured interview and observations. Respondents (principal and teachers) first filled out the questionnaire, which operated afterwards as a starting point for the structured interview in which the answers of the respondents to the questionnaire were explored in more detail. The data analysis in Phase 2 followed the same principles as in Phase 1. Data were first analysed at the level of the individual respondent, and then, in a second step, at the school level. Data from questionnaires and interviews were transcribed and coded, then submitted to interpretative analysis resulting in a summarising, pre-structured document (as in Phase 1). The case reports of the schools were then comparatively analysed.

In the follow-up studies we used the same conceptual framework and a slightly modified methodology (i.e. more exclusive emphasis on interview data) as in the main study. In the rest of this article we limit ourselves to a presentation of the outcomes from the micropolitical analysis.

CATEGORIES OF PROFESSIONAL INTERESTS

In the analysis of the data, five different *categories of professional interests* were identified. We called them: material, organisational, social-professional, cultural-ideological and self interests. Below we discuss and illustrate the categories in more detail. These categories were later also found in studies on the socialisation of beginning teachers (see, for example, Kelchtermans & Ballet, 2002, 2003) and on the merger processes in schools (Kelchtermans et al., 2003).

Micropolitics from material interests

Teachers and principals have a rather clear idea about the material, financial and infrastructural facilities that need to be available for proper job performance (for example, copier facilities; funding for extra-mural activities or the purchase of specific learning materials; a staff room for informal contacts between colleagues or desk facilities to prepare lesson plans, mark pupils' assignments, and so on). As such these working conditions operate as material interests. We include in this category also time (in the sense of 'organisationally available time'): time for meeting and planning between teachers or time to participate in in-service training during school hours (see also below: social-professional interests). Hargreaves has studied the micropolitical use of 'time' in schools. He found that the distribution of school time between teachers, classes and subjects reflected the dominant power relations between subject departments. He further observed that planning time, as a facility for teachers to meet during school time in order to work on the imple-mentation of an educational reform, operated in diverse ways, according to the micropolitical agendas of the teachers involved and often contrary to the rationale from which the time had been made available (Hargreaves, 1990, 1992, 1994).

The effectiveness of the educational consultants was found to be closely related to time. Because of the large number of schools they are supposed to support, and because of the wide range of duties they have in central administration (representation in diverse official committees; membership of task forces working on the development of curricula or teaching materials), the time they can actually be present and working in schools is limited. Often their interventions in school took the form of one-shot meetings, without any follow-up and therefore with very little impact on the school's functioning.

The audit procedure includes an explicit and critical analysis of the material and infrastructural conditions in the school. This was used by some school teams intentionally to optimise particular material conditions. In one school, for example, all nursery teachers agreed to use any opportunity during the inspectors' visit in the school to complain about the limited number of small toilets for their pupils. By doing so they hoped the inspectors would include in their report a recommendation to invest in an expansion of these toilets. The nursery teachers had been complaining about this for years to their school board, but without any success. Priority had been given to investing in more computers to be used in the fifth and sixth grades of the primary school. Therefore the nursery teachers had put all their hope on the authority of the inspectors' report to find their need taken seriously. Getting the extra toilets thus became the object of purposeful micropolitical action, using the inspectors' visit for their own agenda.

Yet, the toilets issue was not only a material interest, but also reflected a clear educational concern. The nursery teachers were frustrated about the amount of time that was lost in providing toilet visits with their young pupils (aged between 2.5 and 5 years). The waiting and queuing time during that endeavour was lost for educationally valuable activities, they argued. Finally, the issue had even become a cultural and symbolic matter: the repeated neglect or turning down of the nursery teachers' request by the school board was interpreted as an indication of the lack of recognition and acknowledgement of nursery education and therefore of the nursery teachers. The struggle to get the extra toilets thus became a public claim for recognition of their work and their professionalism.

This *symbolic meaning* of material working conditions was also observed in the eagerness with which several schools took up recommendations in the audit report on infrastructure (sports infrastructure, furniture or learning materials). This can of course be partly explained by the fact that these recommendations are rather unequivocal and relatively easy to deal with (assuming, of course, that the necessary funding is available). Because of the latter, school boards often tend to quickly deal with the material recommendations, as a way to show their 'good will' to take up the recommendations and thus appeal to the inspectorate's mildness and patience in their coping with the more difficult recommendations (such as, for example, improving collegial collaboration; using a differentiated pedagogy to meet the differences in educational needs of the pupils; and so on).

Micropolitics from organisational interests

Apart from a number of legal prescriptions, schools have a large autonomy in matters of internal organisation and structure. Yet, in the ongoing negotiation and decision-making processes different interests from different school members may interfere, conflict or converge. Organisational interests, then, have to do with procedures, roles, positions, contract conditions and formal task descriptions.

In School B1, one of the teachers had hoped for an explicit and positive appraisal of her work by the inspectors as a positive element in her application for getting tenure. She feared the competition from a younger colleague in this strive for tenure. This teacher expressed deep disappointment about the audit report that focused on the entire school, without mentioning any appraisal of individual teachers' work. Thus her technical and critical comments on the inspectorate and the audit procedure in fact can only be properly understood against the background of her own individual (micropolitical) agenda (getting a tenure contract). The example also illustrates how this individual agenda determines both the teacher's perception and evaluation of the quality control procedure and ultimately her willingness to accept and take up the inspectors' recommendations for improvement.

Organisational interests are also at stake in (beginning) teachers' suspicion and lack of trust in an educational consultant whose advice was asked by and given to the principal in decisions about extending their contracts. Although their job definition does not allow them to, consultants sometimes provided this 'service' to 'buy off' their entrance to the school. Letting themselves get involved in the principal's human resources policy, however, had as a downside for the consultants the loss of teachers' trust in their impartiality. Teachers then were less willing to engage themselves in efforts for change and improvement, initiated and supported by the consultant.

A both more dramatic and more complex example could be observed in School B7, where the principal – who had been heavily criticised by his teachers in their interviews with the inspectors – kept his honour and sent in his resignation. One of the team members afterwards got appointed as the new principal, but for him it was very difficult to gain authority among his former colleagues. The audit report, however, provided the opportunity to rearrange the allocation of the teachers to the different grades and to replace the teacher of the first grade by a colleague more competent in working with young children. The report was thus used as an external argument for and justification of unpopular decisions by a principal who – in spite of his formal hierarchical position – had not yet sufficiently established his authority as a leader.

Another illustration of organisational interests at play was observed in School B6, where the inspector was asked by the principal to come and present the (very critical) report to the team. The team members experienced the public presentation of the report by the inspector as humiliating and as a denial of their professionalism, and reacted very angry to the inspector. So he took the blame and the criticism, but the principal – who actually agreed with the report – did not have to state his opinion in public, thus maintaining a more positive relation with his team as well as a more serene basis for developing improvement actions to deal with the reports' recommendations.

Organisational interests are also at stake in the work of the educational consultants. In secondary schools, for example, one distinguishes between, on the one hand, 'subject-consultants', who support teachers from a particular subject department in a school (and only them), and on the other, 'school-consultants', whose work aims at initiating and supporting processes of more overall school development. This strict distinction in their job definition often creates 'conflicts of territory' between the different consultants working in the same school, since they all want to safeguard the specificity of their job (and by doing so also the justification for their position and professional identity). This organisational interest of the consultants thus gets into conflict with the school's complex needs for support and therefore does not exactly add to the recognition and appreciation of the educational consultants' professionalism by the school staff.

Micropolitics from social-professional interests

The character and the quality of the professional relations among members of a school team constitute a very important category of professional interests (see e.g. Smylie & Brownlee-Conyers, 1992; Clement & Vandenberghe, 2000; Kelchtermans, 2006). Good professional and personal relationships with the colleagues, with whom one has to work every day, rank highly among the desirable working conditions of teachers. And the same applies to the relationship with principals, parents and external institutions. These relationships constitute valuable sources of social recognition, job satisfaction and motivation. Teachers, but also principals (especially in primary schools), appear to be very sensitive to this matter. Because relationships are so important, they also become micropolitically very relevant. Several micropolitical strategies, like gossip, smearing and particular forms of humour, explicitly address these relationships or the mutual perception of organisation members.

We already mentioned the fact that principals use inspectors or consultants in order to strengthen their own authority. In schools with 'weak' principals, we found that the principal was often more inclined to subscribe to the evaluation by the inspectors than the teachers were. In School B3, for example, the audit had a strong positive effect (in the short term) on the social climate and the relations among the school team. The reason for this, however, was the arrogant and authoritarian attitude of one of the inspectors during the audit. This caused so much anger and frustration among the staff that they were strongly motivated to make sure that in the follow-up audit a positive assessment would be achieved. Thus, here operated a mechanism of 'all against one', which positively affected the professional relationships and – eventually – the development of the school.

Also in other cases it was found that the inspectors' attitude during the audit strongly influenced the teachers' willingness to use the audit as a starting point for improvement. Inspectors who take an authoritarian attitude make teachers feel like they are not taken seriously professionally and this in the end triggers reactions of resistance and rejection towards the audit. The opposite also holds: a humane, yet still critical attitude by the inspectors results in fewer feelings of stress and uncertainty among the staff and thus contributes to a more positive, accepting attitude towards the report and an increased willingness to use it as a start for further improvement.

Since the internal support structure in schools and teachers' participation in in-service training are also part of the whole quality policy, our case studies also include data on these issues. The micropolitical role of social-professional interests also became apparent in the way staff members deal with opportunities for in-service training (INSET). In the decision to participate in in-service training, we found that not only personal or professional interest in the subject were relevant, but that also other interests were calculated in a kind of 'cost-benefit-balance'. Three types of costs were found to play a part: time costs, social-professional costs and social application costs.

If the in-service training takes place after school hours, participation is paid for in terms of leisure time. In-service training during school hours does not cost leisure time, but can bring with it important 'social-professional costs'. Especially for smaller primary schools, it is not easy to find substitutes for the participants in the INSET. This most often means that either the principal or other colleagues have to take on an extra burden (taking over the class of the absent colleague), in order to allow for the others to participate in the INSET. If duties of supervising the playground or school bus already weigh heavily on the staff, this extra cost may become too high and make teachers decide to give up the INSET. The risk of their participation in the INSET being paid off with conflicts or irritations with colleagues is too high a price. We labelled a final type of 'cost' 'social application costs'. If the participants fear that colleagues will negatively react to their application of what they learned in the INSET in their own classroom practice, this 'cost' may take away their motivation to either participate at all or to implement new insights or practices in the classroom (leaving the INSET ultimately with hardly any real effect on practice).

Micropolitics from cultural-ideological interests

'Cultural-ideological interests' refer to the set of (more or less explicit) values and goals one aims for as an individual and the norms that guide life and work in the school as an organisation (school culture). These types of interests thus have to do with the issue of the more or less collectively shared idea about what 'good education' is. As such they constitute the norm for the staff members' professional actions in the school. These cultural norms – or more precisely, this normative culture – is on the one hand the result of negotiation processes in the past (e.g. habits, 'sensitive topics', implicit rules and procedures, and so on). In order to be effective, however, these normative ideas need on the other hand to be constantly confirmed or modified in the complex social processes of sense-making in day-to-day life in schools. This sense-making among staff members operates at the same time as a negotiation process through which particular norms, values and goals achieve the status of priorities or legitimate and binding elements of the school culture. In essence the cultural-ideological interests therefore concern the 'definition of the organisation', the process through which it becomes clear what kind of school one wants it to be and how this normative idea is to be put into practice (see also the example earlier of the school board that preferred to invest in more computer facilities for the fifth and sixth grade, rather than increasing the number of toilets for kindergarten pupils).

Because of their value-laden character, measures aiming at the improvement of 'educational quality' in the school inevitably run into this category of interests: to what extent are the normative ideas on 'quality education' by the government compatible with the organisational culture and the individual teachers' ideas on good education and how is that to be achieved?

Linked to this, we observed that the audit procedure by the inspectorate also operates as a form of 'hidden curriculum'. The audit procedure not only 'controls' but at the same time also communicates particular ideas and norms about good education and how they are to be achieved. Because in the audit procedure, the inspectors systematically explore the issues of collegial collaboration, the use of different teaching methods, the initiatives for supporting pupils with special needs, and so on, they clearly convey the message that all these issues are part of what the government considers to be important in school education. As such the audit procedure simultaneously both informs and sets a norm. However, this norm is not self-evidently accepted by all staff members. Principals very often indicated that to them the message from the audit was revealing and clarifying: 'at least I know what the government expects from a good school'. Depending on the situation of the school, the autonomy and professionalism of the leadership and staff, this 'hidden curriculum' had different effects. Some schools would strive to fit as neatly as possible with the expectations (compliance), whereas others would develop a more sharp awareness that their normative beliefs diverge from what seems to be the norm and that they thus will need to provide an explicit and carefully grounded justification for the choices in their educational practice. This will then rather lead to resistance, protest, discussion and a questioning of the audit results.

A clear example of cultural-ideological interests can be found in School A3, where the visit by the inspectorate gave rise to a (renewed) discussion about certain options in the educational project of the school. School A3 traditionally put a strong focus on cognitive goals and academic achievement. Yet, a minority of the staff didn't wholeheartedly share this traditional emphasis and argued for a broader set of goals, including also pupils' socio-emotional development, creativity and more artistic goals. Those teachers (a minority in the team) felt supported by the 'hidden curriculum' in the audit procedure that clearly subscribes to the idea of 'development of the entire person of each pupil'. And so they re-opened the discussion about the educational project of the school (after the audit was over). They thus hoped to use the audit report as a powerful argument to modify the school's policy and priorities. The majority in the school team (including the principal), however, did 'read' the conclusions of the audit report differently. Their conclusion was that they had apparently failed to convincingly account for and communicate to the inspectors the value of their 'cognitive emphasis' in education. Since to them the problem was only a matter of effective communication, all that had to be done was making the school's options more explicit. The internal discussion – in which the school board also got involved – finally ended with a rewriting of the school's educational project (and the brochure for the parents in which it was presented) in the sense that the cognitive option was more extensively presented and accounted for. The 'traditionalist' faction within the school had won this struggle over the 'definition of the school' and formalised its victory in the document on the educational project.

Another illustration was seen in the confrontation between an educational consultant and one school. The very directive approach (including very restrictive processes of follow-up) by the consultant made the staff stand aloof. The staff members repeated time and again that they themselves wanted and would determine whether and to what extent they would participate in and implement the consultant's 'programme'. So, although the consultant's professional expertise in the matter was not disputed, the latent threat of losing autonomy seems sufficient for some teachers to react with aloofness. The norm 'we decide as a team what we want to do and how, and nobody else should come and tell us what to do' operated as a kind of regulative and normative idea. Eventually this means that interventions of the educational consultants hardly had any effect and that the entire staff persisted in a collective attitude of resistance and refusal.

Questioning the legitimacy and validity of the audit procedure is another illustration of the category of cultural-ideological interests. Teachers or principals then complain that the procedure does too little justice to the particularities of the school's situation or its specific educational project. If the audit by the inspectorate really wants to operate as a powerful impetus for quality-improving changes in the school's organisation or in the teaching and learning processes (as was the purpose of the Decree), then it is of crucial importance that the audit procedure (and its final report) are acknowledged by the school staff as a valid and reliable evaluation of the school's efforts and achievements. Schools must recognise themselves in the image that they see mirrored in the report (including the value choices that they make in their practices). If this is not the case, there is little chance that staff will be willing to take up the recommendations in the report. More probably schools will engage in 'window dressing', superficial and formal modifications (e.g. purely administrative or infrastructural changes) without real impact in the classroom practice, without real professional development of the teachers or school development.

Micropolitics from self-interests

The normative ideas about 'good education' and 'good teaching'/'good leadership' within the staff of a school are partly collectively shared, but in some ways also idiosyncratic. Teaching as a profession is only to a limited extent a technical issue of putting into practice the appropriate pedagogical strategies and tools to achieve good classroom management and effective learning outcomes. Apart from that, the person of the teacher and the particular quality of the educational relationship with the pupils are as important for good education as the technical knowledge and skills (see e.g. Ball & Goodson, 1985; Nias, 1989; Kelchtermans, 1993, 1996, 2007). As Nias (1989, pp. 202–203) has put it, 'the teacher as a person is held by many within the profession and outside it to be at the centre of not only the classroom but also the educational process. By implication, therefore, it matters to teachers themselves, as well as to their pupils, who and what they are. Their self-image is more important to them as practitioners than is the case in occupations where the person can easily be separated from the craft'.

Individual teachers thus have a more or less clear idea about what matters to them personally in teaching and what kind of teacher they want to be. This consti-tutes their sense of professional identity or their 'professional self-understanding', as we have argued elsewhere (Kelchtermans, 1993, 1996, 2007). This self-under-standing results from the experiences teachers have during their career, although some core elements often date back as far as the teacher's own years as a pupil. In the self-understanding, we have argued, one can distinguish several, intertwined components. There is not only a descriptive *self-image* but also the personal normative idea of what one has to do in order to be a proper teacher (*task perception*) as well as one's evaluative and emotional judgement about the extent to which one is successful (*self-esteem*). Further, one's motives to choose teaching as a career (*job motivation*) as well as one's expectations about the future (*future perspective*) are components of that self-understanding. If policy measures (stemming from either outside or inside the school) constitute a threat to this self-understanding, this will lead to micropolitical action, because the teacher will try to safeguard his/her task perception or self-esteem.

In other words, safeguarding and possibly restoring the self-image, the self-esteem, one's task perception, job motivation and future perspective are important to teachers and principals in the context of quality policy (like the inspectors' visit or the work with the educational consultant). As such they constitute interests concerning their professional 'selves', *self interests* (not to be confused with 'selfish interests').

Self interests are at stake, for example, when there is a tension between the individual teacher's task perception and the dominant normative ideas in the staff (see above). Also, if teachers in their contacts with the inspectors feel humiliated or not properly recognised as competent professionals, they often experience a strong need to restore their self-esteem. From that experience their refusal to accept or acknowledge the results of the audit becomes understandable.

We already mentioned the example of the principal resigning after the negative audit report was presented (School B7). In School B2 the audit also had a very negative impact on the principal's self-esteem, because he had hoped for an explicit appreciation of his work. In School B3 the self-esteem of several team members had been negatively affected by the arrogant attitude of one inspector during the interview. Restoring that self-esteem became a central concern for those teachers. From that negative experience they found it very hard to accept the conclusions of the report and feared to have to live through a similar experience again when the inspectors would do their follow-up audit. Elsewhere we have already explained the moral and political roots of these self-doubts and how strongly they affected teachers' actions and development (Kelchtermans, 1996, 2007). The same conclusions can be drawn in the context of external quality services.

The persistent expectation by many teachers of receiving individual feedback from the inspectors (who are formally no longer entitled to provide it!) as well as suggestions for improvement of their classroom practice, can also be understood in terms of self interests. The desire to get individual feedback hides a request for social and explicit recognition and appreciation: 'Am I (still/already) doing well as a teacher/principal?' Especially after visits of the inspectors in their classrooms, teachers really want to get some kind of (preferably positive) evaluative comments. If the inspectors do not provide any feedback or comment (as is – strictly speaking – prescribed by their job definition), this may contribute to teachers' feelings of uncertainty, self-doubt and powerlessness (see also Kelchtermans, 1996, 2007; Van den Berg, 2002). This illustrates how a general policy measure aiming at improving educational quality (i.e. the strict separation of control and support of educational quality), may result in increased stress and self-doubts for individual teachers. Because, if educational quality becomes such a public issue, it can hardly come as a surprise that the people who are the first ones to provide it show more intense concerns about their professional practice. Thus it is self-evident to see a growing need for acknowledgement and positive feedback, in a job that is fundamentally characterised by complexity, uncertainty and therefore a sense of vulnerability (see Kelchtermans, 1996, 2007).

The analysis of teachers' and principals' experience of and dealing with the quality policy shows that the existence and interventions of the external quality services provoke particular micropolitical processes that to a large extent determine the actual impact of those interventions and eventually the policy measures. The micropolitical 'reading' of the quality services through the lens of one's professional interests implies that teachers and principals interpretatively filter the interventions. Their interests and concerns (agenda) often reach beyond, and are more complex and pressing than, the striving for more educational quality. Our micropolitical analysis thus confirms the fact that the effect and impact of external quality services ultimately depends on the specific processes of meaningful interaction between the characteristics of the external quality services and the perceptions, interests and goals of school staff in the particular context of that school (contextualisation). "The internal dynamics of organisational life are often energised by external interventions (…) but the implementation of such changes is mediated by the established culture and history of the institution and existent patterns of influence and control" (Ball, 1994a, p. 3823).

As such, in policy implementation there is *always happening at the same time both more and less than was envisaged*. 'Less' happens because the measures turn out to be always somewhat less effective in terms of the goals they were supposed to achieve. However, 'more' also happens, because the implementation of the policy triggers unintended and unanticipated effects (dynamics and processes in the schools), that may be both positive and negative in terms of the policy makers' goals. Marshall and Anderson, reviewing the influence of the social studies approach in the study of educational policy, argue that this approach provoked a shift in the relationship between the macro-policy arena and its local or 'street-level' impact. "Traditional models have viewed the policy filtering process as flawed but capable of being rationalised through better implementation models. Cultural studies suggest that micropolitics at the local level involve complex forms of cultural and political resistance, accommodation, and compliance rooted in the informed intentionality of social actors" (Marshall & Anderson, 1994, pp. 173–174). Our study clearly illustrates this claim.

DISCUSSION

With the Decree on Inspectorate and Educational Consultants (1991), the Flemish government put in practice two professional bodies with complementary tasks in the evaluation and improvement of educational quality. Although the policy rationale was very clear and its legitimacy not disputed, our analysis of the actual implementation reveals that the Decree has had different and more complex consequences than had been envisaged by the policy makers.

The analysis from a micropolitical perspective shows that the achievement of the policy goals gets caught up in the processes of sense-making and translation to the local context of the school. In this interpretive process the professional interests (conceived of as desirable working conditions) of the people involved play a central role. This 'getting caught up', however, does not necessarily mean that the actual implementation of policy measures is *per se* counter-productive. It does mean, though, that the interaction between policy measures, on the one hand, and the practices of schools and teachers when implementing them, on the other, is a complex issue that unfolds in non-evident and unpredictable ways.

Implementing policy measures is thus not to be reduced to the execution of technical prescriptions. One important reason for this is the intrinsic value-laden character of decisions in educational policy. Every measure inevitably reflects a particular idea about good education and how this is best to be implemented. And this normative position can and will be disputed, since there is no self-evident consensus about educational goals and how they are to be achieved (see e.g. Hargreaves, 1994).

Second, teachers and principals who take themselves seriously as professionals will evaluate and interpret policy measures in terms of their own professional normative system. Their idea about what constitutes good education and what conditions are needed to achieve it will largely determine whether and to what extent they will comply with the measures or, on the contrary, react with aloofness or even resistance.

Closely linked to this is a third reason. The staff members of a school most often do not constitute a monolithic block of like-minded individuals. It is more likely that (groups of) staff members differ in their opinion about good education and more particularly about the way this is to be achieved and therefore the issue of good education – at least implicitly or to some degree – constitutes an ongoing debate in schools. In order to develop a good, effective and stimulating local policy, school leaders have to create opportunities in which these differences in opinion can be made explicit and discussed. Among other things, this is important in order to avoid conflicting cultural-ideological and social-professional interests inhibiting or negatively influencing the teachers' work.

Our study has shown the value of the micropolitical perspective in disentangling and understanding the processes of interpretation in schools that influence the actual enactment of policy measures (i.e. the policy on external quality control). In our approach we emphasised the actors' agency and sense-making as a social construction. It would be interesting, however, to expand the micropolitical reading of policy implementation practices and link it with the role of policy discourses in these processes of interpretation (see e.g. Jephcote & Davies, 2004). For example, the performativity discourse, that has become very dominant in education policy and practice, is clearly both constitutive for and reflected in the policy measures on educational quality (see e.g. Blake et al., 2000; Sachs, 2001; Jeffrey, 2002; Ball, 2003). However, a combination of both perspectives is beyond the scope of this article.

For central policy makers an important conclusion from our study is that they ought to be both sufficiently ambitious and sufficiently modest in their efforts to steer actual practices in the school system. Because the government remains responsible for providing good education for all citizens, she ought to cherish her ambition to achieve this goal as completely as possible through different forms of steering. Yet, at the same time she cannot but be modest, based on the knowledge that policy measures (especially in as value-laden a field as education) will always be interpreted by the local actors and that this interpretation ultimately will determine the policy implementation. Furthermore, the latter is a condition implied in the idea of teachers and principals as the 'professionals' who make education work. So, in the end the government cannot but trust the commitment and competencies of the actors in the schools, since ultimately, it is the staff in schools that will determine how education is actually shaped and established through the relationship they develop with the pupils, for whom they are responsible. And also in this relationship, there is always both more and less happening than policy makers (are able to) plan and imagine.

NOTES

[1] This chapter has been published earlier as: Kelchtermans, G. (2007). Macropolitics caught up in micropolitics. The case of the policy on quality control in Flanders. *Journal of Education Policy, 22,* 471-491. Reprinted with the much appreciated permission of the publisher.

[2] More information on the Flemish educational system and the role of the inspectorate can be found on http://www.ond.vlaanderen.be

[3] This judgement can take three forms: positive, conditionally positive, or negative. 'Positive' means that the school can carry on as an accredited institute for six years (until the next audit). 'Conditionally positive' implies that a limited number of flaws have been identified. Schools are advised to remedy them and will be visited by the inspectors again within about a year. In the – very rare – case of a 'negative' evaluation the school has to engage in an urgent and drastic improvement plan or it may lose both its accreditation and its funding by the government.

REFERENCES

Achinstein, B. (2002). Conflict amid community: The micropolitics of teacher collaboration. *Teachers College Record, 104*, 421–455.

Altrichter, H., & Salzgeber, S. (2000). Some elements of a micro-political theory of school development. In H. Altrichter & J. Elliott (Eds.), *Images of educational change* (pp. 99–110). Buckingham and Philadelphia: Open University Press.

Ball, S. (1987). *The micropolitics of the school: Towards a theory of school organization.* London: Methuen.

Ball, S. (1994a). Micropolitics of schools. In T. Husén & T. N. Postlethwaite (Eds.), *The international encyclopaedia of education* (2nd ed., Vol. 7, pp. 3821–3826). Oxford: Pergamon.

Ball, S. (1994b). *Education reform. A critical and post-structural approach.* Buckingham: Open University Press.

Ball, S. (2003). The teacher's soul and the terrors of performativity. *Journal of Education Policy, 18*(2), 215–228.

Ball, S., & Goodson, I. (Eds.). (1985). *Teachers' lives and careers.* London and Philadelphia: Falmer Press.

Blake, N., Smeyers, P., Smith, R., & Standish, P. (2000). *Education in an age of nihilism.* London and New York: RoutledgeFalmer.

Blase, J. (Ed.). (1991). *The politics of life in schools. Power, conflict, and cooperation.* Newbury Park, CA, London and New Delhi: Sage.

Blase, J. (1997). The micropolitics of teaching. In B. J. Biddle, et al. (Eds.), *International handbook of teachers and teaching* (pp. 939–970). Dordrecht: Kluwer Academic Publishers.

Blase, J. (1998). The micropolitics of educational change. In A. Hargreaves, A. Lieberman, M. Fullan, & D. Hopkins (Eds.), *International handbook of educational change* (pp. 544–557). Dordrecht: Kluwer Academic Publishers.

Blase, J., & Anderson, G. (1995). *The micropolitics of educational leadership. From control to empowerment.* New York: Teachers College Press.

Clement, M., & Vandenberghe, R. (2000). Teachers' professional development: A solitary or collegial (ad)venture? *Teaching and Teacher Education, 16*, 81–101.

Coburn, C. E. (2001). Collective sense making about reading: How teachers mediate reading policy in their professional communities. *Education Evaluation and Policy Analysis, 23*(2), 145–170.

Coburn, C. (2006). Framing the problem of reading instruction: Using frame analysis to uncover the microprocesses of policy implementation. *American Educational Research Journal, 43*, 343–379.

Daniëls, K., Kelchtermans, G., Vandenberghe, R., & Kemps, T. (2002). De doorluchtigheid van de doorlichting. Kanttekeningen bij een decennium Decreet op inspectie en pedagogische begeleiding [Commenting on the first decade of implementing the Decree on Inspectorate and Educational Consultants]. *Impuls voor Onderwijsbegeleiding, 33*(1), 21–25.

Daniëls, K., & Kemps, T. (2001). *Schooldoorlichting in het Vlaams Secundair Onderwijs. Een kwalitatief onderzoek naar de bijdrage van doorlichting tot schoolontwikkeling* [The audit by the inspectorate in secondary education] (Leuven, K.U.Leuven—Centrum voor Onderwijsbeleid en—vernieuwing).

Denzin, N. K., & Lincoln, Y. (Eds.). (1994). *Handbook of qualitative research.* Thousand Oaks, CA: Sage.

Devis, I. (1998). *Analyse en effecten van doorlichting, begeleiding en nascholing in Vlaamse basisscholen [Effectiveness of policy on educational quality: inspectorate and educational consultants in primary schools]* (Leuven, K.U.Leuven—Centrum voor Onderwijsbeleid en—vernieuwing).

Fullan, M., & Stiegelbauer, S. (1991). *The new meaning of educational change.* New York: Teachers College Press.

Geerts, K. (2002). *De effectiviteit van het beleid inzake kwaliteitszorg: De doorlichting door de inspectie in het basisonderwijs [The effectiveness of the policy on educational quality: the audit by the inspectorate in primary education]* (Leuven, K.U.Leuven—Centrum voor Onderwijsbeleid en—vernieuwing).

Hargreaves, A. (1990). Teachers' work and the politics of time and space. *International Journal of Qualitative Studies in Education, 3*, 303–320.

Hargreaves, A. (1992). Time and teachers' work: An analysis of the intensification thesis. *Teachers College Record, 94*(1), 87–108.

Hargreaves, A. (1994). *Changing teachers, changing times. Teachers' work and culture in the postmodern age.* London: Cassell.

Hargreaves, A., Lieberman, A., Fullan, M., & Hopkins, D. (Eds.). (1998). *International handbook of educational change.* Dordrecht: Kluwer Academic Publishers.

Hopkins, D. (2001). *School improvement for real.* London and New York: RoutledgeFalmer.

Hoyle, E. (1982). Micropolitics of educational organizations. *Educational Management and Administration, 10*(2), 87–98.

Jeffrey, B. (2002). Performativity and primary teacher relations. *Journal of Education Policy, 17*(5), 431–546.

Jephcote, M., & Davies, B. (2004). Recontextualizing discourse: An exploration of the workings of the meso level. *Journal of Education Policy, 19*(5), 547–564.

Kelchtermans, G. (1993). Getting the story, understanding the lives. From career stories to teachers' professional development. *Teaching and Teacher Education, 9*(5/6), 443–456.

Kelchtermans, G. (1996). Teacher vulnerability. Understanding its moral and political roots. *Cambridge Journal of Education, 26*(3), 307–323.

Kelchtermans, G. (2006). Teacher collaboration and collegiality as workplace conditions. A review. *Zeitschrift für Pädagogik, 52*(2), 220–237.

Kelchtermans, G. (2007). Teachers' self-understanding in times of performativity. In L. F. Deretchin & C. J. Craig (Eds.), *International research on the impact of accountability systems. Teacher education yearbook XV* (pp. 13–30). Lanham, MD: Rowman & Littlefield Education.

Kelchtermans, G., & Ballet, K. (2002). The micropolitics of teacher induction. A narrative-biographical study on teacher socialisation. *Teaching and Teacher Education, 18*(1), 105–120.

Kelchtermans, G., & Ballet, K. (2003). Micropolitical literacy: Reconstructing a neglected dimension in teacher development. *International Journal of Educational Research, 37*, 755–767.

Kelchtermans, G., Janssen, V., & Vandenberghe, R. (2003). *Structuurverandering of schoolontwikkel-ing? Over schaalvergroting in basisscholen* [Structural change or school development? On the merger of primary schools]. Deurne: Wolters Plantyn.

Kelchtermans, G., & Vandenberghe, R. (1998). *Internal use of external control and support for quality improvement.* Paper presented at the annual meeting of the American Educational Research Association, San Diego. ERIC ED 425 495/EA 029271.

Kelchtermans, G., Vandenberghe, R., & Devis, I. (2000). De effectiviteit van inspectie, pedago-gische begeleiding en nascholing [The effectiveness of inspectorate, educational consultants and in-service training]. *Tijdschrift voor Onderwijsrecht en Beleid, 1999–2000*(3), 153–168.

Little, J. W. (1990). The persistence of privacy: Autonomy and initiative in teachers' professional relations. *Teachers College Record, 91*(4), 509–536.

Malen, B. (1994). The micropolitics of education: Mapping the multiple dimensions of power relations in school politics. *Journal of Educational Research, 9*(5/6), 147–167.

Marshall, C., & Anderson, G. L. (1994). Rethinking the public and private spheres: Feminist and cultural studies perspectives on the politics of education. *Journal of Education Policy, 9*(5/6), 169–182.

Merriam, S. (1998). *Qualitative research and case study applications in education.* San Francisco: Jossey-Bass.

Miles, M., & Huberman, M. (1994). *Qualitative data analysis. An extended sourcebook.* Thousand Oaks, CA: Sage.

Nias, J. (1989). *Primary teachers talking. A study of teaching as work.* London and New York: Routledge.

Sachs, J. (2001). Teacher professional identity: Competing discourses, competing outcomes. *Journal of Educational Policy, 16*(2), 149–161.

Schein, E. H. (1985). *Organizational culture and leadership: A dynamic view.* San Francisco: Jossey-Bass.

Smylie, M. (1994). Redesigning teachers' work: Connections to the classroom. In L. Darling-Hammond (Ed.), *Review of research in education* (Vol. 20, pp. 129–177). Washington, DC: American Educational Research Association.

Smylie, M., & Brownlee-Conyers, J. (1992). Teacher leaders and their principals: Exploring the devel-opment of new working relationships. *Educational Administration Quarterly, 28*(2), 150–184.

Staessens, K. (1993). Identification and description of professional culture in schools. *International Journal of Qualitative Studies in Education, 6*(2), 111–128.

Troman, G. (1999). Researching primary teachers' work: Examining theory, policy and practice through interactionist ethnography. In M. Hammersley (Ed.), *Researching school experience* (pp. 33–50). London and New York: Falmer.

Troman, G., Jeffrey, B., & Beach, D. (2006). *Researching education policy: Ethnographic experiences*. London: Tufnell Press.

Van den Berg, R. (2002). Teachers' meanings regarding educational practice. *Review of Educational Research, 72*(4), 577–625.

Vandenberghe, R., & Van der Vegt, R. (1992). *Scholen in de vernieuwingsarena [Schools in the reform arena*. Leuven-Apeldoorn: Garant.

Vandenberghe, R., Kelchtermans, G., Brion, A., & Vanhoudt, J. (1997). *Evaluatie van het beleid inzake kwaliteitszorg. Analyse en effecten van begeleiding, nascholing en inspectie [Evaluation of the policy on educational quality]*. Research report OBPWO project 95.08, Centrum voor Onderwijsbeleid en—vernieuwing, K.U.Leuven.

Verstegen, R. (2004). Recht als context en als instrument voor onderwijsbeleid [Law as context and instrument for education policy]. In G. Kelchtermans (Ed.), *De stuurbaarheid van onderwijs. Tussen kunnen en willen, mogen en moeten* (pp. 57–88). Leuven: Universitaire Pers Leuven.

Yin, R. (1989). *Case study research. Design and methods*. Beverly Hills and London: Sage.

FURTHER READINGS

Achinstein, B. (2002). *Community, diversity, and conflict among schoolteachers. The ties that blind*. New York and London: Teachers College Press.

Ballet, K., & Kelchtermans, G. (2008). Workload and willingness to change. Disentangling the experience of intensified working conditions. *Journal of Curriculum Studies, 40*, 47–67.

Blase, J., & Anderson, G. (1995). *The micropolitics of educational leadership. From control to empowerment*. New York: Teachers College Press.

Coburn, C. (2006). Framing the problem of reading instruction: Using frame analysis to uncover the microprocesses of policy implementation. *American Educational Research Journal, 43*, 343–379.

Hopkins, D. (2001). *School improvement for real*. London and New York: Routledge-Falmer.

Kelchtermans, G. (2007). Professional commitment beyond contract. Teachers' self-understanding, vulnerability and reflection. In J. Butcher & L. McDonald (Eds.), *Making a difference: Challenges for teachers, teaching, and teacher education* (pp. 35–53). Rotterdam: Sense Publishers.

Geert Kelchtermans
Center for Educational Policy and Innovation
K.U.Leuven, Belgium

JAMES G. LADWIG & JENNIFER M. GORE

RE-READING THE STANDARDS AGENDA

An Australian Case Study

INTRODUCTION

Welcome to the NSW Institute of Teachers.
The Institute was established to support quality teaching in all NSW schools.
Its charter is to advance the status and standing of the teaching profession.
The Institute works to support the career-long development of teachers and to
assure both the profession and the community of the quality of teacher
education programs.[1]

The above text is taken from the home web page of the New South Wales Institute of Teachers, established in 2004 by an Act of the New South Wales State parliament. At once declaring its intent and its scope, this introduction reveals the aspirations and differential judgement of those who believe, or would have others believe, that the NSW Institute of Teachers (hereafter the Institute) in this one state of Australia can deliver what it promises. With respect to teachers, the Institute hopes to advance the status and standing of an ostensible profession and to support quality teaching practice. With respect to teacher education, the Institute seeks to assure 'the profession' and 'community' of quality. In this one brief declaration, the recent territorial expansion of disciplinary institutional practices related to teaching in New South Wales is evident. New South Wales is, of course, not alone in such developments.

A global trend, supposedly oriented at increasing the quality and accountability of teachers and manifest in standards for the accreditation of teachers and teacher education institutions, has at its base a mis-recognition of what constitutes quality, how quality can and should be measured, and what forms of accountability can be linked with gains for students, their teachers, or society more broadly. Many calls for standards, like those above, are made in the name of increasing professionalism with the experiences and practices of other 'professions' frequently cited as points of comparison but with minimal recognition of some of the fundamental ways in which teaching differs. In this chapter, drawing on events in New South Wales, we expose flaws in the underlying rationality of the standards agenda, point out some of its contradictions, and outline issues that need to be taken into account if the agenda is to have any educational benefit. The issues addressed range across structural, procedural and, most importantly, substantive matters.

M. Simons, M. Olssen and M.A. Peters (eds.), *Re-Reading Education Policies: A Handbook Studying the Policy Agenda of the 21ˢᵗ Century, 722–734.*
© 2009 Sense Publishers. All rights reserved.

We argue that, on the one hand, the techniques of surveillance and compliance involved in the processes associated with these kinds of standards clearly employ the same techniques of power identified in Foucauldian analyses of governmentality (Dean, 1999; Popkewitz, 1991; Popkewitz, 1998; Rose, 1998). In this light, there is little question that the new teacher institutions function to internalise specific power relations and practices within the bodies of teachers. On the other hand, the institutionalisation of professional standards for teachers relies on mechanisms of credentialing. In this light, it is clear that the now-international push for developing teacher standards is an example of the dynamics of expanding states as identified in analyses of world-cultural institutions (Meyer, Ramirez & Soysal, 1992). Taken together, one predictable outcome of these new institutions of teacher professionalism will be to have little effect on improving teaching, despite self-reports of the credentialed. While the bluster and flurry of publicly broadcasted moves designed to promote teaching may well continue the myth of educational progress, there is good reason to believe that the way standards have been institutionalised will do little to advance the educational experiences of students.

While this general argument is not a particularly new conclusion on the work of teacher institutes and the advancement of technologies behind standards for teacher credentialing, the NSW case does offer an opportunity to explain how there can be such a clear disjunction between the claims made for the Institute's standards and the reality of their institutionalisation. Hence, after providing a brief context for these developments in Australia, we provide a more detailed description of what is involved in the credentialing offered by the NSW Institute of Teachers as a means of showing how its claims to support quality teaching are really little more than wishful optimism. While it may eventuate that the teachers in NSW do use the Institute mechanisms to improve teaching, that possibility is by no means made more probable in the Institute's expansion of technologies of the self (Foucault, 1988). That is, for example, while it is clear that the Institute's requirement for new teachers to demonstrate that they meet the Institute's standards will require forms of surveillance and self-subjection, it is not clear that these technologies will necessarily result in actions that might be called an improvement in teaching.

To be fair, we should note that, even within Australia, developments in New South Wales are not particularly unique. Very similar standards to those adopted by the NSW Institute of Teachers have been adopted in six of the eight states and territory jurisdictions, and many sets are virtually identical to the others. Thus we are not overstating the ubiquity of the Australian turn to credentialing teachers beyond initial tertiary institution training. The simple fact that this turn has occurred is evidence of a vertical expansion of credentialing for the teaching profession, expansion for longer periods of time throughout the course of a career, as the standards are designed for teachers with different amounts of experience and levels of accomplishment.

This pattern of expansion simply fits that identified by the earliest analyses of credentialing and the concomitant de-coupling of the credential from that which it is supposed to represent. Collins (1979) identified credentialing as an explanation of educational expansion, where the cultural markets of schooling pursued educational credentials, leading to credential inflation, irrespective of whether or not the credential actually meant more was learned. This logic has been elaborated by Labaree (1999, 2006) who more starkly questions the learning signified by educational credentials.

The de-coupling that we suggest is evident in the development of teacher standards will be clearer with reference to how de-coupling was first identified and explained. In their seminal papers on education as an institution, John Meyer and Brian Rowan highlighted the need to recognise the ritual and ceremonial basis of much of what educational institutions do (Meyer, 1997; Meyer and Rowan, 1977). In their specific discussion of de-coupling, Meyer and Rowan (1997) noted that organisations would attempt to maintain close alignment between structures and activities but that this reliance could go too far, revealing inefficiency and inconsistencies that would challenge the legitimacy of the organisation itself. From this point, Meyer and Rowan postulated:

> Because attempts to control and coordinate activities in institutionalised organisations lead to conflicts and loss of legitimacy, elements of structure are decoupled from activities and from each other (p. 357).

And in blunt note, they followed:

> The advantages of decoupling are clear. The assumption that formal structures are really working is buffered from the inconsistencies and anomalies involved in technical activities. Also, because integration is avoided disputes and conflicts are minimised, and an organisation can mobilise support from a broader range of external constituents (p.357).

Written more than three decades ago, with volumes of other accounts of schooling and teaching documenting what would readily be recognised by teachers as a fundamental modus operandi of schooling (Mayer, Luke and Luke, 2008), whereby structures and activities do not align, it is somewhat surprising to see the fervour with which Australian teacher institutes are pronouncing the hopes of standards. Below, we will illustrate just how accurate Meyer and Rowan's (1977) postulation was.

TEACHER PROFESSIONALISATION AND THE EMERGENCE OF THE INSTITUTE

As with many reforms in the Australian context, the development of the NSW Institute of Teachers followed from a government review of, *inter alia*, 'the quality of teachers and teaching'. The terms of reference also included 'the implications of technology for pedagogy', 'behaviour management in schools and classrooms,' and 'the practicum and the professional experience of teachers' as issues to be addressed by the Review.

These reviews are essentially committees charged with the task of gathering some evidence about the state of whatever the government puts into the review's 'terms of reference' and then making recommendations to the government about how to fix whatever problems the review finds (which often, not surprisingly, match the presumptions behind the review in the first place). This particular

Review was chaired by a well known (within Australia) and senior educator, Gregor Ramsey, and its report has thus become known within NSW as 'The Ramsey Review' (Ramsey, 2000). While review committees conduct their own research, public consultation is a major mode of gathering information for such reviews. This one was no exception with over 100 organisations making (written) submissions and around 80 organisations and individuals offering direct consultations, plus a similar number of individual submissions.

The centrepiece of the Review's recommendations turned to the then-internationally popular option: establishing a professional institute for teachers. The first of seventeen recommendations heralded this conclusion, recommending:

> That the New South Wales Government establish an Institute of Teachers whose primary purpose is to enhance the level of professionalism of teachers and teaching. The Institute [is] to be responsible for:

> the establishment and promulgation of performance standards at designated stages of development as a teacher, together with standards of ethical practice for teachers (...) [there were nine other sub-points to recommendation One] (Ramsey, 2000, p. 147).

Here we find the simple turn from enhancing professionalism to linking standards with their institutionalisation in NSW. That is, we see a local version of the now internationally ubiquitous idea that putting words on paper and establishing bureaucratic mechanisms to deliver the meaning of those words will yield improvements. Remembering that the Institute and standards emerged from a review of the 'quality of teachers and teaching', a critical question is by what mechanisms will such promulgation of standards to improve the quality of teachers or teaching? The predictable first move of the Ramsey Review, given the international and political context, was to establish an Institute and teaching standards. But what connection to quality do the standards have?

The NSW Professional Teaching Standards are split into four 'stages' – sequenced under the presumption that years of tenure are linked to increased levels of 'professionalism.' The NSW Institute Standards run in four stages: from 1) graduate teacher, 2) professional competence, 3) professional accomplishment, to 4) professional leadership. The Ramsey Review had recommended three stages, but the eventual form of the standards added the first 'graduate teacher' level. So it is that teachers in NSW who entered the profession after the development and institutionalisation of the standards, known as 'new-scheme' teachers, have been busily documenting evidence to show that they are competent. It is interesting to note that existing teachers were deemed to meet the standards at the level of 'professional competence' and are exempted from mandatory accreditation processes. This 'grandfather clause' in the implementation of the standards was clearly a political move to smooth acceptance of the standards by existing teachers and their Unions.

Since these standards are to be applied by all employers of teachers, the procedures for meeting the standards vary according to who pays the teachers' wages. To give a sense of the possible scale of the task involved in accrediting teachers in NSW, consider that the largest single employer of teachers in the State is the public system, which employs approximately 100,000 teachers, about half of whom are 'permanent teachers.' In 2006 (the most recent year for which there is a public report of these matters), some 677 teachers were accredited at the 'Professional Competence' level of the Institute's Professional Teaching Standards and another 2,198 so-called 'new-scheme' teachers were trained in how to gain accreditation.[2] To date, the Institute has not formalised processes for meeting any of the upper stages of the standards, but clearly many new-scheme teachers have already done what was needed to be deemed competent at the first level beyond graduation from a teacher education program.

Becoming accredited as meeting the standards of professional competence, once employed, essentially involves three processes: 1) generating and documenting evidence of meeting the standards (written evidence compiled by the applicant under the direction of a school-based teacher leader); 2) undergoing observation of their teaching (done by the local designated teacher-leader); and, 3) obtaining a supportive report signed by the school's principal and his or her direct manager (a district level director). On what bases are these various points of reference meant to offer evidence of the candidate's competence or quality? Clearly, the evidence is assigned, or presumed to be assignable, to the teacher who is seeking accreditation. The paperwork and observations relate to a person. However, to be deemed to be of quality, we argue that the guidance from the professional standards is ambiguous. To give a sense of this ambiguity, consider how the standards are defined.

Grouped into three 'domains,' ('Professional Knowledge,' 'Professional Practice,' and 'Professional Commitment'), the Institute Standards list seven constitutive 'elements':

– Teachers know their subject/content and how to teach that content to their students;
– Teachers know their students and how students learn;
– Teachers plan, assess and report for effective learning;
– Teachers communicate effectively with their students;
– Teachers create and maintain safe and challenging learning environments through the use of classroom management skills;
– Teachers continually improve their professional knowledge and practice; and,
– Teachers are actively engaged members of their profession and the wider community (see NSW Institute for Teachers, 2005, p. 3).

While these elements are broken down further into 'aspects' in the Institute documentation, their wording denotes a particular slippage. That is, even with those elements clearly addressing the act of teaching (e.g. Element 4 suggesting that 'teachers communicate effectively with their students'), the question remains as to just what counts as high quality in meeting these elements? In the example just named, what counts as 'effective' in communication with students?

Taking this observation one step further, for this Element, three aspects are addressed in the standards and at the 'Professional Competence' stage they are articulated as the teacher being able to:

- Explain goals, content, concepts and ideas clearly and accurately to students;
- Use questions and classroom discussion effectively to probe students' understanding of the content; and,
- Respond to student discussion to promote learning and encourage other students to contribute (NSW Institute of Teachers, 2005, p. 9).

Here we have a more detailed elaboration of what effective communication is supposed to look like, but what does the wording of these aspects actually suggest? Each of them names qualities that need to be judged in relation to a centrally designed and documented syllabus and some idea of what counts as 'promoting learning'. Each of them requires substantial professional judgement. But none of them articulates a level of specificity which requires taking a stance on long standing and on-going debates about how to teach and how to engage students. That is, if one observing principal expects teachers to apply pedagogical modes that might be termed 'traditional', what is judged to be effective and clear could well be very different if the observing principal expects 'constructivist' pedagogy. Herein lies the ambiguity.

While the NSW Institute of Teachers' Professional Teaching Standards are bureaucratically and unambiguously assigned to the individual teacher, the person, they are much more ambiguous on just what that teacher is expected to do in order to be deemed competent. They are, in a sense, professionally neutral on matters of pedagogy.

Placed back into the context of how they are applied, it is clear that self-reported documentary evidence and potentially quite infrequent observations may or may not reflect what that teacher does behind the closed door of his or her classroom – a fact unlikely to be lost on those new-scheme teachers who seek accreditation. Whereas Ball (2000, 2004, this volume) is concerned about the degree to which the institutionalised surveillance mechanisms established to govern teachers might carry significant negative psychic effects, the implementation of the NSW Professional Teaching Standards, we argue, is likely to be less threatening. That is, in the NSW context, the bureaucratic mechanisms established for supposedly enhancing the 'professionalism of teachers and teaching,' can be enacted as the embodiment of banal paper documentation in a system of public representation and positioning, in the sense that, given their lack of specificity and ambiguity, they represent little serious challenge. In this context, compliance may well occur without much effect on the regular teaching practices of teachers.

In the name of professionalisation, developing standards, specifying good practice, and establishing accountability mechanisms are not in and of themselves problematic impulses. Indeed, without explicit criteria as to what counts as legitimate, acceptable, and desirable practice within a profession, practitioners are likely to operate in haphazard and idiosyncratic ways. Monitoring and improving quality within a field of practice requires such strategies. However, as history readily reveals, "no discourse is inherently oppressive or liberatory" (Sawicki, 1991). If the standards discourse translates into vague, populist statements of what matters in teaching (see Popkewitz (2000) on the functioning of popularism in relation to the governance of teachers) and is coupled with weak mechanisms for monitoring achievement of those standards, then the push for professionalisation, as enacted in NSW thus far, seems hard to justify.

The specification of standards will not realize their potential in improving teachers or teaching when the standards are ambiguously articulated, simplistically employed, or employed in such a way as to detract from the energy needed to teach well. How standards are institutionalised in teaching institutes, in teacher education programs, and in the work of schools, is critical to how the standards actually function. What is clear is that the very techniques adopted in the name of professionalisation have no guaranteed effects. For example, if the main push for 'new-scheme' teachers is to put together paper documents and artificial lessons for the accreditation process, this may well provide a means by which teachers learn how to put on a public face that is quite distant from their real practice. Impression management through writing and doing what is expected for accreditation can result in the exact opposite of what the standards are meant to achieve in terms of professionalisation. Indeed, teachers as workers may learn to perform for their supervisors, in ways that further distance them from taking responsibility for the quality of their own professional practice. An example of how these institutionalised arrangements can play out is illustrated by Burroughs (2001) in relation to the US National Board of Professional Teaching Standards (NBPTS): "NBPTS certification is as much an evaluation of a teacher's writing about his or her teaching as it is an evaluation of the teaching itself" (p. 223). In this sense, Ball's (2000) concern that a form of performativity has been applied to teachers is correct here – but since the specification of standards in NSW is as broad as it is, whether or not NSW teachers experience any particular tension in this process seems highly questionable.

To genuinely impact on professionalism, standards need to be defensible, accessible, and translatable into practice; that is they need to be meaningful and rigorous. Consider for example, that of all the state and territory standards for teaching, only one designates the specific quality of the nature of intellectual work expected by students: the Queensland standards require that students should be intellectually challenged (see http://www.qct.edu.au/standards/index.html). Consider also, that in the NSW Teaching Standards there is something of a deferral in relation to what might have been a codification of professional knowledge. Take Element 1, noted above, where the appeal is for teachers to know their subject/content and how to teach it. Specification of the content is left to a separate government body, the NSW Board of Studies, that has authority over school syllabuses. Specification of how to teach that content is left to what is implied or stated in syllabus documents and the interpretation of individual teachers. While there are significant complexities in specifying how to teach, it appears the standards, as articulated, place higher value on appearance rather than substance.

So it is that we see a strong potential, in the development of these standards, for the NSW variant of the international push to institutionalise standards for teachers to become much more and much less than intended. That we see them as *less* than intended should be evident from our discussion above – they certainly offer no guarantees of impact on teacher or teaching quality. The standards are also *more* than intended in the sense that they clearly function as a mechanism of bio-power, a mechanism for sorting and disciplining teachers in specific ways, applying specific techniques of power that could well lead to the internalisation of power in which teachers are the observed inmates of a panoptic 'professional' body. Since it is the corporeal teacher that is observed, credentialed and registered, individually, the mechanisms implied in the development of the standards are very similar in form to those identified in Foucault's analysis of prisons and the creation of docile bodies (Foucault, 1977).

At the same time, however, just what effects this surveillance will have will depend very much on how employers pick up the challenge of applying the standards. But the potential of creating a population of teachers who comply when watched with whatever pedagogical philosophy the local observer wants is clear. The question raised here, then, is what will be the lasting effects once the credential has been obtained, when no one is watching? Since the standards themselves are, we argue, poorly-specified, it is perhaps simply the acceptance of surveillance itself that will be achieved.

WHY WORRY ABOUT THESE STANDARDS?

Comparing the experience of teaching standards in the US to those present above, we see clear reason to question the recent push for teaching standards in NSW. In the USA, David Labaree (2000) identified three factors in the widespread resistance to standards in American education as "a commitment to local control of schools, a commitment to expansion of educational opportunity, and a commitment to form over substance in the way we think about educational accomplishment" (Labaree, 2000, p. 29). His analysis was oriented at standards for student achievement in the US context, but it is interesting to test the same factors for their role in the setting and implementation of teaching standards in Australia (and specifically) NSW.

A desire for local control (or what Labaree encapsulates in the expression 'Don't tell me what to do') is certainly endemic in both the State/Federal organisation of education in Australia, such that each state has independently developed its own standards for teaching and, to date, national attempts to specify teaching standards have failed. The impulse for local control is perhaps even more acutely characteristic of universities, the home of teacher education programs, where attempts to implement standards for teaching or teacher education are typically read as impositional on academic freedom and inadequate and/or political rather than professional in intent. The resistance Labaree refers to is specifically targeted at government attempts to 'interfere' in local affairs. Given the governmental involvement in the development of standards throughout Australia, a strong history of unionism in education, and widespread scepticism toward many government initiatives, it is not surprising to find some resistance among teachers and academics to the push for teaching standards. Translating a similar scepticism among 'new-scheme' teachers to the local functioning and application of the NSW Standards within schooling requires little imagination. Complying with the surveillance required by the standards while also resisting any supervisor's interpretation of the standards seems a likely scenario where serious professional disagreement about what counts as quality teaching occurs. Professional debate and learning are less likely outcomes.

The commitment to expanding educational opportunity, that Labaree identifies as a second factor in the resistance to educational standards, translates into what he calls a "Don't get in my way" message. Here, Labaree contrasts a nostalgic pining for a golden age when standards were high and getting through school was tough with a contemporary push to provide educational access for all. Applied to teaching standards, there is a somewhat nostalgic discourse associated with teaching of yesteryear in which the rigours of the school inspector and assertions of quality reverberate. As Labaree points out for the US context and as can be applied in Australia, schools and teaching were very different decades ago with fewer students gaining access, and memorisation as a primary indicator of student achievement. At the same time, there certainly have been efforts to recruit increasingly more diverse graduates into teaching with the offering of alternative pathways and widely publicised looming teacher shortages. The implications of these efforts for classroom practice when the standards applied to those classrooms do little to define just what sort of pedagogy is considered to be of high quality are also clear. It is, after all, quite possible to articulate more specific standards of teaching than those offered by the NSW standards. Just as one example, consider that Newmann and his colleagues did precisely that when defining 'Authentic Pedagogy' (Newmann and Associates, 1996).

The third factor identified by Labaree as explaining resistance to standards is what he describes as a focus on form over substance in education, in which time in school and credentials are valued over academic performance. As Labaree puts it, "we have consciously created an education system based on attaining formal markers of success – grades, credits, and degrees – rather than one based on acquiring substantive knowledge" (p. 30). This same emphasis can be identified in relation to teaching in Australia whereby in teacher education programs and in professional development initiatives, perhaps because identifying and measuring quality has been difficult, what has mattered most is the number of courses or field experiences prior to graduation or the hours of professional learning, rather than the substance or quality of those learning experiences for teachers. It is this misguided emphasis that has most clearly characterised attempts to implement standards for teaching in Australia. The vague nature of many standards statements is symptomatic of the impulse to have formal standards and accountability rather than a genuine effort to enhance the quality of teaching. As noted above, the NSW Institute of Teachers' Professional Teaching Standards themselves reveal this same focus on form over substance. Despite the explicit call for standards to promote improved quality in teaching, it is clear that the impulse toward bureaucratic credentialing (the form) has had significant influence over the more thorny issue of taking a stand on what counts as pedagogical quality (the substance).

Consider some of the specific criticisms of the development of teaching standards in the US. Major challenges to the National Board of Professional Teaching Standards (NBPTS), for instance, include a concern that the Board will produce a competitive rather than collegial environment among teachers, leading to a hierarchy within the profession that is antithetical to the Board's own vision

(King, 1994) and that assessment procedures associated with the standards will lead to certification and normalisation rather than celebrating diversity and creative difference and in any case fail to distinguish quality or capture its complex nature. Serafini (2002) categorises the main challenges (read criticisms) to the Board as concerns about the assessment process, the legitimisation of particular forms of teaching over others and normalising effects of standardising 'accomplished' teaching, concerns about the commodification of the credential associated with certification, and concerns about whether the standards will actually increase the quality of classroom teaching. King (1994) also refers to the vagueness of the standards and their functioning as a slogan system.

For us, many of these concerns are nearly identical to those we hold for the NSW Teaching Standards. However, our concern is also different in that the form of normalisation implied by the NSW Standards seems to be not so much about limiting diversity and difference among teaching practices through an explicit naming of a narrow range of what is acceptable (as is implied by King's concern about diversity above). Rather, the NSW Standards seem to invite a distinct lack of professional disagreement, thereby normalising a dullness of professional judgement and an uncritical disposition. If the standards articulated some more specific pedagogical standards, (such as those found in Authentic Pedagogy, as but one example), then the implementation of the standards would invite justifiable professional debate, disagreement and critique.

Serafini (2002) questions whether standards *can* raise teacher performance or simply limit teacher control and professional autonomy. Herein lie some of the problems with the field. The setting of standards for teaching as part of a professionalisation agenda, particularly in terms of the codification of a unique body of knowledge, is seen by many within education as being at odds with the notion of autonomy that is also a central characteristic of professions. If standards are, or are perceived to be, overly prescriptive then the limits to teachers' control, and the constriction of difference, are clear. In that context, any attempt to specify teaching quality through observable behaviours is subject to scathing accusations of 'technicism' (cf., Menter, Brisard, and Smith, 2006) which are all the more acute in a field with a strong (if underdeveloped) anti-positivist streak (Ladwig, 1996). Ball's (2004) concerns with standards in the UK seems motivated from a response to such overly prescriptive performativity regimes.

But at the other extreme of minimal prescription, where we place the NSW Standards, the mechanisms associated with accreditation in relation to the standards are also not particularly productive and meaningful as an approach to supporting teachers in achieving high quality performances. The order of things articulated in the standards is at issue here – in NSW they are motherhood statements, vagaries, which offer little to guide genuine improvement in quality teaching. In a 'profession' where standards have previously been rather arbitrary or unspecified, and are seen to remain that way, it would not be surprising that autonomy (limited though it may be) will remain the primary source of teachers' sense of themselves as professionals. In this context, standards seemed destined to have weak effects, primarily achieving increased impression management as teachers meet accreditation requirements while fundamentally continuing to do what they already do.

So it is that we have to ask if much has really been learned from the international experience of developing teaching standards around the globe, much less from early analyses of education as an institution. In relation to the issue of de-coupling, it is clear that the certification of teachers in NSW is based on the development of a credential that will carry some market value in its own right. Whether or not the credential actually signifies 'professional competence' remains to be seen. The chance of credential inflation developing is evident both in the intended vertical expansion of the credential (the higher levels of certification intended as teachers move through their careers are precisely a vertical expansion of the credential market), and in the degree to which obtaining the base credential becomes a mass phenomenon, as any teacher can voluntarily seek accreditation. To date, more than 1700 NSW teachers have been certified at the initial level, and there is no report of anyone being de-certified. Just as Meyer and his colleagues pointed out how such institutional arrangements work well to maintain the ceremony and myth of progress and advancement without raising questions about the validity of that myth, the legitimacy of the NSW standards will remain taken-for-granted as long as no one seeks to link the standards to the actual quality of teaching.

Further, where criticisms of the early push for standards in the US are not surprising, it is disappointing that so little seems to have been learned as standards are being implemented on the other side of the planet. It should of course not surprise us that this is so. As Foucault reminds us:

> We can obviously describe a given society's school apparatus or its set of educational apparatuses, but I think that we can analyse them effectively only if we do not see them as an overall unity, only if we do not try to derive them from something like the Statist unity of sovereignty. We can analyse them only if we try to see how they interact, how they support one another, and how this apparatus defines a certain number of global strategies on the basis of multiple subjugations (of child to adult, progeny to parents, ignorance to knowledge, apprentice to master, family to administration, and so on). All these mechanisms and operators of domination are the actual plinth of the global apparatus that is the school apparatus. So, if you like, we have to see the structures of power as global strategies that traverse and use local tactics of domination (Foucault, 2003, pp. 45–46).

Here we would suggest that analyses of teacher standards and professionalism require a specific analysis of how they are articulated and implemented in particular contexts – hence our attention to detail and our references to contexts like the US and the UK. And yet, we also recognise that the now global push to develop standards for teachers and establish institutes for teacher credentialing carries with it a global strategy based on the subjugation of teachers. Where the NSW Teaching Standards have clearly been articulated in a manner designed to avoid the criticisms applied to overly prescriptive criteria, they have still applied to teachers the basic techniques of self-surveillance so well deployed by schools around the planet. As teachers in NSW subject themselves to mechanisms ostensibly designed to move them from apprentice to master (NSW teachers have to pay to be certified), they adopt the techniques of power that internalise that subjugation. For now, these NSW standards seem relatively benign. Whether or not they remain so is an open question requiring yet another level of vigilant observation.

NOTES

[1]   http://www.nswteachers.nsw.edu.au/ accessed 6 May 2008.
[2]   These figures are taken from the NSW Department of Education and Training 2006 Annual Report: available from https://www.det.nsw.edu.au/media/downloads/reports_stats/annual_reports/yr2006/detar06_full.pdf

REFERENCES

Ball, S. (2000). Performativities and fabrications in the education economy: Towards the performative society? *Australian Educational Researcher, 27*(2), 1–23.

Ball, S. (2004). *Education reform as social barbarism: Economism and the end of authenticity.* Scottish Educational Research Association annual conference. Perth.

Burroughs, R. (2001). Composing standards and composing teachers: The problem of national board certification. *Journal of Teacher Education, 52*(3), 223–232.

Collins, R. (1979). *The credential society: An historical sociology of education and stratitifcation.* London: Academic Press.

Dean, M. (1999). *Governmentality : Power and rule in modern society.* London: Sage.

Foucault, M. (1977). *Discipline & punish: The birth of the prison* (A. Sheridan, Trans.). New York: Viking Press.

Foucault, M. (1988). *The history of sexuality: The care of the self* (R. Hurley, Trans.). New York: Vintage.

Foucault, M. (2003). *Society must be defended: Lecures at Collège de France, 1975–1976* (D. Macey, Trans.). New York: Picador.

Gore, J. M. (1993). *The struggle for pedagogies: Critical and feminist discourses as regimes of truth.* New York & London: Routledge.

King, M. B. (1994). Locing ourselves in: National standards for the teaching profession. *Teaching and Teacher Education, 10*(1), 95–108.

Labaree, D. F. (1999). *How to succeed in school without really learning: The credentials race in American education.* New Haven, CT: Yale University Press.

Labaree, D. F. (2000). Resisting educational standards. *Phi Delta Kappan, 82*(1), 28–33.

Labaree, D. F. (2006). *Education, markets, and the public good.* New York: Routledge.

Ladwig, J. G. (1996). *Academic distinctions: On the theory and methodology of the radical sociology of school knowledge.* New York: Routledge.

Mayer, D., Luke, C., & Luke, A. (2008). Teachers, national regulation and cosmopolitanism. In A. M. Phelan & J. Sumsion (Eds.), *Critical readings in teacher education: Provoking absences* (pp. 79–98). Rotterdam: Sense Publishers.

Menter, I., Brisard, E., & Smith, I. (2006). Making teachers in Britain: Professional knowledge for initial teacher education in England and Scotland. *Educational Philosophy and Theory, 38*(3), 269–286.

Meyer, J. W. (1977). The effects of education as an institution. *American Journal of Sociology, 83*(1), 55–77.

Meyer, J. W., Ramirez, F. O., & Soysal, Y. (1992). World expansion of mass education, 1870–1980. *Sociology of Education, 65*(2), 128–149.

Meyer, J. W., & Rowan, B. (1977). Institutionalised organisations: Formal structures as myth and ceremony. *American Journal of Sociology, 83*(2), 340–363.

Newmann, F. M., & Associates. (1996). *Authentic achievement: Restructuring schools for intellectual quality.* San Francisco: Jossey-Bass.

NSW Institute of Teachers. (2005). *Professional teaching standards.* Retrieved September 26, 2006, from http://www.nswteachers.nsw.edu.au/Main-Professional-Teaching-Standards.html

Petrosky, A. (1994). Schizophrenia. The National Board for Professional Teaching Standards: Raising the bar. *English Journal, 83*(7), 33–42.

Popkewitz, T. S. (1998). *Struggling for the soul: The politics of education and the construction of the teacher.* New York: Teachers College Press.

Popkewitz, T. S. (2000). The denial of change in educational change: Systems of ideas in the construction of national policy and evaluation. *Educational Researcher, 29*(1), 17–29.

Popkewitz, T. S. (1991). *A political sociology of educational reform: Power/Knowledge in teaching, teacher education, and research.* New York and London: Teachers College Press.

Ramsey, G. (2000). *Quality matters. Revitalising teaching: Critical times, critical choices.* Sydney: NSW Department of Education and Training.

Rose, N. (1998). *Inventing our selves: Psychology, power, and personhood.* Cambridge: Cambridge University Press.

Sawicki, J. (1991). *Disciplining Foucault: Feminism, power, and the body.* New York: Routledge.

Serafini, F. (2002). Possibilities and challenges: The National Board for Professional Teaching Standards. *Journal of Teacher Education, 53*(4), 316–327.

FURTHER READINGS

Collins, R. (1979). *The credential society: An historical sociology of education and stratification.* London: Academic Press.

Foucault, M. (2003). *Society must be defended: Lecures at Collège de France, 1975–1976* (D. Macey, Trans.). New York: Picador.

Mayer, D., Luke, C., & Luke, A. (2008). Teachers, National Regulationand Cosmopolitanism. In A. M. Phelan, & J. Sumsion (Eds.), *Critical readings in teacher education: Provoking absences* (pp. 79–98). Rotterdam: Sense Publishers.

Meyer, J. W., Ramirez, F. O., & Soysal, Y. (1992). World expansion of mass education, 1870–1980. *Sociology of Education, 65*(2), 128–149.

Newmann, F. M., & Associates. (1996). *Authentic achievement: Restructuring schools for intellectual quality.* San Francisco: Jossey-Bass.

Popkewitz, T. S. (2000). The denial of change in educational change: Systems of ideas in the construction of national policy and evaluation. *Educational Researcher, 29*(1), 17–29.

James G Ladwig
Institute of Advanced Study for Humanity
University of Newcastle, Australia

Jennifer Gore
School of Education
University of Newcastle, Australia

LYNN FENDLER

TEACHER PROFESSIONALISATION AS A DOUBLE-EDGED SWORD

Regulation/Empowerment in U.S. Educational Policies

INTRODUCTION

Professionalisation has been problematic for a long time. Bledstein (1976) levelled a provocative critique of the culture of professionalism, charging professionals with elitism and corruption: "The culture of professionalism has allowed Americans to achieve educated expressions of freedom and self-realisation, yet it has also allowed them to perfect educated techniques of fraudulence and deceit" (Bledstein, 1976, p. 334). While Bledstein was writing in the field of Sociology, Labaree (1992) provided an equally compelling critique of teacher professionalisation in the field of Education. Labaree's analysis showed us that teaching has become increasingly rationalised through processes of credentialism and codification of knowledge. Furthermore, Labaree argued, the particular form of rationalisation that has beset teacher professionalisation has included a particular form of raced and gendered privilege. Bemoaning these trends in professionalisation, Labaree wrote, "the teacher professionalisation movement has the potential for doing more harm than good in its impact on U.S. education" (p. 124). Labaree and others (see e.g., Popkewitz, 1993; Hatch, 1988; Veysey, 1988; Freidson, 1984) have long recognised that teacher professionalisation is fraught with contradictions of purpose and crises of governance.

This chapter follows from and extends the work of Labaree, Popkewitz, Freidson, Hatch, and Veysey by setting out from the premise that teacher professionalisation is complicated and contradictory on many levels. I draw extensively on these previous analyses, and for purposes of this chapter, bring their critical, historical, and genealogical sensibilities to bear on two current policy-oriented organisations, namely the National Board for Professional Teaching Standards (NBPTS) and Teachers for a New Era (TNE). I have chosen to focus on these two organisations because they are prime sources of policy that currently constitute teacher professionalisation, they are influential and far-reaching in scope, and they describe themselves as being established on behalf of teachers by teachers and teacher educators. By focusing on these two organisations, my analysis does not position the teaching profession in structural opposition to the state or the market. Instead, as a strategy of re-reading, my analysis highlights ways in which sanctioned pro-teacher organisations participate in inextricably interwoven trends of regulation and empowerment.

M. Simons, M. Olssen and M.A. Peters (eds.), Re-Reading Education Policies: A Handbook Studying the Policy Agenda of the 21ˢᵗ Century, 735–753.

An examination of the policy language put forward by these two professionalisation organisations has led me to posit three domains of teacher professionalisation policy that operate for both good and bad, as a double-edged sword:

- Standards-based reforms
- Peer governance
- Elevation of social standing

All three of these domains may seem to most people to be unequivocally desirable and worthy of professional aspirations; all three of these domains are included in most teacher professionalisation literature, regardless of whether that literature comes from schools, universities, foundations, or government agencies. At first impression, it may seem entirely obvious that teachers would benefit under conditions of standards-based reforms, peer governance, and improved social standing. Nevertheless, throughout this analysis I will argue that each of these three domains is comprised of a complex interweaving of affordances and constraints, the combination of which constitutes a mixed bag of results. In no way do I mean to imply that professionalisation for teachers is a bad thing, and neither do I cast aspersions on teaching as a profession, or on the NBPTS or TNE. My foremost concern, in fact, is to emphasise the recognition and respect for good teaching and teachers. It is in this spirit that I offer a critical analysis of particular policy documents: to show how certain policy discourses of teacher professionalisation have tended to work for both good and bad in subtle and unanticipated ways.

NBPTS AND TNE

Before launching into the analysis of regulation and empowerment, brief introductions of these two focal U.S. professionalisation organisations are in order.

National Board of Professional Teaching Standards (NBPTS)

Established in 1987 following a call by Albert Shankar, then president of the American Federation of Teachers[1] (AFT), the NBPTS serves teachers as a regulatory body the way the American Medical Association (AMA) serves physicians. Like Teachers for a New Era, NBPTS has been supported by the Carnegie Corporation, a philanthropic organisation.[2] The current NBPTS Board of Directors is chaired by a former state governor and includes eleven teachers, the former Deputy Director for the Ford Foundation, a speech-language pathologist, an attorney, four university administrators, a member of the National School Board, the national presidents of both the AFT and the NEA, three officers of different local teachers' unions, a school librarian, and a School Improvement Specialist.

The NBPTS has a short, three-point mission statement:

- Maintaining high and rigorous standards for what accomplished teachers should know and be able to do
- Providing a national voluntary system certifying teachers who meet these standards
- Advocating related education reforms to integrate National Board Certification in American education and to capitalise on the expertise of National Board Certified Teachers.

(http://www.nbpts.org/about_us/mission_and_history/mission)

NBPTS is known to U.S. teachers primarily through its Board Certification function. In order to become Board Certified, teachers must meet the standards of the NBPTS by passing an examination and submitting a portfolio that documents teaching performances and other professional accomplishments. The fee for obtaining NBPTS certification is now just over US$3,000. Some U.S. states (primarily those located in the southeast portion of the country) offer generous financial incentives to teachers by subsidising all certification fees and guaranteeing a salary increase for teachers who complete Board Certification requirements. As of January 2007, there were 55,306 NBPTS Board Certified teachers in the United States (of a total of about 3.6 million teachers nationally).

The two primary critiques of NBPTS currently are that 1) teachers of color fail NBPTS certification examinations at a disproportionate rate, and 2) NBPTS Board Certified teachers tend to leave the teaching profession soon after being certified. Many leave the classroom and move on to administrative and educational governance positions.

Teachers for a New Era (TNE)

The Carnegie, Annenberg, and Ford Foundations collaborated to administer a "landmark initiative" designed to "strengthen K-12 teaching by developing state-of-the-art programs at schools of education." In 2002, TNE provided multi-million dollar grants to five schools of education, and now eleven institutions are recipients of TNE grant support.[3] The TNE guiding principles for design of teacher education reforms are:

- Leadership on the part of the presidents of supported institutions that elevates the role and importance of schools of education within the university community and a design that builds on research evidence;
- Top-level collaboration between university faculty in the arts and sciences with the school of education faculty to ensure that prospective teachers are well grounded in specific disciplines and provided a liberal arts education; and

– Establishment of teaching as a clinical profession, with master teachers mentoring students in a formal two-year residency as they make the transition from college to classroom.

(http://www.teachersforanewera.org/index.cfm?fuseaction=home.principles)

TNE reform projects in these institutions are ongoing, and it is too early to draw any conclusions about the long-term effects of the policy. So far, the major impacts of TNE initiatives in colleges and universities have been 1) increased participation of disciplinary departments (such as Biology, Chemistry, Geology, English, History, and Mathematics) in teacher education programs. For example, under the auspices and funding of TNE, representatives from the disciplines meet regularly with teacher educators to discuss curriculum, assessment, and requirements for completion of degree programs; 2) increased attention to teachers in their first two years of teaching, the period which is referred to as the "teacher induction" phase. There have been, for example, many new university course offerings and professional development opportunities that go beyond the teacher preparation years, and university supervision of teachers now extends through the first two years of teaching; and 3) intensified focus on program evaluation and documentation of program effectiveness, measured primarily in terms of improvements in pupils' standardised test scores.

NBPTS and TNE are organisations specific to the United States; however, an analysis of their characteristics will reveal that these organisations exemplify some professional practices and patterns of governance that are shaping teacher professionalisation in many other places as well.

STANDARDS-BASED REFORMS

The idea of standards-based reforms (including policies pertaining to pedagogy, certification, and evaluation) for purposes of professional advancement is not new in education or other fields. There is disagreement about the desirability of standards-based reform for teaching. Much teacher-focused literature welcomes standards-based reforms as an indicator of professional advancement (see, e.g., Flanagan, 2007); however, other teacher education literature is more critical, often taking the perspective that standards and professionalisation are in conflict. For example, Al-Hinai (2007), in his analysis of teacher professionalism in Oman wrote, "Generally, the Western literature in the field of teacher professionalism is quite consistent in stating that reform jeopardises teacher's professionalism. (...) Thus, current reform initiatives are seen as weakening rather than strengthening teacher professionalism" (p. 42). Newby (2007) from the standpoint of teacher education, offered a nuanced proposal saying that *entry standards* should not be reformed, but that "we should energetically consider raising standards of qualification *once within the profession*" (p. 118, emphasis in original).

Strategically re-reading policies on professionalisation, I will not subscribe to any of those previous positions. I do not take the position that there is any essential relationship between standards and professionalisation. My critical strategy for re-reading is to point out and analyse historical features of current professionalisation standards, and to regard them in terms of a double-edged sword. In particular, I suggest that current policies for teacher professionalisation reflect epistemological bases that in turn reflect broader historical developments, namely an intensification of rationalisation, and a historically specific meaning of *science*.

Intensification of rationalisation

The progressive rationalisation of teaching over the past 100 years has already been well documented in educational research. Drawing from parallel analyses in history, sociology, and political science, educational researchers have studied how education in general, and teaching in particular, have become understood more and more in terms of atomistic components, fixed knowledge concepts, and law-like principles. Popkewitz (1993), for example, wrote, "A widespread rationalisation of school processes occurred not through direct state intervention but, rather, through epistemologies associated with local school administration" (p. 267). Similarly, emphasising the classical opposition between rationalisation and bureaucratisation, Labaree (1992) wrote:

> while opposing bureaucratisation, the [teacher professionalisation] movement promises to enhance the rationalisation of classroom instruction. The difference is that bureaucratisation focuses on organisation in the narrow sense of the word, locating power in a hierarchy of offices and thus effecting outcomes by command from supervisor to subordinate; whereas rationalisation focuses on organisation in the broader sense – as process -embedding power in the principles of formal rationality that shape the discourse and procedures by which people guide their actions (Labaree, 1992, p. 147).

Educational literature has clearly documented the rationalisation of teaching practices in the late twentieth century. What we can see in more recent standards-based reforms is that rationalisation impulses have become even more intensive and more pervasive. In 1988, it was reasonable for Andrew Abbott to assert that there were professional fields in which knowledge remained outside the realm of rationalisation. Abbott wrote, "some professions work with knowledge that is highly rationalisable, as does engineering, while others, like psycho-therapy, do not" (Abbott, 1988, p. 178). However, professional domains that had previously been exempt from thoroughgoing rationalisation have recently been permeated and shaped by the intensification of rationalisation in nearly all areas of life. For example, the language of the TNE Prospectus indicates a policy expectation that teacher professionalisation standards will extend beyond departments of teacher education and into all other university departments:

> When conscientiously addressed in light of the requirements necessary to enfranchise a professional teacher, it is likely that fundamental questions will arise about the adequacy of design of academic major programs in the arts

and sciences, or about the program of general and liberal education for all students (TNE Prospectus, p. 11).

The intensification of rationalisation also appears in the form of increased attention to detail; it might even be called micromanaging. In educational policy for curriculum planning we see both the specification of minute levels of detail in curriculum documents, and also the delegation of curriculum design to being a sub-specialty separate from teaching. For example, curricular directives that used to be written in relatively general terms of elementary, middle, and high school expectations have become more differentiated and explicated at tinier levels of detail. Currently, curricular policies are not only specified according to grade-level, they are also frequently stipulated in terms of weekly benchmarks, and sometimes even daily objectives for any given classroom. In Michigan, for example, previously general curricular frameworks were later specified into curricular benchmarks for each grade level, and then most recently further specified as "pacing guides" that state explicit curricular expectations for each class on a day-by-day basis.

The separation of curriculum design from teaching is related to the increased specificity of curriculum documents. Curricula are being written with increasing levels of detail and specificity, and the language of curriculum is being rationalised in terms of transnational discourses of accountability, testing, student achievement, and remediation. In the process, curriculum design and planning has become a professional specialisation that is more and more remote from teachers and classrooms.

When the writing of curriculum becomes its own professional specialisation, we see another double-edged sword. The professionalisation of curriculum writing recognises a domain of educational expertise and elevates the legitimacy of curriculum specialists. At the same time, the professionalisation of curriculum design relegates teaching practices to a paraprofessional status; the more detailed and specific the curricular demands, the less judgment is called for on the part of teachers. According to Abbott (1988), when professional work responsibilities are delegated in these ways, the impact has consistently been to degrade the profession:

> Clear examples are the gradual delegation of conveyancing and costing to managing clerks by solicitors and of drafting to draftsmen by architects, *as well as the separation of curriculum planning from classroom teaching,* and that of systems design from computer programming. In every case, the eventual result has been the degradation of what had been professional work to nonprofessional status, sometime accompanied by the degradation of those who do the work (Abbott, 1988, pp. 125–126, emphasis added).

The intensification of rationalisation in educational policies is a double-edged sword in teacher professionalisation policy because on the one hand, the specificity of discourse lends legitimacy to teaching expertise. In other words, the increased specificity calls attention to levels of detail that have always been part of teaching but not necessarily recognised or appreciated. Increased specificity also provides a forum for participation and discussion. That is, while it is difficult to argue with curricular mandates that are as vague and general as "All children will develop critical thinking skills," it is easier to take issue with a more specific standard or benchmark. A curricular mandate such as "All students will be able to explain the causes of World War I" is more controversial. Specific curricular standards such as this one have provoked some substantive conversations among teachers, parents, and administrators. These narrower standards are less susceptible to multiple interpretations. In this way, there may be advantages to increased specificity and rationalisation of educational practices, at least to the extent that they are recognised as such by those who are subjected to them. That is one edge of the sword.

At the same time, however, the intensification of rationalisation and attention to detail has the effect of usurping at least some part of the non-routine, context-dependent capacity for judgment traditionally afforded to professionals. Of course, administrative oversight of teachers varies greatly from site to site, and this variation allows for a wide range of possibilities for the degree to which teachers exercise individual judgments in their interpretation and implementation of curriculum. But insofar as curriculum is codified in detail, there is a concomitant expectation that teachers will exercise less judgment in their respective classrooms. Intensified rationalisation of teaching has meant increased specialisation of professional responsibilities. Increased specialisation has had the effect of delegating some teaching responsibilities to sites far removed from the classroom. This delegation has shifted professional responsibilities from the non-routine toward the routine.[4] This is the other edge of the sword.

Herein lies the double-edged sword of standards-based reforms. Increased rationalisation promotes educational expertise in a manner that resembles the way medical specialisations promote expertise in sub-specialties. At the same time, increased rationalisation has rendered the responsibilities of teaching into sub-specialities, each of which is understood to be more routine and less demanding of personal judgment. Previous versions of teacher professionalisation rested on the assumption that teachers would have relationships with the students in their classrooms that included awareness of their emotions, sensitivities, and idiosyncrasies; professionalism then implied the exercise of judgment for what would be best for a particular student in any given moment. Of course, teachers still do these things. At the same time, in policy language, the current version of professional judgment by teachers is mediated by intensified rationalisation, including levels of detail and delegation of specialisations.

New meanings for science

In addition to the intensification of rationalisation for professionalisation, current policy discourses also reflect historically specific uses of scientific epistemologies. Like rationalisation, scientific discourse now extends beyond controlled and experimental contexts and into areas that had previously been regarded as exempt from a scientific gaze. The gradual encroachment of a scientific purview into most areas of life is a well-documented characteristic of modern times.[5] Also like rationalisation, what we see in current professionalisation policies is a radical extension of that purview. In the language of TNE and NBPTS, there is a continuation of the belief – however reluctantly held – that science bestows legitimacy, and the most powerful arguments in support of teacher professionalisation are those that most closely conform to the language and methodologies of the natural sciences.

Since *A Nation At Risk*,[6] there has been in the United States a frenzy of activity that attempts to raise the achievement levels of students in the areas of mathematics and science. It seems that, in this frenetic pursuit of excellence, the fanaticism for science has spilled over from being a school subject matter to becoming the epistemological basis on which educational phenomena ought to be investigated.

U.S. Federal policies governing funding for educational research have been striving for years to impose requirements for the exclusive use of experimental scientific methods. For one example, What Works Clearinghouse stipulates criteria for scientific research in education.[7] Those criteria are based almost exclusively on a book published in 1963.[8] In another remarkable move to professionalise teachers, the state of Michigan recently added the curricular mandate that all elementary teacher candidates must now complete a course in statistical methods as a required part of their teacher preparation programs.[9] This is a strangely anachronistic trend these days when researchers in other scientific fields, from physics to anthropology, have been moving away from Newtonian epistemological assumptions and embracing research possibilities more closely related to postmodern approaches. Theoretical physics, for example, is concerned with quanta and the interactive effects of space and time. Much current mathematics is researched in terms of chaos theory. Anthropology and other social sciences have been integrating the epistemological perspectives of narrative communication and rhetorical studies. It is curious, then, that educational policy has continued to rely on modes of generating information that have been made obsolete in other scientific fields (see also Labaree, 1992).

Science is generally regarded to be a quickly changing and progressive enterprise. Therefore, it is ironic that so much policy pertaining to educational research would be based on professional standards that were established before computers were in general use and before AIDS was identified. Since the 1970s, and in spite of federal mandates, many educational researchers have been conducting studies in various qualitative and interpretive modes, having long ago realised that research methods that derive from the natural sciences may be useful for quantifiable descriptive phenomena of education and schooling, but those research approaches are less useful for studying idiosyncratic, dynamic and context-dependent situations like classroom teaching. Whether or not educational researchers make the distinction explicit in their research reports, it is important to remember that classrooms are not laboratories, students do not behave like molecules, and teaching children is not analogous to altering the Ph of garden soil or building a suspension bridge.

Not only is science invoked more frequently in recent professionalisation discourses, science language is also interwoven with other populist and sectarian positions to construct legitimation for particular interests. The language of recent professionalisation policy echoes broader historical trends. Popular opinion in the United States, for example, seems to have a love-hate attitude toward scientific expertise. On the one hand, policy documents and initiatives are explicit in their requirements for scientific and evidence-based practices and evaluations, but the language of rigorous science is hedged with anti-intellectual populist appeals. Noting the peculiarly egalitarian claims expressed in U.S. cultural practices compared to other countries, Hatch (1988) wrote, "the same democratic culture that makes professional status so alluring also remains deeply suspicious of the claims and pretensions of professionals" (p. 5).

Furthermore, the definition of what can be called *scientific* has changed dramatically over time as different ways of producing knowledge emerge. As many sociologists have noted, there are recurring historical tensions between expertise and democracy, and current teacher professionalisation policies are exemplary of these complicated and messy historical tensions. Examples of the historically specific role of popular science in professionalisation policy language can be seen in the Prospectus for TNE:

> The design principles and engagement issues arise from a process of induction. They have been shown in most cases by credible demonstration to contribute to increases in teaching effectiveness. Where the empirical evidence is weak, they represent consensus views of leading researchers and practitioners, based upon experience and reason, about a secure basis for building teaching effectiveness (TNE Prospectus, p. 9).

In the example above, we can see in the policy language a strained effort to insist upon a scientific basis for teaching, even as the document also acknowledges that the findings from empirical research are not helpful. The TNE language continues by distinguishing "research evidence" from "experience":

> [an exemplary teacher education program] should be based upon credible evidence, which includes sound research as well as compelling experience. Flowing from this research-based treatment, a college or university based program of instruction can arise from consideration of the means by which teaching effectiveness can be increased (p. 9).

A final telling excerpt from TNE illustrates the particular role scientific evidence is expected to play in the professionalisation of teaching:

> Although the qualitative, quantitative, and experimental research base for teacher education can be characterised as modest, it must nonetheless intelligently inform program design (TNE Prospectus, p. 9).

PEER GOVERNANCE

Abbott (1988) asserted that in the United States and Great Britain, most professionals have not enjoyed autonomy. That is, most professionals have always worked in larger organisations that are administered by those outside the profession, a situation that Abbott calls heteronomous professionalism. Freidson (1984) came to the same conclusion as Abbott; both argued that in general, professionals have not been self-governing in their working conditions, and that some professions have never been autonomous. Adding a dash of facetiousness to his description of professional governance, Freidson (1984) wrote:

> Looking at the traditional professions – medicine, law, the military, the clergy, and (connected with the clergy historically) university teaching -we see that three of the five never involved self-employment, though professionals in these fields did not necessarily enter into a wage contract. Instead, they operated with the understanding that they could obtain an income from collecting bribes, loot, tithes, rents, student fees, etc. (Freidson, 1984, p. 9).

So with that in mind, the common references to "teacher autonomy" must be understood in a relative sense, and I will provide a critical re-reading of professional governance here. Teachers, like most other professionals (with the possible exception of dentists), generally work in multi-faceted institutions with administrators, and are generally not in charge of their own working conditions.

In this section I will use the term peer governance to indicate the conditions in which teachers have an active voice in the regulation and governance of their professionalisation activities. My critical analysis focuses on Deleuze's *societies of control* as a way to discern some characteristics of peer governance in teacher professionalisation policies.

Societies of control

Rather than argue about professionalisation in traditionally structural terms of autonomy and subordination, I would like to call attention to a mode of professional governance that Deleuze (1992) has termed "societies of control." Deleuze's analysis does not take a structural approach, meaning it does not assume an institutional separation between those who govern and those who are governed. Rather, Deleuze examines relations of power in which governance can be exercised in many forms by different people and various mechanisms. Deleuze's major purpose in his analysis is to draw a provocative distinction between "societies of control" and "societies of discipline."[10] I find Deleuze's theory generative as a means to understand mechanisms of governance of professional activities in which the relations of power do not conform to traditional patterns of domination and subordination. Furthermore, Deleuze's theory affords some critical leverage for exploring ways in which professions discipline themselves in more or less intentional ways.

Among other things, when he characterises current conditions of governance, Deleuze sounds a death knell for traditional modern institutions of social organisation:

> The administrations in charge never cease announcing supposedly necessary reforms: to reform schools, to reform industries, hospitals, the armed forces, prisons. But everyone knows that these institutions are finished, whatever the length of their expiration periods. It's only a matter of administering their last rites and of keeping people employed until the installation of the new forces knocking at the door. These are the *societies of control*, which are in the process of replacing the disciplinary societies (Deleuze, 1992, p. 4, emphasis in original).

Here Deleuze suggests that new or emerging patterns of power relations are sufficiently distinct from the relations of modernity, that a society of discipline no longer pertains to all aspects of society, and that the emerging power relations constitute societies of control. I understand Deleuze's control society as different from a disciplinary society in three respects. To summarise briefly:

- Both discipline and control societies are characterised by the self-monitoring gaze, but in a control society the monitoring is more frequent and continuous than in a disciplinary society.
- Regulations and standards in a disciplinary society tend to be fairly centralised and long-lasting; however, standards in a control society are more hetero-geneous and quickly changing.
- A disciplinary society afforded the promise of closure or completion of a project; however, a control society offers no possibility of closure or completion.

More frequent monitoring. The first salient aspect of the disciplinary society that is now different in the control society is in the nature and rhythm of its regulatory mechanisms. In a disciplinary society, the outcome, or product may be evaluated only once, perhaps by a final exam or quality control unit at the end or completion of a session. At the end of the term or assembly line, students or factory products are inspected, tested, and evaluated. The members of a disciplinary society are self-disciplined and productive members of society. In terms of teacher profession-alisation, this pattern is evident in the previous practice of certifying teachers once and for all.

According to Deleuze, monitoring in a control society is more frequent than in a disciplinary society. A control society is characterised by continuous monitoring: "Indeed, just as the corporation replaces the factory, *perpetual training* tends to replace the school, and *continuous control* to replace the examination" (Deleuze, 1992, p. 5, first emphasis in original; second emphasis added). In schools, there is evidence of a shift from grading on the basis of a final exam to grading many more frequent tests throughout the semester. Smaller, weekly papers are replacing the "one big" research paper required in previous decades. Interactionism as a pedagogical technique constitutes continuous monitoring; the discourse directs attention to each turn of dialogue – each "interaction" in a way that is more frequent than previous lecture-based or discussion-based pedagogies. The shift in frequency of monitoring is evident in fields other than education, including the move in economics when a fixed gold standard was replaced by floating rates of exchange; in criminology electronic tracking devices are locked onto "prisoners" rather than having prisoners locked up in a (fixed place) prison; and in business, marketing in the form of continuous multi-media advertising is replacing brand-name loyalty and market niches.

More kinds of accountability. The second aspect is in the heterogeneity of standards in a control society. Standards in a disciplinary society could be regarded as relatively centralised or uniform. In contrast, a control society is one in which "standards and demands can come from anywhere at any time, in any form" (Ball, 1999). For example, a school curriculum is no longer accountable only to school-board criteria of education. School curricula are now also answerable to local businesses, churches, parents' groups, social service providers, psychiatrists, and police forces. In order to manage a classroom, teachers must be familiar with a wide range of experts in order to make appropriate referrals for children to social services, parent representatives, community liaisons, and legal services. Education must be understood to serve a multicultural, multilingual, and culturally fragmented constituency. In some places, school governance includes the participation of representatives from the McDonalds or Taco Bell franchises that operate in the school lunchrooms (Kaplan, 1996).

Hatch (1988) provides some specific examples of the heterogeneity of standards that is common across professional domains:

> In our own day, the ascendancy of the professions is accompanied by equally strident attack from at least four quarters: from consumer groups who complain of escalating professional fees and unequal distribution of professional service; from critics of professional schools who lament an exclusively utilitarian curriculum; from those who fault the strictly academic standards of access to the professions; and from those who find that professionalism serves to reinforce and extend the inequalities of American society (Hatch, 1988, p. 5).

An example of the heterogeneity of standards can also be seen in the TNE Prospectus:

> Teachers should be perceived as representatives of a profession. Their professional authority will rest in a significant extent upon their ability to demonstrate that they are themselves educated persons. Therefore, teacher candidates must be expected to know more in the way of subject matter than just what they are charged with teaching. Teacher candidates must command general education, liberal education, and the liberal arts. Goals in these areas

should be clearly specified, perhaps in greater detail than for other postsecondary students, and their competencies should be assessed (TNE Prospectus, p. 11).

In this excerpt we can see that teachers and teacher candidates will now be evaluated not only on their effectiveness in teaching others, but also on their mastery of liberal arts fields as well.[11]

Never-ending improvement. According to Deleuze, the final contrast between the discipline society and the control society is in the possibility for completion. In a disciplinary society, one could graduate or be promoted to another rank. However, in a control society, completion is not an option:

> In the disciplinary societies, one was always starting again (...), while in the societies of control one is never finished with anything--the corporation, the educational system, the armed services being metastable states coexisting in one and the same modulation, like a universal system of deformation (Deleuze, 1992, p. 5).

The notion of "never finished" is inscribed in lifelong learning and continuing education programs that have been promoted as mechanisms for professionalisation. One never graduates; one never completes an education; one is continually in the process of professionalising. Considerable literature has now been devoted to lifelong learning and lifelong education, both from the point of view of advocacy and that of critique. The most recent (2001) International Handbook of Lifelong Learning contains forty chapters, most of which regard lifelong learning as a generally positive thing (although some chapters are quite critical of aspects of lifelong learning). In his introduction to the handbook, Sheehan (2001) wrote:

> So important is the concept [of lifelong learning], it should be seen by all of us as representing a new philosophy of education and training, one that aims to facilitate a coherent set of links and pathways between work, school and education, and recognise the necessity for government to give incentives to industry and their employees so they can truly 'invest' in lifelong learning (Sheehan, 2001, p. xi).

Finally, TNE policies stipulate that teacher preparation education no longer ends with certification, but now it must be extended to include a residency period (again, another move to make teacher education resemble medical education):

> [TNE] will consider the teacher candidate's first two years of full-time regular service in the teaching profession as a residency period requiring mentorship and supervision. During this induction period, faculty from the higher education institution, inclusive of arts and sciences faculty, will confer with the teacher on a regular basis, arrange for observation of the teacher's clinical practice, and provide guidance to improve practice (TNE Prospectus, p. 13).

These features of the control society – never-finished, heterogeneous standards, and continuous monitoring – are evident in professionalisation policies that constitute peer governance.[12] All three of these features are double edged. On the one hand, it would be a wonderful thing if everyone continued to learn, grow, and change throughout life. At the same time, when such pursuits are mandated by policy regulations rather than motivated by intellectual curiosity, then engagements in lifelong learning may turn into vacuous credential-seeking. Furthermore, of course educational pursuits should be responsive to a wide range of social interests; however, when standards become overly diffuse, then it becomes virtually impossible to make headway in any direction. Finally, when continuous monitoring serves to support the extension of educational opportunities with increased attention to focus and detail, then such monitoring can be a source of information and clarity for program development. However, continuous monitoring can also become a distraction. When the paperwork associated with responding to continuous monitoring becomes a time-consuming task in itself, then educators spend more time on paperwork and less time on teaching and learning.

ELEVATION OF SOCIAL STANDING

Professionalisation policies for teachers generally promise an improved social standing for teachers. Teaching and teacher education in the United States are traditionally perceived as "lowly" in status (from both inside and outside of the profession), so professionalisation is generally understood as a policy to support upward social mobility.[13] In this section, I focus on professional empowerment for teachers, noting that even empowerment turns out to be a double-edged sword.

For teachers, professionalisation generally implies an improvement in social status. However, Veysey (1988) made some provocative observations about inconsistencies in the use of the term *professional*. He noted that we do not use the term "professional physicist" because in the case of physicists, a high social status is already implied, and the term professional adds no value. Similarly, Veysey noted that poets, whose occupation is highly intellectual and specialised, disdain the designation *professional* because it connotes a degradation of their status as artists. In universities, professional schools are commonly distinguished from academic disciplines. In his historical examination of higher education, Veysey reminds us that professions have had different kinds of relationships to universities. In the nineteenth and twentieth centuries, teacher education elevated its social standing by shifting the site of preparation from teacher training institutes, to normal schools, and finally to universities. Most recently, however, this trend seems to be reversing itself in the United States as university-based teacher education is being seriously challenged, and in some cases replaced by specialised corporate teacher preparation programs.[14] More dimensions of ambiguities of teacher professionalisation are apparent in inconsistencies in the use of the term, and in the history of shifting relationships between higher education and teacher professionalisation.

More evidence of the shift away from the university as the primary site for teacher preparation can be found in the policies of TNE. The TNE prospectus calls teaching a "clinical practice profession" (p. 12), a phrase clearly modelled on medical education. "Excellent teaching is a clinical skill" the TNE prospectus goes on to say (p. 12), and schools are referred to as clinics. TNE promotes the idea that teacher preparation ought to be conducted in clinical settings, by which they mean in schools.

University-based teacher preparation is being diminished in the context of alternative certification routes and increased emphasis on schools as sites of clinical practice. At the same time, there is simultaneously a surprising move to make schoolteachers more like university faculty members and also to have teachers actually become university faculty members. Teacher professionalisation means that teachers are doing more research, both during their initial teacher certification programs and also in graduate programs and continuing education courses. Since professionalisation in most fields is based on the production and dissemination of a knowledge base, research has become a hallmark of professionalisation, particularly in (higher) education. In the 1980s, teacher education underwent professional restructuring that included increased demands to conduct and publish research. Similarly, we now see higher expectations for teachers to do research in the contexts of their own schools and classrooms. Teacher research is known by many terms in different venues (e.g., action research, practitioner research, reflective teaching), and it is a regular feature of teacher preparation and professional development. Another twist in the shifting relationship between professionalisation and higher education are policies that classroom teachers be hired by universities as faculty members. Presumably as a way of elevating the social standing of teachers, TNE policy explicitly advocates that teachers be hired by universities:

> Through some appropriate process of selection, experienced excellent teachers should be recognised as faculty colleagues along with other teacher educators in higher education. Some form of qualified faculty appointment may recognise their status, e.g., clinical faculty, professor of practice, or adjunct professor (TNE Prospectus, p. 13).

It is easy to see how doing more research and joining university faculties would serve to move teachers up in the world. Doing research has been an indispensable component of the formation of professional bodies, and in general, university professors are endowed with higher social capital than school teachers are. However, these trends are also double edged. When teachers become more like university faculty, the standing of teacher educators may be improved, but the standing of teachers *qua* teachers is degraded. Insofar as teachers professionalise themselves by becoming more like another professional group, the social standing of teachers is not improved.

Finally, professionalisation efforts to elevate the social status of teachers can be seen in terms of Cruikshank's (1999) will to empower. Although empowerment is almost universally assumed to be a step in the right direction, Cruikshank's Foucaultian analysis calls our attention to ways in which even empowerment is double-edged.

In her book, Cruikshank analyses the ways empowerment works to produce citizens. If we take her analysis and substitute *professionals* for *citizens,* then we can gain some critical purchase on the workings of empowerment:

> Like any discourse, the discourses of empowerment are learned, habitual, and material (...). It is quite natural to seek the cause of political problems in order to prescribe a cure. It is my hope that readers (...) will find it harder to pin a political problem on the lack of *professionalisation*. I hope that in its stead we will interrogate what there is in the will to empower, the technologies of *professionalisation*, and arts of government by which the various kinds of *professionals* we have are constituted (Cruikshank, 1999, p. 123; italicised words added in place of the original *citizen, citizenship*, and *citizens*).

Cruikshank (1999) sees empowerment as yet another kind of discipline: "I link the operationalisation of social scientific knowledge to what Theresa Funiciello calls 'the professionalisation of being human' or what Foucault called 'bio-power'" (Cruikshank, 1999, p. 20). If we start from the conviction that teaching is neither more nor less worthy than educational administration, then it becomes possible to see that policies and practices that are designed to make teachers *become like something else* are still forms of governance and normalising, even if we call those practices *empowerment.*

CONCLUSION

Professionalisation serves several masters: it empowers teachers to participate in educational governance, it provides a venue for regulation at ever deeper levels of detail and specificity, it provides a warrant for assessment and a theme for accountability, it raises expectations and hence aspirations for advancement, and it makes teaching seem to be affiliated with more prestigious organisations such as physicians, lawyers, and veterinarians. I hope this argument has shown that regulation is not always bad, and empowerment is not always good, and professionalisation has no necessarily positive or negative value for teachers or other concerned educators. Professionalisation, as a complex interweaving of regulation and empowerment, embodies a confusing morass of affordances and limitations that have a mixed-bag effect on teachers, teaching, and teacher education.

When we regard professionalisation from a variety of critical perspectives, then previous arguments that advocate or decry professionalisation policies can be seen as overly simplistic. Such polemical stances – whether celebrating or vilifying professionalisation – miss the opportunity to look critically at a variety of possible implications of professionalisation that range from beneficial to detrimental or ineffectual. Standards, peer governance, and social standing are only three of many dimensions entailed in professionalisation policies that merit careful scrutiny and further critical analysis.

NOTES

[1] This is one of two national teachers' unions in the United States, the other one being the National Education Association.

[2] NBPTS, the National Board of Professional Teaching Standards, was formed in 1986 to provide professional leadership for educators by educators. As stated in the NBPTS 2008 Guide:"The National Board for Professional Teaching Standards has contracted with Educational Testing Service (ETS) to conduct the National Board Certification® process. ETS develops and produces the assessment materials; develops and operates systems for processing candidate applications, materials, and scores; and reports candidate results. This project is funded in part with grants from the U.S. Department of Education and the National Science Foundation. Through September 2007, NBPTS has been appropriated federal funds of $167.7 million, of which $151.9 was expended. Such amount represents approximately 32 percent of the National Board Certification project. Approximately $325.6 million (68 percent) of the project's cost was financed by non-federal sources." (http://www.nbpts.org/userfiles/File/2008_Guide_Web_PDF_final.pdf)

[3] The eleven recipient institutions are Bank Street (NY), California State (Northridge), U. of Virginia, Boston College, Florida A&M, Stanford, U. of Connecticut, U. of Texas (El Paso), U. of Washington, U. of Wisconsin (Milwaukee), and my own institutional home, Michigan State University.

[4] In some traditions of educational research, this shift from non-routine to routine is referred to as "deskilling." I do not use this term here because I regard the shift from non-routine tasks to routine tasks not as one of reducing or eliminating the skills required for teaching, but rather, as a shift in the sorts of skills that are expected and required of teachers in current historical conditions of professionalization.

[5] See, for example, Foucault, 1970; Heilbron, Magnusson & Witrock, 1998; Jones, 1990; Nelson, Megill & McCloskey, 1987; Porter, 1995.

[6] *A Nation at Risk: The Imperative For Educational Reform* is the 1983 report of the National Commission on Excellence in Education convened by then US President Ronald Reagan. This report has formed the basis for a sense of urgency to reform the US educational system, which was portrayed in the report as lagging miserably behind the rest of the world in its capacity to educate students.

[7] See, for example, the research requirements for funding by U.S. government sources at What Works Clearinghouse, http://www.whatworks.ed.gov/.

[8] Campbell & Stanley, 1963.

[9] This policy initiative has baffled even the most die-hard advocates of the use of statistical methods in educational research.

[10] By choosing those terms of contrast, Deleuze is apparently suggesting an alternative to Foucault's theories of discipline. For more on what Foucault means by discipline, see, for example, his *Discipline and Punish: The Birth of the Prison,* Vintage, 1979.

[11] Again, I do not mean to imply that this is necessarily a good thing or a bad thing; I am calling attention to features of professional governance.

[12] Ellsworth's (1996) notion of "situated response-ability" [sic] pertains to a teacher's accountability, and it has some partial relation to peer governance in professionalization endeavors.

[13] For thorough discussions of this phenomenon, see especially Labaree, 1998, 2000 and 2006.

[14] The development of non-university-based teacher education in the United States is often referred to as an "alternative certification" route. See, for example, the National Center for Alternative Certification, http://www.teach-now.org/.

REFERENCES

Abbott, A. (1988). *The system of professions: An essay on the division of expert labor.* Chicago: University of Chicago Press.

Al-Hinai, A. M. (2007). Culture and teacher professionalism. In T. Townsend & R. Bates (Eds.), *Handbook of teacher education: Globalization, standards and professionalism in times of change* (pp. 41–52). Dordrecht: Springer.

Bledstein, B. J. (1976). *The culture of professionalism: The middle class and the development of higher education in America.* New York: Norton.

Campbell, D. T., & Stanley, J. C. (1963). *Experimental and quasi-experimental designs for research.* Boston: Houghton Mifflin.

Cruikshank, B. (1999). *The will to empower: Democratic citizens and other subjects.* Ithaca, NY: Cornell University Press.

Deleuze, G. (1992). Postscript on the societies of control. *October, 59,* 3–7.

Ellsworth, E. (1996, Spring). Situated response-ability to student papers. *Theory into Practice, 35*(2), 138–143.

Flanagan, N. (2007). Teacher professionalism: Diamonds on the souls of her shoes. In R. H. Ackerman & S. V. Mackenzie (Ed.), *Uncovering teacher leadership: Essays and voices from the field* (pp. 89–92). Thousand Oaks, CA: Corwin Press.

Foucault, M. (1970). *The order of things: An archaeology of the human sciences.* New York: Random House.

Freidson, E. (1984). The changing nature of professional control. *Annual Review of Sociology, 10,* 1–20.

Hatch, N. O. (1988). Introduction: The professions in a democratic culture. In N. O. Hatch (Ed.), *The professions in American history* (pp. 1–13). Notre Dame, IN: University of Notre Dame Press.

Heilbron, J., Magnusson, L., & Wittrock, B. (Eds.). (1998). *The rise of the social sciences and the formation of modernity: Conceptual change in context, 1750–1850.* Boston: Kluwer Academic Publishers.

Jones, R. (1990). Educational practices and scientific knowledge: A genealogical reinterpretation of the emergence of physiology in post-revolutionary France. In S. J. Ball (Ed.), *Foucault and education: Disciplines and knowledge* (pp. 78–104). New York: Routledge.

Labaree, D.F. (1992). Power, knowledge, and the rationalization of teaching: A genealogy of the movement to professionalize teaching. *Harvard Educational Review, 62*(2), 123-154.

Labaree, D. F. (1998). Educational researchers: Living with a lesser form of knowledge. *Educational Researcher, 27*(8), 4–12.

Labaree, D. F. (2000). On the nature of teaching and teacher education: Difficult practices that look easy. *Journal of Teacher Education, 51*(3), 228–233.

Labaree, D. F. (2006). *The trouble with ed schools.* New Haven, CT: Yale University Press.

Nelson, J. S., Megill, A., & McCloskey, D. N. (Eds.). (1987). *The rhetoric of the human sciences: Language and argument in scholarship and human affairs.* Madison, WI: University of Wisconsin Press.

Newby, M. (2007). Standards and professionalism: Peace talks? In T. Townsend & R. Bates (Eds.), *Handbook of teacher education: Globalization, standards and professionalism in times of change* (pp. 113–125). Dordrecht: Springer.

Popkewitz, T.S., (1993). U.S. teacher education reforms: Regulatory practices of the state, university, and research. In T.S. Popkewitz (ed.), *Changing Patterns of Power: Social Regulation and Teacher Education Reform* (pp. 263-301). Albany, NY: SUNY Press.

Porter, T. M. (1995). *Trust in numbers: The pursuit of objectivity in science and public life.* Princeton, NJ: Princeton University Press.

Teachers for a New Era Evidence Team. (2007). *Rethinking teacher education: From teacher learning to student learning.* Symposium presented at AERA, Chicago, IL. Retrieved from http://www.teachersforanewera.org/

Veysey, L. (1988). Higher education as a profession: Changes and continuities. In N. O. Hatch (Ed.), *The professions in American history* (pp. 15–32). Notre Dame, IN: University of Notre Dame Press.

Wilson, A. (1999). Creating identities of dependency: Adult education as a knowledge-power regime. *International Journal of Lifelong Education, 18*(2), 85–93.

FURTHER READINGS

Abbott, A. (1988). *The system of professions: An essay on the division of expert labour.* Chicago: University of Chicago Press.

Bledstein, B. J. (1976). *The culture of professionalism: The middle class and the development of higher education in America.* New York: Norton.

Cruikshank, B. (1999). *The will to empower: Democratic citizens and other subjects.* Ithaca, NY: Cornell University Press.

Hatch, N. O. (Ed.). (1988) *The professions in American history.* Notre Dame, IN: University of Notre Dame Press.

Heilbron, J., Magnusson, L., & Wittrock, B. (1998) (Eds.). *The rise of the social sciences and the formation of modernity: Conceptual change in context, 1750–1850.* Boston: Kluwer Academic Publishers.

Lynn Fendler
Department of Teacher Education
Michigan State University, USA

RITA FOSS LINDBLAD & SVERKER LINDBLAD

THE POLITICS OF PROFESSIONALISING TALK ON TEACHING

Boundary Work and Reconfigurations of Teaching and Teachers

INTRODUCTION

Teachers and their work are in focus in this text – or more precisely ways of talking about teaching as a profession. Definitions of teachers and teachers' work in professionalising talk are here examined as a result of various forms of *boundary work* where different actors struggle over the meanings and values of what it means to teach and to be a teacher. As with other such attempts, this boundary work involves an intellectual style for presenting what constitutes the unique work of teachers and teaching and has the purpose of creating a public image of what it is that demarcates it from other occupational work and activities. This boundary work is *political* – producing or challenging distinctions between 'professional' and 'non-professional' ways of teaching and what bearings this differences should have within schools and educational systems. By this, boundary work has the possible power of making a difference in people's lives within these spheres.

In such boundary work of creating and defending, as well as attacking existing demarcations, teachers are just one of many stakeholders, and the objectives of construed content are likewise numerous and varied. Besides teachers, politicians, administrators and researchers of different theoretical orientations and institutional affiliations are active participants here. Thus, definitions and demarcations of the teaching profession are results of the work of a number of agents, which despite their shifting focus are united in a shared interest of enrolling 'science' and 'scientific knowledge' into their arguments and intellectual universes.

There are, and have been, changes over time but the conceptual links between the meanings of 'profession' on the one hand, and different institutional or intellectual links to 'science'[1] and 'scientific knowledge' on the other hand have been with us from 'the beginning.' Given this, a brief historical overview of the social construction of the boundary work of professions gives us opportunities to capture how the politics of professionalising talk on teaching relates to shifting trends in the understanding of science and society. This also provides us with opportunities to address more general issues about the how's and why's in professionalising talks on teaching and to deepen our understanding of the politics involved. More precisely, we are addressing two overarching questions: Firstly, what are the main ideas of 'teachers as professionals' and what are their origins and specificities? Secondly, what are the relations between shifting trends in the

M. Simons, M. Olssen and M.A. Peters (eds.), Re-Reading Education Policies: A Handbook Studying the Policy Agenda of the 21ˢᵗ Century, 754–773.

organisation of education and schooling and teachers' professional authority and what are the significances of the present situation of ongoing boundary works? In order to shed some light on these questions we present a way to unpack professional distinctions and to deal with their changing meanings over time and contexts.

SCIENCE, BOUNDARY WORK, AND TEACHING AS A PROFESSION

The legitimating power of 'science' cannot be underestimated in contemporary societies where no welfare state institution or professional can act with authority without some sort of licence from the knowledge-producing machinery of science. In a broad sense, science (or scientific knowledge production) has become the hallmark of quality. Or to put it differently, science has become the symbolic sign of intellectual authority. But it is an authority which has changed meanings over the years, as the recently altered meanings of the label 'the Knowledge Society' indicates. From its early optimistic meanings in Druckner (1969) and Bell (1973) the Knowledge Society concept of for example Böhme & Stehr (1986) has more cautious, or even pessimistic, connotations. Today's dependences on the sciences and on scientific knowledge has to confront also some of the more disastrous effects of what scientific and technological knowledge have produced (as the atomic bomb, climate changes etc.).The meanings of 'Knowledge Society' has by this departed from much of its previous trust in science as enlightenment and changed into notions of a new sort of economical and political dependences (what usually is referred to as the knowledge economy).

Despite (or maybe in accordance with) this, the power of the science label is visible in many different ways in the spheres of education: in the division of labour and in the hierarchical structuring of educational systems, where salary and social prestige are expected to increase with more training in scientific and scholarly thinking and methods. It is also visible in the ways in which educational activities have been categorised as opposite – or subordinated – to those of science (as for example the well-known practice/theory divide or dominant understandings of the relations between research and education) and, not least, in the ways in which educational practices are governed by knowledge-inscribed practices and technologies. Broad spectra of evaluations and rankings, for example the TIMSS (Trends in International Maths and Science Studies) and PIRLS (Progress in International Reading Literacy Studies), all rely heavily on scientific methods, techniques and conceptualisations of how educational practices could be measured, judged as well as governed within as well as outside the classroom.

However, as has been shown by several historians and sociologists of knowledge, the victory of 'science' as a leading intellectual institution was not won by means of its 'truth' or even its 'efficiency', but by means of boundary work done by scientists to establish truth as well as efficiency as the characteristics which made it distinct from non-scientific activities. Interestingly, and according to Thomas Gieryn (1983), the ultimate victory of science was not won in competition with religion alone. It was won also in competition with Victorian mechanical technicians and engineers, who by the end of the 18th century strongly criticised natural scientists for being too speculative and producing knowledge with little practical impact (which must also be regarded as having been the case in those days). But scientists fruitfully managed to use stylistic resources to contrast science with non-science, where the distinction vis-à-vis religion was as important as the distinction vis-à-vis mechanics.

Contrary to religion, the practical uses of science were said to be found in: its ability to inspire technological progress and material conditions of nations; its empirical nature based on experimentation and observations of the facts of nature; and the belief in science as a sceptical and objective activity, free from interest as well as emotions. In contrast to mechanics, science was considered to be what is applicable, while mechanics was thought of as implementing the applications. The result of this boundary work was a science conceptualised as theoretical and systematic, whose political and practical value derived from its consequences and not from its essence.

The public victory of these conceptions of science paved the way for successful practices in terms of the expansion of expertise in new domains, for the possibility of monopolising resources and the authority achieved, and for protecting autonomy. And over time, boundary work within and beyond science became part of the making of an increasing differentiation within academia, changing science into:

> (...) 'separate' institutional and professional niches through continuing processes of boundary work designed to achieve an apparent differentiation of goals, methods, capabilities and substantive expertise (Gieryn, op. cit., p. 783).

Thus, such boundary work is vital for a profession – be it science, medicine, law or teaching – and necessary for claiming and maintaining intellectual authority in a field of practice. This is also the case for professionalisation projects with ambitions to achieve expansion, monopolisation, and autonomy (e.g. Sarfatti Larson, 1977) where multiple meanings and aspects of 'science' still are central.

But 'science' is also producing boundaries, of inclusions as well as exclusions. This can be exemplified within the history of education: applying the work of Basil Bernstein (2000), the organisation of schooling and teaching is linked to science in three different ways. (a) Based on differentiation in academic territories we find the reproduction of disciplines and boundary work in the selection and defending of school subjects and the authority to teach in these subjects. But in the hands of teachers, who are lacking the authority of research competence, the hierarchy between schools and universities is maintained. (b) Based on research on learning and development we note boundary work to produce a recognised expertise on pedagogy in the development of the child to a responsible citizen, but while the professional expertise of the educationalist scholar is recognised in its all right, the expertise of the teacher is seen as dependent on the expertise produced by the educational sciences. (c) Based on organisational and management theories we note boundary work on how to run and evaluate schools, but here again we find the same asymmetry in symbolic powers and dependences on scientific legacy. Thus, the construction of different kind of teachers and models of school management is to a great extant constituted on bases of institutionalised differences within the organisation of the sciences, as well as on a trust in its legacy. In addition, however, today we find a fourth kind of emerging relations to the sciences, in the (d) ongoing boundary work stating that teachers by their 'own knowledge' are having the authority to be a profession based on teachers' (or teacher educators') clinical expertise. This science-practice link is usually claimed to be new in kind (as for example when used in relation to the Schön (1983) conception of "teacher as a reflective practitioner") and, when related to ongoing boundary work, it put as much pressure on change, as it claims authority to the tasks and duties of teachers and teaching. The issue concerns this time the epistemic dimension of teachers work, and who will have the power and capacities to clarify the content as well as the uses of this body of knowledge.

In these four ways we find different ways of enrolling the sciences in the professionalising talks of teaching. Sometimes these enrolments involves strategies that support each other, sometimes they contradict each other. Our argument here is not about the strategies as such, however. Our point is to demonstrate that the stabilisation, or the destabilisation, of the meanings and authority of teaching as a profession is based on processes of boundary work over scientific authority of some sort, through some organisational and institutional pathway.

HOW TO PROCEED – UNPACKING PROFESSIONAL DISTINCTIONS

During the last century the 'classical' professions, such as medicine and law, have been followed by a number of occupations striving for similar status. Thus, in the 1960s Harold L. Wilensky (1964) noted ongoing professionalisation ambitions among a large set of occupations – such as teachers – and pointed out that the profession concept would embrace almost every job with some kind of specialised knowledge, presumably without professional authority, however. Such an expansion of the profession concept was counteracted in the profession literature by scholars such as Amitai Etzioni (1969). Here, a demarcation line was drawn between professions and semi-professions. In the latter category we find occupations that have some characteristics in common with the professions but lack other characteristics. Thus, semi-professionals were excluded from those occupations that were given the name of 'professions' and, given this distinction, it seemed unlikely that teachers would ever achieve professional status. Teachers were not characterised as autonomous decision-makers and were not accountable to the profession but to their supervisors or policy-makers. Teachers did not govern the school organisation. They were outside of the profession borderline according to this politics of professionalising talk.

However, in the 1980s and 1990s notions of teachers as professionals were again put on the agenda in many parts of the world. At this time the expression 'the teaching profession' came into common use among teachers as well as among researchers and policy makers (e.g. Labaree, 1992; Lundström, 2007). For instance the US National Foundation for the Improvement of Education stated in 1996:

> The teaching profession, from within, has been transforming itself from a semi-profession to a real profession, one based on knowledge and the responsible application of that knowledge.[2]

When utterances like this come out in the plural, their performative character becomes strong, and they can be expected to be part of a collective construction of new kinds of beings. It is naturalised talk where 'the professional teacher' is not only an intellectual construction, but also a teacher with a bodily shape. In the words of Ian Hacking (2001, p. 48):

> Categories of people come into existence at the same time as kinds of people come into being to fit those categories, and there is always a two-way interaction.

Accordingly, we might expect that there should be teachers who 'fit,' and who actually are also made up to fit, the category in question. Not necessarily (or even probably) in a complete way, but at least partially. We may ask who these people are, under what descriptions they appear, and, most importantly, what the mechanisms and practices are that have made them emerge as a category.

Asking these questions reveals our nominalist perspective, claiming that the very act of naming has inventive powers and can make circumstances and objects that did not exist before become real, as stated above by Hacking. Not by magic, but by the potential ability to change the perception of what the act of naming designates. When realising that the work of teachers today frequently is spoken of in professional terms, the problem – or mystery – here is of course that 'profession' is not new as a category, only 'new' with reference to this occupational group. What must be unpacked is what this altered meaning of 'profession' signals within the contexts in which it is situating itself. These are contexts that have been subscribed with as many changes as have those of the profession.

CHANGES IN MEANING – CHANGES IN CONTEXT

So, what do we mean when we talk about professions and professional work? And, more relevantly from our point of view, how are we to understand the talk of teachers as professionals? While the meanings of professions and professional work has long been a central question in the social sciences, where professional theory is recognised as a research field of its own, with history, traditions, and differences, questions concerning teachers as professionals are newer and have never had a central position in the social sciences generally, nor in the field of professional research. However, notions on teaching as a science-based professional work have since long had a central role in the educational sciences (e.g. in Durkheim's lectures on the evolution of educational thought, 1904/1977) where educational science was recognised as having central and critical, and even emancipating functions. The production of adequate (and applicable) scientific knowledge was thought of as important for realising the democratic goals of schooling by making it more effective, from the point of view of the 'learner' as well as from the point of view of the 'nation'.

But, the present situation is different. As shall be shown, today's talk of teaching as a profession occurs at a time when previous thoughts about the meaning of the professions generally has been replaced by new, and at first glance less prestigious, ones. However, a second look may indicate new grounds for what it means to be prestigious in the life, work, and world of professionals and professions. In the next section, we will present an overview of discourses on professions and professionalism as it might be viewed from the horizon of their theoretical underpinnings, and from the view of changed realities for those who was, or was not, included within this category. Again, the category of 'the professional' addresses some specific kinds of people that will, or will not, fit within the category. But what brought these categories into life?

Professional theories and the exclusion/inclusion of teaching

The interest in questions about what it means to be a profession and a professional has dominantly been focussed on the professions in medicine and law and professional theories, dominantly with sociological origins, have to some extant hold on to these domains over the years. Such a focus has also been important for conceptualisations of professions and professional work, for instance in relation to the distinctive traits of 'real professions' in contrast to ordinary occupations. Thus, in scholarly debates on professions and their social importance, the definitions of such traits have been of vital concern. In what can be considered as traditional accounts, the professions are presented as having specific traits linked to scientific or scholarly progress and competence and to their serving of clients and promotion of social reforms in the interest of the public (e.g. Tawney, 1921).

The discussion within the discourse of professional traits has a long history but can be summarised as follows: In order to become a professional, specialised higher education and training in the professional body of knowledge is needed, as is legal status as a professional organisation. Members of a profession, defined in this way, were seen as having a (legitimate) monopoly in access to professional knowledge, and their working position was considered to be autonomous and supported by legal status – subordinated only to the ethical codices of the profession. Professions with such characteristics were also understood as being sheltered from competition from other occupations, and their social recognition was considered to be built on trust and on rewarding remuneration. With such traits, the professionals stood out as altruistic heroes of modern society, utilizing the progress of science and professional experience as they served society in their field of authorised expertise. It goes without saying that the professional was a male with a masculine ethos.

In somewhat similar ways the professions turn up in functionalist/positivist social analyses. For instance, Émile Durkheim (1890/1957) touched upon it in relation to his studies on the social division of labour and social integration in modernising societies, where he came to stress the importance of the creation and institutionalisation of moral bonds and norms within a modernity that was seen as threatened by the spread of moral disorder. Society was, for Durkheim, in need of professionals between the state and the majority of individuals in order to stabilise change in a profound way. Talcott Parsons (1939), in a similar functionalist perspective of obtaining social cohesion and trust, underlined the smooth functioning of professions as vital to modern societies. The professions trained and active within the universities were, according to Parsons, not only a historically unique feature of modern society, but also special in comparison to other groups, such as business managers, given e.g. the professions' mix of scientific rationality and lack of self-interest in relation to clients.

For reasons that may appear obvious, these understandings of professions and professional life seem antique. The world as well as the understandings and organising of the professions have changed and the theoretical underpinnings of defining professions have been object of several criticisms.

Firstly, the validity of claimed altruistic traits of and by the professions was not only questioned, it was turned on its head (e.g. Abbot, 1988). It was argued that the professions are characterised by self-interest in their obtaining and maintaining a privileged position, socially as well as financially, and by striving for market closure. Despite and seemingly unaffected by a substantial number of other critical voices, professional boundary work has been regarded by other occupations as a very successful strategy for prestige and control. Thus, quite a few occupations have more or less successfully been working to be incorporated into the professions – e.g. engineers, architects and accountants etc. (see e.g. Burrage & Torstendahl, 1990) – by fulfilling such traits as those presented above, for instance advanced education, professional organisation, ethical codices etc. These collective actors have developed professional projects (Sarfatti Larson, 1977) with ambitions to achieve professional status.

Secondly, the trait approach is questioned for lacking theoretical significance. The traits presented above – even in taxonomic form – are descriptive with a normative twist. Such traits can be used to make distinctions between professions and non-professions, but offer little in terms of explanatory or theoretical back-up. Given this, it can be argued that the trait approach too readily is giving the professions scope to define themselves and is leaving no explanatory room for capturing asymmetries in power and conflicting interests (e.g. Johnson, 1972).

Thirdly, most sociological theories of professions have taken issues of competence and rationality for granted as an important claim for professional status. However, recent ways to understand professions focus on the knowledge issue in new ways. Thomas Broman (1995), for instance, criticises ways (such as by Abbot, 1988) of defining a profession without considering the intrinsic relation between professional theory and practice. Thus, Broman gives his argument an epistemological critical edge and states:

> The power yielded by professionals (...) derives uniquely from a set of claims that scientific theory can and does guide practice and the institutional and educational structures developed in accordance with those claims (Broman, 1995, p. 837).

Along with the lost trust in these beliefs, new understandings of the history and specificity of the professions have emerged. An influential intellectual resource in this shift has of course been Michel Foucault, and especially his notions of knowledge and power such as those presented in e.g. Discipline and Punish (1977). Jan Goldstein (1984) is a presenter of this 'Foucauldian' approach where professional knowledge is important as a component of disciplining systems and where professionalism appears more as a social and political effect than as an achievement of knowledge and competence in the ordinary sense.

> Professionalism, as rewritten by Foucault, becomes a 'new 'micro-physics' of power, indeed the quintessentially modern mode of wielding power. Hence, it is hardly surprising that the 'disciplines/professions' grew up, as Foucault repeatedly points out in close collaboration with the state, making use of those bureaucratic and 'police' networks which had been spun out of the modern state to check, observe, and preserve the population systematically (Goldstein, 1984, pp. 176–177).

Important here is the constitution of professional knowledge in professional practice. Knowledge is a power at work in professional practice – in the authorised preservation and administration of the population where e.g. the knowledge of lawyers and doctors became constituted as much on what was 'good' for the patient/client as on what was 'the public good' of the national states. Prisons, hospitals as well as mental hospitals all bear witness of the close connections between the emergence of professional knowledge, the makings of new categories of people and the power structures of the state.

This notion of power/knowledge in professionalism is also of vital importance to an understanding of the social and cultural relativism of professional practice where the meanings of 'competent and rational' change over time and contexts. These shifts are orchestrated by shifts in behaviour and tend to occur when new kinds of professional beings have already emerged, or are in their becoming. Valerie Fournier (1999) argues in a similar way and says that professional practice is at work where the conditions of autonomy have already been inscribed in particular forms of conduct. One example is today's notions of 'professional competence' as something that presuppose active knowledge of as much doings as of knowing. Based on this she concludes:

> (...) being a professional is not merely about absorbing a body of scientific knowledge but is also about conducting and constituting oneself in an appropriate manner (Fournier, 1999, p. 287).

It is within the complexity of this power/knowledge nexus that the mystery of the professionalising talk of teaching – as presented in the beginning of this chapter –

could be addressed. Previous omissions, as well as present inclusions, of teaching within the vocabulary of professions may be seen as consequences of more or less successful strategies to mobilise resources of control over, as well as within, labour processes generally. With Fournier, the appeal to professionalism acts as a disciplinary mechanism of some sort and with some targets that are possible to identify within the specific organisation of present-day societies.

Today's way of conducting work, along with changes in the labour market, sets new scenarios for professionals, for their claims of professionality as well as for its governance. Thus, Fournier situates her arguments of professional acting in the economic, cultural and technological context of a postmodern move towards flexible strategies of capital accumulation (e.g. Harvey, 1989). She sees the appeal to professionalism as one of the strategies that are deployed to control the increasing margin of indeterminacy or flexibility in work. With a similar approach Julia Evetts (2006) deals with recent profession discourses as normalising and governing the new professions in the service sector.

This short review of different ways of rethinking professions reveals that the definition of professions has been, and is, controversial in several ways and has also been constituted differently in different times. The review shows that past as well as present discourses are impregnated by more general attempts to deal with social changes. This means that no understandings of the politics that governs – and is governed by – the professionalising talk can ignore its intimate relation to the ways in which its subject matter relates to the thoughts about the world and the situations within it. But the subject matter of a Durkheimian, Parsonian or even Foucauldian reading of professionalism could, we guess, be expected to differ from those readings of professionalism that we now witness regarding the tasks of teachers and teaching.

Professionalising talk on teaching – boundary work and educational restructuring.

Even though today professionalising talk on teaching share some stylistic features of previous boundary works of professionalism (such as the epistemic claims of a specific body of knowledge), the present situations has also some specificities that indicates new scenarios for education as well as for the educational sciences generally. However, there are signs that point to the possibility that the professionalising talk of teaching is more of a restructuring tool within an already restructured socio-political landscape of education and educational sciences; than it is a sign of that the work of teachers now has won increased recognition, authority and autonomy. In the following we are putting forward what these signs and their critical instances are.

The first, important critical instance for understanding the significances of the professionalising talk of teachers is *the very definition of professionalism*. Going back to 1973, June Purvis complained about the lack of research on teaching as a profession. This was a lack by definition. Schoolteachers were instead concept-ualised as semi-professionals or marginal professionals in the dominating discourse on professions at that time. There were, of course, studies on teachers such as those by Winnifred Waller (1932) and Dan Lortie (1969). However, as presented somewhat later by Lortie (1975) in his seminal work on teachers, what characterises teachers is that they are *not* professionals, as they lack the kind of professional ethos and technological culture that is distinctive for lawyers and physicians. There is, we will say, no indication that this situation has changed. Instead, and as we already have pointed out, the invasion of a professional terminology within common language, educational research journals and policy texts from the 1980s and onwards indicate that the claimed entry of teachers into a collective of professionals – the professionalising talk of teaching – is an essential constituting part of making new categories of teachers who are able to fit into new preconditions of work.

A common way to talk about this new circumstances is in terms of educational restructuring and, as it seems, this is were the boundary work of teachers as professionals is situating itself. The epistemic as well as geopolitical contours given to this *situatedness* is the second critical instance for understanding the significances of the professionalising talk on teaching. Educational restructuring is giving contours to the how's and why's of the professionalising talk of teaching and the boundary-works it is involving.

Firstly, this educational restructuring is taking place world-wide and is usually referring to elements such as marketisation, new public management, and de-regulation and gets much of its significances from the consequences of macro-political and economical changes (such as globalisation). It means a clear de-centring of educational policies, from the state to the vernacular and with dislocated centres-peripheries, also including the increase in the power of international and supranational agents (such as the EU and the OECD). A starting point for this period is often labelled neo-liberalism referring to the marketisation initiated in England by the late 1970s – occurring at about the same time as the beginning of the Swedish decentralisation measures and the Irish secularisation of schooling (cf. Goodson & Lindblad, 2008) – and later on turning into 'the middle way' in England or the emergence of a quality agenda in Sweden.

Secondly, the intimate relation between educational restructuring and the professionalising talk of teaching shows itself as a discursive homogeneity. From an historical point of view, *the trajectories into restructuring* – though narrated somewhat different in different national settings contexts – share a focussed interest in teaching as a professional arena of competences, its problems and its possible futures. From a geo-political point of view we find an Anglo-Saxon hegemony in 'international' research discourses on teacher professionalism. To our experience voices outside the Anglo-Saxon domain with few exceptions had little impact on profession discourses, even if they were written in English.[3] This circumstance indicates a geo-political homogenisation of current research communities where three sets of arguments considered of importance for the teaching profession in reconfiguration dominates the arguments:

- General arguments on *societies and institutions in transition* where more or less 'free-floating intellectuals' – such as Benedict Anderson (2002), Pierre Bourdieu (1988), Manuel Castells (1998), Anthony Giddens (1988) and others – comment on and analyse ongoing social and cultural changes, which in turn are part in the reconstruction of the teaching profession as it is vital for given voice and meanings to its social and political contexts.
- Arguments on *education policy changes* or travelling policies, referring to e.g. world movements, translations of policy discourses, as well as changes in governance in different contexts – e.g. Stephen J. Ball (1990), Basil Bernstein (2000), Roger Dale (1997), Sharon Gewirtz (2002), Thomas S. Popkewitz 2000, and others. This literature is often critical of neo-liberalism or performativity in education and is sometimes putting forwards alternatives in terms of democratic accountability and views, sometimes, also professionalism in itself as such an alternative.
- Arguments with a focus on *changes in teaching practices and professional knowledge* adjusting to changing conditions for schooling or performing schooling in revision referring to professional trust (e.g. Lennart Svensson, 2006) and accountability and competence (e.g. Linda Darling Hammond, 1998). These arguments are sometimes explicitly doing boundary work discussing alternative routes concerning teaching and teacher identity (Judyth Sachs, 2001; John Beck & Michael F. Young, 2005).

In sum we note a pattern of homogenising discursive positioning used in constructions of the teaching profession in educational research combining arguments on institutional and socio-political changes as well as patterns of professional practices in transition.

However, whatever (and whoever) comes into our view, the objectives of the knowledge produced makes a difference as it translates and *re-locates* the meanings of educational restructuring and teacher professionalism, which is our third critical instance for understanding the professionalising talk on teaching. Here, we note a number of texts locating the issues of educational restructuring and teacher professionalism to the spheres of teaching and schooling. We find texts dealing with the epistemic construction of "postmodern teachers" (Hargreaves, 1994), professional teachers capable of handling school reforms (Little, 1995) and managing their professional communities (McLaughlin & Talbert, 2001) where the boundary-work involves the epistemic constructions of 'competent and capable teachers of our times'. But there are also those who gives the issue of educational restructuring and the professionalisation of teachers a more openly political edge. Geoff Whitty (2000) is one example and can be dealt with more in detail here. He focuses on relations between the state and the teaching profession in England and considers teaching to be a profession going from licensed autonomy – managing their affairs – to a regulated autonomy:

> (...) a view emerged in the 1970s that teachers had abused this licensed autonomy to the detriment of their pupils and society (Whitty, 2000, p 283).

Whitty is here presenting a number of distinctions and categorisations concerning teachers and their professional authority – questioning a fixed set of criteria for what counts as a profession, making distinctions between the politics of professionalism and professionality, here also identifying distinctions in terms of extended and restricted professionality (c.f. Hoyle, 1974), as well as in management and trust. Through the use of these distinctions Whitty engage himself, together with others, to move a boundary – towards a "democratic professionalism" as a strategic alliance between professionals and their clients:

> So, if altruism and public service remain high on our professional agenda, the next re-formation of teacher professionalism will surely need to be one in which we harness teachers' professional expertise to a new democratic project for the twenty-first century (Whitty, 2000, p 292).

Another, and common, example is the professionalising talk that locates itself within the spheres of educational policy and is addressing questions of educational performances. From the US context: Marilyn Cochran-Smith and Mary Kim Fries (2001) analyse the politics in discourses on teacher education reform from this perspective. For Cochran-Smith and Fries the emphasis on outcomes is floating, having different implications in opposite agendas of professionalisation and deregulation and in the politics of teacher education reform. Their argument about the necessity to widening a 'professional' space in teacher education gives the boundary-work a somewhat different – and pragmatic – contour.

Given this focus on education performances we move over to current research discourses, where performances, or outcomes, or evaluation are playing a vital part in relation to teachers' work. Referring to Bernstein, in times of educational restructuring arguments on evaluation is having a tailwind, while research on curriculum and pedagogy is often regarded as being out of date if it does not present evidence on how to reach certain outcomes (e.g. Black & Dylan, 1998; Hargreaves, 2000). But such a performative turn implies as well that we will hear critical voices questioning this talk in terms of e.g. performativity (Ball, 2000) or the shifting political uses of league tables (e.g. Steiner-Khamsi, 2004). The issues involved in the professionalising talk of teaching are as complex as those involved in the issues of educational restructuring and the ways in which knowledge on the issues are being produced are varying with those of its producers.

Given current boundary work on the teaching profession, we also note a specific kind of professionalising talk favoured mostly by teacher educators and teacher organisations, but being articulated and produced as much inside as outside the traditional stakeholders of university based educational research. Partly, it is a talk directed at politicians and administrators, stressing the importance of teachers' practical professional knowledge or clinical knowledge. Partly it is talk directed to university disciplines, stating that their scientific authority caries less weight than that of the "reflective practitioner" or the "tacit knowledge" within the profession. In both ways this position reminds us of that of the mechanics questioning scientific boundary work in the 18th century as presented by Gieryn (1983). Thus, today, another aspect of boundary work is taking place inside a restructuring university. In university politics we are noting battles between research traditions, disciplines and faculties over what counts as science for the teaching profession, but, as we shall show, these new 'battlefields' has now also come to include the content and power of educational research within dramatically extended research arenas.

Boundary work and the politics of knowledge – the reconfiguration of teaching and teachers

Among the many voices taking part in the agenda-setting discourses on the professionalising talk on teaching, it is possible to identify three major actors, supra-national organisations, national policy-makers and administrators, plus researchers, each essential for understanding the twisted and political nature of the professionalising talk of teaching. All three are also essential for understanding the complexity of the fabrications of the professionalising talk of teaching, e.g. in terms of what will count as professional competence and professional work.

To begin with, supra-national organisations such as the OECD and the World Bank are promoting various kinds of decentralisation and deregulation, as well as international comparisons of educational performance. Their often heard voice (Lingard & Ozga, 2007) does not imply that their politics on education and teaching is implemented in national and local contexts (concerning the World Bank, see e.g. Hunter & Brown, 2000) in a straight-forward way, but their impact on national policies has nevertheless increased. For the OECD, the teaching profession has been on the agenda over a number of years where the teaching population is classified and sorted in relation to age, salary, qualifications etc., all done in a way similar to that of national states dealing with statistics as a basis for administrating their population and their affairs (cf. Popkewitz & Lindblad, 2001). What is more important here, however, is that in various ways the OECD is researching teachers and their work in terms of professional qualifications and demands from changing schooling scenarios (OECD, 2001) and in relation to student outcomes, which means that a central part of the knowledge produced by the OECD and its agencies is translating the affairs of education, schooling, and teaching into very specific epistemic forms and objectives. The OECD states:

Most of the research has examined the relationship between measures of student performance, most commonly standardised test scores, and readily measurable teacher characteristics such as qualifications, teaching experience, and indicators of academic ability or subject-matter knowledge. Such research generally indicates that there is a positive relationship between these measured teacher characteristics and student performance, but perhaps to a lesser extent than may have been expected. A point of agreement among the various studies is that there are many important aspects of teacher quality that are not captured by the commonly used indicators such as qualifications, experience and tests of academic ability. The teacher characteristics that are harder to measure, but which can be vital to student learning include the ability to convey ideas in clear and convincing ways; to create effective learning environments for different types of students; to foster productive teacher-student relationships; to be enthusiastic and creative; and to work effectively with colleagues and parents (OECD 2005, p. 2).

In this quote we learn about a set of categories that the OECD on the one hand is using in order to capture the outcomes of education systems and on the other hand is using to categorise teachers in terms of merits and indicators of professional qualities such as subject matter knowledge and work life experiences. Furthermore, we note that the OECD expands the latter domain into categorisations of teachers' ways of working with students and with parents. These expanded categorisations are assumed to improve the correlation between teachers' characteristics and students' performances. Stated otherwise we find a specific kind of boundary work on part of the OECD – based on its incorporated research activities and growing international databases – proclaiming supreme knowledge about what matters in education (i.e. performances) and what matters in teachers' professional work. Scientific authority by means of scientific methods and techniques has become intrinsic to the supra-national organisation itself. And, as a potential mediator between science and the teaching profession, the OECD directs its interest in both in very specific directions. Not only are its increasingly large comparative data bases dependent on highly qualified (and specific) systems of expertise, but it also translates the operations and activities of schools and teaching into categories which fit these forms of expertise in a very specific way, e.g. in terms of statistics of student performances and by that demanding teachers to master statistics in order to do rational work. In this we can see clear resemblances between the knowledge produced about teaching and its contexts, and the particular forms which its politics have taken for governance and regulation.

Secondly, system actors such as policy-makers and top administrators – sometimes including teacher organisations – are doing mixed kinds of boundary work in various national and international contexts. What is at stake here are changing demands on the teaching profession, recruitment to the profession and its qualifications, but also what counts as professional authority and what lacks authority among e.g. politicians. Feuer, Towne & Shavelson (2002) illustrate this when they refer to the US situation at the turn of the century, where they find attempts to define – in law – scientifically valid quantitative and qualitative methods which the educational should adhere to in order to be conceived of as scientific. This is an example of boundary work telling that authority based on science is not an affair solely of the sciences, but an affair also for the US administration. Feuer et al. adduce:

Academic scientists are usually startled to find the arcane of their craft inserted in law; but surprise turns to anxiety when the law appears to instruct them on methodology and to tie public funding of research to specific modes of inquiry (Feuer et al., 2002, p. 5).

The US government and affiliates are attempting to define what counts as scientific research in education, thus drawing a demarcation line between what counts as scientific knowledge and non-scientific knowledge, based on categorisations such as experimentation and quantitative analyses of the effectiveness of intervention outcomes. This research politics is criticised by several researchers e.g. Erickson & Guiterrez (2002) questioning the understanding of science at the US government.

The US context – as presented here – is perhaps a bit extreme, but similar tendencies are present in different parts of Europe – questioning the scientific authority of present research cultures related to teacher education and the teaching profession (see e.g. Wolter et al, 2004) and proposing scientific authority based on e.g. analyses of educational outcomes and on international comparisons such as those proposed by the OECD.

Turning to the last kind of actors – the researchers – we have noted that they were already in place among the two previous kinds of actors – within supranational organisations and incorporated into political and administrative frameworks. Here, they are very much part of the boundary work concerning the relations between science and the teaching profession (or its scientific as well as social and political foundations), which, of course, also includes researchers within the most classic institution, the university and its professionals (presented in the previous section). This is an institution with dramatic changes. Over the last three or four decades its expansion has been enormous, but in a world where science now has transformed into a socio-cultural category with no possibility to demarcate between what is science and what is society (Drori, Meyer et al., 2003) university-based knowledge production has changed accordingly (see Gibbons et al., 1994; Etzkowitz & Leydesdorff; 2000).

CONCLUDING COMMENTS: PROFESSIONALISING TALK ON TEACHING *AS* POLICY AND POLITICS

Teachers work has long been a central subject in politics as well as in policy-making, but the efforts and aims to 'professionalise' the occupation is of more recent origin, as is the general talk of teachers as professionals. Our historical journey on these issues has aimed to give an overview of various literatures in the field, and, more specifically, aimed to highlight the political nature of questions about the professional status and characteristics of teaching, captured by the term 'boundary work.' We have pointed to the central role of 'science' as an important mediator in raising the intellectual authority of teaching, and we have claimed that it is important also as a source and tool in processes of educational governance. We have also pointed to the social and political nature of the sciences and its conceptualisations. Given this, our overview of the professionalising talk on teaching, and our intention to unpack some of its main ideas, assumptions, and distinctions, has allowed us to reach some conclusions about the present situation of naturalised – taken for granted – talk of teaching as a profession.

Firstly, we could conclude that present talk about teaching as a profession is futuristic, e.g. construing teacher qualifications and behaviours which are supposed to be needed, for today and the near future. The professional concept has become a demarcation between what are considered to be old-fashioned behaviours and new ones, between what has been and what is yet to come.

Secondly, even though there are many stakeholders involved, there seem to be clear convergences between them about how to define the present situation and its challenges: for example, the work of teaching is generally regarded as increasingly dependent on science-based tools and knowledge; for managing such things as school reforms, student outcomes and more complex interactions between the schools and their environments, e.g. in terms of regression analyses on social background and ethnicity in relation to school performances.

As there seems to be little of epistemic controversy among the stakeholders, we can, *thirdly*, note strong tendencies of homogenisation in discourses on teaching and the meaning of schooling. Some decades ago this would be talked about as a convergence of paradigms in the educational sector, where supranational organisations, national system actors (who have previously been seen as *the* central policy-makers) and educationalist researchers engage in exploring the same research agenda, with similar tools and shared research problems.

However, what could be understood as a significant change is, *fourthly*, changes in the research agenda itself; how it situating itself in contemporary societies as a transition in the processes of policymaking and as a shift in the politics of scientific knowledge production generally, as exemplified in terms of the contested performative turn in education as well as in educational research.

Our overview has shown that the present situation of professionalising talk on teaching is taking place in times of educational restructuring and tends in several ways to be sharing some of the restructuration characteristics, such as accountability, transparency and evaluation.

Thus, the de-centering of policy-making could be viewed as a potential explanatory clue for understanding the emergence of professionalising talk on teaching, and for the specific epistemic profiles in this talk. We argue that new forms and technologies for governance inscribed in the processes of educational restructuring involve an expansion of the policy-making apparatus and its actors. This is a transition in the processes of policy-making, where previous boundaries between teachers' work, science, and policy tend to erode. It is also a shift in the politics of scientific knowledge where questions of intellectual authority are preceded in new ways, now involving boundary work on the conception of science, and its institutional place of residence as well. This also makes the professionalising talk of teaching itself a boundary object (see Bowker & Star, 2000), whose plasticity allows it to bridge and stabilise the activities between actors and stakeholders in times of educational restructuring.

NOTES

[1] We use the concept 'science' in its broadest sense and including the spectrum from the humanities, to the natural, social, cultural, and engineering sciences.

[2] As presented 2008-05-13 at http://www.neafoundation.org/publications/charge/section1.htm

[3] This research review was part of the PROFKNOW project, financed by the EU 6th framework programme. The reviews were carried out by research partners in seven countries, including the authors of this text.

REFERENCES

Abbott, A. (1988). *The system of professions: An essay on the division of expert labour*. Chicago: University of Chicago Press.

Adams, A., & Tulasiewicz, W. (1995). *The crisis in teacher education: A European concern?* London: Falmer Press.

Andersen, B. (2002). *Imagined communities: Reflections on the origin and spread of nationalism*. London: Verso.

Ball, S. J. (1990). *Politics and policymaking in education*. London: Routledge.

Beach, D. (Ed.). (2005). *Welfare state restructuring in education and health care: Implications for the teaching and nursing professions and their professional knowledge*. Report No 2 from the Profknow project. Retrieved from www.profknow.net

Beck, J., & Young, M. F. D. (2005). The assault on the professions and the restructuring of academic and professional identities: A Bernsteinian analysis. *British Journal of Sociology of Education, 26*(2), 183–197.

Bell, D. (1973). *The coming of post-industrial society*. New York: Basic Books.

Bernstein, B. (2000). *Pedagogy, symbolic control and identity: Theory, research and critique*. Oxford, NY: Lanham, Rowman and Littlefield.

Black, P., & Dylan, W. (1998). Inside the black box: Raising standards through classroom assessment. *Phi Delta Kappan, March 1998*, 7–74.

Bowker, G. C., & Star, S. L. (2000a). *Sorting things out: Classification and its consequences*. Cambridge, MA: MIT Press.

Bourdieu, P. (1988). *The 'Globalisation' myth and the European welfare state*. In P. Bourdieu & R. Nice (Eds.), *Acts of resistance: against the new myths of our time*. New York: Then New Press.

Broman, T. (1995). Rethinking professionalisation: Theory, practice, and professional ideology in eighteenth-century German medicine. *The Journal of Modern History, 67*(4), 835–872.

Burrage, M., & Torstendahl, R. (Eds.). (1990). *Professions in theory and history: Rethinking the study of the professions*. London: Sage.

Böhme, G., & Stehr, N. (1986). *The knowledge society: The growing impact of science on social relations*. Dordrecht: Kluwer.

Castells, M. (1998). *The information age: Economy, society and culture: The end of millennium*. Oxford: Blackwell.

Cochran-Smith, M., & Fries, M. K. (2001). Sticks, stones, and ideology: The discourse of reform in teacher education. *Educational Researcher, 30*(8), 3–15.

Dale, R. (1997). The state and the governance of education: An analysis of the restructuring of the state-education relationship. In A. H. Halsey, H. Lauder, P. Brown & A. S. Wells (Eds.), *Education: Culture, economy and society*. Oxford: Oxford University Press.

Darling-Hammond, L. (1998). Teachers and teaching: Testing policy hypotheses from a National Commission report. *Educational Researcher, 27*(1), 5–15.

Druckner, P. F. (1969). *The knowledge society*. New Society.

Durkheim, E. (1957). *Professional ethics and civic morals*. London: Routledge and Kegan Paul. (Lectures 1890–1900 in Bordeaux)

Durkheim, E. (1904/05, in English 1977). *The evolution of educational thought: Lectures on the formation and development of secondary education in France* (P. Collins, Trans.). London: Routledge & Kegan.Paul (Lectures 1904–1905 at the University of Paris).

Erickson, F., & Guiterrez, K. (2002). Culture, rigor, and science in educational research. *Educational Researcher*, *31*(8), 21–24.

Etzkowitz, H., & Leydesdorff, L. (2000). The dynamics of innovation: From national systems and 'mode 2' to a triple helix of university–industry–government relations. *Research Policy*, *29*(2), 109–123.

Etzioni, A. (Ed.). (1969). *The semi-professions and their organization*. Free Press.

Evetts, J. (2006). Introduction: Trust and professionalism: Challenges and occupational changes. *Current Sociology*, *54*, 515–531.

Feuer, M., Towne, L., & Shavelson, R. (2002). Scientific culture and educational research. *Educational Researcher*, *31*(8), 4–14.

Foss Lindblad, R., & Lindblad, S. (2006). Knowledge at work: On the politics of knowledge in the reconfiguration of the teaching profession. In T. S. Popkewitz, et al. (Eds.), *"The future is not what it appears to be". Pedagogy, genealogy and political epistemology*. Stockholm: HLS förlag.

Foucault, M. (1977). *Discipline and punish: The birth of the penitentiary*. London: Tavistock.

Fournier, V. (1999). The appeal to "Professionalism" as a disciplinary mechanism. *Social Review*, *47*(2), 280–307.

Friedson, E. (2001). *Professionalism, the third logic: On the practice of knowledge*. Chicago: University of Chicago Press.

Gerwitz, S. (2002). *The managerial school: Post-welfarism and social justice in education*. London: Routledge.

Gibbons, M., Limoges, C., Nowotny, H., Schwartzman, S., Scott, P., & Trow, M. (1994). *The new production of knowledge*. London: Sage.

Giddens, A. (1988). *The third way: The renewal of social democracy*. Oxford: Polity Press.

Gieryn, T. F. (1983). Boundary-work and the demarcation of science from non-science: Strains and interests in professional ideologies of scientists. *American Sociological Review*, *48*(6), 781–795.

Goldstein, J. (1984). Foucault among the sociologists: The "Disciplines" and the history of the professions. *History and Theory*, *23*(2), 170–192.

Goodson, I., & Lindblad, S. (Eds.). (2008). *Crossprofessional studies on nursing and teaching in Europe*. Manus to report No 6 from the Profknow project (To be published at www.profknow.net).

Hacking, I. (2002). *Historical ontology*. Cambridge, MA: Harvard University Press.

Hargreaves, A. (1994). *Changing teachers, changing times: Teachers' work and culture in the postmodern age*. London: Cassell.

Hargreaves, D. (2000). *Teaching as an research based profession. Prospects and possibilities*. In B. Moon, J. Butcher, & E. Bird (Eds.), *Leading professional development in education*. London: Routledge.

Harvey, D. (1989). *The condition of postmodernity*. Cambridge, MA: Blackwell.

Hofstetter, R., & Schneuwly, B. (2001). *Educational science in Switzerland. Evolution and outlooks. Centre for science and technology studies*. Bern: Center for Science and Technology Studies 2001 2001/6.

Hoyle, E. (1974). Professionality, professionalism and control in teaching. *London Education Review*, *3*(2), 13–19.

Hunter, W., & Brown, D. S. (2000). Politics of human capital investment in Latin America. *Comparative Political Studies*, *33*(1), 113–143.

Johnson, T. (1972). *Professions and power*. London: Macmillan.

Knorr-Cetina, K. (1999). *Epistemic cultures: How the sciences make knowledge*. Cambridge, MA: Harvard University Press.

Labaree, D. (1992). Power, knowledge, and the rationalisation of teaching: A genealogy of the movement to professionalise teaching. *Harvard Educational Review*, *62*(2), 123–154.

Latour, B., & Woolgar, S. (1986). *Laboratory life: The construction of scientific facts*. Princeton, NJ: Princeton University Press.

Lingard, B., & Ozga, J. (Eds.). (2007). *Education policy and politics*. London: Routledge.

Little, J. W. (1993). Teachers' professional development in a climate of educational reform. *Educational Evaluation and Policy Analysis, 15*(1), 29–51.

Lortie, D. C. (1969). The balance of control and autonomy in elementary-school teaching. In A. Etzioni (Ed.), *The semi-professions and their organization.* New York: Free Press.

Lortie, D. C. (1975). *Schoolteacher: A sociological study.* Chicago: University of Chicago Press.

Lundström, U. (2007). *Gymansielärare – perspektiv på arbete och yrkesutveckling vid millennieskiftet.* Umeå: Umeå University Press.

McLaughlin, M., & Talbert, J. (2001). *Professional communities and the work of high school teaching.* Chicago: University of Chicago Press.

Norrie, C., & Goodson, I. (2005). *A literature review of welfare state restructuring in education and health care in European contexts.* Report 1 from the Profknow project. Retrieved from www.profknow.net

OECD. (2001). *Education policy analysis.* Centre for Educational Research and Innovation. Paris: Author.

OECD. (2005). *Teachers matter: Attracting, developing and retaining effective teachers.* Paris: Author.

OECD. (2006). *Education at a glance.* OECD Indicators. Paris: Author.

Papagiannis, G. J., Easton, P. A., & Owens, J. T. (1992). *The school restructuring movement in the USA: An analysis of major issues and policy implications.* Paris: UNESCO.

Parsons, T. (1939). The professions and social structure. *Social Forces, 17,* 457–467.

Popkewitz, T. S. (2000). *Educational knowledge: Changing relationships between the state, civil society, and the educational community.* New York: SUNY.

Popkewitz, T., & Lindblad, S. (2001). Estatísticas educacionais como um sistema de razao: Relacoes entre governo da educacao e inclusao e exclusao sociais. *Educacao & Sociedade, 22,* 111–148.

Purvis, J. R. (1973). Schoolteaching as a professional career. *The British Journal of Sociology, 24*(1), 43–57.

Ranson, S. (2007). Public accountability in the age of neo-liberal governance. In B. Lingard & J. Ozga (Eds.), *Education policy and politics.* London: Routledge.

Sachs, J. (2001). Teacher professional identity: Competing discourses, competing outcomes. *Journal of Education Policy, 16*(2), 149–161.

Sarfatti Larson, M. (1977). *The rise of professionalism: A sociological analysis.* Berkeley, CA: University of California Press.

Schön, D. A. (1983). *The reflective practitioner: How professionals think in action.* New York: Basic Books.

Steiner- Khamsi, G. (Ed.). (2004). *The global politics of educational borrowing & lending.* New York: Teachers College Press.

Svensson, L. G. (2006). New professionalism, trust and competence: Some conceptual remarks and empirical data. *Current Sociology, 54*(4), 579–593.

Tawney, R. H. (1921). *The acquisitive society.* New York: Harcourt Brace.

Troman, G. (1996). The rise of the new professionals? The restructuring of primary teachers' work and professionalism. *British Journal of Sociology of Education, 17*(4), 473–487.

Waller, W. (1932). *The sociology of teaching.* New York: Wiley.

Warwick, P., & Cunningham, P. (2006). Progressive alternatives? Teachers' experience of autonomy and accountability in the school community. *Education 3–13, 34*(1), 27–36.

Whitty, G. (2000). Teacher professionalism in new times. *Journal of In-Service Education, 26*(2), 281–295.

Wilensky, H. (1964). The professionalization of everyone. *American Journal for Sociology, 70*(2), 137–158.

Wolter, S., Keiner, E., Palomba, D., & Lindblad, S. (2004). OECD examiners' report on educational research and development in England. *European Educational Research Journal, 3*(2), 510–526.

Wright, E. O. (1997). *Class counts: Comparative studies in class analysis.* Cambridge: Cambridge University Press.

FURTHER READINGS

Broman, T. (1995). Rethinking professionalization: Theory, practice, and professional ideology in eighteenth-century German medicine. *The Journal of Modern History, 67*(4), 835–872.

Böhme, G., & Stehr, N. (1986). *The knowledge society: The growing impact of science on social relations.* Dordrecht: Kluwer.

Friedson, E. (2001). *Professionalism, the third logic: On the practice of knowledge.* Chicago: University of Chicago Press.

Goldstein, J. (1984). Foucault among the sociologists: The "Disciplines" and the history of the professions. *History and Theory, 23*(2), 170–192.

Gieryn, T. F. (1983). Boundary-work and the demarcation of science from non-science: Strains and interests in professional ideologies of scientists. *American Sociological Review, 48*(6), 781–795.

Parsons, T. (1939). The professions and social structure. *Social Forces, 17*, 457–467.

Rita Foss Lindblad
Department of Education
University of Gothenburg, Sweden

Sverker Lindblad
Department of Education,
University of Gothenburg, Sweden

AUTHOR INFORMATION

MICHAEL W. APPLE is the John Bascom Professor of Curriculum and Instruction and Educational Policy Studies at the University of Wisconsin – Madison (USA). He teaches courses in curriculum theory and research and in the sociology of curriculum. His major research interests lie in the relationship between culture and power in education. He has written extensively on the relationship between differential power and educational policy and practice. Among his recent books are *Educating the "Right" Way: Markets, Standards, God, and Inequality*; *The State and the Politics of Knowledge*; and the 25th anniversary 3rd edition of *Ideology and Curriculum*.

STEPHEN J. BALL is a Fellow of the British Academy, member of Academy of Social Sciences, and Karl Mannheim Professor of Sociology of Education, Institute of Education, University of London, UK. His main work is in the field of 'policy sociology'; the use of sociological theories and methods to analyse policy processes and outcomes. His specific research interests focus upon the effects and consequences of the education market in a variety of respects including; the impact of competition on provider behaviour; the class strategies of educational choosers; the participation of private capital in education service delivery and education policy; and the impact of 'performativity' on academic and social life. He has recently completed a three year ESRC Research Fellowship. His theoretical influences draw primarily from Foucault and Bourdieu. A selection of publications: 2008, *The education debate: policy and politics in the 21st Century*, Bristol, Policy Press; 2007, *Education plc: private sector participation in public sector education*, London, Routledge; 2006; *Education Policy and Social Class: Selected Works* (World Library of Educationalists), London, Routledge; 2003, *Class Strategies and the Education Market: the middle class and social advantage*, London, Routledge Falmer.

GERT BIESTA is Professor of Education at the Stirling Institute of Education, University of Stirling, Scotland, UK and Visiting Professor for Education and Democratic Citizenship at Örebro University and Mälardalen University, Sweden. He is editor-in-chief of *Studies in Philosophy and Education*. He conducts theoretical and empirical research and is particularly interested in relationships between education, democracy and democratisation. Recent books include *Derrida & Education* (co-edited with Denise Egéa Kuehne; Routledge 2001); *Pragmatism and Educational Research* (with Nicholas C. Burbules; Rowman & Littlefield 2003); *Beyond Learning: Democratic Education for a Human Future* (Paradigm Publishers 2006); *Improving Learning Cultures in Further Education* (with David James; Routledge 2007) and *Democracy, Education and the Moral Life* (co-edited with Michael Katz and Susan Verducci; Springer 2008). For more information see www.gertbiesta.com

MIKE BOTTERY is Professor of Education and Director of Research Degrees in the Institute for Learning, University of Hull, England. His main research interests are concerned with the values underpinning the policies and practice of education, and of other public sector activities, and his research has embraced both theoretical explorations and empirical investigations. He has published seven single-authored books to date, as well as numerous peer-refereed articles.

XAVIER BONAL holds a degree in Economics from the Autonomous University of Barcelona (UAB) and a doctorate in Sociology from the same university. He is Professor assigned of the Sociology Department of the UAB since 1997. He has been director of the research group 'Analysis of Social Policies Seminar' (SAPS) and is a member of the Interdisciplinary Group on Educational Policies (GIPE). He has carried out several researches in the field of Sociology of Education and Educational Policies. Likewise he has worked extensively on education, poverty and social inequalities. Since 2006 he is Deputy Ombudsman for Children's Rights in Catalonia.

SIMON BRADFORD is a sociologist in the School of Sport and Education at Brunel University, London, and Director of the Centre for Youth Work Studies at Brunel University. His research interests include the history of professional identities in youth work, social policy affecting young people and the development of youth practices and culture, particularly cyber-culture and gaming. He is currently writing about policy for the development of professional training for English youth workers in the 1940s and 1950s and about the contested involvement of universities in this work.

ELIZABETH BULLEN is a senior lecturer in the School of Communication and Creative Arts at Deakin University, Melbourne, Australia. Her research on education and educational policy issues has been published in the *Policy Futures in Education, Journal of Education Policy* and *British Educational Research Journal*. Her other research explores ideological discourses in narratives for young people and the extent to which they support or contradict contemporary educational policy agendas.

ALAN CRIBB is Professor of Bioethics and Education in the Centre for Public Policy Research at King's College London, UK. He has a particular interest in developing interdisciplinary scholarship that links philosophical, social science and professional concerns and has pursued this interest through writing about health and education.

ROGER DALE is a Professor in the Centre for Globalisation, Education and Societies in the Graduate School of Education at the University of Bristol, England. With Susan Robertson, he co-founded the journal Globaisation, Societies and Education. His main interest is in the changing relationships between capitalism and modernity as these are revealed through the development of transnational education policy, in particular of 'European Education Policy'. He is currently Scientific Coordinator of the EU's Network of Experts in Social Science and Education.

ROSEMARY DEEM is Professor of Education, Research Director for Social Sciences and Law at Bristol University and an Academician of the UK Academy of Social Sciences. From 2001-2005 she jointly-edited *The Socological Review*. Research interests include higher education management/leadership, governance & organisational cultures; world-class universities; the relationship between research and teaching; education policy; inequality in educational settings and qualitative methods. Recent publications include, *Knowledge, Higher Education and the New Managerialism: The Changing Management of UK Universities* (with S. Hillyard and M. Reed, 2007) (Oxford: Oxford University Press), *Geographies of Knowledge, Geometries of Power: Higher Education in the 21st Century. World Year Book of Education 2008* (Ed. with Epstein, D., R. Boden, F. Rizvi, and S .Wright, 2007) (New York: RoutledgeFalmer).

RICHARD EDWARDS is Professor of Education at The Stirling Institute of Education, Scotland. He has researched and published extensively in the area of adult education and lifelong learning, drawing on a broadly poststructuralist perspective. His most recent book is, with Robin Usher, *Globalisation and Pedagogy, Space, Place and Identity*, 2008 (London: Routledge).

ANDREAS FEJES is Associate Professor and Senior Lecturer in Education at Linköping University, Sweden. His research explores lifelong learning and adult education in particular drawing on poststructuralist theory. He recently published (as editor together with Katherine Nicoll) the book *Foucault and lifelong learning: Governing the subject* (London: Routledge) and his articles recently appeared in *Journal of Education Policy, Educational Philosophy and Theory, International Journal of Lifelong Education, Teaching in Higher Education, Studies in the Education of Adults and the International Journal of Higher Education in the Social Sciences*. He is also the secretary of the *European Society for Research on the Education of Adults*.

LYNN FENDLER is an Associate Professor in the Department of Teacher Education at Michigan State University, USA, where she teaches courses in educational philosophy, curriculum studies, continental theories, and research epistemologies. Her research interests include genealogical critique, historiography, rhetorical studies of pedagogy, and the philosophy of food. Her recent publications include a history of the bell curve (with Irfan Muzaffar in *Educational Theory*) and Why Generalisability is not Generalisable (*Journal of the Philosophy of Education*). Her book on Michel Foucault (forthcoming 2010) will appear as part of the Continuum Library of Educational Thought (Richard Bailey, series editor).

JOHANNAH FAHEY is a Research Fellow at Monash University, Australia. She has a PhD in cultural studies from Macquarie University, Australia. She is interested in poststructuralist theories of language and textuality; postcolonial models of subjectivity, corporeality and ethnicity; mobility and psycho-affective pedagogies of globalisation; and contemporary Australian visual arts. Her latest co-authored book is *Haunting the Knowledge Economy*. Her earlier book is *David Noonan: Before and Now*. She is currently working on a new book called *Globalizing the Research Imagination*.

SHARON GEWIRTZ is Professor of Education in the Centre for Public Policy Research at King's College London, UK. She has been involved in research in the sociology of education for 20 years during which time she has published extensively on the themes of policy change, teachers' work and social justice.

HENRY A. GIROUX currently holds the Global TV Network Chair Professorship at McMaster University, Ontario, Canada. His primary research areas are: cultural studies, youth studies, critical pedagogy, popular culture, media studies, social theory, and the politics of higher and public education. He has published numerous books and articles. His most recent books include: *The Terror of Neoliberalism (2004)*; *Take Back Higher Education* (2004) (co-authored with Susan Giroux); *Against the New Authoritarianism (2005)*; *Beyond the Spectacle of Terrorism (2005)*; *America on the Edge*: *Henry Giroux on Politics, Culture and Education (2006)*; *and The University in Chains: Confronting the Military-Industrial-Academic Complex (2007)*.

SOTIRIA GREK is a Research Fellow at the Centre for Educational Sociology, University of Edinburgh. Her research interests include education governance, education and Europeanization, analysis of educational policy discourse and the political economy of education.

VALERIE HEY is a sociologist who works in an interdisciplinary way across the fields of cultural, feminist and poststructuralist theory. She has written accounts about education influenced by subcultural theory and ethnography and is currently developing ideas about the structuring of class, gender sociality and identity in late modernity. She is currently a Professor at Brunel University in the School of Sport and Education and will take up a chair in education at the University of Sussex in September 2007 within the Sussex Institute.

GEERT KELCHTERMANS (1962) is a professor of education at the Katholieke Universiteit Leuven (Belgium), where he chairs the Centre for Educational Policy and Innovation. In 1993 he obtained his PhD with a narrative-biographical study on teachers' professional development. He has widely published on teacher development, reflective practice, micro-politics in schools, educational reform, policy implementation and qualitative research methodology, both in international journals and edited books. He also sits on the editorial board several journals, among which *Teaching and Teacher Education; Teachers & Teaching: Theory and Practice; International Journal of Qualitative Studies in Education; Teacher Education Quarterly.*

JANE KENWAY is Professor of global education studies at Monash University and a Fellow of the Academy of the Social Sciences in Australia. Her research expertise is in educational policy in the context of wider social and cultural change. A particular focus of her research is on educational reform and issues of knowledge, power and identity. Among her many books are *Consuming Children* (with Bullen), *Masculinity Beyond the Metropolis* (with Kraack and Hickey-Moody) and *Haunting the Knowledge Economy* (with Bullen, Fahey and Robb). Offering fresh interpretations of enduring educational issues and anticipating educational trends long before others, she is widely recognised as one of the most provocative thinkers in education.

MAREK KWIEK, director of the Center for Public Policy of Poznan University, Poland. His research interests include globalization and higher education, European educational policies, welfare state reforms, and philosophy of education. He has published 80 papers and 8 books, recently *The University and the State: A Study into Global Transformation* (Frankfurt/New York: Peter Lang, 2006). A higher education policy expert to the European Commission, USAID, OECD, World Bank, UNESCO, OSCE, and the Council of Europe. A participant in a dozen international research projects. A Fulbright "New Century Scholar" 2007-2008 ("Higher Education in the 21st Century") and an advisory board member in *Higher Education Quarterly, European Educational Research Journal*, and *Globalisation, Societies and Education.*

MARTIN LAWN is a Professorial Research Fellow at the Centre for Educational Sociology at the University of Edinburgh. He is the Editor of the European Educational Research Journal and publishes on European educational policies, socio-historical studies in international comparison and the histories of educational research.

RITA FOSS LINDBLAD got her PhD in Theory of Science and is a senior lecturer in Education at the University of Gothenburg. Her research is focussing on the social organisation of knowledge and learning in contemporary societies. This includes a special interest in its political dimensions, where issues of gender, class, ethnicity and sexuality are important, as are issues of policies, educational systems and their epistemic configurations. At present she is researching higher education and lifelong-learning on the one hand and professionalism on the other hand. The interest is motivated by their actuality and their complex linking's to the politics of education.

SVERKER LINDBLAD is professor in Education (*Pedagogik*) at the University of Gothenburg. He was one of the founders of the Nordic Educational Research

Association and President of the European Educational Research Association. Lindblad coordinated a European Union research project on Education Governance and Social Inclusion/Exclusion and is now finalising research on Professional Knowledge under Restructuring in Europe. Lindblad is doing research on international statistics and supra-national governing of education, e.g. in terms of comparative studies and ranking lists. With a similar stance he is now developing research on the politics of learning in classroom interaction.

BOB LINGARD is currently Professor in the School of Education at The University of Queensland, Australia. He researches globalization and education policy, school reform, gender and schooling and pedagogies. His most recent books include, *Leading Learning* (Open University Press, 2003) with Debra Hayes, Martin Mills and Pam Christie, *Teachers and Schooling Making a Difference* (Allen and Unwin, 2006) also with those co-authors, *The RoutledgeFalmer Reader in Education Policy and Politics* (Routledge, 2007), edited with Jenny Ozga. He has two in-press books, *Transforming Learning in Schools and Communities* (Continuum), edited with Stewart Ranson and Jon Nixon, and *Educating Boys: Policies, Pedagogies and Practices* (Palgrave), authored with Wayne Martino and Martin Mills. He is currently working on a book, *Globalizing Education Policy* for Routledge with Fazal Rizvi.

SIMON MARGINSON is a Professor of Higher Education in the Centre for the Study of Higher Education at the University of Melbourne, Australia. His research and writing investigate higher education and policy on higher education in the context of globalisation. Current projects are focused on the social and economic security of international students, the comparative study of university strategies in the global environment especially in the Asia-Pacific, policy on innovation and the knowledge economy, and problems of creativity. He has worked on several papers for the OECD including the 2007 thematic review of tertiary education in the Netherlands, and *Globalisation and Higher Education* (with Marijk van der Wende). Among his books are *Markets in Education* (1997) and *The Enterprise University* (with Mark Considine, 2000) and the collection *Prospects of Higher Education: Globalization, market competition, public goods and the future of the university* (Sense, 2007).

KA HO MOK is Associate Dean and Professor of the Faculty of Social Sciences, The University of Hong Kong (HKU). Before he joined the HKU, he was the Founding Director and Chair Professor of the Centre for East Asian Studies, University of Bristol. Professor Mok has research and published extensively in the fields of comparative education policy, public policy and governance, and social development studies in contemporary China. His most recent books include *Changing Governance and Public Policy in East Asia* (London: Routledge, 2009) and *Education Reform and Education Policy in East Asia* (London: Routledge, 2006). He is also Editor of *Journal of Asian Public Policy* and Book Series Editor of *Comparative Development and Policy in Asia* (London: Routledge).

KATHY NICOLL is a senior lecturer in Education at the Stirling Institute of Education, University of Stirling, Scotland, UK. Her research explores post-compulsory and professional education and policy in particular drawing on poststructuralist theory. She has recently published *Rhetoric and Educational Discourse: Persuasive Texts?* (with R. Edwards, N. Solomon and R. Usher, 2004), *Flexibility and Lifelong Learning: Policy, Discourse and Politics* (2006) and an edited collection (with A. Fejes, 2008) entitled *Foucault and Lifelong Learning: Governing the subject.*

MARK OLSSEN is Professor of Political Theory and Education Policy in the Department of Political, International and Policy Studies, University of Surrey. His most recent books are *Toward A Global Thin Community: Nietzsche, Foucault, and the Cosmopolitan Commitment*, Paradigm Press, Boulder and London, published 2009; and *Michel Foucault: Materialism and Education*, Paradigm Press, Boulder and London, published in May 2006. He also recently published, in 2004, with John Codd and Anne-Marie O'Neill of Massey University, New Zealand, a *book titled Education Policy: Globalisation, Citizenship, Democracy, (Sage,* London); an edited volume *Culture and Learning: Access and Opportunity in the Classroom* (IAP Press, New York); with Michael Peters and Colin Lankshear, *Critical Theory and the Human Condition: Founders and Praxis,* and from Rowman and Littlefield, New York, *Futures of Critical Theory: Dreams of Difference*, also with Michael Peters and Colin Lankshear. He has published extensively in leading academic journals in Britain, America and in Australasia.

MICHAEL A. PETERS is professor of education in Department of Educational Policy Studies at the University of Illinois at Urbana-Champaign. He is the author of some thirty books and edited collections, including most recently, *Building Knowledge Cultures: Education and Development in the Age of Knowledge Capitalism* (with Tina Besley) (Rowman & Littlefield, 2006), *Deconstructing Derrida: tasks for the New Humanities* (with Peter Trifonas) (Palgrave, 2005), *Education, Globalization and the State in the Age of Terrorism* (Paradigm Publishers, 2004). His research interests center on educational philosophy and theory, educational policy, and higher education.

LUDWIG A. PONGRATZ is Professor of General Pedagogy and Adult Eduation at the Darmstadt Technical University (Germany). His publications and research concentrate primarily on the history of pedagogic theory and the methodology of pedagogy, critical theory and educational philosophy, school pedagogy and adult education. His research includes empirical studies alongside his historical and conceptual works. He is the author of many aticles and books and edited collections in these fields, including most recently: *Gerechtigkeit und Bildung* (with Michael Wimmer and Roland Reichenbach) (2007); *The Learning Society from the Perspective of Governmentality* (with Jan Masschelein, Maarten Simons and Ulrich Bröckling) (2006); *Nach Foucault – Diskurs- und machtanalytische*

Perspektiven der Pädagogik (with Wolfgang Nieke, Michael Wimmer and Jan Masschelein, 2004).

THOMAS S. POPKEWITZ, The University of Wisconsin-Madison, USA, studies the systems of reason that govern educational reforms and research. His studies are concerned with historical and contemporary schooling both in the US and comparatively. This books include *The Political Sociology Of Educational Reform* (1991), *Struggling for the Soul; The politics of education and the construction of the teacher* (1998), and *Cosmopolitanism and the Age of School Reform: Science, Education And Making Society By Making The Child.* (2008), that latter exploring historically present reforms of teaching, teacher education and the sciences of education as practices that generate principles of exclusion and inclusion. He has also explored historically and comparatively issues of globalization in, for example, *Inventing the modern self and John Dewey: Modernities and the traveling of pragmatism in education* (2005).

SHAUN RAWOLLE is a lecturer in education at Charles Sturt University Australia. He has recently completed his PhD on Bourdieu, the mediatization of education policy and national versions of the knowledge economy. His book publications include the edited book, *Educational Imaginings: On the play of texts and contexts* (Australian Academic Press, 2003), co-edited with Jennifer A. Vadeboncoeur. His journal publications include 'Cross-field effects and temporary social fields: A case study of the mediatisation of recent Australian knowledge economy policies', *Journal of Education Policy*, 20(6); and 'Globalising policy sociology in education: working with Bourdieu', *Journal of Education Policy*, 20(6), with Bob Lingard and Sandra Taylor. Funding for this publication was provided through Charles Sturt University's Writing-Up Award fund.

SUSAN ROBERTSON is Professor Sociology of Education in the Graduate School of Education, University of Bristol. She is the Coordinator of the Centre for Globalisation, Education and Societies at the University of Bristol, and the founding co-editor of the journal *Globalisation, Societies and Education*. Susan has developed an interdisciplinary approach to examine the transformation of education as a result of processes of globalization and regionalization. She has also written extensively on teachers' labour.

TERRI SEDDON is Professor of Education at Monash University, Melbourne Australia. She is currently researching the way changes in work and society, especially greater global interconnectedness and the drive to a knowledge economy and learning society, are diversifying learning spaces and educational work in and beyond formalised education and training. Her books include *Context and Beyond (1993), Pay, Professionalism and Politics: Reforming Teachers? Reforming Education?* (1996), *Beyond Nostalgia: Reshaping Australian Education* (2000, with Lawrie Angus), and *Education Research and Policy: Steering the Knowledge-Based Economy (*2006, with Jenny Ozga and Tom Popkewitz*)*. She is currently completing *Disturbing Work: Approaching Agency* (2009, with Lea Henriksson and Beatrix Niemeyer) that considers changes in work, learning and working life in human services work.

MAARTEN SIMONS is Professor at the Centre for Educational Policy and Innovation and the Centre for Philosophy of Education, Catholic University of Leuven, Belgium. His research interests are educational policy and political philosophy with special attention on governmentality and schooling, autonomy and higher education and performativity in education. Together with Jan Masschelein he is the author of *Globale Immunität. Ein kleine Kartographie des Europaischen Bildungsraum* (2005, Berlin/Zurich, Diaphanes). He is the co-editor of the books *Europa anno 2006. E-ducatieve berichten uit niemandsland.* (2006, Acco), *The learning society from the perspective of governmentality* (2007, Blackwell), *De schaduwzijde van onze welwillendheid* (2008, Acco), and the special issue *The university revisited: questioning the public role of the university in the European knowledge society* (2007, Studies in Philosophy and Education), and the author of several articles in journals and edited books.

HEINZ SÜNKER is Professor of Social Pedagogy and Social Policy/Department of Bildungs- and Social Sciences at the University of Wuppertal (Germany). He studied German literature and language, philosophy, protestant theology and pedagogy at the universities of Münster and Heidelberg; he got his PhD and his habilitation at the university of Bielefeld. Main areas of research and publication: Critical social theory, Western Marxism, theory and history of social work and social policy, sociology and politics of education, theory of Bildung, childhood studies, German fascism.

AINA TARABINI is lecturer at the Sociology Department of the *Universitat Autònoma de Barcelona-Spain* (UAB). She is a member of the research group 'Analysis of Social Policies Seminar' (SAPS) since the year 2002, where she has worked in the projects "Globalization and inequalities in Latin America" and "Beyond Targeting the Poor: Education, development and anti-poverty policies in South America." In 2008 she was awarded a PhD on Sociology from the UAB for her work in the field of Education, Poverty and Development. Her principal research topics are globalization and education politics; education, inequality and poverty; and education and international development.

LEON TIKLY is Professor in Education and Deputy Director of Research at the Graduate School of Education, University of Bristol. Leon is Director of a DfID funded Research Programme Consortium (RPC) on Implementing Education Quality in Low Income Countries (EdQual) (http://www.edqual.org). The consortium includes partners based in the UK, Africa, South Asia and Latin America. He is also currently directing an evaluation of the UK government's *Aiming High: Raising African Caribbean Achievement project*; is involved in a state of the art literature review on globalisation and education with colleagues in the GSoE; and, on a project looking at leadership and the management of change in rural and township schools in South Africa. His main research interests include: the quality of education in low income countries; globalisation and education in low income countries; the achievement of Black and minority ethnic learners in the UK; South African education; the management of change.

CARLOS ALBERTO TORRES is professor of social sciences and comparative education at the University of California Los Angeles. He is the Founding Director of the Paulo Freire Institutes in Sao Paulo, Brazil, Buenos Aires, Argentina and UCLA. He has been a visiting professor in universities in North America, Latin America, Europe, Asia and Africa, lectured across the globe and recently completed a ten-year term as Director of the Latin America Center at UCLA. He has published countless academic essays and over 50 books including *Social Theory and Education* (with Raymond Morrow), *The University, State & Markets: The Political Economy of Globalization in the Americas and Democracy, Education and Multiculturalism: Dilemmas of Citizenship in a Global World*. He has also published a novel and book of poetry. His collected works will be published by Columbia University Press in 2008.

RICHARD VAN HEERTUM is currently a visiting assistant professor in the education departments at CUNY/College of Staten Island. He recently completed his Ph.D. in education and cultural studies at the University of California Los Angeles, where his dissertation focused on cynicism and democracy. He also has a MA in Economics. He has published over 10 academic essays, including works in Policy Futures in Education, Interactions, McGill Journal of Education and a number of anthologies and has published extensively in the popular press. He previously served as the Program Officer for the Paulo Freire Institute at UCLA.

AGNÈS VAN ZANTEN is a sociologist and senior researcher at the Centre National de la Recherche Scientifique. She works at the *Observatoire Sociologique du Changement*, a research centre of Sciences-Po Paris. She is also the director of RAPPE (*Réseau d'Analyse Pluridisciplinaire des Politiques Educatives*), an international network on educational policy. Her main research areas are the reproduction and transformation of social advantage in education, elite education, the organisational and professional dynamics of schools and educational policy. Her most recent publications include *L'école de la périphérie* (Paris, PUF, 2001), *Les politiques d'éducation* (Paris, PUF, coll. « Que sais-je ? », 2004) *Sociologie de l'école* (with M. Duru-Bellat, Paris, A. Colin, 2006) and *Dictionnaire de l'éducation* (Paris, PUF, 2008). Website: http: //osc.sciences-po.fr

LESLEY VIDOVICH is Professor of Education at the University of Western Australia, Australia. Her primary research focus is the field of education policy and practices – both in the schooling and higher education sectors – with a special interest in education policy development in a context of globalisation and internationalisation. She has been involved in research in Europe, Asia and Africa, as well as Australia, and has just commenced a comparative research study which includes North

American sites. She has recently completed an Australian Research Council Grant project on higher education policies and practices in Mainland China, Hong Kong Special Administrative Region and Singapore. Her largest volume of published work has been on accountability/quality policy and curriculum policy.

KENNETH WAIN teaches philosophy of education and moral and political philosophy at the University of Malta and is former dean of it's Faculty of Education. His first book *Philosophy of Lifelong Education* was published by Croom Helm (London) in 1987. Since then he has published extensively on lifelong learning, lifelong education, and the learning society, and on poststructuralist approaches to ethics, politics and education in different academic journals and book chapters. In 2004 he published *The Learning Society in a Postmodern World* with Peter Lang (New York) and is currently completing a book on Rousseau and education for a series on critical thinkers in education.

YUSEF WAGHID is Dean of the Faculty of Education at Stellenbosch University, South Africa. He has been professor in the Department of Education Policy Studies at Stellenbosch University since 2002 and chair of this department since 2003. He is editor of the South African Journal of Higher Education and a member of the Philosophy of Education Society of Great Britain, the American Educational Research Association and the Central Research Committee of Stellenbosch University. He is also an executive member of the South African Association for Research and Development in Higher Education. His interests includes the Analytical and evaluative inquiry vis-à-vis democratic citizenship education, and focussing on teaching and learning, educational policy and higher education transformation. He is the author of several articles in international journals and (edited) books.

AUTHOR INDEX

SUBJECT INDEX

Breinigsville, PA USA
21 June 2010
240285BV00002B/19/P